The SAGE Handbook of

Applied Memory

The SAGE Handbook of
Applied Memory

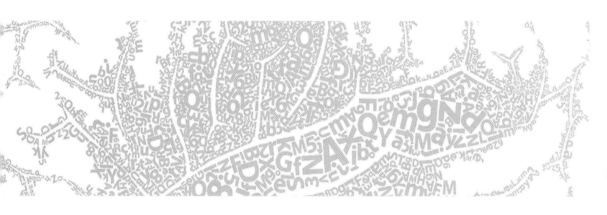

Edited by

Timothy J. Perfect and
D. Stephen Lindsay

Los Angeles | London | New Delhi
Singapore | Washington DC

Los Angeles | London | New Delhi
Singapore | Washington DC

SAGE Publications Ltd
1 Oliver's Yard
55 City Road
London EC1Y 1SP

SAGE Publications Inc.
2455 Teller Road
Thousand Oaks, California 91320

SAGE Publications India Pvt Ltd
B 1/I 1 Mohan Cooperative Industrial Area
Mathura Road
New Delhi 110 044

SAGE Publications Asia-Pacific Pte Ltd
3 Church Street
10-04 Samsung Hub
Singapore 049483

Editor: Michael Carmichael
Assistant editor: Keri Dickens
Production manager: Cenveo Publisher Services
Marketing manager: Alison Borg
Cover design: Wendy Scott
Typeset by: Cenveo Publisher Services
Printed in Great Britain by Henry Ling Limited,
at the Dorset Press, Dorchester, DT1 1HD

Editorial arrangement and Preface © Timothy J. Perfect and
    D. Stephen Lindsay 2014
Chapter 1 © Bennett L. Schwartz 2014
Chapter 2 © Neil W. Mulligan 2014
Chapter 3 © Gilles O. Einstein and Mark A. McDaniel 2014
Chapter 4 © D. Stephen Lindsay 2014
Chapter 5 © Douglas H. Wedell and Adam T. Hutcheson 2014
Chapter 6 © Jackie Andrade 2014
Chapter 7 © Eryn J. Newman and Maryanne Garry 2014
Chapter 8 © Colleen M. Kelley 2014
Chapter 9 © Klaus Fiedler and Mandy Hütter 2014
Chapter 10 © Steven M. Smith 2014
Chapter 11 © Kathleen B. McDermott, Kathleen M. Arnold,
    and Steven M. Nelson 2014
Chapter 12 © Eli Vakil 2014
Chapter 13 © Robyn Fivush and Theodore E. A. Waters 2014
Chapter 14 © Michael Ross and Emily Schryer 2014
Chapter 15 © Stanley B. Klein and Christopher R. Nelson 2014
Chapter 16 © William Hirst, Alin Coman, and Dora Coman 2014
Chapter 17 © Natalie A. Wyer 2014
Chapter 18 © Geoffrey Haddock 2014
Chapter 19 © Shanker Krishnan and Lura Forcum 2014
Chapter 20 © Sean M. Lane and Tanya Karam-Zanders 2014
Chapter 21 © Robert F. Belli 2014
Chapter 22 © Colin M. MacLeod, Tanya R. Jonker, and
    Greta James 2014
Chapter 23 © K. Anders Ericsson and Jerad H. Moxley 2014
Chapter 24 © Christopher Hertzog and Ann Pearman 2014
Chapter 25 © John Dunlosky and Sarah K. Tauber 2014
Chapter 26 © Janet Metcalfe 2014
Chapter 27 © Morris Goldsmith, Ainat Pansky, and
    Asher Koriat 2014
Chapter 28 © Dorthe Berntsen and Lynn A.Watson 2014
Chapter 29 © Chris J.A. Moulin and Celine Souchay 2014
Chapter 30 © Pär Anders Granhag, Karl Ask, and
    Erik Mac Giolla 2014
Chapter 31 © Ronald P. Fisher, Nadja Schreiber Compo,
    Jillian Rivard, and Dana Hirn 2014
Chapter 32 © Tim Valentine 2014
Chapter 33 © Scott D. Gronlund and Curt A. Carlson 2014
Chapter 34 © Amy Bradfield Douglass and Lorena Bustamante
    2014
Chapter 35 © Gabrielle F. Principe, Andrea Follmer Greenhoot,
    and Stephen J. Ceci 2014
Chapter 36 © James C. Bartlett 2014
Chapter 37 © Aldert Vrij 2014

© First published 2014

Library of Congress Control Number: 2013938425

British Library Cataloguing in Publication data
A catalogue record for this book is available from the
British Library

ISBN 978-1-4462-0842-7

Contents

Notes on Editors and Contributors

EDITORS

Timothy Perfect is Professor of Experimental Psychology at Plymouth University. He received his Ph.D. from the University of Manchester in 1989, and worked at Liverpool and Bristol Universities before joining Plymouth University in 1999. His research focuses on theory and application in long-term memory. He has been on the editorial boards of *Memory*, and *Applied Cognitive Psychology*, and is on the governing boards of the *Society for Applied Research in Memory and Cognition*, and the *Experimental Psychology Society*. Prior to taking on this volume he has co-edited three other books: *Models of Cognitive Aging*, *Applied Metacognition*, and *The Handbook of Applied Cognition*, *2nd edition.* He is clearly a glutton for punishment.

D. Stephen (Steve) Lindsay is Professor of Psychology at the University of Victoria, British Columbia, Canada. He received a BA from Reed College in 1981 and a Ph.D. from Princeton University in 1987. Most of his research explores the cognitive processes by which individuals attribute thoughts, images, and feelings to particular sources (e.g., memory, knowledge, inference). He served as Editor of *Journal of Experimental Psychology: General* from 2002 to 2007, and recently began a term as an Associate Editor of *Psychological Science.* Prior to co-editing this volume, he co-edited two other books on human memory. He is also a glutton (ambiguity intended).

CONTRIBUTORS

Jackie Andrade was educated in the UK at Cambridge and Manchester. She worked with Alan Baddeley at the MRC Applied Psychology Unit in Cambridge, followed by 12 years at the University of Sheffield. She has been Professor of Psychology at Plymouth University since 2007. Her approach to research is to develop psychological theories that help solve real-world problems, including drug and food craving, trauma memory, dental anxiety, and awareness in anaesthesia. Her current focus is the role of working memory and imagery in motivation. She co-authored *Instant Notes in Cognitive Psychology*, and edited *Working Memory in Perspective* and *Memory: Critical Concepts in Psychology*.

Kathleen Arnold is a postdoctoral associate in the Department of Psychology and Neuroscience at Duke University. She received her Ph.D. from Washington University in St. Louis in 2013. Her research interests center around human memory and learning with a special interest in test-potentiated learning, or the effects of retrieval on future encoding.

Karl Ask is Associate Professor of Psychology at the University of Gothenburg, Sweden, and is one of the founding members of the research unit for Criminal, Legal, and Investigative Psychology (CLIP). He received his Ph.D. in 2006. His research interests include witness psychology, investigative psychology, emotion, social cognition, and the processes of credibility judgments and guilt attributions. He is frequently involved in the education of police officers and other legal professions on various topics in legal psychology.

James C. Bartlett received his Ph.D. from Yale University in 1975 and has spent most of his career at the School for Behavioral and Brain Sciences at the University of Texas at Dallas. There he has served as Professor and in several administrative and leadership roles including Associate Dean of the School of Human Development, Dean of Graduate Studies and Research, Speaker of the Faculty, and Chair of the University of Texas System Faculty Advisory Council. He currently directs the UT Dallas doctoral program in Cognition and Neuroscience. A fellow of the Association for Psychological Science and the UT Dallas Center for Vital Longevity, his research projects address the factors of age, expertise, and individual differences in perception and memory for complex objects, patterns, and events including faces, visual scenes, melodies, and chessboard displays.

Robert F. Belli is Director of the Survey Research and Methodology Program, and Professor of Psychology, at the University of Nebraska–Lincoln. He received his Ph.D. from the University of New Hampshire in 1987. Belli's research interests focus on autobiographical and eyewitness memory, and the quality of retrospective reports in surveys, having authored scores of articles on these topics. He served as North American Editor of the journal *Applied Cognitive Psychology* from 2004–2009. Belli is co-editor of *Calendar and Time Diary Methods in Life Course Research*, and editor of *True and False Recovered Memories: Toward a Reconciliation of the Debate*.

Dorthe Berntsen is a Professor of Psychology at Aarhus University in Denmark. She received her education and training, including her Ph.D., from the Aarhus University. Her research focuses on autobiographical memory. Her work in autobiographical memory covers research on traumatic memories, involuntary (spontaneously arising) memories, and cultural life scripts, which are culturally shared expectations about the order and timing of life events in a prototypical life course. Recently, she has studied the interplay between memories for the past and images of possible events in the personal future. She is the leader of Center on Autobiographical Memory Research [CON AMORE], which is a Center of Excellence funded by the Danish National Research Foundation.

Lorena Bustamante attended Bates College where she majored in Psychology with a focus on social psychology. During her senior year, she completed a year-long thesis analyzing the interactions between investigators and eyewitnesses during investigative sessions. Bustamante presented her preliminary thesis findings and implications at the annual AP-LS conference in San Juan, Puerto Rico. She currently lives in Boston and works at an internal strategy consulting group.

Curt A. Carlson has been Assistant Professor at Texas A&M University – Commerce since graduating with his Ph.D. (cognitive psychology) from the University of Oklahoma in 2008. His M.S. in psychology also is from OU, and his B.S. in psychology is from the University of Nebraska–Lincoln. His approach to research involves taking methods, empirical findings, and theoretical perspectives from the basic research literature and using them to answer significant applied problems. Specifically, he conducts research within the domains of perception, attention, decision-making, and especially memory. His focus is on the dual influences of recognition memory: recollection and familiarity. Curt is especially interested in the impact that distinctive processing has on these processes vis-à-vis eyewitness identification.

Stephen J. Ceci earned his Ph.D. at the University of Exeter, England, researching memory development. He has continued for the past three decades studying various aspects of children's recollections, with a focus on their eyewitness reports. Since 1991 he has been the Helen L. Carr Chaired Professor of Developmental Psychology at Cornell University. Among his awards, he has been the recipient of the APA and APS Lifetime Contribution Awards for the Application of Science.

Alin Coman is Assistant Professor of Psychology and Public Affairs at Princeton University. He received his Ph.D. from New School for Social Research. His research explores how the effects of cognitive mechanisms, biases, and distortions are attenuated or facilitated by the social dynamics that guide human interactions. More specifically, he studied socio-cognitive processes that allow for the formation of collective memories. His research has been published in a variety of journals and book chapters.

Dora Coman is a member of the Cognitive Science Laboratory at the New School for Social Research. Her interests are the ways in which memory for medical information impacts medical decision-making. She is currently specializing in clinical psychology.

Nadja Schreiber Compo is Associate Professor of Psychology at Florida International University and the Co-Director of the Legal Psychology Graduate Program. She received her Ph.D. from the Westfälische Wilhelms-Universität Münster, Germany. Her research focuses on investigative interviewing, especially the interviewing of vulnerable witnesses. She is both interested in potentially detrimental and beneficial interviewing techniques and their underlying cognitive and social mechanisms to improve the quality and quantity of witness and victim recall. She is further interested in studying other "players" in the legal field, for example, real-world investigators' and legal professionals' perceptions, attitudes, and behaviours in the context of translational research.

Amy Bradfield Douglass is Professor of Psychology at Bates College. She has been on the faculty at Bates since receiving her Ph.D. from Iowa State University in 2001. Her major research area is eyewitness identifications, particularly social factors that influence witnesses' identification choices and testimony-relevant memory reports (e.g., confidence). Other research interests include juror perceptions of eyewitnesses and the interaction between investigative interviewers and eyewitnesses. She is currently serving as an Associate Editor of *Law and Human Behavior*, published by the American Psychological Association.

John Dunlosky is Professor of Psychology at Kent State University. His major area of interest is the study of metacognition as it pertains to improving education across the lifespan. He is the co-founder of the International Association of Metacognition, co-authored the textbook *Metacognition*, and has co-edited several books on metacognition.

Gilles O. Einstein is the William R. Kenan, Jr., Professor of Psychology at Furman University. He received his Ph.D. in 1977 from the University of Colorado. His research focuses on the processes involved in prospective remembering, how these processes break down in important real-world situations, and how they are affected by aging. He is on the editorial board of *Psychology and Aging*, and he and Mark McDaniel are co-authors of *Memory Fitness: A Guide for Successful Aging* and *Prospective Memory: An Overview and Synthesis of an Emerging Field*.

K. Anders Ericsson Ph.D. is presently Conradi Eminent Scholar and Professor of Psychology at Florida State University. After his Ph.D. in Sweden, he collaborated with the Nobel Prize winner in Economics, Herbert A. Simon, on verbal reports of thinking, leading to their classic book *Protocol Analysis: Verbal Reports as Data* (1984). Currently he studies the measurement of expert performance in domains, such as music, chess, medicine, and sports, and how expert performers attain their superior performance by acquiring complex cognitive mechanisms and physiological adaptations through extended deliberate practice. He has edited several books on expertise, the influential *Cambridge Handbook of Expertise and Expert Performance* and the recent *Development of Professional Expertise*. He is a Fellow of the Center for Advanced Study in the Behavioral Sciences, of the American Psychological Association and the Association for Psychological Science, and a member of the Royal Swedish Academy of Engineering Sciences.

Klaus Fiedler holds a Chair in Social Psychology at the University of Heidelberg, Germany. His research interests cover various topics, such as language and social cognition, affect and behavior regulation, judgment and decision making, inductive inference, and the analysis of adaptive cognition from a cognitive-environmental theory perspective. In several journal articles, he has also contributed to methodological problems in behavioral science. Klaus Fiedler has been Associate Editor of several journals, including the *Psychological Review*, the *Journal of Experimental Social Psychology*, and, presently, the *Journal of Experimental Psychology: General*.

Ronald P. Fisher earned his Ph.D. from The Ohio State University (1973) and is currently Professor of Psychology at Florida International University (since 1978). His major areas of interest include eyewitness memory (interviewing techniques to enhance memory; understanding inconsistency in witness recollection) and detecting deception, and he has contributed several articles and book chapters in these areas. He has co-authored *Memory-Enhancing Techniques for Investigative Interviewing: The Cognitive Interview*. He is currently the editor of the *Journal of Applied Research in Memory and Cognition*.

Robyn Fivush is the Samuel Candler Dobbs Professor of Developmental Psychology at Emory University, where she has been on the faculty since 1984. She received her Ph.D. from the Graduate Center of The City University of New York in 1983 and was a Postdoctoral Fellow at the Center for Human Information Processing, University of California at San Diego from 1983 to 1984. She is associated faculty with the Department of Women's Studies and a Senior Fellow in the Center for the Study of Law and Religion. Her research focuses on early memory with an emphasis on the social construction of autobiographical memory and the relations among memory, narrative, identity, trauma, and coping. She has published over 150 books, book chapters, and articles.

Lura Forcum is a doctoral student in marketing at Indiana University's Kelley School of Business. Her major areas of interest are persuasion and social media. Prior to her Ph.D. studies, she worked in public relations promoting the research findings of universities and research organizations.

Maryanne Garry is Professor of Psychology at Victoria University of Wellington. She received her Ph.D. in 1993 from the University of Connecticut, has published widely on the ways people can come to remember what never happened, and has worked with judges, police, and lawyers on the legal applications of this research.

Morris Goldsmith is Professor of Psychology at the University of Haifa. He completed his B.A. studies in Psychology at the University of California, Los Angeles, and received his Ph.D. in Cognitive Psychology from the University of Haifa. He has been a member of the Department of Psychology of at the University of Haifa since 1997, and is presently serving as Department Chair. He is also a member of the Institute of Information Processing and Decision Making (IIPDM). His research focuses on the interaction between cognitive and metacognitive processes in memory and learning and, in particular, the role of metacognitive monitoring and control processes in the strategic regulation of memory accuracy and informativeness. Other research interests include the interaction between attention and perceptual organization in visual cognition.

Pär Anders Granhag is Professor of Psychology at the University of Gothenburg (Sweden). He is the Funding Director of the Research Unit for Criminal, Legal, and Investigative Psychology (CLIP). He has conducted research on legal psychology for 20+ years and published over 200 scientific reports on various topics, such as eyewitness testimony, deception detection, and children's testimony.

Andrea Follmer Greenhoot is an Associate Professor of Psychology and co-director of the doctoral program in Developmental Psychology at the University of Kansas. She earned her Ph.D. at the University of North Carolina at Chapel Hill, with an emphasis on the development of memory for personal experiences. Her research looks at how children, adolescents, and adults make sense of and remember highly stressful or traumatic past experiences, and how these memories are related to mental health and well-being.

Scott D. Gronlund is Professor of Psychology and the Roger and Sherry Presidential Professor at the University of Oklahoma. His undergraduate degree in psychology is from UC Irvine, and his Ph.D. is from Indiana University. Before arriving at the University of Oklahoma he completed a postdoctoral fellowship at Northwestern University. Scott and his students apply basic memory research to solve real-world problems. This has included work on the impact of automation on cognitive performance, situation awareness, and prospective memory, especially with air traffic controllers. His current focus involves eyewitness identification, especially the role of the lineup. Scott prepared an Amicus Brief for the US Supreme Court for petitioner Kevin Keith. He is on the Editorial Board of the *Journal of Experimental Psychology: Applied* and is a Fellow of the Association for Psychological Science (APS).

Erik Mac Giolla is a Ph.D. student at the University of Gothenburg. He completed his B.A. at the National University of Ireland, Galway, before moving to Gothenburg where he earned an M.A. in philosophy and a M.Sc. in psychology. Since 2011 he has been a member of The Research Unit for Criminal, Legal and Investigative Psychology (CLIP). He has a broad interest in forensic psychology, and has been involved in projects within the themes of eyewitness psychology, deception detection, and investigative interviewing.

Geoff Haddock is a Professor of Psychology at Cardiff University. He received his Ph.D. from the University of Waterloo in 1995. After completing a post-doctoral fellowship at the

University of Michigan, he moved to the United Kingdom and held lectureships at Exeter and Bristol Universities before moving to Cardiff in 2001. His major area of interest is the study of attitudes and attitude change; he also maintains research interests in the self and time perception. He is co-author of *The Psychology of Attitudes and Attitude Change* (2010) and co-editor of *Psychology of Attitudes: Key Readings* (2012; both published by Sage). He is currently Associate Editor of the *Journal of Experimental Social Psychology*, having previously fulfilled this role for *Personality and Social Psychology Bulletin*, the *British Journal of Social Psychology*, and the *British Journal of Psychology*.

Christopher Hertzog is Professor of Psychology at the Georgia Institute of Technology. His major research interests concern adult cognitive development, especially individual differences in intelligence, memory, and metacognition. He has used experimental methods and longitudinal studies to evaluate the predictors of cognitive performance and cognitive change in old age, including metacognitive beliefs, activity, and personality. He has expertise in applications of multi-level regression and structural regression models in psychological science. He is a fellow of the American Psychological Association, the Association for Psychological Science, and the Gerontological Society of America. In 2012 he received the Baltes Distinguished Research Contribution Award from the APA's Division 20 (Adult Development and Aging).

Dana Hirn is a graduate student in the legal psychology program at Florida International University. She completed her undergraduate degrees in psychology and criminal justice at the University of Wisconsin–Milwaukee. Her research addresses questions concerning investigative interviewing, specifically developing techniques to better understand and elicit memories for decisions. Her second major research interest is working to "bridge the gap" between legal psychology researchers and law enforcement practitioners in the area of cooperative witness interviewing. Additional work interests include exploring the effects of rapport building and use of video models during child witness interviews.

William Hirst is Professor of Psychology at the New School for Social Research. He has worked on the topics of attention, amnesia, and, most recently, social aspects of collective and individual memory. He is widely published, with four edited books and over 100 publications.

Adam T. Hutcheson is Assistant Professor at Georgia Gwinnett College. He received his Ph.D. from the University of South Carolina in 2007 and continued to serve as an instructor and research there until 2012. His research focuses on spatial cognition and the effects of virtual environments on the estimation of distance and direction. This research has implications for many new technologies such as global positioning systems, augmented reality, and video games.

Mandy Hütter is currently a post-doctoral Researcher at the Chair of Social Psychology at the University of Heidelberg, Germany. She studied psychology at the University of Tübingen, Germany, from which she graduated in 2008. Mandy Hütter received her doctoral degree from the University of Freiburg, Germany, in 2010. Her research interests cover evaluative processes and attitude formation in general, and evaluative conditioning in particular, judgment and decision making, and group processes.

Greta James is a Ph.D. candidate in the Department of Psychology at the University of Waterloo, where she also received her undergraduate degree in Anthropology and Psychology and her master's degree in Psychology. Her major area of interest is the study of memory and decision-making, including her published work on understanding of probability. Other research interests include the study of research participants' use of and memory for information provided to them by researchers.

Tanya R. Jonker is a Ph.D. candidate and a Vanier Canada Graduate Scholar in the Department of Psychology at the University of Waterloo. She obtained her undergraduate degree at the University of the Fraser Valley in British Columbia where she was awarded the Governor General's Silver Medal. She obtained her master's degree at Waterloo, where she continues to research human memory. Recent published work has examined a contextual account of retrieval-induced forgetting.

Tanya Karam-Zanders is a doctoral candidate in Cognitive and Developmental Psychology at Louisiana State University. She previously obtained an M.A. in Cognitive and Social Processes from Ball State University. Her primary area of research interest concerns how emotion affects memory. Other areas of interest include how retrieval processes impact memory representations and the role of memory in social cognition.

Colleen M. Kelley is Associate Professor of Psychology at Florida State University. Her work has centered on determining the cues that are the bases for memory and metacognitive judgments, and understanding memory control processes such as retrieval and deliberate forgetting. She is currently a member of the steering committee of the International Association of Metacognition, and has served on the editorial boards of a number of journals. She is a fellow of the American Psychological Association and the Association for Psychological Science. She has a B.A. from Reed College and Ph.D. from Stanford University.

Stanley B. Klein is Professor at the University of California, Santa Barbara. He has been on the faculty since 1990. Prior to that, he taught at the University of Illinois and at Trinity University. His areas of interest include human memory, neuropsychology, social psychology, the self, evolutionary psychology, and philosophy.

Asher Koriat is Professor of Psychology at the University of Haifa. He completed his B.A. and M.A. studies at Hebrew University of Jerusalem in Psychology and Philosophy, and received his Ph.D. from the University of California, Berkeley. He taught at the Hebrew University in Jerusalem, and has been a member of the Department of Psychology at the University of Haifa since 1977. He is currently the Head of the Institute of Information Processing and Decision Making (IIPDM). His research has covered such topics as memory processes and organization, metacognitive monitoring and control, reading and text-processing, and mental representations and their transformations. Some of his recent work on metacognition has touched upon such themes as subjective experience and consciousness, intuition, and the interaction between conscious and unconscious processes in cognition and behavior.

Shanker Krishnan is Professor of Marketing at the Kelley School of Business, Indiana University. Prior to joining Indiana, he completed his Ph.D. from the University of Arizona in 1991. Shanker's research focuses on the intersection of consumer memory and marketing. Specific projects focus on implicit memory for information, memory interference processes, and role of memory in brand equity, brand associations, and brand extensions. He has published over 25 papers on these topics in marketing, advertising, and psychology journals.

Sean M. Lane is Associate Professor of Psychology at Louisiana State University. He received his Ph.D. in Experimental Psychology from Kent State University. His research has examined both basic and applied aspects of learning and memory. His major area of interest concerns factors affecting the efficacy of retrieval processes, especially those involved in source memory. Other research interests include eyewitness suggestibility, memory beliefs, the impact of emotional arousal on memory, and the application of findings from learning and memory research to educational settings.

Colin M. MacLeod is Professor and Chair in the Department of Psychology at the University of Waterloo. Prior to moving to Waterloo in 2003, he was for 25 years Professor of Psychology at the University of Toronto. He received his Ph.D. from the University of Washington in 1975. His major research interests have been in long-term memory and in attention, most recently focusing on how overt production benefits memory. This research has been continuously supported by the Natural Sciences and Engineering Research Council of Canada. He is former Editor of the *Canadian Journal of Experimental Psychology* and of *Memory & Cognition*.

Mark A. McDaniel is Professor of Psychology at Washington University in St. Louis, and Co-Director of the Center for Integrative Research on Cognition, Learning and Education. He received his Ph.D. from University of Colorado in 1980. His research is in the general area of human learning and memory, with an emphasis on encoding and retrieval processes in retrospective and prospective memory. His applied research includes studies on elaborative study techniques and enhancing learning through testing (repeated retrieval), with much of this latter work being conducted in classrooms. His prospective memory work has included identifying signatures of prospective memory performance in normal and pathological aging and potential interventions. McDaniel is on the editorial boards of *Educational Psychology Review, Journal of Applied Research in Memory and Cognition,* and the *Journal of Experimental Psychology: Learning, Memory, and Cognition*. He is just finished serving as president of Division 3 of the American Psychological Association.

Kathleen B. McDermott is Professor of Psychology at Washington University in St. Louis. Her research program focuses on human memory, especially the efficacy of retrieval in enhancing later memory and the relation between remembering and imagining.

Janet Metcalfe, Ph.D., is Professor of Psychology and of Neurobiology and Behavior at Columbia University. Her research focuses on both behavioral and brain imaging studies concerned with how people – children, young adults, elders, and people with schizophrenia and Asperger's syndrome – know what they know and use that metaknowledge to control behavior. Her work addresses hot and cool emotional self-regulation, as well as strategies of learning and agency. The matter of inquiry that underpins all of Dr. Metcalfe's work is to understand the mechanisms underlying how people are able to willfully control their own thoughts, feelings, actions, and learning. She is co-author, with Dunlosky, of *Metacognition*, and jointly edited *Metacognition: Knowing about Knowing, The Missing Link in Cognition: Origins of Self-Reflective Consciousness*, and *Agency and Joint Attention*.

Chris J. A. Moulin is a Cognitive Neuropsychologist holding a Chaire d'Excellence at the University of Bourgogne, Dijon, France (LEAD-CNRS (UMR 5022)). He conducted his Ph.D. at Bristol under the supervision of Tim Perfect and Alan Baddeley, before holding various posts at the University of Reading, University of Bristol, and University of Leeds. Chris's major research interest is the interaction between consciousness and long term memory, in particular metacognition and subjective experiences of retrieval. He is Editor of two Sage Major Works: *Human Memory* and *Neuropsychology* (with Alastair Smith).

Jerad H. Moxley is a Ph.D. student in the Department of Psychology at Florida State University.

Neil W. Mulligan is Professor of Psychology and Director of the Ph.D. program in cognitive psychology at the University of North Carolina at Chapel Hill. He received his Ph.D. from UNC in 1994, and has also been on the faculty at Southern Methodist University and Illinois State University. His major area of research is human memory, with a focus on implicit memory, encoding processes in memory, and attention and memory. He is currently the Associate Editor of the *Journal of Memory and Language*, and has previously served as Associate Editor of *Memory & Cognition*, and *Experimental Psychology*.

Christopher R. Nelson was a student at the University of California, Berkeley. He since has gone on to bigger and better things and currently runs a rare guitar store in Los Angeles areas and moonlights in a local band.

Steven M. Nelson is a Research Scientist in Psychology at Washington University in St. Louis. He received his Ph.D. in Neuroscience from Washington University in 2009. He is interested in how parietal lobe regions contribute to memory retrieval and the application of cognitive neuroscience to testing-related research.

Eryn J. Newman received her Ph.D. from Victoria University of Wellington in 2013. She has published several papers on memory distortions, cognitive biases, and false beliefs. She is especially interested in the ways that tangential, nonprobative information can boost people's confidence that even false claims are true. She is currently doing postdoctoral work at the University of California, Irvine.

Ainat Pansky is Professor at the Department of Psychology at the University of Haifa and a member of the Institute of Information Processing and Decision Making (IIPDM). She completed her B.A. studies in Psychology and Computer Science, as well as her Ph.D. studies, at Bar-Ilan University. Her early work focused on numerical cognition and selective attention. Her current research focuses mainly on memory accuracy and distortion over time, memory and metamemory, effects of misleading post-event information, and influences of early memory testing on eyewitness memory.

Ann Pearman is a Research Scientist in the School of Psychology at Georgia Institute of Technology as well as a licensed Clinical Psychologist. Her major area of interest is in the study of the meaning of memory complaints in older adults. Other research interests include the study of personality and its effect on cognition across the adult lifespan as well as the interaction of emotion and stress in everyday functioning in later life.

Gabrielle F. Principe is a Professor and Chair of the Department of Psychology at the College of Charleston. She received her Ph.D. in Developmental Psychology from the University of North Carolina at Chapel Hill and later completed a postdoctoral fellowship at Cornell University. Her research, which examines the development of memory in young children, has been federally funded by the National Institutes of Health. Her new book is entitled *Your Brain on Childhood: The Unexpected Side Effects of Classrooms, Ballparks, Family Rooms, and the Minivan* (Prometheus, 2011).

Jillian Rivard is a graduate student of Legal Psychology at Florida International University. She received her Master's Degree in Forensic Psychology from Roger Williams University in 2009. She is interested in the factors influencing interviewing in both criminal investigations and intelligence gathering contexts. Her current research focuses on the effects of blind versus informed interviewing with cooperative witnesses.

Michael Ross is Professor Emeritus at the University of Waterloo. He joined the Waterloo psychology department upon receiving his Ph.D. from the University of North Carolina in 1971. Trained as a social psychologist, Ross has pursued various research interests, including mainstream topics in social psychology as well as the psychology of memory. In recent years, his interests in memory have focused on cognitive aging, perhaps in response to his own transition to senior citizen. His outlook on cognitive aging is quite optimistic. He argues that psychological research tends to underestimate older people's everyday cognitive abilities.

Emily Schryer received her Ph.D. in Social Psychology at the University of Waterloo. Her research examines sociocultural factors that influence successful adaption to aging. She studies the relationship between cognitive appraisals of autobiographical experiences and age differences in emotional, cognitive, and physical well-being. In a second line of research she examines how individuals adapt to changes in cognitive capacity with age. Her research studies how younger and older adults compensate for changes (real and perceived) in cognitive functioning on everyday memory tasks and how factors such as perceived self-efficacy, motivation, and task difficulty influence older and younger adults' use of compensation strategies.

Bennett L. Schwartz is Professor of Psychology and Fellow of the Honors College at Florida International University in Miami, Florida. He has been on the FIU faculty since receiving his Ph.D. from Dartmouth College in 1993. His main area of research is metamemory. In particular, he has studied the nature of the tip-of-the-tongue phenomenon and its relation to both retrieval and conscious experience. He has also conducted research on applications of memory research to education and episodic memory in non-human primates. He is author of the textbook, *Memory: Foundations and Applications, 2nd edition* (2014) and has co-edited several books.

Steven M. Smith is Professor of Psychology at Texas A&M University. He received his Ph.D. from University of Wisconsin in 1979, and he has been on the Texas A&M faculty since 1980. His major areas of interest are human memory, metacognition, and creative cognition. He has done interdisciplinary research on creative cognition in engineering design, human-computer interaction, and patent law, and he has served as an expert witness on eyewitness memory in numerous cases. He is co-author of books on creative thinking, including *Creative Cognition: Theory, Research and Applications*, and he is co-editor of *The Creative Cognition Approach*.

Celine Souchay is a CNRS Researcher at the University of Bourgogne, Dijon, France (LEAD-CNRS (UMR 5022)). She conducted her Ph.D. in Tours, France under the direction of Michel Isingrini. She held post-docs in Montreal, Canada, and Strasbourg, France, before taking a lectureship at the University of Plymouth, England. She moved to the University of Leeds in 2005. Celine's main interest is in metamemory and, in particular, the Feeling of Knowing, which she has researched in healthy ageing, dementia, Parkinson's disease, schizophrenia, and autism. She was guest editor at *Cortex* (Special Issue on Recollection) and *Memory* (Special Issue on Episodic Memory in Healthy Aging).

Uma (Sarah) Tauber is an assistant professor at Texas Christian University. She earned her Ph.D. from Colorado State University and completed a post-doctoral research fellowship at Kent State University. Her major area of interest is in understanding how people self regulate their learning, with a particular emphasis on how aging in adulthood influences self regulation.

Eli Vakil is Professor and former Departmental Chairman in the Department of Psychology and the Head of the Memory and Amnesia lab at the Gonda Multidisciplinary Brain Research Center at Bar Ilan University. He is also Director of the Rehabilitation Center for Veterans After Traumatic Brain-Injury (TBI) in Jaffa, Israel. He received his Ph.D. in Clinical Neuropsychology from the City University of New York in 1985. He worked at the Head Trauma Program at the Institute of Rehabilitation Medicine in New York University Medical Center, and in the Rekanati National Institute for the Rehabilitation of the Head-Injured Person in Israel. Prof. Vakil has served as a board member of the International Neuropsychological Society (INS) and as an Associate Editor of the *Journal of the International Neuropsychological Society* (JINS). He has published extensively in the area of memory and memory disorders in various populations (e.g., TBI, Parkinson's disease, and the elderly).

Tim Valentine obtained his Ph.D. from the University of Nottingham in 1986. He worked at the Universities of Manchester and Durham before being appointed to a Chair at Goldsmiths, University of London in 1997. He is an author of more than 80 publications on human face recognition and eyewitness identification. He has provided advice on eyewitness identification evidence in criminal cases, including the Lockerbie bomb. Recent research projects include investigation of video identification procedures, identification from CCTV imagery, street identification, and evaluation of a new method for constructing facial composites.

Aldert Vrij is Professor of Applied Social Psychology at the University of Portsmouth (UK). His main research interests are (i) nonverbal and verbal correlates of deception and (ii) people's ability to detect deceit. He received grants from the British Academy, Economic and Social Research Council, Engineering and Physical Sciences Research Council, Federal Bureau of Investigation, Innovation Group, Leverhulme Trust, Nuffield Foundation, and Dutch, British, and American Governments, totalling more than £2,200,000. His research has a strongly applied quality, and he works closely with practitioners (police, security services, and insurers), both in terms of conducting collaborative research and in disseminating the research findings via seminars and workshops. He has published 400 articles and seven books on the above topics, including his 2008 book *Detecting Lies and Deceit: Pitfalls and Opportunities* (published by Wiley), a comprehensive overview of research into nonverbal, verbal, and physiological deception and lie detection.

Theodore E. A. Waters completed his dissertation in Psychology at Emory University studying with Dr. Robyn Fivush. He is currently a post-doctoral research fellow at the University of Minnesota's Institute of Child Development. His research interests include the functions of autobiographical memory, the development of individual differences in autobiographical memory/narrative and relations between those constructs and psychological well-being. Currently, he is researching the influences of early attachment experience on adult autobiographical memory and narrative.

Lynn A. Watson is a post doctoral Researcher at the Center on Autobiographical Memory Research at Aarhus University, Denmark. She received her Ph.D. from the University of St Andrews in 2008 and has also worked at the University of Exeter. Her area of interest lies in the role of autobiographical memory during clinical disorders such as depression and PTSD and she has recently published a number of articles in this field along with her collaborator for the chapter in this volume. Her current goal is to help develop the scientific exchange of ideas related to the concept of autobiographical memory between cognitive and clinical psychologists alike.

Douglas H. Wedell is Professor of Psychology at the University of South Carolina. He received his Ph.D. from the University of California, Los Angeles, in 1984, spent time at the University of Illinois as a Post Doctoral Fellow and Visiting Assistant Professor before coming to South Carolina in 1989. His major focus of research concerns how context affects cognitive processing and representations across judgment, decision making, and spatial memory tasks. His interests in spatial memory were first stimulated by conversations and collaborations with his late colleague, Dr. Gary Allen. He currently directs a National Science Foundation sponsored research education program for undergraduates, Summer Research Experience in Cognitive and Brain Sciences, at the University of South Carolina.

Natalie A. Wyer is Associate Professor of Psychology at the University of Plymouth. She has worked in Plymouth since 2004 after holding academic positions at the University of Bristol and the Free University of Amsterdam. Her research interests focus generally on social cognition and more specifically on how both individuals and dyadic relationships are represented in memory, as well as on unconscious processes involved in social behaviour.

Preface

Timothy J. Perfect and D. Stephen Lindsay

It is dangerous in the preface of a book dedicated to the psychology of memory to claim a clear recollection about its origins. Given that we are both interested in source memory and unconscious plagiarism, if one of us did claim a specific recollection, the other might well be able to point to evidence to undermine that belief. Perhaps it is safest to acknowledge the many influences that led to this book.

Intellectually, the origins of this book can be traced back to Bartlett's (1932) book *Remembering* with its focus on the social and reconstructive aspects of memory, and to Neisser's (1978) rallying cry at the first Practical Aspects of Memory conference for more research on "interesting or socially important aspect[s] of memory." One consequence of that speech was the expansion of the breadth of research on human memory, represented by the breadth of chapters in the present volume. If Bartlett and Neisser are the distal influence on this volume, then the proximal influences are the many other inspirational researchers and colleagues who have worked, and continue to work, on applied topics in memory. Particularly influential in this regard were a series of international meetings dedicated to research on memory and its application. The second Practical Aspects of Memory conference (held in Swansea in 1987) was the first international conference TJP ever attended (as a wide-eyed postgraduate student trying to check out name badges for familiarity – a clear recollection is seeing Gus Craik, but failing to locate Robert Lockhart anywhere nearby). The excitement of hearing about topics such as metamemory, eyewitness memory, source memory, and autobiographical memory directly from the leaders in the field was undoubtedly formative in shaping his future research direction. For DSL, a major catalyst was hearing, in the early 1990s, the story of a senior citizen whose daughter had, over the course of two years of trauma-memory-oriented "therapy", developed memories of horrific sexual abuse. Our enthusiasm for these topics has also been maintained by our involvement in a series of biannual meetings of the Society for Applied Research in Memory and Cognition at which the majority of the topics included in this volume have been discussed.

Our aim in crafting this handbook was to capture the breadth of research on applied aspects of human memory. However, in so doing, we wanted to ensure a strong connection with mainstream research and theorising. This book is not an attempt to reopen the debate between proponents of the "laboratory" and the "everyday memory" approaches as to whether memory should best be studied in the laboratory or in the field. We have adopted a liberal interpretation of the term "applied" in our handbook as meaning "of applied value", rather than deriving a meaning based on where the research was carried out. While the term "of applied value" would make for a clunky title to our handbook, it conveys our interest in applying knowledge about memory to situations encountered in the real world. By this, we mean a fleshed out version of the term "memory", which is more than merely the number of items remembered: it reflects what is recalled, things that are recalled (or forgotten), how it feels to recall, what is the social purpose of sharing a memory, and how we can help ensure we remember and so forth. These are all aspects of human memory of applied value because they drive behaviour, just as much as the number of things that are recalled and forgotten. This applies whether the knowledge arises from theoretically motivated studies carried out in the laboratory, or from studies seeking to test ideas in real-world settings, and it applies whether that knowledge is in the form of a detailed theory or a set of empirical findings. With this overarching principle in mind, we solicited contributions that fell into four broad areas. In the order they appear in the current volume, these are: 1) Everyday memory; 2) Social and individual differences in memory; 3) Subjective experience of memory and; 4) Eyewitness memory. Having started out with this clear distinction in our minds, of course the reality is that most of the chapters we received cover a number of issues that could lead to them being relocated within the handbook. To provide a single example, Chapter 34 on social influences on eyewitness memory by Bradfield Douglass and Bustamante is in the "Eyewitness memory" section, but could just as easily be located in the "Social and individual differences in memory" section. But it also covers aspects of subjective experience and memory, and represents discussion of an everyday memory situation, and so could also appear in those sections. In the end, we were left having to make some difficult boundary calls on individual chapters. We hope that readers are sufficiently encouraged to read beyond their core area to see the value in all the excellent chapters we have received.

Our difficulty in appropriately placing some of the chapters illustrates our second aim in bringing together these topics into a single handbook: cross-fertilisation. Academic researchers have a tendency to work within a single framework. By this we mean that they tend to explore the same questions, use the same methodologies, attend the same conferences, use the same technical terminology and publish in the same journals (which reinforce the same practices). Anyone who has ever tried to publish a paper using a non-traditional paradigm within a field, or to publish a work guided by one paradigm in a journal that caters to another, will know how difficult this can be. Consequently, in order to advance in a field, researchers often have quite a narrow view. We sought to bring together researchers on a single theme (memory research of applied value) but with a variety of different approaches. In so doing, we hoped to broaden the perspective of researchers who were originally drawn to one topic in this volume, but were attracted by the obvious overlap with other areas and other approaches. Ultimately, the success of this volume is down entirely to the quality of the contributions, and we have been fortunate to solicit an excellent collection of chapters for this volume, and for this we thank all those involved. We also thank our excellent team of senior editorial colleagues who were enormously helpful in the editorial process. We are also grateful to Michael Carmichael, who has maintained his enthusiasm and support for this project for many years.

Everyday Memory

Memory for People: Integration of Face, Voice, Name, and Biographical Information

Bennett L. Schwartz

From the day we are born, we are immersed in a world with other people, both familiar and unfamiliar. Thus, the ability to recognize and remember other people is and has been critical to human beings and is likely to have played a role in the evolution of human cognition (Adachi, Chou, & Hampton, 2009; Macguinness & Newell, 2014). In this chapter, I review the data on memory for people: for their faces, their voices, their individual characteristics, and their names. This research comes from a variety of perspectives: cognitive neuroscience research, everyday memory, evolutionary psychology, neuropsychology, perception research, and traditional experimental psychology. The goal here is to synthesize this research into a coherent whole. Is there some common representation for individual people, for example, that binds together our memory of their faces, their voices, their names, their history, and their characteristics? These latter questions have only been partially addressed, but an attempt will be made to answer them here.

One of the crucial distinctions in memory for people is the distinction between familiar people and new or unfamiliar people (see Bahrick, 1984; Johnston & Edmonds, 2009, for a review). Familiar people include those

we know personally and those we know vicariously, such as athletes, celebrities, and politicians. Unfamiliar people are those we have just seen for the first time. In fact, it is a continuum, ranging from the highly familiar (e.g., a close family member) to the somewhat familiar (a casual acquaintance at work) to the unfamiliar (someone who just passed you on the street of a large city). Following Johnston and Edmonds (2009), it is the current hypothesis that we use different mechanisms to discriminate among familiar people than to recognize facial and other characteristics of new people. From a functional perspective, this is important. We have a history with familiar people, for good or bad. That is, we know we can trust our mother, but we know we cannot trust our boss. This comes about from many interactions with these people as individuals. Therefore, we must be able to recognize these people quickly and accurately. New or unfamiliar people may represent promise or threat. They must be learned quickly and added to the system that represents people. Therefore, for familiar people, the focus will be on models of representation and retrieval. For unfamiliar people, the focus will be on models of encoding (Johnston & Edmonds, 2009). Of course, recognizing unfamiliar people is important in one highly studied area of memory, namely eyewitness memory. Other chapters in this volume will address eyewitness memory, so I will mostly leave that topic for others.

BRIEF HISTORICAL OVERVIEW

Historically, memory for people has been divided into separate areas. There are researchers who study face memory (Bruce, Henderson, Newman, & Burton, 2001), a small number of researchers who study voice memory (Mullennix, Ross, Smith, Kuykendall, Conard, & Barb, 2011), researchers who study memory of people's personal characteristics (Kole & Healy, 2011), and researchers who study memory for names (Evrard, 2002). However, recently, there have been attempts to integrate the research into a common approach based on memory for individual people (e.g., Hanley & Cohen, 2008; O'Mahoney & Newell, 2012). As Hanley and Cohen discuss, memory for people is not like memory for other objects. In most cases, we do not have to recognize individual objects – a hammer is a hammer, a water glass is a water glass. Rather we must simply recognize an item as being part of a class of objects. Of course, we may have a favorite pen, a favorite mug, or a favorite wrench, but these are the exceptions, not the rule. However, in almost all cases, we must recognize individual people as individual people, and not as an exemplar of a particular category of people. Again, there may be exceptions, such as an athlete need not recognize an individual opponent, but rather just recognize him or her as being part of the other team. Indeed, Yovel, Halsband, Pelleg, Farkash, and Gal (2012) found that neonatology nurses were no better at identifying individual newborns than were control participants because such nurses seldom need to focus on faces of infants as individuals (parents will take comfort in those identity bracelets). But in most contexts, we do need to do so. Our first line

of person recognition is their facial appearance. So much of this review will focus on faces, rather than other aspects of "personhood." But the point remains – people must be recognized as individuals not as part of a class of objects.

Memory for faces has been of interest to psychology for a long time, particularly from the perspective of eyewitness memory (Münsterberg, 1908). Earwitness memory, however, is a much more recent interest (Clifford, 1980; Yarmey, Yarmey, & Yarmey, 1994). Witness memory is most often interested in a specific set of circumstances – a brief encounter, under stress, with a stranger. However important to legal circumstances, such memory is not the norm for people as they live their lives. More often, we must recognize well-known faces of family, friends, or work colleagues, or we must remember the names of casual acquaintances based on well-lit exposure to their faces and adequate hearing of their voices. Professors, for example, are occasionally greeted by former students in restaurants, bookstores, and other places. Unlike the eyewitness situation, this is a brief encounter with a familiar person, which does not occur during a stressful situation. Do we recognize these people and can we remember their names?

Another important historical development in memory for persons is the seminal model of face memory of Bruce and Young (1986). They were interested in how we represent familiar faces in long-term memory (see Figure 1.1). The model postulates a module known as the face recognition unit (FRU). FRUs are specialized devices designed to quickly and accurately assess whether a face is familiar or not. FRUs are connected to Person Identity Nodes (PINs). PINs are the central memory representations for individual people, containing information about the person's relation to the perceiver, his or her occupation, nationality, and other such biographic information. Important in the Bruce and Young model is that names are stored separately, in another node (the Name code node). It is the independent representation of

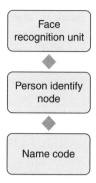

Figure 1.1   A simplified version of the face recognition model developed by Bruce and Young (1986).

name information that creates the situation in which we can recognize a familiar person, know quite a bit about them, but not be able to recall their name (e.g., Hanley & Chapman, 2008). Bruce and Young's model was influential in face memory research and continues to direct research today (Hanley & Cohen, 2008; Schweinberger & Burton, 2011).

Another important historical research trend comes from neuropsychological research on prosopagnosia, or face agnosia (Bauer, 1984). Prosopagnosia represents a neurological condition in which only face recognition is impaired, but other forms of visual object recognition are intact. In reality, such "pure" patients are rare for any neuropsychological profile. Research on prosopagnosia has focused on whether or not there is a special neural mechanism for recognizing faces that is different from recognizing other objects (Tanaka & Farah, 1993). If so, we would expect an occasional patient to show a relatively "pure" pattern. Research on prosopagnosia and recent neuroimaging studies suggests that there are unique neural mechanisms in the human cortex that are responsible for the recognition of familiar faces, as some prosopagnosic patients show impairments remarkably close to the expected pattern of impaired face recognition without impairment to other forms of visual object recognition (Moscovitch & Moscovitch, 2000).

Memory for proper names has also been a topic of interest for some time (Cohen & Faulkner, 1986). Central to the study of memory for proper names is the observation that we may often forget or misremember names of people well known to us (Hanley, 2011). That is, we may recognize a person's face and may remember factual information about them, such as their profession, but we fail to access their proper name. Indeed, face–name associations are often memories for which we have tip-of-the-tongue (TOT) experiences (Hanley, 2011; Yarmey, 1973). Thus, the oft-experienced phenomenon of being in a TOT experience for the name of a person you know well has also driven research on memory for people. At first glance, it appears that person memory is successful at integrating some forms of information (e.g., face recognition with personal knowledge), but poor at integrating other forms of information (faces with names). We will return to this issue later in the chapter.

Thus, four major trends have driven research on memory for people. They are the research on eyewitness (and earwitness) memory, the Bruce and Young (1986) model of face recognition, research on prosopagnosia, and the research on retrieval difficulties of known proper names. With these trends in mind, it is time to move to a discussion of the current theoretical and empirical debates in person memory. We start with research on face recognition.

MEMORY FOR FACES: IS FACE MEMORY SPECIAL?

Whether face recognition occurs via a special mechanism or through normal object recognition has been a debated topic for some time (Farah, Wilson, Drain, & Tanaka, 1998). Over the last ten years, however, a preponderance of the evidence now supports the contention that face memory is special – that there are specific neurocognitive mechanisms for the rapid recognition and learning of human faces as compared with other kinds of stimuli. There is an important terminological distinction here – face perception refers to the rapid identification of face stimuli as faces, whereas face recognition here refers to the identification of individuals from their faces. In this section, we will consider the evidence that supports the view that face recognition is served by a unique system. Most of this research will therefore draw on the recognition of familiar faces.

Most studies suggest that people are good at recognizing familiar faces even across various transformations whereas unfamiliar faces are quite difficult to recognize after transformation. For example, Bruck, Cavanagh, and Ceci (1991) asked participants to match college yearbook photos of classmates with the current images of those people. Despite 25 years of aging, the participants showed high accuracy in matching the 22-year-old faces with the 47-year-old faces. Hole, George, Eaves, and Razek (2002) showed that familiar faces could be recognized across a variety of computer-generated transformations, such as inversion and vertical and horizontal stretching. Moreover, people are good at recognizing familiar faces across transformations of age, hair style, camera angle, and a host of other variables, although often poor at recognizing unfamiliar faces across these transformations (Megreya & Burton, 2006) (see Figure 1.2). These findings have a number of practical implications. For example, they suggest that including photographs on identification cards may not particularly help in identifying identity thieves, as clerks and others may not be good at matching the face handing them the card with the face on the card (Kemp, Towell, & Pike, 1997).

Megreya and Burton (2006) argued that the special mechanism for face recognition is specific to familiar faces, and that unfamiliar faces are processed by normal mechanisms of object recognition (also see McKone, Kanwisher, & Duchaine, 2007). Their reasoning is based on the data with the matching of inverted faces. The inversion effect refers to the observation that people are poor at recognizing inverted (upside-down) faces relative to the inversion of common objects (Valentine, 1988; Yin, 1969). The standard explanation is that faces are matched by holistic face-specific mechanisms, which are disrupted by inversion, whereas normal object recognition is not. This has been taken as evidence that there is a specific face-specific recognition mechanism (McKone et al., 2007; Hanley & Cohen, 2008). Interestingly, Megreya and Burton found that unfamiliar faces showed less decrement in performance when the faces were inverted than when familiar faces were inverted, and that individual differences in performance with unfamiliar faces was positively correlated with performance on non-face objects, but that there was no correlation between non-face objects and familiar faces. As a consequence, Megreya and Burton argue that specific face-recognition mechanisms exist for familiar faces, but that unfamiliar faces use the same mechanisms as non-face objects.

Neuroscience research suggests that we have specialized neural mechanisms that have evolved specifically for face learning and face recognition. Neuroscientists have identified an area of the brain known as the fusiform face area (Kanwisher, McDermott, & Chun, 1997; McKone et al., 2007; Macguinness & Newell, 2014; Sergent, Ohta, & MacDonald, 1992). The fusiform face area (FFA) is located on the ventral surface of the temporal lobe, adjacent to the medial temporal lobe area. Although there is some debate as to how specific the FFA is to face recognition, most research now suggests that the area is involved in the recognition of familiar faces (and face-like objects) after an object has already been perceived as a face. That is, the FFA is an area for identifying familiar faces (Liu, Harris, & Kanwisher, 2010; Ewbank & Andrews, 2008). A separate area of the brain – the occipital face area (OFA) appears to be responsible for making the initial identification of a face as being a face, regardless of its familiarity (Liu et al., 2010) (see Figure 1.3). Thus, neuroanatomy supports the idea that there are

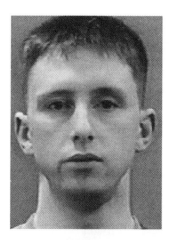

Figure 1.2 Try to find the face among the ten below that match the face above. It is there but is surprisingly difficult to find. From Megreya and Burton (2006). Memory & Cognition. Reprinted with permission.

differences between recognizing familiar and other objects. However, some research disputes that the FFA is unique to face perception; these researchers argue that the FFA is sensitive to other stimuli in addition to faces, and therefore it is inaccurate to refer to it as an area that specializes in face recognition alone (Haxby, Hoffman, & Gobbini, 2000; Minnebusch, Suchan, Köster, & Daum, 2009). Nonetheless, the bulk of the neuroimaging research points to the FFA as a distinct area for recognizing familiar faces (Liu et al., 2010).

Neuropsychological research consistently shows that it is possible to show dissociations between deficits in face recognition (prosopagnosia) and other kinds of object recognition (object agnosia). For example, Sergent and Signoret (1992) examined a population of diagnosed prosopagnosics.

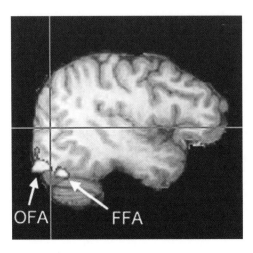

Figure 1.3   fMRI image of the right cortex. FFA = fusiform area; OFA = occipital face area. Reprinted with permission from Ewbank and Andrews (2008). *Neuroimage*, 40, 1857–1870.

They found that the prosopagnosics were superior at recognizing makes of cars than they were at identifying familiar faces. In a double-dissociation study, Moscovitch and Moscovitch (2000) examined prosopagnosic patients and patients diagnosed with object agnosia. The object agnosics were normal at face recognition, but showed deficits in object recognition. In contrast, the prosopagnosic patients showed deficits in facial recognition but not object recognition. Tippett, Miller, and Farah (2000) examined a patient who performed fine on visual tests, including object recognition, but had a selective deficit in learning to recognize new faces. Tippett et al. defined this patient as prosopamnesic, as this patient's problems were with learning new faces rather than recognizing familiar faces. More recently, Busigny and Rossion (2011) identified a prosopagnosic patient with severe deficits with recognizing faces, but who did not show object recognition deficits even when those deficits tapped into global processing. Global processing here means that faces are perceived as a whole, rather than a sum of specific parts. In each of the patients studied, the deficit was limited to faces and not seen for other visual stimuli. Thus, the data from prosopagnosic patients support a selective mechanism for face memory.

Even though prosopagnosics may have severe deficits in consciously recognizing faces, there is evidence that they are processing faces at a non-conscious level. Bauer (1984) found that prosopagnosics showed increases in galvanic skin responses (GSR) for famous faces, even when they could not recognize them as being famous. That is, there was an implicit process that was recognizing the faces and causing the physical reaction, even though the patient was not consciously aware that the face was famous. An interesting contrast is with Capgras Syndrome patients (Hirstein & Ramachandran, 1997). Capgras Syndrome is a neurological condition in which patients think that their family and friends have been replaced with identical-looking doubles. It is associated with destruction of white matter that connects the FFA with areas of the limbic system, which may add the "feeling" of familiarity (Ramachandran & Blakeslee, 1998). Capgras patients recognize people who are familiar and can identify who they look like, even though they do not think the person is the actual person they resemble. Hirstein and Ramachandran suggested that because the faces are no longer accompanied by a feeling of familiarity, patients think the face belongs to an imposter. Breen, Caine, and Coltheart (2000) showed that Capgras patients did not show normal galvanic skin responses to normal faces even when they knew whose face it was. It is possible that this galvanic skin response is correlated with the feeling of familiarity. Thus, there is a dissociation here between prosopagnosics and Capgras patients; prosopagnosics fail to recognize familiar faces but show a GSR, whereas Capgras patients recognize familiar faces (although they deny the identity of those faces) but fail to show a GSR. This dissociation is supportive of the idea of a special mechanism for face recognition.

There are rare cases of developmental prosopagnosia, a condition in which individuals have normal vision and normal social functioning, but show a selective deficit in face recognition (Duchaine & Nakayama, 2006). Recent fMRI research shows less activity in the FFA of developmental prosopagnosics than in normal controls when identifying familiar faces than when viewing other visual material (Furl, Garrido, Dolan, Driver, & Duchaine, 2011). Thus, the emerging trend from work with developmental prosopagnosics is more evidence to support that there are unique neural regions devoted to face recognition.

To summarize this research: Neuropsychological research has identified many prosopagnosic patients who show selective deficits in face recognition even though they do not have deficits in the recognition of other objects. There are also some patients with contrasting phenomena. Their face recognition is normal, but they have either a deficit in object recognition (object agnosia) or they fail to attach an experience of familiarity to a recognized face (Capgras Syndrome). Neuroimaging studies reveal unique areas of the brain that appear to be active predominantly in the act of face recognition. Thus, cognitive, neuropsychological, and neuroimaging research all lead to the same conclusion: the human brain has a unique system for recognizing familiar faces.

DIFFERENCES BETWEEN FAMILIAR FACES AND UNFAMILIAR FACES

Consider an experiment in which an image of a face is presented, and the participant is asked if the face is one previously seen (i.e., "old") or one not previously seen (i.e., "new"). In this standard old–new recognition test, a face may be judged "old" even if there is no other knowledge about the face other than the person remembers seeing the face previously (that is, a familiarity response). However, familiarity exists on a continuum from very familiar (your spouse's face) to moderately familiar (the face of the person

who works downstairs) to completely unfamiliar (a person you have never met). Unfortunately, little research directly addresses the continuum from familiarity to unfamiliar – rather it is the endpoints that interest researchers most (but see Megreya & Burton, 2006). As was apparent in earlier sections, most research suggests that the recognition of faces as objects distinct from others objects occurs by qualitatively different processes from the quantitative differences in judging a particular face to be familiar or not.

Johnston and Edmonds (2009) list a number of factors that can affect face recognition, both with respect to recognizing a face as "old," or in matching two views of the same face (see Table 1 in Johnston and Edmonds). These factors include the view or angle at which the face is seen, the expression on the face, the context in which the face is seen, whether the face is distinctive and the salience of internal features (i.e., eyes, noses, mouth, etc.) relative to external features (hair, ears, etc.). Johnston and Edmonds argue that a number of these factors affect the recognition of familiar and unfamiliar faces in different manners. Facial expressions, for example, have no positive or negative effect on the recognition of familiar faces, but a change in facial expression can increase errors in a matching task of unfamiliar faces. The salience of internal features will help make a familiar face more recognizable, but does not affect the recognition of unfamiliar faces. Based on this reasoning, Johnston and Edmonds argue that different mechanisms must underlie the recognition of familiar and unfamiliar faces.

For example, consider a study by De Haan and van Kollenburg (2005) who examined how internal and external facial features affect recognition of familiar and unfamiliar faces. They were also interested in how the left hemisphere of the brain and the right hemisphere of the brain differentially processed faces. In the experiment, participants judged whether two sequentially presented faces, viewed from different angles, were the same face or not. Half of the presented pairs were the same person, and half were not. They found that when faces were presented in the right visual world (which therefore were initially processed by the left hemisphere) differences emerged between familiar and unfamiliar faces. Recognition of unfamiliar faces based on internal features was slower and less accurate than recognition of familiar faces based on internal features. This pattern was not seen in faces presented in the left visual world (which therefore were initially processed by the right hemisphere). Recognition of external features (hair, ears, etc.) was not affected by any of the variables in either hemisphere. Thus, this study supports the notion that familiar and unfamiliar faces are processed in different ways, as the effect of internal features was greater for familiar than unfamiliar faces.

O'Donnell and Bruce (2001) also found that manipulating internal features affected recognition of familiar faces. They trained participants to recognize some faces by repeated exposure. They then compared trained (familiar) faces with untrained (unfamiliar) faces. For the unfamiliar faces, participants used external features to make same/different judgments, but for familiar faces, participants used internal features (e.g., eyes) to make the judgments, also supporting the distinction in processing between familiar and unfamiliar faces.

What about learning new faces? How does a face go from being unfamiliar to familiar? Clearly, a face must start off unfamiliar but then as we see and interact with the person, the face (and the person) becomes someone "familiar." Given that the mechanism for recognizing unfamiliar faces and familiar faces appears to be so different, it would be of interest to discover when and how a face transitions from one set of recognition processes to another. Surprisingly, little research has actually been directed at this question (but see Johnston & Edmonds, 2009). The research reviewed here suggests that the process is one of focusing on holistic aspects of the face's appearance rather than attention to particular, and changeable, features.

To support the theory that growing familiarity is associated with more holistic processing, Clutterbuck and Johnston (2005) familiarized participants with the faces of previously unknown people. As the participants' exposure to the faces grew, they were more able to discriminate internal features of those faces. This pattern matched the pattern seen with already well-known (famous faces). Burton, Jenkins, Hancock, and White (2005) showed that participants were better at recognizing an "average" of 20 exposed views of a particular face than they were at recognizing any particular view. Thus, even though the "average" had not been one of the learning trials, participants were better at recognizing it than a previously seen image of that face. Thus, the act of making a face familiar is getting a holistic, time-invariant representation of the face. Coin and Tiberghien (1997) reviewed research that shows that memory for faces is better if participants process faces in terms of personality judgments and other "deep" processing than if they process faces in terms of features. To summarize, Johnston and Edmonds (2009) make a convincing case that the process by which familiar faces become familiar involves attending to holistic features that make the face recognizable across a host of transformations.

There was a line of research that suggested that priming people to focus on holistic/global features leads to better face memory than priming people to focus on configural/local features. However, later research casts doubt on the early conclusions. In the original study, MacRae and Lewis (2002) showed participants a video in which they saw a perpetrator rob a bank. Later they showed the participants a series of "Navon" figures for 5 minutes (see Figure 1.4) (Navon, 1977). Some participants were oriented toward global processing and were asked to identify the big letter, whereas other participants were oriented toward local processing and were asked to identify the smaller letters. Finally, they were asked to identify the bank robber from a photographic line-up of people. Those that were oriented toward global processing

Figure 1.4 A Navon figure (Navon, 1977). Do you see a lot of small "A"s (local processing) or one big H (global processing)?

did significantly better than those oriented toward local processing or to a neutral control condition. Thus, causing people to shift to global or holistic processing allows them to recognize new faces better. However, Perfect, Weston, Dennis, and Snell (2008) noted that the original Navon effect shows that people are generally more attuned to the global effect in the Navon letters, seeing the big letter before the many smaller letters. Thus, they wondered if it was the ease of processing that allowed better face memory in the global condition rather than the priming of global features. Thus, Perfect et al. included a condition in which the Navon stimuli promoted local processing rather than global processing, as had been used by MacRae and Lewis. That is, they used stimuli that created a "local precedence" effect rather than the Navon "global" precedence effect. When participants were then asked to focus on the local level in the Navon stimuli, their performance in the face recognition task was as good as it was with global processing of globally oriented Navon stimuli. Thus, they argue the Navon effect is more about automatic processing than it is about holistic processing.

To summarize, most of the research supports the idea that faces are encoded and represented by mechanisms that are unique

to faces and largely qualitatively different from the mechanisms for the recognition of other objects. This assertion seems particularly true for familiar faces. I suspect that one of the challenges for face memory research over the next decade is to explore in greater depth the transformation of a face stimulus from new and unfamiliar to one that is easily recognized (i.e., Megreya & Burton, 2006).

VOICE RECOGNITION

As teenagers, whenever one of my brother's friends called on the telephone, I could invariably fool them into thinking that I was my brother. Despite being fooled by my prank several times already, some of my brother's friends continued to confide in my assumed identity over the telephone. However, our family resemblance notwithstanding, none of his friends ever confused us visually. Research has shown that we can identify others by voice alone, and, in some cases, it may be important, but voice recognition usually is less accurate than visual recognition (Hanley & Cohen, 2008; O'Mahoney & Newell, 2012). A major difference is that face recognition takes place visually across a spatial domain, whereas voice recognition takes place in the auditory system across a temporal domain. Although this may be obvious, it leads to different mechanisms for face and voice recognition.

Empirical studies confirm the superiority of face recognition to voice recognition. For example, Hanley, Smith, and Hadfield (1998) found that participants were more likely to judge the faces of famous people as being familiar than the corresponding voices of famous people. Moreover, faces were better cues than voices at eliciting information about the person. This is true even when the faces are blurred to lower visual recognition (Hanley & Damjanovic, 2009). Research, however, has shown that we can accurately determine gender from voice, and we can determine mood from voice (Stevens, 2004). However, identifying specific individuals is inferior to identifying individuals from their faces.

Neuropsychology has identified patients with phonoagnosia, a selective deficit in recognizing specific human voices but without a deficit in identifying other sounds (Van Lancker, Cummings, Kreiman, & Dobkin, 1988; Neuner & Schweinberger, 2000). Neuner and Schweinberger examined three patients with phonoagnosia. They found that the patients were no different from controls at distinguishing sounds other than voices. However, when they were asked to recognize individual voices, they could not perform above chance levels. Similarly, Van Lancker et al. examined patients who were unable to distinguish which familiar voices went with which person, though they were able to discriminate unfamiliar voices as being dissimilar. These neuropsychological findings suggest that, like face recognition, there may be unique networks in the brain responsible for voice recognition.

Stevens (2004) used fMRI technology to examine the neural underpinnings of voice recognition. Stevens was interested in whether recognition of voices differed in its neurological profile from that of memory for words. In his behavioral task, six different voices presented a series of words to participants. For half of the participants, the task was to recognize whether a word just spoken was the same word that was spoken two words earlier. For the other half of the participants, the task was to recognize if a voice that just spoke was the same voice that had spoken two words earlier. Stevens found that areas in the left temporal lobe were more active in voice recognition than word recognition, but that areas in the left frontal and parietal lobes were more active in the word recognition task than in the voice recognition task. The most distinct area in voice recognition was seen in the posterior cingulate cortex, the most posterior region of the prefrontal cortex (see Figure 1.5). This area is particularly relevant in the current context as the posterior cingulate has also been implicated in recognizing familiar names

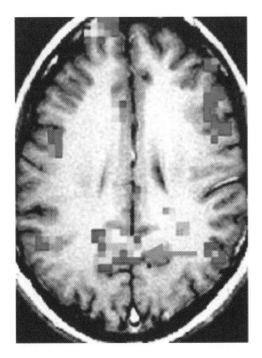

Figure 1.5   The arrows point to the critical region of the posterior cingulate. Adapted from Stevens (2004), Figure 4. Reprinted with permission from Stevens (2004), *Cognitive Brain Research*, 18, 162–171.

(Maddock, Garrett, & Buonocore, 2001) and in recognizing familiar faces (Shah et al., 2001). Thus, it is likely that the posterior cingulate brings together information about people and integrates it into a common experience of familiarity or recognition. As the posterior cingulate cortex has extensive connections with limbic system structures (some consider it part of the limbic system), it may be involved in the subjective experience of familiarity when we hear a familiar voice or see a familiar face.

INTEGRATION OF VOICE AND FACE MEMORY

Hearing a new voice, like seeing a new face, is not a "blank slate." We can immediately begin to categorize the person based on the voice we hear. Upon hearing a new voice, we can categorize a person along a number of dimensions include age, sex, native language, and perhaps even ethnicity or regional identity. Research on the integration of voice and face memory has capitalized on our immediate categorization to explore the nature of the integration. That is, it is possible in the lab to manipulate these relations. What happens, for example, when a female voice is presented coming out of a male face? Or the voice of one famous person is superimposed onto the face of another famous person?

Schweinberger, Robertson, and Kaufmann (2007) examined voice recognition of familiar and unfamiliar people, either accompanied by a matching face or a non-matching face. For familiar, but not for unfamiliar, voices, voice recognition was impaired when a presented face did not match the presented voice. That is, if participants were familiar with the person, the mismatched face impaired their ability to recognize that person's voice. Freeman and Ambady (2011) required participants to make speeded judgments as to whether a face was male or female. Accompanying the face was a voice. Half of the voices matched the face in terms of the range of pitch usually seen for males and females, and half of the voices were mismatched. Mismatched voices and faces resulted in increased response times in the gender judgment task. Moreover, participants' hands hesitated before moving to the button to indicate the correct gender when the voice did not match the face. Nonetheless, the face cues almost always overpowered the voice cues in making gender matches. In addition, De Gelder and Vroomen (2000) showed that sad faces were judged to be less sad when they were accompanied by a happy voice rather than a sad voice. Thus, clearly voices and faces are integrated temporally before such decisions are made. Koizumi et al. (2011) found, however, that anxious people tended to judge a face as anxious regardless of whether the voice or the face or both was exhibiting anxiety. Thus, in anxious people, the integration may be biased in favor of whichever modality expresses that anxiety.

Neuroimaging data suggest pathways for the integration of voice and face information. In particular, it is known that face recognition takes place in regions of the occipital lobe and the FFA in the temporal lobe. Other studies have linked voice recognition to areas in the left temporal lobe, adjacent to auditory processing areas as well as the posterior cingulate in the prefrontal lobe (Stevens, 2004). Campanella and Belin (2007) reviewed the existing neuroscience literature on voice/face integration. They concluded that the research points to the posterior cingulate (specifically, the retrosplenial cortex) as well as regions in the anterior temporal that integrate voice and face information into a common percept of an individual person. Joassin, Pesenti, Maurage, Verreckt, Bruyer, and Campanella (2011) examined face recognition, voice recognition, and face–voice association recognition while using fMRI scanning. They found that the areas unique to the associative task were the left angular gyrus (parietal lobe, adjacent to the occipital lobe) and the right hippocampus. The involvement of the hippocampus suggests that memory representations are present that link voice and face in the representation of a person. Thus, at this point there is accumulating evidence to suggest both the cognitive mechanisms and neural underpinnings of the integration of voice and face information.

MEMORY FOR PERSONAL INFORMATION

Critical in the representation of an individual are their personal characteristics. In addition to a person's name, face, and voice we must also remember the specifics of their personality, their relationship to ourselves, and other aspects of the person, such as dietary restrictions or health issues. Indeed, in keeping with the theme that aspects of personhood are better remembered than corresponding details for other objects, Mesoudi, Whiten, and Dunbar (2006) found that facts about people were better remembered than facts about objects. In the face domain, we have seen how familiar faces and unfamiliar faces are treated differently by our memory systems. This is also the case for information about a particular person. Kole and Healy (2011) asked participants to learn new facts about either familiar people (friends and family) or unfamiliar people. Although the new information was completely fictional, participants learned more rapidly new information about familiar people than unfamiliar, and the participants retained the new information longer for familiar people. Thus, familiarity puts a spotlight on biographical information as well as facial information (similar to the self-reference effect, see Klein and Nelson, Chapter 15, this volume).

PERSON IDENTITY: WHAT'S IN A NAME?

Think of a famous person, the president or prime minister of your native country. Think of his or her face, voice, gait, build, etc. You probably know a few facts about this person; their political party, if they have been a successful leader, where they went to college, what political positions they held before they reached the top. All these things tell you a lot about this person, their character, their future, and their past. But what additional information do the names "Barack Obama," "David Cameron," "Julia Gillard," "Enda Kenny," "Portia Simpson-Miller," or "John Key" (to stick to English-speaking examples) tell us about that person? There is nothing in the names that necessarily tell us about their politics, their educational background, or even what they look like. Perhaps names tell us just a bit about gender or ethnic or regional backgrounds, but little beyond that. Nonetheless, knowing a person's name is important social knowledge and critical in

the representation of people in memory. Thus, in order to understand the nature of memory for persons, we must also examine memory for names and how they are integrated with other aspects of person memory (Cohen & Faulkner, 1986).

In Western culture, as we have just seen, names are completely arbitrary in their association with the person. Thus, to use canonical examples, few people with the last name of Potter are actually potters (or wizards, for that matter), nor are many Taylors actually tailors. Indeed, neither surname (last names) nor given names (first names) usually have any real connection with a person's appearance, voice, profession, or attributes. Even parents who choose eccentric names for their children cannot anticipate what their child is going be like (e.g., Rain Phoenix). In contrast, nicknames often capture some trait of the person, either related to his or her physical appearance or personality (e.g., "Scarface," "Red," "Sleepy," "Dances with Wolves"). Brédart and Valentine (1998) examined people's ability to recall the names of cartoon characters. Some of the characters were chosen because their name was linked to some aspect of their character, whereas other cartoon characters had typical arbitrary names. Brédart and Valentine found that participants had many more retrieval failures for the arbitrary names than they did for the descriptive names, despite the fact that the characters were equally familiar. McWeeney, Young, Hay, and Ellis (1987) argued that names are poorly remembered exactly because of their arbitrary association to individuals. Indeed, in McWeeney et al.'s experiment, participants were more likely to remember the word "baker" if it had been used to describe a person's profession than if it had been used as their surname. Recent research suggests that people are less aware of the difficulties of learning names. Tauber and Rhodes (2010) found that judgments of learning for names were overconfident – more so than their overconfidence for occupations. Tauber and Rhodes suggested that this overconfidence for name learning may also contribute to poor memory for names.

Consider a person you know well, but is not a close friend or relative, perhaps someone who works in a nearby office. You recognize her face, you recognize her voice, you know her approximate age, you know her occupation, you know her ethnicity, you have spoken to her about her family, and you had a short discussion of where she went on vacation last summer. Now consider entering an elevator with her. You say hello and attempt to retrieve her name and fail to do so, despite all this knowledge you have of this woman. This is a common experience and one that increases as we age (Evrard, 2002; Hanley, 2011). We may experience a tip-of-the-tongue state (TOT) that tells us we certainly know the name even if we cannot retrieve it.

TOTs are defined as the feeling of temporary inaccessibility (Schwartz & Metcalfe, 2011). That is, TOTs are feelings that we have some information stored in memory, but we cannot retrieve it at the moment. There are two critical aspects of a TOT. There is retrieval failure, which is common for proper names, and then there is the metacognitive awareness of the retrieval failure, which comes in the form of a TOT experience. It is important to distinguish the feeling of temporary inaccessibility (experience) from the inability to retrieve a known word or other target (retrieval failure) in understanding TOTs. Schwartz and Metcalfe (2011) review the dissociations that can exist between TOTs and retrieval failure.

Two views predominate in thinking about TOTs. In one view, TOTs directly reflect unretrieved knowledge and therefore inform us about the nature of phonological retrieval (e.g., Gollan & Brown, 2006). In this view, sometimes called the direct access view, TOTs are more common for proper names because phonological cues are necessary to retrieve names, whereas in many situations, only other cues (e.g., a person's face) are present. Thus, because proper names may not be used as much

as common nouns, they may have weaker phonological strength in memory, and are therefore more likely to be items for which we have retrieval failure.

In the other view, the metacognitive-heuristic view, TOTs are subjective experiences that result from monitoring processes, which are correlated with retrieval (Schwartz & Metcalfe, 2011). In this latter view, information that is related to the likelihood of having learned a person's name will increase the likelihood that they will experience a TOT when the person does not retrieve the name. Having information related to but not directly linked to the name will induce an experience of a TOT. Because having more information about a person is likely to be correlated with also having a representation of the person's name, this monitoring leads TOTs to be accurate predictors of retrieval. In this view, we have many TOTs for proper names because we have so much other information about individual people. The access to this person information informs us that we ought to be able to retrieve the target name.

Consider one study that examines TOTs for proper names (Brennen, Baguley, Bright, & Bruce, 1990). Brennen et al. asked participants to retrieve the names of famous people by asking general information questions about the person. For example, one of their questions was "In a Disney film, who played the musical governess of the Von Trapp children?" (Julie Andrews). If participants recalled the correct name, they moved on to the next question. However, if they did not recall it, they were asked if they were in a TOT and then given a second opportunity to recall the name. For some of the unrecalled items, a photo of the target person was shown whereas for other unrecalled items, the initial of the target person was shown. Brennen et al. found that including the photo did not increase the likelihood that TOTs would be resolved. However, seeing the initials of the person (e.g., J. A.) did facilitate more retrieval. That is, only phonological information cued the retrieval of the phonological name. Additional information in the form of a picture did not aid resolution. This supports the idea that it is access to phonological information or lack thereof that makes it difficult to retrieve proper names.

However, the Brennen et al. (1990) study cannot distinguish between the two models of TOTs themselves. In the Brennen et al. study, the additional information was administered after the TOT judgment was made. Thus, the presentation of the faces or the initials could not affect the likelihood of causing a TOT, rather only what allows retrieval failures to be resolved. Thus, this study is silent on the issue of whether the direct access view or the heuristic-metacognitive view better explains TOT experiences, although it does stress the importance of phonological information in retrieval failure of names.

What does it mean in terms of a model of person memory, however? The data suggest that the representation of names is not strongly associated to other aspects of the representation of a person. It is likely that it is easier to form strong associations between faces, voices, elaborated semantic information, and episodic events, than it is for any of these features to become associated with names. In terms of a model, such as the Bruce and Young (1986) model, names are inherently less strongly connected to face recognition units (FRU) or voice recognition units. In terms of the practical aspects of retrieval, phonological cues (first letter of first name) are better cues than faces or facts about a person.

The exception to these findings is the names of very familiar people. We seldom fail to retrieve, for example, the names of our spouses, parents, children, and best friends. That is, names that are frequently used are highly accessible and thus easy to retrieve. Brédart, Brennen, Delchambre, McNeill, and Burton (2005) found that naming familiar colleagues was faster than making other decisions about those people (their nationality or highest degree). Once again, familiarity plays a large role. Names of familiar people may be more closely linked to the representation of that person than names of less familiar people.

CONCLUSION

We now know a great deal about face memory, voice memory, and the memory of proper names. For face memory, there is an important distinction between familiar faces and unfamiliar faces, and there are special neural mechanisms in place for face memory. However, although familiarity is a continuum from the very familiar (spouse, parents, children) to the completely new (strangers passed on city streets), most of the research focuses on familiarity as a categorical variable. More research is required to examine how a face (or person) transitions from the object-recognition mechanisms responsible for new faces to the specific face-recognition mechanisms responsible for familiar faces. We have a harder time identifying an individual from his or her voice than we do from his or her face, but we can identify people by their voice. Names are particularly difficult to retrieve because, except for very familiar people, we do not get much retrieval practice for names so that the phonology is often difficult to retrieve. Names may be more difficult to access than other forms of person memory because they are largely arbitrarily related to the person.

Recognition of other people is of vital importance to us as individual people. It is a form of memory that was most likely shaped by evolutionary processes (Klein, Cosmides, Gangi, Jackson, Tooby, & Costabile, 2009). Crucial to memory for people is the ability to be able to integrate disparate information about a particular person. We need to know what a person looks like, how they talk, how they move, if they are trustworthy, if they are smart, what knowledge they have, and what we should call them. If I think that John is a good basketball player and invite him on my team, when, in fact, he is awkward and short, I've made a costly mistake. If I then address him by the wrong name, I may likely lose a potential friend. Thus, keeping information about individuals straight is functionally, if not evolutionarily, important.

Bruce and Young's (1986) influential model of face recognition acknowledged the importance of integrating such information into a common representation of a person. However, in the 25 years since, most of the research has examined only some aspects of person memory, namely face memory, voice memory, or at best, the integration of two features, such as face and name, or face and voice. I think that one of the challenges of the next 25 years of person memory research is to advance and test models that examine "memory for persons" rather than face memory, voice memory, and name memory.

REFERENCES

Adachi, I., Chou, D. P., & Hampton, R. R. (2009). Thatcher effect in monkeys demonstrates conservation of face perception across primates. *Current Biology, 19*, 1273–1279.

Bahrick, H. P. (1984). Memory for people. In J. E. Harris and P. E. Morris (Eds.), *Everyday memory, actions, and absentmindedness.* London: Academic Press, 19–34.

Bauer, R. (1984). Autonomic recognition of faces and names in prosopagnosia. *Neuropsychologia, 22*, 457–469.

Brédart, S., Brennen, T., Delchambre, M., McNeill, A., & Burton, A. M. (2005). Naming very familiar people: When retrieving names is faster than retrieving semantic biographical information. *British Journal of Psychology, 96*, 205–214.

Brédart, S., & Valentine, T. (1998). Descriptiveness and proper name retrieval. *Memory, 6*, 199–206.

Breen, N, Caine, D., & Coltheart, M. (2000). Models of face processing and delusional misidentification: A critical review. *Cognitive Neuropsychology, 17*, 55–71.

Brennen, T., Baguley, T., Bright, J., & Bruce, V. (1990). Resolving semantically-induced tip-of-the-tongue states for proper names. *Memory & Cognition, 18*, 339–347.

Bruce, V., Henderson, Z., Newman, C., & Burton, A. (2001). Matching identities of familiar and unfamiliar faces caught on CCTV images. *Journal of Experimental Psychology: Applied, 7*, 207–218.

Bruck, M., Cavanagh, P., & Ceci, S. J. (1991). Fortysomething: Recognizing faces at one's 25th reunion. *Memory and Cognition, 19*(3), 221–228.

Bruce V., & Young A. W. (1986). Understanding face recognition. *British Journal of Psychology, 77*, 305–327.

Burton, A. M., Jenkins, R., Hancock, P. J. B., & White, D. (2005). Robust representations of face recognition: The power of averages. *Cognitive Psychology, 51*, 256–284.

Busigny, T., & Rossion, B. (2011). Holistic processing impairment can be restricted to faces in acquired prosopagnosia: Evidence from the global/local Navon effect. *Journal of Neuropsychology, 5*, 1–14.

Campanella, S., & Belin, P. (2007). Integrating face and voice in person perception. *Trends in Cognitive Sciences, 11*, 535–543.

Clifford, B. R. (1980). Voice identification by human listeners: On earwitness reliability. *Law and Human Behavior, 4*, 373–394.

Clutterbuck, R., & Johnston, R. A. (2005). Demonstrating how unfamiliar faces become familiar using a face matching task. *European Journal of Cognitive Psychology, 17*, 97–116.

Cohen, G., & Faulkner, D. (1986). Memory for proper names: Age differences in retrieval. *British Journal of Developmental Psychology, 4*, 187–197.

Coin, C., & Tiberghien, G. (1997). Encoding activity and face recognition. *Memory, 5*, 545–568.

De Gelder, B., & Vroomen, J. (2000). The perception of emotions by ear and eye. *Cognition and Emotion, 14*, 289–311.

De Haan, E. H. F., & van Kollenburg, E. N. M. (2005). Lateralised processing of the internal and external facial features of personally familiar and unfamiliar faces: A visual half-field study. *Cognitive Processing, 6*, 189–195.

Duchaine, B. C., & Nakayama, K. (2006). Developmental prosopagnosia: A window to content-specific face processing. *Current Opinion in Neurobiology, 16*, 166–173.

Evrard, M. (2002). Ageing and lexical access to common and proper names in picture naming. *Brain and Language, 81*, 174–179.

Ewbank, M. P., & Andrews, T. J. (2008). Differential sensitivity for viewpoint between familiar and unfamiliar faces in human visual cortex. *Neuroimage, 40*, 1857–1870.

Farah, M. J., Wilson, K. D., Drain, M., & Tanaka, J. N. (1998). What is "special" about face perception? *Psychological Review, 105*, 482–498.

Freeman. J. B., & Ambady, N. (2011). When two become one: Temporally dynamic integration of the face and voice. *Journal of Experimental Social Psychology, 47,* 259–263.

Furl, N., Garrido, L., Dolan, R. J., Driver, J., & Duchaine, B. (2011). Fusiform gyrus face selectivity relates to individual differences in facial recognition ability. *Journal of Cognitive Neuroscience, 23,* 1723–1740.

Gollan, T., & Brown, A. S. (2006). From tip-of-the-tongue (TOT) data to theoretical implications in two steps: When more TOTs means better retrieval. *Journal of Experimental Psychology: General, 135,* 462–483.

Hanley, J. R. (2011). Why are the names of people associated with so many phonological retrieval failures? *Psychonomic Bulletin & Review, 18,* 612–617.

Hanley, J. R., & Chapman, E. (2008). Partial knowledge in a tip of the tongue state about two and three-word proper names. *Psychonomic Bulletin & Review, 15,* 156–160.

Hanley, J. R., & Cohen, G. (2008). Memory for people: Faces, names, and voices. In G. Cohen and M. Conway (Eds), *Memory in the Real World* (3rd edn.) New York: Psychology Press.

Hanley, J. R., & Damjanovic, L. (2009). It is more difficult to retrieve a familiar person's name and occupation from their voice than from their blurred face. *Memory, 17,* 830–839.

Hanley, J. R., Smith, S. T., & Hadfield, J. (1998). I recognise you but I can't place you: An investigation of familiar-only experiences during tests of voice and face recognition. *Quarterly Journal of Experimental Psychology, 51A,* 179–195.

Haxby, J. V., Hoffman, E. A., & Gobbini, M. I. (2000). The distributed human neural system for face perception. *Trends in Cognitive Sciences, 4,* 223–233.

Hirstein, W., & Ramachandran, V. S. (1997). Capgras syndrome: a novel probe for understanding the neural representation and familiarity of persons. *Proceedings of the Royal Society of London, 264,* 437–444.

Hole, G. J., George, P. A., Eaves, K., & Razek, A. (2002). Effects of geometric distortions on face recognition performance. *Perception, 31,* 1221–1240.

Joassin, F., Pesenti, M., Maurage, P., Verreckt, E., Bruyer, R., & Campanella, S. (2011). Cross-modal interactions between human faces and voices involved in person recognition. *Cortex, 47,* 367–376.

Johnston, R. A., & Edmonds, A. J. (2009). Familiar and unfamiliar face recognition: A review. *Memory, 17,* 577–596.

Kanwisher, N., McDermott, J., & Chun, M. M. (1997). The fusiform face area: a module in human extrastriate cortex specialized for face perception. *Journal of Neuroscience, 17,* 4302–4311.

Kemp, R., Towell, N., & Pike, G. (1997). When seeing should not be believing: Photographs, credit cards and fraud. *Applied Cognitive Psychology, 11,* 211–222.

Klein, S. B., Cosmides, L., Gangi, C. E., Jackson, B., Tooby, J., & Costabile, K. A. (2009). Evolution and episodic memory: An analysis and demonstration of a social function of episodic recollection. *Social Cognition, 27,* 283–319.

Koizumi, A., Tanaka, A., Imai, H., Hiramatsu, S., Hiramoto, E., Sato, T., & de Gelder, B. (2011). The effects of anxiety on the interpretation of emotion in the face–voice pairs. *Experimental Brain Research, 213,* 275–282.

Kole, J. A., & Healy, A. F. (2011). Memory for details about people: familiarity, relatedness, and gender congruency. *Memory & Cognition, 39,* 637–648.

Liu, J., Harris, A., & Kanwisher, N. (2010). Perception of face parts and face configurations: An fMRI study. *Journal of Cognitive Neuroscience, 22,* 203–211.

MacRae, C. N., & Lewis, H. L. (2002). Do I know you? Processing orientation and face recognition. *Psychological Science, 134,* 194–196.

Macguinness, C., & Newell, F. (2014). Recognising others: Adaptive changes to person recognition throughout the lifespan. In B. L. Schwartz, M. L. Howe, M. P. Toglia, and H. Otgaar (Eds), *What is adaptive about adaptive memory?* Oxford: Oxford University Pres. pp. 231–257.

Maddock, R. J., Garrett, A. S., & Buonocore, M. H. (2001). Remembering familiar people: the posterior cingulate cortex and autobiographical memory retrieval. *Neuroscience, 104,* 667–676.

McKone, E., Kanwisher, N., & Duchaine, B. C. (2007). Can generic expertise explain special processing for faces? *Trends in Cognitive Sciences, 11,* 8–15.

McWeeny, K. H., Young, A., Hay, D. C., & Ellis, A. W. (1987). Putting names to faces. *British Journal of Psychology, 78,* 143–149.

Megreya, A. M., & Burton, A. M. (2006). Unfamiliar faces are not faces: Evidence from a matching task. *Memory & Cognition, 34,* 865–876.

Mesoudi, A., Whiten, A., & Dunbar, R. (2006). A bias for social information in human cultural transmission. *British Journal of Psychology, 97,* 405–423.

Minnebusch, D. A., Suchan, B., Köster, O., & Daum, I. (2009). A bilateral occipitotemporal network mediates face perception. *Behavioural Brain Research, 198,* 179–185.

Moscovitch, M., & Moscovitch, D. (2000). Super face inversion effects for isolated internal or external features, and for fractured faces. *Cognitive Neuropsychology, 17,* 201–219.

Mullennix, J. W., Ross, A., Smith, C., Kuykendall, K., Conard, J., & Barb, S. (2011). Typicality effects on memory for voice: Implications for earwitness testimony. *Applied Cognitive Psychology, 25*, 29–34.

Münsterberg, H. (1908). *On the witness stand.* New York: Doubleday.

Navon, D. (1977). Forest before trees: The precedence of global features in visual perception. *Cognitive Psychology, 9*, 353–383.

Neuner, F., & Schweinberger, S. R. (2000). Neuropsychological impairments in the recognition of faces, voices, and personal names. *Brain & Cognition, 44*, 342–366.

O'Donnell, C., & Bruce, V. (2001). Familiarisation with faces selectively enhances sensitivity to changes made by the eyes. *Perception, 30*, 755–764.

O'Mahoney, C., & Newell, F. N. (2012). Integration of faces and voices, but not faces and names, in person recognition. *British Journal of Psychology, 103*, 73–82.

Perfect, T. J., Weston, N. J., Dennis, I., & Snell, A. (2008). The effects of precedence on Navon-induced processing bias in face recognition. *The Quarterly Journal of Experimental Psychology, 61*, 1479–1486.

Ramachandran, V. S., & Blakeslee, S. (1998). *Phantoms in the brain.* New York: William Morrow.

Schwartz, B. L., & Metcalfe, J. (2011). Tip-of-the-tongue (TOT) states: Retrieval, behavior, and experience. *Memory & Cognition, 39*, 737–749.

Schweinberger, S. R., & Burton, A. M. (2011). Person perception 25 years after Bruce and Young (1986): An introduction. *British Journal of Psychology, 102*, 695–703.

Schweinberger, S. R., Robertson, D., & Kaufmann, J. M. (2007). Hearing facial identities. *The Quarterly Journal of Experimental Psychology, 60*, 1446–1456.

Sergent, J., Ohta, S., & MacDonald, B. (1992). Functional neuroanatomy of face and object processing. A positron emission tomography study. *Brain, 115*, 15–36.

Sergent, J., & Signoret, J-L. (1992). Varieties of functional deficits in prosopagnosia. *Cerebral Cortex, 5,* 375–388.

Shah, N. J., Marshall, J. C., Zafiris, O., Schwab, A., Zilles, K., Markowitsch, H. J., & Fink, G. R. (2001). The neural correlates of person familiarity. A functional magnetic resonance imaging study with clinical applications. *Brain, 124*, 804–815.

Stevens, A. A. (2004). Dissociating the cortical basis of memory for voices, words and tones. *Cognitive Brain Research, 18*, 162–171.

Tanaka, J., & Farah, M. (1993). Parts and wholes in face recognition. *Quarterly Journal of Experimental Psychology (A) 46*, 225–245.

Tauber, S. K., & Rhodes, M. G. (2010). Metacognitive errors contribute to the difficulty in remembering proper names. *Memory, 18*, 522–532.

Tippett, L. J., Miller, L. J., & Farah, M. J. (2000). Prosopamnesia: A selective impairment in face learning. *Cognitive Neuropsychology, 17,* 241–255.

Valentine, T. (1988). Upside-down faces: A review of the effect of inversion upon face recognition. *British Journal of Psychology, 79,* 471–491.

Van Lancker, D. R., Cummings, J. L., Kreiman, J., & Dobkin, B. H. (1988). Phonagnosia: A dissociation between familiar and unfamiliar voices. *Cortex, 24*, 195–209.

Yarmey, A. D. (1973). I recognize your face but I can't remember your name: Further evidence on the tip-of-the-tongue phenomenon. *Memory & Cognition, 3*, 287–290.

Yarmey, A. D., Yarmey, A. L., & Yarmey, M. J. (1994). Face and voice identifications in showups and lineups. *Applied Cognitive Psychology, 8*, 453–464.

Yin, R. K. (1969). Looking at upside-down faces. *Journal of Experimental Psychology, 81*, 141–145.

Yovel, G., Halsband, K., Pelleg, M., Farkash, N., & Gal, B. (2012). Can massive but passive exposure to faces contribute to face recognition abilities? *Journal of Experimental Psychology: Human Perception and Performance, 38*, 285–289.

2

Memory for Pictures and Actions

Neil W. Mulligan

In a first course on Cognitive Psychology or Human Memory, students quickly discover that memory research relies heavily on verbal materials, typically quite simple verbal materials like lists of words. The earliest formal studies of memory by Ebbinghaus, the student learns, may not have used real words but they did use word-like materials (nonsense syllables). In modern research, as well, verbal materials predominate. Students come across many experiments in which participants are presented with a study list of words, followed by a retention interval, followed by a test, in which the participant attempts to recall the words (perhaps with the aid of other verbal memory cues) or recognize the words intermixed with still other verbal materials (the distracter items on a recognition test).

The most famous results in the field stem from studies using simple verbal materials. The classic levels-of-processing effect demonstrating that deep, semantic encoding is superior to shallow encoding, was initially demonstrated in experiments using word lists (Craik & Tulving, 1975). The generation effect, the finding that self-generated materials are remembered better than materials passively perceived, was first demonstrated and almost always studied with simple verbal materials (Mulligan & Lozito, 2004; Slamecka & Graf, 1978). Classic studies of the serial position effect, characterizing the separable manipulability of primacy and recency effects, and undergirding the distinction between short-term and long-term memory, were conducted with word lists (Atkinson & Shiffrin, 1968). The principle of encoding specificity was predicated on experiments using word pairs (Tulving & Thomson, 1973). Research on implicit memory (unintentional or unconscious influences of memory) largely relies on verbal materials (Mulligan, 2003). Likewise, neuropsychological studies of memory often use simple verbal materials to contrast the memory of control subjects and amnesic patients. Neuroimaging research makes use of the same paradigms, and consequently materials, as traditional behavioral memory research, rendering the cognitive neuroscience of memory heavily inflected by verbal processing (Eichenbaum, 2011).

Although much has been learned using verbal materials, it is natural for students to wonder if our understanding of human memory would be changed if other types of materials were considered. Are the principles and effects uncovered in memory research reflective of human memory in general or are they limited by the nature of the verbal materials used in the typical experiment? Despite the predominance of verbal materials, researchers have certainly considered this question, conducting many experiments using other types of materials. In some cases, the researchers were interested in whether other types of materials enhanced memory compared with verbal materials. In other cases, researchers were interested in whether the principles that govern memory for verbal materials generalize to nonverbal materials. Indeed, a number of researchers have wondered whether the "rules" of memory are qualitatively different for other types of materials (Cohen, 1981; Engelkamp, 1998; Standing, 1973; Zimmer, Cohen, Guynn, Engelkamp, Kormi-Nouri, & Foley, 2001).

In this chapter, we will discuss two domains in which nonverbal materials were used, research using pictures and research using actions. First, we will consider how these materials affect memory compared with verbal materials. Second, we will consider if the principles of memory are similar for these and verbal materials with respect to five effects from the memory literature. In particular, we will consider developmental and age effects, to determine if memory for pictures and actions demonstrates the same trajectories (in childhood and late adulthood) as memory for verbal materials. We will consider serial position effects in recall, especially primacy effects, to determine the extent to which classic results from verbal learning generalize to pictorial and action materials. We also examine two important encoding factors, the levels-of-processing manipulation and divided attention, to see if these factors influence memory for pictures and actions as they do verbal memory. These effects were chosen for two reasons. First, they are robustly displayed in memory for verbal materials. Second, these effects have been suggested as especially important for examining potential differences between memory for verbal and nonverbal materials. In particular, researchers have often suggested that pictures and actions lead to more

automatic forms of encoding than do verbal materials, and that these particular memory effects are likely candidates for uncovering differences across verbal and nonverbal materials (Cohen, 1981; Engelkamp, 1998; Stenberg, 2006; Zimmer et al., 2001).

These issues are especially important for applications of memory research to important real-world domains such as memory remediation in impaired populations, educational practice, and advertising. Applied memory research using pictorial information and actions has often been motivated by the possibility that these forms of information have a special status in memory, leading to greater memory encoding with less overt, controlled rehearsal (e.g., Ally, Gold, & Budson, 2009; Cohen, 1989; MacKay & Smith, 2006). It is important to evaluate this underlying supposition so that basic research might more profitably guide application.

MEMORY FOR PICTURES

The notion that pictures and imagery enhance memory has a long history in ancient writings in philosophy and rhetoric, and the earliest recorded mnemonic devices (e.g., the method of loci) are based on imagery (Yates, 1966). The earliest experiments on imagery concur, showing that images are better remembered than rotely rehearsed words (Kirkpatrick, 1894). Memory for pictures can be astoundingly good. For example, Standing (1973) presented participants with 10,000 pictures for a few seconds each, and found later recognition accuracy rates of 83 percent. Brady, Konkle, Alvarez, and Oliva (2008) demonstrated that participants retain highly detailed memory for large number of pictures, showing that we do not simply remember the gist of pictures (e.g., the name of the object) but we also retain substantial perceptual detail.

These studies demonstrate impressive memory for pictorial information but they do not allow us to directly compare memory for words and pictures nor determine the extent to which memory for the two types of materials might qualitatively differ. For example, it is not always clear what the verbal equivalent might be for a picture of a natural scene. Consequently, if memory for some set of pictures differs from some set of verbal material, it is difficult to know if the difference is due to the nature of the materials (pictures versus words) or to some other factor, like the complexity of the picture or the paucity of perceptual detail in the verbal stimulus. Furthermore, despite the impressive levels of picture recognition, other studies imply that recognition memory for pictures and words might not be tremendously discrepant. Shepard (1967) had participants study long lists of words or pictures of common objects and found accuracy rates on a recognition test of 88 percent for the words and

96 percent for the pictures, an advantage favoring the pictures but not dramatically so.

To allow more direct comparison of memory for pictures and words, researchers have generally used images (line drawings or pictures of real objects) that have unambiguous names (see Figure 2.1 for examples from Snodgrass & Vanderwart, 1980). Researchers can then compare memory for pictures that elicit high levels of name agreement with memory for the verbal labels of the pictures. In a typical experiment, participants are presented with an intermixed list of pictures and words and are later asked to recall the words or picture names. Memory is usually better for items presented as pictures, a result known as *the picture-superiority effect* (Paivio & Csapo, 1973). This picture-superiority effect is quite general, occurring across a number of encoding instructions

Figure 2.1   Some example pictures from the Snodgrass and Vanderwart (1980) norms.

and memory tests. For example, the effect occurs whether the pictures and words are presented in the same study list, or whether one group sees a list composed of all pictures and another group see an all-word list. The effect also occurs under both intentional and incidental encoding instructions. In the former, participants are explicitly informed about an upcoming memory test and are asked to intentionally learn the materials. In the latter, participants are simply given a task to carry out on the presented stimuli but are not informed of any impending memory test. The effect occurs when participants are asked to overtly name each picture or word, and when verbal naming is discouraged by presenting the items at a very quick rate. The effect occurs on a number of memory tests in addition to free recall. In a recognition test, participants see a list of old items mixed in with new items and must decide which of the test items are from the study list. Items studied as pictures produce higher recognition memory than items studied as words, a result obtained regardless of whether the test items are presented as pictures or words. Cued recall and serial-order recall tests also exhibit the picture-superiority effect (see Crutcher & Beer, 2011, for a recent review).

The picture-superiority effect has applied as well as theoretical relevance. Ally et al. (2009) found enhanced memory for pictures in patients with mild Alzheimer's disease and mild cognitive impairment, suggesting that pictures and images could serve as important memory aids in these populations. In healthy aging as well, pictures maintain their potency (as is detailed below), suggesting that using pictures and images may enhance memory function in normal as well as pathological aging. Advertising research demonstrates that consumers often exhibit better memory for brand names when the ads include images or logos of the brand, an example of picture-superiority effect in an applied setting (e.g., Childers & Houston, 1984; MacKay & Smith, 2006). Finally, educational researchers have often touted the importance of pictorial information as

a memory aid in learning even abstract mathematical and scientific concepts (e.g., Newcombe, 2010).

Interestingly, the superiority of picture memory has an auditory analog. Crutcher and Beer (2011) found better memory for environmental sounds compared with the verbal labels for the sounds. The sounds were brief (1–2 s) audio clips of natural and man-made sounds such as thunder or a ringing bell. As with pictures used in this type of research, the sounds were chosen because they elicited high levels of name agreement. Participants heard a sequence of the sounds or heard the verbal labels for the sounds (i.e., a list of words). As in the case of pictures, participants were more likely to recall the names of the sounds than the verbal labels (a sound-superiority effect).

Despite the impressive generality of the picture-superiority effect, there are some important limitations. For example, certain encoding instructions can eliminate the effect. If participants are asked to draw a picture of the object denoted by the word or simply imagine the object, the picture-superiority effect is eliminated. This indicates that overt or covert imagery processing for verbal materials can increase memory to the level found with pictures. The sound-superiority effect is similar. Crutcher and Beer (2011) included a third group exposed to the verbal labels but asked to imagine the environmental sounds denoted. This group produced the same level of recall as the sound group, indicating that the sound-superiority effect can be eliminated if the verbal group engages in imagistic processing of the sound. In the applied domain, a similar result has been reported. When pictures were added to an advertisement using low-imagery text, memory for the ad was enhanced. However, pictures added to ads with high-imagery text produced no such benefit (Unnava & Burnkrant, 1991). High-imagery text induces a degree of internal imagistic processing that renders an external image redundant.

Deep encoding tasks can also eliminate the picture-superiority effect. Durso and

Johnson (1980) had subjects encode words or pictures with various orienting tasks. In the shallow-encoding condition, participants simply named the item or identified the last letter of the word (or verbal label for pictures). In the deep condition, participants answered a meaningful question about the word or object. Participants in the shallow condition exhibited the normal picture-superiority effect whereas those in the deep condition exhibited equal memory for words and pictures. This indicates that semantic encoding, like imagery encoding, is capable of raising word recall to the level of picture recall.

Despite these limitations, it is clear that pictures produce superior memory than verbal materials under many conditions. However, this does not tell us whether the principles of memory uncovered with verbal materials are characteristic of pictorial materials. In the following sections, we focus on several classic findings from research with verbal materials to determine if the same findings apply when the materials are pictorial. The particular effects that we focus on speak to the automatic versus controlled nature of the encoding of verbal and pictorial information. This is most relevant because, to the extent that claims of qualitative difference between verbal and nonverbal memory are made, they often are based on the notion that a nonverbal form of information (e.g., pictures) is encoding more automatically than are verbal materials (see discussion in Cohen, 1981; Engelkamp, 1998; Stenberg, 2006; Zimmer et al., 2001). The findings discussed below are often attributed to controlled or strategic encoding processes for verbal information. To the extent that nonverbal materials entail more automatic forms of encoding, we might expect these effects to be eliminated or at least diminished with respect to verbal materials.

Development Trends

A robust and long-standing result from research using verbal materials is that memory improves through childhood into young adulthood. This result is often attributed to the adult's superior use of controlled encoding strategies (Hasher & Zacks, 1979; Schneider, 2011). If pictures are more automatically encoded than words, then developmental effects may not be as pronounced for pictorial compared with verbal materials. However, this does not appear to be the case. If anything, developmental trends for pictures are more pronounced than for verbal materials.

A typical result is reported by Defeyter, Russo, and McPartlin (2009), who presented words and pictures to groups of children age 7, 9, or 11 years old and to a group of young adults. Memory was assessed with a test of recognition using memory. All groups exhibited a picture-superiority effect except the youngest group. Recognition accuracy increased across the age groups both for words (the typical developmental effect found with verbal materials) and for pictures. Furthermore, the developmental effect was larger for pictures than words. Other researchers report the same result (Ritchey, 1980; Whitehouse, Maybery, & Durkin, 2006) or find a similar developmental effect for pictures and words (and consequently, a comparable picture-superiority effect for children and adults; Bevan & Steger, 1971). These results indicate that memory for both pictures and words exhibits a robust increase with age through childhood into early adulthood. There is no indication that picture memory is less susceptible to developmental effects – just the contrary. To the extent that developmental effects differ for words and pictures, they appear to be greater in the latter case.

Age Effects

Older and younger adults typically exhibit differences in recall and recognition memory, a result frequently attributed to differences in strategic or controlled encoding processes (Craik & Rose, 2012; Hasher & Zacks, 1979). Although much of the research on memory and aging uses simple verbal materials, there are a number of studies using pictures, affording the opportunity to determine if the age effect found with verbal materials generalizes to pictorial stimuli. As with developmental effects, if pictures afford more automatic encoding, then we might expect age effects to be minimized with these materials. Such a view also implies that the picture-superiority effect would be enhanced in older compared with younger adults. As was the case with developmental differences, the extant research shows no support for this possibility, instead demonstrating similarity in age effects for words and pictures.

A typical study is reported by Maisto and Queen (1992), in which healthy older (mean age of 68 years) and younger adults (mean age of 21 years) studied a list of pictures or words. Young adults later remembered more items than the older adults (the typical age effect), and both groups exhibited the usual picture-superiority effect. Most importantly, the effect of age on memory was comparable for words and pictures, and the groups exhibited a comparable picture-superiority effect (Keitz & Gounard, 1976; Winograd, Smith, & Simon, 1982). The foregoing studies used the common strategy of comparing simple line drawings of easily named objects with the verbal labels of the objects. Park, Puglisi, and Smith (1986) report that robust age differences can also be found with more naturalistic and complex pictures (photographs from magazines). In a delayed recognition test, younger adults recognized more of the pictures than did older adults, a result that held consistently for pictures varying in complexity and detail (Russo & Parkin, 1993). Consequently, the presence of a robust age effect on pictorial materials extends from simple, easily named line drawings to complex pictorial information found in photographs of natural and social scenes.

In general, memory changes in later adulthood appear to exhibit the same pattern for words and pictures. The robust effect of age on memory generalizes from verbal materials to pictures, and the effect appears to be of a comparable magnitude.

Serial Position Effects

When participants recall a list of items, the serial position in the study list has an important impact on later recall. In particular, the first few items in a series are typically better recalled than other items, a result referred to as *the primacy effect*. In addition, if the recall test immediately follows the study list, the last few items are typically better recalled than middle items, *the recency effect*. If recall is delayed with a brief period of distraction, the recency effect is typically eliminated but the primacy effect is maintained. Jointly, the effects of primacy and recency are referred to as *serial position effects*, a fundamental characteristic of human recall. Research on serial position effects typically makes use of simple verbal materials (e.g., word lists) so it is natural to wonder if pictures produce the same characteristic effects. Furthermore, in the traditional analysis of serial position effects, the primacy effect is attributed to strategic rehearsal processes, and its presence and size are taken as indicators of the extent to which strategic rehearsal has taken place (Atkinson & Shiffrin, 1968).

Direct comparisons indicate that pictures and words exhibit similar serial position effects. Madigan, McCabe, and Itatani (1972) presented subjects with short lists of words or pictures for immediate or delayed recall. The immediate tests exhibited primacy and recency effects of the same magnitude for words and pictures, whereas delayed recall exhibited a primacy but not recency effect, and this pattern was comparable for words and pictures (Bonk & Healy, 2010; Richardson, 1978). Dempster and Rohwer (1983) examined recall of pictures and words in children in grades 3, 6, and 9 for both immediate and delayed free recall. For immediate recall, the primacy effect was comparable for pictures and words through all grade levels, although for the younger grades, pictures produce a somewhat weaker recency effect than did words. Across several studies and age groups, the results consistently showed that pictures and verbal labels produce equivalent primacy effects.

The Levels-of-Processing Effect

A classic result in research using verbal materials is that words encoded in terms of their semantic features produce better recall and recognition than words encoded in terms of surface-level or perceptual features (Craik & Tulving, 1975). Although this effect is subject to important limitations based on the nature of the retrieval cues (e.g., Morris, Bransford, & Franks, 1977; Mulligan & Picklesimer, 2012), the levels-of-processing effect in standard memory tests such as recall and recognition is quite large and highly replicable. With regard to pictorial materials, several studies find a levels-of-processing effect, although there is some evidence that the effect is smaller for pictures than for words.

Foos and Goolkasian (2008) provide an extensive analysis of levels-of-processing effects in which each study word or picture was presented with either a shallow encoding question (focusing on a perceptual attribute of the item) or a deep encoding question (regarding category membership). Deep encoding produced better memory than shallow encoding for both pictures and words. Furthermore, when the memory test was free recall, the size of the levels-of-processing effect was comparable for pictures and words. When the memory test was recognition, the levels-of-processing effect was somewhat greater for words than pictures. However, no matter what the level of processing or memory test, pictures produced better memories than words. In contrast, the study by Durso and Johnson (1980) mentioned earlier, demonstrated a levels-of-processing effect that was larger for words than pictures, and found that the picture-superiority effect was eliminated

under deep encoding. In a related manipulation, Ritchey (1980) varied the amount of semantic elaboration by manipulating the complexity of a categorization decision made during the encoding of words and pictures. This enhanced recall for both pictures and words, but did so to a greater degree for words. These studies suggest that levels-or-processing effects may be attenuated for pictures compared with words.

Divided Attention

Ancient practical manuals on memory and rhetoric begin with the fundamental assumption that successful memory starts with attention (Yates, 1966). Likewise, the earliest modern researchers, such as Ebbinghaus and James, emphasize that attentional state during learning is a key determinant of retention. Empirical research concurs: distraction during memory encoding impairs (usually greatly impairs) later memory (see Mulligan, 2008, for a review). Of course, the bulk of the research on attention and memory has made use of verbal materials. A consideration of research using pictorial materials gives us no reason to question that attention plays a similar role in the encoding of pictures.

A typical result is reported by Parkin and Russo (1990, Experiment 1) in which participants were presented with line drawings of familiar objects in one of three condition. The full attention group named the pictures without any distracting secondary task. Two other groups named the pictures while simultaneously monitoring a sequence of tones, categorizing each as a high, medium, or low tone. For one of the groups, the presentation rate of the tones was slow (an easy divided-attention condition); for the other group, the tones were presented more rapidly (a hard divided-attention condition). The full attention group later recalled the most, followed by the easy divided-attention group, with the hard divided-attention group recalling the least (see Russo & Parkin, 1993 for a similar result). This pattern of results is quite consistent with the graded effects of divided attention on verbal materials (Mulligan, 2008). The deleterious effects of divided attention extend to more complex drawings (Park et al., 1986) as well as pictures of natural scenes (Wolfe, Horowitz, & Michod, 2007). Pottage and Schaefer (2012) found similar divided-attention effects on memory for neutral and emotional pictures.

One last study deserves mention. Talmi, Schimmack, Paterson, and Moscovitch (2007) presented subjects with pictures under full-attention or under one of two divided-attention conditions. In both divided-attention conditions, the distracter tasks entailed detecting tones played over headphones. The researchers used instructions to vary the emphasis placed on memory encoding versus the distracter task. In the first divided-attention condition, participants were told that paying attention to the pictures and responding to the tone detection task were equally important (50–50 emphasis). In the second divided-attention condition, the participants were told that the tone detection task was more important than the pictures, although the participant was still to maintain eye fixation on the pictures (tone emphasis). On a later recall test, memory for emotionally neutral pictures produced a graded effect of attentional emphasis. Recall was greatest in the full attention condition, next in the 50–50 condition, and worst when the emphasis was placed on the distracter task. This closely mirrors the results of studies on attentional emphasis using emotionally neutral verbal materials (Craik, Govoni, Naveh-Benjamin, & Anderson, 1996). With regard to attention, picture memory is not just generally similar to verbal memory but is similar even at a more fine-grained level.

Summary

Picture materials exhibit robust effects of age early in life (developmental trends) and later in life (age effects). Likewise, pictures demonstrate serial position effects,

levels-of-processing effects, and divided-attention effects. Considering studies in which pictures and comparable verbal materials have been compared, all of the factors that influence verbal memory also influence picture memory to about the same degree. With regard to the factors considered at present, memory for pictures seems to be generally similar to verbal memory. The one exception is the levels-of-processing effect, which often produces smaller effects on pictures than words. We will return to this last point after discussing memory for actions.

MEMORY FOR ACTIONS

The enhancing effects of action on memory were not appreciated as early as were the effects of images. It was not until the 1980s that researchers began to systematically assess the effects of physical action on memory (see Engelkamp, 1998, for review). In a typical study, participants are presented with a set of sentences or phrases describing simply actions (e.g., *knock on the door* or *break the pencil*). During the encoding phase of the experiment, participants either carry out actions, observe an experimenter carry out actions, or simply listen to action sentences. Carrying out actions usually produces better memory than either observing or listening to the actions, a result called the *enactment effect*.

In light of the known effects of imagery, it was important for early research to determine whether the apparent effect of action might instead be due to imagining the action in the course of planning to carry it out. Engelkamp and Krumnacker (1980; reported in Engelkamp, 1998) included an additional group of participants who imagined the actions, and found that imagining did not eliminate the enactment effect. Subsequent research has shown the enactment effect to be quite general. It is found on a variety of memory tests. On free recall tests, enactment typically produces superior recall of both whole sentences as well as sentence parts. Enactment enhances the recall of both nouns and verbs in sentences – that is, enactment enhances memory for the action as well as any objects acted upon. Tests of recognition memory exhibit the enactment effect, as do tests of cued recall, in which one part of the sentence (e.g., the verb) is used as a cue to recall other parts of the action sentence (e.g., the object) (Engelkamp, 1998).

The enactment effect also generalizes across various subject populations. As is typical with memory research, the bulk of the studies have been conducted with healthy young adults. However, the enactment advantage is also found with healthy older adults and with children as young as 1st grade (Foley & Ratner, 2001; Saltz & Dixon, 1982; Zimmer & Cohen, 2001). Mentally retarded adults produce an enactment effect, as do children with autism spectrum disorder (Cohen & Bean, 1983; Lind & Bowler, 2009). Adults with memory disorders also exhibit an enactment effect, including patients with Alzheimer's disease, Korsakoff syndrome, and amnestic mild cognitive impairment (Daprati, Nico, Saimpont, Franck, & Sirigu, 2005; Karantzoulis, Rich, & Mangels, 2006).

Research on action memory often emphasizes the importance of the motor component in producing the enactment effect. For example, the effect does not require the manipulation of actual objects. When people mime an action without actually handling an object (e.g., making the motion to bounce a pretend basketball), memory is enhanced compared with a verbal encoding condition just as it is when participants perform the action with a real object (e.g., bouncing a real basketball). Indeed, the size of the enactment effect is equivalent whether real objects are used or not (Engelkamp & Zimmer, 1997). This indicates that tactile feedback provided by the manipulation of objects is not critical to the enactment effect. Likewise, visual information does not appear to be critical. Mulligan and Hornstein (2003) found an enactment advantage even when participants were blindfolded, indicating that visual feedback

does not drive the effect. Similarly, Kormi-Nouri (2000) reports that blind participants demonstrate an enactment effect, further arguing against a role for visual feedback.

Consistent with this notion is the finding that reenactment during retrieval can enhance action memory. In a study by Engelkamp, Zimmer, Mohr, and Sellen (1994; see also Mulligan & Hornstein, 2003) subjects either listened to a series of action sentences or enacted them. A later recognition test consisted of a list of old and new action sentences. Participants either simply read the test item or acted it out prior to rendering a recognition decision. For items that had previously been encoded via enactment, enacting the sentence during the test produced better recognition accuracy than reading the sentence, a phenomenon labeled the reenactment effect. For items that had been verbally encoded at study, there was no benefit (or decrement) for enacting the sentence at test compared with reading it. Engelkamp et al. (1994) interpreted these results in terms of the encoding-specificity principle (Tulving & Thomson, 1973), arguing that the recapitulation of motor information would not enhance memory unless motor information was encoded at study and used during retrieval. Mulligan and Hornstein (2003) replicated the reenactment effect even when participants were blindfolded during retrieval, indicating that the reenactment effect is really due to motor recapitulation and not to the recapitulation of the visual information that accompanies reenactment.

The effect of action on memory has also been explored in applied research. Cohen (1989) provided the earliest analysis of the applied utility of actions for learning. Based on the view that actions are encoded more automatically than verbal materials, Cohen argued that action memory has important implications for curricular development. Likewise, as was the case with pictorial materials, actions have been suggested as a means for memory remediation in memory impaired populations (e.g., Mimura Komatsu, Kato, Yoshimasu,

Moriyama, & Kashima, 2005), as well as a means to preserve memory performance in healthy aging (Cohen, Sandler, & Schroeder, 1987; Feyereisen, 2009). In all cases, the animating notion is that actions are encoded in qualitatively different ways from verbal materials, prompting researchers to wonder whether these materials might be advantageous for groups with diminished ability to encode materials in effortful, strategic ways.

Developmental Trends

One early (and oft cited) study of action memory and development came to the conclusion that action memory shows little effect of age, in contrast to verbal materials, which show large developmental effects (Cohen & Stewart, 1982). This has been taken as evidence that actions are automatically encoding, and thus minimally affected by age, whereas verbal materials are subject to strategic rehearsal, and so are more sensitive to developmental effects. However, there are reasons to be concerned about this study because the verbal materials were individual words but the enacted materials were sentences. Differences in the materials (words versus sentences) may have produced the difference in results rather than enactment, per se. A more apt comparison is between action sentences that are not enacted and the same action sentences enacted. In addition, the enactment condition of Cohen and Stewart's study exhibited a small but non-significant increase in mean recall across age groups, raising questions about whether action memory really fails to produce developmental effects.

Another early examination of the enactment effect in children came to a different conclusion. Saltz and Dixon (1982) presented children (age 5–7) and adults with a list of sentences that they either acted out or merely listened to. Later, participants recalled more of the sentences in the enactment than listen condition (the normal enactment effect) and adults recalled more than children (the typical

developmental effect). Furthermore, there was an interaction between age and encoding condition, but in the opposite direction to that reported in Cohen and Stewart (1982): the age effect was larger in the enactment condition. Alternatively stated, the enactment effect was larger for adults than children. Similarly, Kormi-Nouri, Moniri, and Nilsson (2003) examined memory in children in grades 2, 4, and 6 who either listened to action sentences or performed actions, some of which used objects and others of which did not. Older children recalled more than younger children and all groups exhibited an enactment effect. Again, the developmental effect was greater for both types of enactment (with and without objects) than for the purely verbal condition replicating the results of Saltz and Dixon (1982). Generally speaking, when the action and verbal conditions use the same sentential materials, there is little evidence that enactment diminishes the developmental effect (and may actually enhance it) (Foley & Ratner, 2001).

Age Effects

At the other end of the lifespan, memory for actions clearly demonstrates age effects that are at least qualitatively similar to those found with verbal materials. For example, Earles (1996) examined memory for action sentences that were either enacted or simply heard. Younger adults recalled more than older adults, but both groups exhibited an enactment effect of the same magnitude, indicating an equivalent effect of age for actions and verbal material (Cohen et al., 1987). Feyereisen (2009) extended this analysis by including a third encoding condition in which the actions were observed by the participant. Both recognition memory and cued recall exhibited the usual enactment effects, in which enactment produced better memory than either listening or observing. Likewise, younger adults had better memory on the recognition and recall tests than did older adults. Finally, consistent with the results of Earles (1996), there was no interaction between age and encoding condition, indicating no differential age effects for actions, either enacted or observed (Mangels & Heinberg, 2006). Other studies have even reported a larger age effect in the enactment than listen condition (Dijkstra & Kaschak, 2006), consistent with the notion that age effects are at least no smaller for actions than verbal materials.

Finally, it should be noted that early studies by Bäckman and Nilsson (1984, 1985) reported that the effects of age are smaller (or entirely absent) for actions compared with verbal materials, another of the results initially taken in favor of the automaticity view of action encoding. However, many subsequent studies have made it clear that enactment can produce both robust age effects, and age effects equivalent to (or larger than) those found with comparable verbal materials (Feyereisen, 2009). More importantly, this same research group (Rönnlund, Nyberg, Bäckman, & Nilsson, 2003) subsequently came to the conclusion that memory for actions exhibits the same age effect as memory for verbal materials. These authors found several potential reasons why some earlier studies appeared to show reduced (or no) age effects for actions, including the possibility of ceiling effects in action recall of the young, floor effects in some of the older groups, and differences in participant selection criteria. This study introduced a large scale (N=1000) experiment demonstrating that age effects across the adult lifespan were equivalent for actions and verbal materials. In sum, the bulk of the research implies that action memory produces age effects equivalent to those produced by verbal materials.

Serial Position Effects

Cohen's (1981) initial exploration of action memory focused heavily on the primacy effect. Participants were given a sequence of short study lists (of 15 items) each followed by an immediate recall test. For some lists, the participants listened to a set of words, listened to a set of action sentences, performed a set of actions, or watched the experimenter perform the actions. After all the study-test blocks were completed, the participants were given a final free recall test in which they recalled materials from all the lists. On the immediate recall tests, the verbal conditions and the observe condition all produced the typical serial position effects: greater recall of the first items (the primacy effect) and the last few items (recency effect) compared with mid-list items. The enactment condition, in contrast, produced no significant primacy effect, although it did produce a recency effect. When questioned post-experimentally about encoding strategies, participants reported that during enactment lists, they did not actively try to remember the actions but for the verbal lists, they reported overt rehearsal. The lack of a primacy effect and participant reports about differential rehearsal strategies were taken by Cohen as indicating that enactment is a nonstrategic encoding process. However, it should be noted that this view is complicated by the final recall test, in which all conditions showed an equivalent primacy effect (along with no recency effect as is expected when recall is delayed), a point to which we will return shortly.

The pattern uncovered by Cohen (1981) has been replicated a number of times: immediate recall of short lists produces a primacy and recency effect for verbal items but not for enacted items (see Schatz, Spranger, Kubik, & Knopf, 2011, for a recent review). But the interpretation of this apparent difference may not be straightforward, as indicated by Cohen's (1981) result concerning delayed recall. Primacy effects in delayed recall are thought to reflect the same encoding processes as primacy effects in immediate recall, so the presence of a normal primacy effect at a delay for enacted items is problematic for the simple notion that these items are not strategically rehearsed. Likewise, Engelkamp (1998, pp. 109–113) reviews evidence indicating that for long lists of actions (e.g., 40 or 80 items), substantial primacy effects are evident even on immediate recall tests. For long lists, the average time between an item's presentation and the time of test is considerably longer than for short lists, even when the long list is followed by an immediate test. Consequently, the emergence of primacy effects for long lists of actions may be tantamount to the emergence of these effects at a delay when short lists were used. It seems likely that the pattern of similarities and differences in primacy effects between enacted and verbal items reflects not simply an encoding difference but an interaction between encoding differences and differential retrieval strategies that are applied at different retention intervals (Seiler & Engelkamp, 2003).

Levels of Processing

Cohen's (1981) initial study of the enactment effect not only examined serial position effects, but also the impact of levels of processing on action memory using shallow orienting questions (e.g., *How much noise is involved in doing the following task?*) and deep orienting questions (e.g., *How frequently is the following task performed in everyday life?*). On each study trial, participants were presented with one of the orienting questions, heard the action phrase, observed or carried out the action, and then answered the orienting question using a rating scale. Later recall of the observed actions was greater in the two deep encoding conditions than in the shallow conditions, the typical levels-of-processing effect. In contrast, recall of enacted items was unaffected by levels of processing. Subsequent research partially agrees with Cohen (1981) by showing that the effect of levels of processing is diminished in action memory, but the research also shows that there is at least some effect of levels of processing for enacted items. For example, Nilsson and Craik (1990) found that recall of both enacted items and verbal items exhibited a levels-of-processing effect, although the

effect was larger for verbal items (see also Zimmer & Engelkamp, 1999). Thus, there is at least some effect of levels of processing on enacted items although the effect is muted compared with the effect found with verbal materials.

In addition, there is very little difference in recall between enacted items and verbal items under deep encoding (Nilsson & Craik, 1990; Zimmer & Engelkamp, 1999). This elimination of the enactment effect under deep encoding is reminiscent of findings with the picture-superiority effect (Durso & Johnson, 1980). As was the case with picture memory, this has been taken as evidence that enacted items are deeply or conceptually encoded by default. As Zimmer and Engelkamp (1999) put it, "in order to perform an action upon verbal command, subjects have to understand the action." Relatively deep conceptual analysis of the sentence is required simply to carry out the task, whereas listening to an action sentence (or passively observing an action) does not demand such conceptual analysis.

Additional support for this notion comes from a study of serial position effects carried out by Seiler and Engelkamp (2003). These researchers found that when verbal items are encoded with a deep encoding task, the serial position curve in immediate recall changes to closely resemble serial position curves found with enacted items. That is, the verbal items no longer exhibit a primacy effect. Furthermore, when enacted items are paired with the same deep encoding task, the appearance of their serial position curve does not change, implying that overt instructions to conceptually encode the item are redundant with the conceptual processing that is "naturally" carried out with such items.

Divided Attention

There are relatively few studies on attention and action memory, but all report that memory for enacted items is disrupted by divided attention during encoding. Bäckman,

Nilsson, and Chalom (1986) presented participants with a list of action sentences with instructions to listen or enact. Attention was either undivided during encoding, or divided by having subjects count backwards by threes while listening to or performing the action sentences. Divided attention significantly impaired recall for both types of items. Engelkamp and Zimmer (1996) examined memory for enacted and verbal items with real or imaginary objects, and report the same result. In both studies, some experiments report that the effect of divided attention was equivalent for enacted and verbal items, and other experiments found that the divided attention effect was somewhat larger for verbal items (although in all cases the effect of divided attention on enacted items was significant).

An additional study (Kormi-Nouri, Nilsson, & Bäckman, 1994) examined memory for enacted items only, and found that divided attention produced a robust effect on memory. In this study, actions with real objects were encoded under full or divided attention. Later, the object name from each sentence was used as a memory cue, and participants were asked to recall either the verb from the sentence or the color of the object that was used for the enactment. Dividing attention during encoding reduced cued recall whether one retrieved conceptual information about the original event (i.e., the verb) or perceptual information (i.e., the object color), indicating that the negative effect of divided attention on memory for actions is not limited to any single aspect of the event. In sum, it is clear that divided attention reduces memory for actions as it does for verbal materials, and largely to the same degree.

Summary

Compared with pictorial material, there is more scope to claim that memory for actions differs from memory for verbal materials, although there are important points of similarity. First, developmental and age effects appear to be quite similar for actions and verbal materials with both types of material showing substantial effects that are comparable in size. Next, the effect of divided attention is quite robust for both verbal materials and actions. With regard to levels of processing, the basic effect is present for both actions and verbal materials but the effect is clearly larger for verbal materials. Finally, the primacy effect in immediate recall is missing for short lists of actions. This is a clear difference between verbal and action memory, although as noted earlier, subject to important limitations (i.e., only for short lists and immediate recall). Furthermore, when both verbal and enacted items are deeply encoded, the difference in primacy effects disappears. In sum, the pattern of differences does not lend support to the notion that actions are governed by wholly different mnemonic principles than those uncovered with research into verbal materials, but differences remain to be explained.

CONCLUSION

Although memory research is dominated by the use of verbal materials, researchers have examined other materials as well. We have considered two types of nonverbal materials, pictures and actions. It is clear that under many circumstances, both pictures and actions produce better memory than comparable verbal materials. In this sense, it might be claimed that an overreliance on verbal materials causes us to underestimate human memory at least quantitatively. This is an important point and one upon which applied researchers should capitalize. But a more important issue is whether principles that emerge from research with verbal materials generalize to other materials. Is memory for pictures or actions qualitatively different from memory for verbal materials? We chose to address this question with respect to five effects from the verbal memory literature (developmental trends, age effects, the primacy effect, the levels-of-processing effect, and divided-attention effects) both because these effects are robust and because these effects speak to the question of automaticity of encoding, one of the ways that the encoding of nonverbal materials has been suggested to differ from the encoding of verbal materials.

In the domain of picture memory, it is clear that all of these effects have been documented, rendering picture memory similar to verbal memory at least in these regards. Only with respect to the levels-of-processing effect is there an indication of difference, but this difference is again quantitative rather than qualitative, with some studies reporting that the levels-of-processing effect is diminished with pictures compared with verbal materials. For action memory, similarities with verbal memory were found on developmental, age, and divided-attention effects, but differences emerged on primacy and levels-of-processing effects. In both cases, actions tend to produce smaller effects than do verbal materials. Interestingly, accounts of picture and action memory suggest the same potential reason for the smaller levels-of-processing effects, and its complement result, smaller (or eliminated) picture-superiority and enactment effects under deep encoding. A claim that is often made is that both actions and pictures induce greater conceptual processing than occurs with comparable verbal materials (Seiler & Engelkamp, 2003; Stenberg, 2006; Zimmer & Engelkamp, 1999). Consequently, orienting tasks that emphasize semantic encoding are largely redundant with the encoding that already occurs for pictures and actions, producing little increase in performance under deep encoding with these materials. Given that verbal materials do not routinely induce deeper, conceptual analyses, the semantic orienting task has greater scope to enhance later recall. This produces both a larger levels-of-processing effect for verbal materials and a reduced advantage for pictures or actions compared with verbal materials. As noted above, obligatory deep encoding for actions may also account for

the difference in primacy effects, as action sentences encoded with a semantic orienting task exhibit the same serial position effects as actions do regardless or orienting task.

These final points indicate that there are, of course, differences in the encoding of action or pictures on the one hand, and verbal materials on the other. It appears that the encoding of these nonverbal materials more routinely entails analysis of conceptual information, so on this dimension at least, it might be argued that actions and pictures are encoded more automatically than verbal materials. However, this seems to be a difference in degree not kind, given that a semantic orienting task for verbal materials results in quite similar patterns of performance.

REFERENCES

Ally, B. A., Gold, C. A., & Budson, A. E. (2009). The picture superiority effect in patients with Alzheimer's disease and mild cognitive impairment. *Neuropsychologia*, *47*, 595–598. doi:10.1016/j.neuropsychologia.2008.10.010

Atkinson, R. C., & Shiffrin, R. M. (1968). Human memory: A proposed system and its control processes. In K. W. Spence and J. T. Spence, *The psychology of learning and motivation* (Vol. 2), (pp. 89–195). New York: Academic Press.

Bäckman, L., & Nilsson, L. (1984). Aging effects in free recall: An exception to the rule. *Human Learning: Journal of Practical Research & Applications*, *3*, 53–69.

Bäckman, L., & Nilsson, L. (1985). Prerequisites for lack of age differences in memory performance. *Experimental Aging Research*, *11*, 67–73.

Bäckman, L., Nilsson, L., & Chalom, D. (1986). New evidence on the nature of the encoding of action events. *Memory & Cognition*, *14*, 339–346.

Bevan, W., & Steger, J. A. (1971). Free recall and abstractness of stimuli. *Science*, *172*, 597–599. doi:10.1126/science.172.3983.597

Bonk, W. J., & Healy, A. F. (2010). Learning and memory for sequences of pictures, words, and spatial locations: An exploration of serial position effects. *The American Journal of Psychology*, *123*, 137–168.

Brady, T. F., Konkle, T., Alvarez, G. A., & Oliva, A. (2008). Visual long-term memory has a massive storage capacity for object details. *PNAS Proceedings of the National Academy of Sciences of the United States of America*, *105*, 14325–14329. doi:10.1073/pnas.0803390105

Childers, T. L., & Houston, M. J. (1984). Conditions for a picture-superiority effect on consumer memory. *Journal of Consumer Research*, *11*, 643–654. doi:10.1086/209001

Cohen, R. L. (1981). On the generality of some memory laws. *Scandinavian Journal of Psychology*, *22*, 267–281. doi:10.1111/j.1467-9450.1981.tb00402.x

Cohen, R. L. (1989). Memory for action events: The power of enactment. *Educational Psychology Review*, *1*, 57–80. doi:10.1007/BF01326550

Cohen, R. L., & Bean, G. (1983). Memory in educable mentally retarded adults: Deficit in subject or experimenter? *Intelligence*, *7*, 287–298. doi:10.1016/0160-2896(83)90019-3

Cohen, R. L., & Stewart, M. (1982). How to avoid developmental effects in free recall. *Scandinavian Journal of Psychology*, *23*, 9–15. doi:10.1111/j.1467-9450.1982.tb00408.x

Cohen, R. L., Sandler, S. P., & Schroeder, K. (1987). Aging and memory for words and action events: Effects of item repetition and list length. *Psychology and Aging*, *2*, 280–285. doi:10.1037/0882-7974.2.3.280

Craik, F. I. M., & Rose, N. S. (2012). Memory encoding and aging: A neurocognitive perspective. *Neuroscience and Biobehavioral Reviews*, *36*(7), 1729–1739. doi:10.1016/j.neubiorev.2011.11.007

Craik, F. I. M., & Tulving, E. (1975). Depth of processing and retention of words in episodic memory. *Journal of Experimental Psychology: General*, *104*, 268–294.

Craik, F. I. M., Govoni, R., Naveh-Benjamin, M., & Anderson, N. D. (1996). The effects of divided attention on encoding and retrieval processes in human memory. *Journal of Experimental Psychology: General*, *125*, 159–180.

Crutcher, R. J., & Beer, J. M. (2011). An auditory analog of the picture superiority effect. *Memory & Cognition*, *39*, 63–74. doi:10.3758/s13421-010-0015-6

Daprati, E., Nico, D., Saimpont, A., Franck, N., & Sirigu, A. (2005). Memory and action: An experimental study on normal subjects and schizophrenic patients. *Neuropsychologia*, *43*, 281–293. doi:10.1016/j.neuropsychologia.2004.11.014

Defeyter, M. A., Russo, R., & McPartlin, P. L. (2009). The picture superiority effect in recognition memory: A developmental study using the response signal procedure. *Cognitive Development*, *24*, 265–273. doi:10.1016/j.cogdev.2009.05.002

Dempster, F. N., & Rohwer, W. D. (1983). Age differences and modality effects in immediate and final free recall. *Child Development*, *54*, 30–41. doi:10.2307/1129858

Dijkstra, K., & Kaschak, M. P. (2006). Encoding in verbal, enacted and autobiographical tasks in young and older adults. *The Quarterly Journal of Experimental Psychology*, *59*, 1338–1345. doi:10.1080/17470210600695092

Durso, F. T., & Johnson, M. K. (1980). The effects of orienting task on recognition, recall, and modality confusion of pictures and words. *Journal of Verbal Learning and Verbal Behavior*, *19*, 416–429.

Earles, J. L. (1996). Adult age differences in recall of performed and nonperformed items. *Psychology and Aging*, *11*, 638–648. doi:10.1037/0882-7974.11.4.638

Eichenbaum, H. (2011). *The cognitive neuroscience of memory* (2nd ed.). New York: Oxford University Press.

Engelkamp, J. (1998). *Memory for actions*. Hove, UK: Psychology Press/Taylor & Francis.

Engelkamp, J., & Zimmer, H. (1996). Organisation and recall in verbal tasks and in subject-performed tasks. *European Journal of Cognitive Psychology*, *8*, 257–273.

Engelkamp, J., & Zimmer, H. D. (1997). Sensory factors in memory for subject-performed tasks. *Acta Psychologica*, *96*, 43–60.

Engelkamp, J., Zimmer, H. D., Mohr, G., & Sellen, O. (1994). Memory of self-performed tasks: Self-performing during recognition. *Memory & Cognition*, *22*, 34–39.

Feyereisen, P. (2009). Enactment effects and integration processes in younger and older adults' memory for actions. *Memory*, *17*, 374–385. doi:10.1080/09658210902731851

Foley, M. A., & Ratner, H. H. (2001). The role of action-based structures in activity memory. In H. D. Zimmer, M. Guynn, R. Cohen, J. Engelkamp, R. Kormi-Nouri, and M. Foley (Eds.), *Memory for action: A distinct form of episodic memory?* (pp. 112–135). New York: Oxford University Press.

Foos, P. W., & Goolkasian, P. (2008). Presentation format effects in a levels-of-processing task. *Experimental Psychology*, *55*, 215–227. doi:10.1027/1618-3169.55.4.215

Hasher, L., & Zacks, R. T. (1979). Automatic and effortful processes in memory. *Journal of Experimental Psychology: General*, *108*, 356–386.

Karantzoulis, S., Rich, J. B., & Mangels, J. A. (2006). Subject-performance tasks improve associative learning in amnestic mild cognitive impairment. *Journal of the International Neuropsychological Society*, *12*, 493–501. doi:10.1017/S1355617706060632

Keitz, S. M., & Gounard, B. R. (1976). Age differences in adults' free recall of pictorial and word stimuli. *Educational Gerontology*, *1*, 237–241. doi:10.1080/0360127760010303

Kirkpatrick, E. A. (1894). An experimental study of memory. *Psychological Review*, *1*, 602–609. doi:10.1037/h0068244

Kormi-Nouri, R. (2000). The role of movement and object in action memory: A comparative study between blind, blindfolded and sighted subjects. *Scandinavian Journal of Psychology*, *41*, 71–75. doi:10.1111/1467-9450.00173

Kormi-Nouri, R., Moniri, S., & Nilsson, L. (2003). Episodic and semantic memory in bilingual and monolingual children. *Scandinavian Journal of Psychology*, *44*, 47–54. doi:10.1111/1467-9450.00320

Kormi-Nouri, R., Nilsson, L., & Bäckman, L. (1994). The dual-conception view reexamined: Attentional demands and the encoding of verbal and physical information in action events. *Psychological Research/Psychologische Forschung*, *57*, 42–46. doi:10.1007/BF00452994

Lind, S. E., & Bowler, D. M. (2009). Recognition memory, self–other source memory, and theory-of-mind in children with autism spectrum disorder. *Journal of Autism and Developmental Disorders*, *39*, 1231–1239. doi:10.1007/s10803-009-0735-2

MacKay, K. J., & Smith, M. C. (2006). Destination advertising: Age and format effects on memory. *Annals of Tourism Research*, *33*, 7–24. doi:10.1016/j.annals.2005.07.002

Madigan, S., McCabe, L., & Itatani, E. (1972). Immediate and delayed recall of words and pictures. *Canadian Journal of Psychology/Revue Canadienne De Psychologie*, *26*, 407–414. doi:10.1037/h0082448

Maisto, A. A., & Queen, D. E. (1992). Memory for pictorial information and the picture superiority effect. *Educational Gerontology*, *18*, 213–223. doi:10.1080/0360127920180207

Mangels, J. A., & Heinberg, A. (2006). Improved episodic integration through enactment: Implications for aging. *Journal of General Psychology*, *133*, 37–65. doi:10.3200/GENP.133.1.37-65

Mimura, M., Komatsu, S., Kato, M., Yoshimasu, H., Moriyama, Y., & Kashima, H. (2005). Further evidence for a comparable memory advantage of self-performed tasks in Korsakoff's syndrome and nonamnesic control subjects. *Journal of the International Neuropsychological Society*, *11*, 545–553. doi:10.1017/S1355617705050654

Morris, C. D., Bransford, J. D., & Franks, J. J. (1977). Levels of processing versus transfer appropriate processing. *Journal of Verbal Learning and Verbal Behavior*, *16*, 519–533.

Mulligan, N. W. (2003). Memory: Implicit versus explicit. In L. Nadel (Ed.), *Encyclopedia of cognitive science* (pp. 1114–1120). London: Nature Publishing Group/MacMillan.

Mulligan, N. W. (2008). Attention and memory. In H. L. Roediger (Ed.), *Learning and memory: A comprehensive reference* (pp. 7–22). Oxford: Elsevier.

Mulligan, N. W., & Hornstein, S. L. (2003). Memory for actions: Self-performed tasks and the reenactment effect. *Memory & Cognition*, *31*, 412–421.

Mulligan, N. W., & Lozito, J. P. (2004). Self-generation and memory. In B. H. Ross (Ed.), *Psychology of learning and motivation* (pp. 175–214). San Diego, CA: Elsevier Academic Press.

Mulligan, N. W., & Picklesimer, M. (2012). Levels of processing and the cue-dependent nature of recollection. *Journal of Memory and Language*, *66*, 79–92. doi:10.1016/j.jml.2011.10.001

Newcombe, N.S. (2010). Picture this: Increasing math and science learning by improving spatial thinking. *American Educator*. Summer 2010, 29–43.

Nilsson, L., & Craik, F. I. (1990). Additive and interactive effects in memory for subject-performed tasks. *European Journal of Cognitive Psychology*, *2*, 305–324. doi:10.1080/09541449008406210

Paivio, A., & Csapo, K. (1973). Picture superiority in free recall: Imagery or dual coding? *Cognitive Psychology*, *5*, 176–206. doi:10.1016/0010-0285(73)90032-7

Park, D. C., Puglisi, J. T., & Smith, A. D. (1986). Memory for pictures: Does an age-related decline exist? *Psychology and Aging*, *1*, 11–17. doi:10.1037/0882-7974.1.1.11

Parkin, A. J., & Russo, R. (1990). Implicit and explicit memory and the automatic/effortful distinction. *European Journal of Cognitive Psychology*, *2*, 71–80.

Pottage, C. L., & Schaefer, A. (2012). Visual attention and emotional memory: Recall of aversive pictures is partially mediated by concurrent task performance. *Emotion*, *12*, 33–38. doi:10.1037/a0024574

Richardson, J. T. (1978). Memory for pictures and words, and the negative recency effect. *Perceptual and Motor Skills*, *47*, 967–970.

Ritchey, G. H. (1980). Picture superiority in free recall: The effects of organization and elaboration. *Journal of Experimental Child Psychology*, *29*, 460–474. doi:10.1016/0022-0965(80)90107-1

Rönnlund, M., Nyberg, L., Bäckman, L., & Nilsson, L. (2003). Recall of subject-performed tasks, verbal tasks, and cognitive activities across the adult life span: Parallel age-related deficits. *Aging, Neuropsychology, and Cognition*, *10*, 182–201. doi:10.1076/anec.10.3.182.16449

Russo, R., & Parkin, A. J. (1993). Age differences in implicit memory: More apparent than real. *Memory and Cognition*, *21*, 73–80.

Saltz, E., & Dixon, D. (1982). Let's pretend: The role of motoric imagery in memory for sentences and words. *Journal of Experimental Child Psychology*, *34*, 77–92.

Schatz, T. R., Spranger, T., Kubik, V., & Knopf, M. (2011). Exploring the enactment effect from an information processing view: What can we learn from serial position analyses? *Scandinavian Journal of Psychology*, *52*, 509–515. doi:10.1111/j.1467-9450.2011.00893.x

Schneider, W. (2011). Memory development in childhood. In U. Goswami and U. Goswami (Eds.), *The Wiley-Blackwell handbook of childhood cognitive development (2nd ed.)*. (pp. 347–376) Hoboken, NJ: Wiley-Blackwell.

Seiler, K. H., & Engelkamp, J. (2003). The role of item-specific information for the serial position curve in free recall. *Journal of Experimental Psychology: Learning, Memory, and Cognition*, *29*, 954–964. doi:10.1037/0278-7393.29.5.954

Shepard, R. N. (1967). Recognition memory for words, sentences, and pictures. *Journal of Verbal Learning & Verbal Behavior*, *6*, 156–163. doi:10.1016/S0022-5371(67)80067-7

Slamecka, N. J., & Graf, P. (1978). The generation effect: Delineation of a phenomenon. *Journal of Experimental Psychology: Human Learning and Memory*, *4*, 592–604.

Snodgrass, J. G., & Vanderwart, M. (1980). A standardized set of 260 pictures: Norms for name agreement, image agreement, familiarity, and visual complexity. *Journal of Experimental Psychology: Human Learning and Memory*, *6*, 174–215.

Standing, L. (1973). Learning 10,000 pictures. *The Quarterly Journal of Experimental Psychology*, *25*, 207–222. doi:10.1080/14640747308400340

Stenberg, G. (2006). Conceptual and perceptual factors in the picture superiority effect. *European Journal of Cognitive Psychology*, *18*, 813–847. doi:10.1080/09541440500412361

Talmi, D., Schimmack, U., Paterson, T., & Moscovitch, M. (2007). The role of attention and relatedness in emotionally enhanced memory. *Emotion*, *7*, 89–102. doi:10.1037/1528-3542.7.1.89

Tulving, E., & Thomson, D. M. (1973). Encoding specificity and retrieval processes in episodic memory. *Psychological Review*, *80*(5), 352–373.

Unnava, H. R., & Burnkrant, R. E. (1991). An imagery-processing view of the role of pictures in print advertisements. *Journal of Marketing Research*, *28*, 226–231. doi:10.2307/3172811

Whitehouse, A. J. O., Maybery, M. T., & Durkin, K. (2006). The development of the picture-superiority effect. *British Journal of Developmental Psychology*, *24*, 767–773. doi:10.1348/026151005X74153

Winograd, E., Smith, A. D., & Simon, E. W. (1982). Aging and the picture superiority effect in recall. *Journal of Gerontology*, *37*, 70–75.

Wolfe, J. M., Horowitz, T. S., & Michod, K. O. (2007). Is visual attention required for robust picture memory? *Vision Research*, *47*, 955–964. doi:10.1016/j.visres.2006.11.025

Yates, F. A. (1966). *The art of memory*. Chicago, IL: University of Chicago Press.

Zimmer, H. D., & Cohen, R. L. (2001). Remembering actions: A specific type of memory? In H. D. Zimmer, M. Guynn, R. L. Cohen, J. Engelkamp, R. Kormi-Nouri, and M. A. Foley (Eds.), *Memory for action: A distinct form of episodic memory?* (pp. 3–24). New York: Oxford University Press.

Zimmer, H. D., Cohen, R. L., Guynn, M., Engelkamp, J., Kormi-Nouri, R., & Foley, M. A. (Eds.) (2001). *Memory for action: A distinct form of episodic memory?* New York: Oxford University Press.

Zimmer, H. D., & Engelkamp, J. (1999). Levels-of-processing effects in subject-performed tasks. *Memory & Cognition*, *27*, 907–914.

3

Prospective Memory and Aging: When it Becomes Difficult and What You Can Do About It[1]

Gilles O. Einstein and Mark A. McDaniel

Prospective memory refers to memory tasks in which one has to remember to perform an intended action at some point in the future, such as remembering to buy a loaf of bread on the way home, remembering to take the cake out of the oven, and remembering to perform one's back exercises. This contrasts with the more typically studied retrospective memory in which one is prompted to remember a particular past event. Examples of retrospective memory include remembering a list of words learned in an experiment, remembering what you ate for lunch yesterday, and remembering the plot of a movie that you saw two weeks ago. In this chapter, we present an overview of the research on prospective memory and aging. In doing so, we identify different kinds of prospective memory tasks, theorize about the cognitive processes involved in performing these tasks, and discuss whether these processes are especially vulnerable to forgetting for all people and for older adults in particular. We also develop applied implications for improving prospective remembering in these situations.

PREVALENCE AND IMPORTANCE OF PROSPECTIVE MEMORY IN THE REAL WORLD

Prospective memory is an integral part of our daily lives. On any given day, we may need to remember to take medication, to give a colleague a message, and to pick up a child from tennis practice. To get a rough sense of the frequency of prospective memory tasks, relative to retrospective memory tasks in everyday life, we often ask college-age students and older adults to indicate "the last thing you remember forgetting." We then categorize their responses as either prospective or retrospective memory failures. Consistently, we find that a majority of the memory failures for both college-age students and older adults are prospective in nature.

Reason (1990), in reviewing human error in the work place, proposed that prospective memory failures are among the most common causes of workplace accidents. Dismukes (2008: 412) argued that many airline accidents are the result of highly experienced pilots being susceptible to unexpected events like distractions or changes in routine and failing "to remember to perform a fairly simple procedural step that they had executed on thousands of previous occasions" According to the World Health Organization (2003: xiii), medication adherence for chronic diseases "is a worldwide problem of striking magnitude." Although there are many reasons for poor adherence (less than 50 percent in developed countries and lower than that in undeveloped countries), nonadherence is often the result of forgetfulness (Stone, 2001) and research has shown that cognitive functioning is associated with adherence (e.g., Insel, Morrow, Brewer, & Figueredo, 2006).

Interestingly, although there have been thousands of studies conducted on retrospective memory and aging, up until about 30 years ago, there was virtually no research on prospective memory and aging. Significant strides in our understanding of prospective memory and aging have been made over this period, however, and we highlight the major advances in this chapter.

PROSPECTIVE MEMORY POSES A SPECIAL PROBLEM FOR RETRIEVAL AND SOME THEMES OF THIS CHAPTER

One of the intriguing distinctions between prospective and retrospective memory tasks is that they have different retrieval requirements. The prospective memory task of remembering to give your friend Joe a message superficially resembles the very often studied retrospective memory task of remembering that the word "table" was paired with the word "dog" (i.e., a cued recall task). In both, one needs to remember the cue and the associated response. In a laboratory test of retrospective memory, however, there is always a request by an external agent to recollect a prior episode; thus, at some point the participant is given the word "dog" and explicitly asked to recall the word that was

associated with it. In contrast, in most prospective memory situations, there is not a request for a memory search. In other words, when you see Joe, there is no one there to specifically prompt you to search your memory for the message that was associated with Joe. So, somehow, attention has to switch from processing Joe as a friend to retrieving the intention to give him a message. An interesting issue is to understand how the cognitive system accomplishes this retrieval process.

Much of the interest in prospective memory emanated from Craik's (1986) seminal conceptualization of retrospective and prospective memory tasks and of age-related memory deficits (see also initial reviews and experiments in the area by Harris, 1984, and Harris & Wilkins, 1982). Consistent with the different retrieval requirement for prospective memory developed above, Craik suggested that memory tasks could be ordered in terms of the amount of self-initiated retrieval required. As can be seen in Figure 3.1, recognition is considered to have low self-initiated retrieval demands (or to be high in environmental support), because recognition provides the target item itself as a cue for retrieval; cued recall would require more self-initiated retrieval; free recall would require even more self-initiated retrieval because there are no

Tasks low in self-initiated retrieval – tasks that should produce small age-related deficits

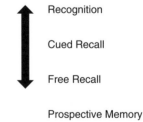

Recognition

Cued Recall

Free Recall

Prospective Memory

Tasks high in self-initiated retrieval – tasks that should produce large age-related deficits

Figure 3.1   Amount of self-initiated retrieval required for various memory tasks in Craik (1986).

cues given other than specification of the temporal-spatial context for the target event. Prospective memory was seen by Craik as having the highest self-initiated retrieval because there is not only an absence of cues, but in addition, one has to remember to remember. Thus, because of this high degree of self-initiated retrieval, prospective memory should generally be more difficult than retrospective memory tasks.

Craik (1986) further suggested that conditions of high self-initiated retrieval (low environmental support) require extensive processing resources and there are age-related declines in processing resources. Thus, age deficits in memory should be a function of the amount of self-initiated retrieval required. Specifically, memory tests low in self-initiated retrieval (high environmental support) should produce small age-related deficits, whereas memory tasks high in self-initiated retrieval (low environmental support) should produce large age-related deficits. On this view, prospective memory should generally be difficult and especially so for older adults.

Another factor that makes prospective memory tasks difficult is that they typically need to be performed in the midst of performing other activities or satisfying other goals (e.g., buying a loaf of bread while driving home and while also thinking about how to organize the discussion section of a paper; taking medication while engaged in the goals of preparing and eating breakfast and getting ready for work; and remembering to give a message to a friend while also politely greeting and engaging the friend). If remembering to perform intentions was not imbedded in other activities (e.g., if the sole goal of our journey was to buy bread), then there would be little forgetting. Given that our prospective memory demands are often intermixed with the demands of other ongoing tasks, it would be helpful to have reminders that can help us disengage from the ongoing activities at the appropriate times. In the ideal case, one would want to use an external device that could trigger remembering at the appropriate time. For example, if your task is to buy bread on the way home, there are GPS devices that can track your location and send you a signal when you are approaching the store. Because many of us do not have these devices or are not compulsive about programming them, we often need to rely on our cognitive processes.

In terms of using our cognitive processes, one solution would be to rely on monitoring processes to maintain the intention until the appropriate time for performing the action. Another solution would be to identify and rely on cues to help bring the intention back to mind. One theme in this chapter is that monitoring is a capacity consuming process that is quickly exhausted and easily distracted and thus is especially sensitive to forgetting and particularly so in older adults. Following Bargh and Chartrand's (1999) proposal that there are severe limits in the extent to which we can maintain conscious control over behavior, we believe that it is difficult (as well as costly) for the cognitive system to sustain monitoring processes over extended retention intervals and especially so in the face of distractions (i.e., while performing other activities). Moreover, aging interferes with this ability to maintain attentional control, and this is likely to make it especially difficult for older adults to effectively disengage from the ongoing task at the appropriate moment (Coubard, Ferrufino, Boura, Gripon, Renaud, & Bherer, 2011).

Recent research (Shelton, McDaniel, Scullin, Cahill, Singer, & Einstein, 2011) suggests that cognitive exertion or fatigue interferes with the ability of older-old adults (those over 72 years old) to sustain monitoring processes. Given this basic limit in our cognitive system's ability to maintain an intention in awareness, another theme in this chapter is that it is critical to establish external cues that can trigger spontaneous retrieval of the intended action. In Craik's (1986) terminology, this would provide more environmental support for prospective remembering. Moreover, there is increasing evidence that these relatively automatic spontaneous retrieval processes are spared with age (Dywan & Jacoby, 1990; Jacoby, 1992; see McDaniel & Einstein, 2011). Thus, we believe that prospective memory is especially vulnerable to failure (and especially so for older adults) when there are no external cues that can stimulate retrieval of the intention and when people must instead rely on monitoring processes.

A particularly dramatic (and tragic) example of our limited capability at sustaining monitoring to support prospective remembering is a situation that has been reported a number of times in the popular press. The scenario is that a parent sets off for work in the morning with his or her infant strapped in the car seat in the back of the car. This parent's usual routine is to drive straight to work, as typically the other parent takes the child to day care. For that day, however, the parent has planned to drop off the child at the day care on the way in to work, which involves a slight departure in the usual route to work (perhaps a different turn at an intersection close to work). While en route the child falls asleep, and the parent gets absorbed in thinking about other things, such as the demands that await at work. The parent drives straight to work, and leaves the child locked in a hot car for the day with horrific consequences. Typically, these are loving parents who have every intention of taking the child to day care (see www.4rkidssake.org/mikeysstory.htm for a more complete account of one such tragedy). Yet, once the child falls asleep, there are no external cues to trigger retrieval of the intention. Accordingly, sustained maintenance or monitoring of the intention is required to successfully remember to take the child to day care. Despite strong motivation to remember to take the child to day care, continuous monitoring is unlikely to be reliably supported by the cognitive system. It would be better to rely on external cues, such as placing the diaper bag in the front seat when the infant is in the car, to trigger retrieval of the intention. We will amplify our discussion

of prospective memory cues and spontaneous retrieval in later sections.

EARLY RESEARCH AND PARADIGMS FOR STUDYING PROSPECTIVE MEMORY IN THE LABORATORY

Initially, the prediction that prospective memory tasks would be especially difficult for older adults was tested in semi-naturalistic paradigms. Typically in these paradigms subjects would be in the laboratory participating in an experiment for some other purpose. The experimenter would then instruct subjects that upon leaving the laboratory, they should telephone the experimenter at specified times over several days. In other paradigms, subjects might be instructed to mail a postcard back to the laboratory on a certain day of the week for several weeks. These studies invariably found that older adults performed as well or better than younger adults (see Phillips, Henry, & Martin, 2008). Given the expectation that older adults should show a dramatic decline in prospective memory, researchers were somewhat puzzled by this result. Although there is not complete agreement on the interpretation of this high performance by older adults on naturalistic prospective memory tasks, the explanations have suggested that older adults are more motivated to perform well in naturalistic settings (Aberle, Rendell, Rose, McDaniel, & Kliegel, 2010), are more likely to rely on external reminders like calendars (e.g., Moscovitch, 1982), and/or have less busy and more regular or routine lifestyles (Wilson & Park, 2008).

The inability to control important variables across younger and older adults in naturalistic settings stimulated us (Einstein & McDaniel, 1990) to develop a laboratory paradigm for studying prospective memory. With a laboratory prospective memory paradigm, the use of external strategies could be prevented, motivation levels and ongoing task demands could be equated, and prospective memory could be studied in carefully controlled conditions that allow more refined analysis of the cognitive processes, just as researchers had been able to do with retrospective memory. Our general orientation was to keep participants busily engaged in an ongoing task, while also trying to remember on their own some additional activity. We reasoned that this parallels real-world situations in which people are busily engaged with daily activities during the time in which they are supposed to remember their intended action. Participants were engaged in an ongoing task such as rating a set of words. In addition, participants were asked to press a designated key at some specified point later in the experiment. For example, participants might be asked to press the *Enter* key when they saw the word *table*. The target word *table* occurred only a few times across many word rating trials, and prospective memory performance was measured by the proportion of times participants responded when *table* occurred. Before describing the findings from these laboratory paradigms, we note a further distinction in prospective memory.

Following the groundbreaking work of Harris (1984), Einstein and McDaniel (1990) proposed that there were variations in prospective memory tasks that had important implications for aging effects. In timed-based prospective memory tasks, one performs the intended action at a certain time or after a period of time has elapsed. For example, one might have to remember to pick up one's child at three in the afternoon, or one might have to remember to take cookies out of the oven after 10 minutes have elapsed. Other prospective memory tasks are event-based. In these tasks, one must remember to perform the intended action when an external event occurs. For example, one might have to remember to give a colleague a message later in the day when encountering that colleague. An important difference between time-based and event-based tasks is that in the time-based task, there is no obvious and specific external cue that might prompt remembering the intended

action. Thus, time-based tasks especially fit Craik's (1986) criteria for a memory task high in self-initiated retrieval and accordingly should produce robust age-related decline.

There are a handful of laboratory studies that have examined time-based prospective memory for younger and older adults (e.g., d'Ydewalle, Luwel, & Brunfaut, 1999). For example, Einstein et al. (1995) instructed subjects to remember to press a designated key every 5 minutes while performing an unrelated ongoing activity. Responses were considered correct if the response was within 1 minute of the target time. Table 3.1 shows that older adults were half as likely as younger adults to remember to perform the prospective memory activity. Middle-aged adults, those from 35 to 49, also remembered to perform the prospective memory task at a high level (thus the news is good for those in this middle-aged group). Using a much narrower response window (7 seconds in Table 3.1), Park, Hertzog, Kidder, Morrell, and Mayhorn (1997) found similar significant declines for older adults in time-based prospective memory (see also Kvavilashvili, Kornbrot, Mash, Cockburn, & Milne, 2009; Mioni & Stablum, 2013). For laboratory time-based tasks, then, the picture appears clear. As anticipated by Craik's initial ideas, older adults show a consistent and robust decline in prospective memory (see Henry, MacLeod, Phillips, & Crawford , 2004, for a meta-analysis confirming age-related declines on time-based prospective memory tasks).

Table 3.1 Time Based: Proportion of correct prospective responses that occurred within the designated time window

	Einstein et al., 1995	Park et al., 1997
	(1 minute response window)	(7 second response window)
Age Group		
Young	.65	.89
Older	.32	.62
Middle Aged	.82	

APPLIED IMPLICATIONS FOR TIME-BASED PROSPECTIVE MEMORY TASKS

From an applied perspective, a finding reported in Einstein et al. (2005) is noteworthy. Specifically, for time periods that are distal from the target time, the frequency of clock monitoring for younger and older adults was fairly equivalent. By contrast, for the time period just preceding the target time, younger but not older adults substantially increased their monitoring frequency. That is, older adults do not seem to monitor strategically in time-based prospective memory tasks, and this may in part underlie the age-related decline in time-based prospective memory. Accordingly, a fruitful avenue for further applied research would be to see if older adults can be trained to strategically monitor in situations in which they are not able to set an external timer. Along these lines, in the ongoing Exercise and Cognitive Training (EXACT) trial at Washington University, a component of an eight-week prospective memory training regimen for older adults includes instruction and practice on strategic clock monitoring for time-based prospective memory.

Yet, more frequent monitoring proximal to the target time does not ensure high levels of prospective memory performance (e.g., Harris & Wilkins, 1982). Even when participants monitored the clock within ten seconds of the target time, Harris and Wilkins found that participants still sometimes forgot to perform the response (about a quarter of the time), thereby indicating that it is surprisingly easy to get reabsorbed by ongoing activities and lose track of one's intention. Consequently, another technique for improving time-based prospective memory is to try to convert the time-based task to an event-based task (see the following section) by associating the intention with external cues. For instance, instead of conceptualizing one's task as remembering to take medication at a particular time (say 8 am), one could

associate the intention with starting the coffee pot in the morning (something one of the authors does as he first awakens). Of course, one could also rely on external timers.

In considering the applied implications of the current laboratory research, one clear limitation must be noted. The real world provides a much richer and related set of cues for many prospective memory tasks than does the laboratory. Moreover, time-based tasks often encompass much longer intervals than the 5- to 10-minute intervals implemented in laboratory experiments. In a semi-naturalistic experiment, Kvavilashvili and Fisher (2007) instructed younger and older adults to telephone the experimenters a week later within a one-hour interval. Older adults performed as well as younger adults on this time-based task, despite being instructed not to use external aids. Subjects' daily introspections indicated that they were frequently reminded of the time-based task during encounters in the environment (e.g., passing by their phone). It appears that these naturally occurring event-based reminders may have kept the intention more activated and readily retrievable, or may have fostered a richer array of associations between the environment and the intention (leading to repeated reminders). Thus, at least some everyday time-based tasks may naturally be enriched with environmental (event) cues, cues that could mitigate forgetting in these time-based tasks. We turn now to a consideration of purely event-based prospective memory tasks.

AGING AND PERFORMANCE ON EVENT-BASED PROSPECTIVE MEMORY TASKS

The work with event-based prospective memory tasks has revealed a more complex and intriguing story. A priori, the expected age-related patterns are not so clear-cut. On the one hand, compared with a time-based PM task, an event-based task would appear to be lower in self-initiated retrieval because there is an environmental event that could cue retrieval of the intended action. If so, then minimal or no age differences would be anticipated. On the other hand, in the event-based task, one still has to remember to remember. That is, there is no external agent requesting or stimulating an attempt to remember. On this analysis, event-based prospective memory should reveal age differences just as time-based prospective memory does. In a review of the literature, Henry et al. (2004) identified 48 experiments examining age and event-based prospective memory. In general, they found a significant age-related decrement (see also Kliegel, Jager, & Phillips, 2008). These reviews reinforce the impression of many researchers that prospective memory is especially sensitive to the effects of age and consequently many memory researchers today believe that "prospective memory failure generally increases with age" (Craik, 2003, p. 13).

Yet, a number of researchers find equivalent prospective memory for younger and older adults on event-based tasks (Cherry & LaCompte, 1999; Einstein & McDaniel, 1990; Einstein, McDaniel, Richardson, Guynn, & Cunfer, 1995; Kvavilashvili et al., 2009; Reese & Cherry, 2002; Vogels, Dekker, Brouwer, & de Jong, 2002), and we believe that there are sufficient experiments reporting no age differences to take this finding seriously (see McDaniel & Einstein, 2007, for a more complete review). This mixed pattern of results suggests that the processes involved in prospective remembering are more complex than originally thought, and we develop this position in the next sections.

MULTIPROCESS THEORY OF PROSPECTIVE MEMORY

A prominent issue in understanding prospective memory and aging is the question of why are there significant age differences in some laboratory event-based prospective memory tasks but not others. To answer this question, we (McDaniel & Einstein, 2000) proposed the multiprocess theory of prospective memory. This view is based on the overarching assumption that remembering to perform actions in the future is critical to our lives. We assume, therefore, that it would be adaptive to have a flexible system that uses a variety of mechanisms to support prospective remembering. One process might be a more strategic, self-initiated process such as monitoring for the target event (Smith, 2003) or actively maintaining the intention while performing the ongoing task (West & Craik, 1999). Another process, however, might be a more spontaneous retrieval process that is initiated by the target event (e.g., reflexive associative processes, McDaniel et al., 2004). On the multiprocess view, age differences are expected on event-based tasks in which resource-demanding monitoring or self-initiating processes are necessary or are engaged. Age differences are not expected when spontaneous retrieval is more prominent.

There are likely a number of factors that influence whether event-based prospective memory will require monitoring or self-initiating processes versus more spontaneous or reflexive retrieval processes (Einstein et al., 2005; McDaniel & Einstein, 2000). We suggest that a prominent factor underlying the inconsistency in the literature regarding age effects and event-based prospective memory is the relation of the ongoing task to the target event. Specifically, we suggest that processing of the target event can be *focal* to the processing engaged by the ongoing task (i.e., the ongoing task directs attention to the target event and especially those features that were processed at encoding or planning), or processing of the target event may be *non-focal* to the processing required by the ongoing task. An everyday example of a focal cue would be encountering and pausing to converse with the friend to whom you intended to give a message (see Einstein & McDaniel, 2005, for additional examples). An example of a nonfocal cue would be a grocery store (for stopping to buy bread) located a bit off the road when you are traveling in rush hour traffic (and thus attending closely to the other cars).

The multiprocess theory assumes that the occurrence of a focal cue is likely to trigger spontaneous retrieval of the intention (i.e., the occurrence of the cue is likely to stimulate retrieval when no attentional or working memory resources are being devoted to maintaining the intention). The theory anticipates that the occurrence of a nonfocal cue is unlikely to trigger spontaneous retrieval and therefore that monitoring (actively searching for the nonfocal target and/or maintaining the attention in awareness) is necessary for successful retrieval in these situations. Monitoring is assumed to draw on executive attentional and/or working memory resources. A recent series of experiments provided strong support for these predictions. In a particularly compelling experiment, Scullin, McDaniel, Shelton, and Lee (2010; Experiment 4) highly discouraged monitoring on the part of their participants and presented them either with a focal cue (the task was to press a designated key when they saw the word *crossbar*) or a nonfocal cue (the task was to press a designated key when they saw a word beginning with the letter *c*). The experimenters discouraged monitoring by emphasizing the importance of the ongoing task (a lexical decision task), by presenting only a single prospective memory target, and by not presenting that target until the 501st lexical decision trial. Previous research had shown that monitoring declines over the course of the ongoing task and particularly so when prospective memory targets are not encountered (Harrison & Einstein, 2010; Loft, Kearney, & Remington, 2008). And indeed, by the last 100 trials, the results showed no evidence for monitoring in the focal condition (i.e., no slowing on the ongoing task relative to a control condition that did not have a prospective memory intention). Consistent with the multiprocess theory, presenting a focal target on the 501st

trial led to high prospective memory performance (73 percent), thereby suggesting that spontaneous retrieval is likely with focal cues. By contrast, in the nonfocal condition, where there was evidence of only low levels of monitoring, prospective memory performance was low (18 percent), thereby suggesting that monitoring is required for nonfocal cues.

In another set of experiments, Scullin, McDaniel, and Einstein (2010) manipulated monitoring levels by sometimes presenting cues that were related to the prospective memory target events (e.g., if the prospective memory target event was *water*, related cues were words like *splash* and *faucet*) a few trials prior to the occurrence of the target events. These cues served to alert participants that prospective memory targets were forthcoming and significantly enhanced monitoring levels. Consistent with the multiprocess theory, however, the increased monitoring levels improved prospective memory only with nonfocal cues. In the focal condition, there was high prospective memory performance in the absence of monitoring, and increased monitoring (resulting from the presentation of cues) did not enhance prospective memory performance. Taken together, these results indicate that prospective memory retrieval is dependent on monitoring with nonfocal cues but can occur spontaneously with focal cues. Consistent with this interpretation, Brewer, Knight, Marsh, and Unsworth (2010) found that working memory capacity was associated with nonfocal, but not focal, prospective memory performance.

Although we believe that spontaneous retrieval is likely with focal cues, we do not mean to imply that the occurrence of a focal cue will always lead to spontaneous retrieval of the intention. Indeed, as we have proposed elsewhere (McDaniel & Einstein, 2000), we believe that spontaneous retrieval is a probabilistic process that likely depends on a number of factors beyond the overlap in the features that are processed at encoding (during planning) and retrieval.

Although further research is needed to clearly determine the moderating influences, there is currently evidence that spontaneous retrieval with focal cues is more likely when the target event is distinctive (McDaniel & Einstein, 1993), when there is a strong association between the target event and the intended action (McDaniel, Guynn, Einstein, & Breneiser, 2004), when the target event is not highly associated with other events and actions (McDaniel & Einstein, 1993), and when one's ongoing task activities are not overly demanding at the time the focal cue occurs (i.e., when our attention is not highly divided; Harrison, Mullet, Whiffen, Ousterhout, & Einstein, in press).

The findings with focal and nonfocal cues presented above lead to predictions about when you will and will not find age differences in prospective memory. We assume that relatively automatic spontaneous retrieval processes are spared with normal aging and that monitoring draws on working memory processes that decline with age (McDaniel & Einstein, 2011). Thus, the multiprocess theory prediction is that age differences should be larger on tasks that require capacity consuming monitoring processes, and two meta-analyses are in-line with this prediction. Henry et al. (2004) classified, in a post hoc fashion, the event-based laboratory prospective memory studies into those that seemed to impose higher levels of controlled strategic demand (i.e., monitoring) and those that were supported by more spontaneous processes. They found that the tasks associated with higher strategic demand showed large age decline, whereas the tasks thought to be supported by relatively more spontaneous processes showed minimal age-related decline. In a more recent meta-analysis of 46 experiments, Kliegel, Jager, and Phillips (2008) compared the effect size associated with age in those studies that used nonfocal cues with those that used focal cues. In line with the multiprocess theory prediction and the Henry et al. meta-analysis they found significantly larger age effects with nonfocal cues relative to focal cues. Nonetheless,

although reduced in magnitude, there was still a significant age effect with focal cues, and Kliegel et al. concluded that their results supported only a weak version of the multiprocess theory (see Uttl, 2008, for a different interpretation).

Although suggestive, one problem in using meta-analyses to evaluate whether spontaneous retrieval is preserved with normal aging is that some of the experiments classified as using focal cues actually encouraged a monitoring approach to the prospective memory task. For example, the prospective memory task in two of the "focal" experiments (Cohen, West, & Craik, 2001) asked participants to perform an action in response to any of 24 focal cues. Previous research has shown that using more than a couple of cues encourages extensive monitoring (Cohen & Gollwitzer, 2008), and thus it is unlikely that prospective remembering in the studies classified as using focal cues reflected only spontaneous retrieval.

To evaluate more clearly whether spontaneous retrieval processes are preserved in older adults, Mullet, Scullin, Hess, Arnold, Scullin and Einstein (in press) directly compared the performance of younger and older adults on a focal and nonfocal prospective memory task. To our knowledge, this is the first experiment that examined age effects on focal and nonfocal prospective memory tasks that were equated in monitoring difficulty and that carefully measured monitoring. The ongoing task in this experiment was a lexical decision task, and in the nonfocal condition participants were asked to press a designated key when they saw a word beginning with the letter p. In the focal condition, participants were asked to press a designated key when they saw the word *printer*. To discourage monitoring, the experimenter emphasized the importance of the ongoing task and deemphasized the importance of the prospective memory task. With a nonfocal cue, Mullet et al. (in press) found evidence of monitoring in all of the age groups, and there were age-related declines in prospective memory performance. With a focal cue, the exciting result was that there was no evidence of monitoring and yet high prospective memory by all participants, even in the old-old participants (those over 70 years of age).

This finding of preserved spontaneous retrieval in older adults was also obtained in other experiments using a very different paradigm. Specifically, Mullet et al. (in press) tested younger and older participants in an intention interference paradigm in which they were asked to perform a prospective memory task (e.g., press the Q key whenever they saw the word *animal*) in the context of an image-rating task. Importantly, participants were then told to suspend their prospective memory intention while completing an intervening lexical decision task. Because the intention was suspended during this phase, there was no incentive to monitor. Nonetheless, during the lexical decision task, the experimenters presented the prospective memory cue (i.e., *animal*), and inferred spontaneous retrieval from slowed lexical decision responses to prospective memory cues. The idea is that slowed responses indicate that the information related to the prospective memory intention was popping into mind and interfering with a speedy lexical decision response (Cohen, Kantner, Dixon, & Lindsay, (2011). In two experiments, younger and older adults showed significant, and statistically similar, slowing when the prospective memory cue was presented. Collectively, these results suggest that older adults are as likely as younger adults to spontaneously retrieve an intention when they encounter a focal prospective memory cue.

APPLIED IMPLICATIONS: EVERYONE BUT ESPECIALLY OLDER ADULTS SHOULD CONNECT INTENDED ACTIONS TO FOCAL CUES WHENEVER POSSIBLE

Often, when forming intentions, we form only general intentions such as when we tell ourselves that we need to telephone a friend, take a vitamin supplement, or plan to exercise. Conceptualized in this manner, these intentions focus on the intended action, and they do not connect the action to a focal cue that can trigger remembering. Thus, in these situations, remembering is more dependent on monitoring processes, which we have seen are fragile. Generalizing from the laboratory to real-world settings, it seems important to develop focal cues to facilitate retrieval of intended actions. In addition to showing that focal cues lead to higher prospective memory performance (relative to nonfocal cues), the current evidence is that these spontaneous retrieval processes are spared in older adults. Thus, an important applied implication of this research is that everyone, and especially older adults, should capitalize on spontaneous retrieval processes to accomplish their prospective memory demands.

This thinking has been captured in Gollwitzer's (1999) formulation of implementation intentions. Despite forming strong intentions, Gollwitzer believes that we often fail to follow through on them because we forget to think of them at the appropriate point in time. According to Gollwitzer, the problem is that we tend to form general intentions and are thus dependent on conscious processes (like monitoring) to retrieve the intention at the desired time. Instead, he believes that we should reframe our goals into implementation intentions, which are specific "if–then" plans that connect goal-directed responses to the anticipated target cues (i.e., focal cues). Implementation intentions take the form of "When situation x arises, I will perform response y" (p. 494). Thus, instead of forming the general intention "I will take my vitamin supplement," we should tell ourselves, "When I have breakfast at the kitchen table in the morning, I will take my vitamin supplement." Gollwitzer's (1994) interpretation of the demonstrated benefits of this strategy is that implementation intentions allow people to switch from "conscious and effortful control" of their intentions (such as monitoring) to being "automatically controlled" by the presence of the target events, which spontaneously cue the intended actions (p. 494). With an implementation intention, the idea is that the cues associated with breakfast (e.g., your bowl of cereal, your kitchen table) become associated with the intention, and processing these cues will spontaneously trigger retrieval of the intention to take your medication.

Research has shown impressive benefits of using implementation intentions in both laboratory (McDaniel, Howard, & Butler, 2008; McDaniel & Scullin, 2010; McFarland & Glisky, 2012) and naturalistic settings (Gollwitzer & Brandstatter, 1997; Orbell, Hodgkins, & Sheeran, 1997; Sheeran & Orbell, 1999). In one naturalistic experiment, Orbell et al. (1997) examined whether forming an implementation intention would help women remember to perform self-examinations of their breasts, which was thought to improve the chances of early detection of breast cancer. One group simply formed the intention whereas the other group formed an implementation intention. Thus, instead of forming the general intention "I will self-examine my breasts," participants in the implementation intention condition linked that action to a particular situation or focal cue (e.g,, "When I take a shower in the morning, I will self-examine my breasts"). When queried a month later, women in the implementation intention condition were over three times more likely to report that they had performed breast self-examinations. Despite equivalent levels of motivation between the groups, the implementation intention apparently helped trigger retrieval of the intention to perform the action at an appropriate time.

Consistent with emerging results suggesting that spontaneous retrieval processes are spared in older adults, implementation intentions have been shown to be very effective with older adults. Working with older adults, Liu and Park (2004) found that implementation intentions substantially improved adherence on a 3-week blood glucose monitoring regimen relative to control groups that either extensively rehearsed

the intention or thought at length about the value of blood glucose testing (see also Chasteen, Park, & Schwarz, 2001). Further, even though spontaneous retrieval processes appear to be at risk in older adults in the very mild stages of Alzheimer's disease (AD) (McDaniel, Shelton, Breneiser, Moynan, & Balota, 2011), implementation intentions may help bootstrap the functioning that remains. In an initial experiment with a handful of participants (13 very mild AD patients in the control and 10 in the implementation intention condition), implementation intentions increased prospective memory performance in a demanding laboratory task (Virtual Week, Rendell, & Craik, 2000) from .08 for those not given implementation intentions to .15 (Shelton, Lee, Scullin, Rose, Rendell, & McDaniel, 2012). The absolute levels of prospective memory were still quite low for the AD patients using implementation intentions, but it may be that with a more extensive encoding regimen for the implementation intention, higher levels of prospective memory could be observed.

One caveat associated with using implementation intentions is that one needs to be aware that the anticipated contextual cues that stimulate retrieval of the intention can change. For example, if we form the intention to take a vitamin supplement and we imagine the triggering situation as "eating a bowl of cereal at the kitchen table," there will likely be problems in remembering to take our medication when those cues are no longer present such as when we are out of town (and eating eggs in the hotel restaurant). Dismukes (2008) has pointed out that changing cues can have devastating consequences in aviation contexts. For example, pilots normally set the flaps on the plane to takeoff position prior to taxiing to the runway, and this is an action that is deeply cued by the events normally occurring at that time. Because of freezing weather conditions, however, pilots must occasionally defer that action until after taxiing onto the runway. At this point, the typical cues for setting the flaps to takeoff position are

no longer present, and the action is susceptible to forgetting. While providing many
advantages for prospective remembering,
relying on typical external cues can cause
problems when the cues that normally trigger retrieval of the intention action are not
present. In these cases, it seems important to
"reset" your implementation intention for the
new situation or to rely on external reminding devices.

INTRODUCING DELAYS BETWEEN PROSPECTIVE MEMORY RETRIEVAL AND RESPONDING

Standard prospective memory laboratory
tasks generally allow performance of the
intended action immediately upon cue presentation. In other words, participants are
instructed to press the designated response
key as soon as the target item occurs. Immediately performing a response after having
retrieved it is not always possible in everyday
situations. For example, upon seeing your
neighbor and remembering that you need
to give her a message, the neighbor may be
in the midst of a conversation with another
person. In this case, politeness dictates that
you delay delivering the message until there
is a pause in the conversation. Or, you may
retrieve the intention to take your medication
when you are in the bedroom, but must delay
taking the medication until you walk to the
kitchen to get the medicine bottle. A priori,
it is unclear how age will affect performance
in these delayed-execute situations. On the
one hand, the delays are often very brief, a
matter of seconds, and such brief delays may
not be very challenging for older adults. On
the other hand, there is ample theoretical
and empirical work suggesting that keeping
current concerns activated is a core function of working memory (Engle, Tuholski, Laughlin, & Conway, 1999), and that
working memory resources decline with age
(Park, Lautenschlager, Hedden, Davidson,
Smith, & Smith, 2002; Salthouse, 1991).

Older adults may also be more distractible
(Hasher & Zacks, 1988). Taken together,
these views suggest that brief delays may be
very problematic for older adults.

To examine this issue, Einstein, McDaniel,
Manzi, Cochran, and Baker (2000) developed
a delay-execute laboratory paradigm. As can
be seen in Figure 3.2, in this paradigm subjects read a series of short three-sentence
paragraphs. Following the paragraph, there
was a series of tasks. First, there were several
synonym items to answer and then several
trivia questions. And following the trivia
questions was a comprehension question
directed at the just-read paragraph. In the
immediate prospective memory conditions,
subjects were instructed to press a designated
key whenever they encountered a particular
target word and critically, the target word,
when it occurred always appeared in the
three-sentence paragraph and was presented

Ongoing task – Paragraph comprehension (this
sequence was repeated for 20 trials)

1. A three-sentence paragraph was presented
   one sentence at a time.
2. Participants performed a brief multiple-
   choice synonym task.
3. Participants answered two multiple-choice
   trivia questions.
4. Participants answered a multiple-choice
   comprehension question about the initial
   three-sentence paragraph.

Prospective memory task

A prospective memory target cue
(TECHNIQUE or SYSTEM) occurred in
some of the three-sentence paragraphs.

Immediate prospective memory condition –
participants were asked to make the
prospective memory response as soon as
they saw TECHNIQUE or SYSTEM.

Delay-execute condition – upon seeing
TECHNIQUE or SYSTEM, participants were
asked to delay their prospective memory
response until they encountered the trivia
questions.

**Figure 3.2   Sequence of events for the
Delay-Execute Task (from Einstein et al.,
2000).**

in capital letters so it was always a very salient cue. The salient cue produced virtually perfect retrieval in these conditions. The critical conditions were those in which subjects were instructed to delay executing the intended action until they encountered the trivia question.

In a series of experiments, Einstein and McDaniel and colleagues (Einstein et al., 2000; McDaniel, Einstein, Stout, & Morgan, 2003) showed that older adults display robust and dramatic declines in performance on this task. With delays as brief as 5 seconds, older adults remembered to execute the action less than half the time (remember that memory was virtually perfect for both younger and older adults when they were allowed to respond immediately). This low level of performance occurred even when the 5-second delay was unfilled with any distracter activity (see Figure 3.3 for results from McDaniel et al., 2003). As can be seen from Figure 3.3, the low level of performance for older adults was in sharp contrast to younger adults' performance. Younger adults responded at least 80 percent of the time even after a 15-second filled delay and nearly 90 percent of the time after the 5-second unfilled delay.

Why is maintaining intentions for 5–30 seconds a major problem for older adults? One possibility is that older adults are less aware of the fleeting nature of passively stored information (a meta-memory problem)? This factor may play a role as McDaniel et al. (2003) showed that older adults instructed to rehearse the intended activity over the brief delay somewhat improved their prospective memory performance (see Figure 3.3). However, the rehearsal-instructed older adults still did not achieve performance levels displayed by noninstructed younger adults. This suggests that perhaps reduced working memory resources with age produce difficulty in maintaining the activation of retrieved intentions.

According to Kane and Engle (2003), a central function of working memory is controlling attention and keeping thoughts (such as intentions) activated in the face of distraction. Thus compromised working memory ability could create difficulties in maintaining rehearsal while performing other activities. This may not be the whole story either because, as previously mentioned, with 5-second unfilled delays older adults still displayed a dramatic decline

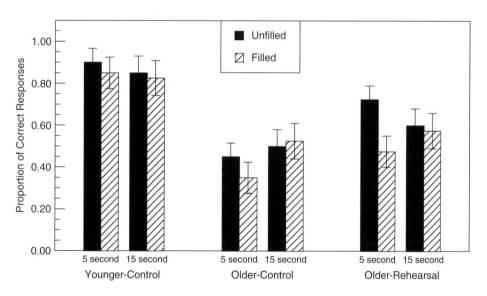

Figure 3.3 Mean proportion of delayed-execute responses for control young and old and rehearsal-instructed older adults (McDaniel et al., 2003).

in performance relative to younger adults. Still another possibility is that older adults have difficulty reformulating their plans once the intention cannot be performed at that moment. Any or all of these factors might influence the decline for older adults in delayed-execute tasks.

APPLIED IMPLICATIONS OF DELAYS IN PERFORMING INTENDED ACTIONS

Regardless of the exact explanation, brief delays after retrieving an intention pose serious problems for prospective memory in general but especially for older adults (see also Kelly & Hertzog, 2010; Rendell, Ozgis, & Wallis, 2004). Once retrieved and a delay is encountered, we are dependent on fragile monitoring processes for keeping the intention activated until we can perform it. A consistent theme in this chapter is that monitoring is difficult to maintain and easily distracted, and this is particularly the case for older adults. Although retrieved intentions often seem vivid and indelible, we need to realize that these thoughts can be quickly lost from focal awareness. For example, many of us have had the experience of forming the intention to send an attachment via email to a friend. As we get absorbed with the task of writing a cover note, however, we sometimes lose this intention (which was the sole reason for sending the email in the first place) and send the message without the attachment. Thus, one recommendation for older adults, but also for younger adults, is "to do it or lose it." So, the next time you get the thought to include an attachment in an email, don't wait until you have finished your message but instead make that the first thing that you do.

Sometimes, however, we cannot avoid a delay. For example, the telephone may ring just before we attach the attachment in the email. In those cases, we recommend that you set up an external cue to alert you to the fact that you still have an intention to complete (perhaps a quickly jotted note or reminding yourself either by crossing your fingers or by putting a nearby object in an unusual location such as a book in the middle of the floor).

Even experienced prospective memory researchers sometimes underestimate the pernicious effects of short delays on prospective memory. Just a few weeks ago, one of the authors of this chapter drove to the dry cleaners to pick up shirts. As he got out of the car, he laid his sunglasses on the driver's seat. Being aware of the research and fully realizing that this could be a problem, he formed the conscious intention to remember to remove the sunglasses before getting back in the car. He also consciously tried to keep that intention in mind over the brief interval that it took to pick up the shirts. As you might guess, after a brief chat with the clerk at the dry cleaners, he was no longer thinking about his sunglasses one minute later when he jumped into the driver's seat and broke the sunglasses into two pieces. (Fortunately, he had insurance that allows one replacement – and he will not trust his monitoring processes again!)

HABITUAL PROSPECTIVE MEMORY TASKS

Another type of prospective memory situation that poses challenges for all, but especially for older adults, is habitual prospective memory tasks. In habitual prospective memory tasks, the intended activity is one that is performed on a regular or systematic basis. Older adults have a number of important habitual prospective memory tasks, perhaps the most prominent being medication regimens. With habitual prospective memory tasks, however, the main difficulty for older adults may be the *retrospective* memory problem of remembering whether or not the action has already been performed. Einstein, McDaniel, Smith, and Shaw (1998) developed a laboratory habitual prospective memory paradigm to investigate age-related changes in habitual prospective memory. In this experiment, participants busily performed eleven 3-minute tasks and in addition were asked to press a designated key about 30 seconds into each task. Einstein et al. found that omission errors for older adults declined as the prospective memory task became more habitual. Importantly, as the trials progressed, a new kind of error emerged for older adults. As the prospective memory task became more habitual, older adults demonstrated increasing repetition errors, whereas younger adults demonstrated very low levels of repetition errors (see Figure 3.4). That is, as the prospective memory task became more habitual, older adults had difficulty remembering whether or not they had performed the activity, and consequently often repeated the activity.

Einstein et al.'s (1998) instructions encouraged subjects to repeat the intended action if they were not sure whether they had performed it in the first place. In a follow up study, McDaniel, Bugg, Ramuschkat, Kliegel, and Einstein (2009) varied whether instructions encouraged omission or repetition errors. In this experiment, regardless of the instructional bias, as the prospective memory task became habitual, older adults persisted in demonstrating repetition errors. Extending this finding to the real world, older adults may have problems in a habitual task like medication taking, and these could lead to potentially serious overmedication. At this point, it is uncertain what kind of processing problems support repetition errors for older adults in habitual prospective memory tasks. Older adults may have problems with output monitoring such that as the activity becomes more routine they increasingly have difficulty remembering whether or not they performed the activity (Marsh, Hicks, Cook, & Mayhorn, 2007). Older adults may also have problems with source monitoring, such that they remember performing the activity but that memory dissociates from the spatial and temporal context (Hashtroudi, Johnson, & Chrosniak, 1989). Older adults may also have problems with reality monitoring (McDaniel, Lyle, Butler, & Dornburg, 2008) such that they cannot distinguish thoughts about the activity from actual performance of the activity.

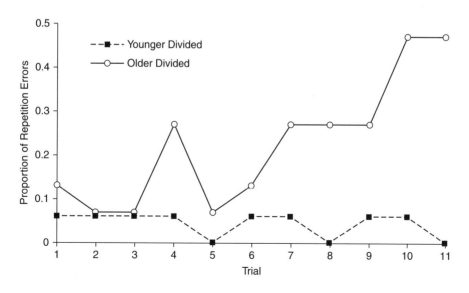

Figure 3.4 Mean proportion of repetition errors in Einstein, McDaniel, Smith, and Shaw (1998).

APPLIED IMPLICATIONS OF HABITUAL TASKS

This research highlights the importance of providing aids for older adults who have important habitual prospective memory demands. For medication taking, a common external aid would be a pillbox in which the daily regime is placed in boxes identified by different days of the week. Such pillboxes may not always serve their purpose, however. In some cases it appears that older adults do not trust the information provided by the pillbox. That is, when encountering an empty box for the day the older adult, rather than thinking that he or she took the medication, may believe that he or she did not fill the pillbox in the first place. Thus, in some cases it may be necessary to implement a particular motor strategy to overcome problems with habitual prospective memory. In McDaniel et al. (2009), some older subjects were instructed to place their hand on their head when performing the prospective memory activity. The idea here is that the unusual motor activity produces a rich memory trace that is then well remembered and associated with the particular context. Under these instructional situations, older adults did not display the repetition errors that the noninstructed older adults did. Thus, age-related problems with habitual prospective memory tasks can be overcome either with external aids or by making the action more complex so that it is performed less automatically and is thus more likely to be remembered.

PROSPECTIVE MEMORY UNDER BUSY CONDITIONS

One intuition that most people have is that we are more likely to forget to perform actions in the future when we are busy. Indeed, there is ample evidence that dividing attention interferes with prospective memory performance (e.g., Einstein, Smith, McDaniel, & Shaw, 1997; Marsh & Hicks, 1998) and even when people use implementation intentions (McDaniel & Scullin, 2010). There is also evidence that dividing attention is particularly disruptive for older adults (Einstein et al., 1997). These studies do not, however, specify the exact processes that are disrupted by busy conditions.

Given that monitoring processes are known to be attentionally demanding (e.g., Scullin, McDaniel, & Einstein, 2010; Smith, 2003), it seems clear that when we are busy, we are less able to sustain an effective monitoring process. It is also possible, however, that busy conditions interfere with cue-driven spontaneous retrieval processes. The idea here is that focal cues that have been associated with intended actions might be less likely to cause retrieval of the intended action into conscious awareness under highly demanding conditions, perhaps because focusing attention involves setting a higher threshold for allowing new thoughts into awareness (Conway & Pleydell-Pearce, 2000; Einstein & McDaniel, 2008, 2010). This thinking is in line with research showing that involuntary memories (i.e., autobiographical memories that come to mind spontaneously) are more likely to occur when the attentional system is not highly focused.

Recently, Harrison et al. (in press) directly examined whether dividing attention interferes with spontaneous retrieval of prospective memories. They asked subjects to perform an ongoing lexical decision task while also at times performing a concurrent random number generation task, which has been shown to require extensive central executive resources. The prospective memory task was to press a designated key whenever a particular target word occurred. Critically, the instructions encouraged reliance on spontaneous retrieval processes by strongly discouraging monitoring. Monitoring was discouraged by telling participants that the main goal of the research was to examine performance on the ongoing lexical decision and random number generation tasks. Further, participants were told that the prospective memory target would only occur for 5 percent of the participants and thus not to focus on that task, but that they should make the appropriate response if they should happen to see it. These instructions were effective as there was no evidence of monitoring (i.e., no evidence that subjects slowed down when they had a prospective memory intention relative to a control block when they did not have a prospective memory intention). In two experiments, the results showed that performing a random number generation task concurrently with the lexical decision task significantly lowered prospective memory performance.

It appears that busy conditions compromise prospective remembering by interfering with both spontaneous retrieval processes and monitoring processes. Thus, external cues that are effective under standard attentional conditions become less effective under busy conditions.

Another feature of Harrison et al.'s (in press) experiments is that dividing attention did not disrupt prospective memory when the target event was a highly salient cue. Specifically, when the target event was presented in large, red capital letters and the nontarget items occurred in small, black lowercase letters, prospective memory performance was nearly perfect, regardless of whether attention was divided or not. Thus, perceptually distinctive events seem to be noticed and lead to retrieval of intended actions regardless of current attentional demands.

IMPLICATIONS OF BUSY CONDITIONS FOR PROSPECTIVE MEMORY

Given that both monitoring and spontaneous retrieval processes are affected under busy conditions, one should realize that prospective remembering is especially vulnerable in these situations. Indeed, although fairly rare, surgical doctors and nurses occasionally leave a foreign object (e.g., an instrument) in a person's body (Gawande, Studdert, Orav,

Brennan, & Zinner, 2003). Interestingly, one of strongest predictors of this kind of error is the demanding conditions of an emergency surgery. Thus, we should be aware that prospective memory is especially susceptible to forgetting under these conditions and particularly so for older adults, and we should try to use highly salient external cues (like perceptually distinctive cues or reminding devices) under these conditions.

COMPLEX PROSPECTIVE MEMORY AND THE IMPORTANCE OF PLANNING

Laboratory research of prospective memory has mostly focused on relatively simple prospective memory tasks that require little to no planning (for tractability and for purposes of experimental control). In the real world, however, prospective memory tasks can be complex such that several interlinked intended actions are planned in the service of accomplishing an overarching goal. For instance, accomplishing the goal of mailing items to your daughter involves planning and remembering to take those items to work, remembering to buy packing materials, and remembering to stop by the post office on the way home from work. As a start to investigating the planning processes of younger and older adults in these more complex prospective memory tasks, Kliegel, McDaniel, and Einstein (2000) adopted a laboratory sub-goal scheduling task, the six-element task. In the typical six-element task, subjects work on the tasks with the constraints that certain tasks cannot be worked on in consecutive sequence, there is not enough time to finish all tasks, and the first items in each task are worth more than later items (Shallice & Burgess, 1991). The challenge for the subject is to schedule the order in which tasks are worked on, to work on every task, and to not spend too much time on any one task.

In the Kliegel et al. (2000) paradigm, planning and intention formation were examined by asking subjects to plan aloud how they would perform the six-element task. Then approximately half an hour later in the experiment (during a questionnaire task), subjects had to remember to initiate the six-element task. A major finding was that there was an age-related decline in plan quality, in terms of the specificity and elaborateness of the plans. Younger adults were more likely than older adults to specify reasons for the order in which they would perform the six sub-tasks (in the six-element task), and to develop cues for when to interrupt one sub-task and move to the next task. The second major finding was that better quality plans were in turn associated with greater success at remembering to initiate the six-element task and with success in performing the six-element task, that is, in interrupting one of the six sub-tasks and moving on to other sub-tasks. More recent research with this paradigm has established a causal connection between plan quality and the level of performance on this complex prospective memory task (Kliegel, Martin, McDaniel, Einstein, & Moor, 2007). Thus, appropriate planning appears to be an important determinant of successful completion of complex prospective memory tasks, with older adults showing deficits in their plan quality.

APPLIED IMPLICATIONS FOR COMPLEX TASKS

People can improve performance on complex prospective memory tasks by appropriate planning. Kliegel et al. (2007) found that providing explicit guidance in formulating plans for the six-element task, guidance that included explicit instructions to incorporate the cue for initiating the six-element task into the plan nearly doubled the frequency with which people remembered to initiate the six-element task. The effect was as robust for older adults as for younger adults. Further, when the plan guidance also encouraged people to specify switching heuristics for the six sub-tasks, older adults especially showed

improvement in interrupting sub-tasks and moving on to other sub-tasks. Older adults might thus be assisted in complex prospective memory tasks by providing explicit planning guidance on particular tasks they find most challenging. We speculate, however, that interventions that inform older adults (and younger adults) about the features of appropriate plans would be more broadly useful, because such interventions would in principle allow older adults to generate plans for whatever complex task they encountered. Developing and evaluating such an intervention awaits further research.

CONCLUSION

A feature of prospective memory tasks is that retrieval is self-initiated. That is, when the opportunity for performing an intended action occurs, there is no one there to get you to initiate a search of memory for the action that you planned to perform. Given that these opportunities tend to occur while we are busily engaged in other activities, we can easily fail to remember to perform an intended action at the appropriate point in time (despite complete retrospective memory for the intention). There is evidence that we can use multiple processes to support prospective remembering, including controlled monitoring processes and spontaneous retrieval processes that are triggered by environmental cues.[2]

The evidence shows that prospective memory is more susceptible to forgetting when we are more dependent on capacity consuming monitoring processes (e.g., with nonfocal cues, when delays are encountered, when we have not established focal cues through planning). It has also been established that such monitoring functions draw on working memory resources and decline with age (Park et al., 2002). Monitoring processes are also subject to fatigue and easily distracted. Thus, whenever possible, we suggest using external reminders and/or in the spirit of forming implementation intentions (Gollwitzer, 1999), connect the to-be-performed action with an anticipated focal cue. The idea is that future processing of the focal cue will stimulate spontaneous retrieval of the intended action, and there is growing exciting evidence that this process is relatively spared in older adults.

NOTES

1 We thank Gus Craik and Steve Lindsay for helpful suggestions on an earlier version of this paper.

2 We assume also that we sometimes retrieve our prospective memory intentions through controlled searches of memory for unfinished planned activities, and we assume that the processes involved in this kind of retrieval are captured by retrospective memory retrieval processes like those involved in cued recall tasks.

REFERENCES

Aberle, I., Rendell, P. G., Rose, N., McDaniel, M. A., & Kliegel, M. (2010). The age prospective memory paradox: Young adults may not give their best outside of the lab. *Developmental Psychology, 46*, 1444–1453.

Bargh, J. A. & Chartrand, T. L. (1999). The unbearable automaticity of being. *American Psychologist, 54*, 462–479.

Brewer, G. A., Knight, J. B., Marsh, R. L., & Unsworth, N. (2010). Individual differences in event-based prospective memory: Evidence for multiple processes supporting cue detection. *Memory & Cognition, 38*, 304–311.

Chasteen, A. L., Park, D. C., & Schwartz, N. (2001). Implementation intentions and facilitation of prospective memory. *Psychological Science, 12*, 457–461.

Cherry, K. E., & LeCompte, D. C. (1999). Age and individual differences influence prospective memory. *Psychology and Aging, 14*, 60–76.

Cohen, A. L., & Gollwitzer, P. M. (2008). The cost of remembering to remember: Cognitive load and implementation intentions influence ongoing task performance. In M. Kliegel, M. A. McDaniel, and G. O. Einstein (Eds.), *Prospective memory: Cognitive,*

neuroscience, developmental, and applied perspectives (pp. 367–390). Mahwah, NJ: Erlbaum.

Cohen, A-L., Kantner, J., Dixon, R. A., & Lindsay, D. S. (2011). The intention interference effect: The difficulty of ignoring what you intend to do. *Experimental Psychology, 58*, 425–433.

Cohen, A.-L., West, R., & Craik, F. I. M. (2001). Modulation of the prospective and retrospective components of memory for intentions in younger and older adults. *Aging, Neuropsychology, and Cognition, 8*, 1–13.

Conway, M. A., & Pleydell-Pearce, C. W. (2000). The construction of autobiographical memories in the self-memory system. *Psychological Review, 107*, 261–288.

Coubard, O. A., Ferrufino, L., Boura, M., Gripon, A., Renaud, M., & Bherer, L. (2011). Attentional control in normal aging and Alzheimer's disease. *Neuropsychology, 25*, 353–367.

Craik, F. I. M. (1986). A functional account of age differences in memory. In F. Klix and H. Hagendorf (Eds.), *Human memory and cognitive capabilities: Mechanisms and performances* (pp. 409–422). North Holland: Elsevier Science Publishers.

Craik, F. I. M. (2003). Aging and memory in humans. In J. H. Byrne (Ed.), *Learning and memory* (2nd ed., pp. 10–14). New York: Macmillan Reference USA.

Dismukes, R. K. (2008). Prospective memory in aviation and everyday settings. In M. Kliegel, M. A. McDaniel, and G. O. Einstein (Eds.), *Prospective memory: Cognitive, neuroscience, developmental, and applied perspectives* (pp. 411–431). Mahwah, NJ: Erlbaum.

d'Ydewalle, G., Luwel, K., & Brunfaut, E. (1999). The importance of on-going concurrent activities as a function of age in time- and event-based prospective memory. *European Journal of Cognitive Psychology, 11*(2), 219–237.

Dywan, J., & Jacoby, L. L. (1990). Effects of aging on source monitoring: Differences in susceptibility to false fame. *Psychology and Aging, 5*, 379–387.

Einstein, G. O., & McDaniel, M. A. (1990). Normal aging and prospective memory. *Journal of Experimental Psychology: Learning, Memory and Cognition, 16*, 717–726.

Einstein, G. O., & McDaniel, M. A. (2008). Prospective memory and metamemory: The skilled use of basic attentional and memory processes. In A. Benjamin (Ed). *The psychology of learning and motivation* (pp.145–173). San Diego, CA: Elsevier.

Einstein, G. O., & McDaniel, M. A. (2010). Prospective memory and what costs do not reveal about retrieval processes: A commentary on Smith, Hunt, McVay, and McConnell (2007). *Journal of Experimental*

Psychology: Learning, Memory, & Cognition, 36, 1082–1088.

Einstein, G. O., McDaniel, M. A., Manzi, M., Cochran, B., & Baker, M. (2000). Prospective memory and aging: Forgetting intentions over short delays. *Psychology and Aging, 15,* 671–683.

Einstein, G. O., McDaniel, M. A., Richardson, S. L., Guynn, M. J., & Cunfer, A. R. (1995). Aging and prospective memory: Examining the influences of self-initiated retrieval processes. *Journal of Experimental Psychology: Learning, Memory and Cognition, 21,* 996–1007.

Einstein, G. O., McDaniel, M. A., Smith, R. E., & Shaw, P. (1998). Habitual prospective memory and aging: Remembering intentions and forgetting actions. *Psychological Science, 9,* 284–288.

Einstein, G. O., McDaniel, M. A., Thomas, R., Mayfield, S., Shank, S., Morrisette, N., & Brenheiser, J. (2005). Multiple processes in prospective memory retrieval: Factors determining monitoring versus spontaneous retrieval. *Journal of Experimental Psychology: General, 134,* 327–342.

Einstein, G. O., Smith, R. E., McDaniel, M. A., & Shaw, P. (1997). Aging and prospective memory: The influence of increased task demands at encoding and retrieval. *Psychology and Aging, 12,* 479–488.

Engle, R.W., Tuholski, S. W., Laughlin, J. E., & Conway, A. R. A. (1999). Working memory, short-term memory, and general fluid intelligence: A latent variable approach. *Journal of Experimental Psychology: General, 128,* 309–331.

Gawande, A. A., Studdert, D. M., Orav, E. J., Brennan, T. A., & Zinner, M. J. (2003). Risk factors for retained instruments and sponges after surgery. *New England Journal of Medicine, 348*(3), 228–235.

Gollwitzer, P. M. (1999). How can good intentions become effective behavior change strategies? *American Psychologist, 54,* 493–503.

Gollwitzer, P. M. & Brandstatter, V. (1997). Implementation intentions and effective goal pursuit. *Journal of Personality & Social Psychology, 73*(1), 186–199.

Harris, J. E. (1984). Remembering to do things: A forgotten topic. In J. E. Harris and P. E. Morris (Eds.), *Everyday memory, actions, and absent-mindedness* (pp. 71–92). New York: Academic Press.

Harris, J. E., & Wilkins, A. J. (1982). Remember to do things: A theoretical framework, and an illustrative experiment. *Human Learning, 1,* 123–136.

Harrison, T. L., Mullet, H. G., Whiffen, K. N., Ousterhout, H., & Einstein, G. O. (in press). Prospective memory: Effects of divided attention on spontaneous retrieval. *Memory & Cognition.*

Harrison, T. L., & Einstein, G. O. (2010). Prospective memory: Are preparatory attentional processes necessary for a single focal cue? *Memory & Cognition, 38*(7), 860–867.

Hasher, L., & Zacks, R. T. (1988). Working memory, comprehension, and aging: A review and a new view. In G. Bower (Ed.), *The psychology of learning and motivation* (pp. 193–225). New York: Academic Press.

Hashtroudi, S., Johnson, M. K., & Chrosniak, L. D. (1989). Aging and source monitoring. *Psychology and Aging, 4,* 106–112.

Henry, J. D., MacLeod, M. S., Phillips, L. H., & Crawford, J. R. (2004). A meta-analytic review of prospective memory and aging. *Psychology and Aging, 19,* 27–39.

Insel, K., Morrow, D., Brewer, B., & Figueredo, A. (2006). Executive function, working memory, and medication adherence among older adults. *Journal of Gerontology: Psychological Sciences, 61B,* 102–107.

Jacoby, L. L. (1992). A process dissociation framework: Separating automatic from intentional uses of memory. *Journal of Memory and Language, 30,* 513–541.

Kane, M. J., & Engle, R. W. (2003). Working-memory capacity and the control of attention: The contributions of goal neglect, response competition, and task set to Stroop interference. *Journal of Experimental Psychology: General, 132,* 47–70.

Kelly, A. J., & Hertzog, C. (2010, April). Delay-execute prospective memory and aging: Differences in monitoring? Poster presented at the Cognitive Aging Conference, Atlanta, GA.

Kliegel, M., Jager, T., & Phillips, L. H. (2008). Adult age differences in event-based prospective memory: A meta-analysis on the role of focal versus nonfocal cues. *Psychology and Aging, 23,* 203–208.

Kliegel, M., Martin, M, McDaniel, M. A., Einstein, G. O., & Moor, C. (2007). Realizing complex delayed intentions in young and old adults: The role of planning aids. *Memory & Cognition, 35,*1735–1746.

Kliegel, M., McDaniel, M. A., & Einstein, G. O. (2000). Plan formation, retention, and execution in prospective memory: A new approach and age-related effects. *Memory & Cognition, 28,* 1041–1049.

Kvavilashvili, L., & Fisher, L. (2007). Is time-based prospective remembering mediated by self-initiated rehearsals? Effects of incidental cues, ongoing activity, age, and motivation. *Journal of Experimental Psychology: General, 136,* 12–132.

Kvavilashvili, L., Kornbrot, D. E., Mash, V., Cockburn, J., & Milne, A. (2009). Differential effects of age on prospective and retrospective memory tasks in young, young –old, and old –old adults. *Memory, 17,* 180–196.

Liu, L. L., & Park, D. C. (2004). Aging and medical adherence: The use of automatic processes to achieve effortful things. *Psychology & Aging, 19,* 318–325.

Loft, S., Kearney, R., & Remington, R. (2008). Is task interference in event-based prospective memory dependent on cue presentation? *Memory & Cognition, 36,* 139–148.

Marsh, R. L., & Hicks, J. L. (1998). Event-based prospective memory and executive control of working memory. *Journal of Experimental Psychology: Learning, Memory, and Cognition, 24,* 336–349.

Marsh, R. L., Hicks, J. L, Cook, G. I., & Mayhorn, C. B. (2007). Comparing older and younger adults in an event-based prospective memory paradigm containing an output monitoring component. *Aging, Neuropsychology, and Cognition, 14,* 168–188.

McDaniel, M. A., Bugg, J. M., Ramuschkat, G. M., Kliegel, M., & Einstein, G. O. (2009). Repetition errors in habitual prospective memory: Elimination of age differences via complex actions or appropriate resource allocation. *Aging, Neuropsychology, and Cognition, 16,* 563–588.

McDaniel, M. A., & Einstein, G. O. (1993). The importance of cue familiarity and cue distinctiveness in prospective memory. *Memory, 1,* 23–41.

McDaniel, M. A., & Einstein, G. O. (2000). Strategic and automatic processes in prospective memory retrieval: A multiprocess framework. *Applied Cognitive Psychology. Special Issue: New perspectives in prospective memory, 14,* S127–S144.

McDaniel, M. A., & Einstein, G. O. (2007). *Prospective memory: An overview and synthesis of an emerging field.* Thousand Oaks, CA: Sage.

McDaniel, M. A., & Einstein, G. O. (2011). The neuropsychology of prospective memory in normal aging: A componential approach. *Neuropsychologia, 49,* 2147–2155.

McDaniel, M. A., Einstein, G. O., Stout, A. C., & Morgan, Z. (2003). Aging and maintaining intentions over delays: Do it or lose it. *Psychology and Aging, 18,* 823–835.

McDaniel, M. A., Guynn, M. J., Einstein, G. O., & Breneiser, J. (2004). Cue-focused and reflexive-associative processes in prospective memory retrieval. *Journal of Experimental Psychology: Learning, Memory, and Cognition, 30,* 605–614.

McDaniel, M. A., Lyle, K., Butler, K. M., & Dornburg, C. C. (2008). Age-related deficits in reality monitoring of action memories. *Psychology and Aging, 23,* 646–656.

McDaniel, M. A., Howard, D. W., & Butler, K. M. (2008). Implementation intentions facilitate prospective memory under high attention demands. *Memory & Cognition, 36,* 716–724.

McDaniel, M. A., & Scullin, M. K. (2010). Implementation intention encoding does not automatize prospective memory responding. *Memory & Cognition, 38,* 221–232.

McDaniel, M. A., Shelton, J. T., Breneiser, J. E., Moynan, S., & Balota, D. A. (2011). *Focal and nonfocal prospective memory performance in very mild dementia: A signature decline. Neuropsychology, 25,* 387–396.

McFarland, C. P., & Glisky, E. L. (2012). Implementation intentions and imagery: Individual and combined effects on prospective memory among young adults. *Memory & Cognition, 40*(1), 62–69.

Mioni, G. & Stablum, F. (2013). Monitoring behavior in a time-based prospective memory task: The involvement of executive functions and time perception. *Memory.* Advance online publication. doi:10.1080/09658211.2013.801987.

Moscovitch, M. (1982). A neuropsychological approach to memory and perception in normal and pathological aging. In F. I. M. Craik and S. Trehub (Eds.), *Advances in the study of communication and affect: Vol. 8. Aging and cognitive processes* (pp. 55–78). New York: Plenum Press.

Mullet, H. G., Scullin, M. K., Hess, T. J., Scullin, R. B., Arnold, K. M., & Einstein, G. O. (in press). Prospective memory and aging: Evidence for preserved spontaneous retrieval with exact but not related cues. *Psychology and Aging.*

Orbell, S., Hodgkins, S. & Sheeran, P. (1997). Implementation intentions and the theory of planned behavior. *Personality & Social Psychology Bulletin, 23*(9), 945–954.

Park, D. C., Hertzog, C., Kidder, D. P., Morrell, R. W., & Mayhorn, C. B. (1997). Effect of age on event-based and time-based prospective memory. *Psychology and Aging, 12,* 314–327.

Park, D. C., Lautenschlager, G., Hedden, T., Davidson, N. S., Smith, A. D., & Smith, P. K. (2002). Models of visuospatial and verbal memory across the adult life span. *Psychology and Aging, 17,* 299–320.

Phillips, L. H., Henry, J. D., & Martin, M. M. (2008). Adult aging and prospective memory: The importance of ecological validity. In M. Kliegel, M. A. McDaniel, and G. O. Einstein (Eds.), *Prospective memory: Cognitive, neuroscience, developmental, and applied perspectives* (pp. 161–185). Mahwah, NJ: Erlbaum.

Reason, J. T. (1990). *Human error*. Cambridge, New York: Cambridge University Press.

Reese, C. M., & Cherry, K. E. (2002). The effects of age, ability, and memory monitoring on prospective memory task performance. *Aging, Neuropsychology, and Cognition, 9*, 98–113.

Rendell, P. G., & Craik, F. I. M. (2000). Virtual and actual week: Age-related differences in prospective memory. *Applied Cognitive Psychology. Special Issue: New perspectives in prospective memory, 14*, S43–S62.

Rendell, P. G., Ozgis, S., & Wallis, A. (2004, April). Age-related effects in prospective remembering: The role of delaying execution of retrieved intentions. Paper presented at the 10th Cognitive Aging Conference, Atlanta, Georgia.

Salthouse, T. A. (1991). *Theoretical perspectives on cognitive aging*. Hillsdale, NJ: Lawrence Erlbaum.

Scullin, M. K., McDaniel, M. A., & Einstein, G. O. (2010). Control of cost in prospective memory: Evidence for spontaneous retrieval processes. *Journal of Experimental Psychology: Learning, Memory, & Cognition, 36*, 190–203.

Scullin, M. K., & McDaniel, M. A., Shelton, J. T., & Lee, J. H. (2010). Focal/nonfocal cue effects in prospective memory: Monitoring difficulty or different retrieval processes? *Journal of Experimental Psychology: Learning, Memory, & Cognition, 36*, 736–749.

Shallice, T. & Burgess, P. (1991). Deficits in strategy application following frontal lobe damage in man. *Brain, 114*, 727–741.

Sheeran, P. & Orbell, S. (1999). Augmenting the theory of planned behavior: Roles for anticipated regret and descriptive norms. *Journal of Applied Social Psychology, 29*, 2107–2142.

Shelton, J. T., McDaniel, M. A., Scullin, M. K., Cahill, M. J., Singer, J. S., & Einstein, G. O. (2011). Cognitive exertion and subsequent intention execution in older adults. *Journal of Gerontology: Psychological Sciences, 66B* (2), 143–150.

Shelton, J., Lee, J. H., Scullin, M., Rose, N., Rendell, P., & McDaniel, M. A. (2012, April). Implementation intentions boost prospective memory in very mildly demented older adults. Poster presented at the 14th Cognitive Aging Conference, Atlanta, Georgia.

Smith, R. E. (2003). The cost of remembering to remember in event-based prospective memory: Investigating the capacity demands of delayed intention performance. *Journal of Experimental Psychology: Learning, Memory, & Cognition, 29*, 347–361.

Stone, V. E. (2001). Strategies for optimizing adherence to highly active antiretroviral therapy: lessons from research and clinical practice. *Clinical Infectious Diseases, 33*(6), 865–872.

Uttl, B. (2008). Transparent meta-analysis of prospective memory and aging. *PloS ONE, 3*, e1568.

Vogels, W. W. A., Dekker, M. R., Brouwer, W. H., & de Jong, R. (2002). Age-related changes in event-related prospective memory performance: A comparison of four prospective memory tasks. *Brain & Cognition, 49*(3), 341–362.

West, R., & Craik, F. I. M. (1999). Age-related decline in prospective memory: The roles of cue accessibility and cure sensitivity. *Psychology and Aging, 14*, 264–272.

Wilson, E. A. H., & Park, D. (2008). Prospective memory and health behaviors: Context trumps cognition. In M. Kliegel, M. A. McDaniel, and G. O. Einstein (Eds.), *Prospective memory: Cognitive, neuroscience, developmental, and applied perspectives* (pp. 391–410). Mahwah, NJ: Erlbaum.

World Health Organization (2003). Adherence to long-term therapies: Evidence for action. Retrieved from http://apps.who.int/medicinedocs/en/d/Js4883e/5.html

4

Memory Source Monitoring Applied

D. Stephen Lindsay

How does the mind/brain differentiate fact from fancy, perception from inference? How do we distinguish creating a novel tune from remembering someone else's melody? How do we discriminate memories of what we witnessed at the scene of a crime from memories of a co-witness's description of what happened? The central premise of the source-monitoring framework (SMF) is that the origins of our sensations, thoughts, images, and feelings are not abstractly and unambiguously specified and labelled a priori but rather are inferred by the mind/brain (usually very rapidly and without conscious reflection) on the basis of their content in the course of our experiencing them. Most of the time the inferences are correct, but often the accessed information is insufficient to support a source attribution and occasionally a mental event from one source is misattributed to another. In the realm of gustatory experience, for example, inputs from the nose are routinely misattributed to the tongue; lacking olfaction it is reportedly difficult to distinguish an apple from a potato, but when one savours an orange pippin the lovely flavour sensations seem to come from the mouth. As another perceptual example,

what we see, hear, feel, or smell can be influenced by our expectations; if you are waiting for Don to telephone and your iPhone rings you may mistake Patrick's voice for Don's, especially if the connection quality is poor or there is lots of background noise or you are momentarily distracted as you take the call.

Research and theorizing informed by the SMF has focused primarily on mental events that are attributed to memory.[1] The majority of work on the SMF has had to do with mental events that are attributed to memory for specific experiences in the personal past, that is, to episodic memory. A smaller literature informed by (or at least consistent with) the SMF has examined attributions to knowledge or what Newman, Garry, Bernstein, Kantner, and Lindsay (2012) recently termed (in reference to comedian Stephen Colbert's term) "truthiness." Thus the purview of the current chapter is applied implications of source monitoring in the domains of autobiographical memory and belief. Before discussing those applied issues I will provide some general background on the SMF (see Mitchell & Johnson, 2009, and Lindsay, 2008, for more extensive exegeses of the SMF itself).

A BRIEF OVERVIEW OF THE SOURCE-MONITORING FRAMEWORK

The SMF has roots in Frederick Bartlett's seminal 1932 work *Remembering*. It also shares ideas with a variety of more recent theoretical perspectives, including Larry Jacoby's "attributional" approach to the subjective experience of remembering (e.g., Jacoby, Kelley, & Dywan, 1989), Bruce Whittlesea's elaboration of the attribution approach, SCAPE (e.g., Whittlesea, 2003), Koriat and Goldsmith's (e.g., 1996) work on monitoring and control processes, Tulving's (e.g., 1982) ideas about synergistic ecphory and conversion processes, and Michael Ross's (e.g., 1989) work on theories of the self and autobiographical memory. But the immediate parent of the SMF was Marcia Johnson and Carol Raye's (1981) reality monitoring (RM) model.

The motivation for the RM model grew out of research in the 1970s that, partly inspired by Bartlett (1932), explored the roles of knowledge and belief in sculpting remembrance (e.g., Bransford & Johnson, 1972). This research showed that people often mistake details that they had inferred/imagined during an event as things they had directly perceived during the event. For example, having read "The spy threw the secret document into the fireplace," subjects sometimes remembered having read "The spy burned the secret document" (even though they had not been told that there was a fire in the fireplace) (Johnson, Bransford, & Solomon, 1973). The RM model had to do with differentiating between memories of "real" (i.e., perceptually experienced) past events versus memories of imagined or inferred past events. It emphasized quantitative aspects of recollections. The core assumption is that memories of perceptual experiences are, on average, more perceptually vivid and contextually embedded and have fewer memorial indicators of effortful internal generation than do memories of imagined events, so people are biased to perceive recollections that are high on

perceptual detail and embeddedness and low on indications of effortful cognitive operations as memories of real events, and they tend to attribute memories that are lacking in vividness and embeddedness and rich in markers of cognitive operations to imagination. A key claim of the RM model is that the distributions of memories of real and imagined events overlap, such that (for example) we sometimes recollect a peculiarly vivid product of fantasy that we are hence liable to misidentify as a memory of an actual event. The RM model also allowed for a more reflective, post-access process that catches some such errors on the basis of their qualitative content. For example, an extraordinarily vivid recollection of flying might at first feel like a memory of a real event but then correctly be identified as a memory of a dream because one knows one cannot fly unaided. But according to the RM model most attributions to reality versus imagination/thought are made without conscious reflection in the course of experiencing the recollection, not as a deliberate post-retrieval decision-making process.

The source-monitoring framework (Johnson, Hashtroudi, & Lindsay, 1993; Lindsay, 2008) differs from the RM model in several ways. Whereas the RM model essentially dichotomized memories into two categories (real or imagined),[2] "source" is a multidimensional construct with indefinitely many possibilities. Suppose, for example, that you recall an episode in which you learned a joke. Aspects of the source of that recollection include when and where you encountered the joke, the medium in which the joke was presented, the agent who delivered the joke, etc. The notion of "source" overlaps with, but is somewhat more broad and vague than, the notion of "context." The distinction between an event and its source is often fuzzy because aspects of source participate in constituting the event and its meaning (e.g., the import of a statement depends, in part, on who utters it). As Hintzman (2011, p. 257) noted, "Which aspect counts as item and which as context derives more from the perspective of the researcher than from the way memory actually works."

Whereas the RM model emphasized quantitative bases for discriminating memories of actual versus imagined events, the SMF emphasizes the qualitative content of the information evoked by cues (although quantitative characteristics also influence attributions in the SMF). The central idea is that we recognize (or fail to recognize, or misrecognize) aspects of memory sources in ways that are analogous to how we recognize (or fail to recognize or misrecognize) stimuli in ongoing perception (see also Payne & Blackwell, 1998). Because people rarely reflect on and label aspects of source while they are experiencing events (e.g., presumably you are not repeating to yourself "It's the 27th of August at 3:30 pm and I'm sitting in my office reading Steve Lindsay's chapter"), we can rarely directly "retrieve" abstract source designations but rather must infer them from cues in the accessed information[3]. The accessed memory information about a joke, for example, might include fragmentary records of the sound of the teller's voice. Perhaps the acoustic signal would be so clear that you would immediately recognize the speaker as your friend Marty (always good for a joke) without being aware of doing any "monitoring" at all – you'd "just" remember Marty telling you the joke, as you would "just" recognize Marty if he walked in the door. In both cases, the available information is used to infer identity. Under other conditions, perhaps the remembered acoustic information would be too impoverished to enable you to identify the speaker of the remembered utterance yet provide enough information for you to infer that the jokester was male or at least that you learned the joke by hearing someone tell it rather than by reading it.

The multiple features or aspects that make up an event are only loosely bound, and which ones are accessed at a particular moment depends on multifaceted interactions between current and past cognitive processing. Thus often we can access rich cues to some aspects of source but few cues to other aspects of source. You might, for example, confidently recollect being in your office when you heard the joke, and yet have no idea who told the joke. Sometimes deliberative, post-access searches of memory can uncover additional memorial cues to source, enabling us accurately to recognize dimensions of source that previously we could not identify.

People are susceptible to source-monitoring errors when a mental event has characteristics that are typical of another source; just as when answering the phone you might mistake one friend's voice for another's if the two happen to sound similar, so too you would be susceptible to misremembering which of them had uttered a particular statement. Such source misattributions are especially likely if current orientation or expectations bias remembers toward the wrong source.

Source attributions can also be affected by biases as to the strength of memories from particular sources. For example, in three studies by Johnson, Raye, Foley, and Foley (1981), subjects heard some words and had to generate other words on their own, and were later shown a mix of words they had heard, words they had generated, and new words. When subjects false alarmed to words spoken by neither partner, they more often attributed those words to their partner than to themselves. This bias presumably arose because subjects remembered little about those words (after all, they were new words) and presumed that they would remember them better if they had generated them themselves (see Hoffman, 1997).

Time is a particularly challenging aspect of source monitoring. People often have difficulty specifying when a past event occurred, particularly across a range of plausible candidate times during which the person was in a given context. You may, for example remember an excruciating childhood moment when you put your tongue on a frozen metal post; the content of the memory may include many cues to time of year, time of day, and place, but if you spent your entire childhood in that place it may be very difficult to say which year it was. If the place was in the school yard at recess, that probably helps to constrain the day of the week. And if the event was somehow associated with what Neisser (1982) called a benchmark event (e.g., first day at school, change of domicile) then you may be able to site the event in time quite precisely. But often it is difficult to place past events in time with much precision. Perhaps this is because time per se is not a causal agent; it is events that are embedded in and hence correlated with time that have effects, not time itself.

In everyday life, accurate source monitoring is not always at the top of our priorities. If you are entertaining friends with an anecdote, your story may seamlessly mingle accurate episodic details with products of imagination, belief, and desire. Your goals in such a situation may have to do more with impression management and persuasion than with source monitoring. Similarly, if your aim is to solve a problem, your thinking is likely to blend retrieval of past solutions with generation of new ones with little reflection as to their provenance. On the witness stand, in contrast, accurate source monitoring may become front and center, enabling you to do a better job of separating fact from fancy.

These ideas about source monitoring are supported by findings from studies in which people were exposed to information from different sources and then later tested (in various ways) on their ability to differentiate information from those two sources. Consistent with the SMF, errors on such tasks tend to be more common if the two sources are perceptually and/or semantically similar or if the same orienting task had been used to encode items from each source (e.g., Lindsay & Johnson, 1989a; Lindsay, Johnson, & Kwon, 1991). Dividing attention at study or a long study-test delay can impair subsequent source-monitoring (SM) performance to a greater extent than subsequent old/new discrimination (Jacoby, Woloshyn, & Kelley, 1989; cf. Troyer, Winocur, Craik, & Moscovitch, 1999; Kelley & Lindsay, 1993; Lane,

2006). Dividing attention at test can also increase false-memory errors presumably by impairing source monitoring (e.g., Knott & Dewhurst, 2007; Zaragoza & Lane, 1998). Orienting subjects to attend to source at test typically reduces (and sometimes eliminates) source-monitoring misattributions (e.g., Oeberst & Blank, 2012).

LIMITATIONS OF THE SMF

In principle, a well-specified theory of source monitoring should be able to predict the probability of SM errors under any given well-defined set of conditions. But in practice the SMF is too vague and incomplete to support such estimates. Indeed, even predicting whether two conditions will differ in accuracy can be difficult. Suppose, for example, that subjects witness an event and then receive misleading suggestions regarding details in the event that are presented in ways that either make them very similar to the witnessed event or make them quite distinct (while holding overall memorability of the suggestions approximately constant). Should the rate of reporting suggestions differ in the two conditions? Only if test instructions motivate subjects to try to exclude the post-event information; if subjects assume that the post-event information is a legitimate source of answers then there is no reason for them to more often report that information in a high-similarity situation than in a low-similarity situation. Source confusability comes into play only if conditions encourage subjects to differentiate information from different sources.

A related limitation is that we know little about how different dimensions of source interact with one another to determine overall similarity. In an early study, we showed that subjects are more likely to misremember who said what if both of two potential speakers were young women than if one was a young woman and the other an older man. We also observed that source misattributions were more common if the utterance concerned a topic that both speakers had addressed than if it concerned a topic spoken of by only one speaker. In that particular study these two types of similarity appeared to be roughly additive, but in other situations they might interact. The point is that we need more empirical work to explore how multiple dimensions of source act together to determine confusability. Lacking a priori ways to define similarity, the SMF becomes difficult to falsify (see Lindsay & Johnson, 2001).

The vast majority of studies of the SMF have involved situations in which only two sources are in play. Very often, subjects are explicitly asked to differentiate between the two or to base responses on only one of the sources. But in everyday life when thoughts and images come to mind there are indefinitely many potential sources; the situation may offer cues to but does not tightly constrain the field of potential sources. Little is known about source monitoring in such naturalistic situations. Nonetheless, as discussed below, there are many reasons to believe that source-monitoring processes play key roles in a wide variety of everyday applied situations.

APPLIED ASPECTS OF THE SMF

According to the SMF, people go through life making moment-to-moment inferences and attributions as to the sources of the thoughts and images that come to mind (at situationally varying levels of precision). Such attributions have implications for action. Thus applications of the SMF are ubiquitous. Did I take my medications today, or did I just think about taking them (or was that yesterday anyway)? Did I unload the shotgun or did I merely intend to unload it? Was that claim about Obama being an alien in the *New York Times* or in the *National Enquirer*? Did I see a stop sign and broken glass at the accident scene, or did I hear about those details from another witness? Is this guy the mugger, or is his face familiar because

I saw him somewhere else? Do this patient's symptoms indicate scabies, or is my perception of the case being biased by prior cases? Was the razor held by the black guy, or is a racist stereotype causing that image to come to mind so fluently? Have I always held this view on abortion or am I reducing cognitive dissonance? Did I just compose this catchy melody, or am I remembering someone else's tune? Have I always been liberal-minded, or are transfer-appropriate-processing phenomena and my self-theory biasing my remembered past? Does "Hickok" come to mind because it is the correct answer to the question about Buffalo Bill's last name or because I was recently exposed to the name "Hickok?" Are these statistics problems inherently easy, or is it that I've done them so many times before that they seem easy? (See Kelley & Lindsay, 1993.) In the following I summarize some of the research on some of these applied questions.

Eyewitness misinformation effect

Elizabeth F. Loftus pioneered the modern study of eyewitness memory and introduced a three-stage procedure in which subjects first view an event (e.g., a slide show depicting an accident in which a car hits a pedestrian, including a number of critical event details), are then exposed to verbal misleading suggestions regarding some of the critical details in that event (e.g., that an intersection had been marked by a yield sign when a stop sign had appeared in the event), and finally are tested on memory for critical details about which misleading suggestions had versus had not been suggested. Across a wide variety of materials and procedures, subjects often err by reporting misleading suggestions rather than witnessed details.

Loftus initially attributed the effects of misleading post-event information to an updating mechanism. The idea was that when post-event information was encountered subjects retrieved their memorial representation of the original event and (with some probability) replaced the representation of the witnessed detail (e.g., stop sign) with a representation of the suggested detail (e.g., yield sign). Such a process would have two profound implications. First, to the extent that updating occurred, witnessed details would no longer be available in memory – subjects would not be able to remember the critical detail regardless of how memory was cued. Second, the representation of the suggested detail would be an integral part of the original memory representation, no different from representations of witnessed details.

The Loftus updating process can be questioned on a number of grounds. Indeed, it can be asserted as fact that most if not all of the effect in standard misinformation studies does not reflect such a mechanism. For one thing, as noted above such effects can be greatly diminished and perhaps eliminated when tested in different ways. For another, suggestions presented *before* an event is witnessed can produce misinformation effects on reports of event details that seem analogous to those produced by post-event information, even though updating makes no sense with pre-event suggestions (Holliday & Hayes, 2002; Lindsay & Johnson, 1989b). Also, suggestions do not have to have been apprehended as being "about" the witnessed event; relevant details from one story can intrude into reports of another (Allen & Lindsay, 1998; Lindsay, Allen, Chan, & Dahl, 2004). Questions can also be raised about the adaptiveness of a system that irrevocably discards old knowledge when new information is encountered; privileging such information makes more sense. And my impression is that psychologists have only the vaguest idea of what it means to say that "the" representation of an event can be retrieved, edited, and restored for subsequent retrieval and play-back. Finally, as explained by Watkins (1990), it is methodologically challenging to build a convincing case for non-availability, and much easier to champion arguments in terms of retrieval and/or output monitoring/conversion processes (cf. Hintzman, 2011; Sederberg, Gershman, Polyn, & Norman, 2011).

From the perspective of the SMF, the interesting question is under what conditions subjects are likely to confuse memories of suggested details as memories of witnessed details. Results from the sorts of tests used by Loftus and others in early research were ambiguous because subjects might knowingly base their reports on information drawn from the extra-experimental source. Then-typical procedures implied to subjects that the extra-experimental information was accurate, so there was no reason for them to avoid using it. Zaragoza and Koshmider (1989) and Lindsay and Johnson (1989a) showed that assessing subjects on a source-monitoring test, in which they were asked to specify the source or sources of their test answers, eliminated the suggestibility effect obtained with a yes/no recognition test. But subsequent research revealed that when conditions made it difficult for subjects to distinguish between memories of witnessed event details and memories of extra-event suggestions subjects sometimes appeared genuinely to believe that they had witnessed suggested details (e.g., Zaragoza & Lane, 1994). Provided test instructions discourage subjects from knowingly relying on extra-event information, manipulations that make memories of suggested details less discriminable from memories of witnessed details increase the likelihood of such errors (e.g., Lindsay, Hagen, Read, Wade, & Garry, 2004).

Lindsay (1990) reported a misinformation experiment in which test instructions clearly (and correctly) warned them that any question-relevant detail that had been mentioned in the extra-event information was a misleading suggestion and therefore should *not* be reported (à la Larry Jacoby's "opposition" procedure). When suggestions had been presented shortly before the test instructions (such that memories of suggestions were highly accessible and easily distinguishable from memories of the witnessed event, which had been viewed two days earlier), subjects did not report suggestions at above-baseline rates. This shows that subjects understood and attempted to follow the opposition instructions. But when the suggestions had been presented two days earlier under conditions that made memories of suggestions highly confusable with memories of event details, subjects quite often falsely reported suggestions as things they had witnessed in the event (see also Eakin, Schreiber, & Sergent-Marshall, 2003).

More recently, Oeberst and Blank (2012) used a multistage procedure in which subjects view an event, are exposed to misinformation, take a standard test (on which they often err by reporting misinformation instead of the corresponding event details), and then receive "enlightenment" before taking a final test in which they are asked to remember both what they observed in the event and what (if anything) they encountered in the extra-event information. That is, subjects were told that they had been exposed to misleading suggestions regarding some of the details and were asked to remember content from both sources (see Belli, Lindsay, Gales, & McCarthy, 1994, for a procedure that shared some of these features). In three experiments Oeberst and Blank found that the large misinformation effect their subjects evinced on the standard test was greatly reduced or eliminated by the enlightenment procedure. Whether or not a misinformation effect survives "enlightenment" should, from the SMF perspective, depend on the extent to which subjects can identify the sources of their memories of suggestions and their memories of event details when motivated to do so, which in turn depends on the interaction between how memory is cued and how the material from the two sources (and other potentially interfering material) was encoded. Future research using Oeberst and Blank's procedure has the potential to help sharpen our knowledge of those interactions.

Recovered memories of childhood sexual abuse

The mid-1990s saw a heated controversy regarding cases in which individuals reported that they had "recovered" memories of childhood sexual abuse of which they had previously been unaware. Psychologists on one side argued that such reports were often caused by suggestive approaches to therapy, whereas psychologists on the other side dismissed such claims as unjustified by the available science and motivated by desires to deny the reality of childhood sexual abuse (see Lindsay & Briere, 1997, for a middle-ground position piece on this complex and sensitive network of issues).

This debate inspired memory researchers to conduct studies testing the hypothesis that suggestive procedures can lead adults to believe that they had experienced significant events in childhood that, really, had not occurred. In the first published study of this sort, Loftus and Pickrell (1995) cued subjects to remember several childhood events that the researchers had learned about from the subjects' siblings, along with a pseudoevent (getting lost in a shopping mall) that the sibling indicated had not occurred. About a quarter of their subjects appeared to come to believe that the suggested event really happened. Subsequent studies demonstrated apparent false memories for knocking over a punch bowl at a wedding (e.g., Hyman, Husband, & Billings, 1995), being bitten by a dog (Porter, Birt, Yuille, & Lehman, 2000), riding in a hot air balloon (Wade, Garry, Read, & Lindsay, 2002), and putting Slime in a teacher's desk (Desjardins & Scoboria, 2007; Lindsay, Hagen, Read, Wade, & Garry, 2004), among various other distinctive events (e.g., Hart & Schooler, 2006; Scoboria, Mazzoni, Jarry, & Bernstein, 2012; Scoboria, Wysman, & Otgaar, 2012).

No experiment has tested the hypothesis that suggestions can lead individuals to develop compelling false memories or beliefs of being sexually abused by a parent. There are many reasons to believe that hypothesis is true, provided the suggestive influences are sufficiently powerful (see Newman & Garry's chapter on false memory, Chapter 7, in this volume). But there are also reasons to believe that healthy people have a range of effective defences against the formation of such consequential false memories. Most research on false memories has emphasized evidence that false memories occur, but it is also important to make clear that very often subjects successfully resist suggestive influences, especially if the suggested events are perceived as implausible, the subject lacks schema for the suggested events, and/or the suggestive influences are weak (e.g., Pezdek, Blandon-Gitlin, Lam, Hart, & Schooler, 2006). A large number of variables interact to determine the likelihood that a particular person will develop a particular false belief/memory. A dozen years ago, Don Read and I wrote,

> We are far short of a detailed understanding of the way the various factors that determine the strength of suggestive influences combine with one another and interact with the content of the suggestions and with individual differences. Specific claims regarding the likelihood that a particular constellation of suggestive influences would lead to particular kinds of false memory reports in specific individuals must await the development of such an understanding.
> (Lindsay & Read, 2001, p. 81)

I expect that we still have a long wait ahead.

Photographs and source monitoring

Wade et al. (2002) used a variant of the familial information false narrative procedure in which subjects were shown several childhood photos of themselves and family members and asked to remember the occasion when the photo was taken. Mixed among the photos was one in which a picture of the subject and a family member had been photoshopped into the basket of a hot-air balloon floating high aloft. Half of the subjects eventually appeared to believe that they had taken such a ride (even though the familial informant said they had not in fact done so).

Photos are not necessarily more inductive of false memories than are narratives – indeed, evidence from Garry & Wade (2005) suggests the opposite – but under the right conditions photos can be very suggestive indeed. Lindsay et al. (2004) asked subjects

to recall three elementary-school-related events, two of which had been reported by parents and the third of which parents said had never occurred. The pseudoevent involved the subject and a friend putting Slime in their grade 1 or 2 teacher's desk. Subjects were encouraged to try to remember this event in numerous ways over a period of about a week. Half of them were given a copy of the class group photo for that year as an aid to remembering. Among those who tried to remember without a photo, 23 percent were judged to come to believe that they remembered the suggested event. Among those given the photo, 66 percent were judged to believe they remembered putting Slime in the teacher's desk. There are probably several different ways in which photos contribute to false memories, but I believe that the most important is that they scaffold imagination of the suggested event. Without the photo, subjects can only vaguely imagine what it would have been like, but with the photo they can form detailed images of themselves, their accomplice, and their teacher, and those images may begin to feel like memories.

Garry and her co-workers have shown that not only can photographs contribute to the formation of false memories of the distant past, they can also affect judgments regarding concurrent information in the present. For example, Strange, Garry, Bernstein, and Lindsay (2011) showed subjects newspaper headlines with or without photographs that were related to but did not depict the headline event (e.g., a photo of Tony Blair giving a speech to parliament, with the headline "Blair defends botched Baghdad rescue mission"). For each news event, subjects indicated whether they (a) remembered learning about that event from the media, (b) knew they had heard about that event in the media but didn't recollect doing so, or (c) thought they had not learned of the news event in the media. A small proportion of the headlines were made up. For both real and made-up headlines, subjects were more likely to indicate that they thought they had learned about the event when the headline was accompanied by a photo than when it was presented without a photo. Similarly, Newman, Garry, Bernstein, Kantner, and Lindsay (2012) found that non-probative photographs increased the "truthiness" of a variety of kinds of statements. For example, subjects were more likely to endorse the true/false statement "The liquid metal inside a thermometer is magnesium" if the statement was accompanied by a picture of a thermometer. Here again, we believe that pictures scaffold participants' attempts to imagine the claim being true, nudging them in the direction of believing it.

Forced fabrication

Maria Zaragoza and Jennifer Ackil developed a procedure in which subjects are required to answer questions about details in a video that were not in fact shown in that video (e.g., Ackil & Zaragoza, 1995, 2011). For example, subjects might be asked "What kind of weapon was the thief carrying?" when the thief had not been shown carrying a weapon. Subjects are typically strongly resistant to this demand, and only produce specific answers when pushed to do so and even then do so with many verbal hedges that make it clear that they feel that they are guessing, not remembering. Yet, fascinatingly, after a delay of days or weeks these same subjects quite often appear to believe that they had indeed witnessed in the event the details they had so reluctantly generated in the forced confabulation phase. It is important for forensic interviewers (and especially those working with children) to understand the risks of encouraging subjects to guess or speculate (Poole & Lamb, 1998; Principe, Greenhoot, & Ceci, Chapter 35, this volume).

Mugshot pre-exposure effect and unconscious transference (aka bystander misidentification)

Police sometimes ask witnesses to look through mugshots of prospective suspects, as a way of focusing their investigations

and getting leads. If subsequent investigative work yields inculpating evidence, or if the proto-suspect is not able to provide a compelling alibi (which, it turns out, is quite difficult to do – see Olson & Wells, 2012), then police may run a lineup identification test with that person as the suspect. Unfortunately, exposing witnesses/subjects to a mugshot of an innocent prospective suspect before presenting a lineup including that suspect increases the chance that witnesses/subjects will mistakenly identify that suspect as the culprit (see meta-analysis by Deffenbacher, Bornstein, & Penrod, 2006). This "transference" effect is especially large if neither the mugshots nor the lineup included the culprit. Also, the effect is greater when the innocent suspect is falsely identified from the mugshots, but it occurs even if no such initial identification is made. This effect may partly reflect failures of source monitoring. That is, when viewing the lineup subjects may mistakenly attribute the familiarity of the pre-exposed innocent suspect to the witnessed event rather than to the mugshots.

Researchers have also tested the hypothesis that witnesses may confuse their memories of an innocent bystander as memories of the perpetrator of a crime. Compared with evidence on ill effects of mugshots, the evidence for such "unconscious transference" effects is more mixed. Deffenbacher et al. (2006) argued that the extant findings support the reality of such an effect, but there are reasons to believe that some of the existing studies involve "change blindness" rather than unconscious transference. "Change blindness" (e.g., Potter, 1976) occurs when a viewer fails to notice a marked change in the environment, such as failing to notice that an actor's scarf disappears from one camera angle to the next (Simons & Levin, 1997). Davis, Loftus, Vanous, and Cucciare (2008) presented evidence that change blindness can masquerade as unconscious transference when viewers mistakenly believe that the culprit and bystander are one and the same person. Subjects watched a video in which an innocent person was shown walking down the liquor aisle in a grocery store; the view of that person was briefly obstructed by a big stack of cardboard boxes. Then a different person emerged into view on the same trajectory as the first person. This second person then stole a bottle of liquor. Later, subjects often erroneously identified the innocent shopper as the culprit. Many subjects failed to notice that the person had changed, and those who did not notice were especially likely to falsely identify the innocent person. It seems likely that similar identity confusions have played a role in producing apparent bystander misidentification effects in some other studies as well (e.g., Ross, Ceci, Dunning, & Toglia, 1994). Nonetheless, there are also good reasons to believe that genuine source-monitoring confusions sometimes contribute to bystander misidentification effects (e.g., Perfect & Harris, 2008).

Unconscious plagiarism/ cryptomnesia

I have a yellowed newspaper clipping of an Ann Landers article from the late 1980s, in which the famed advice columnist followed up on an earlier piece in which she had published a poem sent in by a reader who recruited Ann's help in discovering the poet's identity. Four people wrote to Ann explaining how and when and why they had written the poem; perhaps one of them had actually done so. Comparable anecdotes of plagiarism abound, with cases involving musicians, poets, scientists, et alia (see Gregory, 1923, for some early observations, and Perfect & Stark, 2008, for a review). Such false claims of creation could be explained in a variety of ways, but the most interesting possibility is that at least some of the claimants had false memories of creating the work in question.

Brown and Murphy (1989) developed a procedure to study these issues that has been widely adopted (with due citation). First, the subject participates in an idea-generation phase with one or more other persons (confederates or fellow subjects). Later, subjects are asked to recall the ideas that they

contributed during the collaboration phase, and they are also asked to generate additional brand new ideas of their own. Two indices of plagiarism are derived: Recall-own errors, in which subjects report that they generated ideas that others had provided during the collaboration phase, and generate-new errors, in which subjects present as new creations ideas that had been reported (by them or someone else) in the collaboration phase.

As Perfect and Stark (2008) noted, recall-own errors and generate-new errors differ qualitatively. Screening out previously generated ideas from the generate-new phase essentially relies on old/new recognition; any idea generated during the collaboration phase should be excluded regardless of the specific source. In contrast, screening out ideas that others had generated during the recall-own task requires a finer grained source-monitoring judgment. Consistent with this distinction, manipulations of source similarity have been shown to affect recall-own errors but not generate-new errors (Landau & Marsh, 1997).

Stark and Perfect (2006, 2007, 2008; Stark, Perfect, & Newstead, 2005) found that asking subjects to improve ideas generated in the collaboration phase dramatically increased recall-own errors. The effect of working on improvements does not reduce to a matter of mere memory strength, because asking subjects to form vivid visual images of ideas (which boosted memory strength to the same extent as thinking about improvements) did not increase recall-own errors. Using a clever design in which subjects both generated improvements and received (bogus) feedback about idea quality, Perfect and Stark (2008) reported evidence that it is the process of generating improvements (not perceived idea quality) that inflates generate-own plagiarism. Thus there is something about thinking about improvements to an idea that increases the risk of later thinking the idea was one's own all along. This may help explain why collaborations so often yield disputes about authorship; working to improve another's idea may later make that idea feel very much one's own.

Mental health

In a 1988 chapter, Marcia Johnson explored the idea that psychotic delusions and hallucinations arise from major breakdowns in the same reality monitoring processes whose more benign errors give rise to everyday memory distortions and misperceptions in healthy individuals. By the time of this writing, a substantial number of articles have reported studies of individuals with and without schizophrenia tested on source-memory tests. Interest has focused on interactions between diagnostic group and type of test. In the first such article, Harvey (1985) reported evidence that patients diagnosed with schizophrenia had problems in differentiating memories of saying a word from memories of thinking a word, whereas those diagnosed with mania had problems in discriminating memories from two external sources. Unfortunately, however, there has been great inconsistency in results across studies. The inconsistency is probably at least partly due to the fact that studies with patients often have small numbers, but my impression is that researchers have also roiled the waters somewhat by using a variety of different tasks and procedures and terminologies. Achim and Weiss (2008) reported a meta-analysis of 27 studies comparing schizophrenic and control groups on various source-monitoring tasks. They expected to find that patients would be particularly impaired on self/other discriminations (what they termed "reality monitoring") relative to discriminations between thoughts and actions or discriminations between two external sources, but the degree of impairment on all of those tasks was moderate and equivalent. Nor do schizophrenics consistently demonstrate greater-than-usual rates of false memories in DRM procedures, but they do show a striking tendency to be overconfident in errors and underconfident in correct responses (e.g., Moritz, Woodward, Jelinek, & Klinge, 2008). This suggests that the SM deficit associated with schizophrenia is not due to extraordinarily "strong" memories of thoughts/images in this population but rather to poor metacognitive calibration of confidence.

A number of studies have examined relationships between false memory errors and individual difference measures. Unfortunately, most such studies have samples that are too small to get much traction in such analyses. One of the variables that has most consistently correlated with false memories is responses on the Dissociative Experiences Scale (e.g., Gallo, 2010; Hyman & Billings, 1998; Porter et al., 2000). Another is age: Pre-schoolers are more susceptible to source confusions than are older children and young adults (e.g., Lindsay, 2002; Principe, Greenhoot, & Ceci, Chapter 35, this volume), and source-monitoring difficulties increase late in the lifespan (e.g., Mitchell, Johnson, & Mather, 2003).

REDUCING SM ERRORS

The likelihood of SM errors can be reduced by attention. Attending reflectively to aspects of source during an event (e.g., noting to oneself which things one is witnessing and which things one is inferring; noting and reflecting on the where and the who and the how of events as they happen) has been shown to enhance SM. And dividing attention at study impairs SM. Those attentional factors seem very likely to matter in the real world as well as in studies. Likewise attending to dimensions of source while memory is being used and scrutinizing memory for source-relevant cues are likely to reduce error rates. False alarms can further be reduced by setting a high threshold on what is accepted as a memory of an actual event (at the cost of increased rates of erroneously identified memories of actual events as memories of inferences, etc.). But source misattributions likely cannot be driven to zero, because it is adaptive and efficient and suits the organism's purposes to gloss and blur information across multiple sources (see Newman & Lindsay,

2009; Schacter, 2012). Reconstructive processes that blend products of inference, bias, expectation, and imagination with products of retrieval serve us well most of the time. For one thing, these processes likely support our senses of self (e.g., Williams & Conway, 2009). More fundamentally, without such reconstructive mechanisms our ability to recollect our own pasts (and envision our futures) would be grossly impoverished. Reconstructive processes enable us to use partial and imperfect cues to re-envision the past as it probably was. Our recollections often stray from the "literal" truth of the past but generally capture the essence of what happened with effective fidelity. Sometimes relatively minor memory errors (e.g., thinking that you saw Paul yesterday when it was really the day before) can be profoundly consequential (e.g., by undermining his perfectly valid alibi). And sometimes conditions conspire to foster grossly false beliefs or illusory memories (as when a person comes to believe that he or she was abducted by space aliens or subjected to outlandish and improbable satanic ritual abuse), but in healthy individuals such false memories are unlikely unless the person is exposed to prolonged and multifaceted suggestive influences. In brief, reconstructive remembering does us more good than harm. If that wasn't the case our memories would have evolved differently.

FUTURE DIRECTIONS

As noted in the earlier section on limitations, the source-monitoring framework is not sufficiently well-defined to enable specific predictions in complex situations. For example, the framework holds that all else being equal, confusions between memory sources will be more common for sources that are highly similar than for sources that are dissimilar (provided that performance is above floor and below ceiling and that the task motivates subjects to differentiate between sources), but when all else is not

equal, predictions are less clear. This is in part simply a reflection of the difficulty of developing psychological models of similarity (Decock & Douven, 2011). The problem is compounded by variations across condition in individuals' motivation, orientation, attention, goals, criteria, etc. at study and at test. SM performance may also be affected by material in memory prior to study and by material learned between study and test, potentially in ways that interact with experimental manipulations. All of this makes precise prediction difficult.

Most SM studies involve discriminations between two rival sources (e.g., which of two actors said "Fish?" Did you generate the word "motel" from a stem or did you merely read that word? Did you read that the spy burned the document, or did you just infer that?) (Often some items were not studied and subjects have the option of responding Source A, Source B, or new.) In everyday life, potential sources of thoughts, images, and feelings are not so well-defined and narrowly constrained. The interaction between your past, your current orientation, and your environment causes thoughts and images to come to mind moment by moment and as they do you make attributions at various levels of specificity (grain size) from a huge gamut of potential sources. Maybe, for example, you read something about the concept of similarity and the phrase "likeness and likelihood" pops to mind. That could be a new idea, or it could be something you heard or read at some time in some context. Maybe automatic source-monitoring processes have filled in some of those dimensions, such that it seems simply to come to mind as something you read years ago (a remarkable chapter by Richard Shweder, 1977). My point here is that although it seems reasonable to extend the SMF to these naturalistic situations in which potential sources are not pre-defined there have been very few if any tests of the framework in such situations.

The SMF has emphasized source attributions that are made during the course of or after retrieval, but people also use source to constrain searches of memory. Try, for example, to remember a high-school episode involving a phone call. Give it a go – these illustrations are always more fun if you try them. Probably you can recall a high-school phone episode without having memories of recent phone calls come to mind – you can largely constrain the memories that come to mind to your high-school years, an example of source-constrained cued recall. Likely the constraint is imperfect – maybe a high-salience recent memory of a phone call will intrude, or one from junior high or college years. For present purposes the point is merely that it would be interesting to know more about source-constrained recall and how it interacts with SM processes that unfold as thoughts and images come to mind. (For ideas about source-constraint in recognition, see Alban & Kelley, 2012; Jacoby, Shimizu, Daniels, & Rhodes, 2005; Kantner & Lindsay, 2013.)

Marcia Johnson situates ideas about SM in the broader context of her multiple-entry modular memory (MEM) theory. MEM has an ambitiously broad scope.

Perhaps the hottest arena for future research on SM has to do with the brain structures and functions that underlie source monitoring. Brain-imaging techniques have been used to study SM for at least two decades, and in recent years the quality and informativeness of that work has increased substantially (see Johnson, Raye, Mitchell, & Ankudowich, 2011, and Mitchell & Johnson, 2009, for reviews). Very briefly (and relying heavily on these reviews), it appears that various kinds of mental processing have lasting effects on the specialized brain regions that perform those processes (e.g., the fusiform gyrus for high-level representations of faces); hippocampal processes (modulated by the amygdale and various subparts of the prefrontal cortex [PFC]) bind together different features during encoding. Appropriate cues evoke information from representational areas, with that information converging in parietal regions. PFC appears to be involved in deliberative efforts to retrieve additional information from representational information and in attributing information to particular sources. If sufficiently detailed, distinctive, and coherent information converges in the parietal cortex, it gives rise to the subjective experience of recollecting a prior experience. Much remains to be learned about the brain functions that give rise to subjective experiences of knowing, remembering, solving, etc., but the rate of progress on these questions appears to be accelerating tremendously.

CONCLUSION

The thoughts and images that crowd the mind have multiple sources – products of perception, inference, schemata, and episodic memory interweave in the tumbling stream of thought. A person who made no differentiation between vision and visualization, between fact and fancy, would not long survive. We have evolved abilities to attribute mental events to likely sources, and most of the time those (largely unconscious) attribution processes serve us well. Mental events that feel like memories usually are based largely on memory; events that seem to be happening "out there" in the environment usually are, etc. The inferences we make about what probably happened blend near-seamlessly with memories of what did happen, and those inferences are usually essentially accurate. But at times a mental event will have characteristics of a source other than its true source, and on such occasions people are vulnerable to source-monitoring errors. Such errors can be deeply consequential in a wide gamut of real-world domains.

NOTES

1   For one of several exceptions, see Johnson and Sherman's (1990) chapter on imagined future events, which in some ways presaged recent proposals as to the overlap between mechanisms of mental time travel backward and forward (e.g., Schacter, 2012).

2   Johnson and Raye and their co-workers applied the RM model to several subtypes of this basic dichotomy, but the fundamental distinction was a dichotomy between sources having more versus less of certain characteristics.

3   This claim is with reference to the first time one recollects a particular past episode; subsequent recollections of the same episode may well include records of initial source attributions (cf. Hintzman, 2011).

REFERENCES

Achim, A. M., & Weiss, A. P. (2008). No evidence for a differential deficit of reality monitoring in schizophrenia: A meta-analysis of the associative memory literature. *Cognitive Neuropsychiatry, 13,* 369–384. doi:10.1080/13546800802299476

Ackil, J. K., & Zaragoza, M. S. (1995). Developmental differences in eyewitness suggestibility and memory for source. *Journal of Experimental Child Psychology, 60,* 57–83. doi:10.1006/jecp.1995.1031

Ackil, J. K., & Zaragoza, M. S. (2011). Forced fabrication versus interviewer suggestions: Differences in false memory depend on how memory is assessed. *Applied Cognitive Psychology, 25,* 933–942. doi:10.1002/acp.1785

Alban, M. W., & Kelley, C. M. (2012). Variations in constrained retrieval. *Memory & Cognition, 40,* 681–692. doi:10.3758/ 1158 s13421-012-0185-5

Allen, B. P., & Lindsay, D. S. (1998). Amalgamations of memories: Intrusions of information from one event into reports of another. *Applied Cognitive Psychology, 12,* 277–285.

Bartlett, F. C. (1932). *Remembering: A study in experimental and social psychology.* New York: Macmillan.

Belli, R. F., Lindsay, D. S., Gales, M. S., & McCarthy, T. T. (1994). Memory impairment and source misattribution in postevent misinformation experiments with short retention intervals. *Memory and Cognition, 22,* 40–54.

Bransford, J. D., & Johnson, M. K. (1972). Contextual prerequisites for understanding: Some investigations of comprehension and recall. *Journal of Verbal Learning & Verbal Behavior, 11,* 717–726. doi:10.1016/S0022-5371(72)80006-9

Brown, A. S., & Murphy, D. R. (1989). Cryptomnesia: Delineating inadvertent plagiarism. *Journal of Experimental Psychology: Learning, Memory, and Cognition, 15,* 432–442. doi:10.1037/0278-7393.15.3.432

Davis, D., Loftus, E. F., Vanous, S., & Cucciare, M. (2008). 'Unconscious transference' can be an instance of 'change blindness'. *Applied Cognitive Psychology, 22,* 605–623. doi:10.1002/acp.1395

Decock, L., & Douven, I. (2011). Similarity after Goodman. *Review of Philosophy and Psychology, 2,* 61–75. doi:10.1007/s13164-010-0035-y

Deffenbacher, K. A., Bornstein, B. H., & Penrod, S. D. (2006). Mugshot exposure effects: Retroactive interference, mugshot commitment, source confusion, and unconscious transference. *Law & Human Behavior, 30,* 287–307. doi:10.1007/s10979-006-9008-1

Desjardins, T., & Scoboria, A. (2007). "You and your best friend Suzy put Slime in Ms. Smollett's desk": Producing false memories with self-relevant details. *Psychonomic Bulletin & Review, 14,* 1090–1095. doi:10.3758/BF03193096

Eakin, D. K., Schreiber, T. A., & Sergent-Marshall, S. (2003). Misinformation effects in eyewitness memory: The presence and absence of memory impairment as a function of warning and misinformation accessibility. *Journal of Experimental Psychology: Learning, Memory, and Cognition, 29,* 813–825. doi:10.1037/0278-7393.29.5.813

Gallo, D. A. (2010). False memories and fantastic beliefs: 15 years of the DRM illusion. *Memory & Cognition, 38,* 833–848. doi:10.3758/MC.38.7.833

Garry, M., & Wade, K. A. (2005). Actually, a picture is worth less than 45 words: Narratives produce more false memories than photographs do. *Psychonomic Bulletin & Review, 12,* 359–366. doi:10.3758/BF03196385

Gregory, J. C. (1923). Memory, forgetfulness, and mistakes of recognition in waking and dreaming, *Monist, 33,* 15–32.

Hart, R. E., & Schooler, J. W. (2006). Increasing belief in the experience of an invasive procedure that never happened: The role of plausibility and schematicity. *Applied Cognitive Psychology, 20,* 661–669. doi:10.1002/acp.1218

Harvey, P. D. (1985). Reality monitoring in mania and schizophrenia: The association of thought disorder and performance. *Journal of Nervous and Mental Disease, 173,* 67–73. doi:10.1097/00005053-198502000-00001

Hintzman, D. L. (2011). Research strategy in the study of memory: Fads, fallacies, and the search for the "coordinates of truth". *Perspectives on Psychological Science, 6,* 253–271. doi:10.1177/1745691611406924

Hoffman, H. G. (1997). Role of memory strength in reality monitoring decisions: Evidence from source attribution biases. *Journal of Experimental Psychology: Learning, Memory, and Cognition, 23,* 371–383. doi:10.1037/0278-7393.23.2.371

Holliday, R. E., & Hayes, B. K. (2002). Automatic and international processes in children's recognition memory: The reversed misinformation effect. *Applied Cognitive Psychology, 16,* 1–16. doi:10.1002/acp.789

Hyman, I. E. Jr., & Billings, F. (1998). Individual differences and the creation of false childhood memories. *Memory, 6,* 1–20. doi:10.1080/741941598

Hyman, I. E. Jr., Husband, T. H., & Billings, F. (1995). False memories of childhood experiences. *Applied Cognitive Psychology, 9,* 181–197. doi:10.1002/acp.2350090302

Jacoby, L. L., Kelley, C. M., & Dywan, J. (1989). Memory attributions. In H. Roediger and F. M. Craik (Eds.), *Varieties of memory and consciousness: Essays in honour of Endel Tulving* (pp. 391–422). Hillsdale, NJ England: Lawrence Erlbaum Associates, Inc.

Jacoby, L. L., Shimizu, Y., Daniels, K. A., & Rhodes, M. G. (2005). Modes of cognitive control in recognition and source memory: Depth of retrieval. *Psychonomic Bulletin & Review, 12,* 852–1197. doi:10.3758/BF03196776.

Jacoby, L. L., Woloshyn, V., & Kelley, C. M. (1989). Becoming famous without being recognized: Unconscious influences of memory produced by dividing attention. *Journal of Experimental Psychology: General, 118,* 115–125. doi:10.1037/0096-3445.118.2.115

Johnson, M. K. (1988). Discriminating the origin of information. In T. F. Oltmanns and B. A. Maher (Eds.), *Delusional beliefs* (pp. 34–65). Oxford: John Wiley & Sons.

Johnson, M. K., Bransford, J. D., & Solomon, S. K. (1973). Memory for tacit implications of sentences. *Journal of Experimental Psychology, 98,* 203–205. doi:10.1037/h0034290

Johnson, M. K., Hashtroudi, S., & Lindsay, D. (1993). Source monitoring. *Psychological Bulletin, 114*(1), 3–28. doi:10.1037/0033-2909.114.1.3

Johnson, M. K., & Raye, C. L. (1981). Reality monitoring. *Psychological Review, 88,* 67–85.

Johnson, M. K., Raye, C. L., Foley, H. J., & Foley, M. A. (1981). Cognitive operations and decision bias in reality monitoring. *The American Journal of Psychology, 94,* 37–64. doi:10.2307/1422342

Johnson, M. K., Raye, C. L., Mitchell, K. J., & Ankudowich, E. (2012). The cognitive neuroscience of the true and false memories. In R. F. Belli (Ed.), *True and false recovered memories: Toward a reconciliation of the debate* (pp. 15–52). New York: Springer Science + Business Media. doi:10.1007/978-1-4614-1195-6_2

Johnson, M. K., & Sherman, S. J. (1990). Constructing and reconstructing the past and the future in the present. In E. T. Higgins and R. M. Sorrentino (Eds.), *Handbook of motivation and social cognition: Foundations of social behavior* (pp. 482–526). New York: Guilford Press.

Kantner, J. & Lindsay, D. (2013). Top-down constraint on recognition memory. *Memory & Cognition, 41,* 465–479. doi:10.3758/s13421-012-0265-6

Kelley, C. M., & Lindsay, D. (1993). Remembering mistaken for knowing: Ease of retrieval as a basis for confidence in answers to general knowledge questions. *Journal of Memory and Language, 32,* 1–24. doi:10.1006/jmla.1993.1001

Knott, L. M., & Dewhurst, S. A. (2007). The effects of divided attention at study and test on false recognition: A comparison of DRM and categorized lists. *Memory & Cognition, 35,* 1954–1965. doi:10.3758/BF03192928

Koriat, A., & Goldsmith, M. (1996). Monitoring and control processes in the strategic regulation of memory accuracy. *Psychological Review, 103,* 490–517. doi:10.1037/0033-295X.103.3.490

Landau, J. D., & Marsh, R. L. (1997). Monitoring source in an unconscious plagiarism paradigm. *Psychonomic Bulletin & Review, 4,* 265–270. doi:10.3758/BF03209404

Lane, S. M. (2006). Dividing attention during a witnessed event increases eyewitness suggestibility. *Applied Cognitive Psychology, 20,* 199–212. doi:10.1002/acp.1177

Lindsay, D. S. (1990). Misleading suggestions can impair eyewitnesses' ability to remember event details. *Journal of Experimental Psychology: Learning, Memory, and Cognition, 16,* 1077–1083.

Lindsay, D. S. (2002). Children's source monitoring. In H. L. Westcott, G. Davies, and R. H. C. Bull (Eds.), *Children's testimony: Psychological research and forensic practice* (pp. 83–98). Chichester, UK: John Wiley and Sons.

Lindsay, D. S. (2008). Source monitoring. In H. L. Roediger, III (Ed.), *Cognitive psychology of memory. Vol. 2 of Learning and memory: A comprehensive reference*, 4 vols. (J. Byrne, Editor), pp. 325–347. Oxford: Elsevier.

Lindsay, D. S., Allen, B. P., Chan, J. C. K., & Dahl, L. C. (2004). Eyewitness suggestibility and source similarity: Intrusions of details from one event into memory reports of another event. *Journal of Memory and Language, 50,* 96–111.

Lindsay, D. S., & Briere, J. (1997). The controversy regarding recovered memories of childhood sexual abuse: Pitfalls, bridges and future directions. *Journal of Interpersonal Violence, 12,* 631–647.

Lindsay, D. S., Hagen, L., Read, J. D., Wade, K. A., & Garry, M. (2004). True photographs and false memories. *Psychological Science, 15,* 149–154.

Lindsay, D. S., & Johnson, M. K. (1989a). The eyewitness suggestibility effect and memory for source. *Memory and Cognition, 17*, 349–358.

Lindsay, D. S., & Johnson, M. K. (1989b). The reversed eyewitness suggestibility effect. *Bulletin of the Psychonomic Society, 27*, 111–1139.

Lindsay, D. S., & Johnson, M. K. (2001). False memories, fuzzy trace theory, and the source monitoring framework. *Learning and Individual Differences, 12*, 145–161.

Lindsay, D. S., Johnson, M. K., & Kwon, P. (1991). Developmental changes in memory source monitoring. *Journal of Experimental Child Psychology, 52*, 297–318.

Lindsay, D. S., & Read, J. D. (2001). The recovered memories controversy: Where do we go from here? In G. Davies and T. Dalgleish (Eds.), *Recovered memories: Seeking the middle ground* (pp. 71–94). London: Wiley.

Loftus, E. F., & Pickrell, J. E. (1995). The formation of false memories. *Psychiatric Annals, 25*, 720–725.

Mitchell, K. J., & Johnson, M. K. (2009). Source monitoring 15 years later: What have we learned from fMRI about the neural mechanisms of source memory? *Psychological Bulletin, 135*, 638–677.

Mitchell, K., Johnson, M. K., & Mather, M. (2003). Source monitoring and suggestibility to misinformation: Adult age-related differences. *Applied Cognitive Psychology, 17*, 107–119.

Moritz, S., Woodward, T., Jelinek, L., & Klinge, R. (2008). Memory and metamemory in schizophrenia: A liberal acceptance account of psychosis. *Psychological Medicine, 38*, 825–832.

Neisser, U. (1982). Snapshots or benchmarks? In U. Neisser (Ed.) *Memory observed*. New York: W.H. Freeman.

Newman, E., Garry, M., Bernstein, D. M., Kantner, J., & Lindsay, D. S. (2012). Non-probative photographs (or words) inflate truthiness. *Psychonomic Bulletin & Review*.

Newman, E., & Lindsay, D. S. (2009). False memories: What the hell are they for? *Applied Cognitive Psychology, 23*, 1105–1121.

Oeberst, A., & Blank, H. (2012). Undoing suggestive influence on memory: The reversibility of the eyewitness misinformation effect. *Cognition, 125*, 141–159.

Olson, E. A. & Wells, G. L. (2012). The alibi-generation effect: Alibi-generation experience influences alibi evaluation. *Legal and Criminological Psychology, 17*, 151–164. doi:10.1111/j.2044-8333.2010.02003.x

Payne, D. G., & Blackwell, J. M. (1998). Truth in memory: Caveat emptor. In S. J. Lynn and K. M. McConkey (Eds.), *Truth in memory* (pp. 32–61). New York: Guilford Press.

Perfect, T., & Harris, L. (2003). Adult age differences in unconscious transference: Source confusion or identity blending? *Memory & Cognition, 31*, 570–580.

Perfect, T. J., & Stark, L. J. (2008). Tales from the Crypt … omnesia. In J. Dunlosky and R. A. Bjork (Eds.), *Handbook of metamemory and memory* (pp. 285–314). New York: Psychology Press.

Pezdek, K., Blandon-Gitlin, I., Lam, S., Hart, R., & Schooler, J. W. (2006). Is knowing believing? The role of event plausibility and background knowledge in planting false beliefs about the personal past. *Memory & Cognition, 34*, 1628–1635.

Poole, D. A., & Lamb, M. E. (1998). *Investigative interviews of children: A guide for helping professionals*. Washington, DC: American Psychological Association. doi:10.1037/10301-000

Porter, S., Birt, A. R., Yuille, J. C., & Lehman, D. R. (2000). Negotiating false memories: Interviewer and rememberer characteristics relate to memory distortion. *Psychological Science, 11*, 507–510. doi:10.1111/1467-9280.00297

Potter, M. C. (1976). Short-term conceptual memory for pictures. *Journal of Experimental Psychology: Human Learning and Memory, 2*, 509–522. doi:10.1037/0278-7393.2.5.509

Ross, D. F., Ceci, S. J., Dunning, D., & Toglia, M. P. (1994). Unconscious transference and lineup identification: Toward a memory blending approach. In D. Ross, J. D. Read, and M. P. Toglia (Eds.), *Adult eyewitness testimony: Current trends and developments* (pp. 80–100). New York: Cambridge University Press. doi:10.1017/CBO9780511759192.005

Ross, M. (1989). Relation of implicit theories to the construction of personal histories. *Psychological Review, 96*, 341–357. doi:10.1037/0033-295X.96.2.341

Schacter, D. L. (2012). Adaptive constructive processes and the future of memory. *American Psychologist, 67*, 603–613. doi:10.1037/a0029869

Scoboria, A., Mazzoni, G., Jarry, J. L., & Bernstein, D. M. (2012). Personalized and not general suggestion produces false autobiographical memories and suggestion-consistent behavior. *Acta Psychologica, 139*, 225–232. doi:10.1016/j.actpsy.2011.10.008

Scoboria, A., Wysman, L., & Otgaar, H. (2012). Credible suggestions affect false autobiographical beliefs. *Memory, 20*, 429–442. doi:10.1080/09658211.2012.677449

Sederberg, P. B., Gershman, S. J., Polyn, S. M., & Norman, K. A. (2011). Human memory reconsolidation can be explained using the temporal context model. *Psychonomic Bulletin & Review, 18*, 455–468. doi:10.3758/s13423-011-0086-9

Shweder, R. A. (1977). Likeness and likelihood in everyday thought: Magical thinking in judgments about personality. *Current Anthropology, 18*, 637–658. doi:10.1086/201974

Simons, D. J., & Levin, D. T. (1997). Change blindness. *Trends in Cognitive Sciences, 1*, 261–267. doi:10.1016/S1364-6613(97)01080-2

Stark, L., & Perfect, T. J. (2006). Elaboration inflation: How your ideas become mine. *Applied Cognitive Psychology, 20*, 641–648. doi:10.1002/acp.1216

Stark, L., & Perfect, T. J. (2007). Whose idea was that? Source monitoring for idea ownership following elaboration. *Memory, 15*, 776–783. doi:10.1080/09658210701643042

Stark, L., & Perfect, T. (2008). The effects of repeated idea elaboration on unconscious plagiarism. *Memory & Cognition, 36*, 65–73.

Stark, L., Perfect, T. J., & Newstead, S. E. (2005). When elaboration leads to appropriation: Unconscious plagiarism in a creative task. *Memory, 13*, 561–573. doi:10.1080/09658210444000232

Strange, D., Garry, M., Bernstein, D. M., & Lindsay, D. S. (2011). Photographs cause false memories for the news. *Acta Psychologica, 136*, 90–94.

Troyer, A. K., Winocur, G., Craik, F. M., & Moscovitch, M. (1999). Source memory and divided attention: Reciprocal costs to primary and secondary tasks. *Neuropsychology, 13*, 467–474. doi:10.1037/0894-4105.13.4.467

Tulving, E. (1982). Synergistic ecphory in recall and recognition. *Canadian Journal of Psychology/ Revue Canadienne De Psychologie, 36*, 130–147. doi:10.1037/h0080641

Wade, K. A., Garry, M., Read, J., & Lindsay, S. (2002). A picture is worth a thousand lies: Using false photographs to create false childhood memories. *Psychonomic Bulletin & Review, 9*, 597–603. doi:10.3758/BF03196318

Watkins, M. J. (1990). Mediationism and the obfuscation of memory. *American Psychologist, 45*(3), 328–335. doi:10.1037/0003-066X.45.3.328

Williams, H. L., & Conway, M. A. (2009). Networks of autobiographical memories. In P. Boyer and J. V. Wertsch (Eds.), *Memory in mind and culture* (pp. 33–61). New York: Cambridge University Press. doi:10.1017/CBO9780511626999.004

Whittlesea, B. A. (2003). On the construction of behavior and subjective experience: The production and evaluation of performance. In J. S. Bowers and C. J. Marsolek (Eds.), *Rethinking implicit memory* (pp. 239–260). New York: Oxford University Press.

Zaragoza, M. S., & Koshmider, J. W. (1989). Misled subjects may know more than their performance implies. *Journal of Experimental Psychology: Learning, Memory, and Cognition, 15*, 246–255. doi:10.1037/0278-7393.15.2.246

Zaragoza, M. S., & Lane, S. M. (1994). Source misattributions and the suggestibility of eyewitness memory. *Journal of Experimental Psychology: Learning, Memory, and Cognition, 20*, 934–945. doi:10.1037/0278-7393.20.4.934

Zaragoza, M. S., & Lane, S. M. (1998). Processing resources and eyewitness suggestibility. *Legal and Criminological Psychology, 3*(Part 2), 305–320. doi:10.1111/j.2044-8333.1998.tb00368.x

5

Spatial Memory:
From Theory to Application

Douglas H. Wedell and Adam T. Hutcheson

Spatial memory has been investigated across diverse environments and under numerous cognitive constraints. This research has provided the basis for understanding the cognitive and neural underpinnings of remembering places in space. We review these findings with a particular focus on how they may apply to problems of spatial memory posed by technological advances that are fundamentally changing the way people process spatial information. While there are a myriad of applications tied to spatial memory processing, we primarily consider those linked to technological innovations, as these provide exciting new frontiers for exploration. Before beginning our review, we provide an overview of three technologies of particular interest: 1) the widespread use of virtual environments, 2) the implementation of augmented reality, and 3) the widespread use of global positioning systems.

VIRTUAL ENVIRONMENTS (VEs)

Research on spatial memory has traditionally used real-world settings of various orders of magnitude to test participants' spatial abilities. However, these environments pose problems related to controlling elements of experimental design. It may be difficult to find environments that suit the needs of the study, whether because of size, environmental features, availability, or familiarity. In contrast, VEs, such as those found in video games and military training simulators, provide an excellent testing ground for spatial memory. VEs make it possible to generate completely novel worlds that simulate the kinds of real world environmental features that people encounter without the limitations of those environments. Spatial memory results from VEs tend to be very similar to those from real environments, with the only consistent difference being greater underestimation of distance in VEs compared with real environments (Jansen-Osmann & Berendt, 2002).

Whereas researchers first used VEs for greater experimental control of the environment, the case can now be made that understanding how spatial memory applies to VEs is of inherent interest. This is because VEs are becoming the primary environment we experience in some cases. For example, medical surgery is now guided by VE renditions, as is the piloting of drone planes. Thus, it is important to pay close attention to how VEs are perceived and remembered. Chen and Stanney (1999) have identified many ways that VEs can be used as navigational aids. Importantly, VEs can remove the difficulties of translating information between maps and wayfinding, providing a viewer centered representation to the individual that may facilitate exploration of the environment. As these technologies become more available to the public on a daily basis, it becomes incumbent on researchers to understand navigation through VEs and how their features may best be utilized in aiding spatial memory and navigation.

AUGMENTED REALITY (AR)

An even newer technology that has immediate applications is AR. Mapping the egocentric perspective of environmental object layouts found in VEs onto views of actual environments, AR technology places virtual objects and markers within a real-world viewpoint. This technology allows users to place a virtual marker in an environment and then use the camera on their cellular phone to locate the marker in their visual field. A recent development in AR technology comes from Google in the form of a pair of glasses that overlay information from an on-board computer to aid the user in various tasks. The tool of AR technology brings to the fore the key research question of how verbal and other enhanced information is integrated with spatial information in creating cognitive spatial maps that guide interactions with the environment. Hence, it is important to consider applications of integration of different modalities of information in applications to AR technology.

GLOBAL POSITIONING SYSTEMS (GPS) AND SATELLITE-VIEW MAPS

Anyone with a dedicated GPS or a smartphone now has access to very sophisticated technology for determining one's position within the environment. People routinely use these devices when navigating in unfamiliar places. GPS devices provide maps that change as one's position changes. GPS units equipped with auditory cues may help people find locations in ways that we could not dream of only a few decades ago (Loomis, Golledge, Klatsky, & Marston, 2007). One exciting application of this research is in aiding visually impaired individuals during wayfinding.

Despite their popularity, there may be drawbacks to using GPS as a means of wayfinding. Ishikawa, Fujiwara, Imai, and Okabe (2008) found that GPS users took longer to navigate, showed more errors, and constructed poorer cognitive maps than traditional map users or individuals who navigated just by using direct experience with the environment. If people are attending to the GPS, they may not be encoding useful information about the environment that is needed for developing accurate spatial memory. Considering the rapid and dedicated infusion of this technology into all aspects of daily life, it will be important to understand how these technically advanced spatial navigation devices can both aid and hinder spatial memory and successful navigation in a complex environment.

BASIC ISSUES AND APPROACHES TO STUDYING SPATIAL MEMORY

Although our approach to the literature is primarily from a psychological viewpoint, there are implications of this research across diverse disciplines, such as geography, anthropology, linguistics, neurosciences, and computer science. We overview these approaches, highlighting key historical trends and issues. In the bulk of our review, we describe contemporary spheres of inquiry divided into four basic themes: 1) the nature of spatial representations, 2) distortions of spatial memory, 3) dynamic spatial memory, and 4) individual differences.

Several recurrent issues will be woven together throughout our discussion of the spatial memory literature. First is the issue of scale: Do the same mechanisms of spatial memory that apply to remembering locations in small spaces also apply to remembering locations in large spaces? Second is how memory is utilized in navigation: How does one update location, estimate distance, and make course corrections? Third is the issue of how to integrate information gathered from different perspectives, egocentric or viewer-centered perspectives and allocentric or map-like representations. Finally, we consider the issue of how analog and categorical representations of spatial information are combined in various spatial memory tasks. As we review the literature, we encourage the reader to consider how the technological advances described above may influence performance in spatial memory tasks in these different ways.

FIELDS RELATED TO SPATIAL MEMORY

In cognitive studies of spatial memory, the key research issues concern the nature of the representation of information and the processes used to encode, retrieve, manipulate, transform, and respond to that information. Other disciplines examine how these processes may apply to specific domains. Geographers have examined the role of spatial cognition and information systems and real-world navigation. For example, they have developed complex digital layered maps that have been used in locating lost persons in forests by law enforcement in an attempt to make the process of navigating unfamiliar areas more efficient (Heth & Cornell, 2007). Linguists have conducted collaborative research examining the links between language and spatial concepts and representations. Linguistic descriptions of spatial relations provide many of the tools for mentally constructing a representation of spatial

arrangements and environments (Beirwisch, 1996). The best forms of communicating these relationships may well depend on cultural conventions, as explored within the discipline of anthropology. For example, field anthropologists have shown how human cognitive mapping abilities relate to the hunting of migratory animals (Istomin & Dwyer, 2009).

The neural basis of spatial cognition and memory has long been an important area of research. With the development of neuroimaging techniques, cognitive-neuroscience researchers have made great strides in validating and expanding neural models of spatial cognition and memory developed from comparative research to human spatial cognition (Burgess, Maguire, & O'Keefe, 2002). Finally, a growing and broad area of application for spatial memory research derives from technological advances in the computer sciences that pose human factors engineering problems related to how devices may best utilize spatial interfaces. Wide-ranging areas such as the use of interactive tabletop computer displays (Kim & Maher, 2008), navigation within programs (Guerlain, 2007), and the military use of VE training simulators (Templeman & Sibert, 2007) all depend heavily upon an understanding of human spatial cognition and memory.

HISTORICAL LANDMARKS

From response learning to cognitive maps

Edward C. Tolman is recognized as the father of modern spatial memory research. His research program centered on the question of whether organisms navigate using stimulus–response associative mechanisms, as posited by the behaviorists of the day, or whether they use map-like spatial representations that describe relationships among features of the environment, a view that Tolman championed. Numerous studies conducted in this vein have indicated that organisms extract a rich representation of the spatial relationships in the environment that can be efficiently and effectively transformed when necessary (Olton, 1978; Tolman, 1948). This cognitive map framework provided an explanation of how complex spatial relationships may be stored in memory. It appears in the literature under numerous guises, sometimes called schema representations or survey knowledge (Taylor & Tversky, 1992). Tolman and subsequent researchers have shown how cognitive maps can be used by both humans and nonhuman animals to produce flexible and adaptive behaviors within complex spatial environments. A key question for future research is how modern technological tools may alter, enhance, or detract from the cognitive spatial maps people form.

Recognition of modality specific memory

Despite the early advances of Tolman's ideas for cognitive maps, cognitive psychologists of the 1960s tended to posit amodal representations of memory. However, research in the 1970s led to a general acceptance of modality specific memory stores. An important advancement to the understanding of spatial abilities arose from the introduction of the working memory model (Baddeley & Hitch, 1974), which proposed two independent rehearsal spaces, the phonological loop for auditory verbal information and the visuospatial sketchpad for visual and spatial information. Contemporary researchers take it as a given that there are specific working memory resources dedicated to manipulation and temporary storage of visuospatial information. Importantly, AR technologies may change the working memory demands of spatial memory processing, as linked information can be visualized directly rather than having to be retrieved from long-term memory and held in short-term memory.

Researchers have attempted to determine what types of flexible activities can be applied to spatial representations. Shepard and Metzler (1971) demonstrated in a seminal study that people were able to mentally rotate objects. Mental rotation abilities are important from an applied perspective, with research focusing on surgical training (Peters & Battista, 2008) and video game expertise (Spence & Feng, 2010). Along similar lines of inquiry, Kosslyn and colleagues conducted several seminal studies of mental scanning and zooming that implied that the mind treats remembered images in a similar analog fashion to how it perceives the corresponding visual stimuli (Kosslyn, Ball, & Reiser, 1978). While this research placed short-term and long-term analog spatial memory representations on a firm footing, it was not without its critics. Pylyshyn (1973) argued that these "analog" demonstrations did not rule out an explanation in terms of an underlying propositional representation of spatial information. Within the propositional framework, spatial representations can be described in an amodal form with relational operators that code relevant spatial information, such as "on top of," "to the right of," or "close to." Although neuroimaging data provide further evidence of the existence of modality specific visuospatial representations in the brain (Farah, 1984; Kosslyn, Ganis, & Thompson, 2001), it is also clear that propositional or categorical encoding of spatial information is an important component of spatial memory.

Exploring the neural circuitry of spatial memory

In their seminal book, *The Hippocampus as a Cognitive Map*, O'Keefe and Nadel (1978) focused on the hippocampus as a key neural structure responsible for spatial memory processing. Their research is credited with the discovery of place cells, which are active whenever an organism is in a specific location within its environment. Support for the key role of the hippocampus in forming cognitive maps comes from Morris and Parslow

(2004) using the now standard Morris water maze, which requires that the animal use a metric coordinate system to encode location. Rats with hippocampal lesions showed large deficits in navigation to platforms hidden under the surface of the water as compared with controls, implying that critical place information was blocked by the lesions.

Further support for the key role of the hippocampus in spatial navigation comes from research on taxi drivers, whose right posterior hippocampus contained more gray matter volume than controls (Maguire et al., 2000; Maguire, Woollett, & Spiers, 2006). However, research from lesion studies in humans and nonhuman animals has demonstrated a more complex picture regarding the hippocampus and spatial memory. Spatial memories can sometimes be maintained in the face of large hippocampal lesions, and neural damage that does not include parahippocampal cortex typically does not impair spatial memory for long familiar environments (Moscovitch, Nadel, Winocur, Gilboa, & Rosenbaum, 2006). Furthermore, former taxi drivers with hippocampal damage due to Alzheimer's disease still showed knowledge for spatial locations they knew before the onset of the disease (Rosenbaum, Gao, Richards, Black, & Moscovitch, 2005). These findings suggest a broader spatial memory network, with the hippocampus needed to bind information across network components.

In line with this idea, parietal and frontal cortices have also been found to be linked to spatial memory. Recent studies using functional magnetic resonance imaging and transcranial magnetic stimulation in humans have also allowed researchers to investigate the role of the parietal cortex in spatial cognition and have demonstrated it to be an essential component for comprehending where objects are within the visual field (Sack, 2009). Furthermore, the frontal cortex may play a critical role in the processing of spatial memories through its relationship to working memory representation and processing (Kessels, Postma, Wijnalda, & de Haan, 2000).

There is also clear evidence of a specialized parahippocampal place area that plays a critical role in scene recognition, and is activated when viewing large-scale places, such as cityscapes, as well as small-scale places, such as rooms (Epstein, Harris, Stanley, & Kanwisher, 1998).

SPHERES OF INQUIRY

The nature of spatial representations

Tolman's (1948) seminal research established cognitive spatial maps as a fundamental representation of spatial information in both humans and nonhuman animals. Pursuing this approach, Downs and Stea (1973) examined the steps involved in acquiring and using cognitive maps. First, the perceiver *acquires* information about the general layout of the environment through perception. This layout is *encoded* as a cognitive map (i.e., a set of interrelated locations that include distance and direction information) and *stored* in long-term memory. Later, when it is *recalled*, the cognitive map must be *decoded* in order to use necessary relational properties between geographic entities within the environment.

Lynch (1960) postulated that people remember the layout of cities through five environmental features: paths, edges, districts, nodes, and landmarks. Because people use paths to navigate, their representation of the environment is typically path bound. The egocentric perspective of navigation paths provides a great deal of information about the size of environmental features. In studying differences between acquiring information through maps and navigation, Thorndyke and Hayes-Roth (1982) proposed that map learning results in survey knowledge, an allocentric representation that provides access to the relationships among environmental features as a unitary whole. In contrast, learning through navigation results in route knowledge, an egocentric view that relies on knowing a sequence of behaviors when encountering the environmental features. When asked to transform learned spatial layouts into the opposite perspective, people show increased errors, supporting the general conclusion that spatial memory performance is decremented when one must transform the representation encoded in memory. One implication of this line of research is that while the structure of an environment may contribute to people getting lost, another large factor stems from developing incomplete cognitive maps or use of incorrect spatial strategies during navigation (Carlson, Hölscher, Shipley, & Dalton, 2010).

Memory for spatial information is also affected by retrieval factors. Montello, Richardson, Hegarty, and Provenza (1999) asked participants who learned locations through direct experience to either point to those locations or turn their bodies toward those locations. Even though the method of acquisition was the same in both conditions, participants who were asked to use a pointing device to indicate direction to the location showed higher error rates than those who were asked to turn their bodies. These results support the conclusion that the representation of spatial layout can change given the demands of the task at retrieval. Future research needs to address how the use of GPS devices and AR technology in navigation affects spatial memories. Will these be enhanced or decremented by the ease of navigation and the ready access to information?

Typically, maps can be considered allocentric or viewpoint independent, showing the interrelationships of the different elements in the environment as a configuration. But of course, the environment is typically encountered from an egocentric or viewer-based perspective. When facing a landmark, one must determine which way to turn. To utilize the cognitive map, one must match one's orientation toward landmarks to a given location on the map, a kind of "you are here" position. Then as one moves through an environment, one must continue to transform the egocentrically encountered information into a form that allows it to be integrated with the allocentric internal map. The interplay between egocentric and allocentric representations has been well studied in recent years (Mou, McNamara, Rump, & Xiao, 2006; Shelton & McNamara, 1997; Waller, 2006). From this research, it is clear that under the right circumstances, both egocentric and allocentric representations of space are encoded during learning of the environmental layout. People prefer to make judgments about views that they have directly experienced, but when asked about a novel view, they can generate the imagined view required to solve the task. As new technologies such as virtual environments and augmented reality become more accessible to researchers, studies will clarify the role of these technologies in the use of and preference for different representations in spatial tasks.

While researchers have generally emphasized the cognitive map-like perceptual representation of space in memory, there is evidence that response-based representations are also used to encode memory. When rats are not trained from different orientations in the Morris water maze, they show response based errors in their swimming behavior (Brandeis, Brandys, & Yehuda, 1989). However, when learning the locations from different orientations, the rat quickly learns to swim relative to distal cues rather than follow a predominant motoric response. Developmental perspectives suggest that spatial layouts are first learned in the form of route knowledge, reflecting directions relative to landmarks along the way, and only through extensive experience does one develop the survey knowledge characteristic of cognitive spatial maps (Siegel & White, 1975).

In addition to encoding cognitive maps and associative sequences, propositional and categorical codes are also available and are presumably widely used. When trying to locate one's keys, it seems most reasonable to begin by thinking propositionally. For example, one might think of being recently in the kitchen and placing the keys down on the counter by the stove. Kitchen, counter, and stove are all categorical markers that allow us to navigate through the spatial memory of the larger environment (i.e., house) quite efficiently. These types of categories and relational properties, such as "left of" and "below," are critical verbal descriptions that allow us to localize objects. As discussed later, the categorization process can often lead to a distortion of the remembered location for an object. As a simple example of types of potential errors, consider which is further west, Reno or San Diego? Most people would incorrectly indicate that San Diego is further west, as San Diego is in California, which is west of Nevada, the state in which Reno is located (Stevens & Coupe, 1978). Thus, categorical memory, while robust and accessible, can sometimes lead to inferring erroneous spatial relationships. Studies of the interplay between spatial memory and language have produced a rich body of research literature that indicates a strong influence of verbalization on spatial representation in memory (Noordzij & Postma, 2005; Rinck, 2005; Zwaan & Radvansky, 1998). An unexplored area of research is the effect of augmented reality and GPS on the use of verbal characteristics of space. Will people's ability to describe where one landmark is in relation to another improve if they have access to portable interactive mapping technology?

Distortions of spatial memory

We have considered the various ways spatial information may be represented in memory. When using spatial memory, presumably different types of representations may be retrieved and acted upon. As with many cognitive tasks, the errors observed in spatial memory tasks can be very informative in revealing the processes and representations being used. In this section we focus on research that has attempted to explain the basis for the many systematic distortions observed in spatial memory tasks.

Schema based distortions

Tversky (1993) proposed two explanations for frequent errors found in spatial memory studies. First, she noted that cognitive maps are not rigid templates for environmental layouts, but rather they are more like a cognitive collage. People learn small pieces of environments very well. When spending time in one particular location, one experiences the relative positions of objects within the environment from specific egocentric viewpoints. When one navigates to different locations, one learns the relative positions of objects in that environment. What happens when one is subsequently asked to make judgments of location across these two districts? Presumably, one must quickly create a larger cognitive map from the previously existing smaller cognitive maps. The resulting constructed map will naturally have areas of high fidelity and low fidelity. This constructive view of cognitive mapping then argues that errors in spatial memory occur because the new representation is like a patchwork quilt rather than a seamless, accurate map.

Tversky (1993) also noted that errors occur when mentally representing well known environments. She argued that these result from the use of schemas or *spatial mental models*, which store expectations about position, orientation, and size of features. These learned expectations then lead to the use of heuristics that enhance efficiency in responding to the required task but may distort memories for spatial layouts. Use of spatial mental models often leads to regularizing the configuration, such as aligning the configuration with cardinal directions, smoothing out irregular boundaries, etc.

Taylor and Tversky (1992) further discuss how people tend to rely on hierarchical grouping of landmarks to help them organize environmental features. For example, they may think of the mountains, trees, and rivers as being natural features and will remember those locations as a group configuration. Similar clustering will occur with buildings, streets, and other manmade landmarks. These clustering rules are derived in part from gestalt principles of organization. More generally, the idea that people use spatial mental models to organize spatial information in memory is consistent with the proposition of other researchers that spatial information is encoded at two levels, coarse and fine-grain, and that the coarse, categorical representation leads to systematic distortions in memory.

Location memory

A particularly productive way to consider distortions of spatial memory locations is within the framework of the category-adjustment model developed by Huttenlocher and colleagues (Huttenlocher, Hedges, & Duncan, 1991). The category-adjustment model assumes that locations are encoded at the level of fine-grain memory, reflecting angular and metric properties of the representation, and at the level of categorical memory, reflecting a grosser partitioning of the space. Spatial categories can be represented by boundaries, such as the wall between the kitchen and the living room, and also by prototypes, corresponding for example to the central tendency of the category (i.e., the center of the kitchen). These fine-grain and categorical memory representations differ not only in their level of detail, but also in how robust and accessible the memories are. Although highly accurate, fine-grain memory is posited to be fragile and forgotten quickly. The coarser categorical memory, by contrast, is highly robust and accessible. The category-adjustment model posits that the individual attempts to recall locations through retrieval of the fine-grain memory representation. However, to the degree that the fine-grain memory is uncertain, the remembered location is shifted toward the corresponding category prototype. Accordingly, research has demonstrated that forgetting induced by delays or interference tasks results in estimates that are more dependent on categorical encoding and hence reflect greater bias toward category prototypes

(Fitting, Wedell, & Allen, 2007b; Hund & Plumert, 2002; Huttenlocher et al., 1991). Although the influence of category prototypes results in systematic bias in recall, it reduces overall memory error and is thereby considered to reflect adaptive behavior.

Researchers have begun to tease apart whether these effects occur at encoding or retrieval stages of processing. Research by Sargent, Dopkins, and Philbeck (2011) is supportive of the idea that spatial categories can be reorganized at retrieval. The pattern of angular bias they found implied that rotating the participant's egocentric orientation to the task field led to the establishment of new spatial categories centered on the new heading. Sampaio and Wang (2009) found strong evidence supporting a retrieval basis for category bias, such that reproduced locations showed the usual bias toward the prototype but recognition tests of location did not. The issue of whether category influences are formed when first encountering the environment or are determined by the current context has implications for the use of GPS, AR, and VEs. Hutcheson and Wedell (2012), in a VE task, found differences in the bias when remembering locations from an egocentric or allocentric viewpoint, implying that the viewpoint presented by the VE is a strong determinant of the nature of the bias. These effects may be important when applied to VE applications of flying planes or locating mines or persons.

Distance memory

Memory biases also apply to judgments of components of spatial location, such as remembered distances and angles. As discussed by Montello (1997) many factors can affect distance estimates. Measurement techniques can lead to specific bias patterns. Having participants draw maps forces them to think about the overall layout of the environment rather than just a single distance between two points, and may lead to regularization of distances (Tversky, 1993). Requiring participants to give verbal or physical estimates of distance with a learned metric may be problematic as it provides only relative rather than absolute accuracy. Other researchers have had participants reproduce the distance between two points in a nonsymbolic way, such as experiencing a blindfolded walk between two marks on the floor and then being asked to walk back to the first mark. This technique works well only for a small number of estimations. Methods for maximizing accuracy of recall distances have practical implications for eyewitness testimony, in which remembered distances may be important determinants of who is at fault. Research shows that people not only recognize events more poorly as distance increases but that they are also inaccurate in remembering the distance to the event itself (Lindsay, Semmler, Weber, Brewer, & Lindsay, 2008).

Environmental and situational factors may affect distance memory. Increasing the time it takes to travel the distance or the effort required to reach a destination often results in an overestimation of distance (Montello, 1997). Multiple studies have found that partitions across spatial categories can have a large influence on estimated distance. People remember distances that cross spatial regions as greater than like distances within a spatial region (Allen & Kirasic, 1985; Sadalla, Staplin, & Burroughs, 1979). The number of turns one takes along a path can be a powerful influence on the perception and memory of distance. The route angularity effect, as it has become known, is the finding that the more turns a person encounters along a path, the longer the person remembers the path to be. This effect can be present in both real and virtual environments used to test spatial abilities (Jansen-Osmann & Berendt, 2002; Sadalla & Magel, 1980). Hutcheson and Wedell (2009) demonstrated in a VE how the route angularity effect is consistent with using number of turns as a heuristic to estimating distance when fine-grain memory for the traveled path is disrupted by either a concurrent task at encoding or a filled delay after traversing the route. These results help to explain why the route angularity effect is

not observed when the memory demands of the task are low.

Angle memory

Angular estimates are frequently used to assess spatial memory, as when blindfolded participants are asked to point to locations in an array they have memorized, or when one is asked to point in the direction of as unseen specific location after navigating different paths (Waller, Knapp, & Hunt, 2001). Memory for angles may also be applied to surfaces encountered in an environment (angles of inclination and declination) along with direction in the horizontal plane (azimuth).

An important issue reflecting measurement of angles in memory is whether these are expressed directly through motor movements or must be translated into a verbal expression, such as a measure of degrees. Creem and Profitt (1998) found that when participants made responses within a few seconds of viewing, motor estimates of inclination were very accurate but verbal estimates were strongly biased upward. They interpreted these results as reflecting two memory systems. The motor system briefly stores information for guiding actions and functions within an egocentric frame that provides rapid and precise responding. The verbal system is based on explicit memory, requires effortful computation, is flexible and long lasting but is subject to biases.

While there is good evidence supporting the distinction between motor and verbal response systems in many perceptual tasks, research by Haun, Allen, and Wedell (2005) suggests that the systems may not be as distinct as first posited by Creem and Proffitt (1998). Using a wider range of inclination angles and also measuring azimuth, their results were consistent with previous results in that motor estimates were more accurate and less biased than verbal estimates. However, inconsistent with the idea of two completely separate systems, they found significant bias for motor estimates that was of the same pattern as found for verbal estimates and consistent with Huttenlocher et al.'s (1991) category-adjustment model.

Research also suggests that estimation of angles in real world settings may depend on contextual factors. Estimates of steepness of hills are influenced by the presence of a friend (Schnall, Harber, Stefanucci, & Proffitt, 2008), and also by glucose intake (Schnall, Zadra, & Proffitt, 2010). What might the effects of VE depictions and AR information be on memory for steepness of the terrain we encounter?

Verbal descriptions of space

A final area of consideration for understanding distortions of spatial memory is the role of verbal descriptions. People are quite sensitive to the various kinds of statements made when describing a route that would allow them to reach a desired location. They need to know the temporal/spatial order of landmarks and how to respond to those landmarks while avoiding confusion during the description to maintain mutual knowledge (Allen, 2000). Ferguson and Hegarty (1994) found that the type of landmarks provided in a written description of space to a person can change the accuracy for recalling spatial layout. Their study shows that important "anchor" landmarks are used to maintain spatial memories for environmental layout regardless of whether the description is written in route or survey terminology, whether or not they were given a map, whether the anchor landmarks were described first, or the level of detail provided. Thus some features of spatial memory generated from verbal descriptions appear more malleable than others.

Once again eyewitness testimony may be an important area to explore how verbal reports influence memory for spatial layouts. Research on the verbal overshadowing effect finds that verbal reports may degrade later retrieval of memories for experienced stimuli (Meissner, Brigham, & Kelley, 2001). This may provide researchers with a firm basis for explaining real world errors in spatial memory for learned locations. Additionally,

AR applications are an important arena for exploring the interface of verbal and spatial descriptions of layouts.

Dynamic spatial memory

As we gain experience in an environment, our spatial memories may change to incorporate new information. Wayfinding, or the process of mentally and physically navigating toward a desired location, is particularly relevant to understanding applications of spatial memory, as this is a key applied task. According to Siegel and White's (1975) research on wayfinding, a person acquires route knowledge by learning a sequence of turns at specific landmarks. Over time, the person begins to form a more map-like representation of the environment, referred to as survey knowledge. This type of representation is more flexible than route knowledge, as it is less reliant on proximal landmarks and may use distal cues, such as celestial bodies or large faraway buildings, to maintain a sense of heading. In some environments, one may need to maintain a sense of distance and direction traveled even if one cannot see relevant environmental cues, a process referred to as spatial updating. For example, when the power goes out at home, one may find oneself in total darkness and have to locate another light source without visual cues. Remembering that there are candles in the kitchen, one can get up off of the couch and slowly move to where one believes the kitchen door is located. This action may start with an initial heading based on the angular assessment of starting point and destination point. As travel proceeds, one must be careful to determine distance traveled to avoid bumping into obstacles. At any given point, course adjustments may be needed along with consideration of the relative location of objects in the environment. People's ability to carry out these types of tasks suggests that spatial updating is robust and possibly automated.

A common way to test spatial updating is to blindfold participants and have them perform a triangle completion task, as illustrated in Figure 5.1. From the starting position, experimenters guide participants forward, then through a turn and another forward leg of the triangle. At this point participants are asked to turn and walk back to the starting position on their own while still blindfolded. As shown in Figure 5.1, three measures of performance are typically obtained: angular error, distance error, and absolute error. To successfully complete this task requires that the participant maintains a sense of distance and direction traveled by understanding how much muscular exertion has been required (kinesthetic cues) and how much motion has been perceived using the movement of fluid in the ears' semicircular canals (vestibular cues). Studies using this method have found that participants with sight tend to have more difficulty with this task than congenitally blind participants. While people generally can get close to the targeted destination using only kinesthetic and vestibular cues, sighted individuals use visual cues to correct for

errors as they update their location (Klatzky, Loomis, Beall, Chance, & Golledge, 1998).

Two basic processes have been posited to explain how updating is accomplished. One account assumes that spatial updating is a continuous cognitive act that occurs during navigation and that requires spatial working memory resources (Sholl & Fraone, 2004; Wang et al., 2006). The second assumes that spatial updating occurs after navigation is completed and a location is prompted, referred to as offline updating (Hodgson & Waller, 2006). Although both of these accounts predict the requirement of cognitive resources, they make different predictions about the time course for using those resources. There currently is support for both of these spatial updating processes, depending on task constraints. Allen, Kirasic, Rashotte, and Haun (2004) compared updating in younger and older adults using a triangle completion task in which participants either walked the paths (kinesthetic and vestibular cues) or rode a wheel chair through the paths (vestibular cues only). The results indicate that kinesthetic-based updating is more robust across aging than vestibular-based updating, with working memory measures significantly predicting nearly all the age related variance in signed direction and distance errors. Thus, cognitive resources appear to be needed for updating when environmental feedback is held at a minimum.

Both wayfinding and spatial updating often require people to change orientation to their cognitive maps in order to find their target location. Even when an environment feature is learned from a fixed orientation, a person may need to locate it from a different orientation. Research in this area demonstrates that when asked about the location of a landmark from a rotated perspective, people can do this as well, but performance is often resource dependent (Presson, DeLange, & Hazelrigg, 1989; Sholl & Nolin, 1997). Future research should investigate the impact of the use of advanced technologies on this resource intensive perspective taking task. Will use of VEs and GPS help or hurt abilities to reorient

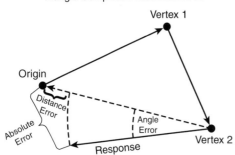

Figure 5.1 Illustration of the triangle completion task and related measures. The blindfolded participant starts at the origin and is guided to the first vertex, turned, and guided to the second vertex. At this point, participants must turn and walk to where they believe they started. The absolute error is the distance from the origin to where participants stopped. This can be decomposed into angle error and distance error.

to the environment? Will unburdening working memory resources through the use of AR provide the needed resources to aid in this task?

Finally, we note how the category-adjustment model described earlier can relate to navigation. Fitting, Wedell, and Allen (2009) studied how participants navigated a rat icon though a simulated Morris water maze to find a hidden platform while varying the number and location of cues. They found clear evidence that participants formed cue-based categories to guide their navigation toward the remembered locations, as indicated by heading error bias and bias near the end of the path. In another study, Fitting et al., (2007a) had participants remember locations in a 3 m arena and also found cue-based bias. These studies suggest that at least in these sparse environments, cues may be used to create spatial categories and that navigation tends to proceed toward the center of the spatial category in which the location is situated. However, in a recent study, Hutcheson and Wedell (2012) found that size of the environment may matter. When participants had to remember locations encoded via a map view by navigating to them within a large scale VE, manipulation of distal cue placement once again resulted in bias patterns that indicated cue-based categories. However, unlike the smaller scale results, cues did not correspond to category prototypes but rather to category boundaries. Thus, when cues are distal and viewed using an egocentric orientation within a large space, they may function primarily to orient one to the space and hence form natural boundaries or category partitions.

Individual differences

Sex differences in spatial abilities have been widely studied for decades. The finding that males tend to outperform females in mental rotation tasks, navigation tasks, and other spatial tasks related to mental imagery is quite robust (Halpern, 2000). When using self-report measures to get a sense of the strategies used in wayfinding, women tend to use route knowledge more than men, especially as familiarity with the environment increased. Men tend to show less spatial anxiety, better sense of direction, and greater willingness to try shortcuts, suggestive of more complete cognitive maps (Lawton, 2001; Prestopnik & Roskos-Ewoldsen, 2000). Explanations for these differences often center on hormonal influences (Silverman & Phillips, 1993) or enhancement of abilities through specialized training such as video game play (Spence & Feng, 2010), which is more common in males.

Occupations and activities that may promote individual differences in spatial abilities need to be further documented in the literature. Individuals who use American Sign Language tend to be better at mental imagery than those who do not (Emmorey & Kosslyn, 1996). More recently there has been a spate of research investigating how video gamers may enhance spatial abilities through brain related changes (Spence & Feng, 2010). From the research on expertise, it is clear that experts in a domain have access to better schemas for problem solving than novices, who focus on the physical properties of the stimulus rather than the underlying principles of the problem (Glaser, 1984). Likewise, researchers who study location memory should strive to understand the effects associated with jobs that require the use of spatial representations, such as architecture, engineering, and product design. A better understanding of how expertise affects spatial memory is needed, with an emphasis on mechanisms through which this is achieved.

CONCLUSION

As we move into an age in which complex navigational devices are small enough to fit in our pockets or in a pair of glasses, spatial memory researchers must adapt old theoretical principles to new problems. The general public has access to technology only considered in science fiction a few decades ago. This increased instant access to a wide array of spatial information may have both detrimental and beneficial consequences. Increased reliance on navigation tools may lead to poorer overall spatial memory, as less attention is paid to where one is going and what are the relevant landmarks. On the other hand, well designed information enhancement can lead to more efficient navigation and free up working memory resources that aid in spatial memory integration. Future research is critical to understanding how human spatial memory will function in this new information era.

REFERENCES

Allen, G. L. (2000). Principles and practices for communicating route knowledge. *Applied Cognitive Psychology, 14,* 333–359.

Allen, G. L., & Kirasic, K. C. (1985). Effects of the cognitive organization of route knowledge on judgments of macrospatial distance. *Memory & Cognition, 13,* 218–227.

Allen, G. L., Kirasic, K. C., Rashotte, M. A., & Haun, D. B. M. (2004). Aging and path integration skill: Kinesthetic and vestibular contributions to wayfinding. *Perception & Psychophysics, 66,* 170–179.

Baddeley, A. D., & Hitch, G. J. (1974). Working memory. In G. Bower (Ed.), *The psychology of learning and motivation* (Vol. 8, pp. 47–89). New York: Academic Press.

Beirwisch, M. (1996). How much space gets into language? In P. Bloom, M. A. Peterson, L. Nadel, and M. F. Garrett (Eds.), *Language and Space* (pp. 31–76). Cambridge, MA: MIT Press.

Brandeis, R., Brandys, Y., & Yehuda, S. (1989). The use of the Morris Water Maze in the study of memory and learning. *International Journal of Neuroscience, 48,* 29–69.

Burgess, N., Maguire, E. A., & O'Keefe, J. (2002). The human hippocampus and spatial and episodic memory. *Neuron, 35,* 625–641.

Carlson, L. A., Hölscher, C., Shipley, T. F., & Conroy Dalton, R. (2010). Getting lost in buildings. *Current Directions in Psychological Science, 19,* 284–289.

Chen, J. L., & Stanney, K. M. (1999). A theoretical model of wayfinding in virtual environments: Proposed strategies for navigational aiding. *Presence: Teleoperators & Virtual Environments, 8,* 671–686.

Creem, S. H., & Proffitt, D. R. (1998). Two memories for geographical slant: Separation and interdependence of action and awareness. *Psychonomic Bulletin & Review, 5,* 22–36.

Downs, R. M., & Stea, D. (1973). *Theory.* In R. M. Downs and D. Stea (Eds.), Image and Environment (pp. 1–13). Chicago, IL: Aldine Press.

Emmorey, K., & Kosslyn, S. M. (1996). Enhanced image generation abilities in deaf signers: A right hemisphere effect. *Brain and Cognition, 32,* 28–44.

Epstein, R., Harris, A., Stanley, D., & Kanwisher, N. (1999). The parahippocampal place area: Recognition, navigation, or encoding? *Neuron, 23,* 115–125.

Farah, M. J. (1984). The neurological basis of mental imagery: a componential analysis. *Cognition, 18,* 245–272.

Ferguson, E. L., & Hegarty, M. (1994). Properties of cognitive maps constructed from texts. *Memory & Cognition, 22,* 455–473.

Fitting, S., Allen, G. L., & Wedell, D. H. (2007a). Remembering places in space: A human analog study of the Morris Water Maze. In T. Barkowsky, M. Knauff, G. Ligozat, and D. R. Montello (Eds.), *Spatial cognition V: Reasoning, Action, Interaction,* LNAI 4387 (pp. 59–75). Berlin: Springer-Verlag.

Fitting, S., Wedell, D. H., & Allen, G. L. (2007b). Memory for spatial location: Cue effects as a function of field rotation. *Memory and Cognition, 35,* 1641–1658.

Fitting, S., Wedell, D. H., & Allen, G. L. (2009). Cue effects on memory for location when navigating spatial displays. *Cognitive Science, 33,* 1267–1300.

Glaser, R. (1984). Education and thinking: The role of knowledge. *American Psychologist, 39,* 93–104.

Guerlain, S. (2007). Software navigation design. In G. L. Allen and G. L. Allen (Eds.), *Applied spatial cognition: From research to cognitive technology* (pp. 317–337). Mahwah, NJ: Lawrence Erlbaum Associates Publishers.

Halpern, D. F. (2000). *Sex differences in cognitive ability.* New York: Psychology Press.

Haun, D. B. M., Allen, G. L., & Wedell, D. H. (2005). Bias in spatial memory: a categorical endorsement, *Acta Psychologica, 118,* 149–170.

Heth, C., & Cornell, E. H. (2007). A geographic information system for managing search for lost persons. In G. L. Allen and G. L. Allen (Eds.), *Applied spatial cognition: From research to cognitive technology* (pp. 267–284). Mahwah, NJ: Lawrence Erlbaum Associates Publishers.

Hodgson, E., & Waller, D. (2006). Lack of set size effects in spatial updating: Evidence for offline updating. *Journal of Experimental Psychology: Learning, Memory and Cognition, 32*, 854–866.

Hund, A. M., & Plumert, J. M. (2002). Delay-induced bias in children's memory for location. *Child Development, 73*, 829–840.

Hutcheson, A. T., & Wedell, D. H. (2009). Moderating the route angularity effect in a virtual environment: Support for a dual memory representation. *Memory and Cognition, 37*, 514–521.

Hutcheson, A. T., & Wedell, D. H. (2012). From maps to navigation: The role of cues in finding locations in a virtual environment. *Memory & Cognition, 40*(6), 946–957.

Huttenlocher, J., Hedges, L. V., & Duncan, S. (1991). Categories and particulars: Prototype effects in estimating spatial location. *Psychological Review, 98*, 352–376.

Ishikawa, T., Fujiwara, H., Imai, O., & Okabe, A. (2008). Wayfinding with a GPS-based mobile navigation system: A comparison with maps and direct experience. *Journal of Environmental Psychology, 28*, 74–82.

Istomin, K. V., & Dwyer, M. J. (2009). Finding the way: A critical discussion of anthropological theories of human spatial orientation with reference to reindeer herders of northeastern Europe and Western Siberia. *Current Anthropology, 50*, 29–49.

Jansen-Osmann, P., & Berendt, B. (2002). Investigating distance knowledge using virtual environments. *Environment & Behavior, 34*, 178–193.

Kessels, R. C., Postma, A., Wijnalda, E. M., & de Haan, E. F. (2000). Frontal lobe involvement in spatial memory: Evidence from PET, fMRI, and lesion studies. *Neuropsychology Review, 10*, 101–113.

Kim, M., & Maher, M. (2008). The impact of tangible user interfaces on designers' spatial cognition. *Human–Computer Interaction, 23*, 101–137.

Klatzky, R. L., Loomis, J. M., Beall, A. C., Chance, S. S., & Golledge, R. G. (1998). Spatial updating of self-position and orientation during real, imagined, and virtual locomotion. *Psychological Science, 9*, 293–298.

Kosslyn, S. M., Ball, T., & Reiser, B. J. (1978). Visual images preserve metric spatial information: Evidence from studies of image scanning. *Journal of Experimental Psychology: Human Perception and Performance, 4*, 47–60.

Kosslyn, S. M., Ganis, G., & Thompson, W. L. (2001) Neural foundations of imagery. *Nature Reviews Neuroscience, 2*, 635–642.

Lawton, C. A. (2001). Gender and regional differences in spatial referents used in direction giving. *Sex Roles, 44*, 321–337.

Lindsay, R. L., Semmler, C., Weber, N., Brewer, N., & Lindsay, M. R. (2008). How variations in distance affect eyewitness reports and identification accuracy. *Law and Human Behavior, 32*, 526–535.

Loomis, J. M., Golledge, R. G., Klatsky, R. L., & Marston, J. R. (2007). Assisting wayfinding in visually impaired travelers. In G. L. Allen and G. L. Allen (Eds.), *Applied spatial cognition: From research to cognitive technology* (pp. 267–284). Mahwah, NJ: Lawrence Erlbaum Associates Publishers.

Lynch, K. (1960). *The image of the city.* Cambridge, MA: MIT Press.

Maguire, E. A., Gadian, D. G., Johnsrude, I. S., Good, C. D., Ashburner, J., Frackowiak, R. S. J., & Frith, C. D. (2000). Navigation-related structural change in the hippocampi of taxi drivers. *Proceedings of the National Academy of Sciences USA, 97*, 4398–4403.

Maguire, E. A., Woollett, K., & Spiers, H. J. (2006). London taxi drivers and bus drivers: A structural MRI and neuropsychological analysis. *Hippocampus, 16*, 1091–1101.

Meissner, C. A., Brigham, J. C., & Kelley, C. M. (2001). The influence of retrieval processes in verbal overshadowing. *Memory & Cognition, 29*, 176–186.

Montello, D. R. (1997). The perception and cognition of environmental distance: Direct sources of information. In S. C. Hirtle and A. U. Frank (Eds.), *Spatial Information Theory: A theoretical basis for GIS. Proceedings of COSIT 1997* (pp. 297–311). Berlin: Springer-Verlag.

Montello, D. R., Richardson, A. E., Hegarty, M., & Provenza, M. (1999). A comparison of methods for estimating directions in egocentric space. *Perception, 28*, 981–1000.

Morris, R. G., & Parslow, D. (2004). Neurocognitive components of spatial memory. In G. L. Allen and G. L. Allen (Eds.), *Human spatial memory: Remembering where* (pp. 217–247). Mahwah, NJ: Lawrence Erlbaum Associates Publishers.

Moscovitch, M., Nadel, L., Winocur, G., Gilboa, A., & Rosenbaum, R. S. (2006). The cognitive neuroscience of remote episodic, semantic and spatial memory. *Current Opinion in Neurobiology, 16*, 179–190.

Mou, W., McNamara, T. P., Rump, B., & Xiao, C. (2006). Roles of egocentric and allocentric spatial representations in locomotion and reorientation. *Journal of Experimental Psychology: Learning, Memory, and Cognition, 32*, 1274–1290.

Noordzij, M. L., & Postma, A. (2005). Categorical and metric distance information in mental representations derived from route and survey descriptions. *Psychological Research, 69*, 221–232.

O'Keefe, J., & Nadel, L. (1978). *The hippocampus as a cognitive map.* Oxford: Oxford University Press

Olton, D. S. (1978). Mazes, maps, and memory. *American Psychologist, 34,* 583–596.

Peters, M., & Battista, C. (2008). Applications of mental rotation figures of the Shepard and Metzler type and description of a mental rotation stimulus library. *Brain and Cognition, 66,* 260–264.

Presson, C. C., DeLange, N., & Hazelrigg, M. D. (1989). Orientation specificity in spatial memory: What makes a path different from a map of the path? *Journal of Experimental Psychology: Learning, Memory, and Cognition, 15,* 887–897.

Prestopnik, J. L., & Roskos-Ewoldsen, B. (2000). The relations among wayfinding strategy use, sense of direction, sex, familiarity, and wayfinding ability. *Journal of Environmental Psychology, 20,* 177–191.

Pylyshyn, Z. W. (1973). What the mind's eye tells the mind's brain: A critique of mental imagery. *Psychological Bulletin, 80,* 1–24.

Rinck, M. (2005). Spatial situation models. In P. Shah and A. Miyake (Eds.), *The Cambridge handbook of visuospatial thinking* (pp. 334–382). Cambridge: Cambridge University Press.

Rosenbaum, R., Gao, F., Richards, B., Black, S. E., & Moscovitch, M. (2005). 'Where to?' Remote memory for spatial relations and landmark identity in former taxi drivers with Alzheimer's disease and encephalitis. *Journal of Cognitive Neuroscience, 17*(3), 446–462.

Sack, A. T. (2009). Parietal cortex and spatial cognition. *Behavioural Brain Research, 202,* 153–161.

Sadalla, E. K., & Magel, S. G. (1980). The perception of traversed distance. *Environment and Behavior, 12,* 65–79.

Sadalla, E. K., Staplin, L. J., & Burroughs, W. J. (1979). Retrieval processes in distance cognition. *Memory & Cognition, 7,* 291–296.

Sampaio, C., & Wang, R. F. (2009). Category-based errors and the accessibility of unbiased spatial memories: A retrieval model. *Journal of Experimental Psychology: Learning, Memory, and Cognition, 5,* 1331–1337.

Sargent, J., Dopkins, S., & Philbeck, J. (2011). Dynamic category structure in spatial memory. *Psychonomic Bulletin & Review, 18,* 1105–1112.

Schnall, S., Harber, K. D., Stefanucci, J. K., & Proffitt, D. R. (2008). Social support and the perception of geographical slant. *Journal of Experimental Social Psychology, 44,* 1246–1255.

Schnall, S., Zadra, J. R., & Proffitt, D. R. (2010). Direct evidence for the economy of action: Glucose and the perception of geographical slant. *Perception, 39,* 464–482.

Shelton, A. L., & McNamara, T. P. (1997). Multiple views of spatial memory. *Psychonomic Bulletin & Review, 4,* 102–106.

Shepard, R. N., & Metzler, J. (1971). Mental rotation of three-dimensional objects. *Science, 171,* 701–703.

Sholl, M. J., & Fraone, S. K. (2004). Visuospatial working memory for different scales of space: Weighing the evidence. In G. Allen (Ed.), *Human spatial memory* (pp. 67–100). Mahwah, NJ: Lawrence Erlbaum Associates.

Sholl, M. J., & Nolin, T. L. (1997). Orientation specificity in representations of place. *Journal of Experimental Psychology: Learning, Memory, and Cognition, 23,* 1494–1507.

Siegel, A. W., & White, S. H. (1975). The development of spatial representations of large-scale environments. *Advances in Child Development and Behavior, 10,* 10–55.

Silverman, I., & Phillips, K. (1993). Effects of estrogen changes during the menstrual cycle on spatial performance. *Ethology & Sociobiology, 14,* 257–269.

Spence, I., & Feng, J. (2010). Video games and spatial cognition. *Review of General Psychology, 14,* 92–104.

Stevens, A., & Coupe, P. (1978). Distortions in judged spatial relations. *Cognitive Psychology, 10,* 422–437.

Taylor, H. A., & Tversky, B. (1992). Spatial mental models derived from survey and route descriptions. *Journal of Memory and Language, 31,* 261–292.

Templeman, J. N., & Sibert, L. E. (2007). Immersive simulation of coordinated motion in virtual environments: An application to training small unit military tactics, techniques, and procedures. In G. L. Allen and G. L. Allen (Eds.), *Applied spatial cognition: From research to cognitive technology* (pp. 339–372). Mahwah, NJ: Lawrence Erlbaum Associates.

Thorndyke, P. W., & Hayes-Roth, B. (1982). Differences in spatial knowledge acquired from maps and navigation. *Cognitive Psychology, 14,* 560–589.

Tolman, E. C. (1948). Cognitive maps in rats and men. *Psychological Review, 55,* 189–208.

Tversky, B. (1993). Cognitive maps, cognitive collages, and spatial mental models. In A. U. Frank and I. Campari (Eds.), *Spatial Information Theory: A theoretical basis for GIS.* (pp. 14–24). Berlin: Springer-Verlag.

Waller, D. (2006). Egocentric and nonegocentric coding in memory for spatial layout: Evidence from scene recognition. *Memory & Cognition, 34,* 491–504.

Waller, D., Knapp, D., & Hunt, E. (2001). Spatial representations of virtual mazes: The role of visual fidelity and individual differences. *Human Factors: The Journal of Human Factors and Ergonomics Society, 23*, 147–158.

Wang, R. F., Crowell, J. A., Simons, D. J., Irwin, D. E., Kramer, A. F., Ambinder, M. S., Thomas, L. E., Gosney, J. L., Levinthal, B. R., & Hsieh, B. B. (2006). Spatial updating relies on an egocentric representation of space: Effects of the number of objects. *Psychonomic Bulletin and Review, 13*, 281–286.

Zwaan, R. A., & Radvansky, G. A. (1998). Situation models in language comprehension and memory. *Psychological Bulletin, 123*, 162–185.

6

Working Memory Beyond the Laboratory

Jackie Andrade

Working memory is the ability to temporarily store and transform information to support other cognitive functions. When a friend tells you their telephone number, you use working memory to keep it in mind while you find a pencil or enter it into your own phone. When you check the map while driving an unfamiliar route, you use working memory to keep in mind the path to your destination and update your progress along that path. When shopping on a tight budget, you use working memory to tally the costs of the items in your shopping basket. Applied research has featured strongly in the development of our understanding of working memory. As you can see from these examples, working memory plays a key role in everyday complex cognitive activities. The range of applied working memory research is very broad. A search of the journal *Applied Cognitive Psychology*, for papers published since 2000 that include the term "working memory" in their title, produced topics ranging from sense of direction (Wen, Ishikawa, & Sato, 2011), ballet moves (Cortese & Rossi-Arnaud, 2010), scholastic achievement (Gathercole, Pickering, Knight, & Stegmann, 2004), police officers' decisions to shoot (Kleider, Parrott, & King, 2010), and parachuting (Leach & Griffith, 2008). This review will show how

the working memory model (Baddeley & Hitch, 1974; Baddeley, 1986, 2000) has guided research on such everyday activities and abilities, and how everyday problems have informed the development of working memory theory and provided a test-bed for assessing the success of that theory. It is not feasible to cover the entire breadth of applied working memory research in a single chapter, so we shall focus on two abilities that are at the heart of human existence: language and imagination.

HISTORICAL OVERVIEW

Short-term and long-term memory

The idea of working memory grew from research into the structure of memory. This research aimed to explain the subjective impression that our continued awareness of what has just occurred, which William James described as the "feeling of the specious present" (James, 1918, p. 647), differs from our ability to retrieve "knowledge of a former state of mind after it has already once dropped from consciousness" (James, 1918, p. 648). Memory was assumed to comprise a primary or short-term store that temporarily retained limited amounts of information (e.g., Miller's magic number of 7 plus or minus 2 chunks of information; Miller, 1956), which were then either displaced by new information and forgotten, or transferred through rehearsal to a secondary or long-term memory system that was relatively permanent and had unlimited storage capacity. Hebb (1949) suggested a neural basis for this binary memory system, with short-term memory resulting from temporary activation of neural connections between clusters of cells and long-term memory resulting from permanent synaptic changes.

Working memory

Short-term memory was typically researched by comparing the effects of task and stimulus variables on immediate, ordered recall of short lists of words with free recall of long lists (e.g., Baddeley, 1966a, b), to test whether short-term memory reflected the operation of a distinct short-term memory store (e.g., Waugh & Norman, 1965) or a single memory system (e.g., Melton, 1963; Norman, 1968; Shiffrin & Schneider, 1977). However, it was often also assumed that the short-term store functioned as a "working memory" (e.g., Atkinson & Shiffrin, 1968, p. 92), playing a key role in cognitive functions such as encoding of new information into long-term memory, language comprehension, and memory retrieval. In other words, short-term memory *used* information as well as merely storing it.

Baddeley and Hitch (1974) tested this assumption that the ability to temporarily store short sequences of information relied on the same, limited-capacity "working memory" system that served as a workspace for manipulating information during reasoning and comprehension tasks. Their results cast serious doubt on the idea of a common system fulfilling these short-term recall and working memory functions. Retaining loads of six digits, close to the capacity of short-term memory, had a

relatively small effect on comprehension and reasoning performance, not the large effect that would be expected if a single system, capable of storing only around seven digits at a time, were needed for those tasks too.

In response to these findings, Baddeley and Hitch proposed a tripartite model of working memory that explained how temporary storage could be accomplished at the same time as tasks like reasoning and recall. Their model comprised two temporary stores that had limited capacity and were specialised for storing and rehearsing visuospatial and speech-based information. The processing component of the model, the central executive, could carry out the processing needed for successful reasoning and comprehension even when the temporary stores were fully loaded. It also provided a route into long-term memory for patients like KF (Warrington & Shallice, 1969; Shallice & Warrington, 1970) with impaired short-term recall of digits but apparently intact long-term memory.

Working memory updated

The most recent instantiation of this model (Baddeley, 2000; Baddeley, Allen, & Hitch, 2011) contains four components: the *phonological loop* temporarily stores speech-based, acoustic and rhythmical information; the *visuospatial sketchpad* temporarily stores visual and spatial information; the *central executive* processes that information; and the *episodic buffer* stores "bound" representations, which could be multimodal representations containing acoustic and visuospatial information from the phonological loop and visuospatial sketchpad, or information retrieved from long-term memory. It is via the episodic buffer that long-term knowledge supports short-term recall, enabling us to retain sequences of known words better than sequences of nonsense words and enabling patients with amnesia to temporarily retain far more information from stories than could feasibly be held in the phonological loop (Baddeley, 2000). In Baddeley et al.'s (2011) version of the model, information from long-term memory, the visuospatial sketchpad, and the phonological loop reaches the central executive via the episodic buffer.

Approaches to working memory

Broadly speaking, the focus of working memory research in Europe has been specifying the operation of the modality-specific short-term memory components, that is, the phonological loop and visuospatial sketchpad. This focus has translated into applied research testing the role of visual versus verbal processes in real-world situations. In North America, the focus has been on individual differences in working memory function, and working memory has been measured in terms of ability to store and process information simultaneously (Daneman & Carpenter, 1980; Engle, Tuholski, Laughlin, & Conway, 1999). The introduction of the episodic buffer to Baddeley's model, providing a multimodal store supporting executive processing, has brought this approach closer to North American models (e.g., Saults & Cowan, 2007). The next part of this chapter shows how the historically North American approach has been applied to scholastic achievement, and how the more European approach has been applied to testing the specific role of verbal short-term memory in language learning.

WORKING MEMORY AND EDUCATIONAL ACHIEVEMENT

Educational achievement

Daneman and Carpenter (1980) in the US reasoned that reading shares many of the same processes needed for performing well on their working memory span task. Working memory span tasks provide a measure of overall working memory capacity by measuring ability to process and store information simultaneously. In reading, one needs to process the syntax and semantics of sentences, and store and continuously update this information. A sentence like "The owner of the puppy called Bob a genius" presents a challenge because the reader starts constructing a mental model of someone with a puppy called Bob, and then has to update or replace this model by one in which there are two people, the owner of the puppy and someone called Bob (who may or may not be a genius). Daneman and Carpenter hypothesised that storing, manipulating, and updating linguistic, semantic, and pragmatic information during reading would load heavily on working memory. In line with their predictions, they found that working memory span predicted reading ability, listening comprehension, and verbal SAT scores. Simple verbal short-term memory did not, supporting the argument that being able to process and store information concurrently is a key skill for academic attainment.

In the UK, Gathercole et al. (2004) showed strong relationships between children's working memory span and their scores on national tests of literacy and numeracy at age 7. By 14 years, literacy scores were no longer related to working memory, but strong relationships remained between working memory and performance on tests of mathematics and science.

Language acquisition

Learning vocabulary
Although simple verbal short-term memory did not predict scholastic achievement in Daneman and Carpenter's study, it does predict an early, and very important, skill. Work by Gathercole and Baddeley in the UK showed strong relationships between young children's ability to repeat multisyllabic nonsense words – a measure of the capacity of their phonological store – and the size of their vocabulary in English, their native language. For example, Gathercole

and Baddeley (1989) measured vocabulary knowledge using the British Picture Vocabulary Scale and found that nonword repetition at age 4 predicted vocabulary scores at age 5, even when age 4 vocabulary and the contribution of general intelligence measured by Raven's coloured matrices were partialed out. Subgroups of this sample of children, matched for nonverbal IQ and age but differing in verbal short-term memory ability, were tested on their ability to learn new words. The two groups of children were equally good at learning familiar names for toys, for example, "Simon" and "Peter", but the children with higher short-term memory ability were much better at learning novel names for the toys, like "Pimas" and "Miton", supporting the argument that verbal short-term memory is necessary for learning new words (Gathercole & Baddeley, 1990a). Children with delayed language development typically have disproportionately poor verbal short-term memory (Gathercole & Baddeley, 1990b), with the short-term memory deficits persisting after language ability has reached that of typically developing children (Bishop, North, & Donlan, 1996).

Studies of foreign language learning show that verbal short-term memory remains important for language learning in adulthood. For example, impairment of the phonological loop has no effect on memory for familiar words but reduces ability to learn foreign words (Baddeley, Papagno, & Vallar, 1988). Similar findings have been reported in participants without brain damage when the phonological loop is temporarily blocked by simultaneously articulating an irrelevant word over and over (Papagno, Valentine, & Baddeley, 1991).

Learning syntax

Moving into an educational setting, Service (1992) found that Finnish schoolchildren's ability to repeat nonwords predicted their grades in English language two and a half years later, even when mathematics grades had been partialed out. Language was assessed by measures of comprehension and

production, raising the question of whether short-term memory contributes solely to vocabulary learning or also to grammar learning. This question has not yet been clearly answered. Syntax and vocabulary knowledge are closely related in natural languages (Bates & Goodman, 1997) and several studies have found that effects of verbal short-term memory on grammar learning mirror the effects on vocabulary learning. For example, English-speaking adults learned Welsh vocabulary and a component of Welsh grammar, the soft mutation, better when they were encouraged to rehearse Welsh phrases than when the phonological loop was blocked by concurrent articulation of an irrelevant phrase (Ellis & Sinclair, 1996). Williams and Lovatt (2003) found correlations between verbal short-term memory and proficiency at learning an artificial "micro-language". In typically developing children, verbal short-term memory is related to the complexity of spontaneous speech and story-telling around the ages of 3 and 4 (Adams & Gathercole, 1995, 1996). Children with impaired verbal short-term memory may have poor grammar learning as well as poor vocabulary learning (Speidel, 1993).

Alan Baddeley and I attempted to disentangle the contributions of verbal short-term memory to vocabulary and grammar learning by using an artificial grammar with a very limited vocabulary of only five items. Experimental manipulations of verbal short-term memory affected grammar learning: encouraging rehearsal of grammatical strings improved grammar learning and blocking rehearsal through concurrent articulation of irrelevant material impaired it. However, this was only the case when the vocabulary, as well as the grammar, was novel. Teaching participants the five novel "words" beforehand removed the effect of verbal short-term memory manipulations (Andrade & Baddeley, 2011). Our results supported the conclusions of Service and Kohonen (1995) that the relationship between verbal short-term memory and grammar learning is entirely explained by the mediating relationship between short-term memory and vocabulary learning. However, the debate is not yet resolved because there is evidence that a role for verbal short-term memory in grammar learning may emerge in more experienced learners, once vocabulary knowledge has reached a critical level. In bilingual Quebec, French and O'Brien (2008) tested French-speaking children's learning of English after approximately 100 hours of English tuition and exposure to English through television programmes. Verbal short-term memory predicted children's learning of English grammar even after controlling for their knowledge of English vocabulary.

Based on the extensive evidence for a positive relationship between verbal short-term memory and vocabulary learning in children and adults, Baddeley, Gathercole, and Papagno (1998) argued that the phonological loop evolved for the purpose of language learning. Temporarily storing or rehearsing unfamiliar sequences of sounds helps to weld them together so they are easier to store as a chunk in long-term memory. The extent to which short-term memory also helps us to weld together related items in sentences is unclear. It may be the case that short-term memory makes a direct contribution to grammar learning, as French and O'Brien suggested, or that it makes an indirect contribution because learning of words and phrases, which is dependent on verbal short-term memory, bootstraps learning of more abstract syntax (Ellis, 1996). Whatever the outcome, this debate shows how the working memory model has aided our understanding of the processes underlying language acquisition, and how studying language acquisition "in the wild" is helping to produce a clearer specification of how working memory supports language learning.

Educational achievement revisited

Working memory is essential to scholastic achievement because it aids two fundamental processes, learning language and learning to read, as well as contributing to general intelligence (Conway, Kane, & Engle, 2003). Recent work by Gathercole and Alloway (2008) highlights another important role, namely the influence of working memory on children's ability to make the best use of learning opportunities in the classroom. Through observational studies of interactions between teachers and children, they showed how children with poor short-term memory ability struggle to follow instructions, monitor their own performance, and keep on track with tasks. Long, complex instructions for completing a task or for moving from one activity to another can pose a challenge for children with poor short-term memory. Gathercole and Alloway (2008) cite the example of a 6-year old called John whose teacher asked his class to "Put your sheets on the green table, arrow cards in the packet, put your pencil away and come and sit on the carpet" (p. 57). John remembered only the first step in the sequence. He moved his sheets but did not do anything else until he realised that the class was sitting on the carpet, whereupon he joined them. In another example of short-term memory failure leading to what could easily be classed as bad behaviour, 8-year-old Rhys was asked to lead the other children to line up at the door ready for the lunch break. Instead of waiting by the door, he walked out of the classroom.

Children with poor working memory ability are not only hampered in their ability to learn fundamental information and skills, they are also likely to struggle to engage in the tasks that will help them learn and are at risk of being labelled by teachers as children who do not listen or are "in a world of [their] own" (p. 62). Gathercole and Alloway (2008) recommend helping children overcome their working memory constraints by looking for warning signs of children failing to follow instructions or giving up on tasks, reducing working memory loads in the classroom by using posters to remind children of key information and familiar material to illustrate new concepts, and helping children to develop skills that support memory, for example writing notes, asking for help, or rehearsing key points.

These examples show how the concept of working memory has been applied to education. This research has focused on the central executive and phonological loop components of Baddeley's model. It has shown the importance of processing and storage capacity for general attainment, and the specific role of verbal short-term memory in language learning. Similar findings have been obtained in educational settings, using school tests as outcome measures, and in the laboratory. Gathercole and Alloway's research shows how the working model provides a useful framework for classifying the cluster of problems experienced by children who struggle to keep track in classroom settings, and suggests solutions to those problems.

MENTAL IMAGERY AND PSYCHOPATHOLOGY

The working memory model has been applied to problems of psychopathology. This research has focused more on the visuospatial sketchpad than on the phonological loop and central executive. Visuospatial working memory is interesting in clinical psychology because it supports visual imagery (Baddeley, 1986; Baddeley & Andrade, 2000; Logie, Zucco, & Baddeley, 1990) and visual imagery plays a key role in diverse clinical disorders (Holmes & Mathews, 2010). Post-traumatic stress disorder or PTSD is an important example of imagery contributing to the development and maintenance of a disorder, with patients experiencing vivid and intrusive imagery in the form of "flashbacks" to the traumatic event (e.g., Holmes, Grey, & Young, 2005), but imagery is prominent in other disorders too. People with social anxiety typically imagine themselves failing in public situations (Hirsch, Meynen, & Clark, 2004); those with spider phobia imagine fear-inducing encounters with spiders (Pratt,

Cooper, & Hackmann, 2004); while those with health anxiety imagine illness and its consequences (Muse, McManus, Hackmann, Williams, & Williams, 2010).

Imagery in clinical disorders is frequently multisensory. For example, in a study of craving in alcohol dependence by Kavanagh, May, and Andrade (2009), respondents pictured themselves drinking, imagined the taste and smell of their favourite drink, and imagined the sensation of swallowing alcohol, reporting an average of 2.3 sensory modalities in their imagery. However, experimental research on imagery in clinical disorders has focused on visual imagery, for several reasons. One is to make use of the working memory model as a framework to guide study design. Although Baddeley speculated that there might be temporary storage systems like the phonological loop and visuospatial sketchpad for information in other modalities, this possibility has received little research attention with the exception of a small amount of research on short-term memory for olfactory information (e.g., Andrade & Donaldson, 2007; White, 1998). A second reason is that visual imagery is very commonly reported whereas other modalities may be more specific to particular situations. For example, Lilley, Andrade, Turpin, Sabin-Farrell, and Holmes (2009) interviewed patients awaiting treatment for post-traumatic stress symptoms and found that most images, for most patients, were predominantly visual. Similarly, visual imagery is reported in craving across a wide range of substances and activities, but other modalities vary, so smokers report imagining the taste and smell of cigarettes whereas hockey players imagine the sound and bodily feel of playing hockey when they are craving their favourite sport (May, Andrade, Kavanagh, & Penfound, 2008). However, it is the experience of visual imagery that most strongly predicts craving strength, whether for alcohol (Kavanagh et al., 2009) or for sport (May et al., 2008).

Reducing distress during emotional recollection: from laboratory to consulting room

A model for applied psychology

Much of the working memory research exploring imagery in psychopathology has taken an experimental approach, comparing the effects on visual imagery of visuospatial loads against verbal or auditory control tasks. This domain illustrates a model of applied psychology in which a theoretical model, in this case Baddeley's working memory model, provides a framework for exploring real-world problems, first in laboratory-based analogue[1] studies, and subsequently in clinical settings with patients. These real-world studies feed back into theory development, providing new ideas and challenges as well as testing that theories developed in the laboratory generalise to everyday human behaviours.

Theoretical research on mental imagery

Let us begin with the theoretical aspect. Baddeley and Andrade (2000) tested the role of working memory in imagery by studying people's reports of the vividness of their mental images. In a series of experiments, we asked participants to hold in mind a recently presented tune or pattern, or to create an image from a written cue, for example to imagine the sound of a conversation or the appearance of a rose garden. Participants generated and maintained each image unhampered by a secondary task, while counting aloud to load the phonological loop, or while tapping a pattern on a keypad to load the visuospatial sketchpad. They then rated the vividness of their image on a scale of 0, no image at all, to 10, image as clear and vivid as normal hearing or vision. As we predicted, visual images were less vivid with the concurrent visuospatial task than with the concurrent verbal task, while the converse was true for auditory images (Figure 6.1).

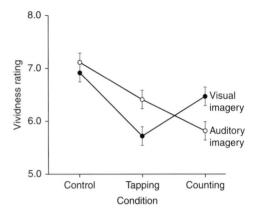

Figure 6.1   Combined data from five experiments showing effects of spatial and verbal concurrent tasks (tapping and counting respectively) on mean rated vividness of visual and auditory imagery, with standard error bars. Reprinted from Andrade, J. (2001b). The contribution of working memory to conscious experience. In J. Andrade (Ed.) *Working Memory in Perspective.* Hove, UK: Psychology Press. Original data were reported in Baddeley and Andrade (2000).

Vividness of images in both modalities also showed general effects of concurrent tasks and of long-term knowledge. Participants in general were able to imagine familiar sights and sounds (a cat climbing a tree, the sound of a baby crying) more vividly than novel sights and sounds (an elephant eating peas, a jelly being squashed), despite people intuitively predicting that the opposite would be true. One interpretation of these findings is that working memory stores representations combining multimodal sensory information and information retrieved from long-term memory, and that general task loads reduce its capacity to do so. Baddeley (2000) introduced the episodic buffer to the working memory model as a separate storage module for this type of multimodal information.

The episodic buffer has not been incorporated into the research programmes reviewed below, but new lines of research are now testing the impact of working memory-based imagery interventions on the consolidation and reconsolidation of long-term memories. The approach is informed by research showing that, after a memory is encoded, it remains labile for a few hours; changes in brain state due to stress or sleep, for example, influence how strongly the memory is laid down in this "consolidation" period (Cahill & McGaugh, 1998; Walker, Brakefield, Hobson, & Stickgold, 2003). Recall of the memory renders it malleable again and the process of consolidation is repeated, hence "reconsolidation" (Nader & Hardt, 2009; Walker et al., 2003). The fragility of the memory during consolidation and reconsolidation makes it vulnerable to cognitive interventions. The research discussed below shows how cognitive tasks that interfere with visual imagery may help to prevent or ameliorate traumatic memories, and potentially raises new questions about the relationship between working memory and long-term memory, feeding back into theory development.

Applying the working memory model to the problem of treating trauma

A first step towards relating a working memory model of imagery to the clinical problem of PTSD was to test the impact of a visuospatial interference task on imagery for emotional pictures. We used a side-to-side eye movement task as our visuospatial interference task to relate our findings to what was then a fairly new and contentious treatment for PTSD called Eye Movement Desensitization and Reprocessing or EMDR (Shapiro, 1995). Eye movements are an effective task for selectively loading the temporary visual storage and spatiomotor rehearsal processes of the visuospatial sketchpad because they involve visual interference, as the eyes move rapidly across the visual field, and spatiomotor loads to control the movement of the eyes (Lawrence, Myerson, & Abrams, 2004; Postle, Idzikowski, Della Sala, Logie, & Baddeley, 2006). We wondered if this load contributed to the claimed clinical effectiveness of EMDR.

Using a similar procedure to our theoretical studies (Baddeley & Andrade, 2000), we asked nonclinical participants to view newspaper photos of distressing events and then to hold an image of the event in mind for a few seconds, during which they performed no other task, the eye movement task, or another comparison task such as tapping a pattern on a keypad or counting aloud (Andrade, Kavanagh, & Baddeley, 1997). As predicted, visuospatial tasks reduced vividness of these visual images more than a verbal task. Eye movements had a somewhat stronger effect than pattern tapping, which we attributed to the visual interference of shifting gaze across a scene in addition to the spatiomotor control needed in both tasks. A particularly interesting finding was that effects on participants' ratings of the emotion they felt when imagining the stimuli were very similar to the effects of interference on image vividness. By manipulating the working memory processes supporting mental imagery, we could also manipulate participants' affective responses, suggesting that simple concurrent tasks might be helpful for temporarily reducing distress in therapeutic settings where clients are asked to bring to mind distressing images.

Working memory, imagery, and emotion

Recent theoretical work has given a role for working memory in the experience of emotion, based on findings that working memory loads reduce emotional responses to affective stimuli (van Dillen & Koole, 2007; van Dillen, Heslenfeld, & Koole, 2009). However, at the time of the research reported in Andrade et al. (1997), there was no theoretical basis for linking working memory and emotion. With the exception of Lang's bioinformational theory of imagery (Lang, 1979), there was also little understanding of how imagery and emotion might be related. Subsequent laboratory research into these relationships has in part been a response to the clinical problems and applied research described above, showing how applied problems help drive the development of the theories that might help to solve them. Bywaters, Andrade, and Turpin (2004) confirmed that vividness of imagery was strongly and positively correlated with emotionality of the scenes being imagined, while Holmes and Mathews (2005) manipulated imagery experimentally by asking participants to imagine or verbally think about potentially anxiety-provoking scenarios. Anxiety increased more following the imagery task than following the verbal thinking task, confirming that imagery can induce emotional change more effectively than other types of cognition. Holmes and her colleagues have since shown that training in positive imagery can improve mood in patients with depression (Holmes, Lang, & Shah, 2008).

Reducing the distress of personal memories and fears

In the final experiment in the Andrade et al. (1997) series, we moved from presenting the material to be imaged, to asking participants to imagine events from their own past; in other words, to recollect emotional autobiographical memories as vividly as possible. Side-to-side eye movements again reduced the vividness and emotionality of participants' memories, showing that even personally salient, long-established memories are susceptible to effects of imagery interventions on recollection. Van den Hout, Muris, Salemink, and Kindt (2001) extended these findings by showing that eye movements during recall of an emotional personal memory have similar effects on the vividness and emotionality of immediately subsequent recollections of that memory, even though those subsequent recollections are performed without a concurrent task. In this study, the subsequent recollection occurred immediately after the recollection with eye movements. The longevity of these effects has not yet been established, with some studies suggesting that the effects are temporary (e.g., Kavanagh, Freese, Andrade, & May, 2001; Lilley et al., 2009) and others showing that they last as long as a week (Gunter &

Bodner, 2008); in other words, that interference affected reconsolidation of the memory.

These studies focused on manipulating visuospatial loads (e.g., Kavanagh et al., 2001; Lilley et al., 2009; van den Hout et al., 2001) or general working memory loads (e.g., Gunter & Bodner, 2008). Kemps and Tiggemann (2007a) tested the specific working memory prediction that the degree of interference with vividness would depend on the match between the modality of the image and the modality of the task. They found the crossover interaction that is the signature of involvement of the phonological loop and visuospatial sketchpad. Eye movements reduced the vividness of visual autobiographical images relative to articulatory suppression (counting aloud), whereas articulatory suppression reduced the vividness of auditory autobiographical images relative to eye movements. Similar effects were observed for the emotion ratings, confirming the close relationship between imagery and emotion that was discussed above, and showing how the contents of working memory influence one's current emotional state.

Problematic imagery relates not only to vivid recollections of distressing events, but also to images of things we fear happening in the future, for example losing one's job or being told by a doctor that we have a terminal illness. Engelhard and colleagues (2010a, 2011a) showed that side-to-side eye movements reduced the vividness and emotionality of these images of feared future events, or "flashforwards", compared with a no-task control condition. These findings offer the promise that the results of laboratory research on working memory and emotional imagery might be applicable across the range of clinical disorders in which distressing imagery features, and not only to those where the images are of past events that have actually been experienced.

Developing an analogue of exposure treatment

As the next step towards applying working memory to imagery in clinical conditions, we developed a protocol in which participants recalled an emotional memory, rated it for vividness and emotionality with or without a concurrent task, and then did the same again repeatedly, so that each memory was recalled and rated a total of eight times in each task condition (Kavanagh et al., 2001). The reason for doing this was to mimic the repeated exposure to an emotional stimulus or memory that is needed to habituate emotional responses in exposure treatments. Side-to-side eye movements again reduced vividness and emotionality of happy and distressing personal memories. A clay-modelling task (Stuart, Holmes, & Brewin, 2006) produced similar effects (Andrade, Bosworth, & Baugh, 2012a), consistent with a general role for visuospatial working memory rather than a specific effect of eye movements.

Clinical applications: treating reactions to trauma

This research confirmed that working memory contributes to the vividness and emotionality of personal memories. A question remained about whether interference with working memory could reduce distress even in patients recalling traumatic experiences, or whether highly emotional memories are resistant to interference. Lilley et al. (2009) replicated Kavanagh et al.'s (2001) procedure, with repeated exposures and ratings, to compare the effects of side-to-side eye movements with counting aloud and no-task control conditions, on patients' recollections of "hot spots" from their trauma memories. As predicted by the working memory interpretation of emotional imagery effects, eye movements reduced vividness and emotionality compared with counting aloud (to control for phonological loop involvement) or doing nothing else.

Taken together, these findings suggest that visuospatial tasks may be useful tools for reducing distress during exposure treatments for PTSD and other anxiety disorders. For imaginal exposure to work effectively, clients need to be able generate a clear, detailed image or recollection, so there is a risk that

reducing image vividness might also reduce the efficacy of treatment. Kavanagh et al.'s (2001) findings do not support this concern, as reductions in emotion occurred across the study period from baseline to one-week follow-up, and were no smaller in the eye movement condition but this finding needs replication. Gunter and Bodner (2008), on the other hand, did find lasting changes in distress following eye movements, but these were reductions in distress, not the increases that one would expect if eye movements were impeding habituation. Our interpretation of the findings is that eye movements help clients to engage in cognitive therapy by reducing distress and preventing full-blown flashbacks. They are a "response aid" to help clients control their distress levels, akin to wearing gloves during exposure treatment for snake phobia (Kavanagh et al., 2001; Lilley et al., 2009). Alternatively, the combination of recall and interference may cause the memory to be reconsolidated in a less distressing form (Brewin, Gregory, Lipton, & Burgess, 2010).

Selective interference versus general distraction

Key to our approach is the assumption that the working memory model can help us find interventions to selectively target the processes of interest, without imposing a large general resource load that would impair clients' ability to concentrate on what the therapist is asking them to do. Gunter and Bodner (2008) challenged this interpretation of the eye movement findings, arguing that the observed reductions in distress were caused by general distraction rather than selective interference. In support of their argument, they showed that eye movements and an auditory shadowing task had equivalent effects on vividness and emotionality when matched for general working memory load (Experiment 3). In support of our argument, other authors have shown that increasing the general task load does not increase the impact on recollection (Engelhard, van Uijen, & van den Hout, 2011; van den Hout et al., 2010). The debate continues, and highlights the importance of establishing task loads by testing the impact of interference tasks on performance of a neutral control task such as reaction time (Engelhard, van den Hout, & Smeets, 2011) or memory span (Andrade, Pears, May, & Kavanagh, 2012c).

Developing a cognitive vaccine against PTSD

Holmes and her colleagues used tasks from the working memory literature to test Brewin's model of the development of intrusive imagery in PTSD (Brewin, Dalgleish, & Joseph, 1996). Brewin argued that extreme distress prevents the normal stripping away of sensory information from memories, leaving trauma memories that are rich in sensory detail, vulnerable to being triggered by environmental cues but difficult to retrieve voluntarily, and detached from the contextual anchors that label them as memories rather than current experiences, hence the experience of retrieval as a flashback rather than recollection (Brewin et al., 2010). Holmes, Brewin, and Hennessy (2004) argued that if encoding of sensory detail can be impaired, then memories will be less rich in sensory detail and less likely to intrude spontaneously. Their findings supported their argument. Participants who watched a film of road traffic accidents subsequently reported fewer intrusive memories of scenes viewed while performing a visuospatial task than either performing no task (Stuart et al., 2006) or a verbal task (Holmes et al., 2004). Most interestingly of all, similar benefits are observed when interference tasks are employed *after* exposure to the traumatic material, suggesting that working memory contributes to the consolidation of memories and not simply to their initial encoding (Holmes, James, Coode-Bate, & Deeprose, 2009). This finding raises the possibility of "vaccinating" people who have experienced a traumatic event against developing the intrusive memories of the event that are thought to contribute to the development and maintenance of PTSD.

Working memory, motivation, and desire

In 2005, David Kavanagh, Jon May, and I published a cognitive theory of desire, Elaborated Intrusion theory (EI theory; Kavanagh, Andrade, & May, 2005). At the heart of EI theory was the assumption that the feeling of desire, or craving in a drug-use context, resulted from the operation of working memory processes to maintain information about the desired activity in consciousness. In contrast to most other theories of craving, EI theory assumed that environmental, physiological, cognitive, and mood cues are triggers for, rather than proximal causes of, craving and desire. These cues increase the likelihood of experiencing an apparently spontaneous, intrusive thought about the activity ("I need a drink", for example). This thought, when elaborated, leads to an episode of desire, and the process of elaboration loads heavily on working memory. General working memory resources are used in retrieving desire-related information from long-term memory, and in using that information to construct mental images of achieving one's desire that are rich in sensory detail. We might imagine biting into a bar of chocolate and feeling it melt in our mouth, or taking a first sip of our favourite drink. This sensory imagery is emotionally charged, conveying some of the pleasure or relief of the actual activity. The positive emotional tone encourages further imagery but the ultimate impact of craving imagery is negative, as images of satisfaction enhance awareness of our current deficit state.

Experimental tests of EI theory built on observations that craving for drugs such as alcohol and nicotine, and for everyday substances like food and drink, involved visual imagery as well as imagery of taste, smell, and bodily sensations, but did not involve auditory imagery (Kavanagh et al., 2009; May, Andrade, Panabokke, & Kavanagh, 2004; May et al., 2008). In working memory terms, we hypothesised that craving imagery loads the visuospatial sketchpad more than the phonological loop. Tests of this hypothesis compared the effects of visuospatial loads, such as clay modelling, or competing visual imagery, against auditory imagery or verbal task loads. Relative to auditory loads, visuospatial imagery or tasks reduce craving for cigarettes (May, Andrade, Kavanagh, & Panabokke, 2010; Versland & Rosenberg, 2007) and food (Andrade, May, & Kavanagh, 2012b; Kemps & Tiggemann, 2007b).

Laboratory work on EI theory has progressed hand in hand with applied research into the craving experiences of alcohol-dependent clients (Kavanagh et al., 2009; Statham et al., 2011), which confirms the role of imagery, and the development of a new treatment for alcohol dependency. Functional Imagery Training (called Functional Decision Making in Andrade et al., 2012b) extends Miller and Rollnick's (2002) motivational interviewing approach, where clients are encouraged to think about and rehearse their reasons for change. The important difference is that, in Functional Imagery Training, clients are encouraged to identify potential immediate benefits of changing their behaviour. Rather than consider the long-term benefits to health of abstinence or moderate drinking, they focus on smaller but more concrete, proximal, and *imageable* benefits such as being able to drive themselves home after a night out or taking their children to football training without a hangover. Clients are asked to imagine these benefits as vividly as possible, and to rehearse their images repeatedly, building actual episodic memories into their imagery after successful attempts at abstinence. Functional Imagery Training has yet to be evaluated in a clinical trial, but illustrates the application of a working memory-based theory to a real-world problem and its potential solution.

EVALUATION OF THE WORKING MEMORY MODEL AS A TOOL FOR APPLIED RESEARCH

Applications of the working memory model have been extensive; this review has only scratched the surface. Heathcote (2005), for example, offers a completely different treatment, exploring the role of working memory in tasks such as using a computer or controlling air traffic. Contributors to the applied perspectives section of *Working Memory in Perspective* (Andrade, 2001a) discussed adult ageing (Phillips & Hamilton, 2001), consciousness (Andrade, 2001b), and child development (Jarrold, 2001) in addition to the language (Adams & Willis, 2001) and imagery (Pearson, 2001) topics included here. The examples of recent research on parachuting and ballet moves have not been mentioned since their introduction in the first paragraph.

I focused on educational attainment because that area of research illustrates how working memory is fundamental for learning to understand and produce language, to read, and to follow instructions in order to benefit from education. This research has combined laboratory studies, individual differences studies, and real-world observations in such a way that theoretical and applied research are intimately entwined. The working memory model was based on laboratory tests of assumptions about the role of short-term memory in everyday cognitive tasks. It was used to guide research into memory and achievement in educational settings, which has led to suggestions for improved teaching practices (Gathercole & Alloway, 2008) and new theoretical work on language acquisition (Baddeley et al., 1998) and intelligence (Conway, Kane, & Engle, 2003).

The second focus of this chapter was clinical applications of working memory, because the role of mental imagery in the maintenance of disorders, and the development of new treatments involving imagery "rescripting", is currently a hot topic in clinical psychology (Hackmann, Bennett-Levy, & Holmes, 2011). Research on working memory and psychopathology shows a similar cycle between applications of theory to real-world problems, which in turn raise new challenges that inform theory development, such as the problem of how imagery motivates behaviour (Andrade et al., 2012b) and what cognitive processes occur during memory consolidation (Holmes et al., 2009).

The working memory model has informed this clinically applied research in two ways. First, it has provided a framework for analysing the problem. For example, it suggested the interpretation of eye movement effects in EMDR as effects of loading the visuospatial sketchpad. Second, it has provided a set of tools for testing hypotheses about the problem, in the form of tasks that selectively load verbal or visuospatial short-term memory systems. One could argue that a careful task analysis would be sufficient, as it is not particularly surprising that visual tasks interfere with other visual tasks more than they interfere with verbal tasks. The importance of having a theory to guide research is that is tells you where to look and what to focus on. The eye movement task used in EMDR involves tracking the therapist's finger as it moves rapidly to and fro. Satisfactory performance requires following instructions, keeping on track, and ignoring distracting stimuli as well as moving one's eyes. The hypothesis that any effect happens because the task loads the visuospatial sketchpad leads researchers to focus on the visual interference and spatiomotor control elements of the task and control for other task variables (e.g., Andrade et al., 1997, Experiment 1). Knowing what to focus on is particularly beneficial for helping to simplify real-world problems into testable hypotheses. Of course, if the theory is wrong then you will look in the wrong place and focus on the wrong things, which is why the interchange between theoretical and applied research is so important. Theories need to be subjected to strong testing in the laboratory and in the field if they are to be useful for solving real-world problems. The debate covered in the section entitled "Selective interference versus general distraction", about whether eye movements reduce distress because they are distracting or because they interfere selectively with visual imagery, illustrates the usefulness of having a theory-based set of tools: the working memory model provides directions and constraints, specifying the need to match general processing loads and manipulate modality-specific loads in order to solve the problem.

IMPORTANT AREAS FOR FUTURE RESEARCH

Contributors to *Working Memory in Perspective* (Andrade, 2001a) valued Baddeley's working memory model for its breadth, specificity, and central place in cognitive psychology. The research reviewed above shows that these qualities are still important. The breadth of the model, in terms of combining visuospatial and auditory processing as well as general, executive processes, has allowed it to be applied to domains as different as language acquisition and psychopathological mental imagery. Compared with the traditional North American view of working memory as the ability to store and process information simultaneously, Baddeley's model more clearly specifies how information processing is combined with short-term storage of different sorts of information. This specificity has been useful for designing experiments to test the contribution of visual imagery to emotion, because verbal concurrent tasks can be used to control for general processing effects while visual tasks selectively block the processes that support visual imagery (see the section entitled "Mental imagery and psychopathology", above, for examples). The central place of the model in cognitive psychology is still important for helping to maintain the close intercourse between applied and theoretical research. Explaining intrusive imagery in terms of working memory processes, for example, has raised new avenues for research in terms of the cognitive and neurobiological processes underpinning memory consolidation and reconsolidation (e.g., Holmes et al., 2009; Van den Hout et al., 2011).

The introduction of the episodic buffer to the working memory model (Baddeley,

2000) potentially threatened these virtues of the model for applied research. The capacity and mode of operation of the new buffer were not yet well specified and it appeared unduly powerful, leaving little for the visuospatial sketchpad and phonological loop to do (see Andrade, 2001c) and, because of this, forcing a reinterpretation of dual task experimental work such as much of that reviewed in this chapter. In Baddeley (2000) all three storage systems – the episodic buffer, visuospatial sketchpad, and phonological loop – communicated directly with the central executive, so it was not clear whether a visual stimulus, for instance, would be stored by the episodic buffer or visuospatial sketchpad. Baddeley, Allen, and Hitch (2011) have revised the model to address this sort of uncertainty. The visuospatial sketchpad and phonological loop now feed visuospatial or verbal representations into the epidodic buffer. This is an important improvement because it brings a closer rapprochement between this model and American models featuring general purpose temporary storage capacity (e.g., Saults & Cowan, 2007) and it gives a clear role to the modality-specific stores. Interference with the visuospatial sketchpad or phonological loop will change the nature of the representation in the episodic buffer. If it is the visual sensory details that make a particular trauma image troubling, then a competing visuospatial load will render the representation in the episodic buffer less distressing by shifting the balance of sensory information from visual to other modalities. The image is changed, not simply made less vivid. Reconsolidation of this changed image in memory should help increase the controllability and reduce the intrusiveness of the image. This concept of reconsolidation, and the possibility of permanently altering maladaptive autobiographical memories by manipulating recollection, is an exciting new direction in experimental psychopathology.

There has been good progress in episodic buffer research since 2000, covering experimental, neuropsychological, and neuroscience studies of feature binding (e.g., Baddeley et al., 2011) and the influence of long-term memory on working memory performance (e.g., Darling et al., 2012). An important direction for future research will be developing tasks that specifically measure episodic buffer capacity or selectively interfere with the episodic buffer, and are simple enough to be used in applied contexts. Assuming this can be done, the new working memory model has the potential to guide future research to explain how working memory and long-term knowledge and memories interact in everyday tasks and problems.

NOTE

1 Analogue studies are studies with nonclinical participants that are designed to test hypotheses about aspects of clinical problems or treatments.

REFERENCES

Adams, A-M. & Gathercole, S. E. (1995). Phonological working memory and speech production in preschool children. *Journal of Speech and Hearing Research, 38*(2), 403–414.

Adams, A-M. & Gathercole, S. E. (1996). Phonological working memory and spoken language development in young children. *Quarterly Journal of Experimental Psychology, 49A*(1), 216–233.

Adams, A-M. & Willis, C. (2001). Language processing and working memory: A developmental perspective. In J. Andrade (Ed.). *Working memory in perspective*. Hove, UK: Psychology Press.

Andrade, J. (Ed., 2001a). *Working memory in perspective*. Hove, UK: Psychology Press.

Andrade, J. (2001b). The contribution of working memory to conscious experience. In J. Andrade (Ed.). *Working memory in perspective* (pp. 60–78). Hove, UK: Psychology Press.

Andrade, J. (2001c). The working memory model: Consensus, controversy, and future directions. In J. Andrade (Ed.), *Working memory in perspective* (pp. 281–310). Hove, UK: Psychology Press.

Andrade, J. & Baddeley, A. D. (2011). The contribution of phonological short-term memory to artificial grammar learning, *Quarterly Journal of Experimental Psychology, 64*, 960–974.

Andrade, J., Bosworth, S., & Baugh, S-J. (2012a). Effects of clay modelling on vividness and emotionality of autobiographical memories. *Journal of Experimental Psychopathology, 3*(2), 146–157.

Andrade, J. & Donaldson, L. (2007). Evidence for an olfactory store in working memory? *Psychologia, 50,* 76–89.

Andrade, J., Kavanagh, D., & Baddeley, A. (1997). Eye movements and visual imagery: A working memory approach to the treatment of post-traumatic stress disorder. *British Journal of Clinical Psychology, 36,* 209–223.

Andrade, J., May, J., & Kavanagh, D. J. (2012b). Sensory imagery in craving: From cognitive psychology to new treatments for addiction. *Journal of Experimental Psychopathology, 3*(2), 127–145.

Andrade, J., Pears, S., May, J., & Kavanagh, D. J. (2012c). Use of a clay modeling task to reduce chocolate craving. *Appetite, 58,* 955–963.

Atkinson, R. C. & Shiffrin, R. M. (1968). Human memory: a proposed system and control processes. In K. W. Spence and J. D. Spence (Eds.), *The psychology of learning and motivation* (Vol. 2). New York: Academic Press.

Baddeley, A. D. (1966a). Short-term memory for word sequences as a function of acoustic, semantic, and formal similarity. *Quarterly Journal of Experimental Psychology, 18,* 362–365.

Baddeley, A. D. (1966b) The influence of acoustic and semantic similarity on long-term memory for word sequences. *Quarterly Journal of Experimental Psychology, 18,* 302–309.

Baddeley, A. (2000). The episodic buffer: A new component of working memory? *Trends in Cognitive Science, 4*(11), 417–423.

Baddeley, A. D. (1986). *Working memory.* Oxford: Oxford University Press.

Baddeley, A. & Andrade, J. (2000). Working memory and the vividness of imagery, *Journal of Experimental Psychology: General, 129*(1), 126–145.

Baddeley, A. D. & Hitch, G. J. (1974) Working Memory. In G. H. Bower (Ed.), *The psychology of learning and motivation,* Vol. 8, pp. 47–89. New York: Academic Press.

Baddeley, A. D., Allen, R. J., & Hitch, G. J. (2011). Binding in visual working memory: The role of the episodic buffer. *Neuropsychologia, 49,* 1393–1400.

Baddeley, A. D., Gathercole, S. E., & Papagno, C. (1998). The phonological loop as a language learning device. *Psychological Review, 105*(1), 158–173.

Baddeley, A. D., Papagno, C., & Vallar, G. (1988) When long-term learning depends on short-term storage. *Journal of Memory and Language, 27,* 586–595.

Bates, E. & Goodman, J. C. (1997). On the inseparability of grammar and the lexicon: Evidence from acquisition, aphasia and real-time processing. *Language and Cognitive Processes, 12,* 507–584.

Bishop, D. V. M., North, T., & Donlan, C. (1996) Nonword repetition as a behavioural marker for inherited language impairment: Evidence from a twin study. *Journal of Child Psychology and Psychiatry, 37,* 391–403.

Brewin, C. R., Dalgleish, T., & Joseph, S. (1996). A dual representation theory of post-traumatic stress disorder. *Psychological Review, 103,* 670–686.

Brewin, C. R., Gregory, J. D., Lipton, M., & Burgess, N. (2010). Intrusive images in psychological disorders: Characteristics, neural mechanisms, and treatment implications. *Psychological Review, 117,* 210–232.

Bywaters, M., Andrade, J., & Turpin, G. (2004). Determinants of the vividness of visual imagery: The effects of delayed recall, stimulus affect and individual differences, *Memory, 12,* 479–488.

Cahill, L. & McGaugh, J. L. (1998). Mechanisms of emotional arousal and lasting declarative memory. *Trends in Neurosciences, 21*(7), 294–299.

Conway, A. R. A., Kane, M. J., & Engle, R. W. (2003). Working memory capacity and its relation to general intelligence. *Trends in Cognitive Sciences, 7,* 547–552.

Cortese, A. & Rossi-Arnaud, C. (2010). Working memory for ballet moves and spatial locations in professional ballet dancers. *Applied Cognitive Psychology, 24*(2), 266–286.

Daneman, M. M. & Carpenter, P. (1980). Individual differences in working memory and reading. *Journal of Verbal Learning & Verbal Behavior, 19,* 450–466.

Darling, S., Allen, R. J., Havelka, J. Campbell, A., & Rattray, E. (2012). Visuospatial bootstrapping: Long-term memory representations are necessary for implicit binding of verbal and visuospatial working memory. *Psychonomic Bulletin & Review, 19,* 258–263.

Ellis, N. C. (1996). Sequencing in SLA: Phonological memory, chunking, and points of order. *Studies in Second Language Acquisition, 18,* 91–126.

Ellis, N. C. & Sinclair, S. G. (1996). Working memory in the acquisition of vocabulary and syntax: Putting language in good order. *Quarterly Journal of Experimental Psychology, 49A*(1), 234–250.

Engelhard, I. M., van den Hout, M. A., Janssen, W. C., & van der Beek, J. (2010a). Eye movements reduce vividness and emotionality of "flashforwards". *Behaviour Research and Therapy, 48,* 442–447.

Engelhard, I. M., van den Hout, M.A., Dek, E.C.P., Giele, C. L., van der Wielen, J-W., Reijnen, M.J., & van Roij, B. (2011a). Reducing vividness and emotional intensity of recurrent "flashforwards" by taxing working memory: An analogue study, *Journal of Anxiety Disorders, 25*, 599–603.

Engelhard, I. M., van den Hout, M. A., & Smeets, M. A. M. (2011b). Taxing working memory reduces vividness and emotionality of images about the Queen's Day tragedy. *Journal of Behavior Therapy and Experimental Psychiatry, 42*, 32–37.

Engelhard, I. M., van Uijen, S. L., & van den Hout, M. A. (2010b). The impact of taxing working memory on negative and positive memories. *European Journal of Psychotraumatology, 1*, 5623.

Engle, R. W., Tuholski, S. W., Laughlin, J. E., & Conway, A. R. A. (1999). Working memory, short-term memory, and general fluid intelligence: A latent-variable approach. *Journal of Experimental Psychology: General, 128*, 309–333.

French, L. M. & O'Brien, I. (2008). Phonological memory and children's second language grammar learning. *Applied Psycholinguistics, 29*(3), 463–487.

Gathercole, S. E. & Alloway, T. P. (2008). *Working memory and learning: A practical guide for teachers*. London: Sage.

Gathercole, S. E. & Baddeley, A. D. (1989). Evaluation of the role of phonological STM in the development of vocabulary in children: A longitudinal study. *Journal of Memory and Language, 28*, 200–213.

Gathercole, S. E. & Baddeley, A. D. (1990a). The role of phonological memory in vocabulary acquisition: A study of young children learning new names. *British Journal of Psychology, 81*, 439–454.

Gathercole, S. E. & Baddeley, A. D. (1990b). Phonological memory deficits in language-disordered children: Is there a causal connection? *Journal of Memory and Language, 29*, 336–360.

Gathercole, S. E., Pickering, S. J., Knight, C., & Stegmann, Z. (2004). Working memory skills and educational attainment: Evidence from national curriculum assessments at 7 and 14 years of age. *Applied Cognitive Psychology, 18*(1), 1–16.

Gathercole, S. E., Willis, C., Baddeley, A. D., & Emslie, H. (1994). The Children's Test of Nonword Repetition: A test of phonological working memory. *Memory, 2*, 103–127.

Gunter, R. W. & Bodner, G. E. (2008). How eye movements affect unpleasant memories: Support for a working-memory account. *Behaviour Research and Therapy, 46*, 913–931.

Hackmann, A., Bennett-Levy, J., & Holmes, E. A. (2011). *Oxford guide to imagery in cognitive therapy*. Oxford: Oxford University Press.

Heathcote, D. (2005). Working memory and performance limitations. In A. Esgate and D. Groome. *An introduction to applied cognitive psychology*. Hove, UK: Psychology Press.

Hebb, D. O. (1949). *Organization of behavior*. New York: Wiley.

Hirsch, C., Meynen, T., & Clark, D. (2004). Negative self-imagery in social anxiety contaminates social interactions, *Memory, 12*, 496–506.

Holmes, E. A., Brewin, C. R., & Hennessy, R. G. (2004). Memory, trauma films, information processing, and intrusive memory development. *Journal of Experimental Psychology: General, 133*, 3–22.

Holmes, E. A. & Mathews, A. (2005). Mental imagery and emotion: A special relationship? *Emotion, 5*, 489–497.

Holmes, E. A. & Mathews, A. (2010). Mental imagery in emotion and emotional disorders. *Clinical Psychology Review, 30*, 349–362.

Holmes, E. A., Grey, N., & Young, K. A. D. (2005). Intrusive images and "hotspots" of trauma memories in posttraumatic .stress disorder: An exploratory investigation of emotions and cognitive themes. *Journal of Behavior Therapy and Experimental Psychiatry, 36*, 3–17.

Holmes, E. A., James, E. L., Coode-Bate, T., & Deeprose, C. (2009). Can playing the computer game 'tetris' reduce the build-up of flashbacks for trauma? A proposal from cognitive science. *PLoS ONE, 4*(1), e4153, doi:4110.1371/journal.pone.0004153

Holmes, E. A., Lang, T. J., & Shah, D. M. (2008). Developing interpretation bias modification as a "cognitive vaccine" for depressed mood: Imagining positive events makes you feel better than thinking about them verbally. *Journal of Abnormal Psychology, 118*, 76–88.

James, W. (1890/1918). *The principles of psychology*, vol. I. London: Macmillan and Co. Ltd.

Jarrold, C. (2001). Applying the working memory model to the study of atypical development. In J. Andrade (Ed.) *Working memory in perspective*. Hove, UK: Psychology Press.

Kavanagh, D. J., Freese, S., Andrade, J., & May, J. (2001). Effects of visuospatial tasks on desensitization to emotive memories, *British Journal of Clinical Psychology, 40*, 267–280.

Kavanagh, D. J., Andrade, J., & May, J. (2005). Imaginary relish and exquisite torture: The Elaborated Intrusion theory of desire, *Psychological Review, 112*(2), 446–467.

Kavanagh, D. J., May, J., & Andrade, J. (2009). Tests of the elaborated intrusion theory of craving and desire: Features of alcohol craving during treatment for an alcohol disorder, *British Journal of Clinical Psychology, 48*, 241–254.

Kemps, E. & Tiggemann, M. (2007a). Reducing the vividness and emotional impact of distressing autobiographical memories: The importance of modality-specific interference, *Memory, 15*, 412–422.

Kemps, E. & Tiggemann, M. (2007b). Modality-specific imagery reduces cravings for food: An application of the Elaborated Intrusion theory of desire to food craving. *Journal of Experimental Psychology: Applied, 13*(2), 95–104.

Kleider, H. M., Parrott, D. J., & King, T. Z. (2010). Shooting behaviour: How working memory and negative emotionality influence police officer shoot decisions. *Applied Cognitive Psychology, 24*(5), 707–717.

Lang, P. J. (1979). A bio-informational theory of emotional imagery. *Psychophysiology, 16*, 495–512.

Lawrence, B. M., Myerson, J., & Abrams, R. A. (2004). Interference with spatial working memory: An eye movement is more than a shift of attention. *Psychonomic Bulletin and Review, 11*, 488–494.

Leach, J. & Griffith, R. (2008). Restrictions in working memory capacity during parachuting: A possible cause of 'no pull' fatalities. *Applied Cognitive Psychology, 22*(2), 147–157.

Lilley, S., Andrade, J., Turpin, G., Sabin-Farrell, R., & Holmes, E. A. (2009). Visuo-spatial working memory interference with recollections of trauma, *British Journal of Clinical Psychology, 48*, 309–321.

Logie, R. H., Zucco, G. M., & Baddeley, A. D. (1990). Interference with visual short-term memory. *Acta Psychologica, 75*, 55–74.

May, J., Andrade, J., Kavanagh, D., & Panabokke, N. (2010). Visual imagery tasks suppress craving for cigarettes. *Behaviour Research and Therapy, 48*, 476–485.

May, J., Andrade, J, Panabokke, N., & Kavanagh, D. (2004). Images of desire: Cognitive models of craving. *Memory, 12*(4), 447–461.

May, J., Andrade, J., Kavanagh, D., & Penfound, L. (2008). Imagery and strength of craving for eating, drinking and playing sport. *Cognition and Emotion, 22*(4), 633–650.

Melton, A. W. (1963). Implications of short-term memory for a general theory of memory. *Journal of Verbal Learning and Verbal Behavior, 2*, 1–21.

Miller, G. A. (1956). The magical number seven plus or minus two: Some limits on our capacity to process information. *Psychological Review, 63*, 81–97.

Miller, W. R. & Rollnick, S. (2002). *Motivational interviewing: Preparing people for change* (2nd ed.). New York: Guilford Press.

Muse, K., McManus, F., Hackmann, A., Williams, M., & Williams, M. (2010). Intrusive imagery in severe health anxiety: Prevalence, nature and links with memories and maintenance cycles. *Behaviour Research and Therapy, 48*, 792–798.

Nader, K. & Hardt, O. (2009). A single standard for memory: the case for reconsolidation. *Nature reviews. Neuroscience, 10*(3), 224–234.

Norman, D. A. (1968). Toward a theory of memory and attention. *Psychological Review, 75*(6), 522–536.

Papagno, C., Valentine, T., & Baddeley, A. D. (1991). Phonological short-term memory and foreign-language vocabulary learning. *Journal of Memory and Language, 30*, 331–347.

Pearson, D. J. (2001). Imagery and the visuo-spatial sketchpad. In J. Andrade (Ed.), *Working memory in perspective*. Hove, UK: Psychology Press.

Phillips, L. H. & Hamilton, C. (2001). The working memory model in adult aging research. In J. Andrade (Ed.) *Working memory in perspective*. Hove, UK: Psychology Press.

Postle, B. R., Idzikowski, C., Della Sala, S., Logie, R. H., & Baddeley, A. D. (2006). The selective disruption of spatial working memory by eye movements. *Quarterly Journal of Experimental Psychology, 59*, 100–120.

Postman, L. & Phillips, L. W. (1965). Short-term temporal changes in free recall. *Quarterly Journal of Experimental Psychology, 17*, 132–138.

Pratt, D., Cooper, M. J., & Hackmann, A. (2004). Imagery and its characteristics in people who are anxious about spiders. *Behavioural and Cognitive Psychotherapy, 32*, 165–176.

Saults, J. S. & Cowan, N. (2007). A central capacity limit to the simultaneous storage of visual and auditory arrays in working memory. *Journal of Experimental Psychology: General, 136*, 633–684.

Service, E. (1992). Phonology, working memory, and foreign-language learning. *Quarterly Journal of Experimental Psychology, 45A*(1), 21–50.

Service, E. & Kohonen, V. (1995). Is the relation between phonological memory and foreign language learning accounted for by vocabulary acquisition? *Applied Psycholinguistics, 16*, 155–172.

Shallice, T. & Warrington, E. K. (1970). Independent functioning of verbal memory stores: A neuropsychological study. *Quarterly Journal of Experimental Psychology, 22*, 261–273.

Shapiro, F. (1995). *Eye movement desensitisation and reprocessing*. New York: Guilford Press.

Shiffrin, R. M. & Schneider, W. (1977). Controlled and automatic human information processing. II. Perceptual learning, automatic attending and a general theory, *Psychological Review, 84*, 127–190.

Speidel, G. E. (1993). Phonological short-term memory and individual differences in learning to speak: A bilingual case study. *First Language, 13*, 69–91.

Statham, D. J., Connor, J. P, Kavanagh, D. J., Feeney, G. F. X., Young, R. McD., May, J., & Andrade, J. (2011). Measuring alcohol craving: Development of the Alcohol Craving Questionnaire. *Addiction, 106*, 1230–1238.

Stuart, A. D. P., Holmes, E. A., & Brewin, C. R. (2006). The influence of a visuospatial grounding task on intrusive images of a traumatic film. *Behaviour Research and Therapy, 44*, 611–619.

Van den Hout, M. A., Engelhard, I. M., Beetsma, D., Slofstra, C., Hornsveld, H., Houtveen, J., & Leer, A. (2011). EMDR and mindfulness: Eye movements and attentional breathing tax working memory and reduce vividness and emotionality of aversive ideation. *Journal of Behavior Therapy and Experimental Psychiatry, 42*, 423–431.

Van den Hout, M. A., Engelhard, I. M., Smeets, M. A. M. et al. (2010). Counting during recall: Taxing of working memory and reduced vividness and emotionality of negative memories. *Applied Cognitive Psychology, 24*, 303–311.

Van den Hout, M., Muris, P., Salemink, E., & Kindt, M. (2001). Autobiographical memories become less vivid and emotional after eye movements. *British Journal of Clinical Psychology, 40*, 121–130.

Van Dillen, L. F. & Koole, S. L. (2007). Clearing the mind: A working memory model of distraction from negative mood. *Emotion, 7*, 715–723.

Van Dillen, L. F., Heslenfeld, D.J., & Koole, S.L. (2009). Tuning down the emotional brain: An fMRI study of the effects of cognitive load on the processing of affective images. *NeuroImage, 45*, 1212–1219.

Versland, A. & Rosenberg, H. (2007). Effect of brief imagery interventions on craving in college student smokers. *Addiction Research and Theory, 15*(2), 177–187.

Walker, M. P., Brakefield, T., Hobson, J. A., & Stickgold, R. (2003). Dissociable stages of human memory consolidation and reconsolidation, *Nature, 425*(October), 8–12.

Warrington, E. K. & Shallice, T. (1969). The selective impairment of auditory verbal short-term memory. *Brain, 92*, 885–896.

Waugh, N. C. & Norman, D. A. (1965). Primary memory. *Psychological Review, 72*, 89–104.

Wen, W., Ishikawa, T., & Sato, T. (2011). Working memory in spatial knowledge acquisition: Differences in encoding processes and sense of direction. *Applied Cognitive Psychology, 25*(4), 654–662.

White, T. L. (1998). Olfactory memory: The long and short of it. *Chemical Senses, 23*, 433–441.

Williams, J. N. & Lovatt, P. (2003). Phonological memory and rule learning. *Language Learning, 53*, 67–121.

7

False Memory

Eryn J. Newman and Maryanne Garry

After Sally Blackwell identified him as the man who raped her, Clarence Von Williams was sentenced to 50 years in prison. But Von Williams did not commit the crime, a man named Jon Simonis did (Loftus & Ketcham, 1991). After the September 2001 US terrorist attacks, George W. Bush remembered watching television outside a Florida classroom and seeing the first plane hit the tower. But Bush could not have learned about it like this – no footage was available at that time (Greenberg, 2004). After spending months in therapy, Sheri Storm remembered that as a child, she was sexually abused by her father. But Sheri later learned that other patients under the care of the same therapist had come to remember similar events – and she now says the abuse never happened (Lambert & Lilienfeld, 2007). These memory errors differ in context, scale, and consequence, but they share a common thread: in each case, people have made an error in judging the origin of a mental experience, ultimately calling it a memory when it was not.

We know from our everyday experiences that our memories are not intact, rigid records of the past. Many of us have experienced an event with a friend, only to remember it quite differently from them later on. Many of us have debated with family members about who was present at some event and who was not. We all have anecdotes that illustrate the point that remembering an event is not like finding and playing a YouTube video, and psychological research fits with this view. Bartlett (1932) provided one of the earliest demonstrations of the malleability of memory. He asked a group of British students to read a Native North American story, and then recall it. As people attempted to recall the story, errors crept into their reports. But the most striking finding was the pattern of errors that people produced: they distorted details of the story in line with their own knowledge and experience. They reworked elements of the story to be more familiar, misremembering a canoe rather than a rowboat, and a fishing trip instead of a seal hunt. In describing this demonstration, Bartlett emphasized the reconstructive nature of memory, proposing that people weren't simply playing back what they had read, but reconstructing details from the story. He suggested that people remember details as being more typical and familiar than they really are because people craft what they remember so it fits with how they made sense of the story in the first place. That is, they tend to engage in what Bartlett called an "effort after meaning," in which people pursue information that fits with their understanding of an event (see also Bergman & Roediger, 1999, for a replication). Today, a large body of work demonstrates that prior knowledge can shape memory (Anderson & Pichert, 1978; Bower, Black, & Turner, 1979; Bransford & Franks, 1971; Bransford & Johnson, 1972; Brewer & Treyens, 1981; Johnson, Bransford, & Solomon, 1973; see also Lewandowsky, Stritzke, Oberauer, & Morales, 2005).

What does Bartlett's (1932) simple demonstration tell us about what happened to Sally Blackwell, George Bush, and Sheri Storm? On the one hand, it suggests that prior knowledge can change what we recollect from what we originally encountered into a more familiar version that fits with how we understand the world. But prior knowledge does not just mold information so it is more familiar, it can also lead people to fill in the gaps and add details that were never present. For example in one study, when people read a passage describing the famous blind and deaf author Helen Keller, they often recalled details that fit with their knowledge of Helen Keller, but were never actually present in the passage. For instance, people recalled reading that she was blind – which of course is true, but that fact was never stated in the passage. This study showed that prior knowledge can lead people to remember beyond what they actually experience (see also Bower, Black, & Turner, 1979; Bransford & Franks, 1971; Brewer & Treyens, 1981; Johnson, Bransford, & Solomon, 1973).

Taken together, these studies tell us that memories are not an objective, unyielding imprint of the past, but a subjective, pliable patchwork of experience, thoughts, and daydreams. Still, critics might ask how these demonstrations of people distorting mere details of a story can help us understand how others might misremember details of a crime, a shocking public event, or even an entire event. As we shall see, these memory distortions are often remarkably similar to their more mundane counterparts.

FALSE MEMORIES FOR DETAILS OF EVENTS

Misinformation and its consequences for memory

At the trial of Clarence Von Williams, Sally Blackwell described how she came to realize that Von Williams was her attacker. Blackwell told the court that the morning after the attack, she had spoken to Lois Von Williams, Clarence's wife. Sally and Lois worked together, and Sally had telephoned Lois to inform her that she would be off work that day. The only other connection Sally had with the Von Williams is that she attended a dinner party with them a few weeks earlier. After the phone call with Lois, Sally talked to her boyfriend, who convinced her that the perpetrator must be someone she knew. He listed situations where she may have encountered her attacker – "the grocery store or at church … at a party somewhere … " (Loftus & Ketcham, 1991, p. 189). As soon as her boyfriend mentioned the word "party," Sally realized who her attacker was – it was Clarence Von Williams, the husband of her co-worker and the same man she had met at a dinner party a few weeks earlier (for more on this case, see Loftus & Ketcham, 1991). Could the phone call to Lois Von Williams and subsequent suggestions from her boyfriend have altered Sally Blackwell's memory somehow?

To investigate questions such as this one, researchers often use a three-stage procedure. First, people watch an event – usually a movie or slideshow – that typically depicts a crime. For example, in one study people watched a man steal a wallet out of a woman's bag and put it in his jacket pocket (Okado & Stark, 2005). Second, after a short delay designed to let memories decay, people read information about that event. What they do not know is that the information is riddled with inaccuracies. This postevent information (PEI) is crafted to expose some people (but not others) to misleading suggestions about certain aspects of the event. For example, some people read that the man "took her wallet and hid it in his pants pocket" but others read that he "took her wallet and hid it in a pocket." Typically, PEI is manipulated within-subjects, so that everyone reads some misleading information. In a third and final phase, researchers test people's memory for what they originally saw. The key question is whether people tend to incorporate inaccurate details from the misleading question into their memory for the accident. The answer is yes. Those who receive misleading information about the event are more likely to report that inaccurate information on the subsequent memory test. The finding that people incorporate inaccurate PEI into their memory reports is known as the misinformation effect (Loftus & Hoffman, 1989; Tousignant, Hall, & Loftus, 1986). Over the last four decades, hundreds of experiments conducted in laboratories all over the world have demonstrated that people often unwittingly adopt misleading suggestions as their own memories. Although here we focus on how information after an event can shape people's memory reports, information that people encounter before an event can also shape memory (see Carmichael, Hogan, & Walter, 1932).

How can misinformation invade memory?

The misinformation effect is a robust phenomenon and has been demonstrated with a variety of materials, altering memory reports in minor and dramatic ways – changing (for example) the color of a car, brand of soft drink, and even features of someone's appearance (Jenkins & Davies, 1985; Loftus, 1977; Takarangi, Parker, & Garry, 2006; see Loftus, 2005 for a review). Even subtle changes to the wording of a question can be misleading. Simply changing the verb used to ask about a motor vehicle accident can systematically influence people's estimates of speed: people reported that cars were traveling at higher speeds when asked, "How fast were the cars going when they smashed

into each other?" than when smashed was replaced with bumped, hit, collided, or contacted (Loftus & Palmer, 1974). Thus, misleading information does not have to be overtly suggestive in order to distort people's memory.

PEI can alter memory reports in more dramatic ways too, inserting objects that were never really there, adding broken glass, buildings, and wounded animals to a witnessed event (Loftus, 1975; Loftus & Zanni, 1975; Nourkova, Bernstein, & Loftus, 2004). In one study, when people were queried in a way that presumed the presence of an object, they apparently came to remember things that they never actually saw. People who were asked if they saw "the broken headlight" said they did more often than people who were asked whether they saw "a broken headlight" (Loftus & Zanni, 1975). Another study shows that even more subtle leading questions can insert objects. People were asked, "How fast was the white sports car going while traveling along the country road?" or "How fast was the white sports car going when it passed the barn while traveling along the country road?" Although the task was to estimate speed, simply encountering the phrase "passed the barn" was enough to lead subjects to report having seen a barn in the original event (Loftus, 1975).

Real-life cases such as those of Clarence Von Williams tell us that once adopted, misinformation can "stick, leading people to report their distorted memories in court weeks or even years later. Research squares with this observation. In one study, people reported misleading information up to one and a half years after viewing an event (Zhu et al., 2012). Moreover, even when misinformation is corrected, people can continue to believe the initial inaccurate version. When misinformation about the Iraq War was retracted by various media outlets, many Americans still thought the initial inaccurate reports were true – approximately 30 percent falsely remembered that there was evidence of Weapons of Mass Destruction (Lewandowsky et al., 2005). Taken together, these findings show that misinformation can invade people's memory via a subtle change to a verb, adding a definite rather than indefinite article, and by disguising an object in a sentence that queries the subject about something else. Other researchers have planted misinformation by asking subjects to read a narrative describing the event that they witnessed – although we might expect subjects to read the narrative carefully for accuracy, the misinformation still infiltrates their memory reports. Moreover this research tells us that misinformation doesn't just alter details in our memory, it can add information to memory that was never there in the first place.

Where does misinformation come from?

In the real world, there are many sources of misinformation. Misleading PEI does not need to come from an authoritative experimenter, nor be intentional, to hurt memory. Talking to co-witnesses after an event, viewing media reports, or retelling an experience to friends or officials are all opportunities for PEI to creep into memory reports. Indeed, a growing literature shows that witnesses can misinform each other (Bodner, Musch, & Azad, 2009; French, Garry, & Mori, 2008; Gabbert, Memon, & Allan, 2003; Paterson & Kemp, 2006). In the typical "co-witness" experiment, people participate in a modified version of the traditional three-stage misinformation effect procedure. First, pairs of people each watch what is ostensibly the same event – but in reality, each sees a different version of the event. This deception has been achieved in a variety of ways, including showing people slightly different camera views, editing a version of each event and using optical trickery to project a different version to each person (French et al., 2008; Gabbert et al., 2003). In one study, pairs of people viewed an event filmed from two different angles, such that, for example, both see a woman taking something from a drawer

but only one can see what she took. In the second phase, the pairs discussed what they saw. Because they saw different versions of the event, the discussion provided a chance for each to suggest misleading PEI. In the third phase, people were tested, separately, for their memory of the original event. This study showed the typical pattern of results: even when tested individually, people often report having seen details that were communicated by their co-witness (French et al., 2008; Gabbert et al., 2003; Paterson & Kemp, 2006; Wright, Self, & Justice, 2000; see also Meade & Roediger, 2002). This line of research suggests that simply sharing our experience with someone else can be an opportunity for misinformation to invade memory.

More recently, researchers have examined the effects of PEI in other arenas, such as education and advertising. In one experiment highlighting the consequences of misinformation in an educational setting, people studied various historical topics such as the French revolution, and then watched popular films related to those topics (Butler, Zaromb, Lyle, & Roediger, 2009). The films depicted some details accurately, but also contained misleading information – details that were inconsistent with what people had read. One week later, on a memory test for the passages, people often misremembered details from the movie as being details they had read in the text. Other studies have demonstrated similar effects in advertising, showing that, when people reviewed fake ads for Disneyland asking them to remember childhood visits meeting Bugs Bunny, many became more confident that they really did meet Bugs (Braun, Ellis, & Loftus, 2002). As you might have guessed, the ad was misleading: Bugs Bunny belongs to Universal Studios, not Disney.

Perhaps the most surprising way misinformation can invade memory is through our own retellings about an event. What dangers are likely when witnesses are pressed to provide details they did not see? One possibility is that they might guess about how events might have happened. But guessing and describing can act as misinformation, so that details people first offer as guesses can later corrupt their memory for the event (Ackil & Zaragoza, 1998; Zaragoza, Payment, Ackil, Drivdahl, & Beck, 2001). In one clever study, people watched a short clip from a Disney movie. Afterwards, people responded to two types of questions: questions about details they actually witnessed, and questions about details they never saw. The interviewer asked some people (but not others) to answer both types of questions, even if it meant guessing. One week later, a different interviewer asked which details everyone had actually seen in the original event – along with a warning that the first interviewer had questioned them incorrectly, asking them about some details that weren't actually in the movie. But even with the warning, people reported seeing details from their made-up speculations about the event, even though just a week ago they knew that information was a guess (Zaragoza et al., 2001; see also sleeper effect, Hovland & Weiss, 1951; Kumkale & Albarracín, 2004).

Considered as a whole, this research tells us that misinformation can invade our memory in a variety of ways and through diverse sources in a range of contexts. But under what conditions are we susceptible to misinformation?

What are the boundary conditions for the misinformation effect?

How well people remember the original event

Under some conditions it is especially easy for misinformation to creep into people's memory for an event. In particular, as memory for the event becomes weaker, it becomes more susceptible to misleading PEI. In one study, people received misleading information 20 minutes, one day, two days, or one week after they witnessed an event. People were most misled at the longest delays, when time had allowed people's memory for the original event to fade (Loftus, Miller,

& Burns, 1978; see also Frost, Ingraham, & Wilson, 2002). As the delay increases people are also more likely to say that they really remembered seeing the misleading details (Frost, 2000). Put another way, as the delay between the event and misinformation phases increases, the likelihood that people report misleading details also increases (Loftus et al., 1978).

The idea of centrality of information can also be useful in appreciating how PEI can invade memory. In one study, when adults watched a (simulated) shoplifting, they were better at remembering central details (such as a stolen bottle of wine) than peripheral details (such as the color of a bystander's shirt); they were also less likely to be misled about central details than peripheral details (Wright & Stroud, 1998; see also Sutherland & Hayne, 2001). But even though ideas about "central" and "peripheral" details seems intuitive, there are problems with these notions. For one thing, the distinction is circular: people remember central details better than peripheral ones, and details are often defined as central because they are remembered better than details that are peripheral. Moreover, what scientists mean by central or peripheral varies across studies and circumstances. Is a detail central because it is large, or because people see it for a long time, or because it is important to how the event unfolds? Whether an item is defined as central or peripheral can also change depending on the surrounding event context and the person's knowledge of the event, which may change over time. Whether a gunman was wearing a blue or yellow New York Yankees shirt might be a peripheral detail – until an hour later, when the police arrest a man wearing a yellow New York Yankees shirt. Finally, people sometimes fail to notice seemingly obvious things that happen right in front of them, a phenomenon known as inattentional blindness. In one well-known study, roughly half the people asked to watch a basketball game and count the passes among the teammates did not notice when a woman dressed in a gorilla costume walked through the middle of the game, stopped to thump her chest, and then walked out of view (Simons & Chabris, 1999). When it comes to notions of centrality, this and other similar findings throw a ... gorilla wrench into the works.

Features of the misinformation

Social cues can also affect people's susceptibility to misinformation. When the misinformation messenger seems particularly credible, inaccurate PEI is more likely to creep into people's memory. Findings from co-witness research fits with this idea: witnesses who believe that another witness saw an event for longer are more likely to adopt that witness' inaccurate suggestions (Gabbert, Memon, & Wright, 2007). The same pattern occurs when a co-witness speaks first in a discussion (Gabbert, Memon, & Wright, 2006; but see Lindsay, 2007, for why that particular report is ambiguous; see also Hewitt, Kane, & Garry, 2013). Characteristics of the discussion partners can also bear on whether PEI is incorporated into memory. In one study, people watched an event and then discussed it with a stranger or their romantic partner. Those who heard PEI from their romantic partner were more misled than those who heard it from a stranger (French et al., 2008). Even an accent can affect whether people take on PEI. In one study subjects rated how powerful and socially attractive a speaker sounded. When the speaker sounded powerful, subjects were equally misled regardless of how socially attractive they thought the speaker was. But when the speaker did not sound powerful, social attractiveness affected their susceptibility to misleading information: people were more misled when they thought the speaker was socially attractive (Vornik, Sharman, & Garry, 2003). Thus, social factors that make the source of PEI seem more credible can lead subjects to be more likely to incorporate misinformation into their reports (see also Dodd & Bradshaw, 1980).

In addition, factors that make PEI feel more familiar can make it easier for misinformation to take hold. Repeating inaccurate details can enhance the misinformation effect – regardless of whether the repeated details are attributed to multiple eyewitnesses or just one (Foster, Huthwaite, Yesberg, Garry, & Loftus, 2012; Zaragoza & Mitchell, 1996). Elaborating on certain features of misinformation can also lead people to be more likely to remember suggested details. People who are asked to consider what a detail looked like or how a detail contributed to the overall meaning of the event are more likely to adopt misinformation as part of their memory when tested later (Drivdahl & Zaragoza, 2001; Zaragoza, Mitchell, Payment, & Drivdahl, 2011).

Monitoring where information came from

Research suggests that a feeling of familiarity plays a large role in the impact of misleading suggestions, as does the ability to track the sources of information about the target event. At test, people have the task of deciding whether they saw an item in the original event, or whether it comes to mind for some other reason. They might ask themselves, "Does my memory of the stop sign come from the questions I answered, or did I see a stop sign in the event?" To answer their own question, people must rely on a bundle of cognitive mechanisms that help us keep track of our mental life and decide what is real, through a process called source monitoring (Johnson, Hashtroudi, & Lindsay, 1993; Lindsay, 2008; Lindsay, Chapter 4, this volume). These processes evaluate possible memories to determine if they have the characteristics – the who, what, when, where, and how – typical of real events. If the target memory clears this bar, we experience it as a real memory. If it falls short of the bar, we may experience it as a memory of a thought or a dream, or as a product of current imagination. The height of the bar is flexible, and where we put it depends on the demands of the situation and our goals.

Thankfully, healthy people are capable of efficient source monitoring, or else we would live in a world of profound delusion where thoughts, movies, and genuine experience all seem equally real. But occasionally we make mistakes. For instance, we sometimes take shortcuts, setting the bar too low and making bad source monitoring decisions. Other times, when our mental events share many of the characteristics associated with genuine experience, they can come close to the bar and it becomes too difficult to tell whether these mental events are memories. As a consequence, we sometimes call a false memory a real memory.

With a weak memory for the original event, and after spending time thinking about features of the misinformation (such as what it looks like), the suggested detail may feel more familiar than the detail people originally saw. That is, the misinformation may feel like its source was genuine experience. Moreover, if people remember that a detail came from a credible misinformation messenger then they might be especially inclined to trust the feeling of familiarity, lowering the bar and being less likely to ask themselves if they really saw that detail in the original event. Research on source monitoring fits with this account. People examine the sources of their memories at different levels of analysis depending on the situation, relying on a quick automatic feeling of familiarity to tell them whether something is a memory or using a more analytical, reasoned approach if the situation calls for it (Johnson et al., 1993; Lindsay, 2008).

As source monitoring becomes easier, people are typically less misled. Under some conditions it is especially difficult for misinformation to creep into memory. For instance, if the PEI introduces a detail that blatantly contradicts what people remember seeing in the event, then they are unlikely to confuse that detail as being something they saw earlier. That is, if a New York baseball fan saw a perpetrator wearing a t-shirt bearing his beloved Yankees logo, and the PEI suggests the perpetrator wore the shirt of his cross-town rivals, the witness would probably reject the suggestion (see Loftus, 1991). As it becomes easier to disentangle what information comes from the original event and what is the product of misleading suggestion, people can better ward off PEI – especially if people are warned about potential inaccuracies. In one study, people watched and listened to a narrated event, and then heard PEI in the same room and from the same narrator, two days before they took the test (Lindsay, 1990). But others heard the PEI on a different day, in a different room, and from a different narrator – and while they were standing up – minutes before taking the test. Before the memory test, everyone was told that the PEI was incorrect, so they should not report anything from it on the test. Those who encountered the PEI under very different conditions (in the well-lit room, standing up, just a few minutes ago) were better able to identify the source of that information and so did not recall it on the test. In other words, if people can track the sources of their memories easily and they are told to watch out for errors, they can better avoid misleading suggestions (see also research on warnings: Butler et al., 2009; Eakin, Schreiber, & Sergent-Marshall, 2003; Tousignant et al., 1986). In general, warnings are most effective when they occur before the PEI, because people can carefully scrutinize subsequent information and protect themselves from misleading suggestions. Nonetheless, some instructions after PEI can reduce the effects of hearing inaccurate details (Echterhoff, Hirst, & Hussy, 2005; Oeberst & Blank, 2012).

Considered as a whole, the vast misinformation effect literature shows that information we encounter after an event can invade us, as Loftus said, "like a Trojan horse, precisely because we do not detect its influence" (Loftus, 2007, p. 4). It is the ease with which it hides in plain sight that makes it so dangerous, and its consequences so serious.

FLASHBULB MEMORIES

Some events are particularly laden with emotion and have consequences on a wide scale. For instance, like George W. Bush, most of us can think back to the moment we learned of the World Trade Center attacks of 2001. Some of us can think back and remember how we learned about the OJ Simpson verdict, or where we were when the space shuttle Challenger exploded. These memories come to mind with a peculiar vividness, a feeling that we are being transported back to the moment, and high confidence that we can answer correctly the question we often ask each other: Where were you when …? (Brown & Kulik, 1977; Neisser & Harsch, 1992; Talarico & Rubin, 2003; Weaver, 1993). Is that confidence warranted?

Brown and Kulik (1977) named these vivid, detailed "where were you when …" recollections "flashbulb memories" (FBM), and attributed them to a special "now print!" mechanism, concluding that these events left an accurate, long-lasting record in memory. Although FBMs often come to mind with a sense of reliving and high confidence, subsequent research showed that these phenomenological experiences do not perfectly map onto accuracy (Schmolck, Buffalo, & Squire, 2000; Talarico & Rubin, 2003; Weaver & Krug, 2004). For instance, in one study people reported how they heard about the Challenger explosion approximately 24 hours after the event, and then two and a half years later (Neisser & Harsch, 1992). Collecting people's reports soon after the event allowed the researchers to examine how accurate people were over time (on the assumption that the one-day-old memory reports were highly likely to be accurate). If flashbulbs are the result of some special mechanism that engraves a long lasting memory, then people should be quite consistent over time. But memory reports did not show this kind of pattern. In fact, nobody was entirely consistent; only 7 percent of people were very consistent and even they were not entirely accurate. A quarter of people recalled completely different circumstances of learning about the Challenger when they were queried again two and a half years later. For example, one subject initially reported being "in my religion class and some people

walked in and talked about it." After a delay of two years, the same subject reported hearing the news "in my freshman dorm with my roommate and we were watching TV" (p. 9).

This pattern of results has been replicated for a variety of events, ranging from deaths of politicians and royalty to the terrorist attacks of 9/11. In these studies, researchers typically survey people shortly after a surprising and emotional public event, and ask them to report in detail the circumstances in which they learned about the event – how they heard about the event, where they were, what they were doing, who told them and how they felt at the time. Following the initial report, people then report their memories at different delays. The key question is whether these reports are consistent. Just as with memories of the Challenger, over two decades of research shows that FBMs often change over time, and sometimes depart from reality in dramatic ways (Hirst et al., 2009; Schmolck, Buffalo, & Squire, 2000).

How do these memories compare to everyday memories? Compared with everyday memories, over time they feel more vivid, and create more of a feeling of being back into the moment than everyday memories. Moreover, people are more inclined to believe their FBMs than everyday memories – even though their accuracy declines at a similar rate (Talarico & Rubin, 2003; see also Weaver, 1993 for a similar pattern in confidence, although cf. Kvavilashvili, Mirani, Schlagman, Erskine, & Kornbrot, 2010, for evidence that sometimes FBMs can have better test–retest reliability than a matched control event). That people believe their flashbulb memories is not surprising; we know that mental products that are full of perceptual details are more likely to be categorized as real events than those lacking perceptual details (see Reality Monitoring; Johnson & Raye, 1981; Johnson, 2006).

Most of the time in this context an error has little consequence. But other times, when memories are the subject of court battles they can have crushing consequences. The literature covered thus far looks at changes to memory for events that happened. Details of the witnessed event changed, details and context of the flashbulb changed – even dramatically. But usually people remember the core event correctly; there was a crime, the main events of 9/11. Could memory distortion happen on a more grand scale? Could people come to remember events that did not happen rather than just misremembering the details?

FALSE MEMORIES FOR ENTIRE EXPERIENCES

The case of Sheri Storm and other retractors called for answers from psychological science: how is it that people could recall terrible childhood events, only to conclude that their memory was not only inaccurate, but a complete fabrication? Before considering how people might come to remember events that never occurred we must first put these cases in some historical context.

In the 1980s and early 1990s cases like Sheri Storm started emerging from patients undergoing approaches to psychotherapy that included an emphasis on attempts to uncover suspected memories of childhood trauma. The aim of this clinical practice was to uncover traumatic memories from childhood, memories that had been banished from conscious awareness by a mechanism called repression (for a review on the repression controversy, see McNally, 2003). Although there was little empirical evidence of such a mechanism (see Holmes, 1990) many well-intentioned but misguided clinicians asked clients to engage in dubious, potentially dangerous, practices such as imagining what might have happened (Poole, Lindsay, Memon, & Bull, 1995). Often they encouraged repeated use of these techniques. As the number of recovered memory cases started increasing, many psychological scientists became concerned that attempts to uncover buried memories could in fact be creating illusory memories rather than helping people recall real experiences (Loftus, 1993).

Although earlier research led many scientists to be skeptical about trauma-memory-oriented therapy, convincing evidence of where Sheri Storm and others went awry demanded new paradigms. Could people systematically come to remember wholly false experiences?

CAN THESE TECHNIQUES PRODUCE FALSE MEMORIES FOR ENTIRE EVENTS?

To examine this question, researchers wondered if people would develop completely false memories with the same techniques used by therapists trying to uncover suspected memories of childhood trauma. For instance, in one study subjects reviewed descriptions of four childhood events and tried to recall them over two sessions (Loftus & Pickrell, 1995). Three of the descriptions were provided by parents and detailed events that really occurred. But the fourth event – getting lost in the mall – was created by the researchers and never actually happened. For example, one subject read that "You, your mom, Tien, and Tuan all went to the Bremerton K-Mart. You must have been 5 years old at the time … and somehow lost your way in the store. Tien found you crying to an elderly Chinese woman" (p. 721). The question was whether simply trying to recall a suggested event could lead normal healthy adults to develop a false memory for an experience that never occurred. After two interviews within the space of approximately two weeks 25 percent of subjects remembered details about the suggested event. Even after the debriefing one subject who could not believe the event was false said "I totally remember walking around those dressing rooms and my Mom not being in the section she said she'd be in …" (Loftus & Pickrell, 1995, p. 723).

This finding was not unique to getting lost in a mall. In studies that followed, people came to remember spilling punch at a wedding, being attacked by an animal, being saved by a lifeguard, and taking a hot air balloon ride (Heaps & Nash, 2001; Hyman, Husband, & Billings, 1995; Porter, Yuille, & Lehman, 1999; Wade, Garry, Read, & Lindsay, 2002). On average, across 20 studies, people developed images or memories of these false events 36 percent of the time.[1] In some of these studies researchers coded whether people came to remember images (also labeled partial false memories) or complete false memories (where subjects showed evidence of genuinely feeling as though they were remembering the false event). On average, across 12 studies that made this distinction, people developed images of the false event 19 percent of the time and complete false memories 20 percent of the time.

Can people come to remember implausible events?

The rate at which people recall these suggested events varies with the nature of the suggested event and how elaborate the suggestion is. But some questioned whether people would ever come to remember events that were seen as implausible. For instance, in one study although people came to remember being lost in a mall, none developed false memories of having a rectal enema – an event that they knew little about, and thus was probably difficult for them to imagine as they attempted to recall one (Pezdek, Finger, & Hodge, 1997). Pezdek et al. concluded that people would come to remember plausible events, but they would be far less likely to develop false memories for implausible events.

Yet later research showed that a little knowledge could shift plausibility and boost people's belief that an event initially rated as implausible, may have happened (Mazzoni, Loftus, & Kirsch, 2001). In the first session of this study, subjects rated the plausibility of a series of life events and whether those events had happened to them in childhood. In a second session, some subjects read articles about a plausible target event (choking as a child), and some subjects read articles about an implausible target event (witnessing a

demonic possession). The articles described the target event and noted that it was a common phenomenon. In the following session, subjects completed a survey about their fears. The survey was actually bogus and people's responses were always used as evidence that they had a fear of the target event. In the final session, subjects made the same ratings as session one.

There are two key findings from this study. First, reported plausibility was malleable: reading the narrative and receiving the fear survey results led people to rate witnessing a demonic possession as being more plausible than they had in session one. Second, although the demonic possession event remained relatively implausible, people became more confident that they had witnessed one – a confidence boost similar to that of the choking event (see also Sharman & Scoboria, 2009, for evidence that confidence and memory can increase for high and low plausibility events). These findings fit with real-life cases and give us some insight into the mechanisms that might explain how people remember being abducted by aliens and witnessing satanic cults, events that we might classify as low plausibility or even implausible (Clancy, 2005; Loftus & Ketcham, 1994).

Can photos lead people to remember false events?

Having people read a narrative about a childhood event is not the only way to plant an entirely false memory. In order to help cue recall during therapy, clients are sometimes asked to review photos in family albums (e.g. Weiser, 2004). But this tool can be especially dangerous when the event that people are pursuing is false. Instead of asking people to read narratives, in one study researchers asked subjects to review childhood photos while trying to recall four childhood events (Wade et al., 2002). Three of the photos depicted the subject engaged in a real family event. A fourth photo was doctored so that the subject was in a hot air balloon with a family member – an event that never happened. Across three interviews subjects worked at recalling details about the events; by the third interview, half of the subjects remembered at least some details about the balloon ride (Wade et al., 2002). Images can distort memory for recent events as well. When researchers digitally altered video footage of an event to make it look like people stole money during an experiment, people were three times more likely to sign an official form corroborating the cheating behavior than those who did not see the doctored video footage (Wade, Green, & Nash, 2010).

Of course, in real life it would be rather sinister to edit photos or videos to suggest that someone experienced an event they did not. Would a real childhood photo produce similar effects? To address this question, people tried to recall three childhood events, one of which was false: putting a gooey Slime toy in a grade school teacher's drawer (Lindsay, Hagan, Read, Wade, & Garry, 2004). One group of people worked at recalling the events by hearing narratives, but another group heard the narratives along with a class photograph from the year each narrative described. Whereas just under half the people who saw only the narrative appeared to come to remember the false event, more than three-quarters of those who worked at recalling events with a narrative and a class photo apparently remembered it. Although the class photos did not provide evidence the event really happened, they did give people additional information that should have helped scaffold imagery of the false event – who was involved in the execution of the prank, the victim who discovered Slime, and so on. Indeed, their memory ratings square with this idea. Those who saw photographs had higher confidence, as well as feelings of reliving and remembering for the false event compared with subjects who did not see a photo. Other lines of work emphasize the role of imagery in producing false memories (Dobson & Markham, 1993; Hyman &

Pentland, 1996; Johnson, Foley, Suengas, & Raye, 1988; cf. Heaps & Nash, 1999). For example, Hyman and Billings (1998) found that the higher subjects scored on a self-report measure of mental imagery the more likely they were to developed false memories. Together, this research documents the power of photos – even seemingly innocuous untampered photos – to plant entirely false memories experiences we have never had.

THE POWER OF IMAGINATION

Many of the lost-in-the-mall studies used a combination of trauma-memory-oriented therapy techniques to build false memories, but other work suggests that even when these techniques are used in isolation they can be dangerous. A number of studies have now documented the power of imagination to boost belief that one had experienced an event in childhood. In one study exploring the effects of imagination, people participated in a three-phase procedure (Garry, Manning, Loftus, & Sherman, 1996). In the first phase, people made confidence ratings for whether they had experienced a range of life experiences before the age of 10 (for example, that they had broken a window with their hand). In the second phase, people imagined some low-likelihood events but not others. Finally, the experimenter fed people a cover story that she had lost their original ratings and asked them to complete the confidence measure again. When people spent just a short time imagining an event they originally rated as unlikely, they became more confident that it occurred, an effect known as imagination inflation. Later research showed that this increase in confidence is not unique to the act of imagination: explaining how an event could have occurred or simply paraphrasing a claim about a childhood event can boost people's belief that they experienced events in their childhood (Garry et al., 1996; Sharman, Garry, & Beuke, 2004; Sharman, Manning, & Garry, 2005). The common thread in these activities is that they encourage elaboration about the event – as people add details, people and sensory information, the imagined event feels more like a real memory.

Does imagination merely help people remember real events?

An alternative explanation for imagination inflation is that these techniques do not make fictitious events seem real, but are simply helping people to remember events that really did happen. To control for this explanation, several studies have examined the effect of imagination on a set of known, verifiable events (Goff & Roediger, 1998; Seamon, Philbin, & Harrison, 2006; Thomas & Loftus, 2002). In one study, experimenters took subjects on a campus walk and had them perform some acts but only imagine performing others (Seamon et al., 2006). Some of those acts were familiar such as waving from the top of some steps, and some were bizarre such as proposing marriage to a Pepsi machine. The next day, subjects took another campus walk and imagined performing some of the actions from session one and some new actions they had never encountered. Two weeks later, subjects completed a memory test asking them which actions they performed or imagined in session one. Imagining acts only once in session two often led people to falsely report performing them in session one. Moreover, imagination didn't just lead to false memories for familiar actions like waving at some steps, imagination sometimes led people to remember bizarre actions such as proposing to a Pepsi machine. The Seamon et al. (2006) study tells us that imagination can lead people to falsely remember performing recent acts, even those that are distinct from everyday experience – you might have expected people would have an easy time rejecting the notion that they proposed to the Pepsi machine (although the fact that they had performed some bizarre acts as part of the experiment likely played a role in fostering these errors).

Together this work tells us that inflation can happen for recent events that researchers know are false, but could inflation also occur for childhood experiences that researchers know are false? The answer is yes. In one study, imagination increased people's belief that they had a skin sample taken from their finger as part of a health check as a child – a false event created by the researchers (Mazzoni & Memon, 2003). What's more, compared with those who simply read about the skin removal event, subjects who imagined the event were four times more likely to report a false memory of experiencing the event as a child. Taken together these studies demonstrate the power of imagination to systematically distort autobiographical belief and memory for everyday through to bizarre events that never happened.

HOW DO PEOPLE FALL VICTIM TO ENTIRELY FALSE MEMORIES?

So how does a suggestion combined with a recovered-memory therapy (RMT) technique grow into a false memory for an event that never occurred? Although there are a number of models of false memory development, researchers would agree that plausibility and belief promote their growth (Hyman & Kleinknecht, 1999; Mazzoni et al., 2001). As we have noted above, both plausibility and belief are malleable. An event that is initially rated as implausible can come to seem more plausible and people's belief that an event occurred can grow via imagination or other forms of elaboration (Garry et al., 1996; Mazzoni et al., 2001). But in order to have a false memory per se, people must make a source monitoring error, and confuse the details they extracted from narratives or photos, and related thoughts and images that came to mind as a result of reviewing these materials, as being a consequence of real experience. They must experience these mental contents as memories.

A number of factors work in concert to make source monitoring errors likely in these studies and in trauma-memory-oriented therapy. That the suggestion is attributed to a family member in these studies (or the therapist in a clinical setting) may serve to boost the credibility of the suggestive narrative or photos and perhaps consequently boost the credibility of the information that people bring to mind. Moreover, people repeatedly attempt to recall the events, using techniques that facilitate elaboration about the event. We know that repetition fuels feelings of familiarity and that elaborating can add additional perceptual and semantic details that make a mental event feel more like a memory (see Johnson, 2006, for a review). Third, when people come to evaluate these mental events it is difficult, particularly because the events they are judging are old (from their childhood) and much more difficult to distinguish from imagined events (Johnson et al., 1988).

Considered together, these factors are a recipe for false memories. Even with the best intentions, using them to dig up a possible buried event from long ago can be dangerous. Some people who came out of therapy with detailed memories of traumatic childhood events went on to pursue criminal charges against family members only to later learn that their memories were in fact false; they experienced their mistaken memories as though they were real. (Bernstein & Loftus, 2009; see also McNally, Lasko, Clancy, Macklin, Pitman, & Orr, 2004, for evidence that people's physiological responses to true and false memories are sometimes indistinguishable.)

DO FALSE MEMORIES FALL OUT OF A FLAWED MEMORY SYSTEM?

In this chapter, we examined the false memories that invade us – those that creep past our cognitive defense system. But not all false memories go undetected. Many of us can bring to mind an experience that, with a bit of reflection, we know cannot possibly be true. We remember seeing Santa climb down the chimney, feeding a family pet that died before we were born, or see ourselves from an external, observer's perspective when bringing to mind a cherished childhood memory (see Mazzoni, Scoboria, & Harvey, 2010). Whether we catch them or not, why do we have a memory system that allows us to create these illusory versions of reality?

Instead of considering false memories as a flaw in an imperfect system, recently researchers have considered false memories from a more functional perspective (Howe, 2011; Newman & Lindsay, 2009; Schacter, Guerin, & St. Jacques, 2011). Having a system that allows us to concoct illusory versions of reality also allows us to do many important cognitive acts such as thinking into the future and reconsidering our past – a kind of counterfactual thinking (Schacter & Addis, 2007; Suddendorf & Corballis, 1997). In fact, there is growing evidence that people use past experiences as raw materials for future thinking (Addis, Wong, & Schacter, 2007; Szpunar, Watson, & McDermott, 2007). But to use memory for future thinking requires reconstruction, rather than playing back; one must be able to recombine elements from past events to create novel future scenarios – people must be able to build a kind of false memory for the future (Schacter & Addis, 2007). A memory system that allows us to reconstruct, rather than play back, is prone to error – but it also gives us the capacity to consider not only alternative pasts or how an event might have occurred, but also to consider our possible futures. Without this flexibility, we might be stuck with a past we cannot reconsider or revise and a future we can't anticipate or pre-experience.

NOTE

1 We calculated weighted means from the following studies (Desjardins & Scoboria, 2007; French, Sutherland, & Garry, 2006; Garry & Wade, 2005; Heaps & Nash, 2001; Hyman & Billings, 1998; Hyman, Husband, & Billings, 1995; Hyman & Pentland, 1996;

Lindsay, Hagen, Read, Wade, & Garry, 2004; Loftus & Pickrell, 1995; Mazzoni & Memon, 2003; Ost, Foster, Costall, & Bull, 2005; Pezdek, Finger, & Hodge, 1997; Porter, Yuille & Lehman, 1999; Wade, Garry, Read, & Lindsay, 2002).

REFERENCES

Ackil, J. K., & Zaragoza, M. S. (1998). Memorial consequences of forced confabulations: Age differences in susceptibility to false memories. *Developmental Psychology, 34*, 1358–1372.

Addis, D. R., Wong, A. T., & Schacter, D. L. (2007). Remembering the past and imagining the future: Common and distinct neural substrates during event construction and elaboration. *Neuropsychologia, 45*, 1363 –1377.

Anderson, R. C., & Pichert, J. W. (1978). Recall of previously unrecallable information following a shift in perspective. *Journal of Verbal Learning and Verbal Behaviour, 17*, 1–12.

Bartlett, F. C. (1932). *Remembering: A study in experimental and social psychology.* Cambridge: Cambridge University Press.

Bergman, E., & Roediger, H. L., III (1999). Can Bartlett's repeated reproduction experiments be replicated? *Memory & Cognition, 27*, 937–947.

Bernstein, D. M., & Loftus, E. F. (2009). The consequences of false memory for food preferences and choices. *Perspectives on Psychological Science, 4*, 135–139.

Bodner, G. E., Musch, E., & Azad, T. (2009). Reevaluating the potency of the memory conformity effect. *Memory & Cognition, 37*, 1069–1076.

Bower, G. H., Black, J. B., & Turner, T. J. (1979). Scripts in memory for text. *Cognitive Psychology, 11*(2), 177–220.

Bransford, J. D., & Franks, J. J. (1971). The abstraction of linguistic ideas. *Cognitive Psychology, 2*, 331–350.

Bransford, J. D., & Johnson, M. K. (1972). Contextual prerequisites for understanding: Some investigations of comprehension and recall. *Journal of Verbal Learning & Verbal Behaviour, 11*(6), 717–726.

Braun, K. A., Ellis, R., & Loftus, E. F. (2002). Make my memory: How advertising can change our memories of the past. *Psychology and Marketing, 19*, 1–23.

Brewer, W. F., & Treyens, J. C. (1981). Role of schemata in memory for places. *Cognitive Psychology, 13*, 207–230.

Brown, R., & Kulik, J. (1977). Flashbulb memories. *Cognition, 5*, 73–99.

Butler, A. C., Zaromb, F., Lyle, K. B., & Roediger, H. L., III (2009). Using popular films to enhance classroom learning: The good, bad, and the interesting. *Psychological Science, 20*, 1161–1168.

Carmichael, L., Hogan, H. P., & Walter, A. A. (1932). An experimental study of the effect of language on the reproduction of visually perceived form. *Journal of Experimental Psychology, 15*, 73–86.

Clancy, S. (2005). *Abducted: How people come to believe they were kidnapped by aliens.* Cambridge, MA: Harvard University Press.

Desjardins, T., & Scoboria, A. (2007). 'You and your best friend Suzy put Slime in Ms. Smollett's desk': Producing false memories with self-relevant details. *Psychonomic Bulletin and Review, 14*, 1090–1095.

Dobson, M., & Markham, R. (1993). Imagery ability and source monitoring: Implications for eyewitness memory. *British Journal of Psychology, 84*, 111–118.

Dodd, D. H., & Bradshaw, J. M. (1980). Leading questions and memory: Pragmatic constraints. *Journal of Verbal Learning & Verbal Behavior, 19*(6), 695–704.

Drivdahl, S. B., & Zaragoza, M. S. (2001). The role of perceptual elaboration and individual differences in the creation of false memories for suggested events. *Applied Cognitive Psychology, 15*(3), 265–281.

Eakin, D. K., Schreiber, T. A., & Sergent-Marshall, S. (2003). Misinformation effects in eyewitness memory: The presence and absence of memory impairment as a function of warning and misinformation accessibility. *Journal of Experimental Psychology: Learning, Memory, and Cognition, 29*, 813–825.

Echterhoff, G., Hirst, W., & Hussy, W. (2005). How eyewitnesses resist misinformation: Social postwarnings and the monitoring of memory characteristics. *Memory & Cognition, 33*, 770–782.

Foster, J. L., Huthwaite, T., Yesberg, J. A., Garry, M., & Loftus, E. F. (2012). Repetition, not number of sources, increases both susceptibility to misinformation and confidence in the accuracy of eyewitnesses. *Acta Psychologica, 139*, 320–326.

French, L., Garry, M., & Mori, K. (2008). You say tomato? Collaborative remembering leads to more false memories for intimate couples than for strangers. *Memory, 16*, 262–273.

French, L., R. Sutherland, and M. Garry. 2006. "Discussion affects memory for true and false childhood events." *Applied Cognitive Psychology 20*: 671–680.

Frost, P. (2000). The quality of false memory over time: Is misinformation "remembered" or "known"? *Psychonomic Bulletin & Review, 7*(3), 531–536.

Frost, P., Ingraham, M., & Wilson, B. (2002). Why misinformation is more likely to be recognised over time: A source monitoring account. *Memory, 10*(3), 179–185.

Gabbert, F., Memon, A., & Allan, K. (2003). Memory conformity: Can eyewitnesses influence each other's memories for an event? *Applied Cognitive Psychology, 17*, 533–543.

Gabbert, F., Memon, A., & Wright, D. B. (2006). Memory conformity: Disentangling the steps towards influence during a discussion. *Psychonomic Bulletin & Review, 13*, 480–485.

Gabbert, F., Memon, A., & Wright, D. B. (2007). I saw it for longer than you: The relationship between perceived encoding duration and memory conformity. *Acta Psychologica, 124*, 319–331.

Garry, M., Manning, C. G., Loftus, E. F., & Sherman, S. J. (1996). Imagination inflation: Imagining a childhood event inflates confidence that it occurred. *Psychonomic Bulletin & Review, 3*, 208–214.

Garry, M., & Wade, K. A. (2005). Actually, a picture is worth less than 45 words: Narratives produce more false memories than photographs do. *Psychonomic Bulletin & Review, 12(2)*, 359–366.

Goff, L., & Roediger, H. (1998). Imagination inflation for action events: Repeated imaginings lead to illusory recollections. *Memory & Cognition, 26*, 20–33.

Greenberg, D. L. (2004). President Bush's false 'flashbulb' memory of 9/11/01. *Applied Cognitive Psychology, 18*, 363–370.

Heaps, C., & Nash, M. P. (1999). Individual differences in imagination inflation. *Psychonomic Bulletin & Review, 6*, 313–318.

Heaps, C. M., & Nash, M. (2001). Comparing recollective experiences in true and false autobiographical memories. *Journal of Experimental Psychology: Learning, Memory, and Cognition, 27*, 920–930.

Hewitt, L. Y., Kane, R., & Garry, M., (2013). Speaking Order Predicts Memory Conformity After Accounting for Exposure to Misinformation. *Psychonomic Bulletin and Review, 20*, 558–565. doi: 10.3758/s13423-013-0377-4.

Hirst, W., Phelps, E. A., Buckner, R. L., Budson, A. E., Cuc, A., Gabrieli, J. D. E., Johnson, M. K., Lyle, K. B., Lustig, C., Mather, M., Mitchell, K. J., Meksin, R., Ochsner, K. N., Schacter, D. L., Simons, J. S., & Vaidya, C. J. (2009). Long-term retention of the terrorist attack of September 11: Flashbulb memories, event memories, and the factors that influence their retention. *Journal of Experimental Psychology: General, 138(2)*, 161–176.

Holmes, D. (1990). The evidence for repression: An examination of sixty years of research. In J. Singer (Ed.), *Repression and dissociation: Implications for personality, theory, psychopathology, and health* (pp. 85–102). Chicago, IL: University of Chicago Press.

Hovland, C. I., & Weiss, W. (1951). The influence of source credibility on communication effectiveness. *Public Opinion Quarterly, 15*, 635–650.

Howe, M. L. (2011). The adaptive nature of memory and its illusions. *Current Directions in Psychological Science, 20*, 312–315.

Hyman, I. E., Jr. & Billings, F. J. (1998). Individual differences and the creation of false childhood memories. *Memory, 6*(1), 1–20.

Hyman, I. E., Husband, T. H., & Billings, F. J. (1995). False memories of childhood experiences. *Applied Cognitive Psychology, 9*, 181–197.

Hyman, I. E., Jr. & Kleinknecht, E. E. (1999). False childhood memories: Research, theory, and applications. In L. M. Williams and V. L. Banyard (Eds.), *Trauma and memory* (pp. 175–188). Thousand Oaks, CA: Sage Publications.

Hyman, I. E., Jr. & Pentland, J. (1996). The role of mental imagery in the creation of false childhood memories. *Journal of Memory and Language, 35*(2), 101–117.

Jenkins, F., & Davies, G. (1985). Contamination of facial memory through exposure to misleading composite pictures. *Applied Cognitive Psychology, 70*, 164–176.

Johnson, M. K. (2006). Memory and reality. *American Psychologist, 61*, 760–771.

Johnson, M. K., Bransford, J. D., & Solomon, S. K. (1973). Memory for tacit implications of sentences. *Journal of Experimental Psychology, 98*, 203–205.

Johnson, M. K., Foley, M. A., Suengas, A. G., & Raye, C. L. (1988). Phenomenal characteristics of memories for perceived and imagined autobiographical events. *Journal of Experimental Psychology: General, 117*, 371–376.

Johnson, M. K., Hashtroudi, S., & Lindsay, D. S. (1993). Source monitoring. *Psychological Bulletin, 114*(1), 3–28.

Johnson, M. K., & Raye, C. L. (1981). Reality monitoring. *Psychological Review, 88*(1), 67–85.

Kumkale, G. T., & Albarracin, D. (2004). The sleeper effect in persuasion: A meta-analytic review. *Psychological Bulletin, 130*, 143–172.

Kvavilashvili, L., Mirani, J., Schlagman, S., Erskine, J. A. E., & Kornbrot, D. E. (2010). Effects of age on phenomenology and consistency of flashbulb memories of September 11 and a staged control event. *Psychology and Aging, 25*(2), 391–404.

Lambert, K., & Lilienfeld, S. (2007, October/November). Brain stains. *Scientific American Mind*, 51.

Lewandowsky, S., Stritzke, W. G. K., Oberauer, K., & Morales, M. (2005). Memory for fact, fiction, and misinformation. *Psychological Science, 16*(3), 190–195.

Lindsay, D. S. (1990). Misleading suggestions can impair eyewitnesses' ability to remember event details. *Journal of Experimental Psychology: Learning, Memory, and Cognition, 16*, 1077–1083.

Lindsay, D. S. (2007). Order effects in collaborative memory contamination? Comment on Gabbert, Memon, and Wright (2006). *Psychonomic Bulletin & Review, 14*, 1010.

Lindsay, D. S. (2008). Source monitoring. In H. L. Roediger, III (Ed.), *Cognitive psychology of memory. Vol. 2 of Learning and memory: A comprehensive reference*, 4 vols. (J. Byrne, Editor) (pp. 325 –348). Oxford: Elsevier.

Lindsay, D. S., Hagen, L., Read, J. D., Wade, K. A., & Garry, M. (2004). True photographs and false memories. *Psychological Science, 15*(3), 149–154.

Loftus, E. F. (1975). Leading questions and the eyewitness report. *Cognitive Psychology, 7*, 560–572.

Loftus, E. F. (1977). Shifting human color memory. *Memory & Cognition, 5*, 696–699.

Loftus, E. F. (1991). Made in memory: Distortions of recollection after misleading information. In. G. Bower (Ed.), *Psychology of learning and motivation, 27*, 187–215. NY: Academic Press.

Loftus, E. F. (1993). The reality of repressed memories. *American Psychologist, 48*, 518–537.

Loftus, E. F. (2005). Planting misinformation in the human mind: A 30-year investigation of the malleability of memory. *Learning & Memory, 12*, 361–366.

Loftus, E. F. (2007). Memory distortions: Problems solved and unsolved. In M. Garry and H. Hayne (Eds.), *Do justice and let the sky fall: Elizabeth Loftus and her contributions to science, law, and academic freedom* (pp.1–14). Hillsdale, NJ: Erlbaum.

Loftus, E. F., & Hoffman, H. G. (1989). Misinformation and memory: The creation of memory. *Journal of Experimental Psychology: General, 118*, 100–104.

Loftus, E. F., & Ketcham, K. (1991). *Witness for the defense: The accused, the eyewitness, and the expert who puts memory on trial.* New York: St. Martin's Press.

Loftus, E. F., & Ketcham, K. (1994). *The myth of repressed memory.* New York: St. Martin's Press.

Loftus, E. F., Miller, D. G., & Burns, H. J. (1978). Semantic integration of verbal information into a visual memory. *Journal of Experimental Psychology: Human Learning and Memory, 4*, 19–31.

Loftus, E. F., & Palmer, J. C. (1974). Reconstruction of automobile destruction: An example of the interaction between language and memory. *Journal of Verbal Learning and Verbal Behavior, 13*, 585–589.

Loftus, E. F., & Pickrell, J. (1995). The formation of false memories. *Psychiatric Annals, 25*, 720–724.

Loftus, E. F., & Zanni, G. (1975). Eyewitness testimony: The influence of wording of a question. *Bulletin of the Psychonomic Society, 5*, 86–88.

Mazzoni, G. A. L., Loftus, E. F., & Kirsch, I. (2001). Changing beliefs about implausible autobiographical events: A little plausibility goes a long way. *Journal of Experimental Psychology: Applied, 7*, 51–59.

Mazzoni, G. A. L., & Memon, A. (2003). Imagination can create false autobiographical memories. *Psychological Science, 14*, 186–188.

Mazzoni, G., Scoboria, A., & Harvey, L. (2010). Non-believed memories. *Psychological Science, 21*(9), 1334–1340.

McNally, R. J. (2003). *Remembering trauma.* Cambridge, MA: Belknap Press/Harvard University Press.

McNally, R. J., Lasko, N. B., Clancy, S. A., Macklin, M. L., Pitman, R. K., & Orr, S. P. (2004). Psychophysiological responding during script-driven imagery in people reporting abduction by space aliens. *Psychological Science, 15*, 493–497.

Meade, M. L., & Roediger, H. L. (2002). Explorations in the social contagion of memory. *Memory & Cognition, 30*, 995–100.

Neisser, U., & Harsch, N. (1992). Phantom flashbulbs: False recollections of hearing news about Challenger. In E. Winograd and U. Neisser (Eds.), *Affect and accuracy in recall: Studies of "flashbulb memories"* (pp. 9–31). Cambridge: Cambridge University Press.

Newman, E. J., & Lindsay, D. S. (2009). False memories: What the hell are they for? *Applied Cognitive Psychology, 23*, 1105–1121.

Nourkova, V. V., Bernstein D. M., & Loftus, E. F. (2004). Echo of explosions: Comparative analysis of recollections about the terrorists attacks in 1999 (Moscow) and 2001 (New York City). *Psychological Journal, 24*, 64–72.

Oeberst, A., & Blank, H. (2012). Undoing suggestive influence on memory: The reversibility of the eyewitness misinformation effect. *Cognition, 125*(2),141–159.

Okado, Y., & Stark, C. E. L. (2005). Neural activity during encoding predicts false memories created by misinformation. *Learning & Memory, 12*, 3–11.

Ost, J., Foster, S., Costall, A., & Bull, R. (2005). False reports of childhood events in appropriate interviews. Memory, 13(7), 700–710.

Paterson, H. M., & Kemp, R. I. (2006). Comparing methods of encountering post-event information: The power of co-witness suggestion. *Applied Cognitive Psychology, 20*, 1083–1099.

Pezdek, K., Finger, K., & Hodge, D. (1997). Planting false childhood memories: The role of event plausibility. *Psychological Science, 8*, 437–441.

Poole, D. A., Lindsay, D. S., Memon, A., & Bull, R. (1995). Psychotherapy and the recovery of memories of childhood sexual abuse: U.S. and British practitioners' opinions, practices, and experiences. *Journal of Consulting and Clinical Psychology, 63*, 426–437.

Porter, S., Yuille, J. C., & Lehman, D. R. (1999). The nature of real, implanted, and fabricated memories for emotional childhood events: Implications for the recovered memory debate. *Law and Human Behavior, 23*, 517–537.

Schacter, D. L., & Addis, D. R. (2007). Constructive memory: The ghosts of the past and future. *Nature, 445*, 27.

Schacter, D. L., Guerin, S. A., & St. Jacques, P. L. (2011). Memory distortion: An adaptive perspective. *Trends in Cognitive Sciences, 15*, 467–474.

Schmolck, H., Buffalo, E. A., & Squire, L. R. (2000). Memory distortions develop over time: Recollections of the O.J. Simpson trial verdict after 15 and 32 months. *Psychological Science, 11*, 39–45.

Seamon, J. G., Philbin, M. M., & Harrison, L. G. (2006). Do you remember proposing marriage to the Pepsi machine? False recollections from a campus walk. *Psychonomic Bulletin & Review, 13*, 752–756.

Sharman, S. J., Garry, M., & Beuke, C. J. (2004). Imagination or exposure causes imagination inflation. *American Journal of Psychology, 117*, 157–168.

Sharman, S. J., Manning, C. G., & Garry, M. (2005). Explain this: explaining childhood events inflates confidence for those events. *Applied Cognitive Psychology, 19*, 67–74.

Sharman, S. J., & Scoboria, A. (2009) Imagination equally influences false memories of high and low plausibility events. *Applied Cognitive Psychology, 23*, 813–827.

Simons, D. J., & Chabris, C. F. (1999). Gorillas in our midst: Sustained inattentional blindness for dynamic events. *Perception, 28*, 1059–1074.

Suddendorf, T., & Corballis, M. C. (1997). Mental time travel and the evolution of the human mind. *Genetic, Social, & General Psychology Monographs, 123*, 133–167.

Sutherland, R., & Hayne, H. (2001). The effect of postevent information on adults' eyewitness reports. *Applied Cognitive Psychology, 15*, 249–263.

Szpunar, K. K., Watson, J. M., & McDermott, K. B. (2007). Neural substrates of envisioning the future. *Proceedings of the National Academy of Sciences, 104*, 642–647.

Takarangi, M. K. T., Parker, S. L., & Garry, M. (2006). Modernizing the misinformation effect: The development of a new stimulus set. *Applied Cognitive Psychology, 20*, 1–8.

Talarico, J. M., & Rubin, D. C. (2003). Confidence, not consistency, characterizes flashbulb memories. *Psychological Science, 14*, 455–461.

Thomas, A. K., & Loftus, E. F. (2002). Creating bizarre false memories through imagination. *Memory & Cognition, 30*, 423–431.

Tousignant, J. P., Hall, D., & Loftus, E. F. (1986). Discrepancy detection and vulnerability to misleading postevent information. *Memory & Cognition, 14*, 329–338.

Vornik, L. A., Sharman, S. J., & Garry, M. (2003). The power of the spoken word: Sociolinguistic cues influence the misinformation effect. *Memory, 11*, 101–109.

Wade, K. A., Garry, M., Read, J. D., & Lindsay, D. S. (2002). A picture is worth a thousand lies: Using false photographs to create false childhood memories. *Psychonomic Bulletin & Review, 9*, 597–603.

Wade, K. A., Green, S. L., & Nash, R. A. (2010). Can fabricated evidence induce false eyewitness testimony? *Applied Cognitive Psychology, 24*, 899–908.

Weaver, C. A., III. (1993). Do you need a "flash" to form a flashbulb memory? *Journal of Experimental Psychology: General, 122*, 39–46.

Weaver, C. A., III., & Krug, K. S. (2004). Consolidation-like effects in flashbulb memories: Evidence from September 11, 2001. *American Journal of Psychology, 117*, 517–530.

Weiser, J. (2004). Photo therapy techniques in counselling and therapy—Using ordinary snapshots and photo-interactions to help clients heal their lives. *Canadian Art Therapy Association Journal, 17*, 2353.

Wright, D. B., Self, G., & Justice, C. (2000). Memory conformity: Exploring misinformation effects when presented by another person. *British Journal of Psychology, 91*, 189–202.

Wright, D. B., & Stroud, J. N. (1998). Memory quality and misinformation for peripheral and central objects. *Legal and Criminological Psychology, 3*, 273–286.

Zaragoza, M. S., & Mitchell, K. J. (1996). Repeated exposure to suggestion and the creation of false memories. *Psychological Science, 7*, 294–300.

Zaragoza, M. S., Mitchell, K. J., Payment, K., & Drivdahl, S. (2011). False memories for suggestions: The impact of conceptual elaboration. *Journal of Memory and Language, 64*(1), 18–31.

Zaragoza, M. S., Payment, K. E., Ackil, J. K., Drivdahl, S. B., & Beck, M. (2001). Interviewing witnesses: Forced confabulation and confirmatory feedback increase false memories. *Psychological Science, 12*(6), 473–47.

Zhu, B., Chen, C., Loftus, E. F., He, Q., Chen, C., Lei, X., Lin, C., & Dong, Q. (2012). Brief exposure to misinformation can lead to long-term false memories. *Applied Cognitive Psychology, 26*, 301–307.

8

Forgetting

Colleen M. Kelley

Cases of forgetting can be dramatic and even startling. For example, a colleague and I were collaborating on a number of experiments and we talked about even more experiments that went undone. During a discussion one afternoon, we hit upon a particularly wonderful idea for a study that would illustrate that the fluency or ease of generating ideas is one basis for remembering. My colleague was so excited that he promptly turned to his computer and typed a logical name for the experiment into the editor for the software he used to program experiments. Lo, an entire program opened up on the screen. Not only had he previously given an experiment this same name, it was the same experiment we now wanted to test. And not only had he already programmed the experiment, he'd already run the whole experiment! The data were a bit of a bomb, but the fact that we were so taken with the idea of the experiment (both times) may illustrate a related phenomenon, namely, that the ease of generating ideas may be mistaken for brilliance.

Everyday experience makes it painfully clear that we all too often forget things we'd like to remember and remember things we'd like to forget. People forget intentions, such as to put the wash in the dryer, to take something out of the freezer for dinner, or to send a birthday card. The consequences are frustration and inefficiency when people forget intentions or where they parked their car, or mild social awkwardness when they forget a name or that they already told the same story to a class. But the consequence of forgetting are sometimes tragic, as in several cases of parents who have forgotten to drop off their infants at daycare on the way to work and then left them in hot cars (see Einstein & McDaniel, Chapter 3, this volume).

Despite the negative consequences, forgetting may nonetheless be generally adaptive. The poet Caryn Goldberg writes movingly of forgetting the tenth anniversary of discovering that she had breast cancer, grateful "to have forgotten what I can never forget" because her thoughts were on an upcoming trip, the early flowering spring, and how good meatballs would be for dinner. Life goes on and with time the likelihood that a particular memory is needed is diminished. In fact, the very shape of the forgetting curve, with initial rapid loss of access to memories, followed by a prolonged period of slower forgetting, mirrors the demands the environment places on access to memories over time (Anderson & Schooler, 1991). We may be exquisitely adapted to an environment where the probability that an event will recur is highest immediately after it has occurred and so it is useful that it is easily accessed, but with an increasing delay there is less and less of a chance that the particular event will recur, and so less and less of a need to remember it (for an adaptive, evolutionarily informed theory of exactly *what* we need to remember, see Nairne, 2010).

The topic of forgetting is as large and wide-ranging as the topic of memory in general, so this review is necessarily selective. My aim is to review three major theories of the cause of forgetting. Most of the work on these accounts has been laboratory based and has emphasized theory over application, but at the end of each section I provide some brief reflections on practical implications. I first review disrupted consolidation as a modern incarnation of decay theory; then forgetting due to competition from other memories, as in interference and retrieval-induced forgetting; and finally, forgetting due to the loss of retrieval cues with changes of context. I also touch briefly on the possibility of motivated or intentional forgetting. These forgetting mechanisms are not mutually exclusive and a complete account of forgetting will require multiple mechanisms that reduce access to memories or completely obliterate them.

BIOLOGICAL THEORIES OF FORGETTING: DISRUPTED CONSOLIDATION

Muller and Pilzecker (1900; for a review and excerpted translations from the German, see Lechner, Squire, & Byrne, 1999; also Dewar, Cowan, & Della Sala, 2007) proposed that experienced events perseverate for a short time. Participants in their experiments studied pairs of syllables, and reported that the syllabic pairs involuntarily came to mind repeatedly between training sessions. Muller and Pilzecker noted common examples of perseveration such as when recently heard songs or recently worked on scientific

problems come to mind repeatedly, particularly when one is not occupied by some other effortful tasks and proposed that such perseveration is important for *consolidation* of the initial memory. Specifically, they proposed that effortful activity within about ten minutes of an event disrupted the process of consolidation, leading to forgetting, and presented as evidence a number of studies that found better memory for lists of syllables when people were given a short period with no mentally effortful task, compared with even very dissimilar activities such as describing landscape paintings. Muller and Pilzecker named the phenomenon *retroactive inhibition*.

Later physiological studies of memory in animals established that a process of consolidation must occur after a memory is encoded for that memory to be expressed after a delay. Consolidation can be disrupted in animals with electroconvulsive shock, drugs that disrupt protein synthesis, or surgical removal of the hippocampus, if those manipulations fall within a certain time window after the to-be-remembered event. Once that time is past, the memory appears to be immune to those disrupting treatments (McGaugh, 2000), although a newer theory of reconsolidation (Sara, 2000) proposes that when a memory is retrieved, it must be consolidated anew, and re-enters a stage of vulnerability to factors that disrupt consolidation.

The human data relevant to consolidation include studies of patients undergoing electroconvulsive shock therapy (ECT) for the treatment of profound depression or people who suffer head injuries or concussions. Patients experiencing ECT or concussion often have better memory for events farther back in time than for events immediately preceding the ECT or concussion, a pattern known as the temporal gradient of retrograde amnesia (for a review, see Brown, 2002). Although retrograde amnesia often recovers over time, the recovery is usually not complete, and events closest in time to the trauma are not recovered. The temporal gradient of amnesia has been interpreted as evidence that older memories were fully consolidated whereas more recent ones were still in the process of being consolidated when the amnesia-inducing event occurred (for a review, see Squire, 2006).

McGaugh (2000) asked why human and animal memories consolidate so slowly, noting that it cannot be the case that the biological machinery of consolidation is necessarily very slow, because working memories and even memories lasting minutes to hours are established very quickly. He proposed that slow consolidation serves an adaptive function in that it allows endogenous processes set off by the initial experience to modulate the durability of the memory. In particular, events that are emotionally arousing produce adrenal stress hormones, epinephrine, and cortisol, and these hormones enhance memory for emotional experiences in both animals and humans (McGaugh, 2004). The release of norepinephrine in the basolateral amygdala is critical for the modulation of consolidation in widespread systems of the brain, including the hippocampus, cortex, and caudate nucleus. In research with humans, consolidation processes are often invoked to account for why differences in memory for emotional versus neutral events sometimes emerge only after a delay, particularly a 24-hour delay that includes sleep (Payne & Kensinger, 2010; Sharot, Verfaellie, & Yonelinas, 2007; Walker & van der Helm, 2009).

Consolidation is also invoked when memory or a newly learned skill is better after sleep than after an equivalent amount of time spent awake. Jenkins and Dallenbach (1924) and Ekstrand (1967) argued that consolidation is disrupted by encoding new events into memory and that sleep provides a respite from new encoding. An alternative interpretation of the memory-enhancing effects of sleep is that it allows a process of replaying networks that were active during the original event (Euston, Tatsuno, & McNaughton, 2007; Ji & Wilson, 2007; Wilson & McNaughton, 1994). Forgetting might occur over the

long-term if such reactivation did not occur (Squire & Alvarez, 1995).

Opportunities for a night's sleep after learning verbal material and motor skills improves retention, but even short naps following learning retard forgetting compared with a period of wakefulness (for a review, see Diekelmann & Born, 2010). Post-event sleep reduces interference effects, even when the interfering information is presented just prior to testing the original information (Ellenbogen, Hubert, Jiang, & Stickgold, 2009). Importantly, the beneficial effects of sleep for reducing forgetting appear selective in that sleep enhances memories that have future relevance. Wilhelm, Diekelmann, Molzow, Ayoud, Molle, and Born (2011) had people memorize word pairs to a criterion, learn the locations of objects, or learn a finger-tapping sequence. When participants were told to expect a future test, sleep reduced forgetting, but not when the test was unexpected. One might question whether people who expected a test attempted to rehearse the material or practice the skill. Key evidence against a differential rehearsal process and for the role of sleep in consolidation was that only people who expected a future retrieval test showed an increase in slow oscillation activity and sleep spindles during slow-wave sleep following learning, and furthermore, there was a robust correlation between biological markers of sleep-related consolidation and retention, but again, only for people who expected a retrieval test.

Emotional information is especially likely to have future relevance for people and provides another case in which sleep reduces forgetting of relevant information. Sleep reduces forgetting of central aspects of emotional experiences, but not neutral background material. Payne, Stickgold, Swanberg, and Kensinger (2008) showed people photographs containing negative objects (a dead body, a car accident) or neutral objects, all placed on neutral backgrounds. Memory was tested after 30 minutes (in the morning or evening to control for circadian effects), or after 12 hours containing a night's sleep or a normal waking day. Time spent awake led to similar forgetting of negative objects and neutral objects. In contrast, time spent asleep selectively preserved memory for negative objects (there was a nonsignificant *increase* in memory) but not for the neutral backgrounds.

Wixted (2004) revisited the original studies of Muller and Pilzecker, which proposed that the consolidation of new experiences is disrupted when any effortful mental cognition follows the original experience in the context of the neuroscience of consolidation. Of course, one alternative to the disruptive effects of subsequent learning compared with a period of "mental quietude" is that participants were rehearsing or spontaneously reflecting back on the studied material during the period of mental quietude. As Wixted noted, later researchers attempted to prevent rehearsal in the rest condition by engaging participants in conversation, or having them read newspapers or rate cartoons (McGeoch & McDonald, 1931), which violates the period of mental quietude with new learning, a fact that may have gone unappreciated because the new learning was incidental. Wixted argued that the hypothesis that learning is disrupted by subsequent effortful mental activity fits well with the neuroscience of consolidation.

Cowan, Beschin, and Della Salla (2004) proposed that the disruptive effect of post-learning mental effort would be particularly evident in amnesiacs, as amnesia likely reflects impaired mechanisms of consolidation. Cowan et al. taught amnesic participants and age-matched controls a list of words, then either took them to a quiet room to lie down for ten minutes or kept them in the testing room doing a series of neuropsychological tests. After the filled delay, amnesic patients lived up to their diagnosis and recalled almost none of the list of words, whereas amnesiacs taken to the quiet room after learning showed quite substantial recall of the list. Similar benefits from the unfilled quiet time occurred when memory for stories was tested after an hour. During the longer

interval, the experimenter noted that some participants fell asleep, which was associated with particularly enhanced retention. The age-matched controls also showed enhanced retention when the delay was unfilled compared with filled, although the benefit was not as large as for the amnesiacs. Similar beneficial effects of an unfilled quiet interval post-learning are found in patients with mild cognitive impairment (Cowan, Beschin, Perini, & Della Sala, 2003). Later studies explored the parameters of type of interfering task (Dewar, Della Sala, Beschin & Cowan, 2010) and timing of the nonspecific interference (Dewar, Garcia, Cowan, & Della Salla, 2009). Families of the amnesiacs were so impressed by the memories established by the post-encoding quiet time that they reported trying to use the same technique at home to help their family member remember key events (Dewar et al., 2010). Dewar et al. termed their effect "nonspecific interference" and tied it to Muller and Pilzecker's idea that the consolidation of a new memory is disrupted by encoding new events.

What might be the biological underpinnings of the disruptive effects of new learning following an encoded event? Mednick, Cai, Shuman, Anagnostaras, and Wixted (2011) argue that consolidation of previously encoded events is disrupted whenever the hippocampus encodes new information. Perhaps slow-wave sleep (SWS) is not a crucial neural state for consolidation, but merely one of a number of situations when the hippocampus is closed to new encoding, but critically, not closed to the replay of recently experienced patterns of neural activity that represent the consolidation of newly learned information. The consolidation of hippocampal-dependent memories might occur opportunistically whenever the hippocampus is not otherwise occupied by encoding ongoing new experiences. Periods of quiet rest might simply be another opportunity for consolidation, as new encoding is dampened during states of quiet wakefulness.

Mednick et al. (2011) speculated that the hippocampus operates in two modes: encoding new information versus replaying old information out into the cortex for long-term system consolidation. Acetylcholine, which is lower during quiet wakefulness and SWS may "flip the switch" on the hippocampus from an encoding mode to a consolidation mode. Exposure to novel stimuli or events that signify threat or reward raises acetylcholine, which may flip the hippocampus to encoding mode. Thus, the timing of quiet wakefulness and sleep as opposed to novel and emotional stimuli following events could well determine whether the events will be consolidated and remembered or forgotten over time.

Applications of consolidation theory

One of the most important applications of consolidation theory may turn out to be more deliberate use of sleep to slow forgetting. Educators realize that sleep deprivation hurts learners' ability to attend and encode, but have perhaps thought less about the need for sleep post-learning. Expert musicians who want to maximize the effectiveness of practice sessions are meticulous about maintaining regular sleep (for a review of expertise see Ericsson & Moxley, Chapter 23, this volume), and it could be that their work at the extremes of performance has allowed them to discover the role of sleep in the consolidation of learning, as well as for optimal attention during training. Importantly, naps also confer benefits, although it will be important to establish whether that is due to recovery from the general sleep deprivation that afflicts participants, or is due to specific processes during sleep.

Whether times of quiet wakefulness also allow for memory consolidation as well as sleep is less well established, but they too could prove to have practical implications for improving memory and reducing forgetting, as illustrated in the work of Cowan, Dewar, Della Salla, and colleagues with amnesiacs and those who suffer with mild cognitive impairment. Modern life provides few moments of "mental quietude": Indeed, the stream of information often feels more like a fire hose. Moments of quiet wakefulness might be important for people undergoing intense new learning, as well as people who have impaired consolidation processes.

Disruption of consolidation may prove useful when memories are *too* accessible and repeatedly intrude into consciousness. Intrusive memories or "flashbacks" occur after particularly shocking events and can impede normal activities. A laboratory analog of traumatic events is to show participants films of gory traffic accidents depicting injury and deaths, which provoke a relatively large number of intrusive images in the ensuing week. Emily Holmes and colleagues reasoned that consolidation of images from such a film could be disrupted by performance of a demanding visual task within hours of viewing the film. Playing the game Tetris for ten minutes either half an hour (Holmes, James, Coode-Bate, & Deeprose, 2009) or four hours (Holmes, James, Kilford, & Deeprose, 2010) after viewing the accident film greatly reduced the incidence of involuntary memories recorded by participants in the following week, whereas playing a Pub Quiz game did not. Holmes and colleagues speculated that the visual-spatial demands of Tetris differentially disrupt consolidation or reconsolidation of the visual images of the traumatic film, but leave general conceptual memory of the film intact. It holds promise as a sort of "cognitive vaccine" against the flashbacks that characterize post-traumatic stress disorder.

COMPETITION CAUSES FORGETTING: INTERFERENCE THEORY AND RETRIEVAL-INDUCED FORGETTING

Research on specific interference in memory followed closely on the heels of Muller and Pilzecker's studies of the disruptive effects of general mental effort following learning.

Greater inter-task similarity of subsequently learned tasks to an original event led to worse memory for the original event. For example, McGeoch and McDonald (1931) varied the similarity of intervening lists to an originally learned list of adjectives, and found worse recall of the original list after learning a list of synonyms, compared with a list of numbers.

Researchers quickly embraced the paradigm of paired associate learning, as similarity could be varied more precisely. In paired associate learning, lists of pairs of items such as words (A–B, e.g., *dog–basket*) must be learned such that participants recall the target B when presented with the cue A. Learning different responses to the same stimuli in successive lists (A–B, A–D, e.g., *dog–basket, dog–brick*) is the interference condition, compared with the control condition in which a single list is learned, or when a list of unrelated items are learned (A–B, C–D, e.g., *dog–basket, spoon–brick*). The learning of the A–D pairs typically impairs performance for the earlier A–B pairs, which is called retroactive inhibition or interference; and the learning of the A–B pair also impairs performance for the A–D pairs, which is called proactive inhibition or interference. Forgetting was easily induced in the laboratory by such interference, with more forgetting after multiple lists than a single list and so researchers embraced interference as the major cause of forgetting (McGeoch, 1932).

The initial theory of retroactive inhibition was that the newly learned associates to the A cue created competition at the time of recall. McGeoch cited the occurrence of intrusion errors (recalling the D response while attempting to recall the initially learned B response) as evidence for such competition, although he also noted that the competition could lead to each response blocking the other, and so the responses would not even be accessed. McGeoch's theory assumed that all responses were still available even when response competition had reduced recall of the A–B list.

Proactive interference is a particularly powerful source of forgetting. In both free recall and the cued-recall laboratory paradigms, the greater the number of lists learned on prior days, the greater the forgetting of a more recently learned list, particularly for longer retention intervals such as 24 hours. The proactive interference is massive and, strikingly, occurs even when the lists are dissimilar to the critical final list, so even for paired associate lists of the form A–B, C–D, E–F, and so forth (Keppel, Postman, & Zavortink, 1968). Such proactive interference was evident in Ebbinghaus's self-study of memory, where his forgetting of lists of nonsense syllables over a 24-hour period sometimes exceeded 80 percent. When a participant was tested on a single list, forgetting over 24 hours was only about 20 percent, and the amount of forgetting increased regularly with the number of prior lists learned in an experiment (Underwood, 1957).

But what could account for forgetting over 24 hours for participants who studied only a single list, particularly in the experiments that used nonsense syllables? Materials studied in the laboratory were distinctly different from the participants' lives outside the laboratory, and so it was hard to imagine what real life-events were creating interference. Underwood and Postman (1960) attempted to identify sources of proactive and retroactive interference in the language used and encountered outside the laboratory. To do so, they varied the materials studied in the laboratory to be more or less word-like, and so potentially more or less interfered with by words encountered outside the laboratory. The results did not fit with interference as a cause of forgetting: Items learned to a criterion were forgotten equally whether they were similar or dissimilar to language that would be encountered outside the laboratory (Postman, 1961; Underwood & Keppel, 1963). A second blow against proactive interference as the sole mechanism of forgetting outside the laboratory came from Underwood and Ekstrand's (1966) study of proactive interference when learning an

A–B list was distributed across four days or massed in a single day. Remarkably, when practice on the A–B list was distributed across four days, there was much less forgetting of the A–D list than when practice of the A–B list was massed.

Despite such failures to understand why forgetting of even distinctive experimental materials occurred with 24 hours of experience outside the laboratory, the powerful effects of interfering materials in inducing forgetting continues to be a mechanism of forgetting in many theories of memory. The competition mechanism at the heart of interpretations of interference came to be conceptualized as cue overload (Watkins & Watkins, 1975). In memory models, the retrieval competition during the search of memory is captured by the ratio-rule, where the probability of retrieving a particular memory given a particular cue is a function of the strength of that particular memory divided by the sum of the strengths of all other memories associated to the cue (Shiffrin, 1970, see also the fan effect in Anderson, 1974).

In the influential SAM/REM (search of associative memory/retrieving effectively from memory) models, retrieval of a memory is a two-stage process that incorporates competition between memories. In the first phase, a retrieval cue such as "words studied in this experiment" is used to activate or sample a set of memories. The probability of sampling a particular memory is a function of its strength relative to the strengths of all other memories in the search set. Sampling is followed by recovery of those items into consciousness in a process that is dependent on the absolute strength of the item, rather than the relative strength of the item compared with its competitors. Absolute strength is a function of variables such as attention during encoding, number of repetitions, time allowed for encoding, and type of analysis applied to items.

An important exception to problems retrieving a memory due to competition among memories is when the various memories associated with a cue are integrated and interconnected (Reder & Anderson, 1980). Access to a memory is *improved* rather than *impaired* when the memory is integrated with other memories. The facilitation occurs even in classic A–B, A–D interference studies (for a review, see Anderson & McCulloch, 1999), and is typically associated with awareness of the relationship between the A–B and A–D lists. Reder and Anderson conceptualized the integration as creating a web of associations among different memories that could then mutually support retrieval, rather than individually compete in response to a cue.

Recently, Wahlheim and Jacoby (2013) showed that awareness of the relationship between a current item and an item on a prior list in an A–B, A–D interference paradigm produces facilitation at the level of individual pairs. During study of the second list, participants were told to indicate when an A–D pair reminded them of the A–B pair on the prior list. If participants were reminded of the A–B pair they showed facilitation in memory for A–D on the final test. In contrast, for pairs where reminding did not occur, participants showed interference in memory for A–D, relative to control pairs. Conscious reminding creates a recursive representation, in that the experience of the second event (A–D) contains the memory of being reminded of the first event (A–B), which allows people to judge the recency as well as frequency of events (Hintzman, 2004). More broadly, conscious reminding provides a mechanism by which people update their model of the world by detecting change (Hintzman, 2011).

DOES REMEMBERING CAUSE FORGETTING? THE CASE OF RETRIEVAL-INDUCED FORGETTING

In a seminal paper, Anderson, Bjork, and Bjork (1994) took a closer look at the evidence of strength dependent competition among memories linked to a cue. They noted that remembering may itself cause forgetting. For example, retrieving a memory strengthens the existing representation or adds a new representation to memory, and so according to the ratio rule, the likelihood that other memories associated with the same cue could be recalled will be reduced. However, in some cases, strengthening a memory through some means other than retrieving it does *not* produce impairment of other memories. Anderson et al. noted that classic studies of retroactive interference such as that by Barnes and Underwood (1959) had people learn the second list in an AB–AD design by the method of anticipation, by presenting the A item and asking them to guess the appropriate response on the first trial, then see the correct response as feedback. Perhaps it is not so much the presentation of new associations to the A cue that creates retroactive interference, but the requirement to practice retrieving new associations that led to forgetting.

To test the idea that retrieval produces forgetting of competitors, Anderson et al. (1994) invented the retrieval-induced forgetting paradigm. People studied a set of category names and six exemplars, such as Fruit–Orange, Fruit–Lemon, Fruit–Banana. In the second phase of the experiment, for some categories half the items were presented for retrieval practice, using the category plus a stem of the target word (Fruit–OR___). This procedure creates items for which retrieval was practiced (RP+), and items from the same categories for which retrieval was not practiced (RP–), as well as categories for which no exemplars underwent retrieval practice and so serve as baseline (Nrp). On the final test, participants were cued with the various category names to recall all the studied exemplars. Retrieval practice enhanced RP+ items compared with baseline items, but led to a forgetting of other unpracticed items in the same category (RP– items).

Although the overall pattern is consistent with the ratio-rule of strength dependent competition, in that testing of the RP+ items increases the strength of the association between category cues and practiced

exemplars, and so provides more competition when people attempt to use the category cue to retrieve RP– exemplars, other aspects of the data were not. Categories consisted of either strong exemplars as in the case of Fruit–Orange, or weak exemplars, such as Tree–Hickory. If impairment of RP– items were caused by strength-dependent competition, there should be more strengthening of RP+ items from weak categories, and hence more impairment of recall of RP– items from weak categories. However, retrieval practice enhanced strong and weak items to the same degree, but impaired retrieval of RP– items more for the strong items than for the weak items. Across experiments, only strong competitors suffered impairment from retrieval practice of other members of the category. Weak competitors showed no impairment, and often showed facilitation, which is contrary to a simple ratio-rule model of competition.

To account for the pattern of retrieval-induced forgetting of RP– items, Anderson et al. (1994) proposed that whenever memories interfere during attempts to retrieve a target memory, those memories are suppressed or inhibited. Later experiments found that the inhibition lasts at least 20 minutes, but is generally gone after 24 hours (Chan, 2009; MacLeod & Macrae, 2001). The very representation of the memory may be inhibited, such that even an independent cue (not the cue studied with the item, but an extra-list cue with an associative relationship to the to-be-remembered target) fails to retrieve the memory (Anderson & Spellman, 1995). The suppression of competitors appears to be a specific byproduct of retrieval, and does not necessarily occur when the items are strengthened in ways other than retrieval practice, such as by extra presentations (Bauml, 1996) or by retrieval of the category name given an exemplar (e.g., FR____–ORANGE; Anderson, Bjork, & Bjork, 2000). The strength-dependent competition instantiated in the ratio rule would predict otherwise.

Retrieval-induced forgetting has been replicated many times and with many different kinds of materials, and has been applied to a wide-ranging set of applications. Anderson (2003) argues that retrieval-induced forgetting is the major mechanism by which we forget, and that many prior studies of forgetting that have been used to argue for relative strength competition between memories actually measured retrieval-induced forgetting. Nonetheless, the claim that retrieval-induced forgetting represents inhibition of a memory representation rather than strength-dependent competition is not completely settled.

Verde (2012) reviews the status of four key predictions of the inhibition theory of retrieval-induced forgetting. First, is retrieval-induced forgetting dependent on interference during retrieval, such that only strong competitors are suppressed because only they cause interference during retrieval practice? There are cases where retrieval-induced forgetting occurs for weak as well as strong competitors (cf. Jakab & Raaijmakers, 2009; Williams & Zacks, 2001). Second, does retrieval-induced forgetting lead to inhibition of the RP– items even when they are cued with extra-list cues? Simple cue-overload and relative strength competition from the RP+ memories should not extend to extra-list or independent cues, yet retrieval-induced forgetting does occur with extra-list cues. However, some have argued that people augment the independent cues with the original cue during the final test (Camp, Pecher, Schmidt, & Zeelenberg, 2009) and so they are using a cue that is "overloaded," rather than a truly independent cue. Such spontaneous use of the original cue may only be possible when there is an association between it and the independent cue (Huddleston & Anderson, 2012). Further challenges to the notion that the representations of the RP– have been inhibited come from the fact that those items can be accessed using other cues, such as word fragment completion or word fragment cued recall (Butler, Williams, Zacks, & Maki, 2001). Perfect, Stark, Tree, Moulin, Ahmed, and Hutter (2004) presented a unique face along with each category-exemplar pair during study, and then presented the category names without the faces as cues during retrieval practice. They found no evidence of retrieval-induced forgetting when recall was cued with the face on the final test.

The third key prediction of the inhibition theory of retrieval-induced forgetting reviewed by Verde was: Is retrieval-induced forgetting truly retrieval dependent? Fourth, is forgetting truly independent of strengthening of competitive memories by means other than retrieval? Relative strength models predict that any method of strengthening competitive memories, either via retrieval practice or via better encoding of RP+ items, would be to the detriment of RP– items. Strengthening items via repeated study does not necessarily reduce access to unstrengthened items (Ciranni & Shimamura, 1999), although it can, even when covert retrieval during re-study is unlikely (Verde, 2009).

As noted above, Anderson et al. found no retrieval-induced forgetting when retrieval practice was of the category, rather than the exemplar (e.g., FR___–ORANGE), even though such category retrieval practice should have strengthened the category–exemplar associations of practiced items, and so reduced recall of RP– items. Raaijmakers and Jakab (2012) noted that retrieval of the category when cued with exemplars may have been too simple a task in Anderson et al. (1994), which led to minimal strengthening of the Fruit–Orange association. Raaijmakers and Jakab made retrieval more difficult and found that retrieval of the category when given an exemplar did indeed decrease recall of RP– exemplars when cued with the category name, in accord with strength dependent competition models. Raaijmakers and Jakab also used a version of the SAM model (Raaijmakers & Shiffrin, 1981) that relies on relative strength as a source of forgetting to successfully model the results of Anderson et al. (2000), by assuming that competitive retrieval practice strengthens practiced items much more than noncompetitive retrieval practice or additional study trials.

In summary, there is a current controversy about whether retrieval-induced forgetting can be explained by strength dependent competition or demands a new construct of inhibition (Raaijmakers & Jakab, 2013). Whether retrieval-induced forgetting produces inhibition of items that compete for retrieval, or whether it is a process that produces particularly strong competitive memories will probably require more precise measures than recall (Bauml, Zellner, & Vilimek, 2005), as well as the use of more precise predictions derived from modeling (Verde, 2009).

To further explore how executive control over memory retrieval can produce forgetting, Anderson and Green (2001) invented the think–no think paradigm. Participants first studied a set of pairs of cue-targets words to a criterion. In a second phase, they engaged in retrieval practice of the "think" pairs, recalling the targets when presented with the cues. However, they were signaled to not recall other items even though the cues were presented repeatedly. These "no think" items showed a dose dependent loss of accessibility on a final test, when cued with either the original cue or an independent extra-list cue. The forgetting to the extra-list cue was interpreted as a case of inhibition of the representation of the "no think" items.

What do people do when told not to remember on the no think trials? Clearly one strategy is to think of something else, which might produce retrieval competition. Hertel and Calcatera (2005) showed that people are better able to comply with the no think instructions if they are given substitute thoughts to focus on during a no think trial, such as learning to think of "vehicle" when cued with "security" rather than the studied target "officer," which could produce forgetting due to relative strength competition. Levy and Anderson (2008) asked participants what strategies they used on the "no think" trials and found a variety of reports, including thinking of something else, retrieving a personal memory, perceptual focusing on the cue word, and "mind blanking." Different strategies may produce later forgetting of

the no think target according to different mechanisms, which is a promising avenue for research (for a review, see Anderson & Huddleston, 2011).

Applications of competition theory

Competition among memories linked to a particular cue is an important source of forgetting, whether due to simple strength-based competition or competition among memories when one is retrieved at the expense of others. Retrieval of some memories is a particularly potent source of forgetting other memories and the effects are not restricted to simple verbal materials but scale up to autobiographical memories. Coman, Manier, and Hirst (2009) had New York residents selectively retrieve their memories of September 11 and the destruction of the World Trade Center. Un-retrieved (RP–) memories from categories of experience where retrieval of other memories had been practiced suffered retrieval-induced forgetting in the form of slower recognition latencies, and a similar effect occurred even in free-flowing conversations between two people. Hearing someone recount a particular aspect of a shared event may induce retrieval of one's own memory and so create retrieval-induced forgetting.

Competition among memories can cause massive forgetting even of emotional and distinctive material. Smith and Moynan (2008) attempted to capture the situation where across an extended period, such as a childhood summer camp, a single distinctive negative episode (of abuse) is surrounded by recurring positive and neutral events (camp-outs, sing-alongs, swimming, games). Could those recurring events bias retrieval away from the negative event? Participants initially encoded 24 categorized lists of words by rating them for typicality. Three critical lists were either negative (diseases, curse words, death-related), or neutral, and the rest were filler lists. Then, in the interference condition, people were exposed repeatedly to the filler lists but not the critical lists (people in the control condition did nonverbal tasks unrelated to any of the categories). Finally, people were asked to recall all the categories. Forgetting of the critical lists due to interference from the far more accessible filler lists was substantial. Recall of the death category dropped from over 70 percent in the control condition to less than 10 percent in the interference condition (Experiment 2).

Motivated forgetting of unpleasant or even traumatic events could arise from deliberate attempts to suppress retrieval of a memory, as in the think–no think paradigm. Anderson and Huddleston (2011) speculate that deliberate suppression would be particularly useful when people want to forget an event but must continue to live with reminders of it, as when a child continues to live with a parent who has abused him or her. Processes and strategies seen in the no-think paradigm such as shifting attention to other thoughts, inhibition, or control over entering retrieval mode could reduce the likelihood of remembering a traumatic event even in the presence of a cue. A person with psychogenic amnesia showed far more forgetting of no think items in the think–no think procedure than did control participants (Tramoni, Aubert-Khalfa, Guye, Ranjeva, Felician, & Ceccaldi, 2009), even to independent cues, which may be a case of particular expertise in suppressing retrieval.

In educational contexts, we generally want to improve memory rather than forget, and both relative strength competition and retrieval-induced forgetting can be eliminated at the point of encoding by increased integration. When students can form an integrated situation model of a text, practicing retrieval of a subset of material enhances retrieval even of the unpracticed material, particularly after a 24-hour delay (Chan, 2009; for a review of the benefits of testing, see McDermott, Arnold, & Nelson, Chapter 11, this volume). But for students who struggle with a text and never achieve an integrated representation, quizzes on a subset of the material could enhance tested facts at the expense of related material, at least over the short-term. Thus the comprehension difficulties of poorer students could be compounded by memory problems due to interference.

CONTEXT CHANGE AS A THEORY OF FORGETTING

Memory retrieval is cue-driven and access to memories is optimal when the cues at retrieval are those that were encoded at test (Tulving & Thomson, 1973) particularly when the cue is not overloaded with relations to other items. The final theory of forgetting reviewed here holds that context changes between the experience of an event and the later attempt to retrieve the event, and so retrieval of the event suffers because of the missing contextual cues. Context is an extremely broad term, referring to internal and external information consciously experienced that is extra to the core of the event, including the temporal context such as time of day or time of year, environmental contexts including location, the presence of other people, internal contexts such as hunger, fatigue, mood, or psychoactive drug states, and ongoing trains of thoughts such as daydreaming (for a review of environmental context effects, see Smith, Chapter 10, this volume). Global contexts are slow-changing factors such as environment and internal states such as mood, hunger, and fatigue. Local contexts change more rapidly, and include the task being performed, reflections or memories prompted by a prior word in an experiment or even the background colors or background photos present on the screen. Any of these aspects of context can serve as a cue for retrieval, and the absence of any one contextual cue can reduce the probability of retrieval of core information about an event.

As is true of consolidation and interference theory, context change as a cause of forgetting has a long history. W. R. Wilson (cited in Smith & Guthrie, 1921) found that testing participants' memory for lists of non-sense syllables in the same location (in the laboratory or out of doors) or with pepper-mint oil that had been present during study led to better memory than when the location or ambient odor was changed between study and test. McGeoch's (1942) interference theory of forgetting included changed con-text as a mechanism for forgetting (see also McGovern, 1964).

Smith and Vela (2001) found the effect size in environmental context reinstate-ment studies to be approximately $d = .23$, with larger effect sizes when the retention intervals were longer (one day to a week, $d = .63$), and when the means of encoding material originally did not provide alterna-tive associative relations to aid retrieval (d represents the difference between two means divided by the standard deviation of the data). When more contextual elements differ between encoding and retrieval there is more forgetting. Studies that changed environmental context and the experimenter showed more forgetting ($d = .62$) than studies that changed environmental context but kept the same experimenter ($d = .26$). Several of the studies varied encoding and retrieval in particularly immersive ways: Godden and Baddeley (1975) had divers learn a list of words sitting 20 feet underwater or on the beach, and found better memory when the test was in the same rather than a different context ($d = .91$). Likewise, being tested at home for a list of words presented in the laboratory reduced recognition memory sub-stantially ($d = 1.06$; Canas & Nelson, 1986). Isarida and Isarida (2004) manipulated envi-ronmental context, task context (the tasks of doing addition problems or moving beans among cups with chopsticks was interposed between sets of studied words), or both between study and free recall of a list of words. The context reinstatement effect size for the combined cues of environment and task was much larger ($d = .80$) than the addi-tive effects of environment alone ($d = .35$) and task alone ($d = .02$). Contextual cues

appear to have multiplicative effects on the likelihood of successful retrieval.

Even when context has been changed between encoding and retrieval, people can mentally reinstate the original context and gain back the loss of memories due to con-text change (Smith, 1979). Such mental reinstatement of context is an important part of deliberate memory search (Burgess & Shallice, 1996). However, people do not engage in context reinstatement to the fullest extent possible, given that experimenter-guided context reinstatement produces sub-stantial gains in memory. There are likely important individual differences and devel-opmental differences in the strategic use of mental context to guide retrieval.

Just as mentally reinstating context can be used to enhance remembering, mentally changing one's context can be used to enhance forgetting. Directed forgetting refers to a phenomenon in which people are asked to memorize a list of words, and then told "that was just for practice, forget that list and get ready for the real list." The partici-pants then memorize a second list of words, but after a delay, they are surprised with a request to recall the first list of words. In comparison with a Remember control group that is told after the first list "That was the first list of words to remember, get ready for the next list," participants in the Forget con-dition show worse memory for the first list.

Directed forgetting is quite a puzzle, and in an effort to gain insight into the mecha-nism that produces such intentional forget-ting, Lili Sahakyan (reported in Sahakyan & Kelley, 2002) obtained protocols from participants who showed directed forgetting, and noticed that people reported attempting to "clear their heads" by thinking of some-thing totally unrelated to the experiment. One participant reported that she thought about her sister's upcoming wedding, and her own plans to travel home to be fitted for her bridesmaid's dress. These reports represented a self-directed mental context change. In several experiments, Sahakyan and Kelley

(2002) showed that a mental context change between studying lists of words evoked by instructions to imagine "what you would do if you were invisible" or to "draw the rooms in your parents' house and sketch out the furniture" led to forgetting of the first list of words when recall was requested after studying the second list of words, and the magnitude of forgetting was similar to that obtained by directed forgetting instructions. The imaginary changes of context, either spontaneously used as a means of forgetting by participants in directed forgetting experiments, or evoked by experimental instructions, led to worse memory because of the mismatch between the encoding context and the context present at test. Better encoding of context with items *increases* the amount of directed forgetting (Sahakyan, Delaney, & Waldrum, 2008). As in the case of environmental context effects, greater change of mental contexts produces greater forgetting (Delaney, Sahakyan, Kelley, & Zimmerman, 2010). Mind-wandering to very different contexts may be particularly disruptive to memory for what just happened in a meeting or conversation.

Many models of memory hold that temporal and spatial context is routinely encoded along with the content of an event (Anderson & Bower, 1972; Raaijmakers & Shiffrin, 1981). To account for why forgetting increases over time, some models assume context changes more after a long time than a short time, modeling context as a pool of elements that are randomly fluctuating in and out of an active state (Bower, 1972; Estes, 1955). The context at the time of encoding is assumed to be the most effective retrieval cue, but the context cue at test differs more with a longer passage of time. For example, Mensink and Raaijmakers (1988) incorporated contextual fluctuation or context drift over time into a SAM-like model that accounts for many phenomena from interference studies. A second source of forgetting in their model is the strength-dependent competition between memories during the process of retrieval.

The temporal context model or TCM (Howard & Kahana, 2002) is a model of context effects on memory in which contextual change is not due to random drift, but rather, studying an item in an experiment leads to the retrieval of its pre-experimental context, which then drives contextual change. Each newly studied item retrieves its pre-experimental context (seeing the word "apple" might make you think of the last time you ate an apple), and the retrieved context is then incorporated into the current representation of context in the experiment. When an item is recalled at test, its pre-experimental context and studied context is also retrieved. This retrieved context then serves as the retrieval cue for the next attempt. TCM can account for several interesting dynamics during recall. For example, because contiguous items share context during encoding, after retrieving an item and its context the next item to be recalled is more likely to have been at a lag of $n + 1$ or $n - 1$ during encoding than more distant lags (the lag CRP function). The model also accounts for the forward bias in recall order, in that the most likely next item to be recalled is the item that was originally studied at lag $n + 1$. This forward bias occurs because the context when item n is studied is more similar to the context when item $n + 1$ is studied than when earlier items were studied because studying item n drives context change as its pre-experimental context is added to the ongoing contextual representation for item $n + 1$. The TCM model scales up from item context to more global contexts (for a review, see Kahana, Howard, & Polyn, 2008). A recent version of TCM incorporates representations of more global context with slowly changing features that would represent contextual differences such as being hungry one day but not another in a multi-session experiment (Sederberg, Gershman, Polyn, & Norman, 2011). Key to all versions of TCM is that experiences drive changes in mental context over time and greater context change, rather than time itself, produces forgetting.

Applications of contextual change theory

Contextual change across a lifespan involves a scale of change that far exceeds laboratory demonstrations and encompasses additional dimensions such as changes to one's self-concept. Moffitt and her colleagues (2010) recently discovered that nearly half of all people who once suffered from a major psychiatric disorder such as depression, anxiety, alcohol or drug abuse forget those episodes when asked about them during a clinical interview. Moffitt et al. (2010) proposed that such forgetting happens particularly for people who experience a single episode of a disorder and then move on to a period of improved mental health. Current views of the self may differ so much from past views of the self that memories of the earlier psychiatric disorder are forgotten.

In a study that had people review events recorded in old diaries, Lindsay and Read (2006) found similar cases of people forgetting major childhood events including events that extended over time such as holding different political views or being depressed. The changes in context from childhood to adulthood include where one lives, roles (middle-schooler versus professional; child versus parent), the important people in one's life, and the context provided by recent experiences. Given that memory cues have multiplicative rather than additive effects, loss of multiple cues can lead one to forget even major life-events.

One application of the context theory of forgetting is in the domain of eyewitness testimony. Context reinstatement is a key part of the Cognitive Interview, a method of interviewing eyewitnesses invented by Geiselman and Fisher that leads to much better recall of correct information with relatively small increases in the recall of incorrect details (see Fisher, Schreiber Compo, Rivard, & Hirn, Chapter 31, this volume; Fisher, Geiselman, & Amador, 1989; Geiselman, Fisher, MacKinnon, & Holland, 1985; Memon, Meissner, & Fraser, 2010).

Older adults benefit even more from the Cognitive Interview than do younger adults, which might reflect an age-related deficit in active retrieval processes such as reinstating context.

ONE FORGETTING MECHANISM OR MORE?

The mechanisms of forgetting reviewed here are not exclusive, and it is likely that more than one is needed for a complete theory of forgetting, as in most current cognitive models of memory. The physiological evidence for decay and processes of disrupted consolidation are on a different level of analysis from cognitive processes such as competition and loss of contextual cues. It would be remarkable if the human brain operated according to very different biological memory mechanisms from other mammalian species. However, some of the human behavioral data interpreted as evidence for disrupted consolidation may be alternatively described as due to other cognitive processes, as noted by Cowan et al. (2004). For example, moving amnesiacs to a quiet dark room after learning a list of words may dramatically increase the distinctiveness of the context in which the list appeared and reduce interference from other tasks in the experiment. Lewandowsky, Ecker, Farrell, and Brown (2012) model a number of effects that are classic to consolidation theory including the temporal gradient of retroactive interference and illustrate how those effects are compatible with a model where loss of temporal distinctiveness over time determines forgetting. Sederberg et al. (2011) show how variations in context can account for patterns of memory errors that some have taken as an indication of alterations made to memories during reconsolidation (Hupbach, Gomez, Hardt, & Nadel, 2007). Conflicts between accounts of forgetting should ultimately sharpen our understanding of forgetting both theoretically and practically.

REFERENCES

Anderson, J. R. (1974). Retrieval of propositional information from long-term memory. *Cognitive Psychology, 6*, 451–474.

Anderson, J. R., & Bower, G. H. (1972). Recognition and retrieval processes in free recall. *Psychological Review, 79*, 97–123.

Anderson, J. R., & Schooler, L. J. (1991). Reflections of the environment in memory. *Psychological Science, 2*, 396–408.

Anderson, M. C. (2003). Rethinking interference theory: Executive control and the mechanisms of forgetting. *Journal of Memory and Language, 49*, 215–445.

Anderson, M. C., Bjork, E. L., & Bjork. R. A. (1994). Remembering can cause forgetting: Retrieval dynamics in long-term memory. *Journal of Experimental Psychology: Learning, Memory, and Cognition, 20*, 1063–1087.

Anderson, M. C., Bjork, E. L., & Bjork. R. A. (2000). Retrieval-induced forgetting: Evidence for a recall-specific mechanism. *Psychonomic Bulletin & Review, 7*, 522–530.

Anderson, M. C., & Green, C. (2001). Suppressing unwanted memories by executive control. *Nature, 410*, 366–369.

Anderson, M. C., & Huddleston, E. (2011). Towards a cognitive and neurobiological model of motivated forgetting. In Belli, R. F. (Ed.), *True and false recovered memories: Toward a reconciliation of the debate*. Nebraska Symposium on Motivation, Volume 58, New York: Springer, pp. 53–120.

Anderson, M. C., & McCulloch, K. C. (1999). Integration as a general boundary condition on retrieval-induced forgetting. *Journal of Experimental Psychology: Learning, Memory, and Cognition*, 25, 608–629.

Anderson, M. C., & Spellman, B. A. (1995). On the status of inhibitory mechanisms in cognition: Memory retrieval as a model case. *Psychological Review, 102*, 68–100.

Barnes, J. M., & Underwood, B. J. (1959) "Fate" of first-list associations in transfer theory. *Journal of Experimental Psychology, 58*, 97–105.

Bauml, K -H. (1996). Revisiting an old issue: Retroactive interference as a function of the degree of original and interpolated learning. *Psychonomic Bulletin & Review, 3(3)*, 380–384.

Bauml, K -H., Zellner, M., & Vilimek, R. (2005). When remembering causes forgetting: Retrieval-induced forgetting as recovery failure. *Journal of Experimental Psychology: Learning, Memory, & Cognition, 31*, 1221–1234.

Bower, G. H. (1972). Stimulus-sampling theory of encoding variability. In E. Martin and A. Melton (Eds.), *Coding theory in learning and memory*. New York: Academic Press.

Brown, A. (2002). Consolidation theory and retrograde amnesia in humans, *Psychonomic Bulletin & Review, 9*, 403–425.

Burgess, P. W., & Shallice, T. (1996). Confabulation and control of recollection. *Memory, 4*, 359–411.

Butler, K. M., Williams, C. C., Zacks, R. T., & Maki, R. H. (2001). A limit on retrieval-induced forgetting. *Memory & Cognition, 27*, 1314–1319.

Camp, G., Pecher, D., Schmidt, H. G., & Zeelenberg, R. (2009). Are independent probes truly independent? *Journal of Experimental Psychology: Learning, Memory, and Cognition, 35*, 934–942.

Canas, J. J., & Nelson, D. L. (1986). Recognition and environmental context: The effect of testing by phone. *Bulletin of the Psychonomic Society, 24*, 407–409.

Chan, J. C. K. (2009). When does retrieval induce forgetting and when does it induce facilitation? Implications for retrieval inhibition, testing effect, and text processing. *Journal of Memory and Language, 61*, 153–170.

Ciranni, M. A. L., & Shimamura, A. P. (1999). Retrieval-induced forgetting in episodic memory. *Journal of Experimental Psychology: Learning, Memory, and Cognition, 25*, 1403–1414.

Coman, A., Manier, D., & Hirst, W. (2009). Forgetting the unforgettable through conversation: Socially shared retrieval-induced forgetting of September 11 memories. *Psychological Science, 20*, 627–633.

Cowan, N. Beschin, N., & Della Salla, S. (2004). Verbal recall in amnesiacs under conditions of diminished retroactive interference. *Brain, 127*, 825–834.

Cowan, N., Beschin, N., Perinia, M., & Della Sala, S. (2005). Just lying there, remembering: Improving recall of prose in amnesic patients with mild cognitive impairment by minimizing interference. *Memory, 13*, 435–440.

Delaney, P. F., Sahakyan, L., Kelley, C. M., & Zimmerman, C. A. (2010). Remembering to forget: The amnesic effect of daydreaming. *Psychological Science, 21*, 1036–1042.

Dewar, M. T., Cowan, N., & Della Salla, S. (2007). Forgetting due to retroactive interference: A fusion of Muller and Pllzecker's (1900) early insights into everyday forgetting and recent research on anterograde amnesia. *Cortex, 43*, 616–634.

Dewar, M., Della Salla, S, Beschin, N., & Cowan, N. (2010). Profound retroactive interference in anterograde amnesia: What interferes? *Neuropsychology*, *24*, 357–367.

Dewar, M., Garcia, Y., Cowan, N., & Della Sala, S. (2009). Delaying interference enhances memory consolidation in amnesic patients. *Neuropsychology*, *23*, 27–634.

Diekelmann, S., & Born, J. (2010). The memory function of sleep. *Nature Reviews Neuroscience*, *11*, 114–126.

Ekstrand, B. R. (1967). Effect of sleep on memory. *Journal of Experimental Psychology*, *75*, 64–72.

Ellenbogen, J. M., Hulbert, J. C., Jiang, Y., & Stickgold, R. (2009). The sleeping brain's influence on verbal memory: Boosting resistance to interference. *PLOS ONE*, *4*, 1–4.

Estes, W. K. (1955). Statistical theory of spontaneous recovery and regression. *Psychological Review*, *62*, 145–154.

Euston, D. R., Tatsuno, M., & McNaughton, B. L. (2007). Fast-forward playback of recent memory sequences in prefrontal cortex during sleep. *Science*, *318*, 1147–1150.

Fisher, R. P., Geiselman, R. E., & Amador, M. (1989). Field test of the cognitive interview: Enhancing the recollection of actual victims and interviewees of crime. *Journal of Applied Psychology*, *74*, 722–727.

Geiselman, R. E., Fisher, R. P., MacKinnon, D. P., & Holland, H. L. (1985). Eyewitness memory enhancement in the police interview: Cognitive retrieval mnemonics versus hypnosis. *Journal of Applied Psychology*, *70*, 401–412.

Godden, D. R., & Baddeley, A. (1975).Context-dependent memory in two natural environments: On land and underwater. *British Journal of Psychology*, *66*, 325–331.

Hertel, P. T., & Calcaterra, G. (2005). Intentional forgetting benefits from thought substitution. *Psychonomic Bulletin & Review*, *12*, 484–489.

Hintzman, D. L. (2004). Judgment of frequency versus recognition confidence: Repetition and recursive reminding. *Memory & Cognition*, *32*, 336–350.

Hintzman, D. L. (2011). Research strategy in the study of memory: Fads, fallacies, and the search for the "coordinates of truth". *Perspectives on Psychological Science*, *6*, 253–271.

Holmes, E. A., James, E. L., Coode-Bate, T., & Deeprose, C. (2009). Can playing the computer game "Tetris" reduce the build-up of flashbacks for trauma? A proposal from cognitive science. *PLOS ONE*, *4*, e4153.

Holmes, E. A., James, E. L., Kilford, E. J., & Deeprose, C. (2010). Key steps in developing a cognitive vaccine against traumatic flashbulbs: Visuospatial Tetris versus verbal Pub Quiz. *PLOS ONE*, *5*, e13706.

Howard, M. W., & Kahana, M. J. (2002). A distributed representation of temporal context. *Journal of Mathematical Psychology*, *46*, 269–299.

Huddleston, E., & Anderson, M. C. (2012). Reassessing critiques of the independent probe method for studying inhibition. *Journal of Experimental Psychology: Learning, Memory, and Cognition*, *38*(5), 1408–1418. doi 10.1037/a0027092.

Hupbach, A., Gomez, R., Hardt, O., & Nadel, L. (2007). Reconsolidation of episodic memories: A subtle reminder triggers integration of new information. *Learning & Memory*, *14*, 47–53.

Isarida, T., & Isarida, T. K. (2004). Effects of environmental context manipulated by the combination of place and task on free recall. *Memory*, *12*, 376–384.

Jakab, E., & Raaijmakers, J. G. W. (2009). The role of item strength in retrieval-induced forgetting. *Journal of Experimental Psychology: Learning, Memory, and Cognition*, *35*, 607–617.

Jenkins, J. G., & Dallenbach, K. M. (1924). Oblivescence during sleep and waking. *American Journal of Psychology*, *35*, 605–612.

Ji, D. Y., & Wilson, M. A. (2007). Coordinated memory replay in the visual cortex and hippocampus during sleep. *Nature Neuroscience*, *10*, 100–107.

Kahana, M. J., Howard, M. W., & Polyn, S. M. (2008). Associative retrieval processes in episodic memory. In H. L. Roediger III (Ed.), *Cognitive psychology of memory*. Vol. 2 of *Learning and memory: A comprehensive reference*, 4 vols. (J. Byrne, Ed.). Oxford: Elsevier.

Keppel, G., Postman, L., & Zavortink, B. (1968). Studies of learning to learn VIII: Influence of massive amounts of training upon learning and retention of paired-associate lists. *Journal of Verbal Learning and Verbal Behavior*, *7*, 790–796.

Lechner, H. A., Squire, L. R., & Byrne, J. H. (1999). 100 years of consolidation—Remembering Muller and Pilzecker. *Learning & Memory*, *6*, 77–87.

Levy, B. J., & Anderson, M. C. (2008). Individual differences in the suppression of unwanted memories: The executive deficit hypothesis. *Acta Psychologica*, *127*, 623–635.

Lewandowsky, S., Ecker, U. K. H., Farrell, S., & Brown, G. D. A. (2012). Models of cognition and constraints from neuroscience: A case study involving consolidation. *Australian Journal of Psychology*, *64*, 37–45.

Lindsay, D. S., & Read, J. D. (2006). Adults' memories of long-past events. In G. -G. Nilson, and N. Ohta (Eds.), *Memory and Society: Psychological Perspectives* (pp. 51–72). Hove, UK: Psychology Press.

MacLeod, M. D., & Macrae, C. N. (2001). Gone but not forgotten: The transient nature of retrieval-induced forgetting. *Psychological Science*, *12*, 148–152.

McGaugh, J. L. (2000). Memory—A century of consolidation. *Science, 287,* 248–251.

McGeoch, J. A. (1932). Forgetting and the law of disuse. *Psychological Review, 39,* 352–370.

McGeoch, J. A. (1942). *The psychology of human learning.* New York: Longmans, Green.

McGeoch, J. A., & McDonald, W. T. (1931). Meaningful relation and retroactive inhibition. *The American Journal of Psychology, 43,* 579–588.

McGovern, J. B. (1964). Extinction of associations in four transfer paradigms. *Psychological Monographs: General and Applied, 78*(16), 1–21.

Mednick, S. C., Cai, D. J., Shuman, T., Anagnostaras, S., & Wixted, J. T. (2011). An opportunistic theory of cellular and systems consolidation. *Trends in Neurosciences, 34,* 504–514.

Memon, A., Meissner, C. A., & Fraser, J. (2010). The Cognitive Interview: A meta-analytic review and study space analysis of the past 25 years. *Psychology, Public Policy, and Law, 16,* 340–372.

Mensink, G. J. M., & Raaijmakers, J. G. W. (1988). A model of interference and forgetting. *Psychological Review, 95,* 434–455.

Moffitt, T. E., Caspi, A., Taylor, A., Kokaua, J., Milne, B. J., Polanczyk, G., & Poulton, R. (2010). How common are common mental disorders. Evidence that lifetime prevalence rates are doubled by prospective versus retrospective ascertainment. *Psychological Medicine, 40,* 899–909.

Nairne, J. S. (2010). Adaptive memory: Evolutionary constraints on remembering. In B. H. Ross (Ed.), *The psychology of learning and motivation,* Vol. 53, (pp.1–32). Burlington: Academic Press..

Payne, J. D., & Kensinger, E. A. (2010). Sleep's role in the consolidation of emotional episodic memories. *Current Directions in Psychological Science, 19,* 290–295.

Payne, J. D., Stickgold, R., Swanberg, K, & Kensinger, E. A. (2008). Sleep preferentially enhances memory for emotional components of scenes. *Psychological Science, 18,* 781–788.

Perfect, T. J., Stark, L. Tree, J. J., Moulin, C. J. A., Ahmed, L., & Hutter, R. (2004). Transfer appropriate forgetting: The cue-dependent nature of retrieval induced forgetting. *Journal of Memory and Language, 51,* 399–417.

Raaijmakers, J. G. W., & Jakab, E. (2012). Retrieval-induced forgetting without competition. Testing the retrieval-specificity assumption of the inhibition theory. *Memory & Cognition, 40,* 19–27.

Raaijmakers, J. G. W., & Jakab, E. (2013). Rethinking inhibition theory: On the problematic status of the inhibition theory for forgetting. *Journal of Memory and Language, 68,* 98–122.

Raaijmakers, J. G. W., & Shiffrin, R. M. (1981). Search of associative memory, *Psychological Review, 88,* 93–134.

Reder, L. M., & Anderson, J. R. (1980). A partial resolution of the paradox of interference: The role of integrating knowledge. *Cognitive Psychology, 12,* 447– 472.

Sahakyan, L., Delaney, P. F., & Waldrum, E. R. (2008). Intentional forgetting is easier after two "Shots" than one. *Journal of Experimental Psychology: Learning, Memory, and Cognition, 34,* 408–414.

Sahakyan, L., & Kelley, C. M. (2002). A contextual change account of the directed forgetting effect. *Journal of Experimental Psychology: Learning, Memory, and Cognition, 28,* 1064–1072.

Sara, S. J. (2000). Retrieval and reconsolidation: Toward a neurobiology of remembering. *Learning & Memory, 7,* 73–84.

Sederberg, P. B., Gershman, S. J., Polyn, S. M, & Norman, K. A. (2011). Human memory reconsolidation can be explained using the temporal context model. *Psychonomic Bulletin & Review, 18,* 455–468.

Sharot, T., Verfaellie, M., & Yonelinas, A. P. (2007). How emotion strengthens the recollective experience: A time-dependent hippocampal process. *PLOS ONE, 10,* 1–10.

Shiffrin, R. M. (1970). Memory search. In D. A. Norman (Ed.), *Models of memory* (pp. 375–447), Academic Press: New York.

Smith, S. M. (1979). Remembering in and out of context. *Journal of Experimental Psychology: Human Memory & Learning, 5,* 460–471.

Smith, S. M., Glenberg, A., & Bjork, R. A. (1978). Environmental context and human memory. *Memory & Cognition, 6,* 342–353.

Smith, S., & Guthrie, E. R. (1921). *General psychology in terms of behavior.* New York: D. Appleton and Company.

Smith, S. M., & Moynan, S. C. (2008). Forgetting and recovering the unforgettable. *Psychological Science, 19,* 462–468.

Smith, S. M., & Vela, E. (2001). Environmental context-dependent memory: A review and meta-analysis. *Psychonomic Bulletin & Review, 8,* 203–220.

Squire, L. R. (2006). Lost forever or temporarily misplaced? The long debate about the nature of memory impairment. *Learning & Memory, 13,* 522–529.

Squire, L. R., & Alvarez, P. (1995). Retrograde amnesia and memory consolidation: A neurobiological perspective. *Current Opinion in Neurobiology, 5,* 169–177.

Tramoni, E., Aubert-Khalfa, S., Guye, M., Ranjeva, J. P., Felician, O., & Ceccaldi, M. (2009). Hypo-retrieval and hyper-suppression mechanisms in functional amnesia. *Neuropsychologia, 47*, 611–624.

Tulving, E., & Thomson, D. M. (1973). Encoding specificity and retrieval processes in episodic memory. *Psychological Review, 80*, 352–373.

Underwood, B. J. (1957). Interference and forgetting. *Psychological Review, 64*, 49–60.

Underwood, B. J., & Ekstrand, B. R. (1966). An analysis of some shortcomings in the interference theory of forgetting. *Psychological Review, 73*, 540–549.

Underwood, B. J., & Keppel, G. (1963). Retention as a function of degree of learning and letter-sequence interference. *Psychological Monographs, 77*, Whole No. 567.

Underwood, B. J., & Postman, L. (1960). Extra-experimental sources of interference in forgetting. *Psychological Review, 67*, 73–95.

Verde, M. F. (2009). The list-strength effect in recall: Relative-strength competition and retrieval inhibition may both contribute to forgetting. *Journal of Experimental Psychology: Learning, Memory and Cognition, 35*, 205–220.

Verde, M. F. (2012). Retrieval-induced forgetting and inhibition: A critical review. In B. H. Ross (Ed.), *The psychology of learning and motivation, Vol. 56* (pp. 47–80). New York: Academic Press.

Wahlheim, C. N., & Jacoby, L. L. (2013). Remembering change: The critical role of recursive remindings in proactive effects of memory. *Memory and Cognition, 41*(1), 1–15.

Walker, M. P., & van der Helm, E. (2009). The role of sleep in emotional brain processing. *Psychological Bulletin, 135*, 731–748.

Watkins, O. C., & Watkins, M. J. (1975). Buildup of proactive inhibition as a cue-overload effect. *Journal of Experimental Psychology: Human Learning and Memory, 104*, 442–452.

Wilhelm, I., Diekelmann, S., Molzow, I., Ayoud, A., Molle, M., & Born, J. (2011). Sleep selectively enhances memory expected to be of future relevance. *The Journal of Neuroscience, 31*, 1563–1569.

Williams, C. C., & Zacks, R. T. (2001). Is retrieval-induced forgetting an inhibitory process? *American Journal of Psychology, 114,* 329–354.

Wilson, M. A., & McNaughton, B. L. (1994). Reactivation of hippocampal ensemble memories during sleep. *Science, 265*, 676–679.

Wixted, J. T. (2004). The psychology and neuroscience of forgetting. *Annual Review of Psychology, 55*, 235–269.

9

Memory and Emotion

Klaus Fiedler and Mandy Hütter

INTRODUCTION

The topic of this chapter, memory and emotion, is ideally suited to substantiate Kurt Lewin's notion that there is nothing more practical than a good theory – affording a reasonable motto for a handbook of applied memory. Numerous findings on affect and cognition have face validity or content validity for practically important questions in such diverse fields as social influence, stereotyping, education, law, achievement, and health. Empirical discoveries and practical insights from all these areas reflect the fertility and explanatory power of distinct theories that enabled this research. Conversely, the evidence gathered in applied domains has greatly increased the development of more refined theories and research paradigms.

The goal of the present chapter is to provide an overview of theoretical and applied work on memory and emotion, in a way that highlights the practical value of a theory-driven approach. To meet this goal, we first outline a sensible theoretical framework before we present an overview of empirical evidence on applied memory research. A final section will be concerned with a discussion of the adaptive functions of affective-cognitive behavior regulation and a prospect

on future directions of research. However, first of all, a brief look at the historical origins is in order to understand the broader issues that motivate contemporary research and theorizing.

HISTORICAL PRECURSORS OF MODERN RESEARCH ON MEMORY AND EMOTION

In ancient philosophy (Plato) and the enlightenment (Kant, Schopenhauer) emotions were conceived as hard-to-control impulses that rational and ethical beings should learn to resist and to channel appropriately. This view on emotion as a rival of proper thought and veridical memory also underlies Freud's (1915/1957) psychodynamic approach to repressed and subliminal memories. In contrast to this negative image of emotions as causes of irrationality and affective disorder, Darwin's (1998) seminal writings (first published in 1872) were primarily concerned with valuable adaptive functions served by emotions. His "principle of serviceable associated habits" states that expressive movements that occur in emotion (like concealing movements in shame) are of "service" to the organism. While these adaptive functions appear to be performed consciously, they can become routinized through habit and so firmly fixed that they are elicited automatically by the emotion-eliciting conditions (cf. Manstead, 2012), even when detached from their original purpose. This idea re-appears in contemporary research on mood priming suggesting that emotional states and even subtle emotional cues facilitate the processing of mood-congruent information.

Darwin's "principle of antithesis" states that emotion expression inhibits the expressive movements of opposing emotional states, thus invoking regulatory processes. A dog with hostile intentions, for instance, makes itself appear physically large in order to scare its rival. When the same dog in an affectionate state makes itself appear physically small, this only serves to accentuate the contrast of hostile and affectionate situations (Manstead, 2012). This example nicely illustrates the communicative and informative function of emotions that late became the focus of Schwarz and Clore's (2007) affect-as-information approach.

Darwin's third "principle of direct action of the nervous system," together with William James' (1884) idea that bodily reactions may precede the conscious experience of emotions, can be considered precursors of modern embodiment approaches (Damasio, 1994; Niedenthal, 2007). These approaches emphasize the importance of somatic experience and feelings in specific sensory modalities as mediators of affect and cognition.

Darwin (1998), McDougall (1908), and Watson (1919), who all stressed the universality of basic emotions (Tomkins, 1992), regarded emotions as distinct antecedent conditions that determine and delimit cognitive functions. In contrast, the soon arising constructionist approach (cf. Harlow & Stagner, 1933) assumed that cognitive constructions shape and mediate the genesis of emotions, as later articulated in Schachter's (1964) attribution theory. Today, a bi-directional causal assumption that cognition and emotion influence each other in multiple ways is commonly taken for granted, motivating, for example, a rapidly growing research program on affective behavior regulation conceived as a dialectical interplay of cognitive, affective, and environmental influences on behavior (Gross, 2007; Koole, 2009).

CONCEPTUAL AND TERMINOLOGICAL CONVENTIONS

There is wide consensus now to use the term "affect" as a generic, super-ordinate term for all kinds of affective processes and states. The term "emotion" refers to more specific affective states associated with particular emotion-eliciting stimuli. If the eliciting stimulus or situation is dangerous or threatening, the resulting emotion is anxiety or horror but not sadness or embarrassment.

In contrast, the term "mood" refers to more diffuse and enduring affective states. Moods are broader in meaning and not bound to specific eliciting stimuli, making them more likely to carry over to a broader class of situations and behavioral targets. A melancholic mood can taint the entire world with pessimistic connotations; an elated mood can cause generalized optimism. It is this broad meaning of mood states that justifies the crude distinction of "positive" and "negative" moods. Its unbounded independence of eliciting conditions creates the potential of moods to carry over to many real-life behaviors and judgment targets.

The term "feeling" finally refers to affective stimuli stemming from proprioceptive feedback, immediate body experience, or meta-cognitive monitoring of one's cognitive processes. The experience of facial or somatic muscle feedback is an example of a body feeling. Fluency or familiarity associated with recognition would be a cognitive feeling. Feelings may not be experienced consciously. Yet, even subtle and short feelings may be powerful enough to elicit similar behavioral effects as full-blown emotions or mood states.

CLASSES OF EMPIRICAL FINDINGS

The vast majority of studies on affect, cognition, and behavior regulation (Blanchette & Richards, 2010; Gross, 2002; Martin & Clore, 2001; Taylor, 1991) are concerned with three broad classes of empirical phenomena:

1. Studies dealing with *valence asymmetries* often reveal a negativity bias, reflecting enhanced attention allocated to aversive or dangerous stimuli. However, many other studies exhibit a processing advantage of positive stimuli. Finding the crucial moderators of positivity and negativity effects presents a challenging theoretical and practical question.
2. Research on *mood-congruency* examines the interaction between stimulus valence and the individual's mood state. The generic finding is a processing advantage of information congruent with the individual's current emotional states; it can be found at all stages of cognitive processing, from attention and perception to encoding, inference making, retrieval, and resulting functions of judgment, decision making, and manifest behavior. The general idea is that positive affective states facilitate the processing of positive information, whereas negative affective states support the processing of negative information. The basic principle of mood congruency can also account for mood-state-dependency (Eich, 1989) as a special case, whereby the individual's affective state facilitates the recall of information that has been encoded in, and is thus associated with, the same affective state.
3. Different cognitive and behavioral styles are associated with positive and negative mood states. As a general rule, positive (happy, elated) moods foster top-down processing and knowledge-driven holistic and creative inferences, whereas negative (depressed, melancholic) states trigger stimulus-driven bottom-up processing and conservative inferences (Bless & Fiedler, 2006; Clore, Schwarz, & Conway, 1994). Processing requirements of the task therefore moderate the relation between affect and cognition.

THEORETICAL CONCEPTIONS

Being able to account for these three major classes of empirical phenomena – mood asymmetries, congruency effects, and mood-dependent processing styles – is a chief criterion for the viability of pertinent theories (cf. Martin & Clore, 2001).

Early approaches to deal with memory and emotion (cf. Bower, 1981; Isen, Shalker, Clark, & Karp, 1978) have adopted the theoretical metaphor of an associative network, trying to explain mood congruency in terms of spreading association. Assuming that activation emanating from mood-related nodes spreads over to concepts and stimulus nodes of the same affective tone seemed to offer a simple and straightforward explanation of mood congruency. However, although associative principles afford a necessary component of any comprehensive theory, the notion of an associative network cannot in and of itself explain the asymmetry of positive and negative affect, the direct, memory-independent influence of affect on social judgments, and the evidence on processing-style effects in different affective states.

Motivated by these limitations of purely associative accounts, the affect-as-information approach (Clore et al., 1994; Schwarz & Clore, 2007) was proposed to account for direct mood influences on social judgments in terms of a heuristic process. Survey respondents judged their life satisfaction to be higher on sunny than on rainy days, as if they were misattributing their current affective reaction to the weather to their life success (Schwarz & Clore, 1983). Reminding them of the weather as an external cause discredited the informative value of their affective state, thus eliminating its impact on life satisfaction and other judgment targets. Misattribution of extraneously caused affective states is a crucial condition of the mood-as-information conception.

This approach can be expanded to cover valence asymmetries and mood effects on cognitive style. Assuming that positive states signal benevolent situations and encouragement to "go," whereas negative states signal danger and malevolent situations and warnings to "wait" or "stop" provides a natural account of the intuitive and creative style observed in positive mood, as compared with the hesitating and conservative style in negative states.

We suggest an even broader and less restrictive theoretical framework that is consistent with most assumptions of the mood-as-information approach but distinct in its premises and its scope. Taking a functional-theory perspective (Bless & Fiedler, 2006; Fiedler, 2001), we interpret emotion and memory in terms of two complementary adaptive functions, *assimilation* and *accommodation*. As explicated by Piaget (1954), accommodation is a stimulus-driven bottom-up function that updates internal structures to cope with environmental chances and threats. Assimilation, in contrast, is a knowledge-driven top-down function that imposes internal structures (knowledge, inferences, goals) onto the external world, regardless of normative and ecological stimulus constraints.

Simply defining accommodation and assimilation as externally versus internally determined adaptation processes is slightly misleading, because both components are involved in all processing stages. The actual defining features of the two adaptive functions are summarized in Table 9.1. Accommodation is the degree to which performance on a task depends on accurate bottom-up processing of the given task input and the utilization of approved social and task-specific processing rules. Assimilation is the degree to which task performance may profit from top-down inferences that assimilate the given input to older knowledge structures, and the use of self-determined rules and operators that may deviate from normative rules.

Both components are to some degree involved in any cognitive operation, regardless of whether it is triggered by the perception of the external world or memory of internally represented information. For example, reading involves stimulus-driven careful decoding of given letter strings (accommodation) but also knowledge-driven inferences and guessing strategies that go well beyond the decoded letters (assimilation). Yet, most tasks vary greatly in their relative emphasis on assimilation and accommodation.

Both adaptive strategies may be met with success (e.g., when accommodation results in accurate psychophysical estimates, or when assimilation produces a creative invention) or fail (e.g., when limited capacity prevents accommodation to stimulus details or when assimilation causes dysfunctional norm violations). Moreover, it may not always be possible to scale a set of tasks on both adaptive dimensions. However, whenever it is possible to order two or more tasks as relatively more accommodative or assimilative, the theoretical framework leads to clear-cut predictions concerning the influence of mood on memory.

The central assumption is that positive states (or affective cues) support assimilation whereas negative states (or affective cues) support accommodation. This assumption offers an immediate account for the different cognitive and behavioral styles triggered by different affective states or cues. Indeed, the terms "accommodative" and "assimilative" sound like phenomenological descriptions of the detailed and cautious style exhibited in negative mood and the unconventional and creative style exhibited in positive mood. Moreover, since mood congruency itself reflects an assimilative process (i.e., an assimilation of memory contents and target stimuli to the individual's internal state),

Table 9.1

Adaptive function	Information contents	Procedural rules
Accommodation	Performance depends on accurate processing of given input …	… and on utilization of approved social norms and task-specific rules
Assimilation	Performance depends on knowledge-driven inferences beyond the given input …	… and on the use of self-determined operators that may deviate from existing norms

this framework offers a natural explanation for the asymmetrically stronger congruency effects in positive as compared with negative mood. With regard to valence asymmetries, it can explain why a negativity advantage during early perceptual stages (e.g., accommodation to input from a detection task) turns into a positivity bias in later stages involving knowledge-driven assimilative inferences.

Many implications of this theoretical framework are consistent with the predictions of the mood-as-information approach. Nevertheless, the assimilation-accommodation framework is less restrictive than, and its implications go beyond, the mood-as-information approach in several respects. The assimilation-accommodation framework is not confined to situations in which affect manipulations are subtle and equivocal enough to allow for affect misattribution. It does not exclude findings from many studies in which mood states can be obviously attributed to an external event or manipulation (such as film clips or failure). Moreover, it allows for congruency effects in genuine memory performance and not just heuristic response biases. It also offers an explanation for the empirical fact that congruency effects are clearly weaker or sometimes totally disappear in negative affective states, which is hard to reconcile with the notion that affective cues in general serve an informational function. The assimilation–accommodation framework predicts a number of processing-style effects that do not reflect an informative function of mood cues (like eliminated priming effects in negative mood; Storbeck & Clore, 2008). And last but not least, this framework implies that positive and negative affective states have similar influences as other factors that trigger assimilation and accommodation, such as high versus low construal level (Trope & Liberman, 2010), promotion versus prevention focus (Higgins, 2008), or familiar versus novel environments (Bischof, 1975). It therefore facilitates the theoretical interpretation

and integration of the affect-cognition link within a comprehensive meta-theoretical framework.

REVIEW OF EVIDENCE

The empirical review presented in the remainder of this chapter will contain four major sections, devoted to social cognition, law, education, and regulation of affect and behavior. Each section will open up new fields of application but also introduce distinct theoretical ideas and empirical laws that are best explained in the specific applied context. The topic of the next section, social cognition, is ideally suited to present and explain the basic asymmetry of positive and negative affect. The section on eyewitness memory nicely illustrates the reconstructive nature of memory. Applications in the educational context highlight the important role of memory organization. Finally, health-related research speaks to emotion regulation processes and adaptive behavior.

Social perception, social influence, and attitude learning

A prominent theme in social-cognition research is valence asymmetries. Several theories stress the importance of recognizing negative stimuli faster than positive stimuli (Cannon, 1932; Taylor, 1991), and the higher weight given to negative than positive information in social judgment (Fiske, 1980; Fiedler, Walther, & Nickel, 1999; Skowronski & Carlston, 1989). Despite this vigilance for negative stimulation, people tend to think positively about themselves (Boucher & Osgood, 1969; Matlin & Stang, 1978; Taylor & Brown, 1988; Baumeister, Tice, & Hutton, 1989) and to avoid or ignore negative stimuli (Brandtstädter, Voss, & Rothermund, 2004; Voss, Rothermund, & Brandtstädter, 2008).

Mobilization and minimization

In an influential model by Taylor (1991), this co-existence of negativity and positivity biases was explained as reflecting two processing stages. Attending to and detecting negative and potentially dangerous environmental stimuli is functional during an early mobilization stage, which serves an accommodative function. During a subsequent minimization stage, then, higher mental operations are employed to reduce the aversive stimulation and negative implications in an assimilative process.

Early negativity effects

Using a Stroop-like task involving color naming of adjectives, Pratto and John (1991) provided strong evidence for automatic vigilance, a stimulus-driven mechanism that automatically directs attention to unpleasant stimuli. The time required to name the ink color of a stimulus word was longer for negative than for positive words, presumably because negative stimulus contents interfere with color naming. Furthermore, participants showed more frequent incidental learning of negative compared with positive stimuli. Despite this attention-grabbing power of negative stimuli, it is however possible that negative stimuli are inhibited from entering consciousness (Holmes, 1974, 1990), as evident in perceptual defense or repression. For instance, baseball fans remember success of their team more vividly than failures (Breslin & Safer, 2011).

Asymmetries of positive and negative valence have also been studied in the face-in-the-crowd paradigm, in which participants have to detect a distinct target face embedded in a matrix of distracter faces. Several studies seemed to demonstrate a recognition advantage of angry faces embedded in a set of otherwise positive faces. Because the time needed to find a friendly face increased with display size whereas recognition time for threatening faces was unaffected, the negative superiority was interpreted as an automatic pop-out effect (e.g., Hansen & Hansen, 1988; Öhman, Lundqvist, & Esteves, 2001;

but see Juth, Lundqvist, Karlsson, & Öhman, 2005; Purcell, Stewart, & Skov, 1996).

Negativity effects revisited

Closer inspection and more refined study designs revealed that the evidence for a negativity effect on selective attention tasks is less clear-cut than expected from Pratto and John (1991). Using the drift-rate parameter in diffusion analysis as a measure of cognitive-processing speed in a speeded classification task with bi-colored geometric figures, Voss et al. (2008) found that colors associated with losses were processed slower than colors associated with gains. Other research suggests that Pratto and John's (1991) negativity advantage may be peculiar to enhanced arousal of negative stimuli (Keil & Ihssen, 2004; Schimmack, 2005), or to highly anxious participants (Bar-Haim, Lamy, Pergamin, Bakermans-Kranenburg, & van IJzendoorn, 2007).

Recently, more refined study designs controlled for confounding perceptual features like the V-shape of angry eyebrows or white teeth in smiling faces that may be responsible for conflicting results in face-in-the-crowd research (see Becker, Anderson, Mortensen, Neufeld, & Neel, 2011). Contrary to the seemingly well-established anger-superiority effect, the positive faces enjoyed a processing advantage. Moreover, there was no evidence for a pre-attentive popping-out of angry faces, as the latencies needed to discover angry faces in the crowd were not invariant when the size of the face matrix was manipulated. Instead, Becker et al. (2011) found that the fast processing of happy background faces can explain the often cited fast recognition of angry target faces.

The evidence for a positivity bias in the face-in-the-crowd paradigm is consistent with other recent findings motivated by the density hypothesis (Unkelbach, Fiedler, Bayer, Stegmüller, & Danner, 2008). Based on the central assumption of higher density and greater interconnectedness of positive than negative stimuli in memory, several studies have found faster speeded classification and stronger affective priming effects for positive than for negative stimuli. Moreover, the strength of these effects could be predicted by the density value of particular stimuli, as assessed through multi-dimensional scaling.

As a rule, the minimization of hedonically unpleasant stimuli increases to the extent that the task conditions allow for assimilative inferences, reframing, and self-determined interpretation. Granting sufficient meta-cognitive control, negative experiences may be prevented strategically or ignored deliberately (e.g., Brandtstädter et al., 2004) to shield the self from unpleasant feedback and devaluation (e.g., Taylor & Brown, 1988; Baumeister et al., 1989; for a comprehensive review, see Baumeister, Bratslavsky, Finkenauer, & Vohs, 2001). Complementary, the generalized preference for positive ideas and conclusions – the so-called Pollyanna principle (Matlin & Stang, 1978) – is, for example, reflected in higher occurrence rates of positive than negative words in language (Boucher & Osgood, 1969).

Formation of attitudes

Valence asymmetries have also been found in the formation of attitudes. The tendency to avoid unpleasant stimuli can produce a negativity bias when information sampling from aversive sources is truncated so that negative initial impressions or stereotypes cannot be corrected (Denrell, 2005; Fazio, Eiser, & Shook, 2004). As a consequence of the minimization of negative input through selective avoidance, the low frequency of occurrence renders negative behaviors more diagnostic than positive behaviors (Ajzen, 1971; Eisinger & Mills, 1968). Thus, observing somebody lying on a single occasion has more impact on the belief that the person is dishonest than a single instance of telling the truth has on the belief that the person is honest (Skowronski & Carlston, 1989). Because of this epistemic asymmetry, negative observations trigger deeper processing and receive more weight in attitude formation and social judgments than positive observations (Fiske, 1980).

Evaluative conditioning is an experimental analog of attitude learning, whereby the mere co-occurrence of neutral, conditioned stimuli (CS) and valence-laden, unconditioned stimuli (US) leads to a shift in the evaluation of the CS toward the same valence as the US. Evaluative conditioning is particularly relevant to applied research on stereotyping, prejudice, or consumer settings, in which products are presented together with pleasant stimuli like celebrity endorsers. This paradigm often produces stronger conditioning effects after negative than after positive pairings (Baeyens, Eelen, & van den Bergh, 1990; Hütter, Sweldens, Stahl, Unkelbach, & Klauer, 2012; Levey & Martin, 1975). Moreover, when the valence of the US changes after the conditioning procedure (US revaluation), the CS is also affected but more so after negative than positive US revaluation (Walther, Gawronski, Blank, & Langer, 2009).

Negative evaluations thus appear to be more persistent and to have higher impact than positive evaluations. Hence, evaluative conditioning constitutes a largely accommodative, stimulus-driven process that may, however, be modulated by assimilative processes. Direction and size of conditioning effects depend on the self-generated relations between CS and US. For example, when facial stimuli allow participants to construe a friend-relation between CS and US, a regular EC effect is evident in CS taking on the same valence as US. However, pairing the same stimuli can induce a CS valence opposite to the US valence when the two faces are construed as belonging to enemies (Fiedler & Unkelbach, 2011).

Measurement of attitudes

Direct questionnaire measures of attitudes have been criticized as being prone to Pollyanna effects and motivated biases toward positive self-representation. As countermeasures to deal with these problems, indirect measures have been proposed that allow for less assimilation and rely instead on more accommodative, stimulus-dependent speeded classification and approach-avoidance tasks. Prominent examples are implicit association tests (Greenwald, McGhee, & Schwartz, 1998), affective priming (Fazio, Sanbonmatsu, Powell, & Kardes, 1986), or simple motor tasks that call for pulling (approach) or pushing (avoidance) motor responses (e.g., with a joy stick; Brendl, Markman, & Messner, 2005) relative to attitude objects presented on a computer screen. Recent evidence suggests, though, that such indirect measures are also subject to more voluntary and strategic control than expected (De Houwer, 2001; Fiedler, Bluemke, & Unkelbach, 2009; Teige-Mocigemba & Klauer, 2008).

Social judgment

The social judgment literature is replete with mood-congruency and processing-style effects in such diverse paradigms as person perception, stereotyping, persuasion, self-related judgments, cooperation, and deception. Mood-congruency effects were found in autobiographical memory (Salovey & Singer, 1989), memory for flavor (Pliner & Steverango, 1994), evaluations of consumer items (Forgas & Ciarrochi, 2001), confabulations of patients (Bajo, Fleminger, & Kopelman, 2010), reactions to (im)politeness (Forgas, 1999), interpretations of relationship conflicts (Forgas, 1994), evaluations of commercials (Kamins, Marks, & Skinner, 1991), and judgments of life satisfaction (Schwarz & Clore, 1983; Strack, Schwarz, & Gschneidinger, 1985). These congruency effects tend to be much stronger for positive than negative affect, consistent with the fact that mood congruency is an assimilative function fostered by positive mood. Moreover, the likelihood and strength of congruency effects increases when memory or the judgment task is unrestricted and constructive (Forgas, 1995), that is, the more room there is for assimilation.

Processing style effects are reflected in stronger top-down influences in positive mood but stronger bottom-up influences in negative mood. In positive compared with negative mood, people are more prone to make stereotypical judgments (Bodenhausen, 1993; Bodenhausen & Lichtenstein, 1987), to follow trust expectancies (Lount, 2010), to rely on guessing based on scripted knowledge (Bless, Clore, Schwarz, Golisano, Rabe, & Wolk, 1996), to generate false memories (Storbeck & Clore, 2005), to use abstract rather than concrete language (Beukeboom & Semin, 2006), to profit from self-generation effects in learning (Fiedler, Nickel, Asbeck, & Pagel, 2003), to flexibly attend to global or local stimulus aspects (Huntsinger, Clore, & Bar-Anan, 2010), and to produce group-polarization effects (Forgas, 1999).

Persuasion

Several experiments have tested the impact of mood on recipients processing styles in persuasive communication. For instance, Bless, Bohner, Schwarz, and Strack (1990) had their participants write a report on a happy or a sad life event for mood manipulation. They were then presented with a persuasive message advertising an increase in student service fees that either contained weak or strong arguments. Participants in sad mood were persuaded by cogent arguments but disapproved of weak arguments. When participants were in elated moods, argument quality had little influence. While this insensitivity to message quality was often attributed to lower effort expenditure in positive mood, further analyses showed that the number of cognitive responses was not reduced in positive mood. Given that the manipulation of argument strength was not based on logical or empirical truth but on consensual agreement, another plausible explanation is that recipients in positive mood were less conformist and less dependent on majority opinions.

Consistent with this notion, Ziegler and Diehl (2011) found that, relative to negative mood, positive mood led to deeper processing of arguments provided by minorities (versus majorities) and by untrustworthy (versus trustworthy) sources. Open-mindedness and independence of conformist norms is a typical property of an assimilative processing style in positive mood. Another property is taking the freedom to follow one's hedonic goals. Central to Wegener and Petty's (1994) hedonic contingency model, indeed, is the assumption that people in positive mood may simply not process unpleasant arguments that might interfere with their elated affective state.

Eyewitness-memory and face recognition

Human memory is crucial and consequential when court trials have to rely on eyewitness testimony, in the absence of physical proofs of the defendant's guilt or innocence. It is thus no surprise that eyewitness memory is one of the most important domains of applied memory research. Numerous DNA exoneration cases – convicted people whose innocence was later proven through DNA analysis – testify to the fallibility of human memory as a major cause of false convictions (Wells, Malpass, Lindsay, Fisher, Turtle, & Fulero, 2000). Given the intense emotions experienced by many witnesses of crimes, the impact of emotional states on eyewitness memory constitutes a prominent research topic.

Face recognition
A recognition test that calls for accurate discrimination between actually presented stimuli and a large number of foils constitutes an accommodative task: sticking to the stimulus input, which must not be confused with assimilative inferences that go beyond the information given. Consistent with the notion that negative affective states support accommodation, negative mood during encoding was found to facilitate the discrimination of faces in a recognition test (Hills, Werno, & Lewis, 2011; Teitelbaum & Geiselman, 1997). Positive mood again led to a congruency bias toward remembering happy faces better than sad faces (Hills et al., 2011), reflecting the selective elaboration of mood-congruent faces.

The assimilative encoding style in positive mood also fosters holistic encoding. Participants in a study by Bridge, Chiao, and Paller (2010) read happy or sad narratives while viewing the faces to be remembered later. During recognition, the encoding context was either retained or obscured (by presenting the faces in an inverted spatial orientation). Consistent with the notion that positive affect facilitates deep contextualized encoding of holistic information, conceivable as assimilative encoding, Bridge et al. (2010) found better recall of faces encoded in happy settings when the context was retained. However, a recognition advantage of faces encoded in sad settings was obtained when the context was obscured so that recognition decisions had to rely on accommodative encoding of concrete physiognomic features of the original stimulus faces proper.

False memories
One intriguing implication of a more assimilative, holistic, and top-down driven processing style is that positive (compared with negative) mood should produce more false memories (Roediger & McDermott, 1999). When presented with a recognition probe that was not included in the stimulus list but that bore a strong relation to the semantic theme of the list, people in positive mood should be more likely than people in negative states to make constructive errors. Moreover, assimilative response sets should induce higher confidence under positive mood than accommodative response sets under negative mood. Both predictions were supported by Storbeck and Clore (2005).

Applying the same rationale to eyewitness reports, a more liberal response bias that is typical for positive mood should increase the incorrect recognition of non-experienced lures (false alarms), even when correct recognition of actually experienced stimuli (hits) may also profit from positive affective cues. Because eyewitness recognition suffers from too liberal a response bias, the net result should be impaired eyewitness performance (due to mainly false positives) in positive mood. Support for this contention was found by Forgas, Laham, and Vargas (2005) in a study of eyewitnesses' verbal reports. Participants in positive mood incorporated more false positives in their reports than participants in negative mood.

State dependency

An eyewitness study conducted by Rainis (2001) speaks to the impact of mood-state-dependency on face recognition (Eich, 1989). Re-establishing a similar affective state at recognition as during the original observation stage improved the accuracy of eyewitness testimony. The affective influence on memory was again enhanced in positive affective states. Recognition of faces encoded in negative states was generally weak, presumably because the highly aversive pictures used to induce negative affect (depicting concentration camps or road accidents), presented in the same modality as the stimulus faces, interfered with an efficient encoding process, consistent with Taylor's (1991) minimization principle. Indeed, when affective recognition states were induced semantically rather than pictorially, a state-dependent memory advantage was also observed for negative affect. Thus, creating a matching "semantic context" seems to afford a useful remedy to emotional stress, compensating for the impairment of emotional distracters.

Memory for affectively extreme stimuli

In the eyewitness literature, it is commonly presupposed that memory for highly aversive and stressful events is impaired. The available evidence, however, is less clear-cut (Christianson, 1992). On the one hand, the inverted U-shape of the Yerkes–Dodson law predicts that witness performance first increases from low to medium arousal and then decreases when arousal becomes too strong (Teigen, 1994). An accommodative focus on danger and threat interferes with context memory (Christianson & Loftus,

1991; Ochi, 2005). On the other hand, affectively intensive experiences may produce strong and endurable flashbulb memories (Winograd & Neisser, 1992), which are also reflective of accommodation. Whether strong affect improves or impairs subsequent memory depends on several boundary conditions, such as the encoding context, the type and delay of the memory test, and the amount of detail required (cf. Christianson, 1992).

The phenomenon of repressed memories (Loftus, Garry, & Hayne, 2008) supports this hybrid message. On the one hand, the incisive experience of being raped or abused is unlikely to be forgotten. On the other hand, it is claimed that extremely threatening and intolerable experiences may be actively purged or blocked from consciousness. However, there is hardly any cogent evidence for the validity of this widely shared claim about amnesia for threatening events (Loftus et al., 2008; Rofé, 2008), beyond the well-established general evidence for inferior recall and recognition of unpleasant events (Depue, Curran, & Banich, 2007; Erdelyi, 2006).

The lack of evidence for complete repression of incisive autobiographical episodes is compatible with the finding that intense negative affect may reduce memory for real crimes (Ihlebaek, Løve, Eilertson, & Magnussen, 2003). To study the impact of relatively high degrees of fear, Valentine and Mesout (2009) assessed heart-rate changes and questionnaire measures of state anxiety in visitors to the horror labyrinth of the London Dungeon. Dependent measures were cued-recall of descriptive attributes of the scary person in the horror labyrinth (sex, age, height, hair color, clothing, etc.) and identification of the scary person in a nine-person photo line-up. High-state anxiety led to a marked decrease in memory performance, as manifested in fewer correctly reported person descriptors, more incorrectly reported details, and fewer correct identifications.

The role of affect in academic learning

Theoretically, the relationship between positive versus negative mood and task-related performance and motivation should depend on the relative degree to which a task calls for accommodation and assimilation. Negative mood should enhance performance when the task requires accommodation, careful assessment of stimulus details, and conservative response strategies. In contrast, positive mood should facilitate performance on assimilative tasks that invite holistic and intuitive processing, unorthodox creativity, and liberal response strategies.

Indeed, a negative-mood advantage was found for learning tasks involving careful attention and thorough processing, such as correlation judgments from scatter diagrams (Sinclair & Mark, 1995), recognition accuracy (Storbeck & Clore, 2005), and careful consideration of all possibilities in reasoning tasks (Oaksford, Morris, Grainger, & Williams, (1996). A positive-mood advantage, in contrast, was obtained in assimilative tasks involving creativity (Baas, De Dreu, & Nijstad, 2008), memory organization (Bless, Hamilton, & Mackie, 1992), top-down processing (Lee & Sternthal, 1999), developing trust (Lount, 2010), and intuitive inferences from small amounts of information (Fiedler, Renn, & Kareev, 2010).

Episodic memory for words and pictures

In the academic-learning realm, too, the relative advantage of positive and negative mood should depend on the degree to which the learning task involves careful conservation of stimulus details and/or creative elaboration and generative inferences. Thus, a negative-mood advantage can be expected for reproductive tasks, such as learning of vocabulary or historical dates, monitoring of orthography and grammar, or careful numerical calculation. However, because even basic mental operations rely on active

elaboration and idiosyncratic integration (Mandler, 2011), it is no surprise that learning can greatly profit from the assimilative functions fostered by positive moods. A key finding here is that positive mood facilitates clustering of categorized coding of stimulus lists (Fiedler, Pampe, & Scherf, 1986; Lee & Sternthal, 1999), which is crucial to effective retrieval. Positive mood also enhanced the speed and accuracy of mathematical thinking (Bryan & Bryan, 1991), whereas the conservative style of students in negative mood restricted the learning transfer to new situations (Brand, Reimer, & Opwis, 2007).

Creativity and problem solving

Mental operations are called creative if their output is substantially different from the task input, reflecting an assimilative transformation that goes beyond the mere (accommodative) conservation of the information given. Not surprisingly, therefore, positive mood was found to foster creative performance on many different tasks. In a study by Isen, Daubman, and Nowicki (1987), for instance, positive mood decreased the time required to solve Duncker's candle problem, a "classical" task to assess the ability to overcome functional fixedness (discovering that matchboxes can also be used to construct a platform on the wall). Analogous findings were obtained for many other operational measures of creativity. For instance, positive mood led to more original, uncommon responses to verbal association tasks (Isen, Johnson, Mertz, & Robinson, 1985), according to association norms. Or, Rowe, Hirsh, Anderson, and Smith (2007) reported that positive mood enhanced performance on a remote association test, due to loosened reins on inhibitory control resulting in increased breadth of attention allocation.

A meta-analysis by Baas et al. (2008) corroborated and refined this contention. Creativity was most enhanced in positive states that foster approach tendencies and promotion focus (e.g., happiness), but not in positive states that lack these assimilative functions (e.g., relaxation). Creativity decreased in negative states that trigger avoidance and prevention focus (fear, anxiety). Less accommodative negative moods (e.g., sadness) did not affect creativity.

Adaptive functions of cognitive-emotional regulation

The adaptive regulation of behavior depends on a twofold – informational and motivational – function of affective states. People use their momentary affective states as information about the world. They utilize their mood resulting from sunny or rainy weather to estimate their life satisfaction (Schwarz & Clore, 1983). But moods also contribute to ending unpleasant and dysfunctional affective states and to re-establishing healthy and motivating states. In good mood people strive for mood maintenance whereas in sad mood they make every effort to repair or terminate their unpleasant state (Baumeister, Heatherton, & Tice, 1994). Maintaining positive mood not only serves a hedonic function. According to the mood-as-a-resource hypothesis (Aspinwall, 1998; Trope & Neter, 1994), it also functions as a buffer against short-term affective costs of negative information in favor of long-term gains.

Affective priming and short term processes triggered by affective cues

Mood effects can be elicited not only by hedonically significant events but also by subtle, short-term affective cues. One experimental paradigm to investigate the adaptive functions of affective cues is affective priming (e.g., Fazio et al., 1986; Klauer, 1998; Klauer & Musch, 2003). In this paradigm, participants have to evaluate positive and negative targets preceded by positive or negative primes. If prime and target match in valence, the response to the target is typically facilitated (*congruent* condition). If they differ in valences, responding to the target can be decelerated (*incongruent* condition).

Priming can be regarded as an experimentally induced assimilation effect, whereby the prime initiates a top-down expectancy that influences the accommodative response to the target stimulus. Consistent with this notion, priming effects are enhanced in positive mood (Bless & Fiedler, 1995) and may be completely eliminated in negative mood (Storbeck & Clore, 2008). Similarly, stronger flanker effects were found in positive than in negative mood (Rowe et al., 2007). The flanker task is to categorize a central stimulus (e.g., < or >) flanked by matching or mismatching context stimuli (e.g., > > < > > or > > > > >). As in priming response latencies are typically shorter for matching trials. Although priming is considered adaptive but flanker effects as impairment, they both reflect similar assimilative functions.

The asymmetry of positive and negative affect in evaluative priming is even visible at the level of individual trials. When latencies (and accuracies) for specific trial pairs were reported, the valence–congruity advantage was mainly due to positive-prime–positive-target trials but hardly visible for negative–negative trials (Fiedler, Bluemke, & Unkelbach, 2011; Unkelbach et al., 2008). Thus, the congruity effects elicited by short-term affective cues (i.e., primes) resemble those elicited by the participants' long-term affective states.

Asymmetric priming effects have been related to the regulation of well-being and health. Robinson and von Hippel (2006) demonstrated that stronger positive than negative priming effects are indicative of high life satisfaction. Other recent publications point toward the potential use of affective priming in the context of therapeutic interventions (Evans, 2010; Bargh & Shalev, 2012). The idea underlying these claims is that affective priming in clinical settings can serve to heighten clients' temporary mood and their receptiveness for treatment and that priming-based interventions can be carried out unobtrusively, at minimal reactance.

CONCLUSION

The empirical findings and theoretical insights we have presented in this chapter do not provide a comprehensive review of all published research on emotion and memory. Following Kurt Lewin's maxim that there is nothing more practical than a good theory, we have concentrated on those aspects of applied memory research that reflect the adaptive functions of the individual's affective states. In doing so, we have found, conversely, that applied memory studies provide impressive convergent evidence for the notion that the complementary functions of assimilation and accommodation afford a sensible theoretical framework for the integration of research on emotion, memory, and behavior regulation.

ACKNOWLEDGEMENT

The research and scientific work underlying this chapter was supported by a Koselleck Grant of the Deutsche Forschungsgemeinschaft awarded to the first author (Fi 294 / 23-1). Correspondence concerning this chapter should be addressed to kf@psychologie.uni-heidelberg.de or to mandy.huetter@psychologie.uni-heidelberg.de.

REFERENCES

Ajzen, I. (1971). Attribution of dispositions to an actor: Effects of perceived decision freedom and behavioral utilities. *Journal of Personality and Social Psychology, 18,* 144–156.

Aspinwall, L. G. (1998). Rethinking the role of positive affect in self-regulation. *Motivation and Emotion, 22,* 1–32.

Baas, M., De Dreu, C. W., & Nijstad, B. A. (2008). A meta-analysis of 25 years of mood-creativity research: Hedonic tone, activation, or regulatory focus? *Psychological Bulletin, 134,* 779–806.

Baeyens, F., Eelen, P., & Van den Bergh, O. (1990). Contingency awareness in evaluative conditioning: A case for unaware affective-evaluative learning. *Cognition and Emotion, 4,* 3–18.

Bajo, A., Fleminger, S., & Kopelman, M. (2010). Confabulations are emotionally charged, but not always for the best. *Journal of the International Neuropsychological Society, 16,* 975–983.

Bargh, J. A., & Shalev, I. (2012). The substitutability of physical and social warmth in daily life. *Emotion, 12*(1), 154–162.

Bar-Haim, Y., Lamy, D., Pergamin, L., Bakermans-Kranenburg, M. J., & van IJzendoorn, M. H. (2007). Threat-related attentional bias in anxious and non-anxious individuals: A meta-analytic study. *Psychological Bulletin, 133,* 1–24.

Baumeister, R. F., Bratslavsky, E., Finkenauer, C., & Vohs, K. D. (2001). Bad is stronger than good. *Review of General Psychology, 5,* 323–370.

Baumeister, R. F., Heatherton, T. F., & Tice, D. M. (1994). *Losing control: How and why people fail at self-regulation.* San Diego, CA: Academic Press.

Baumeister, R. F., Tice, D. M., & Hutton, D. G. (1989). Self-presentational motivations and personality differences in self-esteem. *Journal of Personality, 57,* 547–579.

Becker, D. V., Anderson, U. S., Mortensen, C. R., Neufeld, S. L., & Neel, R. (2011). The face in the crowd effect unconfounded: happy faces, not angry faces, are more efficiently detected in single- and multiple-target visual search tasks. *Journal of Experimental Psychology: General, 140,* 637–59.

Beukeboom, C. J., & Semin, G. R. (2006). How mood turns on language. *Journal of Experimental Social Psychology, 42,* 553–566.

Bischof, N. (1975). A systems approach toward the functional connections of attachment and fear. *Child Development, 46,* 801–817.

Blanchette, I., & Richards, A. (2010). The influence of affect on higher level cognition: A review of research on interpretation, judgement, decision making and reasoning. *Cognition and Emotion, 24,* 561–595.

Bless, H., Bohner, G., Schwartz, N., & Strack, F. (1990). Mood and persuasion: A cognitive response analysis. *Personality and Social Psychology Bulletin, 16,* 331–345.

Bless, H., Clore, G. L., Schwarz, N., Golisano, V., Rabe, C., & Wolk, M. (1996). Mood and the use of scripts: Does a happy mood really lead to mindlessness? *Journal of Personality and Social Psychology, 71,* 665–679.

Bless, H., & Fiedler, K. (1995). Affective states and the influence of activated general knowledge. *Personality and Social Psychology Bulletin, 21,* 766–778.

Bless, H., & Fiedler, K. (2006). Mood and the regulation of information processing and behavior. In J. P. Forgas and J. P. Forgas (Eds.), *Affect in social thinking and behavior* (pp. 65–84). New York: Psychology Press.

Bless, H., Hamilton, D. L., & Mackie, D. M. (1992). Mood effects on the organization of person information. *European Journal of Social Psychology, 22,* 497–509.

Bodenhausen, G. V. (1993). Emotion, arousal, and stereotypic judgments: A heuristic model of affect and stereotyping. In D. M. Mackie and D. L. Hamilton (Eds.), *Affect, cognition, and stereotyping: Interactive processes in group perception* (pp. 13–37). San Diego, CA: Academic Press.

Bodenhausen, G. V., & Lichtenstein, M. (1987). Social stereotypes and information-processing strategies: The impact of task complexity. *Journal of Personality and Social Psychology, 52,* 871–880.

Boucher, J., & Osgood, C. E. (1969). The Pollyanna hypothesis. *Journal of Verbal Learning and Verbal Behavior, 8,* 1–8.

Bower, G. H. (1981). Mood and memory. *American Psychologist, 36,* 129–148.

Brand, S., Reimer, T., & Opwis, K. (2007). How do we learn in a negative mood? Effects of a negative mood on transfer and learning. *Learning and Instruction, 17,* 1–16.

Brandtstädter, J., Voss, A., & Rothermund, K. (2004). Perception of danger signals: The role of control. *Experimental Psychology, 51,* 24–32.

Brendl, C., Markman, A. B., & Messner, C. (2005). Indirectly measuring evaluations of several attitude objects in relation to a neutral reference point. *Journal of Experimental Social Psychology, 41*(4), 346–368.

Breslin, C. W., & Safer, M. A. (2011). Effects of event valence on long-term memory for two baseball championship games. *Psychological Science, 22,* 1408–1412.

Bridge, D. J., Chiao, J. Y., & Paller, K. A. (2010). Emotional context at learning systematically biases memory for facial information. *Memory & Cognition, 38,* 125–133.

Bryan, T., & Bryan, J. (1991). Positive mood and math performance. *Journal of Learning Disabilities, 24,* 490–494.

Christianson, S. (1992). Emotional stress and eyewitness memory: A critical review. *Psychological Bulletin, 112,* 284–309.

Christianson, S., & Loftus, E. F. (1991). Remembering emotional events: The fate of detailed information. *Cognition and Emotion, 5,* 81–108.

Cannon, W. B. (1932). *The wisdom of the body.* New York: Norton.

Clore, G. L., Schwarz, N., & Conway, M. (1994). Affective causes and consequences of social information processing. In R. S. Wyer and T. K. Srull (Eds.), *The handbook of social cognition* (2nd ed.). Hillsdale, NJ: Lawrence Erlbaum Associates.

Damasio, A. R. (1994). *Descartes' error: Emotion, reason, and the human brain.* New York: Putnam.

Darwin, C. (1998). *The expression of the emotions in man and animals* (3rd ed.). Oxford: Oxford University Press.

De Houwer, J. (2001). A structural and process analysis of the Implicit Association Test. *Journal of Experimental Social Psychology, 37,* 443–451.

Denrell, J. (2005). Why most people disapprove of me: Experience sampling in impression formation. *Psychological Review, 112,* 951–978.

Depue, B. E., Curran, T., & Banich, M. T. (2007). Prefrontal regions orchestrate suppression of emotional memories via a two-phase process. *Science, 317,* 215–219.

Eich, E. (1989). Theoretical issues in state dependent memory. In H. Roediger, F. M. Craik, H. Roediger and F. M. Craik (Eds.), *Varieties of memory and consciousness: Essays in honour of Endel Tulving* (pp. 331–354). Hillsdale, NJ: Lawrence Erlbaum Associates, Inc.

Eisinger, R., & Mills, J. (1968) Perception of the sincerity and competence of a communicator as a function of the extremity of his position. *Journal of Experimental Social Psychology, 4,* 224–232.

Erdelyi, M. (2006). The unified theory of repression. *Behavioral and Brain Sciences, 29,* 499–511.

Evans, I. M. (2010). Positive affective priming: A behavioral technique to facilitate therapeutic engagement by families, caregivers, and teachers. *Child & Family Behavior Therapy, 32,* 257–271.

Fazio, R. H., Eiser, J. R., & Shook, N. J. (2004). Attitude formation through exploration: Valence asymmetries. *Journal of Personality and Social Psychology, 87,* 293–311.

Fazio, R. H., Sanbonmatsu, D. M., Powell, M. C., & Kardes, F. R. (1986). On the automatic activation of attitudes. *Journal of Personality and Social Psychology, 50,* 229–238.

Fiedler, K. (2001). Affective states trigger processes of assimilation and accommodation. In L. L. Martin and G. L. Clore (Eds.), *Theories of mood and cognition: A user's guidebook* (pp. 86–98). Mahwah, NJ: Erlbaum.

Fiedler, K., Bluemke, M., & Unkelbach, C. (2009). Exerting control over allegedly automatic associative processes. In J. Forgas, R. Baumeister and D. Tice (Eds.), *The psychology of self-regulation* (pp. 249–269). New York: Psychology Press.

Fiedler, K., Bluemke, M., & Unkelbach, C. (2011). On the adaptive flexibility of evaluative priming. *Memory & Cognition, 39,* 557–572.

Fiedler, K., Nickel, S., Asbeck, J., & Pagel, U. (2003). Mood and the generation effect. *Cognition and Emotion, 17,* 585–608.

Fiedler, K., Pampe, H., & Scherf, U. (1986). Mood and memory for tightly organized social information. *European Journal of Social Psychology, 16,* 149–164.

Fiedler, K., Renn, S., & Kareev, Y. (2010). Mood and judgments based on sequential sampling. *Journal of Behavioral Decision Making, 23,* 483–495.

Fiedler, K., & Unkelbach, C. (2011). Evaluative conditioning depends on higher-order encoding processes. *Cognition and Emotion, 25,* 639–656.

Fiedler, K., Walther, E., & Nickel, S. (1999). The auto-verification of social hypotheses: Stereotyping and the power of sample size. *Journal of Personality and Social Psychology, 77,* 5–18.

Fiske, S. T. (1980). Attention and weight in person perception: The impact of negative and extreme behavior. *Journal of Personality and Social Psychology, 38,* 889–906.

Forgas, J. P. (1994). Sad and guilty? Affective influences on the explanation of conflict episodes. *Journal of Personality and Social Psychology, 66,* 56–68.

Forgas, J. P. (1995). Mood and judgment: The affect infusion model (AIM). *Psychological Bulletin, 117,* 39–66.

Forgas, J. P. (1999). On feeling good and being rude: Affective influences on language use and request formulations. *Journal of Personality and Social Psychology, 76,* 928–939.

Forgas, J. P., & Ciarrochi, J. (2001). On being happy and possessive: The interactive effects of mood and personality on consumer judgments. *Psychology & Marketing, 18,* 239–260.

Forgas, J. P., Laham, S. M., & Vargas, P. T. (2005). Mood effects on eyewitness memory: Affective influences on susceptibility to misinformation. *Journal of Experimental Social Psychology, 41,* 574–588.

Freud, S. (1915/1957). Repression. In J. Strachey (Ed.), *The standard edition of the complete psychological works of Sigmund Freud* (Vol. 14, pp. 146–158). London: Hogarth Press.

Greenwald, A. G., McGhee, D. E., & Schwartz, J. L. K. (1998). Measuring individual differences in implicit cognition: The Implicit Association Test. *Journal of Personality and Social Psychology, 74,* 1464–1480.

Gross, J. J. (2002). Emotion regulation: Affective, cognitive, and social consequences. *Psychophysiology, 39,* 281–291.

Gross, J. J. (Ed.). (2007). *Handbook of emotion regulation.* New York: Guilford Press.

Hansen, C. H., & Hansen, R. D. (1988). Finding the face in the crowd: An anger superiority effect. *Journal of Personality and Social Psychology, 54,* 917–924.

Harlow, H. F., & Stagner, R. (1933). Psychology of feelings and emotions: II. Theory of emotions. *Psychological Review, 40,* 184–195.

Higgins, E. (2008). Regulatory fit. In J. Y. Shah, W. L. Gardner, J. Y. Shah and W. L. Gardner (Eds.), *Handbook of motivation science* (pp. 356–372). New York: Guilford Press.

Hills, P. J., Werno, M. A., & Lewis, M. B. (2011). Sad people are more accurate at face recognition than happy people. *Consciousness and Cognition: An International Journal, 20,* 1502–1517.

Holmes, D. S. (1974). Investigations of repression: Differential recall of material experimentally or naturally associated with ego threat. *Psychological Bulletin, 81,* 632–653.

Holmes, D. S. (1990). The evidence for repression: An examination of sixty years of research. In J. L. Singer (Ed.), *Repression and dissociation: Implications for personality theory, psychopathology, and health* (pp. 85–102). Chicago, IL: University of Chicago Press.

Huntsinger, J. R., Clore, G. L., & Bar-Anan, Y. (2010). Mood and global–local focus: Priming a local focus reverses the link between mood and global–local processing. *Emotion, 10,* 722–726.

Hütter, M., Sweldens, S., Stahl, C., Unkelbach, C., Klauer, K. C. (2012). Dissociating contingency awareness and conditioned attitudes: Evidence of contingency-unaware evaluative conditioning. *Journal of Experimental Psychology: General, 141,* 539–557.

Ihlebaek, C., Løve, T., Eilertson, D. E., & Magnussen, S. (2003). Memory for a staged criminal event witnessed live and on video. *Memory, 11,* 319–327.

Isen, A. M., Daubman, K. A., & Nowicki, G. P. (1987). Positive affect facilitates creative problem solving. *Journal of Personality and Social Psychology, 52,* 1122–1131.

Isen, A. M., Johnson, M. M., Mertz, E., & Robinson, G. F. (1985). The influence of positive affect on the unusualness of word associations. *Journal of Personality and Social Psychology, 48,* 1413–1426.

Isen, A. M., Shalker, T. E., Clark, M., & Karp, L. (1978). Affect, accessibility of material in memory, and behavior: A cognitive loop? *Journal of Personality and Social Psychology, 36,* 1–12.

James, W. (1884). What is an emotion? *Mind, 19,* 188–205.

Juth, P., Lundqvist, D., Karlsson, A., & Öhman, A. (2005). Looking for foes and friends: Perceptual and emotional factors when finding a face in the crowd. *Emotion, 5,* 379–395.

Kamins, M. A., Marks, L. J., & Skinner, D. (1991). Television commercial evaluation in the context of program induced mood: Congruency versus consistency effects. *Journal of Advertising, 20,* 1–14.

Keil, A., & Ihssen, N. (2004). Identification facilitation for emotionally arousing verbs during the attentional blink. *Emotion, 4,* 23–35.

Klauer, K. C. (1998). Affective priming. In W. Stroebe and M. Hewstone (Eds.), *European Review of Social Psychology* (pp. 67–103). New York: John Wiley and Sons.

Klauer, K. C., & Musch, J. (2003). *Affective priming: Findings and theories.* In K. C. Klauer and J. Musch (Eds.), The psychology of evaluation: Affective processes in cognition and emotion (pp. 7–49). Mahwah, NJ: Lawrence Erlbaum.

Koole, S. L. (2009). The psychology of emotion regulation: An integrative review. *Cognition and Emotion, 23,* 4–41.

Kuhl, J. (2000). A functional-design approach to motivation and self-regulation: The dynamics of personality systems interactions. In M. Boekaerts, P. R. Pintrich and M. Zeidner (Eds.), *Handbook of self-regulation* (pp. 111–169). San Diego, CA: Academic Press.

Lee, A. Y., & Sternthal, B. (1999). The effects of positive mood on memory. *Journal of Consumer Research, 26,* 115–127.

Levey, A. B., & Martin, I. (1975). Classical conditioning of human "evaluative" responses. *Behaviour Research and Therapy, 13,* 221–226.

Loftus, E. F., Garry, M., & Hayne, H. (2008). Repressed and recovered memory. In E. Borgida, S. T. Fiske, E. Borgida and S. T. Fiske (Eds.), *Beyond common sense: Psychological science in the courtroom* (pp. 177–194). Malden, UK: Blackwell Publishing.

Lount, R. B. (2010). The impact of positive mood on trust in interpersonal and intergroup interactions. *Journal of Personality and Social Psychology, 98,* 420–433.

Mandler, G. (2011). From association to organization. *Current Directions in Psychological Science, 20,* 232–235.

Manstead, A. R. (2012). A history of affect and emotion research in social psychology. In A. W. Kruglanski and W. Stroebe (Eds.), *Handbook of the history of social psychology* (pp. 177–198). New York: Psychology Press.

Martin, L., & Clore, G. (Eds.) (2001). *Theories of mood and cognition: A user's guidebook.* Mahwah, NJ: Lawrence Erlbaum Associates Publishers.

Matlin, M. W., & Stang, D. J. (1978). *The Pollyanna principle. Selectivity in language, memory, and thought.* Cambridge, MA: Schenkman.

McDougall, W. (1908). The principal instincts and the primary emotions of man. In *An introduction to social psychology* (pp. 45–89). London: Methuen & Co.

Niedenthal, P. M. (2007). Embodying emotion. *Science, 316,* 1002–1005.

Oaksford, M., Morris, F., Grainger, B., & Williams, J. G. (1996). Mood, reasoning, and central executive processes. *Journal of Experimental Psychology: Learning, Memory, and Cognition, 22,* 476–492.

Ochi, K. (2005). The effects of emotional arousal on the memory of eyewitnesses and victims. *Japanese Psychological Review, 48,* 299–315.

Öhman, A., Lundqvist, D., & Esteves, F. (2001). The face in the crowd revisited: A threat advantage with schematic stimuli. *Journal of Personality and Social Psychology, 80,* 381–396.

Piaget, J. (1954). *The construction of reality in the child.* New York: Free Press.

Pliner, P., & Steverango, C. (1994). Effect of induced mood on memory for flavors. *Appetite, 22,* 135–148.

Pratto, F., & John, O. P. (1991). Automatic vigilance: The attention grabbing power of negative social information. *Journal of Personality and Social Psychology, 61,* 380–391.

Purcell, D. G., Stewart, A. L., & Skov, R. B. (1996). It takes a confounded face to pop out of a crowd. *Perception, 25,* 1091–1108.

Rainis, N. (2001). Semantic contexts and face recognition. *Applied Cognitive Psychology, 15,* 173–186.

Robinson, M. D., & von Hippel, W. (2006). Rose-colored priming effects: Life satisfaction and affective priming. *Journal of Positive Psychology, 1,* 187–197.

Roediger, H., & McDermott, K. B. (1999). False alarms and false memories. *Psychological Review, 106,* 406–410.

Rofé, Y. (2008). Does repression exist? Memory, pathogenic, unconscious and clinical evidence. *Review of General Psychology, 12,* 63–85.

Rowe, G. G., Hirsh, J. B., Anderson, A. K., & Smith, E. (2007). Positive affect increases the breadth of attentional selection. *PNAS Proceedings of the National Academy of Sciences of the United States of America, 104,* 383–388.

Salovey, P., & Singer, J. A. (1989). Mood congruency effects in recall of childhood versus recent memories. *Journal of Social Behavior & Personality, 4,* 99–120.

Schachter, S. (1964). The interaction of cognitive and physiological determinants of emotional state. In L. Berkowitz (Ed.), *Advances in experimental social psychology* (Vol. 1, pp. 49–79). New York: Academic Press.

Schimmack, U. (2005). Attentional interference effects of emotional pictures: Threat, negativity, or arousal? *Emotion, 5,* 55–66.

Schwarz, N., & Clore, G. L. (1983). Mood, misattribution, and judgments of well-being: Informative and directive functions of affective states. *Journal of Personality and Social Psychology, 45,* 513–523.

Schwarz, N., & Clore, G. L. (2007). Feelings and phenomenal experiences. In A. W. Kruglanski and E. Higgins (Eds.), *Social psychology: Handbook of basic principles* (2nd ed.) (pp. 385–407). New York: Guilford Press.

Sinclair, R. C., & Mark, M. M. (1995). The effects of mood state on judgemental accuracy: Processing strategy as a mechanism. *Cognition and Emotion, 9,* 417–438.

Skowronski, J. J., & Carlston, D. E. (1989). Negativity and extremity biases in impression formation: A review of explanations. *Psychological Bulletin, 105,* 131–142.

Storbeck, J., & Clore, G. L. (2005). With sadness comes accuracy; with happiness, false memory: Mood and the false memory effect. *Psychological Science, 16,* 785–791.

Storbeck, J., & Clore, G. L. (2008). The affective regulation of cognitive priming. *Emotion, 8,* 208–215.

Strack, F., Schwarz, N., & Gschneidinger, E. (1985). Happiness and reminiscing: The role of time perspective, affect, and mode of thinking. *Journal of Personality and Social Psychology, 49,* 1460–1469.

Taylor, S. E. (1991). Asymmetrical effects of positive and negative events: The mobilization–minimization hypothesis. *Psychological Bulletin, 110,* 67–85.

Taylor, S. E., & Brown, J. D. (1988). Illusion and well-being: A social psychological perspective on mental health. *Psychological Bulletin, 110,* 67–85.

Teige-Mocigemba, S., & Klauer, K. C. (2008). Automatic evaluation? Strategic effects on affective priming. *Journal of Experimental Social Psychology, 44,* 1414–1417.

Teigen, K. (1994). Yerkes-Dodson: A law for all seasons. *Theory & Psychology, 4,* 525–547.

Teitelbaum, S., & Geiselman, R. (1997). Observer mood and cross-racial cognition of faces. *Journal of Cross-Cultural Psychology, 28,* 93–106.

Tomkins, S. S. (1992). *Affect, imagery, consciousness: Vol. 4. Cognition: Duplication and transformation of information.* New York: Springer.

Trope, Y., & Liberman, N. (2010). Construal-level theory of psychological distance. *Psychological Review, 117,* 440–463.

Trope, Y., & Neter, E. (1994). Reconciling competing motives in self-evaluation: The role of self-control in feedback seeking. *Journal of Personality and Social Psychology, 66,* 646–657.

Unkelbach, C., Fiedler, K., Bayer, M., Stegmüller, M., & Danner, D. (2008). Why positive information is processed faster: The density hypothesis. *Journal of Personality and Social Psychology, 95,* 36–49.

Valentine, T., & Mesout, J. (2009). Eyewitness identification under stress in the London Dungeon. *Applied Cognitive Psychology, 23,* 151–161.

Voss, A., Rothermund, K., & Brandtstädter, J. (2008). Interpreting ambiguous stimuli: Separating perceptual and judgmental biases. *Journal of Experimental Social Psychology, 44,* 1048–1056.

Walther, E., Gawronski, B., Blank, H., & Langer, T. (2009). Changing likes and dislikes through the backdoor: The US-revaluation effect. *Cognition and Emotion, 23,* 889–917.

Watson, J. B. (1919). A schematic outline of the emotions. *Psychological Review, 26,* 165–196.

Wegener, D. T., & Petty, R. E. (1994). Mood management across affective states: The hedonic contingency hypothesis. *Journal of Personality and Social Psychology, 66,* 1034–1048.

Wells, G. L., Malpass, R. S., Lindsay, R. L., Fisher, R. P., Turtle, J. W., & Fulero, S. M. (2000). From the lab to the police station: A successful application of eyewitness research. *American Psychologist, 55,* 581–598.

Winograd, E. & Neisser, U. (Eds.). (1992). *Affect and accuracy in recall: Studies of 'flashbulb' memories.* New York: Cambridge University Press.

Ziegler, R., & Diehl, M. (2011). Mood and multiple source characteristics: Mood congruency of source consensus status and source trustworthiness as determinants of message scrutiny. *Personality and Social Psychology Bulletin, 37,* 1016–1030.

10

Effects of Environmental Context on Human Memory

Steven M. Smith

INTRODUCTION

Returning to a place after many years of absence can bring memories to mind that may have seemed to be long-lost. Remembering experiences often begins with remembering where we were when the events occurred. How do the environmental contexts of experiences affect what we learn and remember? And how can an understanding of environmental context-dependent memory be used to benefit people?

An *environment* refers to one's physical surroundings, such as the immediately perceptible and navigable space in which one is immersed. Whereas no individual object or stimulus should be considered an environment, they are nonetheless *parts* of environments, and collections of objects and stimuli can make up important elements of environments. The environment in which one's experiences occur, or more precisely, one's mental representation of that environment is an *environmental context*, a representation of a place that can be instantiated by an environment that is physically present, one that is remembered, one that is cued or suggested by various stimuli

(such as a photo, a video, or a virtual reality device), or an environment that is imagined. Environmental contexts have been defined operationally in many ways by various researchers, but central to the research that will be considered here are the effects of places in which experiences occur. Although stimuli such as color, type font, mood state, and associated words can be elements of episodic contexts, they are not places where experiences occur, nor do they reliably trigger mental representations of places the way that pictures or movies do. This discussion will focus on places or environments associated with events, and their effects on learning and memory.

The present chapter will review a long history of investigations of effects of environmental contexts on memory, examining a variety of operational definitions of environmental contexts. Theoretical treatments of contextual influences on memory will be discussed, and some applied uses of context cues will be described, primarily in terms of education, aging, clinical applications, and eyewitness memory. Finally, some as-yet-unanswered questions about environmental context and memory will be discussed.

HISTORICAL OVERVIEW: EXPERIMENTAL STUDIES OF ENVIRONMENTAL CONTEXT AND HUMAN MEMORY

The past hundred years of experimental psychology research has produced a steady trickle of studies that have examined, sometimes in colorful and imaginative ways, the effects of environmental contexts on memory. If an environmental context is a mental representation, then how can environmental context be defined operationally? Throughout the long history of studies of context-dependent memory there has never been a consensus of opinion with regards to this subject. Historically, operational definitions have tended to center around global types of context, that is, contexts that are common to entire episodes of events, although there have been notable exceptions (e.g., Dulsky, 1935; Pan, 1926). The initial studies of context-dependent memory began with non-human animals, an area of research that is burgeoning a century later, but interest quickly turned to studies of humans. After a brief description of a few of the early studies with non-human animals, there will be an historical review of twentieth-century research on environmental context effects on human memory.

Early studies with non-human animals

Some of the earliest of the reported experiments were those done by John B. Watson (1907), who studied maze-learning in laboratory rats that had learned an experimental maze, and were given retention trials with the maze oriented in the lab the same way as it had been during learning trials, or oriented in different directions in the same lab. Although negotiating the maze involved the same learned sequence of turns in the different treatment conditions, Watson was quite surprised to find worse performance for those whose maze orientation was altered

from the way it had been at learning, relative to the originally oriented maze. Even more surprising was the finding that shifts in the orientation of the learned maze relative to the laboratory had detrimental effects even on blind rats whose eyes had been surgically removed. Clearly, these pitiful creatures had learned about some subtle environmental features that became part of their maze-learning, and alterations in those features at test disrupted their memories.

The finding that changes in environmental cues that were incidental to learned tasks (e.g., maze-running) had detrimental effects on retention were reported for other animals observed in the laboratory, such as sparrows (Porter, 1906) and pigeons (Hunter, 1911). Other types of changes in incidental environmental contexts, such as changes in the ambient illumination, the position of the experimenter relative to the maze, or rotation of a canvas top of the maze that had one side open, also had detrimental effects of retention (Carr, 1917). Carr summarized these studies by stating, "Any sensorimotor act cannot be regarded as an isolated independent function; the act was learned within a wider sensory environment, and it never ceases to be wholly free from those conditions either during or after its development" (p. 291). Since those early experiments, a great deal of research has studied and explicated the effects of environmental contexts on learning and memory, including effects on generalization, extinction, and renewal (recovery of extinguished learning) in laboratory animals (e.g., Balsam & Tomie, 1985; Bouton, 1991, 1993; Fanselow, 1990; Riccio, Richardson, & Ebner, 1984; Spear, 1979).

Twentieth-century studies with humans

Experiments examining the effects of environmental context on human memory began not long after the first reports with non-human subjects. Smith and Guthrie (1921) described two unpublished experiments by

W. R. Wilson that studied environmental context-dependent memory in humans. The first involved learning four sequences of ten nonsense syllables; two lists were learned inside a laboratory, and two were learned out of doors. Relearning of the four lists was done 72 hours later, half in the laboratory, and half out of doors. Thus, two lists were relearned in the same environmental context in which they had been originally studied, and two were tested in altered environmental contexts. Smith and Guthrie (1921, p. 112) stated,

> In eight of the ten subjects there was greater saving in each case where relearning occurred in the same surroundings in which the first learning had taken place. Two subjects showed in one of their four series a greater saving where relearning had occurred under dissimilar conditions.

In the second experiment the odor of oil of peppermint, versus an absence of the odor was used to operationally define environmental contexts. That experiment again showed context-dependent memory effects in relearning, using a typing task to assess learning and retention. Thus, these two experiments, which manipulated global environmental contexts (i.e., each context corresponded to an entire target list of items) in very different ways, both found that unfamiliar materials were better remembered when study contexts were reinstated, a finding now referred to as a context reinstatement effect.

Other early experiments of global context-dependent memory in humans included a study by Burri (1931), who used the presence or absence of a small audience to operationally define environmental contexts. Burri found that paired associates were better recalled and relearned when the study environmental context, in the form of an audience versus no audience, was reinstated at test. A study by Abernethy (1940) used combinations of two factors, classroom and instructor, to operationally define global environmental contexts in a classroom study of exam scores. Exam scores were highest when students were tested in the same classroom and with the same instructor that had been present during the corresponding lecture, were worst when both room and instructor changed with intermediate performance if only one element changed. These very early studies, which used rooms, outdoor environments, instructors, audiences, and odors to operationally define global contexts, supported findings of global environmental context-dependent memory seen in non-human animals. Since this work, an array of manipulations has been used to operationally define environmental contexts in studies of humans involving global contexts, including radically different rooms (e.g., Smith, Glenberg, & Bjork, 1978), aquatic versus dry environments (Godden & Baddeley, 1975, 1980), and a dry lounge versus a quiet dark flotation tank designed for "sensory deprivation" experiments (Smith & Sinha, 1987). Another approach has been to manipulate a single prominent feature of an environment, such as a noticeable odor (e.g., Cann & Ross, 1989) or background music (e.g., Balch, Bowman, & Mohler, 1992; Smith, 1985). Each of these types of global environmental contexts has been used to demonstrate context reinstatement effects.

Bilodeau and Schlosberg (1951) examined context-dependent interference reduction, rather than reinstatement effects. The basic idea behind interference reduction experiments is that interference-based forgetting, such as retroactive and proactive interference, may depend on the environmental contexts of original and interpolated learning sessions. They, hypothesized that material learned in one environmental context should only minimally interfere with material learned in a different context, relative to learning both original and interpolated material in a single context. The first reported test of this interference reduction hypothesis (Nagge, 1935) failed to show the effect when laboratory rooms were used as environmental contexts. Bilodeau and Schlosberg (1951), however, noted that in Nagge's experiment, both the original and interpolated lists of syllables were presented with the same type of apparatus, a memory drum, making the contexts, from the subject's perspective, highly similar. Bilodeau and Schlosberg (1951), therefore, covaried the apparatus and modes of stimulus presentation with the more general features of global environmental contexts, and their study was the first to report context-dependent interference reduction effects. Others, using variations of their methods, have also reported interference reduction effects (e.g., Greenspoon & Ranyard, 1957; Strand, 1970), a reliable effect, according to a meta-analysis (Smith & Vela, 2001). It is not clear what aspects or elements of environmental contexts must vary for subjects to perceive them as qualitatively different, but researchers should be advised that the apparatus and stimulus modality may serve as important elements in a subject's perceptions and mental representations of environmental contexts.

Just as the necessary and sufficient elements of environmental contexts are not clearly understood, it is also the case that context reinstatement is possible even in the absence of appropriate environmental stimuli. Smith (1979) showed that it is not always necessary to physically reinstate the environmental context of events in order to stimulate memory of those events. Rather, it is possible to mentally reinstate environmental contexts one has experienced, and to use the mentally reinstated contexts as memory cues for events that occurred in those contexts. Subjects tested in unfamiliar surroundings, who were instructed to imagine their study environmental contexts, were able to recall as many critical list words as those whose study environments were physically reinstated. This mental reinstatement of physical environmental contexts was found to be less effective when the use of many similar study contexts made the appropriate study environment difficult to remember. These findings also show that assessing the effects of environmental manipulations, at least for human subjects, is complicated by participants' differential tendencies and abilities to mentally manipulate their own environments through the power of imagination.

Effects of mental reinstatement of context are central to an important application of context effects, eyewitness memory, which will be considered later in this chapter.

Failures to find effects of environmental context manipulations on memory have been reported almost since the time that the first positive findings were reported in the early twentieth century. For example, Reed (1931) found that posture (i.e., sitting versus standing up), manipulated as a contextual cue at learning and at test, had no effect on recall. Giving final exams to students in various psychology classes either in their regular classroom versus in an unfamiliar room, Farnsworth (1934) reported finding no effect of the test room. As already noted, Nagge (1935) found no interference reduction effect using rooms as contexts. A null effect reported by Smith et al. (1978) appeared to have found the key to what moderates environmental context-dependent memory effects; this study noted that although robust effects were found when a free recall test was given, no effect was found on recognition memory tests (See Figure 10.1). A short time later, Godden and Baddeley (1980) confirmed this hypothesis; the context-dependent memory effect they had previously reported for scuba divers taking a recall test (Godden & Baddeley, 1975) was not found when a recognition memory test was used to assess retention (See Figure 10.2).

The subject was further confused when Saufley, Otaka and Bavaresco (1985) reported repeated failures to find environmental context-dependent memory in several experiments involving class exams in different rooms, and Fernandez and Glenberg (1985) reported several experiments in which recall of word lists was not affected by room manipulations. These failures, and others, showed clearly that changing rooms and testing memory are not sufficiently specified conditions for producing robust environmental context reinstatement effects.

Smith and Vela (2001) conducted a meta-analysis that reviewed nearly a century of research on the effects of global manipulations of incidental environmental contexts

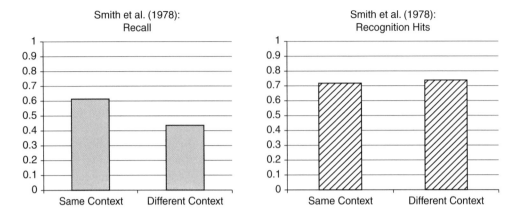

Figure 10.1   Smith et al. (1978) found a significant context effect for recall, but not for recognition memory.

on human memory. Across 93 effect sizes calculated from 75 experiments reported in 41 published articles the average effect size was $d = .28$, a modest but reliable effect. Smith and Vela also identified moderating factors, which had a reliable influence on the magnitude of context effects. For example, larger effect sizes were found for studies that used longer delays prior to testing memory. One of the most revealing findings of that meta-analysis separated experiments based on the degree of inter-item associative processing of memory targets that was encour-

aged at study; those that clearly encouraged non-associative processing at study produced a mean effect size of $d = .33$, whereas those that encouraged associative encoding averaged $d = .13$, a significantly smaller effect. Interestingly, significant positive effects were found for both recall and recognition, indicating that finding incidental environmental context-dependent memory effects depends on principles that were less obvious than the type of memory test used. These principles, or our best understanding of them, will be discussed later in this chapter.

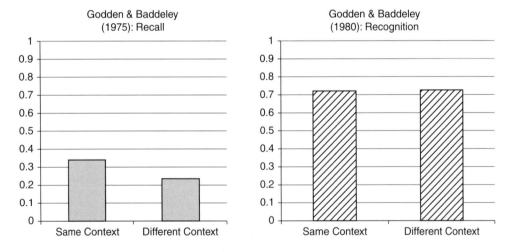

Figure 10.2   Godden and Baddeley (1975) found a significant context effect for recall, but Godden and Baddeley (1980) found no effect for recognition memory.

Pan (1926) manipulated different types of contextual stimuli that accompanied a list of studied word pairs, including context words printed above and below the memory targets, context numbers, or no contexts. Most interesting, however, was Pan's experiment in which subjects studied a list of 24 pictures of male and female faces, each paired with an unfamiliar name; recall of the name paired with each face was tested 48 hours later. At study, each face–name pair was placed on a different picture postcard, and on each card was a picture of a park, building, statue, or a similar type of public place in the city of Chicago. At test, a duplicate set of cards with faces but no names was shown, and subjects tried to recall the name associated with each face. On the recall test, half of the faces were shown with the same pictorial contexts that were originally paired with those faces, and half were tested with new pictorial contexts. Pan found a substantial difference in recall between the two conditions; names tested with the corresponding faces in their originally studied contexts were recalled at a 20 percent greater rate than those tested with new pictorial contexts, a classic context reinstatement effect. Pan also found that changing contexts caused more forgetting for material in the early stages of learning, as compared with better learned material. Pan's study bore a remarkable resemblance to modern studies of environmental context-dependent memory, foreshadowing experimental methods used many decades later.

Although Pan's stimulus materials were local in the sense that each target item was paired with a single picture postcard, they were nonetheless environmental contexts in the sense that each photo was a representation of a physical environment. Thus, each postcard served as a cue for a mental representation of an environment. Physical environments clearly serve the same function, with respect to human representations of environments. Environmental contexts need not be global; local environments can serve the same function, supporting mental representations of environments, whether those

contexts become associated with one or many events. This idea will be discussed later in terms of cue overload or fan effects.

Many studies of context effects have varied elements of environments, but not actual environments or representations of environments. Such studies varied elements such as colors (e.g., Dulsky, 1935) or combinations of colors and screen locations (e.g., Murnane & Phelps, 1993; Wright & Shea, 1991).

THE CURRENT STATE OF KNOWLEDGE FOR THEORY AND RESEARCH

We now turn to the current state of knowledge about environmental context's effects on human memory. This discussion will include methods that are currently used for experimentally manipulating environmental contexts, theoretical principles such as the outshining hypothesis, the cue overload principle, and the roles of recollection and familiarity in context-dependent memory, and context-dependent implicit memory. Also discussed will be the neuroscience of contextual memory, the effects of environmental contexts on early development and aging, and the role of context in clinical treatments.

Methods for manipulating contexts

One direction that experimental studies of context-dependent memory have taken is to make the environments in question radically different from each other, in the tradition of Godden and Baddeley (1975, 1980), who used dry docks versus underwater for different environmental contexts. For example, Thompson, Williams, L'Esperance, and Cornelius (2001), using experienced skydivers as participants, had a list of words studied either on the ground or in the air while skydiving, and had participants recall words either in the study context or in the other context. They observed an effect, but performance was so poor for the skydiving conditions that conditions involving watching videotapes of skydiving, rather than actually being in the air, increased the context-dependent memory effect. Thompson et al.'s attempts to make environmental conditions as different as possible in the different treatment conditions fit with previous such attempts (e.g., Godden & Baddeley, 1975; Smith et al., 1978; Smith & Sinha, 1987). Such studies that compare memory in radically different environments usually show robust environmental context-dependent memory effects, although poor performance in certain environments can cause the effects to be asymmetric.

A different approach has been to ask whether a change in some specific factor or environmental feature is sufficient for finding an effect on memory. Keeping physical environments constant, some have varied the presence or absence of one odor or another (e.g., Aggleton & Waskett, 1999; Cann & Ross, 1989; Parker & Gellatly, 1997), the presence of one musical piece or another (Balch et al., 1992; Smith, 1985), the alteration of one feature of background music (tempo versus timbre, Balch & Lewis, 1996), or the flavor of gum being chewed (Baker, Bezance, Zellaby, & Aggleton, 2004; Johnson & Miles, 2007, 2008). Some researchers have examined context-dependence using independent manipulations of specific factors, such as odor and music (Parker & Gellatly, 1997), or chewing gum and flavor (Johnson & Miles, 2008). Independent manipulations of room environments and a second factor, such as music (Parker & Gellatly, 1997) or task (Isarida & Isarida, 1999), have also been studied.

Currently, the predominant method for effectively manipulating environmental contexts in memory studies is the use of artificial or virtual environments, such as pictures, computer screen configurations, video recordings, or virtual reality devices. Methods involved for computer-generated environmental contexts were pioneered by Murnane and Phelps (e.g., Murnane & Phelps, 1993; Murnane, Phelps, & Malmberg, 1999), who used configurations of computer screen features, such as location, font color, and background color as contexts in most of their experiments. One experiment by Murnane et al. (1999) involved what they termed "rich visual contexts," which consisted of:

> pictures of scenes containing a focal object on which it was sensible to display words. These included a television in a living room, a sign on the side of a desert road, a banner trailing from an airplane, a delivery truck parked in front of a building, and a chalkboard in a school classroom. (p. 409)

Eight word pairs were shown in association with each pictorial context. The simpler contexts that Murnane and Phelps used increased familiarity on a recognition test, that familiarity simply increased both hits and false alarms, not contributing to an improvement in discriminating old from new words on a speeded recognition test. Reinstatement of the rich visual contexts used by Murnane et al., however, improved hits significantly more that it increased false alarms, what Murnane et al. (1999) termed "context-dependent discrimination."

Others using digital representations of environments include Hayes, Nadel, and Ryan (2007), who used pictures of visually rich scenes to study context-dependent recognition of previously seen objects, using photos of scenes from inside of houses, such as an object on a countertop or a table. Hollingworth (2009) presented realistic pictures of scenes, such as a kitchen or a weightlifting room to test context effects on recognition. Hockley (2008) used as contexts pictures of scenes of natural landscapes, seascapes, and buildings to examine the effect of these contexts on recognition, reporting that that the effects were greater for more complex contexts than for simpler ones, such as color backgrounds. All of these studies have shown context-dependent discrimination effects, that is, greater increases in hits than false alarms as a function of reinstatement, although the mean differences produced by these experiments have been fairly small.

Particularly powerful effects of context reinstatement were reported by Smith and

Manzano (2010), who used video-recorded scenes as environmental contexts. The video scenes were 5-second amateur movies of places unfamiliar to the participants, but the scenes showed familiar situations, including, for example, movie clips from a crowd outdoors at a college campus, diners at a delicatessen, and a soccer game. The scenes had movement, action, and sounds, making these video contexts multimodal. A single to-be-learned word was superimposed over each video context (See Figure 10.3). Smith and Manzano tested free recall of the studied words, and found reinstatement effects in which contextually cued recall levels were as much as 50 percent higher than the non-reinstated condition. Clearly, visually rich contexts can produce reliable context cuing, and multimodal videos, which include dynamic sounds and actions, evoke particularly powerful effects. Video contexts have also produced context-dependent memory effects in paired associates recall (Smith, Handy, & Angello, 2010) and recognition memory (Shahabuddin & Smith, 2009).

A final issue about current methods for manipulating contexts concerns the distinction between an environmental contextual stimulus and a generic associative stimulus. Although it seems likely that anyone would agree that a particular room or an underwater setting would clearly qualify as an environmental context, it is not as clear that other operational definitions qualify as such. Although stimuli that represent environments, such as pictures of environments, video-recordings of places, or virtual reality

Figure 10.3 Smith and Manzano (2010) used as contextual stimuli 5-second videotaped scenes of places. Verbal stimuli for participants to learn were shown superimposed over the video contexts.

environments, can evoke varying degrees of feelings of environmental immersion, they do so only in an indirect way that necessarily involves the participants' projection of themselves into those virtual environments. Does a typewritten word printed near a to-be-remembered word qualify as an environmental context? Is a type font a type of environmental context? A face printed near a memory target? Some definitions stretch the limits of what seems like an environment, and reduce the definition of an environmental context to include any associated material whatsoever. Future research must struggle with this concept if we are to have a consensus about what is versus is not truly an environmental context.

Outshining and overshadowing

Overshadowing of environmental context refers to a failure to encode environmental material because one's limited attention is devoted to other information at encoding. Outshining, a similar phenomenon, refers to a failure at test to use environmental cues, even if they have been encoded. Although these principles were originally used to explain early failures to find environmental reinstatement effects with typical recognition tests (e.g., Godden & Baddeley, 1980; Jacoby, 1983; Smith et al., 1978), subsequent findings of context effects in recognition (e.g., Dalton, 1993; Krafka & Penrod, 1985; Smith & Vela, 1992) showed that the type of test was not the key to explaining findings versus failures of context effects. Nonetheless, outshining and overshadowing have been supported by research showing that contextual information may not be encoded or used at test when non-contextual material is given greater attention.

What determines whether one cue or another is better or worse for evoking a specific episodic memory? Although there are numerous factors that can determine the effectiveness of a particular memory cue, such as the integration of a cue with its target,

or its distinctiveness, the focus of discussion in regards to the outshining hypothesis has been cue specificity; better cues are those that better specify the associated target. For example, Smith (1986) showed that the environmental context was a better cue for a list of words when the encoding task minimized the formation of more specific inter-item associations among to-be-remembered words, a pattern that was replicated in the overall meta-analysis by Smith and Vela (1992) discussed above. Consequently, Smith and Vela (1992) tested recognition memory for a single person who had staged a live event, thereby precluding the encoding of inter-item associations among memory targets. That study found significant effects of environmental context reinstatement on recognition of that one person in a photo-spread, a finding consistent with the cue-specificity version of the outshining hypothesis.

A test of the outshining hypothesis was reported by McDaniel, Anderson, Einstein, and O'Halloran (1989). In several experiments they tested the influence of various encoding strategies on environmental context-dependent memory, using dissimilar rooms to manipulate environmental contexts at test. The encoding strategies involved encoding sentences by forming (versus not forming) mental images in various ways, by using (versus not using) a self-referential encoding strategy, or by organizing (versus not organizing) groups of target sentences. Each of these strategies encouraged the encoding of effective mnemonic cues, including visual images, inter-item associations, or the participants' selves. McDaniel et al. (1989) found that conditions that promoted the elaborative encoding of effective non-contextual cues were least likely to find effects of environmental reinstatement, whereas encoding tasks that did not involve visual imagery, inter-item organization, or self-reference were most likely to show the effect of environmental context on memory. These results are consistent with the outshining hypothesis, that global, incidental environmental context cues are less effective when better memory cues are present at test.

Both the overshadowing and outshining effects described here emerge from an embodied cognition perspective, that is, the notion that human memory stems from a need to maintain mental representations of currently experienced environments (e.g., Glenberg, 1997). This embodied view posits that both perceptual and memory systems share the same cognitive resources to manage current environmental stimuli. People disengage their perceptual processing of environmental stimuli in order to make cognitive resources available for memory and other conceptual processes. For example, Glenberg, Schroeder, and Robertson (1998) found that remembering was improved when participants in their study averted their gaze from their environment. Perfect et al. (2008) found that instructing eyewitnesses to close their eyes while remembering either a videotaped or a live/staged event resulted in better memory for detail of the witnessed events. In these studies, suppressing processing of their immediate environment allowed people to devote more of their shared pool of cognitive resources to difficult memory tasks. Therefore, when encoding or recollection focuses on interitem associations among members of a memorized list, processing of the immediate environment is diminished, resulting in smaller effects of the environment on encoding and retrieval.

Cue overload/fan effects

One version of the outshining principle relates to the cue overload effect (e.g., Watkins & Watkins, 1975), also known as the fan effect (Anderson, 1974). The principle that explains cue overload and fan effects is the idea that a memory is more likely to be evoked by an associated cue that has fewer competing targets, and retrieval of that particular memory target becomes less likely the more overloaded the cue is with memory targets (or the greater the size of that cue's fan). A global environmental context with many associated memory targets

should, therefore, be a less effective memory cue than a local context that has only a few associated targets. Thus, an outshining effect should be observed if an overloaded environmental context cue is accompanied by better cues that are less overloaded. Contexts with fewer associated memory targets should be less susceptible to outshining effects, and should therefore show a greater likelihood of producing context reinstatement effects.

The interaction of environmental context manipulations with fan size has been tested by several studies. Examining context-dependent recognition as a function of one versus three different presentation backgrounds, Rutherford (2004) found that reinstatement in the three-contexts condition (i.e., the less overloaded cue condition) exerted a greater effect than did the one-context condition (i.e., the more overloaded context cue). The reinstatement effects that Rutherford reported, however, were quite small even in the less overloaded condition. A similar study by Isarida, Isarida, and Okamoto (2005) compared two versus six color-contexts, and found that less overloaded color-contexts led to a greater reinstatement effects in recognition.

A more dramatic interaction of context reinstatement with fan size was reported by Smith and Manzano (2010), who used one versus three versus fifteen target words per video context, and measured the effect of context reinstatement on recall (See Figure 10.4). Smith and Manzano found a significant context-reinstatement effect even for the most overloaded condition in which there were fifteen words per video context, with an effect size of $d = 1.00$. For the smaller fan size of three words per context the effect was even greater ($d = 2.18$), and for the smallest fan size, the magnitude of the effect of video context reinstatement on recall was remarkable ($d = 3.02$).

Recollection and familiarity

Recollection and familiarity are the two terms commonly used to denote qualitatively different memory processes. Familiarity refers to a rapid cognitive process, the result of which is a graded impression of a previous

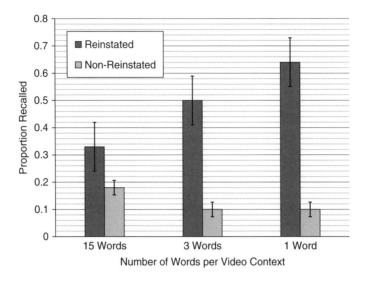

Figure 10.4   Mean proportions recalled as a function of test scene reinstatement and number of words per scene (from Smith & Manzano, 2010).

experience. One can know very quickly whether an object or face or name is familiar or novel, even if that feeling of familiarity produces no memorial content beyond the strength of the feeling of familiarity. In contrast, recollection is a slower memory process, one that brings to mind additional content, such as associated material, or the contextual elements that are bound to a memory. Respecification of the context or source of a remembered event is one way to define recollection. Which of these two memory processes, familiarity or recollection, is affected by environmental contexts?

Murnane and Phelps (e.g., 1993) studied the effects of visually simple screen contexts on recognition memory judgments. In their experiments, participants typically were required to give yes-no recognition responses within a few seconds of memory prompts. These experiments reported numerous findings of context-dependent recognition, defined by the authors as increases in hits and false alarms as a function of context reinstatement at test. These effects were distinguished from context-dependent discrimination effects, which they defined as cases in which context reinstatement increased hits more than false alarms. The pattern of

Murnane and Phelps' results clearly favors a familiarity explanation; that is, previously experienced contexts seen at test increase the global familiarity of both new and old test items.

Other attempts at dissociating the effects of context manipulations on familiarity versus recollection in recognition have been published. For example, Macken (2002) used a *remember–know* paradigm, and found that context-dependent discrimination was found only for *remember* judgments, and not for *know* responses. Hockley (2008) likewise found that words presented on a recognition test showed a context-dependent discrimination effect, but only when target words had been intentionally encoded in association with their study contexts. Again, these effects occurred only for *remember* responses, and not for *know* responses. Hockley pointed out that the same pattern is seen in any associative recognition task, in which recollection plays an important role.

Given that visually simple previously viewed contexts merely increase the judged familiarity of items on a recognition test, and that context-dependent discrimination effects in recognition are found only when items are intentionally associated with their study contexts, or when contexts are visually rich, it seems safe to conclude that recollection must be involved when test contexts evoke memories of events or items that were encoded in those contexts. A sense of familiarity can be evoked by familiar contexts on a recognition test, but such familiarity does not appear to impart the ability to discriminate new test items from old ones.

Context-dependent implicit memory experiments might also be explained by distinguishing the roles of unconscious familiarity and conscious recollection on the memory test. Several failures to find effects of environmental contexts on implicit memory tests have been reported. Jacoby (1983) found no effects of room manipulations on perceptual recognition, a primarily data-driven implicit memory task. Parker, Gellatly, and Waterman (1999) also found no effects of environmental context manipulations on implicit memory tests that are considered to be primarily perceptually-driven, word fragment completion and anagram solution. Using indoors versus outdoors as environmental contexts, McKone and French (2001) found context-dependence on an explicit stem-cued recall test, but not when stem-cued recall was used as an implicit test. Other studies, however, have found significant effects of environmental manipulations on implicit memory tests. Smith, Heath, and Vela (1990) found such effects on an implicit homophone spelling test. Likewise, Parker et al. (1999) found that implicit memory tests that are primarily conceptually driven, namely, category generation and general knowledge questions, did show effects of room manipulations.

Do environmental context manipulations influence implicit memory? Parker, Dagnall, and Coyle (2007) replicated Parker et al.'s (1999) context-dependent effect with a conceptually driven implicit memory test, but they showed that when participants who claimed to have used explicit memory strategies on the test were weeded out, the effect disappeared. Likewise, Mulligan (2011) found environmental context-dependent effects on an implicit category production

test, but the effect was confined to test-aware participants, as identified on a post-test questionnaire. In sum, it appears that the pattern of findings for environmental context-dependent implicit memory can be explained by the degree that explicit recollection was used at the time of the test. This conclusion is consistent with findings that show that context-dependent discrimination in recognition testing is due to the role of recollection.

Familiarity as a memory process may have little to do with contextually evoked memories, but the familiarity of studied material may be an important factor in the dependence of memory on environmental context. Pan (1926) was the first to directly examine this hypothesis. Using paired associates recall, Pan reported that the detrimental effect of a new context at recall was inversely related to the degree of learning, indicating that the least familiar (or poorest learned) was the most susceptible to context-dependent forgetting. Dalton (1993), who examined the effects of room contexts on face recognition, found that context changes impaired recognition only for unfamiliar faces, and not for faces that participants had seen before the study phase of the experiment. Russo, Ward, Guerts, and Scheres (1999) replicated Dalton's findings, showing that reinstated room contexts caused recognition discrimination effects for both faces and for words.

APPLICATIONS OF ENVIRONMENTAL CONTEXT EFFECTS ON MEMORY

Eyewitness memory

An important application of environmental context-dependent memory effects, and the most researched one, concerns methods for enhancing eyewitness memory. Smith and Vela (1992) showed that eyewitnesses' ability to identify the actor of an unexpected staged event was better if the witnesses were returned to the environment where the event was staged. Krafka and Penrod (1985), using a combination of physical and mental context reinstatement conditions, showed that convenience store clerks were better at identifying a previously encountered customer. Using a "guided memory" method that involved mental reinstatement of context plus some details of a witnessed incident, Malpass and Devine (1981) found that witnesses were better at identifying the actors of a staged vandalism with the guided memory enhancement, relative to a control condition that had no context reinstatement. The effectiveness of mental reinstatement of contexts led to its incorporation in a procedure known as the cognitive interview, which is widely used to enhance the memories of eyewitnesses (e.g., Fisher, Schreiber Compo, Rivard, & Hirn, Chapter 31, this volume; Fisher & Geiselman, 1992; Geiselman, Fisher, MacKinnon, & Holland, 1985).

Neuroscience of context

The nature of contextual binding and its role in episodic memory has been an issue of great interest. One focus of research investigations has been the roles of various brain regions, particularly the ventromedial prefrontal cortex and the mediotemporal (hippocampal, parahippocampal, and perirhinal) cortex, in the episodic binding of events, objects, and contexts (e.g., Ciaramelli & Spaniol, 2009; Davachi, 2006; Diana, Yonelinas, & Ranganath, 2007; Hayes, Nadel, & Ryan, 2007). These studies show how medial temporal lobe structures are critically important in episodic memory formation, and that domain-general binding mechanisms are supported by the hippocampus, and domain-specific mechanisms exist within the perirhinal and parahippocampal cortices (Davachi, 2006). Thus, the role of environmental context effects in the treatment of patients with medial temporal disorders may have some applied value.

Development and aging

Infancy and childhood

Effects of environmental context on human memory have been studied primarily using college-aged adults, but there have also been studies of context-dependence in infants and in elderly adults. Carolyn Rovee-Collier and her colleagues pioneered the study of context effects on long-term memory in infants (e.g., Borovsky & Rovee-Collier, 1990; Butler & Rovee-Collier, 1989; Hayne, Greco-Vigorito, & Rovee-Collier, 1993; Hayne, Rovee-Collier, & Borza, 1991). These studies typically use an operant conditioning paradigm in which, for example, a string connects the supine infant's foot to an overhead mobile, and the infant learns to kick that foot to move the mobile, a rewarding outcome. As environmental contexts, crib bumper pads with very different patterns, or different rooms in the infant's home are manipulated. A typical finding is that a change in context impairs recognition after three to five days (e.g., Butler & Rovee-Collier, 1989; Rovee-Collier, Griesler, & Earley, 1985). These context effects are quite robust, even for infants younger than 8 months of age (see Rovee-Collier & Hartshorn, 1999), and clearly reject the idea that learning and memory during infancy is context-independent because of immature hippocampal formation in such young infants.

Although there have been few studies of effects of environmental context during childhood beyond infancy, context-dependent memory was examined in one important study of school-aged children. Jensen, Harris, and Anderson (1971) examined a large sample of children in grades 2, 4, 6, 8, and 10, using a serial recall paradigm. A list of eight nonsense syllables was studied in one room, and 24 hours later students were given a retention test, either in the same environmental context where learning had occurred, or in a very different schoolroom. Jensen et al. (1971) predicted that the environmental manipulations would affect retention more for younger children than for older ones, based on the idea that older but not younger children would have learned to ignore ambient contextual stimuli . However there was a reliable reinstatement effect that was the same for all age levels. Thus, the dependence of memory on incidental environmental contexts can be seen throughout childhood.

Aging and context

There has been great interest in aging and memory binding, that is, associative processes that combine contexts with items and events that occur in those contexts (e.g., Howard, Kahana, & Wingfield, 2006; Kessels, Hobbel, & Postma, 2007; Old & Naveh-Benjamin, 2008; Park, Puglisi, & Sovacool, 1984). In a meta-analysis, Spencer and Raz (1995) found support for the theory that aging is associated with deficits in terms of binding experiences with their contexts; they concluded that age-related memory deficits are reliably greater in memory for contextual information than for content. The brain mechanisms implicated in these age-related memory deficits include the medial temporal/hippocampal region, which binds events into memory traces via temporal contiguity, and functions somewhat automatically for consciously attended materials. The frontal lobes, which direct strategic information processing in an effortful manner, are also implicated in age-related declines in contextual binding (e.g., Old & Naveh-Benjamin, 2008).

Paradoxically, elderly eyewitnesses show greater performance gains than younger ones in terms of memory for details of a witnessed event with the use of the cognitive interview, which relies heavily on mental reinstatement of context to enhance eyewitness memory, as shown by a meta-analysis by Memon, Meissner, and Fraser (2010). This differential benefit for the elderly is explained by the contextual support hypothesis (e.g., Craik, 1994; Craik, Byrd, & Swanson, 1987), which states that older adults increasingly rely on environmental support for long-term memory cues. Given the well-established binding

deficits that older adults show, one would expect that context reinstatement should have *less* of an effect for the elderly, not more. The paradox is resolved, however, by understanding that these binding deficits are in large part due to lack of initiative to intentionally use contextual cues, both at encoding and at test. Whereas younger people tend to initiate intentional encoding of context and mental reinstatement of context cues, older adults are more likely to do so only when they are instructed, or when perceptual cues are provided that tend to initiate such intentional strategies.

Clinical applications

There have been numerous studies relating psychological disorders to contextual binding, such as deficient contextual binding in schizophrenics (e.g., Badcock, Chhabra, Maybery, & Paulik, 2008; Lamy, Goshon-Kosover, Harari, Levkovitz, & Aviani, 2008; McClure, Barch, Flory, Harvey, & Siever, 2008; Talamini & Meeter, 2009); these studies show context processing deficits specific to schizophrenia. Patients with depression have also been studied with respect to contextual binding (e.g., Balardin et al., 2009; Barch, Yodkovik, Sypher-Locke, & Hanewinkel, 2008; Lamy et al., 2008; Levens & Gotlib, 2009). For example, Lamy et al. (2008) found that implicit memory for spatial context was impaired in clinically depressed patients, suggesting an implicit memory impairment for spatial context in depression. Balardin et al. (2009) found mild depressive symptoms interfered with the effects of context encoding instructions in older adults.

A great deal of research has examined the role of environmental context, in both humans and non-human animals, in the acquisition and treatment of phobias and conditioned fear (e.g., Bouton & Bolles, 1979; Bouton & Ricker, 1994; Brooks & Bouton, 1994; Culver, Stoyanova, & Craske, 2011). Fear conditioned to an environmental context, and extinguished in another context, will return when the original context is reinstated (e.g., Bouton & Bolles, 1979). Clinical treatment of fear, such as exposure therapy, also can be dependent on the treatment context; human participants treated for fear of spiders were less fearful when they returned to the treatment context, as compared with those tested in a new context (e.g., Mineka, Mystkowski, Hladek, & Rodriguez, 1999). Instructions to mentally reinstate the treatment context likewise reduce fear in phobics who have received treatment (Mystkowski, Craske, Echiverri, & Labus, 2006).

Educational applications

The applied use of environmental context cues in education and learning is not clear. On the one hand, exam scores for students tested in their regular lecture hall versus in a different classroom usually do not show effects of the test environment (Saufley, Otaka, & Bavaresco, 1985, but see Abernethy, 1940). On the other hand, it is not at all clear whether students learn the bulk of exam material in the classroom, or elsewhere, such as a study place in the library or at home. One unpublished study controlled for study location (Mellgren, 1984), arranging for extra study sessions either in the regular classroom (where the exam was subsequently given) or in a different classroom. Extra study benefited all participants' exam scores, but more so for students whose extra study occurred in the test classroom.

IDENTIFICATION OF PROMISING AND IMPORTANT AREAS FOR FUTURE RESEARCH

Although we have learned a great deal from a long history of research on the effects of environmental contexts on human memory, there are many questions that remain unanswered, and numerous promising directions

for future research. A brief listing of a few of the unanswered questions and promising directions for research follows.

We do not know enough about remembering contexts. In most published research, contexts have been viewed as cues for accessing other material, whereas source memory has been thought of as a means of differentiating one episodic memory from another. Generally, in contextual cuing, one is given (or not given) a cue to determine its effect on producing associated content. In studies of source memory, the associated source material must be retrieved to assess something about already accessed content. These two areas of research need to be better integrated, since they seem to be two sides of the same coin. If a physical cue is withheld, does the rememberer think to recall contexts as a way of recalling events? If source is difficult to access, what are the effects of source reinstatement? Starns and Hicks (2008) examined binding of item and context, and compared that with binding among different types of context information to see, for example, if reinstating object information increased recognition memory for contextual attributes, and whether participants could distinguish between intact and recombined pairings of object and contextual information on an associative recognition test. Such research combines two existing lines of work, namely, contextual cuing and source memory, and represents a promising direction for future research.

Another promising direction for future research is the creation and study of artificial contexts. Published work has already shown the efficacy of pictures and videorecordings of environments for producing strong context reinstatement effects. Virtual reality devices may also provide powerful tools for creating realistic immersive and embodied environments. Such devices have already been used to study both basic (e.g., Radvansky & Copeland, 2006) and applied (e.g., García-Palacios, Hoffman, Carlin, Furness, & Botella, 2002) research questions. This area of research could lead to digital support tools that are useful in a number of ways, such as diagnosing or treating clinical disorders, or for enhancing learning and training.

Decontextualization, that is, learning in ways that do not depend on contextual cues, is another promising direction for future research. Much semantic and conceptual knowledge can be optimally used if it does not rely on specific contexts; how can such decontextualized knowledge be acquired and developed? This question touches on how episodic memories eventually give rise to semantic memories (Tulving, 1972; Tulving, 1983). One of the first researchers of environmental context, Pan (1926), showed that well-learned material was less context-dependent than poorly learned material. Furthermore, Smith and Rothkopf (1984) found some evidence that varying contexts during learning can benefit retention of classroom material. Future research should return to these early findings to learn more about the process of knowledge decontextualization, which could be particularly important in terms of retaining and transferring knowledge acquired through education and training.

Related to training and performance issues is the *home-field advantage*, that is, the benefit for individuals and teams in sport competitions who are playing at their home field, court, or stadium, relative to playing at the opposing team's field. This advantage is not a myth; teams consistently win over 50 percent of the home games played under a balanced home and away schedule (Courneya & Carron, 1992). Researchers have identified several possible factors for the home-field advantage, including influences of the crowd (e.g., motivational support from spectators, influences on referees), home rule factors, travel (e.g., jet lag), and familiarity. The importance of familiarity has been examined in terms of how recently a team has relocated, and differences in playing surfaces (e.g., Pollard, 1986, 2002), but research has not focused on the role of environmental context-dependent memory. It is conceivable that memory of training, specific skills, or planned plays could be affected by environmental memory cues associated with home playing fields.

Are context cues privileged, that is, are they automatically encoded, without the need for attentional resources? If so, is contextual information automatically bound to events and experiences? Automatic encoding and binding of truly incidental environmental information would make contexts qualitatively different from other types of stimuli. If so, then neuroimaging might reveal mental representations of contexts that would be distinguishable from the way the brain represents other types of associatively bound information. Privileged material could be particularly useful as mnemonic scaffolding in education and training situations. In addition, as previously noted, older adults' failures to spontaneously use context cues can be remedied through instructions and perceptually obvious cues; provision of contextual support could be an important tool for addressing age-related memory deficits.

CONCLUSION

Although many different operational definitions of "context" have been used to manipulate and study the role of environmental contexts in human memory, it can be concluded that experiences tend to become associated with the environments in which they occur, and that environmental contexts can serve as retrieval cues for events that occurred in those contexts. Such context reinstatement effects have been observed in non-human animals, infants, children, and adults.

Not only physical reinstatement of environments, but mental reinstatement of contexts can also cause reinstatement effects. That is, imagining or thinking about environments that are not physically present can cue memories associated with the imagined contexts. Thus, it is not the physical environment, itself, that is bound to events, but rather *mental representations* of environments that are associated with *mental representations* of events and experiences that occur in those contexts. This fact is one of the major reasons that experimental manipulations may not have significant cuing effects; that is, those tested in new environments are not necessarily confined to their test environments, but can use non-ambient cues to retrieve memories. The ability to mentally access non-ambient environmental cues is a retrieval strategy that may not be used by less sophisticated subjects, explaining why infants and non-human animals show such reliable effects of experimentally manipulated environments.

Further complicating our understanding of environmental context effects is that not all memory cues are equal. Cues that are better integrated with memory targets are more effective than those that are poorly-integrated with memories. The more overloaded a context cue is (i.e., the larger a response fan it has), the less effective it is for evoking a particular target memory. Simple contexts are less effective as cues than contexts that are richer in content. When more effective non-contextual cues are used at recall, that is, better integrated and less overloaded cues that are richer in content, then simple incidental global environmental context cues have less of an effect on memory.

Both unconscious familiarity and conscious recollection appear to be affected by contextual manipulations. Contextually cued familiarity, however, does not lead to memory of associatively bound content, but rather increases familiarity of both studied and non-studied items in recognition. Contextual cues appear to enhance memory via recollection, which relies on associative binding of contextual information with studied or experienced events. Thus, context cues may have weaker effects on the memories of individuals who are poorer at associative binding, such as schizophrenic individuals and the elderly.

REFERENCES

Abernethy, E. M. (1940). The effect of changed environmental conditions upon the results of college examinations. *Journal of Psychology, 10*, 293–301.

Aggleton, J. P., & Waskett, L. (1999). The ability of odours to serve as state-dependent cues for real-world memories: can Viking smells aid the recall of Viking experiences? *British Journal of Psychology, 90*, 1–7.

Anderson, J. R. (1974). Retrieval of propositional information from long-term memory. *Cognitive Psychology, 6*, 451–474.

Badcock, J. C., Chhabra, S., Maybery, M. T., & Paulik, G. (2008). Context binding and hallucination predisposition. *Personality and Individual Differences, 45*, 822–827.

Baker, J. R., Bezance, J. B., Zellaby, E., & Aggleton, J. P. (2004). Chewing gum can produce context-dependent effects upon memory. *Appetite, 43*, 207–210.

Balardin, J. B., Vedana, G., Ludwig, A., de Lima, D. B., Argimon, I., Schneider, R., Luz, C., Schröder, N., & Bromberg, E. (2009). Contextual memory and encoding strategies in young and older adults with and without depressive symptoms. *Aging & Mental Health, 13*(3), 313–318.

Balch, W. R., Bowman, K., & Mohler, L. A. (1992). Music-dependent memory in immediate and delayed word recall. *Memory & Cognition, 20*, 21–28.

Balch, W., & Lewis, B. S. (1996). Music-dependent memory: The roles of tempo change and mood mediation. *Journal of Experimental Psychology: Learning, Memory, and Cognition, 22*(6), 1354–1363.

Balsam, P. D., & Tomie, A. (Eds.) (1985). *Context and learning.* Hillsdale, NJ: Erlbaum.

Barch, D. M., Yodkovik, N., Sypher-Locke, H., & Hanewinkel, M. (2008). Intrinsic motivation in schizophrenia: Relationships to cognitive function, depression, anxiety, and personality. *Journal of Abnormal Psychology, 117*(4), 776–787.

Bilodeau, I. M., & Schlosberg, H. (1951). Similarity in stimulating conditions as a variable in retroactive inhibition. *Journal of Experimental Psychology, 41*, 199–204.

Borovsky, D., & Rovee-Collier, C. (1990). Contextual constraints on memory retrieval at six months. *Child Development, 61*, 1569–1583.

Bouton, M. E. (1991). Context and retrieval in extinction and in other examples of interference in simple associative learning. In L. Dachowski and C. F. Flaherty (Eds.), *Current topics in animal learning: Brain, emotion, and cognition* (pp. 25–53). Hillsdale, NJ: Erlbaum.

Bouton, M. E. (1993). Context, time, and memory retrieval in the interference paradigms of Pavlovian learning. *Psychological Bulletin, 114*, 80–99.

Bouton, M. E., & Bolles, R. C. (1979). Contextual control of the extinction of conditioned fear. *Learning and Motivation, 10*, 445–466.

Bouton, M. E., & Ricker, S. T. (1994). Renewal of extinguished responding in a second context. *Animal Learning and Behavior, 22*(3), 317–324.

Brooks, D. C., & Bouton, M. E. (1994). A retrieval cue for extinction attenuates response recovery (renewal) caused by a return to the conditioning context. *Journal of Experimental Psychology: Animal Behavior Processes, 20*(4), 366–379.

Burri, C. (1931). The influence of an audience upon recall. *Journal of Educational Psychology, 22*, 683–690.

Butler, J., & Rovee-Collier, C. (1989). Contextual gating of memory retrieval. *Developmental Psychology, 22*(6), 533–552.

Cann, A., & Ross, D. A. (1989). Olfactory stimuli as context cues in human memory. *American Journal of Psychology, 102*, 91–102.

Carr, H. (1917). Maze studies with the white rat. I. Normal animals, *Animal Behavior, 7*, 259–275.

Ciaramelli, E., & Spaniol, J. (2009). Ventromedial prefrontal damage and memory for context: Perceptual versus semantic features. *Neuropsychology, 23*, 649–657.

Courneya, K. S., & Carron, A. V. (1992). The home-field advantage in sport competitions: A literature review. *Journal of Sport and Exercise Psychology, 14*, 28–39.

Craik, F. I. M. (1994). Memory changes in normal aging. *Current Directions in Psychological Science, 5*, 155–158. doi:10.1111/j.1467-8721.1994.tb00166.x

Craik, F. I. M., Byrd, M., & Swanson, J. M. (1987). Patterns of memory loss in three elderly samples. *Psychology & Aging, 2*, 79–86. doi:10.1037/0882-7974.2.1.79

Culver, N. C., Stoyanova, M., & Craske, M. G. (2011). Clinical relevance of retrieval cues for attenuating context renewal of fear. *Journal of Anxiety Disorders, 25*, 284–292.

Dalton, P. (1993). The role of stimulus familiarity in context-dependent recognition. *Memory & Cognition, 21*, 223–234.

Davachi, L. (2006). Item, context, and relational episodic encoding in humans. *Neuropsychology, 18*, 693–700.

Diana, R. A., Yonelinas, A. P., & Ranganath, C. (2008). The effects of unitization on familiarity-based source memory: Testing a behavioral prediction derived from neuroimaging data. *Journal of Experimental Psychology: Learning, Memory, and Cognition, 34*(4), 730–740.

Dulsky, S. G. (1935). The effect of a change of background on recall and relearning. *Journal of Experimental Psychology, 18*, 725–740.

Fanselow, M. S. (1990). Factors governing one-trial contextual conditioning. *Animal Learning and Behavior, 18*, 264–270.

Farnsworth, P. R. (1934). Examinations in familiar and unfamiliar surroundings. *Journal of Social Psychology, 5*, 128–129.

Fernandez, A., & Glenberg, A. M. (1985). Changing environmental context does not reliably affect memory. *Memory & Cognition, 13*, 333–345.

Fisher, R. P., & Geiselman, R. E. (1992). *Memory enhancing techniques for investigative interviewing: The cognitive interview*. Springfield, IL: Charles C. Thomas.

García-Palacios, A., Hoffman, H., Carlin, A., Furness, T. A., & Botella, C. (2002). Virtual reality in the treatment of spider phobia: A controlled study. *Behaviour Research and Therapy, 40*, 983–993.

Geiselman, R. E., Fisher, R. P., MacKinnon, D. P., & Holland, H. L. (1985). Eyewitness memory enhancement in the police interview: Cognitive retrieval mnemonics versus hypnosis. *Journal of Applied Psychology, 70*(2), 401–412.

Glenberg, A. M. (1997). What memory is for. *Behavioral & Brain Sciences, 20*, 1–55.

Glenberg, A. M., Schroeder, J. L., & Robertson, D. A. (1998). Averting the gaze disengages the environment and facilitates remembering. *Memory & Cognition, 26*, 651–658.

Godden, D. R., & Baddeley, A. D. (1975). Context-dependent memory in two natural environments: On land and underwater. *British Journal of Psychology, 66*, 325–331.

Godden, D. R., & Baddeley, A. D. (1980). When does context influence recognition memory? *British Journal of Psychology, 71*, 99–104.

Greenspoon, J., & Ranyard, R. (1957). Stimulus conditions and retroactive inhibition. *Journal of Experimental Psychology, 53*, 55–59.

Hayes, S. M., Nadel, L., & Ryan, L. (2007). The effect of scene context on episodic object recognition: Parahippocampal cortex mediates memory encoding and retrieval success. *Hippocampus, 17*(9), 873–889.

Hayne, H., Greco-Vigorito, C., & Rovee-Collier, C. (1993). Forming contextual categories in infancy. *Cognitive Development, 8*, 63–82.

Hayne, H., Royce-Collier, C., & Borza, M. A. (1991). Infant memory for place information. *Memory & Cognition, 19*, 378–386.

Hockley, W. E. (2008). The effects of environmental context on recognition memory and claims of remembering. *Journal of Experimental Psychology: Learning, Memory, and Cognition, 34*, 1412–1429.

Hollingworth, A. (2009). Two forms of scene memory guide visual search: Memory for scene context and memory for the binding of target object to scene location. *Visual Cognition, 17*, 273–291.

Howard, M. W., Kahana, M. J., & Wingfield, A. (2006). Aging and contextual binding: Modeling recency and lag-recency effects with the temporal context model. *Psychonomic Bulletin & Review, 13*, 439–445.

Hunter, W. S. (1911). Some labyrinth habits of the domestic pigeon. *Journal of Animal Behavior, 1*, 278–304.

Isarida, T., & Isarida, T. K. (1999). Effects of contextual changes between class and intermission on episodic memory. *Japanese Journal of Psychology, 69*, 478–486.

Isarida, T., Isarida, T. K., & Okamoto, K. (2005). Influences of cue overload on background-color context effects in recognition. *Japanese Journal of Cognitive Psychology, 3*, 45–54.

Jacoby, L. L. (1983). Perceptual enhancement: Persistent effects of an experience. *Journal of Experimental Psychology: Learning, Memory, & Cognition, 9*, 21–38.

Jensen, L. C., Harris, K., & Anderson, D. C. (1971). Retention following a change in ambient contextual stimuli for six age groups. *Developmental Psychology, 4*, 394–399.

Johnson, A. J., & Miles, C. (2007). Evidence against memorial facilitation and context- dependent memory effects through chewing gum. *Appetite, 48*, 394–396.

Johnson, A. J., & Miles, C. (2008). Chewing gum and context-dependent memory: The independent roles of chewing gum and mint flavor. *British Journal of Psychology, 99*, 293–306.

Kessels, R. P. C., Hobbel, D., & Postma, A. (2007). Aging, context memory and binding: a comparison of "what, where and when" in young and older adults. *The International Journal of Neuroscience, 117*(6), 795–810.

Krafka, C., & Penrod, S. (1985). Reinstatement of context in a field experiment on eyewitness identification. *Journal of Personality & Social Psychology, 49*, 58–69.

Lamy, D., Goshen-Kosover, A., Aviani, N., Harari, H., & Levkovitz, H. (2008). Implicit memory for spatial context in depression and schizophrenia. *Journal of Abnormal Psychology, 117*(4), 954– 61.

Levens, S. M., & Gotlib, I. H. (2009). Impaired selection of relevant positive information in depression. *Journal of Abnormal Psychology, 118*(4), 757–66.

Macken, W. J. (2002). Environmental context and recognition: The role of recollection and familiarity.

Journal of Experimental Psychology: Learning, Memory, and Cognition, 28, 153–161.

Malpass, R. S., & Devine, P. G. (1981). Guided memory in eyewitness identification. *Journal of Applied Psychology, 66*, 343–350.

McClure, M. M., Barch, D. M. Flory, J. D., Harvey, P. D., & Siever, L. J. (2008). Context processing in schizotypal personality disorder: Evidence of specificity of impairment to the schizophrenia sSpectrum. *Journal of Abnormal Psychology, 117*(2), 342–354.

McDaniel, M. A., Anderson, C. D., Einstein, G. O., & O'Halloran, C. M. (1988). Modulation of environmental reinstatement effects through encoding strategies. *American Journal of Psychology, 102*, 523–548.

McKone, E., & French, B. (2001). In what sense is implicit memory "episodic"? The effect of reinstating environmental context. *Psychonomic Bulletin & Review, 8*(4), 806–811.

Mellgren, R. L. (1984). The classroom as context. Paper presented at the convention of the Southwestern Psychological Association, New Orleans, LA.

Memon, A., Meissner, C. A., & Fraser, J. (2010). The cognitive interview: A meta-analytic review and study space analysis of the past 25 years. *Psychology, Public Policy, and Law, 16*(4), 340–372.

Mineka, S. M., Mystkowski, J. L., Hladek, D., & Rodriguez, B. I. (1999). The effects of changing contexts on return of fear following exposure therapy for spider fear. *Journal of Consulting and Clinical Psychology, 67*(4), 599–604.

Mulligan, N. W. (2011). Conceptual implicit memory and environmental context. *Consciousness and Cognition, 20*, 737–744.

Murnane, K., & Phelps, M. P. (1993). A global activation approach to the effect of changes in environmental context on recognition. *Journal of Experimental Psychology: Learning, Memory, and Cognition, 19*, 882–894.

Murnane, K., Phelps, M. P., & Malmberg, K. (1999). Context-dependent recognition memory: The ICE theory. *Journal of Experimental Psychology: General, 128*, 403–415.

Mystkowski, J. L., Craske, M. G., Echiverri, H. M., & Labus, J. S. (2006). Mental reinstatement of context and return of fear in spider-fearful participants. *Behavior Therapy, 37*, 49–60.

Nagge, J. W. (1935). An experimental test of the theory of associative interference. *Journal of Experimental Psychology, 18*, 663–682.

Old, S. R., & Naveh-Benjamin, M. (2008). Differential effects of age on item and associative measures of memory: A meta-analysis. *Psychology and Aging,* *23,* 104–118.

Pan, S. (1926). The influence of contextual conditions upon learning and recall. *Journal of Experimental Psychology, 9,* 468–491.

Park, D. C., Puglisi, J. T., & Sovacool, M. (1984). Picture memory in older adults: Effects of contextual detail at encoding and retrieval. *Journal of Gerontology, 39,* 213–215.

Parker, A., Dagnall, N., & Coyle, A. (2007). Environmental context effects in conceptual explicit and implicit memory. *Memory, 15,* 423–434.

Parker, A., & Gellatly, A. (1997). Moveable cues: A practical method for reducing context dependent forgetting. *Journal of Applied Cognitive Psychology, 11,* 163–173.

Parker, A., Gellatly, A., & Waterman, M. (1999). The effect of environmental context on memory: Dissociation between perceptual and conceptual implicit tests. *European Journal of Cognitive Psychology, 11,* 555–570.

Perfect, T. J., Wagstaff, G. F., Moore, D., Andrews, B., Cleveland, V., Newcombe, S., Brisbane, K., & Brown, L. (2008). How can we help witnesses to remember more? It's an (eyes) open and shut case. *Law and Human Behavior, 32,* 314–324. doi:10.1007/s10979-007-9109-5

Pollard, R. (1986). Home advantage in soccer: A retrospective analysis. *Journal of Sports Sciences, 4,* 237–248.

Pollard, R. (2002). Evidence of a reduced home advantage when a team moves to a new stadium. *Journal of Sports Sciences, 20,* 969–973.

Porter, J. P. (1906). Further study of the English sparrow and other birds. *American Journal of Psychology, 17,* 248–271.

Radvansky, G. A., & Copeland, D. E. (2006). Walking through doorways causes forgetting: Situation models and experienced space. *Memory & Cognition, 34,* 1150–1156.

Reed, H. J. (1931). The influence of a change of conditions upon the amount recalled. *Journal of Experimental Psychology, 14,* 632–649.

Riccio, D. C., Richardson, R., & Ebner, D. L. (1984). Memory retrieval deficits based upon altered contextual cues: A paradox. *Psychological Bulletin, 96,* 152–165.

Rovee-Collier, C., & Hartshorn, K. (1999). Long-term memory in human infants: Lessons in psychobiology. In C. Rovee-Collier & K. Hartshorn (Eds.), *Advances in the study of behavior, Vol. 28* (pp. 175–245)by, San Diego, CA: Academic Press.

Rovee-Collier, C., Griesler, P. C., & Earley, L. A. (1985). Contextual determinants of retrieval in three-month-old infants. *Learning and Motivation, 16,* 139–157.

Russo, R., Ward, G., Guerts, H., Scheres, A. (1999). Context effects in recognition memory for unfamiliar faces. *Journal of Experimental Psychology: Learning, Memory and Cognition, 25,* 488–499.

Rutherford, A. (2004). Environmental context-dependent recognition memory effects: An examination of ICE model and cue-overload hypotheses. *Quarterly Journal of Experimental Psychology, 57A,* 107–127.

Saufley, W. H., Jr., Otaka, S. R., & Bavaresco, J. L. (1985). Context effects: Classroom tests and contextual independence. *Memory & Cognition, 13,* 522–528.

Shahabuddin, S., & Smith, S. M. (October, 2009). Context-dependent recognition memory. Presented at ARMADILLO, Rice University, Houston, TX.

Smith, S., & Guthrie, E. R. (1921). *General psychology in terms of behavior.* New York: Appleton.

Smith, S. M. (1979). Remembering in and out of context. *Journal of Experimental Psychology: Human Learning & Memory, 5,* 460–471.

Smith, S. M. (1985). Background music and context-dependent memory. *American Journal of Psychology, 6,* 591–603.

Smith, S. M. (1986). Environmental context-dependent recognition memory using a short-term memory task for input. *Memory & Cognition, 14,* 347–354.

Smith, S. M., Glenberg, A., & Bjork, R. A. (1978). Environmental context and human memory. *Memory & Cognition, 6,* 342–353.

Smith, S. M., Handy, J., & Angello, G. (November, 2010). Video context-dependent memory for Swahili–English word pairs. Presented at the meeting of the Psychonomic Society, St. Louis, MO.

Smith, S. M., Heath, F. R., & Vela, E. (1990). Environmental context-dependent homophone spelling. *American Journal of Psychology, 103,* 229–242.

Smith, S. M., & Manzano, I. (2010). Video context-dependent recall. *Behavior Research Methods, 42,* 292–301; doi:10.3758/BRM.42.1.292.

Smith, S. M., & Rothkopf, E.Z. (1984). Contextual enrichment and distribution of practice in the classroom. *Cognition & Instruction, 1,* 341–358.

Smith, S. M., & Sinha, A. K. (1987). *Effects of brief immersion in a flotation tank on memory and cognition* (Tech. Rep. No. CSCS-004). College Station, TX: Texas A&M University, Committee for the Study of Cognitive Science.

Smith, S. M., & Vela, E. (1992). Environmental context-dependent eyewitness recognition. *Applied Cognitive Psychology, 6,* 125–139.

Smith, S. M., & Vela, E. (2001). Environmental context-dependent memory: A review and meta-analysis. *Psychonomic Bulletin & Review, 8,* 203–220.

Spear, N. E. (1979). Experimental analysis of infantile amnesia. In J. F. Kihlstrom and F. J. Evans (Eds.), *Functional disorders of memory* (pp. 75–101). Hillsdale, NJ: Erlbaum.

Spencer, W. D., & Raz, N. (1995). Differential effects of age on memory for content and context: A meta-analysis. *Psychology & Aging, 10,* 527–539.

Starns J. J., & Hicks, J. L. (2008). Context attributes in memory are bound to item information, but not to one another. *Psychonomic Bulletin & Review, 15*(2), 309–314.

Strand, B. Z. (1970). Change of context and retroactive inhibition. *Journal of Verbal Learning & Verbal Behavior, 9,* 202–206.

Talamini, L. M., & Meeter, M. (2009). Dominance of objects over context in a mediotemporal lobe model of schizophrenia. *PlOS ONE, 4*(8):e6505.

Thompson, L. A., Williams, K. L., L'Esperance, P. R., & Cornelius, J. (2001). Context-dependent memory under stressful conditions: The case of skydiving. *Human Factors, 43*(4), 611–619.

Tulving, E. (1972). Episodic and semantic memory. In E. Tulving and W. Donaldson (Eds.), *Organization of memory* (pp. 382–402). New York: Academic Press, Inc.

Tulving, E. (1983). *Elements of episodic memory.* New York: Oxford University Press.

Watkins, O. C., & Watkins, M. J. (1975). Buildup of proactive inhibition as a cue-overload effect. *Journal of Experimental Psychology: Human Learning & Memory, 104,* 442–452.

Watson, J. B. (1907). Kinesthetic and organic sensations: their role in the reactions of the white rat to the maze. *Psychological Review: Monograph Supplements,* Whole No. 33, *8*(2), 1–101.

Wright, D. L., & Shea, C. H. (1991). Contextual dependencies in motor skills. *Memory & Cognition, 19,* 361–370.

11

The Testing Effect

Kathleen B. McDermott, Kathleen M. Arnold, and Steven M. Nelson

I'm curious to see if in a year from now, I can remember EVERYTHING from my birthday week. So I started yesterday.
Started what exactly? Not memorizing, actually. Reviewing.
Long term memory is all about reviewing.
(Feb 3, 2012 blogpost, Climbformemory.org by Nelson Dellis, 2011, 2012 US Memory Champion)

The basic principle behind US Memory Champion Nelson Dellis's approach to remembering described above is that the best way to remember information over the long term is to practice retrieval of that information in the interim. Specifically, as studied in the laboratory, the *testing effect* refers to the finding that "subjects tested between the initial learning episode and the final test given over the material outperform subjects only given the final test" (Glover, 1989, p. 392). Figure 11.1 demonstrates the basic finding, which can be shown between participants (as described by Glover) or within participants such that a subset of the studied items are tested initially and the others are not. Note that this positive effect of prior tests occurs even in the absence of experimenter-provided feedback.

Over time, the definition of the testing effect has morphed somewhat to include the observation that an initial retrieval practice (or "test") is so powerful that it can actually enhance later memory more than an additional study phase (e.g., Kornell & Son, 2009). Although that comparison is a particularly impressive demonstration of the power of retrieval to enhance subsequent retention, we here restrict the use of the term "testing effect" to the no-test comparison, following Glover (1989). There are a multitude of ways to demonstrate that retrieval practice benefits later memory, however, and we do touch upon some of these other methods, albeit briefly.

HISTORY

In an early demonstration of the testing effect, Gates (1917) set out to test the intuition of Bacon, who (300 years previously) had posited that "If you read a piece of text through twenty times, you will not learn it by heart so easily as if you read it ten times while attempting to recite from time to time and consulting the text when your memory fails" (Bacon 1620/2000, p. 143). In his empirical test of Bacon's conjecture, Gates asked grammar school students to spend nine

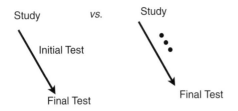

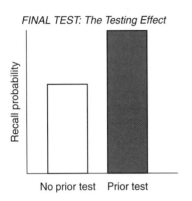

Figure 11.1   The "Testing Effect" is demonstrated when performance on a final test differs as a function of whether an initial test (without feedback) occurred. Typically the effect is beneficial, although there are exceptions.

minutes attempting to learn 16 nonsense syllables (or, in another experiment, biographical facts). Each student was assigned to one of five groups, which differed according to how the nine-minute learning period was spent. Students in the first group tried to learn the material by reading and re-reading it for the full nine minutes. The other groups spent varying amounts of time reading and reciting (i.e., self-testing, or, as Gates said, in "recitation or voluntary recall of what has been learned" (p. 1)). The primary finding was that the greater the percent of time spent in recitation (from 0 to 20 to 40, 60, or 80 percent of the total time) the greater the proportion of information recalled a few hours later.

In considering the results of his studies, Gates (1917, p. 267) quotes Katzaroff (1908): "in the readings, the subject is passive, calm, indifferent; in recitations he is active, he has to seek, he rejoices when he has found and

is irritated at the syllables which evade his recall." As is considered later in the chapter, the exact cognitive processes leading to the testing effect are still under debate, but theorizing about the power of retrieval to enhance memory has a long history.

Over 20 years after Gates's landmark study, another impressive large-scale classroom experiment on the role of retrieval practice was undertaken by Spitzer (1939), who asked 3605 sixth-grade students in Iowa to spend eight minutes reading short (approx. 600-word) fact-heavy articles on the topics of "bamboo" and "peanuts." Most students took two tests, and Spitzer manipulated the retention interval between reading and the initial test and that between the first and second test. The second test was unexpected by the students. Several key findings emerged. When the time interval between reading the article and taking the test was held constant, students receiving their second test outperformed those receiving their first test. Another observation is that very little forgetting occurred from the first to the second test: Testing seemed to dramatically slow the rate of forgetting, despite a long interval (in many conditions two weeks) between tests.

Glover's (1989) article entitled "The 'testing' phenomenon: Not gone but nearly forgotten" rejuvenated interest in the phenomenon, as did Carrier and Pashler's (1992) "The influence of retrieval on retention," in which it was demonstrated convincingly that the testing effect cannot be attributed to simple re-presentation of the information. Consider a manipulation in which subjects are given a set of material to learn, after which they either attempt to remember the material or do some other activity for an equivalent amount of time. Then everyone is asked to recall the material. Might the group that took an initial test outperform the control group simply because some of the items were re-encountered during the intervening test phase? That is, is there anything special about retrieval, or is any re-presentation sufficient to produce the benefit? Carrier and Pashler demonstrated that testing has benefits beyond the effects of simple re-presentation. They compared performance in a condition in which subjects restudied cue-target word pairs for ten seconds each and one in which they attempted retrieval of the target when given the cue for five seconds and then restudied the pair for five seconds. The pairs that were tested (five seconds) and then restudied (five seconds) were better recalled on a later test, indicating that attempting retrieval offered something over and above simple re-presentation of the information in terms of its effects on later memory.

Below, we consider various features of the testing effect. Specifically, if a single test is good, are more tests better? Does feedback influence the impact of testing? Does testing one set of concepts affect memory for related, non-tested concepts? Does a retrieval attempt influence later encoding attempts? What are the theoretical approaches to thinking about the testing effect? What are the implications for learning in the classroom? We consider these questions in turn, with a particular emphasis on the topic of how retrieval attempts impact later encoding opportunities (i.e., test-potentiated learning). This topic receives more in-depth focus than the others, as it has not received as much recent attention as the others, which have been reviewed elsewhere (Roediger & Butler, 2011; Roediger & Karpicke, 2006a; Roediger, Putnam, & Smith, 2011).

A SINGLE TEST HELPS, BUT MORE TESTS ARE BETTER

If taking a single test enhances later memory, can multiple successive tests help more? As will be seen, the answer seems to be yes. Allen, Mahler, and Estes (1969) addressed this question by giving subjects five or ten study trials in a paired-associate learning paradigm using three-letter words paired with two-digit numbers (e.g., *cat–13*). They were then given zero, one, or five test trials without feedback. Twenty-four hours later,

everyone returned for a final set of tests. Here we focus on the first test trial of Day 2. As shown in Figure 11.2, the proportion correct (for the ten-study trial condition) was greatest for the items that had received five test trials, intermediate for the one-test condition, and lowest for the zero-test condition. Similar patterns were seen for items receiving five study trials, although overall performance was worse. Allen et al. (1969, p. 465) noted that "overnight retention loss was substantially reduced by the effect of a single [test] trial after training on Day 1 and was almost completely eliminated by a sequence of five [test] trials after training on Day 1". In short, they obtained a testing effect, and the benefit was magnified when more initial tests had occurred.

Wheeler and Roediger (1992) presented subjects with a series of 60 slides showing pictures of objects and then (a few minutes later) tested some subjects three successive times, some once, and some not at all. The tests were *forced recall* tests, in which people were given answer sheets with 60 lines and instructed to fill in answers for all 60 lines. That is, they were to remember as many of the 60 pictures as possible but if unable to remember all 60 to guess to fill the 60 spaces. A week later, all subjects took three successive forced recall tests.

Interest here focuses on the first recall test after the delay. How did performance differ as a function of the prior number of tests? Again, as in Allen et al. (1969), the condition with three initial tests produced the most correct responses, the one-test condition performed intermediately, and the zero-test condition the worst (see Figure 11.2).

Were the subjects in the three-test condition simply producing more correct items on the forced recall test (e.g., as guesses), or did they actually remember more items? Subsequent data with free recall suggest that more tests do boost the likelihood of remembering. For example, McDermott (2006) asked subjects to encode 18 lists of 15 semantically associated words, each list converging on a single, non-presented word

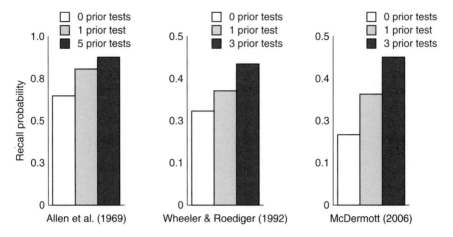

Figure 11.2   More prior tests (without feedback) elicited greater probabilities of later paired associate recall (Allen et al., 1969), forced recall (Wheeler & Roediger, 1992), and free recall (McDermott, 2006). Selected conditions from each article.

(e.g., they heard *bed, rest, awake*, etc., but not *sleep*, Roediger & McDermott, 1995). The more initial retrieval attempts taken, the greater the likelihood of final free recall of studied words when subjects were asked to remember as much as possible without guessing (.44, .33, and .21 for three, one, or zero prior tests, respectively, as shown in Figure 11.2).

Further, when a modified version of Tulving's (1985) remember/know procedure was used, subjects assigned the most remember responses to the condition in which three prior tests had occurred and the least for the no-test condition (i.e., the probability of a remember judgment was .25, .17, and .14 for the three-test, one-test and zero-test conditions, respectively, McDermott, 2006).

It should be noted that not every measure of memory shows improvement with prior testing, though. For example, the improvement in final recall was accompanied by an increased likelihood of false recall of critical non-presented words (e.g., sleep, .37, .35, and .27 for three, one, and zero initial tests, respectively, McDermott, 2006). Hence, although tests enhanced memory (in terms of boosting later accurate recall), this benefit was offset by an increased likelihood of false recall. Similar findings have

been obtained for multiple-choice testing, as reviewed below.

FEEDBACK

The concept of feedback has featured prominently in the testing literature and has been the topic of a number of studies that have investigated the conditions in which feedback is most efficacious (Bangert-Drowns, Kulik, & Kulik, 1991; Kulik & Kulik, 1988). Although feedback virtually always improves performance compared with trials where feedback does not follow testing, there are certain types of tests in which feedback is a critical component. One such format is the multiple-choice test. Because people are exposed to incorrect information on these kinds of tests, it is important to ensure that after an answer has been given, the correct alternative is revealed. Roediger and Marsh (2005) demonstrated that lures, presented in the context of a multiple-choice exam, can supply false knowledge if the person believes the lure is indeed the correct answer. Additionally, the presentation of more lures (two versus four versus six) results in a higher likelihood that the person will produce the error on a final test. This study has obvious implications in educational settings because although testing is a powerful form of learning, negative consequences can arise when incorrect information is provided as a possible answer. Feedback provides a means by which to remedy the negative effects of multiple-choice testing (Butler & Roediger, 2008). It is important to note that the overall consequences of multiple-choice tests on long-term retention, like other forms of testing, are strongly positive. The benefits of multiple-choice testing outweigh the negative effects that can sometimes result from endorsing lures as the correct answer (Marsh, Roediger, Bjork, & Bjork, 2007).

An important question that has received a great deal of attention is when feedback should be given following a test trial (Butler, Karpicke, & Roediger, 2007; Kulik & Kulik, 1988; Metcalfe, Kornell, & Finn, 2009). Although it seems at first glance that feedback may be more beneficial immediately following a test trial, delaying feedback typically confers more of an advantage at final performance than immediate feedback. For example, Butler and Roediger (2008) showed that a week after learning, the probability of cued recall for students given delayed feedback on their initial tests exceeded performance for those given immediate feedback (.54 and .43, respectively). Both conditions were more efficacious than one in which no feedback had been given (.33) or a no-test control condition (.11). The comparison of these last two points, of course, is a demonstration of the basic testing effect. Feedback enhances later performance, and delaying feedback can be especially beneficial.

Recent work from Finn and Metcalfe (2010) has emphasized not just when feedback should be given, but how. In many situations, individuals play a passive role during feedback as the information is merely presented upon the completion of a trial. However, Finn and Metcalfe determined that feedback fostered long-term retention when individuals played a more active role and attempted to generate the feedback given

incremental hints about the correct answer. This technique, known as scaffolded feedback, emphasizes the role of retrieval practice and self-generation and their advantages following a failed attempt at recall.

Feedback following tests has also been compared across trials in which individuals successfully retrieved the material and trials in which retrieval was unsuccessful (Butler & Roediger, 2008; Pashler, Cepeda, Wixted, & Rohrer, 2005). Although there is a clear benefit to receiving feedback when an item could not be recalled, there is mixed evidence regarding the role of feedback for correct trials. Some have concluded that feedback supplies no benefit when items are correctly retrieved (Pashler et al., 2005). Others have shown that when time on task is held constant, providing feedback after correct responses can have a negative effect because the time it takes to process the feedback could be better spent with further studying or testing (Hays, Kornell, & Bjork, 2010). However, Butler and Roediger (2008) examined whether feedback may impact correct trials as a function of response confidence. Indeed, although feedback did not change final test performance when subjects responded with high confidence, lower confidence responses benefited significantly from feedback (Figure 11.3). Thus, it is perhaps the case that when individuals are correct, but unsure, feedback increases confidence to a level that makes the item less likely to be forgotten. In this way, feedback is not simply about "righting a wrong," but can have additional effects on more general features of decision making such as confidence.

MEMORY FOR RELATED, NON-TESTED INFORMATION IS ALSO ENHANCED

That retrieval practice can enhance later access to the practiced information is certainly of relevance to classroom settings. But if such practice can also enhance later retrieval of related, non-tested information,

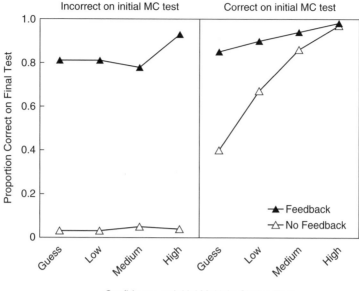

Figure 11.3   On an initial multiple-choice (MC) test, low-confidence correct responses benefited greatly from correct-answer feedback, whereas high-confidence responses were less impacted by the feedback. Adapted from Butler and Roediger (2008).

it would be that much more beneficial. The work reviewed here deals with these issues, under two related literatures.

Chan, McDermott, and Roediger (2006) asked university students to spend 25 minutes reading an article designed to approximate the content of a college-level textbook; the students were told to expect a later memory test. Initial testing involved answering 22 short-answer questions, with no feedback given. A day later, retrieval for related, non-tested questions was facilitated by these initial questions. Further, simply re-reading the facts targeted in the initial questions on day one did not produce the facilitation; a prior retrieval attempt was necessary.

This finding of retrieval-induced facilitation of material related to tested material stands in contrast to a better known finding, retrieval-induced forgetting (Anderson, 2003, Anderson, Bjork, & Bjork, 1994; Bjork, Bjork, & MacLeod, 2006). Briefly, retrieval-induced forgetting has been shown to occur when subjects practice retrieval of

a subset of previously studied information; this practice can diminish the likelihood of related, non-tested information.

Chan (2009) was able to clarify this discrepancy by demonstrating conditions that elicit retrieval-induced forgetting and those that elicit retrieval-induced facilitation. He noted that retrieval-induced forgetting is a short-lived phenomenon (MacLeod & Macrae, 2001) and is eliminated by encoding instructions that encourage integration of the materials (Anderson & McCulloch, 1999). In contrast, Chan et al. (2006), when showing retrieval-induced facilitation, had used a longer delay (24 hours) and revealed the importance of integration during encoding. Chan (2009) put this all together and twice found both retrieval-induced forgetting and retrieval-induced facilitation within a single experiment. As predicted, retrieval-induced forgetting was seen when subjects were not encouraged to integrate materials at encoding and a short retention interval was used. Retrieval-induced facilitation manifested when subjects integrated material at encoding

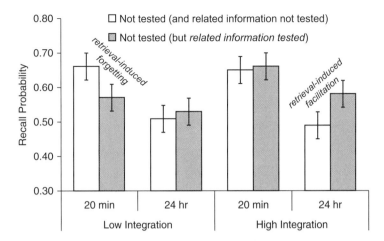

Figure 11.4   Final recall probability for information that had been studied but not previously tested. In one condition (dark bars), related material had been tested, and in the other condition (white bars) related information had not been tested. Testing related information led to retrieval-induced forgetting or retrieval-induced facilitation, depending on level of integration at encoding and retention interval. Adapted from Chan (2009).

and a long retention interval was used. This pattern can be seen in Figure 11.4.

In some sense, this pattern can be considered similar to the testing effect itself, which is time sensitive. That is, the benefit of testing is particularly strong after a long (relative to short) delay (Carpenter, Pashler, Wixted, & Vul, 2008; Halamish & Bjork, 2011; Roediger & Karpicke, 2006b; Runquist, 1983; Slamecka & Katsaiti, 1988; Thompson, Wenger, & Bartling, 1978). Indeed, the testing effect is sometimes not present at very short delays. This influence of retention interval was anticipated by Kühn (1914), who noted that "The advantage of learning with recitation for retention is much greater after a pause of a day than after a pause of a few minutes" (p. 466 as cited in Gates, 1917, p. 9).

This retrieval-induced facilitation literature has parallels to the literature on transfer, which also shows that testing one set of information can help the learner perform in a different domain (Butler, 2010; Kang, McDaniel, & Pashler, 2011; Karpicke & Blunt, 2011; Rohrer, Taylor, & Sholar, 2010). For example, Kang, McDaniel, and Pashler (2011) tested participants on learning

a mathematical function. The participants had to attempt to guess the value of y given x or else they were given x–y values; these conditions have obvious parallels to testing and restudying, although it is perhaps more related to generation of guesses than to testing. Later, the participants were more accurate after having attempted to guess the values (rather than reading them), and this pattern held true even for new x-values that exceeded the range of previously-experienced x–y pairs. In short, an emerging literature suggests that retrieval practice does not simply benefit the information practiced but goes beyond that information to facilitate the accessibility of related concepts.

TESTING ALSO HELPS LATER ENCODING: TEST-POTENTIATED LEARNING

In addition to benefiting long-term retention, testing can also enhance future encoding. Taking an initial test enhances the effect of a subsequent restudy trial, an indirect effect of testing known as test-potentiated learning (Izawa, 1966). That is, taking an initial test prior to restudying the tested material increases the amount of learning that will take place during a subsequent restudy trial. Further, with each additional prior test, the enhancing effect continues to increase (Izawa, 1970).

Although there was a flurry of research on this topic in the late 1960s and early 1970s (e.g., Izawa, 1966, 1971; Lachman & Laughery, 1968; LaPorte & Voss, 1975; Rosner, 1970; Royer, 1973; Young, 1971), interest in the topic lapsed for many years and has only recently come to the fore again (Arnold & McDermott, 2013a, 2013b; Grimaldi & Karpicke, 2012; Hays, Kornell, & Bjork, 2012; Huelser & Metcalfe, 2012; Karpicke, 2009; Karpicke & Roediger, 2007b; Richland, Kornell, & Kao, 2009). In this section, we briefly review the limited research that has been done thus far on test-potentiated learning, but before reviewing the literature, we first clearly define what we mean by the term.

Definition

We define test-potentiated learning as the additional, or enhanced, benefit of restudying that occurs as a result of taking prior test(s). That is, test-potentiated learning is any additional learning that occurs during restudy that would not otherwise have occurred had no initial test(s) been taken. Given this definition, there are two possible ways in which tests may indirectly enhance the benefit of a subsequent study trial: they may enhance the retention of already learned items (i.e., items that could be recalled on the initial tests) and/or they may enhance the encoding of unlearned items (i.e., items that could not be recalled on the initial tests).

The first indirect benefit of testing is similar to the testing effect in that both effects improve the retention of items that have been recalled on an initial test. The difference between these two effects is that the testing effect is a direct effect of retrieving the items,

whereas the test-potentiated learning effect is an indirect effect that is mediated through a subsequent encoding trial. That is, a testing effect can occur without a subsequent study or feedback trial (e.g., Roediger & Karpicke, 2006b), whereas a subsequent study opportunity is necessary to obtain a test-potentiated learning effect.

Although a testing effect can occur without feedback, it can be enhanced when feedback is given, especially when items are retrieved with low confidence (see Figure 11.3; Butler, Karpicke, & Roediger, 2008). That is, the effect of retrieving an item on retention of that item can be enhanced by subsequent study. Test-potentiated learning would indicate the converse is also true. The effect of a subsequent study trial on retention of an item can be enhanced by first retrieving that item. Parsing apart these two parallel effects is not trivial, and most research on feedback has focused only on the effect of feedback on tests, not the reverse.

The second way initial tests may potentiate learning is by enhancing the encoding of previously unlearned items during a subsequent study trial. That is, attempting but failing to retrieve an item may increase the probability that it will be learned in a following study trial. Evidence supporting this aspect of test-potentiated learning has been found. Using conditional probability, Izawa (1968, 1969) provided preliminary evidence for this component of test-potentiated learning in a multi-trial cued recall paradigm. She measured conditional probability averaged over multiple study trials. On average, a larger proportion of previously unlearned items were learned during restudy trials in conditions with more interspersing test trials. Arnold and McDermott (2013a) expanded on Izawa's findings by comparing conditional probability on individual restudy trials. As can be seen in Figure 11.5, Arnold and McDermott found that a larger proportion of items were retrieved for the first time following a given restudy trial in conditions with more interspersing tests, although this effect diminished as more items were learned.

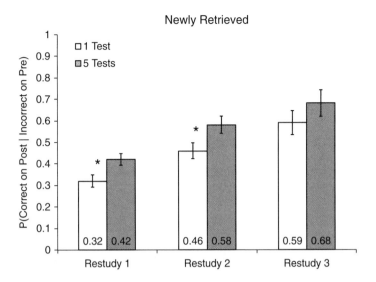

Figure 11.5 Proportion of items not recalled on pre-restudy tests that were correctly retrieved on post-restudy tests after Restudies 1, 2, and 3 as a function of the number of interspersed tests. Adapted from Arnold and McDermott (2013a).

Research on test-potentiated learning

As was previously mentioned, several researchers studied test-potentiated learning in the 1960s and 1970s. Most notably, Izawa (Izawa, 1966, 1967, 1968, 1969, 1970, 1971) studied this effect in multi-trial cued recall paradigms in many experiments. Her typical paradigm involved participants learning pairs of items (e.g., BIY–97) in conditions with different numbers of test trials interspersed between study trials. She then measured the proportion of errors participants made on the first test following each study trial and found that, in general, errors decreased at a faster rate in conditions with more interspersed test trials. She concluded from these results that tests potentiate learning on subsequent study trials. For example, in Experiment 1 in Izawa (1971), she used five conditions, each with a different number of interspersing tests (1–5 tests) between study trials. Figure 11.6 illustrates the results from two of the conditions, 2 Tests and 5 Tests, displayed as a function of the proportion of correctly recalled items and the number of preceding study trials. In the 5 Tests condition, items were learned at a

faster rate, which, according to Izawa, indicates that the tests potentiated learning on the subsequent study trials.

However, this interpretation should be re-examined in light of more recent research on the testing effect that shows that tests themselves can directly enhance future recall (e.g., Roediger & Butler, 2011). Also relevant is work on the spacing effect, which indicates that increasing the spacing between study trials (as happens when the number of test trials increases) can also enhance learning (for a review, see Cepeda, Pashler, Vul, Wixted, & Rohrer, 2006). From the results illustrated in Figure 11.6, it is unclear if the advantage seen in the 5 Tests condition is a result of direct effects of the test trials themselves, from indirect, potentiating effects of the tests, from a combination of both direct and indirect effects, and/or from a spacing effect. As mentioned earlier, in some of her experiments, Izawa (1968, 1969) supplemented the results with conditional probability analyses, which is stronger evidence that the advantage in the 5 Tests condition is at least partially due to test-potentiated learning. Further, in at least one study, she used

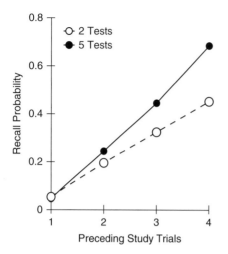

Figure 11.6   Recall probability as a function of the number of tests between study trials and the number of preceding study trials. Recall probability was higher when more tests were taken between study trials. Adapted from Izawa (1971).

conditional probability analyses while controlling for spacing (Izawa, 1968) suggesting that the effect is not due to increased spacing between study trials. However, she did not indicate that this additional analysis was necessary for determining if test-potentiated learning had occurred. Several researchers

who followed up on her work continued to interpret a steeper learning curve or greater final recall in conditions with more interspersed tests as sufficient evidence for determining that test-potentiated learning was present (e.g., Karpicke, 2009; Karpicke & Roediger, 2007a; LaPorte & Voss, 1975; Young, 1971).

An alternative way to study test-potentiated learning was introduced by Arnold and McDermott (2013b). In their paradigm, the test-potentiated learning effect can be isolated from the testing effect by using control conditions in which the material is not restudied. The difference in final recall between conditions with and without a restudy trial given the same number of initial test(s) indicates the degree to which restudying benefits the learner. If the benefit (i.e., the difference) is larger in conditions with more prior tests, then it can be assumed that the additional test(s) enhanced the effect of the restudy trial. This comparison is illustrated in Figure 11.7. In two experiments using free recall tests, Arnold and McDermott found that the benefit of the restudy trial was larger when tests had been taken prior to the restudy trial. This suggests that the tests potentiated learning during the

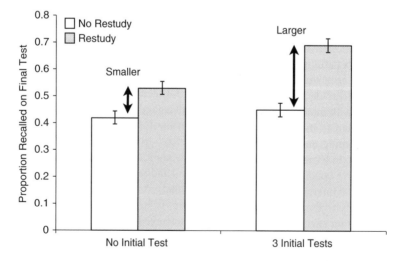

Figure 11.7   Test-potentiated learning. The benefit of a restudy opportunity is greater when a prior test preceded that restudy opportunity. Adapted from Arnold and McDermott (2013b).

restudy trial. However, these results do not indicate whether this test-potentiated learning effect was due to enhanced retention of already learned items, enhanced learning of not-yet-learned items, or a combination of both.

Another approach some researchers have used to study test-potentiated learning has been to use a paradigm in which no initial study trial is given (e.g., Kornell, Hays, & Bjork, 2009). In this case, participants are given a cue (e.g., *whale*) and are asked to guess the correct target (e.g., *mammal*). Attempting (and failing) to guess the target before studying the cue–target pair increases the probability that the target will be retrieved on a later test relative to a condition in which no initial guess is made (see also Slamecka & Fevreiski, 1983). Because there is no initial study, learning the target must occur on the subsequent study trial. However, because participants are attempting to generate rather than to retrieve the target item, this effect seems more appropriately termed generate-potentiated learning (Arnold & McDermott, 2013b), and, at this time, it is unclear how this effect is related to test-potentiated learning.

Theories of test-potentiated learning

How might retrieving or attempting to retrieve an item facilitate subsequent encoding of that item? Several theories have been put forth in an attempt to answer this question. Below we briefly describe the most prominent theories and their supporting evidence. These theories are not mutually exclusive, and several mechanisms may underlie test-potentiated learning.

The first theory put forth to explain test-potentiated learning was introduced by Izawa (1971) and was based on Estes's (1955a, 1955b) stimulus fluctuation model. Izawa called her theory the Test Trial Potentiating Model and explained the effects of testing in terms of changes in fluctuation of stimulus elements, or tiny fragments of the universe that compose a target. According to this model, testing has two main effects: 1) keeping stimulus elements that have already

been conditioned to the cue in an available state and thus preventing forgetting; and 2) moving unconditioned stimulus elements to an available state at a faster rate than normal so that more of them can become conditioned to the cue during a subsequent study opportunity. She provided evidence that her model could accurately predict the rate at which pairs of items would be learned in conditions with varying numbers of interspersed tests.

Izawa's (1971) model came out of the verbal learning and animal learning traditions, and therefore she approached test-potentiated learning from a behavioral point of view. In contrast, a metacognitive explanation of test-potentiated learning comes from a more modern cognitive tradition and takes into consideration the learners' mental states and how testing may change their approach to studying. This metacognitive theory of test-potentiated learning can come in many forms, but the basic tenet is that testing changes learners' metacognitive knowledge, which in turn changes the strategies they use during restudy in such a way as to enhance learning. Pyc and Rawson (2010) introduced one such metacognitive theory, the mediator-effectiveness hypothesis, which, though originally proposed as a testing effect theory, can also be used to explain test-potentiated learning. This hypothesis posits that when learners use mediators (i.e., cues, words, or phrases that connect targets with cues) to help them learn paired items, testing prior to restudying allows learners to develop more effective mediators. Effective mediators are defined as ones that learners can remember when presented with the cue and that help learners remember the correct target. For example, when trying to learn the Swahili–English word pair *wingu–cloud*, "wing" could serve as an effective mediator because wings allow birds to fly through clouds. Taking prior tests allows learners to determine which mediators are effective and which ones should be replaced by more effective mediators during subsequent study. Testing therefore potentiates subsequent learning by changing learners' understanding of their ability to recall the targets and thus changing their strategy during restudy.

Although the mediator-effectiveness hypothesis is specific to paired-associate paradigms, not all metacognitive-based theories are paradigm specific. A straightforward hypothesis that can be applied to many different learning situations is that testing informs learners about what they do and do not know well (Thompson, Wenger, & Bartling, 1978). During a subsequent restudy trial they can then use memory for what they have previously recalled to guide their study so that they focus on items that would benefit most, that is, items not previously recalled. Arnold and McDermott (in preparation) have recently found some evidence supporting this hypothesis. They had subjects learn Russian–English word pairs by taking either one test or five tests between study trials. Each restudy trial was self-paced such that participants could spend as much or as little time as they wanted on each item. Although participants in both conditions spent approximately the same amount of time studying items they correctly recalled on the prior test, participants who had taken five interspersed tests between study trials spent significantly more time studying items they had not recalled on the test prior to restudying. This suggests that taking the additional tests changed participants' study strategies such that they spent additional time studying items that would presumably benefit the most from restudy.

Another explanation of the test-potentiated learning effect, at least in free recall, is that testing can improve the organization of recalled items, which enhances subsequent encoding by providing a context in which to incorporate new items. Multiple researchers in the 1960s and 1970s proposed an organizational explanation for test-potentiated learning (e.g., Donaldson, 1971; Lachman & Laughery, 1968; Rosner, 1970). They posited that enhanced organization allows to-be-learned items to be more effectively incorporated with already learned items. More recent research has found supporting evidence that testing does indeed improve organization and

that this improvement underlies the testing effect (Zaromb & Roediger, 2010). That is, enhanced organization improves retention. Future work is needed to determine if this finding can be extended to show that the enhanced organization also improves subsequent encoding.

Nelson, Arnold, Gilmore, Najjar, Finn, and McDermott (2013) have proposed a new hypothesis for test-potentiated learning that posits that testing increases study-phase retrieval, or remindings (Greene, 1989; Hintzman, 2004, 2011), during subsequent restudy opportunities. That is, learning is enhanced because testing increases the extent to which retrieval processes are engaged during restudy. Retrieving previous exposures to the target item (i.e., either a previous study trial and/or a prior test trial) during restudy enhances the probability that the item will be retrieved on a later test. Nelson et al. (2013) proposed this hypothesis because they found evidence using functional Magnetic Resonance Imaging (fMRI) that there was greater activation within the left posterior inferior parietal lobule when restudying items that had been previously tested relative to restudying items that did not have an initial retrieval attempt. This specific region has been implicated previously in successful recognition memory (McDermott, Szpunar, & Christ, 2009; Nelson, et al., 2010), suggesting that when studying previously tested items learners are more likely to engage retrieval processes than when studying other items. However, this evidence is preliminary, and future research that directly tests remindings during restudy phases is needed to further explore this hypothesis.

Theories of the testing effect

Although the testing effect has been researched extensively in recent years, the field still lacks a thorough understanding of why retrieval enhances retention. Over the years, several theories have been proposed to explain this effect, and, although a number of these theories have strong empirical support, no one theory has become the dominant explanation. One possible reason for this is that many of these theories are not mutually exclusive. Evidence in support of one theory does not necessarily negate the validity of another. In this section, we will briefly describe several of the most prominent testing effect theories.

One explanation of the testing effect is that retrieval produces deep, effortful processing (Bjork, 1975; Carpenter & DeLosh, 2006; Gardiner, Craik, & Bleasdale, 1973; Pyc & Rawson, 2009). According to this theory, retrieval functions in a similar manner to deep processing at encoding (e.g., Craik & Tulving, 1975), and it is this deep processing that enhances memory. It follows from this theory that the more effortful the retrieval, the deeper the processing, and therefore the testing effect should be enhanced when retrieval is more difficult (Bjork, 1994; Roediger & Karpicke, 2006a). Several lines of research have found support for this theory, which Bjork (1994) has termed *desirable difficulties*. For instance, the testing effect is larger when initial retrieval takes more time (Gardiner et al., 1973), when fewer retrieval cues are provided at initial test (e.g., Carpenter & DeLosh, 2006), when the initial test is delayed (e.g., Pyc & Rawson, 2009; Whitten & Bjork,1977), and when the initial tests require recall rather than recognition (e.g., Kang, McDermott, & Roediger, 2007).

A related theory is that testing elaborates on the existing memory trace and produces new retrieval routes thus enhancing future retrieval (e.g., Bartlett, 1977; Bjork, 1975, 1988; Carpenter, 2009; McDaniel & Masson, 1985). The basic idea is that in the process of retrieving the target item, related concepts are activated, and these related concepts can later serve as additional retrieval cues. Results from several experiments have provided support for this theory by showing that when the cues at initial retrieval encourage diverse or elaborative processing, the testing effect is enhanced. For instance, Carpenter (2009)

had participants study strongly associated (e.g., Toast–Bread) and weakly associated (e.g., Basket–Bread) cue–target pairs. After initial study, participants either restudied the cue–target pairs or were presented with the cues and attempted to retrieve the targets (no feedback was given). After a 5-minute delay, participants were given a final free recall test. Targets that had been tested were more likely to be recalled if they had been paired with a weakly related cue than a strongly related cue. In contrast, when the cue–target pairs had been restudied, there was no difference between final recall of targets paired with weak or strong cues. Carpenter suggested these results indicate that testing with weakly associated cues encourages more elaborative processing, which in turn enhances future retrieval.

Another explanation of the testing effect is based on the concept of transfer-appropriate processing, the idea that encoding will benefit retrieval in so much as the processes engaged at encoding match those required at retrieval (Morris, Bransford, & Franks, 1977). This can be applied to the testing effect because testing during learning engages processes that closely match processes needed at final test (Roediger & Karpicke, 2006a). Counter to this theory is the finding that the testing effect is larger if the initial test is a recall rather than a recognition test, no matter the type of final test (e.g., Kang, et al., 2007). That is, an initial cued recall test leads to better final performance than an initial recognition test, even if the final test is a recognition test.

Bjork and Bjork (1992) developed the new theory of disuse, a theory that incorporates many of the previously discussed ideas in a more formal way. According to this theory, there are two types of strength: storage strength, which refers to the strength of the memory trace of an item, and retrieval strength, which refers to the ease with which an item can be retrieved. According to this theory, the effect of retrieval on storage strength is inversely related to retrieval strength. That is, if retrieval strength is high (e.g., if an item has been studied very recently), then retrieving the item will have little impact on its storage strength. Conversely, if retrieval strength is low and therefore retrieving is effortful, retrieval will greatly enhance storage strength.

The relation between storage strength and retrieval strength is illustrated in an experiment conducted by Gardiner et al. (1973). They read subjects the definitions of 50 low-frequency words; subjects attempted to retrieve each word. After a short delay, subjects were given a surprise final recall test in which they attempted to recall all of the defined words. Words that had been retrieved slowly during the initial phase (i.e., those that initially had low retrieval strength) were more likely to be recalled on the final test than those that had been retrieved quickly (i.e., those that initially had high retrieval strength). The new theory of disuse would explain this result as follows. Initially retrieving words that had low retrieval strength increased storage strength more than did initially retrieving words that had high retrieval strength. Therefore, words that required more effort to retrieve during the initial phase received a bigger boost to storage strength and were therefore better remembered on the final test.

Applications in the classroom

The foregoing review should make it clear that retrieval practice impacts subsequent memory, at least in laboratory settings. Does this principle hold in real-life classroom settings with class content? Emerging evidence suggests that it does (for reviews see Bangert-Drowns et al., 1991; McDaniel, Roediger, & McDermott, 2007).

Much of the literature relevant to this question has not used real classroom content but instead either simulated classrooms or real classrooms with extraneous research materials (Carpenter, Pashler, & Cepeda, 2009; Duchastel & Nungester, 1982; Sones & Stroud, 1940). A growing effort is being made to examine how real-life performance in classrooms with the core curricular materials is affected by low stakes, in-class tests, or quizzes.

For example, McDaniel, Anderson, Derbish, and Morrisette (2007) tested students enrolled in an online university level psychology course. The students were either quizzed weekly or given the same information in additional reading. Weekly quizzing (unlike additional reading) resulted in gains on the unit exam (see also McDaniel, Wildman, & Anderson, 2012).

Experiments within middle school classrooms have recently been carried out as well. Students in a sixth-grade social studies class who received in-class multiple-choice quizzes throughout the semester performed better on the chapter exams and end-of-semester exams for the items that had been quizzed (relative to those not quizzed, Roediger, McDaniel, McDermott, & Agarwal, 2011). Similar results were obtained in an eighth-grade science classroom as well (McDaniel, Agarwal, Huelser, McDermott, & Roediger, 2011). A recent practice guide for educators highlighted the contribution that retrieval practice can make toward learning (Pashler et al., 2007).

Although there is good evidence that in-class tests can boost performance on later exams, many questions remain: What types of test work best? How many initial tests are necessary to see gains? When should feedback be given? How much can retrieval practice aid transfer to related topics? These questions and more await future work.

CONCLUSION

One of the most powerful ways to enhance the likelihood of later recall of recently learned information is to test oneself on that information or related information. The power of testing can be seen in the absence of feedback, at long delays, for information not itself tested but related to the tested information. Further, retrieval practice impacts subsequent study. Emerging evidence suggests that this may be a largely untapped method for enhancing student learning in the classroom.

ACKNOWLEDGEMENTS

Work on this chapter was funded in part by a James S. McDonnell Foundation Bridging Brain, Mind, and Behavior Collaborative Activity Award, an Institute of Education Sciences award R305A110550, National Institute of General Medical Sciences award 5T32GM081739, and the Washington University McDonnell Center for Systems Neuroscience.

REFERENCES

Allen, G. A., Mahler, W. A., & Estes, W. K. (1969). Effects of recall tests on long-term retention of paired associates. *Journal of Verbal Learning & Verbal Behavior, 8*, 463–470.

Anderson, M. C. (2003). Rethinking interference theory: Executive control and the mechanisms of forgetting. *Journal of Memory & Language, 49*, 415–445.

Anderson, M. C., Bjork, R.A., & Bjork, E. L. (1994). Remembering can cause forgetting: Retrieval dynamics in long-term memory. *Journal of Experimental Psychology: Learning, Memory, & Cognition, 20*, 1063–1087.

Anderson, M. C., & McCulloch, K. C. (1999). Integration as a general boundary condition on retrieval-induced forgetting. *Journal of Experimental Psychology: Learning, Memory, and Cognition, 25*, 608–629.

Arnold, K. M., & McDermott, K. B. (2013a). Test-potentiated learning: Distinguishing between direct and indirect effects of tests. *Journal of Experimental Psychology: Learning, Memory, and Cognition, 39*(3), 940–945 .

Arnold, K. M., & McDermott, K. B. (2013b). Test-potentiated learning in free recall. *Psychonomic Bulletin & Review, 20*, 507–513.

Arnold, K. M., & McDermott, K. B. (in preparation). Does metacognition contribute to test-potentiated learning?

Bacon, F. (2000). *Novum organum* (L. J. M. Silverthorne, Trans.). Cambridge: Cambridge University Press (Original work published in 1620).

Bangert-Drowns, R. L., Kulik, J. A., & Kulik, C. L. C. (1991). Effects of frequent classroom testing. *Journal of Educational Research, 85*, 89–99.

Bartlett, J. C. (1977). Effects of immediate testing on delayed retrieval: Search and recovery operations with four types of cue. *Journal of Experimental Psychology: Human Learning and Memory, 3*, 719–732.

Bjork, E. L., Bjork, R. A., & MacLeod, M. D. (2006). Types and consequences of forgetting: intended and unintended. In L.-G. Nilsson and N. Ohta (Eds.), *Memory and society: Psychological perspectives* (pp. 134–158). New York: Routledge and Psychology Press.

Bjork, R. A. (1975). Retrieval as a memory modifier: An interpretation of negative recency and realted phenomenon. In R. L. Solso (Ed.), *Information processing and cognition* (pp. 123–144). New York: John Wiley.

Bjork, R. A. (1988). Retrieval practice and the maintenance of knowledge. In M. M. Gruneberg, P. E. Morris, and R. N. Sykes (Eds.), *Practical aspects of memory: Current research and issues* (Vol. 1, pp. 396–401). New York: Wiley.

Bjork, R. A. (1994). Memory and metamemory considerations in the training of human beings. In J. Metcalfe and A. Shimamura (Eds.), *Metacognition: Knowing about knowing* (pp. 185–205). Cambridge, MA: MIT Press.

Bjork, R. A., & Bjork, E. L. (1992). A new theory of disuse and an old theory of stimulus fluctuation. In A. F. Healy, S. Kosslyn and R. Shiffrin (Eds.), *From learning processes to cognitive processes: Essays in honor of William K. Estes* (Vol. 2, pp. 35–67). Hillsdale, NJ: Lawrence Erlbaum Associates, Inc.

Butler, A. C. (2010). Repeated testing produces superior transfer of learning relative to repeated studying. *Journal of Experimental Psychology: Learning, Memory, and Cognition, 36*, 1118–1133.

Butler, A. C., Karpicke, J. D., & Roediger, H. L., III. (2007). The effect of type and timing of feedback on learning from multiple-choice tests. *Journal of Experimental Psychology. Applied, 13*, 273–281.

Butler, A. C., Karpicke, J. D., & Roediger, H. L. (2008). Correcting a metacognitive error: Feedback increases retention of low-confidence correct responses. *Journal of Experimental Psychology, Learning, Memory, and Cognition, 34*, 918–928.

Butler, A. C., & Roediger, H. L., III. (2008). Feedback enhances the positive effects and reduces the negative effects of multiple-choice testing. *Memory & Cognition, 36*, 604–616.

Carpenter, S. K. (2009). Cue strength as a moderator of the testing effect: The benefits of elaborative retrieval. *Journal of Experimental Psychology: Learning, Memory, and Cognition, 35*, 1563–1569.

Carpenter, S. K., & DeLosh, E. L. (2006). Impoverished cue support enhances subsequent retention: Support for the elaborative retrieval explanation of the testing effect. *Memory & Cognition, 34*, 268–276.

Carpenter, S. K., Pashler, H., & Cepeda, N. J. (2009). Using tests to enhance 8th grade students' retention of U.S. history facts. *Applied Cognitive Psychology, 23*, 760–771.

Carpenter, S. K., Pashler, H., Wixted, J. T., & Vul, E. (2008). The effects of tests on learning and forgetting. *Memory & Cognition, 36*, 438–448.

Carrier, M., & Pashler, H. (1992). The influence of retrieval on retention. *Memory & Cognition, 20*, 633–642.

Cepeda, N. J., Pashler, H., Vul, E., Wixted, J. T., & Rohrer, D. (2006). Distributed practice in verbal recall tasks: A review and quantitative synthesis. *Psychological Bulletin, 132*, 354–380.

Chan, J. C. K. (2009). When does retrieval induce forgetting and when does it induce facilitation? Implications for retrieval inhibition, testing effect, and text processing. *Journal of Memory and Language, 61*, 153–170.

Chan, J. C. K., McDermott, K. B., & Roediger, H. L., III. (2006). Retrieval-induced facilitation: Initially nontested material can benefit from prior testing of related material. *Journal of Experimental Psychology: General, 135*, 553–571.

Craik, F. I. M., & Tulving, E. (1975). Depth of processing and the retention of words in episodic memory. *Journal of Experimental Psychology: General, 104*, 268–294.

Donaldson, W. (1971). Output effects in multitrial free recall. *Journal of Verbal Learning and Verbal Behavior, 10*, 577–585.

Duchastel, P. C., & Nungester, R. J. (1982). Testing effects measured with alternate test forms. *Journal of Educational Research, 75*, 309–313.

Estes, W. K. (1955a). Statistical theory of distributed phenomena in learning. *Psychological Review, 62*, 369–377.

Estes, W. K. (1955b). Statistical theory of spontaneous recovery and regression. *Psychological Review, 62*, 145–154.

Finn, B., & Metcalfe, J. (2010). Scaffolding feedback to maximize long-term error correction. *Memory & Cognition, 38*, 951–961.

Gardiner, J. M., Craik, F. I. M., & Bleasdale, F. A. (1973). Retrieval difficulty and subsequent recall. *Memory & Cognition, 1*, 213–216.

Gates, A. I. (1917). Recitation as a factor in memorizing. *Archives of Psychology, 6*.

Glover, J. A. (1989). The 'testing' phenomenon: Not gone but nearly forgotten. *Journal of Educational Psychology, 81*, 329–399.

Greene, R. L. (1989). Spacing effects in memory: Evidence for a two-process account. *Journal of Experimental Psychology: Learning, Memory, and Cognition, 15*, 371–377.

Grimaldi, P. J., & Karpicke, J. D. (2012). When and why do retrieval attempts enhance subsequent encoding? *Memory & Cognition, 40*, 505–513.

Halamish, V., & Bjork, R. A. (2011). When does testing enhance retention? A distribution-based interpretation of retrieval as a memory modifier. *Journal of Experimental Psychology: Learning, Memory, and Cognition, 37*, 801–812.

Hays, M. J., Kornell, N., & Bjork, R. A. (2010). The costs and benefits of providing feedback during learning. *Psychonomic Bulletin & Review, 17*, 797–801.

Hays, M. J., Kornell, N., & Bjork, E. L. (2012). When and why a failed test potentiates the effectiveness of subsequent study. *Journal of Experimental Psychology: Learning, Memory, and Cognition, 39*(1), 290–296.

Hintzman, D. L. (2004). Judgment of frequency versus recognition confidence: Repetition and recursive reminding. *Memory & Cognition, 32*, 336–350.

Hintzman, D. L. (2011). Research strategy in the study of memory: Fads, fallacies, and the search for the 'oordinates of truth'. *Perspectives on Psychological Science, 6*, 253–271.

Huelser, B. J., & Metcalfe, J. (2012). Making related errors facilitates learning, but learners do not know it. *Memory & Cognition, 40*, 514–527.

Izawa, C. (1966). Reinforcement-test sequences in paired-associate learning. *Psychological Reports, 18*, 879–919.

Izawa, C. (1967). Function of test trials in paired-associate learning. *Journal of Experimental Psychology, 75*, 194–209.

Izawa, C. (1968). Effects of reinforcement, neutral and test trials upon paired-associate acquisition and retention. *Psychological Reports, 23*, 947–959.

Izawa, C. (1969). Comparison of reinforcement and test trials in paired-associate learning. *Journal of Experimental Psychology, 81*(3), 600–603.

Izawa, C. (1970). Optimal potentiating effects and forgetting-prevention effects of tests in paired-associate learning. *Journal of Experimental Psychology, 83*, 340–344.

Izawa, C. (1971). Massed and spaced practice in paired-associate learning: List versus item distributions. *Journal of Experimental Psychology, 89*, 10–21.

Kang, S. H. K., McDaniel, M. A., & Pashler, H. (2011). Effects of testing on learning of functions. *Psychonomic Bulletin & Review, 18,* 988–1005.

Kang, S. H. K., McDermott, K. B., & Roediger, H. L. (2007). Test format and corrective feedback modify the effect of testing on long-term retention. *European Journal of Cognitive Psychology, 19,* 528–558.

Karpicke, J. D. (2009). Metacognitive control and strategy selection: Deciding to practice retrieval during learning. *Journal of Experimental Psychology: General, 138,* 469–486.

Karpicke, J. D., & Blunt, J. R. (2011). Retrieval practice produces more learning than elaborative studying with concept mapping. *Science, 331,* 772–775.

Karpicke, J. D., & Roediger, H. L. (2007a). Expanding retrieval practice promotes short-term retention, but equally spaced retrieval enhances long-term retention. *Journal of Experimental Psychology: Learning, Memory, and Cognition, 33,* 704–719.

Karpicke, J. D., & Roediger, H. L. (2007b). Repeated retrieval during learning is the key to long-term retention. *Journal of Memory and Language, 57,* 151–162.

Katzaroff, D. (1908). Rôle de la récitation comme facteur de la mémorisation. *Archives de Psychologie, 7,* 224–259.

Kornell, N., Hays, M. J., & Bjork, R. A. (2009). Unsuccessful retrieval attempts enhance subsequent learning. *Journal of Experimental Psychology: Learning, Memory, and Cognition, 35,* 989–998.

Kornell, N., & Son, L. K. (2009). Learners' choices and beliefs about self-testing. *Memory, 17,* 493–501.

Kulik, J. A., & Kulik, C. C. (1988). Timing of feedback and verbal learning. *Review of Educational Research, 58,* 79–97.

Lachman, R., & Laughery, K. R. (1968). Is a test trial a training trial in free recall learning? *Journal of Experimental Psychology, 76,* 40–50.

LaPorte, R. E., & Voss, J. F. (1975). Retention of prose materials as a function of postacquisition testing. *Journal of Educational Psychology, 67,* 259–266.

MacLeod, M. D., & Macrae, C. N. (2001). Gone but not forgotten: The transient nature of retrieval-induced forgetting. *Psychological Science, 12,* 148–152.

Marsh, E. J., Roediger, H. L., Bjork, R. A., & Bjork, E. L. (2007). The memorial consequences of multiple-choice testing. *Psychonomic Bulletin & Review, 14,* 194–199.

McDaniel, M. A., Agarwal, P. K., Huelser, B. J., McDermott, K. B., & Roediger, H. L. (2011). Test-enhanced learning in a middle school science classroom: The effects of quiz frequency and placement. *Journal of Educational Psychology, 103*(2), 399–414.

McDaniel, M. A., Anderson, J. L., Derbish, M. H., & Morrisette, N. (2007). Testing the testing effect in the classroom. *European Journal of Cognitive Psychology, 19,* 494–513.

McDaniel, M. A., & Masson, M. E. J. (1985). Altering memory representations through retrieval. *Journal of Experimental Psychology: Learning, Memory, and Cognition, 11,* 371–385.

McDaniel, M. A., Roediger, H. L., & McDermott, K. B. (2007). Generalizing test-enhanced learning from the laboratory to the classroom. *Psychonomic Bulletin & Review, 14,* 200–206.

McDaniel, M. A., Wildman, K. M., & Anderson, J. L. (2012). Using quizzes to enhance summative-assessment performance in a web-based class: An experimental study. *Journal of Applied Research in Memory and Cognition, 1,* 18–26.

McDermott, K. B. (2006). Paradoxical effects of testing: Repeated retrieval attempts enhance the likelihood of later accurate and false recall. *Memory & Cognition, 34,* 261–267.

McDermott, K. B., Szpunar, K. K., & Christ, S. E. (2009). Laboratory-based and autobiographical retrieval tasks differ substantially in their neural substrates. *Neuropsychologia, 47,* 2290–2298.

Metcalfe, J., Kornell, N., & Finn, B. (2009). Delayed versus immediate feedback in children's and adults' vocabulary learning. *Memory & Cognition, 37,* 1077–1087.

Morris, C. D., Bransford, J. D., & Franks, J. J. (1977). Levels of processing versus transfer appropriate processing. *Journal of Verbal Learning & Verbal Behavior, 16,* 519–533.

Nelson, S.M., Arnold, K.M., Gilmore, A.W., & McDermott, K.B. (2013). Neural signatures of test-potentiated learning in parietal cortex. *Journal of Neuroscience, 33,* 11754-11762.

Nelson, S. M., Cohen, A. L., Power, J. D., Wig, G. S., Miezin, F. M., Wheeler, M. E., et al. (2010). A parcelation scheme for human left lateral parietal cortex. *Neuron, 67,* 156–170.

Pashler, H., Bain, P., Bottge, B., Graesser, A., Koedinger, K., McDaniel, M. A., et al. (2007). Organizing instruction and study to improve student learning. In I. o. E. S. National Center for Education Research, US Department of Education (Ed.), http://ncer.ed.gov

Pashler, H., Cepeda, N. J., Wixted, J. T., & Rohrer, D. (2005). When does feedback facilitate learning of words? *Journal of Experimental Psychology. Learning, Memory, and Cognition, 31,* 3–8.

Pyc, M. A., & Rawson, K. A. (2009). Testing the retrieval effort hypothesis: Does greater difficulty correctly recalling information lead to higher levels of memory? *Journal of Memory and Language, 60,* 437–447.

Pyc, M. A., & Rawson, K. A. (2010). Why testing improves memory: Mediator effectiveness hypothesis. *Science, 330,* 335.

Richland, L. E., Kornell, N., & Kao, L. S. (2009). The pretesting effect: Do unsuccessful retrieval attempts enhance learning? *Journal of Experimental Psychology: Applied, 15,* 243–257.

Roediger, H. L., & Butler, A. C. (2011). The critical role of retrieval practice in long-term retention. *Trends in Cognitive Sciences, 15,* 20–27.

Roediger, H. L., III, & Marsh, E. J. (2005). The positive and negative consequences of multiple-choice testing. *Journal of Experimental Psychology: Learning, Memory, and Cognition, 31,* 1155–1159.

Roediger, H. L., & Karpicke, J. D. (2006a). The power of testing memory: Basic research and implications for educational practice. *Perspectives on Psychological Science, 1,* 181–210.

Roediger, H. L., & Karpicke, J. D. (2006b). Test-enhanced learning: Taking memory tests improves long-term retention. *Psychological Science, 17,* 249–255.

Roediger, H. L., McDaniel, M. A., McDermott, K. B., & Agarwal, P. K. (2011). Test-enhanced learning in the classroom: Long-term improvements from quizzing. *Journal of Experimental Psychology: Applied, 17,* 382–395.

Roediger, H. L., & McDermott, K. B. (1995). Creating false memories: Remembering words not presented in lists. *Journal of Experimental Psychology: Learning, Memory, and Cognition, 21,* 803–814.

Roediger, H. L., Putnam, A. L., & Smith, M. A. (2011). Ten benefits of testing and their applications to educational practice. *Psychology of Learning and Motivation, 55.*

Rohrer, D., Taylor, K., & Sholar, B. (2010). Tests enhance the transfer of learning. *Journal of Experimental Psychology: Learning, Memory, and Cognition, 36,* 233–239.

Rosner, S. R. (1970). The effects of presentation and recall trials on organization in multitrial free recall.

Journal of Verbal Learning and Verbal Behavior, 9, 69–74.

Royer, J. M. (1973). Memory effects for test-like events during acquisition of foreign language vocabulary. *Psychological Reports, 32,* 195–198.

Runquist, W. N. (1983). Some effects of remembering on forgetting. *Memory & Cognition, 11,* 641–650.

Slamecka, N. J., & Fevreiski, J. (1983). The generation effect when generation fails. *Journal of Verbal Learning and Verbal Behavior, 22,* 153–163.

Slamecka, N. J., & Katsaiti, L. T. (1988). Normal forgetting of verbal lists as a function of prior testing. *Journal of Experimental Psychology: Learning, Memory, and Cognition, 14,* 716–727.

Sones, A. M., & Stroud, J. B. (1940). Review, with special reference to temporal position. *Journal of Educational Psychology, 31,* 665–676.

Spitzer, H. J. (1939). Studies in retention. *Journal of Educational Psychology, 30,* 641–656.

Thompson, C. P., Wenger, S. K., & Bartling, C. A. (1978). How recall facilitates subsequent recall: A reappraisal. *Journal of Experimental Psychology: Human Learning & Memory, 4,* 210–221.

Tulving, E. (1985). Memory and consciousness. *Canadian Psychologist, 26,* 1–12.

Wahlheim, C. N., & Jacoby, L. L. (2013). Remembering change: The critical role of recursive remindings in proactive effects of memory. *Memory & Cognition, 41,* 1–15.

Wheeler, M. A., & Roediger III, H. L. (1992). Disparate effects of repeated testing: Reconciling Ballard's (1913) and Bartlett's (1932) results. *Psychological Science, 3,* 240–245.

Whitten, W. B., & Bjork, R. A. (1977). Learning from tests: Effects of spacing. *Journal of Verbal Learning & Verbal Behavior, 16,* 465–478.

Young, J. L. (1971). Reinforcement-test intervals in paired-associate learning. *Journal of Mathematical Psychology, 8,* 58–81.

Zaromb, F. M., & Roediger, H. L. (2010). The testing effect in free recall is associated with enhaned organizational processes. *Memory & Cognition, 38,* 995–1008.

12

Breakdowns in Everyday Memory Functioning Following Moderate-to-Severe Traumatic Brain Injury (TBI)

Eli Vakil

INTRODUCTION

Traumatic brain injury (TBI) is a major epidemiological problem in Western countries that causes a wide range of emotional, behavioral, and cognitive difficulties. Memory impairment is one of the most disturbing consequences of such an injury, because of its effect on a wide range of daily life activities, return to work, and social interactions. It is also the most frequent complaint by individuals with TBI and their families (Arcia & Gualtieri, 1993). For the person with memory problems simple daily activities require constant effort and become very exhausting (Wilson, 2002). There is evidence of impaired learning and memory even ten years after severe TBI (Zec et al., 2001). Therefore, it is not surprising that among the various cognitive impairments following TBI, memory is the most studied issue (Goldstein & Levin, 1995). The goal of this chapter is to review the literature on the effects of moderate-to-severe TBI on memory in adults, and how it impacts various aspects of everyday functioning. Severity of trauma defined as being mild, moderate or severe is based on the Glasgow Coma Scale (which evaluates the severity of coma), duration of loss of consciousness and Post Traumatic Amnesia (PTA, which tests immediate memory and orientation to time and space) (Williamson, Scott, & Adams, 1996). There are two major reasons for the decision to focus in this chapter on moderate-to-severe rather than on mild TBI. The first is that memory impairment following moderate-to-severe injury is very pronounced and has significant implications for everyday functioning. The second reason is the difficulty with differential diagnosis following mild injuries.

PREVALENCE OF TBI

According to the Centers for Disease Control and Prevention, based on data gathered from 2002 to 2006, 1.7 million people in the US suffer from TBI annually (Faul, Xu, Wald, & Coronado, 2010). Under the age of 35, TBI is the primary cause of mortality and chronic disability (Sosin, Sacks, & Holmgreen, 1990). Falls tend to be the most common cause of head injuries in infants and young children as well as in the elderly population, whereas motor vehicle accidents are the leading cause of head injuries in the other age groups (Williamson et al., 1996).

NEUROPATHOLOGY

Following TBI, abnormalities on MRI scans have been commonly found in the mesial temporal and lateral frontal lobes, and ventricular enlargement is a frequent symptom (Avants, Duda, Kim, Zhang, Pluta, & Gee, 2008). It often leads to diffuse axonal injury (Ommaya & Gennarelli, 1974), in which the frontal and temporal lobes are found to be the most vulnerable cortical areas (Adams, 1975). Thus, it is not surprising that Vakil (2005) concluded that the literature indicates that the profile of memory deficits in patients with TBI resembles that of patients with frontal injury rather than that of patients with mid-temporal amnesia. A significant correlation was found between changes in the white matter measured with Diffusion Tensor Imaging (DTI) and cognitive functioning (Kraus, Susmaras, Caughlin, Walker, Sweeney, & Little, 2007). More specifically, DTI measures were associated with learning and memory indices (Palacios et al., 2011). Atrophy of the hippocampus, which has a critical role in memory, has also been observed following severe TBI, due to either anoxia and/or high intra-cranial pressure (Bigler, Johnson, Anderson, & Blatter, 1996).

In addition to the severity and location of the injury as predictors of memory outcome following TBI, "cognitive reserve" was also found to be a predictor. This concept was introduced in order to explain repeated findings that similar brain pathologies have resulted in different clinical outcomes (Stern, 2002). This model assumes that people with higher cognitive reserve, determined for example by higher IQ, education, occupational attainment, and socioeconomic status, could cope better with brain pathology by more efficient usage of cognitive potential. Based on studies conducted subsequent to the introduction of the reserve concept, it became more evident that a person's premorbid cognitive abilities provide differential reserve against age-related changes or brain injury (for a review, see Bigler, 2006). For example, children with a history of learning difficulties showed more severe memory and attention difficulties as a result of TBI compared with controls and children with TBI with no history of learning difficulties (Farmer, Kanne, Haut, Williams, Johnstone, & Kirk, 2002).

COGNITIVE IMPLICATIONS OF TBI

TBI results in a wide range of cognitive deficits in addition to learning and memory. The most pronounced include executive functions, processing speed, and attention (Azouvi, Vallat-Azouvi, & Belmont, 2009). As mentioned above, the frontal lobes are most vulnerable following TBI, and the behavioral sequelae of TBI are consistent with frontal lobe injury (Stuss & Gow, 1992). Damage to the frontal lobes causes impairments in the executive functions of self-directive behavior, planning, decision-making, judgment, and self-perception and self-monitoring (Tranel, Anderson, & Benton, 1994), all of which interact with memory. Using Moscovitch's (1994) terminology "working-with-memory", the frontal lobes support the memory system by applying top-down processes such as implementation of strategy, organization, and conceptual elaboration at encoding as well as at retrieval. The fact that, in addition to memory, TBI affects a wide range of cognitive processes has very important implications. Impaired executive functions could be expressed in real-world difficulties in decision making, perseveration, confabulation, etc.

One illustrative example that is an important aspect of the social reintegration of TBI patients is driving: fitness to drive is dependent on the integration of several intact cognitive processes. Thus, for rehabilitation as well as for medico-legal purposes, it is important to be able to predict fitness to drive following TBI. Under the assumption that at least the perceptual-motor skills are preserved, the procedural aspects of driving are expected to be preserved following TBI (Brouwer, Withaar, Tant, & Van Zomeren, 2002). However, judging fitness to drive is not a trivial thing, because driving is a complex task that involves several cognitive processes in addition to the pure ability to acquire a skill. In their review, Brenner, Homaifar, and Schultheis (2008) suggest that fitness to drive could be affected by impaired processing speed, attention, executive functions, visualspatial skills, and visual memory.

MEMORY ASSESSMENT

The literature examining the effects of TBI on memory may be divided into three basic approaches. The first is in the context of an experimental design in a laboratory setting, typically studying an isolated memory process (e.g., priming). The second approach is in a context of neuropsychological evaluation, typically using a standardized test battery (e.g., the *Wechsler Memory Scale –* working memory). See Vakil (2012) for a presentation of the various memory measures classified on the basis of several dimensions: time frame, perceptual modality, process, and retrieval conditions. The third approach is testing an everyday task that is assumed to involve one or more memory processes (e.g., face–name association, social interactions, driving). These three approaches could be viewed as a continuum ranging from the evaluation of a purer memory process to more complex tasks contaminated with several memory and possibly other cognitive processes. At the same time it could

be viewed as a tradeoff, by which these approaches range respectively from less to more ecologically valid tests of memory, or a tradeoff in the opposite direction, from more to less pure memory measure.

Thus, although the present focus is primarily on studies of the third approach, studies of the other two categories will be reviewed as well, where the results have practical and functional implications. An echo of this continuum may be found in the neuropsychological assessment literature. Vakil (2012) presents a model in which the various assessment means available for the clinician are ranked from those based on the analysis of pure cognitive processes (i.e., cognitive tests) to those that are based on observation of behavior in real-life situations. Examples of an intermediate set of tests on this continuum are the "behavioral tests" developed by Wilson and colleagues in an attempt to improve the ecological validity of neuropsychological assessment. These tests (e.g., Rivermead Behavioural Memory Test –RBMT; Wilson, Cockburn, & Baddeley, 1985) use real-life tasks and items (e.g., remembering new names).

Among the various goals of neuropsychological assessment, Vakil (2012) mentions two applied goals: "functional assessment", which is the evaluation of the day to day functional implications of the head trauma, and "design of rehabilitation program", which aims to assist setting goals for rehabilitation in order to maximize the patient's functional potential. In Wilson's (2002) opinion, the sampling of real-life situations makes "behavioral tests" better in assessing a person's daily functioning and for planning rehabilitation than the standard tests that focus on the analysis of pure cognitive processes, because they sample real-life situations.

MEMORY AND DAILY LIVING

Almost all aspects of our daily living are dependent on our memory. Furthermore, since memory is not a unitary system, various aspects of daily activities can be affected by impairment of different aspects of memory. For example, interpersonal skills are critical for adequate vocational, marital, and social functioning (Hawley & Newman, 2010), and are significantly impaired following TBI. Social skills consist of several cognitive processes including executive functions, self-awareness, and different aspects of memory. Imagine that you are meeting with a group of old friends at a reunion. Any number of memory failures could disrupt your ability to maintain a friendship. You might be unable to follow a complex conversation across multiple speakers (working memory), forget their names (face–name association as one example of impaired learning and forgetting rate), be unable to report the "gist" of a movie you have just watched (semantic memory), forget shared past experiences (autobiographical memory), confuse who said what (source memory), or forget to return their phone calls (prospective memory), all of which could be very embarrassing. Thus, the effect of TBI on these aspects of memory will be reviewed because of their impact on everyday functioning.

Working memory

Baddeley's (2003) model of working memory involves two slave systems, the phonological loop and the visuospatial sketchpad, that respectively keep on line verbal and visuospatial information. The episodic buffer integrates the information from these two slave systems and mediates between working memory and long term memory. Additionally, there is a central executive component thought to control and manipulate on-line information.

Several studies have shown altered brain activity of patients with TBI while performing a working memory task. Christodoulou et al. (2001) tested patients with TBI on a modified version of a frequently used working memory task: Paced Auditory Serial Addition Task – PASAT. This task requires maintenance and manipulation of information on line. Participants hear numbers (1 to 9) at a rate of one every 2 seconds and are asked to continuously add up the last two numbers and if the sum is 10 to lift their right index finger. The results showed that compared with healthy controls, the patients made significantly more errors on the task. The fMRI activity of the patients' group while performing the task was more widely spread than that of the controls. The authors' interpretation of these findings is that the patients needed to recruit larger brain areas in order to cope with the task.

Perlstein et al. (2004) tested mild, moderate, and severe TBI patients with the n-back test of working memory under event-related fMRI. In this test stimuli are presented sequentially and participants are asked to indicate when the current stimulus (i.e., letter) is identical to the stimulus from n steps earlier. The distance (i.e., n) between stimuli, which could range from zero to three, determines the difficulty level of the task: zero when the target was any stimulus that matches a pre-specified stimulus, and three when the target was any stimulus that matches the one presented three trials back.

The behavioral results showed that the moderate-to-severe patients were less accurate than the mild patients and controls with the impairment dependent on the task load: impairment was observed at the high loads (i.e., $n = 2$ and 3) but not at the low loads (i.e., $n = 0$ and 1). The neuroimaging data of the control group replicated previous findings that found increased brain activity in areas associated with working memory (e.g., dorsolateral prefrontal cortex, parietal cortex, and Broca's area), as a function of the task load. The TBI patients did not show the expected pattern, which was interpreted as a disturbance of the working memory related brain network. Kasahara et al. (2011) have also used the n-back task with patients that sustained TBI (mostly moderate-to-severe injuries). Consistent with the results by Perlstein et al. (2004), the impairment compared with controls was associated with the difficulty level of the task. The neuroimaging data showed that activation of the left inferior parietal gyrus (LIPG) in the patient group was significantly lower than that of the control group, and vice versa with the activation of the right inferior frontal gyrus (RIFG). Furthermore, while accuracy on the n-back task was associated with LIPG activation in controls, in patients it was associated with RIFG activation. The authors interpreted these results to indicate a connectivity problem, between the LIPG and RIFG in the patient group, which results in the working memory deficits observed in these patients.

Vallat-Azouvi, Weber, Legrand, and Azouvi (2007) tested patients with severe TBI with a wide range of tasks tapping the various components of working memory. Results showed that the TBI group was not significantly different from the control group on measures of the two slave systems, the phonological loop (e.g., digit span forward and backward) and the visuospatial sketchpad (e.g., Corsi Block-tapping test, forward and backward). However, the patients were impaired on tasks tapping the central executive (e.g., Brown–Peterson paradigm, verbal and visual modalities with and without interference).

These findings are consistent with previous reports that following TBI dual-task processing (which is a critical function in the central executive) is very impaired (Azouvi, Couillet, Leclercq, Martin, Asloun, & Rousseaux, 2004). The tasks used in the previously reported studies, the PASAT (Christodoulou et al., 2001) and the n-back test (Kasahara et al., 2011; Perlstein et al., 2004) require on-line control and manipulation of the stimuli, and are therefore viewed as tapping primarily the central executive. This is consistent with Vallat-Azouvi et al.'s (2007) conclusion about the sensitivity of the central executive to TBI. A similar conclusion was reached based on a meta-analysis conducted by Park, Moscovitch and Robertson (1999), which showed that following TBI patients had difficulties with divided attention tasks when effortful, but not automatic, processes are required.

Working memory is essential for complex cognitive tasks that require holding on-line and manipulating several sources of information simultaneously, such as in a conversation, or problem solving (Baddeley, 2003; Perlstein et al., 2004). Imagine being engaged in a discussion with several participants. In order to take an active part in the discussion, you need to keep in mind what is said by each participant while simultaneously working out in your mind your response or contribution to the discussion. Such a situation requires holding on line and manipulating several pieces of information, which is exactly the role of the central executive. As demonstrated above (Kasahara et al., 2011; Perlstein et al., 2004), the higher the memory load (in this example determined by number of participants), or the greater the need to integrate over longer periods of time, the more vulnerable patients with TBI would be.

Dysfunction of the central executive also explains difficulties in problem solving following TBI, because of the effort required holding on-line simultaneously all the components of a problem. The Tower of Hanoi puzzle is a prototypical task studying cognitive problem solving (Anderson, Albert, & Fincham, 2005). In this task disks are arranged according to size with the largest disk at the bottom of the extreme left peg (#1). The task is to move the disks with minimum steps to the right-most peg (#3) while following several rules (i.e., only one disk at a time can be moved, and no disk can be placed on a smaller one). Compared with controls, the learning rate of this task was slower in terms of the number of moves required to solve the puzzle (Vakil, Gordon, Birnstok, Aberbuch, & Groswasser, 2001). Head, Raz, Gunning-Dixon, Williamson, and Acker (2002) have shown that learning to solve the task is associated with working memory capacity. Working memory is necessary for keeping the rules in mind while solving the puzzle, considering the alternative legitimate moves, and planning subsequent moves. The Tower of Hanoi puzzle can be viewed as a simulation of numerous real-life problem-solving situations such as planning an event or shopping for multiple items, while having to keep in mind certain "rules" or limitations (e.g., time available, budget limit), considering the alternative options, and planning (e.g., planning route, planning time, and schedule).

Learning and forgetting rate

Because of the dependence of forgetting rate on the quality of learning, these two aspects of memory are discussed together. Using a wide range of tests learning rate has been consistently found to be impaired whether verbal (Wright, Schmitter-Edgecombe, & Woo, 2010) or visual material (Shum, Harris, & O'Gorman, 2000) is presented. Most of the studies using standard memory tests report an accelerated forgetting rate following TBI. However, these findings cannot be conclusive, because initial learning is also impaired in this population.

A study that controlled for initial learning reached the conclusion that encoding, rather than retention, is primarily affected by TBI (DeLuca, Schultheis, Madigan, Christodoulou, & Averill, 2000). When baseline was controlled for by additional learning trials, the forgetting rate, as measured after 30 and 90 minutes, did not differ significantly between the patient and the control groups. Nevertheless, the end result is that learning rate and forgetting rate are impaired as a result of TBI. As noted by the authors, these results have encouraging implications for rehabilitation. It suggests that despite the memory difficulties, given sufficient opportunity for rehearsal, retention of material over time could be normally preserved.

Face naming is one of the most difficult things to learn because of the arbitrary nature of face–name associations (Groninger, 2000). Several studies have reported improvement in face–name association with memory-impaired patients using various strategies such as visual imagery, method of vanishing cues, and name. Manasse, Hux, and Snell (2005) trained five patients with severe TBI for face–name association. In the first phase, nine traditional one-on-one sessions of training were conducted (three sessions a week for three weeks). In these sessions participants were presented with a photograph of a staff member while the researcher directed their attention to special facial features (e.g., "Notice whether the person is wearing glasses"). In addition, participants were asked to repeat after the researcher the staff member's name. This was followed by the participant reading an imagery statement associated with the name (e.g., for Jim "Imagine Jim working out at the gym"). The second phase – the "real-world training" lasted for 15 days, with two interactions a day conducted by the staff members whose names had to be remembered. The effectiveness of three cuing conditions was evaluated: name restating, phonemic cueing (i.e., staff member provides the initial sound of his/her name), and visual imagery (i.e., the staff member repeated the imagery statement from the first phase associated with his/her name). Overall treatment in both phases targeted six staff members' names. The results clearly showed a significant improvement in face–name association following training, as compared with base-line performance. The finding with the most significant implications for rehabilitation is that the one-to-one training did not generalize to real-world situations. However, face–name association was evident following training in a real-world setting with the to-be-named staff members. Further research is needed in order to address the question of whether the face–name association training reported in this study would transfer to other stimuli such as association between people (couples) or association between places (country–capital city). However, this study highlights the importance of training in real-world settings in order to facilitate the functional implications of training.

Semantic memory

In everyday life we are exposed to a massive amount of information and are not expected to remember all the details of a story we heard or a movie we watched, but rather to retain the most important parts of it. The fuzzy-trace theory distinguishes between two types of mental representations, *verbatim* and *gist*. The former captures the exact stimuli (e.g., words or numbers), while the latter captures the essence of the information presented (Reyna & Brainerd, 2011). In an attempt to test whether patients who sustained TBI are capable of extracting and remembering the gist of a story, Vakil, Arbell, Gozlan, Hoofien, and Blachstein (1992) used a standard memory test for a story (i.e., the *Logical Memory* subtest of the WMS). In the first phase 50 undergraduate students were given the story (listed as 24 units of information according to the manual) and were asked to rank the importance of each unit in the story on a scale of 1 to 3 from least to most important, respectively. Consequently, the 24 units of the story were divided into three; the eight most important units with the most points, the next eight important units, and the eight least important units. In the second phase, 40 individuals with moderate-to-severe TBI and 40 controls (who did not participate in the first phase) were tested on the story immediately, after 40 minutes, and after a one-day delay. As expected, it was found that the control group recalled and retained more units of information over time than the group with TBI. But more importantly, it was found that unlike controls, patients did not show differential delayed recall according to the relative importance of the information in the story (i.e., better retention over time of the more important information units). Interestingly, patients did not differ from controls when judging the relative importance of the units of information of the story. These findings led the researchers to conclude that TBI patients' difficulty is not with semantic knowledge per se, but rather with utilization of this knowledge in the memory process.

Consistent with these findings, Carlesimo, Sabbadini, Loasses, and Caltagirone (1997) presented participants with sets of 16 drawings either semantically related (exemplars of four categories) or unrelated. Free recall, cued recall, and recognition were tested after 30 seconds' and after 60 minutes' delay. The results showed that while the immediate-delay decay was comparable between the TBI and control groups in the free recall of the unrelated drawings, the decay was significantly steeper for the patient group under the cued recall and free recall of the related drawings. The source of the difference is that the controls, but not the patients, took advantage of the semantic relations between the items. As in the previous research by Vakil (1992) reported above, semantic memory impairment probably reflects the difficulty in implementation of semantic knowledge to support memory. This deficit might stem from a working-memory problem, particularly the central executive component that enables the manipulation and recombination of elements.

For a patient with such a deficit, going back to school or college might be contra-indicated, since the ability to summarize and extract the most important information from reading material is critical. The inability to remember important elements of a discussion, a book just read, or a movie just watched could be quite frustrating and embarrassing. Because of its importance, several rehabilitation programs focus their training on "Gist reasoning". A recent example is the report by Vas, Chapman, Cook, Elliott, and Keebler (2011), which applied a very structured training program, "Strategic Memory and Reasoning Training – SMART" to patients following TBI. In 12 sessions (15–18 hours) the SMART program trains individuals in a hierarchical fashion to extract the most important elements of information and to generalize or abstract its meaning. The training includes application of the learned strategies to real-life situations. In their study Vas et al. reported that the SMART training improved gist-reasoning even when measured six months later. Another important finding is that the effect of training was generalized to untrained areas, including the working memory measure of listening span and rating (using a social integration scale) of increased participation in daily activities.

Autobiographical memory deficits

Difficulties with autobiographical memory and memory for early acquired knowledge of public events are highly pervasive among patients who suffer from TBI (Carlesimo et al., 1998). Knight and O'Hagan (2009) used a test of famous faces to distinguish between semantic and episodic autobiographical memories. The former requires general knowledge of the person independent of a specific event or context. However, the latter requires memory of a specific episode (context dependent) associated with the famous person. There is evidence that these two forms of memory are mediated by different brain structures. Episodic memory is primarily dependent on the functioning of the hippocampus and adjacent structures while representation of semantic memory extends to other areas of the temporal lobes and the neocortex (Moscovitch, Nadel, Winocur, Gilboa, & Rosenbaum, 2006). Knight and O'Hagan (2009) predicted that because semantic knowledge has a widespread representation in the neocortex, it would be less vulnerable to TBI than episodic memory, which is represented in much more restricted brain areas. In their study, Knight and O'Hagan (2009) presented cards to participants with names printed on them. They were asked to sort them into two piles – "famous" and "not famous". Then for the names sorted as famous, they were asked whether they could recall a personal memory related to that name. For example, if a participant classified Princess Diana's picture as famous and in addition could recall watching her wedding on television that would be considered an episodic memory. However, if he just says that he remembers her from

television or newspapers, that would be considered a semantic memory. As predicted, the TBI group was impaired compared with controls on the episodic task but not the semantic task. Coste et al. (2011) found that patients following TBI were impaired in retrieval of both episodic as well as semantic autobiographical memories. Nevertheless, consistent with Knight and O'Hagan (2009), patients were more impaired in retrieval when specific details were required (i.e., episodic) compared with retrieval of general events (i.e., semantic). Furthermore, it was found that difficulty in accessing specific details is associated with impairment of the "updating" aspect of executive functions (i.e., running span). The implications for real-life functioning is that patients with TBI would be able to follow a conversation when famous events or names are mentioned, yet they would have difficulties associating personal experiences with these events or people. From the perspective of memory remediation, training could focus on this difficulty in drawing attention to the details of an experienced event and emphasizing the personal relevance or significance of such an event.

Prospective memory

According to Groot, Wilson, Evans, and Watson (2002), "Prospective memory involves remembering to perform previously planned actions at the right time or within the right time interval or after a certain event takes place while being involved in other activities" (p. 645). Mateer, Sohlberg, and Crinean (1987) reported that patients with head trauma and their families viewed prospective memory as the most problematic memory forgetting experience. Based on their review of the literature and meta-analysis, Shum, Levin, and Chan (2011) concluded that patients who sustained TBI are impaired compared with controls in time (i.e., to perform a planned action at a certain time) and event-based (i.e., to perform a planned action following a certain event such as when someone knocks on the door) prospective memory. Prospective memory was associated with executive functions and severity of TBI as measured by length of post-traumatic amnesia (PTA) (Fleming, Riley, Gill, Gullo, Strong, & Shum, 2008). A rehabilitation program for prospective memory was reported by Fleming, Shum, Strong, and Lightbody (2005). Three individuals with TBI were trained for eight weeks on various cognitive processes associated with prospective memory. This included training of self-awareness by assessing it and providing feedback. Then patients were trained in using a diary efficiently, including note-taking and cues. That also included the use of organizational devices such as alarms, watches, and computers. To enhance generalization of the strategies learned, they were implemented in real-life situations with the assistance of family members. The effectiveness of the training was reflected in the comparison of the pre- to post-intervention performance on formal prospective memory testing. In addition, the training led to more frequent post-training, as compared with pre- training, use of a diary.

In their review, Shum et al. (2011) concluded that although the reports on treatment of prospective memory look promising, they have some experimental flaws, such as small sample sizes and short follow-up periods. In their review, Ellis and Kvavilashvili (2000) claim that prospective memory is a critical cognitive ability necessary for independent living. This type of memory reflects much of our need and use of memory in our daily activities (e.g., returning phone calls, keeping appointments, taking medications, paying bills).

Context and source memory

Schacter, Harbluk, and McLachlan (1984) introduced the distinction between item and source memory. Item memory is the memory for the information asked explicitly to be learned and remembered, while source memory refers to the contextual information of an item or event that was not explicitly expected to be learned and remembered (e.g., temporal order or modality of presentation). Source memory is tested explicitly when a person is asked directly about contextual information. However, contextual information can be tested implicitly as well. The facilitation due to correspondence of context of the information across learning and retrieval – a context effect – provides an implicit measure of memory for context (Vakil, Openheim, Falck, Aberbuch, & Groswasser, 1997). Patients with TBI have been consistently found to be impaired when memory for context was tested explicitly (i.e., source memory), but not impaired when tested implicitly through a context reinstatement effect (e.g., Vakil et al., 1997, re: modality of presentation – visual versus auditory word recall).

Source memory has an important role in many aspects of our social interactions, such as remembering who said what. Misattribution of information to a person, place, or time could have embarrassing consequences. But at the same time, based on the studies reviewed above, patients with TBI could implicitly benefit from contextual cues (i.e., context effect). So far, this benefit has been demonstrated in a laboratory setting. The effectiveness of reinstatement of contextual environment in real-life settings needs to be demonstrated in this patient population in order for it to be a used as a compensatory strategy in rehabilitation.

Skill learning

The ability to use old skills or to learn new skills has very significant implications for employment and rehabilitation following TBI. Several studies have reported that well-practiced skills acquired prior to injury are preserved (Schmitter-Edgecombe & Nissley, 2000). But what about the ability to acquire new skills after the injury? This question has been addressed using a range of laboratory tasks. Among the most frequently used skill learning tasks are the Serial Reaction Time (SRT) task and the Tower of Hanoi Puzzle. In the SRT task a red light appears in one of four squares arranged horizontally on the computer screen. Participants are asked to press as fast as possible one of the four horizontal numerical keys on the keyboard that corresponds to the position of the red light. Participants are not told that there is a sequence of 12 positions that repeats itself. The indication for motor sequence learning is reduction of reaction time across trials and more importantly, increase in reaction time upon changing the learned sequence. Most studies that have used the SRT task with TBI patients reported that patients had difficulty with sequence learning (Vakil, Kraus, Bor, & Groswasser, 2002). The Tower of Hanoi Puzzle, as described above, is a cognitive skill learning task. Patients with TBI were impaired in learning the task, as measured by the number of moves required to solve it (Vakil et al., 2001).

Schmitter-Edgecombe and Beglinger (2001) tested patients with TBI on a search-detection task. In this task, a category name (e.g., animal) is presented on the screen and followed by a display of two words in two rows (forming a 2 × 2 rectangle). Participants were asked to press on a numeric keyboard with similar 2 × 2 layout, on the corresponding location of the correct category exemplar (e.g., goat). Contrary to findings with the previous two skill learning tasks, the patients were able to reach automaticity, although at a slower rate than controls. Vakil (2005) pointed out that sequencing (SRT) and problem solving (Tower of Hanoi Puzzle) are more dependent on the intactness of the frontal lobes than the search-detection task. Thus, the vulnerability of the frontal lobes to TBI could explain this pattern of results.

Much of our routine activity is performed automatically as a result of continuous repetitions and practice (e.g., brushing teeth, utilization of instruments). There are also new skills that we are expected to learn at various points in our life (learning to drive or to play a musical instrument). Sandhaug, Andelic, Berntsen, Seiler, and Mygland (2012) have trained people with TBI on computer-based skills using either a random or blocked training schedule. Although both training schedules yielded significant improvement, only people in random training showed transfer to another task. This finding has important implications for rehabilitation when attempting to teach new skills such as a new computer program.

Self-awareness

Lack of awareness following TBI could be a primary result of the injury (i.e., anosognosia) or a secondary result that is a psychological reaction (i.e., denial) to the injury or a combination of both (Azouvi et al., 2009). Poor self-awareness of cognitive and daily functioning is frequently reported following TBI (Sandhaug et al., 2012). Oddy, Coughlan, Tyerman, and Jenkins (1985) reported that, seven years after onset, only 40 percent of the patients with TBI, whose family members reported that they have memory problems, have acknowledged such problems. Knight, Harnett, and Titov (2005) tested the accuracy of patients with TBI in predicting their performance on a prospective memory task. In this task they were instructed to perform 20 activities in the city (e.g., to take a tire to a service station for repair). Participants were asked to rank on a scale from 1 to 4 how likely it is for them to remember the instructions. Then they watched a video as if they were traveling into the city or walking in a shopping area. They were expected to stop when they reached a place where they were instructed to perform an activity (e.g., at a service station to repair the tire). The results showed that the patients with TBI had an impaired prospective memory (fewer instructions were remembered) compared with controls. In addition, patients were poorer in predicting their performance by over-estimating their memory, indicating low self-awareness.

Jamora, Young, and Ruff (2012) tested the relations between the subjective cognitive complaints to the objective neuropsychological test results of mild and more severe TBI. Their major findings were that the patients with the mild injuries were more aware and more accurate with complaints about their attention deficits, while the patients with moderate to severe injuries were more accurate in estimating their learning and memory deficits. Consistent with this, Livengood, Anderson, and Schmitter-Edgecombe (2010) found that although patients with moderate-to-severe TBI showed impaired memory, self-awareness of their deficit was intact.

While awareness of the impairment could lead to distress and depression (Wilson, 2002), lack of awareness of deficits in general and memory in particular may cause reduced motivation for rehabilitation (Malec & Moessner, 2001). Furthermore, it could lead to unpleasant consequences by setting unrealistic goals (e.g., financial, academic). Thus, increasing awareness should be a primary goal in rehabilitation, in order to enable intervention and change.

REMEDIATION OF MEMORY

Tsaousides and Gordon (2009) distinguish between two basic approaches to memory remediation: those that focus on mnemonic strategies (e.g., visual imagery) and those that focus on compensatory approaches (e.g., electronic devices). The first approach assumes that as a result of massive practice the lost capabilities can be restored at least to some extent. The second approach does not make this assumption, and therefore needs to rely on external aids, and the training is aimed to maximize the utilization of these aids. In addition, Wilson (2002) emphasizes the importance of environmental adaptations in facilitating everyday functioning. For example, labeling (e.g., drawers, doors), placing needed objects in a place that cannot be missed, or arrangement in advance of items in the order to be used (e.g., ingredients for baking a cake).

In their report, the EFNS task force for guidelines on cognitive rehabilitation (Cappa Benke, Clarke, Rossi, Stemmer, & Van Heugten, 2005) divided the studies on memory remediation they reviewed into three categories. First are those studies that aim to develop internal strategies without using external memory aids (e.g., visual imagery). Second are studies that attempted to improve functioning by using non-electronic external memory aids (e.g., diary). And third are those that train the participants in using electronic technology (e.g., pagers). In addition, it should be mentioned that there are memory groups conducted with patients with TBI that integrate several approaches (Wilson & Moffat, 1992).

Several studies have taken the first approach. In an attempt to improve encoding in individuals with memory impairment, Wilson (2002) made the following recommendations: to simplify information, remember one thing at a time, verify that information is understood, make an association between new information and old, distributed practice, and finally active or elaborated encoding (e.g., write down, use imagery).

Several studies have evaluated systematically the effectiveness of the various strategies. Potvin, Rouleau, Senechal, and Giguere (2011) have shown that visual imagery improved prospective memory in patients with moderate-to-severe TBI. Self-imagination (i.e., imagination of an event from a realistic, personal perspective), a relatively new mnemonic strategy, was demonstrated to be more efficient than other strategies (e.g., semantic elaboration and visual imagery) in improving cued recall (Grilli & Glisky, 2011) and prospective memory (Grilli & McFarland, 2011) in individuals with neurological damage including TBI. Goverover, Arango-Lasprilla, Hillary, Chiaravalloti, and DeLuca (2009) have confirmed that just like healthy controls, patients with TBI have demonstrated the spacing effect (better recall of information learning under spaced rather than massed presentation).

Similarly, Lengenfelder, Chiaravalloti, and DeLuca (2007) and Schefft, Dulay, and Fargo (2008) have reported that patients following TBI show the generation effect (better memory of self-generated words than words provided). Moreover, there are studies aimed at improving internal strategies using sophisticated technology. For example, Caglio et al. (2012) described memory improvement following intensive training of a person who sustained TBI on a 3D virtual navigation task. Furthermore, comparing brain activity with fMRI pre and post training, they found increased brain activities in several areas including the hippocampus and parahippocampal areas. These kinds of findings could be utilized in cognitive remediation programs.

Among studies that implemented the second approach, using non-electronic external memory aids, are those of Schmitter-Edgecombe, Fahy, Whelan, and Long (1995) and Ownsworth and McFarland (1999), who trained individuals with TBI to use a notebook or a diary and found that it reduced memory failure in everyday functioning.

There are also studies that took the third approach, i.e., the utilization of electronic devices as memory aids. For example, Gentry, Wallace, Kvarfordt, and Lynch (2008) showed that following short training, community-dwelling individuals with severe TBIefficiently learned to use personal digital assistants for daily tasks. Kirsch, Shenton, and Rowan (2004) describe how an alphanumeric paging system facilitated the use of a daily planner for a patient with memory difficulties following TBI.

It is important to emphasize that the different approaches are not mutually exclusive, but quite the opposite: it is important to combine approaches in order to evaluate which one is most efficient for a particular task. All the methods mentioned above could be implemented either as individual or group training or in combination (Wilson & Moffat, 1992). Group training has many advantages: it increases motivation, helps with acceptance of the impairment, reduces anxiety and depression, and enables honest feedback by

peers, which is better accepted than when given by the therapist (Wilson, 2002).

Generalization is one issue that all remediation approaches have to deal with. The usefulness for everyday functioning of a memory aid or of a strategy learned would be very limited if it was restricted to a particular setting, place, or person. Therefore, part of the training should be directed to increasing its applicability to as wide a range of situations as possible. One of the most efficient approaches to increase generalization and transfer of the strategy acquired is by implementing it as often as possible in various situations, places, and individuals. If this does not happen spontaneously, it should be done intentionally by the trainers and by the trainees (Wilson, 2002). Unfortunately, many of the remediation studies reported in the literature did not test generalization from one type of stimuli to another and to real-world situations. As demonstrated by Manasse et al. (2005), face–name association training was effective only when conducted in a real-world setting, that is, with the staff members whose names were to be remembered.

Tsaousides and Gordon (2009) list several factors that could hamper the effectiveness of the use of compensatory devices or memory remediation in general. Among them are patients' lack of awareness or motivation and appropriateness of the training method. In their review of the literature on cognitive rehabilitation, Cicerone, Langenbahn, and Braden (2011) reached several conclusions regarding remediation of memory deficits. There is evidence for the effectiveness of training memory strategies with individuals suffering from mild memory impairments after TBI. Individuals with moderate or severe memory deficits could benefit from the use of external compensation or external memory aids and errorless training (preventing the person from making errors) for acquiring specific skills. Thus, with milder deficits of memory, training internal strategies (i.e., the first approach) could be helpful. Patients with more severe memory difficulties need to depend on external memory aids (i.e., second and third approaches). Finally, the "holistic approach" to rehabilitation should be mentioned (Ben-Yishay, 1996). According to this approach, cognitive remediation including memory should be addressed in the context of a broader intervention that includes emotional, behavioral, as well as other, cognitive difficulties.

Psychopharmacological treatments

In parallel with the cognitive approaches, there are attempts to test whether medications could offset to some degree the cognitive impairment in general and memory in particular following TBI. Writer and Schillerstrom (2009) reviewed the literature on the use of various psychopharmacological treatments to improve cognitive functioning, including memory, following TBI. A wide range of medications is used, including antidepressant and antipsychotic agents, dopamine-enhancing medications, and acetylcholinesterase inhibitors. Based on their review, they reached the conclusion that the use of dopamine-enhancing medications was consistently supported. Wheaton, Mathias, and Vink (2011) applied a meta-analysis procedure to evaluate the effectiveness of various medications used to improve the behavioral and cognitive consequences of TBI. Their major conclusions were that dopaminergic drugs (i.e., methylphenidate) have a positive effect on behavior such as aggression (Katz Adjustment Scale [KAS], Belligerence subscale: $d = 0.82$; State-Trait Anger Scale: $d = 0.83$; Profile of Mood States: $d = 0.75$), while cholinergic drugs (i.e., donepezil) have a positive effect on cognition, primarily attention (Paced Auditory Serial Addition Test: $d = 2.93$) and memory (WMS: $d = 1.56$).

CONCLUSION

The prevalence of TBI is very high in Western countries. TBI causes behavioral, emotional, and cognitive problems. Memory problems are among the most pronounced and durable disturbing effects of TBI. As demonstrated in this chapter, memory impairment affects a wide range of daily functioning. Following TBI, the frontal lobes are the most vulnerable brain structures (Avants et al., 2008). This is consistent with the conclusion reached in a previous review, that the profile of the memory deficit in patients with TBI resembles that of patients with frontal injury (Vakil, 2005). In other words, the memory impairment is particularly pronounced in tasks that require top-down and effortful processes, implementation of strategy, organization, and conceptual elaboration at encoding as well as at retrieval. Tasks requiring perceptual or automatic processes are relatively preserved. These deficits affect many aspects of daily living such as social integration.

Neuropsychological assessment does not capture fully the impact of memory impairment on everyday functioning. Behavioral tests in addition to clinical interview and questionnaires can improve the ecological validity of the assessment (Wilson, 2002). There are aspects of memory, such as prospective memory and skill learning, which reflect very important aspects of daily living but are not usually included in memory assessment batteries. In recent years we have witnessed the introduction of new sophisticated technology for neuropsychological assessment. This includes the use of virtual reality (VR) and Internet (for a review, see Vakil, 2012). VR and the Internet have become part of today's reality. We shop (e.g., Amazon), socialize (e.g., Facebook), and learn (e.g., Wikipedia) via the Internet. Thus, it is reasonable to assume that tests based on advanced technologies (e.g., 3D pictures) would simulate reality better than the conventional test, thus improving the ecological validity of testing.

Although the focus of this chapter is on the effects of memory impairment on daily living, it should be stressed that daily tasks are complex and involve other cognitive processes in addition to memory, such as executive functions, motor skills, and attention (e.g., driving). There is no doubt that emotional state (e.g., anxiety, depression) impacts as well on performance. Thus, prediction of daily functioning could improve with the assessment of emotional state and other cognitive processes in addition to memory.

The advanced technologies that are now being developed have the potential in the future to play a key role in rehabilitation in general, and in memory remediation in particular. Two such examples are the "Experience Organizer" developed by "IBM" Company and "Life Caching" developed by "TrendWatch" Company. These tools (which can be carried by a person 24 hours a day) have the capability to collect and store pictures and voices. They capture a person's experiences, store them, and enable the display of any segment indexed, for example, by time or person. A person with severe memory problems could use such a tool to go back to a particular day at a particular time and recover exactly what happened at that time. In a case study of a person with acquired brain injury and anxiety disorder, Brindley, Bateman, and Gracey (2011) have used a wearable camera (SenseCam) to support retrieval of autobiographical events. This method was found to be very efficient in supporting recall of anxiety-related trigger events that have a very significant therapeutic value. As a result of these technological advances, healthy individuals rely more and more on sophisticated gadgets and advanced technology (e.g., smartphones). There is no doubt that these technologies could revolutionize the field of memory remediation, and patients with impaired memory could be trained to rely on and take advantage of these advances.

REFERENCES

Adams, J. H. (1975). The neuropathology of head injury. In P. J. Binken and G. W. Bruyn, (Eds.), *Handbook of clinical neurology*, 35–65, New York: Elsevier.

Anderson. J. R., Albert, M. V., & Fincham, J. M. (2005). Tracing problem solving in real time: fMRI analysis of the subject-paced Tower of Hanoi. *Journal of Cognitive Neuroscience, 17*, 1261–1274.

Arcia, E., & Gualtieri, C. T. (1993). Association between patient report of symptoms after mild head injury and neurobehavioural performance. *Brain Injury, 7*, 481–489.

Avants, B., Duda, J. T., Kim, J., Zhang, H., Pluta, J., & Gee, J. C. (2008). Multivariate analysis of structural and diffusion imaging in traumatic brain injury. *Academic Radiology, 15*, 1360–1375.

Azouvi, P., Couillet, J., Leclercq, M., Martin, M., Asloun, S., & Rousseaux, M. (2004). Divided attention and mental effort after severe traumatic brain injury. *Neuropsychologia, 42*, 1260–1268.

Azouvi, P., Vallat-Azouvi, C., & Belmont, A. (2009). Cognitive deficits after traumatic coma. *Progress in Brain Research, 177*, 89–110.

Baddeley, A. (2003). Working memory: Looking back and looking forward. *Nature Review Neuroscience, 4*, 829–839.

Ben-Yishay, Y. (1996). Reflections on the evolution of the therapeutic milieu concept. *Neuropsychological Rehabilitation, 6*, 327–343.

Bigler, E. D. (2006). Traumatic brain injury and cognitive reserve. In Y. Stern (Ed.), *Cognitive reserve: Theory and applications*. Hove, UK: Psychology Press.

Bigler, E. D., Johnson, S. C., Anderson, C. V., & Blatter, D. D. (1996). Traumatic brain injury and memory: The role of hippocampal atrophy. *Neuropsychology, 10*, 333–342.

Brenner, L. A., Homaifar, B. Y., & Schultheis, M. T. (2008). Driving, aging, and traumatic brain injury: Integrating findings from the literature. *Rehabilitation Psychology, 53*, 18–27.

Brindley, R., Bateman, A., & Gracey, F. (2011). Exploration of use of SenseCam to support autobiographical memory retrieval within a cognitive-behavioural therapeutic intervention following acquired brain injury. *Memory, 19*, 745–757.

Brouwer, W. H., Withaar, F. K., Tant, M. L., & Van Zomeren, A. H. (2002). Attention and driving in traumatic brain injury: A question of coping with time-pressure. *Journal of Head Trauma Rehabilitation, 17*, 1–15.

Caglio, M., Latini-Corazzini, L., D'Agata, F., Cauda, F., Sacco, K., Monteverdi, S., Zettin, M., Duca, S. & Geminiani, G. (2012). Virtual navigation for memory rehabilitation in a traumatic brain injured patient. *Neurocase, 18*, 123–131.

Cappa, S. F., Benke, T., Clarke, S., Rossi, B., Stemmer, B., & Van Heugten, C. M. (2005). EFNS guidelines on cognitive rehabilitation: Report of an EFNS task force. *European Journal of Neurology, 12*, 665–680.

Carlesimo, G. A., Sabbadini, M., Loasses, A., & Caltagirone, C. (1997). Forgetting from long-term memory in severe closed-head injury patients: Effect of retrieval conditions and semantic organization. *Cortex, 33,* 131–142.

Carlesimo, G. A., Sabbadini, M., Bombardi, P., Di Porto, E., Loasses, A., & Caltagirone, C. (1998). Retrograde memory deficits in severe closed head injury patients. *Cortex, 34,* 1–23.

Christodoulou, C., DeLuca, J., Ricker, J. H., Madigan, N. K., Bly, B. M., Lange, G., Kalnin, A. J., Liu, W. C., Steffener, J., Diamond, B. J., & Ni, A. C. (2001). Functional magnetic resonance imaging of working memory impairment after traumatic brain injury. *Journal of Neurology, Neurosurgery and Psychiatry, 71,* 161–168.

Cicerone, K. D., Langenbahn, D. M., & Braden, C. (2011). Evidence-based cognitive rehabilitation: Updated review of the literature from 2003 through 2008. *Archives of Physical Medicine and Rehabilitation, 92,* 519–530.

Coste, C., Agar, N., Petitfour, E., Quinette, P., Guillery-Girard, B., Azouvi, P., & Piolino, P. (2011). Exploring the roles of the executive and short-term feature-binding functions in retrieval of retrograde autobiographical memories in severe traumatic brain injury. *Cortex, 47,* 771–786.

DeLuca, J., Schultheis, M. T., Madigan, N. K., Christodoulou, C., & Averill, A. (2000). Acquisition versus retrieval deficits in traumatic brain injury: Implications for memory rehabilitation. *Archives of Physical and Medical Rehabilitation, 81,* 1327–1333.

Ellis, J., & Kvavilashvili, L. (2000). Prospective memory in 2000: Past, present, and future directions. *Applied Cognitive Psychology, 14,* 1–9.

Farmer, J. E., Kanne, S. M., Haut, J. S., Williams, J., Johnstone, B., & Kirk, K. (2002). Memory functioning following traumatic brain injury in children with premorbid learning problems. *Developmental Neuropsychology, 22,* 455–469.

Faul, M., Xu, L., Wald, M. M., & Coronado, V. G. (2010). Traumatic brain injury in the United States: Emergency department visits, hospitalizations, and deaths, 2002–2006. Atlanta, GA: Centers for Disease Control and Prevention, National Center for Injury Prevention and Control.

Fleming, J., Riley, L., Gill, H., Gullo, M. J., Strong, J., & Shum, D. (2008). Predictors of prospective memory in adults with traumatic brain injury. *Journal of the International Neuropsychological Society, 14,* 823–831.

Fleming, J. M., Shum, D., Strong, J., & Lightbody, S. (2005). Prospective memory rehabilitation for adults with traumatic brain injury: A compensatory training program. *Brain Injury, 19,* 1–10.

Gentry, T., Wallace, J., Kvarfordt, C., & Lynch, K. B. (2008). Personal digital assistants as cognitive aids for individuals with severe traumatic brain injury: A community-based trial. *Brain Injury, 22,* 19–24.

Goldstein, F. C., & Levin, H. S. (1995). Post-traumatic and anterograde amnesia following closed head injury. In A. D. Baddeley, B. A. Wilson, and F. N. Watts (Eds.), *Handbook of memory disorders* (pp. 187–209). New York: John Wiley & Sons.

Goverover, Y., Arango-Lasprilla, J. C., Hillary, F. G., Chiaravalloti, N., & DeLuca, J. (2009). Application of the spacing effect to improve learning and memory for functional tasks in traumatic brain injury: A pilot study. *American Journal of Occupational Therapy, 63,* 543–548.

Grilli, M. D., & Glisky, E. L. (2011). The self-imagination effect: Benefits of a self-referential encoding strategy on cued recall in memory-impaired individuals with neurological damage. *Journal of the International Neuropsychological Society, 17,* 929–933.

Grilli, M. D., & McFarland, C. P. (2011). Imagine that: Self-imagination improves prospective memory in memory-impaired individuals with neurological damage. *Neuropsychological Rehabilitation, 21,* 847–859.

Groninger, L. D. (2000). Face-name mediated learning and long-term retention: The role of images and imagery process. *American Journal of Psychology, 113,* 199–219.

Groot, Y. C. T., Wilson, B. A., Evans, J., & Watson, P. (2002). Prospective memory functioning in people with and without brain injury. *Journal of the International Neuropsychological Society, 8,* 645–654.

Hawley, L. A., & Newman, J. K. (2010). Group interactive structured treatment (GIST): A social competence intervention for individuals with brain injury. *Brain Injury, 2,* 1292–1297.

Head, D., Raz, N., Gunning-Dixon, F., Williamson, A., & Acker, J. D. (2002). Age related differences in the course of cognitive skill acquisition: The role of regional cortical shrinkage and cognitive resources. *Psychology and Aging, 17,* 72–84.

Jamora, C. W., Young, A., & Ruff, R. M. (2012). Comparison of subjective cognitive complaints with neuropsychological tests in individuals with mild vs more severe traumatic brain injuries. *Brain Injury, 26,* 36–47.

Kasahara, M., Menon, D. K., Salmond, C. H., Outtrim, J. G., Tavares, J. V., Carpenter, T. A., Pickard, J. D., Sahakian, B. J., & Stamatakis, E. A. (2011).

Traumatic brain injury alters the functional brain network mediating working memory. *Brain Injury, 5,* 1170–1187.

Kirsch, N. L., Shenton, M., & Rowan, J. (2004). A generic, 'in-house', alphanumeric paging system for prospective activity impairments after traumatic brain injury. *Brain Injury, 18,* 725–734.

Knight, R. J., Harnett, M., & Titov, N. (2005). The effects of traumatic brain injury on the predicted and actual performance of a test of prospective remembering. *Brain Injury, 19,* 19–27.

Knight, R. J., & O'Hagan, K. (2009). Autobiographical memory in long-term survivors of severe traumatic brain injury. *Journal of Clinical and Experimental Neuropsychology, 31,* 575–583.

Kraus, M. F., Susmaras, T, Caughlin, B. P., Walker, C. J., Sweeney, J. A., & Little, D. M. (2007). White matter integrity and cognition in chronic traumatic brain injury: A diffusion tensor imaging study. *Brain, 130,* 2508–2519.

Lengenfelder, J., Chiaravalloti, N. D., & DeLuca, J. (2007). The efficacy of the generation effect in improving new learning in persons with traumatic brain injury. *Rehabilitation Psychology, 52,* 290–296.

Livengood, M., Anderson, J. W., & Schmitter-Edgecombe M. (2010). Assessment of memory self-awareness following traumatic brain injury. *Brain Injury, 24,* 598–608.

Malec, J. F., & Moessner, A. M. (2001). Self-awareness, distress, and post acute rehabilitation outcome. *Rehabilitation Psychology, 45,* 227–241.

Manasse, N. J., Hux, K., & Snell, J. (2005). Teaching face–name associations to survivors of traumatic brain injury: A sequential treatment approach. *Brain Injury, 19,* 633–641.

Mateer, C. A., Sohlberg, M. M., & Crinean, J. (1987). Focus on clinical research: Perceptions of memory function in individuals with closed-head injury. *The Journal of Head Trauma Rehabilitation, 2,* 74–84.

Moscovitch, M. (1994). Memory and working with memory: Evaluation of a component process model and comparisons with other models. In D. L. Schacter and E. Tulving (Eds.), *Memory systems 1994.* Cambridge, MA: MIT Press.

Moscovitch, M., Nadel, L., Winocur, G., Gilboa, A., & Rosenbaum, R. S. (2006). The cognitive neuroscience of remote episodic, semantic and spatial memory. *Current Opinion in Neurobiology, 16,* 179–190.

Oddy, M., Coughlan, T., Tyerman, A., & Jenkins, D. (1985). Social adjustment after closed head injury: A further follow-up seven years after injury. *Journal of Neurology, Neurosurgery and Psychiatry, 48,* 564–568.

Ommaya, A. K., & Gennarelli, T. A. (1974). Cerebral concussion and traumatic unconsciousness. *Brain, 97,* 633–654.

Ownsworth, T. L., & McFarland, K. (1999). Memory remediation in long-term acquired brain injury: Two approaches in diary training. *Brain Injury, 13,* 605–626.

Palacios, E. M., Fernandez-Espejo, D., Junque, C., Sanchez-Carrion, R., Roig, T., Tormos, J. M., Bargallo, N., & Vendrell, P. (2011). Diffusion tensor imaging differences relate to memory deficits in diffuse traumatic brain injury. *BMC Neurology, 24,* 1–11.

Park, N. W., Moscovitch, M., & Robertson, I. H. (1999). Divided attention impairments after traumatic brain injury. *Neuropsychologia, 37,* 1119–1133.

Perlstein, W. M., Cole, M. A., Demery, J. A., Seignourel, P. J., Dixit, N. K., Larson, M. J., & Briggs, R. W. (2004). Parametric manipulation of working memory load in traumatic brain injury: behavioral and neural correlates. *Journal of the International Neuropsychological Society, 10,* 724–741.

Potvin, M. J., Rouleau, I., Senechal, G., & Giguere, J. F. (2011). Prospective memory rehabilitation based on visual imagery techniques. *Neuropsychological Rehabilitation, 21,* 899–924.

Reyna, V. F., & Brainerd, C. J. (2011). Dual processes in decision making and developmental neuroscience: A fuzzy-trace model. *Developmental Review, 31,* 180–206.

Sandhaug, M., Andelic, N., Berntsen, S. A., Seiler, S., & Mygland, A. (2012). Self and near relative ratings of functional level one year after traumatic brain injury. *Disability & Rehabilitation, 34,* 904–909.

Schacter, D. L., Harbluk, J. L., & McLachlan, D. R. (1984). Retrieval without recollection: An experimental analysis of source amnesia. *Journal of Verbal Learning and Verbal Behavior, 23,* 593–611.

Schefft, B. K., Dulay, M. F., & Fargo, J. D. (2008). The use of a self-generation memory encoding strategy to improve verbal memory and learning in patients with traumatic brain injury. *Applied Neuropsychology, 15,* 61–68.

Schmitter-Edgecombe, M., Fahy, J., Whelan, J., & Long, C. (1995). Memory remediation after severe closed head injury. Notebook training versus supportive therapy. *Journal of Consulting and Clinical Psychology, 63,* 484–489.

Schmitter-Edgecombe, M., & Beglinger, L. (2001). Acquisition of skilled visual search performance following severe closed-head injury. *Journal of the International Neuropsychological Society, 7,* 615–630.

Schmitter-Edgecombe, M., & Nissley, H. M. (2000). Effects of divided attention on automatic and controlled components of memory after severe closed-head injury. *Neuropsychology, 14,* 559–569.

Shum, D. H. K., Harris, D., & O'Gorman, J. G. (2000). Effects of severe traumatic brain injury on visual memory. *Journal of Clinical and Experimental Neuropsychology, 22,* 25–39.

Shum, D., Levin, H., & Chan, R. C. (2011). Prospective memory in patients with closed head injury: A review. *Neuropsychologia, 49,* 156–165.

Sosin, D. M., Sacks, J. J., & Holmgreen, P. (1990). Head injury-associated deaths from motorcycle crashes. Relationship to helmet use laws. *Journal of the American Medical Association, 264,* 2395–2399.

Stern, Y. (2002). What is cognitive reserve? Theory and research applications of the reserve concept. *Journal of International Neuropsychological Society, 8,* 448–460.

Stuss, D. T., & Gow, C. A. (1992). "Frontal dysfunction" after traumatic brain injury. *Neuropsychiatry, Neuropsychology, and Behavioral Neurology, 5,* 272–282.

Tranel, D., Anderson, S. W., & Benton, A. (1994). Development of the concept of "executive function" and its relationship to the frontal lobes. In F. Boller and H. Spinnler (Eds.), *Handbook of neuropsychology* (vol. 9, pp. 125–148). Amsterdam: Elsevier.

Tsaousides, T., & Gordon, W. A. (2009). Cognitive rehabilitation following traumatic brain injury: Assessment to treatment. *Mount Sinai Journal of Medicine, 76,* 173–181.

Vakil, E. (2005). The effect of moderate to severe Traumatic Brain Injury (TBI) on different aspects of memory: A selective review. *Journal of Clinical and Experimental Neuropsychology, 27,* 977–1021.

Vakil, E. (2012). Neuropsychological assessment: Principles, rationale, and challenges. *Journal of Clinical and Experimental Neuropsychology, 34,* 135–150.

Vakil, E., Arbell, N., Gozlan, M., Hoofien, D., & Blachstein, H. (1992). Relative importance of informational units and their role in long-term recall by closed-head-injured patients and control groups. *Journal of Consulting and Clinical Psychology, 60,* 802–803.

Vakil, E., Gordon, Y., Birnstok, S., Aberbuch, S., & Groswasser, Z. (2001). Declarative and nondeclarative sequence learning tasks: Closed-head injured patients versus control participants. *Journal of Clinical and Experimental Neuropsychology, 23,* 207–214.

Vakil, E., Kraus, A., Bor, B., & Groswasser, Z. (2002). Impaired skill learning in patients with severe closed-head injuries as demonstrated by the serial reaction time (SRT) task. *Brain and Cognition, 50,* 304–315.

Vakil, E., Openheim, M., Falck, D., Aberbuch, S., & Groswasser, Z. (1997). The indirect influence of modality on the direct memory for words and their modality: Closed-head injured patients versus control participants. *Neuropsychology, 11,* 545–551.

Vallat-Azouvi, C., Weber, T., Legrand, L., & Azouvi, P. J. (2007). Working memory after severe traumatic brain injury. *Journal of the International-Neuropsychological Society, 13,* 770–780.

Vas, A. K., Chapman, S. B., Cook, L. G., Elliott, A. C., & Keebler, M. (2011). Higher-order reasoning training years after traumatic brain injury in adults. *Journal of Head Trauma Rehabilitation, 6,* 224–239.

Wheaton, P., Mathias, J. L., & Vink, R. (2011). Impact of pharmacological treatments on cognitive and behavioral outcome in the postacute stages of adult traumatic brain injury: A meta-analysis. *Journal of Clinical and Psychopharmacology, 31,* 745–757.

Williamson, D. J. G., Scott, J. G., & Adams, R. L. (1996). Traumatic brain injury. In R.L. Adams and O. A. Parsons et al. (Eds.), *Neuropsychology for clinical practice: Etiology, assessment, and treatment of common neurological disorders* (pp. 9–64). Washington, DC: American Psychological Association.

Wilson, B. A. (2002). Management and remediation of memory problems in brain-injured adults. In A. D. Baddeley, M. D. Kopelman, & B. A. Wilson (Eds.), *The handbook of memory disorders* (pp. 655–682). Chichester, UK: John Wiley & Sons.

Wilson, B. A., Cockburn, J., & Baddeley, A. D. (1985). *The Rivermead Behavioural Memory Test manual.* Bury St Edmunds, UK: Thames Valley Test Company.

Wilson, B. A., & Moffat, N. (1992). The development of group memory therapy. In B. A. Wilson and N. Moffat (Eds.), *Clinical management of memory problems* (2nd ed.), (pp. 243–273). London:. Chapman & Hall.

Wright, M. J., Schmitter-Edgecombe, M., & Woo, E. (2010). Verbal memory impairment in severe closed head injury: The role of encoding and consolidation. *Journal of Clinical and Experimental Neuropsychology, 32,* 728–736.

Writer, B. W., & Schillerstrom, J. E. (2009). Psycho-pharmacological treatment for cognitive impairment in survivors of traumatic brain injury: A critical review. *Journal of Neuropsychiatry Clinical Neurosciences, 21,* 362–370.

Zec, R. F., Zellers, D., Belman, J., Miller, J., Matthews, J., Ferneau-Belman, D., & Robbs, R. (2001). Long-term consequences of severe closed head injury on episodic memory. *Journal of Clinical and Experimental Neuropsychology, 23,* 671–691.

Social and Individual Differences in Memory

13

Sociocultural and Functional Approaches to Autobiographical Memory

Robyn Fivush and Theodore E. A. Waters

Autobiographical memory is that uniquely human form of memory that ties our self to our past, that creates a sense of continuity and coherence to our lives, and that forms a life story that defines who we are, how we became this way, and who we will become. Autobiographical memory is, quite simply, our sense of identity across time. Perhaps somewhat surprisingly, autobiographical memory as a topic of research within the broader category of memory has a relatively short history. Although philosophers and psychologists have long been interested in memory of the personal past, there was sparse empirical investigation of everyday memory, especially as compared with the extensive research on memory in the laboratory. In 1977, Brown and Kulik published a seminal paper on flashbulb memories, memories of consequential real-world public events, that provided new methods for studying autobiographical memory under more controlled conditions. Accuracy was a major focus of this research, and, of course, accuracy remains an important question especially in forensic contexts, as discussed in multiple chapters in this handbook. In 1982, Dick Neisser called for a more ecologically valid approach to memory research. In this chapter, we respond to Neisser's call for

ecological validity, and focus attention on a set of ecologically motivated questions about autobiographical memory, namely, why do we recall our past experiences at all, and why does it matter? We address Baddeley's (1988) now famous question about autobiographical memory, "But what the hell is it for?" Stemming from both sociocultural and functional approaches, we argue that autobiographical memory emerges from and contributes to ongoing social interactions, is socially and culturally mediated, and serves to define self, maintain relationships, and direct behavior over time.

DEFINING AUTOBIOGRAPHICAL MEMORY

To begin, we must clearly define the type of memory we are discussing. In 1972, Tulving made a distinction between two types of declarative, or consciously available, memory. Semantic memory is memory unanchored from space and time, essentially knowledge about the world (e.g., Paris is the capital of France). Episodic memory, in contrast, is tied to a specific time and place and thus includes specific details about an event (e.g., the time I went to the top of the Eiffel tower in Paris). For Tulving, episodic memory included both being located at a specific time and place and autonoetic consciousness, an awareness of the self as having experienced the event. We argue here, as elsewhere (Fivush, 2010), that these two components of episodic memory, locating an event in time and place and autonoetic consciousness, are separable, and whereas the former is episodic, only the latter allows for autobiographical memory.

Autobiographical memory is first and foremost about the self (Conway & Pleydell-Pearce, 2000; Fivush, 1988). For a memory to be autobiographical, there must be an awareness of a self in the present recalling a self in the past. This, in turn, involves constructing a subjective perspective, an understanding that one recalls an experience from one's own unique perspective that is understood to be different from another's perspective (Fivush, 2010; Fivush & Nelson, 2006). This perspective is marked not only by recalling the external events, but integrating this with the internal "landscape of consciousness" (Bruner, 1990) that includes information about thoughts, emotions, motivations, and desires. It is through internal state language that events are linked subjectively through time, connected through the continuity of internal consciousness, and thus become autobiographical memories, in the sense that they are personally significant and meaningful (James, 1890; Fivush & Nelson, 2006; Schectman, 2003).

It is important to emphasize that this is a developmental argument. That is, early in development, young children do not have the ability to take a subjective perspective on any personally experienced event; they are unaware that others may have a different representation or perspective from their own (see Fivush & Nelson, 2006, for full discussion). During the preschool years, as children engage in parentally structured reminiscing, they gradually acquire this ability. Once this ability is acquired, it is internalized such that the individual engages in constructing subjective perspective whether they talk about this particular event or not; it is a generalized ability that develops from these early socially mediated interactions. Thus the argument we flesh out here is how children come to develop the needed skills for subjective perspective, and how this depends on early engagement in parent–child reminiscing.

Second, whereas episodic memories are a collection of single past events, autobiographical memories are linked together into a personal history that relates self through past, present, and future, forming a personal timeline, or a life narrative (Habermas & Bluck, 2000; McAdams, 2001). Note that many memories remain episodic, in that we retain memories of many inconsequential events at least over short periods of time, but for an episodic memory to become autobiographical and integrated into one's sense of personally significant memories, it must take on this kind of subjective perspective.

Further, theorists agree that autobiographical memory includes other types of knowledge structures in addition to single episodes (e.g., Barsalou, 1988; Brewer, 1988; Conway & Pleydell-Pearce, 2000; Nelson & Fivush, 2004; Rubin, 2006), including autobiographical facts (e.g., where and when I was born), generic personal memory or scripts (recurring events that form personal schematic representations, such as Sunday dinners with family), life periods (e.g., when I was in high school), and life themes (e.g., education), all hierarchically organized into an autobiographical self. Thus, autobiographical memory, unlike episodic memory, is about the self in relation to others over time. This formulation, in turn, suggests that autobiographical memory is related to sociocultural practices that unite what we remember with who we are.

SOCIOCULTURAL PERSPECTIVES ON AUTOBIOGRAPHICAL MEMORY

Stemming from Vygotsky's (1978) theory of sociocultural development, Nelson and

Fivush (2004) provided a model of the development of autobiographical memory that emerges from, and contributes to, social and cultural interactions. More specifically, Vygotsky argued that all human activity is culturally mediated, in that cultures provide the tools and the motivations for the development of specific skills deemed necessary to become a competent member of the culture. A good example is literacy. In industrialized cultures, infants are surrounded by the cultural tools of literacy virtually from birth. Letters and numbers on crib mobiles, infant clothing, picture books, and refrigerator magnets, in tandem with alphabet and number songs and poems, draw the infant into a world in which literate activities are valued and the forms and functions of literacy are modeled. Autobiographical memory is also a culturally mediated skill that serves specific social and cultural functions. Again, especially in Western industrialized cultures, it is necessary to be able to provide a coherent account of self through autobiographical narratives (Nelson, 2003; McAdams, 2001). Whether it is telling Daddy what you did in the park today, sharing of weekend activities with schoolmates, writing an essay to get into college, or meeting a potential romantic partner, individuals are expected to be able to tell their stories.

Sociocultural approaches highlight the key role that language and narrative play in autobiographical memory. Whereas memories of our personal experiences do not rely on language per se, in that memories are encoded and recalled in multiple modalities (Rubin, 2006) and even non-verbal animals and infants can recall specific episodes from their past (see Roberts, 2002, for a review), autobiography is mediated by language. Language allows for two factors critical in the development of autobiographical memories. First, language allows the individual to share their memories with others in social interaction. It is through social sharing that memories take on a subjective perspective, the idea that a memory is "owned" (Fivush & Nelson, 2006; James, 1890). Even if experiencing the same ostensible event, in social interaction, the individual can ascertain that others may not recall the event in the same way; different facts, and especially different evaluations, come to light (e.g., I loved the roller coaster but my brother was scared). It is the capability for subjective perspective that emerges from sharing our experiences with others in language that transitions episodic memory from something that happened to an autobiographical memory of something that happened *to me*. Thus, developmentally, as children engage in parentally structured reminiscing about their personal past, they develop an understanding of the possibility of multiple perspectives on an experience, and this understanding transforms the system. Even for experiences that are never spoken of, the ability to understand that one recalls one's own experiences from a particular perspective allows those memories to be subjective and autobiographical.

Beginning early in development, young children are already participating in sharing their memories with others, in the form of parentally guided reminiscing about the shared past. These early interactions set the stage for a developmental trajectory that leads to individual differences in autobiographical memory, some of which are related to gender and culture (see Nelson & Fivush, 2004; and Wang & Ross, 2007, for overviews). Parental sharing and structuring of autobiographical memory continues throughout adolescence, as individual autobiographical memories coalesce into a life narrative (Habermas & Bluck, 2000).

Second, in the process of reminiscing with others, language highlights the canonical narrative forms that autobiographical memories take. Narrative forms move beyond a chronological recounting of what occurred to include subjective perspective and evaluation, thus providing culturally mediated tools for framing how and why individuals behave as they do (Linde, 1993; Ricouer, 1991). At the most global level, Wang (in press) describes how cultural values of independence and interdependence define an individual's sense of self as autonomous or related, and how this self-definition modulates autobiographical memory; individuals from more independent cultures recall more specific, more detailed, and more self-referenced autobiographical narratives, whereas individuals from more interdependent cultures recall more generic, less detailed, and more relationally oriented autobiographical narratives. Although a full discussion of cultural differences in autobiographical memory is beyond the scope of this chapter, we note here that a great deal of research has demonstrated differences both in parent–child reminiscing and in adult autobiographical narratives in line with cultural values of self and relationships across multiple Eastern cultures, Latino cultures, and European cultures (see Wang & Ross, 2007, and Hirst, Coman, & Coman, Chapter 16, this volume, for more extensive discussions of the cultural differences in autobiographical memory). These cultural differences provide a background against which we must understand any individual autobiography.

In addition to providing narrative forms for single events, cultures further define what a life should look like, that is, the content and timing of specific cultural milestones, in the form of a canonical biography (Habermas & Bluck, 2000), or life script (Berntsen & Rubin, 2004), that provides a set of typically occurring life events, such as entering school, graduation, marriage, parenthood, retirement, and the typical time at which these events occur. Importantly the life script does not simply provide a canonical narrative of what *will* occur in a typical life, but it provides expectations of what *should* occur. If one's own life experiences follow the life script, one need not explain, but if one does not follow the life script, explanation of the deviation is expected. For example, people do not need to explain why they married in their twenties and had children, but they do need to explain why they married for the first time in their fifties or why they never married and chose not to have children. Thus, the cultural life script provides evaluative, as

well as normative, frames for an individual autobiography.

Similarly, master narratives (Harbus, 2011; Thorne & McLean, 2002) also provide evaluative frames. Master narratives are culturally accepted templates for interpreting experiences. For example, in American culture, the "rags to riches" master narrative provides a life story that values hard work that leads to reward. McAdams (2004) describes two major master narratives prevalent in American culture, redemption and contamination. In redemption narratives, the individual experiences a significant setback, but then uses this setback as a springboard for growth. Good examples of redemption narratives are recovery narratives; the addict hits bottom, but is able to use this experience not only to end the addiction, but to grow in self-awareness and ultimately to help others. In contrast, the contamination narrative also begins with a setback, but the individual simply spirals down from this experience into despair. These various cultural forms for recalling the personal past are communicated through language, in the course of local conversations and cultural artifacts, including memories, novels, films, and television (Fivush, Habermas, Waters, & Zaman, 2011; Harbus, 2011).

Outside of developing within a language using community, individuals would have memories of what happened. Through developing within a language using community, memories transition to evaluative stories about self and others interacting in a social and cultural world in which actions have consequences and selves have meaning. For example, deaf children growing up in hearing households, and thus without the benefit of ongoing language interactions, have less dense memories of their childhoods (Weigle & Bauer, 2000), develop narrative skills later, and tell less detailed autobiographical narratives even into adolescence, well after they enter a language using community (Rathman, Mann, & Morgan, 2007).

Thus the sociocultural approach underscores that it is through the process of sharing memories with others through language that personal memories take on the possibility of a canonical narrative form and an evaluative and subjective stance. Again, this is a developmental argument. Early in development, children learn these skills through parentally structured reminiscing, but once learned, they are internalized and the individual is capable of providing subjective perspective and canonical narrative form on any memory, whether socially shared or not. Thus the argument is that social sharing is necessary to get the system started. It also remains the case that as memories are shared with others, in childhood or adulthood, they are reshaped and re-evaluated through social sharing (see Hirst, Coman, & Coman, Chapter 16, this volume, for a full discussion of how memories are shaped in and by social interactions). The sociocultural approach to autobiographical memory further highlights that memories of the self are not simply socioculturally mediated, but are intricately related to how autobiographical memories are used in sociocultural contexts. This aligns quite well with recent functional approaches to autobiographical memory.

FUNCTIONS OF AUTOBIOGRAPHICAL MEMORY

The functions of autobiographical memory have received increasing attention over the last two decades, with growing consensus on three functional domains: self, social, and directive (Bluck, 2003; Bluck & Alea, 2011; Bluck, Alea, Habermas, & Rubin, 2005), all of which impact psychological adjustment (see Waters, 2013; for a review). The self function refers to the major role autobiographical memories play in helping us understand who we are, and to create a stable and enduring representation of our selves over time (e.g., Bluck, 2003; Wilson & Ross, 2003). The social function involves using autobiographical memory to create and maintain intimacy through sharing personal memories, as well as creating a stable representation of a shared history between individuals (Bluck et al., 2005; Fivush, Haden, & Reese, 1996; Hyman & Faries, 1992; Waters, Bauer, & Fivush, submitted). The directive function refers to the use of autobiographical memories to foster decision making, or to help navigate difficult situations (Pillemer, 1998, 2003). Bluck and colleagues have attempted to validate these theoretical functions of autobiographical memory through the examination of the factor structure of a questionnaire designed to assess the functions most frequently served by autobiographical memories (i.e., the Thinking About Life Events questionnaire). Results have supported the proposed use of autobiographical memories for self, social, and directive functions (e.g., Bluck & Alea, 2011).

Research on emotion and memory points to another possible function of autobiographical memory, that of emotion regulation (Pillemer, 2009). Pillemer, Ivcevic, Gooze, and Collins (2007) found that we use memories of positive accomplishments in the service of increasing self-esteem, and we use memoires of more negative emotional experiences to plan for, or to avoid, negative events in the future, thus using our memories to regulate current emotion. Fivush (2007) has argued that a critical function of sharing negative experiences with others in reminiscing is to help create a more explanatory framework of the event that, in turn, alleviates the experienced distress. She reviews longitudinal research demonstrating mothers who help their children construct more coherent, emotionally explanatory narratives of stressful events subsequently have children who show higher levels of emotional regulation and psychological well-being.

Integrating across sociocultural and functional approaches to autobiographical memory suggests that it would be fruitful to consider how functions of autobiographical memory are both shaped by and contribute to social interactions. More specifically, in the remainder of this chapter, we examine the ways in which we use our memories to create a sense of self, to maintain relationships with others, and to direct our behaviors, and how this occurs in socioculturally mediated interactions that define what kind of self we should be, what kind of relationships we should have, and what kinds of goals we should pursue. We examine these questions at two critical developmental time points, the preschool years when autobiographical memory emerges, and adolescence, when individuals construct a life narrative. Although our focus is on these two ages, we refer to autobiographical memory research across the lifespan.

THE EMERGENCE OF AUTOBIOGRAPHICAL MEMORY

The development of verbal recall

Some forms of memory clearly begin in utero, and even one-year-olds have the ability to recall specific experiences (see Bauer, 2007, for a review). However, given our theoretical framework and the fact that verbal recall is a hallmark of autobiographical memory, our focus is on verbal recall across childhood. Intriguingly, the ability to verbally recall the past occurs quite soon after children begin talking. By about 16 months of age, children will begin to make references to past events, although these references are fleeting and tend to be about quite recent events (see Fivush, 2007, for a review). Yet even at this early age, parents will expand and elaborate on children's recall to create more of a story. For example, young children may look up from play and say "berries." The mother will say, "Yes, we had berries for breakfast this morning. Weren't they delicious? You ate them all up." By about 20 to 24 months of age children will respond to specific questions about the past, but usually just with a word or two or a confirmation, such as responding "berries" when asked "What did we eat for breakfast?" Between 30 and 36 months of age, children begin providing

more information in response to specific questions about the past, and they begin showing more evidence of verbally recalling events that occurred in the more remote past. In fact, Fivush, Gray, and Fromhoff (1987) demonstrated that children as young as 30 months of age could recall accurate details of experiences that occurred as long as 3 to 6 months in the past, but they generally needed a lot of questions and prompts in order to recall sparse details.

Between 3 and 5 years of age, children become more verbally competent at recalling the past. They not only recall more information with fewer prompts (Hamond & Fivush, 1991; Hudson, 1990), they begin to organize their recall into more coherent narrative forms. Although 3-year-olds barely provide a coherent account of a past event, by age 5 most children can stay on topic and provide some evaluative and elaborative information about what occurred, describing component actions in a reasonably clear chronological order (see Reese, Haden, Baker-Ward, Bauer, Fivush, & Ornstein, 2011, for a full description of coherence and its development). However, there remain large individual differences in children's recall, and, indeed, individual differences in the density, coherence, and elaboration of autobiographical memories remain throughout the lifespan (Bauer, 2007). We note here that some of these differences are related to gender; a full discussion of gender is beyond the scope of this chapter, but we return to this issue briefly at the end of the chapter (see also Fivush & Zaman, in press).

Maternal reminiscing style

Given this developmental trajectory and the substantial individual differences in autobiographical recall, the question arises as to how early social interactions around remembering may influence the forms and functions of early autobiographical memory. A substantial body of research has now established that there are significant differences in how mothers (with much less research on fathers; see Fivush & Zaman, in press) structure reminiscing interactions with their young preschool children (see Fivush, Haden, & Reese, 2006, for a full review). Some mothers are more elaborative than others, co-constructing narratives that are longer and more detailed. More highly elaborative mothers also include more emotional content than do less elaborative mothers. When their young child does not recall much information, highly elaborative mothers expand on their questions, providing more context and more details, essentially helping their child to build a story of what occurred. In contrast, less elaborative mothers simply repeat the same questions over and over, with little modeling of a more elaborated coherent form of recall.

An elaborative reminiscing style is consistent over time as children grow older (Reese, Haden, & Fivush, 1993) and consistent across siblings within the family (Haden, 1998). Importantly, however, mothers who are highly elaborative when reminiscing are not necessarily more talkative when book reading or playing with their children, or when they are engaging in general caretaking activities (Haden & Fivush, 1996). Thus, maternal reminiscing style seems a special strategy that mothers use when talking about the past.

Critically, both longitudinal and intervention research indicates that mothers who are more highly elaborative when reminiscing with their young preschoolers have children who begin to tell more detailed and more coherent narratives by the end of the preschool years (see Fivush et al., 2006, for a review). Notably, although many other developmental skills play a role in the development of autobiographical memory, including language, temperament, and executive function skills, maternal reminiscing style predicts unique variance in developing autobiographical memory skills throughout early childhood (Fivush et al., 2006), and continues to predict autobiographical memory into adolescence. Adolescents whose mothers had been more elaborative when they were preschoolers have an earlier age of first memory (Jack, McDonald, Reese, & Hayne, 2009) and have a more elaborated life narrative (Reese, Yan, Jack, & Hayne, 2010) than adolescents whose mothers were less elaborative when they were young.

A caution across this research, even when longitudinal, is the issue of causality. A possible interpretation is that, since mothers are consistent in reminiscing style across development, it is concurrent relations and not longitudinal relations that are critical. Two findings argue against this interpretation. One, there are a few longitudinal studies where current reminiscing style is statistically controlled and previous maternal reminiscing style still predicts child outcome (see Fivush et al., 2006, for a review of these studies). Two, there are a couple of intervention studies, in which mothers are instructed to be more elaborative and, compared with non-instructed control groups, children of instructed mothers show more coherent and accurate memories at follow-up assessments (Boland, Haden, & Ornstein, 2003; Peterson, Jesso, & McCabe, 1999). Thus, there is good evidence that children are learning to tell more elaborated coherent narratives of their personal past through engaging in more elaborative maternal reminiscing. But, to again echo Baddeley (1988), what is it for?

Early functions of autobiographical reminiscing

Turning to the emerging functions of autobiographical memory, we must make a distinction between explicit functions and implicit functions (Pillemer, 2009). As mentioned earlier in this chapter, while there is a burgeoning literature on the functions of autobiographical memory, this literature focuses on adults, and virtually nothing has assessed function directly in childhood. Moreover, at these very early ages, we would not expect children to have the reflective abilities necessary for being explicit about how they might use their memories. Thus, in thinking about functions of mother–child reminiscing we must consider both the functions that the mother believes this reminiscing serves, as well as the actual functions reminiscing may serve in children's developing understanding of self, relationships, and emotions.

Very little research has assessed maternal beliefs about reminiscing or what functions this activity may serve. Kulkofsky, Wang, and Koh (2009) have shown that mothers report reminiscing with their preschool children frequently, at least on a daily basis. More pertinent to our arguments here, in both open-ended interviews and specific questionnaire measures, mothers report reminiscing about the past for all the functional reasons identified in the adult literature. The most frequent reason mothers provide and endorse is to maintain relationships, to help their children solve current problems, and to regulate their children's emotions. Helping their children build an identity is also endorsed but to a lesser extent. Importantly, Kulkofsky et al. (2009) also found that mothers who endorse more of a relationship function for reminiscing also reminisce with their preschoolers in more elaborative and evaluative ways, supporting the link between actual behavior and its functions.

While establishing a link between maternal behavior and functional goals, it is equally important to ascertain whether maternal reminiscing actually accomplishes these functions. In general, the research has shown links between a more elaborative coherent maternal reminiscing style and children's developing sense of self, relationships, and emotions. In terms of self-understanding, mothers who are more elaborative when reminiscing with their young preschoolers have children who display a more coherent and integrated self-concept by the end of the preschool years (Bird & Reese, 2006; Welch-Ross, Fasig, & Farrar, 1999). In addition, mothers who use more internal state language when reminiscing have preschoolers who are better able to coherently describe their own personality traits (Wang, Doan, & Song, 2010). These relations seem to extend across childhood. Mothers who are more elaborative during the preschool years have

adolescents who report higher levels of self-esteem (Reese et al., 2010).

Links between reminiscing and social functions of autobiographical memory early in development have mostly been assessed via attachment. Attachment is conceptualized as the emotional bond between caregiver and child (see Cassidy & Shaver, 1999, for an overview). Mothers who engage in sensitive caregiving have children who are securely attached; these children learn that the world is a safe and secure place, that they are loved, and that they will be taken care of. In contrast, mothers who do not engage in sensitive caregiving have children who are insecurely attached, who are not sure if they will be cared for, and do not believe the world to be a safe and secure place. These early attachment bonds are critical for developing relationships throughout the lifespan. Secure children develop better prosocial skills than insecure children, and more harmonious and satisfying peer relationships in childhood and adulthood (Schneider, Atkinson, & Tardif, 2001), and, indeed, are more likely to maintain healthy romantic relationships in adulthood (Treboux, Crowell, & Waters, 2004; Shaver & Mikulincer, 2002). Through reminiscing about the shared past, children learn how to conceptualize relationships through time. There is substantial evidence both that a secure attachment relationship contributes to more elaborated mother–child reminiscing and that more elaborated mother–child reminiscing contributes to the maintenance of a secure attachment relationship (Laible, 2004; Oppenheim, Nir, Warren, & Emde, 1997).

Related to findings on attachment and reminiscing is research on emotional understanding and reminiscing. It is as yet not clear whether emotional regulation is a separable function of autobiographical memory or a function that is related to the self, social, and directive functions, but however conceptualized, it is quite clear that maternal reminiscing is highly related to children's developing emotional understanding and regulation skills (see Fivush, 2007, and Fivush et al., 2006, for reviews). Mothers who are more elaborative and focus more on internal state language when reminiscing with their preschool children have children who, both concurrently and longitudinally, show higher ability to appropriately label emotions, to understand the causes of emotions (e.g., why someone might be sad or angry), and have better skill sets for regulating negative emotions (e.g., proactive coping strategies such as planning and restructuring). More elaborative maternal reminiscing is also related to children's developing moral reasoning and conscience development (Laible, 2004).

Some of these emotion regulation skills are also related to the directive functions of autobiographical memory, in that emotion regulation skills include the ability to plan for situations that might lead to aversive emotions. However, the directive function of autobiographical memory has received little research attention in preschoolers. There is some emerging evidence that by age 4, children are able to use memory to plan a future event, in the form of episodic foresight (Atance & Martin-Ordas, in press), but the specific links to maternal reminiscing have not been made.

In summary, maternal reminiscing style is clearly related to the development of structure and function in children's autobiographical memory. Mothers who are more elaborative when reminiscing with their preschoolers have children who develop more detailed and coherent autobiographical memories, and these effects extend into adolescence. More elaborative mothers also facilitate the development of a more coherent sense of self, a more secure attachment relationship, and higher levels of emotional regulation. By the end of the preschool years, children have internalized these styles, and have begun their individual autobiographical journey.

THE LIFE NARRATIVE: DEVELOPMENTS IN ADOLESCENCE AND BEYOND

While the construction, and co-construction, of specific autobiographical narratives can be seen as early as the preschool years, the ability to integrate several specific episodes in autobiographical memory emerges much later (Habermas & Bluck, 2000). This more cognitively complex ability is made possible by several developments in cognitive skills, as well as developmental advances in identity, seen in adolescence (Erikson, 1968). These developments manifest themselves in two skills that emerge in early adolescence and continue to develop across the teenage years and into adulthood. The first is the ability to construct a coherent life story/autobiography (Habermas & Bluck, 2000), essentially linking single autobiographical memories into life periods and themes that provide an overarching narrative of one's entire life. The second is the ability to draw inferences about the self/identity by linking autobiographical memories together, such as using one event to understand another event, or linking several disparate events together to create an explanation of current circumstances (autobiographical reasoning; Habermas, 2011).

The critical cognitive developments in early adolescence that allow for the construction of the life story and autobiographical reasoning include developments in temporal understanding and causal reasoning that facilitate more complex organization of autobiographical memories (Fivush et al., 2011). Temporal reasoning is obviously essential for constructing a timeline of one's own life, which undergirds a life narrative, and causal reasoning contributes to a more complex understanding of how events are linked together across time. While sparse, the research on the development of understanding of time suggests that the ability to understand and order events chronologically is a relatively late developmental achievement. Friedman, Reese, and Dai (2009) showed that only by middle childhood were children able to accurately locate and sequentially order events occurring more than a few weeks previously. And, quite surprisingly, mastery of conventional time, in terms of a Western calendar, is not fully acquired until the beginning of adolescence (Friedman, 1993).

In terms of causal reasoning, the ability to reason and gain a deeper understanding of self by using autobiographical memories emerges in pre-adolescence (Fivush et al., 2011). As the understanding of what constitutes a person evolves from easily observed habits and preferences to more enduring psychological characteristics, autobiographical reasoning provides one avenue for the discovery or attribution of psychological characteristics to oneself, as well as to others. By middle adolescence children begin to conceive of individual traits as having roots in early experiences and memories (Selman, 1980). Feldman, Bruner, Kalamar, and Renderer (1993) found that older adolescents, but not younger adolescents, interpreted protagonists' motives as both situational and rooted in specific biographic experiences. Pasupathi, Mansour, and Brubaker, (2007) have argued that this ability to reason about enduring personal characteristics leads to the construction of explanatory autobiographical narratives aimed at accounting for behaviors/events that are both "like me" and "not like me." The ability to use autobiographical memories to explain away inconsistent behavior suggests that adolescents are both aware of these inconsistencies and view them as requiring explanation because they interfere with the creation of a stable and internally consistent life story.

Beyond the development of specific cognitive skills that allow for more complex organization of autobiographical memories, adolescents are also highly motivated and encouraged to construct a life story to serve newly emerging self and social functions. Early in adolescence, children growing up in Western cultures are called upon to construct temporally and causally organized explanatory frameworks of who they are to share with others, as well as to better understand themselves. From English class and personal statements for college, to the practice of keeping a diary, adolescents are enculturated into valuing their own unique history, their perspective on their past, and being able to share it with others. These cultural tools allow adolescents to create an explanatory

account for a variety of social and psychological changes occurring in adolescence, what Erikson (1968) termed the "Identity Crisis." As adolescents' social world begins to shift more dramatically away from the home and into peer groups and the formation of new friendships, the need for an integrated and explanatory life story increases. A life story allows for people who do not have a shared history to quickly communicate personal information and develop intimacy. With the developmental precursors and the motivation to construct a life story in place, the development of the life story becomes possible.

The emergence of the life narrative

Several researchers have tracked the development of the life story from its most rudimentary beginnings as the rough ordering of lifetime periods all the way to a sophisticated temporally ordered and causally connected account of one's experiences, what McAdams (e.g., 1996, 2001) calls the life story. As soon as children are able to order the events of their lives competently they begin to tell life stories. Reese et al. (2010) found that, by the beginning of the adolescent period, children are able to break down their lives into temporally and thematically organized chapters, often focusing on school periods (e.g., elementary school, then junior high), although these rudimentary stories develop quite dramatically across adolescence.

The qualitative differences in the life stories told by adolescents has been operationalized as "global coherence" (Habermas & de Silveira, 2008). Habermas and Bluck (2000) describe several dimensions that comprise global coherence, including temporal , causal, and thematic coherence. Habermas and de Silveira (2008) examined the development of these constructs from 8 to 20 years of age. Temporal coherence reflects the organization of the life story along a discernible timeline, and sees its largest jump between 8 and 12 years of age. Whereas 8-year-olds typically produce unconnected and incoherent accounts of their lives, 12-year-olds produce temporally ordered histories of their lives, but still provide little elaboration. Causal coherence, the inclusion of sophisticated causal links between events and self, shows its largest increase between 12 and 16. By 16, participants include and elaborate on motivational and psychological themes in the life story and attempt to use the events of their lives to explain how they came to be who they are. Thematic coherence, the degree to which the events of one's life are linked in an explicit and plausible manner, sees its largest increase in late adolescence between 16 and 20. At 20, the life story has expanded beyond an account of the past leading up to the present, to an account of the past that has projections into the future. Themes like career and personal goals, hopes, and dreams make their first appearance, and suggest that between ages 16 and 20 adolescents develop the ability to use their autobiographical memory to not only reason about the past, but also to reason about the future.

Interestingly, variables like intelligence and frequency of biographical practices (e.g., journaling) contributed minimally to the developmental changes in the coherence variables. However there is some suggestive evidence that the ways in which mothers help structure life narratives with their adolescents may facilitate adolescents' developing life story coherence. Habermas, Negele, and Brenneisen-Mayer (2010) showed that, when asked to co-narrate the child's life story together, mothers of 10-year-olds focused on helping the child construct a coherent temporal time line, whereas mothers of 12- and 14-year-olds focused more on helping their child construct causal connections among the events of their lives. By age 16 and 20, mothers focused more on thematic evaluations and biographical coherence, suggesting that mothers were sensitive to where their children were in terms of creating more coherent life stories, and worked to help their children construct life story coherence in developmentally appropriate ways. Thus, similar to the preschool years when social interactions help shape the emergence of autobiographical memory, we continue to see social interaction, in the form of parental scaffolding, shaping the emergence of a coherent life story in adolescence.

The development of the life story also involves more global influences through culturally mediated, normative expectations of what constitutes an autobiography, or what Habermas and Bluck (2000) term the cultural concept of biography. Several studies have examined the development of specific features of the cultural concept of biography, specifically the form and function of beginnings and endings to life narratives (Habermas, Ehlert-Lerche, & de Silveira, 2009) and the cultural life script (Berntsen & Rubin, 2004). Studies in both Germany and Denmark have shown that narrative devices marking the beginning of a life and concluding a life story with projections into the future increase dramatically as children enter adolescence (Bohn & Berntsen, 2008; Habermas et al., 2009). This suggests that around the transition into adolescence children become aware of the cultural norms for starting a life story (e.g., that you start with birth, not from your earliest memory) as well as finishing a life story (e.g., looking forward to future goals).

The cultural life script further describes culturally shared expectations regarding the temporal order of normative significant life events (Berntsen & Rubin, 2004). Events fitting within a cultural life script include an appropriate age norm and a cultural expectation that the event will occur (i.e., getting married or your first love) and most often deal with life transitions. Research has consistently found little variability in the contents of the cultural life script across Western, and some non-Western, samples (e.g., Habermas, 2007; Haque & Hasking, 2010). As children develop across late childhood and into adolescence their knowledge of the cultural life script increases (Bohn & Berntsen, 2008; Habermas, 2007). Knowledge of the cultural life script has also been shown to predict the global coherence of life stories, but not the coherence of specific life events (Bohn &

Berntsen, 2008). This suggests that adolescents do indeed use the cultural life script to help structure, organize, and connect events within their life story. Thus, we see that the emergence of the life narrative in adolescence is facilitated both in local interactions, with maternal reminiscing style continuing to be an important factor in autobiographical memory development, as well as in larger cultural mediation, in the form of life scripts and master narratives.

Evolving functions of autobiographical memory

With the formation of the life narrative, the functions of autobiographical memory mature and become more explicit. Whereas in early childhood, elaborated autobiographical memories are related to developments of self, relationships, and emotional regulation, with adolescence and the ability to more effectively reflect on one's own functioning, autobiographical memories begin to take on the explicit self, social, and directive functions described earlier in this chapter. Studies using questionnaire measures to assess how participants ranging from college students to the elderly use their memories have shown that individuals endorse using autobiographical memory to serve these functions (e.g., Bluck et al., 2005; Alea & Bluck, 2007). Surprisingly little research, however, has examined how functions might be expressed or used within autobiographical narratives themselves.

Specific to the self function, whereas there is broad consensus that autobiographical memory is related to self-definition, there is actually little empirical research examining how this function might be expressed or communicated to others through narrative. One line of related research focuses instead on individual meaning-making within autobiographical narratives, as a measure of how the memory functions to define meaning or purpose for the self. Although there is no accepted definition of

exactly what constitutes meaning-making in autobiographical memory, researchers have taken a broad approach examining a variety of independent constructs (Waters, Shallcross, & Fivush, 2013). Specifically, meaning-making has been conceptualized as the creation of more coherent narratives (Reese et al., 2011), the use of internal state language describing thoughts and emotions (Fivush & Baker-Ward, 2005), and through reflection on lessons learned about the self and the world (Mclean & Pratt, 2006; see Fivush, Bohanek, Zaman, & Grapin, 2012, for a full discussion).

Examining individual autobiographical narratives, McLean, Breen, and Fournier (2010) found that in early adolescence meaning-making, measured as self-reflective evaluation, was negatively related to well-being, but that by late adolescence the relation had reversed and meaning-making was positively related to well-being. In contrast, Bohanek and Fivush (2010) found that meaning-making, measured as internal state language and coherence, was related to fewer behavioral problems in 13- to 16-year-olds, but this relation held only for boys, not for girls. The type of meaning may also matter. Waters et al. (2013) found that young adults (18 to 20 years of age) who created more negative meaning in their narratives of highly negative experiences (essentially creating contamination sequences) showed higher levels of psychological distress related to the event.

At the level of the life story, meaning-making is often discussed in terms of life themes based on master narratives, as discussed earlier, such as redemption, contamination, and personal growth. In general, middle-aged adults who tell life stories with more themes of redemption (negative experiences turning out positively), self-report higher levels of life satisfaction (Bauer, McAdams, & Sakaeda, 2005). Participants who tell life stories with more contamination themes (good things go bad, and stay bad), show higher levels of depression and lower self-esteem (Adler, Kissel, & McAdams, 2006). Individuals who tell life narratives with more themes of growth and change exhibit higher levels of ego development (Pals, 2006). Beyond themes of redemption, contamination, and growth, Baerger and McAdams (1999) found that individuals with more coherent life stories were less depressed and had higher satisfaction with life. The patterns suggest that during adolescence, as autobiographical memories are consolidating into a life story, and adolescents struggle with personal identity issues, meaning-making may actually have some detrimental concomitants, but as individuals mature into middle age, meaning-making appears to have mostly beneficial consequences.

Across adulthood, autobiographical memory also serves social functions. For example, Alea and Bluck (2007) examined the social function by asking participants to recall memories about their romantic partner and examining changes in feelings of intimacy with that partner (see also Alea & Vick, 2010). They found that recalling relationship events produced increases in feelings of warmth and closeness, suggesting that those memories served a social function. Further, they found that these effects did not change across the lifespan as they were present in groups of young adults and seniors. Kuwabara and Pillemer (2010) examined the directive function autobiographical memories served in relation to donation behavior in a sample of undergraduate students. Students who were prompted to think of memories associated with their current school were more likely to donate to their school rather than another charity, compared with controls who did not recall a memory from of their current school, even if the memories they recalled were negative.

To date, little research has considered how different types of memories may be related to different functions, that is, how the structure and functions of autobiographical memory may be related (but see Rasmussen & Berntsen, 2009). We have recently begun to examine this more directly in our lab in young adults (see Waters, 2012, for a full review). Waters, Bauer, and Fivush (submitted) examined how narratives of single, recurring, and extended events might be differentially related to autobiographical functions. Using both narrative and questionnaire measures, single events were found to serve more of a self and directive function, recurring events served more of a social function, and extended events were comparatively high on all three functions. Waters (2013) further examined the relations between the self, social, and directive functions of autobiographical memories and psychological well-being. Individuals who reported higher use of their autobiographical memories to serve self, social, and directive functions also reported higher levels of purpose in life and more positive social relationships, indicating that memories used to serve more functional goals were related to higher levels of psychological well-being. These findings also call attention to the fact that any given memory may serve multiple functions simultaneously. This is an important direction for future research.

Overall, beginning in adolescence, we can track the formation and development of the life story. The life story is mediated in both local interactions and through cultural tools that provide the forms, and possibly the functions, of autobiographical narratives. During early adolescence, when the life story is in formation, there seems to be inconsistent relations between more coherent narratives and higher functionality, especially as measured by higher levels of well-being more generally. By late adolescence and early adulthood, individuals who tell more coherent narratives of their lives show higher levels of well-being. Most interesting, Waters (2013) has demonstrated that the more individuals use their memories in the service of self, social, and directive goals, the higher their levels of well-being. Thus, the link between autobiographical narratives and well-being seems to be due to the ways in which these memories function for the individual.

CONCLUSION

In this chapter, we provided an overview of sociocultural and functional approaches to autobiographical memory. The research shows links between social interaction and the emergence and coalescence of auto-biographical memory from early childhood through adolescence and emerging adult-hood. Moreover, the research demonstrates emerging relations between what individuals recall and how they use these memories to serve self, social, and directive functions. Yet there are several issues that we were not able to address, either due to space constraints or scarcity of research.

First is the issue of accuracy. As we alluded to in the introduction to this chapter, our focus was on the functional meaning of autobiographical memories, rather than on their accuracy. Still, we must acknowledge that accuracy remains a critical variable in autobiographical memory research. Future research would benefit greatly from an integration of functional and veridical approaches to memory. There are clearly costs and benefits to memory accuracy. While inaccuracy allows for behaviors inconsistent with one's sense of self to be forgotten or "revised" to better fit the life story, inaccuracy could prove problematic for directing future behavior in an adaptive way. As we discuss throughout this chapter, autobiographical memories are largely a social construction, and accuracy, or inaccuracy, may also influence listeners' reactions in both positive and negative ways.

Second is the issue of gender. There is substantial research indicating that autobiographical memory differs by gender, with females producing more vivid, elaborated, and emotionally imbued autobiographical memories than males, although it is important to emphasize that gender differences are more likely to be found in some contexts than in others (see Fivush et al., 2006; Fivush & Zaman, in press, for reviews). There is also evidence that these differences emerge early in development and may be influenced by differences in parental reminiscing style. Both mothers and fathers are more elabora-tive and emotionally expressive when remi-niscing with daughters than with sons, and longitudinal studies suggest that these early differences are related to emerging differ-ences in how boys and girls recall their experiences (Fivush & Zaman, in press). How functional aspects of autobiographical memory may be related to gender has been understudied, although, in general, research-ers have not found gender differences in how memories are used (e.g., Bluck et al., 2005; Waters, Bauer, & Fivush, submitted; but see Alea & Bluck, 2007). An important avenue for future research is to more fully examine gendered patterns of remembering.

Third is the issue of culture. As discussed in the introductory sections of this chapter, autobiographical memory varies by culture, as is predicted by the sociocultural model. There is ample empirical evidence of how both individual memories and the life story varies by culture, which was beyond the scope of this chapter (see Hirst, Coman, & Coman, Chapter 16, this volume; Wang & Ross, 2007 for excellent reviews). However, how these cultural differences in autobio-graphical memory may be related to differ-ences in how memories are used functionally is still unknown and a promising direction for future research.

Finally, we did not include research on autobiographical memory and aging. Research has consistently shown that as we age our freely recalled autobiographi-cal memories become more positive (see Walker, Skowronski, & Thompson, 2003, for a review). Also, our memories during late adolescence stay with us as specific and emotional events (e.g., Pillemer, Goldsmith, Panter, & White, 1988). Meanwhile, the events we recall after this critical period of autobiographical memory and identity devel-opment tend to be more generalized (Pillemer et al., 1988). Further, as we approach middle age and beyond, themes in the life story acquire new correlates such as generativity

(McAdams, 2004). These findings suggest that across development the social function may become more prevalent, especially following identity and life story development in adolescence, which is strongly associated with the self function. Whether our propensity to use new memories for any given function changes across the lifespan as the developmental and sociocultural context changes remains an open question. It is also unclear if the function an autobiographical memory comes to serve is stable across the lifespan, or if the functional approach to autobiographical memory should consider a more dynamic process.

Even acknowledging the limits of our review, and several open questions, the patterns presented here are compelling. Individuals hold their personal memories dear, yet why humans spend so much time reminiscing about their past has been a puzzle. The sociocultural approach to autobiographical memory has led to important findings about how autobiography is shaped in both local social interactions and by culturally provided tools that define the form and the functions of personal memory that allows individuals to develop a sense of self-continuity and social bonds critical to be a culturally competent adult. A functional approach has led to discoveries about how we use our memories in everyday life to serve these important cultural functions – to define a self over time, to create and maintain relationships with others, to regulate emotion, and to direct our future behavior. To answer Baddeley (1988), autobiographical memory is for many things, and, interestingly enough, is more about who we are and where we come from than what we remember.

REFERENCES

Adler, J., Kissel, E., & McAdams, D. P. (2006). Emerging from the CAVE: Attributional style and the narrative study of identity in midlife adults. *Cognitive Therapy and Research, 30,* 39–51.

Alea, N., & Bluck, S. (2007). I'll keep you in mind: The intimacy function of autobiographical memory. *Applied Cognitive Psychology, 21,* 1091–1111.

Alea, N., & Vick, S. C. (2010). The first sight of love: Relationship-defining memories and marital satisfaction across adulthood. *Memory, 18,* 730–742.

Atance, C. M., & Martin-Ordas, G. (in press). Projecting the self into the future. In P. J. Bauer and R. Fivush (Eds.), *The handbook of children's memory development.* New York: Wiley-Blackwell.

Baddeley, A. D. (1988). But what the hell is it for? In M. M. Grunebert, P. Morris, and R. N. Sykes (Eds.), *Practical aspects of memory: Current research and issues, Vol. 1: Memory in everyday life* (pp. 3–18). Oxford: John Wiley & Sons.

Baerger, D. R., & McAdams, D. P. (1999). Life story coehrence and its relations to psychological well-being. *Narrative Inquiry, 9(1),* 69–96.

Barsalou, L. W. (1988). The content and organization of autobiographical memories. In U. Neisser and E. Winograd (Eds.), *Remembering reconsidered: Ecological and traditional approaches to the study of memory.* New York: Cambridge University Press.

Bauer, P. J. (2007). *Remembering the times of our lives: Memory in infancy and beyond.* Mahwah, NJ: Lawrence Erlbaum Associates.

Bauer, J. J., McAdams, D. P., & Sakeda, A. R. (2005). Interpreting the good life: Growth memories in the lives of mature, happy people. *Journal of Personality and Social Psychology, 88,* 203–217.

Berntsen, D., & Rubin, D.C. (2004). Cultural life scripts structure recall from autobiographical memory. *Memory and Cognition, 32,* 427–442.

Bird, A., & Reese, E. (2006). Emotional reminiscing and the development of an autobiographical self. *Developmental Psychology, 42,* 613–626.

Bluck, S. (2003). Autobiographical memory: Exploring its functions in everyday life. *Memory, 11(2),* 113–124.

Bluck, S., Alea, N., Habermas, T., & Rubin, D. C. (2005). A tale of three functions: The self-reported uses of autobiographical memory. *Social Cognition, 23(1),* 91–117.

Bluck, S., & Alea, N. (2011). Crafting the TALE: Construction of a measure to assess the functions of autobiographical remembering. *Memory, 19(5),* 470–486.

Bohanek, J. G., & Fivush, R. (2010). Personal narratives, well-being, and gender in adolescence. *Cognitive Development, 25,* 368–379.

Bohn, A., & Berntsen, D. (2008). Life story development in childhood: The development of life story coherence abilities and the acquisition of cultural life scripts from late middle childhood to adolescence. *Developmental Psychology, 44,* 1135–1147.

Boland, A. M., Haden, C. A., & Ornstein, P. A. (2003). Boosting children's memory by training mothers in the use of an elaborative conversational style as an event unfolds. *Journal of Cognition and Development, 4,* 39–65.

Brewer, W. F. (1988). Memory for randomly sampled autobiographical events. In U. Neisser and E. Winograd (Eds.), *Remembering reconsidered: Ecological and traditional aproaches to the study of memory* (pp. 21–90). New York: Cambridge University Press.

Brown, R., & Kulik, J. (1977). Flashbulb memories. *Cognition, 5,* 73–99.

Bruner, J. (1990). *Acts of meaning.* Cambridge, MA: Harvard University Press.

Cassidy, J., & Shaver, P. R. (1999). *Handbook of attachment: Theory, research and clinical applications.* New York: Guilford.

Conway, M.A., & Pleydell-Pearce, C.W. (2000). The construction of autobiographical memories in the self-memory system. *Psychological Review, 107,* 261–288.

Erikson, E. H. (1968). *Identity: Youth and crisis.* New York: Norton.

Feldman, C., Bruner, J., Kalmar, D., & Renderer, B. (1993). Plot, plight, and dramatism: Interpretation at three ages. *Human Development, 36,* 327–342.

Fivush, R. (1988). The functions of event memory: Some comments on Nelson and Barsalou. In U. Neisser and E. Winograd (Eds.), *Remembering reconsidered: Ecological and traditional approaches to memory* (pp. 277–282). New York: Cambridge University Press.

Fivush, R. (2007). Maternal reminiscing style and children's developing understanding of self and emotion. *Clinical Social Work, 35,* 37–46.

Fivush, R. (2010). The development of autobiographical memory. *Annual Review of Psychology, 62,* 559–582.

Fivush, R. & Baker-Ward, L. (2005). The search for meaning: Developmental perspectives on internal state language in autobiographical memory. *Journal of Cognition and Development, 6,* 455–462.

Fivush, R., Bohanek, J. G., Zaman, W., & Grapin, S. (2012). Gender differences in adolescents' autobiographical memories. *Journal of Cognition and Development, 13,* 295–319.

Fivush, R., Gray, J. T., & Fromhoff, F. A. (1987). Two year olds talk about the past. *Cognitive Development, 2,* 393–409.

Fivush, R., Habermas, T., Waters, T. E. A., & Zaman, W. (2011). The making of autobiographical memory: Intersections of culture, narratives and history. *International Journal of Psychology, 46,* 321–345.

Fivush, R., Haden, C. A., & Reese, E. (2006). Elaborating on elaborations: The role of maternal reminiscing style in cognitive and socioemotional development. *Child Development, 77,* 1568–1588.

Fivush, R., & Nelson, K. (2006). Parent–child reminiscing locates the self in the past. *British Journal of Developmental Psychology, 24,* 235–251.

Fivush, R., & Zaman, W. (in press). Gender and autobiographical consciousness. In P. J. Bauer and R. Fivush (Eds.), *The handbook of children's memory development.* New York: Wiley-Blackwell.

Friedman, W. J. (1993). Memory for the time of past events. *Psychological Bulletin, 113,* 44–66.

Friedman, W., Reese, E., & Dai, J. (2009). Children's memory for the times of events from the past years. *Applied Cognitive Psychology, 23,* 1–17.

Habermas, T. (2007). How to tell a life: The development of the cultural concept of biography across the lifespan. *Journal of Cognition and Development, 8,* 1–31.

Habermas, T. (2011). *The development of autobiographical reasoning in adolescence and beyond: New directions for child and adolescent development, No. 131.* San Francisco, CA: Jossey-Bass.

Habermas, T., & Bluck, S. (2000). Getting a life: The emergence of the life story in adolescence. *Psychological Bulletin, 126,* 748–769.

Habermas, T., Ehlert-Lerche, S., & de Silveira, C. (2009). The development of the temporal macrostructure of life narratives across adolescence: Beginnings, linear narrative form, and endings. *Journal of Personality, 77*(2), 527–560.

Habermas, T., & de Silveira, C. (2008). The development of global coherence in life narratives across adolescence: Temporal, causal, and thematic aspects. *Developmental Psychology, 44,* 707–721.

Habermas, T., Negele, A., & Brenneisen-Mayer, F. (2010). "Honey, you're jumping about" – Mothers' scaffolding of their children's and adolescents' life narratives. *Cognitive Development, 25*(4), 339–351.

Haden, C. A. (1998). Reminiscing with different children: Relating maternal stylistic consistency and sibling similarity in talk about the past. *Developmental Psychology, 34,* 99–114.

Haden, C. A., & Fivush, R. (1996). Contextual variation in maternal conversational styles. *Merrill-Palmer Quarterly, 42,* 200–227.

Hamond, N. R., & Fivush, R. (1991). Memories of Mickey Mouse: Children recount their trip to Disneyworld. *Cognitive Development, 6,* 433–448.

Harbus, A. (2011). Exposure to life writing as an impact on autobiographical memory. *Memory Studies, 4,* 206–220.

Haque, S., & Hasking, P. A. (2010). Life scripts for emotionally charged autobiographical memories: A cultural explanation of the reminiscence bump. *Memory, 18,* 712–729.

Hudson, J. A. (1990). The emergence of autobiographic memory in mother–child conversation. In R. Fivush and J. A. Hudson (Eds.), *Knowing and remembering in young children* (pp. 166–196). New York: Cambridge University Press.

Hyman, I. E., & Faries, J. M., (1992). The functions of autobiographical memory. In M.A. Conway, D.C. Rubin, H. Spinnler and J.W.A. Wagenar (Eds.), *Theoretical perspectives on autobiographical memory* (pp. 207–221). The Netherlands: Kluwer Academic.

Jack, F., MacDonald, S., Reese, E., & Hayne, H. (2009). Maternal reminiscing style during early childhood predicts the age of adolescents' earliest memories. *Child Development, 80,* 496–505.

James, W. (1890). *The principles of psychology.* New York: Dover.

Keyes, C. L. M., & Magyar-Moe, J. L. (2003). The measurement and utility of adult subjective well-being. In S. J. Lopez and C. R. Snyder (Eds.), *Positive psychological assessment: A handbook of models and measures* (pp. 411–425). Washington, DC: American Psychological Association.

Kulkofsky, S., Wang, Q., & Koh, J. B. K. (2009). Functions of memory sharing and mother–child reminiscing behaviors: Individual and cultural variations. *Journal of Cognition and Development, 10,* 92–114.

Kuwabara, K. J., & Pillemer, D. B. (2010). Memories of past episodes shape current intentions and decisions. *Memory, 18*(4), 365–374.

Laible, D. (2004). Mother–child discourse surrounding a child's past behavior at 30 months: Links to emotional understanding and early conscious development at 36 months. *Merrill-Palmer Quarterly, 50,* 159–180.

Linde, C. (1993). *Life stories: The creation of coherence.* New York: Oxford University Press.

McAdams, D. P. (1996). Personality, modernity, and the storied self: A contemporary framework for studying persons. *Psychological Inquiry, 7,* 295–321.

McAdams, D. P. (2001). The psychology of life stories. *Review of General Psychology, 5,* 100–122.

McAdams, D. P. (2004). The redemptive self: Narrative identity in America today. In D. R. Beike, J. M. Lampinen, and D. A. Behrend (Eds.), *The self and memory* (pp. 95–116). New York: Psychology Press.

McLean, K., Breen, A., & Fournier, M. (2010). Constructing the self in early, middle and late adolescent boys: Narrative identity, individuation, and well-being. *Journal of Research on Adolescence, 20,* 166–187.

McLean, K. C., & Pratt, M. W. (2006). Life's little (and big) lessons: Identity statuses and meaning-making in the turning point narratives of emerging adults. *Developmental Psychology, 42,* 714–722.

Neisser, U. (1982). *Memory observed: Remembering in natural contexts.* San Francisco, CA: Freeman.

Nelson K. (1993). The psychological and social origins of autobiographical memory. *Psychological Science, 4,* 7–14.

Nelson, K. (2003). Narrative and self, myth and memory. In R. Fivush and C. Haden (Eds.), *Connecting culture and memory: The social construction of an autobiographical self.* Hillsdale, NJ: Erlbaum.

Nelson, K., & Fivush, R. (2004). The emergence of autobiographical memory: A social cultural developmental theory. *Psychological Review, 111,* 486–511.

Oppenheim, D., Nir, A., Warren, S., & Emde, R. N. (1997). Emotion regulation in mother–child narrative co-construction: Associations with children's narrative and adaptation, *Developmental Psychology, 33,* 284–294.

Pals, J. L. (2006). The narrative identity processing of difficult life experiences: Pathways of personality development and positive self-transformation in adulthood. *Journal of Personality, 74,* 2–31.

Pasupathi, M., Mansour, E., & Brubaker, J. R. (2007). Developing a life story: Constructing relations between self and experience in autobiographical narratives. *Human Development, 50,* 85–110.

Peterson, C., Jesso, B., & McCabe, A. (1999). Encouraging narratives in preschoolers: An intervention study. *Journal of Child Language, 26,* 49–67.

Pillemer, D. B. (1998). *Momentous events, vivid memories.* Cambridge, MA: Harvard University Press.

Pillemer, D. B. (2003). Directive functions of autobiographical memory: The guiding power of the specific episode. *Memory, 11*(2), 193–202.

Pillemer, D. B. (2009). Twenty years after Baddeley (1988): Is the study of autobiographical memory fully functional? *Applied Cognitive Psychology, 23,* 1193–1208.

Pillemar, D. B., Goldsmith, C. R., Panter, A. T., & White, S. H. (1988). Very long-term memories of the first year in college. *Journal of Experimental Psychology: Learning, Memory and Cognition, 14,* 709–715.

Pillemer, D. B., Ivcevic, Z., Gooze, R. A., & Collins, K. A. (2007). Self-esteem memories: Feeling good about achievement success, feeling bad about relationship distress. *Personality and Social Psychology Bulletin, 33,* 1292–1305.

Rasmussen, A. S., & Berntsen, D. (2009). Emotional valence and the functions of autobiographical memories: Positive and negative memories serve different functions. *Memory and Cognition, 23,* 1137–1152.

Rathmann, C., Mann, W., & Morgan, G. (2007). Narrative structure and narrative development in deaf children. *Deafness and Education International, 9,* 187–196.

Reese, E., Haden, C. H., Baker-Ward, L., Bauer, P. J., Fivush, R., & Ornstein, P. A. (2011). Coherence in personal narratives: A multidimensional model. *Journal of Cognition and Development, 12,* 1–38.

Reese, E., Haden, C. A., & Fivush, R. (1993). Mother–child conversations about the past: Relationships of style and memory over time. *Cognitive Development, 8,* 403–430.

Reese, E., Yan, C., Jack, F., & Hayne, H. (2010). Emerging identities: Narrative and self from early childhood to early adolescence. In K.C. McLean and M. Pasupathi (Eds.), *Narrative development in adolescence: Creating the storied self* (pp. 23–44). New York: Springer-Verlag.

Ricoeur, P. (1991). Life in quest of narrative. In D. Wood (Ed.), *On Paul Ricoeur: Narrative and interpretation* (pp. 20–33). London: Routledge.

Roberts W. A. (2002) Are animals stuck in time? *Psychological Bulletin, 128,* 473–89.

Rubin, D. C. (2006). The basic-systems model of episodic memory. *Perspectives on Psychological Science, 1,* 277–311.

Schectman, M. (2003). Empathic access: The missing ingredient in personal identity. In R. Martin and J. Barresi (Eds.), *Personal identity* (pp. 238–259). Oxford: Oxford University Press.

Schneider, B., Atkinson, L., & Tardif, C. (2001). Parent–child attachment and children's peer relations: A quantitative review, *Developmental Psychology, 37,* 86–100.

Selman, R. L. (1980). *The growth of interpersonal understanding: Developmental and clinical analyses.* New York: Academic Press.

Shaver, P. R. & Mikulincer, M. (2002). Attachment-related psychodynamics. *Attachment & Human Development, 4,* 133–161.

Thorne, A. & McLean, K. C. (2002). Gendered reminiscence practices and self-definition in late adolescence. *Sex Roles, 46,* 267–277.

Treboux, D., Crowell, J. & Waters, E. (2004). When "new" meets "old": Configurations of adult attachment representations and their implications for marital functioning. *Developmental Psychology, 40,* 295–314.

Tulving, E. (1972). Episodic and semantic memory. In E. Tulving and W. Donaldson (Eds.), *Organization of memory* (pp. 382–403). New York: Academic Press.

Vygotsky, L. S. (1978). *Mind in society: The development of higher psychological processes.* Cambridge, MA: Harvard University Press.

Walker, W. R., Skowronski, J. J., & Thompson, C. P. (2003). Life is good – and memory helps to keep it that way. *Review of General Psychology, 7,* 203–210.

Wang, Q. (in press). The cultured self and remembering. In P. J. Bauer and R. Fivush (Eds.), *The handbook of children's memory development.* New York: Wiley-Blackwell.

Wang, Q., Doan, S. N., & Song, Q. (2010). Talking about internal states in mother–child reminiscing influences children's self-representations: A cross-cultural study. *Cognitive Development, 25,* 380–393.

Wang, Q. & Ross, M. (2007). Culture and memory. In: *Handbook of cultural psychology* (pp. 645–667). S. Kitayama and D. Cohen (Eds.), New York: Guilford Press.

Waters, T. E. A. (2012). Functions of autobiographical memory in single and recurring events: Relations to well-being. *Unpublished Dissertation.*

Waters, T. E. A. (2013). Relations between the functions of autobiographical memory and psychological well-being. *Memory.* DOI: 10.1080/09658211.2013.778293

Waters, T. E. A., Bauer, P. J., & Fivush, R. (submitted). Autobiographical memory functions for single, recurring, and extended events.

Waters, T. E. A., Shallcross, J. F., & Fivush, R. (2013). The many facets of meaning-making: Comparing multiple measures of meaning-making and their relations to psychological distress. *Memory, 21*(1), 111–124.

Weigle, T.W. & Bauer, P. J. (2000). Deaf and hearing adults' recollections of childhood and beyond. *Memory, 8,* 293–310.

Welch-Ross, M. K., Fasig, L., & Farrar, M. J. (1999). Predictors of pre-schoolers' self-knowledge: Reference to emotion and mental states in mother–child conversation about past events. *Cognitive Development, 14,* 401–422.

Wilson, A. E., & Ross, M. (2003). The identity function of autobiographical memory: Time is on our side. *Memory, 11*(2), 137–149.

14

What Everyone Knows About Aging and Remembering Ain't Necessarily So

Michael Ross and Emily Schryer

It seems that just about everyone is certain that remembering declines in old age. This belief is a core feature of the aging stereotype (Hummert, Garstka, Shaner, & Strahm, 1994). Cartoonists amuse their readers with scenarios featuring forgetful seniors. Amazon sells many popular books on aging and memory, as well as software and "brain games" designed to help older people maintain their memory. Various dietary supplements are promoted as effective in preventing age-related memory loss. Also, research psychologists have conducted thousands of studies relating normal aging to memory. Although psychological research provides more nuanced findings than other sources, the data generally support the aging stereotype. Even after controlling for vocabulary, education, depression, gender, marital, and employment status, age significantly predicts performance on many tests of memory (West, Crook, & Barron, 1992).

Psychologists have related aging to different types of memory. Compared with younger adults, older adults typically perform worse on laboratory tests of source, episodic, working, and prospective memory (d'Ydewalle, Bouckaert, & Brunfaut, 2001; Henry, MacLeod, Phillips, & Crawford, 2004; Johnson, Hashtroudi, & Lindsay, 1993; Salthouse, 1991; Schacter, Osowiecki, Kaszniak, Kihlstrom, & Valdiserri, 1994; Zacks, Hasher, & Li, 2000). Older adults are also more likely to report false memories than younger adults are (Hashtroudi, Johnson, & Chrosniak, 1989; Jacoby, 1999; Jacoby & Rhodes, 2006; Norman & Schacter, 1997; Ross, Spencer, Blatz, & Restorick, 2008).

In the current chapter, we discuss ramifications of these research findings for age differences in everyday remembering. The implications would appear to be bleak. For example, if episodic and prospective memory decline in old age, we might expect to find that aging baby boomers frequently forget to take their medications, miss medical appointments, and lose their cars in parking lots.

Our analysis will be more optimistic than the laboratory research findings seem to suggest. We argue that normal aging does not sentence older people to decades of forgetfulness. Older adults' everyday remembering exceeds expectations based on their performance in the laboratory. To help understand the discrepancy, we turn to a distinction proposed by Baltes (1997). Baltes differentiated the mechanics (e.g., working memory capacity) from the pragmatics (e.g., learned expertise) of performance on cognitive tasks. Memory tasks in the lab largely measure the mechanics of memory. Researchers examine the capacity and structure of memory and how these aspects of memory change across the lifespan. Psychologists have learned a great deal about the mechanics of memory in more than a century of laboratory research.

There are two major differences, however, between laboratory tasks and remembering in everyday life that have implications for recall, and perhaps especially for memory in old age. First, everyday memory often allows for pragmatics, the application of learned expertise. People can often choose what to remember and how to remember it. Second, aspects of people's everyday behavior and the environment in which it occurs can facilitate recall.

In the current chapter, we examine the relation between aging and everyday memory. We show that the relationship can sometimes differ quite considerably from lab findings. We do not argue that lab findings or theories of aging and memory are invalid. Rather, we examine the context and nature of everyday recall with the goal of identifying factors that might offset or even reverse the age-related declines in the mechanics of memory revealed in lab research. We evaluate three specific features of everyday remembering that potentially facilitate recall: constancies, repetition, and the outsourcing of memories. We then discuss research on everyday remembering, which reveals that older adults are more capable in normal surroundings than the laboratory findings would seem to imply. When older adults do forget in everyday life, we suggest that remembering could be enhanced by alterations to the pragmatics of remembering and the structure of the environment. We conclude by offering ways of improving everyday remembering in both older and younger adults.

EVERYDAY REMEMBERING

In everyday life, remembering depends only partly on the mechanics of memory (Baltes, 1997; Freund & Riediger, 2003; Sunderland, Watts, Baddeley, & Harris, 1986) and whether people remember is much more significant than how they remember. We consider aspects of everyday life that facilitate remembering.

Constancy and repetition

For many people in Western cultures, everyday life is characterized by constancies and repetitions that simplify remembering. Behavioral routines are an important example. Most people do not regularly forget the location of their toothbrushes, in part, because they place their brushes in the same location and retrieve them at least once a day. Most people also keep kitchen items in a consistent location rather than, for example, varying the placement of their cups and saucers on a daily basis. Moreover, they repeatedly access these locations to retrieve needed items. The use of constancy reflects the pragmatics of everyday memory. People create behavioral routines and environments that promote remembering.

Rememberers also benefit from behavioral routines and constancies that are not entirely of their own devising. Students' class schedules and employees' work schedules tend to be constant from week to week. Characteristics of other people (e.g., faces, names, addresses, phone numbers, postal codes, birthdays, and anniversaries) and groups (e.g., names, national and religious celebrations) are relatively stable. As time passes, people have repeated exposure to these schedules, percepts, labels, numbers, rituals, and dates. The task of remembering this information is quite different from remembering similar information in the lab, which is often tested after a single exposure.

Constancy also characterizes locations and structures in people's environment. The places that people commonly frequent, including grocery stores, pharmacies, restaurants, and work settings, tend to stay in the same locations and their internal organization (e.g., the location of vegetables in the supermarket) remains quite stable. In laboratory research, people's spatial memory ability declines in old age (e.g., Kirasic, 2000; Perlmutter, Metzger, Nezworski, & Miller, 1981), but even spatially challenged individuals likely learn to negotiate their stable environments with repetition.

Outsourcing

Individuals can outsource remembering. For many people, Google Search and Wikipedia have become resources for semantic information, supplementing or even replacing the storage of memories in individual minds (Sparrow, Liu, & Wegner, 2011). Google Search and Wikipedia are to semantic memory what online calendars, smartphones, and GPS systems are to episodic and prospective memory. People program their smartphones to send reminders of appointments, as well as to store phone numbers and addresses. It is unnecessary to store such information in mental memory.

A person might remember a doctor's appointment because she spontaneously retrieves the date and time of the appointment from memory, just as a student recalls information on an exam or a research participant recalls words from the list that she read earlier. Alternatively, a person might remember a doctor's appointment because her online calendar sent a reminder of the appointment to her smartphone. If she arrives for the appointment at the correct time, we would normally say that she remembered, regardless of how she recalled it. Also, the ready availability of GPS systems means that it is less necessary to retain driving routes in mental memory. GPS systems should provide a useful supplement to stable environments in helping older people maintain their ability to negotiate their way around a city in the face of declines in spatial memory.

Many of the external reminders in the above paragraph require initiative – people must program their phones and cue their GPS systems. Other forms of everyday reminders require less initiative. Some home appliances flash advice and reminders. One of us owns a clothes dryer that reminds users to clean the lint filter. Many newer cars have computers that signal when service is required. Professionals provide clients with email or telephone reminders of upcoming appointments.

Although sophisticated hardware and software is in the ascendancy, old standbys such as a pen and paper remain useful. When people need to remember a phone number they can try to commit it to memory, as they are often required to do even in laboratory analogues of everyday remembering (e.g., West & Crook, 1990). Alternatively, they could simply write down the number. Similarly, people can use plastic pill containers with compartments labeled for each day of the week to help them remember both to take their medicines and avoid overdosing, rather than rely on their memories or sophisticated external devices.

Finally, everyday remembering is sometimes a joint enterprise rather than the solo activity it typically is in the lab. People can outsource memories to other people (Wegner, Erber, & Raymond, 1991). Spouses can divide their memory responsibilities, with one being responsible for remembering, for example, to retrieve their children from daycare after work and the other remembering to shop for dinner. Also, individuals can jointly retrieve names, phone numbers, biographical memories, and so forth. There is a limited amount of research on collaborative remembering, but it is evident that two heads are superior to one, whether the heads are old or young (e.g. Ross et al., 2008).

Active versus passive outsourcing

Some sources of external support depend on self-initiative and others do not. It is possible that, relative to younger adults, older people will be more likely to take the initiative to rely on external sources. Successful aging involves, in part, learning to use external resources to compensate for declines in mental capacities (Baltes, 1997; Freund & Riediger, 2003). It is also possible, however, that older adults will initiate external strategies less frequently or effectively, especially if their use taxes cognitive resources that are diminished with age (Baltes & Baltes, 1990). With age, strategies that require little effort and are less dependent on self-initiation (e.g., environmental constancy) may become increasingly important.

Research evidence

Our analysis of aspects of everyday life that support remembering suggests that lab results showing that younger adults perform better than their older counterparts on standard tests of memory may not generalize to everyday life. We review research on everyday remembering to examine whether this is the case. We then review research on factors that might account for differences between remembering in the lab and remembering in everyday life.

EVERYDAY MEMORY PERFORMANCE

There are many self-report questionnaires that assess everyday memory performance. Older adults generally report more memory failures than younger adults do (Hertzog & Pearman, Chapter 24, this volume). However, the negative relation between age and self-reported memory lapses in everyday life tends to be modest. Indeed some researchers found no relation (Hertzog & Pearman, Chapter 24, this volume) and others that self-reported memory failures declined with age (Rabbit & Abson, 1990; Rabbitt, Maylor, McInnes, Bent, & Moore, 1995).

The validity of self-reports of memory successes and failures has not been established. Psychologists have known for a long time that people's subjective assessments of their everyday memory performances correlate poorly

with laboratory tests of memory (e.g., Kliegel & Jager, 2006; Perlmutter, 1978; Sunderland, Harris, & Baddeley, 1983; Sunderland et al., 1986). By comparison, there are few studies in which self-assessments of everyday memory performance are used to predict direct observations of everyday memory performance. The studies that do exist suggest that the relationship is sometimes statistically significant, but modest (Hertzog & Pearman, Chapter 24, this volume; Sunderland et al., 1986).

A few researchers have conducted daily diary studies to obtain more direct evidence of everyday memory performance in older and younger adults. Although diary studies potentially provide more valid information than self-report questionnaires, the data still depend on self-reports, the samples and methodologies differ across studies, and the findings are contradictory. Cavanaugh, Grady, and Perlmutter (1983) asked a small sample of participants (12 older adults and 12 younger adults) to record memory failures (e.g., forgetting names) immediately after their occurrence for four days. Older adults reported more memory lapses than younger adults did. Cavanaugh et al. (1983) did not assess the number of memory tasks that participants confronted; conceivably, older adults had more to remember on a daily basis. Consequently it is unclear whether older adults experienced a higher proportion of memory lapses than younger adults did.

Schryer (2012, Study 1) conducted an online study of everyday memory performance with older adults and university-aged participants. Her study was similar to that of Cavanaugh et al. (1983), except that she used a larger sample and assessed the percentage of specific, everyday memory tasks on which forgetting occurred (e.g., locating keys, taking medication, attending appointments). Older adults reported forgetting both a smaller number and percentage of these common memory tasks than younger adults did.

Burke, Mackay, Worthley, and Wade (1991) asked participants to record TOT (tip of the tongue) memory errors in a daily diary.

Older and middle-aged adults reported more TOT errors than younger participants did. However, participants' probability of resolving their TOTs was high and did not differ significantly by age. Older participants did report taking longer to resolve their TOTs than younger participants did. Participants in all age groups were most likely to report that they resolved the TOTs when the words simply popped into mind. Older adults were no more likely than younger adults to report resolving their TOTs by using external resources such as books or other people.

Burke et al. (1991) also examined the relation between type of words and TOTs. Of particular interest here, the number of TOTs for names of acquaintances increased with age (we say more about name recall below). The age difference in TOTs for names of acquaintances might be due, at least in part, to recency of usage. Older adults reported less recent contact with their TOT acquaintances than participants in the other age groups.

The Burke et al. (1991) diary study did not allow for an assessment of the proportion of total instances of remembering that yielded TOTs. In a subsequent lab study, Burke et al. (1991) tested for TOTs in response to a series of questions designed to elicit responses involving non-object names, object names, adjectives, verbs, place names, and famous people. In terms of absolute numbers, older people responded with more TOTs only when responding to questions designed to elicit the names of famous people. The researchers did not investigate whether this age effect was related to age differences in recency of contact with the famous names. Also, as the authors acknowledged, age differences in familiarity with targets across different types of words may obscure the interpretation of the findings.

The most compelling assessments of everyday memory involve direct observation. Almost all published studies that include direct observation focus on prospective memory. Prospective memory is both straightforward to study (e.g., researchers assess

whether participants phone them at scheduled times) and common in everyday life.

On laboratory tests of prospective memory, older adults typically perform worse than younger adults do (see Einstein & McDaniel, Chapter 3, this volume, for a review). Although researchers occasionally report no age differences in prospective memory (e.g., Einstein & McDaniel, 1990), we are unaware of any published studies in which older adults perform better than younger adults in the lab.

The data from everyday tests of prospective memory are the mirror image of the laboratory findings (Phillips, Henry, & Martin, 2008). Researchers typically report either no age differences or, more commonly, that older adults perform better. Researchers who ask participants to phone the experimenter on specific dates have reported that older adults outperform younger adults (Devolder, Brigham, & Pressley, 1990; d'Ydewalle & Brunfaut, 1996; Maylor, 1990; Moscovitch, 1982). Older adults are more likely than younger adults to remember to mail a postcard to the experimenter each day (Patton & Meit, 1993), or press a button on an electronic organizer at certain times of the day (Rendell & Craik, 2000; Rendell & Thomson, 1993, 1999). Also, compared with younger adults, older adults are less likely to miss medical and mental health appointments, as indicated by records of missed appointments (Frankel, Farrow, & West, 1989; Gallucci, Swartz, & Hackerman, 2005; Neal et al., 2001). People may miss appointments for reasons other than forgetfulness, but the data do not support the stereotypes or lab findings that older individuals are especially forgetful.

Researchers have offered several explanations for the paradox that prospective memory declines with age in the lab but improves with age in more naturalistic settings. These explanations include that older adults are more motivated than their younger counterparts to complete prospective memory tasks in everyday life, that older adults lead more structured and predictable lives, and that older adults are more likely to use external memory aids. The last two explanations are consistent with our analysis of aspects of everyday recall that facilitate remembering. Prospective memory researchers suggest that these features of everyday prospective remembering are particularly advantageous to older rememberers. We review research designed to test each of these explanations.

Motivation

Research conducted in the lab and in everyday life may elicit different degrees of motivational commitment from younger and older adults. Younger adults may be particularly unmotivated when performing experimenter-derived prospective memory tasks in everyday life (Aberle, Rendell, Rose, McDaniel, & Kliegel, 2010; Ihle, Schnitzspahn, Rendell, Luong, & Kliegel, 2012; Patton & Meit, 1993; Phillips et al., 2008; Rendell & Craik, 2000; Schnitzspahn, Ihle, Henry, Rendell, & Kliegel, 2011). Younger adults in these studies are often university undergraduates who receive course credit for participating. As credit is typically not linked to their level of performance, younger adults may feel little need to adhere to experimental instructions in the face of competing activities. Older volunteers may be more likely regard the task as a social contract between themselves and the experimenter and its successful completion as important.

The motivational interpretation has been evaluated directly in three recent studies. Aberle et al. (2010) varied whether or not they provided an incentive for participants to send text messages at specific times on five consecutive days. In the incentive condition, participants' chances of winning a lottery increased when they sent the messages at the correct times. Older adults outperformed younger adults in the absence of an incentive, but this age difference disappeared when the researchers offered an incentive for performance. The incentive improved younger adults' performance but had no effect on older adults.

Although the data are intriguing, the findings do not resolve the paradox. It is unclear whether the increased opportunity to win the lottery was as motivating for older as for younger participants. Also, even with the incentive younger participants performed no better than older adults. The researchers still failed to replicate the laboratory finding that younger adults exhibit superior prospective memory.

In a second study, Schnitzspahn et al. (2011) found that older adults reported marginally more motivation ($p < .09$) than younger adults and outperformed them on a naturalistic prospective memory task (texting the experimenter). When Schnitzspahn et al. controlled for reported motivation in their analyses, it reduced but did not eliminate the age advantage in prospective memory.

Finally, Ihle et al. (2012) asked participants to provide daily reports of tasks that they intended to perform the following day. Participants rated the importance of each task. At the end of each subsequent day, participants reported whether they had completed their planned actions. For extremely important tasks, almost all participants followed through on their intentions and there was no age difference in completion rates. For less important tasks, older adults were more likely to complete their planned actions than younger adults were.

On the basis of current findings, a motivational account does not explain the paradox. Whereas younger adults consistently outperform older adults in the lab, they perform no better and often worse than older adults on prospective memory tasks in naturalistic settings even when they are highly motivated and the tasks are embedded in their daily lives rather than initiated by researchers.

Lifestyle

According to a second account of the paradox, older adults lead more organized and predictable lives than their younger counterparts do (Maylor, 1995; Phillips et al., 2008;

Rendell & Craik, 2000). Consequently, older adults can more readily integrate an additional prospective memory task into their daily routines. There is mixed evidence for this lifestyle account. In a study of medication adherence, Park et al. (1999) found that older participants reported leading less busy lives than younger participants did. Bailey, Henry, Rendell, Phillips, and Kliegel (2010) asked participants to respond on a personal data assistant (PDA) to semi-random prompts throughout the day. Older and younger adults did not differ in the extent to which they reported ongoing activities when prompted. Rendell and Thomson (1999) compared the memory performance of working, retired, and home-based older adults on a task in which participants had to press a sequence of buttons on a PDA four times per day. Participants' performance did not differ according to their occupational status.

Finally, Schnitzspahn et al. (2011) found that younger adults reported being more absorbed in ongoing daily tasks than older adults and also performed less well on a naturalistic prospective memory task (texting the experimenter). This age difference in absorption could reflect age differences in the nature of the tasks or in the distractibility of participants. Statistically controlling for absorption eliminated age differences in task performance. Schnitzspahn et al.'s findings provide preliminary evidence of the potential relevance of absorption, but again fail to show evidence of superior performance in naturalistic tasks by younger adults.

External memory aids

The most popular explanation for the paradox, by far, is that older adults recognize the unreliability of their memory and make use of external reminders to cue their memories (e.g., inscribe the dates of scheduled tasks in calendars rather than depend on memory). Phillips et al. (2008) describe this conjecture as the "prevailing wisdom" in the literature. This common conjecture raises two related questions. Are older adults generally more likely than younger adults to outsource their memories to external aids? Are external memory aids more beneficial for older than younger adults?

The hypothesis that older adults will be more likely to use readily available memory aids is consistent with Selective Optimization and Compensation (SOC) theory (Baltes, 1997; Freund & Baltes, 2002; Li, Lindenberger, Freund, & Baltes, 2001). SOC theory suggests that older adults seek alternative means to maintain functioning when faced with declines in capability. The use of aids is an example of a strategy that adults could use to offset age-related declines in memory mechanics.

Some researchers have suggested that using memory aids can greatly reduce or eliminate cognitive deficits associated with aging (Bäckman & Dixon, 1992; de Frias & Dixon, 2005). Craik's environmental support theory (Craik, 1986, 1992) implies that memory aids may be particularly beneficial to older people. According to environmental support theory, individuals reconstruct memories from self-initiated internal cues when little environmental support is available to help cue memories. Self-initiated retrieval is an effortful, resource-demanding process that becomes more difficult in older age. If external memory aids provide strong cues at the time of recall, then age differences in memory performance should diminish.

Use of external memory aids

On self-report measures, adults of all ages recount extensive use of external memory aids. Intons-Peterson and Fournier (1986) asked university students how often they would use memory aids in various situations involving memory (e.g. directions to a friend's house). Participants reported that they would use some kind of aid in 91 percent of the cases and preferred external memory strategies to internal ones. In another study, middle-aged respondents (mean age 42) reported frequent use of external memory aids (Harris, 1980).

Some researchers use the Memory Compensation Questionnaire (MCQ) (Dixon, de Frias, & Bäckman, 2001) to measure self-reports of everyday memory strategies. In longitudinal studies of older participants' responses to this measure, individuals reported using external memory aids more often and internal memory strategies less often as they aged (e.g., Dixon & de Frias, 2004). In studies comparing the responses of university students to those of older adults, older respondents reported greater use of memory compensation strategies on the MCQ, and especially more use of external memory aids (Schryer & Ross, in press).

The age difference in use of external memory aids obtained on self-report questionnaires tends to disappear when respondents are asked the frequency with which they used a memory aid to help them with a specific task. In a number of naturalistic studies of prospective memory, participants reported their use of memory strategies at the conclusion of the studies (Aberle et al., 2011; d'Ydewalle & Brunfaut, 1996; Patten & Meit, 1993; Rendell & Thompson, 1999). The results are variable, but do not support the expectation that older adults spontaneously rely more on external memory aids than younger adults do. Instead, older adults reported using external memory aids less or as often as younger adults did.

Maylor (1990) conducted perhaps the most extensive study of the use of aids in an everyday prospective memory task. Participants, who were 52 to 95 years old, were asked to call the experimenter at a specific time over the course of four days. Participants were also asked to record the strategies they used to remember the phone calls. Maylor failed to find an age difference in the frequency with which respondents reported using internal (e.g., memory alone) versus external cues (e.g., alarm clocks).

All of these studies rely on self-reports to measure participants' use of memory aids. The validity of these reports is unknown. A number of researchers have directly observed participants' spontaneous use of external memory aids in laboratory contexts. Einstein and McDaniel (1990) varied whether older and younger adults were encouraged to create their own memory aids for a prospective memory task. Participants in the aid condition had 30 seconds to create a memory aid if they wished to do so. Older and younger adults were highly and equally likely to create and use external memory aids. Morrow, Leirer, Carver, Tanke, and McNally (1999) studied optional note taking and message repetition, while older and younger adults listened to detailed health messages that they would later recall. Most participants chose to take notes and repeat the messages, regardless of age. Henry, Rendell, Phillips, Dunlop, and Kliegel (2012) examined the frequency with which older and younger participants checked a "To Do" list during the context of a virtual board game involving prospective memory tasks. Older and younger adults accessed the list equally often. Schryer and Ross (in press) varied whether or not participants could take notes while listening to a series of brief, straightforward phone messages that they would be asked to recall later. In two studies, only about 50 percent of the older participants and slightly more younger adults took notes on the messages. In neither study was there a statistically significant age difference in the likelihood of taking notes.

The research findings on spontaneous use of memory aids present their own paradox. Given that that older adults regard their memory as deteriorating (e.g., Hertzog & Pearman, Chapter 24, this volume), it seems reasonable to assume that they will make greater use external memory aids. Consistent with this reasoning, older adults report more extensive use of external memory aids on self-report questionnaires such as the MCQ. However, direct observation of strategy use in laboratory experiments indicates that older adults are no more likely than younger adults to rely on external memory aids. The evidence suggests that either participants' answers to retrospective self-report questionnaires are misleading or that the laboratory results do not accurately reflect people's use of memory aids in everyday life. In the absence of directly relevant data, a plausible argument could be offered for either alternative.

In self-report questionnaires, participants recall the frequency with which they engage in various behaviors. Frequency judgments are estimates based, in part, on generalizations from the recall of readily accessible exemplars; people are not especially accurate in their overall assessments of frequency (Bradburn, Rips, & Shevel, 1987). Older adults' estimates of their frequency of external memory aid use may be influenced by a variety of factors in addition to actual use, including their stereotypes of aging, as well as beliefs about how they ought to behave (Ross, 1989). Stereotypes of aging and beliefs about appropriate behavior may lead older adults to unintentionally inflate their use of external memory aids on self-report questionnaires. From this perspective, the findings from self-report questionnaires are misleading and lab studies involving direct observation of strategy usage may be more revealing of people's everyday behavior.

Alternatively, perhaps people's spontaneous use of external aids in the lab does not reflect their use of memory aids in naturalistic settings. Each of the lab studies focused on a single external aid (most often, but not exclusively, note taking) and a single memory task. A more representative sampling of aids and tasks would provide more compelling data. Also, the general lack of an age difference in use of memory aids could be due, in part, to ceiling effects. In most studies other than Schryer and Ross (in press), both younger and older adults made extensive use of available aids. Schryer and Ross examined recall of short, mundane phone messages of the sort people receive on a daily basis. In this context, both older and younger participants seemed to under-utilize memory aids. Perhaps the lowered use of external memory aids is reflective of participants' everyday responses to phone messages.

Psychologists have assumed that older people would be more likely to use memory aids because they are aware of their memory deficiencies and the potential value of external aids. Are people who could potentially benefit most from aids indeed more likely to use them? This question can be addressed at the level of individual differences, regardless of age. In Schryer and Ross's (in press) studies, only some of the participants (older and younger) who were allowed to take notes on the phone messages did so. What differentiates people who take notes from those who do not? Conceivably, older and younger adults who have previously performed relatively poorly on a memory task are particularly likely to use a readily available aid when the task recurs.

To assess whether people's decision to use external aids reflects their prior performance, Schryer and Ross (in press), Study 2) related older and younger adults' unaided recall of phone messages in the first phase of the study to their choice to use permissible note taking to recall messages in the second phase. Regardless of age, participants who recalled fewer details on the first trial were no more likely to use a memory aid on the second trial. This finding should be considered preliminary until it is replicated, but the data suggest that the individuals within each age group who could most benefit from using memory aids are not more likely to use them.

In summary, the data are currently inconclusive, but fail to provide consistent support for the "prevailing wisdom" that older adults make greater use of external memory aids than younger adults do. The findings from the lab studies consistently contradict the self-reports of research participants and the expectations of theorists and researchers. In our efforts to understand one puzzle (the divergent prospective memory findings in the lab versus the field) we encounter another puzzle. If nothing else the data indicate that, as is often the case, psychologists cannot simply rely on their common sense intuitions. In researching seemingly obvious assumptions, we sometimes find surprises. Further research is needed to resolve the puzzles.

Effectiveness of external memory aids

Next we examine the limited research on the effects of external memory aids on the recall of younger and older adults. Relative to younger adults, do older adults benefit more from the use of external memory aids as Craik's (1986, 1994) environmental support theory would predict?

Several studies show the usefulness of external aids such as pagers, smartphones, and Google Calendar for individuals with impaired memories (e.g., McDonald, Haslam, Yates, Gun, Leeder, & Sayers, 2011; Svoboda & Richards, 2009; Wilson, Emslie, Quirk, & Evans, 2001). These researchers studied participants of various ages but did not examine whether the effectiveness of external aids varied with age.

There are also a few lab studies in which researchers assessed the effectiveness of memory aids in the context of normal aging. Einstein and McDaniel (1990) found that participants who used a memory aid performed better on a prospective memory task; the gain was equivalent for younger and older adults. Other researchers have found similar results on retrospective memory tasks. Burack and Lachman (1996) presented participants with word lists. Some participants were required to write down the items and others were not permitted to do so. When subsequently recalling the list, participants in the note-taking condition were prohibited from looking at their notes. Note taking enhanced recall to a similar degree in both age groups. Also, younger participants exhibited superior recall with or without prior use of aids. Morrow et al. (1999) found that note taking and repetition improved recall of health messages to a similar extent in older and younger adults. Younger adults outperformed their older counterparts regardless of aid usage. As in Burack and Lachman's (1996) study, participants could not use their notes at the time of recall.

In Schryer and Ross's (in press) studies, note taking was permitted in some conditions and not others. Participants who took notes on phone messages could refer to their notes when subsequently reporting the messages to the experimenter, as would be the case in everyday recall of phone messages. When note taking was prohibited, younger adults subsequently reported more core details (information necessary to act on the message) of the phone messages than older adults did. When note taking was permitted, Schryer and Ross found that older adults' reporting of core details improved dramatically whereas that of younger adults either did not change (Study 1) or improved only marginally (Study 2). The message recall task was more challenging in the second study (there were more phone messages to remember), which may explain why note taking was somewhat beneficial even for younger adults.

The laboratory research suggests that older adults benefited as much (Burack & Lachman, 1996; Einstein & McDaniel, 1990; Morrow et al., 1999) or more (Schryer & Ross, in press) from external memory aids as younger adults did. Only Schryer and Ross allowed participants to consult their notes at the time of recall. The greater benefit of this aid for older adults is consistent with Craik's (1986, 1992) theory that environmental support at the time of recall is especially advantageous to older adults.

OUTSOURCING REVISITED

Psychologists have only recently focused research attention on external memory aids. Traditionally researchers have been more concerned with understanding the structure of memory than with memory strategies (Hintzman, 2011). When psychologists do study strategies, they generally focus on internal tactics, such as mnemonics, rehearsal, imaging, categorization, and chunking (e.g., Bottiroli, Cavallini, & Vecchi, 2008; Lachman & Andreoletti, 2006; Lachman, Andreoletti, & Pearman, 2006; Lustig & Flegal, 2008;

Verhaeghen, Marcoen, & Goossens, 1992; West & Crook, 1990).

Researchers are likely attracted to internal tactics because they involve intriguing mental procedures that sometimes have long intellectual histories (e.g., the method of loci dates back to ancient Rome). By comparison, the study of external aids such as note taking seems boring. As we have seen, however, what seems obvious (e.g., that older adults make greater use of aids) is not always obviously correct.

By focusing on internal strategies for training better memories, researchers may miss opportunities to promote more effective and lasting improvements in remembering for adults of all ages. Internal strategies, such as the method of loci, are difficult to learn, do not generalize readily to other relevant tasks or everyday activities, and are often ignored subsequent to training (Burack & Lachman, 1996; Rebok, Carlson, & Langbaum, 2007; Verhaeghen et al., 1992). Also, internal strategies may become less successful in old age (Verhaeghen et al., 1992).

External strategies should be more effective than internal strategies for older people, because external strategies do not depend as highly on cognitive resources. The research that we have reviewed indicates the effectiveness of external memory aids for both younger and older adults. Schryer and Ross's (in press) research also suggests that individuals may under-utilize external aids, but there is a need for research in which their use in everyday life is directly observed in the context of both prospective and retrospective memory. Also, most of the relevant lab research has focused on note taking and all of it involves the self-initiated use of external aids. There is a need to examine the value of other external aids for memory, such as behavioral routines and environmental constancies.

Despite our enthusiasm for outsourcing as a means of enhancing everyday memory, we acknowledge that there are potential limitations and costs associated with depending on external sources of remembering. When people rely on external sources they may stop storing information in and retrieving it from their own memories. Sparrow et al. (2011) found that people who regularly access information from the internet showed reduced recall for the information itself and increased recall for where the information could be found. Anecdotally, many people report similar experiences with inputting telephone numbers into their cell phones. They subsequently rely on their cell phones to generate numbers and are unable to recall numbers on their own. Consequently, if the Internet is down or people misplace or forget their cell phones, they are temporarily inconvenienced. The inconvenience is not too great, however, as back-up systems such as phone books still exist.

Similarly, if individuals depend on behavioral routines, stable environments, or other people to remember, they may experience confusion and forgetting if any of these features are lost (e.g., a change in residence or death of a spouse). The more people rely on these external features, the greater the potential impact of their loss. Older adults who depend on these features for remembering will be vulnerable to changes (Ames, 1993; Davis, Moritz, Neuhaus, Barclay, & Gee, 1997; Ferraro, 1983).

There are also potential disadvantages to navigating with GPS systems. GPS systems can be distracting and lead to driving errors (Kun, Paek, Medenica, Memarović, & Palinko, 2009), as well as provide directions inconsistent with drivers' intentions (Hipp, Schaub, Kargl, & Weber, 2010). We are not aware of research that examines whether these difficulties are exacerbated with age, but the potential for distractibility seems particularly problematic for older drivers. We suspect that the benefits of GPS systems outweigh the costs and that simple changes in behavior would reduce the problems for adults in any age group (e.g., audio guidance alone may be safer than visual guidance; Jensen, Skov, & Thiruravichandran, 2010).

Although we have emphasized the value of modern technology, it is important to note that people have been outsourcing remembering for millennia – probably at least since a Stone Age person first scratched symbols on cave walls. In the distant past, Hebrew scholars memorized the Talmud and oral law so that it could be transmitted from generation to generation (Stratton, 2000). Due to historical events and the introduction of writing, the written text of the Talmud and oral law gradually replaced the memorized text. Similarly, books, art, maps, and photographs have long served as external repositories of memories (Yates, 1966). The trend to a greater reliance on external sources continues with newer, more convenient external sources replacing or complementing their predecessors.

We suggest that, in general, people may rely too little not too much on external sources of remembering. They sometimes fail to record appointments in their calendars, and may be overly confident of their memories. Also, people may fail to make sufficient use of behavioral routines that would aid remembering, such as always placing their keys or purses or glasses in the same spots in their house. Professionals could more regularly transmit external reminders to their clients as the time for scheduled appointments approaches, especially when missed appointments are costly to the service provider or client. Also, developers and architects could take remembering more into account as they construct our environments. For example, parking garages and lots could often be altered in ways that would provide external prompts for remembering. Different levels or areas should look different (e.g., be painted in different colors). In parking garages, rows, parking spots, and levels often have different numbers and labels to help people locate their cars, but drivers should be reminded to look at the numbers on exiting their vehicles and note the location of their vehicle relative to salient landmarks. Moreover drivers could be encouraged to record the relevant information on paper or smartphones or share it with their passengers, rather than presume that they will remember.

RECALL OF PROPER NAMES

One important memory context in which memory pragmatics such as outsourcing may be of limited use is the recall of proper names. A failure to recall proper names is the most common cognitive complaint among the aged (Cohen & Faulkner, 1986; Maylor, 1997). Laboratory and diary research confirms that older adults have greater difficulty recalling proper names than younger adults do. In several laboratory studies, researchers report that the effect of aging on the recall of proper names is no greater than its effect on many other aspects of recall (e.g., recall of common names, semantic information, or faces) (Maylor, 1997; Rendell, Castel, & Craik, 2005). However, other researchers report disproportionately greater age impairment for proper names (e.g., James, 2004).

Whether or not recall of proper names is disproportionately affected by age, it does pose a problem for older people. Proper name recall is often more difficult for both older and younger adults than, for example, recall of common names or semantic information (Maylor, 1997). Even if age-related forgetting of proper names is comparable to other memory losses, a main effect for age would mean that older people are indeed having considerable trouble remembering people's names (Maylor, 1997). Second, when people forget common names they can often provide an alternative, acceptable word or phrase, but there is often no satisfactory substitute for a person's name. Therefore, memory lapses for proper names are often more noticeable and embarrassing than memory lapses for common names (Maylor, 1997). Third, older adults may potentially know more people in their personal lives (think for example of how many extended families expand over time as children are born, marry, and have children) and have used their names less recently than younger adults. Thus, older people confront a more difficult memory task in everyday life than their younger counterparts do. Fourth, older adults are slower to produce correct naming responses (Maylor, 2007; Salthouse, 1991). In everyday life, people often have to produce names quickly as they seek to address or introduce others. In short, a variety of factors conspire to render the recall of proper names particularly problematic for older people.

There has been no published research in which name recall is directly observed outside of the lab. Outside of the lab, it should sometimes be possible to offset age-related declines in recall of proper names with memory pragmatics. For example, people can use external sources such as contact lists to record the names of acquaintances' spouses and family members. Also, with the help of others, older adults can rehearse the names of family members and acquaintances that they are likely to encounter at upcoming social events.

It is difficult, however, to compensate fully for the effects of aging on name recall. For example, older people may experience frustrating and embarrassing memory lapses when they unexpectedly meet an acquaintance or family member whose name they have not retrieved recently. It is not easy to prepare for unexpected encounters.

CONCLUSION

Do older adults exhibit worse everyday memory than their younger counterparts, as stereotypes and laboratory research would suggest? Most of the relevant research focuses on prospective memory and the answer, at least in this domain of memory, appears to be "no." Do older adults have better everyday prospective memory than younger adults? The answer to this question may depend on the definition of prospective memory. The answer is likely "no" if we restrict our definition to mental capacity. The answer is "yes" if we define prospective memory in terms of whether people are likely to act on their earlier intentions (e.g., to go to the dentist), regardless of how they

do so. If, as Woody Allen suggested, the secret to success is showing up, then older adults would appear to be more successful than their younger counterparts.

Do older adults generally use external memory aids more frequently than younger adults, as many psychologists seem to suppose? Current research does not provide a clear answer to this question. More important, perhaps, there is strong, consistent evidence that external memory aids are very useful for adults of all ages. Historically, psychologists have shown greater interest in psychologically intriguing internal strategies for remembering (e.g., classic memory mnemonics) than in external strategies such as note taking. In the context of practical efforts to improve remembering, we suggest that psychologists put aside their enthusiasm for internal strategies and more actively encourage the use of external sources of remembering. When remembering is important, adults of all ages should use such aids rather than rely on their own retrospective and prospective memories. External memory aids dramatically improve people's ability to reconstruct the past and act on their intentions.

In discussing the prospective memory findings we focused on the paradox that prospective memory declines with age in the lab but improves with age in more naturalistic settings. The "obvious" explanations received at best tepid research support. The research is limited, however, and it seems fair to say that if no single explanation for the paradox has been ruled in, none has been excluded either. The research has focused on factors that might enhance older adults' or impair younger adults' prospective memory performance outside of the lab. The premise of the research and theorizing in this domain often appears to be that the superior performance of older adults in everyday life is anomalous, an artifact due to differences in motivation, life style, or memory aid usage (Phillips et al., 2008). Whether the findings from lab or field research are anomalous depends on the eye of the beholder, however. Even in the lab, it is possible to decrease or eliminate age differences in memory with various experimental manipulations, including the time of day at which memory is tested and the presence or absence of stereotype threat (May, Hasher, & Stoltzfus, 1993; Thomas & Dubois, 2011).

Moreover, one could argue that the prospective memory paradox, although intellectually intriguing, is not all that important from a practical perspective. Far more significant is the evidence that older adults seem to perform as well as or better than younger adults on everyday prospective memory tasks. The lab results on prospective memory do not generalize to everyday life and that is good news for older adults.

REFERENCES

Aberle, I., Rendell, P. G., Rose, N. S., McDaniel, M. A., & Kliegel, M. (2010).The age prospective memory paradox: Young adults may not give their best outside of the lab. *Developmental Psychology, 46,* 1444–1453.

Ames, D. (1993). Depressive disorders among elderly people in long-term institutional care. *Australian and New Zealand Journal of Psychiatry, 27,* 379–391.

Bäckman, L. & Dixon, R. A. (1992). Psychological compensation: A theoretical framework. *Psychological Bulletin, 112,* 259–283.

Bailey, P. E., Henry, J. D., Rendell, P.G., Phillips, L. H., & Kliegel, M. (2010). Dismantling the "age-prospective memory paradox". The classic laboratory paradigm simulated in a naturalistic setting. *The Quarterly Journal of Experimental Psychology, 63,* 646–652.

Baltes, P. B. (1997). On the incomplete architecture of human ontogeny: Selection, optimization, and compensation as foundation of developmental theory. *American Psychologist, 52,* 366–380.

Baltes, P. B., & Baltes, M. M. (1990). Psychological perspectives on successful aging: The model of selective optimization with compensation. In P. B. Baltes and M. M. Baltes (Eds.), *Successful aging: Perspectives from the behavioral sciences* (pp. 1–34). New York: Cambridge University Press.

Bottiroli, S., Cavallini, E., & Vecchi, T. (2008). Long-term effects of memory training in the elderly: A longitudinal study. *Archives of Gerontology and Geriatrics, 47,* 277–289.

Bradburn, N. M., Rips, L. J., & Shevell, S. K. (1987). Answering autobiographical questions: the impact of memory and inference on surveys. *Science, 236,* 157–161.

Burack, O. R., & Lachman, M. E. (1996). The effects of list-making on recall in young and elderly adults. *The Journals of Gerontology: Series B, 51B,* 226–233.

Burke, D. M., Mackay, D. G., Worthley, J. S., & Wade, E. (1991). On the tip of the tongue: What causes word finding failures in young and older adults? *Journal of Memory and Language, 30,* 542–579.

Cavanaugh, J. C., Grady, J. G., & Perlmutter, M. (1983). Forgetting and use of memory aids in 20 to 70 year olds' everyday life. *The International Journal of Aging & Human Development, 17,* 113–122.

Cohen, G., & Faulkner, D. (1986). Memory for proper names: Age differences in retrieval. *British Journal of Developmental Psychology, 4,* 187–197.

Craik, F. I. M. (1986). A functional account of age differences in memory. In F. Klix and H. Hangendorf (Eds.), *Human memory and cognitive capabilities: Mechanisms and performances* (pp. 409–422). Amsterdam: Elsevier-North-Holland.

Craik, F. I. M. (1992). Memory changes in normal aging. *Current Directions in Psychological Science, 3,* 155–158.

d'Ydewalle, G., Bouckaert, D., & Brunfaut, E. (2001). Age-related differences and complexity of ongoing activities in time- and event-based prospective memory. *The American Journal of Psychology, 114,* 411–423.

d'Ydewalle, G., & Brunfaut, E. (1996). Are older subjects necessarily worse in prospective memory tasks? In M. Georga, E. Manthouli, E. Besevegis and A. Kokkevi (Eds.), *Contemporary psychology in Europe: Theory, research and applications* (pp. 161–172). Gottingen, Germancy: Hegrefe & Huber.

Davis, M. A., Moritz, D. J., Neuhaus, J. M., Barclay, J. D., & Gee, L. (1997). Living arrangements, changes in living arrangements and survival among community dwelling older adults. *American Journal of Public Health, 87,* 371–377.

de Frias, C. M., & Dixon, R. A. (2005). Confirmatory factor structure and measurement invariance of the Memory Compensation Questionnaire. *Psychological Assessment, 17,* 168–178.

Devolder, P. A., Brigham, M. C., & Pressley, M. (1990). Memory performance awareness in younger and older adults. *Psychology and Aging, 5,* 291–303.

Dixon, R. A., & de Frias, C. M. (2004). The Victoria longitudinal study: From characterizing cognitive aging to illustrating changes in memory compensation. *Aging, Neuropsychology, and*

Cognition. Special Issue: Longitudinal studies of cognitive aging, 11, 346–376.

Dixon, R. A., de Frias, C. M., & Bäckman, L. (2001). Characteristics of self-reported memory compensation in older adults. *Journal of Clinical and Experimental Neuropsychology, 23,* 650–661.

Einstein, G. O., & McDaniel, M. A. (1990). Normal aging and prospective memory. *Journal of Experimental Psychology: Learning, Memory and Cognition, 16,* 717–726.

Ferraro, K. F. (1983). The health consequences of relocation among the aged in the community. *Journal of Gerontology, 38,* 90–96.

Frankel, S., Farrow, A., & West, R. (1989). Non-attendance or non-invitation? A case-control study of failed outpatient appointments. *British Medical Journal, 298,* 1343–1345.

Freund, A., M., & Baltes, P. B. (2002). Life-management strategies of selection, optimization and compensation: Measurement by self-report and construct validity. *Journal of Personality and Social Psychology, 82,* 642–662.

Freund, A. M., & Riediger, M. (2003). Successful aging. In R. M. Lerner, A. Easterbrooks and J. Mistry (Eds.), *Comprehensive handbook of psychology: Volume 6: Developmental psychology* (pp. 601–628). New York: Wiley.

Gallucci, G., Swartz, W., & Hackerman, F. (2005). Impact of the wait for an initial appointment on the rate of kept appointments at a mental health center. *Psychiatric Services, 56,* 344–346.

Hashtroudi, S., Johnson, M. K., & Chrosniak, L. D. (1989). Aging and qualitative characteristics for perceived and imagined complex events. *Psychology and Aging, 5,* 119–126.

Henry, J. D., MacLeod, M. S., Phillips, L. H., & Crawford, J. R. (2004). A meta-analytic review of prospective memory and aging. *Psychology and Aging, 19,* 27–39.

Henry, J. D. Rendell, P. G., Phillips, L. H., Dunlop, L., & Kliegel, M. (2012). Prospective memory reminders: A laboratory investigation of initiation source and age effects. *The Quarterly Journal of Experimental Psychology, 65,* 1274–1287.

Hintzman, D. L. (2011). Research strategy in the study of memory: Fads, fallacies, and the search for the "coordinates of truth". *Perspectives on Psychological Science, 6,* 253–271.

Hipp, M., Schaub, F., Kargl, F., & Weber, M. (2010). Interaction weaknesses of personal navigation devices. Proceedings of the Second International Conference on Automotive User Interfaces and Interactive Vehicular Applications, November 11–12, Pittsburgh, PA.

Hummert, M. L., Garstka, T. A., Shaner, J. L., & Strahm, S. (1994). Stereotypes of the elderly held by young, middle-aged and elderly adults. *The Journal of Gerontology, 49,* 240–249.

Ihle, A., Schnitzspahn, K., Rendell, P. G., Luong, C., & Kliegel, M. (2012). Age benefits in everyday prospective memory: The influence of personal task importance, use of reminders and everyday stress. *Aging, Neuropsychology, and Cognition, 19,* 84–101.

Intons-Peterson, M. J., & Fournier, J. (1986). External and internal memory aids: When and how often do we use them? *Journal of Experimental Psychology: General, 115,* 267–280.

Jacoby, L. L. (1999). Ironic effects of repetition: Measuring age-related differences in memory. *Journal of Experimental Psychology: Learning, Memory, and Cognition, 25,* 3–22.

Jacoby, L. L., & Rhodes, M. G. (2006). False remembering in the aged. *Current Directions in Psychological Science, 15,* 49–53.

James, L. E. (2004). Meeting Mr. Farmer versus meeting a farmer: Specific effects of aging on learning proper names. *Psychology and Aging, 19,* 515–522.

Jensen, B. S., Skov, M. B., & Thiruravichandran, N. (2010). Studying driver attention and behaviour for three configurations of GPS navigation in real traffic driving (pp. 1271–1280). Proceedings of the 28th international conference on human factors in computing systems, April 10–15, Atlanta, GA.

Johnson, M. K., Hashtroudi, S., & Lindsay, D. S. (1993). Source monitoring. *Psychological Bulletin, 114,* 3–28.

Kirasic, K. C. (2000). Age differences in adults' spatial abilities, learning environment layout, and wayfinding behavior. *Spatial Cognition and Computation, 2,* 117–134.

Kliegel, M., & Jäger, T. (2006). Can the Prospective and Retrospective Memory Questionnaire (PRMQ) predict actual prospective memory performance? *Current Psychology, 25,* 182–191.

Kun, A. L., Paek, T., Medenica, Z., Memarović, N., & Palinko, O. (2009). Glancing at personal navigation devices can affect driving: Experimental results and design implications. Proceedings of the First International Conference on Automotive User Interfaces and Interactive Vehicular Applications, Sep 21–22, Essen, Germany.

Lachman, M. E., & Andreoletti, C. (2006). Strategy use mediates the relationship between control beliefs and memory performance for middle-aged and older adults. *The Journals of Gerontology: Series B, 61,* 88–94.

Lachman, M. E., Andreoletti, C., & Pearman, A. (2006). Memory control beliefs: How are they related to memory improvement? *Social Cognition, 43,* 359–385.

Li, K. Z. H., Lindenberger, U., Freund, A. M., & Baltes, P. B. (2001). Walking while memorizing: Age-related differences in compensatory behavior. *Psychological Science, 12,* 230–237.

Lustig, C., & Flegal, K. E. (2008). Targeting latent function: Encouraging effective encoding for successful memory training and transfer. *Psychology and Aging, 23,* 754–764.

May, C. P., Hasher, L., & Stoltzfus, E. R. (1993). Optimal time of day and the magnitude of age differences in memory. *Psychological Science, 4,* 326–330.

Maylor, E. A. (1990). Age and prospective memory. *The Quarterly Journal of Experimental Psychology A: Human Experimental Psychology, 42,* 471–493.

Maylor, E. A. (1995). Age-related changes in memory. In M. L. Johnson (Ed.), *The Cambridge handbook of age and ageing.* Cambridge: Cambridge University Press.

Maylor, E. A. (1997). Proper name retrieval in old age: Converging evidence against disproportionate impairment. *Aging, Neuropsychology, and Cognition, 4,* 211–226.

McDonald, A., Haslam, C., Yates, P., Gun, B., Leeder, G., & Sayers, A. (2011). Google Calendar: A new memory aid to compensate for prospective memory deficits following acquired brain injury. *Neuropsychological Rehabilitation: An International Journal, 21,* 784–807.

Morrow, D. G., Leirer, V. O., Carver, L. M., Tanke, E. D., & McNally, A. D. (1999). Effects of aging, message repetition, and note-taking on memory for health information. *The Journals of Gerontology: Series B, 54B,* P369–P379.

Moscovitch, M. (1982). A neuropsychological approach to memory and perception in normal and pathological aging. In F. I. M. Craik and S. Trehub (Eds.), *Aging and cognitive processes* (pp. 55–78). New York: Plenum Press.

Neal, R. D., Lawlor, D. A., Allgar, V., Colledge, M., Ali, S., Hassey, A., Portz, C., & Wilson, A. (2001). Missed appointments in general practice: Retrospective data analysis from four practices. *British Journal of General Practice, 51,* 830–832.

Norman, K. A., & Schacter, D. L. (1997). False recognition in younger and older adults: Exploring the characteristics of illusory memories. *Memory and Cognition, 25,* 838–848.

Park, D.C., Hertzog, C., Leventhal, H., Morell, R. W., Leventhal, E., Birchmore, D., et al. (1999). Medication adherence in rheumatoid arthritis patients: Older is wiser. *Journal of American Geriatrics Society, 47,* 172–183.

Park, D. C., Smith, A. D., Dudley, W. N., & Lafronza, V. N. (1989). Effects of age and a divided attention task presented during encoding and retrieval on memory. *Journal of Experimental Psychology: Learning, Memory and Cognition, 15,* 1185–1191.

Patton, G. W., & Meit, M. (1993). Effect of aging on prospective and incidental memory. *Experimental Aging Research, 19,* 165–176.

Perlmutter, M. (1978). What is memory aging the aging of? *Developmental Psychology, 14,* 330–345.

Perlmutter, M., Metzger, R., Nezworski, T., & Miller, K. (1981). Spatial and temporal memory in 20 and 60 year olds. *The Journal of Gerontology, 36,* 59–65.

Phillips, L. H., Henry, J. D., & Martin, M. (2008). Adult aging and prospective memory: The importance of ecological validity. In M. Kliegel, M. McDaniel and G. Einstein (Eds.), *Prospective memory: Cognitive, neuroscience, developmental and applied perspectives* (pp. 161–185). New York: Taylor & Francis Group.

Rabbit, P., & Abson, V. (1990). "Lost and found": some logical and methodological limitations of self-report questionnaires as tools to study cognitive ageing. *British Journal of Psychology, 81,* 1–16.

Rabbitt, P. Maylor, E., McInnes, L., Bent, N., & Moore, B. (1995). What goods can self-assessment questionnaires deliver for cognitive gerontology? *Applied Cognitive Psychology, 9,* 127–152.

Rebok, G. W., Carlson, M. C., & Langbaum, J. B. S. (2007). Training and maintaining memory abilities in healthy older adults: Traditional and novel approaches. *Journal of Gerontology, 62*B, 53–61.

Rendell, P. G., Castel, A.D., & Craik, F. I. M. (2005). Memory for proper names in old age: A disproportionate impairment? *The Quarterly Journal of Experimental Psychology, 58(A),* 54–71.

Rendell, P. G., & Craik, F. I. M. (2000). Virtual week and actual week: Age-related differences in prospective memory. *Applied Cognitive Psychology. Special Issue: New Perspectives in Prospective Memory, 14,* S43–S62.

Rendell, P. G., & Thomson, D. M. (1993). The effect of ageing on remembering to remember: An investigation of simulated medication regimens. *Australian Journal of Ageing, 12,* 11–18.

Rendell, P. G., & Thomson, D. M. (1999). Aging and prospective memory: Differences between naturalistic and laboratory tasks. *The Journals of Gerontology: Series B, 54B,* 256–269.

Ross, M. (1989). Relation of implicit theories to the construction of personal histories. *Psychological Review, 96,* 341–357.

Ross, M., Spencer, S. J., Blatz, C. W., & Restorick, E. (2008). Collaboration reduces the frequency of false memories in older and younger adults. *Psychology and Aging, 23,* 85–92.

Salthouse, T. A. (1991). Mediation of adult age differences in cognition by reductions in working memory and speed of processing. *Psychological Science, 23,* 179–183.

Schacter, D. L., Osowiecki, D., Kaszniak, A. W., Kihlstrom, J. F., & Valdiserri, M. (1994). Source memory: Extending the boundaries of age-related deficits. *Psychology and Aging, 9,* 81–89.

Schnitzspahn, K. M., Ihle, A., Henry, J. D., Rendell, P. G., & Kliegel, M. (2011). The age-prospective memory-paradox: An exploration of possible mechanisms. *International Psychogeriatrics, 23,* 583–592.

Schryer, E., (2012). *Do older and younger adults use and benefit from memory aids?* (Unpublished doctoral dissertation). University of Waterloo, Waterloo, Ontario.

Schryer, E., & Ross, M. (in press). The use and benefits of memory aids by older and younger adults. *Applied Cognitive Psychology.*

Sparrow, B., Liu, J., & Wegner, D. M. (2011). Google effects on memory: Cognitive consequences of having information at our fingertips. *Science, 333,* 776–778.

Stratton, G. M. (2000). The mnemonic feat of the "Shass Pollak". In U. Neisser and I. E. Hyman (Eds.), *Memory observed* (2nd ed.) (pp. 393–396). San Francisco, CA: W. H. Freeman and Company.

Sunderland, A., Harris, J. E., & Baddeley, A. D. (1983). Do laboratory tests predict everyday memory? A neuropsychological study. *Journal of Verbal Learning and Verbal Behavior, 22,* 341–357.

Sunderland, A., Harris, J. E., & Gleave, J. (1984). Memory failures in everyday life following severe head injury. *Journal of Clinical Neuropsychology, 6,* 127–142.

Sunderland, A., Watts, K., Baddely, A. D., & Harris, J. E. (1986). Subjective memory assessment and test performance in elderly adults. *Journal of Gerontology, 41,* 376–384.

Svoboda, E., & Richards, B. (2009). Compensating for anterograde amnesia: A new training method that capitalizes on emerging smartphone technologies. *Journal of the International Neuropsychological Society, 15,* 629–638.

Thomas, A. K., & Dubois, S. J. (2011). Reducing the burden of stereotype threat eliminates age differences in memory distortion. *Psychological Science, 22,* 1515–1517.

Verhaegan, P., Marcoen, A., & Goossens, L. (1992). Improving memory performance in the aged through mnemonic training: A meta-analytic study. *Psychology and Aging, 7,* 242–251.

Wegner, D. M., Erber, R., & Raymond, P. (1991). Transactive memory in close relationships. *Journal of Personality and Social Psychology, 61,* 923–929.

West, R. L., & Crook, T. H. (1990). Age differences in everyday memory: Laboratory analogues of telephone number recall. *Psychology and Aging, 5,* 520–529.

West, R., Crook, T. H., & Barron, K. L. (1992). Everyday memory performance across the lifespan: Effects of age and noncognitive individual differences. *Psychology and Aging, 7,* 72–82.

Wilson, B. A., Emslie, H. C., Quirk, K., & Evans, J. J. (2001). Reducing everyday memory and planning problems by means of a paging system: A randomised control crossover study. *Journal of Neurology, Neurosurgery & Psychiatry with Practical Neurology, 70,* 477–482.

Yates, F. A. (1966). *The art of memory.* London: Routledge & Kegan Paul.

Zacks, R. T., Hasher, L., & Li, K. Z. H. (2000). Human memory. In F. I. M. Craik and T. A. Salthouse (Eds.), *The handbook of aging and cognition* (2nd ed.). Mahwah, NJ: Lawrence Erlbaum Associates, Inc.

15

The Effects of Self-Reference on Memory: A Conceptual and Methodological Review of Inferences Warranted by the Self-Reference Effect

Stanley B. Klein and Christopher R. Nelson

We have three goals in this chapter. First, we argue that the main construct under discussion – the self – is a multifaceted entity that does not easily submit to clear and precise description. As we hope to make clear, the aspect of self studied by most investigators is actually a subset of the cognitive and neural underpinnings of "self" and not the self of first-person subjectivity. Second, we take a look at what currently is the dominant theoretical treatment of human long-term memory – the systems approach (e.g., Foster & Jelicic, 1999) – and examine how the construct of "self" is situated in this theoretical framework. Finally, we review the best-known paradigm for exploring the role of self in memory – the self-reference effect (SRE) manipulation. We argue that, similar to the other constructs in play (i.e., self and memory), there is not one Self-Reference Effect, but rather a family of related SREs that are influenced by a variety of variables and contexts.

We conclude that great care is required when investigators attempt to draw inferences about the self from tests employing the SRE, since (a) while the SRE provides insight into memory-based self-knowledge, it does not warrant any conclusions about the self of conscious awareness (these two aspects of self – e.g., James, 1890 – are conflated in most self/memory studies: e.g., Klein, 2012a, 2012b), and (b) when employing the self-reference effect paradigm to test the relation between self and memory, conclusions one has license to draw rest heavily on a variety of factors including, but not limited to, the memory system(s) being utilized by the task, the type of stimulus items employed, the degree of familiarity with task referents, and the conditions adopted as controls.

These considerations are important. The Self-Reference Encoding Task has been widely adopted by researchers with both applied and theoretical concerns, as well as serving as a standard paradigm for drawing inferences about a number of practical memory processes, such as the role of self/memory in disease processes (e.g., depression, schizophrenia), learning techniques, and marketing strategies.

THE SELF AND ITS RELATION TO MEMORY

The self and memory share a complicated relation. On the one hand, the act of experiencing a personal memory presupposes a sense that the memory is not just any memory, but my memory. At the same time, knowledge of self, by most accounts, is based on the content of memory. The apparent circularity of this relation, and the ensuing infinite regress it portends, has long been recognized both by philosophers (e.g., Locke, 1690/1731; Schectman, 1996; see Bernecker, 2010, for review), and psychologists (e.g., James, 1890; see Klein, 2001, 2010, for review).

THE SELF

Different ways of knowing the self

Most psychologists and philosophers studying the self fail to differentiate between aspects of and the ways in which we use the word self. Klein and Gangi (2010) suggested that Russell's (1912/1992) distinction between knowledge by *acquaintance* and knowledge by *description* provides a way to break the conceptual impasse posed by the definitional entanglement between self and memory. Russell proposed that we have knowledge by acquaintance when we know something via direct personal contact (sensory or introspective) and exhibit that knowledge by using appropriately referential terms when we communicate with others. With respect to the self, this is seen in the ease with which we talk about the self as well as understand talk about self by others.

However, when we attempt to make explicit what it is we refer to by the word "self" – when asked to *describe* what the word "self" means – problems quickly arise. Despite centuries devoted to the task, it has proven notoriously difficult to provide a set of propositions capable of transforming our acquired knowledge into a satisfying description of what a self *is*.

How, for example, can one explain experienced identity of the self over time – that is, the diachronic self? Locke (1690/1731) argued that a continuity of consciousness (what we now would call episodic long-term memory) might do the trick, but issues soon raised by Thomas Reid and others philosophers (e.g., Butler, 1736/1819; Reid, 1785) called attention to serious problems with Locke's criterion (see below, for review and discussion, see Dainton, 2008; Shoemaker & Swinburne, 1984; Slors, 2001). Equally vexing problems arise when we attempt to explain the perceived phenomenological unity of the self at a single moment in time – the synchronic self. Specifically, how do we account for the ways in which a diversity of images, sensations, and thoughts appear to merge into a single, unified experience of self-awareness (the so called "binding" problem of conscious awareness; e.g., Dainton, 2008; Lowe, 1996; Lund, 2005)?

These, and a host of other contentious ontological issues involving the word "self" (e.g., consciousness, subjectivity, self-awareness, free will, explanatory gap, mind/body, subject/object, personal continuity, etc.) make clear that describing what we are talking about when we use the word "self" is a task for which insufficient progress has been made (for reviews, see Dainton, 2008; Eccles, 1994; Johnstone, 1970; Lund, 2005; Madell, 1984; Schechtman, 1996; Shoemaker & Swinburne, 1984; Strawson, 2009; Vierkant, 2003; for an historical review of problems arising in the use of the term "self", see Sorabji, 2006).

While this might seem a cause for great concern among psychologists – William James (1890) argued that the self is the fundamental unit of analysis for a science of mental life, the problem about which everything else revolves (e.g., James, 1890, p. 221) – such concern is not readily apparent from perusal of articles in contemporary (non-analytic) psychological literatures (e.g., social, cognitive, developmental, neuropsychological, brain imaging; for review, see Klein 2010, 2012a, 2012b). The number of research papers exploring self-related processes has been proliferating at a staggering pace. Commenting in 1971 on the explosion of articles on the self appearing in the 20 years since the behaviorist movement in America gradually had given way to traditional appreciation of the importance of inferring mental structures from the behavior of persons (e.g., Klein & Kihlstrom, 1998; Niesser, 1967), Gergen (1971) recorded an astonishing 2,000 studies published on the self during the previous two decades. Approximately 25 years later, John Kihlstrom and colleagues (Kihlstrom, Cantor, Albright, Chew, Klein, & Niedenthal, 1988) identified dozens of "hot" research areas in which the word self served as prefix (thus occupying the central position with regard to the topics addressed): e.g., self-awareness, self-concept, self-control, self-handicapping, self-reference, self-schema, and self-image.

But what exactly is the "self" that serves as the object of this diverse set of predicates? What is *it* that is being conceptualized, esteemed, referenced, regulated, and handicapped? Although this question has led to a number of psychological models of self, dating back more than 100 years (e.g., Calkins, 1915; Conway, 2005; Greenwald, 1981; James, 1890; Kihlstrom et al., 1988;

Kihlstrom & Klein, 1994; Neisser, 1988), it is extremely difficult to find a coherent and convincing descriptive account of the self, per se. Rather, these papers largely describe the neurological and cognitive mechanisms that appear causally responsible for the knowledge available to the self of subjective experience.

The neural self of science and the subjective self of first person phenomenology

In this section we turn attention to what can be asserted with reasonable confidence about the self. Specifically, we discuss what Klein (2012a) calls the *epistemological self* – the behavioral, affective, cognitive, and neural systems assumed to be causally responsible (at least in part) for providing the subjective self with knowledge of whom and what it is (for reviews, see Klein, 2004, 2010, 2012b; Strawson, 2009). We then point to an apparent incompatibility between treating the self as *both* the subject of experience (i.e., an object) and the agent of experience (i.e., a subject; for more detailed treatment, see Earle, 1972; Klein, 2012b; Strawson, 2009; Zahavi, 2005). This latter aspect of self we have called the *ontological self* (e.g., Klein, 2004, 2012a).

It is a fact of scientific inquiry and personal experience that the self of an individual is able to learn about the individual in which it is situated and even experience itself as a knower (for a classic treatment, see, James, 1890; more modern accounts can be found in Crispin, Smith, & Macdonald, 1998; Klein, 2004; Rosenthal, 1986). Scientific accounts of the mechanisms, databases, and search engines that allow information about the self to be acquired, stored, and retrieved are flourishing in academic psychology, even if troubling ontological issues remain mostly unaddressed (e.g., Klein, 2012a, 2012b; Klein & Gangi, 2010).

In particular, considerable progress has been made describing the cognitive and neurological bases of the epistemological self (e.g., Conway, 2005; Kihlstrom & Klein, 1994, 1997; Klein, Cosmides, Tooby, & Chance, 2002; Klein & Gangi, 2010; Neisser, 1988). This is because, unlike ontological questions, the epistemological self – that is, neurological bases of self-knowledge – are empirically testable, and thus amenable to scientific analysis. By contrast, the ontological self, the self of personal experience, is too poorly understood to bear the definitional adequacy required of the terms of a causal relation between self and memory (e.g., Earle, 1955; Hasker, 1999; Klein, 2012a; Strawson, 2009). Not surprisingly, many researchers (intentionally or otherwise) side-step this difficulty, relying on their readers' familiarity with the term "self" (i.e., the self of subjective experience), derived from years of knowledge by acquaintance, to confer a sense of confidence that he or she knows to what it is the author refers. But the basic problem remains – we do not know what it is we are talking about when we apply the label "self" (nor, as detailed in Klein, in press a, is the term open to being grasped and thus labeled via scientific objectification). This is a serious problem.

Compounding the difficulty surrounding study of the self is that many researchers fail to fully appreciate that the self as subjectivity – what we are calling the ontological self – is not the object of their experimental studies. Indeed, it cannot be the object of their studies. Objectivity is based on the assumption that an act or object exists independent of any individual's awareness of it (e.g., Earle, 1955; Foster, 1991; Nagel, 1974); that is, it is something "other" than the self. When objectivity is the stance adopted by the self to study itself, the self must, by necessity, be directed toward what is not the self but rather to some "other" that serves as the self's object (e.g., Earle, 1972; Husserl, 1964; Lund, 2005; Klein, 2012a, 2012b; Nagel, 1974; Zahavi, 2005). To study myself as an object, I must transform myself into an "other", into a "not-self".

Thus, the self is not, and cannot be, an object for itself and still maintain its subjectivity.

Paradoxically, we can achieve objectivity of the ontological self only at the cost of losing awareness of our self as a subjective center (for detailed treatment, see Klein, 2012a, 2012b). Given these considerations, the ontological self would seem a particularly poor candidate for scientific exploration – an enterprise predicated on understanding objects and their relations. Science is the world of publically observable and physically measureable objects and events. Since nothing can be an object for the self unless it is "other" to the self, it follows that the self cannot objectively apprehend itself as itself (Earle, 1972; Foster, 1991; Lund, 2005; Nagel, 1974; Zahavi, 2005). Scientific analysis therefore has the unintended consequence of eliminating the object under discussion – the ontological self – from the discussion.

Nor is the ontological self something one can locate via inference. I do not posit myself nor do I have to guess that I exist. I am immediately aware of my self as myself, as a unique subjectivity (e.g., Earle, 1972; Husserl, 1964; Lund, 2005). And I am immediately aware of my feelings, beliefs, memories, knowledge, decisions, judgments, and acts (i.e., the domain of psychological processes, which constitute the epistemological self) as *mine*. These things cannot force themselves, via some scientifically accepted mechanism of physical forces, to be known (Earle, 1955; Klein, in press).

Given these concerns, some (e.g., epiphenomenalists, eliminative materialists) have tried to banish the ontological self from investigation, to argue that it is an illusion, the anachronistic myth of a folk-psychology that rapidly is being replaced by advances in the neurosciences (most of which await future discovery – hence the "promissory note" aspect of the eliminativist program; e.g., Churchland, 1986; for a critique, see Hasker, 1999). But after the dust of promised reductive analyses clears, a simple question remains – to or for *whom* is the self an illusion? There is a mystery here and it will not go away by sweeping it under a metaphysical rug.

Summing up thus far, our stance is this: We will ultimately not make progress coming to terms with our object of inquiry – the Self – until we acknowledge (in Jamesian fashion) that the self is a *multiplicity* – both as pertains to (a) two intimately related, yet metaphysically separable aspects of the term "self" (i.e., ontological versus epistemological), as well as (b) within each of these two self aspects. The claim of componential plurality holds strongly for the epistemological self (for recent review, see Klein & Gangi, 2010). Whether it holds for the ontological self as well is subject of considerable debate (e.g., Dainton, 2008; James, 1909/1996; Lund, 2005; Strawson, 2009). Regardless, the takeaway message is this – until we not only recognize, but fully embrace the different "types" of selves we routinely conjoin in both our thought and research (for reviews, see Klein, 2012b; Strawson, 2009), progress on what Chalmers (1966) has described as the "hard question" likely will remain elusive.

Types of epistemological self-knowledge: A partial taxonomy

As noted in the previous section, there are a diversity of self-predicated terms that have received empirical attention in psychology. For example, neuropsychological studies of self suggest that the singular self of everyday experience actually is informed by a number of different, functionally isolable neuro-cognitive systems (e.g., Klein, 2004, 2010; Neisser, 1988; Stern, 1985). These include, but are not limited to:

1. Episodic memories of one's life events.
2. Semantic summary representations of one's personality traits.
3. Semantic knowledge of facts about one's life.
4. An experience of continuity through time: The "I" experienced now is connected to the "I" experienced at previous points (as well as later points) in one's life. Episodic memory is known to contribute heavily to this ability.
5. A sense of personal agency and ownership: The belief – or experience – that "I" (agency) am the

cause of "my own" (ownership) thoughts and actions.
6. The ability to self-reflect: To form meta-representations where the agent is the self, and make inferences on the basis of those representations.
7. The physical self: The ability to represent and recognize (e.g., in mirrors, photographs) one's body.

While in normal individuals, sources of self-knowledge work together to help create our sense of self as a subjective unity (e.g., Damasio, 1999; White, 1991), taken separately none of these systems are either logically or empirically necessary to maintain the experience of the self as a singular, subjective point of view (for reviews, see Klein, 2010, 2012b).

MEMORY

This section of the chapter is focused on epistemological self-knowledge derived from memory (i.e., points 1, 2, and 3 above). Accordingly, understanding of the relation between types of self-knowledge and memory needs to be made explicit. In what follows we provide an account of our position.

How is self-referential knowledge represented in and retrieved from memory? We have chosen to address these questions within the context of the position that long-term memory consists in multiple systems (for review of the memory systems debate, see Foster & Jelicic, 1999).

Tulving's (1983, 1985, 1993) widely adopted idea of memory systems distinguishes two types or systems within declarative long-term memory memory: episodic and semantic (see also Cermak, 1984; Furlong, 1951; Moscovitch, Yaschyshyn, Zeigler, & Nadel, 2000; Parkin, 1993). Semantic memory contains relatively generic, context-free knowledge about the world, such as *Grapes are edible, 2 + 2 = 4* and *Sacramento is the capital of California*. Semantic memory usually lacks a source tag: that is, it is experienced as knowledge without regard to where and when that knowledge was obtained (e.g., Gennaro, 1996; Perner &

Ruffman, 1994; Tulving, 1983, 1993; Wheeler, Stuss, & Tulving, 1997). Semantic memory typically makes no reference to the self; it can, however, contain propositions expressing facts about the self (e.g., *I was born in New York*), just as it can about other things in the world. But this information is known in the same way that one knows that *2 + 2 = 4*; it is not recollected or re-experienced vis à vis the context in which it originally was learned.

In contrast to semantic memory, the episodic memory system records events as having been experienced by the self at a particular (and unique) point in space and time; when retrieved, these events are re-experienced in a quasi-perceptual way, with conscious awareness that "this happened to *me*" (e.g., Tulving, 1983, 1993; Wheeler et al., 1997). Every episodic memory, by definition, entails a mental representation of the self as the agent or recipient of some action, or as the stimulus or experiencer of some state. Examples of episodic memory are: *I remember eating chicken for supper yesterday evening*; *I recall having met with Judith last Monday*.

Not surprisingly, it is the episodic component of declarative memory that historically has been the focus of interest for psychologists studying the relation between self and memory. This is because retrieval from episodic memory is assumed to have a self-referential quality thought to be largely absent from other types of memorial experience (i.e., semantic and procedural; for discussion, see Klein, Cosmides, Tooby, & Chance, 2002).

However, as we now know (for reviews, see Klein & Loftus, 1993; Klein, 2004, 2010) semantic memory also contains a variety of self-referential information – thus rendering the assumption that episodic memory and the self share a unique relation tenuous at best. The failure to consider the possibility of self-referential information in both episodic and semantic long-term memory has had important, unintended consequences for many years on how people have interpreted findings from the most influential paradigm for exploring the memorial effects of the self: the Self-Reference Effect.

TESTING THE RELATION BETWEEN MEMORY AND THE SELF: THE SELF-REFERENCE EFFECT

In one of the first demonstrations that information is well remembered when it is considered in relation to the self, Rogers, Kuiper, and Kirker (1977) used Craik and Tulving's (1975) depth of processing methodology to examine the effects of various encoding strategies on incidental recall. Rogers et al. (1977) found that judging trait adjectives for self-descriptiveness ("Describes you?") led to better recall than did structural (e.g., "Printed in capital letters?"), phonemic (e.g., "Rhymes with XXX?"), or semantic (e.g., "Means the same as XXX?") encoding of the same material.

The superior recall and recognition (the effect is found reliably using both methods of interrogating memory; for meta-analytic review, see Symons & Johnson, 1997) for words encoded with respect to the self (the Self-Reference Effect, or SRE) generated much interest because it contradicted the prevailing belief among many psychologists (e.g., Craik & Tulving, 1975; Hyde & Jenkins, 1973) that semantic encoding produced optimal retention within the depth of processing framework. In addition, because the memory of self-referentially encoded material was assumed to be informative about the memorial properties of the self, the Rogers et al. (1977) paradigm seemed to offer a method for exploring the role of the self in memory.

Problems: A divergence of results, explanations and inferences based on SRE studies

The SRE has since been the subject of literally hundreds of investigations, many of which have replicated Rogers et al.'s (1977) findings (e.g., for a review, see Symons & Johnson, 1997). In addition, the self-reference paradigm has been used to explore self-referent encoding under a staggering variety of theoretically interesting conditions. Researchers have examined the mnemonic effectiveness of self-reference as a function of private self-consciousness (e.g., Agatstein & Buchanan, 1984; Hull & Levy, 1979; Nasby, 1985), developmental stage in the aging process (e.g., Gliskey & Marquine, 2009; Sui & Zhu, 2005), creativity (Katz, 1987), autism (e.g., Hare, Mellor, & Azmi, 2007; Henderson et al., 2009), culture (e.g., Zang, Zhu, Zhang, Liu, Fan, & Zhu, 2006; Zhu, Zhang, Fan, & Han, 2007), sex typing (e.g., Mills, 1983), neurological damage (e.g., Grilli & Glisky, 2010), Alzheimer's dementia (e.g., Ruby et al., 2009), meditation (e.g., Han, Gu, Mao, Ge, Wang, & Ma, 2010), ADHD (e.g., Klein, Gangi, & Lax, 2011), stimulus type (e.g., Klein & Loftus, 1988), stimulus valence (e.g., Glisky & Marguine, 2009), neuroticism (Young & Martin, 1981), social schemata and prototypes (e.g., Markus, 1977; Roger, Rogers, & Kuiper, 1979), depression (e.g., Kuiper & Derry, 1982) schizophrenia (e.g., Harvey, Lee, Horan, Ochsner, & Green, 2011), and religion (e.g., Ge, Gu, Ji, & Han, 2009).

Three problems, however, have rendered the self-reference paradigm less theoretically fruitful than it promised to be. First, attempts to extend it have yielded conflicting results. For example, self-referent encoding has been compared with encoding in reference to a well-known other (e.g., one's mother). In some studies, self-referent encoding produced higher recall (e.g., Lord, 1980, Experiment 1), but in others it did not (e.g., Bower & Gilligan, 1979, Experiment 2).

Similarly, when nouns replaced trait adjectives as stimuli, some investigators reported that self-referent encoding led to greater recall than did semantic encoding (e.g., Warren, Chattin, Thompson, & Tomsky, 1983); however, other investigators did not obtain this effect (e.g., Aboud, 1980). These inconsistencies have led some to question whether there really is a recall advantage for information encoded self-referentially. The conclusion of Higgins and Bargh (1987, p. 392) is typical of this sentiment: "In brief, self-reference is neither necessary nor sufficient for memory of input to be facilitated in comparison to a semantic orientation task."

The second problem is that among studies examining the same population varying results are found. For example, some investigators employing the SRE to test the relation between self and memory in autism have found some evidence of SREs (e.g., Hare et al., 2007; Lombardo et al., 2010) while others have not (e.g., Henderson et al., 2009; Lind & Bowler, 2008). Similar discrepancies are found in other domains in inquiry (e.g., in testing whether SREs are present prior to age eight, Halpin, Puff, Mason, & Martson, 1984, obtained null results of SRE manipulations while Sui & Zhu, 2005, reported positive SREs).

A third problem is that investigators are unable to agree on the mechanisms mediating the effect. The SRE has been proposed to reflect the operation of a variety of cognitive processes, including elaboration (e.g., Keenan & Baillet, 1980; Klein & Loftus, 1988; Rogers et al., 1977), organization (Klein & Kihlstrom, 1986; Klein & Loftus, 1988), evaluation (Ferguson, Rule, & Carlson, 1983; Zajonc, 1980), cognitive cueing (Bellezza, 1984), and distinctiveness (Bruss, 1986; Friedman & Pullyblank, 1982). None of these proposals has emerged as definitive, partly because of the lack of a consistent pattern of results against which to evaluate them. In the absence of a clear understanding of the SRE, results obtained with the self-reference paradigm have been less useful in explicating the role of the self in memory than was originally expected.

A proposed resolution

In 1989, Klein, Loftus, and Burton demonstrated that much of the controversy surrounding self-reference stemmed from a failure to distinguish between SREs produced in different experimental contexts. Specifically, two different self-referent encoding tasks have been used to produce the SREs reported in the literature: A descriptive task (i.e., "Describes you?"), in which participants decide whether a stimulus word is self-descriptive, and an autobiographical task (i.e., "Recall a time when"), in which participants retrieve an autobiographical memory related to a stimulus word. The two tasks have been used interchangeably both between and within self-reference studies. For example, some studies comparing the mnemonic effectiveness of self-reference with other-reference use descriptive tasks (e.g., Ferguson et al., 1983; Kuiper & Rogers, 1979), others use autobiographical tasks (e.g., Brown, Keenan, & Potts, 1986; Miall, 1986), and still others include both tasks in the same experiment (e.g., Bower & Gilligan, 1979; Friedman & Pullyblank, 1982).

Similar intermixing of tasks is found among studies investigating the processes mediating the SRE. Some studies rely exclusively on descriptive tasks to explore self-reference (e.g., Ferguson et al., 1983; Kendzierski, 1980; Rogers et al., 1977), some use autobiographical tasks (e.g., Bellezza, 1984; Bruss, 1986; Klein & Loftus, 1988), and others draw conclusions from studies that include both tasks (e.g., Bower & Gilligan, 1979; Klein & Kihlstrom, 1986).

Klein et al. (1989) argued that this treatment of descriptive and autobiographical tasks as equivalent methods for studying the SRE was responsible for much of the difficulty both in demonstrating consistent effects of self-reference and in specifying the processes mediating the effect. The interchangeable use of these tasks reflected an assumption that they function similarly, but the only empirical basis for their assumed equivalence was a study by Bower and Gilligan (1979, Experiment 2). For each of a list of trait adjectives, Bower and Gilligan's subjects either decided whether the trait was self-descriptive or searched memory for a personal experience in which they had manifested the trait. The descriptive and autobiographical tasks produced comparable recall enhancement. It is important to note, however, that many factors are known to facilitate recall; thus, it is difficult to argue for process equivalence solely on the basis of recall equivalence.

Klein and colleagues presented evidence that descriptive and autobiographical tasks involve different cognitive processes, and showed how much of the variability in the SRE literature results from a failure to appreciate this difference. A large part of the difference between these two forms of the SRE task involves the memorial system mediating the request for epistemological self-knowledge. Klein and colleagues have amassed a large body of evidence over the last two decades that demonstrates that the "Describes you" variant of the SRE test entails the activation and retrieval of self-relevant information from semantic memory, whereas the "autobiographical" form of the task accesses self-relevant knowledge from episodic memory. The two primary forms of the SRE task thus activate and access different aspects of self-knowledge contained in different systems of memory (for reviews, see Klein, 2004; Klein & Loftus, 1993; Klein, Robertson, Gangi, & Loftus, 2008).

Klein et al. (1989) proposed that when SRE investigations are segregated on the basis of these two distinct self-reference effects, a clearer picture of the role of the self in memory emerges. In a series of studies, they first replicated Bower and Gilligan's (1979) finding that descriptive and autobiographical tasks yield comparable recall. They then presented evidence that although episodic retrieval is required for the SRE obtained with the autobiographical task, it was not involved in performance of the descriptive task. Finally, they offered evidence against the possibility that descriptive and autobiographical tasks rely on a common process other than autobiographical retrieval to achieve their comparable mnemonic effectiveness.

To illustrate these points, consider a recent paper by Klein, Lax, and Gangi (2011), who demonstrate that when self-referential recall is examined in young adults with ADHD, small changes in task instructions can yield large changes in recall performance. In their first study, participants were asked the standard SRE question – "Does this trait word describe you"? Under these conditions, ADHD participants produced a recall profile statistically indistinguishable from that produced by age-matched controls. However, in Study 2, the self-referential question was changed. Participants now were requested to retrieve a personal recollection (presumably from episodic memory) in which their behavior exemplified the presented trait words. Under these conditions, ADHD participants showed a weaker effect of self-reference on recall and evidenced significantly less organization in their recall compared with Study 1 (more on organization and the SRE below). So, whether ADHD participants demonstrate a self-referential recall advantage depends on whether the stimulus traits are processed with respect to semantic self-knowledge (Study 1) or with respect to episodic self-knowledge (Study 2).

Accordingly, a far more consistent picture of the literature on self- versus other-reference can be seen when the studies are grouped according to the task used in the investigation. In every study in which encoding in reference to a well-known other has involved autobiographical retrieval (e.g., "Recall an incident in which your mother exemplified this trait"), other-reference has produced recall comparable to that obtained with self-reference (Bower & Gilligan, 1979, Experiment 2; Brown et al., 1986, Experiment 5; Chew, 1983, Experiment 3; Miall, 1986).

In contrast, with a few exceptions (Friedman & Pullyblank, 1982, Experiment l; Kuiper & Rogers, 1979; Maki & McCaul, 1985), the use of descriptive tasks for making judgments about well-known

others (e.g., "Does this trait describe your mother?") has produced recall inferior to that found with self-reference (Bradley & Mathews, 1983; Chew, 1983, Experiment 2; Ferguson et al., 1983; Friedman & Pullyblank, 1982, Experiments 2 and 3; Karylowski & Buczek, 1984, Experiment 1; Kuiper & Derry, 1982, Experiment 2; Lord, 1980, Experiment 1).

A lack of consistency has also plagued studies testing whether self-reference enhances memory for nouns. Early demonstrations of the SRE (e.g., Kuiper & Rogers, 1979; Rogers et al., 1977) used trait adjectives as stimulus material, and the effects were universally obtained. Attempts to obtain the effect using nouns, however, have produced discrepant results. Some studies replicated the SRE with nouns (e.g., Klein & Kihlstrom, 1986; Warren et al., 1983), but others have not (e.g., Aboud, 1980; Maki & McCaul, 1985).

Grouping these studies according to the task used also introduces greater consistency into the literature. The SREs with nouns typically are obtained with self-reference tasks promoting autobiographical retrieval (Brown et al., 1986, Experiments 5 and 6; Klein & Kihlstrom, 1986; Klein & Loftus, 1988; Warren et al., 1983; but see Bellezza, 1984, 1986). Studies failing to obtain SREs, however, have used self-reference tasks not requiring autobiographical retrieval, such as descriptive tasks (Aboud, 1980; Klein & Kihlstrom, 1986) and tasks in which subjects create a mental image of themselves interacting with the noun (Karylowski & Buczek, 1984, Experiment 2; Lord, 1980, 1987; Maki & McCaul, 1985, Experiment 2; Pressley, Levin, Kuiper, Bryant, & Michener, 1982, Experiment 2). Even within a set of studies, different findings from the same population (e.g., people with ADHD) are obtained when the self-referential processing task is varied with regard to the specific format of the encoding question employed.

Yet another problem is that amount of familiarity with a task-referent (i.e., the person –self versus other – to whom the encoding task judgments are directed) can determine the type of memory system involved in task performance even when the task requirements nominally remain the same (e.g., Klein et al., 1992). For example, even within the context of SRE tasks comparing trait judgments of self and other (e.g., "Describes you? vs. "Describes Bob?"; for example, Bower & Gilligan, 1979; Kuiper & Rogers, 1979), one cannot assume that semantic trait-knowledge is being activated by task demands. Familiarity with the "other" plays a crucial role (for review of the evidence, see Klein & Loftus, 1993; Klein et al., 1992; Klein et al., 2008).

When the to-be-judged other is well-known or familiar, one can be reasonably assured that trait judgments are being made via access to semantic trait knowledge. By contrast, when the comparison other is one for whom familiarity is only partial, episodic recollections of the other's trait-relevant behaviors are more likely to play the major role in judgments of trait applicability (e.g., Klein & Loftus, 1993; Klein, Cosmides, Tooby, & Chance, 2002).

Thus, although there are some exceptions, a far more coherent picture of SRE research emerges when the findings are separated into those resulting from autobiographical tasks and those resulting from descriptive tasks. While this classification scheme does not serve as the sole explanation for the differential effects of these tasks on other-referent and noun recall, the order it introduced into a research literature that had appeared unpredictable can provide direction to the theoretical understanding of these phenomena.

The mechanisms mediating the effects of self-reference on memory

So, what causes the SRE? As reviewed, a large number of processes have been suggested over the years. However, as a result of a meta-analytic review of over 50 studies, two have emerged as the most likely contenders – the elaborative processing hypothesis and the organizational processing hypothesis (for review, see Klein & Loftus, 1988; Symons & Johnson, 1997).

The elaborative processing hypothesis

Perhaps because the SRE initially was demonstrated using the depth-of-processing methodology, most investigators explained the effect in terms of Craik and Tulving's (1975) elaborative processing model of memory facilitation (e.g., Brown, Keenan, & Potts, 1986; Keenan & Baillet, 1980; Kendzierski, 1980; Kuiper & Rogers, 1979; Rogers et al., 1977). Elaborative processing refers to operations that result in the encoding of information specific to an individual item (e.g., Craik, 1979; Einstein & Hunt, 1980; Klein & Kihlstrom, 1986). That is, elaborating a word entails the formation of multiple associations between it and extralist material in memory (e.g., Bellezza, Cheesman, & Reddy, 1977).

Elaborating the word "dance," for example, may involve encoding it along with information such as "taking ballet lessons" and "going to the senior prom," whereas the word "music" may prompt the encoding of information such as "buying a cd" and "playing the piano." The process of drawing on item-specific information in memory to embellish the encoded representation of a word benefits recall by creating multiple routes for retrieval; in addition, it supports inference-based reconstruction in case retrieval efforts fail (e.g., Anderson, 1983; Klein & Loftus, 1988).

According to the elaboration hypothesis, tasks that promote the best retention should be those that encourage subjects to engage in the greatest amount of trace elaboration during encoding (e.g., Anderson & Reder, 1979; Craik & Tulving, 1975). The recall superiority of self-referent over structural and semantic encodings thus may be interpreted as indicating that self-reference is superior to these tasks in its potential for creating an elaborate memory trace (e.g., Keenan & Baillet, 1980; Kendzierski, 1980; Rogers et al., 1977).

The organizational processing hypothesis

In 1986, Klein and Kihlstrom proposed that organization, rather than elaboration, may be responsible for the SRE. In contrast to elaborative processing, organizational processing results in the encoding of associations among list words by leading subjects to think about the stimulus words in relation to one another. This relational information can include word-to-word associations and associations that emerge when words share a common category label (e.g., Battig & Bellezza, 1979).

Thus, the words "dance" and "music" can be organized both as direct associates of one another and under the category label "things connected with parties." The process of organizing a list of words augments recall by establishing interitem associative paths in memory that can be used during retrieval (e.g., Srull, 1983) and category labels that can act as retrieval cues for category members (e.g., Tulving & Pearlstone, 1966).

Organizational processing can be assessed by examining the extent to which associated words are clustered during recall. A high degree of clustering is assumed to indicate the use of relational information as a basis for organizing stimulus words in memory (e.g., Hunt & Einstein, 1981). Klein and Kihlstrom found support for this hypothesis in a series of studies. Specifically, they showed that if self-reference tasks (autobiographical self-referential encoding of nouns – for example, body parts, a form of self-knowledge that William James, 1890, argued is central to one's self-concept) were compared with semantic tasks that also encouraged organization (e.g., requiring the same noun stimuli to be categorized as internal or external body parts), self and semantic tasks produced comparable recall and organization. Organization was assessed using a measure of category clustering, the details of which can be found in Klein and Kihlstrom (1986). Under these conditions, the self-referent recall advantage vanished.

The elaborative + organizational processing hypothesis

In a study designed specifically to clarify the respective contributions of elaboration and organization to self-referential recall, Klein and Loftus (1988) demonstrated that self-reference differs from comparison encoding tasks in that it establishes an encoded representation having *both* item-specific (i.e., elaborative) and relational (i.e., organizational) information. Whether this two-factor encoding ultimately is more memorable than encodings induced by comparison tasks, however, depends both on stimulus conditions and on the task chosen for comparison. Specifically, when stimulus material makes item-specific information salient (e.g., Hunt & Einstein, 1981), tasks promoting relational information will be most useful to recall. Accordingly, self-reference will be superior to an elaborative task, but not to an organizational task. When stimulus material draws attention to relational information (e.g., Hunt & Einstein, 1981), tasks inducing encoding of item-specific information will benefit recall the most; consequently, the relative effectiveness of comparison tasks will be reversed. In this instance, self-reference will be more facilitating than an organizational task, but not more facilitating than an elaborative task.

A conclusion to be drawn from these results is that the effects of self-reference on recall cannot be accounted for by a single type of processing: Both elaborative and organizational processes appear to be involved, but which will play the larger role in recall cannot be predicted without an understanding of the conditions that determine the relative importance of at encoding (Klein & Loftus, 1988; strong support for this conclusion comes from Symons & Johnson's, [1997], meta-analytic review).

A dual-process explanation of self-referent encoding has implications for understanding the manner in which information processed in relation to the self may be represented in memory. Considerable research has shown that a stimulus may be represented in memory by both item-specific and relational information (e.g., Begg, 1978; Einstein & Hunt, 1980), but the type of information encoded depends on the type of processing the stimulus receives. Because both elaborative and organizational processes appear to occur during self-referent encoding, the resulting memorial representation should incorporate both item-specific and relational information.

In sum, the elaborative/organizational dual process explanation has received wide support (e.g., Symons & Johnson, 1997) and appears a viable processing explanation regardless of whether traits (e.g., Klein & Kihlstrom, 1986, Experiment 1; Klein et al., 2011) or nouns (e.g., Burns, Burns, & Hwang, 2011; Klein & Loftus, 1988) serve as the to-be-remembered items.

CONCLUSION

In recent years, research involving the SRE has gradually shifted from identifying mechanism to employing the SRE as a research tool to examine the nature of the self and its relation to memory. Assumptions about underlying mechanisms producing the SRE have largely been left unstated and unstudied. This, in turn, has led to conceptual confusion and a lack of clarity about the meaning of effects obtained. Specifically, to what do data obtained using SRE tasks refer?

In this chapter we have highlighted several areas of consideration that should be embraced by anyone choosing to adopt the SRE paradigm as way of gaining insight into the functioning of self in a particular population (e.g., developmental, neurological, clinical, personality subtype, etc.). We offer, by way of conclusion, the following considerations that investigators should be aware of when using the paradigm:

1. It is important, when using the SRE, to test the self and its representation in memory, to be aware that different task variables (e.g., traits vs. nouns), task referents (e.g., self vs. other; self vs. semantic processing), and memory systems (e.g., semantic vs. episodic) may be involved in task performance. And, depending on the nature of the materials being used, a high level of self-referential recall, if obtained, can be due to elaborative, organizational, or both elaborative and organizational processing.

2. The type of memory systems that mediate the SRE will vary as a function of the nature of the self-referential task (e.g., "Descrribes you?" vs. "Autobiographical"). Accordingly, investigators drawing conclusions from the use of the SRE task must be aware of memory systems relevant to task performance. There is no single epistemological source of self-knowledge. Many neural systems can and do play a role. We have touched here on two forms of memory, but, as our review suggests, there are other systems that may come into play (e.g., imagery systems such as tasks asking participants to visually imagine the stimulus in relation to the self; e.g., Brown et al., 1986; Grilli & Glisky, 2010).

   Moreover, even within a type of memory, there can be multiple aspects of self-knowledge that are functionally independent and hence dissociable. For example, Klein and Lax (2010) have shown that semantic self-knowledge can be either factual or dispositional, and that these two forms or self-knowledge are dissociable.

3. The evidence accrued from the SRE paradigm has far more to say about memory systems than the self. Memory systems may contain various forms of knowledge that are self-relevant (e.g., traits such as "I am friendly," facts such as "I was born in New York," and events such as "I recall tripping over a stone during my morning jog"). Each of these epistemological sources of self is informative about neural representations of self-knowledge, but the degree to which such knowledge systems license statements about the ontological self – that is, the self of everyday conscious experience – is far less clear. It is important that investigators be cognizant of limitations in the type and scope of inferences they can make about the self from findings obtained with the SRE. Ultimately what carries as much importance

as the methods and techniques used to address the memorial representations of the epistemological self is the specificity with which the constructs we submit to experimentation capture the essence of what they are intended to describe (e.g., Uttal, 2001).

4. Finally, inferences about the type of memory involved in the *subsequent* recollection of a trait judgment do not necessarily license inferences about the memory systems involved in *initial* performance of the judgment. Specifically, while self-referential trait judgments typically reflect the operation of the semantic system of self-knowledge (e.g., Klein & Loftus, 1988; Klein, Loftus, & Burton, 1989; Klein et al., 1992), the mechanisms mediating the subsequent recall or recognition of those judgments (most often, but not always, episodically based) have, at best, a tenuous relation to the systems mediating the initial judgments. This point often is missed by individuals employing the self-reference paradigm as a means to draw inferences about the self.

REFERENCES

Aboud, F. (1980, June). Self referent memory for concrete and abstract personal adjectives. Paper presented at the meeting of the Canadian Psychological Association, Calgary, Alberta, Canada.

Agatstein, F. C., & Buchanan, D. B. (1984). Public and private self-consciousness and the recall of self-relevant information. *Personality and Social Psychology Bulletin, 10*, 314–325.

Anderson, J. R. (1983). A spreading activation theory of memory. *Journal of Verbal Learning and Verbal Behavior, 22*, 261–295.

Anderson, J. R., & Reder, L. M. (1979). An elaborative processing explanation of depth of processing. In L. S. Cermak and F. I. M. Craik (Eds.), *Levels of processing in human memory* (pp. 385–403). Hillsdale, NJ: Erlbaum.

Battig, W. F., & Bellezza, F. S. (1979). Organization and levels of processing. In C. R. Puff (Ed.), *Memory organization and structure* (pp. 321–346). New York: Academic Press.

Begg, I. (1978). Similarity and contrast in memory for relations. *Memory & Cognition, 6*, 509–517.

Bellezza, F. S. (1984). The self as a mnemonic device: The role of internal cues. *Journal of Personality and Social Psychology, 47*, 506–516.

Bellezza, F. S. (1986). Mental cues and verbal reports in learning. In G. H. Bower (Ed.), *The psychology of learning and motivation* (Vol. 20, pp. 237–273). New York: Academic Press.

Bellezza, F. S., Cheesman, F. L., & Reddy, B. G. (1977). Organization and semantic elaboration in free recall. *Journal of Experimental Psychology: Human Learning and Memory, 3*, 539–550.

Bower, G. H., & Gilligan, S. G. (1979). Remembering information related to one's self. *Journal of Research in Personality, 13*, 420–432.

Bradley, B., & Mathews, A. (1983). Negative self-schemata in clinical depression. *British Journal of Clinical Psychology, 22*, 173–181.

Brown, P., Keenan, J. M., & Potts, G. R. (1986). The self-reference effect with imagery encoding. *Journal of Personality and Social Psychology, 51*, 897–906.

Bruss, G. (1986). Categorization of orienting referents and the self-reference effect. Unpublished Masters Thesis, Illinois State University, Normal.

Bunge, M.A. (2010). *Matter and mind: A philosophical inquiry.* New York: Springer.

Burns, D. J., Burns, S. A., & Hwang, A. J. (2011). Adaptive memory: Determining the proximate mechanisms responsible for the memorial advantage of survival processing. *Journal of Experimental Psychology: Learning, Memory, and Cognition, 37*, 206–218.

Calkins, M. W. (1915). The self in scientific psychology. *Psychological Bulletin, 12*, 495–524.

Cermak, L. S. (1984). The episodic-semantic memory distinction in amnesia. In. L. R. Squire and N. Butters (Eds.), *Neuropsychology of memory* (pp. 45–54). New York: Guilford Press.

Chalmers, D. J. (1996). *The conscious mind: In search of a fundamental theory.* New York: Oxford University Press.

Chew, B. R. (1983). Selective recall of self- and other-referenced information. Unpublished doctoral dissertation, Harvard University, Cambridge.

Churchland, P. S. (1986). *Neurophilosophy: Toward a unified science of the mind-brain.* Cambridge, MA: MIT Press.

Conway, M. A., (2005). Memory and the self. *Journal of Memory and Language, 53*, 594–628.

Craik, F. I. M. (1979). Human memory. *Annual Review of Psychology, 30*, 63–102.

Craik, F. I. M., & Tulving, E. (1975). Depth of processing and the retention of words in episodic memory. *Journal of Experimental Psychology: General, 11*, 268–294.

Crispin, W, Smith, B. C., & Macdonald, C. (Eds.) (1998). *Knowing our own minds.* Oxford: Oxford University Press.

Dainton, B. (2008). *The phenomenal self*. New York: Oxford University Press.

Damasio, A. R. (1999). *The feeling of what happens: Body and emotion in the making of consciousness*. Orlando, FL: Harcourt, Inc.

Dennett, D. C. (1996). *Kinds of minds*. New York: Basic Books.

Earle, W. (1955). Objectivity: An essay on phenomenological ontology. New York: The Noonday Press.

Earle, W. E. (1972). *The autobiographical consciousness*. Chicago, IL: Quadrangle Books.

Eccles, J. C. (1994). *How the self controls its brain*. New York: Springer-Verlag.

Einstein, G. O., & Hunt, R. R. (1980). Levels of processing and organization: Additive effects of individual item and relational processing. *Journal of Experimental Psychology: Human Learning and Memory*, *6*, 588–598.

Ferguson, T. J., Rule, G. R., & Carlson, D. (1983). Memory for personally relevant information. *Journal of Personality and Social Psychology*, *44*, 251–261.

Foster, J. (1991). *The immaterial self*. New York: Routledge.

Foster, J. K., & Jelicic, M. (1999). *Memory: Systems, process, or function?* New York: Oxford University Press.

Friedman, A., & Pullyblank, J. (1982, November). Remembering information about oneself and others: The role of distinctiveness. Paper presented at meeting of the Psychonomic Society, Minneapolis, MN.

Furlong, E. J. (1951). *A study in memory*. New York: Thomas Nelson & Sons Ltd.

Ge, J., Gu, X., Ji, M., & Han, S. (2009). Neurocognitive processes of the religious leader in Christians. *Human Brain Mapping*, *30*, 4012–4024.

Gennaro, R. J. (1996). *Consciousness and self-consciousness*. Phildelphia, PA: John Benjamins Publishing Co.

Gergen, K. J. (1971). *The concept of self*. New York: Holt, Rinehart, & Winston, Inc.

Glisky, E. L., & Marguine, M. J. (2009). Semantic and self-referential processing of positive and negative trait adjectives in older adults. *Memory*, *17*, 144–157.

Greenwald, A. G. (1981). Self and memory. In G. H. Bower (Ed.), *The psychology of learning and motivation* (Vol. 15, pp. 201–236). New York: Academic Press.

Grilli, M. D., & Glisky, E. L. (2010). Self-imagining enhances recognition memory in memory-impaired individuals with neurological damage. *Neuropsychology*, *24*, 698–710.

Halpin, J. A., Puff, C. R., Mason, H. F., & Martson, S. P. (1984). Self-reference and incidental recall by children. *Bulletin of the Psychonomic Society*, *22*, 87–89.

Han, S., Gu, X., Mao, L., Ge, J., Wang, G., & Ma, Y. (2010). Neural substrates of self-referential processing in Chinese Buddhists. *Social, Cognitive & Affective Neuroscience*, *5*, 332–339.

Hare, J. H., Mellor, C., & Azmi, S. (2007). Episodic memory in adults with autistic spectrum disorders: Recall for self- versus other-experienced events. *Research in Developmental Disabilities*, *28*, 317–329.

Harvery, P-O., Lee, J., Horan, W. P., Ochsner, K., & Green, M. F. (2011). Do patients with schizophrenia benefit from a self-referential memory bias? *Schizophrenia Research*, *127*, 171–177.

Hasker, W. (1999). *The emergent self*. Ithaca, NY: Cornell University Press.

Henderson, H. A., Zahka, N. E., Kojkowski, N. M., Inge, A. P., Schwartz, C. B., Hileman, C. M., Coman, D. C., & Mundy, P. C. (2009). Self-referenced memory, social cognition, and symptom presentation in Autism. *Journal of Child Psychology and Psychiatry*, *50*, 853–861.

Higgins, E. T., & Bargh, J. A. (1987). Social cognition and social perception. *Annual Review of Psychology*, *38*, 369–425.

Hull, J. G., & Levy, A. S. (1979). The organizational functions of the self: An alternative to the Duval and Wicklund model of self-awareness. *Journal of Personality and Social Psychology*, *37*, 756–768.

Hunt, R. R., & Einstein, G. O. (1981). Relational and item-specific information in memory. *Journal of Verbal Learning and Verbal Behavior*, *20*, 497–514.

Husserl, E. (1964). *The phenomenology of internal time-consciousness*. Bloomington, IN: Indiana University Press.

Hyde, T. S., & Jenkins, J. J. (1973). Recall for words as a function of semantic, graphic and syntactic orienting tasks. *Journal of Verbal Learning and Verbal Behavior*, *12*, 471–480.

James, W. (1890). *Principles of psychology (Vol.1)*. New York: Henry Holt and Company.

James, W. (1909/1996). *A pluralistic universe*. Lincoln, NE: University of Nebraska Press.

Johnstone, H. W. (1970). *The problem of the self*. University Park, PA: The Pennsylvania State University Press.

Karylowski, J., & Buczek, M. (1984, August). Cognitive representation of self and others: Words and images. Paper presented at the 92nd Annual convention of the American Psychological Association, Toronto.

Katz, A. N. (1987). Self-reference in the encoding of creative-relevant traits. *Journal of Personality*, *55*, 97–120.

Keenan, J. M., & Baillet, S. D. (1980). Memory for personally and socially significant events. In R. S. Nickerson (Ed.), *Attention and performance* (Vol. 8, pp. 651–669). Hillsdale, NJ: Erlbaum.

Kendzierski, D. (1980). Self-schemata and scripts: The recall of self-referent and scriptal information. *Personality and Social Psychology Bulletin, 6,* 23–29.

Kihlstrom, J. F, Cantor, N., Albright, J. S., Chew, B. R., Klein, S. B., & Niedenthal, P. M. (1988). Information processing and the study of the self. In L. Berkowitz (Ed.), *Advances in experimental social psychology* (Vol. 21, pp. 145–177). New York: Academic Press.

Kihlstrom, J. F., & Klein, S. B. (1994). The self as a knowledge system. In R. S. Wyer and T. K. Srull (Eds.), *Handbook of social cognition (Vol 1), Basic processes* (pp. 153–208). Hillsdale, NJ: Erlbaum.

Klein, S. B. (2004). The cognitive neuroscience of knowing one's self. In M. A. Gazzaniga (Ed.), *The Cognitive Neurosciences III* (pp. 1007–1089). Cambridge, MA: MIT Press.

Klein, S. B. (2010). The self: As a construct in psychology and neuropsychological evidence for its multiplicity. *WIREs Cognitive Science, 1,* 172–183.

Klein, S. B. (2012a). The two selves: The self of conscious experience and its brain. In M. R. Leary and J. P. Tangney (Eds.), *Handbook of self and identity* (2nd ed.) (pp. 617–637). New York: Guilford Press.

Klein, S. B. (2012b). The self and its brain. *Social Cognition, 30,* 474–516.

Klein, S. B. (in press). *The two selves: Metaphysical commitments and functional independence.* New York, NY: Oxford University Press.

Klein, S. B., Cosmides, L., Tooby, J., & Chance, S. (2002). Decisions and the evolution of memory: Multiple systems, multiple functions. *Psychological Review, 109,* 306–329.

Klein, S. B., & Gangi, C. E. (2010). The multiplicity of self: Neuropsychological evidence and its implications for the self as a construct in psychological research. *The Year in Cognitive Neuroscience 2010: Annals of the New York Academy of Sciences, 1191,* 1–15.

Klein, S. B., German, T. P., Cosmides, L., & Gabriel, R. (2004). A theory of autobiographical memory: Necessary components and disorders resulting from their loss. *Social Cognition, 22,* 460–490.

Klein, S. B., & Kihlstrom, J. F. (1986). Elaboration, organization, and the self-reference effect in memory. *Journal of Experimental Psychology: General, 115,* 26–38.

Klein, S. B., & Lax, M. L. (2010). The unanticipated resilience of trait self-knowledge in the face of neural damage. *Memory, 18,* 918–948.

Klein, S. B., Lax, M. L., & Gangi, C. E. (2010). A call for an inclusive approach to the Social Cognitive Neurosciences. *Social Cognition, 28,* 747–755.

Klein, S. B., Lax, M. L., & Gangi, C. E. (2011). Memory and self-knowledge in young Adults with ADHD. *Self and Identity, 10,* 213–230.

Klein, S. B., & Loftus, J. (1988). The nature of self-referent encoding: The contributions of elaborative and organizational processes. *Journal of Personality and Social Psychology, 55,* 5–11.

Klein, S. B., & Loftus, J. (1993). The mental representation of trait and autobiographical knowledge about the self. In T. K. Srull and R. S. Wyer (Eds.), *Advances in social cognition* (Vol. 5, pp. 1–49). Hillsdale, NJ: Erlbaum.

Klein, S. B., Loftus, J., & Burton, H. A. (1989). Two self-reference effects: The importance of distinguishing between self-descriptiveness judgments and autobiographical retrieval in self-referent encoding. *Journal of Personality and Social Psychology, 56,* 853–865.

Klein, S. B., Loftus, J., & Kihlstrom, J. F. (2002). Memory and temporal experience: The effects of episodic memory loss on an amnesic patient's ability to remember the past and imagine the future. *Social Cognition, 20,* 353–379.

Klein, S. B., Loftus, J., Trafton, R. G., & Fuhrman, R. W. (1992). The use of exemplars and abstractions in trait judgments: A model of trait knowledge about the self and others. *Journal of Personality and Social Psychology, 63,* 739–753.

Klein, S. B., Robertson, T. E., & Delton, A. W. (2010). Facing the future: Memory as an evolved system for planning future acts. *Memory & Cognition, 38,* 13–22.

Klein, S. B., Robertson, T. E., & Delton, A. W. (2011). The future-orientation of memory: Planning as a key component mediating the high levels of recall found with Survival processing. *Memory, 19,* 121–139.

Klein, S. B., Robertson, T. E., Gangi, C. E., & Loftus, J. (2008). The functional independence of trait self-knowledge: Commentary on Sakaki (2007). *Memory, 16,* 556–565.

Kuiper, N. A., & Derry, P. A. (1982). Depressed and nondepressed content self-reference in mild depressives. *Journal of Personality, 50,* 67–80.

Kuiper, N. A., & Rogers, T. B. (1979). Encoding of personal information: Self–other differences. *Journal of Personality and Social Psychology, 37,* 499–514.

Lind, S., & Bowler, D. (2008). Episodic memory and autonoetic consciousness in Autistic spectrum disorders: The roles of self awareness, representational abilities and temporal cognition. In J. Boucher and D. Bowler (Eds.), *Memory in autism* (pp. 166–187). New York: Cambridge University Press.

Locke, J. (1731). *An essay concerning human understanding*. London: Edmund Parker (original work published 1690).

Lombardo, M. V., Chakrabarti, B., Bullmore, E. T., Sadek, S. A., Pasco, G., Wheelwright, S. J., Suckling, J., & Baron-Cohen, S. (2010). Atypical neural self-representation in Autism. *Brain, 133*, 611–624.

Lord, C. G. (1980). Schemas and images as memory aids: Two modes of processing social information. *Journal of Personality and Social Psychology, 38*, 257–269.

Lord, C. G. (1987). Imagining the self and others: Reply to Brown, Keenan, and Potts. *Journal of Personality and Social Psychology, 53*, 445–450.

Lowe, E. J. (1996). *Subjects of experience*. Cambridge: Cambridge University Press.

Lund, D. H. (2005). *The conscious self*. Amherst, NY: Humanity Books.

Madell, G. (1984). *The identity of the self*. Edinburgh: Edinburgh University Press.

Maki, R. H., & McCaul, K. D. (1985). The effects of self-reference versus other reference on the recall of traits and nouns. *Bulletin of the Psychonomic Society, 23*, 169–172.

Markus, H. (1977). Self-schemata and processing information about the self. *Journal of Personality and Social Psychology, 35*, 63–78.

McCaul, K. D., & Maki, R. H. (1984). Self-reference versus desirability ratings and memory for traits. *Journal of Personality and Social Psychology, 47*, 953–955.

Miall, D. S. (1986). Emotion and the self: The context of remembering. *The British Journal of Psychology, 77*, 389–397.

Mills, C. J. (1983). Sex-typing and self-schemata effects on memory and response latency. *Journal of Personality and Social Psychology, 45*, 163–172.

Metzinger, T. (2009). *The ego tunnel: The science of mind and the myth of the self*. New York: Basic Books.

Moscovitch, M., Yaschyshyn, T., Ziegler, M., & Nadel, L. (2000). Remote episodic memory and retrograde amnesia: Was Tulving right all along? In E. Tulving (Ed.), *Memory, consciousness, and the brain: The Tallinn conference* (pp. 331–345). Philadelphia, PA: Psychology Press.

Nagel, T. (1974). What is it like to be a bat? *Philosophical Review, 83*, 435–450.

Nasby, W. (1985). Private self-consciousness, articulation of the self-schema, and recognition memory for trait adjectives. *Journal of Personality and Social Psychology, 49*, 704–709.

Neisser, U. (1967). *Cognitive psychology*. New York: Appleton-Century-Crofts.

Neisser, U. (1988). Five kinds of self–knowledge. *Philosophical Psychology, 1*, 35–39.

Parkin, A. J. (1993). *Memory: Phenomena, experiment and theory*. Cambridge, MA: Blackwell.

Perner, J., & Ruffman, T. (1994). Episodic memory and autonoetic consciousness: Developmental evidence and a theory of childhood amnesia. *Journal of Experimental Child Psychology, 59*, 516–548.

Polanyi, M. (1967). *The tacit dimension*. Garden City, NY: Anchor Books.

Pressley, M., Levin, J. R., Kuiper, N. A., Bryant, S. L., & Michener, S. (1982). Mnemonic versus nonmnemonic vocabulary-learning strategies: Additional comparisons. *Journal of Educational Psychology, 74*, 693–707.

Rogers, T. B., Kuiper, N. A., & Kirker, W. S. (1977). Self-reference and the encoding of personal information. *Journal of Personality and Social Psychology, 35*, 677–688.

Rogers, T. B., Rogers, P. J., & Kuiper, N. A. (1979). Evidence for the self as a cognitive prototype: The "false alarms effect". *Personality and Social Psychology Bulletin, 5*, 53–56.

Rosenthal, D. M. (1986). Two concepts of consciousness. *Philosophical Studies, 49*, 329–359.

Ruby, P., Collette, F., Argembau, A. D., Peters, F., Degueldre, C., Balteau, E., Luxen, A., Maquet, P. & Salmon, E. (2009). Perspective taking to access self-personality: What's modified in Alzheimer's disease. *Neurobiology of Aging, 30*, 1637–1651.

Russell, B. (1912/1992). *The problems of philosophy*. Mineola, NY: Dover Publications.

Schechtman, M. (1996). *The constitution of selves*. Ithaca, NY: Cornell University Press.

Shoemaker, S., & Swinburne, R. (1984). *Personal identity*. Oxford: Basil Blackwell Ltd.

Slors, M. (2001). *The diachronic mind: An essay on personal identity, psychological continuity and the mind–body problem*. Boston, MA: Kluwer Academic Publishers.

Sorabji, R. (2006). *Self: Ancient and modern insights about individuality, life, and death*. Chicago, IL: The University of Chicago Press.

Srull, T. K. (1983). Organizational and retrieval processes in person memory: An examination of processing objectives, presentation format, and the possible role of self-generated retrieval cues. *Journal of Personality and Social Psychology, 44*, 1157–1170.

Strawson, G. (2009). *Selves*. New York: Oxford University Press.

Sui, J., & Zhu, Y. (2005). Five-year olds can show the self-reference advantage. *International Journal of Behavioral Development, 29*, 382–387.

Symons, C. S., & Johnson, B. T. (1997). The self-reference effect in memory: A meta-analysis. *Psychological Bulletin, 121*, 371–394.

Terrace, H. S., & Metcalfe, J. (Eds.) (2005). *The missing link in cognition: Origins of self-reflective consciousness.* New York: Oxford University Press.

Tulving, E. (1983). *Elements of episodic memory.* New York: Oxford University Press.

Tulving, E. (1985). Memory and consciousness. *Canadian Psychology/ Psychologie Canadienne, 26*, 1–12.

Tulving, E. (1993). What is episodic memory? *Current Directions in Psychological Science, 2*, 67–70.

Tulving, E., & Pearlstone, Z. (1966). Availability versus accessibility of information in memory for words. *Journal of Verbal Learning and Verbal Behavior, 5*, 381–391.

Tulving, E., & Schacter, D. L. (1990). Priming and human memory systems. *Science, 247*, 301–306.

Uttal, W. R. (2001). *The new phrenology.* Cambridge, MA: MIT Press.

Vierkant, T. (2003). *Is the self real?* London: Transaction Publishers.

Warren, M. W., Chattin, D., Thompson, D. D., & Tomsky, M. T. (1983). The effects of autobiographical elaboration on noun recall. *Memory & Cognition, 11*, 445–455.

Wheeler, M. A., Stuss, D. T., & Tulving, E. (1997). Toward a theory of episodic memory: The frontal lobes and autonoetic consciousness. *Psychological Bulletin, 121*, 331–354.

White, S. L. (1991). *The unity of the self.* Cambridge, MA: MIT Press.

Young, O. C. D., & Martin, M. (1981). Processing of information about self by neurotics. *British Journal of Clinical Psychology, 20*, 205–212.

Zahavi, D. (2005). *Subjectivity of selfhood: Investigating the first-person perspective.* Cambridge, MA: MIT Press.

Zhang, L., Zhou, T., Zhang, J., Liu, Z., Fan, J., & Zhu, Y. (2006). In search of the Chinese self: An fMRI study. *Science in China: Series C Life Sciences, 49*, 89–96.

Zhu, Y., Zhang, L., Fan, J., & Han, S. (2007). Neural basis of cultural influence on self-representation. *NeuroImage, 34*, 1310–1316.

16

Putting the Social Back into Human Memory

William Hirst, Alin Coman, and Dora Coman

Since their initial foray into the experimental study of human memory, psychologists have been perplexed about how to come to terms with the obvious influence social interactions can have on memory. Consider the widely disparate stances taken by some of the founding figures of experimental psychology. Wundt (1912/1973), for instance, despaired at the deeply socially encrusted nature of memory and felt that psychologists could not study it, at least experimentally. He assigned the study of memory to the realm of *Volkpyschologie*. Ebbinghaus (1885/1913), on the other hand, saw a possibility for an experimental psychology of memory, made tractable, he thought, by stripping away the influence that meaning, associations, and social interactions have on memory and studying what one reviewer of his book *Memory* referred to as its "raw material." Taking a different tack, Bartlett (1932) acknowledged the social nature of memory, but, in a move quite different from both Wundt's and Ebbinghaus's, insisted that psychologists both investigate memory experimentally and do so in a social context. Indeed, he thought that little would be learned about memory unless one explored it in the context in which it occurs. Finally, there was Vygotsky, who, like Bartlett, acknowledged the social – and,

in Vygotsky's case, historical – influences on memory (Vygotsky, 1972). He focused his efforts largely on understanding how these influences mediate memorizing and remembering.

This chapter is about recent research that has begun to unravel how to study social influences on memory. This research essentially seeks to put the social back in social cognition, to use the memorable title of a book published 16 years ago (Nye & Brower, 1996). To a large extent, while acknowledging that memory is socially influenced, since the mid-1950s, with the introduction of an information-processing approach to the study of memory, psychology has mainly followed the lead of Ebbinghaus. For those espousing this approach, the place for a study of social influences seemed, at best, a side-bar affair, especially if, as Johnson-Laird (1988) admirably and boldly stated, that theories of mental processes should be expressed in forms that can be modeled in a computer program. But this modeling tool has certain limitations. Computer programs do not have social lives, and they do not, by and large, interact with each other. In some ways, they seem the wrong medium through which to model mentation. In his classic articulation of the at-the-time budding field of cognitive psychology, Neisser (1967) assigned to cognitive psychologists the job of tracing the flow of information from input through the "information-processing machine" to output. Following the lead of philosophers advancing computational functionalism, he dismissed the importance of studying the hardware of the machine. And although he ended his book by discussing Bartlett, he did so without fully acknowledging the social concerns animating Bartlett's exploration of memory. To be sure, social influences could be viewed as retrieval cues or embedded in the schemata out of which memories were reconstructed, but what ultimately needed to be investigated were the structures of memory, the way memories were represented "in the head," and the processes that worked on these representations. A clear line was drawn between what was out there in the world and what took place in the mind. Psychologists, by and large, study the latter and treat the former merely as input into the system.

EXTENDED MIND AND DISTRIBUTED COGNITION

The computational functionalism driving Neisser's manifesto for a cognitive psychology now seems quaint, for at least two reasons. First, few would claim today that the hardware does not matter. But, more importantly, by insisting that the mind *is* a Turing machine, those adopting this approach seem blind, or at least, indifferent, to the social nature of humans. People interact with each other constantly, build communities, and have long histories of traditions and rituals. Sociologists, anthropologists, and other social scientists have long recognized that one cannot take the social out of the humans (e.g., Geertz, 1973). If people did not live in a social world, then, they would argue, human intelligence, linguistic facility, and mnemonic abilities would probably not be fully manifest. From this perspective, it

seems futile to build a psychology that does not acknowledge the importance of the social. Some recent work by philosophers of cognitive science seems to agree. These philosophers argue that mind must be extended beyond the surface of the skin, viewing cognition as distributed across a network of individuals and environment rather than resting within the head of an individual person.

If external resources, such as media, cultural institutions, or social networks continuously scaffold cognition, the argument goes, then scholars cannot easily separate the individual from these resources (Clark, 2010; Hutchins, 1995; Sutton, Harris, Keil, & Barnier, 2010; Wilson, 2005). Scaffolds are as much a part of the mind as what happens inside the head.

Consider Bateson's (1979) blind man navigating through the world with a cane. To explain the blind man's navigation, cognitive neuroscientists might investigate cortical activity and treat any input from the outside world in terms of cortical input. Some researchers might want to go beyond an exclusive focus on cortical activity and include in their explanations the origins of cortical inputs, for instance, the activation occurring at the nerve endings of the fingers holding the cane. The configuration of these nerve endings might be important, for instance, inasmuch as different configurations might produce different patterns of cortical input. A proponent of an extended mind would ask: Why not go beyond the surface of the skin and include the cane? Unquestionably, the nature of the cane – for instance, its rigidity – is as much a factor in the blind man's ease of navigation as the configuration of nerve endings or the processing in the cortex. There is no a priori reason to exclude the cane from explanations. For proponents of an extended mind, the most principled approach would include the cortex, the fingertips, and the cane.

In a similar way, those postulating an extended mind want to include external influence in their explanations (Wilson & Clark, 2009). Even the simple presence of a similar other can affect (specifically increase) the accessibility of memories (Shteynberg, 2010). Consider the conversations in which remembering often takes place (Hirst & Echterhoff, 2012). Although one can, in some instances, distinguish between the retrieval of a memory and its conversion into an expression of this memory, often in the form of some type of verbal communication (Tulving, 1983), in many instances, it is impossible to separate the memory from its expression (Barnier, Sutton, Harris, & Wilson, 2008; Echterhoff & Hirst, 2012). Jane's conversation with her mother about her date might differ in content from her conversation with her girlfriend about the same date. Jane may sometimes intentionally censor what she says to her mother, but in many instances, she may simply talk to her mother in a free-flowing manner, without any sense of censoring herself. The nuances of the ending of the date may simply not come to mind because that is not what her mother is interested in or asks her about. On the other hand, details about the end of the date may figure centrally in Jane's conversation with her girlfriend. These details may be what the girlfriend is interested in and what she asks Jane about. In her conversations, Jane is simply tuning her remembering to her audience. From this perspective, what is remembered is governed by what is communicated. Remembering is, if you like, communicating.

SCHEMATA

To the extent that psychological theories incorporated social influences into their modeling, they do so mainly by building on Bartlett's discussion of *schemata*, the organized representation of knowledge. According to Bartlett, memories grow out of schemata, and social influence acts on memorizing and remembering through schemata. Bartlett illustrated this point by discussing how the Swazis, a small group of Bantu who raise cattle, possessed

extraordinary memories for past cattle auctions, even though, when tested on other material, their memory seemed to be quite ordinary. The Swarzis's cattle schemata probably lead to the improved mnemonic performance. Moreover, as psychologists have repeatedly shown, these schemata do not simply buttress memories, as in the case of the Swazis, but can also distort them. In an early study, for instance, Allport and Postman (1947) showed that, after seeing a picture of a crowded subway, people will falsely remember that the black man in the picture was wielding a switch blade, when in truth it was a white man.

Wertsch (2002, 2008) has explored the schemata that communities possess, what he calls schematic narrative templates. He is interested in the way that they shape what community members remember about their collective, historical past. Wertsch has shown through careful interviewing, for instance, that Russians often render historical episodes employing the following template: 1) Russia is peaceful and does not interfere with others; (2) A foreign enemy treacherously attacks Russia without provocation; (3) Russia is almost fully defeated as it suffers from the enemy's attempts to destroy it as a civilization; (4) Through heroism, and against all odds, Russia and its people triumph and succeed in expelling the foreign enemy, thus justifying its status as a great nation. The Russian rendering of the Napoleonic invasion and defeat, for instance, nicely reflects this template. Other nations have different templates. For instance, as Wertsch also documented, the US has several, quite different templates, for example, "the mystique of Manifest Destiny" and the "reluctant hegemon."

SOCIAL INTERACTION

Schemata no doubt provide a means of understanding, at least in part, how social influences shape memory. They do not, however, provide the theoretical tools needed to address the insights of those espousing an extended mind. Schemata safely rest within the head. Those interested in the extended mind want to understand how others – and external objects – can scaffold remembering.

Sociologists have nicely articulated many of the social influences of material culture and social practices on memorizing and remembering, examining, for instance, memorials and commemorations (Olick & Robbins, 1998), or urban geography (Nora, 1992). In both instances, material artifacts – the physicality of the memorial, the parades that mark the commemoration, or the streets and buildings of the city – guide memorizing and remembering. In other instances, it is the social practices, such as the rituals of speeches and the placements of wreaths on Memorial Day, that serve as vehicles for shaping memory.

We want to focus here on an ephemeral social practice, that is, conversations about the past. We will take up the issue of social practices more generally toward the end of this chapter, but, at present, it is probably best to focus on a single, widespread means by which external influences can shape memory. Conversations are ephemeral social influences because they are gone as soon as they happen. When broadly conceived, so that one includes one-directional exchanges as well as dialogic ones, they are undoubtedly ubiquitous. Moreover, they are unquestionably social in nature. A conversational participant's interaction with another is guided by the social conventions surrounding conversations (Grice, 1975), by the social relationships among conversational participants, and by expectations and goals negotiated by the conversational participants. Clearly, their effect on memory is worth studying. In addressing the study of conversational remembering, we want to focus on three sets of questions:

1. How does conversational remembering differ from remembering in isolation? Does one remember more, less, and in either case, how does what is remembered differ from what might be remembered in isolation?

2. What is the effect of speaking about the past in a conversation on one's own memory? We include this question because what one says is determined in large part by the audience one is addressing. Consequently, although the effect is "internal" to the speaker, it is inevitably social, because what the speaker says is, in part, socially determined.

3. What is the effect of speaking about the past in a conversation on the memories of other conversational participants?

REMEMBERING WITHIN A CONVERSATION

Conversations are usually collaborative efforts, and, to a large extent, the remembering that occurs within a conversation can also be conceived as collaborative. To be sure, one participant in a conversation could intentionally mislead others or work to disrupt the successful retrieval of a memory, but in most instances, people work together to reconstruct the past.

Collaborative facilitation

As a collaborative effort, one might expect that more is remembered within a conversation than is remembered separately, what is often referred to as *collaborative facilitation*. And indeed, in studies contrasting the amount recalled as a group with how much people recall individually, collaborative facilitation is usually found (Meudell, Hitch, & Kirby, 2006). It obviously arises in part because not all the original material is equally memorable across participants, and hence, some of the participants may contribute to the group recounting something that would not appear in other members' recall. But there are other reasons as well.

Transactive memory
People will often divide a memory task among themselves so as to distribute the burden of memorizing and remembering,

thereby forming a *transactive memory system* (Wegner, 1987). Participants often divide responsibility according to perceived expertise. Transactive memory systems can be found in close relationships, work teams, and professional relationships (see Hollingshead & Brandon, 2003). For instance, because of their use of transactive memory systems, dating couples, which presumably have exquisite knowledge about each other, exhibit better aggregate memory than do pairs of unacquainted individuals (Hollingshead, 1998). When people know that information will be accessible at a future date, they appear not to make the same effort at memorizing the material than if they feel its future accessibility is not ensured. As a result, people will have more difficulty subsequently remembering studied information if they believe it will be available on the World Wide Web than if they believe that it will be erased as soon as it is read (Sparrow, Liu, & Wegner, 2011).

Cross-cueing

One might expect that what one person in a conversation says might cue the memory of another person, thereby offering an aid to memory that would not exist when remembering in isolation. Surprisingly, such cross-cueing is not easily observed (e.g., Meudell, Hitch, & Boyle, 1995). Experimenters, however, may have failed to uncover evidence for cross-cueing because it is masked by disruptions occurring while participants collaboratively remember rather than because it does not occur (Congleton & Rajaram, 2011).

Collaborative inhibition

Just because a group may remember more than an individual would remember in isolation, it does not follow that the group will remember all that individuals in the group are capable of remembering. That is, group recounting is not the sum of the individual capacities of the group members,

what is known as *collaborative inhibition*. The explanations for collaborative inhibition are many. It could, for instance, be attributed to social loafing or "free-riding." However, when personal accountability and motivation are manipulated to control for social loafing, collaborative inhibition still remains robust (Weldon, Blair, & Huebsch, 2000).

A more universally applicable explanation, the *retrieval disruption hypothesis*, asserts that collaborative inhibition occurs, at least in part, because one group member's pursuit of an effective retrieval strategy disrupts the use of retrieval strategies that may be more effective for other group members (Basden, Basden, Bryner, & Thomas, 1997). As a result, some group members may not be able to undertake their most effective retrieval strategy. In such an instance, they may recall less during the group recounting than they would if recalling by themselves.

Tests of retrieval disruption often contrast conditions in which the organizational representation of the to-be-remembered material is more or less likely to be shared across group members. The more organizational representations differ across participants, the more likely it is that different retrieval strategies will be effective for different participants, and, consequently, the more collaborative inhibition. On the other hand, with similar organizational representations across group members, collaborative inhibition should be diminished or disappear. When Finlay, Hitch, and Meudell (2000) ensured that the organizational structure was similar across group members, they failed to observe collaborative inhibition. Building on similar lines of reasoning, one would expect, and finds, that the size of the group matters (Basden, Basden, & Henry, 2000). Members of large groups are more likely to have diverse mnemonic representations than members of small groups. Moreover, groups of familiar individuals should be and are less likely to exhibit collaborative inhibition when recounting as a group than are unrelated individuals (e.g., Andersson, 2001).

In addition, same-group members should be more likely to have similar mnemonic representations than different-group members. Finally, Meade, Nokes, and Morrow (2009) contrasted collaborative remembering of scenarios involving the navigation of planes. Non-expert pilots exhibited the standard collaborative inhibition, whereas expert pilots recalling with other expert pilots produced a group recall score that was actually greater than the nominal score. Presumably, the expert pilots shared the same organization and knowledge about flying.

Selective remembering in a group recounting can also occur because group members are more likely to recollect aloud shared memories than unshared memories (Stasser & Titus, 1987). In order to document this *information sampling bias*, Stasser, Wittenbaum, and their colleagues taught participants about a political candidate and then assembled small groups to discuss with each other what they knew about the candidate. Whereas all participants in the group knew certain facts about the candidate, each participant also knew several unique facts, that is, facts that only they knew. Participants in the group recounting were more likely to fail to recall their uniquely held memories than their shared ones (for a review, see Wittenbaum & Park, 2001). As Stasser and colleagues reasoned (see Stasser & Titus, 1987), a group will fail to discuss an item only if all members fail to mention it. As a result, when memories are shared, there is a greater probability that they will be mentioned by at least one group member than when they are uniquely held (see Wittenbaum, Hollingshead, & Botero, 2004, for a review of alternative explanations).

Finally, selective remembering can arise because of audience tuning. Marsh (2007) has distinguished recalling from retelling. In a standard, laboratory-based recall experiment, participants are explicitly told to remember all that they can remember as accurately as possible. Marsh reserved the term *recall* for this activity. In everyday life, however, people may simply wish to retell a story about the past, without trying to be either accurate or complete. This *retelling* can be shaped by conversational goals. For instance, recollections for which the goal is to entertain contain fewer story events and more intrusions than factual retellings (Dudukovic, Marsh, & Tversky, 2004). Moreover, the entertaining stories are less accurate, more likely to be told in the present tense, contain more emotion words and fewer disfluencies (e.g., uhs) than factual retellings (Pasupathi, Stallworth, & Murdoch, 1998). It has also been shown that speakers conveyed more, particularly more novel and more elaborated, information to an attentive as opposed to a distracted listener (Pasupathi et al., 1998). Moreover, people will recount more details, such as everything involved in a trip to the doctors, when talking to a hypothetical Martian, who presumably knows little about how things work on Earth, than when talking to a peer, who presumably knows a lot more (Vandierendonck & Van Damme, 1988). Furthermore, a story told to peers contains more interpretations about the content of the story than if told to an experimenter, when participants largely stuck to the "facts" (Hyman, 1994). There is also experimental work establishing that when helping another identify a specific person among a group of individuals, people will emphasize the target's positive qualities if they know the listener likes the target, and the target's negative qualities if they know the speaker dislikes the target (Echterhoff, Higgins, & Levine, 2009; also see the chapter by Fisher, Schreiber Compo, Rivard, & Hirn, Chapter 31, this volume, on cognitive interviewing, which can serve as a means of overcoming the selectivity of remembering).

THE EFFECT OF SPEAKER ON SPEAKER'S MEMORY

Saying-is-believing effect

The way speakers tune to their audience can reshape the speakers' memory, a change known as *saying-is-believing* effect (Higgins & Rholes, 1978; for a review, see Echterhoff et al., 2009). In studies of this effect, participants are presented with a story in which a character is described in ambiguous terms ("Donald uses coupons, buys things on sale, avoids donating money or lending money to friends." Donald could, therefore, be labeled as either "thrifty" or "stingy"). Subsequently, they are told to describe Donald to an audience that either likes or dislikes him. The results reveal that participants described Donald as "thrifty" to the favorable audience and as "stingy" to the unfavorable audience. Importantly, in a final recall test, where participants are told to recall the *initial* description, they remember the character in a manner consistent with the tuned message. The participants will come to remember what they said to their audience rather than what they originally learned about Donald (Echterhoff et al., 2009).

An important facilitating factor for this memory bias is whether participants are motivated to create a *shared reality* with the audience. By shared reality scholars refer to the experienced commonality between one's own and others' representations and evaluations of the world (Echterhoff et al., 2009). To explore the relation between shared reality and the saying-is-believing effect, Echterhoff, Higgins, Kopietz, and Groll (2008) asked German participants to describe the target person to a Turkish audience (a minority out-group in Germany) or to a German audience. Both the Turkish audience and the German audience either liked the target or disliked him. Participants tuned their message to both the Turkish audience and to their German audience, thereby exhibiting audience tuning irrespective of the composition of the audience. However, whereas the Germans' tuning to the German audience restructured their memory, as measured in the final recall, no such restructuring was observed for the Turkish audience. A key difference between the two conditions was in the motive underlying audience tuning: on

the one hand, participants wanted to create a shared reality with a German in-group audience, while on the other hand they were complying with (politeness) norms with the Turkish out-group audience. This motivation is what created the conditions for the saying-is-believing effect in the German-audience condition.

Within individual retrieval induced forgetting (WIRIF)

Extant research has established that the act of retrieval – as when a speaker recounts to an audience a past event – not only strengthens the retrieved memories, but, in certain conditions, also results in the induced forgetting of related, but unmentioned, memories (for a review see, Anderson & Levy, 2009). In studies using this paradigm, participants are first asked to study category-exemplar pairs (e.g., fruit–apple, fruit–orange, clothes–dress, clothes–pants). Next, they receive selective practice through a stem completion task for half of the items from half of the categories (e.g., clothes–d____). Finally, in a cued recall task, the participants are asked to remember the initially presented word pairs. The retrieval practice phase creates three conditions: Rp+, items that receive retrieval practice (e.g., clothes–dress); Rp–, items that are not practiced, but are related to those practiced (e.g., clothes–pants); and Nrp, items that are not practiced, nor are they related to the practiced items (e.g. fruit–apple, fruit–orange). A practice effect occurs when Rp+ items are remembered better than Nrp items, whereas induced forgetting occurs when the recall proportion of Rp– items is smaller than that of Nrp items. The mechanism putatively responsible for the induced forgetting effect is inhibition: as one attempts to retrieve an item from memory, related items compete for activation, which triggers the inhibitory processes that result in subsequent forgetting of the competitor items (Anderson & Levy, 2009). To the extent that the rememberer in this paradigm can be considered a speaker, the research suggests that selective remembering can induce forgetting for unmentioned items related to what is remembered. Indeed, in studies in which the selective practice takes the form of a speaker selectively remembering within a conversation, retrieval induced forgetting (RIF) is clearly observed (Cuc, Koppel, & Hirst, 2007). Here the person remembering in the conversation can be viewed as a speaker, the one producing a recollection. Others in the conversation are listeners, attending to the speaker remembering. To be sure, as time passes in a conversation, a speaker can become a listener and vice versa. However, the utterances of an individual across the conversation can be viewed as tapping the effect of speakers on their own memory. The selective remembering of a participant in a conversation produces RIF to levels similar to or greater than what is found in more controlled studies (Cuc et al., 2007).

THE EFFECT OF SPEAKER ON LISTENER'S MEMORY

Social contagion

The extensive work on the postevent misinformation effect clearly demonstrates that speakers can implant memories into listeners, a phenomenon also known as *social contagion* (Loftus, 1979). In one set of experiments exploring social contagion, two participants study different versions of a story so that each version contains "misleading information," at least as far as the other participant is concerned. In the experimental condition, the two participants jointly remember the story in a conversation, while in the control condition, each participant remembers the story by herself. Finally, in both conditions, a final recognition or recall phase follows. Participants often falsely recognize the misleading information recounted by their conversational partner. One participant, in this case,

the person speaking the misleading information "contaminates" the other's memory. These findings have been replicated with different types of stimulus materials: stories (Loftus & Palmer, 1976), pictures (Wright, Self, & Justice, 2000), and videos (Gabbert, Memon, & Allan, 2003). The possibility of social contagion is particularly worrisome in situations where false memories have serious consequences, such as eyewitness testimony (Loftus, 1993).

Social contagion is commonly explored in situations when the information that the participants study is slightly different. In this way, establishing influence is straightforward: if an item uniquely presented to participant A emerges in the conversation, and further in participant B's recollection, then social contagion is said to occur. However, this class of situations does not take into account the fact that social contagion might take more nuanced forms. For example, when groups of individuals are exposed to the same event, each individual might form slightly different memories of the event. Could communicating with one another about the event result in a shared representation among the group members? Investigating already established groups (families of four members), Cuc, Manier, Ozuru, and Hirst (2006) found that joint remembering increased the overlap between the group members' memories of a story relative to a control condition. More importantly, the emerging mnemonic consensus was shaped by the dominant narrator – the family member who introduced the most units of information in the conversation. The dominant narrator need not be perceived as an expert in order for him or her to influence this shared representation of the past (Brown, Coman, & Hirst, 2009).

Socially shared retrieval-induced forgetting (SSRIF)

In the section discussing the influence a speaker can have on the speakers' memories, we reviewed evidence that selective remembering in a conversation leads to induced forgetting for the speaker. Does it also induce forgetting in the listener? Given what a speaker says, we can classify memories as Rp+ (stated by the speaker and attended to by the listener), Rp– (not mentioned by the speaker; for speaker, related to what she said; for listener, related to what the speaker said, but not to anything the listener said) and Nrp (not mentioned and unrelated to what anyone said; see Coman, Manier, & Hirst, 2009 for a more detailed classification). Will we find that listeners remember Rp– items worse than the Nrp items, a pattern Cuc et al. (2007) referred to as *socially shared retrieval-induced forgetting* (SSRIF)? A large number of studies have found just this pattern (for a review see Stone, Coman, Brown, Koppel, & Hirst, 2012). Cuc et al. (2007) argued that it emerges because listeners concurrently, but covertly, retrieve with the speaker. This concurrent, covert retrieval creates the conditions for listeners to experience similar retrieval-induced forgetting as the speakers.

In support of this claim, Cuc et al. (2007) found SSRIF when listeners monitored the speaker for accuracy, but not when they monitored for the fluidity with which the speaker recollected. The former presumably requires concurrent retrieval, whereas the latter may not. Following a similar line of reasoning, Koppel, Wohl, Meksin, and Hirst (2012) showed that SSRIF was reduced when listeners perceived a speaker as an expert rather than a poorly prepared non-expert, arguing that the listener trusts the expert and hence is inclined not to make the effort to monitor for accuracy. Koppel et al. (2013) also showed the reverse effect, that is, more SSRIF when listeners were warned that the speaker was untrustworthy (e.g., possessing a "hidden agenda"). Now listeners should be inclined to monitor for accuracy. Koppel et al. (2013) also assessed social contagion, studying both RIF and social contagion as within subject factors. They replicated the finding that social contagion increases if the source of the contagion is viewed as an expert

(e.g., Brown, Coman, & Hirst, 2009; Dodd & Bradshaw, 1980) and decreases when warned against (Echterhoff, Hirst, & Hussy, 2005; Echterhoff, Groll, & Hirst, 2007). The argument is that when a speaker is trusted, listeners do not make the effort to monitor for the source of a memory, and hence are susceptible to social contagion. When a speaker is not trusted, listeners will make the effort, thereby limiting social contagion. These findings speak to the complexity and impact of social influences on people's memory: With perceived expertise, social contagion increased, while SSRIF decreased. With a warning, social contagion decreased, while SSRIF increased.

Both WIRIF and SSRIF can be found for a wide range of stimulus materials and situations, including critical elements of a story (Stone, Barnier, Sutton, & Hirst, 2010), scientific material (Coman, Coman, & Hirst (2013); Koppel et al., 2013), emotional material (Barnier, Hung, & Conway, 2004; Coman, Manier, & Hirst, 2009;) and autobiographical memories (Coman, Manier, & Hirst, 2009; Stone, Barnier, Sutton, & Hirst, 2012). Laboratories other than Hirst's have also reported SSRIF (Barber & Mather, 2012).

MEMORY PROPAGATION: PRACTICE EFFECTS AND INDUCED FORGETTING

Conversations that people have with one another are rarely confined to a single exchange, at a specific time and place. In the real world, people experience an event and then repeatedly talk about the event with others. At an individual level, these repeated interactions will fundamentally shape what individuals remember and forget. At a larger social level, the repeated conversation could lead to a convergence among interacting individuals on a shared representation of the past.

Employing a social-interactionist methodology, Coman and Hirst (2012) examined how practice effects and RIF propagate through a small sequence of social interactions. They investigated how listening to a lecture on the legalization of euthanasia reshapes memories of learned material and whether the influence of the lecture propagates into a conversation and then through the conversation to a final recall test. In the experiment (see Figure 16.1), after an initial attitude assessment, participants studied arguments for and against legalization of euthanasia, which were grouped into categories, such as, for instance, scientific implications or legal implications (Study phase). Two arguments in each category were in favor of legalization, while the other two were against legalization. In a slideshow presentation, participants were then exposed to a person arguing for legalization of euthanasia, offering half of the arguments from half of the categories presented during the study phase (Person-Pro Practice Phase; all practiced arguments were in favor of euthanasia). This selective presentation created the three conditions necessary to observe induced forgetting (Rp+, Rp–, and Nrp). A cued recall test then followed (Pre-conversational recall). Two participants were then paired and asked to recount the arguments they had studied in the Study phase

(Conversational Recall phase). The pairs were made up so that participants had either similar attitudes toward the legalization of euthanasia (pro-pro, anti-anti), or dissimilar ones (pro-anti). Subsequent to the conversation, the participants received a final recall test (Post-conversational Recall) and a final attitude assessment.

By following the practice effects and induced forgetting effects triggered by Person-Pro in the pre-conversational recall, conversational recall, and post-conversational recall, Coman and Hirst sought to understand whether the effect of Person-Pro propagated through this small sequence of interactions. The results revealed some interesting findings, chief amongst which were:

1 Practice effects and SSRIF can occur even for a one-directional interaction, such as a Powerpoint presentation, in that Person-Pro induced forgetting as assessed in participants' pre-conversational recall, regardless of participants' attitudes toward the legalization of euthanasia;

2 The practice effects and SSRIF induced by Person-Pro propagated in subsequent conversations between similar (but not dissimilar) others and, through the conversation, influenced what was subsequently remembered in the final memory test; and

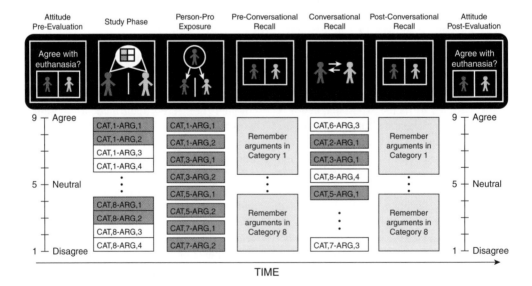

Figure 16.1 Phases of the experimental procedure in Coman and Hirst (2012).

3 Practice effects and SSRIF led to increased mnemonic convergence between the two participants' memories, as assessed by the overlap in their memories in the Post-conversational recall relative to the Pre-conversational recall.

Coman and Hirst (2012) examined a small sequence of social interactions between two people, but as mentioned earlier, our social worlds involve much more complex interactions. Coman, Kolling, Lewis, and Hirst (2012) extended these empirical findings to large networks of individuals with multiple interactions by using agent-based simulations (Axelrod, 1997; Epstein, 2006). This class of computer simulations is based on the idea that macro-scale complex dynamics could be understood as emergent phenomena that grow out of small-scale local interactions among autonomous agents. The simulation is designed to model artificial societies composed of agents that correspond to human societies composed of individuals. The model requires the specification of: (1) agent characteristics (e.g., agent's memory; (2) agent's interactions (e.g., networks of conversations among agents); and (3) interaction outcomes, (e.g., how agents influence one another following communication between them). Subsequent to the specification of these features, agents are allowed to interact with one another with the purpose of understanding the emergent properties of the system. For example, by employing Agent-Based Simulations (ABM), one could understand the emergence of collective violence (Lim, Metzler, & Bar-Yam, 2007; Epstein, 2006) and propagation of information (Watts, 2004). Following this methodology, Coman et al.'s strategy was to extract the principles observed in their empirical data (Coman & Hirst, 2012) and to implement these principles in ABMs.

With this in mind, Coman et al. (2012) built an ABM in which a large network of agents first "studied" material and "encoded" it in memory, then listened to Person-Pro's arguments and then "communicated" to one another repeatedly. The study phase

set the level of initial activation for the agent's memory. Based on the empirical data described above, this study phase did not lead to a similar representation across agents. Coman et al. then explored whether the conditions under which subsequent agent interactions produced convergence. Interaction, either with Person-Pro or with other agents, increased the activation for items recalled during the interaction and decreased activation for other items, with a greater decrease for those more closely related to recalled items. This differential decrease captured the induced forgetting effect. Coman et al. based activation updates on values obtained in their empirical study (Coman & Hirst, 2012). We found that 1) community size and number of conversations among agents impact convergence, such that smaller networks reach greater convergence with fewer conversations compared with larger networks, and 2) the conversational network structure is influences the degree of convergence, with denser networks reaching convergence faster than less dense ones (Coman et al., 2012). This framework is the first that we know of in which psychologically grounded memory models are implemented in ABMs to explore the dynamics of knowledge diffusion, with the goal of understanding the significant parameters driving the formation of shared representations.

Collective memory

Although we have so far framed our discussion in terms of the effect of communication on memory, we could easily have framed it in terms of the formation and maintenance of collective memory. Since Halbwachs (1950), the study of collective memory has mainly been undertaken by sociologists, historians, political scientists, and anthropologists. Their interest is understandable, since, just as autobiographical memories can ground individual identity, so can collective memories serve as the foundation of the identity of a community, be it as small as a couple or as large as a nation. A major reason why psychologists have rarely figured in the discussion is that social scientists, such as sociologists, tend to be interested in the way society promotes and maintains collective memory, whereas psychologists are interested in the individual mechanisms underlying the formation and promotion of collective memories (see Hirst & Manier, 2008; Olick & Robbins, 1998). This difference in emphasis can lead to different definitions of collective memories: They are either the sociologically oriented "patterns of publicly available symbols" (Olick & Robbins, 1998) or the psychologically oriented "memories shared across individuals in a community" (Hirst & Manier, 2008). Only recently have the two different perspectives attempted to find a common ground (DiMaggio, 1997; Sutton et al., 2010; see Hirst & Fineberg, 2012, for an application to Belgian collective memory).

The literature we have reviewed so far indicates that practice effects, social contagion, and retrieval-induced forgetting all have the ability to shape not just individual memory, but to promote convergence across individuals onto a shared representation of the past. They act on both speaker and listener in similar ways, and as a result, shape the memories of speaker and listener in similar ways. Social contagion, for instance, implants a memory held by the speaker into the listener, thereby producing a shared memory. And retrieval-induced forgetting leads both speaker and listener to forget in particular the unmentioned memories that are closely related to memories that have been recalled.

Practice effects, social contagion, and retrieval-induced forgetting, then, may be representative of the cognitive mechanisms underlying the formation of a collective memory. These claims about the formation of collective memory, of course, begin at the micro-level, with the individual processes governing individual memory performance. Through the interplay among practice effects,

social contagion, and retrieval-induced forgetting, socially interacting individuals come to share their renderings of the past. But what about macro-level discussions of collective memory? Social scientists have, of course, had a great deal to say about the characteristics of, for instance, national collective memories, or historical memories. To the extent that psychology is employed to characterize collective memory, the effort usually borrows from the psychodynamic lexicon. Thus, there are extensive discussions about how societies "repress" past traumas (e.g., Caruth, 1996). The use of cognitive vocabulary is much more limited. Cognitive psychologists, nevertheless, have made some efforts to characterize collective memory at a macro-level. Let us provide three examples.

Generation effects

As Mannheim (1952) noted in his studies of the sociology of knowledge, each generation possesses a distinctive set of memories particular to that generation. That is not to say that other generations might not have similar memories, but the memories of one generation are more accessible to members for that generation than they are to members of other generations. Schuman and Scott (1989) provided a rigorous methodology for specifying generational memories. They asked participants to list the three most important historical memories in, for instance, the last 50 years. Different generations provided different memories, with each generation providing memories, in the main, of public events that figured in late adolescence or early adult life. For instance, those in their late teens or early twenties during the Korean War tended to list it in their top three, while younger and older participants tended not to. Similarly, for those in their late teens and early twenties during the late 1960s and early 1970s, the Vietnam War figured centrally. On the other hand, it should be stressed that some memories of public events reach across generations, for example, World War II (Koppel et al., 2013). Why some memories are generationally specific, while others are not remains unclear at present.

As to the generationally specific memory, a number of cognitive explanations exist. By and large, they build on the cognitive explanations offered for the reminiscence bump (Rathbone, Moulin, & Conway, 2008). This is a similar phenomenon to the generation effect, but deals with autobiographical memories rather than memories of public events. Thus, if asked to say the first autobiographical memory that comes to mind when given a word to free-associate from, people will tend to remember events from their late adolescence and early adulthood: their first day at college, their wedding, their graduation from high school. Some researchers claim that these autobiographical events are encoded in a more robust, detailed, or elaborate manner, perhaps because they are distinctive or important for identity development. Similarly, Belli (1998) has argued that public events during this time are better and more elaborately encoded, for similar reasons, and hence figure more centrally in any list of "important public events." However, in a study of event memories of the terrorist attack of September 11, 2001, Meksin and Hirst (2005) reported that those who were in their late adolescence or early adulthood actually had worse memories for the event itself (e.g., the names of the airlines involved) one week, 11 months, and 35 months after the attack than did respondents over 35 years of age. These results suggest that the memory held by the younger generation may have changed over time in a manner that allows them to go from being less memorable to being more memorable, less accessible to more accessible. The generality of this pattern is difficult to determine, however, inasmuch as it has only been examined in the context of 9/11.

Dating public memories

People will often date events in their private lives using public events as landmarks (e.g., "I went to Europe before the war broke out."). Brown et al. (2009) have explored this phenomenon by first asking participants to recall a specific autobiographical memory that words such as *automobile*, *ball*, and *river* brought to mind. They then asked participants to date the event (day and year) and to verbalize their thoughts as they were completing the task. Brown et al. coded these protocols as to whether they referred to personal events (e.g., "around when I got married"), to historical events (e.g., "after the war"), or to pop, sports, or cultural events (e.g., "after the Horowitz Carnegie Hall concert"). If autobiographical events were dated by referring to historical events, Brown et al. said that participants were "living in history." Despite testing participants from many countries, they observed "living in history" in only two of their samples: Bosnians and Turks living in Izmir, following a terrible earthquake. People seem only to employ historical events as temporal landmarks for autobiographical memories when the events are disruptive to daily life. Even something as significant as the terrorist attack of September 11 did not serve as a temporal landmark for New Yorkers. Personal and public timelines did not intersect in most instances.

Flashbulb memories

Brown et al.'s (2009) research focuses on dating events on a timeline. But there is a class of events where the public and private do appear to intersect, if not when dating an event, then at least in terms of the connection people feel to the public event. The terrorist attack of 9/11 is one of these, but there are a host of others: the assassination of John F. Kennedy, the death of Princess Diana, the resignation of Margaret Thatcher (see Brown & Kulik, 1977; Kvavilashvili, Mirani, Schlagman, & Kornbrot, 2003; Hirst et al., 2009). These are public events, but people remember vividly and confidently the circumstances in which they learned of the event, the latter often referred to as *flashbulb memories*. Flashbulb memories are not formed for all public events of consequence.

We dare say that few Americans have flash-bulb memories of learning of the nomination of Samuel Alito for a Justice of the Supreme Court, but his appointment will have long and dramatic consequences. Nevertheless, for some public events – the characteristics of which are only beginning to be determined – the private and the public intersects (see Luminet & Curci, 2009).

Although early studies of flashbulb memories focused on the characteristics and accuracy of the autobiographical memories formed of reception events, more recent studies have turned to memory for the events themselves. What are the memories partici-pants have of the event? If there is a consen-sual memory, then the study of the memory of these events becomes the study of the formation of collective memories. Are these memories accurate? What do people remem-ber about these events? How can we predict what they would remember?

Although the study of memory for public events is in its infancy, one clear observa-tion is emerging. Although these events are usually of extraordinary historical impor-tance, they are not remembered accurately – and what is remembered reflects the social practices surrounding the event more than anything intrinsically memorable about the event. Consider the terrorist attack of 9/11. In a three-year follow-up study, Hirst et al. (2009) found that participants from across the United States showed a dramatic decline in event memory from the first week after the attack to 11 and 35 months after the attack. After a week, participants answered questions about the facts of 9/11 accurately 88 percent of the time, on average, but only 77 percent of the time after 11 months. Performance did not decline between 11 and 35 months.

What people remembered reflected how the event was told through public media. Participants remembered the number of planes and the crash sites, details of the attack that appear in almost every render-ing of the story. They failed to remember the names of the airlines and the location of President Bush, things often not men-tioned in accounts of the attack. For instance, the extensive Wikipedia account of the "September 11 attacks" does not mention that Bush was in Florida at the time of the attacks (http://en.wikipedia.org/wiki/September_11_attacks). Moreover, whereas many written summaries of the event will name the flights, in order to avoid confusion and keep the various planes involved distinct, brief summaries do not. Accounts designed for children clearly state that there were four planes and that the planes crashed into the World Trade Center, the Pentagon, and "a field," but no mention is made of the airlines names (nor the location of the President; see, for instance, www.classbrain.com/artfree/publish/cat_index_17.shtml).

There is a close correspondence between how much the media covers a public event and how well it is remembered. As we noted, memory for the facts of 9/11 seemed to asymptote after 11 months: Memories *generally* did not get better, but they also did not get worse. This pattern is in marked contrast to the pattern of forgetting observed for the facts about the Challenger explo-sion. Bohannon and Symons (1992) reported that memory here tended to decline steadily over a three-year period. Hirst et al. (2009) contrasted the rate of forgetting of the facts of these two events with the coverage of the events, as tracked by Lexus/Nexus. A decline in press coverage nicely predicts the rate of forgetting.

A clear example of the effect of media is what Hirst et al. (2009) dubbed the *Michael Moore effect*. In Moore's film about the terrorist attack, *Fahrenheit 911*, Bush was shown sitting in a Florida elementary school classroom reading to the attendant students *My Pet Goat*, despite having been told of the attack by an aide. In the Hirst et al. survey, memory for Bush's location went from 60 percent accuracy after 11 months to 91 percent after 35 months for those who saw the film.

These observations nicely illustrate why one must view memory as "extending beyond the surface of the skin," as we suggested it must be in the introduction to this chapter. What people remember about public events, such as 9/11, appears to have less to do with the events' intrinsic characteristics, such as their emotional salience, than the social practices that govern whether a memory will be continually rehearsed. As a consequence, what people remember is as much a reflection of what happens in the world as it is about internal mechanisms.

shape and reshape memories in a way that promotes the formation of collective memories. Individual memory, of course, does not have to work this way. Computer memories, for instance, do not have this characteristic flexibility. Yet the seeming flaws of human memory – what makes computers seem superior to many of us – are just those facets of memory that allow for the formation and maintenance of collective memories (Hirst & Echterhoff, 2012). Only by focusing on the social aspects of memory could one begin to understand the virtues of mnemonic flaws.

CONCLUSION

We began this chapter by asking how psychologists should study social influences of memory: Resign themselves to the complexity of the topic and avoid studying them, control for them, or investigate them head on? The chapter could be viewed as an argument for studying them "head on." Indeed, it has strongly asserted that without understanding social influences we will never understand why people remember what they do, why people come to share similar renderings of the past, and why human memory possesses the flaws that undoubtedly characterize it. These so-called flaws can take on different meaning when they are viewed as means of promoting collective memories. A number of evolutionary psychologists have stressed how human behavior and cognition, such as their complex syntax (Hurford, 2011) and their high level of intelligence (Humphrey, 1976), have been shaped by the need of humans to adapt to complex social situations. The contribution of practice effects, social contagion, and induced forgetting in promoting the formation of collective memory suggests that we might add memory to this list of social adaptations (see Hirst, 2010; Hirst & Brown, 2012): The mechanisms of human memory are exquisitely tuned to social influences so that others can

REFERENCES

Allport, G. W., & Postman, L. (1947). *The psychology of rumor*. New York: Henry Holt.

Anderson, M. C., & Levy, B. J. (2007). Theoretical issues in inhibition: Insights from research on human memory. In D. S. Gorfein and C. M. MacLeod (Eds.), *Inhibition in cognition* (pp. 81–102). Washington, DC: American Psychological Association.

Anderson, M. C., & Spellman, B. A. (1995). On the status of inhibitory mechanisms in cognition: Memory retrieval as a model case. *Psychological Review, 102,* 68–100.

Andersson, J. (2001). Net effect of memory collaboration: How is collaboration affected by factors such as friendship, gender, and age? *Scandinavian Journal of Psycholology, 42,* 367–375.

Axelrod, R. (1997). *The complexity of cooperation: Agent-based models of competition and collaboration*. Princeton, NJ: Princeton University Press.

Barber, S. J., & Mather, M. (2012). Forgetting in context: The effects of age, emotion, and social factors on retrieval induced forgetting. *Memory & Cognition, 40,* 874–888.

Barnier, A. J., Hung, L., & Conway, M. A. (2004). Retrieval-induced forgetting of emotional and unemotional autobiographical memories. *Cognition & Emotion, 18,* 457–477.

Barnier, A. J., Sutton, J., Harris, C. B., & Wilson, R. A. (2008). A conceptual and empirical framework for the social distribution of cognition: The case of memory. *Cognitive Systems Research, 9,* 33–51.

Bartlett, F. (1932). *Remembering: A study in experimental and social psychology*. New York: Cambridge University Press.

Basden, B. H., Basden, D. R., Bryner, S., & Thomas, R. L. III. (1997). A comparison of group and individual remembering: Does collaboration disrupt retrieval strategies? *Journal of Experimental Psychology: Learning, Memory & Cognition, 23,* 1176–1189.

Basden, B. H., Basden, D. R., & Henry, S. (2000). Cost and benefits of collaborative remembering. *Applied Cognitive Psychology, 14,* 497–507.

Bateson, G. (1979). *Mind and nature: A necessary unity (Advances in systems theory, complexity, and the human sciences)*. New Jersey, NJ: Hampton Press.

Belli, R. F. (1998). The structure of autobiographical memory and the event history calendar: Potential improvements in the quality of retrospective reports in surveys. *Memory, 6,* 383–406.

Block, N., & Fodor, J. (1972). What psychological states are not. *Philosophical Review, 81*(2), 159–181.

Bohannon, J. N., & Symons, V. L. (1992). Flashbulb memories: Confidence, consistency, and quantity. In E. Winograd and U. Neisser (Eds.), *Affect and accuracy in recall: Studies of "flashbulb" memories* (pp. 65–91). New York: Cambridge University Press.

Brown, A. D., Coman, A., & Hirst, W. (2009). The role of narratorship and expertise in social remembering, *Social Psychology, 40,* 113–129.

Brown, N. R., Lee, P. J., Krsiak, M., Conrad, F. G., Havelka , J., & Reddon, J. R. (2009). Living in history: How war, terrorism, and natural disaster affect the organization of autobiographical memory. *Psychological Science, 20,* 399–405.

Brown, R., & Kulik, J. (1977). "Flashbulb memories". *Cognition, 5*(1), 73–99.

Caruth, C. (1996). *Unexplained experience: Trauma, narrative, and history*. Baltimore, MD: Johns Hopkins University Press.

Casasanto, D. (2009). Embodiment of abstract concepts: Good and bad in right- and left-handers. *Journal of Experimental Psychology: General, 138*(3), 351–367.

Charness, N. (1976). Memory for chess positions: Resistance to interference. *Journal of Experimental Psychology: Human, Learning & Memory, 2*(6), 641–653.

Clark, A. (2010). *Supersizing the mind: Embodiment, action, and cognitive extension*. New York: Oxford University Press.

Coman, A., & Hirst, W. (2012). Cognition through a social network: the propagation of practice and induced forgetting effects. *Journal of Experimental Psychology: General*. In press.

Coman, D., Coman, A., & Hirst, W. (2013). Memory accessibility and treatment decision making for significant others. The role of socially shared retrieval induced forgetting. In Frontiers in Behavioral Neuroscience, 7, 72. doi: 10.3389.

Coman, A. Kolling, A. Lewis, M., & Hirst, W. (2012). Mnemonic convergence: from empirical data to large-scale dynamics. *Lectures in Computer Science, 7227,* 256–265.

Coman, A., Manier, D., & Hirst, W. (2009). Forgetting the unforgettable through conversation: socially-shared retrieval-induced forgetting of September 11 memories. *Psychological Science, 20,* 627–633.

Congleton, A., & Rajaram, S. (2011). The influence of learning methods: Prior repeated retrieval enchances retrieval organization, abolishes collaborative inhibition, and promotes post-collaborative memory. *Journal of Experimental Psychology: General, 140,* 535–551.

Cuc, A., Koppel, J., & Hirst, W. (2007). Silence is not golden: A case for socially-shared retrieval-induced forgetting. *Psychological Science, 18,* 727–733.

Cuc, A., Ozuru, Y., Manier, D., & Hirst, W. (2006). On the formation of collective memories: The role of a dominant narrator. *Memory & Cognition, 34,* 752–762.

DiMaggio, P. (1997). Culture and cognition. *Annual Review of Sociology, 23,* 263–287.

Dodd, D. H., & Bradshaw, J. M. (1980). Leading questions and memory: Pragmatic constraints. *Journal of Verbal Learning and Verbal Behavior, 19,* 695–704.

Dudukovic, N. M., Marsh, E. J., & Tversky, B. (2004). Telling a story or telling it straight: The effects of entertaining versus accurate retellings on memory. *Applied Cognitive Psychology, 18,* 125–143.

Ebbinghaus, H. (1913). *Memory: A contribution to experimental psychology*. New York: Teachers College, Columbia University (original work published in 1885).

Echterhoff, G., Groll, S., & Hirst, W. (2007). Tainted truth: Overcorrection for misinformation influence on eyewitness memory. *Social Cognition, 25,* 367–409.

Echterhoff, G., Higgins, E. T., Kopietz, R., & Groll, S. (2008). How communication goals determine when audience tuning biases memory. *Journal of Experimental Psychology: General, 137,* 3–21.

Echterhoff, G., Higgins, E. T., & Levine, J. M. (2009). Shared reality: Experiencing commonality with others' inner states about the world. *Perspectives on Psychological Science, 4,* 496–521.

Echterhoff, G., Hirst, W., & Hussy, W. (2005). How eyewitnesses resist misinformation: Social postwarnings and the monitoring of memory characteristics. *Memory & Cognition, 30,* 770–782.

Epstein, J. (2006). *Generative social science: Studies in agent-based computational modeling.* Princeton, NJ: Princeton University Press.

Finlay, F., Hitch, G. J., & Meudell, P. R. (2000). Mutual inhibition in collaborative recall: Evidence for a retrieval-based account. *Journal of Experimental Psychology: Learning, Memory, and Cognition, 26,* 1556–1567.

Flavell, J. H. (1987). Speculation about the nature and development of metacognition. In F. Weinert and R. Kluwe (Eds.), *Metacognition, motivation, and understanding* (pp. 21–29). Hillsdale, NJ: Lawrence Erlbaum.

Gabbert, F., Memon, A., & Allan, K. (2003). Memory conformity: Can eyewitnesses influence each other's memories for an event? *Applied Cognitive Psychology, 17,* 533–544.

Geertz, C. (1973). *The interpretation of culture: Selected essays.* New York: Basic Books.

Grice, P. (1975). Logic and conversation. In P. Cole and J. Morgan (Eds.), *Syntax and semantics* (Vol 3). New York: Academic Press.

Halbwachs, M. (1950). *Collective memory* (F. J. Ditter, V. Y. Ditter, Trans). New York: Harper & Row.

Higgins, E. T., & Rholes, W. S. (1978). Saying is believing: Effects of message modification on memory and liking for the person described. *Journal of Experimental Social Psychology, 14,* 363–378.

Hirst, W. (2010). A virtue of memory: The contribution of mnemonic malleability to collective memory. In P. A. Reuter-Lorenz, K. Baynes, G. R. Mangun and E. A. Phelps (Eds.), *The cognitive neuroscience of the mind: A tribute to Michael. S. Gazzaniga* (pp. 139–154). Cambridge, MA: MIT Press.

Hirst, W., & Brown, A. (2012). On the virtues of an unreliable memory: Its role in grounding sociality. In G. Semin and G. Echterhoff (Eds.), *Grounding sociality: Neurons, minds, and culture,* (pp. 95–114). New York: Psychology Press.

Hirst, W., & Echterhoff, G. (2012). Remembering in conversations: The social sharing and reshaping of memory. *Annual Review of Psychology, 63,* 55–79.

Hirst, W., & Fineberg, I. A. (2012). Psychological perspective on collective memory and national identity: The Belgian case. *Memory Studies,* in press.

Hirst W., & Manier D. (2008). Towards a psychology of collective memory. *Memory, 16,* 183–200.

Hirst, W., Phelps, E. A., Buckner, R. L., Budson, A. E., Cuc, A., et al. (2009). Long-term retention of the terrorist attack of September 11: Flashbulb

memories, event memories, and the factors that influence their retention. *Journal of Experimental Psychology: General, 138,* 161–176.

Hollingshead, A. B. (1998). Communication, learning, and retrieval in transactive memory systems. *Journal of Personality & Social Psychology, 34,* 423–442.

Hollingshead, A. B., & Brandon, D. P. (2003). Potential benefits of communication in transactive memory systems. *Human Communication Research, 29,* 607–615.

Humphrey, N. K. (1976). The social function of intellect. In P. P. G. Bateson and R. A. Hinde (Eds.), *Growing points in ethology.* New York: Cambridge University Press.

Hurford, J. M. (2011). *The origins of grammar.* New York: Oxford University Press.

Hutchins, E. (1995). *Cognition in the wild.* Cambridge, MA: MIT Press.

Hyman, I. E. (1994). Conversational remembering: Story telling with a peer versus for an experimenter. *Applied Cognitive Psychology, 8,* 49–66.

Johnson-Laird, P. (1987). How could consciousness arise from the computations of the brain? In C. Blakemore and S. Greenfield (Eds.), *Mindwaves.* Oxford: Basil Blackwell.

Koessler, S., Engler, H., Riether, C., & Kissler, J. (2009). No retrieval induced forgetting under stress. *Psychological Science, 20,* 1356–1363.

Koppel, J., Wohl, D., Meksin, R., & Hirst, W. (2013). The role of expertise and resistance in moderating socially shared retrieval-induced forgetting. *Social Cognition,* under review.

Kvavilashvili, L., Mirani, J., Schlagman, S., & Kornbrot, D. (2003). Comparing flashbulb memories of September 11 and the death of Princess Diana: Effects of time delays and nationality. *Applied Cognitive Psychology, 17,* 1017–1031.

Lim, M., Metzler, R., & Bar-Yam, Y. (2007). Global pattern formation and ethnic/cultural violence. *Science, 317*(5844), 1540–1544.

Lindsay, D. S., Hagen, L., Read, J. D., Wade, K. A., & Garry, M. (2004). True photographs and false memories. *Psychological Science, 15,* 149–154.

Loftus, E. F. (1979). *Eyewitness testimony.* Cambridge, MA: Harvard University Press.

Loftus, E. F. (1993). The reality of repressed memories. *American Psychologist, 48,* 518–537.

Loftus, E. F., & Palmer, J. C. (1974). Reconstruction of automobile destruction: An example of the interaction between language and memory. *Journal of Verbal Learning and Verbal Behavior, 13,* 585–589.

Luminet, O., & Curci, A. (Eds.) (2009). *Flashbulb memories: New issues and new perspectives*. New York: Psychology Press.

Mannheim, K. (1952). *Essays on the sociology of knowledge*. New York: Oxford University Press.

Marsh, E. J. (2007). Retelling is not the same as recalling: Implications for memory. *Current Directions in Psychological Science, 16,* 16–20.

Meade, M. L., Nokes, T. J., & Morrow, D. G. (2009). Expertise promotes facilitation on a collaborative memory task. *Memory, 17,* 39–48.

Meksin, R., & Hirst, W. (2005, January). Generational effects on memory for the terrorist attack of September 11, 2001. Paper presented at the meeting of the Society of Applied Research on Memory and Cognition, Wellington, New Zealand.

Meksin, R., & Hirst, W. (2012, March). A 10-year follow-up of a study of memory for the terrorist attack of September 11, 2001. Paper presented at the meeting of the Eastern Psychological Association, Pittsburgh, PA.

Meudell, P. R., Hitch, G. J., & Boyle, M. M. (1995). Collaboration in recall: Do pairs of people cross-cue each other to produce new memories? *Quarterly Journal of Experimental Psychology A: Human Experimental Psychology, 48,* 141–152.

Neisser, U. (1967). *Cognitive psychology*. New York: Meredith.

Nora, P. (Ed.) (1992). *Les Lieux de memoire* (Vol 7). Paris: Gallimard.

Nye, J., & Brower, A. M. (1996). *What's social about social cognition? Research on socially shared cognition in small groups*. Thousand Oaks, CA: Sage Publications, Inc.

Olick, J. K., & Robbins, J. (1998). From "collective memory" to the historical sociology of mnemonic practices. *Annual Review of Sociology, 24,* 105–140.

Pasupathi, M., Stallworth, L. M., & Murdoch, K. (1998). How what we tell becomes what we know: Listener effects on speakers' long-term memory for events. *Discourse Processes, 26,* 1–25.

Rajaram, S., & Pereira-Pasarin, L. P. (2010). Collaborative memory: Cognitive research and theory. *Perspectives on Psychological Science, 5,* 649–663.

Rathbone, C. J., Moulin, C. J., & Conway, M. A. (2008). Self-centered memories: The reminiscence bump and the self. *Memory & Cognition, 36*(8), 1403–1414.

Roediger, H. L., Meade, M. L., & Bergman, E. (2001). Social contagion of memory. *Psychonomic Bulletin and Review, 8,* 365–371.

Schuman, H. S., & Scott, J. (1989). Generations and collective memories. *American Sociological Review, 54,* 359–381.

Shteynberg, G. (2010). A silent emergence of culture: The social tuning effect. *Journal of Personality and Social Psychology, 99,* 683–689.

Sparrow, B., Liu, J., & Wegner, D. M. (2011). Google effects on memory: Cognitive consequences of having info at our fingertips. *Science, 333,* 776–778.

Squire, L. R. (2004). Memory systems of the brain: A brief history and current perspective. *Neurobiology of Learning and Memory, 82,* 171–177.

Stasser, G., & Titus, W. (1987). Effects of information load and percentage of shared information on the dissemination of unshared information during group discussion. *Journal of Personality and Social Psychology, 53,* 81–93.

Stone, C. B., Barnier, A. J., Sutton, J., & Hirst, W. (2012a). Forgetting our personal past: Socially shared retrieval-induced forgetting for autobiographical memories. *Journal of Experimental Psychology: General*. In press.

Stone, C. B., Coman, A., Brown, A. D., Koppel, J., & Hirst, W. (2012b). The sound – and mnemonic consequences – of silence. *Perspectives on Psychological Science, 7,* 39–53.

Sutton, J., Harris, C., Keil, P., & Barnier, A. (2010). The psychology of memory, extended cognition, and socially distributed remembering. *Phenomenology and the Cognitive Sciences, 9*(4), 521–560.

Tulving, E. (1983). *Elements of episodic memory*. New York: Oxford University Press.

Vandierendonck , A., & Van Damme, R. (1988). Schema anticipation in recall: Memory process or report strategy? *Psychological Research, 50,* 116–122.

Vygotsky, L. S. (1978). *Mind in society: The development of higher psychological processes*. Cambridge, MA: Harvard University Press.

Watts, D. J. (2004). The new science of networks. *Annual Review of Sociology, 30,* 243–270.

Wegner, D. M. (1987). Transactive memory: A contemporary analysis of group mind. In B. Mullen and G. R. Goethals (Eds.), *Theories of group behavior, Springer Series of Social Psychology* (pp. 185–208). New York: Springer-Verlag.

Weldon, M. S., Blair, C., & Huebsch, D. (2000). Group remembering: Does social loafing underlie collaborative inhibition? *Journal of Experimental Psychology: Learning, Memory & Cognition, 26,* 1568–1577.

Wertsch, J. V. (2002). *Voices of collective remembering*. New York: Cambridge University Press.

Wertsch, J. V. (2008). Collective memory and narrative templates. *Social Research, 75,* 133–156.

Wilson, R. A. (2005). Collective memory, group minds, and the extended mind thesis. *Cognitive Processing, 6,* 227–236.

Wilson, R. A., & Clark, A. (2009). How to situate cognition: Letting nature take its course. In P. Robbins and M. Aydede (Eds.), *The Cambridge handbook of situated cognition* (pp. 55–77). New York: Cambridge University Press.

Wittenbaum, G. M., Hollingshead, A. B., & Botero, I. C. (2004). From cooperative to motivated information sharing in groups: Moving beyond the hidden profile paradigm. *Communication Monographs, 71,* 286–310.

Wittenbaum, G. M., & Park, E. S. (2001). The collective preference for shared information. *Current Directions in Psychological Science, 10,* 70–73.

Wright, D. B., Self, G., & Justice, C. (2000). Memory conformity: Exploring misinformation effects when presented by another person. *British Journal of Psychology, 91,* 189–202.

Wundt, W. (1912/1973). *An introduction to psychology.* New York: Arno Press.

17

When I Think of You: Memory for Persons and Groups

Natalie A. Wyer

Humans are inherently social animals, and as such a great deal of their cognitive resources are devoted to establishing, maintaining, and occasionally terminating social relationships. Thinking about other people consumes a lot of our mental lives. The raw material for such thoughts, of course, derives in part from our memories of those people, making the question of how we learn, store, retrieve, and use information about others an important one.

How does memory for others differ from memory for non-social information? Or does it differ at all? Social memory, of course, shares a great deal with memory in other domains. Memory for other people can be episodic (I remember the time that Steve refused to ask for directions) or semantic (I know that Steve is stubborn) in nature. Attention allocated to social information at encoding has a strong influence on the likelihood that information can later be retrieved. And social memory, like other aspects of memory, is prone to error and bias as the result of factors such as salience, pre-existing expectancies or schemas, and post hoc suggestion.

However, there are a number of factors that, arguably, make social memory special. Although non-social information is, at times, personally relevant, memory for other people is likely to be more so. Our memories for others are often based on events in which we ourselves have been involved. Social interactions during which representations of others are formed and elaborated often involve a degree of self-involvement that is not characteristic of other experiences.

In addition, social information is often complex and open to interpretation. In contrast to objects and events that are fairly easy to assess objectively (I remember that the car was a Volvo; I remember that my steak came with a side of mashed potatoes), social events are often more ambiguous (Was she ignoring me or did she just not hear what I said?). This ambiguity has a number of implications for what is later recalled, as one's interpretation of an event at the time it occurs (itself influenced by one's current goals and mood, among numerous other factors) may influence how it is reconstructed later.

In part because social information is more ambiguous, it is subjected to greater spontaneous elaboration than is factual information. In order to understand the meaning of a person's behavior, one must not only identify what the behavior is (Jack walked up the hill) but why it was done (he wanted to fetch a pail of water) and what that might mean about the actor (he was thirsty). Non-social targets are not typically perceived as having motivation or intentions, or to possess internal states that can be understood by observing their movement or operation.

There are, of course, cases where animals or objects (e.g., cars or computers) are imputed with a "will" and treated as if they were human, but such cases are typically recognized as irrational. Drawing such inferences from human action is, on the other hand, normally regarded as entirely reasonable and appropriate. The end result of this greater level of elaboration is likely to be a stronger (though not necessarily more accurate) recollective experience.

The aim of this chapter is to provide an overview of the current state of play in person memory research. Following a brief history of the beginnings of person memory research, attention will be turned to summarizing the major findings that emerged from the first 20 years of research on person memory, concluding with a more detailed discussion of more recent empirical and theoretical developments in the field.

In framing this discussion, it is useful to first differentiate among different targets of social memory. Empirical research has focused on two primary types of target: unknown individuals and unknown groups. Typically, experimental participants are asked to form first impressions of an individual and/or a group by learning different kinds of information about them. Less common is research into memory for familiar or known others and groups. One key issue that remains relevant throughout this chapter is the extent to which findings obtained from laboratory studies that expose participants to social information about hypothetical others within perfectly controlled environments are relevant to understanding memory for others about whom much is already known, and about whom information is typically learned in a much different way.

our life stories out of a series of social relationships (Gergen & Gergen, 1988), and knowledge of others involved in those relationships forms an important reference point for how we know ourselves. Yet despite the fundamentally social nature of many day-to-day as well as self-defining memories, traditional memory researchers have seldom investigated the question of how we remember others (and our relationships with them).

Nevertheless, research on person memory exploded in the 1980s, largely conducted by social psychologists who embraced the so-called cognitive revolution. During that time, dozens if not hundreds of studies were carried out in which research participants were routinely presented – typically under the guise of a study on "impression formation" – with a series of statements about a fictitious person. These statements described the target as behaving in different ways: sometimes friendly, sometimes rude, sometimes intelligent, sometimes rather daft. Though researchers did occasionally inquire about participants' impressions, this was inevitably accompanied by a "surprise recall" test in which memory for the earlier-presented behaviors was tested.

Although it would be hard to argue convincingly that these exercises mirror the normal experience one has when learning about another person, such studies provided insights into the fundamental processes involved in impression formation, and identified several factors that influence not only how much people can remember about others, but also the content of those memories and the influence that they have on judgments. Let us now consider each of these factors in turn.

PERSON MEMORY 101: THE FUNDAMENTALS

Remember the old days?

Our most important memories are, most often, those that involve others. We create

Encoding processes in person memory

Why are you telling me this? Processing goals and person memory

Some of the earliest work on person memory investigated the seemingly simple question of what people remember when their goal is to use information to form an impression of another person compared with when their goal is to memorize the same information. Intuitively, one might expect that studying a list of sentences with the expectation of being asked to recall them later would produce maximum levels of recall. It was somewhat surprising, then, that studies consistently found a memory advantage when people reviewed behavioral information with the goal of forming an impression, compared with the goal of memorizing it. For example, a study by Hamilton, Katz, and Leirer (1980) demonstrated that participants given a goal to memorize a list of behavioral descriptions were later able to recall 25 percent of the information; in contrast, participants who were asked to use the same descriptions to form an impression of the person described were able to recall 33 percent (see also Devine, Sedikides, & Fuhrman, 1989).

What is it about the goal to form an impression that leads to superior memory? Several factors have been proposed and tested. One possibility is that, given the goal of impression formation, perceivers draw inferences from behavioral descriptions (e.g., inferring that Peter is "intelligent" after reading that he "solved the *Sunday Times* crossword puzzle"). When the same inference is drawn from a number of behaviors, the inferred trait can later serve as a cue to recall associated behaviors ("I remember that Peter solved the crossword puzzle … what were those other intelligent things that he did?"). Support for this account derives from examinations of the order in which statements are recalled: in many cases (e.g., Hastie & Kumar, 1979), the order of participants' recall protocols reflects organization (i.e., clustering) by the trait implied by recalled behaviors.

Like the goal to form an impression, the goal to prepare for a future interaction can also boost the memorability of a target's behavior. Devine et al. (1989) compared a variety of processing goals for their effects on the recallability and organization of behaviors attributed to a target. Like forming an impression of a target, expecting to interact with that target led to greater levels of recall compared with memorizing information about the target or comparing the target with the self or a friend. This suggests not only that anticipating an interaction with someone is likely to prompt spontaneous attempts at impression formation, but that the memory advantage stemming from impression formation is not due to mere depth-of-processing effects (in that case, one would expect a memory advantage for self- and other-comparison instructions relative to memorization instructions).

The power of expectations

One of the most robust findings to emerge from person memory research is that *a priori* expectations about others play a powerful role in determining what we attend to when learning further information about them. Precisely *how* expectations influence memory depends on a number of factors, including both the target about whom information is learned and the method of assessing memory.

Why did you do that? Inconsistency resolution in impression formation

Expectations guide attention not only to information that fits easily into our preconceived notions of what someone will be like, but also to information that blatantly violates those notions. A typical paradigm for investigating both types of memory entails presenting participants with a general description of a target (e.g., personality traits that characterize him or her) before presenting specific behavioral descriptions that are or are not consistent with that description. Using such a paradigm, Srull, Lichtenstein, and Rothbart (1985) established that, when presented with a series of statements that included expectancy-consistent, expectancy-inconsistent, and expectancy-irrelevant items, participants not only showed superior memory for consistent compared with irrelevant items, but even greater recall for the inconsistent items. A recall advantage for inconsistent information has since been replicated numerous times (see Stangor & McMillan, 1992 for a review).

This advantage appears to be due to two factors: First, inconsistent information draws greater attention because it is surprising. Increased attention, in turn, produces deeper processing of the surprising item. Second, and more importantly, perceived inconsistency triggers attributional processing or elaboration in order to find a resolution ("If Peter is intelligent, how is it possible that he can't remember his own phone number? Perhaps he has changed his number recently and hasn't had time to learn the new one yet"; see Hastie, 1984). This additional processing not only creates a stronger memory trace, but may also involve relating the inconsistent information with other information, creating inter-item associations and additional retrieval routes.

Evidence for the operation of an inconsistency-resolution process stems not only from the frequent observation that behavioral items that violate trait expectancies are more likely to be recalled, but also from studies that more directly examine the manner in which these items are processed. Stern, Marrs, Millar, and Cole (1984), for example, observed that, when allowed to read a series of behavioral statements relating to a target at their own pace, participants spent longer reading those that were inconsistent with trait descriptions that had been provided earlier. Moreover, Srull et al. (1985; see also Srull, 1981) examined the effect of introducing inconsistent behaviors on recall of consistent and trait-irrelevant behaviors. Their finding that adding trait-inconsistent behaviors boosted recall of trait-consistent behaviors (but had no effect on recall of trait-irrelevant behavior) suggests that consideration of consistent items was involved in processing of inconsistent items, as would be expected if one were attempting to reconcile the discrepancy in their implications.

Does what we remember determine how we evaluate?

Given the amount of empirical attention paid to encoding and retrieval processes in person memory, one might reasonably assume that the contents of one's memory have important implications for the judgments or evaluations one forms of those he or she remembers. Upon reflection, however, it will be clear that our tendency to preferentially recall information that is *inconsistent* with our impressions undermines a straightforward relationship between memory and judgment.

In reviewing the evidence for a memory-judgment relationship, Hastie and Park (1986) drew the vital distinction between on-line and memory-based judgment. They proposed that, when perceivers have the goal to form an impression of a target, they are likely to begin the process of doing so as soon as they start learning information, and to continue to develop their impressions throughout learning (at least until they are satisfied that they have learned enough). They refer to this as *on-line* impression formation. Once an impression is formed, it can be retrieved independent of the behavioral evidence on which it is based. That is, when asked for their evaluation of the target, they can simply recall the impression they formed without consulting specific behaviors. As a result, the extent to which the kind of information they recall corresponds to the evaluation they report is likely to be low.

In contrast, Hastie and Park posit that there may be conditions where perceivers do not engage in on-line impression formation, but rather form an evaluation only when they are explicitly asked to produce one. In such cases, perceivers are likely to reflect on what they have learned and use the information they recall in order to formulate their impressions. Because judgments in this case are based directly on what is recalled, the correlation between memory and judgment should be high. Indeed, Hastie and Park (1986) report evidence that directly supports this view.

Under what conditions, then, are people likely to rely on what they remember about others to make judgments about them? One key factor in determining the necessity of consulting behavioral episodes to generate judgments about a target is the extent of one's experience with that target. Klein, Loftus, Trafton, and Fuhrman (1992) utilized a priming paradigm to examine whether behavioral episodes were consulted when participants made trait judgments about themselves and others. Specifically, participants were asked to make self- or other-descriptiveness judgments (e.g., Does "selfish" describe John?) immediately prior to being asked to recall a behavioral episode consistent with the judgment (e.g., recall a time when John was selfish). If participants recalled behavioral episodes in order to make the descriptiveness judgment, then they should be faster to report such episodes when asked to recall them. Klein et al.'s (1992) results suggested that behavioral episodes were more likely to be recalled when making descriptiveness judgments on target/trait combinations for which they had less extensive experience. For example, they were more likely to retrieve behavioral episodes to judge their mother on traits that only weakly described her (compared with traits that were highly descriptive of her), or to judge themselves in a novel context (in contrast to a familiar context). Such findings support Hastie and Park's contention that, once a coherent impression has been formed, perceivers are able to retrieve that impression directly from memory without consulting the specific episodes that led to its formation.

Memory for individuals versus groups

While inconsistent information has an advantage when it comes to recalling information about individuals, a different pattern emerges when the target of impression formation is not a single person but rather a group of people. As noted by Hamilton and

Sherman (1996), several key principles that govern how people form impressions (and thus create memories) of individuals do not apply when they form impressions of social groups. Hamilton and Sherman argue that expectations that an individual target of impression formation should display a coherent personality and consistency in their behavior (which prompts attempts to reconcile inconsistencies) do not extend to group targets. When learning about a group, perceivers should expect greater variability and hence respond less to inconsistencies in the behavior of group members.

Indeed, there is substantial evidence that, even when perceivers are provided with trait descriptions of a group, they do not show the same tendency to elaborate on trait-inconsistent information that they do in the case of learning about an individual R. Wyer, Bodenhausen, and Srull (1984), for example, observed a marked difference in the likelihoods of recalling trait-consistent and inconsistent information about individual and group targets: whereas inconsistent behaviors had a distinct advantage when they applied to an individual, they were more poorly recalled if they applied to members of a group. A meta-analysis by Stangor and McMillan (1992) confirms this tendency across a large number of studies.

Further evidence that perceivers process inconsistent information differently when it applies to a group than when it applies to an individual stems from more direct processing measures. The aforementioned tendency for people to spend more time reading behavioral descriptions that violate individual trait expectancies disappears when the same descriptions violate group-based expectancies (Stern et al., 1984). Additionally, Susskind, Maurer, Thakkar, Hamilton, and Sherman (1994) reported that the tendency to generate explanations for expectancy-inconsistent behaviors was limited to cases where the expectancy stemmed from the target's personal attributes rather than from a group she or he belonged to.

Thus, it is clear that information about individuals and groups is processed in different ways, presumably due to perceivers' recognition that groups are more variable than individuals. Yet is it the case that all groups are perceived as more heterogeneous than individuals, and hence are less prone to inconsistency effects, memory-based judgments, and so on? Lickel, Hamilton, Wieczorkowska, Lewis, Sherman, and Uhles (2000) proposed a typology of groups that ranges from highly cohesive units (e.g., a family or sports team) to loose collections of individuals (e.g., people waiting together for the bus). To characterize the difference among these types, Lickel et al. adopted the term "entitativity" (Campbell, 1958) to reflect variations in the extent to which a group might be treated as a single entity – akin to an individual.

Indeed, research is consistent with the notion that some groups – those very high in entitativity – are similar to individuals in the manner in which information about them is stored, retrieved, and used in judgment. For example, McConnell, Sherman, and Hamilton (1997; see also McConnell, Sherman, & Hamilton, 1994) reported that when participants expected a group to be high in entitativity, they showed superior recall of behaviors that had been attributed to it (consistent with findings for recall of an individual's behavior). Moreover, whereas memory and judgment were significantly correlated for low entitativity groups, the same relationship did not emerge for high entitativity groups – suggesting that impressions of these groups were formed on-line (as is typical for individuals). Johnson and Queller (2003) subsequently reported further evidence that perceivers consulted remembered behaviors to make judgments about a group only when the group was low in entitativity. For high entitativity groups, judgments could be made without first recalling the group's behavior – presumably because the judgment had already been formed on-line during the impression formation process.

Retrieval processes

The vast majority of person memory research has focused on identifying factors that influence the quantity and quality of what people recall after learning about a target. Much less attention has been paid to recognition memory; yet, important differences exist between how perceivers recall versus recognize information about others. In their meta-analysis of person memory studies, Stangor and McMillan (1992) compared studies that used free recall versus recognition memory as their dependent measure. Both free recall and recognition sensitivity (i.e., recognition rates corrected for response bias) demonstrate a bias towards remembering more expectancy-incongruent information. However, measures of response bias tend to show a significant tendency for more expectancy-congruent information to be identified. Stangor and McMillan argue that these two findings, taken together, reflect schema-driven processing of behavioral information. When new information is encountered that fits easily within one's existing schemas (in this case, beliefs about a target's personality), there is no need to retain that information in memory as it is essentially redundant with what is already known. In contrast, schema-violating information is retained precisely because it does add new information to what is already known.

Sherman and colleagues (e.g., Sherman, Lee, Bessenoff, & Frost, 1998; Sherman & Frost, 2000) offer a similar conceptualization with their encoding flexibility model. Their research addresses the question of how information that confirms or violates pre-existing group impressions (i.e., stereotypes) is processed, particularly when cognitive resources are taxed. According to their model, the efficiency of stereotypes stems from their ability to facilitate memory for information that is both consistent and inconsistent with them. Consistent information is processed easily because it fits with existing stereotypic schemas. This allows attentional resources to be diverted to more in-depth encoding of stereotype-inconsistent information. This attention allocation is particularly likely to occur when processing capacity is constrained. Under such conditions, stereotypic behaviors are processed rapidly and attention is channelled toward comprehending stereotype-inconsistent behaviors. In testing their model, Sherman and Frost (2000; see also Sherman et al., 1998) found that, under cognitive load, participants were more successful at retrieving stereotype-consistent behaviors during a free recall task – a finding the authors attributed to participants' use of stereotype-based search strategies during retrieval. In contrast, stereotype-inconsistent behaviors had an advantage when it came to a recognition task (in which retrieval strategies were made irrelevant), suggesting that it was the expectancy-*inconsistent* information that was stored more extensively in memory. This suggests that the oft-observed memory advantage for stereotype-consistent information may be driven primarily by retrieval strategies rather than by the depth in which it is initially processed.

Memory for familiar others

Thus far, the discussion has primarily focused on how perceivers form mental representations (and specifically personality impressions) of individuals or groups about whom they have no prior knowledge. In comparison with the wealth of research into that question, research into how we remember others who are more familiar to us is rare (research into memory for the self – discussed at length elsewhere in this volume (see Chapter 13 by Fivush & Waters, and Chapter 15 by Klein & Nelson) – notwithstanding). In the following sections, research into how we remember familiar individuals and groups (to which we do or do not belong) will be reviewed.

Memory for significant others

In large part, research into how we remember significant others is centered on the question of how we remember our own relationships with them. For example, various researchers have developed conceptions of the "relational self" or "self-in-relationship" (e.g., Andersen & Chen, 2002; Aron, McLaughlin-Volpe, Lewandowski, Wright, & Aron, 2004; Agnew, van Lange, Rusbult, & Langston, 1998). Though there are distinctions among various models, they share the central assumption that mental representations of significant others are associated with representations of the self in important ways. For example, Aron, Aron, Tudor, and Nelson (1991) propose that the closeness of an interpersonal relationship is represented as the extent to which one's representation of a relationship partner is subsumed within one's self-representation. In support of such models, people are more likely to mis-remember information about a close other as applying to the self or vice versa (Mashek, Aron, & Boncimino, 2003; see also N. Wyer, 2008). They are also quicker to make self-descriptiveness judgments about traits that are shared with significant others (Aron et al., 1991; see also Smith & Henry, 1996) suggesting that activation of the self- and of close other-representations are likely to coincide.

Indirect evidence regarding how significant others are mentally represented is offered by Chen (2003), who argues that representations of significant others contain not only memories relating to their traits and behaviors, but also beliefs about their mental processes and psychological states. For example, one might store – as part of their representation of a significant other – beliefs about how s/he would feel or act in a particular situation. Maintaining this kind of information allows one to make predictions about the preferences and behavior of significant others.

Relatedly, several recent studies have examined the effects of activating representations of others on perceivers' own goals, emotions, and behaviors. For instance, Fitzsimons and Bargh (2003) reported that participants who were primed with their best friend were later more helpful to someone they had just met. This finding was interpreted as evidence that activating the best friend representation led to the activation of goals related to interacting with that friend. Similarly, research by Morrison, Wheeler, and Smeesters (2007) suggests that people automatically pursue goals for themselves if they are primed with significant others who possess those goals for them. For example, a person whose mother wished them to do well in school might increase their effort at academic tasks after being primed (even nonconsciously) with the concept of "mother".

These findings suggest that mental representations of familiar others encompass much more than abstract trait concepts and concrete behavioral episodes. Rather, more complex beliefs about significant others' mental states, motivations, and interpersonal goals are all stored in our memories of them. Such findings highlight the limitations of early person memory research that examined first impression formation in artificial and highly controlled experimental conditions. Though early impressions of others may well be heavily influenced by behaviors and traits inferred from them, over time our representations are likely to become much more multi-faceted.

Memory for in-groups and out-groups

A central question that has drawn attention from social psychologists within and outside of the social cognition tradition is how people think about groups to which they belong (in-groups) versus those to which they don't (out-groups). This issue has been the subject of entire volumes, thus the current discussion will be limited to a few key aspects that are of particular relevance here.

A robust finding in social cognition is that in-groups are generally perceived as more heterogeneous than out-groups (e.g., Park & Rothbart, 1982). In other words, we tend to view groups to which we belong as being composed of a wide variety of unique

individuals. In contrast, we tend to view groups of which we are not members as composed of people who are "all alike." This "out-group homogeneity bias" has a number of key consequences for how we encode and retrieve information about in-groups and out-groups. In particular, because in-groups are perceived as more variable, information that is inconsistent with one's impressions of the overall group is more easily tolerated and less subject to extensive elaboration than is the equivalent information about an out-group (Ostrom, Carpenter, Sedikides, & Li, 1993). Consequently, preferential recall of expectancy-inconsistent behaviors may not emerge when those behaviors relate to in-group members (e.g., Barduch & Park, 1996).

In addition, people tend to treat evaluatively positive and negative information pertaining to in-group and out-group members in different ways. Instances of negative in-group behavior is subject to elaborative processing to explain it (see Pettigrew, 1979; Chatman & von Hippel, 2001; N. Wyer, 2004) whereas the same information attributed to an out-group is accepted as diagnostic of their character. In a similar vein, people are quicker to conclude that an in-group possesses positive attributes (i.e., they require less behavioral evidence to draw that conclusion) or that an out-group possesses negative attributes (Sherman et al., 1998). As a result, specific behavioral episodes are more likely to be retrieved when they relate to negative in-group judgments or positive out-group judgments, as such cases are more likely to prompt relatively elaborate processing in order to understand how they fit within one's overall impressions of an in-group or out-group.

CONTEMPORARY RESEARCH ON SOCIAL MEMORY

In more recent years, research into person memory has shifted to focus increasingly on implicit and/or automatic processes involved in the formation and change of person impressions. This trend is reflected not only in the emergence of a number of dual-process and dual-systems models (e.g., Smith & DeCoster, 2000; Wilson et al., 2000; Gawronski & Bodenhausen, 2006; Strack & Deutsch, 2004) but a number of empirical advances as well. As summarized below, experimental work has tackled questions ranging from how non-conscious processes influence our processing goals when we encounter new information, to how multiple mental representations of the same target may co-exist in memory.

Implicit versus explicit memory – encoding processes

In daily life, impressions of others are shaped by a variety of factors, which vary in the extent to which they are open to conscious reflection. Unlike participants in experimental studies on impression formation, everyday perceivers rarely devote full attention to the goal of forming a coherent impression of someone based on discrete behavioral episodes. Rather, they may be influenced by fleeting glimpses of behavior, their interpretation of which may be colored by their current mood, goals, and relationship with the target. And, more often than not, the information available is processed under conditions where attention is divided and, occasionally, where processing takes place outside of conscious awareness. Recent research trends have therefore turned to the question of how implicit processes contribute to impression formation.

Implicit and explicit goals to form an impression

Before considering how implicit and explicit processes contribute to the outcome of impression formation, it is worth noting that the very impression formation process may be triggered not only by conscious intentions but also by automatically activated goals. Chartrand and Bargh (1996) used a subtle priming manipulation (namely, unscrambling sentences containing goal-related words) to activate impression formation versus memory goals prior to presenting participants with a series of behavioral statements. Their studies replicated classic studies in person memory (e.g., Hamilton et al., 1980), substituting their priming induction of processing goals for the original explicit goal induction. Remarkably, participants for whom impression formation goals were primed displayed the same patterns of memory as in the original studies where impression formation goals were explicitly induced.

Implicit processes influence impression formation in ways that differ from explicit processes in a number of ways. As noted by Skowronski, Carlston, and Isham (1993), perceivers' impressions of a target may be influenced by trait concepts that have been activated prior to encountering the target (see DeCoster & Claypool, 2004 for a review). For example, classic research by Higgins, Rholes, and Jones (1977; see also Bargh & Pietromonaco, 1982; Srull & R. Wyer, 1979) demonstrated that subtle (even non-conscious) exposure to personality trait terms in one context can influence impressions of a target encountered in an ostensibly unrelated context. In such cases, those trait concepts are not directly attributed to the target – indeed, one may not be aware of the source of a trait's accessibility. Thus, trait-related encoding processes (e.g., organization in terms of implied traits, inconsistency resolution, etc.) may be less likely to take place, and memory for the target may not follow the same patterns as would be expected had the accessible trait been explicitly attributed to the target.

When explicit and implicit person memories diverge

How do impressions formed on the basis of implicit processes differ from those formed on the basis of explicit processes? With the current theoretical emphasis on distinguishing between implicit and explicit processes, it comes as no surprise that such distinctions have found their way into research on person memory and impression formation. One of the major themes emerging from this research relates to the question of whether impressions of the same person that are based on implicit versus explicit processes are consistent with each other. The answer to this question is an unequivocal "not necessarily."

There are two dimensions on which implicit and explicit person impressions may diverge. Firstly, explicit and implicit impressions may be tuned to different criteria for drawing a conclusion about a target person. Whereas explicit processes (e.g., inference and attribution, see Gilbert, Pelham, & Krull, 1988) draw on reasoning about the meaning of another person's behavior, implicit impressions are based on associations between that person and trait or evaluative concepts encountered contemporaneously (often regardless of the objective association between the person and concepts). In an extreme example, Claparède (1995) describes the case of a patient with profound anterograde amnesia, who nevertheless displayed evidence of implicit memory for people. Claparède recalls that the patient was unable to retain explicit episodic memories for their interactions (and indeed was unable to remember him from one meeting to the next). Yet, after an occasion on which Claparède pricked the patient's hand with a pin concealed in his own hand, the patient refused to shake hands on the next occasion of their meeting. When Claparède inquired why, the patient expressed the belief that she might be stuck, despite insisting that she had no memory of having been stuck in the past.

Though anecdotal, this story suggests that implicit beliefs about others may be formed and retained in the absence of explicit memory. In adults with normal memories, implicit impressions also appear to be form independently of explicit beliefs about a person. For example, Rydell, McConnell, Mackie, and Strain (2006) reported evidence that implicit impressions of a target (measured

by the Implicit Association Test (IAT), a response-time based measure of associative strength) were formed on the basis on subliminally presented primes, whereas explicit impressions (measured using rating scales) were formed in response to overt descriptions of the target. When descriptions and primes had differing evaluative connotations, explicit and implicit impressions diverged such that the former was determined by propositional information provided about the target while the latter was dictated by subliminal primes associated with the target. Once formed, implicit evaluations of the target were also more responsive to subliminal priming rather than new overtly presented information; the reverse was true for explicit impressions (see also Rydell & McConnell, 2006). Such findings add support to the notion that a perceiver might store multiple representations of the same target (perhaps in different memory systems), based on different types of experiences or information.

Revising implicit and explicit impressions

The existence of multiple representations of a single target also becomes relevant when considering how impressions of others are changed. Although most research on person memory has focused on how first impressions are formed, it is clear that our initial impressions of others are sometimes flawed, or should be revised in response to new information (e.g., in situations where the target's personality undergoes some change, or new information becomes available). Although early research and theory (e.g., R. Wyer & Unverzagt, 1985; Hamilton & Sherman, 1996) suggested that explicit beliefs are resistant to change – indeed, research on inconsistency resolution would appear to suggest this – recent evidence makes it clear that explicit impressions are actually relatively malleable under many conditions, particularly when the basis for an original impression is undermined or discredited (e.g., Golding, Fowler, Long, & Lotta, 1990). In contrast, the preponderance of evidence seems to imply that implicit impressions are markedly less so.

Although there is variability in the extent to which perceivers acknowledge the capacity of others to change their character (Dweck, Hong, & Chiu, 1993), evidence suggests that the conscious beliefs one holds about another person are susceptible to change given sufficiently persuasive information. At the same time, it seems that people are less able to relinquish the associations with others that they store as part of their original beliefs about them. There are a variety of situations in which one might rationally wish to replace an existing impression with a new one (see N. Wyer, 2010). First, one might learn new information that suggests that an original impression was faulty. As noted above, research by Rydell and colleagues (Rydell & McConnell, 2006; Rydell et al., 2006) indicates that people require far more new information that contradicts their original evaluations of a target in order to change or override stored associations with that target (assessed using implicit measures) than to change their explicitly reported evaluations.

A second case for changing one's impression of a target arises when the target is perceived as undergoing an actual change in character. Gregg, Seibt, and Banaji (2006) investigated the extent to which implicit and explicit impressions of novel social groups could be changed given sufficient information indicating an actual reversal of their dispositions and roles over time. Although participants read an elaborate and compelling narrative describing the events that led to the change in character, Gregg et al. reported that implicit evaluations of the two groups remained unchanged (while explicit impressions accurately reflected the change that had occurred).

A final scenario in which one might expect stored impressions of a social target to change occurs when perceivers learn that the information on which they based their original impressions was faulty. Though early work (e.g., Golding et al., 1990; R. Wyer & Unverzagt, 1985) established that such discoveries led perceivers to readily change their explicit impressions, more recent investigations suggest that even in these cases implicit impressions are quite resilient. For example, Wilson, Lindsey, and Aronson (1998, described in Wilson, Lindsey, & Schooler, 2000) provided participants with profiles of a child molester and a lawyer who was prosecuting him. After forming an initial impression of the two targets, participants learned that the photos that accompanied the profiles had been inadvertently swapped, and hence the face they had first learned was the child molester was in truth the lawyer, and vice versa. Though participants readily changed their explicit reports to accommodate the corrected information, Wilson et al. found that the faces continued to prompt automatic associations with the original evaluation assigned to them (see also Gregg et al., 2006).

Similarly, N. Wyer (2010) presented participants with information about a target implying that he was either a skinhead or a cancer patient. After forming an initial impression of the target, all participants received information either confirming that the target belonged to the category they had learned, or that the target in fact belonged to the other category. For example, participants who initially learned that the target was a skinhead were informed that the original information was inaccurate and that he was actually a cancer patient. Later, participants' explicit judgments of the target (as measured by trait ratings) were in fact based largely on their current beliefs about the target, yet they continued to respond to the target in terms of the original category when assessed by implicit (reaction time) measures – unless they were given the opportunity to re-evaluate the original information on the basis of the new category membership.

Thus, an accumulation of evidence suggests an important distinction between implicit (associative) and explicit (propositional) memory for other people. Judgments of a target person are likely to vary depending upon which memory system they draw. Moreover, associative and propositional memory representations appear to be dramatically different in their responsiveness to new information, leading to the possibility that they will conflict under a variety of conditions.

THEORETICAL APPROACHES TO PERSON MEMORY

A variety of theories have been advanced to account for findings such as those discussed in the preceding sections. Theories of person memory have been greatly influenced by the literature on non-social memory. The advent of the cognitive revolution inspired researchers to adapt, in particular, principles of associative networks and spreading activation. Notably, some of the most influential person memory models are fundamentally associative network models (e.g., Klein et al., 1992; Srull & R. Wyer, 1989).

Srull and R. Wyer (1989) proposed an associative network-based person memory model to account for a wide variety of phenomena in the literature, including organization at recall, superior recall of inconsistent behaviors, and differences in memory for individuals versus groups. Although an in-depth discussion of their model is beyond the scope of this chapter, it is worth highlighting a number of points which are shared by a variety of related models (e.g., Hamilton et al., 1980; Srull, 1981). First, the Srull–Wyer model proposes that representations are built around a central "person node" to which impression-relevant information is associatively linked. The organization of this impression-relevant information is a critical focus on the model.

According to Srull and R. Wyer, perceivers who have the goal to form an impression of a target person's personality will automatically interpret that person's behavior in terms of the personality trait it implies. As evidence

pertaining to a particular trait accumulates, a summary representation of the trait is formed and linked to the person node. Specific behavioral episodes that reflect the trait are then linked to the summary representation. Because of behavioral examples that imply the same trait are all linked to that trait in memory, they are likely to be recalled in sequence as activation travels up and down associative links – resulting in apparent organization by trait in memory (see Klein et al., 1992 for an alternative retrieval-based account). In the case that trait-inconsistent behaviors are encountered, they are not only linked to the summary but also to individual trait-consistent behaviors that are consulted during the process of inconsistency resolution. These additional links provide additional retrieval routes through which inconsistent items may be recalled, resulting in the well-established inconsistency bias in person memory.

While associative network models were prevalent in the 1980s and early 1990s, subsequent theorists turned to other models inspired by work in cognitive psychology. For example, Kunda and Thagard's (1996) model of impression formation rests on assumptions derived from parallel distributed processing models (see also Queller & Smith, 2002) where links among nodes in a network can be either excitatory or inhibitory, and the strength of these links is affected by learning (e.g., of additional behavioral information). In such models, one's representations of individuals or groups are not hierarchically organized (with a central person/group node from which trait and behavioral nodes emanate) but rather are based on distinct patterns of activation that demarcate one person or group from another.

More recently, further models have been developed to account for the growing body of evidence relating to implicit processes in social perception. Such theories are particularly focused on accounting for differences between implicit and explicit beliefs or evaluations about others. The nature of such differences will be discussed in more depth later, but it is worth noting here that contemporary models posit the existence of multiple memory systems that represent information in distinct ways (e.g., Smith & DeCoster, 2000; Wilson et al., 2000), or the operation of distinct types of processing that give rise to different outputs (e.g., Gawronski & Bodenhausen, 2006; Strack & Deutsch, 2004). These theories, while differing in some important features, share the assumption that the impressions that perceivers report may reflect either automatic associations or intentionally retrieved propositional knowledge about the subject.

Recent theoretical advances in person memory

Dual process approaches to person memory

A number of theories have emerged in recent years to account for differences between implicit and explicit evaluations. Some such theories focus on distinguishing between multiple memory systems (e.g., Devine, 1989; Evans & Over, 1996; Smith & DeCoster, 2000; Wilson et al., 2000) while others emphasize the role of distinctive types of information processing (e.g., Gawronski & Bodenhausen, 2006; Sloman, 1996; Strack & Deutsch, 2004).

A proposition common to a number of theories (e.g., Gawronski & Bodenhausen, 2006; Petty, Tormala, Brinol, & Jarvis, 2006) is that explicit responses should reflect perceivers' conscious beliefs (i.e., their understanding of the "truth"), whereas implicit responses are less influenced by a belief's validity and are instead driven by associations that may or may not be grounded in truth. For example, Gawronski and Bodenhausen's (2006) associative-propositional evaluation (APE) model asserts that associative (or implicit) responses are generated without regard to whether the perceiver consciously endorses the response. Similarly, Petty et al.'s (2006) "past attitudes are still there" (PAST) model suggests that initial attitudes are "tagged"

as false once they have been consciously changed. Ironically, however, a disavowed attitude is still likely to be expressed on implicit measures unless the new attitude is sufficiently strong *and* the "false tag" is sufficiently accessible. Though the PAST model is concerned primarily with attitudes, the research that has emerged to test it has primarily examined attitudes towards other people. Such research has suggested that positive and negative evaluations about the same individual can co-exist and essentially balance each other when implicit evaluations are measured. Like research stemming from other models, explicit evaluations tend to support currently held beliefs and are relatively uncontaminated by earlier impressions.

The adaptive significance of remembering others

The capacity to store information about one's environment in memory has obvious adaptive functions. When it comes to non-social information (the location of food sources, the typical changes in weather patterns across the seasons), keeping track of such information is relatively straightforward. Although such agricultural and climatic events may not be perfectly predictable, there is no sense in which they regulate themselves in anticipation of responses by humans. The same cannot be said for human behavior – humans do regulate their behavior in order to achieve personal and collective goals, and thus using past behavior to predict future behavior is more complex.

One of the key adaptive challenges that may have shaped the ways in which we store and retrieve information about others is suggested by theories of social exchange. Humans appear to quite adept at keeping mental records of social contracts, and "cheaters" (i.e., individuals who violate those contracts) are easily recognized (Cosmides, Barratt, & Tooby, 2010). Cosmides and Tooby (1992) suggest that this capacity requires that perceivers are both skilled at recognizing people with whom they've interacted in the past and at retaining "accounts" of costs and benefits derived from those interactions. Indeed, empirical research appears to support this contention, as researchers have found a memory advantage for information about past social contract violations (Buchner, Bell, Mehl, & Musch, 2009; Chiappe, Brown, Dow, Koontz, Rodriguez, & McCulloch, 2004).

The propensity to recall another person's previous behavior lays the foundation for much of what is currently known about person memory. Indeed, early research into person memory was largely devoted to investigating the relationship between memory for specific behavioral episodes and trait inferences based upon those episodes. Theorists such as Klein, Cosmides, Tooby, and Chance (2002; see also Klein, Cosmides, Gangi, Jackson, Tooby, & Costabile, 2009) suggest that the evolution of episodic and semantic memory may have been heavily influenced by social interaction and the need to accurately predict the behavior of others by forming inferences about their personality on the basis of their behavior. This perspective compares personality judgment to first language learning in that it is a complex but automatic process that occurs ubiquitously and without explicit training.

In discussing the adaptive functions of episodic and semantic memory, Klein and colleagues (Klein et al., 2002) make reference to two forms of memories. Inceptive memories include most episodic memory, and reflect a perceiver's original experience of a person, place, or event. Derived memory, in contrast, refers to summary knowledge that is extracted from the experience – knowledge that has been stripped of idiosyncratic details associated with a particular event but that retains its meaning or implications. Klein et al. suggest that these two distinct forms of memory have developed because they serve two distinct functions, and that these functions are particularly relevant to social interaction. When faced with the need to predict a target's behavior in a particular situation, one has two basic options (other than blindly guessing). First, one can consult one's episodic memory for instances that are similar to the situation at hand and base predictions on how the target has behaved in the past. Second, one can retrieve a previously formed trait judgment that is relevant to the situation, and base one's prediction on that. The first option is more systematic and effortful, the second more efficient but error-prone.

REMAINING QUESTIONS AND FUTURE DIRECTIONS

The preceding pages have provided an overview both of early empirical and theoretical work on person memory and of more recent developments. The remainder of this chapter will consider a number of emerging and potential future research questions that are likely to shape the study of person memory in the years to come.

Cultural influences on person memory

Among the fastest growing areas of psychology is the study of how culture shapes various social and cognitive processes (Kitayama & Cohen, 2008; R. Wyer, Chiu, & Hong, 2009). This rapid growth in psychological inquiry reflects the increase in cross-cultural interactions in recent years. Although few studies have (as of now) directly examined cultural differences in person memory, there is ample reason to posit that such differences may exist. A few key examples are described here.

Prior work has identified a fundamental cultural difference in how the self-concept is construed. Cultures that foster an interdependent view of the self are represented in East and South Asia, Latin America, Africa, and parts of Southern Europe, while those that foster an independent view of the self are heavily represented in Western/Northern Europe and North America (Markus & Kitayama, 1991). The former "Eastern" type of construal holds the self as part of one or more larger collectives (e.g., a community, family group, or organization). The latter "Western" type of construal entails a view of the self as essentially an independent and unique entity, less defined by social ties. This difference can have profound effects on a variety of motivational and cognitive outcomes (e.g., Cross, Morris, & Gore, 2002; Haberstroh, Oyserman, Schwarz, Kühnen, & Ji, 2002).

With regard to person memory, a number of effects of self-construal have been suggested. Markus and Kitayama (1991) suggest that those with an interdependent self-construal literally represent significant others as part of the self-concept. Others (e.g., Cross et al., 2002) have found that individuals with interdependent self-construals are more likely to attend to and later recall information about others' relationships as well. Thus, one's culture of origin may not only impact upon how and what they remember about their own relationships, but may also determine how sensitive one is to information about the relationships of others.

Yet, culture may also influence social memory in ways that have not yet been identified. Representatives of different cultures may also differ in the processes they use to extract meaning from one another's behavior (Nisbett, 2003; Chiu & Hong, 2006). For example, in contrast to Westerners, individuals from Asian cultures are chronically disposed to think about themselves in relation to others (Markus & Kitayama, 1991). As a result, Asians may also possess a more general disposition to think about stimuli in relation to others in a variety of content domains. For example, whereas Westerners have a disposition to encode social stimuli in terms of their category membership, Asians encode stimuli on the basis of their relation to one another (Ji, Zhang, & Nisbett, 2004). Some implications of these differences have already been noted, but may extend to other aspects of person memory (e.g., the extent to which one relates new information about a person to previously learned information or to other features of the current situation).

Beyond this tendency towards relational thinking, Asians are also characterized by more holistic processing (Nisbett & Miyamoto, 2005). Holistic thinking is marked by a focus on the features of a stimulus as a configural whole rather than an analysis of the implications of each feature individually. Recent research has established that Western and Asian participants differ in their processing of both face identification (Michel, Rossion, Han, Chung, & Caldara (2006) and emotional expression (Masuda, Ellsworth, Mesquita, Leu, Tanida, & van de Veerdonk, 2008). Moreover, Morris and Peng (1994) noted that Western participants were more likely to draw dispositional inferences from behavior than were Asian participants, which may be a consequence of Asians' tendency to take contextual information into account (i.e., to process holistically). Further studies are needed to more directly test the influence culture on how information about others is stored and retrieved.

Neurological basis of social memory

As in other areas of psychology, the explosion of neuroscience research has given rise to new insights into how information about other people is stored and retrieved from memory. Much of this work has focused on autobiographical memory in particular and the experience of the self in general (e.g., Johnson, Baxter, Wilder, Pipe, Heiserman, & Prigatano, 2002; Kelley, Macrae, Wyland, Caglar, Inati, & Heatherton, 2002; Svoboda, McKinnon, & Levine, 2006) and is therefore left to other authors in this volume for discussion. For the present purposes, a brief overview of key person memory findings within neuroscience is provided.

A fundamental question that has pervaded much of social cognition theory and research is the extent to which social cognition is actually distinct from non-social cognition. Not surprisingly, then, this was among the first questions to be tackled by neuroscience researchers with an interest in social perception. To the gratification of social cognition researchers, Mitchell, Heatherton, and Macrae (2002) provided initial evidence that, indeed, tasks that involved thinking about information in relation to others (e.g., impression formation) recruited different parts of the brain (specifically the medial prefrontal cortex, superior temporal cortex, intraparietal sulcus, and fusiform gyrus) than did thinking about the same information without a social context. Following such findings, Mitchell, Macrae, and Banaji (2004) reported that memory for behavioral information used in the process of impression formation was significantly predicted by activity in the medial prefrontal cortex. Memory for the same information, when used for a non-social task, was predicted by different brain areas (e.g., the hippocampus). Such findings provide essential underpinnings for research into the unique nature of social cognition and person memory (see Mason, Banfield, & Macrae, 2004 for further discussion related to this point).

Contextual factors in person memory

Early in this chapter, the point was made that much of person memory research has been undertaken in highly controlled and hence relatively artificial environments. As person memory research moves forward to tackle new questions, it will be important to consider how memory for others operates in situations that more closely mirror those that we encounter in daily life. Initial steps have been taken towards this end.

For example, Gawronski and colleagues (Gawronski, Rydell, Vervliet, & De Houwer, 2010) have explored the influence of context on the formation and revision of implicit evaluations of others. They propose that one's mental representations of other individuals are contextualized – that is, the context or situation in which information about

another person is learned is stored as part of one's representation. When an evaluation of that person is later required, the match between the present context and the learning context will determine whether a particular set of information influences one's response. Stored information about a target is most likely to influence one's judgments or evaluations of the target when the learning context is re-instated when a response is required (see also Rydell & Gawronski, 2009). Research supporting this view provides a fuller understanding of how mental representations of other individuals may be formed and used in more naturalistic environments. Whereas early person memory research created context-free learning environments, this work makes it clear that as perceivers move from one situation to the next, the extent to which one draws on a particular set of knowledge about another person is also likely to vary.

Another area of research that has provided new insights into how person memory may work in the "real world" has been reported by R. Wyer and Adaval (e.g., Adaval, Isbell, & R. Wyer, 2007; R. Wyer, Adaval, & Colcumbe, 2002). This line of work suggests that perceivers store thematically related information about others in the form of narratives or "stories" about events. Such narrative representations involve links between individual pieces of information that identify their temporal sequence and causal relationships. Individual items (e.g., descriptions of individual behaviors) are, in this case, less likely to be evaluated independently – rather, the entire sequence of events will be evaluated for its overall meaning. The impact of individual items on judgment may therefore vary depending on whether those items form parts of a narrative or are stored as unrelated pieces of information.

The extent to which perceivers derive meaning from a sequence of events was also explored by N. Wyer, Perfect, and Pahl (2010) in their investigation of how adopting a particular processing style influenced participants' recollection of specific verbal and non-verbal behaviors that occurred during a staged encounter with a confederate.

In that work, a holistic or detail-oriented processing style was induced by manipulating psychological distance in an independent task (i.e., by asking participants to plan for activities that would take place in the near versus distant future). Psychological proximity has, in other work, been found to produce detail-oriented processing whereas psychological distance produces holistic processing (Trope & Liberman, 2010). Wyer et al. (2010) found that participants induced to adopt a holistic processing style were more likely to draw meaning from the staged encounter (e.g., inferences about the confederate's personality and goals), whereas those induced to adopt a more detail-oriented processing style tended to retrieve more specific information about the confederate's words and actions. This research provides insights into how differences in processing style (even those temporarily induced) may influence how perceivers retrieve information about events that they have experienced.

CONCLUSION

Interest in person memory – how we encode, store, retrieve, and use information about others – has a substantial history in social psychological research. Yet despite the central role that social interaction plays in day-to-day life, and its probable influence on the very evolution of cognitive systems for storing information, issues relating to person memory have been explored relatively seldom by "mainstream" memory researchers. It is hoped that the overview provided in this chapter – while inevitably incomplete – may serve as an impetus for the development of new lines of research into this important subject.

REFERENCES

Adaval, R., Isbell, L. M., & Wyer, R. S. (2007). The impact of pictures on narrative-based impression formation: A process interference model. *Journal of Experimental Social Psychology, 43*, 352–364.

Agnew, C. R., Van Lange, P. A. M., Rusbult, C. E., & Langston, C. A. (1998). Cognitive interdependence: Commitment and the cognitive representation of close relationships. *Journal of Personality and Social Psychology, 74*, 939–954.

Andersen, S. M., & Chen, S. (2002). The relational self: An interpersonal social-cognitive theory. *Psychological Review, 109*, 619–645.

Aron, A., McLaughlin-Volpe, T., Mashek, D., Lewandowski, G., Wright, S. C., & Aron, E. N. (2004). Including close others in the self. *European Review of Social Psychology, 15*, 101–132.

Aron, A., Aron, E. N., Tudor, M., & Nelson, G. (1991). Close relationships as including other in the self. *Journal of Personality and Social Psychology, 60*, 241–253.

Barduch, L., & Park, B. (1996). The effect of in-group/out-group status on memory for consistent and inconsistent behavior of an individual. *Personality and Social Psychology Bulletin, 22*, 169–178.

Bargh, J. A., & Pietromonaeo, P. (1982). Automatic information processing and social perception: The influence of trait information presented outside of conscious awareness on impression formation. *Journal of Personality and Social Psychology, 43*, 437–449.

Buchner, A., Bell, R., Mehl, B., & Musch, J. (2009). No enhanced recognition memory, but better source memory for faces of cheaters! *Evolution and Human Behavior, 30*, 212–224.

Campbell, D. T. (1958). Common fate, similarity, and other indices of the status of aggregates of persons as social entities. *Behavioral Science, 3*, 14–25.

Chartrand, T. L., & Bargh, J. A. (1996). Automatic activation of impression formation and memorization goals: Nonconscious goal priming reproduces effects of explicit task instructions. *Journal of Personality and Social Psychology, 71*, 464–478.

Chen, S. (2003). Psychological-state theories about significant others: Implications for the content and structure of significant-other representations. *Personality & Social Psychology Bulletin, 29*, 1285–1302.

Chatman, C. M., & von Hippel, W. (2001). Attributional mediation of ingroup bias. *Journal of Experimental Social Psychology, 37*, 267–272.

Chiappe, D., Brown, A., Dow, B., Koontz, J., Rodriguez, M., & McCulloch, K. (2004). Cheaters are looked at longer and remembered better than cooperators in social exchange situations. *Evolutionary Psychology, 2*, 108–120.

Chiu, C. Y., & Hong, Y. Y. (2006). *Social psychology of culture: Principles of social psychology.* New York: Psychology Press.

Claparède, E. (1995). Recognition and selfhood. *Consciousness and Cognition, 4,* 371–378.

Cosmides, L., & Tooby, J. (1992). Cognitive adaptations for social exchange. In J. Barkow, L. Cosmides, and J. Tooby (Eds.), *The adapted mind: Evolutionary psychology and the generation of culture.* New York: Oxford University Press.

Cosmides, L., Barrett, H. C., & Tooby, J. (2010). Adaptive specializations, social exchange, and the evolution of human intelligence. *Proceedings of the National Academy of Sciences, 107,* 9007–9014.

Cross, S. E., Morris, M. L., & Gore, J. S. (2002). Thinking about oneself and others: The relational–interdependent self-construal and social cognition. *Journal of Personality and Social Psychology, 82,* 399–418.

DeCoster, J., & Claypool, H. M. (2004). A meta-analysis of priming effects on impression formation supporting a general model of informational biases. *Personality and Social Psychology Review, 8,* 2–27.

Devine, P. G. (1989). Stereotypes and prejudice: Their automatic and controlled components. *Journal of Personality and Social Psychology, 56,* 5–18.

Devine, P. G., Sedikides, C., & Fuhrman, R. W. (1989). Goals in social information processing: The case of anticipated interaction. *Journal of Personality and Social Psychology, 56,* 680–690.

Dweck, C. S., Hong, Y. Y., & Chiu, C. Y. (1993). Implicit theories and individual differences in the likelihood and meaning of dispositional inference. *Personality and Social Psychology Bulletin, 19,* 644–656.

Evans, J. St. B. T., & Over, D. E. (1996). Rationality in the selection task: Epistemic utility versus uncertainty reduction. *Psychological Review, 103,* 356–363.

Fitzsimons, G. M., & Bargh, J. A. (2003). Thinking of you: Nonconscious pursuit of interpersonal goals associated with relationship partners. *Journal of Personality and Social Psychology, 84,* 148–164.

Gawronski, B., & Bodenhausen, G. V. (2006). Associative and propositional processes in evaluation: An integrative review of implicit and explicit attitude change. *Psychological Bulletin, 132,* 692–731.

Gawronski, B., Rydell, R. J., Vervliet, B., & De Houwer, J. (2010). Generalization versus contextualization in automatic evaluation. *Journal of Experimental Psychology: General, 139,* 682–701.

Gergen, K. J., & Gergen, M. M. (1988). Narrative and the self as relationship. In L. Berkowitz (Ed.), *Advances in experimental social psychology, Vol. 21* (pp. 17–56). New York: Academic Press.

Gilbert, D. T., Pelham, B. W., & Krull, D. S. (1988). On cognitive business: When person perceivers meet persons perceived. *Journal of Personality and Social Psychology, 54,* 733–740.

Golding, J. M., Fowler, S. B., Long, D. L., & Latta, H. (1990). Instructions to disregard potentially useful information: The effects of pragmatics on evaluative judgments and recall. *Journal of Memory and Language, 29,* 212–227.

Gregg, A. P., Seibt, B., & Banaji, M. (2006). Easier done than undone: Asymmetry in the malleability of automatic preferences. *Journal of Personality and Social Psychology, 90,* 1–20.

Haberstroh, S., Oyserman, D., Schwarz, N., Kühnen, U., & Ji, L. J. (2002). Is the interdependent self more sensitive to question context than the independent self? Self-construal and the observation of conversational norms. *Journal of Experimental Social Psychology, 38,* 323–329.

Hamilton, D. L., & Sherman, S. J. (1996). Perceiving persons and groups. *Psychological Review, 103,* 336–355.

Hamilton, D. L., Katz, L. B., & Leirer, V. O. (1980). Organizational processes in impression formation. In R. Hastie, T. M. Ostrom, E. B. Ebbesen, R. S. Wyer, D. L. Hamilton, and D. E. Cadston (Eds.), *Person memory: The cognitive basis of social perception* (pp. 121–154). Hillsdale, NJ: Erlbaum.

Hastie, R. (1984). Causes and effects of causal attribution. *Journal of Personality and Social Psychology, 46,* 44–56.

Hastie, R., & Kumar, A. P. (1979). Person memory: Personality traits as organizing principles in memory for behaviors. *Journal of Personality and Social Psychology, 37,* 25–38.

Hastie, R., & Park, B. (1986). The relationship between memory and judgment depends on whether the judgment is memory-based or on-line. *Psychological Review, 93,* 258–268.

Higgins, E. T., Rholes, W. S., & Jones, C. R. (1977). Category accessibility and impression formation. *Journal of Experimental Social Psychology, 13,* 141–154.

Ji, L. J., Zhang, Z., & Nisbett, R. E. (2004). Is it culture, or is it language? Examination of language effects in cross-cultural research on categorization. *Journal of Personality and Social Psychology, 87,* 57–65.

Johnson, A. L., & Queller, S. (2003). The mental representations of high and low entitativity groups. *Social Cognition, 21,* 101–119.

Johnson, S. C., Baxter, L. C., Wilder, L. S., Pipe, J. G., Heiserman, J. E., & Prigatano, G. P. (2002). Neural correlates of self-reflection. *Brain, 125,* 1808–1814.

Kelley, W. M., Macrae, C. N., Wyland, C. L., Caglar, S., Inati, S., & Heatherton, T. F. (2002). Finding the self? An event-related fMRI study. *Journal of Cognitive Neuroscience, 14,* 785–794.

Kitayama, S., & Cohen, D. (1998). *Handbook of cultural psychology.* New York: Guilford Press.

Klein, S., Cosmides, L., Gangi, C., Jackson, B., Tooby, J., & Costabile, K. (2009). Evolution and episodic memory: An analysis and demonstration of a social function of episodic recollections. *Social Cognition, 27,* 283–319.

Klein, S., Cosmides, L., Tooby, J., & Chance, S. (2002). Decisions and the evolution of memory: Multiple systems, multiple functions. *Psychological Review, 109,* 306–329.

Klein, S. B., Loftus, J., Trafton, J. G., & Fuhrman, R. W. (1992). Use of exemplars and abstractions in trait judgments: A model of trait knowledge about the self and others. *Journal of Personality and Social Psychology, 63,* 739–753.

Kunda, Z., & Thagard, P. (1996). Forming impressions from stereotypes, traits, and behaviors: A parallel-constraint-satisfaction theory. *Journal of Personality and Social Psychology, 103,* 285–308.

Lickel, B., Hamilton, D. L., Wieczorkowska, G., Lewis, A., Sherman, S. J., & Uhles, A. N. (2000). Varieties of groups and the perception of group entitativity. *Journal of Personality and Social Psychology, 78,* 223–246.

Markus, H., & Kitayama, S. (1991). Culture and the self: Implications for cognition, emotion, and motivation. *Psychological Review, 98,* 224–253.

Mason, M. F., Banfield, J. F., & Macrae, C. N. (2004) Thinking about actions: The neural substrates of person knowledge. *Cerebral Cortex, 14,* 209–214.

Mashek, D., Aron, A., & Boncimino, M. (2003). Including other in the self as overlap of cognitive elements: Evidence from source memory confusions. *Personality and Social Psychology Bulletin, 29,* 382–392.

Masuda, T., Ellsworth, P. C., Mesquita, B., Leu, J., Tanida, S., & van de Veerdonk, E. (2008). Placing the face in context: Cultural differences in the perception of facial emotion. *Journal of Personality and Social Psychology, 94,* 365–381.

McConnell, A. R., Sherman, S. J., & Hamilton, D. L. (1994). On-line and memory-based aspects of individual and group target judgments. *Journal of Personality and Social Psychology, 67,* 173–185.

McConnell, A. R., Sherman, S. J., & Hamilton, D. L. (1997). Target entitativity: Implications for information processing about individual and group targets. *Journal of Personality and Social Psychology, 72,* 750–762.

Michel, C., Rossion, B., Han, J., Chung, C-S., & Caldara, R. (2006). Holistic processing is finely tuned for faces of our own race. *Psychological Science, 17,* 608–615.

Mitchell, J. P., Heatherton, T. F., & Macrae C. N. (2002). Distinct neural systems subserve person and object knowledge. *Proceedings of the National Academy of Sciences, 99,* 15238–15243.

Mitchell, J. P., Macrae, C. N., & Banaji, M. R. (2004). Encoding-specific effects of social cognition on the neural correlates of subsequent memory. *Journal of Neuroscience, 24,* 4912–4917.

Morris, M. W., & Peng, K. (1994). Culture and cause: American and Chinese attributions for social and physical events. *Journal of Personality and Social Psychology, 67,* 949–971.

Morrison, K. R., Wheeler, C. S., & Smeesters, D. (2007). Significant other primes and behavior: Motivation to respond to social cues moderates pursuit of prime-induced goals. *Personality and Social Psychology Bulletin, 33,* 1661–1674.

Nisbett, R. E. (2003). *The geography of thought: How Asians and Westerners think differently … and why.* New York: The Free Press.

Nisbett, R. E., & Miyamoto, Y. (2005). The influence of culture: Holistic versus analytic perception. *Trends in Cognitive Science, 9,* 467–473.

Ostrom, T. M., Carpenter, S. L., Sedikides, C., & Li, F. (1993). Differential processing of in-group and out-group information. *Journal of Personality and Social Psychology, 64,* 21–34.

Park, B., & Rothbart, M. (1982). Perception of out-group homogeneity and levels of social categorization: Memory for the subordinate attributes of in-group and out-group members. *Journal of Personality and Social Psychology, 42,* 1051–1068.

Pettigrew, T. F. (1979). The ultimate attribution error: Extending Allport's cognitive analysis of prejudice. *Personality and Social Psychology Bulletin, 5,* 461–476.

Petty, R. E., Tormala, Z. L., Brinol, P., & Jarvis, B. G. (2006). Implicit ambivalence from attitude change: An exploration of the PAST model. *Journal of Personality and Social Psychology, 90,* 21–41.

Queller, S., & Smith, E. R. (2002). Subtyping versus bookkeeping in stereotype learning and change: Connectionist simulations and empirical findings. *Journal of Personality and Social Psychology, 82,* 300–313.

Rydell, R. J., & Gawronski, B. (2009). I like you, I like you not: Understanding the formation of context-dependent automatic attitudes. *Cognition and Emotion, 23,* 1118–1152.

Rydell, R. J., & McConnell, A. R. (2006). Understanding implicit and explicit attitude change: A systems of reasoning analysis. *Journal of Personality and Social Psychology, 91,* 995–1008.

Rydell, R. J., McConnell, A. R., Mackie, D. M., & Strain, L. M. (2006). Of two minds: Forming and changing valence inconsistent implicit and explicit attitudes. *Psychological Science, 17,* 954–958.

Sherman, J. W., & Frost, L. A. (2000). On the encoding of stereotype-relevant information under cognitive load. *Personality and Social Psychology Bulletin, 26,* 26–34.

Sherman, J. W., Lee, A. Y., Bessenoff, G. R., & Frost, L. A. (1998). Stereotype efficiency reconsidered: Encoding flexibility under cognitive load. *Journal of Personality and Social Psychology, 75,* 589–606.

Sherman, J. W., Klein, S. B., Laskey, A., & Wyer, N. A. (1998). Intergroup bias in group judgment processes: The role of behavioral memories. *Journal of Experimental Social Psychology, 34,* 51–65.

Skowronski, J. J., Carlston, D. E., & Isham, J. (1993). Implicit versus explicit impression formation: The differing effects of overt labeling and covert priming on memory and impressions. *Journal of Experimental Social Psychology, 29,* 17–41.

Sloman, S. A. (1996). The empirical case for two systems of reasoning. *Psychological Bulletin, 119,* 3–22.

Smith, E. R., & DeCoster, J. (2000). Dual-process models in social and cognitive psychology: Conceptual integration and links to underlying memory systems. *Personality and Social Psychology Review, 4,* 108–131.

Smith, E. R., & Henry, S. M. (1996). An in-group becomes part of the self: Response time evidence. *Personality and Social Psychology Bulletin, 22,* 635–642.

Srull, T. K., & Wyer, R. S. (1979). The role of category accessibility in the interpretation of information about persons: Some determinants and implications. *Journal of Personality and Social Psychology, 37,* 1660–1672.

Srull, T. K. (1981). Person memory: Some tests of associative storage and retrieval models. *Journal of Experimental Psychology: Human Learning and Memory, 7,* 440–463.

Srull, T. K., & Wyer, R. S. (1989). Person memory and judgment. *Psychological Review, 96,* 58–83.

Srull, T. K., Lichtenstein, M., & Rothbart, M. (1985). Associative storage and retrieval processes in person memory. *Journal of Experimental Psychology: Learning, Memory, and Cognition, 11,* 316–345.

Stangor, C., & McMillan, D. (1992). Memory for expectancy-congruent and expectancy-incongruent information: A review of the social and social-developmental literatures. *Psychological Bulletin, 111,* 42–61.

Stern, L. D., Marrs, S., Millar, M. G., & Cole, E. (1984). Processing time and the recall of inconsistent and consistent behaviors of individuals and groups. *Journal of Personality and Social Psychology, 47,* 253–262.

Strack, F., & Deutsch, R. (2004). Reflective and impulsive determinants of social behavior. *Personality and Social Psychology Review, 8,* 220–247.

Susskind, J., Maurer, K. L., Thakkar, V., Hamilton, D. L., & Sherman, J. W. (1999). Perceiving individuals and groups: Expectancies, dispositional inferences, and causal attributions. *Journal of Personality and Social Psychology, 76,* 181–191.

Svoboda, E., McKinnon, M. C., & Levine, B. (2006). The functional neuroanatomy of autobiographical memory: A meta-analysis. *Neuropsychologia, 44,* 2189–2208.

Trope, Y., & Liberman, N. (2010). Construal level theory of psychological distance. *Psychological Review, 117,* 440–463.

Wilson, T. D., Lindsey, S., & Schooler, T. Y. (2000). A model of dual attitudes. *Psychological Review, 107,* 101–126.

Wyer, N. A. (2008). Cognitive consequences of perceiving social exclusion. *Journal of Experimental Social Psychology, 44,* 1003–1012.

Wyer, N. A. (2010). You never get a second chance to make a first (implicit) impression. *Social Cognition, 28,* 1–19.

Wyer, N. A., Perfect, T. J., & Pahl, S. (2010). Temporal distance and person memory: Thinking about the future changes memory for the past. *Personality and Social Psychology Bulletin, 36,* 805–816.

Wyer, R. S., & Unverzagt, W. H. (1985). The effects of instructions to disregard information on its subsequent recall and use in making judgments. *Journal of Personality and Social Psychology, 48,* 533–549.

Wyer, R. S., Chiu, C-y., & Hong, Y-y. (2009). *Understanding culture: Theory, research and application.* New York: Psychology Press.

Wyer, R. S., Bodenhausen, G. V., & Srull, T. K. (1984). The cognitive representation of persons and groups and its effect on recall and recognition memory. *Journal of Experimental Social Psychology, 20,* 445–469.

Wyer, R. S., Adaval, R., & Colcumbe, S. J. (2002) Narrative-based representations of social knowledge: Their construction and use in comprehension, memory, and judgment. *Advances in Experimental Social Psychology, 34,* 131–197.

18

Memory, Attitudes, and Persuasion

Geoffrey Haddock

The study of attitudes and attitude change (i.e., persuasion) is at the forefront of social psychology. Attitudes are important because they influence how we process information and how we behave. In this chapter, I consider how memory processes, in their broadest sense, are important to the conceptualization of attitudes and our understanding and application of attitudinal phenomena. I start by addressing how theorists have defined the concept of *attitude*. We will see how different researchers postulate different roles for memory in relation to attitudes. The second section of the chapter highlights strands of research in which the field's understanding and application of the attitude concept has been enriched by considering how memory processes influence attitudes. The third section focuses on how memory processes are related to attitude change, while the final section considers how future research on attitudes should continue to be enhanced by integrating memory processes.

WHAT ARE ATTITUDES?

To start, I wish to describe what is meant by the term *attitude*. Here are four definitions that have been offered by prominent researchers. Eagly and Chaiken (1993, p.1) define an attitude as "a psychological tendency that is expressed by evaluating a particular entity with some degree of favor or disfavor." Fazio (1995, p. 247) defines an attitude as "an association in memory between a given object and a given summary evaluation of the object." Petty and Cacioppo (1981, p. 7) define an attitude as "a general and enduring positive or negative feeling about some person, object, or issue." Finally, Schwarz (2007, p. 639) notes that attitudes are "evaluative judgments, formed when needed, rather than enduring personal dispositions." From these definitions, one shared feature is the idea that reporting an attitude involves expressing an *evaluative judgment* about an attitude object. Indeed, it is widely agreed that evaluation is *the* predominant aspect of attitudes (see Banaji & Heiphetz, 2010; Bohner & Dickel, 2011; Maio & Haddock, 2010). However, you can also see that researchers take different views regarding the role of memory in what is represented by an attitude. In particular, there has been considerable debate regarding the degree to which attitudes represent *stable* evaluations that are stored in memory versus temporarily *constructed* dispositions (see Bohner

& Dickel, 2011; Maio & Haddock, 2010, for similar perspectives on this distinction). On the one hand, Fazio, Petty, and colleagues (e.g., Fazio, 2007; Petty, Briñol, & DeMarree, 2007) suggest that an attitude is a stable disposition toward an attitude object that is represented in memory. This perspective of attitudes as stored representations is at the core of these researchers' (and others') models of attitude. Consistent with this perspective, it has been metaphorically suggested that individuals possess a file-drawer of attitudes that can be accessed when required (Bohner & Dickel, 2011; Holland, Verplanken, & van Knippenberg, 2002). On the other hand, researchers such as Schwarz and Bohner (2001; Schwarz, 2007) favor the view that attitudes are evaluations that are formed on the spot, on the basis of accessible and salient information. According to the strong version of this view, individuals "always need to compute a judgment from scratch and can't recall their previous evaluations" (Schwarz & Bohner, 2001, p. 455).

Which of these perspectives is correct? Some researchers have stated that this distinction might not be important. Consistent with Eagly and Chaiken's (1993) view of attitudes as tendencies, Albarracín, Johnson, Zanna, and Kumkale (2005, p. 4) noted that "attitudes can be judgments, memories, or both." As you might expect, proponents of both the stable and constructed views offer evidence in support of their perspective (see Bohner & Dickel, 2011; Maio & Haddock, 2010). Consistent with the constructed view, research has demonstrated that attitudes are malleable in response to seemingly subtle changes to the way questions are presented. For example, variations in question order and question format can elicit differentially favorable attitudes on explicit measures of attitude (Schwarz, 1999; Schwarz & Bohner, 2001). Consistent with the stable perspective, researchers point to evidence regarding the temporal and situational stability of attitudes, and much research has shown that attitudes influence subsequent judgments and behavior, even when there is no active

consideration of the attitude (see Fazio, 2007). For example, Roskos-Ewoldsen and Fazio (1992) found that when participants were briefly presented with an array of attitude objects, they were more likely to visually notice and attend to objects for which they had highly accessible attitudes. This (and other) types of research is taken as evidence that stored object–evaluation associations have important behavioral implications.

The stable versus constructed debate has obvious relevance to the role of memory processes in attitudes. How can this debate be resolved? For many researchers (e.g., Bohner & Dickel, 2011; Fazio, 2007; Maio & Haddock, 2010), the stable versus constructed argument highlights the role of *attitude strength*. As noted by Krosnick and Petty (1995), strong attitudes are more stable over time, more resistant to persuasive appeals, and more likely to influence information processing and behavior. Research has demonstrated the differential implications of strong versus weak attitudes, and some have argued that strong attitudes are those that are more likely to be stored in memory, whereas weak attitudes are those that are more likely to be constructed (see Fazio, 2007; Maio & Haddock, 2010; Visser, Bizer, & Krosnick, 2006).

In sum, researchers share the perception that attitudes reflect evaluations of an object (which refers to anything that can be evaluated on a dimension of favorability – such as a person (Usain Bolt), group (Canadians), social policy (abortion), concept (atheism), or physical entity (my baseball glove)). However, researchers sometimes differ in their views regarding the extent to which attitudes are represented in memory. Next, I wish to introduce three prominent attitude models that highlight the degree to which attitudes can represent stored evaluations. These are the MODE model (Fazio, 1990, 1995, 2007), the Dual Attitudes model (Wilson, Lindsey, & Schooler, 2000), and the Meta-Cognitive Model (Petty et al., 2007). However, before describing the major tenets of these models, it is necessary to introduce the distinction between explicit and implicit conceptualizations of attitude.

EXPLICIT AND IMPLICIT CONCEPTUALIZATIONS OF ATTITUDE

Over the past two decades, the most substantial development in attitudes research concerns the distinction between explicit and implicit conceptualizations of attitude. This distinction has had different meanings in the context of attitudes. At one level, there has been a distinction between the terms *explicit attitudes* and *implicit attitudes*. This distinction has revolved around the idea that individuals might possess evaluations that they have not directly considered (e.g., attitudes about which they lack awareness). That said, numerous researchers (e.g., Fazio & Olson, 2003; Petty, Fazio, & Briñol, 2009; Wegener & Carlston, 2005) have expressed concerns with the idea that individuals might possess attitudes for which they have a complete lack of awareness. This concern is best articulated by Fazio and Olson (2003, p. 302), who asked "How do we know that individuals lack awareness of their attitudes?" (italics added).

In light of these concerns, many researchers have concentrated on the explicit–implicit distinction at the level of attitude measurement, distinguishing between *explicit measures of attitude* and *implicit measures of attitude* (see Fazio & Olson, 2003; Maio & Haddock, 2010; Wegener & Carlston, 2005). At a basic level, this differentiation concerns whether or not an individual is aware that their attitude is being assessed. For example, in measuring self-esteem, an explicit measure might ask an individual's agreement to the item "I have high self-esteem" (Robins, Hendin, & Trzesniewski, 2001), while an implicit measure might be a self-esteem implicit association test (IAT; Greenwald, McGhee, & Schwartz, 1998). Until recently, explicit measures (such as questionnaires and semantic differential measures) were the primary tools for assessing attitudes. However,

based on concerns about socially desirable responding to explicit measures and, more importantly, developments regarding implicit and explicit cognition, attitude researchers developed new, indirect techniques of attitude measurement. These new measures, such as the IAT and the evaluative priming measure (among others), are based on the notion that individuals activate from memory evaluative responses when presented with an attitude object.

The use of implicit and explicit measures has significantly increased the field's basic and applied understanding about attitudes. For example, research has revealed that explicit and implicit measures tend to predict different types of behavior – explicit measures of attitude are particularly effective in predicting deliberative behavior, whereas implicit measures of attitude are particularly effective in predicting spontaneous behavior. In one such application, Dovidio, Kawakami, Johnson, Johnson, and Howard (1997) found that scores on an implicit measure of attitudes toward African Americans best predicted spontaneous non-verbal behaviors (e.g., eye contact, frequency of blinking) with a Black experimenter, whereas scores on an explicit measure best predicted deliberative responses made by participants in response to questions posed by a Black experimenter. Further, the implicit-explicit distinction has led to new developments about the nature of evaluations, and the role of memory in the nature of evaluations (e.g., Gawronski & Bodenhausen, 2006; Rydell & McConnell, 2006; Smith & DeCoster, 2000; Strack & Deutsch, 2004).

ATTITUDES AND MEMORY: SOME GENERAL PERSPECTIVES

Fazio's (1990, 1995, 2007) MODE (Motivation and Opportunity as DEterminants of Behavior) model states that attitudes are object–evaluation associations stored in memory, and that the strength of the stored association reflects the accessibility of the attitude. The MODE model specifies two ways through which attitudes influence behavior. First, when individuals have both sufficient motivation and opportunity, they can base their behavior on a deliberative consideration of their stored attitude and other relevant information. However, if either motivation or opportunity is low, attitude accessibility is important. When an individual has a strong object–evaluation association stored in memory, the automatically activated evaluation elicits attitude-consistent behavior. But when the object–evaluation association is weak, the attitude is not automatically activated and is less likely to predict behavior. An impressive volume of research has provided strong evidence for this model (see Fazio, 1995, 2007; Fazio & Towles-Schwen, 1999). As one example, Fazio and Williams (1986) found that participants with highly accessible attitudes toward Ronald Reagan (when assessed five months before an American presidential election) were subsequently significantly more likely to vote for Reagan compared with participants with less accessible attitudes (even when these attitudes were matched for extremity).

The other models I wish to highlight share the tenet that individuals can possess in memory more than one attitude toward an object. Historically, it was assumed that when an individual's attitude changes, the old attitude disappears and is replaced by the new one (Petty, Tormala, Briñol, & Jarvis, 2006). However, recent developments, largely derived from the distinction between implicit and explicit conceptualizations of attitude, have argued that the old attitude can be retained in memory and influence subsequent judgments and behaviors.

One approach highlighting this perspective is Wilson and colleagues' (2000) Dual Attitudes model. In their model, Wilson et al. (2000) differentiate between implicit and explicit attitudes, and argue that when an attitude changes, the old attitude can be retained in memory, with this attitude becoming more implicit. In their conceptualization,

an implicit attitude has an unknown origin, is activated automatically, and influences implicit responses (Wilson et al., 2000; see Lindsay & Johnson, 1989 for a comparable perspective). Wilson and colleagues argue that the (new) explicit and (old) implicit attitudes are differentially likely to be expressed, and influence behavior, dependent upon motivation and cognitive capacity. When an individual has motivation and cognitive capacity, the model argues that the (new) explicit attitude is more likely to be expressed and guide behavior, but when these conditions are absent the (old) implicit attitude is more likely to be expressed and guide behavior. As such, the model perceives the new and old attitudes as quite independent and having different underlying processes. In support of this framework, Wilson et al. (2000) demonstrated that after a persuasive appeal, participants' evaluations reflected their explicit attitude when the evaluation was made in the absence of time pressure, but that their evaluation reflected their implicit attitude when the evaluation was made under time pressure.

Another recent perspective, the Meta-Cognitive Model (MCM; Petty, 2006; Petty et al., 2006, 2007), shares the Dual Attitudes model's view that when an attitude changes, the old attitude can remain in memory and influence information processing and behavior. Similar to Fazio's model, the MCM takes the perspective that attitudes can reflect object–evaluation associations that are stored in memory. Unlike the Dual Attitudes approach, the MCM suggests that under some conditions (such as when the old and new attitudes are based on the same information), the old and new attitudes are likely to be stored in a single memory system, whereas when they are based on different information, they are likely to be stored in different memory systems. Also, this model is unique by proposing that these object–evaluation links are associated with validity tags – a consideration of whether an individual perceives the object–evaluation link as a valid reflection of their opinion. According to this model, when an attitude changes, the original object–evaluation remains in memory, but becomes linked with a tag stating that it is invalid. However, under some conditions, this tag might not be retrieved, leading both the old and new attitudes to be (mis)perceived as valid, resulting in a state of ambivalence (simultaneous positive and negative evaluations about an attitude object). The model argues that this ambivalence is implicit, since the attitude holder does not actively endorse both the old and new attitude (Petty, 2006). In support of this model, Petty et al. (2006) found that individuals whose attitudes had changed in response to novel information showed evidence of implicit ambivalence, as evidenced by reporting less confident attitudes. Furthermore, implicitly ambivalent individuals were more likely to deeply process attitude-relevant information, a marker of attitude ambivalence (see Maio, Bell, & Esses, 1996).

Taken together, these models highlight key ways in which memory processes are relevant to the study of attitudes. The MODE model is explicit in conceptualizing attitudes as object–evaluation links that are stored in memory. The more recent Dual Attitudes and Meta-Cognitive Models have been extremely influential in generating new insights about the conceptualization of attitudes. In particular, the MCM, and its conceptualization of validity tags and implicit ambivalence, has received strong support and is a substantial advance that has generated many novel questions about how memory processes influence attitudes.

MEMORY AND ATTITUDE-RELEVANT PHENOMENA

In this section of the chapter, I highlight some ways in which memory processes are relevant to attitudes research. I start by addressing how people's mental representation in memory of an object influences their attitude. Second, I discuss how the ease with which people retrieve from memory

attitude-relevant information influences their evaluations. Third, I discuss whether individuals are more likely to retain in memory information that supports or counters their attitude – the so called *congeniality hypothesis*. Fourth, I highlight research that has addressed how memory processes influence how people evaluate new information about their attitudes. Fifth, I highlight attitudes research has benefited from work carried out using individuals with memory impairments. Sixth, I address how changing one's attitude influences an individual's memory for their perceptions regarding how often they have carried out a behavior.

Mental representations of an attitude object

One interesting line of research in the last two decades has assessed how the stability of mental representations of an attitude object influences the favorability and stability of an individual's attitude. According to Attitude Representation Theory (ART; Lord & Lepper, 1999), when reporting an attitude, individuals first activate from memory mental representations of the attitude object; these representations can include the activation of a relevant exemplar. For example, when asked to indicate their attitude toward politicians, the model proposes that individuals retrieve from memory an exemplar. This activated exemplar then shapes the attitude that is expressed. As you might expect, individuals differ in the degree to which they retrieve from memory the same exemplar across time. According to ART, the stability with which individuals retrieve the same exemplar across time has important implications for their reported attitude, with greater exemplar retrieval stability associated with more temporally stable attitudes.

Lord and colleagues have gathered strong evidence in support of their model. In one study, Sia, Lord, Blessum, Thomas, and Lepper (1997) had individuals report their attitudes toward several social categories, including politicians. Participants also indicated a category exemplar. One month later, participants were primed with the political exemplar retrieved at time 1 or a different exemplar, before indicating their attitude toward the category politicians. The results revealed that greater attitude stability was exhibited by participants who had been primed with the same exemplar that they had retrieved at time 1. In other studies, individuals who retrieved different exemplars across time were less likely to behave in a way congruent with their original attitude and were more likely to change their attitudes compared with individuals with temporally stable exemplars (Lord, Paulson, Sia, Thomas, & Lepper, 2004).

Ease of retrieval and attitudes

A long line of research has addressed how retrieving from memory accessible information influences evaluative judgments. Based on Tversky and Kahneman's (1973) research on the availability heuristic, Schwarz, Bless, Strack, Rittenauer-Schatka, and Simons (1991) conducted an experiment in which a group of participants retrieved from memory either a few (6) or many (12) instances in which they had acted assertively, before rating their own level of assertiveness. If these self-ratings are based on the *ease* with which people retrieve instances from memory, higher assertiveness should be associated with retrieving fewer instances, as this task is easier than retrieving from memory many instances. In contrast, if these ratings are based on the *amount* of information accessed from memory, higher assertiveness ratings would be expected among participants who retrieved more instances from memory. Schwarz and colleagues found that judgments of assertiveness were indeed based on the ease with which instances were accessible in memory, unless the subjective experience was rendered non-diagnostic.

More relevant to the present context, studies have assessed how the subjective ease associated with retrieving information from memory influences attitudes. Wänke, Bohner, and Jurkowitsch (1997) asked participants to retrieve from memory either one or ten reasons for (for some participants) or against (for other participants) purchasing a BMW automobile over a Mercedes. Subsequently, participants reported their attitude toward BMWs. The results revealed that attitudes toward BMWs were most favorable when individuals had experienced an easy time retrieving reasons in favor of buying a BMW or many reasons against buying a BMW. A further study in the domain of consumer attitudes revealed that these effects occur when brand knowledge is moderate. When brand knowledge is low or high, people rely on the content of retrieved information (Tybout, Sternthal, Malaviya, Bakamitsos, & Park, 2005).

Ease of retrieval paradigms have been studied in other attitude domains. Haddock (2002) asked participants to retrieve from memory either two or five positive (or two or five negative) attributes about former British Prime Minister Tony Blair. After completing this task, participants indicated their attitude toward Blair. This study revealed that attitudes toward Blair were most positive when participants retrieved from memory either few positive attributes or many negative attributes. Further, ease of retrieval affected attitudes only among individuals low in political interest. Among individuals high in interest, who already possessed in memory a strong attitude toward Blair, the manipulation did not affect attitudes (despite the fact that these participants also found it easier to retrieve from memory two rather than five attributes).

In addition to studying how ease of retrieval impacts attitude favorability, research has assessed how information retrieval affects other types of attitudinal responses. For example, attitude strength judgments are affected by the ease with which individuals retrieve from memory arguments that support or counter their attitude. Haddock, Rothman, and Schwarz (1996) asked participants to retrieve either three or seven arguments that either supported (or opposed) their attitude toward euthanasia. It was found that participants perceived their attitudes as stronger when they had experienced either an easy time retrieving from memory supporting arguments or a difficult time retrieving from memory opposing arguments.

One recent extension of this research has considered how influencing individuals' subjective perceptions of ease impacts the effect of retrieval on attitudes. There has been an assumption that easily retrieved thoughts are seen as reflecting good memory, as well as the thoughts themselves being perceived as valid and trustworthy (Tormala, Petty, & Briñol, 2002). In a clever set of experiments, Briñol, Petty, and Tormala (2006) assessed whether the "ease is good/difficulty is bad" view is malleable, and tested whether making people believe that ease is good or bad would lead to different effects on attitudes. Participants in the "ease is bad" condition were informed that unintelligent people experience ease in thinking, as their thoughts are simplistic (participants in the other condition received opposite information). Consistent with past research, these researchers found when people perceive ease as good, ease of retrieval led to more favorable attitudes. However, when people are led to believe that ease is bad, it resulted in opposite effects on attitudes.

Memory and attitudes for relevant information

One question that has been addressed concerns whether individuals have better memory for information that supports their attitudes compared with information that counters their attitudes. Recent reviews have provided limited evidence in support of the congeniality hypothesis; a meta-analysis by Eagly, Chen, Chaiken, and Shaw-Barnes

(1999) revealed that there is an extremely small effect of attitudes on memory for attitude-consistent information. Following from these conclusions, Eagly, Kulesa, Brannon, Shaw, and Hutson-Comeaux (2000) considered the processes underlying this weak effect, and found that message recipients allocated more attention to counter-attitudinal information, with no preference for congenial information. Eagly et al. (2000) asserted that counter-attitudinal information is processed deeply to help develop counter-arguments to these positions. The resources allocated to this information can lead it to become memorable (Eagly, Kulesa, Chen, & Chaiken, 2001).

Relevant to this research, other work has considered whether the strength of an attitude influences an individual's motivation to seek out (and process) information about the attitude object. Holbrook, Berent, Krosnick, Visser, and Boninger (2005) addressed whether individuals seek out, selectively attend to, and more deeply process information about important attitudes compared with non-important attitudes. In studies using various political attitudes, Holbrook et al. (2005) found that attitude importance yields greater long-term memory (in the form of cued recall and recognition memory) for attitude-relevant information, and that these effects are attributable to selective exposure and enhanced elaboration. Further, consistent with work on the congeniality hypothesis, Holbrook and colleagues found that there was no substantial advantage for remembering attitude-consistent information over attitude-inconsistent information.

Finally, research has considered how differential access to attitude-relevant information from memory influences important outcomes. In research of this type, respondents are asked to retrieve from memory as many attitude-relevant beliefs as possible (see e.g., Wood, 1982; Wood, Kallgren, & Priesler, 1985). This research has revealed that the greater the amount of attitude-relevant information stored in memory, the more likely the attitude is to predict behavior

(Kallgren & Wood, 1986), and the greater the resistance to a counter-attitudinal message (Wood, 1982).

On-line versus memory-based processing

Relevant to the research described in the previous section, another line of work has considered how message recipients evaluate novel information, and the implications of whether attitudes are formed via on-line or memory-based processes (Hastie & Park, 1986). For example, imagine someone is presented with multiple pieces of information about an unfamiliar target person (see Bizer, Tormala, Rucker, & Petty, 2006). In the on-line process, participants evaluate the target after receiving each individual piece of information, and report their overall attitude once all of the information has been presented. In the memory-based process, individuals do not evaluate the target during message acquisition; instead they evaluate the target only after having being presented with all of the individual pieces of information.

Research has considered consequences associated with attitudes formed via on-line versus memory-based processes. For example, attitudes formed via memory-based processes are more consistent with the favorability of the individual pieces of information retrieved immediately before making the judgment (Bizer et al., 2006). In another study, Bassili and Roy (1998) tested whether attitudes toward political policies were derived from on-line versus memory-based processes. These researchers used a priming paradigm in which participants completed pairs of tasks in quick succession, where the focal task involved evaluating a government policy or thinking of an implication of the policy. Bassili and Roy (1998) found that thinking about a policy led to a faster subsequent evaluation of the policy, while individuals who first evaluated the policy were quicker in thinking about an implication of the policy, but only among participants with strong attitudes.

Research has also addressed how on-line versus memory-based processes influence the speed with which individuals report their attitude. Studies have shown that attitudes formed via on-line processes are more accessible than attitudes formed via memory-based processes (see Mackie & Asuncion, 1990; Tormala & Petty, 2001). This is unsurprising, as during the on-line process the message recipient has repeated opportunities to express their attitude. Building on this research, work has considered whether attitudes formed through on-line versus memory-based processes differ in their underlying strength. In one set of studies, Bizer and colleagues (2006) found that attitudes formed via on-line processing were held with greater certainty and were more likely to predict behavior compared with attitudes formed via memory-based processes.

Memory impairments and attitudes

A number of theorists have considered how attitude models can be informed by using as research participants individuals with memory impairments. To the extent that particular memory processes are important in attitudinal phenomena, individuals with memory impairments can be compared with matched controls. Here, I review components of this research, and discuss how it has led to new developments about the nature of attitudes.

To start, research by Klein and colleagues has addressed whether an individual's self-knowledge differs between participants with and without memory impairment. Klein, Rozendahl, and Cosmides (2002) studied whether a patient (DB) suffering from severe amnesia might still retain a sense of self. A series of tests revealed that DB had severe impairments to his episodic and semantic memory. To assess self-knowledge, DB and two matched controls rated themselves on the degree to which they possessed 60 personality attributes. This measure was completed twice, one week apart. Correlations between the ratings provided at the two times indicated that DB's ability to *understand* his self was equal to those of those of the matched controls. Importantly, these results were not attributable to social desirability (e.g., DB only attributing positive attributes to himself at both assessments). Based on these results, Klein and colleagues (2002) argued that trait self-knowledge may be functionally independent of memory systems, suggesting that there is something special about self-knowledge.

This paradigm was expanded into the study of attitudes in research by Haddock, Newson, and Haworth (2011), who tested how individuals in the early stages of Alzheimer's dementia compared with matched controls in their ability to remember their attitudes. The researchers showed participants photos of various objects and asked them to indicate how much they liked each object. Participants expressed their attitudes twice, one week apart. This study found that memory-impaired individuals retained a high level of insight into their attitudes. Interestingly, memory-impaired individuals showed less attitude change toward disliked objects (e.g., rats) compared with liked objects (e.g., cookies). These findings suggest that memory-impaired individuals might have greater insight into what they do not like, and converge with the negativity effect, whereby negative information influences evaluations more strongly than positive information (Baumeister, Bratslavsky, Finkenauer, & Vohs, 2001).

Other research has used different populations to address questions relevant to conceptualizations of attitude. In one interesting example, Lieberman, Ochsner, Gilbert, and Schacter (2001) examined whether behavior-induced attitude change occurs even when people do not recall carrying out the relevant behavior. In a seminal study, Brehm (1956) asked participants to select one of two household items (e.g., a kettle and a toaster) that they had just rated as equally positive. Not

long after making their choice, the selected item (let's say the kettle) and the non-selected item (let's say the toaster) were once again rated. Brehm found that participants became more positive toward the selected item and more negative toward the non-selected item. Brehm argued that this effect was attributable to participants wanting to reduce the inconsistency between their behavior (I picked the kettle over the toaster) and their prior attitudes (I really liked both objects). This dissonance is reduced by changing their post-choice attitude (the kettle is much better than the toaster). The principle is that explicit memory for selecting the chosen option is assumed to be important in eliciting the effect, as the initial behavior (picking the kettle) must be remembered in order for dissonance to occur.

In their research, Lieberman and colleagues (2001) tested whether explicit memory is indeed necessary to elicit behavior-induced attitude change. To do this, they required a paradigm where a person performed a behavior (choosing between two equally liked options) that was subsequently forgotten. With these parameters, the researchers used a sample of individuals with anterograde amnesia (and matched controls). If explicit memory is required for behavior-induced attitude change, individuals with anterograde amnesia should not elicit the Brehm effect, as they should have no explicit memory for having chosen one alternative over the other. In the first part of their experiment, the researchers had participants rank a series of art prints. Participants then selected between two prints that had been judged as equally liked. After a brief delay, participants re-ranked the prints and were asked which print they had selected. As expected, control participants had almost perfect memory of which print they had chosen, whereas amnesiacs responded at chance level. However, despite this memory deficit for behavior, *both* groups showed equal levels of attitude change in the second set of rankings. This suggests that explicit memory is not required to elicit behavior-induced attitude change.

Attitudes and reconstructive memory

Research has considered how our attitudes influence our memory for attitude-consistent versus attitude-inconsistent information. There are also ways in which our attitudes affect our recollection of having performed a behavior. Based on models describing how implicit theories of the self influence the reconstruction of autobiographical memory (see Ross, 1989; Fivush & Waters, Chapter 13, this volume), research has addressed whether individuals' attitudes impact their recollection of how often they have performed a behavior. In one demonstration, Ross, McFarland, and Fletcher (1981) manipulated students' attitudes toward the act of tooth brushing. In the study, all participants were given mock dental hygiene information from a reputable source. Some students were told that brushing your teeth every day was necessary for good dental hygiene, whereas others were told that brushing your teeth every day was bad for dental hygiene. After receiving this information, participants stated how often they had brushed their teeth in the past two weeks. It was found that participants who had read about the costs of tooth brushing reported having brushed their teeth 20 percent less often than those who had read about the benefits of tooth brushing. Ross and colleagues suggest that people like to believe that their attitudes are consistent and that their behavior is consistent with their attitudes. When attitudes are *altered*, people misperceive that they have always had the same attitude and reconstruct their past memories to fit this *perceived* attitude. From an applied perspective, this is relevant to work on how responses to surveys are affected by memory-based processes (see Belli, Chapter 21, this volume).

MEMORY PROCESSES AND PERSUASION

One core area of attitudes research involves how attitudes change in response to persuasive information. Here, I discuss ways in which researchers have studied links between memory and persuasion. In typical research of this type, information is presented to participants about an attitude object that is designed to alter their attitude. In some studies, the attitude object is something about which participants already hold an attitude, such that the information is designed to change the favorability of the respondent's attitude. In other studies, the attitude object might be novel, and the content of the information is designed to shape the respondent's attitude.

A consideration of how memory influences attitude change goes back to seminal models of persuasion. In light of the role of propaganda during World War II, Hovland, Janis, and colleagues initiated empirical research on when and how attitudes are most likely to change (see Hovland, Janis, & Kelley, 1953). These researchers considered how variables such as the message source, characteristics of the message recipient, and aspects of the message itself influence persuasion. To elicit attitude change, these researchers assumed that message recipients needed to attend to, understand, and remember the contents of a persuasive appeal. Following from this model, McGuire (1968) hypothesized numerous stages that message recipients must navigate in order for maximal attitude change to occur. This model proposed that in order to achieve attitude change, the message needed to draw the recipient's attention and be understood, with components of the message being retained in memory.

These early models were influential in the development of the most prominent models of attitude change – the Elaboration Likelihood Model (Petty & Cacioppo, 1981, 1986; Petty & Wegener, 1998a) and the Heuristic-Systematic Model (Chaiken, 1987; Chaiken, Eagly, & Liberman, 1989). Both models share the tenet that motivation and ability influence how people process persuasive information. When people are motivated and able to process a persuasive appeal, they are particularly likely to be persuaded by the contents of an appeal. However, when individuals are less motivated or able to consider the contents of an appeal, they are more likely to be persuaded by cues or heuristics relevant to the message (e.g., if the appeal comes from a credible source, it must be good).

In line with these perspectives, research has addressed the link between memory processes and persuasion. Perhaps the most pertinent work has assessed whether persuasive messages need to be remembered to change attitudes. Initial studies assessing the relation between memory for message content and persuasion revealed limited support for the idea that greater message recall elicits enhanced persuasion (Eagly & Chaiken, 1993). It has been argued that this lack of association is attributable to initial models not accounting for individuals' personal assessments of the strength of the arguments contained within a persuasive appeal (see Petty & Wegener, 1998a; Wegener & Carlston, 2005). For example, if an individual remembers a persuasive argument but believes that it offers weak evidence, it is unlikely to change the recipient's attitude. This led Petty and Wegener (1998a) to conclude that memory for the contents of an appeal is not necessary for attitude change to occur. Instead, theorists argue that a message recipient's *cognitive responses* to the persuasive appeal (i.e., their reactions to the arguments; see Greenwald, 1968; Petty & Cacioppo, 1981) play a predominant role in whether an individual is persuaded by an appeal's contents. Ample evidence has been garnered in support of the important role of cognitive responses as a determinant of persuasion (see Briñol & Petty, 2004; Petty & Cacioppo, 1986; Petty & Wegener, 1998a).

The influence of advertisement sequence

In the real world, message recipients are often presented with multiple messages in a short space of time. For example, when watching television, we are presented with a sequence of advertisements in a row. Similar to how the order in which evidence is presented influences jurors' responses (e.g., Pennington & Hastie, 1992); does our memory of the contents of an advertisement for one product influence our evaluations of a subsequent advertisement for another product?

How *knowledge contrast* influences persuasion was addressed by Tormala and Petty (2007). These researchers explored whether the amount of information in memory from a first persuasive appeal influences persuasiveness of a subsequent target appeal. Based on the literature on assimilation and contrast effects (see Bless & Schwarz, 2010), Tormala and Petty predicted that participants' responses to a target persuasive appeal would depend on the number of arguments in a previous appeal. Specifically, they predicted that when an initial appeal contained many arguments that could be stored in memory, responses to the target ad would be less favorable compared with a condition in which the initial appeal contained few arguments. To test this prediction, participants were presented with persuasive messages about two fictitious stores. Participants were first presented with a message about Smith's store. For participants in the high prior information condition, the message about Smith's contained information about six different departments, whereas in the low prior information condition the message about Smith's contained information about one department. All participants were then given the same information about Brown's store; this message contained information about three different departments. After reading the message about Brown's, participants indicated their attitude toward this store. The results revealed that attitudes toward Brown's were more positive among participants in the low prior information condition. Further, results from a free-recall task revealed that participants recalled from memory more information about Brown's in the low prior information condition.

Matched messages, persuasion, and memory

The last strand of persuasion research I want to discuss has addressed whether people are more likely to remember information from particular types of persuasive appeals. Research on *matching effects* has addressed whether tailoring the contents of an appeal to the individual enhances persuasion. For example, individuals whose attitudes primarily reflect their core personal values are more persuaded by appeals focusing on product quality rather than product image, whereas individuals whose attitudes are most likely to be influenced by their peers are more persuaded by appeals focusing on product image rather than product quality (Snyder & DeBono, 1985).

Matching effects have also been demonstrated when individuals are presented with persuasive information that is affect-based or cognition-based. In one study, Haddock, Maio, Arnold, and Huskinson (2008) assessed whether an affect-based or cognition-based appeal would be differentially persuasive as a function of individual differences in the need for affect (Maio & Esses, 2001) and the need for cognition (Cacioppo & Petty, 1982). These researchers found that receptivity to an affect-based appeal varied as a function of individual differences in need for affect, whereas receptivity to a cognition-based appeal varied as a function of individual differences in the need for cognition.

Recent research on matching has addressed whether matched appeals lead to greater attention being paid to the appeal's content. To test this hypothesis, Haddock and colleagues (2008) had participants read an affect- or cognition-based appeal. Subsequently, participants were presented with a series of sentences and tasked with determining whether each sentence had appeared in the passage they had read. The results revealed that individual differences in need for affect were associated with increased recognition of information from an affect-based (but not cognition-based) message, whereas individual differences in need for cognition were associated with increased recognition of information from a cognition-based (but not affect-based) message. This research suggests that individuals have enhanced memory for persuasive appeals that are congruent with their preference for particular types of information (see also Petty & Wegener, 1998b).

FUTURE QUESTIONS LINKING ATTITUDES AND MEMORY PROCESSES

In this final section of the chapter, I highlight possible future avenues of research where the study of attitudes will continue to be informed by the consideration of memory processes. This discussion is structured on what Greg Maio and I (e.g., Haddock & Maio, 2012; Maio & Haddock, 2010) refer to as the *three witches of attitude:* attitude content, attitude structure, and attitude function. *Attitude content* refers to the cognitive, affect, and behavioral (CAB) components of attitude. At the beginning of the chapter, I noted that an attitude represents an overall evaluation of an object. These evaluations are based on the beliefs, feelings, and behaviors an individual associates with the attitude object. Ample evidence has demonstrated that attitudes can be based on one or more of a combination of the CAB components, depending on factors such as the attitude object and the individual (Maio & Haddock, 2010). *Attitude structure* refers to the notion that an attitude can contain both positive and negative components. For example, an individual might like the taste of chocolate cake, while knowing that it is unhealthy. This bi-dimensional framework is important in that it makes salient the notion that attitudes can be ambivalent. *Attitude function* refers to the psychological needs that are fulfilled by possessing an attitude. Through the years, researchers have theorized that attitudes can fulfill different needs – they can express our values, they can simplify information processing, and they can help us navigate our social environment (see Maio & Haddock, 2010). The three witches offer a useful framework for understanding the continued evolution of the study of attitudes, and how a consideration of memory processes will enhance the construct's evolution.

Starting with the witch of attitude content, research might further consider the degree to which attitudes with different bases are likely to be stored in memory. At the level of individual components, research has suggested that under some conditions, attitudes that are predominantly affect-based are more accessible compared with attitudes based on cognitive information (Giner-Sorolla, 2001). Similarly, attitudes where there is high consistency between the favorability of feelings, beliefs, and actions have shown evidence of enhanced strength, and thus should be more likely to be highly accessible and stored in memory (see Huskinson & Haddock, 2006).

Future research relevant to the content witch might consider whether different memory systems underlie how cognitive, affective, and behavioral information about attitudes are processed. Amodio's Multiple Memory Systems Model (see Amodio & Ratner, 2011) argues that different memory systems – semantic associations, fear conditioning, and instrumental learning – are associated with different physiological structures and underlie implicit social processes. As noted by Amodio and Ratner (2011) and Minarik (2012), these three systems roughly match onto cognitive, affective, and behavioral processes. As applied to the study of attitudes, future research might address whether cognitive, affective, and behavioral attitudinal information is associated with different physiological structures.

Regarding the witch of attitude structure, extant research has considered the degree to which people's attitudes impact their memory for pro- versus counter-attitudinal information. Building upon this work, future

research might address in greater detail the mental representation of ambivalent and non-ambivalent attitudes. Further, given findings on the negativity bias, research might consider whether negative information about an object is more likely to be accessible than positive information, and whether such differences are moderated by the ambivalence of an attitude (see Cacioppo, Bernston, & Gardner, 1997). To date, initial research has revealed that positive and negative associations of ambivalent attitudes are both strong (de Liver, van der Plight, & Wigboldus, 2007).

Finally, turning to attitude functions, research might consider whether attitudes fulfilling a particular function are more likely to be accessible. As one example, an individual whose positive attitude toward (say) abortion reflects their core values (i.e., a value-expressive attitude) should have a more accessible attitude toward this issue than an individual whose equally positive attitude is based on the attitudes held by their close friends (e.g., a social adjustive attitude). Further, following from research on content-based matching effects in persuasion, another strand of research might assess whether individuals are more likely to recognize information from a persuasive appeal that matches the primary function of their attitude. That is, if someone holds a value-expressive attitude, are they more likely to recognize information from a value-based appeal than another type of appeal?

REFERENCES

Albarracín, D., Johnson, B. T., Zanna, M. P., & Kumkale, G. T. (2005). Attitudes: Introduction and scope. In D. Albarracín, B. T. Johnson, and M. P. Zanna (Eds.), *The handbook of attitudes* (pp. 3–19). Mahwah, NJ: Erlbaum.

Amodio, D. M., & Ratner, K. G. (2011). A memory systems model of implicit social cognition. *Current Directions in Psychological Science, 10,* 143–148.

Banaji, M. R., & Heiphetz, L. (2010). Attitudes. In D. T. Gilbert and S. T. Fiske (Eds.), *Handbook of social psychology* (pp. 353–393). Hoboken, NJ: John Wiley & Sons.

Bassili, J. N., & Roy, J -P. (1998). On the representation of strong and weak attitudes about policy in memory. *Political Psychology, 19,* 669–681.

Baumeister, R. F., Bratslavsky, E., Finkenauer, C., & Vohs, K. D. (2001). Bad is stronger than good. *Review of General Psychology, 5,* 323–370.

Bizer, G. Y., Tormala, Z. L., Rucker, D. D., & Petty, R. E. (2006). Memory-based versus on-line processing: Implications for attitude strength. *Journal of Experimental Social Psychology, 42,* 646–653.

Bless, H., & Schwarz, N. (2010). Mental construal and the emergence of assimilation and contrast effects: The inclusion/exclusion model. In M. P. Zanna (Ed.), *Advances in experimental social psychology (Vol. 42,* pp. 319–373). San Diego, CA: Academic Press.

Bohner, G., & Dickel, N. (2011). Attitudes and attitude change. *Annual Review of Psychology, 62,* 391–417.

Brehm, J. (1956). Postdecision changes in the desirability of alternatives. *Journal of Abnormal and Social Psychology, 52,* 384–389.

Briñol, P., & Petty, R. E. (2004). Self-validation processes: The role of thought confidence in persuasion. In G. Haddock and G. R. Maio (Eds.), *Contemporary perspectives on the Psychology of Attitudes* (pp. 205–226). Philadelphia, PA: Psychology Press.

Briñol, P., Petty, R. E., & Tormala, Z. L. (2006). The malleable meaning of subjective ease. *Psychological Science, 17,* 200–206.

Cacioppo, J. T., Gardner, W. L., & Berntson, G. G. (1997). Beyond bipolar conceptualizations and measures: The case of attitudes and evaluative space. *Personality and Social Psychology Review, 1,* 3–25.

Cacioppo, J. T., & Petty, R. E. (1982). The need for cognition. *Journal of Personality and Social Psychology, 42,* 116–131.

Chaiken, S. (1987). The heuristic model of persuasion. In M. P. Zanna, J. M. Olson, and C. P. Herman (Eds.), *Social influence: The Ontario symposium* (Vol. 5, pp. 3–39). Mahwah, NJ: Lawrence Erlbaum.

Chaiken, S., Liberman, A., & Eagly, A. H. (1989). Heuristic and systematic processing within and beyond the persuasion context. In J. S. Uleman and J. A. Bargh (Eds.), *Unintended thought* (pp. 212–252). New York: Guilford Press.

de Liver, Y., van der Pligt, J., & Wigboldus, D. (2007). Positive and negative associations underlying ambivalent attitudes. *Journal of Experimental Social Psychology, 43,* 319–326.

Dovidio, J. F., Kawakami, K., Johnson, C., Johnson, B., & Howard, A. (1997). On the nature of prejudice: Automatic and controlled processes. *Journal of Experimental Social Psychology, 33,* 510–540.

Eagly, A. H., & Chaiken, S. (1993). *The psychology of attitudes.* Orlando, FL: Harcourt Brace.

Eagly, A. H., Chen, S., Chaiken, S., & Shaw-Barnes, K. (1999). The impact of attitudes on memory: An affair to remember. *Psychological Bulletin, 125,* 64–89.

Eagly, A. H., Kulesa, P., Brannon, L. A., Shaw, K., & Hutson-Comeaux, S. (2000). Why counterattitudinal messages are as memorable as proattitudinal messages: The importance of active defense against attack. *Personality and Social Psychology Bulletin, 26,* 1392–1408.

Eagly, A. H., Kulesa, P., Chen, S., & Chaiken, S. (2001). Do attitudes affect memory? Tests of the congeniality hypothesis. *Current Directions in Psychological Science, 10,* 5–9.

Fazio, R. H. (1990). Multiple processes by which attitudes guide behavior: The MODE model as an integrative framework. In M. P. Zanna (Ed.), *Advances in experimental social psychology* (Vol. 23, pp. 75–109). San Diego, CA: Academic Press.

Fazio, R. H. (1995). Attitudes as object–evaluation associations: Determinants, consequences, and correlates of attitude accessibility. In R. E. Petty and J. A. Krosnick (Eds.), *Attitude strength: Antecedents and consequences* (pp. 247–282). Hillsdale, NJ: Erlbaum.

Fazio, R. H. (2007). Attitudes as object–evaluation associations of varying strength. *Social Cognition, 25,* 603–637.

Fazio, R. H., & Olson, M. A. (2003). Implicit measures in social cognition research: Their meaning and use. *Annual Review of Psychology, 54,* 297–327.

Fazio, R. H., & Towles-Schwen, T. (1999). The MODE model of attitude-behavior processes. In S. Chaiken and Y. Trope (Eds.), *Dual process theories in social psychology* (pp. 97–116). New York: Guilford.

Gawronski, B., & Bodenhausen, G. V. (2006). Associative and propositional processes in evaluation: An integrative review of implicit and explicit attitude change. *Psychological Bulletin, 132,* 692–731.

Giner-Sorolla, R. (2001) Affective attitudes are not always faster: The moderating role of extremity. *Personality and Social Psychology Bulletin, 27,* 656–667.

Greenwald, A. G. (1968). Cognitive learning, cognitive response to persuasion, and attitude change. In A. G. Greenwald, T. C. Brock, and T. A. Ostrom (Eds.), *Psychological foundations of attitudes* (pp. 147–170). New York: Academic Press.

Greenwald, A. G., McGhee, D., & Schwartz, J. (1998). Measuring individual differences in implicit cognition:

The Implicit Association Test. *Journal of Personality and Social Psychology, 74*, 1464–1480.

Haddock, G. (2002). It's easy to (dis)like Tony Blair: Accessibility experiences and the favorability of attitude judgments. *British Journal of Psychology, 93*, 257–267.

Haddock, G., & Maio, G. R. (Eds.) (2012). *The psychology of attitudes: Key readings.* London: Sage.

Haddock, G., Maio, G. R., Arnold, K., & Huskinson, T. (2008). Should persuasion be affective or cognitive? The moderating effects of need for affect and need for cognition. *Personality and Social Psychology Bulletin, 34*, 769–778.

Haddock, G., Newson, M., & Haworth, J. (2011). Do memory-impaired individuals remember their attitudes? *British Journal of Social Psychology, 50*, 234–245.

Haddock, G., Rothman, A. J., & Schwarz, N. (1996). Are (some) judgments of attitude strength context dependent? *Canadian Journal of Behavioural Science, 24*, 313–317.

Hastie, R., & Park, B. (1986). The relationship between memory and judgment depends on whether the judgment is memory-based or on-line. *Psychological Review, 93*, 258–268.

Holbrook, A. L., Berent, M. K., Krosnick, J. A., Visser, P. S., & Boninger, D. S. (2005). Attitude importance and the accumulation of attitude-relevant knowledge in memory. *Journal of Personality and Social Psychology, 88*, 749–769.

Holland, R., Verplanken, B., & van Knippenberg (2002). On the nature of attitude-behavior relations: The strong guide, the weak follow. *European Journal of Social Psychology, 32*, 869–876.

Hovland, C. I., Janis, I. L., & Kelley, H. H. (1953). *Communication and persuasion: Psychological studies of opinion change.* New Haven, CT: Yale University Press.

Huskinson, T. L. H., & Haddock, G. (2006). Individual differences in attitude structure and the accessibility of affective and cognitive components of attitude. *Social Cognition, 24*, 453–468.

Kallgren, C. A., & Wood, W. (1986). Access to attitude-relevant information in memory as a determinant of attitude-behavior consistency. *Journal of Experimental Social Psychology, 22*, 328–338.

Klein, S., Rozendahl, K., & Cosmides, L. (2002). A social-cognitive neuroscience analysis of the self. *Social Cognition, 20*, 105–135.

Krosnick, J. A., & Petty, R. E. (1995). Attitude strength: An overview. In R. E. Petty and J. A. Krosnick (Eds.), *Attitude strength: Antecedents and consequences* (pp. 1–24). Hillsdale, NJ: Erlbaum.

Lieberman, M. D., Ochsner, K. N., Gilbert, D. T., & Schacter, D. L. (2001). Do amnesics exhibit cognitive dissonance reduction? The role of explicit memory and attention in attitude change. *Psychological Science, 12*, 135–140.

Lindsay, D. S., & Johnson, M. K. (1989). The eyewitness suggestibility effect and memory for source. *Memory and Cognition, 17*, 349–358.

Lord, C. G., & Lepper, M. R. (1999). Attitude representation theory. In M. P. Zanna (Ed.), *Advances in experimental social psychology* (Vol. 31, pp. 265–343). San Diego: Academic Press.

Lord, C. G., Paulson, R. M., Sia, T. L., Thomas, J. C., & Lepper, M. R. (2004). Houses built on shifting sand: Effects of exemplar stability on resistance to attitude change. *Journal of Personality and Social Psychology, 87*, 733–749.

Mackie, D. E., & Asuncion, A. G. (1990). On-line and memory-based modifications of attitudes: Determinants of message recall–attitude change correspondence. *Journal of Personality and Social Psychology, 59*, 5–16.

Maio, G. R., Bell, D. W., & Esses, V. M. (1996). Ambivalence and persuasion: The processing of messages about immigrant groups. *Journal of Experimental Social Psychology, 32*, 513–536.

Maio, G. R., & Esses, V. M. (2001). The need for affect: Individual differences in the motivation to approach or avoid emotions. *Journal of Personality, 69*, 583–616.

Maio, G. R., & Haddock, G. (2010). *The psychology of attitudes and attitude change.* London: Sage.

McGuire, W. J. (1968). Personality and attitude change: An information-processing theory. In A. G. Greenwald, T. C. Brock and T. A. Ostrom (Eds.), *Psychological foundations of attitudes* (pp. 171–196). San Diego, CA: Academic Press.

Minarik, T. (2012). Context sensitivity in implicit attitudes: The effect of independent context and test modality. Unpublished doctoral dissertation, University of Surrey, UK.

Pennington, N., & Hastie, R. (1992). Explaining the evidence: Tests of the story model for jury decision making. *Journal of Personality and Social Psychology, 62*, 189–206.

Petty, R. E. (2006). A metacognitive model of attitudes. *Journal of Consumer Research, 33*, 22–24.

Petty, R. E., Briñol, P., & DeMarree, K. G. (2007). The Meta-Cognitive Model (MCM) of attitudes: Implications for attitude measurement, change, and strength. *Social Cognition, 25*, 657–686.

Petty, R. E., & Cacioppo, J. T. (1981). *Attitudes and persuasion: Classic and contemporary approaches.* Dubuque, IA: Brown.

Petty, R. E., & Cacioppo, J. T. (1986). The Elaboration Likelihood Model of persuasion. In L. Berkowitz (Ed.), *Advances in experimental social psychology* (Vol. 19, pp. 123–205). New York: Academic Press.

Petty, R. E., Fazio, R. H., & Briñol, P (Eds.) (2009). *Attitudes: Insights from the new implicit measures.* New York, NY: Psychology Press.

Petty, R. E., Tormala, Z. L., Briñol, P., & Jarvis, W. B. G. (2006). Implicit ambivalence from attitude change: An exploration of the PAST Model. *Journal of Personality and Social Psychology, 90,* 21–41.

Petty, R. E., & Wegener, D. T. (1998a). Attitude change: Multiple roles for persuasion variables. In D. T. Gilbert, S. T. Fiske, and G. Lindzey (Eds.), *The handbook of social psychology* (4th ed., Vol. 1, pp. 323–390). Boston, MA: McGraw-Hill.

Petty, R. E., & Wegener, D. T. (1998b). Matching versus mismatching attitude functions: Implications for scrutiny of persuasive messages. *Personality and Social Psychology Bulletin, 24,* 227–240.

Robins, R. W., Hendin, H. W., & Trzesniewski, K. H. (2001). Measuring global self-esteem: Construct validation of a single-item measure and the Rosenberg self-esteem scale. *Personality and Social Psychology Bulletin, 27,* 151–161.

Roskos-Ewoldsen, D. R., & Fazio, R. H. (1992). On the orienting value of attitudes: Attitude accessibility as a determinant of an object's attraction of visual attention. *Journal of Personality and Social Psychology, 63,* 198–211.

Ross, M. (1989). Relation of *implicit theories* to the construction of personal histories. *Psychological Review, 96,* 341–357.

Ross, M., McFarland, C., & Fletcher, G. J. O. (1981). The effect of attitude on recall of past histories. *Journal of Personality and Social Psychology, 40,* 627–634.

Rydell, R. J., & McConnell, A. R. (2006). Understanding implicit and explicit attitude change: A systems of reasoning analysis. *Journal of Personality and Social Psychology, 91,* 995–1008.

Schwarz, N. (1999). Self-reports: How the questions shape the answers. *American Psychologist, 54,* 93–105.

Schwarz, N. (2007). Attitude construction: Evaluation in context. *Social Cognition, 25,* 638–656.

Schwarz, N., Bless, H., Strack, F., Rittenauer-Schatka, H., & Simons, A. (1991). Ease of retrieval as information: Another look at the availability heuristic. *Journal of Personality and Social Psychology, 65,* 195–202.

Schwarz, N., & Bohner, G. (2001). The construction of attitudes. In A. Tesser and N. Schwarz (Eds.), *Blackwell handbook of social psychology, Vol. 1: Intraindividual processes* (pp. 436–457). Oxford: Blackwell.

Sia, T. L., Lord, C. G., Blessum, K. A., Ratcliff, C. D., & Lepper, M. R. (1997). Is a rose always a rose? The role of social category exemplar change in attitude stability and attitude-behavior consistency. *Journal of Personality and Social Psychology, 72,* 501–514.

Smith, E. R., & DeCoster, J. (2000). Dual process models in social and cognitive psychology: Conceptual integration and links to underlying memory systems. *Personality and Social Psychology Review, 4,* 108–131.

Snyder, M., & DeBono, K. G. (1985). Appeals to image and claims about quality: Understanding the psychology of advertising. *Journal of Personality and Social Psychology, 49,* 586–597.

Strack, F., & Deutsch, R. (2004). Reflective and impulsive determinants of social behavior. *Personality and Social Psychology Review, 8,* 220–247.

Tormala, Z. L., & Petty, R. E. (2001). On-line versus memory based processing: The role of need to evaluate in person perception. *Personality and Social Psychology Bulletin, 12,* 1599–1612.

Tormala, Z. L., & Petty, R. E. (2007). Contextual contrast and perceived knowledge: Exploring the implications for persuasion. *Journal of Experimental Social Psychology, 43,* 17–30.

Tormala, Z. L., Petty, R. E., & Briñol, P. (2002). Ease of retrieval effects in persuasion: A self-validation analysis. *Personality and Social Psychology Bulletin, 28,* 1700–1712.

Tversky, A., & Kahneman, D. (1973). Availability: A heuristic for judging frequency and probability. *Cognitive Psychology, 5,* 207–232.

Tybout, A., Sternthal, B., Malaviya, P., Bakamitsos, G., & Park, S-B. (2005). Information accessibility as a moderator of judgments. *Journal of Consumer Research, 32,* 76–85.

Visser, P., Bizer, G. Y., & Krosnick, J. T. (2006). Exploring the latent structure of strength–related attitude attributes. In M. P. Zanna (Ed.), *Advances in experimental social psychology* (Vol. 38, pp. 1–67). San Diego, CA: Academic Press.

Wänke, M., Bohner, G., & Jurkowitsch, A. (1997). There are many reasons to drive a BMW: Does imagined ease of argument generation influence attitudes? *Journal of Consumer Research, 24,* 170–177.

Wegener, D. T., & Carlston, D. E. (2005). Cognitive processes in attitude formation and change. In D. Albarracin, B. Johnson, and M. Zanna (Eds.), *The handbook of attitudes and attitude change* (pp. 493–542). Mahwah, NJ: Erlbaum.

Wilson, T. D., Lindsey, S., & Schooler, T. Y. (2000). A model of dual attitudes. *Psychological Review, 107,* 101–126.

Wood, W. (1982). The retrieval of attitude-relevant information from memory: Effects on susceptibility to persuasion and on intrinsic motivation. *Journal of Personality and Social Psychology, 42,* 798–810.

Wood, W., Kallgren, C. A., & Preisler, R. M. (1985). Access to attitude-relevant information in memory as a determinant of persuasion: The role of message attributes. *Journal of Experimental Social Psychology, 21,* 73–85.

19

Consumer Memory Dynamics: Effects of Branding and Advertising on Formation, Stability, and Use of Consumer Memory

Shanker Krishnan and Lura Forcum

Interest in memory processes within the domain of consumer behavior has a 30-year history. Some of the early writings that sparked this interest stemmed from theories of information processing. An influential book by Bettman (1979) devoted an entire chapter to reviewing memory concepts and developing propositions. Lynch and Srull (1982) echoed the call for emphasizing the role of memory and reviewed theories of memory that may be pertinent in the consumer domain. Concomitantly several empirical efforts established that memory plays an important role in consumer choice (e.g., Biehal & Chakravarti, 1982, 1983) and advertising (Singh & Rothschild, 1983; Singh & Churchill, 1986).

ROLE OF MEMORY

Initial efforts at understanding memory designated its role as an important marketing *outcome* for investigation by consumer behavior researchers. For example, in the domain of advertising, if consumers cannot remember important brand information from an advertisement, the ad may not be very effective in helping consumers make informed decisions. Hence, the focus was on figuring out the causes of poor memory performance and finding ways to improve performance via memory cues (e.g., Keller 1987, 1991).

Other researchers working in the consumer choice domain cast memory in a different role. These researchers argued that consumers often make memory-based choices. For example, consumers may attempt to remember information from an advertisement or their own usage experience when making a choice. These researchers established that choices made from memory differed in many characteristics from stimulus-based choices. Hence, by comparing choice in these two conditions, the role of memory as an important *moderator* of choice was established. For example, Biehal and Chakravarti (1983) used choice outcomes as a dependent variable in a calculator selection scenario. In their experiment, all subjects were shown information about various attributes of several calculators. In a directed-learning condition, subjects learned product information in anticipation of a recall task. In a non-directed-learning condition, they were simply asked to choose the best calculator based on the attribute descriptions. Both sets of subjects were given additional information before being asked to choose a calculator. The results showed that directed-learning subjects were more likely to choose the best calculator, demonstrating that the accessibility of information in memory plays an important role in moderating the effects of information exposure on product choice.

More recently the notion of memory as a constructive process involving the acquisition, storage, and retrieval of information has been developed. Researchers explored whether memory could thus play a role as a *mediator* variable in influencing important outcomes as a function of advertising. For example, Braun (1999) showed that exposure to advertising after an experience influences consumers' product memory and may be incorporated into their brand schema, influencing future purchase decisions. Braun demonstrated that when subjects viewed advertisements that referred to an orange juice brand's taste (versus non-taste information, i.e., how it was procured), their memory of the actual taste was influenced. Although Braun had added vinegar to create an unpleasant taste, exposure to ad claims about the orange juice's pleasant taste led subjects to recall the taste as pleasing.

Perhaps the role that has least often been ascribed to memory is that of an important *independent* variable. A notable exception is a study by Zauberman, Ratner, and Kim (2009), who manipulated special memories, for example, a resort where a couple honeymooned. Using both actual and hypothetical special memories, the authors demonstrated that subjects attempt to prevent the acquisition of new and less-pleasant memories by not returning to a special place. Furthermore, subjects also attempt to protect their special memories by obtaining memory pointers such as souvenirs. However, for the most part memory's role as an independent variable is underutilized and future research should explore this role.

MEASURES OF MEMORY

Given its importance in the consumer domain, researchers have also explored what constitutes an appropriate test of consumer memory. Early studies focused primarily on recall (e.g., Alba & Chattopadhyay, 1985). Because recall scores tend to be very conservative estimates of actual memory, other researchers broadened measures for advertising effectiveness by also focusing on recognition (Singh & Churchill, 1986; Singh & Rothschild, 1983). Recognition memory scores tend to be higher (versus recall) because the stimulus is provided for identification in the presence of distractors. Such measures mirror commercial tests used in marketing practice. For example, Starch recognition scores are commonly used to assess print media such as advertisements in magazines. In contrast, ads in broadcast media such as television are evaluated using memory measures such as day-after recall. While initial debates centered on the relative merits of these measures, subsequent research delineated a specific role for each measure. Recall is considered a more relevant test in situations where consumers attempted to remember brand information without any cues. In contrast, within a store shopping environment where the packaging provides a visual cue and possibly other brand information, recognition processes are more likely implicated in choice. Hence involvement in choice became an important consideration for whether recall (high involvement) or recognition (low involvement) should be used as a measure of memory.

Parallel to advances in psychology there was also an interest in implicit measures of advertising (Krishnan & Shapiro, 1996) and whether these could provide evidence of advertising effects beyond those of (explicit) measures of recall and recognition (Krishnan & Chakravarti, 1993, 1999). Such measures typically show evidence of ad effectiveness without a conscious link, at retrieval, to the original ad information. For example, after exposure to a series of advertisements, including one for a target brand *Imperial*, subjects complete a filler task. Subsequently they are asked to complete a word-stem (Imp_____) or a word-fragment task (I_p_r__l) for several words ostensibly as part of a new study. Higher completion of *Imperial* relative to a control group not exposed to the advertisement provides evidence of priming. In addition, to verify that these memories are truly implicit, researchers typically demonstrate that subjects cannot recognize the target word on an explicit recognition task or that the priming is not correlated with performance on an explicit memory test.

Such tests also paved the way for an increasing focus on memory effects that may be so subtle that they are undetected by traditional tests (Shapiro, 1999). Tracking such effects led to the development of newer measures. Shapiro (1999) examines effects of advertisements on consideration set formation via (implicit) fluency effects. He shows that ads can lead to perceptual or conceptual fluency depending on whether the product is part of a scene or featured by itself. These fluency effects in turn influence the likelihood that the advertised products are considered for choice. Lee (2002) extends these findings to showing effects of advertising on brand choice. She shows that ads that result in perceptual (conceptual) priming lead to higher levels of stimulus-based (memory-based) choice. In a similar vein, Nordhielm (2002) uses a measure of perceptual fluency to test the effects of brand logos on consumers. Repeated exposures to logos make it

easier to process the stimulus without consumer awareness of this facilitation.

Consistent with recent trends in psychology, some researchers have also delved into the use of neuropsychological approaches to studying the mind (e.g.,Yoon, Gutchess, Feinberg, & Polk, 2006). These researchers used functional magnetic resonance imaging (fMRI) measures to show that judgments about products and persons are not processed in a similar fashion. More specifically, processing of products (objects) resulted in greater activation in the left inferior prefrontal cortex, whereas processing of humans triggered greater activation in the medial prefrontal cortex.

As with any new method, there is a substantial learning curve that needs to be surmounted before the promise of new insights can be fully realized. Yet the promise of integrating neuropsychological perspectives with traditional approaches holds much promise for uncovering brand insights (Shiv & Yoon, 2012). Apart from its role in corroborating, validating, and extending insights gleaned from other tools, neuroscience can also stimulate theoretical advances in understanding consumer responses (Plassmann, Ramsøy, & Milosavljevic, 2012).

Other researchers have broadened the set of measures by going beyond cognitive approaches. Chartrand, Huber, Shiv, and Tanner (2008) manipulated goals in a subtle manner resulting in the formation of consumer goals without consumer awareness. Subsequent consumer choice reflected a higher preference for Nike (Hanes) when prestige (thrift) goals were manipulated. Perkins and Forehand (2012) use an Implicit Association Test (IAT) to understand consumer attitude toward brands. Using the IAT they showed that brands can affect consumers by forming implicit associations between the self and the brands.

In addition to treating memory as an object, measures of memory have also included an exploration of the process of memory retrieval. For example, the phenomenological aspects of memory retrieval are captured by the Remember/Know/Guess memory paradigm developed by Tulving (1985) and used by Braun (1999) in consumer research. Remembering is a conscious re-experiencing of the original event, whereas knowing is general knowledge without consciously accessing the past. These measures help us understand whether consumers believe they are accessing their original product experience in making judgments. This is an important distinction because consumers make decisions based on beliefs about their memory; if they believe they are guessing a brand's benefits they may not be inclined to choose that brand. Another measure of how people retrieve brand information is the extent to which their recall shows "clusters" of brands from the same category. More specifically, if consumers switch back and forth across product categories in retrieving brands, they are less efficient with respect to their retrieval processes (Lindsey & Krishnan, 2007). Hence, a clustering measure can be an indicator of how an advertisement leads to efficient retrieval when a consumer is making a choice. These studies demonstrate that accurate, objective recall of information, while important, is not the only influence on consumer behavior. Subjective aspects of memory retrieval may also play an independent role in affecting consumer behavior.

MAINSTREAM RESEARCH STREAMS

Interference effects in advertising

Given the amount of media clutter in today's world it is inevitable that there is a tussle for viewer attention. The fights between Coke and Pepsi, Apple and Samsung, Nestle and Kraft are as much in the stores as in our living rooms. Early research in advertising effects has documented the prevalence of a competitive interference effect (Burke & Srull, 1988; Keller, 1987, 1991). Burke and Srull had subjects view magazine ads

and rate how interesting they found them as well as their likelihood of purchasing a particular product. They varied whether subjects viewed ads for different products, different brands of the same product, or a repetition of the same ad. After viewing the stimuli, subjects were given a surprise recall test on the ads they viewed. Burke and Srull concluded that advertising for competing brands can interfere with consumers' memory of advertised brand information. Thus memory for information from an advertisement is detrimentally affected by ads for other brands within the same category.

Keller (1987) showed subjects sets of print ads with varying levels of competitive interference (either two or four ads for other brands within the same product category) with the goal of either rating the brand or rating the advertisement. Keller found that higher levels of interference weakened the link between the brand and its claims but not between the brand and the subjects' evaluation of the ad. Keller (1991) extends this result by showing the moderating role of number and valence of competing advertisements.

The rationale for this interference effect is based on schema and memory retrieval theories. A consumer's schema is thought to be organized around a hierarchy with product class on top, leading to a set of candidate brand names, and subsequently to the claims made about each brand. Consumers are bombarded with information from multiple brands within the same product class, and this information can block other information from being learned and retrieved. This diminishes the likelihood that the product and brand name will lead to accurate memory of claims. Even if specific claims are recalled, confusion arises about which brand was associated with those claims. Hence, in Burke and Srull's and Keller's studies using fictitious brands, the product class was a prime cause of interference.

In contrast to the fictitious brands used in these studies, consumers usually have previous exposure to brands and may even be users. In such cases, prior familiarity may influence interference outcomes. Kent and Allen (1994) examined this issue by testing interference effects for familiar and unfamiliar brands. They postulated that familiar brands already have a schema and hence attribute claims could have a strong direct link to the brand rather than the product class. This should prevent accessibility failure due to weak activation or confusion. Kent and Allen showed subjects print ads for brands that were either familiar or unfamiliar and were either surrounded by familiar or unfamiliar competing ads before measuring claim recall. Results from their studies indeed confirmed the conjecture that claims about familiar brands were less susceptible to competitive interference.

These results from competitive interference reinforce the common advertising practice of ensuring that competitors' ads do not appear near one another. For example, when buying TV media, Nike can ensure that Adidas ads are not featured in the same program. However this practice, while laudable, assumes that interference does not stem from other sources. For example it is increasingly common to see the same popular celebrity pitching multiple products. Yet common elements such as celebrities, music,

or settings (rather than product category or brand claims) can also lead to interference. Kumar (2000) examined this issue in his research on *contextual* interference. He showed that similar images in ads could cause contextual interference. For example, ads for two different products that both feature a picture of a beach may lead to poor memory for the brand name (brand A) and the specific claims made in the ad (see Figure 19.1). Further, such ads do not have to be for competing brands within a product class, suggesting that the locus of interference is not the product class. Thus interference is a phenomenon caused by similarity of not only products (Burke & Srull, 1988; Keller, 1987) but also execution (Kumar, 2000).

Kumar and Krishnan (2004) further extended these interference findings. In their study, subjects were shown several advertisements in various product categories. The target ad was for either a familiar or unfamiliar brand of sunscreen. The interfering ad was for an unfamiliar brand of iced tea, which featured a picture that was either similar to or different from the picture in the sunscreen ad. Subjects were asked to rate the ads and then given a five-minute filler task, after which they were asked to recall

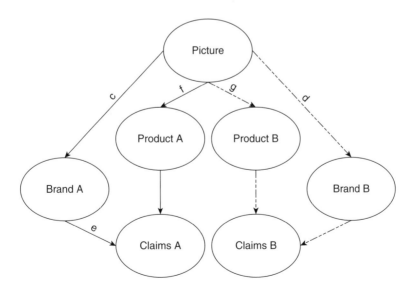

Figure 19.1   The memory retrieval process in interference studies.

brand claims associated with pictures, some of which had appeared in the advertisements. Dependent measures were cued recall of the brand name and claims using the ad image. A second study was similar to the first except that at retrieval, a verbal label for the image (e.g., "beach scene") or for the product category (e.g., "sunscreen") was used rather than the image itself. In this study, there was no interference from the similar ad images. These two studies show that contextual interference occurs when a picture, the basis of similarity between the two ads, is used as a retrieval cue. When the picture is not used as a cue these contextual interference effects disappear.

Kumar and Krishnan thus show that contextual interference can occur for familiar brands. This result qualifies Kent and Allen's (1994) findings that familiar brands are immune to competitive interference effects, and acknowledges the broad scope of interference to include new and familiar brands. Second, these researchers show that contextual interference is caused via a different process. To develop their rationale, they use a particular theory of interference, namely response competition, which has been suggested as a mechanism underlying competitive ad interference (Burke & Srull, 1988; Kent & Allen, 1994). Different associations (brand A versus B) formed with the same stimulus (the picture) compete at recall, thus interference stems from competition between the two different brand names (A versus B) associated with the similar pictures.

In general, memory research in marketing has focused solely on the effects of cues on retrieval of target brands for *individuals* in non-collaborative settings (e.g., part-list cueing studies by Alba & Chattopadhyay 1985, 1986). In many consumer contexts, collaboration is common, such as when watching TV with friends and choosing which brand of pizza to order. Lindsey and Krishnan (2007) examine potential interference effects of collaboration using the part-list cueing paradigm. Their studies contrast memory performance of a collaborative group (three

interacting individuals) with the non-redundant output of a nominal group (three participants tested individually). Subjects were given five minutes to look through a booklet of brands and then undertook a ten-minute filler task before being asked to recall as many of the brands as possible. At recall, subjects were either shown no brand cues or a set of moderately familiar brand cues. The results show the potential inhibitory effect of brand cues in a group setting, which has only recently started to receive attention. Further they show the presence of a double cuing effect in a collaborative memory setting. Individuals in a collaborative context are not only initially exposed to an external cue from an outside source (e.g., TV, radio, etc.), but they also hear these cues verbalized by other group members during retrieval. Double cueing is likely to disrupt their preferred mode of retrieval, leading to memory interference.

Because of the negative consequences of interference researchers have attempted to mitigate these effects. One way to combat the problem of interference is through differentiation of brand cues. Warlop, Ratneshwar, and van Osselaer (2005) demonstrate that distinctive brand name and packaging improve memory for brand information. Specifically, distinctive brand cues allow consumers to make better memory-based quality judgments following a product experience. Further, distinctive cues result in slower declines in the accuracy of such judgments. Thus in categories with many brands where consumers might have difficulty remembering which product is the high-quality one, differentiation can lead to increases in consumer welfare.

A common theme of the research noted above is that interference is "bad" in that it leads to reduced brand memory. A rare exception is Jewell and Unnava's (2003) research that examines the potentially beneficial aspects of interference. While acknowledging that interference is in general detrimental to brand memory, they attempt to identify conditions wherein this principle will not hold. In an advertising context where a brand is attempting to promote new attributes, the challenge is often in helping consumers to forget old attributes associated with this brand. If competitors' ads can help reduce memory for old attributes, this would be a good outcome for the brand. In Jewell and Unnava's study, subjects saw target and filler ads for a real clothing store with either a competitive ad present or no competitive ad. Subjects rated each ad's meaningfulness and persuasiveness before completing a distractor task. The primary dependent variable was their response latencies as they answered "agree" or "disagree" to 50 statements about brand claims (as well as additional items to disguise the purpose of the study). Subjects took longer to agree with brand claims about the target brand when a competitive ad was present. A second study was similar in set-up but the advertisement contained a brand claim relating to a new (rather than existing) product attribute. When a competitive ad was present, subjects learned the new brand attributes to a greater extent. These studies demonstrated that competitive interference can reduce the accessibility of old brand-attribute associations to a degree sufficient to help learn new attribute associations.

Misinformation and false memories

A long history of research in psychology has focused on examining effects of information on creating false memories. In a consumer setting, there is potential that advertising or other kinds of information to which consumers are exposed can lead to false memories. In an influential study, Braun (1999) demonstrated the power of advertising in causing a misinformation effect. As described above, in her studies consumers initially tasted orange juice, with the juice's quality varying across experimental conditions. Subsequently participants were exposed to ad messages that touted the positive qualities of the orange juice brand. At issue was whether participants would rely on their own taste perceptions versus the advertising claims in judging the orange juice brand. Her study indicated that participants' responses were indeed biased by exposure to the ad. Although subjects had actually tasted poor-quality orange juice, the advertising acted as misinformation and led to false memories of having tasted a better quality orange juice.

While the misinformation effects documented by Braun are noteworthy, Cowley and Janus (2004) questioned the pervasiveness of this effect. They reasoned that these findings may be due to the difficulty that subjects have in finding differences between the orange juice varieties. Hence they designed a study to help consumers observe these differences by a) having participants taste grapefruit juice and then see an orange juice ad, and b) assessing consumers' prior familiarity with orange juice. Their results confirmed their speculation that low-familiarity participants were more likely to claim to have tasted an orange-grapefruit juice blend, thus implying that the misinformation has a stronger suggestive influence on consumers with less product familiarity. Consumers with more product familiarity became more accurate after exposure to misinformation, because the false information helped them to separate the advertised qualities of the juice from its actual qualities.

Such effects of misinformation can have an especially strong effect on older adults. Skurnik, Yoon, Park, and Schwarz (2005) exposed older adults to claims about products that were explicitly labeled "false" or "true" and asked them to remember the truth value of the claims either after a 30-minute filler task or after three days. While participants remembered the claims as false when tested immediately, they judged them as true after a three-day delay. Hence the misinformation appears to be judged as true due to its familiarity, devoid of the source of exposure to the information. In a second study, the authors showed a claim to subjects repeatedly, but revealed the truth or falsity of the claim after either one viewing or three viewings of the claim. Subjects were later asked to rate a number of claims as to whether they were "true," "false," or "new." When subjects were not told a claim was false until the third viewing, the claim's familiarity increased, making subjects less likely to remember that a claim was actually false. These findings not only have important public policy implications with regard to advertising and product labeling effects on older adults, but they also attest to the pervasiveness of source monitoring as an explanatory theory (e.g., Johnson, Hashtroudi, & Lindsay, 1993; Pham & Johar, 1997).

While it makes sense to argue that low-knowledge consumers are particularly susceptible to the misinformation effect, Mehta, Hoegg, and Chakravarti (2011) suggest that experts can also fall prey to it. In a new product introduction context it is often difficult to directly compare the features of two different brands. Experts by definition have a lot of information about the product category and may use this superior knowledge to make inferences to fill in the missing information. The result is that experts exhibit a higher level of false recall for features that were not advertised by the brands. The authors demonstrated this in a study in which subjects were shown video game console stimuli with features that were either aligned across stimuli (i.e., "20 GB hard drive" versus "no hard drive") or not aligned (i.e., "Bluetooth enabled" versus no mention of Bluetooth). Subjects were queried on their experience with video game consoles and their sense of accountability (i.e., the feeling that they should be able to give concrete reasons for how they decided on one option versus another to arrive at their product choice). After a filler task, they answered recall questions about the features present in the consoles they viewed, which was the primary dependent variable. Incorrect answers were subdivided into three categories: attempt to align (i.e., recalling a feature present when it was not in an attempt to make the two products more comparable), incorrect value (i.e., recalling a hard drive was 20 GB when it was actually 40), and confusion (i.e.,

recalling a feature present in one console when it was present in the other). While experts were more likely to correctly recall features, they were also more likely to fall victim to attempt-to-align errors, an effect that is driven by experts' greater sense of accountability for explaining their decision-making process. In a subsequent experiment, the authors showed that relieving experts of their sense of accountability – for example by asking them to explain their final decision rather than the process of arriving at that decision – can reduce these errors.

Modern consumption often implicates imagery processing with products such as movies, video games, leisure parks, and many forms of Internet usage. With such products, imagery may be induced during consumption and also in post-consumption behaviors, such as narrating the experience to a friend, posting on blogs, or responding to market research. This raises the question of whether misinformation effects would obtain in such environments. Schlosser (2006) showed that imagery generated from interacting with a product can lead to higher rates of false memories. Subjects viewed a website with either static pictures of a digital camera or an interactive image of the camera and were instructed to either look at whatever they found interesting or to search for particular information. Afterward they were asked to identify which of ten attributes were actually present in the camera they saw. Key dependent variables included the number of accurate responses, false positives, and false negatives when asked which attributes were present. Subjects who saw the interactive image were more accurate in the matching tasks, but they were also more likely to believe an attribute was present when it was not. A second study was similar in its set-up, except that the use of imagery was manipulated by asking half the subjects to visualize the camera and its functions, while the other half were asked to learn about the camera, but not to let their imaginations get the better of them. Subjects who used imagery were more likely to have false memories of features they had seen, a difference that obtained regardless of whether they anticipated a test of what they had learned.

The vividness and realism of imagery generated by video games, for example, has led some firms to advertise their products by placing their logos within the scenery of particular video games. While the violence of some video games might be expected to lead to arousal and greater memory for the information encountered in the game, Jeong, Bohil, and Biocca (2011) show a more complex effect. Their research shows that the arousal generated by violent video games does lead to more positive attitudes toward brands, but poorer memory for brand logos present in the game.

Lakshmanan and Krishnan (2009) find a heightened level of false memories when post-consumption imagery is explicitly encouraged; the rationale is that it is difficult to monitor the true memory of consumption versus the images generated via visualization. In their experiments, subjects were instructed that they would be testing a video game, which had a Mayan civilization theme in its background. Half the subjects were given misinformation about the theme (i.e., that it was Egyptian rather than Mayan). Subjects were also assigned to one of three elaboration conditions regarding a video game tournament. They were encouraged to either not elaborate on the tournament, to visualize themselves in the tournament, or to cognitively elaborate on the tournament. The key dependent variable was a free recall task in which subjects listed single-word responses to what they remembered from the game and then rated these as things they remembered, knew, or guessed. The results showed that subjects in the imagery condition were most likely to falsely recall the Egyptian theme as present in the game.

More recently, Rajagopal and Montgomery (2011) demonstrate a "false experience effect." In their study, subjects were either shown high- or low-imagery advertisements for popcorn (Orville Redenbacher's "Gourmet Fresh" is a fictitious product,

though the brand is real) as well as other filler products. Also, half the subjects sampled popcorn while the other half did not. The primary dependent measures were attitudes toward the brand and product experience beliefs. For product experience beliefs, subjects were given a list of 36 products and asked to indicate any they had tried at least once. Subjects who experienced the high-imagery advertisement but did not sample the popcorn had product attitudes that were as confident and favorable as subjects who had sampled the popcorn. Thus, exposure to an imagery-evoking ad led individuals to (falsely) believe that they had actually used the advertised brand. These findings show that high involvement does not make consumers immune to misinformation effects. In such contexts, high levels of imagery coupled with involvement may actually make source monitoring (separating true from false information) more difficult.

Repetition and spacing effects

It is common knowledge that ad repetition is needed to ensure that consumers have the opportunity to learn and remember brand information. This is particularly critical for unfamiliar brands because consumers know very little about these brands. Campbell and Keller (2003) investigated the moderating effects of familiarity on repetition. They showed subjects an ad for either a familiar or unfamiliar brand of women's clothing or health-care plan, which was repeated one, two, or three times within a half-hour segment of a television news show. Their studies show that repetition results in greater wearout (i.e., the point at which additional exposures of an ad are no longer effective) for an unfamiliar brand than a familiar brand.

The effects of repetitions are known to be contingent on the time interval between exposures. When advertisement repetitions are spaced, rather than massed, memory for ad information is superior. This is known as the spacing effect (e.g., Appleton-Knapp, Bjork, & Wickens, 2005; Janiszewski, Noel, & Sawyer, 2003) and has been shown to be a robust phenomenon. In their meta-analysis of 97 studies, Janiszewski et al. (2003) argue that these studies support two theoretical mechanisms, based on facilitation from involuntary retrieval of information from earlier exposures (retrieval based) and benefit from previous exposures being accessible in memory aiding in processing of subsequent exposures (reconstruction based).

Appleton-Knapp et al. (2005) examined alternative theoretical mechanisms in their experiments. They tested whether spacing of information leads to varied encoding of each repetition (encoding variability hypothesis) versus the act itself of retrieval enhancing memory traces from initial exposures (study phase hypothesis). To test these two hypotheses, subjects were shown booklets of ads to study, followed by a distractor task, and a cued recall test of the brands they had seen. The target ads were arranged so that half the subjects saw the same brand name–slogan pairs (AB–AB, consistent with the study phase hypothesis), while half saw the same slogan paired with more than one brand name (AB–AD, consistent with the encoding variability hypothesis). Spacing of the repetitions of the two target ads was also manipulated, so that zero, two, four, or twelve ads appeared between them. Recall was highest for the AB–AB ads with 12 ads in between them. The authors conclude that the study-phase hypothesis is more accurate in explaining the benefits of spacing in the context of advertising.

Most studies examining this effect focus on memory-related outcomes. Yet, in many consumption situations, consumers may be attempting to learn to perform specific tasks with products wherein usage proficiency may be a more relevant goal. Consider, for example, a consumer learning to use the Nintendo Wii system. She may look through the onscreen instructions a few times to understand and learn the sequence of steps to follow in order to play a game. While playing the game, this knowledge is useful, but may not completely map on to learning how to handle the remote or manipulate the nunchuk. Thus, while she possesses descriptive knowledge of how to perform a specific task using a product feature, she may not have attained proficiency in using it. How would massed versus spaced learning influence learning outcomes related to usage proficiency? Lakshmanan, Lindsey, and Krishnan (2010) examine this question.

In their studies, individuals acquire usage skills for an audio software task either via hands-on practice or via written instructions. In the experiential learning condition, subjects had trials to practice the task; in the verbal learning condition, they read the written instructions. In the spaced learning condition, filler tasks interrupted each trial or exposure to the instructions; there were no interruptions in the massed learning condition. The key dependent variable was usage proficiency, which was operationalized in two ways: the amount of time it took subjects to complete the software task (study 1) as well as the quality of the completed task and transfer learning to a new task (studies 3 and 4). Completion time was shortest for subjects in the massed (versus spaced) learning condition, and among subjects in the massed condition, it was shorter for experiential (versus verbal) learners. Thus, the authors show that massing leads to superior usage proficiency under experiential learning conditions (see Figure 19.2). In other words, repeated practice leads to better usage of a product when these practice attempts are close together in time. The mechanism that appears to be operating is that individuals are able to form a conceptual map of the usage space, which leads to better performance on immediate and transfer learning tasks. Hence not only is their task performance enhanced due to massing but they also have a better understanding of what they are doing. These results suggest that memory researchers need to broaden their focus from conceptual memory to also examine procedural memory.

EXPERIMENT 1: TASK COMPLETION TIME

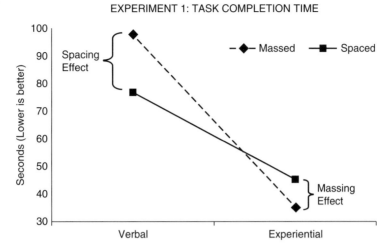

Figure 19.2   A "massing" effect for experiential learning.

PROMISING NEW DIRECTIONS

Sensory attributes

Sensory attributes such as smell, touch, and sound are known to be difficult to encode and recall accurately. Yet many products, such as wine, mattresses, and stereos are purchased on the basis of such attributes. Researchers have begun to explore factors that improve the use of sensory information in memory for product characteristics (Shapiro & Spence, 2002; Krishna, Lwin, May, & Morrin, 2010; Morrin, Lwin, & Krishna, 2011). This is a burgeoning area of study for researchers to explore.

Not only is encoding and recalling sensory aspects of a product challenging, but firms complicate matters further by presenting consumers with potentially biasing advertising information that may conflict with consumers' assessment of a particular attribute. Shapiro and Spence (2002) show that a consumption vocabulary can provide criteria for evaluating the sensory aspects of a product. In their study, subjects were asked to compare stereo brands A and B with market information (a *Consumer Report* review) provided either during or after product trial. A negative review was paired with the higher quality

stereo and a positive review was paired with the lower quality stereo to examine the effect of market information that conflicted with sensory information. Subjects were also given evaluative criteria with or without a rating scheme (a control group received neither criteria nor rating scheme). Subjects who were provided the evaluative criteria and rating scheme while experiencing the stereo were most likely to correctly identify the better quality stereo. Subjects were also more likely to identify the high-quality stereo if they received the *Consumer Report* information while hearing the stereo, rather than afterward. This demonstrates that evaluative criteria help consumers encode sensory attributes more accurately and enable better retrieval of this information. Provision of such criteria thus reduces bias from conflicting advertising information.

Sensory attributes do not always have to complicate consumers' perceptions, however. Krishna et al. (2010) demonstrate that imbuing products with scent can enable consumers to remember product information for a longer period of time (up to two weeks). In two studies, the authors test the effects of scented products (pencils and facial tissues) on subjects' recall of the brand name and product attributes. Both common (pine) and uncommon (tea tree) scents were tested. In the study's first session, subjects viewed an ad for the product as well as a sample of the product; in the second session, recall for the ad was tested. The first and second session occurred either in the same one-hour period, or in two half-hour periods separated by 24 hours or by two weeks. The dependent variable was subjects' unaided recall of the brand name and its attributes. Subjects' recall was equally enhanced by the common scent (versus no scent) in the same-day and 24 hour tests; with a two-week delay, recall was most improved by the uncommon scent. This effect obtains with unaided recall and without reintroducing the scent at the time of recall. The authors demonstrate that this manifests due to the distinctiveness phenomenon: scented products stand out from unscented products.

What happens when consumers are exposed to multiple scented products? Morrin et al. (2011) explored the role of scent in product memory further by examining the mechanism that underlies competitive interference in memory. Noting that the underlying mechanism for interference has received little attention, the authors test whether it stems from inhibition (a new scent prevents an earlier scent from being recalled) or from response competition (information regarding brand A is incorrectly associated with brand B). Morrin et al. found that, for scented products, interference was the result of inhibition and could be ameliorated by providing a scent-based cue at the time of recall.

The topic of memory for sensory attributes is in its infancy, and many important research questions still need to be investigated. Further investigation of how consumers assess the validity of their sensory recall is needed. What alerts them to the fact that their sensory memory is no longer veridical? Additional study of how decision criteria affect sensory recall and how sensory recall occurs in the absence of decision criteria would also be valuable. Krishna et al.'s (2010) distinctiveness hypothesis should also be further examined. What other types of sensory inputs can establish distinctiveness? How are other sensory inputs affected by (or immune to) competitive interference?

Modality

Advertisements and marketing communications transmit information about products and their attributes through multiple modalities: radio ads convey auditory information, while a banner ad on a website conveys visual information. Ads may also attempt to elicit product imagery through different modalities: visual imagery of how a product might appear, auditory imagery of how it might sound, even tactile imagery of how it might feel. Researchers have investigated how multiple modalities influence memory in order to understand how consumers respond to such advertising strategies (Unnava, Agarwal, & Haugtvedt, 1996; Russell, 2002).

Both perception and imagery require cognitive resources. Thus advertisements that trigger both perception and imagery of stimuli from the same modality should result in reduced consumer memory of product attributes (Unnava et al., 1996). In Unnava and colleagues' study, visual and auditory imagery was evoked by an advertisement, which was presented in either visual or auditory format. After subjects were exposed to the target ad (for a fictitious brand of car) and four filler ads, they were administered a questionnaire that included an unaided recall question about the target ad.

Consider a magazine ad for a car that asks consumers to visually imagine others' envious glances at them as they drive by, and that simultaneously presents product attributes for consumers to read about. Unnava and colleagues demonstrate that such ads reduce consumers' elaboration and recall of the advertising content. A radio ad that asks subjects to visualize others' envious looks while product attributes are described, however, does not reduce consumer memory. Thus, when the presentation and imagery modalities matched (i.e., visual presentation and imagery or auditory presentation and imagery), recall for the ad claims was reduced.

Russell (2002) examines the effect of multimodal product information in the context of product placement. Marketing through product placement exposes consumers to products at a variety of levels, from cans of cola visible on a sitcom character's coffee table, to a particular model of car featuring prominently in the plot of a movie. Because television and movies are audiovisual media, viewers are exposed to product information in three different ways, according to Russell: visual information (the product appears on screen, which is the least involving for viewers, who may or may not notice it), auditory information (the product is discussed by characters, which viewers are more likely to notice), and level of plot connection (whether the product is mentioned in passing or figures prominently in the storyline). Russell demonstrates that interactions between these modalities of information have different implications for memory versus persuasion. In her experiment, subjects saw a videotape of a sitcom with either visual or auditory presentation of product information and with either high or low level of plot connection. Afterward, subjects rated the sitcom and then, ostensibly as part of another study, completed brand attitude scales for the products that appeared in the sitcom as well as for filler products. Key dependent variables were aided brand recall (used to test the memory hypotheses) and brand attitude (used to test the persuasion hypotheses). The results demonstrated that the factors that maximized memory for the brand name did not necessarily maximize persuasion. Specifically, when plot connection was incongruous with the modality of product presentation (i.e., plot connection is low, but the presentation modality is auditory, which attracts more viewer attention), consumers were more likely to notice the product as they tried to account for the cause of the mismatch. Thus, the mismatch between plot connection and modality leads to greater memory for the product. However, mismatch does not result in greater persuasion of the product's benefits: matching between plot connection and modality yields greater persuasion.

This developing area of scholarship raises a number of interesting questions regarding modality's connection to memory and regarding connections between memory and persuasion. For example, which modalities are most memorable for which types of products? Are there differences in the duration of memory across modalities? Further investigation into the memory–persuasion link as a function of modalities would also be valuable. Are there circumstances in which memory and persuasion can both be heightened? Or does increased persuasion depend on a high level of memory?

Ease of memory retrieval

Many factors – cognitive load, recency, and distraction, for example – influence whether we find it easy or difficult to retrieve information from memory. However, this ease or difficulty is itself incorporated in how we assess the retrieved information. A few studies (e.g., Wänke, Bohner, & Jurkowitch, 1997; Menon & Raghubir, 2003; Tybout, Sternthal, Malaviya, Bakamitsos, Georgios, & Park, 2005) have explored the influence that ease of retrieval has on our assessment of information recalled from memory. This is yet another research area in which much work remains to be done.

Wänke et al. (1997) showed subjects ads for a BMW that asked them to think of either one or ten reasons to drive a BMW or not to drive a BMW. The dependent measures in the study were general evaluations of and intentions to purchase BMWs. Consistent with the ease-of-retrieval phenomenon, subjects asked to generate ten reasons in favor of driving a BMW formed less positive evaluations of the car than did subjects with the much easier task of generating only one reason. The reverse was also true: subjects asked to generate ten reasons not to drive a BMW formed more positive evaluations of the car than did subjects with the easier task of generating one reason not to drive a BMW. Interestingly, this effect also held when subjects were asked simply to imagine generating one or ten reasons for or against driving a BMW. Thus, both experienced and imagined ease of retrieval influences subjects' attitudes.

Menon and Raghubir (2003) further investigated ease of retrieval by evaluating whether the phenomenon is automatic, uncontrollable, and effortless. In their study, subjects were shown a one-page ad for a Micron computer (unfamiliar to 80 percent of subjects), displaying ten product claims. After viewing the ad, a surprise recall task asked subjects to recall two (easy condition) or eight (difficult condition) of the product claims. The primary dependent variable was whether subjects would recommend the computer to a friend. Evaluations were more favorable in the easy condition than in the difficult condition. Thus, Menon and Raghubir demonstrated that subjects automatically incorporate ease of retrieval information into judgments. They also showed that incorporating this information is uncontrollable since subjects cannot correct for it in response to a warning. Specifically, once subjects incorporated ease of retrieval into their judgments, they were unable to correct for this information if they were informed that others found the task difficult (and thus that negative feelings that arise are attributable to the task rather than the product). Finally, the researchers showed that ease of retrieval is effortless in that it does not require cognitive resources. Whether subjects were under cognitive load (a television program was playing during exposure to the advertisement, but subjects were asked to ignore it) or not, their product evaluations were still influenced by ease of retrieval of the product claims.

Tybout et al. (2005) further refine the understanding of ease of retrieval by demonstrating that at either extreme – highly accessible or highly inaccessible – subjects will evaluate information retrieved from memory on the basis of its content rather than the ease or difficulty of accessing this information. This is because subjects are able to anticipate the ease or difficulty of the retrieval task. However, between these two extremes, when information is moderately accessible, subjects will rely on the ease of retrieving the information as diagnostic in making judgments. In Tybout and colleagues' study, subjects were shown an ad for a familiar (BMW) or unfamiliar (Hyundai) car and then asked to generate one (easy condition) or ten (difficult condition) reasons to drive the car. Afterward, subjects were asked to evaluate the car on a 13-item scale. For the unfamiliar car, when subjects were asked to generate more reasons they were able to do so, but the difficulty of the task did not color their evaluation of the product – they simply evaluated the reasons generated. However, for the familiar car, requesting more reasons increased the difficulty of the task, and subjects' evaluations of the car were influenced.

Future research may benefit from using ease of retrieval as a mediator or moderator in studies of memory. It is also an interesting phenomenon in its own right. Additional work needs to focus on understanding the processes underlying subjective experiences and their impact on decision making (Wänke et al., 1997). Further investigation is also necessary on differences between stimulus-based and memory-based judgments, which will be a revival of that particular comparison. Finally, what factors lead people to expect that information is likely to be accessible or inaccessible in memory?

Affect

Affect plays multiple roles in memory research. It not only influences the ability to remember information (Lee & Sternthal, 1999; Cowley, 2007), but people also seek to recall affect itself (Aaker, Drolet, & Griffin, 2008; Zauberman et al., 2009). This is a complex and nuanced vein of memory research that merits further investigation.

The issue of how affect influences memory has been investigated by Lee and Sternthal (1999) and Cowley (2007). In their studies, Lee and Sternthal manipulated mood by showing subjects humorous or neutral television ads before administering the focal learning task, in which subjects were shown lists of 20 target product brands and five filler brands for ten seconds. Following a ten-minute distractor task, subjects were given a surprise memory task in which they were asked to write down as many of the brands that they could remember. The dependent variable was the number of brands recalled, and subjects who viewed the humorous ads recalled more brands than did those who viewed the neutral ads. Lee and Sternthal show that positive mood increases memory for brand names in two ways: it leads to increased relational elaboration and brand rehearsal. Relational elaboration is the consideration of linkages between a product, its category, and the other items that belong within that category. Consistent with this hypothesis, the authors found that subjects in a positive mood recalled a greater number of brand names, which were clustered according to category membership. They also remembered a greater variety of product categories. Brand rehearsal in this context refers to the repetition of a brand name in one's mind due to the positive mood. Specifically, subjects in a positive mood activate a category node when encoding a particular brand, and this prompts the rehearsal of other brand names in the same category, leading to increased recall. Lee and Sternthal found that subjects in a positive mood were more likely to recall the first three brands presented (compared with those in a neutral mood), indicating a strengthened primacy effect for these subjects. The authors argue that the strengthened primacy was the result of greater brand rehearsal among subjects in the positive mood condition.

What about when we have a poor memory of a particular experience? Consider having a neutral experience at a restaurant and later hearing a friend describe a particularly pleasant experience at the same restaurant. In Cowley's (2007) study, subjects first viewed a short clip of a movie and rated their affective reaction to the film. They were then given the choice of receiving a free DVD of the film they had just seen or another film. The other film options were manipulated so that in the "choose" condition, subjects were likely to choose the film they saw because the other options were unappealing. In the "do-not-choose" condition, subjects were likely to not choose the film they saw because the other options were appealing. Afterward, subjects were shown ads with still images from the movie that featured either humorous dialog or facts about the movie. Following a filler task, subjects rated the film and re-rated their affective reaction to it. Subjects were deemed to have a consistent memory of the film if their initial affective rating matched their later rating. The results show that those who viewed the humorous movie ads, which elicited positive affect, had less consistent memories of their initial affective reaction. Furthermore, the direction of the distortion of their memory depended on whether they chose the film (positive distortion) or did not choose the film (negative distortion). Thus, they inferred their opinion of the movie from their behavior when selecting a DVD, implying that consumers often scrutinize their behaviors ("Have I recommended the movie to a friend?") to infer their original reaction.

Affect can be complex and difficult to recall accurately, according to Aaker et al. (2008). Aaker and colleagues explore memory for mixed emotions. They demonstrate that over time, people tend to recall that mixed emotions were more unipolar – either positive or negative – than they actually were. This shift in valence does not occur with unipolar emotions. The authors tested this by having MBA students rate their reactions (the extent to which their emotions were happy, sad, or mixed) after receiving their graded midterm exam. Two weeks later, subjects were asked to rate the same scale again. Regardless of their exam performance, subjects reported mixed emotions in response to their grades.

However, over time, they recalled their emotions as more unipolar than mixed. Aaker and colleagues also demonstrate that there is a cultural basis for the tolerance of mixed emotions. They conducted a similar experiment with advertisements for a moving company that elicited either happy or mixed emotions. MBA student subjects of Anglo- or Asian-American cultural backgrounds viewed the ad and rated their reaction to the ad, and repeated the rating one and two weeks later. The Asian-American students were more likely to recall their emotions as mixed than the Anglo-American students because of Asian cultural norms that mixed emotions are acceptable. The conflict Anglo-American students felt over mixed emotions led them to recall their reactions as more unipolar as time passed.

This stream of research raises other questions in need of further investigation. How does affect both before and after an experience influence memory of the experience and how enduring are these effects? In the context of mixed emotions, Aaker et al. (2008) argue that implicit theories, which are culturally transmitted, may influence memory decay, which needs refinement and testing. They also point out that there is a connection between felt conflict and mixed emotions that is in need of further examination in order to determine the causal linkages.

Linguistic influences

Recent work on memory has also examined how aspects of language influence memory. For example, the ability to correctly spell a brand name when it is presented auditorily increases memory for the brand (Luna, Carnevale, & Lerman, 2012). The authors argue that this is because correctly spelling the name creates a visual image of the spelling, which is stored in conjunction with the sound of the brand name. This dual coding facilitates recall. Given that many firms use invented words for their products or brands, the authors argue that providing consumers with a word spelled and pronounced in a similar way to the invented word facilitates memory (i.e., the word "rose" would help consumers unfamiliar with "Bose" to spell the brand).

Language can also influence memory through word choice. Individuals seem to be less likely to recall information when it is communicated with certain types of words that negate action. For example, Freeman, Shapiro, and Brucks (2009) show that when marketing messages are based on enactment (i.e., carrying out a particular action, such as smoking behavior), they are more likely to be learned and retrieved than are messages based on non-enactment (i.e., not carrying out a particular action, such as non-smoking behavior).

Individual characteristics

Individuals' traits may also have a role in their memory for brand information. For example, Viswanathan, Torelli, Xia, and Gau (2009) show that a person's level of literacy influences how well they perform on memory tasks such as recognition and stem completion tasks. Individuals with low levels of literacy perform worse because of their difficulty engaging in more abstract styles of thinking. The authors demonstrate that for low-literacy consumers, pictorial representations of brands improve memory for brand information.

Styles of thinking, such as field dependence (the tendency to attend to contextual information) and field independence (the tendency to ignore contextual information) also influence memory for brand information. Ng and Houston (2009) demonstrate that individuals who are field dependent tend to focus on individuating information, and thus remember more detailed, episodic information. Field dependents are also less likely to generalize across product categories and instead form product-specific beliefs. Conversely, individuals who are field independents extract and integrate episodic information in order to form overall brand beliefs in memory. Field independents are more likely to generalize their brand beliefs toward judging brand extensions.

CONCLUSION

Research on memory dynamics in consumer behavior is a robust area of inquiry. Memory has played a multi-faceted role in terms of enriching our understanding of consumer behavior. To assist in the inquiry process, researchers have developed measures that delve into different types of memory as well as memory processes. Using these measures, several important areas of research have contributed to a deep understanding of memory dynamics. In specific, interference effects, misinformation and false memories, and repetition effects have established research streams that contribute to a nuanced understanding of advertising and branding phenomena. Yet there are numerous interesting issues waiting to be tackled. Newer approaches that focus on sensory attributes, affect, and individual characteristics hold particular promise at the intersection of theory development and novelty. Our goal is to point researchers in the right directions in terms of these new research avenues.

REFERENCES

Aaker, J., Drolet, A., & Griffin, D. (2008). Recalling mixed emotions. *Journal of Consumer Research*, *35*(2), 268–278.

Alba, J. W., & Chattopadhyay, A. (1985). Effects of context and part-category cues on recall of competing brands. *Journal of Marketing Research*, *22*(3), 340–349.

Alba, J. W., & Chattopadhyay, A. (1986). Salience effects in brand recall. *Journal of Marketing Research*, *23*(4), 363–369.

Appleton Knapp, S. L., Bjork, R. A., & Wickens, T. D. (2005). Examining the spacing effect in advertising: Encoding variability, retrieval processes, and their

interaction. *Journal of Consumer Research*, *32*(2), 266–276.

Bettman, J. R. (1979). *An information processing theory of consumer choice*. Reading, MS: Addison-Wesley Publishing Company.

Biehal, G., & Chakravarti, D. (1982). Information-presentation format and learning goals as determinants of consumers' memory retrieval and choice processes. *Journal of Consumer Research*, *8*(4), 431–441.

Biehal, G., & Chakravarti, D. (1983). Information accessibility as a moderator of consumer choice. *Journal of Consumer Research*, *10*(1), 1–14.

Braun, K. A. (1999). Postexperience advertising effects on consumer memory. *Journal of Consumer Research*, *25*(4), 319–334.

Burke, R. R., & Srull, T. K. (1988). Competitive interference and consumer memory for advertising. *Journal of Consumer Research*, *15*(1), 55–68.

Campbell, M. C., & Keller, K. L. (2003). Brand familiarity and advertising repetition effects. *Journal of Consumer Research*, *30*(2), 292–304.

Chartrand, T., Huber, J., Shiv, B., & Tanner, R. J. (2008). Nonconscious goals and consumer choice. *Journal of Consumer Research*, *35*(2), 189–201.

Cowley, E. (2007). How enjoyable was It? Remembering an affective reaction to a previous consumption experience. *Journal of Consumer Research*, *34*(4), 494–505.

Cowley, E., & Janus, E. (2004). Not necessarily better, but certainly different: A limit to the advertising misinformation effect on memory. *Journal of Consumer Research*, *31*(1), 229–235.

Freeman, D., Shapiro, S., & Brucks, M. (2009). Memory issues pertaining to social marketing messages about behavior enactment versus non-enactment. *Journal of Consumer Psychology*, *19*(4), 629–642.

Janiszewski, C., Noel, H., & Sawyer, A. G. (2003). A meta analysis of the spacing effect in verbal learning: Implications for research on advertising repetition and consumer memory. *Journal of Consumer Research*, *30*(1), 138–149.

Jeong, E. J., Bohil, C. J., & Biocca, F. A. (2011). Brand logo placements in violent games: Effects of violence cues on memory and attitude through arousal and presence. *Journal of Advertising*, *40*(3), 59–72.

Jewell, R. D., & Unnava, H. R. (2003). When competitive interference can be beneficial. *Journal of Consumer Research*, *30*(2), 283–291.

Johnson, M. K., Hashtroudi, S., & Lindsay, D. S. (1993). Source monitoring. *Psychological Bulletin*, *114*(1), 3–28.

Keller, K. L. (1987). Memory factors in advertising: The effect of advertising retrieval cues on brand evaluations. *Journal of Consumer Research, 14*(3), 316–333.

Keller, K. L. (1991). Memory and evaluation effects in competitive advertising environments. *Journal of Consumer Research, 17*(4), 463–476.

Kent, R. J., & Allen, C. T. (1994). Competitive interference effects in consumer memory for advertising: The role of brand familiarity. *The Journal of Marketing, 58*(3), 97–105.

Kim, Y.-J., Park, J., & Wyer, R. S. (2009). Effects of temporal distance and memory on consumer judgments. *Journal of Consumer Research, 36*(4), 634–645.

Krishna, A., Lwin, May O., & Morrin, M. (2010). Product scent and memory. *Journal of Consumer Research, 37*(1), 57–67.

Krishnan, H. S., & Chakravarti, D. (1993). Varieties of brand memory induced by advertising: Determinants, measures, and relationships. In D. A. Aaker and A. L. Biel (Eds.), *Brand equity & advertising: Advertising's role in building strong brands* (pp. 213–234). Hillsdale, NJ: Laurence Erlbaum Associates.

Krishnan, H. S., & Chakravarti, D. (1999). Memory measures for pretesting advertisements: An integrative conceptual framework and a diagnostic template. *Journal of Consumer Psychology, 8*(1), 1–37.

Krishnan, H. S., & Shapiro, S. (1996). Comparing implicit and explicit memory for brand names from advertisements. *Journal of Experimental Psychology: Applied, 2*(2), 147–163.

Kumar, A., (2000). Interference effects of contextual cues in advertisements on memory for ad content. *Journal of Consumer Psychology, 9*(3), 155–166.

Kumar, A., & Krishnan, H.S. (2004). Memory interference in advertising: A replication and extension. *Journal of Consumer Research, 30*(4), 602–611.

Lakshmanan, A., & Krishnan, H. S. (2009). How does imagery in interactive consumption lead to false memory? A reconstructive memory perspective. *Journal of Consumer Psychology, 19*(3), 451–462.

Lakshmanan, A., Lindsey, C. D., & Krishnan, H. S. (2010). Practice makes perfect? When does massed learning improve product usage proficiency? *Journal of Consumer Research, 37*(4), 599–613.

Lee, A. (2002). Effects of implicit memory on memory-based versus stimulus-based brand choice. *Journal of Marketing Research, 39*(November), 440–454.

Lee, A. Y., & Sternthal, B. (1999). The effects of positive mood on memory. *Journal of Consumer Research, 26*(2), 115–127.

Lindsey, C. D., & Krishnan, H. S. (2007). Retrieval disruption in collaborative groups due to brand cues. *Journal of Consumer Research, 33*(4), 470–478.

Luna, D., Carnevale, M., & Lerman, D. (2013). Does brand spelling influence memory? The case of auditorily presented brand names. *Journal of Consumer Psychology, 23*(1), 36–48.

Lynch, J. G., Jr., & Srull, T. K. (1982). Memory and attentional factors in consumer choice: Concepts and research methods. *Journal of Consumer Research, 9*(1), 18–37.

Mehta, R., Hoegg, J., & Chakravarti, A. (2011). Knowing too much: Expertise-induced false recall effects in product comparison. *Journal of Consumer Research, 38*(3), 535–554.

Morrin, M., Krishna, A., & Lwin, M. O. (2011). Is scent-enhanced memory immune to retroactive interference? *Journal of Consumer Psychology, 21*(3), 354–361.

Menon, G., & Raghubir, P. (2003). Ease of retrieval as an automatic input in judgments: A mere accessibility framework? *Journal of Consumer Research, 30*(2), 230–243.

Muehling, D. D., & Sprott, D. E. (2004). The power of reflection: An empirical xamination of nostalgia advertising effects. *Journal of Advertising, 33*(3), 25–35.

Ng, S., & Houston, M. J. (2009). Field dependency and brand cognitive structures. *Journal of Marketing Research, 46*(2), 279–292.

Nordhielm, C. (2002). The influence of level of processing on advertising repetition effects. *Journal of Consumer Research, 29*(3), 371–382.

Perkins, A., & Forehand, M. R. (2012). Implicit self-referencing: The effect of nonvolitional self-association on brand and product attitude. *Journal of Consumer Research, 39*(1), 142–156.

Pham, M. T., & Johar, G. V. (1997). Contingent processes of source identification. *Journal of Consumer Research, 24*(3), 249–265.

Plassmann, H., Ramsøy, T. Z., & Milosavljevic, M. (2012). Branding the brain: A critical review and outlook. *Journal of Consumer Psychology, 22*(1), 18–36.

Rajagopal, P., & Montgomery, N. V. (2011). I imagine, I experience, I like: The false experience effect. *Journal of Consumer Research, 38*(3), 578–594.

Russell, C. A. (2002). Investigating the effectiveness of product placements in television shows: The role of modality and plot connection congruence on brand memory and attitude. *Journal of Consumer Research, 29*(3), 306–318.

Schlosser, A. E. (2006). Learning through virtual product experience: The role of imagery on true versus false memories. *Journal of Consumer Research, 33*(3), 377–383.

Shapiro, S. (1999). When an ad's influence is beyond our conscious control: Perceptual and conceptual fluency effects caused by incidental ad exposure. *Journal of Consumer Research*, *26*(1), 16–36.

Shapiro, S., & Spence, M. T. (2002). Factors affecting encoding, retrieval, and alignment of sensory attributes in a memory based brand choice task. *Journal of Consumer Research*, *28*(4), 603–617.

Shiv, B., & Yoon, C. (2012). Integrating neurophysiological and psychological approaches: Towards an advancement of brand insights. *Journal of Consumer Psychology*, *22*(1), 3–6.

Singh, S. N., & Churchill, G. A., Jr. (1986). Using the theory of signal detection to improve ad recognition testing. *Journal of Marketing Research*, *23*(4), 327–336.

Singh, S. N., & Rothschild, M. L. (1983). Recognition as a measure of learning from television commercials. *Journal of Marketing Research*, *20*(3), 235–248.

Skurnik, I., Yoon, C., Park, D. C., & Schwarz, N. (2005). How warnings about false claims become recommendations. *Journal of Consumer Research*, *31*(4), 713–724.

Tulving, E. (1985). Memory and consciousness. *Canadian Psychology*, *26*(1), 1–12.

Tybout, A. M., Sternthal, B., Malaviya, P., Bakamitsos, Georgios A., & Park, S. B. (2005). Information accessibility as a moderator of judgments: The role of content versus retrieval ease. *Journal of Consumer Research*, *32*(1), 76–85.

Unnava, H. R., Agarwal, S., & Haugtvedt, C. P. (1996). Interactive effects of presentation modality and message-generated imagery on recall of advertising information. *Journal of Consumer Research*, *23*(1), 81–88.

Viswanathan, M., Torelli, C. J., Xia, L., & Gau, R. (2009). Understanding the influence of literacy on consumer memory: The role of pictorial elements *Journal of Consumer Psychology*, *19*(3), 389–402.

Wänke, M., Bohner, G., & Jurkowitsch, A. (1997). There are many reasons to drive a BMW: Does imagined ease of argument generation influence attitudes? *Journal of Consumer Research*, *24*(2), 170–178.

Warlop, L., Ratneshwar, S., & van Osselaer, S. M. J. (2005). Distinctive brand cues and memory for product consumption experiences. *International Journal of Research in Marketing*, *22*(1), 27–44.

Yoon, C., Gutchess, A. H., Feinberg, F., & Polk, T. (2006), A functional magnetic resonance imaging study of neural dissociations between brand and person judgments. *Journal of Consumer Research*, *33*(1), 31–40.

Zauberman, G., Ratner, R. K., & Kim, B. K. (2009). Memories as assets: Strategic memory protection in choice over time. *Journal of Consumer Research*, *35*(5), 715–728.

20

What Do Lay People Believe about Memory?

Sean M. Lane and Tanya Karam-Zanders

It isn't so astonishing, the number of things that I can remember, as the number of things I can remember that aren't so.
(Mark Twain, 1835–1910)

Why is it that our memory is good enough to retain the least triviality that happens to us, and yet not good enough to recollect how often we have told it to the same person?
(Francois de La Rochefoucauld, 1630–1680)

Although there is little doubt that people appreciate that the ability to remember our past experiences is important for navigating our lives, it is much less clear what people actually *know* about the processes that underlie memory. As is evident from the quotations above, people who are not memory researchers nevertheless do have insight into some aspects of memory. Research, however, has also documented that lay people's beliefs about the workings of memory can be mistaken. In this chapter, we discuss what people believe about how memory works. We begin by reviewing research that has empirically evaluated what lay people know about memory. These studies have been motivated by very different (often applied) questions, but despite their differences, the conclusions across areas are often quite similar. We conclude by describing theoretical and applied issues that are suggested by

these findings and discuss promising areas for future research.

LAY KNOWLEDGE OF MEMORY

Most of what we know about people's ideas about memory prior to the twentieth century comes predominantly from the writings of philosophers and other authors (for extended discussion, see e.g., Danzinger, 2007; Magnussen, Endestad, Koriat, & Helstrup, 2007; Roediger, 1980). For example, as can be seen in the two quotations above, people have been aware for some time of important characteristics of human memory, including the fact that memories can be false (Twain) and that one can distinguish between memory for a fact and memory for its source (de La Rochefoucauld). Although historical beliefs about the processes underlying memory contain elements that have counterparts in modern scientific views of memory, this by no means implies a complete or complex understanding of the topic. Nor does it necessarily imply that the public actually shared such beliefs at the time. Furthermore, there were (and are) cultural differences in beliefs about the nature of memory and what types of things are worth remembering – that is, what Danzinger (2007) calls *mnemonic values* (see also Wang & Ross, 2007). In the remainder of this chapter, we turn our attention to empirical attempts to assess what people believe about memory.

Most empirical research on lay knowledge of memory began in the late 1960s and early 1970s[1] and has continued to grow since that time. Researchers have been interested in what people know about memory for a variety of reasons. Knowledge about memory is thought to affect decisions we make about ourselves, such as what strategies to use when trying to remember information for a later time (e.g., Hertzog & Hultsch, 2000) or whether to believe that what is being remembered corresponds to an actual event rather than something one thought about (e.g., Johnson, Hashtroudi, & Lindsay, 1993). Knowledge might also affect the way we judge other people's memories, such as when we decide one witness to an accident is more credible than another (e.g., Tenney, Spellman, & MacCoun, 2008), or that forgetfulness in an elderly adult is cause for concern (e.g., Erber, 1989). Researchers are also interested in simply knowing whether the findings of the memory literature have been adequately disseminated to the general public (e.g., Simons & Chabris, 2011).

In the following review of research on the topic, we focus on what lay people believe about how memory works and what factors affect its operation. We discuss to a much lesser extent research that asks people to report about their own memory abilities (e.g., Dixon & Hultsch, 1983). The research literature on this topic is not found in any one single research area, and researchers with very different theoretical and applied goals have conducted the relevant studies. This diversity has meant, though, that a broad set of topics has been assessed, and there are similar conclusions that can be drawn across areas. We discuss these different research domains according to their conceptual focus, and divide them into: i) research on general knowledge about memory; ii) knowledge about eyewitness memory factors; iii) memory knowledge related to the repressed memory debate; and iv) knowledge about memory as a component of metacognition.

GENERAL KNOWLEDGE ABOUT MEMORY PROCESSES

Recently, two large-scale studies were conducted in order to develop a better understanding of public beliefs about the general characteristics of memory (Magnussen et al., 2006; Simons & Chabris, 2011). Magnussen et al. (2006) conducted a phone survey of a representative sample of 2000 Norwegians. Across two waves of data collection, a total of 1000 adults answered 13 questions about their understanding of a number of memory topics. Their respondents showed a mix of accurate and inaccurate beliefs. For topics such as the time of earliest memories, the inhibiting effects of collaborative recall, and the notion that dramatic events are remembered better than mundane ones, a majority of participants expressed beliefs consistent with the research literature. The authors suggest that people's beliefs about these topics are accurate because information about them can be learned through normal everyday experience, and thus research simply confirms lay theory. In contrast to the findings of the research literature, the majority of participants believed that olfactory information is remembered better than visual or verbal information, that repression is common for traumatic memories, that young children often remember things better than adults, that memory can be trained, and that long-term memory has a limited capacity. Magnussen et al. suggest that, for these topics, everyday experience is insufficient for people to acquire accurate knowledge or, in some cases, they are simply relying on culturally conveyed beliefs (e.g., repression).

The goal of Simons and Chabris' (2011) survey was to determine the prevalence of misconceptions about memory. They assessed the beliefs of a representative sample of 1500 U.S. citizens on six common misconceptions: Amnesiacs cannot remember their own identity, a confident eyewitness should be enough to convict a defendant, memory works by accurately recording experience like a video recorder, hypnosis is useful for helping witnesses accurately remember, people generally notice when an unexpected event occurs even when their attention is focused elsewhere (change blindness), and memory is permanent. Lay responses were compared with the responses of a group of 16 expert memory researchers who had answered the same questions at a conference. Results revealed the predicted finding. Participants agreed with each misconception by large majorities and experts disagreed unanimously or by large margins. Simons and Chabris also found several trends suggesting that more accurate knowledge was positively related to years of education and to the number of psychology books participants claimed to have read. The authors concluded that their findings suggest that memory researchers have not adequately communicated their findings to the public and that people's misconceptions have implications for education and issues such as juror evaluations of eyewitness memory.

KNOWLEDGE ABOUT FACTORS AFFECTING EYEWITNESS MEMORY

One area that has been the focus of much research concerns what people believe about factors that affect eyewitness memory. Although there has been a longstanding concern that eyewitness accounts can sometimes be mistaken (e.g., Munsterberg, 1908), this concern has grown with the advent of empirical research on the topic (for a review, see Wells & Olson, 2003) and DNA exoneration cases that revealed the role of mistaken eyewitnesses in wrongful convictions (e.g., Scheck, Neufeld, & Dwyer, 2000). One potential legal safeguard under U.S. law

involves the use of expert testimony to help jurors evaluate eyewitness reports (although this is not without controversy, see e.g., Ebbesen & Konecni, 1996). For example, U.S. Federal Rules of Evidence and similar state statutes allow a judge to admit an expert when their testimony is based on sound scientific research, would not prejudice the jurors, and is not commonsense knowledge. The most typical reason given by trial judges for excluding experts is that their testimony would simply duplicate what jurors already know (see, e.g., Schmechel, O'Toole, Easterly, & Loftus, 2006). Because this belief is based on judges' personal opinions, researchers have been interested in testing this assertion empirically.

The majority of research on this topic has used survey methods (although see Cutler, Penrod, & Dexter, 1990; Martire & Kemp, 2009; McAuliff & Bull-Kovera, 2007, for exceptions[2]), and the first studies to assess lay knowledge of eyewitness memory used the Knowledge of Eyewitness Behavior Questionnaire (KEBQ; Deffenbacher & Loftus, 1982). The KEBQ asks participants multiple-choice questions about 12 factors that may influence eyewitness memory accuracy (e.g., the impact of stress, whether the event was violent). In the initial study, Deffenbacher and Loftus administered the survey to a group of undergraduate students and community volunteers. Participants were judged to be knowledgeable about a topic when the overall rate of agreement for the sample was 50 percent or higher. This was the case for four topics (e.g., the impact of stress on memory, the impact of question wording on witness responses, mugshot-induced bias, and the overestimation of event duration), but participants failed to meet this criterion for the other eight topics (e.g., that violence during an event impairs memory, that confidence is not a good predictor of witness accuracy, and that the presence of a weapon impairs perpetrator identification). In addition, they found no significant differences between their student and community samples. Similar findings were obtained by Noon and Hollin (1987) using British student and community samples, and Seltzer, Lopes, and Venuti (1990), who used a modified version of the questionnaire with jurors who had just completed jury duty. The conclusions of the authors of these studies were also highly similar. Jury-eligible adults appear to have poor knowledge of many important factors that affect eyewitness memory, and thus how these factors influence memory is not commonsense.

A second wave of research followed the publication of a survey of eyewitness experts (Kassin, Ellsworth, & Smith, 1989, and subsequently, Kassin, Tubb, Hosch, & Memon, 2001). The primary motivation for these expert surveys concerned whether there was scientific consensus about a number of factors thought to affect the accuracy of eyewitness reports, as this is a critical element in judges' decisions to allow experts to testify about a topic (the "general acceptance" criteria; *Frye v. United States, 1923*). Researchers now had the ability to compare the extent of lay person knowledge about eyewitness memory factors with those of experts using the same survey instrument, as well as ascertain whether any differences between their views concerned topics that met the general acceptance criteria (defined as 80 percent agreement or higher for experts in Kassin et al., 2001). For example, Kassin and Barndollar (1992) provided 21 true–false statements from Kassin et al. (1989) to a student and community sample. Although the beliefs of students and the community members were similar, they significantly differed from the experts on 13 topics (e.g., cross-race bias, effect of lineup instructions). Similarly, Benton, Ross, Bradshaw, and Bradshaw (2006) had a sample of jurors, judges, and law enforcement personnel indicate whether 30 statements taken from the Kassin et al.'s (2001) survey of experts were generally true or false (there was also an "I don't know" option). They further divided these statements into ones that concerned *system variables* (those under the control of the judicial system, such as lineup format; Wells, 1978) and those that concerned *estimator variables*

(those not under control of the judicial system, such as the stress experienced by the witness). The jurors and experts significantly differed on 26 of the topics and of the four topics on which they were similar, only one (alcohol intoxication) was an issue that a substantial proportion of the Kassin et al. (2001) experts had agreed was scientifically reliable enough to present in court. Judges and law enforcement personnel appeared to know more about these issues than did jurors, but still significantly differed from the experts on 18 of the topics. All lay groups agreed with the experts significantly more for system variables than estimator variables. Thus, the authors concluded that there are large gaps between lay knowledge of eyewitness memory factors and what is known from the empirical literature, and that this discrepancy suggests that expert testimony on eyewitness memory could be of assistance to jurors (see Schmechel et al., 2006, for similar conclusions based on a different survey measure).

Across the array of survey studies that have been conducted on the topic of eyewitness memory knowledge, there are differences in sample characteristics, geographic location, type of response required, and the topics that are tested. In an attempt to characterize the pattern of findings across these studies, Desmarais and Read (2011) conducted a meta-analysis of 23 published and unpublished surveys assessing lay knowledge in Australia, Canada, the United Kingdom, and the United States. They focused on 16 topics for which 80 percent or more of the Kassin et al. (2001) experts agreed were reliable enough to present in court. Across the studies, participants correctly agreed with the statements about 67 percent of the time. However, the mean level of agreement for different topics varied dramatically. For topics such as the effect of alcohol intoxication, the influence of attitudes and expectations on memory, and the impact of question wording on eyewitness accuracy, lay knowledge was very similar to that of experts. For topics such as the effect of presentation format of a lineup, the relationship between confidence and accuracy, and hypnotic suggestibility, lay knowledge was much lower.

Supporting the research reviewed above, Desmarais and Read (2011) also found little difference between the knowledge of student and community samples, and knowledge was significantly better for system than estimator variables. Interestingly, the authors also found that lay knowledge accuracy significantly increased from the 1980s to the present, which they speculated might be due to increased coverage of eyewitness memory in the media during that time period. They also found that the response format of the question affected knowledge accuracy, with performance higher for surveys where participants had to indicate agreement with a statement rather than pick a multiple-choice answer (see also Read & Desmarais, 2009). Finally, they note that whether one interprets these results as optimistic or pessimistic with regard to lay knowledge depends on the criterion one adopts (e.g., a simple majority or 80 percent agreement, see also Alonzo & Lane, 2010).

Although surveys are arguably a better way to assess lay knowledge of eyewitness memory than informal assessments (e.g., a judge's belief that a topic would be commonsense to jurors), two recent studies have noted their limitations (Alonzo & Lane, 2010; Read & Desmarais, 2009). Read and Desmarais' study highlights the potential impact of how knowledge judgments are elicited. They surveyed three separate samples of Canadian adults. They argued that prior research might underestimate knowledge because the wording of questions (developed to evaluate expert knowledge) could be confusing to a lay person because of unfamiliar or vague terminology (e.g., *showups*) or because there is a lack of context to understand the question. In the first survey, the authors assessed knowledge using the same statements used in the survey of experts in Kassin et al. (2001) to serve as a baseline. Respondents in the last two surveys answered questions that had been

simplified, and additional information (e.g., definitions) was provided for topics such as memory recovery, repression, and simultaneous/sequential lineups. The authors found that the changes made a dramatic difference such that participants expressed high levels of agreement for most of the topics deemed reliable by the Kassin et al. (2001) experts. Furthermore, questions where lay people disagreed with the experts tended to concern topics for which there were lower levels of agreement among experts. Thus, their results argue that estimates of what people know about eyewitness memory are heavily dependent on how we ask the questions.

Alonzo and Lane (2010) focused on a different issue; namely whether the beliefs expressed about eyewitness memory indicate how people will behave in a situation where those beliefs are potentially relevant. Presumably, the goal in a court case would be to correctly predict whether potential jurors are likely to appropriately account for conditions encountered during witnessing (e.g., stress) or interviewing (e.g., wording of questions) when they are assessing the accuracy of an eyewitness account. Alonzo and Lane note that there are a number of findings in the psychological literature that suggest that juror responses to survey questions may not be predictive of their behavior. For instance, people often to fail to apply knowledge learned in one context when a relevant situation is encountered (a failure to transfer, e.g., Nunes, Schliemann, & Carraher, 1993), they often fail to act in accordance with their stated attitudes (attitude-behavior consistency; for a review see Cooke & Sheeran, 2004), and people sometimes are able to accurately complete a task without being able to articulate how they completed it (implicit or experience-based learning, e.g., Lane, Mathews, Sallas, Prattini, & Sun, 2008; Reber, 1993).

To evaluate the correspondence between expressed beliefs and performance, Alonzo and Lane assessed knowledge in two different ways. First, participants read a series of brief transcripts and rated the accuracy of each eyewitness that was depicted in the testimony. These transcripts varied with respect to whether a particular eyewitness factor was depicted. Across the study, ten scientifically reliable topics (based on 80 percent agreement of Kassin et al., 2001, experts) were varied within the transcripts. Second, participants answered survey questions about 26 topics taken from the Kassin et al. survey (the critical ten topics were intermixed). A control group only completed the survey. Alonzo and Lane found that participants appropriately reduced their ratings of the accuracy of witnesses depicted in the trial transcripts for a number of important factors (e.g., exposure time, unconscious transference). However, the key analysis concerned the *relationship* between transcript performance and expressed beliefs on the survey. They found participants' survey responses did not significantly correlate with their transcript rating for most of the ten topics. The only clear exception concerned participants' understanding of the relationship between confidence and accuracy. Thus, they concluded that the results of survey research might not provide a complete understanding of what jurors know about eyewitness memory and whether they will use that knowledge when judging a witness's testimony.

Both Alonzo and Lane (2010) and Read and Desmarais (2009) highlight additional issues that are relevant not only for assessments of eyewitness memory, but are often a concern for studies that assess lay knowledge of memory more generally. For example, both teams argue that researchers need to specify the depth of knowledge that jurors should possess in order to evaluate eyewitness evidence appropriately. A closely related issue concerns the criteria that are used in individual studies to ascertain whether such knowledge has been achieved, as it varies dramatically across studies (cf., Kassin & Barndollar, 1992; Read & Desmarais, 2009; Schmechel et al., 2006). Thus, the conclusions one might draw from any one dataset could differ dramatically depending on the criteria adopted (Read & Desmarais, 2009).

Furthermore, the finding that responses can differ across different survey wording (Read & Desmarais), or between different assessments of knowledge (Alonzo & Lane, 2010), argues there is a need for a richer examination of what potential jurors know. We return to these issues in a later section of the chapter.

KNOWLEDGE ABOUT MEMORY FACTORS AT ISSUE IN THE RECOVERED MEMORY DEBATE

Evaluations of what people understand about memory processes have also been conducted in the context of research examining issues underlying the recovered (repressed) memory debate. In the late 1980s and early 1990s, a number of cases in the United States and the United Kingdom involved people who claimed to have recovered memories of childhood sexual abuse, often after long periods of having forgotten the episode (see Lindsay & Read, 1994, for an extended discussion). At issue was whether such claims truly involved recovered memories of abuse or whether memories had been created in the context of psychotherapy using suggestive "memory work" techniques (e.g., imagery, hypnosis; Loftus, 1993). As might be expected, this debate was highly emotionally charged as it involved personal, legal (criminal and civil cases), and public policy issues. With time, a consensus appears to have emerged that it is possible to both recover accurate memories and to create illusory memories of events that did not occur (Geraerts et al., 2009; Lindsay & Briere, 1997). Although there have been many different types of research examining issues related to this debate (e.g., Arnold & Lindsay, 2005), we focus on studies that attempted to determine whether people believe that forgetting of childhood sexual abuse is possible, and whether it is possible to have false memories of such an event.

A number of the previously mentioned eyewitness memory survey studies included items about repressed memory (i.e., "Traumatic memories can be repressed for many years and then recovered") and false childhood memories (i.e., "Memories people recover from their own childhood are often false or distorted in some way"), primarily because these items appeared in the Kassin et al. (2001) expert survey. These studies have generally found a fairly high rate of agreement with the notion of repressed memory, but mixed findings for beliefs about false childhood memory. For example, Benton et al. (2006) found 73% agreement with the repressed memory statement in their juror sample, and 35% agreement on false childhood memories (agreement with this latter statement was somewhat higher for judges and law enforcement personnel). Across their three samples, Read and Desmarais (2009) found agreement with the notion of repressed memory was approximately 80 percent and for false childhood memory approximately 67 percent.

Other studies have examined a larger set of beliefs about repressed memory (e.g., Golding, Sanchez, & Sego, 1996). Golding et al. asked a large sample of undergraduate participants whether they would ever believe a repressed memory as well as other issues, including their media exposure to the topic and whether they had any personal experience with repressed memories. Perhaps the finding of greatest interest was that participants' rating of belief in a repressed memory on a 1–10 scale (1 = never, 10 = usually) varied as a function of their exposure to information about the topic. Rated believability increased from no exposure ($M = 5.3$), to exposure in the media alone ($M = 6.2$), to personal experience with recovered memories by themselves or someone they knew ($M = 7.0$). Researchers have also examined whether experience with more mundane situations can increase belief in memory recovery (Naka & Maki, 2006). Japanese students in their study completed a two-part questionnaire. In the first section, they read a story about someone who had forgotten she had copied an exam and later remembered

doing so. Participants were asked about the plausibility of something like this happening and whether they previously had such experiences. In the second part, participants completed a more general memory questionnaire. Belief in recovered memory was quite high (71 percent) as were reports of mundane recovered memories in their own everyday life (72 percent). Most interesting was that their experience with forgetting and remembering in everyday life was positively correlated with their general beliefs in repression and memory recovery. Thus, the authors argue that the genesis of general beliefs about memory recovery may come from people's experiences in everyday life.

The issue of how plausible people find the possibility that a person could experience trauma and later be unable to remember that trauma was the focus of a series of studies on lay knowledge. These studies were motivated by the finding of Pezdek and colleagues (e.g., Pezdek, Blandon-Gitlin, & Gabbay, 2006) that it is difficult to create false memories that are highly implausible using imagery techniques (one of the "memory work" techniques mentioned above). In addition, they argued that childhood sexual abuse is relatively implausible for most people, and thus it is unlikely such memories are created in therapy. To test this assumption, Rubin and Berntsen (2007) asked a representative sample of 495 Danish adults whether it was plausible that a person with emotional problems could be a victim of sexual abuse, yet not remember the incident. Approximately 67 percent of their sample said it was plausible or very plausible. Thus, they concluded that a belief in the plausibility of forgetting of childhood abuse is quite high.

Pezdek and Blandon-Gitlin (2009), however, responded with a survey of college students that included Rubin and Berntsen's question as well as questions about the plausibility of a repressed memory happening to someone they know or to themselves, and the plausibility that they would seek therapy at some point in their lifetime. In their results, they focused on the finding that although

80 percent of their participants found the general statement plausible or very plausible in general, only 25 percent believed this was plausible for them. Thus, they argued that Rubin's prior work greatly overestimates this belief.

In a reply, Rubin and Berntsen (2009) focused on one component of Pezdek and Blandon-Gitlin's findings, namely that when the data were limited to people who said they were likely to go into therapy, the proportion of people who thought they themselves could have been a victim of abuse and not remembered it rose to 61 percent. Thus, among this key group, many people hold this as a plausible belief. Subsequently, Rubin and Boals (2010) replicated this finding in a separate survey sample. Apart from the implications for the recovered memory debate, this series of studies highlights an issue discussed above (Read & Desmarais, 2009), namely, that the way questions are phrased can have a large impact on conclusions that are drawn about lay knowledge of memory.

KNOWLEDGE ABOUT MEMORY AS A COMPONENT OF METACOGNITION

Whereas most of the previously reviewed research examined lay beliefs about memory in the context of relatively applied questions (although the topics tested may have their basis in memory theory), research on metacognition assumes at a theoretical level that people's knowledge about memory and other aspects of cognition can play a major role in how effectively they learn, remember and use information[3] (e.g., Flavell, 1979; Koriat, 1997). Although definitions about what constitutes metacognition vary in their emphasis, it can be described as knowledge and cognition about cognitive phenomena (e.g., Flavell, 1979). The research base on this topic is vast, and many aspects of metacognitive knowledge are reviewed in other chapters in this volume (e.g., Dunlosky & Tauber, Chapter, 25; Goldsmith, Pansky, &

Koriat, Chapter, 27; Hertzog & Pearman, Chapter, 24; Metcalfe, Chapter, 26). Because of this, we have chosen to focus on several areas of metacognitive research that directly assess general beliefs about memory processes (e.g., the nature of forgetting): theory-based metacognitive beliefs; developmental changes in memory beliefs; and beliefs about how memory changes with aging.

Theory-based metacognitive judgments

Researchers in metacognition distinguish between monitoring, which involves judging one's cognitive state (e.g., how well you have learned information), and control, which involves decisions about regulating subsequent processing (e.g., whether to spend additional time studying the material; see Son & Schwartz, 2002 for a review). Thus, the accuracy of monitoring judgments has important consequences for subsequent behavior. Furthermore, monitoring judgments are often made heuristically. For example, people rely heavily on the experience of retrieval fluency to judge how well information has been learned and will later be recalled (e.g., Benjamin, Bjork, & Schwartz, 1998), or how accurately they have answered general knowledge questions (e.g., Kelley & Lindsay, 1993).

More recently, researchers began to examine how heuristics and memory beliefs may separately contribute to monitoring judgments (e.g., Koriat, Bjork, Sheffer, & Bar, 2004; Kornell & Bjork, 2009; Kornell, Rhodes, Castel, & Tauber, 2011). On this view, people make judgments based on mnemonic cues that are generated from the processing of items (*experience-based processes*) or through deliberate use of beliefs about memory or one's own competence[4] (*theory-based processes*, e.g., Koriat et al., 2004). For example, Koriat et al. (2004) found that participants do not appear to take into account the role of retention interval when predicting their future recall of items that they just studied (JOLs), because participants made similar predictions for different delay conditions (ten minutes, one day, or one week) even though their actual recall differed dramatically. Thus, participants appear to be relying on fluency – an experience-based cue – when making their JOLs. In a follow-up experiment, a new set of participants read a description of the first experiment and predicted performance at each retention interval. These participants, presumably relying on their lay theories of memory, accurately predicted the decrease in recall performance across intervals. Thus, participants in the first experiment were apparently not utilizing their (relatively) accurate memory beliefs about the nature of forgetting. Additional experiments suggest that participants do not spontaneously access their beliefs about forgetting unless the relevance of these beliefs is emphasized (e.g., using a within-subjects manipulation of retention interval or by emphasizing forgetting instead of remembering in the JOLs).

Subsequent research has revealed a similar pattern. For example, Kornell and Bjork (2009) found that although participants believe that restudying improves retention, they predict that they will learn little from additional study trials. Similarly, participants believe that repetition improves memory, but underpredict the effects of repeated study on performance (Kornell et al., 2011). This pattern of findings has been termed a "stability bias" in that people appear to neglect the degree to which memories can change over time.

Altogether, this line of research has been instrumental in highlighting a number of important issues about memory beliefs. First, possessing an accurate belief does not guarantee that it will be used to guide memory judgments. In fact, the relatively automatic nature of experience-based cues makes them difficult to override (e.g., Rhodes & Castel, 2008). Second, task characteristics can influence whether people rely on beliefs to inform their judgments (e.g., manipulations that increase the salience of the belief Koriat et al., 2004). Finally, both experience- and

theory-based judgments can be inaccurate (e.g., Kornell et al., 2011).

Developmental changes in memory beliefs

The overall finding of research examining the development of metamemory knowledge in children suggests that although young children (i.e., 5 years of age) have some basic knowledge, their knowledge increases during early schooling and is more advanced by the age of 12 (e.g., see reviews by Schneider & Pressley, 1989; Schneider & Lockl, 2002). One of the earliest studies on the topic was conducted by Kreutzer, Leonard, and Flavell (1975). They used an extensive interview procedure covering a variety of different types of metamemory knowledge with children in kindergarten and first, third, and fifth grades. Their results revealed that even the youngest groups had basic knowledge, such as the fact that information could be lost quickly from short-term memory and that their ability to recall information would be affected by the number of items to be retrieved. However, they found that only the older children had an appreciation for how the relationship between items (i.e., whether they were associated or unrelated) could affect memory performance. Not surprisingly, accuracy improved as a function of age across topics and the older children could more often explain the rationale for their choices. Overall, researchers have tended to attribute the majority of these age-related changes as being due to children's experience in school. Finally, this literature has also revealed that there is a strong relationship between knowledge about strategies and their effective use in recall (for a review, see Schneider & Pressley, 1989).

Early research examining children's metamemory knowledge tended to focus on children's understanding of encoding strategies or task differences, but researchers have recently begun to study children's knowledge of factors that potentially disrupt memory (e.g., London, Bruck, Poole, & Melnyk, 2011; O'Sullivan & Howe, 1995). This type of knowledge has been recently termed *metasuggestibility*: "an awareness of factors and situations that can taint memory and/or event reports" (London et al., 2011, p. 146). In many ways, the pattern of findings in this area is very similar to prior work on metamemory. For instance, older children are much more likely than preschoolers to report that the peripheral details of an event are more likely to be forgotten than central details, and that memory can be influenced by suggestion (O'Sullivan, Howe, & Marche, 1996). Furthermore, even when younger age groups respond appropriately to questions about the outcomes of depicted situations, older children are more likely to provide appropriate explanations for their responses. For example, in London et al. (2011), children aged 6–13 watched a video where a child ended up making a false statement about an event after strong suggestions from an adult. Although children of all ages were aware that the child in the video was remembering something inaccurate, it was not until children were 12–13 years old that most of them described the false statement as having resulted from the adult's pressure. Thus, these findings have implications for interviewing child witnesses, and their ability to understand when the investigator may have influenced their behavior.

Beliefs about aging and memory

Researchers have examined the beliefs that people of all ages hold about the nature of age-related changes in memory (e.g., Cherry, Allen, Jackson, Hawley, & Brigman, 2010; Erber 1989; Hertzog & Hultsch, 2000; see also Hertzog & Pearman, Chapter 24, Ross & Schryer, Chapter 14, this volume). These beliefs have been termed *implicit theories of memory change*, as they appear to be informal constructions and widely shared within a culture (Hertzog & Hultsch, 2000). For example, within western cultures, adults of all ages appear to believe that memory failures will increase from young to older adulthood (e.g., Heckhausen, Dixon, & Baltes, 1989), although older adults tend to place their estimates of when peak memory performance starts to decline later than younger adults do (e.g., Lineweaver & Hertzog, 1998). People also understand that the effects of aging can differ depending on the memory task (e.g., effects of aging are less pronounced for remembering remote than recent events; Lineweaver & Hertzog, 1998). Research also suggests that some beliefs about memory aging can be modified by education (e.g., Cherry et al., 2010), and that these beliefs can impact attributions made about memory lapses by older versus younger adults (e.g., Erber, 1989). Finally, there is some evidence that implicit beliefs may impact memory in older adults such that more positive beliefs about the impact of aging are associated with better performance (e.g., Levy & Langer, 1994; Levy, Zonderman, Slade, & Ferrucci, 2011).

One interesting line of research on this topic connects general beliefs about how aging affects people's memory with more personal beliefs about how one's own memory functioning is affected by age[5] (e.g., Hertzog, 2002). Lineweaver and Hertzog (1998) developed two questionnaires to separately assess people's general and personal beliefs about the impact of aging on memory. In addition, both questionnaires query participants about beliefs regarding how aging affects global (e.g., ability to remember in general) and more specific (e.g., memory for names) memory abilities. The authors found a strong relationship between their general and personal beliefs about memory, such that a predicted score based on participants' general beliefs about memory aging correlated strongly with actual scores for their beliefs about how aging affects their own memory (for related work, see Camp & Pignatiello, 1988). However, analyses also showed that these beliefs were not completely overlapping. Thus, there seems to be value in looking at how general beliefs about memory may impact how people assess their own memories.

SUMMARY

From the foregoing review, it appears that people do know a number of important things about memory. From a fairly young age, we know that information in working memory is quickly forgotten if it is not rehearsed, and that it is easier to try to remember a small set of things than a large set (e.g., Kreutzer et al., 1975). Furthermore, our knowledge base and the ability to provide deeper explanations about factors influencing memory increases throughout childhood (e.g., Schneider & Pressley, 1997; London et al., 2011). Most adults appear to have relatively accurate knowledge about a number of topics, including that our earliest memories date back to around two to five years of age (Magnussen et al., 2006), that dramatic events are often better remembered than mundane ones (e.g., Magnussen et al., 2006), that memory begins to drop from peak level performance in young adulthood beginning at about 40 to 50 years of age (e.g., Lineweaver & Hertzog, 1998), that forgetting is greater over time (Koriat et al., 2004, Exp. 2), and that the confidence of an eyewitness can be inflated by factors that are unrelated to accuracy (e.g., Desmarais & Read, 2011). However, there are a number of topics for which many or most adults either lack knowledge or endorse beliefs that conflict with the scientific literature. For example, many people believe that hypnosis does not increase suggestibility (e.g., Desmarais & Read, 2011), that confidence is a good indicator of eyewitness accuracy (e.g., Benton et al., 2006), that recovered memories from childhood are not often false or distorted (Benton et al., 2006, but see Read & Desmarais, 2009), that amnesia involves forgetting one's identity, and that memory operates like a video recorder (Simons & Chabris, 2011). Other research (McCabe, 2011) suggests that most people do not appreciate that spaced practice is superior to massed practice (see also Kornell, Castel, Eich, & Bjork, 2010) or that testing oneself on material enhances retention more than restudying it.

Although research on lay knowledge of memory has provided some important insights, it has also raised a number of important theoretical and applied questions. These questions include the impact of beliefs on decisions and behavior, what it means to "know" about memory, the degree to which assessments actually reveal knowledge, what people know about other memory topics, where lay knowledge originates, and how knowledge can be changed. We turn next to these issues and their implications.

KEY ISSUES FOR THEORETICAL DEVELOPMENT, APPLICATION, AND FUTURE RESEARCH

How does memory knowledge affect decisions and behaviors?

Nearly all research on lay people's knowledge about memory assumes that it can play an important role in decisions or behavior. However, studies often do not directly evaluate what people know *and* whether they use this knowledge (but see e.g., Alonzo & Lane, 2010; Koriat et al., 2004). For example, most research on eyewitness memory knowledge assesses only the former (Desmarais & Read, 2011; for an exception see, e.g., Cutler et al., 1990). Yet, there is evidence that beliefs can influence what we do. For instance, strong relationships between strategy knowledge, strategy use, and recall performance in children have been obtained in the literature (see Schneider & Pressley, 1997 for a review).

There is also research that directly manipulates memory beliefs (e.g., Winkielman & Schwarz, 2001). Participants in this experiment were asked to retrieve either four or twelve childhood events (which participants find easy and difficult, respectively). They were then told that research had shown that either pleasant or unpleasant life events from childhood were more likely to be forgotten, and subsequently rated their childhood happiness along a number of dimensions.

Participants who retrieved 12 events (a difficult task) were more likely to claim their childhood was happy when they believed pleasant experiences are more difficult to retrieve than when they believed unpleasant experiences are more difficult to retrieve. Thus, participants' beliefs about memory processes changed how they interpreted the subjective experience that accompanied their recall. Along these lines, there is evidence that people's beliefs about how memory changes in older adulthood can affect the implications they draw about memory difficulties (e.g., Erber, 1989).

These findings suggest two paths for future research. First, there is a need for research that attempts to understand the mechanisms underlying the relationship between memory beliefs and subsequent behavior. For example, as demonstrated by Koriat, Bjork, and colleagues (e.g., Koriat et al., 2004), possessing an accurate lay theory of memory does not ensure that people will apply this knowledge appropriately. Consequently, the issue of when memory beliefs will and will not affect people's decisions is of both theoretical and applied interest. A second research question concerns how different types of beliefs about memory might interact to affect behavior. For example, researchers have examined how more general beliefs about memory can affect specific beliefs that people hold about their own memory abilities, and vice versa (Lineweaver & Hertzog, 1998). In this conception, both general and specific beliefs might have both direct and indirect effects on a person's strategy use or behavior.

What do people need to know about memory and how much knowledge is enough?

Regardless of the way memory knowledge is assessed, one critical issue for researchers is: What do lay people need to know about memory, and in what depth? The answer to the first part of this question may seem straightforward. People need to know about aspects of memory that directly bear on tasks they are expected to perform. For example, jurors might be expected to know about factors that could affect eyewitness memory (at least those relevant to a particular case) to make an informed evaluation of witness accuracy. But, as recently argued by Roediger (2008), there appear to be no universal laws of memory that hold across different conditions. In other words, memory "facts" differ according to specific methodological details such as the characteristics of participants in the study or encoding and retrieval conditions. Take for example, the confidence-accuracy item used by Kassin et al. (2001), "An eyewitness's confidence is not a good predictor of his or her accuracy," for which 87 percent of the experts sampled agreed was a reliable enough finding to offer testimony. Yet, research on the topic suggests that the confidence-accuracy relation is likely to vary widely depending on the context (e.g., Lindsay, Read, & Sharma, 1998). When experts endorse questions like this, presumably they understand they are generalizing across conditions, but that would not be a reasonable assumption with respect to lay people. At the very least, this suggests that researchers must assess memory knowledge in ways that reflect its inherent context-dependence (e.g., through the use of scenarios) if people's answers are to be reasonably classified as accurate or not.

The issue of depth of knowledge has been termed *sufficiency* criteria (Alonzo & Lane, 2010) and it can be different for different research domains or even within a domain. For example, research on knowledge of eyewitness memory has focused on whether potential jurors know enough about specific factors to obviate the need for an expert witness (whether it is commonsense, e.g., Schmechel et al., 2006). Researchers have used different criteria for evaluating "adequate" levels of juror knowledge (cf. Benton et al., 2006; Kassin & Barndollar, 1992; Read & Desmarais, 2009), including different target levels of percentage agreement (e.g., 60, 70, or 80 percent) and whether the mean level of agreement for the lay person sample significantly differed from that of the Kassin et al. (2001) experts. In work examining more general knowledge about memory, researchers have compared the beliefs of lay people qualitatively with the findings of the scientific literature (Magnussen et al., 2006) or quantitatively to the judgments of a group of experts (Simons & Chabris, 2011). Although sufficiency criteria can be important for basic research, it is critical for research with an applied focus. Its importance is clear when one recognizes that the implications that are drawn from the same data can differ markedly depending on the criterion that is adopted. Finally, sufficiency criteria can also function as a benchmark for interventions, such as whether an educational program helps people to reach a desired level of knowledge.

How should we assess memory knowledge?

In many of the studies we have reviewed, participants indicated what they knew about memory by agreeing or disagreeing with a survey statement, or by picking one of multiple responses. Although this is not true of every study of lay knowledge (e.g., London et al., 2011), it does suggest that someone could choose a "correct" or "incorrect" response with rather shallow levels of understanding or by guessing (Read & Desmarais, 2009). As in other domains of knowledge, people who express high levels of confidence in such answers might nevertheless know little about the memory processes involved (the illusion of explanatory depth, e.g., Keil, 2003). Furthermore, some questionnaire research on eyewitness memory has been criticized because it is not clear that participants would interpret the questions in ways that are similar to experts (Read & Desmarais, 2009). More broadly, the potential limitations of questionnaire research for understanding memory knowledge have been

discussed extensively (e.g., Alonzo & Lane, 2010; Cavanaugh, Feldman, & Hertzog, 1998; Herrmann, 1982).

Despite these limitations, questionnaire research has many strengths. For example, it provides the most feasible way of directly assessing the knowledge of large representative samples of lay people (e.g., Simons & Chabris, 2011). However, future research in the domain of memory knowledge could benefit from the extensive lessons learned in the broader survey literature (e.g., Schwarz, 1999), including an awareness of the impact of different response alternatives and rating scales, and specific techniques such as qualitative pre-testing that are aimed at identifying potential issues. Furthermore, empirical research on attitude-behavior consistency and associated theories (for a review, see Cooke & Sheeran, 2004) suggest issues that researchers should consider when structuring their questionnaires to maximize the likelihood of detecting relationships between expressed beliefs and target behaviors. We also believe that researchers should consider using interview or related techniques to elicit richer explanations of lay knowledge (in separate experiments or in tandem with questionnaires), as such data has shown to be quite useful in developmental research (e.g., O'Sullivan et al., 1996). In short, we see a role for strong, well-developed questionnaire instruments in a broader research effort to understand what people know about memory.

OTHER DIRECTIONS FOR FUTURE RESEARCH

What do people know about other aspects of memory?

Despite the substantial literature examining memory beliefs, there remain many more topics that are relatively unexplored. We highlight just three topics, beginning with the fact that there has been little research on people's (explicit) beliefs about implicit memory. One possible reason for this is that researchers have often focused on documenting that implicit memory effects are obtained without participants' awareness that they are relying on memory for information learned in a previous episode (e.g., Bowers & Schacter, 1990). Thus, there are studies showing that people do not believe that prior information influenced their behavior in a specific situation (e.g., Northrup & Mulligan, 2012, see also the priming literature, e.g., Harris, Bargh, & Brownell, 2009), but few, if any, on people's general beliefs about the topic. Another relatively unexplored topic involves people's beliefs about how memory is affected by social interaction (although see Magnussen et al., 2006). For example, research has documented the facilitatory and inhibitory effects of collaborative remembering (see e.g., Rajaram, 2011) and how memories are affected by the stories we tell others (e.g., Marsh, 2007). A final topic concerns beliefs about how memory may be affected by technological advances. For example, recent work has suggested that people may emphasize source recall over item recall when they believe that they will have online access to information at a later time (Sparrow, Liu, & Wegner, 2011).

Where does memory knowledge come from?

Presumably, memory knowledge comes from personal experience with remembering, from discussions about memory with other people, from exposure to stories, movies, and news discussions of memory-related topics, and from the process of education. Surprisingly little research has attempted to examine the situations and experiences that give rise to knowledge about memory. There are exceptions, of course. As previously discussed, Naka and Miki (2006) found that participants' experience with forgetting and recovery in everyday circumstances was associated with beliefs about recovered memories of traumatic events. Similarly, Golding et al. (1996) found that beliefs in recovered traumatic memories increased with exposure to

the topic in the media or when participants had recovered a memory or knew someone who had done so. Others have examined how memory-related topics are portrayed in the media, such as television crime dramas (e.g., Desmarais, Price, & Read, 2008). There is also relevant research from the developmental literature, such as work that documents how adults help shape what children learn about the process of autobiographical remembering (e.g., Nelson & Fivush, 2004). Understanding which sources foster accurate or inaccurate conceptions of memory can be of particular use to those attempting to change such knowledge.

Can memory knowledge be changed?

As we have discussed, there is evidence that memory knowledge can impact decisions and behavior (e.g., Winkielman & Schwarz, 2001). Furthermore, it has been argued that incorrect beliefs about memory can impact memory performance (e.g., by making children prone to suggestion or memory construction; London et al., 2011). Because of the potential impact of inaccurate memory knowledge, there is interest in exploring how it might be corrected. In the context of memory knowledge research, there is some evidence that education can play a role. For example, McCabe (2011) examined knowledge about the impact of study strategies on memory and found that accuracy was higher in students exposed to classes that covered the topics. Other researchers have noted that education is sometimes correlated with more accurate knowledge of memory concepts (e.g., Magnussen et al., 2006). Nevertheless, researchers exploring the impact of education on inaccurate memory knowledge would do well to see such efforts in the context of broader research on how to change naive theories about biology, psychology, physics, and other domains (*conceptual change* research, e.g., see Sinatra & Pintrich, 2008). This research suggests that changing lay knowledge about some memory topics is likely to be difficult, and will involve far more than simply exposing people to accurate factual information (e.g., see discussion of the constellation of beliefs thought to be involved in creation of false memories of traumatic events, Lindsay & Read, 1994).

CONCLUSION

What lay people know about memory has been an interest of researchers seeking to understand how potential jurors evaluate eyewitness evidence (e.g., Read & Desmarais, 2009), how clients in therapy might come to believe they have a repressed traumatic memory (e.g., Golding et al., 1996), how knowledge of memory affects people's ability to use their memories effectively (e.g., Koriat et al., 2004), and simply whether people believe common misconceptions (e.g., Simons & Chabris, 2011). Our review suggests that people appear to know many things about how memory actually works, and yet also have beliefs that are mistaken. Though much has been learned, there are many important questions left to answer. We look forward to the next generation of research aimed at a deeper understanding of what people know about memory and the mechanisms by which such knowledge influences important decisions and behavior, as well as the theoretical and applied benefits that are likely to result.

ACKNOWLEDGMENTS

We thank Robert Mathews, Deborah Eakin, Robert Bjork, and Tim Perfect for their comments on an earlier version of this chapter.

NOTES

1 There were a small number of questionnaire studies about people's knowledge of their own memory in the late nineteenth century (e.g., Colegrove, 1899). Questions tended to focus on people's ability to report personal examples of memory concepts (e.g., "Can you state examples of false memories experienced?") or asked them to offer an opinion about factors that affected their own memory (e.g., "What studies have best developed your memory?"; both examples, p. 229).

2 Desmarais and Read (2011) distinguish two methods for assessing lay knowledge of eyewitness memory. *Direct* methods such as surveys ask participants what they know about factors affecting eyewitness memory. *Indirect* methods assess how people use their knowledge, such as evaluating the credibility of witnesses who vary in their initial witnessing conditions (e.g., Cutler et al., 1990). Most studies use one method exclusively.

3 A number of theories of memory also assume a role for beliefs about memory, including the source-monitoring framework (Johnson et al., 1993).

4 Note that theory-based processes rely on knowledge of memory in general as well as idiosyncratic knowledge of one's own memory processes. To date, there has been no attempt to separately assess these two types of knowledge within this framework.

5 The vast majority of research on beliefs about memory and aging has focused on beliefs that older adults hold about their own memory performance (*self-referent beliefs*, e.g., Dixon & Hultsch, 1983).

REFERENCES

Alonzo, J. D., & Lane, S. M. (2010). Saying versus judging: Assessing knowledge of eyewitness memory. *Applied Cognitive Psychology, 24*, 1245–1264.

Arnold, M. M., & Lindsay, D. S. (2005). Remembrance of remembrance past. *Memory, 13*, 533–549.

Benjamin, A. S., Bjork, R. A., & Schwartz, B. L. (1998). The mismeasure of memory: When retrieval fluency is misleading as a metamnemonic index. *Journal of Experimental Psychology: General, 127*, 55–68.

Benton, T. R., Ross, D. F., Bradshaw, E., & Bradshaw, G. S. (2006). Eyewitness memory is still not common sense: Comparing jurors, judges and law enforcement to eyewitness experts. *Applied Cognitive Psychology, 20*, 115–129.

Bowers, J. S., & Schacter, D. L. (1990). Implicit memory and test awareness. *Journal of Experimental Psychology. Learning, Memory, and Cognition, 16*, 404–416.

Camp, C. J., & Pignatiello, M. F. (1988). Beliefs about fact retrieval and inferential reasoning across the adult lifespan. *Experimental Aging Research, 14*, 89–97.

Cavanaugh, J. C., Feldman, J. M., & Hertzog, C. (1998). Memory beliefs as social cognition: A reconceptualization of what memory questionnaires assess. *Review of General Psychology, 2,* 48–65.

Cherry, K. E., Allen, P. D., Jackson, E. M., Hawley, K. S., & Brigman, S. (2010). Knowledge of normal and pathological memory aging in college students, social workers, and health care professionals. *Educational Gerontology, 36,* 281–297.

Colegrove, F. W. (1899). Individual memories. *American Journal of Psychology, 10,* 228–255.

Cooke, R., & Sheeran, P. (2004). Moderation of cognition-intention and cognition-behavior relations: a meta-analysis of properties of variables from the theory of planned behavior. *British Journal of Social Psychology, 43,* 159–186.

Cutler, B. L., Penrod, S. D., & Dexter, H. R. (1990). Juror sensitivity to eyewitness identification evidence. *Law and Human Behavior, 14,* 185–191.

Danzinger, K. (2007). *Marking the mind: a history of memory.* New York: Cambridge University Press.

Deffenbacher, K. A., & Loftus, E. F. (1982). Do jurors share a common understanding concerning eye-witness behaviour? *Law and Human Behavior, 6,* 15–30.

Desmarais, S. L., & Read, J. D. (2011). After 30 years, what do we know about what jurors know? A meta-analytic review of lay knowledge regarding eyewitness factors. *Law and Human Behavior, 35,* 200–210.

Desmarais, S. L., Price, H. L., & Read, J. D. (2008). "Objection your honor! Television is not the relevant authority." Crime drama portrayals of eyewitness issues. *Psychology, Crime & Law, 14,* 225–243.

Dixon, R. A., & Hultsch, D. F. (1983). Structure and development of metamemory in adulthood. *Journal of Gerontology, 38,* 682–688.

Ebbesen, E. B., & Konecni, V. J. (1996). Eyewitness memory research: Probative v. Prejudicial value. *Expert Evidence, 5,* 2–28.

Erber, J. T. (1989). Young and older adults' appraisal of memory failures in young and older adult target persons. *Journal of Gerontology, 44,* 170–175.

Flavell, J. H. (1979). Metacognition and cognitive monitoring: A new area of cognitive-developmental inquiry. *American Psychologist, 34,* 906–911.

Geraerts, E., Lindsay, D. S., Merckelbach, H., Jelicic, M., Raymaekers, L., Arnold, M. M., & Schooler, J. W. (2009). Cognitive mechanisms underlying recovered-memory experiences of childhood sexual abuse. *Psychological Science, 20,* 92–98.

Golding, J. M., Sanchez, R. P., & Sego, S. A. (1996). Do you believe in repressed memories? *Professional Psychology: Research and Practice, 27,* 429–437.

Harris, J. L., Bargh, J. A., & Brownell, K. D. (2009). Priming effects of television food advertising on eating behavior. *Health Psychology, 28,* 404–413.

Heckhausen, J., Dixon, R. A., & Baltes, P. B. (1989). Gains and losses in development throughout adulthood as perceived by different adult age groups. *Developmental Psychology, 25,* 109–121.

Herrmann, D. J. (1982). Know thy memory: The use of questionnaires to assess and study memory. *Psychological Bulletin, 92,* 434–452.

Hertzog, C., (2002). Metacognition in older adults: Implications for application. In T. J. Perfect and B. L. Schwartz (Eds.), *Applied metacognition* (pp. 169–196). New York: Cambridge University Press.

Hertzog, C., & Hultsch, D. F. (2000). Metacognition in adulthood and old age. In F. I. M. Craik, and T. A. Salthouse (Eds.), *The handbook of aging and cognition* (pp. 417–466). Mahwah, NJ: Lawrence Erlbaum Associated Publishers.

Johnson, M. K., Hashtroudi, S., & Lindsay, D. (1993). Source monitoring. *Psychological Bulletin, 114,* 3–28.

Kassin, S. M., & Barndollar, K. A. (1992). The psychology of eyewitness testimony: A comparison of experts and prospective jurors. *Journal of Applied Social Psychology, 22,* 1241–1249.

Kassin, S. M., Ellsworth, P. C., & Smith, V. L. (1989). The "general acceptance" of psychological research on eyewitness testimony: A survey of the experts. *American Psychologist, 44,* 1089–1098.

Kassin, S. M., Tubb, V. A., Hosch, H. M., & Memon, A. (2001). On the "general acceptance" of eyewitness testimony research: A new survey of the experts. *American Psychologist, 56,* 405–416.

Keil, F. C. (2003). Folkscience: Coarse interpretations of a complex reality. *Trends in Cognitive Sciences, 7,* 368–373.

Kelley, C. M., & Lindsay, S. D. (1993). Remembering mistaken for knowing: Ease of retrieval as a basis for confidence in answers to general knowledge questions. *Journal of Memory and Language, 32,* 1–24.

Koriat, A. (1997). Monitoring one's own knowledge during study: A cue-utilization approach to judgments of learning. *Journal of Experimental Psychology: General, 126,* 349–370.

Koriat, A., Bjork, R. A., Sheffer, L., & Bar, S. K. (2004). Predicting one's own forgetting: The role of experience-based and theory-based processes. *Journal of Experimental Psychology: General, 133,* 643–656.

Kornell, N., & Bjork, R. A. (2009). A stability bias in human memory: Overestimating remembering and underestimating learning. *Journal of Experimental Psychology: General, 138,* 449–468.

Kornell, N., Castel, A. D., Eich, T. S., & Bjork, R. A. (2010). Spacing as the friend of both memory and induction in young and older adults. *Psychology and Aging, 25,* 498–503.

Kornell, N., Rhodes, M. G., Castel, A. D., & Tauber, S. K. (2011). The ease of processing heuristic and the stability bias: Dissociating memory, memory beliefs, and memory judgments. *Psychological Science, 22,* 787–794.

Kreutzer, M. A., Leonard, C., & Flavell, J. H. (1975). An interview study of children's knowledge about memory. *Monographs of The Society For Research in Child Development, 40,* 1–60.

Lane, S. M., Mathews, R. C., Sallas, B., Prattini, R., & Sun, R. (2008). Facilitative interactions of model- and experience-based processes: Implications for type and flexibility of representation. *Memory & Cognition, 36,* 157–169.

Levy, B., & Langer, E. (1994). Aging free from negative stereotypes: Successful memory in China among the American deaf. *Journal of Personality and Social Psychology, 66,* 989–997.

Levy, B., Zonderman, A. B., Slade, M. D., & Ferrucci, L. (2012). Memory shaped by age stereotypes over time. *The Journals of Gerontology: Series B: Psychological Sciences and Social Sciences, 67,* 432–436.

Lindsay, D. S., & Briere, J. (1997). The controversy regarding recovered memories of childhood sexual abuse: Pitfalls, bridges and future directions. *Journal of Interpersonal Violence, 12,* 631–647.

Lindsay, D. S., & Read, J. D. (1994). Psychotherapy and memories of childhood sexual abuse: A cognitive perspective. *Applied Cognitive Psychology, 8,* 281–338.

Lindsay, D. S., Read, J. D., & Sharma, K. (1998). Accuracy and confidence in person identification: The relationship is strong with witnessing conditions vary widely. *Psychological Science, 9,* 215–218.

Lineweaver, T. T., & Hertzog, C. (1998). Adults' efficacy and control beliefs regarding memory and aging: Separating general from personal beliefs. *Aging, Neuropsychology, and Cognition, 5,* 264–296.

Loftus, E. F. (1993). The reality of repressed memories. *American Psychologist, 48,* 518–537.

London, K., Bruck, M., Poole, D. A., & Melnyk, L. (2011). The development of metasuggestibility in children. *Applied Cognitive Psychology, 25,* 146–155.

Magnussen, S., Andersson, J., Cornoldi, C., De Beni, R., Endestad, T., Goodman, G.S., Helstrup, T., Koriat, A., Larsson, M., Melinder, A., Nilsson, L., Ronnberg, J., & Zimmer, H. (2006). What people believe about memory. *Memory, 14,* 595–613.

Magnussen, S., Endestad, T., Koriat, A., & Helstrup, T. (2007). What do people believe about memory and how do they talk about memory? In S. Magnussen, and T. Helstrup (Eds.), *Everyday memory* (pp. 5–25). New York: Psychology Press.

Marsh, E. J. (2007). Retelling is not the same as recalling: Implications for memory. *Current Directions in Psychological Science, 16,* 16–20.

Martire, K. A., & Kemp, R. I. (2009). The impact of eyewitness expert evidence and judicial instruction on juror ability to evaluate eyewitness testimony. *Law and Human Behavior, 33,* 225–236.

McAuliff, B. D., & Bull-Kovera, M. (2007). Estimating the effects of misleading information on witness accuracy: Can experts tell jurors something they don't already know? *Applied Cognitive Psychology, 21,* 849–870.

McCabe, J. (2011). Metacognitive awareness of learning strategies in undergraduates. *Memory & Cognition, 39,* 462–476.

Munsterberg, H. (1908). *On the witness stand.* New York: McClure.

Naka, M., & Maki, Y. (2006). Belief and experience of memory recovery. *Applied Cognitive Psychology, 20,* 649–659.

Nelson, K., & Fivush, R. (2004). The emergence of autobiographical memory: A social cultural development theory. *Psychological Review, 111,* 486–511.

Noon, E., & Hollin, C. R. (1987). Lay knowledge of eyewitness behaviour: A British review. *Applied Cognitive Psychology, 1,* 143–153.

Northrup, T., & Mulligan, N. (2013). Conceptual implicit memory in advertising research. *Applied Cognitive Psychology, 27,* 127–136.

Nunes, T., Schliemann, A. D., & Carraher, D. W. (1993). *Street mathematics and school mathematics.* New York: Cambridge University Press.

O'Sullivan, J. T., & Howe, M. L. (1995). Metamemory and memory construction. *Consciousness and Cognition: An International Journal, 4,* 104–110.

O'Sullivan, J. T., Howe, M. L., & Marche, T. A. (1996). Children's beliefs about long-term retention. *Child Development, 67,* 2989–3009.

Pezdek, K., & Blandon-Gitlin, I. (2009). Planting false memories for childhood sexual abuse only happens to emotionally disturbed people … not me or my friends. *Applied Cognitive Psychology, 23,* 162–169.

Pezdek, K., Blandon-Gitlin, I., & Gabbay, P. (2006). Imagination and memory: Does imagining implausible events lead to false autobiographical memories? *Psychonomic Bulletin & Review, 13,* 764–769.

Rajaram, S. (2011). Collaboration both hurts and helps memory: A cognitive perspective. *Current Directions in Psychological Science, 20,* 76–81.

Read, J. D., & Desmarais, S. L. (2009). Lay knowledge of eyewitness issues: A Canadian survey. *Applied Cognitive Psychology, 23,* 301–326.

Reber, A. S. (1993). *Implicit learning and tacit knowledge: An essay on the cognitive unconscious.* New York: Oxford University Press.

Rhodes, M. G., & Castel, A. D. (2008). Memory predictions are influenced by perceptual information: Evidence for metacognitive illusions. *Journal of Experimental Psychology: General, 137,* 615–625.

Roediger, H. L. (1980). Memory metaphors in cognitive psychology. *Memory & Cognition, 8,* 231–246.

Roediger, H. L. (2008). Relativity of remembering: Why the laws of memory vanished. *Annual Review of Psychology, 59,* 225–254.

Rubin, D. C., & Berntsen, D. (2007). People believe it is plausible to have forgotten memories of childhood sexual abuse. *Psychonomic Bulletin & Review, 14,* 767–778.

Rubin, D. C., & Berntsen, D. (2009). Most people who think that they are likely to enter psychotherapy also think it is plausible that they could have forgotten their own memories of childhood sexual abuse. *Applied Cognitive Psychology, 23,* 170–173.

Rubin, D. C., & Boals, A. (2010). People who expect to enter psychotherapy are prone to believing that they have forgotten memories of childhood trauma and abuse. *Memory, 18,* 556–562.

Scheck, B., Neufeld, P., & Dwyer, J. (2000). *Actual innocence.* New York: Random House.

Schmechel, R. S., O'Toole, T. P., Easterly, C., & Loftus, E. F. (2006). Beyond the ken: Testing jurors' understanding of eyewitness reliability evidence. *Jurimetrics, 46,* 177–214.

Schneider, W., & Lockl, K. (2002). The development of metacognitive knowledge in children and adolescents. In T. Perfect, and B. L. Schwartz, (Eds.), *Applied metacognition* (pp. 224–257). New York: Cambridge University Press.

Schneider, W., & Pressley, M. (1989). *Memory development between 2 and 20.* New York: Springer-Verlag Publishing.

Schwarz, N. (1999). Self-reports: How the questions shape the answers. *American Psychologist, 54,* 93–105.

Seltzer, R., Lopes, G. M., & Venuti, M. (1990). Juror ability to recognize the limitations of eyewitness identifications. *Forensic Reports, 3,* 121–137.

Simons, D. J., & Chabris, C. F. (2011). What people believe about how memory works: A representative survey of the U.S. population. *PLoS ONE, 6,* e22757.

Sinatra, G., & Pintrich, P. R. (2003). *Intentional conceptual change.* Mahwah, NJ: Erlbaum.

Son, L. K., & Schwartz, B. L. (2002). The relation between metacognitive monitoring and control. In T. J. Perfect, and B. L. Schwartz (Eds.), *Applied metacognition* (pp. 15–38). New York: Cambridge University Press.

Sparrow, B., Liu, J., & Wegner, D. M. (2011). Google effects on memory: Cognitive consequences of having information at our fingertips. *Science, 333,* 776–778.

Tenney, E. R., Spellman, B. A., & MacCoun, R. J. (2008). The benefits of knowing what you know (and what you don't): How calibration affects credibility. *Journal of Experimental Social Psychology, 44,* 1368–1375.

Wang, Q., & Ross, M. (2007). Culture and memory. In S. Kitayama, and D. Cohen (Eds.), *Handbook of cultural psychology* (pp. 645–667). New York: Guilford Press.

Wells, G. L., (1978). Applied eyewitness testimony research: System variables and estimator variables. *Journal of Personality and Social Psychology, 36,* 1546–1557.

Wells, G. L., & Olson, E. A. (2003). Eyewitness testimony. *Annual Review of Psychology, 54,* 277–295.

Winkielman, P., & Schwarz, N. (2001). How pleasant was your childhood? Beliefs about memory shape inferences from experienced difficulty of recall. *Psychological Science, 12,* 176–179.

21

Autobiographical Memory Dynamics in Survey Research

Robert F. Belli

Asking people to answer survey questions is the basis for critical data collection efforts in the commercial sector, among governmental statistical agencies, and in the social, behavioral, and health sciences. Since the latter half of the twentieth century it has been recognized that limitations in cognitive and memory processes are a critical source of errors in survey reports (Cannell, Fisher, & Bakker, 1965; Cannell, Miller, & Oksenberg, 1981; Cash & Moss, 1972). Such recognition led to formal initiatives in the early 1980s to seek greater insights into the cognitive processes that contribute to survey response errors, with the hope that such understanding would lead to practices to mitigate those errors. The infusion of cognitive science into survey methodological issues in the early 1980s has become known as the cognitive aspects of survey methodology (CASM) movement (Jabine, Straf, Tanur, & Tourangeau, 1984; Jobe & Mingay, 1991), a movement that continues to this day.

The bulk of survey questions either ask for subjective judgments, such as attitude reports, or for factual information. Although subjective judgments have no clear external objective referent on which to base response accuracy, in principle the source of factual information occurs objectively in observable reality, and hence, is open to validation efforts (Bradburn, Sudman, & Wansink, 2004; Fowler, 1995). Importantly, both of these question types involve a variety of cognitive processes, including memory. Consider one subjective judgment example from the Nebraska Annual Social Indicators Survey: "Overall, how satisfied are you with your current financial situation? Would you say you are very satisfied, satisfied, dissatisfied, or very dissatisfied?" Deriving a thoughtful answer to this question requires one to retrieve information on one's current financial situation before making a judgment concerning one's satisfaction. As for factual information, consider a question from the Current Price Index Housing Survey: "How many bedrooms are there in this house?" Again, a memory for the layout of the home would be needed, unless a respondent decides to actually look. Thus, memory processes are still needed when seeking information on current states of affairs.

Of course, there are questions that ask about past events, such as this question from the National Health Interview Survey: "During the past 12 months, how many times have you seen a doctor or other health care professional about your own health at a doctor's office, a clinic, or some other place?" These types of retrospective questions require retrieval from autobiographical memory, and accurate answers require a greater reliance on memory processes in comparison with questions that ask on current states of affairs.

One especially influential response-process model highlights the presence of four cognitive phases – comprehension, retrieval, judgment, and response formatting – in the answering of any survey question (Sudman, Bradburn, & Schwarz, 1996; Tourangeau, 1984; Tourangeau, Rips, & Rasinski, 2000). Comprehension includes seeking to gain an understanding of the intent of the question and its objectives in terms of what will characterize a satisfactory response. Retrieval focuses on accessing pertinent information on which to evaluate an attitude object, or with factual questions, remembering specific events. Judgment includes examining the relevance of the retrieved information, and specifically for attitude questions, combining potentially conflicting valences of retrieved information (e.g., having lost a bundle in the stock market while having a secure job) into a summary evaluation. Finally, response formatting involves selecting the best response among options and determining one's willingness to reveal potentially sensitive or socially undesirable information.

According to this response-process model, retrieval from long-term memory is necessary for every type of question if the question is to be answered thoughtfully. Because a full assessment of memory processes in answering survey questions would take up considerable space, and because the topic of autobiographical memory has a celebrated place among researchers who are interested in applied memory issues, this chapter concentrates on autobiographical processes that are used in answering factual retrospective reports. Nonetheless, broader memory and cognitive processes are also discussed whenever they are relevant to appreciating the full nature of autobiographical memory within the context of survey responses.

MEMORY PUZZLES AND RESPONSE ERRORS

A key motivation that sparked the CASM movement was the desire to understand, and so reduce, puzzling response errors that were considered as the result of limitations in cognitive processing (Krosnick, 1991: Tourangeau et al., 2000). As for retrospective reports, puzzling response errors were observed 1) with questions that asked whether an event happened, such as whether you had voted in the most recent election and 2) on behavioral frequency questions that ask how often or how many times events happened, such as the number of times you visited a physician about your health in a given time period. For reports of whether an event happened, well-researched response errors include *vote overreporting* and *seam effects*; as for puzzles that are associated with answering behavioral frequency questions, a great deal of work has concentrated on *retrieval-strategy identification* and *forward telescoping*. Each of these response errors illustrates the complicated interaction of autobiographical memory dynamics with other processes in the answering of retrospective questions.

Remembering whether

Vote overreporting

One of the oldest known of the response errors is the reporting of having voted in the most recent election when one, in fact, did not (Clausen, 1967; Parry & Crossley, 1950). On average, vote overreporting has been observed to occur among approximately 10 percent of all respondents to the American National Election Studies (ANES) in the seven surveys in which validation efforts have been conducted (Belli, Traugott, & Beckmann, 2001), and it has also been observed cross-nationally (Granberg & Holmberg, 1991; McCutcheon & Belli, 2003; Waismel-Manor & Sarid, 2011). The opposite error, reporting not voting when one actually did is considerably rarer, occurring less than 1 percent on average in the ANES. Two main determinants of overreporting bias have been proffered, one that emphasizes social desirability – it is better to report having voted than to report not having voted (Anderson, Silver, & Abramson, 1988; Bernstein, Chadha, & Montjoy, 2001; Presser, 1990) – and the other that emphasizes failures to report accurately from memory (Abelson, Loftus, & Greenwald, 1992; Belli, Traugott, & Beckmann, 2001).

As for social desirability, a number of studies have found that respondents tend to underreport behaviors that may lead to a negative or undesirable characterization, such as alcohol consumption, smoking, or experiencing bankruptcy (Bradburn, Sudman, & Associates, 1979; Lemmens, Tan, & Knibbe, 1992; Patrick et al., 1994). Respondents also tend to overreport behaviors that may lead to a positive characterization, such as possessing a library card, using a seat belt, attending church (Bradburn, Sudman, & Associates, 1979; Presser & Stinson, 1998: Stulginskas, Verreault, & Pless, 1985), and as noted above, voting. The notion that respondents will be biased to respond in socially desirable ways assumes that there are social norms that govern appropriate behavior and that respondents wish to be evaluated by those conducting the interview in a favorable way (Sudman & Bradburn, 1974; Tourangeau, Rips, & Rasinski, 2000).

Attempts to link vote overreporting solely to social-desirability effects have provided mixed results. Some of these attempts have examined differences in responses across face-to-face, telephone, and self-administered modes of data collection. On one hand, although interviews by telephone are expected to reduce the impact of socially desirable responding in comparison with face-to-face interviews, these modes do not produce reliable differences in claiming one has voted (Abramson & Claggett, 1986; Locander, Sudman, & Bradburn, 1976; Rogers, 1976). On the other hand, as self-administered internet data collections are expected to reduce

social desirability concerns in comparison with telephone interviews, Holbrook and Krosnick (2010) found that a manipulation intended to reduce socially desirable responding reduced reported turnout over the telephone, but not on the internet.

Experiments that have sought to directly manipulate social desirable responding with vote reporting have also provided mixed results. Presser (1990) varied experimentally the wording of questions so that one set of questions provided a "face-saving" opportunity to more readily admit one had not voted. For example, before being asked the standard ANES question on whether they had voted in the last election, half of the respondents were first asked a question on whether they usually voted or not. Presser (1990) reasoned that answering this prior question would provide some respondents with an opportunity to consider themselves as good citizens, reducing the threat to be seen in an unfavorable light if they admitted to have not voted. Nevertheless, the percent of reported turnout in the set of respondents offered the prior question did not significantly differ from those only provided the voter turnout question. More recently, Holbrook and Krosnick (2010) introduced the item count technique (ICT) to reduce reporting voting due to social desirability concerns. With the ICT, respondents are asked about a number of behaviors either in a control condition that does not include the item biased by social desirability, or in a treatment condition that includes the control condition items and the biased item (Droitcour et al., 1991). In both conditions, respondents are to report on the number of items that apply to them, but because a numeric response does not reveal one's status in terms of the biased item in the treatment condition, concerns regarding social desirability ought be reduced. Indeed, as expected, the ICT technique in telephone interviews reduced estimates of voter turnout in comparison with a condition that asked directly whether one had voted.

Other attempts to reduce vote overreporting have considered the problem as fundamentally one of memory error. For example,

Abelson et al. (1992) saw vote overreporting as a potential case of forward telescoping in which past events are "time-compressed" and remembered as having occurred more recently than their actual occurrence (see also Sudman & Bradburn, 1973). Hence, having voted in a prior election could be forward telescoped and remembered as an instance of having voted in the most recent election. However, their attempt to reduce forward telescoping by first asking respondents about having voted in specific prior elections before being asked whether they voted in the most recent election had no impact on reducing the vote overreporting effect.

Although social desirability and memory failure as determinants of vote overreporting may appear to be mutually exclusive, they likely are not. Social desirability concerns may not lead respondents to lie intentionally in the sense that they remember not having voted. But these concerns may lead respondents to report that they had voted in circumstances in which their actual behavior is not remembered, either because of an initial memory failure attempt, or because the available contents of memory were not checked (Abelson, Loftus, & Greenwald, 1992; Belli, Traugott, Young, & McGonagle, 1999; Stocké & Stark, 2007).

Addressing these potential mechanisms of overreporting, Belli et al. (1999) designed a lengthy experimental question with wording that sought to increase the amount of retrievable information from election day that would help to determine whether one had voted or not (Means & Loftus, 1991). This long question also sought to reduce potential source confusions (Johnson, Hashtroudi, & Lindsay, 1993) that can lead to overreporting. These confusions consist of having thought only about voting, or that one usually votes, as evidence that one voted in the last election when one did not.

Belli et al.'s long experimental question was implemented in a national sample without validation, and in a sample from the state of Oregon with validation. In comparison with the standard ANES question,

the experimental question was effective in reducing reported turnout in the national sample, and in reducing overreporting in the Oregon sample. Further, results from the Oregon sample revealed that the very small level of underreporting was not increased by the experimental question, lending evidence that the decrease in reported turnout in the national sample was due solely to a reduction in overreporting. Yet, approximately one month of delay between election day and when the questions are posed is needed for the effectiveness of the experimental question to be seen. This interaction of question effectiveness with retention interval makes sense. As shown by Belli, Traugott, and Beckmann (2001), vote overreporting with the standard ANES question does increase as the time between election day and the date of interview increases. Accordingly, the amount of retrievable episodic detail on what one had done on election day decreases as retention interval increases, and vote overreporting is dependent on not remembering what one had actually done on election day. Hence, the experimental question's success appears to be contingent on circumstances in which respondents would not ordinarily remember their voting behavior in the most recent election, and succumbing at that point to social desirability concerns.

Observations of overreporting among respondents who vary in their level of political involvement provide further support that the influence of social desirability increases, and the reliability of memory decreases, as retention interval lengthens (Stocké & Stark, 2007). Those who report heightened political involvement are more likely to overreport with the standard ANES question, and this overreporting heightens as the interval between election day and the date of interview increases, indicating that overreporting due to social desirability concerns are more pronounced when one's memory fades.

Despite the long experimental question's success, there is uncertainty in the locus of its effectiveness. The response options, which, unlike the yes/no format of the standard

ANES question, may not only reduce source confusions (Lindsay & Johnson, 1989; Zaragoza & Lane, 1994) but also offer "face-saving" responses such as "I thought about voting this time but didn't" and "I usually vote but didn't this time." In an experiment conducted within the 2002 ANES, Duff, Hammer, Park, and White (2007) significantly reduced reported turnout by 8.0 percentage points with a short experimental question that included the standard ANES question stem but the response options of Belli et al. (1999). Moreover, this successful reduction was accomplished with interviews conducted within a month in which the election had taken place, demonstrating that a fairly lengthy retention interval is not needed for a reduction in vote overreporting to be observed.

As illustrated in Table 21.1, comparisons of the effect sizes of short and long experimental versions reveal a dissociation of each version's effectiveness as a function of retention interval. The effect sizes are computed as the difference between reported turnout with the standard question and with the short and long experimental versions, respectively, with positive values indicating the percentage of reported turnout reduced by the experimental versions. Given that elections in the United States occur in early November, the month of interview provides an estimate of the length of retention interval, that is, the amount of time between election day and when the interview took place. Although the impact of the long version increases with increases in retention interval especially between November and the later months, the impact of the short version either remains constant with increases in retention interval or may actually decrease in effectiveness as retention interval increases.

This dissociation between question version and retention interval indicates that vote overreporting is multi-determined, and that the processes that lead to each version's effectiveness are different. The short version appears to be primarily effective for those respondents who would be influenced by social desirability concerns with the decrease in its effectiveness with increases in retention interval as the result of social desirability concerns decreasing with time (see also Holbrook & Krosnick, 2013). As for the long version, its impact may be mostly the result of attacking source confusions and episodic memory failures, which would ordinarily become more pronounced as retention interval length increases. However, very long reference periods (e.g., one year) will likely not leave sufficient event memory to be available for the long version to work (Waismel-Manor & Sarid, 2011). In any case, the likely multi-determinate nature of vote overreporting highlights that retrospective reports in surveys are governed by both the memory limitations and motivational concerns of respondents.

Seam effects

The occurrence of seam effects is restricted to panel surveys. In panel surveys, the same respondents (or representatives from the

Table 21.1 Voter turnout question versions: Effect sizes (in % difference)

		Month of Interview			
Comparison	Study	November	December	January	February
Standard – short	Duff et al., 2007[a]	8.0			
	Belli et al., 2006[b]		7.1	5.9	2.0
Standard – long	Belli et al., 1999[c]	–3.8	9.4	17.6	
	Belli et al., 2006[b]		14.2	14.1	15.2

[a]Data from 2002 American National Election Studies, interviews were completed within 31 days of election day
[b]Data from Survey of Consumers: December 1998, January and February 1999
[c]Data from Survey of Consumers: November and December 1996, January 1997

same household) are asked for retrospective reports in a series of data collections, with each data collection consisting of a fixed reference period length (e.g., a series of one-year data collections). The point of adjacency between two data collections is referred to as the "seam." The seam effect is observed as an elevation of reported status transitions at the seam (e.g., from being employed to unemployed and vice versa) in comparison with points within a given data collection's reference period.

Seam effects have been observed in a number of panel surveys, including the Survey of Income and Program Participation (SIPP; Burkhead & Coder, 1985), the Panel Study of Income Dynamics (PSID; Hill, 1987), and the Income Survey Development Program (Czajka, 1983). Consider the SIPP, in which each data collection covers a four-month reference period, and respondents are asked about whether they have received food stamps and social security benefits for each month of the reference period. The seam effect in the SIPP is illustrated in Figure 21.1. Validation research has observed that whereas between seam transitions are overreported, within data collection transitions are underreported

(Marquis & Moore, 1989; Moore, Marquis, & Bogen, 1996). Similar to vote overreporting, explanations of seam effects include the existence of imperfect memory and additional biasing influences (Callegaro, 2008; Rips, Conrad, & Fricker, 2003).

The bias referred to as "constant wave responding" helps to account for seam effects (Rips et al., 2003). In constant wave responding, respondents provide the same response for all months within a data collection, leading to possible transitions only occurring at the seam. As a bias, constant wave responding occurs as a way to simplify the response task, that is, to provide an answer when one is either unable or unwilling to respond accurately (Krosnick, 1991).

Rips et al. (2003) have proposed a promising model that combines retention interval effects in memory and constant wave responding as an overall explanation of seam effects. Their model holds that the most recent month of a data collection is remembered, and this month serves as an anchor by which the remaining months in that data collection are considered, leading to the likelihood of constant wave responding. Constant wave responding will also occur if

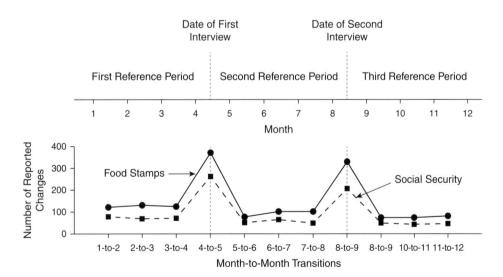

Figure 21.1   Seam bias as revealed from data reported by Burkhead and Coder (1985) in the Survey of Income and Program Participation. Reprinted with permission from Rips, Conrad, and Fricker, ©2003 by the American Association for Public Opinion Research.

respondents entertain implicit theories that their earlier circumstances have not changed from their status in the most recent month or currently (Ross, 1989). Regardless, according to the model of Rips et al., transitions will be increased at the seam, but decreased between months that are queried within the same data collection. In addition, the most accurately reported month will be the most recent in any given data collection.

Although Rips et al. (2003) provide experimental results that support their model, their attempts to control for seam effects have not been completely successful. Rips et al. (2003) compared two methods of questioning. The conventional questioning mirrors the standard approach used in panel surveys in which respondents are asked to report for all temporal periods (either in forward or backward chronological order) of one item before moving on to a second item. In the experimental questioning, respondents first responded to a single temporal period for all items before moving on to the next (either earlier or later) period. Although, as expected, the experimental approach reduced constant wave responding in comparison with the conventional one, results on the accuracy of responses between methods were equivocal. Additional attempts to reduce seam effects have relied on dependent interviewing in which respondents are reminded of their responses to the last data collection before being queried about their current data collection (Jäckle & Lynn, 2007). Dependent interviewing has resulted in reducing seam transitions and increasing within data collection transitions (Moore et al., 2009), but it poses additional challenges and potential problems (Callegaro, 2008).

Remembering how many or how often

Retrieval strategies with behavioral frequency reports

Asking how many times or how often an event has been experienced in a given reference period is considered to be an invaluable measurement tool in marketing and social science survey research, and in governmental statistics research. Hence, collecting retrospective behavioral frequency reports, such as asking how often an item had been purchased in the past month, or how many times one had seen a physician in the past year, is a very common practice in survey research. Accordingly, acquiring accurate behavioral frequency reports has always been considered a priority, and much effort has been devoted to understanding the retrieval strategies that are used in answering behavioral frequency questions.

Three main types of approaches are used to answer behavioral frequency questions: enumeration strategies, rate-based strategies, and providing a general impression (Blair & Burton, 1987; Burton & Blair, 1991; Menon, 1993; Conrad, Brown, & Cashman, 1998). Enumeration is the use of a recall and count strategy. Its use increases when the number of frequencies to report is low, the reference period is short, the events to be reported are distinctive enough to be identified in episodic autobiographical memory, and when respondents are informed to take their time when answering. A rate-based strategy is more likely to be used when the number of frequencies to report is high, when the reference period is long, when events are not distinctive from one another, and when events occur regularly, that is, in a pattern with a predictable periodicity. At times, rates can be directly retrieved, and they may exist in generic autobiographical memory as a typical pattern of occurrence (Menon, 1993). For example, for many people, brushing one's teeth twice a day is a stored rate that exists in generic autobiographical memory.

Often, the reporting of non-distinctive and frequent events is not possible with direct rate retrieval. Respondents may then compute a rate for a portion of the reference period and then extend this rate to the entire reference period, or they may make adjustments to rate information by noting exceptions. Especially when frequent and non-distinctive events are highly irregular in their occurrence, respondents will use a general impression ("it happens a lot") as a guide to developing a numeric response (Conrad et al., 1998).

In circumstances in which events are both distinctive and regular, rate retrieval will be preferred as enumeration is more effortful (Menon, 1993), and such effort increases linearly with each additional event that is retrieved (Conrad et al., 1998). Whether events are activities or emotions is also important. Strategies that rely on remembering specific events or in directly retrieving frequency information are preferred for activities, whereas there is a preference to rely on generic knowledge of the emotions one typically experiences (Brown, Williams, Barker, & Galambos, 2007).

Survey researchers have often assumed that the reliance on episodic memory in an enumeration strategy should lead to better accuracy in comparison with other strategies. In a validation study to test this notion, Burton and Blair (1991) increased the use of an enumeration strategy by insisting that respondents take at least 15 seconds before they provided an answer. In comparison with a control condition, participants in the 15-second condition did enumerate more often during their reporting of higher frequencies, but at a considerable loss in accuracy. Hence, with high-frequency events, enumeration is a non-optimal strategy, and it is best to permit respondents to use non-enumeration strategies – such as rate-based strategies – for frequently occurring events. In general, the use of enumeration will lead to underreporting as respondents will forget instances. The use of rate-based strategies usually leads to overreporting, as respondents will forget exceptions to the usual periodicity of events (Blair & Burton, 1991; Sudman & Bradburn, 1974).

Additional research has determined specific circumstances in which either enumeration or rate retrieval will promote better accuracy in behavioral frequency reports. The use of decomposition, in which a larger category, such as going to restaurants, is broken into several smaller category questions, such as going to Italian restaurants, Chinese restaurants, fast-food restaurants, and so forth, is one method that has revealed differences between enumeration and rate retrieval. Menon (1997) has found that decomposition is beneficial for response accuracy when respondents use an enumeration strategy for irregularly occurring events, but not when respondents use rate retrieval or are faced with regularly occurring events.

In Menon's (1997) research, the types of decomposed categories were first pilot tested for their potential effectiveness before being applied. In addition, only a short one-week reference period was examined, and the decomposition cues were able, at times, to promote an effective enumeration of the low-frequency events that became available via decomposition. In a validation study that examined longer reference periods and frequent irregularly occurring events, Belli, Schwarz, Singer, and Talarico (2000) found that decomposition greatly exacerbated over-reporting and decreased overall accuracy. They theorized that in circumstances in which memory is unreliable, respondents use impression-based heuristics that result in the overestimation of split categories (Fiedler & Armbruster, 1994). Because most behavioral frequency questions do not permit a decomposition approach that encourages effective enumeration strategies, Belli et al. (2000) conclude that decomposition cannot be used as a general approach to improve the accuracy of responses to behavioral frequency questions.

As for the benefits of rate retrieval, situations in which any reliance on memory will be unreliable will again play an important role. Consider, for example, how many hours of television people watch daily. Because television viewing occurs frequently, is largely non-distinctive, and in most people does not have a clear pattern of periodicity, an impression-based estimation strategy is likely used when reporting on daily television viewing. In a clever experiment, Schwarz, Hippler,

Deutsch, and Strack (1985) presented respondents with either a low-frequency (from up to ½ hour, to more than 2½ hours) or a high-frequency (from up to 2½ hours, to more than 4½ hours) scale, and found that the low frequency scale led to significantly lower estimates of daily television consumption. Apparently, the scale options provided participants with potentially diagnostic information concerning their own behavior, as they assumed that the scale had been pragmatically constructed as to conform to a reasonable response distribution for the population to which they belong.

The contextual influence of these response scales, however, is constrained by the inability of respondents to provide a numeric answer using a reliable memory source. Menon, Raghubir, and Schwarz (1995) were able to show that for regularly occurring behaviors that permitted the use of a reliable rate-retrieval strategy, such as washing one's hair, there is no influence of providing participants with different response scales. Such constraints of the contextual features of questionnaires are likely not limited to the use of a rate-based strategy; reliable enumeration strategies in reporting distinctive events also have been shown to be immune to contextual manipulations (see Brown, 1995).

In summary, research into the retrieval strategies that are used in answering behavioral frequency questions has led to considerable insights into the autobiographical memory and estimation processes that are used, and the conditions that influence report accuracy. There are, unfortunately, several applied constraints that limit the impact of this knowledge in boosting the accuracy of retrospective reports in actual surveys. If behavioral reports could be limited to asking about infrequent distinctive events with short reference periods, or of events that have stored rates in generic autobiographical memory, then all would be well. However, many questions on behavioral frequency reports require longer reference periods than would be ideal, and the frequency of occurrence of events, their distinctiveness, and

their regularity, are not universally experienced. Hence, in most situations, respondents will use a variety of retrieval strategies dependent on their own personal experiences and their individual propensities to favor some strategies over others (see also Conrad et al., 1998). Despite there being limitations in using knowledge of retrieval strategies to improve response quality, survey researchers should be vigilant to recognize situations in which such knowledge will be useful.

Telescoping effects

In the asking of behavioral frequencies, a common observation is that the rate of reported events in shorter reference periods is higher than that of longer reference periods (Bachman & O'Malley, 1981; Neter & Waksberg, 1964; Sudman & Bradburn, 1974). A common assumption of these findings is that there is net overreporting in the shorter reference periods. One possible explanation of this overreporting hinges on the notion of forward telescoping as a time compression property of autobiographical memory. With time compression, events are remembered as occurring more recently in time than their actual occurrence (Sudman & Bradburn, 1973). Although there is evidence that events are more likely to be *reported* as having occurred more recently than more remotely in time, evidence that directly favors time compression is lacking.

Instead of an appeal to time compression, telescoping can be explained as an artifact of the common inclusion of a reference period boundary in behavioral frequency questions. As is well known, events are less likely to be remembered as time passes. Moreover, even when remembered, remote events have greater uncertainty as to when they occurred in comparison with more recent events. In other words, the variance in placing events at the time of their occurrence increases as retention interval increases (Baddeley, Lewis, & Nimmo-Smith, 1978). In combination with a reference period boundary, this property of increased variance with increased time will lead to forward telescoping

(Huttenlocher, Hedges, & Prohaska, 1988; Rubin & Baddeley, 1989).

As illustrated in Figure 21.2, consider a behavioral frequency question with a 6-month reference period with variance distributions of two equidistant events from the 6-month boundary, one that occurred at 4 months and the other that occurred at 8 months from the present, with greater variability in dating for the older events. Note that, with regard to these equidistant events, there is greater variance for the more remote 8-month event than the 4-month event, in accordance with Baddeley et al. (1978). The gray area represents the probability that the more remote 8-month event will be remembered (and hence reported) in the reference period, and the black area the probability that the more recent 4-month event will be remembered outside the reference period (and hence not reported). As illustrated, for any given set of two events that are equidistant from the reference period boundary, one more remote and one more recent, there is a greater probability for the remote event to be included in the reference period than for the recent event to be excluded, and net forward telescoping is the result. Also, due to increased forgetting with increased retention intervals, the tendency to overreport for shorter reference periods is greater than for longer ones.

The notion that time estimation is a reconstructive process based on the temporal clues that are present in the memory of an event accounts for the relationship between time location variance and the length of the retention interval. More recent events will typically consist of a greater amount of temporal clues than more remote ones, leading to a better ability to reconstruct when the more recent events had occurred (Friedman, 1993). In general, even for events that are equivalent in length of retention, those that are remembered more fully tend to be dated more accurately in comparison with those that are more poorly remembered (Bartlett & Snelus, 1980; Strube & Neubauer, 1988; Thompson, Skowronski, & Lee, 1988; but see Neter & Waksberg, 1964, for contrary results).

In addition, attempts to reduce forward telescoping appear to be successful by encouraging participants to retrieve more temporal information about an event. A two-time frame procedure, in which participants are first asked for behavioral frequencies at a longer reference period before being asked for a shorter one will lead to fewer reported events in comparison with when a shorter period is used alone (Loftus, Klinger, Smith, & Fiedler, 1990). Similarly, asking participants to date events will lead to fewer events in a given time frame than asking for behavioral frequencies within a reference

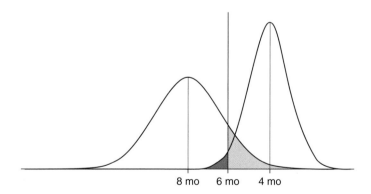

Figure 21.2 Hypothetical distributions in remembering the timing of events that had occurred 4 and 8 months previously, and their respective contribution to a telescoping bias with a 6-month reference period. See text for explanation.

period (Prohaska, Brown, & Belli, 1998). Apparently, in comparison with using a single reference period, both the two-time frame procedure and the asking of dates require participants to engage in a more active reconstructive process in which a greater number of temporal cues are accessed to more precisely locate events in time.

Telescoping exemplifies how imperfections in autobiographical memory processes are governed by the manner in which survey questions are formatted. At first, a fundamental property of autobiographical memory – time compression – was believed responsible. At present, one of the most satisfactory explanations of the occurrence of forward telescoping points to an artifact of the inclusion of a reference period boundary, and that processes associated with autobiographical memory assume a secondary role. Hence, response errors may be puzzling precisely because they occur within the constraining context of how survey questions are typically formatted.

Instead of seeking to mitigate response errors in conventional questionnaire approaches, it may be better to optimize the quality of retrospective reports by using what is known about autobiographical memory as a starting point in designing questionnaires. In the next sections, I examine calendar interviewing methods, which in contrast to conventional questionnaire approaches, have been designed with a focus on the nature of autobiographical memory.

Calendar methods

The standardized-flexible interviewing debate

Conventional questionnaire methods are based on the ideals of standardized interviewing. In standardized interviewing, every respondent is to receive the same stimuli so that any variation in responses is directly measuring the actual variation in respondents' experiences (Fowler & Mangione, 1990; O'Muircheartaigh, 1997). Standardization is to be achieved primarily by having all questions scripted in advance with the task of interviewers being to read the questions exactly as written, and in their predefined order. Additional requirements include that any probing, which may be required to alleviate respondent confusion, is to be performed non-directively.

Interviewers often do not behave in standardized ways, leading to different perspectives on the wisdom of standardized interviewing. Some have argued that restricting interviewer behavior interferes with the benefits of ordinary conversation in clarifying intended meanings (Houtkoop-Steenstra, 2000; Suchman & Jordan, 1990). Others point out that when interviewers behave in non-standardized ways, they are often using tacit knowledge that exists within the parameters of ordinary conversation, which is not unlike the tacit knowledge that pervades all standardized approaches to scientific investigation (Beatty, 1995; Maynard & Schaeffer, 2002). Regardless of which of these points of view one maintains, there is agreement among many that greater flexibility in interviewing can benefit data quality. Schober and Conrad (1997; see also Conrad & Schober, 2000), for example, have shown benefits with a conversational interviewing style in which interviewers are permitted to flexibly convey the meaning of study concepts.

Optimizing autobiographical remembering

The main objective of standardized interviewing is to control for any impact that interviewers may have on contributing to variance in responses, and hence, the method is not intended to optimize the quality of retrospective reports (Belli & Callegaro, 2009). Extending research on the structure of autobiographical knowledge (Barsalou, 1988; Conway, 1996), Belli and colleagues (Belli, 1998; Belli, Shay, & Stafford, 2001; Belli, Smith, Andreski, & Agrawal, 2007) have proposed that optimizing the quality of retrospective reports depends on flexible interviewing methods in which events that are more easily remembered are used as cues to remember events that are more difficult to remember.

Drawing on the properties of the structure of autobiographical knowledge as being hierarchical, temporal, and thematic (categorical), three cuing mechanisms in survey interviews are possible. Taking advantage of hierarchical properties, in top-down cuing, more general events are used as cues to remember more specific ones, such as remembering an employer name serves as a cue to remember specific employment terms such as hourly pay. In sequential cuing, temporal properties of autobiographical knowledge that exist within themes are emphasized, in which remembered events are used as anchors to assist in the remembering of temporally adjacent events that happened earlier or later in time, such as remembering that one worked for employer "y" after having worked for employer "x." In parallel cuing, temporal properties across themes are used in that remembered events in one theme assist in the remembering of nearly contemporaneously occurring events in a different theme, such as remembering that while working for employer "x," one began dating one's future spouse.

Although conventional standardized interviewing methods can take advantage of top-down and limited sequential cuing in how questions are ordered, the constraints imposed by standardization do not permit flexibility in the use of these cues. In contrast, calendar methods, which encourage interviewers to flexibly construct most questions on the spot to target respondents' answering of questionnaire objectives, have the potential to not only optimize the use of these two cuing mechanisms but also to encourage parallel cuing.

Historically, the calendar method was developed by demographers in 1969 to capture the migratory patterns of residents of Mexico (Balán, Browning, Jelin, & Litzler, 1969). Since that time, in addition to demography, the calendar interviewing approach has been used in a broad range of the behavioral,

social, and health sciences (see Belli & Callegaro, 2009; Glasner & van der Vaart, 2009, for reviews). Typically, the calendar method involves the display of a number of different timelines that cover different themes (also called domains), such as residences in which one has lived, persons with whom one has lived, and periods of employment and unemployment one has experienced. The length of reference periods has also varied, from months, to several years, and up to the entire life course. The task of the respondent is to report periods of stability and points of transitions between these periods, such as having worked at "x" for a given period of time, and then starting a job at "y" at a given point in time. Depending on the length of reference periods, the unit of measurement will vary, such that with shorter reference periods, such as a year, interest may center on transitions that occur within a third-of-a month (e.g., changing jobs in the beginning, middle, or end of a specific month), and for a life-course reference period, a calendar year is usually selected as the unit of measurement.

In addition to their potential to enable more complete reconstructions of one's past, the flexible nature of calendar interviewing also may clarify intended meanings and to motivate respondents, although there is also concern that this flexibility can lead to unintended biasing of retrospective reports (Bilgen & Belli, 2010; Callegaro, Yu, Cheng, Liao, & Belli, 2005). Importantly, calendar methods are able to capture the same types of data as conventional standardized interviews regarding whether events happened and how often. To the extent to which calendar methods are able to promote a more accurate reconstruction of when events happened, telescoping biases that result from inclusion of a reference period boundary ought to be minimized.

Direct comparisons of the quality of data that are derived from conventional standardized and calendar methods attest to the benefits of the calendar approach. Table 21.2 lists seven different study comparisons between conventional and calendar methods,

Table 21. 2   Research studies of direct data quality comparisons between calendar and conventional methods

Study	Design	Mode/Medium	Reference period	Results
Panel A: Conventional interviewing in comparison with calendar interviewing				
Engel et al., 2001	Test (Con[a])– Retest (Cal[b])	FtoF[c]/P&P[d]	Life	Cal: reports of more jobs and work time
Belli et al., 2001	Experiment	T[e]/P&P	2 years	Cal: more accurate reports of residential and labor histories; Con: more accurate reports of entitlements
Yoshihama et al., 2005	Quasi-Experiment	FtoF/P&P	Since age 12 years	Cal: more reports of intimate partner violence; elimination of artifactual age-cohort effect
Belli et al., 2007; Belli et al., 2012	Experiment	CATI[f]	Life	Cal: more accurate reports of cohabitation, labor, disability, and health histories; Con: more accurate reports of marital history
Panel B: Conventional data collection in comparison with conventional +calendar data collection				
van der Vaart, 2004	Experiment	FtoF/P&P	8 years	Con + Cal: more accurate reports of number, starting date, and types of educational courses
Van der Vaart & Glasner, 2007a	Experiment	Con: CATI Cal: SAQ[g]/P&P	7 years	Con + Cal: more accurate reports of when pairs of glasses were purchased and their price
Glasner, 2011	Experiment	SAQ/Web	Life	Con + Cal: more reports of unemployment and family leaves, especially for more remote events

[a]Con: Conventional; [b]Cal: Calendar; [c]FtoF: Face to face; [d]P&P: Paper and Pencil; [e]T: Telephone; [f]CATI: Computer-assisted telephone interviewing; [g]SAQ: Self-administered questionnaire

with the exact designs of calendars varying in the mode and media of their administration, and in their length of reference periods. Panel A focuses on studies in which a conventional interviewing method was directly contrasted with the calendar method, and Panel B illustrates studies in which conventional data collection alone had been compared with the inclusion of a calendar as a recall aide to the conventional data collection.

Overall, the use of a calendar outperforms conventional methods in each of these seven studies in terms of the quality of the retrospective data that have been obtained, with data quality measured either as the concordance between retrospective reports and an independent source of validation, or on whether events were reported as having occurred more frequently under the assumption that underreporting is the norm. In addition to this research, Callegaro (2007) observed that seam biases in the Panel Study of Income Dynamics are attenuated (but not eliminated) with calendar interviews. Taken together, these results provide indirect support of advantages in calendar methods on improving autobiographical memory.

Verbal behaviors in calendar methods

To examine more directly whether improvements in calendar interviewing in comparison with conventional methods are due to the greater use of hypothesized memory cues and conversational benefits, research has sought to identify differences in the verbal behaviors engendered in both methods, and whether specific behaviors that indicate memory cuing and conversational repair are associated with improvements in data quality (Belli, Lee, Stafford, & Chou, 2004; Belli, Bilgen, & Al Baghal, 2011; Bilgen & Belli, 2010). As expected, in comparison with conventional interviews, calendar interviews do promote a greater variety of sequential and parallel retrieval cues, and a greater number of conversational behaviors that seek to clarify aspects of the questionnaire and to verify responses. However, calendar interviews are more prevalent in potentially biasing behaviors due to the encouragement of a flexible interviewing approach.

Nascent validation research is seeking to associate the verbal behaviors of calendar interviews with data quality to gain a greater understanding of the respective value of conversational behaviors, motivational aspects, and memory cuing. Most insight is coming from a life course calendar that has asked about residential, relationship, and labor histories (Belli, Bilgen, & Al Baghal, 2013). Patterns of results for conversational behaviors are inconsistent, perhaps due to a flexible interviewing style having both positive and negative impacts on data quality. Motivational behaviors, as exemplified by laughter and digressions – in which participants discuss aspects unrelated to satisfying questionnaire objectives – are associated with greater accuracy for desirable events, such as having been employed, but with poorer accuracy for undesirable events, such as having many marriages. As for retrieval cues, interactions between types of verbal behaviors and the complexity of the respondents' histories have been found. More complex histories are those in which there are a greater number of changing circumstances during one's life, and hence, those that provide a more difficult retrieval task. Memory cuing behaviors are associated with improvements in data quality when the retrieval task is more difficult, but unexpectedly, are associated with decreases in data quality when retrieval is easier.

Unexpected results have been found regarding the impact of memory cuing on the accuracy of reporting of landmark events. Landmark events can be defined as very notable or important personal or public events that are well remembered and that can be dated accurately, which may serve as anchors to assist in the temporal recall of other, non-landmark events (Loftus & Marburger, 1983; Shum, 1998). In some applications of calendar interviews, respondents have been asked to report on personal landmark events. However, the number of reported landmarks has received only very limited evidence of being associated with data quality in calendar interviews (van der Vaart & Glasner, 2007b, 2011). These results point further to the growing realization that the advantages of calendar interviewing in comparison with conventional standardized interviewing rely on a complex interplay of memory, conversational, and motivational factors that we are only beginning to unravel. (See Fisher, Schreiber Compo, Rivard, & Hirn, Chapter 31, this volume, for a similar discussion of the interplay among memory, conversational norms and motivational factors in eyewitness interviewing.)

CONCLUSION

The founders of the CASM movement envisioned a dialogue between disciplines in which both survey methodology and cognitive psychology would benefit (Jabine et al., 1984). With regard to the relationship between survey designs seeking to capture retrospective reports and psychological perspectives on the nature of autobiographical memory, one can see that both disciplines have benefited from the CASM movement.

Given the interest of survey researchers on alleviating response errors in retrospective reports, a greater understanding of the dynamics of autobiographical memory has been helpful. The introduction of question wordings that have been successful in reducing vote overreporting has relied in part on applying theory and evidence from the source monitoring framework; the greater understanding of seam effects and behavioral frequency reports relies on understanding the interplay of memory and estimation processes; and an appropriate modeling of telescoping requires an appreciation of how temporal information is reconstructed. Moreover, benefits that accrue from calendar interviewing can be attributed, at least in part, to utilizing cues that have been proposed to exist in the structure of autobiographical knowledge.

As for future research, we need to embrace the challenges inherent in attempting to disentangle complex processes. First, there must be a more grounded understanding of the similarity and differences of the functions of autobiographical memory in ordinary conversation and in the constrained conversations of survey interviews. Second, better theoretical understanding of autobiographical memory processing requires validation data on which to evaluate the quality of retrospective reports. Finally, we must appreciate the frailties of autobiographical remembering. Using memory in ordinary conversational contexts has a number of functions, but complete accuracy cannot be considered one of them (Bluck, Alea, Habermas, & Rubin, 2005; Newman & Lindsay, 2009). Given the realities of imperfect and false memories, it is not overly surprising that the best efforts to optimize the accuracy of retrospective reports will not always be successful. Hence, within calendar methods, cues cannot be expected to always be effective, and it remains possible that incomplete or false memories may be cue-generated in some situations (Newman & Lindsay, 2009). It is by conducting research that disentangles the interactions among conditions as they impact the quality of retrospective reports that the hopes of the CASM movement as a dialogue between disciplines will become most fully realized.

ACKNOWLEDGMENTS

This material is based upon work supported by the National Science Foundation under Grant No. 1132015. Any opinions, findings, and conclusions or recommendations expressed in this material are those of the author and do not necessarily reflect the views of the National Science Foundation.

REFERENCES

Abelson, R. P., Loftus, E. F., & Greenwald, A. G. (1992). Attempts to improve the accuracy of self reports of voting. In J. M. Tanur (Ed.), *Questions about questions* (pp. 138–153). New York: Russell Sage Foundation.

Abramson, P. R., & Claggett, W. (1986). Race-related differences in self-reported and validated turnout. *Journal of Politics, 48,* 412–422.

Anderson, B. A., Silver, B. D., & Abramson, P. R. (1988). The effects of race of the interviewer on measures of electoral participation by Blacks in SRC National Election Studies. *Public Opinion Quarterly, 52,* 53–83.

Bachman, J. G., & O'Malley, P. M. (1981). When four months equal a year: Inconsistencies in student reports of drug use. *Public Opinion Quarterly, 45,* 536–538.

Baddeley, A. D., Lewis, V., & Nimmo-Smith, I. (1978). When did you last …? In M. M. Gruneberg, P. E. Morris, and R. N. Sykes (Eds.), *Practical aspects of memory* (pp. 77–83). London: Academic Press.

Balán, J., Browning, H. L., Jelin, E., & Litzler, L. (1969). A computerized approach to the processing and analysis of life histories obtained in sample surveys. *Behavioral Science, 14,* 105–114.

Barsalou, L. W. (1988). The content and organization of autobiographical memories. In U. Niesser and E. Winograd (Eds.), *Remembering reconsidered: ecological and traditional approaches to the study of memory* (pp. 193–243). New York: Cambridge University Press.

Bartlett, J. C., & Snelus, P. (1980). Lifespan memory for popular songs. *American Journal of Psychology, 93,* 551–560.

Beatty, P. (1995). Understanding the standardized/ non-standardized controversy. *Journal of Official Statistics, 11,* 147–160.

Belli, R. F. (1998). The structure of autobiographical memory and the event history calendar: Potential improvements in the quality of retrospective reports in surveys. *Memory, 6,* 383–406.

Belli, R. F., Agrawal, S., & Bilgen, I. (2012). Health status and disability comparisons between CATI calendar and conventional questionnaire instruments. *Quality & Quantity, 46,* 813–828.

Belli, R. F., Bilgen, I., & Al Baghal, T. (2013). Memory, communication, and data quality in calendar interviews. *Public Opinion Quarterly, 77,* 194–219.

Belli, R. F., & Callegaro, M. (2009). The emergence of calendar interviewing: A theoretical and empirical rationale. In R. F. Belli, F. P. Stafford, and D. F. Alwin (Eds.), *Calendar and time diary methods in life course research* (pp. 31–52). Thousands Oaks, CA: Sage.

Belli, R. F., Lee, E. H., Stafford, F. P., & Chou, C-H. (2004). Calendar and question-list survey methods: Association between interviewer behaviors and data quality. *Journal of Official Statistics, 20,* 185–218.

Belli, R. F., Moore, S. E., & Van Hoewyk, J. (2006). An experimental comparison of question formats used to reduce vote overreporting. *Electoral Studies, 25,* 751–759.

Belli, R. F., Schwarz, N., Singer, E., & Talarico, J. (2000). Decomposition can harm the accuracy of behavioral frequency reports. *Applied Cognitive Psychology, 14,* 295–308.

Belli, R.F., Shay, W. L., & Stafford, F. P. (2001). Event history calendars and question list surveys: A direct comparison of interviewing methods. *Public Opinion Quarterly, 65,* 45–74. Reprinted (2008) in W. P. Vogt (Ed.), *Selecting research methods* (Vol. 3.): *Methods for coding and measuring data* (pp. 384–411). Thousand Oaks, CA: Sage.

Belli, R. F., Smith, L., Andreski, P., & Agrawal, S. (2007). Methodological comparisons between CATI event history calendar and conventional questionnaire instruments. *Public Opinion Quarterly, 71,* 603–622.

Belli, R. F., Traugott, M. W., & Beckmann, M. N. (2001). What leads to voting overreports? Contrasts of overreporters to validated voters and admitted nonvoters in the American National Election Studies. *Journal of Official Statistics, 17,* 479–498.

Belli, R. F., Traugott, M. W., Young, M., & McGonagle, K. A. (1999). Reducing vote overreporting in surveys: Social desirability, memory failure, and source monitoring. *Public Opinion Quarterly, 63,* 90–108.

Bernstein, R., Chadha, A., & Montjoy, R. (2001). Overreporting voting: Why it happens and why it matters. *Public Opinion Quarterly, 65,* 22–44.

Bilgen, I., & Belli, R. F. (2010). Comparison of verbal behaviors between calendar and standardized conventional questionnaires. *Journal of Official Statistics, 26,* 481–505.

Bradburn, N. M., Sudman, S., & Associates (1979). *Improving interview method and questionnaire design.* San Francisco, CA: Jossey-Bass.

Bradburn, N. M., Sudman, S., & Wansink, B. (2004). *Asking questions: The definitive guide to questionnaire design.* San Francisco, CA: Jossey-Bass.

Brown, N. R. (1995) Estimation strategies and the judgment of event frequency. *Journal of Experimental Psychology: Learning, Memory, and Cognition, 21,* 1539–1553.

Brown, N. R., Williams, R. L., Barker, E. T., & Galambos, N. L. (2007). Estimating frequencies of emotions and actions: A web-based diary study. *Applied Cognitive Psychology, 21,* 259–276.

Blair, E., & Burton, S. (1987). Cognitive processes used by survey respondents to answer behavioral frequency questions. *Journal of Consumer Research, 14,* 280–288.

Bluck, S., Alea, N., Habermas, T., & Rubin, D. C. (2005). A tale of three functions: The self-reported uses of autobiographical memory. *Social Cognition, 23,* 91–117.

Burkhead, D., & Coder, J. (1985). Gross changes in income recipiency from the Survey of Income and Program Participation. *Proceedings of the American Statistical Association, Social Statistics Section,* 351–356.

Burton, S., & Blair, E. A. (1991). Task conditions, response formulation processes, and response accuracy for behavioral frequency questions in surveys. *Public Opinion Quarterly, 55* (1), 50–79.

Callegaro, M. (2007). *Seam effects changes due to modifications in question wording and data collection strategies: A comparison of conventional questionnaire and event history calendar seam effects in the PSID.* (Doctoral dissertation). Retrieved from ProQuest Dissertations and Theses. (Accession Order No. AAT 3252826)

Callegaro, M. (2008). Seam effects in longitudinal surveys. *Journal of Official Statistics, 24,* 387–409.

Callegaro, M., Yu, M., Cheng, F.-W., Liao, D., & Belli, R. F. (2005). Comparison of computerized event history calendar and question-list interviewing methods: A two year hospitalization history study. In *2004 Proceedings of the American Statistical Association, 59th Annual conference of the American Association for Public Opinion Research* (AAPOR) (CD-ROM) (pp. 4746–4753). Alexandria, VA: American Statistical Association.

Cannell, C. F., Fisher, G., & Bakker, T. (1965). Reporting of hospitalization in the Health Interview Survey. *Vital and Health Statistics* (PHS Publication No. 1000, Series 2, No. 6). Washington, DC: US Government Printing Office.

Cannell, C. F., Miller, P. V., & Oksenberg, L. (1981). Research on interviewing techniques. In S. Leinhardt

(Ed.), *Sociological Methodology* (pp. 389–437). San Francisco, CA: Jossey-Bass.

Cash, W. S., & Moss, A. J. (1972). Optimum reporting period for reporting persons injured in motor vehicle accidents. *Vital and Health Statistics* (PHS Publication No. HSM 72-1050, Series 2, No. 50). Washington, DC: US Government Printing Office.

Clausen, A. R. (1967). Response validity: Vote report. *Public Opinion Quarterly, 32,* 1–38.

Conrad, F. G., Brown, N. R., & Cashman, E. R. (1998). Strategies for estimating behavioural frequency in survey interviews. *Memory, 6,* 339–366.

Conrad, F. G., & Schober, M. F. (2000). Clarifying question meaning in a household telephone survey. *Public Opinion Quarterly, 64,* 1–28.

Conway, M. A. (1996). Autobiographical knowledge and autobiographical memories. In D. C. Rubin (Ed.), *Remembering our past: studies in autobiographical memory* (pp. 67–93). New York: Cambridge University Press.

Czajka, J. L. (1983). Subannual income estimation. In D. H. Martin (Ed.), *Technical, conceptual, and administrative lessons of the Income Survey Development Program (ISDP)* (pp. 87–97). New York: Social Science Research Council.

Engel, L. S., Keifer, M. C., & Zahm, S. H. (2001). Comparison of traditional questionnaire with an icon/calendar-based questionnaire to assess occupational history. *American Journal of Industrial Medicine, 40,* 502–511.

Droitcour, J., Caspar, R. A., Hubbard, M. L., Parsley, T. L., Visscher, W., & Ezzati, T. M. (1991). The item count technique as a method of indirect questioning: A review of its development and a case study application. In P. B. Biemer, R. M. Groves, L. E. Lyberg, N. A. Mathiowetz, and S. Sudman (Eds.), *Measurement error in surveys* (pp. 185–210). New York: Wiley.

Duff, B., Hammer, M. J., Park, W-H., & White, I. K. (2007). Good excuses: Understanding who votes with an improved turnout question. *Public Opinion Quarterly, 71,* 67–90.

Fowler, F. J., & Mangione, T., W. (1990). *Standardized survey interviewing. Minimizing interviewer-related error.* Newbury Park, CA: Sage.

Fiedler, K., & Armbruster, T. (1994). Two halfs may be more than one whole: Category-split effects on frequency illusions. *Journal of Personality and Social Psychology, 66,* 633–645.

Fowler, F. J., (1995). *Improving survey questions: Design and evaluation.* Thousand Oaks, CA: Sage Publications.

Friedman, W. J. (1993). Memory for the time of past events. *Psychological Bulletin, 113,* 44–66.

Glasner, T. (2011). *Reconstructing event histories in standardized survey research: Cognitive mechanisms and aided recall techniques.* Amsterdam: Tina Glasner.

Glasner, T., & van der Vaart, W. (2009). Applications of calendar instruments in social surveys: A review. *Quality & Quantity, 43,* 333–349.

Granberg, D., & Holmberg. S. (1991). Self reported turnout and voter validation. *American Journal of Political Science, 35,* 448–459.

Hill, D. H. (1987). Response errors around the seam: Analysis of change in a panel with overlapping reference periods. *Proceedings of the American Statistical Association, Section on Survey Research Methods,* 359–380.

Holbrook, A. L., & Krosnick, J. A. (2010). Social desirability bias in voter turnout reports: Tests using the item count technique. *Public Opinion Quarterly, 74,* 37–67.

Holbrook, A. L., & Krosnick, J. A. (2013). A new question sequence to measure voter turnout in telephone surveys: Results of an experiment in the 2006 ANES pilot study. *Public Opinion Quarterly, 77,* 106–123.

Houtkoop-Steenstra, H. (2000). *Interaction and the standardized survey interview. The living questionnaire.* Cambridge: Cambridge University Press.

Huttenlocher, J., Hedges, L. V., & Prohaska, V. (1988). Hierarchical organization in ordered domains: Estimating the dates of events. *Psychological Review, 95,* 471–484.

Jabine, T. B., Straf, M. L., Tanur, J. M., & Tourangeau, R. (Eds.) (1984). *Cognitive aspects of survey methodology: Building a bridge between disciplines.* Washington, DC: National Academy Press.

Jäckle, A., & Lynn, P. (2007). Dependent interviewing and seam effects in work history data. *Journal of Official Statistics, 23,* 521–551.

Jobe, J. B., & Mingay, D. J. (1991). Cognition and survey measurement: History and overview. *Applied Cognitive Psychology, 5,* 175–192.

Johnson, M. K., Hashtroudi, S., & Lindsay, D. S. (1993). Source monitoring. *Psychological Bulletin, 114,* 3–28.

Krosnick, J. A. (1991). Response strategies for coping with the cognitive demands of attitude measures in surveys. *Applied Cognitive Psychology, 5,* 251–267.

Loftus, E. F., Klinger, M. R., Smith, K. D., & Fiedler, J. (1990). A tale of two questions: Benefits of asking more than one question. *Public Opinion Quarterly, 54,* 330–345.

Lindsay, D. S., & Johnson, M. K. (1989). The eyewitness suggestibility effect and memory for source. *Memory & Cognition, 17,* 349–358.

Locander, W., Sudman, S., & Bradburn, N. (1976). An investigation of interview method, threat and distortion. *Journal of the American Statistical Association, 71,* 269–275.

Loftus, E. F., & Marburger, W. (1983). Since the eruption of Mt. St. Helens, has anyone beaten you up? Improving the accuracy of retrospective reports with landmark events. *Memory & Cognition, 11,* 114–120.

Lemmens, P., Tan, E. S., & Knibbe, R. A. (1992). Measuring quantity and frequency of drinking in a general population survey: A comparison of five indices. *Journal of Studies on Alcohol, 53,* 476–486.

Marquis, K. H., & Moore, J. C. (1989). Some response errors in SIPP with thoughts about their effects and remedies. *Proceedings of the American Statistical Association, Section on Survey Research Methods,* 381–386.

Maynard, D. W., & Schaeffer, N. C. (2002). Standardization and its discontents. In D. W. Maynard, H. Houtkoop-Steenstra, N. C. Schaeffer, and J. van der Zouwen (Eds.), *Standardization and tacit knowledge: Interaction and practice in the survey interview* (pp. 365–397). New York: Wiley.

McCutcheon, A. L., & Belli, R. F. (2003, August). *Social desirability and faulty memory in vote over-reporting: A cross-national comparison of the American and British electorates.* Paper presented at the annual Joint Statistical Meeting, San Francisco.

Means, B., & Loftus, E. F. (1991). When personal history repeats itself: Decomposing memories for recurring events. *Applied Cognitive Psychology, 5,* 297–318.

Menon, G. (1993). The effects of accessibility of information in memory on judgments of behavioral frequencies. *Journal of Consumer Research, 20,* 431–440.

Menon, G. (1997). Are the parts better than the whole? The effects of decompositional questions on judgments with frequent behaviors. *Journal of Marketing Research, 34,* 335–346.

Menon, G., Raghubir, P., & Schwarz, N. (1995). An accessibility-diagnosticity framework for behavioral frequency judgments: The use of response alternatives versus rate of occurrence as sources of information. *Journal of Consumer Research, 22,* 212–228.

Moore, J. C., Bates, N., Pascale, J., & Oken, A. (2009). Tackling seam bias through questionnaire design. In P. Lynn (Ed.), *Methodology of longitudinal surveys* (pp. 73–92). Chichester, UK: Wiley.

Moore, J. C., Marquis, K. H., & Bogen, K. (1996). The SIPP cognitive research evaluation experiment: Basic results and documentation. U. S. Census Bureau Research Report Series (Survey Methodology #2010-04). Retrieved on March 23, 2012 from www.census.gov/srd/papers/pdf/rsm2010-04.pdf

Neter, J., & Waksberg, J. (1964). A study of response errors in expenditures data from household interviews. *Journal of the American Statistical Association, 59,* 18–55.

Newman, E. J., & Lindsay, D. S. (2009). False memories: What the hell are they for? *Applied Cognitive Psychology, 23,* 1105–1121.

O'Muircheartaigh, C. (1997). Measurement errors in surveys: A historical perspective. In L. E. Lyberg, P. P. Biemer, M. Collins, E. de Leeuw, N. Schwarz, and D. Trewin (Eds.), *Survey measurement and process quality* (pp. 1–25). New York: Wiley.

Parry, H. J., & Crossley, H. M. (1950). Validity of responses to survey questions. *Public Opinion Quarterly, 14,* 61–80.

Patrick, D. L., Cheadle, A., Thompson, D. C., Diehr, P., Koepsell, T., & Kline, S. (1994). The validity of self reported smoking: A review and meta-analysis. *American Journal of Public Health, 84,* 1086–1093.

Presser, S., (1990). Can changes in context reduce vote over reporting in surveys? *Public Opinion Quarterly, 40,* 51–65.

Presser, S., & Stinson, L. (1988). Data collection mode and social desirability bias in self-reported church attendance. *American Sociological Review, 63,* 137–145.

Prohaska, V., Brown, N. R., & Belli, R. F. (1998). Forward telescoping: The question matters. *Memory, 6,* 455–465.

Ross, M. (1989). Relation of implicit theories to the construction of personal histories. *Psychological Review, 96,* 341–357.

Rips, L. J., Conrad, F. G., & Fricker, S. S. (2003). Straightening the seam effect in panel surveys. *Public Opinion Quarterly, 67,* 522–554.

Rogers, T. F. (1976). Interviews by telephone and in person: Quality of responses and field performance. *Public Opinion Quarterly, 40,* 51–65.

Rubin, D. C., & Baddeley, A. D. (1989). Telescoping is not time compression: A model of the dating of autobiographical events. *Memory & Cognition, 17,* 653–661.

Schober, M. F., & Conrad, F. G. (1997). Does conversational interviewing reduce survey measurement error? *Public Opinion Quarterly, 61,* 576–602.

Schwarz, N., Hippler, H. J., Deutsch, B., & Strack, F. (1985). Response categories: Effects on behavioral reports and comparative judgments. *Public Opinion Quarterly, 49,* 388–395.

Shum, M. S. (1998). The role of temporal landmarks in autobiographical memory processes. *Psychological Bulletin, 124,* 423–442.

Stocké, V., & Stark, T. (2007). Political involvement and memory failure as interdependent determinants of vote overreporting. *Applied Cognitive Psychology, 21,* 239–257.

Strube, G., & Neubauer, S. (1988). Remember that exam? In M. M. Gruneberg, P. E. Morris, and R. N. Sykes (Eds.), *Practical aspects of memory: Current research and issues* (Vol. 1, pp. 247–252). New York: Wiley.

Sudman, S., & Bradburn, N. (1973). Effects of time and memory factors on response in surveys. *Journal of the American Statistical Association, 68,* 805–815.

Sudman, S., & Bradburn, N. (1974). *Response effects in surveys.* San Francisco, CA: Jossey-Bass.

Suchman, L., & Jordan, B. (1990). Interactional troubles in face-to-face survey interviews. *Journal of the American Statistical Association, 85,* 232–241.

Stulginskas, J. V., Verreault, R., & Pless, I. B. (1985). A comparison of observed and reported restraint use by children and adults. *Accident Analysis & Prevention, 17,* 381–386.

Sudman, S., Bradburn, N., & Schwarz, N. (1996). *Thinking about answers: The application of cognitive processes to survey methodology.* San Francisco, CA: Jossey-Bass.

Thompson, C. P., Skowronski, J. J., & Lee, D. J. (1988). Telescoping in dating naturally occurring events. *Memory & Cognition, 16,* 461–468.

Tourangeau, R. (1984). Cognitive science and survey methods. In T. B. Jabine, M. L., Straf, J. M. Tanur, and R. Tourangeau (Eds.), *Cognitive aspects of survey methodology: Building a bridge between disciplines* (pp. 73–100). Washington, DC: National Academy Press.

Tourangeau, R., Rips, L. J., & Rasinski, K. (2000). *The psychology of survey response.* Cambridge: Cambridge University Press.

van der Vaart, W., & Glasner, T. (2011). Personal landmarks as recall aids in survey interviews. *Field Methods, 23,* 37–56.

van der Vaart, W., & Glasner, T. (2007a). Applying a timeline as a recall aid in a telephone survey: A record-check study. *Applied Cognitive Psychology, 21,* 217–238.

van der Vaart, W., & Glasner, T. (2007b). *The use of landmark events in EHC interviews to enhance recall accuracy.* Report commissioned by the U.S. Bureau of the Census. Washington, DC.

Waismel-Manor, I., & Sarid, J. (2011). Can overreporting in surveys be reduced? Evidence from Israel's municipal elections. *International Journal of Public Opinion Research, 23,* 522–529.

Yoshihama, M., Gillespie, B., Hammock, A. C., Belli, R. F., & Tolman, R. M. (2005). Does the life history calendar method facilitate the recall of intimate partner violence? Comparison of two methods of data collection. *Social Work Research, 29,* 151–163.

Zaragoza, M. S., & Lane, S. M. (1994). Source misattributions and the suggestibility of eyewitness memory. *Journal of Experimental Psychology: Learning, Memory, and Cognition, 20,* 934–945.

22

Individual Differences in Remembering

Colin M. MacLeod, Tanya R. Jonker, and Greta James

Everyone recognizes that memory ability differs across and even within individuals for different kinds of information and under different circumstances. Indeed, we know that these differences can be dramatic: Some people regularly struggle to remember phone numbers, names, and even faces; others, like the *Jeopardy* contestants on television, have a seemingly superhuman dexterity with enormous arrays of facts and knowledge. Ask someone how good their own memory is, though, and they likely will apologetically say "not very good," often followed by pointing to someone that does have a phenomenal memory – or more likely to someone who knows someone who has a phenomenal memory.

What underlies these apparently vast differences in memory? The common answer is *talent* – some people are just born with greater ability. There is indeed evidence of genetic contributions to memory (e.g., de Quervain et al., 2003; Egan et al., 2003), consistent with a role for memory "inheritance." But the fact that this "nature" explanation is very entrenched does not deny a very significant role for "nurture." Practice – intensive deliberate practice over extended time – is, on the evidence, a considerably more reasonable explanation, as Ericsson has persuasively argued (Ericsson & Moxley, Chapter 23, this volume; Ericsson, Krampe, & Tesch-Römer, 1993). Foer's (2011) recent popular book, *Moonwalking with Einstein*, also strongly makes the case for practice in the context of memory improvement techniques.

In this chapter, we address 12 questions about how and why people's memory abilities differ. We chose these 12 because, in our experience, they are the most frequently asked questions in university and public lectures on memory. We will argue overall that the two major factors underlying individual differences in memory are the operation of working memory and the knowledge stored in long-term memory, with additional contributions from motivation and personality. Our primary goals will be to show where the differences in memory ability are worthy of note, what might bring about the differences, and how what we know about these differences enhances our understanding of memory. Psychologists periodically call for better integration of individual differences research into our general theorizing (e.g., Cronbach, 1957): This need is at least as great in the domain of memory as elsewhere (see, e.g., Melton, 1967; Underwood, 1975). Surely the range of memory abilities constitutes a major element of memory that must be explained.

Table 22.1 shows the twelve questions about individual differences in memory that we will try to answer – or at least to summarize what we know. But before we begin answering these central questions, how can we measure memory in the first place?

MEASURING MEMORY

The best known psychometric test designed to measure different memory functions is the Wechsler Memory Scale. Originally developed in 1945 and now in its fourth edition (WMS-IV; 2009), it consists of seven subtests: brief cognitive status exam, spatial addition, symbol span, design memory, logical memory, verbal paired associates, and visual reproduction. These are then combined and reported as five Index Scores: Auditory Memory, Visual Memory, Visual Working Memory, Immediate Memory, and

Table 22.1 Twelve questions about individual differences in remembering

Number	Question
1	Are memory differences just an outgrowth of intelligence differences?
2	Are some people better than others at holding more information in memory at one time?
3	Are some people quicker and more accurate than others at accessing memories?
4	Are some people better than others at dealing with interfering information in memory?
5	Do some people have photographic memories?
6	Do people differ in their use of mental imagery?
7	Do people differ in their susceptibility to false memories?
8	Do people differ in forgetting things that they are supposed to do later?
9	Do people differ in how effectively they study?
10	Do some people remember faces and names better than others?
11	Do some people have earlier or more detailed childhood memories than others?
12	Are men's and women's memories different?

Delayed Memory. When factor-analyzed to determine the underlying traits, the two dominant factors are a general memory factor and an attention/concentration factor (Roid, Prifitera, & Ledbetter, 1988). WMS-IV was designed to accompany the Wechsler Adult Intelligence Scale, fourth edition (WAIS-IV; 2008), which also contains a working memory index made up of two subtests – digit span and arithmetic. The major use of the WMS is as a neuropsychological tool to evaluate people with suspected memory problems, but it can also be used to measure normal memory.

The WMS provides a formal – reliable and valid – measure of memory. But most *research* on memory does not involve the WMS because the concern is often with memory quality, not memory quantity (Koriat & Goldsmith, 1996). This quality (or accuracy) issue pervades the questions that we address, whether we are investigating working memory or long-term memory. The short-term (working) versus long-term memory distinction has long been a key idea in theorizing about memory (Atkinson & Shiffrin, 1968; James, 1890). Working memory (Baddeley, 1986; Baddeley & Hitch, 1974; Cowan, 1988, 2005; Cowan, Rouder, Blume, & Saults, 2012) is the capacity-limited system that actively holds information in memory to permit performance of tasks and to make that information available for further processing. Long-term memory is the system that provides the continuing retention of information, outside of awareness. The information in working memory can come from the environment, from information already in long-term memory, or from their combination.

The longest standing measure of working memory capacity, again a measure of quantity, is span – the maximum amount of information that can be held at one time. This limitation was first identified by Ebbinghaus (1885) and the term "span" was coined by Jacobs (1887). Traditionally, this was digit span, involving repeating back a string of digits in order. An individual's digit span was taken to be the longest string that they could successfully recall. Digit span linked-well with the idea of a short-term memory store that simply held a limited amount of information. But working memory is seen as more dynamic – as active, conscious memory where mental work is done – and so measures of span have changed. Beginning with Daneman and Carpenter's (1980) reading span – where the task was to read and understand a series of sentences while retaining the last word of each sentence – span measures have come to require computation in addition to retention. Conway, Kane, Bunting, Hambrick, Wilhelm, and Engle (2005) provide a good overview of these working memory span tasks.

Long-term memory measures are a much larger and more diverse set, as befits this vast network. We distinguish episodic (personal past) memory from semantic (general knowledge) memory and from procedural (skills) memory (see Tulving, 1985). Episodic memory is typically measured by recall and recognition. In recall, a person is presented with a set of information, and is asked to recollect that information, either without assistance (free recall) or with clues (cued recall). In recognition, items that were or were not studied are presented and the person tries to determine whether each is "old" or "new." These are explicit memory tests, in which the person is aware of trying to remember, as opposed to implicit memory tests, in which the person uses memory without awareness (Graf & Schacter, 1985). Implicit measures typically rely on priming – that prior experience facilitates subsequent experience without awareness. Examples would be faster reading of material previously read, or faster or more successful solution of word fragments (e.g., A - - A - - I N for ASSASSIN) seen previously. Similarly, procedural memory can be measured by more rapid or accurate performance of a previously performed skill. Semantic memory can be measured by priming as well, such as when earlier knowledge related to information currently being processed speeds that processing.

There are many other measures that can be used to assess remembering, from confidence judgments to autobiographical cues and beyond. Many of these also are aimed at quality rather than quantity of memory. It is good to have these measures in mind, and to realize how the richness of memory requires many types of measures.

QUESTION 1: ARE MEMORY DIFFERENCES JUST AN OUTGROWTH OF INTELLIGENCE DIFFERENCES?

In fact, it might be better to think of differences in intelligence as a consequence of memory differences. It is clear from the foregoing that memory and intelligence have to be related: Intelligence tests such as the WAIS-IV include subtests of memory, so that memory performance necessarily contributes to the measurement of overall intelligence. As we will show in Question 2, working memory measures – notably working memory capacity – consistently show a strong relation to intelligence. Indeed, Kyllonen and his colleagues (Colom, Rebollo, Palacios, Juan-Espinosa, & Kyllonen, 2004; Kyllonen, 1996; Kyllonen & Stephens, 1990) argue that working memory is the strongest predictor of intelligence, better than declarative or procedural knowledge or than processing speed. Colom et al. (2004) go further in suggesting that intelligence and working memory may actually be the same construct.

Whether we are remembering or solving problems, working memory is the cornerstone of our mental workspace and long-term memory provides our entire knowledge base. Consequently, memory must be crucial to our intellectual functioning. One could argue, in the context of Horn and Cattell's fluid/crystallized theory of intelligence (Horn & Cattell, 1966), that working memory underlies fluid intelligence (rapid manipulation of information) and long-term memory underlies crystallized intelligence (use of knowledge, or wisdom). Such a characterization makes it clear that memory is central to our intellectual functioning.

QUESTION 2: ARE SOME PEOPLE BETTER THAN OTHERS AT HOLDING MORE INFORMATION IN MEMORY AT ONE TIME?

This, of course, is the issue of working memory capacity, the subject of extensive research (see Andrade, Chapter 6, this volume; Bors & MacLeod, 1996). Certainly, at the extremes, memory span is smaller, as in the learning-disabled (e.g., Torgesen, 1988) and the elderly (Myerson, Emery, White, & Hale, 2003). Simple digit span can detect such extreme differences but is not very useful within the normal adult range (Matarazzo, 1972). Dempster (1981) argued that of the ten frequently considered sources of differences in memory span – rehearsal, grouping, chunking, retrieval strategies, item identification, item ordering, capacity, susceptibility to interference, search rate, and the output buffer – the major one was the speed of identifying presented items. This argument localizes the individual differences in the manipulation of the information rather than in pure storage capacity.

Most work on working memory capacity uses modern span measures, where span is measured during more complex processing, such as reading for understanding or performing complex arithmetic calculations. Engle and Kane (2004) summarize their extensive research as showing that these processing span measures do a very good job of predicting higher-order cognitive capabilities, among them comprehension and most notably general intelligence. Their research on working memory capacity has also implicated fundamental processes of attention and self-control (see, e.g., Kane, Conway, Hambrick, & Engle, 2007).

To illustrate their research program, consider a study by Kane and Engle (2000). They had two groups, one with high and one with low working memory capacity, view short lists and try to recall the items. They manipulated memory load by sometimes adding a finger-tapping task. Not surprisingly, under no load, individuals with low span showed more proactive interference (interference from earlier lists) than did those with high span. The interesting finding was that the two groups performed equivalently under load: Proactive interference increased under load for high-span individuals only, suggesting that they ordinarily use attention to overcome interference but that was not possible under load.

How big is working memory? Researchers agree that the capacity is less than Miller's (1956) "magical number" 7 ± 2, with Cowan's (2010) figure of 4 providing a modern benchmark. This number provides a rough index of how many coherent pieces of information can be held (or referenced in long-term memory) while carrying out computations in working memory, and it is this capacity and the associated executive control processes that vary across individuals. Indeed, capacity and control may not be separate: Greater control may confer greater capacity. The natural follow-up question is whether training can improve working memory – and whether transfer can extend beyond the specific training regimen, even influencing intelligence. There is debate on this (see Klingberg, 2010, for the more positive side; Redick et al., 2013, and Shipstead, Redick, & Engle, 2012, present the more skeptical view). Historically, it has proven very difficult to obtain transfer of training on cognitive skills, but it is early days yet regarding training of working memory and possible transfer to tasks other than the training task.

Kalyuga, Ayres, Chandler, and Sweller (2003) reasonably argue that our finite working memory is the limiting factor in learning new information. Schemas that chunk information into larger units help to reduce working memory load, improving retention of new information. Novices do not yet have these schemas, so detailed instruction helps them to organize the new information into a schema. Experts already have these schemas, so highly guided learning can be harmful – for them, the detailed instruction is redundant, increasing the load on working memory as they try to assimilate information into existing schemas. Kalyuga et al. (2003) dub this the expertise reversal effect (see also McNamara, Kintsch, Songer, & Kintsch, 1996).

We know that working memory capacity and skills relate to many other aspects of psychological functioning. Working memory is central to the development of cognitive abilities in children (Munakata, Morton, & O'Reilly, 2007) and to their decline in the elderly (Hasher & Zacks, 1988), and deficits in working memory may be a marker for early onset Alzheimer's (Rosen, Bergeson, Putnam, Harwell, & Sunderland, 2002). More depressed individuals show a deficit in working memory span but not in simple span, implicating effects of executive control (Arnett, Higginson, Voss, Bender, Wurst, & Tippin, 1999). Even the cost of stereotype threat is partially due to reduced working memory capacity (Schmader & Johns, 2003).

Overall, then, the capacity of working memory and the control processes that operate on its contents are sources of critical individual differences in memory with quite sweeping implications for other aspects of cognition.

QUESTION 3: ARE SOME PEOPLE QUICKER AND MORE ACCURATE THAN OTHERS AT ACCESSING MEMORIES?

This question addresses the communication between working memory and long-term memory. Essentially, working memory is constantly called on to access information in long-term memory both to process inputs from the world and to respond based on experience. Given the sharp limitation of working memory to holding only about four items, it is critical to select only the most

relevant information and to minimize the capacity consumed by irrelevant information. Vogel, McCullough, and Machizawa (2005) have demonstrated that selection efficiency shows considerable variability and that high-capacity individuals are much better than low-capacity individuals at selecting only the relevant items. Intriguingly, low-capacity individuals may actually store more information in working memory, essentially wasting their capacity. This inefficiency could well contribute to diminished success in accessing long-term memory because working memory is "crowded."

In earlier work, Hunt (1978) and colleagues argued that accessing information in long-term memory – even highly familiar information – is an important source of individual differences. Their primary measure was the letter identification task (Posner, Boies, Eichelman, & Taylor, 1969), in which subjects verify as quickly as possible whether two letters have the same name. Physical identity trials (AA, ee) can be verified perceptually without accessing long-term memory, but name identity trials (Aa, eE) require retrieval from long-term memory. Individuals of lower verbal ability as measured by standardized tests showed larger response time differences between physical and name identity trials, indicative of slower access to well-learned information in long-term memory. This pattern was evident for common words as well as for letters (Hunt, Davidson, & Lansman, 1981). When even such overlearned information is slower to retrieve, this has serious consequences: Consider how much it would slow down reading (Palmer, MacLeod, Hunt, & Davidson, 1985).

In working memory, then, those with low spans have trouble selecting and manipulating the relevant information; in long-term memory, those with lower verbal ability (a proxy for fluid intelligence) are slower to access existing information, at least when that information is verbal. These findings articulate well with established findings that processing speed is a critical determinant of performance, and may be a major reason underlying the decline in cognitive ability with advanced age (see Salthouse, 1996).

QUESTION 4: ARE SOME PEOPLE BETTER THAN OTHERS AT DEALING WITH INTERFERING INFORMATION IN MEMORY?

Paradoxically, to remember, we sometimes must forget. Indeed, a critical feature of remembering involves filtering out intruding material, an issue raised in Question 2. Those with high working memory capacity better recall relevant information (Rosen & Engle, 1997; Unsworth, 2010), resist intrusions more effectively (Rosen & Engle, 1998), restrict encoding and maintenance to relevant information (Vogel et al., 2005), and suffer less from proactive interference (Kane & Engle, 2000; Unsworth, 2010). Thus, those with high working memory capacity tend to perform better on tasks that require the restriction of interfering information.

This raises another important question: Does performance differ between those with high and low working memory capacity because of differences in *capacity* or differences in *control*? If differences lie in capacity or available resources alone, one might expect high capacity individuals to be *more* susceptible to interference during retrieval because, in a sense, there is more "space" that can be filled with irrelevant information (for an analogue in attention, see Wilson, Muroi, & MacLeod, 2011). Alternatively, if working memory captures a dimension of executive control (as has been argued by Baddeley & Della Sala, 1996; Baddeley & Hitch, 1974), then one might expect high working memory capacity individuals to be *less* susceptible to interference during retrieval because they have better control over encoding and retrieval processes. In fact, the latter is supported by the data.

Based on the link between working memory and controlling interfering information,

many have argued that inhibition of unwanted or interfering material is beneficial for efficient retrieval (see, e.g., Hasher & Zacks, 1988), and that those with higher working memory capacity have better control processes and are better at this suppression (e.g., Aslan & Bäuml, 2010; Rosen & Engle, 1998). Specifically, during retrieval processes, interfering information is suppressed to facilitate retrieval of the target information. Aslan and Bäuml demonstrated that those with high working memory capacity experienced more difficulties when trying to retrieve information that competed with targets on an earlier task (see also Conway & Engle, 1994; Rosen & Engle, 1998).

A recent study raises an alternative account to the suppression hypothesis. Delaney and Sahakyan (2007) demonstrated that, when instructed to forget a first list and remember a second list, individuals with higher working memory capacity forgot more items from the first list following a context change manipulation that made the first list contextually distinct from the second list. This suggests that individuals with higher working memory capacity might not rely on suppression to reduce interference; instead – or additionally – they might better use context information during encoding and retrieval.

Clearly, high-span individuals cope with interference more effectively than low-span individuals. Those with high working memory capacity may deal more effectively with interfering information because they can better suppress competing material, because they can better recruit critical contextual cues, or some combination of the two.

QUESTION 5: DO SOME PEOPLE HAVE PHOTOGRAPHIC MEMORIES?

In our opening paragraph, we alluded to someone knowing someone who knew someone with an exceptionally good memory. This definitely applies to photographic memory: We have all heard of people with this ability, but few have ever actually met such a person. What would it actually mean to have this ability? Is it just an exceptional memory, or should it be something uniquely pictorial with extraordinary resolution? Certainly, there are people with exceptional memories (see Ericsson & Moxley, Chapter 23, this volume): The most salient case recently is AJ (her initials), a woman who has a prodigious memory for the events of her lifetime, both personal and public (Parker, Cahill, & McGaugh, 2006). Other mnemonists, or memorists as they are sometimes called, have periodically been reported (e.g., Hunt & Love, 1972; Luria, 1968; see Foer, 2011), but none have been claimed to have photographic memory.

A truly photographic memory would contain representations isomorphic to the world that could be retrieved essentially perfectly. It is generally agreed that such an ability does not exist. Instead, what does appear to exist is eidetic imagery, which is more like exceptionally good visual imagery – accurate and detailed (for reviews see Crowder, 2003; Gray & Gummerman, 1975). This ability has long interested researchers (e.g., Allport, 1924; Carmichael, 1925; Kluver, 1928), but gained considerable profile with the work of Haber and Haber (1964, 1988). They studied 150 children in elementary school, briefly showing them a standard set of four pictures and then, after each picture was removed, asking them questions about what they "saw" in memory. About half of the children reported having images, but only 12 (8 percent) seemed to have eidetic imagery. Paivio and Cohen (1979), examining 242 children in grades two and three, produced an almost identical estimate of 8.6 percent. Subsequently, a common test for eidetic imagery became the ability to mentally overlap two meaningless pictures to produce a meaningful one (see Leask, Haber, & Haber, 1969).

Later studies showed this ability to be almost entirely restricted to children under age ten (Giray, Altkin, Vaught, & Roodin, 1976; Richardson & Harris, 1986), and even then to perhaps only 5 percent of children

who can encode pictorial information and recover it, at least for a few minutes, with impressively high resolution (see Hochman, 2010). Intriguingly, there is evidence suggesting that eidetic imagery can "return" in the elderly (Zelhart, Markley, & Bieker, 1985), although the reliability and interpretation of these observations are unclear. It has been suggested that the presence of this ability is related to brain disorders (see Crowder, 2003). What is clear, though, is that whereas eidetic imagery appears to exist in a small subset of children, it is unrelated to – and hence there is no evidence for – photographic memory.

Those children with eidetic imagery may use working memory more effectively, access information in long-term memory more effectively, or both.

QUESTION 6: DO PEOPLE DIFFER IN THEIR USE OF MENTAL IMAGERY?

Mental imagery has always been of interest to those trying to understand memory, no doubt because imaging dramatically improves remembering. Imagery is, according to Intons-Peterson (1992, p. 46) "the introspective persistence of [a sensory] experience, including one constructed from components drawn from long-term memory, in the absence of direct sensory instigation of that experience." Galton (1880) collected and analyzed reports of how – or indeed whether – people experienced mental pictures, and recognized immediately the diversity of visual imagery experience (see also Griffitts, 1927). We know of individuals with extremely good imagery, including Luria's subject, "S" (Luria, 1962), whose overpowering images interfered with his daily functioning, and Stephen Wiltshire, the autistic British architectural artist who, after a single quite brief exposure, can do highly detailed and accurate city and landscape drawings. Moreover, it is well established that mathematics skill benefits from visual imagery ability (Battista, 1990; McGee, 1979).

In fact, there appear to be extensive differences in the ability to form and manipulate visual images in memory (see White, Sheehan, & Ashton, 1977). From the example of eidetic imagery as extremely good imagery, we can move to the self-reports of Galton's subjects, slightly over 10 percent of whom claimed to have no images at all – and were skeptical of others who did report imagery! Figures in the range of 2–5 percent for non-imagers are more routine now (see, e.g., Faw, 2009; Reisberg & Heuer, 2005). Of course, all such data are self-reported, so it could be that the individuals reporting no imagery are simply less willing to label their experience as imagery. Given, however, that the brain areas used in visual imagery correspond closely to those used in vision itself (Kosslyn, 2005; Kosslyn, Ganis, & Thompson, 2009), there is support for imagery being truly visual. At the least, these reports highlight the range of experience.

From Galton (1880) to Betts (1909) to the recent past (White et al., 1977), numerous tests have been developed to measure imagery ability. Some aim to measure ability to manipulate images; some aim to measure image quality (see, e.g., the Vividness of Visual Imagery Questionnaire; Marks, 1973, 1995; see McKelvie, 1995). This is, of course, a thorny measurement problem, given our fundamental inability to observe what is being measured, but tests such as the VVIQ do show some reliability.

Visual imagery is by far the most extensively studied, but other modes of imagery have also been investigated. Hubbard (2010) reviews the literature on auditory imagery, noting that auditory imagery test scores (e.g., the Auditory Imagery Scale of Gissurarson, 1992) correlate quite well with visual imagery test scores. Moreover, there are studies (e.g., Sharps & Price, 1992) to suggest that auditory imagery may benefit memory as much as visual imagery. This would be impressive, given the dramatic memory improvements that occur when people form images (Paivio, 1969).

In sum, there is a vast range in reported imagery ability, which may include a small proportion of individuals who do not experience visual imagery at all. Imaging improves memory substantially relative to rote rehearsal and, together with association, is the basis of almost all successful mnemonic techniques (see Higbee, 1977).

QUESTION 7: DO PEOPLE DIFFER IN THEIR SUSCEPTIBILITY TO FALSE MEMORIES?

False memory involves recollecting an experience or event that did not in fact occur (see Newman & Garry, Chapter 7, this volume). This intriguing field of research is important both theoretically and because it is especially relevant to applied areas such as eyewitness testimony (see Section 4, this volume). Knowing that a person is susceptible to falsely remembering events could prove useful in evaluating the reliability of that person's testimony.

In the experimental setting, a false memory can involve confidently "remembering" a word that was not studied, labeled an "intrusion." However, in a standard free recall test for a list of unrelated words, few intrusions typically occur. The Deese–Roediger–McDermott (DRM; Roediger & McDermott, 1995) paradigm encourages intrusions: Participants study a list of words (e.g., *thread*, *eye*, *sew*) that all are related to a critical unstudied word (e.g., *needle*) and then, on a later test, they frequently err and recall the critical unstudied word. This paradigm has shown strong test–retest reliability, making it is a useful tool for investigating individual differences in false memory (Blair, Lenton, & Hastie, 2002).

Individuals who show more false memory also have lower working memory capacity (e.g., Gerrie & Garry, 2007; Unsworth, 2007; Watson, Bunting, Poole, & Conway, 2005; however, see Salthouse & Siedlecki, 2007), use a more liberal response criterion across different memory tasks (Qin, Ogle, & Goodman, 2008), express more Need for

Cognition (Graham, 2007), and score higher on the Tellegen Absorption Scale, a measure of mental absorption in everyday activities (Drivdahl & Zaragoza, 2001). They also perform more poorly on a battery of intelligence, perception, memory, and face judgment tasks (Zhu et al., 2010). Indeed, Klein and Boals (2001) demonstrated that low working memory capacity individuals are more likely to experience intrusive memories.

Recent accounts concur that poor source monitoring underlies this tendency to experience false memory (e.g., Unsworth & Brewer, 2010a; Winograd, Peluso, & Glover, 1998; see Johnson, Hashtroudi, & Lindsay, 1993, and Lindsay, Chapter 4, this volume). It is a failure of source monitoring to deem an item "studied" when in fact it was not. Unsworth and Brewer (2010b; Unsworth, 2007) argue that high and low working memory capacity individuals differ in their ability to generate items but that they differ even more in their ability to discriminate generated items as being studied items versus intrusions. This editing process is a key part of source monitoring. Unsworth and Brewer (2010a) also demonstrated that working memory capacity and judgments of recency are related to false recall, but these relations were fully mediated by source-monitoring ability.

But is false memory a failure of source monitoring during encoding, retrieval, or both? Dehon, Larøi, and Van der Linden (2011) used the Encoding Styles Questionnaire to determine whether a participant was an "internal" encoder, relying more on schemata or expectations, or an "external" encoder, relying more on stimulus information. According to Dehon et al., high internal encoders rely more on their pre-existing schemata during encoding, leading to more false memories and implicating source monitoring failure during encoding rather than retrieval.

Although the locus of source monitoring differences is not yet clear, approaches to individual differences in false memory seem to converge on this explanation: Those who experience false memory in one domain will likely have difficulties monitoring source information in other domains, such that false memory will be a consistent problem for them.

QUESTION 8: DO PEOPLE DIFFER IN FORGETTING THINGS THAT THEY ARE SUPPOSED TO DO LATER?

Prospective memory refers to the ability to remember to do something at the appropriate time in the future (to differentiate it from retrospective memory, or memory for the past; see Kliegel, McDaniel, & Einstein, 2008; Einstein & McDaniel, Chapter 3, this volume). For example, we may rely on prospective memory to remember to call a family member later in the evening or to take a pill before bed. This ability is quite fundamental when it comes to completing day-to-day tasks.

Individuals differ greatly with respect to memory for future events (e.g., Marsh & Hicks, 1998), and there are clear differences in prospective memory ability between younger and older adults (e.g., Cherry & LeCompte, 1999; West & Bowry, 2005). To explain these differences, it has been argued that those who perform poorly in prospective remembering struggle to recruit preparatory or control attentional resources (Brewer, Knight, Marsh, & Unsworth, 2010; West & Bowry, 2005), and that attentional control declines as one ages (Rose, Rendell, McDaniel, Aberle, & Kliegel, 2010). Specifically, Rose et al. demonstrated that age differences were more pronounced in performance on novel prospective memory tasks and were reduced when tasks were repeated or when the ongoing task highlighted the features of the prospective task. Rose et al. saw this pattern as emphasizing the importance of controlling attention. Brewer et al. (2010) carried out a similar study involving participants with high versus low working memory capacity. The two groups performed similarly when the processing of the prospective task overlapped with the processing of the ongoing task, but those with high working memory capacity performed better when there was no task overlap.

In fact, there is evidence (Maylor, 1993, 1996; see also Hertzog & Pearman, Chapter 24, this volume) that older adults sometimes show superior performance on real-world prospective tasks, such as remembering to attend meetings. It would appear that this is because older adults do not rely as much as younger adults on internal cues, instead using external aids (calendars, diaries, etc.).

An alternative explanation to the attentional resource hypothesis is a monitoring explanation (Marsh & Hicks, 1998). It might not be available attentional resources per se that are crucial; instead, the ability to use efficient monitoring strategies might underlie individual differences in prospective memory (see also Brewer et al., 2010). Savine, McDaniel, Shelton, and Scullin (2012) demonstrated that both personality and cognitive factors underlie prospective memory performance; significantly, their cognitive factors included both the attention and monitoring elements just described. This monitoring deficit harks back to the explanation of false memory, and it is noteworthy that older people are more vulnerable to false memories as well (McCabe, Roediger, McDaniel, & Balota, 2009).

Indeed, prospective memory ability may actually result from the combination of two abilities. Specifically, Smith and Bayen (2004) propose a two-component model: prospective – remembering a task that must be completed, and retrospective – recognizing target events as they happen. In investigating these two components of an event-based prospective memory task, the personality dimension of conscientiousness was positively correlated with the retrospective component whereas working memory capacity was positively correlated with the prospective component (Smith, Persyn, & Butler, 2011; see also Cuttler & Graf, 2007; Smith & Bayen, 2005). Brain imaging data lend further support to roles for both prospective and retrospective components (Reynolds, West, & Braver, 2009).

Overall, it appears that the ability to remember to do things in the future does display significant individual differences. These differences rely in turn on differences in attention and monitoring, and are tied closely to working memory and its capacity.

QUESTION 9: DO PEOPLE DIFFER IN HOW EFFECTIVELY THEY STUDY?

Students and teachers certainly realize that students study differently and that their study regimens influence their learning of and subsequent memory for the material (see Metcalfe, Chapter 26, this volume). Of course, motivation matters: There is evidence that valuing the deep processing that improves memory (cf. Craik & Lockhart, 1972) is well connected to motivation, possibly more than self-reported ability or belief that studying is important (Nolen & Haladyna, 1990). But it is obvious, too, that cognition matters in terms of study strategies. Thomas and Rohwer (1986) identified four characteristics as central to effective studying: specificity (fit between strategies used and course and individual characteristics), generativity (increasing depth of processing), executive monitoring (metamemory used for appraising needs and for selecting and evaluating strategies), and personal efficacy (internal locus of control). With the possible exception of specificity, there are notable individual differences in each of these other factors that could certainly influence study effectiveness.

Although they get better as they move through their education, we know that most students do not employ planful and generative study strategies (Christopoulos, Rowher, & Thomas, 1987). Sadly, effective studying is the exception rather than the rule. Even the total study time that students report spending, although it changes significantly across grade levels, is essentially uncorrelated with achievement. This may well be a failure of metamemory – monitoring again – but likely also reflects insufficient motivation.

With recent moves to translate research on memory to the classroom (e.g., Roediger, Putnam, & Smith, 2011; Rohwer & Pashler, 2010), we can hope to see improved techniques for enhancing learning and memory in the educational system.

QUESTION 10: DO SOME PEOPLE REMEMBER FACES AND NAMES BETTER THAN OTHERS?

Everyone seems to believe that they can remember faces much better than names, but this is likely due to the fact that we ordinarily are recalling names and recognizing faces (Bahrick, Bahrick, & Wittlinger, 1975). Are there real individual differences in this important interpersonal domain? Woodhead and Baddeley (1981) identified subjects whose face recognition had been exceptionally good or bad a few years earlier and gave them three recognition tasks: faces, paintings, and words. Compared with those who had previously recognized faces poorly, those who had previously recognized faces well were better at recognizing faces and paintings but did not differ at recognizing words. This suggests that people who are good at face recognition generally have good visual memory that is separate from verbal memory.

Recently, Bindemann, Avetisyan, and Rakow (2012) have examined individual differences and consistency in identifying unfamiliar faces. By measuring performance repeatedly across several days, they showed that people often made different identification decisions to the same faces and that people who were very accurate on one day could be quite error-prone on another day. Nevertheless, there was a small subset of people who were consistently accurate across days. Their findings fit with the idea that accuracy and consistency are independent components of the ability to match faces, and both are required to predict a person's general face processing skill.

Franklin and Adams (2010) have argued that faces differ from other visual stimuli in that people read complex social meaning into faces. They found that people who were good at decoding emotional messages from expressive faces were more successful at encoding and retrieving neutral faces. Moreover, faces rated as higher in emotionality were better remembered. There are also well-established age differences in face–name association, with older people having considerably more trouble than younger people. Naveh-Benjamin, Shing, Kilb, Werkle-Bergner, Lindenberger, and Li (2009) taught face–name pairs to both age groups under either incidental or intentional learning instructions and found poorer performance by older people on faces, names, and their association under incidental learning, and a specific deficit in older people for the associations under intentional learning. Apparently, there are both general episodic memory deficits and more specific strategic deficits that arise with age.

Faces and names provide a natural testing ground for individual differences in memory. It appears that some people are very good at this, possibly because they encode more accurately and consistently than other people do. This may be a general visual memory superiority or it may hinge on better associative learning, or both of these may play roles. It would seem that both cognitive and social/personality factors are involved.

QUESTION 11: DO SOME PEOPLE HAVE EARLIER OR MORE DETAILED CHILDHOOD MEMORIES THAN OTHERS?

People often share – and hence compare – their earliest memories, and we have each been surprised by how far back some individual(s) can go and how many details they can recollect. We do, however, have to consider whether their memories are real: Apparent differences could reflect differing tendencies to endorse false memories as opposed to real differences in autobiographical memories (see Newman & Garry, Chapter 7; Goldsmith, Pansky, & Koriat, Chapter 27; and Fivush & Waters, Chapter 13, this volume). Reports of memories before the age of three or four likely are false, possibly because the use of relevant memory scripts has not yet developed (see Hudson, Fivush, & Kuebli, 1992). It remains difficult to determine whether reports of very early memories are of the original episode or arise from photographs or stories absorbed later in life.

Parental influence may affect the age of earliest memories. Haden, Ornstein, Rudek, and Cameron (2009) found that mothers who engaged their 18-month-olds with more open-ended elaborative questions, fewer elaborative statements, and more confirmations improved their children's memories for events, in turn leading both to more detailed recollections and to earlier memories. In accord with this, Jack, MacDonald, Reese, and Hayne (2009) found that the tendency of some mothers to elaborate memories rather than repeat them when their children were two to three years old led to earlier memories in their children when they were 12 to 13 years old. Usher and Neisser (1993) also suggest that children may tend to remember later in life only those episodes that the adults saw as important.

Regardless of the earliest age of recall, individuals certainly differ in their ability to recall early memories. A number of variables have been implicated as responsible for this variability. For example, females tend to have earlier memories than males (see Question 12), possibly because of the influence of testosterone on the development of memory ability early in life (Mullen, 1994). Birth order may also affect recall, with age of earliest memory later for younger siblings. A possible explanation could be that parents talk and socialize more with girls and first-born children. Finally, earliest memories tend to be earlier for Caucasians than for Asians, suggesting that culture may also exert some influence (Mullen, 1994).

Theories of how autobiographical memory develops also provide some explanation as to why individuals differ in the extent to which they recall early memories. For example, Howe (2000) argues that the development of autobiographical memory relies on the development of a sense of self, which acts as an organization principle used to reference a memory (but see Hyman & Billings, 1998, for a contrasting view). Indeed, organizational change with development does seem to be an important factor determining childhood memories (see Usher & Neisser, 1993). One reason that adults may forget early memories is because those memories do not fit into our mature organizations; this may also explain why 8-year-olds can remember earlier memories than adults can.

Investigations of infantile amnesia in adults are numerous, but researchers have only recently turned to studying children. Peterson, Warren, and Short (2011) asked children aged 4 to 13 years old for their earliest three memories and then asked them again two years later. Younger children rarely recalled the same memories – even when given cues about the memories that they had recalled previously. Older children were considerably more likely to recall the same memories, and cues to previously recalled memories were successful for them.

There certainly is room for more work on early memories and the extent of detail in those memories; we also need to understand what factors contaminate those memories, and how they do so. Of course, the young child's perceptual system also undoubtedly plays a role in how episodes are processed and hence retained, and the reconstructive nature of recollection also impacts how we remember the beginnings of our lives.

QUESTION 12: ARE MEN'S AND WOMEN'S MEMORIES DIFFERENT?

Differences in memory performance between the sexes do exist. Women generally perform better at verbal memory, episodic recall, and face recognition (e.g., de Frias, Nilsson, & Herlitz, 2006; Krueger & Salthouse, 2010). These sex differences begin early (e.g., Davis, 1999), and remain stable throughout adulthood, even prominent beyond age 85 (de Frias et al., 2006). Women are also better eyewitnesses, typically showing greater accuracy in person and location descriptions than men do (Areh, 2011). Although numerous studies have shown that women have better episodic and verbal memory, generally no sex differences are found in primary memory, semantic memory, or priming (Herlitz, Nilsson, & Bäckman, 1997; see also Maccoby & Jacklin, 1974). Furthermore, when episodic memory tests require visuospatial processing – processing that men are known to excel at – men outperform women (Lewin, Wolgers, & Herlitz, 2001).

Are these sex differences in the encoding or retrieval stage? Krueger and Salthouse (2010) examined memory gains and losses over multiple study-test trials and concluded that differences occur in memory acquisition, rather than in retention. This conclusion is further supported by examining recall and recognition tests where the difference between men and women is equal, suggesting that it lies in encoding processes, not in retrieval processes (Herlitz et al., 1997).

One prominent theory explaining these sex differences asserts that women have a more efficient declarative memory system (e.g., Ullman, 2004), allowing them to rely more heavily on previous experience with language when performing linguistic tasks. This theory is supported by the finding that women perform better than men on a verbal memory task involving familiar-sounding novel words, but do not outperform men when the task involves unfamiliar-sounding novel words (Kaushanskaya, Marian, & Yoo, 2011). Thus, women are better able to recruit their knowledge of language when the stimuli sound familiar. Lewin et al. (2001) argue that the observed sex differences in episodic memory are not the result of superior verbal ability; indeed, the sex difference in episodic recall remains when verbal

ability is controlled (Herlitz, Airaksinen, & Nordström, 1999; Herlitz et al., 1997; Krueger & Salthouse, 2010).

Women also excel at recalling emotional memories (Canli, Desmond, Zhao, & Gabrieli, 2002). They tend to remember more childhood events, but this advantage is restricted to events associated with emotion (Davis, 1999). In general, people remember negatively valenced material better than neutral material, yet neutral material is better remembered if followed by negatively valenced unrelated material (e.g., watching a video with negative content) as opposed to neutral material (Nielson, Yee, & Erickson, 2005). Recently, Wang and Fu (2010) demonstrated that this effect occurs for females but not for males, suggesting that negative affect might influence the memory consolidation process in females only.

The risk in describing sex differences in memory is that this very act of description may make it seem that there are many such differences. But as far as we know, this is not true, and where there are differences, they are relatively subtle. They may also hinge not on differences in the memory system itself, but instead on factors such as motivation, interest, or experience. As is generally the case with group differences, there is much more difference in memory within each gender than there is between the genders.

CONCLUSION

In this chapter, we have endeavored to answer some of the most often asked questions about how people's memories differ. Certainly there are others that we could have included, but our coverage does indicate the richness of individual differences in memory – and their potential impact on everyday behavior. We have also tried to answer the critical theoretical question: What drives individual differences in memory? Our answer rests on the operation of working memory and the knowledge in long-term memory, with contributions from motivation and personality. First and foremost is working memory: It is our mental workspace so it is in constant use. Its capacity and its speed of operation dictate how fluently we can manipulate information, and we have seen its influence throughout the twelve questions. Likening it to fluid intelligence seems entirely appropriate. If we do so, then our crystallized intelligence corresponds to the knowledge in long-term memory. There is huge variation in what people know, and this will necessarily influence what they can do. What brings about that variation? Certainly, our own interests and motivation – our personalities – play pivotal roles in what we choose to learn and how well we learn it and can later recover it from memory. Our prior experience influences what we encode and what we retrieve, such that each of us has, in a very real sense, a different memory system. This is why, when faced with nominally the same event, each of us remembers it somewhat differently: We process it differently based on our experience, and we recollect it differently because what we have encoded, and how we go about retrieving it, is unique.

Cognitive psychologists and other researchers interested in memory should certainly be studying individual differences because it is unquestionably true that we can never have a complete theory of memory without meaningfully incorporating this variation. This is true at the level of explanation: As Underwood (1975) argued, predictions based on individual differences can often provide a test of a general theory. It is also true at the level of application: If we are to predict how an individual will behave when remembering, we need to be able to fine tune our broad understanding of memory by incorporating what we know about this person as opposed to people in general.

REFERENCES

Allport, G. W. (1924). Eidetic imagery. *British Journal of Psychology, 15*, 99–120.

Areh, I. (2011). Gender-related differences in eyewitness testimony. *Personality and Individual Differences, 50*, 559–563.

Arnett, P. A., Higginson, C. I., Voss, W. D., Bender, W. I., Wurst, J. M., & Tippin, J. M. (1999). Depression in multiple sclerosis: Relationship to working memory capacity. *Neuropsychology, 13*, 546–556.

Aslan, A., & Bäuml, K.-H. T. (2010). Individual differences in working memory capacity predict retrieval-induced forgetting. *Journal of Experimental Psychology: Learning, Memory, & Cognition, 37*, 264–269.

Atkinson, R. C., & Shiffrin, R. M. (1968). Human memory: A proposed system and its control processes. In K. W. Spence & J. T. Spence (Eds.), *The psychology of learning and motivation*, Vol. 2 (pp. 89–195). New York: Academic Press.

Baddeley, A. (1986). *Working memory*. Oxford: Clarendon Press.

Baddeley, A. D., & Della Sala, S. (1996). Working memory and executive control. *Philosophical Transactions: Biological Sciences, 351*, 1397–1404.

Baddeley, A. D., & Hitch, G. J. (1974). Working memory. In G. H. Bower (Ed.), *The psychology of learning and motivation* (Vol. 8, pp. 47–89). New York: Academic Press.

Bahrick, H. P., Bahrick, P. O., & Wittlinger, R. P. (1975). Fifty years of memory for names and faces: A cross-sectional approach. *Journal of Experimental Psychology: General, 104*, 54–75.

Battista, M. T. (1990). Spatial visualization and gender differences in high school geometry. *Journal of Research in Mathematics Education, 21*, 47–60.

Betts, G. H. (1909). *The distribution and function of mental imagery*. New York: Columbia University Press.

Bindemann, M., Avetisyan, M., & Rakow, T. (2012). Who can recognize unfamiliar faces? Individual differences and observer consistency in person identification. *Journal of Experimental Psychology: Applied, 18*, 277–291.

Blair, I. V., Lenton, A. P., & Hastie, R. (2002). The reliability of the DRM paradigm as a measure of individual differences in false memory. *Psychonomic Bulletin & Review, 9*, 590–596.

Bors, D. A., & MacLeod, C. M. (1996). Individual differences in memory. In E. L. Bjork and R. A. Bjork (Eds.), *Handbook of perception and cognition, Vol. 10: Memory* (pp. 411–441). San Diego, CA: Academic Press.

Brewer, G. A., Knight, J. B., Marsh, R. L., & Unsworth, N. (2010). Individual difference in event-based prospective memory: Evidence for multiple processes supporting cue detection. *Memory & Cognition, 38*, 304–311.

Canli, T., Desmond, J. E., Zhao, Z., Gabrieli, J. D. E., (2002). Sex differences in the neural basis of emotional memories. *Neurobiology, 16,* 10789–10794.

Carmichael, L. (1925). Eidetic imagery and the Binet test. *Journal of Educational Psychology, 16,* 251–252.

Cherry, K. E., & LeCompte, D. C. (1999). Age and individual difference influence prospective memory. *Psychology and Aging, 14,* 60–76.

Christopoulos, J. P., Rowher, W. D., & Thomas, J. W. (1987). Grade level differences in students' study activities as a function of course characteristics. *Contemporary Educational Psychology, 12,* 303–323.

Colom, R., Rebollo, I., Palacios, A., Juan-Espinosa, M., & Kyllonen, P. C. (2004). Working memory is (almost) perfectly predicted by g. *Intelligence, 32,* 277–296.

Conway, A. R. A., & Engle, R. W. (1994). Working memory and retrieval: A resource-dependent inhibition model. *Journal of Experimental Psychology: General, 123,* 354–373.

Conway, A. R. A., Kane, M. J., Bunting, M. F., Hambrick, D. Z., Wilhelm, O., & Engle, R. W. (2005). Working memory span tasks: A methodological review and user's guide. *Psychonomic Bulletin & Review, 12,* 769–786.

Cowan, N. (1988). Evolving conceptions of memory storage, selective attention, and their mutual constraints within the human information processing system. *Psychological Bulletin, 104,* 163–191.

Cowan, N. (2005). *Working memory capacity.* New York: Psychology Press.

Cowan, N. (2010). The magical mystery four: How is working memory capacity limited, and why? *Current Directions in Psychological Science, 19,* 51–57.

Cowan, N., Rouder, J. N., Blume, C. L., & Saults, J. S. (2012). Models of verbal working memory capacity: What does it take to make them work? *Psychological Review, 119,* 480–499.

Craik, F. I. M., & Lockhart, R. S. (1972). Levels of processing: A framework for memory research. *Journal of Verbal Learning and Verbal Behavior, 11,* 671–684.

Cronbach, L. J. (1957). The two disciplines of scientific psychology. *American Psychologist, 12,* 671–684.

Crowder, R. G. (2003). Eidetic imagery. In J. H. Byrne (Ed.), *Learning & memory* (2nd ed.) (pp. 130–132). New York: Macmillan.

Cuttler, C., & Graf, P. (2007). Personality predicts prospective memory task performance: An adult lifespan study. *Scandinavian Journal of Psychology, 48,* 215–231.

Daneman, M., & Carpenter, P. A. (1980). Individual differences in working memory and reading. *Journal of Verbal Learning & Verbal Behavior, 19,* 450–466.

Davis, P. J. (1999). Gender differences in autobiographical memory for childhood emotional experiences. *Journal of Personality and Social Psychology, 76,* 498–510.

de Frias, C. M., Nilsson, L.-G., & Herlitz, A. (2006). Sex differences in cognition are stable over a 10-year period in adulthood and old age. *Aging, Neuropsychology, and Cognition, 13,* 574–587.

de Quervain, D. J-F., Henke, K., Aerni, A., Coluccia, D., Wollmer, M. A., Hock, C., Nitsch, R. M., & Papassotiropoulos, A. (2003). A functional genetic variation of the 5-HT2a receptor affects human memory. *Nature Neuroscience, 6,* 1141–1142.

Dehon, H., Larøi, F., & Van der Linden, M. (2011). The influence of encoding style on the production of false memories in the DRM paradigm: New insights on individual differences in false memory susceptibility? *Personality and Individual Differences, 50,* 583–587.

Delaney, P. F., & Sahakyan, L. (2007). Unexpected costs of high working memory capacity following directed forgetting and contextual change manipulations. *Memory & Cognition, 35,* 1074–1082.

Dempster, F. N. (1981). Memory span: Sources of individual and developmental differences. *Psychological Bulletin, 89,* 63–100.

Drivdahl, S. B., & Zaragoza, M. S. (2001). The role of perceptual elaboration and individual differences in the creation of false memories for suggested events. *Applied Cognitive Psychology, 15,* 265–281.

Ebbinghaus, H. (1885/1913). *Memory: A contribution to experimental psychology.* New York: Teachers College, Columbia University.

Egan, M. F., Kojima, M., Callicott, J. H., Goldberg, T. E., Kolachana, B. S., Bertolino, A., Zaitsev, E., Gold, B., Goldman, D., Dean, M., Lu, B., & Weinberger, D. R. (2003). The BDNF val66met polymorphism affects activity-dependent secretion of BDNF and human memory and hippocampal function. *Cell, 112,* 257–269.

Engle, R. W., & Kane, M. J. (2004). Executive attention, working memory capacity, and a two-factor theory of cognitive control. In B. H. Ross (Ed.), *The psychology of learning and motivation* (Vol. 44, pp. 145–199). New York: Elsevier Science.

Ericsson, K. A., Krampe, R. T., & Tesch-Römer, C. (1993). The role of deliberate practice in the acquisition of expert performance. *Psychological Review, 100,* 363–406.

Faw, B. (2009). Conflicting intuitions may be based on differing abilities: Evidence from mental imaging research. *Journal of Consciousness Studies, 16,* 45–68.

Foer, J. (2011). *Moonwalking with Einstein.* New York: The Penguin Press.

Franklin, R. G., Jr., & Adams, R. B., Jr. (2010). What makes a face memorable? The relationship between face memory and emotional state reasoning. *Personality and Individual Differences, 49,* 8–12.

Galton, F. (1880). Statistics of mental imagery. *Mind, 5,* 301–318.

Gerrie, M. P., & Garry, M. (2007). Individual difference in working memory capacity affect false memories for missing aspects of events. *Memory, 15,* 561–571.

Giray, E. F., Altkin, W. M., Vaught, G. M., & Roodin, P. A. (1976). The incidence of eidetic imagery as a function of age. *Child Development, 47,* 1207–1210.

Gissurarson, L. R. (1992). Reported auditory imagery and its relationship with visual imagery. *Journal of Mental Imagery, 16,* 117–122.

Graf, P., & Schacter, D. L. (1985). Implicit and explicit memory for new associations in normal and amnesic subjects. *Journal of Experimental Psychology: Learning, Memory, and Cognition, 11,* 501–518.

Graham, L. M. (2007). Need for cognition and false memory in the Deese–Roediger–McDermott paradigm. *Personality and Individual Differences, 42,* 409–418.

Gray, C. R., & Gummerman, K. (1975). The enigmatic eidetic image: A critical examination of methods, data and theories. *Psychological Bulletin, 82,* 383–407.

Griffitts, C. H. (1927). Individual differences in imagery. *Psychological Monographs, 37,* 1–91.

Haber, R. N., & Haber, L. R. (1964). Eidetic imagery: I. Frequency. *Perceptual and Motor Skills, 19,* 131–138.

Haber, R. N., & Haber, L. R. (1988). The characteristics of eidetic imagery. In L. K. Obler and D. Fein (Eds.), *The exceptional brain: Neuropsychology of talent and special abilities* (pp. 218–241). New York: Guilford Press.

Haden, C. A., Ornstein, P. A., Rudek, D. J., & Cameron, D. (2009). Reminiscing in the early years: Patterns of maternal elaborativeness and children's remembering. *International Journal of Behavioral Development, 33,* 118–130.

Hasher, L., & Zacks, R. T. (1988). Working memory, comprehension, and aging: A review and a new view. In G. H. Bower (Ed.), *The psychology of learning and motivation,* Vol. 22 (pp. 193–225). San Diego, CA: Academic Press.

Hasher, L., Goldstein, D., & May, C. P. (2005). It's about time: Circadian rhythms, memory, and aging. In C. Izawa and N. Ohta (Eds.), *Human learning and memory: Advances in theory and application: The 4th Tsukuba international conference on memory* (pp. 199–217). Mahwah, NJ: Lawrence Erlbaum Associates.

Herlitz, A., Airaksinen, E., & Nordström, E. (1999). Sex differences in episodic memory: The impact of verbal and visuospatial ability. *Neuropsychology, 13,* 590–597.

Herlitz, A., Nilsson, L.-G., & Bäckman, L. (1997). Gender differences in episodic memory. *Memory & Cognition, 25,* 801–811.

Higbee, K. L. (1977). *Your memory: How it works and how to improve it.* Englewood Cliffs, NJ: Prentice-Hall.

Hochman, J. (2010). The eidetic: An image whose time has come? *Journal of Mental Imagery, 34,* 1–9.

Horn, J. L., & Cattell, R. B. (1966). Refinement and test of the theory of fluid and crystallized general intelligences. *Journal of Educational Psychology, 57,* 253–270.

Howe, M. L. (2000). *The fate of early memories: Developmental science and the retention of childhood experiences.* Washington, DC: American Psychological Association.

Hubbard, T. L. (2010). Auditory imagery: Empirical findings. *Psychological Bulletin, 136,* 302–329.

Hudson, J. A., Fivush, R., & Kuebli, J. (1992). Scripts and episodes: The development of event memory. *Applied Cognitive Psychology, 6,* 483–505.

Hunt, E. B., Davidson, J., & Lansman, M. (1981). Individual differences in long-term memory access. *Memory & Cognition, 9,* 599–608.

Hunt, E., & Love, L. T. (1972). How good can memory be? In A. Melton and E. Martin (Eds.), *Coding processes in human memory.* Washington, DC: Winston-Wiley.

Hyman, I. E., Jr., & Billings, F. J. (1998). Individual differences and the creation of false childhood memories. *Memory, 6,* 1–20.

Intons-Peterson, M. J. (1992). Components of auditory imagery. In D. Reisberg (Ed.), *Auditory imagery* (pp. 45–71). Hillsdale, NJ: Lawrence Erlbaum Associates.

Intons-Peterson, M. J., Rocchi, P., West, T., McLellan, K., & Hackney, A. (1998). Aging, optimal testing times, and negative priming. *Journal of Experimental Psychology: Learning, Memory, and Cognition, 24,* 362–376.

Jack, F., MacDonald, S., Reese, E., & Hayne, H. (2009). Maternal reminiscing style during early childhood predicts the age of adolescents' earliest memories. *Child Development, 80,* 496–505.

Jacobs, J. (1887). Experiments on prehension. *Mind, 12,* 75–79.

James, W. (1890). *The principles of psychology.* New York: Henry Holt and Co.

Johnson, M. K., Hashtroudi, S., & Lindsay, D. S. (1993). Source monitoring. *Psychological Bulletin, 114,* 3–28.

Kalyuga, S., Ayres, P., Chandler, P., & Sweller, J. (2003). The expertise reversal effect. *Educational Psychologist, 38,* 23–31.

Kane, M. J., & Engle, R. W. (2000). Working-memory capacity, proactive interference, and divided attention: Limits on long-term memory retrieval. *Journal of Experimental Psychology: Learning, Memory, and Cognition, 26,* 336–358.

Kane, M. J., Bleckley, M. K., Conway, A. R. A., & Engle, R. W. (2001). A controlled-attention view of working-memory capacity. *Journal of Experimental Psychology: General, 130,* 169–183.

Kane, M. J., Conway, A. R. A., Hambrick, D. Z., & Engle, R. W. (2007). Variation in working memory capacity as variation in executive attention and control. In A. R. A. Conway, C. Jarrold, M. J. Kane, A. Miyake, and J. N. Towse (Eds.), *Variation in working memory* (pp. 21–46). New York: Oxford University Press.

Kaushanskaya, M., Marian, V., & Yoo, J. (2011). Gender differences in adult word learning. *Acta Psychologica, 137,* 24–35.

Klein, K., & Boals, A. (2001). The relationship of life event stress and working memory capacity. *Applied Cognitive Psychology, 15,* 565–579.

Kliegel, M., McDaniel, M. A., & Einstein, G. O. (Eds.). (2008). *Prospective memory: Cognitive, neuroscience, developmental, and applied perspectives* (pp. 433–439). New York: Taylor & Francis Group/Lawrence Erlbaum Associates.

Klingberg, T. (2010). Training and plasticity of working memory. *Trends in Cognitive Sciences, 14,* 317–324.

Kluver, H. (1928). Studies on the eidetic type and on eidetic imagery. *Psychological Bulletin, 25,* 69–104.

Koriat, A., & Goldsmith, M. (1996). Memory as something that can be counted versus memory as something that can be counted on. In D. Herrmann, C. McEvoy, C. Hertzog, P. Hertel, and M. Johnson (Eds.), *Basic and applied memory research: Practical applications* (Vol. 2, pp. 3–18). Hillsdale, NJ: Erlbaum.

Kosslyn, S. M. (2005). Mental images and the brain. *Cognitive Neuropsychology, 22,* 333–347.

Kosslyn, S. M., Ganis, G., & Thompson, W. L. (2009). Mental imagery. In G. G. Berntson and J. T. Cacioppo (Eds.), *Handbook of neuroscience for the behavioral sciences,* Vol. 1 (pp. 383–394). Hoboken, NJ: John Wiley & Sons.

Krueger, L. E., & Salthouse, T. A. (2010). Differences in acquisition, not retention, largely contribute to sex differences in multitrial word recall performance. *Personality and Individual Differences, 49,* 768–772.

Kyllonen, P. C. (1996). Is working memory capacity Spearman's g? In I. Dennis and P. Tapsfield (Eds.), *Human abilities: Their nature and measurement* (pp. 49–75). Hillsdale, NJ: Lawrence Erlbaum Associates.

Kyllonen, P. C., & Stephens, D. L. (1990). Cognitive abilities as determinants of success in acquiring logic skill. *Learning and Individual Differences, 2,* 129–160.

Leask, J., Haber, R. N., & Haber, R. B. (1969). Eidetic imagery in children: II. Longitudinal and experimental results. *Psychological Monograph Supplements, 3* (whole no. 35).

Lewin, C., Wolgers, G., & Herlitz, A. (2001). Sex differences favoring women in verbal but not in visuospatial episodic memory. *Neuropsychology, 15,* 165–173.

Loftus, E. F. (1993). The reality of repressed memories. *American Psychologist, 48,* 518–537.

Luria, A.R. (1968). *The mind of the mnemonist.* Oxford, UK: Basic Books.

Maccoby, E. E., & Jacklin, C. N. (1974). *The psychology of sex differences.* Palo Alto, CA: Stanford University Press.

Marks , D. F. (1973). Visual imagery differences in the recall of pictures. *British Journal of Psychology, 64,* 17–24.

Marks, D. F. (1995). New directions for mental imagery research. *Journal of Mental Imagery, 19,* 153–167.

Marsh, R. L., & Hicks, J. L. (1998). Event-based prospective memory and executive control of working memory. *Journal of Experimental Psychology: Learning, Memory, & Cognition, 24,* 336–349.

Matarazzo, J. D. (1972). *Wechsler's measurement and appraisal of adult intelligence* (5th ed.). Baltimore, MD: Williams & Wilkins.

Maylor, E. A. (1993). Minimized prospective memory loss in old age. In J. Cerella, J. M. Rybash, W. Hoyer, and M. L. Commons (Eds.), *Adult information processing: Limits on loss* (pp. 529–551). San Diego, CA: Academic Press.

Maylor, E. A. (1996). Does prospective memory decline with age? In M. Brandimonte, G. O. Einstein, and M. A. McDaniel (Eds.), *Prospective memory: Theory and applications* (pp. 173–197). Mahwah, NJ: Lawrence Erlbaum Associates.

McCabe, D. P., Roediger, H. L., McDaniel, M. A., & Balota, D. A. (2009). Aging reduces veridical remembering but increases false remembering: Neuropsychological test correlates of remember-know judgments. *Neuropsychologia, 47,* 2164–2173.

McGee, M. G. (1979). Human spatial abilities: Psychometric studies and environmental, genetic, hormonal, and neurological influences. *Psychological Bulletin, 86,* 889–918.

McKelvie, S. J. (1995). The VVIQ as a psychometric test of individual differences in visual imagery vividness: A critical quantitative review and plea for direction. *Journal of Mental Imagery, 19,* 1–106.

McNamara, D. S., Kintsch, E., Songer, N. B., & Kintsch, W. (1996). Are good texts always better? Interactions of text coherence, background knowledge, and levels of understanding in learning from text. *Cognition and Instruction, 14,* 1–43.

Melton, A. W. (1967). Individual differences and theoretical process variables: General comments on the conference. In R. M. Gagné (Ed.), *Learning and individual differences* (pp. 238–252). Columbus, OH: Merrill.

Miller, G. A. (1956). The magical number seven, plus or minus two: Some limits on our capacity for processing information. *Psychological Review, 63,* 81–97.

Mullen, M. K. (1994). Earliest recollections of childhood: A demographic analysis. *Cognition, 52,* 55–79.

Munakata, Y., Morton, J. B., & O'Reilly, R. C. (2007). Developmental and computational approaches to variation in working memory. In A. R. A. Conway, C. Jarrold, M. J. Kane, A. Miyake, and J. N. Towse (Eds.), *Variation in working memory* (pp. 21–46). New York: Oxford University Press.

Myerson, J., Emery, L., White, D. A., & Hale, S. (2003). Effects of age, domain, and processing demands on memory span: Evidence for differential decline. *Aging, Neuropsychology, and Cognition, 10,* 20–27.

Naveh-Benjamin, M., Shing, Y. L., Kilb, A., Werkle-Bergner, M., Lindenberger, U., & Li, S.-C. (2009). Adult age differences in memory for name–face associations: The effects of intentional and incidental learning. *Memory, 17,* 220–232.

Nielson, K. A., Yee, D., & Erickson, K. I. (2005). Memory enhancement by a semantically unrelated emotional arousal source induced after learning. *Neurobiology of Learning and Memory, 84,* 49–56.

Nolen, S. B., & Haladyna, T. M. (1990). Motivation and studying in high school science. *Journal of Research in Science Teaching, 27,* 115–126.

Paivio, A. (1969). Mental imagery in associative learning and memory. *Psychological Review, 76,* 241–263.

Paivio, A., & Cohen, M. (1979). Eidetic imagery and cognitive abilities. *Journal of Mental Imagery, 3,* 53–64.

Palmer, J., MacLeod, C. M., Hunt, E., & Davidson, J. E. (1985). Information processing correlates of reading. *Journal of Memory and Language, 24,* 59–88.

Parker, E. S., Cahill, L., & McGaugh, J. L. (2006). A case of unusual autobiographical remembering. *Neurocase, 12,* 35–49.

Peterson C., Warren K. L., & Short, M. M. (2011). Infantile amnesia across the years: A 2-year follow-up of children's earliest memories. *Child Development, 82,* 1092–1105.

Posner, M. I., Boies, S. J., Eichelman, W. H., & Taylor, R. L. (1969). Retention of visual and name codes of single letters. *Journal of Experimental Psychology, 79,* 1–16.

Qin, J., Ogle, C. M., & Goodman, G. S. (2008). Adults' memories of childhood: True and false reports. *Journal of Experimental Psychology: Applied, 14,* 373–391.

Redick, T. S., Shipstead, Z., Harrison, T. L., Hicks, K. L., Fried, D. E., Hambrick, D. Z., Kane, M. J., & Engle, R. W. (2013). No evidence of intelligence improvement after working memory training: A randomized, placebo-controlled study. *Journal of Experimental Psychology: General, 142,* 359–379.

Reisberg, D., & Heuer, F. (2005). Visuospatial images. In P. Shah & A. Miyake (Eds.), *The Cambridge handbook of visuospatial thinking* (pp. 35–80). New York: Cambridge University Press.

Reynolds, J. R., West, R., & Braver, T. (2009). Distinct neural circuits support transient and sustained processes in prospective memory and working memory. *Cerebral Cortex, 19,* 1208–1221.

Richardson, A., & Harris, L. J. (1986). Age trends in eidetikers. *Journal of General Psychology, 147,* 303–308.

Roediger, H. L., & McDermott, K. B. (1995). Creating false memories: Remembering words not presented in lists. *Journal of Experimental Psychology: Learning, Memory, & Cognition, 21,* 803–814.

Roediger, H. L. III, Putnam, A. L., & Smith, M. A. (2011). Ten benefits of testing and their applications to educational practice. In J. P. Mestre and B. H. Ross (Eds.), *The psychology of learning and motivation: Vol. 55* (pp. 1–36). San Diego, CA: Elsevier Academic Press.

Rohrer, D., & Pashler, H. (2010). Recent research on human learning challenges conventional instructional strategies. *Educational Researcher, 39,* 406–412.

Roid, G. H., Prifitera, A., & Ledbetter, M. (1988). Confirmatory analysis of the factor structure of the Wechsler Memory Scale – Revised. *Clinical Neuropsychologist, 2,* 116–120.

Rose, N. S., Rendell, P. G., McDaniel, M. A., Aberle, I., & Kliegel, M. (2010). Age and individual difference in prospective memory during a "virtual week": The roles of working memory, vigilance, task regularity, and cue focality. *Psychology and Aging, 25,* 595–605.

Rosen, V. M., & Engle, R. W. (1997). The role of working memory capacity in retrieval. *Journal of Experimental Psychology: General, 126,* 212–227.

Rosen, V. M., & Engle, R. W. (1998). Working memory capacity and suppression. *Journal of Memory and Language, 39,* 418–436.

Rosen, V. M., Bergeson, J. L., Putnam, K., Harwell, A., & Sunderland, T. (2002). Working memory and apolipoprotein E: What's the connection? *Neuropsychologia, 40,* 2226–2233.

Salthouse, T. A. (1996). The processing-speed theory of adult age differences in cognition. *Psychological Review, 103,* 403–428.

Salthouse, T. A., & Siedlecki, K. L. (2007). An individual difference analysis of false recognition. *American Journal of Psychology, 120,* 429–458.

Savine, A. C., McDaniel, M. A., Shelton, J. T., & Scullin, M. K. (2012). A characterization of individual differences in prospective memory monitoring using the Complex Ongoing Serial Task. *Journal of Experimental Psychology: General, 141,* 337–362.

Schmader, T., & Johns, M. (2003). Converging evidence that stereotype threat reduces working memory capacity. *Journal of Personality and Social Psychology, 85,* 440–452.

Sharps, M. J., & Price , J. L. (1992). Auditory imagery and free recall. *Journal of General Psychology, 119,* 81–87.

Shipstead, Z., Redick, T. S., & Engle, R. W. (2012). Is working memory training effective? *Psychological Bulletin, 138,* 628–654.

Smith, R. E., & Bayen, U. J. (2005). The effects of working memory resource availability on prospective memory: A formal modeling approach. *Experimental Psychology, 52,* 243–256.

Smith, R. E., Persyn, D., & Butler, P. (2011). Prospective memory, personality, and working memory. *Experimental Psychology, 219,* 108–116.

Thomas, J. W., & Rohwer, W. D. (1986). Academic studying: The role of learning strategies. *Educational Psychologist, 21,* 19–41.

Torgesen, J. K. (1988). Studies of children with learning disabilities who perform poorly on memory span tasks. *Journal of Learning Disabilities, 21,* 605–612.

Tulving, E. (1985). How many memory systems are there? *American Psychologist, 40,* 385–398.

Ullman, M. T. (2004). Contributions of memory circuits to language: The declarative/procedural model. *Cognition, 92,* 231–270.

Underwood, B. J. (1975). Individual differences as a crucible in theory construction. *American Psychologist, 30,* 128–134.

Unsworth, N. (2007). Individual difference in working memory capacity and episodic retrieval: Examining the dynamics of delayed and continuous distractor free recall. *Journal of Experimental Psychology: Learning, Memory, and Cognition, 33,* 1020–1034.

Unsworth, N. (2010). Interference control, working memory capacity, and cognitive abilities: A latent variable analysis. *Intelligence, 38,* 255–267.

Unsworth, N., & Brewer, G. A. (2010a). Individual differences in false recall: A latent variable analysis. *Journal of Memory and Language, 62,* 19–34.

Unsworth, N., & Brewer, G. A. (2010b). Variation in working memory capacity and intrusions: Differences in generation or editing? *European Journal of Cognitive Psychology, 22,* 990–1000.

Usher, J. A., & Neisser, U. (1993). Childhood amnesia and the beginnings of memory for four early life events. *Journal of Experimental Psychology: General, 122,* 155–165.

Vogel, E. K., McCullough, A. W., & Machizawa, M. G. (2005). Neural measures reveal individual differences in controlling access to working memory. *Nature, 438,* 500–503.

Wang, B., & Fu, X. (2010). Gender differences in the effects of post-learning emotion on consolidation of item memory and source memory. *Neurobiology of Learning and Memory, 93,* 572–580.

Watson, J. M., Bunting, M. F., Poole, B. J., & Conway, A. R. A. (2005). Individual differences in susceptibility to false memory in the Deese–Roediger–McDermott paradigm. *Journal of Experimental Psychology: Learning, Memory, & Cognition, 31,* 76–85.

West, R., & Bowry, R. (2005). Effects of aging and working memory demands on prospective memory. *Psychophysiology, 42,* 698–712.

Wechsler Adult Intelligence Scale, 4th ed. (2008). San Antonio, TX: Pearson.

Wechsler Memory Scale, 4th ed. (2009). San Antonio, TX: Pearson.

White, K., Sheehan, P. W., & Ashton, R. (1977). Imagery assessment: A survey of self-report measures. *Journal of Mental Imagery, 1,* 145–170.

Wilson, D. E., Muroi, M., & MacLeod, C. M. (2011). Dilution, not load, affects distractor processing. *Journal of Experimental Psychology: Human Perception and Performance, 37,* 319–335.

Winograd, E., Peluso, J. P., & Glover, T. A. (1998). Individual difference in susceptibility to memory illusions. *Applied Cognitive Psychology, 12,* 5–27.

Woodhead, M. M., & Baddeley, A. D. (1981). Individual differences and memory for faces, pictures, and words. *Memory & Cognition, 9,* 368–370.

Zelhart, P. F., Markley, R. B., & Bieker, L. (1985). Eidetic imagery in elderly persons. *Perceptual and Motor Skills, 60,* 445–446.

Zhu, B., Chen, C., Loftus, E. F., Lin, C., He, Q., Chen, C., Li, H., Xue, G., Lu, Z., & Dong, Q. (2010). Individual differences in false memory from misinformation: Cognitive factors. *Memory, 18,* 543–555.

23

Experts' Superior Memory: From Accumulation of Chunks to Building Memory Skills that Mediate Improved Performance and Learning

K. Anders Ericsson and Jerad H. Moxley

The superiority of some individuals' performances is clearly shown by their ability to memorize 60,000 digits of pi and their ability to concurrently play multiple chess games without seeing the boards. For many years these exceptional performances led people to assume that such performances could never be attained by people with average ability and thus required innate abilities and talents specific to the domain of expertise. Thus, research focused on early identification of talented children, who would be given the appropriate training to attain their innate potential (for a review, see Ericsson & Charness, 1994).

The talent view of experts' achievements and performances was challenged during the cognitive revolution in psychology by the studies of Chase and Simon (1973a, 1973b), who compared a chess master, a chess expert, and a novice chess player. Their research replicated findings previously published in German and Dutch, which had not become generally known within the main stream of research in psychology in the United States. In an early Russian study Djakow, Petrowski, and Rudik (1927) showed that chess experts had clearly superior memory for chess positions, and in a pioneering study de Groot (1946/1978) showed that chess masters displayed vastly superior memory for briefly presented chess positions. Most importantly, Chase and Simon (1973a, 1973b) demonstrated that this superior memory for chess positions could not be explained by superior general memory ability. The chess masters' vastly superior memory was restricted to positions from actual chess games. When Chase and Simon (1973a, 1973b) presented boards with randomly rearranged chess pieces, the memory performance for these random boards was uniformly low for chess masters and less skilled players.

Subsequent studies have shown that experts have superior memory for representative game situations, but not for recall of random, unstructured stimuli in sports, such as basketball (Allard, Graham, & Paarsalu, 1980), field hockey (Starkes & Deakin, 1984), and volleyball (Bourgeaud & Abernethy, 1987), and in games, such as bridge (Engle & Bukstel, 1978), Othello (Wolff, Mitchell, & Frey, 1984) and GO (Reitman, 1976). The same finding is easily demonstrated in a domain that every citizen is a high performer, namely memory for meaningful text. When Ericsson and Karat (reported in Ericsson & Chase, 1982) presented words in meaningful sentences the participants could recall sentences with around 12–14 words correctly half of time. When the words in these sentences were randomly rearranged and then presented under the same conditions, the participants' recalls were reduced to around six words – within the standard memory performance of seven chunks plus or minus two (Miller, 1956). The latter finding makes some other attributes about experts' memories clear. Acquiring expertise in speaking and understanding English will not give you superior memory for meaningful sentences presented in Chinese compared with randomly arranged sentences, or vice versa. This raises important questions about what can be learned about expert memory and performance that would be useful for anyone interested in improving their own learning and skill acquisition. Is the amount of time engaged in some activity, such as playing chess or working in a given profession, the critical factor in superior memory for stimuli from the corresponding domain of expertise?

In this chapter we will show that exceptional and expert memory is acquired by, at least, two different developmental pathways. The most extreme memory achievements are recorded for seemingly meaningless information such as random digits, and are shown to require the acquisition of memory skills, where encoding mechanisms are actively attained by extended training. In contrast, the superior memory by many types of experts is an incidental consequence of their deliberate acquisition of superior performance in their domain of expertise, such as winning chess

games and finding the best routes as a taxi driver.

Our chapter will start with a historical review of how study of experts' memories was brought into the laboratory and led to the development of the first theories of expertise based on accumulation of a larger number of increasingly complex patterns and chunks. The Simon-Chase theory of expertise (Simon & Chase, 1973) explained the superior memory of experts by their larger chunks maintained in short-term memory (STM). This theory proposed that briefly presented information (displayed for less than 5–8 seconds (Simon, 1974) was exclusively stored in STM. However, it could not account for the finding that experts were able to store information in long-term memory (LTM) (Charness, 1976) and that individuals could develop memory skills to expand their working memory for briefly presented information, such as digits presented at a one per second rate, by relying on storage in LTM (Chase & Ericsson, 1981, 1982). Furthermore, this theory assumes that new patterns and chunks are acquired by "staring" (Simon & Chase, 1973, p. 402) or being exposed to chess positions without any specification of the detailed learning processes leading to better chess performance. Subsequent research has found that it is not the amount of time engaged in domain-related activities that influences the development of superior performance and superior memory (Ericsson, 2006), but the type of activity that matters. In their research on distinguishing the effects on performance from goal-directed practice as opposed to additional experience, Ericsson, Krampe, and Tesch-Römer (1993) proposed the concept of deliberate practice as an activity designed to improve some specific aspects of performance. Most significantly, this work showed that memory for representative stimuli from the domain was increased as an incidental consequence of deliberate practice, because working memory is an integral aspect of expert performance (see Ericsson and Kintsch's (1995) Long-Term Working Memory (LTWM)). In this chapter we will argue that the structure of the superior memory of experts can thus be best understood by describing its development within the context of the acquisition of the expert performance. This approach will provide the most generalizable insights into the acquisition of expert performance and when its development is associated with superior memory.

HISTORICAL REVIEW OF THEORIES OF EXPERT MEMORY

In the 1950s and 1960s researchers were influenced by the new emerging technologies, such as control systems and computers, and started to use these types of systems as models for proposing ideas about the structure of thinking and memory. George Miller (1956) showed that people's STM measured by the amount of information that people could report back after a brief serial presentation seemed invariant across many types of material and was between five and nine chunks (familiar patterns); that is seven ± two. Perhaps the most ground-breaking demonstration supporting the fixed capacity of STM was Chase and Simon's (1973a, 1973b) experimental studies of chess experts. After a brief presentation of a chess position, the chess master could recall the location of some 15–20 chess pieces, but the novice could only recall 4–5 pieces. When Chase and Simon (1973a) analyzed the number of chess configurations (patterns) that the chess master used to reconstruct the chess position from STM, they found that this number was not different from the number of patterns (typically just individual pieces) that the novice used – within the range of five to nine chunks. When recalling the randomly rearranged boards, the chess master was only recalling the same small number of pieces as the novice. This finding validated the idea of a limited capacity STM.

The Simon and Chase (1973) theory of expertise made several assumptions. The first one was that the STM of experts and novices did not seem to differ in capacity to hold chunks even within their domain of expertise. The differences in experts' and novices' immediate recall performances were explained by the experts' ability to recognize larger chunks involving more chess pieces and thus allowing them to recall more pieces with a similar number of chunks. The second assumption concerned how increasingly complex chunks were acquired during extended chess playing to allow players to store associations between configurations of chess pieces (chunks) and appropriate moves, so that they could retrieve the best move from LTM for a presented chess position. Based on data from world class chess players, Simon and Chase (1973) argued that ten years of chess playing would be required to acquire the necessary body of complex chunks to win at international level.

SKILLED MEMORY THEORY: EXPERTS' SUPERIOR MEMORY IS NOT BASED ON CHUNKS STORED IN STM

The assumption that chess experts' superior memory for chess positions reflected storage of chunks in STM was tested by one of Bill Chase's graduate students, Neil Charness (1976). After the brief presentation of a chess position in his experiment, participants were asked to engage in an STM-demanding task such as counting backwards in sevens from a given number, such as 473, for 30 seconds. Charness (1976) also had the chess players remember and recall a second chessboard before they were allowed to recall the chess position presented at the beginning of the memory trial. If the chess position had been maintained only by chunks in STM then these chunks would have been purged from STM to make room for other chunks necessary to complete the assigned task prior to recall. In spite of the interruption, chess experts' recall of the chess position was essentially unaffected (only 6–8 percent decrements), suggesting that the chess position must have been stored in LTM. Further evidence for the need to retrieve the information from LTM was that the chess experts took up to five times longer to retrieve the first chess piece after an interruption, compared with immediate recall without interruption (Charness, 1976; Frey & Adesman, 1976).

The central importance of storage in and retrieval from LTM was also supported by a series of experiments that showed that memory performance could be improved on a task assumed to measure the fixed capacity of STM. The primary task used to measure immediate memory was the digit span, where an auditory series of digits was presented at a rate of one digit every second followed by immediate recall. Chase and Ericsson (1981, 1982) studied the changes in performance of two college students, who started with a normal digit span of around seven digits, and after several hundred hours could recall over 80 and over 100 digits, respectively.

Through systematic process tracking using verbal protocols (Ericsson & Simon, 1993), Chase and Ericsson (1981, 1982) found that the students fundamentally changed how they were performing the task with additional training. The two students' retrospective reports showed that they started out relying on a simple rehearsal strategy – just as other individuals tested on the digit-span task. The first student (SF) discovered that he could improve his performance if he focused on the first three digits as a group and rapidly encoded a semantic association to this group, and then directed his attention to the remaining digits and rehearsed them while he searched for meaningful patterns and association to encode these digits. At the time of recall he would retrieve the first group of three digits from LTM, recall it, and then recall the rest of the digits. With additional practice he would be able to encode the first three three-digit groups before rehearsing the last four to six digits. Eventually he was able to develop retrieval cues to encode several three-digit groups into a "super-group" and then have another "super-group" in a

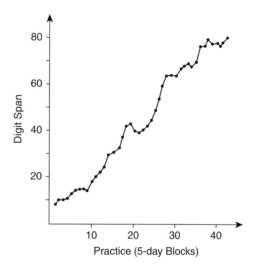

Figure 23.1 Average digit span for SF as a function of practice. Adapted from "Acquisition of a memory skill" by K. Anders Ericsson, William G. Chase, and Steven, Faloon, *Science, 208,* 1181. Copyright 1980 by American Association for the Advancement of Science (AAAS)

hierarchical system (retrieval structure). In Figure 23.1 the increases in performance on the memory span task are shown as function of practice. This is clearly an acquisition of skill, where slow incremental improvements across five to ten sessions are made to the encoding of digit groups and to the encodings using the retrieval structure. This is particularly apparent for the second participant, who eventually attained a digit span of over 100 digits. The first student (SF) explained to the second student (DD) his encoding methods prior to the start of DD's training. One can see a more rapid improvement at the very beginning of training but eventually DD required the same lengthy training to construct his encoding skill and retrieval structure to further improve his performance. It is important to note that the massive improvement for digit span was specific to memory for digits and even after being able recall dozens of digits, SF's memory span for consonants remained unchanged at six letters.

The work on Skilled Memory Theory (Chase & Ericsson, 1981, 1982) shows that individuals can, with practice, improve their memory performance by acquiring domain-specific memory skills even for rapidly presented information. There are several subsequent case studies (see Ericsson, 1985; Ericsson & Kintsch, 1995) and even more importantly studies with large samples of participants have demonstrated impressive memory improvements after extended practice either with instruction (Higbee, 1997; Kliegl, Smith, & Baltes, 1989; Kliegl, Smith, Heckhausen, & Baltes, 1987) or without instruction (Wenger & Payne, 1995).

These basic findings about improved working memory have been replicated and extended outside the domain of traditional memorizing. For instance, Chase and Ericsson (1982) studied a mental multiplication expert (AB). When AB performed long multiplications, such as 3,456 x 3,456 = ?, he would meaningfully encode the intermediate results in LTM and only retrieve them when needed later during the calculation (Chase & Ericsson, 1982). Similarly, Ericsson and Polson (1988) studied a skilled waiter (JC), who was able to remember dinner orders from over eight people without writing anything down. JC used simple retrieval structures based on each customer's place at the table and created separate structures for each type of information, namely salad dressing, type of entrée, temperature for the meat (rare, medium rare, medium, medium well, and well done), and type of starch (rice, fries, or baked potato). Instead of being confused by five different orders of baked potatoes, JC used patterns to encode the starches for all customers, which made memory easier and lowered the risk of errors (Ericsson & Polson, 1988). Finally, reviews of a large number of earlier studies of individuals with exceptional memory showed that the structure and acquisition of their memory performance was consistent with the principles of Skilled Memory Theory (Ericsson, 1985; Wilding, & Valentine, 1997).

In the last decade the research on exceptional memory has been extended to studying individuals who have memorized very

long lists of random numbers – over 10,000 digits of pi. Instead of repeatedly memorizing different lists of digits, memorizing pi requires the memorization of one very long list of digits. Memorizing a long list is challenging because each time a new list of digits is memorized and added to the previously memorized parts, one cannot forget any of the previously memorized digits. Rajan Mahadevan (Ericsson, Delaney, Weaver, & Mahadevan, 2004) had memorized and recalled over 30,000 digits when he established a new Guinness Book World Record in 1984. A large number of different investigators had studied Rajan's memory. These early studies revealed that Rajan had a much higher digit span based on forming groups of ten digits, leading investigators to hypothesize that he had an innately superior basic capacity (Thompson, Cowan, & Frieman, 1993). Subsequent research by Ericsson et al. (2004) found several results that were inconsistent with a superior general basic capacity. For example, when he was presented with different types of stimuli, such as symbols from the top row of a keyboard – !@#$%^, his performance for the initial test session did not significantly differ from that of a control group. However, with additional practice he could attain superior memory performance compared with control participants by associating the new stimuli (symbols) to digits, allowing him to generate associations to his large store of knowledge and encoding techniques. Rajan's encoding methods were consistent with an acquired memory skill based on general mechanisms described in a generalized version of Skilled Memory Theory, namely LTWM (Ericsson & Kintsch, 1995).

Recently Hu, Ericsson, Yang, and Lu (2009) studied the current Guinness Book world record holder, Chao Lu, who had successfully memorized over 67,000 digits of pi. They found results consistent with Skilled Memory Theory and LTWM with a few interesting differences from those of Rajan. Chou Lu's digit span is normal but with self-paced memory tasks he is able to take more time encoding the digits, which allows him use his memory skills and then his memory performance is significantly superior to normal participants. Hu and Ericsson (2012) found that his encoding methods appear to generate very stable and unique encoding based on converting two-digit numbers into nouns and then generating a unique story. Both Rajan and Chao Lu reported that they had engaged in extended memorization of pi for thousands of hours.

Other groups of professionals have engaged in memorization of vast amounts of information, such as taxi drivers and actors – in manner not dissimilar to the extended memorization of pi. For example, London taxi drivers have spent two to four years memorizing the layout of 25,000 streets in London before they can take the examination to attain their licence (Woollett & Maguire, 2010). When taxi drivers are instructed to memorize an unfamiliar environment or map in the laboratory their memory is superior on this task (Kalakoski & Saariluoma, 2001; Woollett & Maguire, 2010), but not on other memory tasks when compared with a control group. In fact, Woollett and Maguire (2009) found in one study that taxi drivers were even systematically inferior to controls for their memory of arrangements of unrelated visual figures and paired associates. Several studies of professional actors have shown that they are not significantly better than college students in memorizing text or lines in a play (Intons-Peterson & Smyth, 1987; Noice, 1993). The actors do not memorize lines by rote but try to understand the character, so the lines becomes a meaningful verbal reaction in situations experienced by that character (Noice & Noice, 2006). More generally, we find that memorization of a large body of information is not associated with a dramatically superior performance to memorize new information for actors and cab drivers as well as for Chao Lu, who memorized the most digits of pi. The only real exception is Rajan Mahadevan, but we know that his memory performance for rapidly presented digits improved dramatically over the several years

that he served as a participant in memory experiments (Thompson et al., 1993).

Several individuals with exceptional memory have been studied with brain scanners while they memorize various types of information (Maguire, Valentine, Wilding, & Kapur, 2003). The collected evidence on the anatomy and size of the brains and the activation during memorization is consistent with the hypothesis that people with exceptional memory performance are not structurally different, but that what differs between them and control participants is their methods for encoding and memorizing the presented stimuli (Ericsson, 2003). Most interestingly, the verbal reports on how the exceptional individuals memorized each type of stimuli were consistent with increased activation in those regions that would be involved in associated processes, such as imagery and retrieval of associated semantic information. Studies of the structure of the brains of London taxi drivers show that gray matter of the hippocampus is increased in the posterior portion and is decreased in the anterior portion (Woollett & Maguire, 2009).

In sum, when experts' and novices' memory performances are compared in memory tasks, such as brief presentations of representative and random stimuli from a domain of expertise, there is most often a significant advantage for experts (Ericsson & Lehmann, 1996). However, the proportional advantage is rather small, around 5–50 percent with a few major exceptions, such as chess and the card game, bridge. The recall of a chess position by a grandmaster in chess can exceed that of a novice by 400 to 500 percent. Similar findings have been observed for self-paced memorization. We noted earlier in this section that taxi drivers were able to memorized new maps and city environments faster than control participants, but that actors did not memorize text faster than control participants. Similarly, Gilhooly, Wood, Kinnear, and Green (1988) found no significant advantage for map experts' recall of non-contour maps compared with novices. In sum, the superior memory of experts in domains of expertise is relatively limited with the exception of a small number of domains, most notably chess.

HOW EXPERTS ACQUIRE SUPERIOR MEMORY: LONG-TERM WORKING MEMORY

The research on skilled and exceptional memory suggests that the superior memories of memory experts are the result of extended practice with the explicit goal of improving memory performance. Vincente and Wang (1998) pointed out that no chess players spend time focusing on intentionally training their memory for chess positions. For chess players "skilled memory is actually only a by-product of chess skill, rather than the other way around" (Vincente & Wang, 1998, p. 48). Research (a study by Ericsson and Harris reported in Ericsson & Oliver, 1989; Gobet & Jackson, 2002) confirms this view and shows that it is possible to improve a person's memory for briefly presented chess positions toward the level of chess masters in around 50 hours without improving chess playing performance. In contrast Simon and Chase (1973) found that it took chess players over ten years to become grandmasters and attain that level of memory performance through studying chess.

Vincente and Wang (1998) proposed that extended perceptual experience of chess positions was the cause of the superior memory and stated "with experience, people learn the strategy that is most economical for the task at hand and thereby focus on the minimal number of distinctive features (invariants) that will successfully discriminate among the events of interest" (p. 36). However, researchers rapidly found that "experts" with extended experience and specialized knowledge frequently did not show a performance superior to their less experienced and skilled peers. For example, highly experienced psychotherapists are not more successful in treating patients than novice

therapists (Dawes, 1994) as measured by the outcomes of therapy. More generally, reviews of decision making (Camerer & Johnson, 1991) and forecasting (Tetlock, 2005) show that experts' decisions and forecasts, such as financial advice on investing in stocks, do not show a reliable superiority over novices and thus cannot have improved with additional experience. Similar lack of improved performance of highly experienced individuals has been documented in several other domains of expertise (Choudhry, Fletcher, & Soumerai, 2005; Ericsson, 2004; Ericsson & Lehmann, 1996).

It is therefore essential to distinguish between individuals, who are viewed as experts by their peers or clients, and individuals who are able to demonstrate their reproducibly superior *expert performance* on the job and under controlled test conditions. Expert performance cannot be an automatic consequence of increased professional experience, so Ericsson et al. (1993) proposed that expert performance is the result of focused training on representative tasks with immediate diagnostic feedback and opportunities for reflection and gradual improvements by repetitive performance on the tasks (cf. deliberate practice). Ericsson et al. (1993) found that differences among violinists at an internationally renowned music academy could be accounted for by the amount of accumulated solitary practice. During solitary practice the violinists would work on weaknesses identified during their weekly meetings with their master teachers and would be repeatedly playing and perfecting parts of challenging music pieces, thus meeting the criteria for deliberate practice.

When expert musicians engage in deliberate practice they need to represent several different types of information, as is illustrated in Figure 23.2. The need to attend to their goals of how they want their music performance to sound to the audience requires that they also are able to listen to how their music performance actually sounds when they play it during practice. Finally they need to be able to identify the differences between

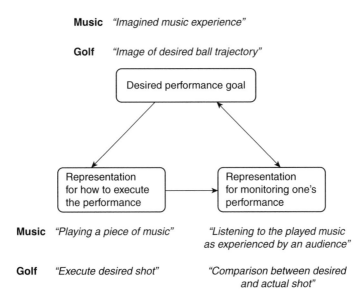

Figure 23.2   Three types of internal representations that mediate expert music performance and the continued improvement during practice. Adapted from "The scientific study of expert levels of performance: General implications for optimal learning and creativity" by K. A. Ericsson in High Ability Studies, 9, 90. Copyright 1998 by European Council for High Ability

their goal and the actual sound so they can make changes to reduce the difference. Similarly, when golfers prepare to make a putt on a green, they image the trajectory of the ball rolling over the slopes and swales on the path to the hole. They then try to hit the golf ball so it makes the envisioned trajectory and can then watch its actual trajectory to assess miscalculations regarding the planned path of the ball.

When experts in many different types of domains engage in deliberate practice or even confront challenging decisions about actions in chess games or on the soccer field they engage in activities that are very demanding on working memory. In order to account for the ability of experts to engage in planning, evaluating their performance, and making changes to their analyses of situations, Ericsson and Kintsch (1995) proposed long-term working memory (LTWM) theory. LTWM is an extension of Skilled Memory Theory and describes mechanisms that permit experts to store information in LTM indexed in such a way that when demand for that information is generated during performance

it will be easily retrieved. Experts acquire memory skills that permit them to maintain access to an extensive base of information through the use of retrieval structures and meaningful encoding. For example when a skilled reader reads a text, they cannot merely rely on short-term memory and the current sentence. Long-term working memory theory argues that skilled readers interpret new sentences in light of their general knowledge and in particular their knowledge of the previously read text. In many narrative texts the reader generates a model of the current situation and this model allows the reader to integrate the new information in memory by updating and changing the model of the current situation (Kintsch, 1998).

The major challenge for developing expanded working memory based on LTWM concerns anticipating future retrieval needs, so when the information is encountered it can be encoded in a manner that allows it to be accessed when needed and relevant. Consequently, as performance improves the skilled performer will attend to a larger number of relevant cues in the current situation, such as the posture and movement cues of a server in tennis. In order to allow for these changes in attended cues and the cognitive processes of the skilled performer, the associated encoding in LTWM will need to be modified, and in some cases altered, to accommodate changes in cognitive processing, performance, and the need for particular changes in relevant information. LTWM is thus not separable from the skilled level of performance and it is an integrated aspect of the acquired skill and thus will be adapted to fit the needs of the skilled performance at the different levels of achievement (Ericsson & Roring, 2007).

THE CHALLENGE OF STUDYING EXPERTS' MEMORY AND ITS GENERALIZABLE CHARACTERISTICS

Our review of theories of expert memory started with Simon and Chase's (1973) theory built on the formal computer models expressed in terms of human information processing theory (Newell & Simon, 1972), where different types of memory systems had fixed unalterable characteristics, such as STM with a fixed limited capacity for storing chunks and LTM with fixed times for storage and retrieval. We then discussed the research on the effect of training in the acquisition of exceptional memory and showed that, after training, times required for storage in LTM do not remain fixed and that it is possible to rely on storage and retrieval from LTM with temporal characteristics in the manner of storage in and retrieval from STM. We reviewed some alternative theoretical accounts of skilled performance on memory tasks after extended training, such as Chase and Ericsson's (1982) Skilled Memory Theory and Ericsson and Kintsch's (1995) LTWM. These theoretical accounts emphasize the over-arching role of acquisition and training and thus do not specify any general constraint on storage times or retrieval times. In contrast to the general capacity models, where capacity of

STM is expressed in terms of a fixed number of stored chunks (patterns) in a domain-general manner (Miller, 1956; Newell & Simon, 1972), LTWM is based on acquired memory skills, where acquired systems of encoding and successful anticipation of future retrieval needs determine whether information is available when needed during performance. This raises the fundamental issue of how accounts of LTWM are constrained and how their structure can be predicted.

Ericsson and Kintsch (1995) proposed that expert memory reflects acquired memory skills that are developed in order to improve the target performance, such as finding the best possible moves for a chess position, and for diagnosing and treating patients. Only by analyzing and describing the superior performance on representative tasks in the domain is it possible to predict the characteristics of the mechanisms that mediate the expert performance and, in particular, experts' acquired expansion of the "functional capacity" of working memory (LTWM). These ideas led Ericsson and Smith (1991) to propose the expert-performance approach, where the superior performance of experts is identified and captured by representative tasks, ideally in the laboratory. By repeatedly reproducing the superior performance under standardized and experimental conditions while collecting process-tracing data, it is possible to identify the mechanisms that mediate this performance. The third and final step concerns explaining how these mechanisms are developed, either by genetic mechanisms and/or as the result of various types of practice activities, such as deliberate practice.

In the remainder of our chapter we will use the expert-performance framework to discuss the structure of expert performance and show that improved memory for some types of information is an important aspect of the acquired skill mediating the performance. This framework of expert performance (Ericsson et al., 1993; Ericsson & Smith, 1991) would allow us to discuss many domains of expertise and their patterns of superior memory performance on presented memory tasks, but in this chapter we will only discuss the domain with the largest effects of expertise on memory performance, namely chess.

EXPERT PERFORMANCE AND EXPERT MEMORY IN CHESS

Chess is one of the foundational domains of the study of expertise (Charness, 1992). As we mentioned earlier we will adopt the expert-performance approach to study superior reproducible performance on representative tasks (Ericsson & Smith, 1991; Ericsson & Ward, 2007). The first step in the expert performance approach is to identify reproducibly superior performance in the domain. The rating system in chess provides an objective measure of the chess player's skill level, which allows for very accurate predictions of which of two chess players will win a game. Two chess games are never the same, so it is difficult to identify the mechanisms that mediate the superior performance of better chess players. Ideally we would like to give the same tasks to all chess players so we can study the detailed processes generating reproducibly superior performance.

Chess performance on representative tasks

The second step in the expert performance approach concerns eliciting the essence of the expert performance with the same set of standardized tasks, ideally presented in the laboratory. De Groot (1946/1978) established the paradigm for expert-performance research by studying world-class chess players (Ericsson & Smith, 1991). De Groot (1946/1978) identified challenging positions in chess games and then presented them to many chess players and asked them to select the best chess move for each position while thinking aloud. The performance on the move-selection task has excellent external validity and is highly

correlated with official chess ratings (Charness, 1991; de Groot, 1946/1978; van der Maas & Wagenmakers, 2005).

If it is possible to reliably reproduce superior chess performance in the laboratory by asking players to select moves for chess positions, then it is also possible to study the cognitive processes that differ between skilled and less skilled players. De Groot (1946/1978) asked the players to think aloud while they selected their moves. During the move-selection task, detailed move planning is found to increase as a function of chess skill at least until the players reach the expert level (Charness, 1981, 1989; de Groot, 1946/1978). Better planning enables world-class players to uncover better chess moves than those that they retrieved from memory based on their initial perception (de Groot, 1946/1978). Planning also minimizes the frequency of mistakes and failures to consider important aspects of the chess position (Saariluoma, 1992).

In order to examine the consequences of a series of moves and counter-moves during planning, a chess player needs an extensive working memory. Chess players can explore a move very deeply, for instance a search of 25 moves ahead has been observed in the laboratory (Campitelli & Gobet, 2004). In addition, to remember the chess board generated after the series of moves and counter-moves the chess player also needs to remember his/her evaluation of other sequences of moves encountered in past searches in order to select the best of possible moves.

To gain an advantage from planning and searching the players need to be able to accurately evaluate chess positions generated at the end of a sequence of moves and counter-moves. Research shows that more highly rated chess players are better able to evaluate positions generated after more moves ahead than less skilled players, whose ability deteriorates quickly with each additional move generated (Holding, 1989; Holding & Pfau, 1985). Cowley and Byrne (2004) found that higher-level players evaluate positions generated at the end of long plans more accurately than less skilled players. The ability of skilled chess players to generate positions at the end of a deep search, and also evaluate that generated position accurately, is an essential characteristic of an acquired memory system that allows accurate and flexible storage and retrieval in LTWM, allowing them to more accurately evaluate these generated chess positions.

A more direct method of demonstrating that skilled chess players are able to maintain all the information about the current chess position and conduct their planning and searches to find the best move in memory is to study chess play and move selection under blindfold conditions, where there is no visible chess board with the pieces. When the likelihood of making an incorrect move is compared with blindfold play and game play under regular conditions, Chabris and Hearst (2003) did not find a significant difference, and Jeremic, Vukmirovic, and Radojicic (2010) found only a very small decrease in play quality when there were limits on the time for selecting moves – rapid chess. Saariluoma and Kalakoski (1998) conducted a particularly interesting study that examined move selection under blindfold conditions in the laboratory. When chess masters were asked to select the best move, the accuracy of move selection was indistinguishable between a regular condition and a blindfold condition. In the blindfold condition the chess pieces were presented one after the other by giving the locations of each of the individual pieces so the chess masters had to mentally construct the position. In contrast, regular tournament players rarely found the best move in the normal or blindfold condition (Saarilouma & Kalakoski, 1998).

Explaining how chess performance (and indirectly memory for chess positions) improves during development

In the same way that performance on move-selection problems is a very good measure of chess skill, it offers an opportunity to improve one's move-selection performance by examining one's cognitive processes for positions where one failed to select the best move. Ericsson et al. (1993) proposed that studying chess games by world-class players would offer an effective method to get feedback. The chess player could simulate playing against the world-class players by trying to select each move and after selecting the move compare their move with the one that the world-class player had selected. Getting immediate feedback about one's move immediately after making the move was predicted to be far more effective than playing a whole chess game and then figuring out if and where one could have made better chess moves. This type of training in selecting moves will force the player to plan ahead and search for the move and thus strain their memory skills for accurately storing chess positions in the expert's working memory (LTWM). Several investigators have collected information on how much time chess players have engaged in various types of chess activities, such as playing chess games, studying in groups, or studying alone. Charness, Tuffiash, Krampe, Reingold, and Vasyukova (2005) found that the amount of solitary study of chess was the most closely correlated activity to chess ratings, where grandmasters had engaged in solitary study for thousands more hours than national level players and club-level players. This effect has been replicated and extended by other studies since. A recent study of Argentinian players found a significant effect of study alone, as well as with a variable that combined chess players with tutoring, studying with other players, and going over matches with the opponent after the games were finished (Gobet & Campitelli, 2007).

Studying aspects of chess expertise by performance on tasks measuring memory

After our description of the development of skilled performance in chess, we will now discuss and explain the results of many studies examining performance on tasks measuring superior memory in chess experts.

The findings of the pioneering studies of memory for briefly presented chess positions were exemplified by Chase and Simon's (1973) chunking theory based on storage in STM. We showed earlier that other investigators, after closer examination, found that memory performance on these tasks could not be explained solely by chunks stored or maintained in STM. Several studies (Frey & Adesman, 1976; Charness, 1976) found virtually unimpaired recall of presented chess positions even if participants had to engage in an STM demanding task prior to recall. These findings require that storage is more stable and requires involvement of LTM, which could be readily explained within Chase and Ericsson's (1982) Skilled Memory Theory (see Ericsson & Staszewski, 1989, for a detailed account) and Ericsson and Kintsch's (1995) LTWM. In recognition of the limitations of chunking theory, Herbert Simon in collaboration with Fernand Gobet proposed a substantial extension of chunking theory called template theory (Gobet & Simon, 1996b). In this theory, chess pieces could be encoded within schemas for very common positions such as opening patterns (called Templates). Consequently, LTWM (Ericsson et al., 2000; Ericsson & Kintsch, 1995) and Templates (Gobet & Simon, 1996b) can account for the findings of recall of regular and random chess boards with brief presentation times by the use of memory structures acquired for the purpose of increasing the quality of selection of the chess moves by better and deeper search and planning.

More careful analyses of recall of random boards showed that skilled chess players recalled more pieces than less skilled players (Gobet & Simon, 1996a) even for randomly rearranged boards. This slight advantage was explained by more skilled players' ability to detect meaningful patterns of a couple of chess pieces even for the randomly arranged boards. The superior recall performance for random boards for skilled over less skilled players is dramatically increased when chess players are given longer study times (Gobet & Simon, 2000; Lories, 1987), or when each chess position is only presented one piece at a time before assembling the board (Saariluoma, 1989). The skilled chess player's ability to encode random boards presented one piece at a time might be difficult to explain within Template theory, but Ericsson et al. (2000) proposed how LTWM would be account for how memory for a sequentially presented random board could be generated and elaborated relying on greater knowledge and superior encoding mechanisms for planning.

In the original study of chess memory Chase and Simon (1973) tested the memory for a chess game with a sequence of chess moves. In one condition the game started from the normal starting position but the sequence of subsequent moves was determined randomly. The grand master player was much stronger at replicating the game than the weaker players. It is not clear how chunking theory (Chase & Simon, 1973) or Template theory (Gobet & Simon, 1996b) could account for this finding, but LTWM would predict that the expert would have developed more effective encoding methods for storing the consequences of generated moves in LTM. Our general argument is that only an analysis of the acquisition of chess skill can provide a theoretical account of the superior performance of the variety of memory tasks, rather than vice versa – the original approach taken by Simon and Chase (1973).

More generally, this type of analysis has been extended to other types of domains of expertise, where research has shown large reproducible differences in performance on representative tasks and where performance has been captured and reproduced in the laboratory and where the mediating mechanisms have been described and studied experimentally (Ericsson & Roring, 2007).

CONCLUSION

In this chapter we started with a description of Simon and Chase's (1973) pioneering theory of expertise. This theory and the supporting experiments on recall of representative situations from games provided an opportunity to study the effects of expertise in the laboratory without the laborious and difficult analysis of differences in performance in the respective domain. Part of the popularity of these studies is that it is easy to present stimuli with chess positions or pictures of a game situation in soccer and field hockey and then score the accuracy of the corresponding recall. It is far more difficult to analyze expert performance in representative situations and identify the best move or moves for a chess position or the best actions for the player with the ball in a soccer game. Superior memory performance of experts is not interesting in itself – especially when the absolute size of the advantage over novices is small. Further superior memory performance of experts is only interesting if it is a valid accurate mediator of the actual expert performance, such as selecting the best moves to win chess games.

The original theory of expertise (Simon & Chase, 1973) offered a theory that predicted that expert performance was a direct function of the complexity of patterns (chunks) and thus connected measurement of memory for briefly presented stimuli to level of performance. In this chapter we showed that several assumptions of the original theory of expertise were incorrect. For example, the time required for storage in LTM does not remain fixed and with acquired memory skills it is possible to rely on storage and retrieval from LTM with temporal characteristics approaching storage in and retrieval from STM. We described the development of alternative theoretical accounts of performance on memory tasks with training, such as Chase and Ericsson's (1982) Skilled Memory Theory and Ericsson and Kintsch's (1995) LTWM. These theoretical accounts emphasize the domain specificity of expert performance and that superior memory performance is limited to the type of material used in training and similarly expanded working memory can only support performance in some particular domain of expertise.

In the remainder of our chapter we described an approach to the study of expertise and expert memory, namely the expert-performance approach, where the focus is to study and describe the expert performance. This approach focuses on the identification of the acquired mechanisms that mediate the superior performance (Ericsson, 2006) including the memory skills that support expanded working memory in this domain. Finally we search for how these mechanisms were developed and refined by effective practice activities.

There are two important take-away messages from the research on expert performance. The bad news is that there appear to be no short-cuts to expert performance in highly competitive domains, such as chess. Every individual needs to construct and acquire the complex skill during a very long period of sustained training and deliberate practice (Ericsson, 2006). There is increasing evidence that many types of training and practice are not effective in building the expert performance and anyone who is interested can now get advice and guidance by professional teachers. The good news is that the research shows that individuals are capable of acquiring a wide range of memory skills including superior working memory to support a given expert performance. We are only starting to understand the necessary types of practice activities (cf. deliberate practice) that can develop the necessary skills for a given area of expert performance. We are starting to collect information on how much training would be necessary to attain changes of the key mediating mechanisms and if such changes can occur more easily at particular periods of child and adolescent development (Ericsson, 2006; Ericsson, Nandagopal, & Roring, 2009). These findings suggest that individuals do not need to be born with innately superior memory or other superior abilities – the specific abilities required for attaining a particular expert performance seem to be constructed and formed during training.

It has been repeatedly shown that acquiring memory skills for some type of information can be attained within 50–200 hours (Ericsson & Kintsch, 1995), but that high levels of expert performance require thousands of hours of deliberate practice (Ericsson, 2006). This is consistent with our review because developing a memory skill to expand functional working memory (LTWM, Ericsson & Kintsch, 1995) is not a matter of simply storing and recalling information but also in developing encoding skills for the relevant encountered information so it can be encoded, stored in LTM, and then automatically retrieved whenever it is relevant to the cognitive processes of the experts. It is also essential that the structure of the expert performance permits planning, monitoring, and modifying in order to execute and improve performance (Ericsson, 2006). Furthermore, it is important that the structure of the performance allows a steady accumulation of new knowledge without significant forgetting. The issue of how some experts can memorize over 60,000 random digits over many months and years raises new theoretical issues about how to control and reduce interference between previously stored digit sequences and new sequences to be memorized (Hu & Ericsson, 2012).

We are finally starting to understand the complexity of attained expert performance and the even more complex acquisition of the gradually emerging structure of expert performance. By accepting the challenge of studying the complex structure and acquisition of expert performance, we will be able to uncover the necessary conditions for its acquisition so we can guide motivated individuals in improving their performance at any level within their selected domain of expertise.

ACKNOWLEDGMENTS

This research was supported by the FSCW/ Conradi Endowment Fund of Florida State University Foundation. The authors want to thank Len Hill for the helpful comments on earlier drafts of the chapter.

REFERENCES

Allard, F., Graham, S., & Paarsalu, M. E. (1980). Perception in sport: Basketball. *Journal of Sport Psychology, 2,* 14–21.

Bourgeaud, P., & Abernethy, B. (1987). Skilled perception in volleyball defense. *Journal of Sport Psychology, 9,* 400–406.

Camerer, C. F., & Johnson, E. J. (1991). The process-performance paradox in expert judgment: How can the experts know so much and predict so badly? In K. A. Ericsson and J. Smith (Eds.), *Towards a general theory of expertise: Prospects and limits* (pp. 195–217). Cambridge: Cambridge University Press.

Campitelli, G., & Gobet, F. (2004). Adaptive expert decision making: Skilled chessplayers search more and deeper. *Journal of the International Computer Games Association, 27,* 209–216.

Chabris, C. F., & Hearst, E. S. (2003). Visualization, pattern recognition, and forward search: effects of playing speed and sight of the position on grandmaster chess errors. *Cognitive Science, 27,* 637–648.

Charness, N. (1976). Memory for chess positions: resistance to interference. *Journal of Experimental Psychology: Human Learning and Memory, 2,* 641–653.

Charness, N. (1981). Aging and skilled problem solving. *Journal of Experimental Psychology: General, 110,* 21–38.

Charness, N. (1989). Expertise in chess and bridge. In D. Klahr and Kotovsky (Eds.), *Complex information processing: The impact of Herbert A. Simon* (pp. 183–208). Hillsdale, NJ: Erlbaum.

Charness, N. (1991). Expertise in chess: The balance between knowledge and search. In K. A. Ericsson and J. Smith (Eds.), *Toward a general theory of expertise: Prospects and limits* (pp. 39–63). New York: Cambridge University Press.

Charness, N. (1992). The impact of chess research on cognitive science. *Psychological Research, 54,* 4–9.

Charness, N., Tuffiash, M., Krampe, T. R., Reingold, E., & Vasyukova, E. (2005). The role of deliberate practice in chess expertise. *Applied Cognitive Psychology, 19*, 151–165.

Chase, W. G., & Ericsson, K. A. (1981). Skilled memory. In J. R. Anderson (Ed.), *Cognitive skills and their acquisition* (pp. 141–189). Hillsdale, NJ: Lawrence Erlbaum Associates.

Chase, W. G. & Ericsson, K. A. (1982). Skill and working memory. In G. Bower (Ed.), *The Psychology of learning and motivation* (Vol. 16, pp 1–58). New York: Academic Press.

Chase, W. G., & Simon, H. A. (1973a). The mind's eye in chess. In W. G. Chase (Ed.), *Visual information processing* (pp. 215–281). New York: Academic Press.

Chase, W. G., & Simon, H. A. (1973b). Perception in chess. *Cognitive Psychology, 4,* 55–81.

Choudhry, N. K., Fletcher, R. H., & Soumerai, S. B. (2005). Systematic review: the relationship between clinical experience and quality of health care. *Annals of Internal Medicine, 142,* 260–273.

Cowley, M., & Byrne, R. M. J. (2004). Chess masters' hypothesis testing. *Proceedings of the Twenty-sixth Annual Conference of the Cognitive Science Society* (pp. 250–255). Mahwah, NJ: Erlbaum.

Dawes, R. M. (1994*). House of cards: Psychology and psychotherapy built on myth.* New York: Free Press.

de Groot, A.D. (1978) *Thought and choice in chess* (2nd English ed.: first Dutch edition published in 1946). The Hague: Mouton Publishers.

Djakow, J. N., Petrowski, N. W., & Rudik, P. A. (1927). *Psychologie des Schachspiels [The psychology of chess].* Berlin: Walter de Gruyter.

Engle, R. W., & Bukstel, L. H. (1978). Memory processes among bridge players of differing expertise. *American Journal of Psychology, 91,* 673–689.

Ericsson, K. A. (1985). Memory skill. *Canadian Journal of Psychology, 39,* 188–231.

Ericsson, K. A. (2003). Exceptional memorizers: Made, not born. *Trends in Cognitive Sciences, 7,* 233–235.

Ericsson, K. A. (2004). Deliberate practice and the acquisition and maintenance of expert performance in medicine and related domains. *Academic Medicine, 10,* S70–S81.

Ericsson, K. A. (2006). The influence of experience and deliberate practice on the development of superior expert performance. In K. A. Ericsson, N. Charness, P. Feltovich, and R. R. Hoffman (Eds.), *Cambridge handbook of expertise and expert performance* (pp. 685–706). Cambridge: Cambridge University Press.

Ericsson, K. A., & Charness, N. (1994). Expert performance: Its structure and acquisition. *American Psychologist, 49(8),* 725–747.

Ericsson, K. A., & Chase, W. G. (1982). Exceptional memory. *American Scientist, 70,* 607–615.

Ericsson, K. A., Delaney, P. F., Weaver, G., & Mahadevan, R. (2004) Uncovering the structure of a memorist's superior "basic" memory capacity. *Cognitive Psychology, 49,* 191–237.

Ericsson, K. A., & Kintsch, W. (1995). Long-term working memory. *Psychological Review, 102,* 211–245.

Ericsson, K. A., & Kintsch, W. (2000). Shortcomings of generic retrieval structures with slots of the type that Gobet (1993) proposed and modeled. *British Journal of Psychology, 91,* 571–590.

Ericsson, K. A., Krampe, R. T., & Tesch-Römer, C. (1993). The role of deliberate practice in the acquisition of expert performance. *Psychological Review, 100,* 363–406.

Ericsson, K. A., & Lehmann, A. C. (1996). Expert and exceptional performance: Evidence on maximal adaptations on task constraints. *Annual Review of Psychology, 47,* 273–305.

Ericsson, K. A., Nandagopal, K., & Roring, R. W. (2009). Toward a science of exceptional achievement: Attaining superior performance through deliberate practice. *Annals of New York Academy of Science, 1172,* 199–217.

Ericsson, K. A., & Oliver, W. (1989). A methodology for assessing the detailed structure of memory skills. In A. Colley and J. Beech (Eds.), *The acquisition and performance of cognitive skills* (pp. 193–215). London: Wiley.

Ericsson, K. A., Patel, V., & Kintsch, W. (2000). How experts' adaptations to representative task demands account for the expertise effect in memory recall: Comment on Vicente and Wang (1998). *Psychological Review, 107,* 578–592.

Ericsson, K. A., & Polson, P. G. (1988). Memory for restaurant orders. In M. Chi, R. Glaser, and M. Farr (Eds), *The nature of expertise* (pp. 23–70). Hillsdale, NJ: Erlbaum.

Ericsson, K. A., & Roring, R. W. (2007). Memory as a fully integrated aspect of skilled and expert performance. *The Psychology of Learning and Motivation, 48,* 351–380.

Ericsson, K. A., & Simon, H. A. (1993). *Protocol analysis: Verbal reports as data* (Rev. Ed.). Cambridge, MA: MIT press.

Ericsson, K. A., & Smith, J. (1991). Prospects and limits in the empirical study of expertise: An introduction. In K. A. Ericsson and J. Smith (Eds.), *Toward a general theory of expertise: Prospects and limits* (pp. 1–38). Cambridge: Cambridge University Press.

Ericsson, K. A., & Staszewski, J. J. (1989). Skilled memory and expertise: Mechanisms of exceptional performance. In D. Klahr and K . Kotovsky (Eds.), *Complex information processing: The impact of Herbert A. Simon* (pp. 235–267). Hillsdale, NJ: Lawrence Erlbaum.

Ericsson, K. A., & Ward. P. (2007). Capturing the naturally occurring superior performance of experts in the laboratory: Toward a science of expert and exceptional performance. *Current Directions in Psychological Science, 16,* 346–350.

Frey, P. W., & Adesman, P. (1976). Recall memory for visually presented chess positions. *Memory & Cognition, 4,* 541–547.

Gilhooly, K. J., Wood, M., Kinnear, P. R., & Green, C. (1988). Skill in map reading and memory for maps. *Quarterly Journal of Experimental Psychology, 40A,* 87–107.

Gobet, F., & Campitelli, G. (2007). The role of domain-specific practice, handedness and starting age in chess. *Developmental Psychology, 43,* 159–172.

Gobet, F., & Jackson, S. (2002). In search of templates. *Cognitive Systems Research, 3,* 35–44.

Gobet, F., & Simon, H. A. (1996a). Recall of random and distorted chess positions: *Memory & Cognition, 24,* 493–503.

Gobet, F., & Simon, H. A. (1996b). Templates in chess memory: A mechanism for recalling several boards. *Cognitive Psychology, 31,* 1–40.

Gobet, F., & Simon, H. A. (2000). Five seconds or sixty? Presentation time in expert memory. *Cognitive Science, 24,* 651–682.

Higbee, K. L. (1997). Novices, apprentices, and mnemonists: Acquiring expertise with the phonetic mnemonic. *Applied Cognitive Psychology, 11,* 147–161.

Holdin, D. H. (1989). Evaluation factors in human tree search. *American Journal of Psychology, 102,* 103–108.

Holdin, D. H., & Pfau, H. D. (1985). Thinking ahead in chess. *American Journal of Psychology, 98,* 271–282.

Hu, Y., & Ericsson, K. A. (2012). Memorization and recall of very long lists accounted for within the Long-Term Working Memory framework. *Cognitive Psychology, 64,* 236–266.

Hu, Y., Ericsson, K. A., Yang, D., & Lu, C. (2009). Superior self-paced memorization of digits in spite of a normal digit span: The structure of a memorist's skill. *Journal of Experimental Psychology: Learning, Memory, and Cognition, 35,* 1426–1442.

Intons-Peterson, M. J., & Smyth, M. M. (1987). The anatomy of repertory memory. *Journal of Experimental Psychology: Learning, Memory, and Cognition, 13,* 490–500.

Jeremic, V., Vukmirovic, D., & Radojicic, Z. (2010). Does playing blindfold chess reduce the quality of game:

Comments on Chabris and Hearst (2003). *Cognitive Science, 34,* 1–9.

Kalakoski, V., & Saariluoma, P. (2001). Taxi drivers' exceptional memory of street names. *Memory & Cognition, 29,* 634–638.

Kliegl, R., Smith, J., & Baltes, P. B. (1989). Testing the limits and the study of adult age differences in cognitive plasticity of a mnemonic skill. *Developmental Psychology, 25,* 247–256.

Kliegl, R., Smith, J., Heckhausen, J., & Baltes, P. B. (1987). Mnemonic training for the acquisition of skilled digit memory. *Cognition & Instruction, 4,* 203–223.

Kintsch, W. (1998). *Comprehension: A paradigm for cognition.* Cambridge: Cambridge University Press.

Lories, G. (1987). Recall of random and non-random chess positions in strong and weak chess players. *Psychologica Belgica, 27,* 153–159.

Maguire, E. A., Valentine, E. R., Wilding, J. M., & Kapur, N. (2003). Routes to remembering: The brains behind superior memory. *Nature Neuroscience, 6,* 90–95.

Miller, G. A. (1956). The magical number seven, plus or minus two: Some limits on our capacity for processing information. *Psychological Review, 63,* 343–355.

Newell, A., & Simon, H. A. (1972). *Human problem solving.* Englewood Cliffs, NJ: Prentice-Hall. *Cognitive Science, 15,* 425–460.

Noice, H. (1993). Effects of rote versus gist strategy on the verbatim retention of theatrical scripts. *Applied Cognitive Psychology, 7,* 75–84.

Noice, H., & Noice, T. (2006). What studies of actors and acting can tell us about memory and cognitive functioning. *Current Directions in Psychological Science, 15,* 14–18.

Reitman, J. S. (1976). Skilled perception in Go: Deducing memory structure from inter-response times. *Cognitive Psychology, 8,* 336–356.

Saariluoma, P. (1989). Chess players' recall of auditorily presented chess positions. *European Journal of Cognitive Psychology, 1,* 309–320.

Saariluoma, P. (1992). Error in chess: The apperception restricting view. *Psychological Research, 54,* 17–26.

Saariluoma, P., & Kalakoski, V. (1998). Apperception and imagery in blindfold chess. *Memory, 6,* 67–90.

Simon, H. A. (1974). How big is a chunk? *Science, 183,* 482–488.

Simon, H. A., & Chase, W. G. (1973). Skill in chess. *American Scientist, 61,* 394–403.

Starkes, J. L., & Deakin, J. (1984). Perception in sport: A cognitive approach to skilled performance. In W. F. Straub and J. M. Williams (Eds.), *Cognitive sport psychology* (pp. 115–128). Lansing, NY: Sport Science Associates.

Tetlock, P. E. (2005). *Expert political judgment: How good is it? How can we know?* Princeton, NJ: Princeton University Press.

Thompson, C. P., Cowan, T. M., & Frieman, J. (1993). *Memory search by a memorist.* Hillsdale, NJ: Erlbaum.

van der Maas, H. L. J., & Wagenmakers, E. J. (2005). A psychometric analysis of chess expertise. *American Journal of Psychology, 118,* 29–60.

Vincente, K. J., & Wang, J. H. (1998). An ecological theory of expertise effects in memory recall. *Psychological Review, 105,* 33–57.

Wenger, M. J., & Payne, D. G. (1995). On the acquisition of mnemonic skill: Application of skilled memory theory. *Journal of Experimental Psychology: Applied, 1,* 194–215.

Wilding, J., & Valentine, E. (1997). *Superior memory.* Hove, UK: Psychology Press.

Wolff, A. S., Mitchell, D. H., & Frey, P. W. (1984). Perceptual skill in the game of Othello. *Journal of Psychology, 118,* 7–16.

Woollett, K., & Maguire, E. A. (2009). Navigational expertise may compromise anterograde associative memory. *Neuropsychologia, 47,* 1088–1095.

Woollett, K., & Maguire, E. A. (2010). The effect of navigational expertise on wayfinding in new environments. *Journal of Environmental Psychology, 30,* 565–573.

Subjective Experience
of Memory

24

Memory Complaints in Adulthood and Old Age

Christopher Hertzog and Ann Pearman

INTRODUCTION

A main question regarding aging and memory complaints is whether they derive from manifestations of actual memory problems, from unfounded beliefs and fears, or from both. Two broad conclusions are supported by the evidence. First, although performance on episodic memory tasks typically declines with age, memory complaints are more reliably correlated with depressive affect and neuroticism than with performance on standardized tests of episodic memory. Second, older adults often but not always voice more memory complaints and concerns than younger and middle-aged adults. What is less clear at present are the processes that generate complaints and whether memory complaints can predict older adults' concurrent or future cognitive status.

The preceding statement may seem quite surprising to clinical neuropsychologists working with older adults. Historically, stated concerns and complaints about one's own memory function have been treated as a diagnostic criterion for Age-Associated Memory Impairment (AAMI: Crook, Bartus, Ferris, & Whitehouse, 1986), cognitive impairment – no dementia (CIND: Plassman et al., 2008), or Mild Cognitive Impairment (MCI: Petersen,

Smith, Waring, Ivnik, Tangalos, & Kokmen, 1999; Winblad, et al., 2004). Should subjective memory complaints be part of the diagnostic criteria for age-related memory problems? In this chapter we selectively review the literature on subjective memory complaints and related constructs, such as memory self-efficacy, in adulthood. Where appropriate, we offer conclusions about gaps in the evidence and knowledge about subjective memory and sketch important areas of future inquiry that could advance the field.

DEFINING AND MEASURING MEMORY COMPLAINTS

Three big issues in making sense of the memory complaint literature are (1) how memory complaint is conceptualized and defined, (2) who is being examined, and (3) how memory complaint is measured.

The construct of memory complaints

The concept of memory complaint reflects how individuals present themselves in clinical settings. Memory complaints are self-reports of problems in remembering desired information in everyday life (e.g., Holsinger, Deveau, Boustani, & Williams, 2007; Kaszniak, 1990; Mascherek, Zimprich, Rupprecht, & Lang, 2011), including concerns about possible deterioration to dementia (e.g., Snitz et al., 2008; Corner & Bond, 2004). A critical question is why individuals do or do not report concerns about everyday memory failures to healthcare professionals.

Actual memory problems are only one influence on complaints. Individuals vary in their proclivity for seeking healthcare services for any symptom (Ramakers, Visser, Bittermann, Ponds, van Boxtel, & Verhey, 2009; Scott & Walter, 2010), including perceived memory problems (Hurt, Burns, Brown, & Barrowclough, 2012). Memory failures may have to reach some kind of critical threshold of functional impairment before individuals seek treatment. Moreover, variables such as loneliness, subjective beliefs about symptoms and illness, and having had a family member with dementia also influence help-seeking behavior (Hurt et al., 2012).

An alternative conception of memory complaints focuses on subjective awareness or perceptions of memory problems. Memory impairment is often accompanied by a lack of awareness of the deficits (anosagnosia; see McGlynn & Schacter, 1989). Brain injury, disease, or trauma that damages the prefrontal cortex can create deficits in the ability to accurately monitor memory failures and to control memory processes (e.g., retrieval searches; Pannu & Kaszniak, 2005). Such deficits may constrain the accuracy of memory complaints in certain patient populations.

Memory complaints can also be viewed as an aspect of beliefs about one's own memory functioning and ability (Gilewski & Zelinski, 1986; Hertzog & Hultsch, 2000). Perceived memory problems can be seen as a negatively framed, failure-oriented aspect of the broader construct of memory self-concept or memory self-efficacy (e.g., Bandura, 1997; Cavanaugh, 2000; Hertzog, Hultsch,

& Dixon, 1989; Berry & West, 1993). More generally, one can view subjective memory as part of a larger, interrelated complex of constructs involving representations of aging and memory for oneself and others, which includes stereotypes and beliefs about memory growth and decline across the lifespan (e.g., Lineweaver & Hertzog, 1998; Ryan & Kwong See, 1993), retrospective perceptions of personal memory change (McFarland, Ross, & Giltrow, 1992), and expectations of future memory problems (Lineweaver & Hertzog, 1998). For instance, individuals with a family history of Alzheimer's disease (AD) often manifest anxiety and concern about possible future memory loss and are prone to interpret everyday memory failures as signifying onset of the disease (e.g., Cutler & Hodgson, 1996; La Rue, Small, McPherson, & Komo, 1996).

Who manifests memory complaints?

Much of the work on memory complaints has focused on adult patient populations suffering from diseases or trauma to the central nervous system that affect memory, such as AD, epilepsy, and multiple sclerosis. An important question in differential diagnosis is whether complaints are actually indicative of other mental health issues, such as clinical depression (Niederehe & Yoder, 1989) or anxiety (Elfgren, Gustafson, Vestberg, & Passant, 2010). In research on adult development and aging, the problem of convenience sampling versus representative sampling is often an issue (e.g., Camp, West, & Poon, 1989), especially if the methods of recruiting participants include explicit solicitation of volunteers to participate in studies of memory or memory problems (Schleser, West, & Boatwright, 1986). Memory complaints may affect volunteering behavior in complex ways that may alter the profile of relationships of complaints to other variables, such as neuroticism.

Early studies of memory complaints were primarily focused on populations in the

United States and the United Kingdom. In the last 20 years, however, the study of memory complaints has spread across the globe. Our review of the literature suggests relatively few differences in the manifestations and patterns of memory complaints across population subgroups (e.g., Sims et al., 2011) or countries (but see Cavallini et al., 2013, and Levy & Langer, 1994, for interesting differences in memory beliefs in other cultures). Hence, we make broad generalizations here about aging and memory complaints without explicit consideration of political, racial, or cultural differences.

Measurement of memory complaints

Measures of memory complaint vary widely in scope and content. National surveys like the Health and Retirement Survey (HRS) have used single-item rating scales to evaluate subjective memory concerns (e.g., Herzog & Rodgers, 1989). Other measures focus more generally on everyday cognitive problems, such as the Cognitive Failures Questionnaire (CFQ; Broadbent, Cooper, FitzGerald, & Parkes, 1982). The CFQ contains a subset of items that assess everyday memory complaints (e.g., Rast, Zimprich, van Boxtel, & Jolles, 2009).

The Memory Functioning Questionnaire (MFQ; Gilewski, Zelinski, & Schaie, 1990) is perhaps the most widely used memory complaints questionnaire that focuses exclusively on memory. It contains a single item about general memory problems but also assesses reported frequency of forgetting in multiple aspects of memory (e.g., names, appointments) over the previous one-week period. The MFQ also specifically assesses problems in remembering information from texts, perceived change in memory function, and the perceived seriousness of memory problems. The Memory Assessment Clinics – Self-Rating Scale (MAC-S; Crook & Larrabee, 1990) and the Memory Assessment Clinics – Memory Complaint Questionnaire

(MAC-Q; Crook, Feher, & Larrabee, 1992) are also widely used. The MAC-S assesses perceived memory ability and frequency of forgetting in a variety of situations, along with four questions about global memory functioning. The MAC-Q measures subjective age-related memory decline.

Finally, more broad-spectrum memory beliefs questionnaires assess subjective memory as part of a larger set of constructs, including perceived control over memory, anxiety about memory, achievement motivation regarding memory, and use of internal and external strategies to support everyday memory (Dixon & Hultsch, 1983; Lachman, Bandura, Weaver, & Elliott, 1995; Lineweaver & Hertzog, 1998).

Cross-sectional findings about memory complaints in adulthood

Important early evidence regarding aging and memory complaints came from large-scale surveys containing a single item assessing memory complaints. Herzog and Rodgers (1989) analyzed data from a representative sample of over 1400 persons with one question about perceived memory problems, rated on a 1 (*inability to recall much information*) to 5 (*no memory difficulties*). Mean ratings were above 4, but age did correlate with rated memory ($r = -.22$). A measure of free recall also weakly correlated ($r = .16$) with self-ratings. Self-rated functional health and gender were the only reliable predictors of self-rated memory with healthy individuals and males rating their memory more positively. Cutler and Grams (1988) also found relationships of age and gender to reported memory problems in a probability sample of almost 15,000 persons ages 55 and older. Again, only self-rated health problems and other limitations on functional independence predicted memory complaints.

Studies using more comprehensive memory questionnaires typically find cross-sectional age differences in subjective memory measures with increasing age associated with lower ratings of memory ability and greater frequency of memory problems, although the effect size is small (e.g., Lineweaver & Hertzog, 1998; Ponds & Jolles, 1996; Zelinski, Gilewski, & Anthony-Bergstone, 1990). In some studies the age effect on memory complaints is not reliably different from zero, despite adequate statistical power (e.g., Hultsch, Hertzog, & Dixon, 1987).

Likewise, the relationship between questionnaire measures of memory complaints and performance on memory tasks has typically been small in magnitude. Beaudoin and Desrichards (2011) conducted a meta-analysis of correlations between rated memory self-efficacy and measures of episodic memory, finding a mean .15 correlation between them. Although memory complaint scales were excluded from their meta-analysis, it is reasonable to guess that the complaints-memory test correlation has a similar magnitude. Many studies failing to link memory performance and subjective memory may have had insufficient sample size to detect a small effect. Furthermore, latent variable models that correct for random measurement error have typically detected reliable cross-sectional correlations of memory and memory beliefs (e.g., Hertzog, Dixon, & Hultsch, 1990; Hertzog, Dunlosky, & Robinson, 2009; Hertzog, Park, Morrell, & Martin, 2000; Jopp & Hertzog, 2007; Lane & Zelinski, 2003; Zelinski & Gilewski, 2004). Clearly, memory complaints do correlate with memory performance, but with a modest effect size.

What else might prevent a stronger correlation between memory complaints and performance? Unfounded memory concerns could be generated by depressive affect, specifically, or neuroticism, more generally. Early on, Kahn, Zarit, Hilbert, and Niederehe (1975) reported that complaints about memory were related to depressive symptoms but not objective memory performance. Multiple other studies since that time have identified a robust depressive affect – memory complaint link (e.g., Crane, Bogner, Brown, & Gallo, 2007; Hänninen,

Reinikainen, Helkala, & Koivisto, 1994; Pond & Jolles, 1996; Verma, Pershad, Kaur, & Bhagat, 1996; Zelinski & Gilewski, 2004). In fact, cross-sectional relationships of memory complaints scales with depression are typically larger in magnitude than the correlations of memory complaints scales with memory performance. There have also been several studies finding that the broader personality construct of neuroticism predicted memory complaints in younger and older adults (Pearman & Storandt, 2004; Pearman, 2009; Verma et al., 1996). Among the multiple facets of neuroticism, only self-consciousness, which is related to self-esteem and embarrassment, reliably predicted memory complaints (Pearman & Storandt, 2005). Perhaps people high in self-consciousness experience memory failures in social settings as particularly distressing, believing that they are being negatively perceived for their memory failures.

Pearman, Gerstorf, and Hertzog (2013) recently evaluated relationships of neuroticism, depressive symptoms (measured by a clinician), and memory task performance to memory complaints in the Berlin Aging Study, which has an atypical rectangular age and gender distribution in persons 70 to 100 years of age and includes many very old adults. Significant relationships of neuroticism, depression symptoms, and subjective age to subjective memory complaints were found, whereas episodic memory measures provided little predictive validity. Such outcomes suggest that depression and neuroticism independently predict memory complaints, even in late older adulthood.

Other aspects of personality and behavioral style may also correlate with memory complaints. Conscientiousness – which taps into personal organization, levels of distractibility, and self-discipline – is negatively related to level of memory complaints in both young and older adults (Pearman, 2009; Pearman & Storandt, 2004; Slavin et al., 2010). Individuals low in conscientiousness may have difficulty with everyday memory tasks because they are poorly organized and are less likely to engage in proactive compensatory memory strategies (e.g., Dixon, de Frias, & Bäckman, 2001).

Given the pattern of relationships reviewed to this point, one can wonder about the construct validity of memory complaints. One basis for validating memory complaints comes from comparisons of self-reports with informant (often spouses and/or children of older adults) reports. The relationships between self- and informant- rated memory vary and depend on several factors, including patient diagnosis (e.g., non-demented, MCI, demented) and non-cognitive variables, such as depression or anxiety in the informant, and the nature of the relationship between the participant and the informant.

For patients with AD and other dementias, informant reports of memory ability are typically more accurate predictors of neuropsychological test performance than patient reports (Buckley, Norton, Deberard, Welsh-Bohmer, & Tschanz, 2010; Chung & Man, 2009; Jorm, 2004; Loewenstein et al., 2001). Few studies have examined the relationship between informant- and self-report of memory problems in non-demented healthy older adults. Sunderland and colleagues (1986) found that informant reports of memory problems had lower predictive validity for memory test performance than self-reported memory problems in their sample of healthy older adults. Buckley et al. (2010) and Chung and Man (2009) found that in normal control groups, higher self-rated memory ability was negatively related with informant ratings of perceived decline (better memory, less decline). However, for patients with MCI or dementia, self-rated memory was not correlated with informant report, possibly due to their anosagnosia. Recently, Volz-Sidiropoulou and Gauggel (2012) studied memory complaints in healthy older adult couples. Underreporting of memory problems when compared with spousal ratings was significantly related to poor memory performance in men but not women.

Longitudinal findings about memory complaints in adulthood

Early in the process of investigating relationships of memory complaints to memory, Herrmann (1982) noted that one constraint on concurrent relations between the two variables might be between-person variability in the criteria used for rating memory complaints. Individual differences in standards for rating the severity of experienced memory problems could limit the magnitude of the relevant cross-sectional correlations. Herrmann suggested collecting longitudinal data and correlating within-person changes in memory with changes in subjective memory complaints or retrospective ratings of change in memory. People, in effect, could serve as their own baseline for assessing change.

Since that time a number of longitudinal studies have assessed whether individual differences in memory change are correlated with changes in memory complaints. Studies have found that longitudinal changes in memory task performance are associated with both initial levels of memory complaints (e.g., Hohman, Beason-Held, Lamar, & Resnick, 2011) and longitudinal changes in memory complaints (e.g., Lane & Zelinski, 2003; Taylor, Miller, & Tinklenberg, 1992). Actual changes in episodic memory also have reliable but weak relations to retrospective perceptions of changes in memory (Lane & Zelinski, 2003), although these effects can be partly explained by implicit internalized theories of age-related memory decline rather than monitoring of actual memory changes (see McDonald-Miszczak, Hertzog, & Hultsch, 1995).

Two recent papers nicely illustrate the benefits of latent growth curve models for examining concurrent changes in memory performance and memory complaints. Mascherek and Zimprich (2011) used 3-wave longitudinal data from the German Interdisciplinary Study on Adult Development on 297 adults (age range 63 to 74) providing complete 3-occasion data in memory and memory complaints. The disattenuated .23

correlation between complaints and memory performance intercepts (corresponding to a cross-sectional correlation) was significant, albeit smaller, than the .39 correlation of age-change slopes.

Parisi et al. (2011) evaluated 5-year longitudinal data on a sample of over 1400 adults, assessing episodic memory (performance on a combination of word list recall and text paragraph recall) and memory complaints. They estimated a .29 partial correlation (controlling for multiple covariates) of initial complaints (measured by the MFQ Frequency of Forgetting scale) and memory performance, compared with a .44 correlation of longitudinal changes in those two variables.

These studies apparently confirm Herrmann's (1982) conjecture that changes in memory complaints are robustly associated with changes in objective memory performance. However, not all latent variable studies using longitudinal data find reliable prediction of changes in memory complaint by changes in memory, despite adequate statistical power (e.g., Lane & Zelinski, 2003; Pearman, Hertzog, & Gerstorf, 2013), and there are insufficient studies in the literature for a meaningful meta-analysis at present.

Recent developments in memory complaints research

Prospective memory complaints

One area of research in memory complaints that has blossomed over the last ten years concerns complaints about prospective memory – remembering to enact or realize behavioral intentions (e.g., Einstein & McDaniel, Chapter 3, this volume). Research on prospective remembering emphasizes the process of retrieving intentions to remember and acting upon those intentions while possibly monitoring the environment for action cues (e.g., Mäntylä, Rönnlund, & Kliegel, 2010; Smith, 2003).

The Betula Longitudinal Study has evaluated both prospective memory (e.g., Mäntylä &

Göran-Nillson, 1997) and subjective prospective memory (Rönnlund, Vestergren, Mäntyla, & Göran-Nilsson, 2011) using the Prospective and Retrospective Memory Questionnaire (PRMQ; Smith, Sala, Lotie, & Maylor, 2000). Rönnlund, Vestergren, Mäntylä, and Göran-Nilsson (2011) found no age differences in the prospective and retrospective PRMQ scales – essentially flat-line functions – from age 60 to age 90. Furthermore, neither PRMQ scale was reliably predicted by objective retrospective or prospective memory, although the measurement of prospective memory was limited to a single binary outcome variable. Rönnlund et al. (2011) did find, however, that depressive symptoms (as measured by the CES-D) and a measure of self-directedness (related to neuroticism and conscientiousness) predicted both PRMQ scales with similar regression weights. Other studies have identified significant but small (.20) correlations of the PRMQ prospective scale with binary prospective memory performance (Kliegel & Jäger, 2006; Mäntylä, 2003) in middle-aged and young-old samples.

Hannon, Adams, Harrington, Fries-Dias, and Gipson (1995) evaluated subjective and objective prospective memory in a sample of persons with closed-head brain injuries and normal adult controls. Prospective memory complaints were measured with a Prospective Memory Questionnaire (PMQ). The brain-injured group reported more prospective memory problems than normal controls. The subjective scales correlated with a short-term prospective memory task; however, they showed even stronger correlations with scores on a depression scale.

Uttl and Kibreab (2011) investigated subjective prospective memory in a sample of 240 undergraduates using multiple measures of laboratory prospective memory and a much broader range of prospective and retrospective memory questionnaires. The PRMQ scales did not correlate reliably with prospective memory variables (−.10 < r < .00), while Hannon et al.'s (1995) PMQ scales did correlate reliably with prospective memory performance, especially a measure requiring individuals to circle target words when encountered within task instructions (all $rs < -.3$). Other newly developed subjective prospective memory scales used by Uttl and Kibreab (2011) also showed some small but significant correlations with prospective memory performance. Like studies of retrospective memory complaints, Uttl and Kibreab (2011) found robust correlations of conscientiousness and neuroticism with measures of subjective prospective memory, with conscientiousness having the larger relationships. Indeed, their hierarchical regression analysis showed that conscientiousness predicted PMQ scale scores independently of retrospective memory performance and neuroticism. They concluded that existing subjective prospective memory scales lack acceptable validity as predictors of prospective memory performance (see also Salthouse, Berish, & Siedlecki, 2004).

Neurobiological correlates of memory complaints

Recent studies have examined relationships between memory complaints and certain neuropathologies, such as white-matter lesions brain atrophy, as well as AD pathology. Not surprisingly, given the inconsistent findings of the other literature on memory complaints, results regarding the neurobiological correlates of memory complaints are also mixed.

White-matter lesions have been shown to be related to age-associated cognitive impairment (Bunce et al., 2010; Gunning-Dixon, Brickman, Cheng, & Alexopoulos, 2009). If memory complaints indeed signal neurodegenerative processes, then older adults with memory complaints should have more white-matter lesions than comparable controls. Minett, Dean, Firbank, English, and O'Brien (2005) found that memory complaints were related to white-matter lesion severity, even when controlling for depression. Similarly, Stewart and colleagues' (2011) longitudinal study found that memory complaints at baseline were related to increases in subcortical white matter lesions over a four-year period.

Memory complaints also correlate with lowered hippocampal-system volume (Jessen et al., 2006; Stewart et al., 2011; van Gunten & Ron, 2004). However, in the van Gunten and Ron study, depression was also related to lower hippocampal volume and the patients did not progress to dementia during follow-up, but did remain depressed. The authors suggested that "the structural brain abnormalities associated with subjective memory impairment may be associated with persistent affective symptoms" (p. 439). However, Van Norden et al. (2008) found that hippocampal volume was related to older adults' objective memory performance and subjective memory, controlling on white-matter lesions and depression.

Risk factors for memory pathology, such as the presence of amyloid plaques, tau tangles are often suggested as predictors of AD presence and/or severity. Barnes, Schneider, Boyle, Bienias, and Bennett (2006) found that level of memory complaints were positively related to the post-mortem presence of both amyloid and tau in older adults with memory complaints. This relationship was partially, but not fully, explained by depression symptoms. However, Antonell et al. (2011) and Schoonenboom et al. (2012) found normal ranges of cerebrospinal fluid AD biomarkers in participants with subjective memory complaints. Amyloid-β (Aβ) deposits in cortex are a better biological marker of probable AD, and recent neuroimaging techniques allow for the non-invasive assays of Aβ in living patients. Perrotin, Mormino, Madison, Hayenga, and Jagust (2012) recently reported that positron emission tomography (PET) targeting Aβ showed differences between individuals with subjective memory complaints and non-complainers, who also differed on an immediate recall test.

Finally, newer studies are beginning to look at functional imaging techniques, such as functional magnetic resonance imaging (fMRI), to evaluate relations of memory complaints to functional activation during memory tasks. Haley, Eagan, Gonzalez, Biney, and Cooper (2011) examined a working memory task (continuous 2-back discriminations) in a sample of middle-aged individuals at risk for cardiovascular disease. Higher memory complaints were associated with worse performance (r = −.30), and complaints correlated with the lower levels of fMRI activation in prefrontal areas often associated with working memory networks. Erk, Spottke, Meisen, Wagner, Walter, and Jessen (2012) also conducted fMRI of episodic and working memory in a subjective memory complaints group (identified by family or spouse reports of memory problems to help avoid contamination by negative affect of the patient). They found greater activation in right hippocampus for control participants over individuals with memory complaints; conversely, they found greater activation in right dorsolateral prefrontal cortex (a region often associated with controlled memory retrieval) in memory complainers. In both cases, degree of activation correlated with recognition memory performance, leading Erk et al. (2012) to conclude that the activation in prefrontal cortex for complainers was functional neural compensation for early preclinical hippocampal dysfunction. Unlike Haley et al. (2011), no differences in brain activation were found in Erk et al.'s working memory task.

Hohman et al. (2011) reported that initial CFQ scores predicted longitudinal decline in performance the California Verbal Learning test (CVLT; a test of multi-trial categorized free recall). They found no initial (cross-sectional) correlations of CFQ with memory. However, the CFQ was reliably associated with structural measures of regional blood flow (as measured by PET) in insula, inferior parietal cortex, and occipital cortex in their cross-sectional sample. CVLT memory scores (but not the CFQ) were associated with activation in prefrontal cortical areas thought to be critical for strategic organization and controlled retrieval on the CVLT (e.g., Alexander, Stuss, & Fansabedian,

2003). Although activation in inferior parietal cortex and occipital regions has been linked to recollection of accurate verbal and perceptual detail during memory tests (e.g., Okada, Vilberg, & Rugg, 2012) and the use of imagery strategies for encoding verbal materials (Leshikar, Hertzog, & Duarte, 2012), it could be the case that the CFQ-correlated regions found by Hohman et al. are associated with non-mnemonic processes that actually suppress cross-sectional CFQ correlations with the CVLT.

Clearly, work on the neurobiological correlates of memory complaints is in its early stages, and there is both insufficient and inconsistent evidence about whether subjective memory complaint is associated with indicators of brain pathology and brain function in older adults. Authors on recent papers using fMRI (e.g., Haley et al., 2011) have argued strongly for the validity of memory complaints based on group differences in brain activation patterns, stating that they have identified brain correlates of early memory change that validate self-reports that are otherwise difficult to corroborate. By this logic, self-reported memory problems by patient or informant could be the initial sign of pending cognitive decline (especially if validated by other measures such as structural indices of hippocampal volume). However, results are heterogeneous across studies, and there is still little consensus in the cognitive neuroscience community about how the networks of brain structures supporting episodic memory actually operate, making it difficult to interpret the various functional imaging outcomes. The argument that structural and functional brain differences between subjectively impaired and normal older adults validate memory complaints as an early warning sign of memory decline are exciting yet premature, but this situation could change rapidly.

Research on memory complaints in geriatric psychiatry

The past ten years of research in the field of geriatric psychiatry has seen a large number of studies that have essentially rediscovered phenomena already reported in the psychological literature. Specifically, numerous studies report that cross-sectional data reveal low correlations of memory complaints to memory performance and that there are much stronger relationships of memory complaints with depression and other measures of negative affect (e.g., Elfgren et al., 2010; Jorm et al., 2004; Slavin et al., 2010).

However some of this literature has focused more specifically on subjective memory complaints as it relates to MCI and dementia. Some studies have generated evidence that memory complaints may correlate with a transition from normal aging to MCI or from MCI to dementias, such as AD. For instance, Schofield, Jacobs, Marder, Sano, and Stern (1997) examined 80 individuals with no memory complaints at baseline in a longitudinal study. At one-year follow-up, 20 individuals had developed memory complaints. New memory complaints were significantly associated with declines in scores on both visuospatial memory as well as episodic memory. In a similar study, Schmand, Jonker, Geerlings, and Lindeboom (1997) examined 2,114 individuals without apparent dementia. At baseline, depressive affect was the variable most strongly associated with baseline subjective memory complaints. However, the presence of dementia at four-year follow-up was predicted by age, baseline cognition, and memory complaints, which suggests that memory complaints may have some predictive validity in terms of the development of dementia.

These findings highlight one of the aforementioned problems with examining memory complaints in clinical versus non-clinical populations. Although anosagnosia becomes prevalent in the middle to late stages of AD, it can and does also occur at earlier disease stages. To the extent that pre-clinical dementia is accompanied by changes in the accuracy of objective self-awareness, actual memory declines may not be manifested in memory complaints. This is why it is recommended that memory complaints be corroborated by an informant or collateral source (Loewenstein et al., 2001; Roberts, Clare, & Woods, 2009) in patient populations. The Informant Questionnaire on Cognitive Decline in the Elderly (IQCODE; Jorm, Scott, & Jacomb, 1989) is the most commonly used measure used to gather collateral source opinion of cognitive decline in older adults. Studies using the IQCODE generally have found it to have better predictive validity in terms of actual decline than participant self-report (Ayalon, 2011; Farias, Mungas, & Jagust, 2005; Isella, Villa, Russo, Regazzoni, Ferrarese, & Appollonio, 2006; Jorm, 2004). Informant reports tend to be less affected than screening measures such as the MMSE by premorbid intelligence and educational status (Isella et al., 2006; Jorm, 2004). However, as mentioned previously, informant reports can be influenced by non-cognitive factors such as mood or anxiety of the participant, the informant, or both (Jorm, 2004; Volz-Sidiropoulou & Gauggel, 2012). Finally, Cacchione and colleagues (2003) found that informants who did not live with the patient or see the patient regularly were significantly less accurate at identifying memory impairment and changes. Regular contact with a person may be required to before informant reports are likely to be helpful in diagnosis.

Explaining the negative affect – memory complaint correlation

The association between neuroticism, depression, and depressive affect with memory complaint is well-established. What is currently needed is more work trying to identify the mechanisms that produce this relationship.

Psychological treatment studies for clinical depressive disorder support the hypothesis that memory complaints are a symptom of depression rather than the reverse. Several studies have found that successful treatment of depression lowers memory complaints (Antikainen et al., 2004; Plotkin, Mintz, &

Jarvik, 1985; Zarit, Gallagher, & Kramer, 1981). For instance, Plotkin et al. (1985) found that the depressed elderly outpatients who responded positively to treatment not only improved in their subjective mood but also decreased their number of memory complaints. Conversely, studies finding training-related improvements in memory and subjective memory typically do not show subsequent changes in depressive affect (Scogin, Storandt, & Lott, 1985; Rasmusson, Rebok, Bylsma, & Brandt, 1999). Although one should be circumspect about issues such as the depth and breadth of memory training studies, the available evidence suggests that depressive affect influences memory complaints, not vice versa.

Exploring the nature of depression in late life may also shed light on its relationship with memory complaint. Cognitive theory, for instance, suggests that people become depressed because of inaccurate, negative biases in their evaluation of themselves and their capabilities (Strunk & Adler, 2009). Negative memory evaluations could be just another form of negative (and inaccurate) self-assessment. Given that memory concerns are highly salient to older adults, memory complaints in older adults with depression should be particularly pronounced, especially when they are questioned about current memory ability. People with depressive symptoms also overestimate the probability of negative future events and show a pessimistic bias (Strunk, Lopez, & DeRubeis, 2006). Consistent with this hypothesis, Crane and colleagues (2007) found that negative cognitive bias, in the form of hopelessness and low self-esteem, fully mediated the relationship between depression and memory complaints.

Similar arguments can be made about neuroticism's relationship with memory complaints. People who are high in neuroticism evaluate their lives with more negativity than people lower in neuroticism and may also be hyperaware of possible memory problems. Kverno (2000) found that people high in neuroticism covertly review threats to themselves, thereby maintaining a negative self-concept. In the context of everyday memory failures, this threat review could actually lead to a better recall of memory failures (e.g., reviewing how an object was lost, or ruminating about where it could be), so that when given a memory questionnaire about ability or frequency of problems, these memory failures would be more readily accessible for a highly neurotic individual than for someone lower in neuroticism.

Construct validity of memory complaints measures

Important questions about the limited predictive validity of memory complaints scales for memory and cognition need to be understood and addressed. As psychologists, we believe it is useful to conceptualize the process by which individuals generate memory complaints (or, more narrowly, responses on memory complaint questionnaire items) and the sources of information accessed and evaluated during that process. A general assumption about memory complaints seems to be that individuals monitor memory successes and failures in everyday life, and then use that monitoring to construct accurate self-representations of their memory problems. How must our conceptions of memory complaints be altered to accommodate the evidence of a limited relationship of memory performance and memory complaints?

Rabbitt, Maylor, McInnes, and Bent (1995) argued that older adults may not report more cognitive lapses than younger adults because of a lower level of environmental demands for memory use in old age. Park et al. (1999) reported that self-reported busyness predicted prospective memory failures in middle age, lending some credence to this argument (but see the failure to replicate by Cuttler & Graf, 2007). Given the difficulties in assessing environmental pressure with respect to memory, Rabbitt et al.'s hypothesis has not yet been adequately tested.

Rabbitt and colleagues also noted that the limited correlations could be an artifact of creating aggregate memory complaint scales that combine responses across multiple domains of memory (e.g., remembering names, faces, phone numbers, and appointments; see also Rabbitt & Abson, 1990). Summing ratings over multiple memory domains could dilute the validity of domain-specific memory complaints. However, there is at present little evidence to support the claim that aggregation over domains is a major issue in validation of memory complaints. For example, differentiating prospective and retrospective memory in both self-ratings and memory tasks does not improve correlations of ratings and tasks, but such evidence is far from definitive.

Another explanation, traditionally framed as a critique of the ecological validity of memory tests, argues that subjective beliefs about memory arise in the context of everyday uses of memory, but that these aspects of everyday memory are inadequately sampled by standard laboratory memory tasks (e.g., Bruce, 1985; Gruneberg, Morris, & Sykes, 1991; for an alternative perspective, see Chaytor & Schmitter-Edgecombe, 2003). From this point of view, the fault is not in the beliefs, but in the task used to validate them.

The existing data offer some support for this view. For example, West, Crook, and Larrabee (1983) found that correlations of memory complaints measures were higher for tasks with face validity for everyday life (e.g., grocery shopping lists), but the improvement over traditional memory tests was relatively minor. Cuttler, Graf, Pawluski, and Galea (2011) found that prospective memory complaints in pregnant women predicted field prospective memory tests (e.g., phoning the laboratory) but not laboratory prospective memory tests. Witt, Glöckner, and Helmstaedter (2011) found better predictive validity with memory complaints of a memory test with a longer four-week retention interval, suggesting that everyday memory complaints may be about longer-term forgetting. Perhaps the most impressive evidence involves differentiation of recollection and familiarity in memory

tests. Debreuil, Adam, Bier, and Gagnon (2007) and Guerdoux, Dressaire, Martin, Adam, and Brouillet (2012) both reported that predictive validity of complaints for memory performance could be enhanced by using process-dissociation procedures in recognition memory tasks to generate better measures of recollection. They argued that recollective failures are more salient in everyday life and hence more likely to influence perceived memory problems.

It does appear that modest gains in validity may be obtained by selecting tasks that align with the types of memory success and failure experiences people encounter. Of course, this is not an easy problem to correct and definitive proof requires better qualitative evidence about the experiential basis for memory complaints. Everyday memory failures are more often prospective than retrospective in nature, and memory successes often require conscientious application of memory-supporting habits, such as the use of external aids (e.g., Cavanaugh, Grady, & Perlmutter, 1983). Vestergren and Nilsson (2011) reported that memory complaints in older adults are attributed to aging, whereas middle-aged adults attribute memory failures to stress and cognitive demands created by multi-tasking. In theory, interview approaches as used in that study could be useful for characterizing the contextual demands that increase risk for memory failures, with possible benefits for improving criterion tasks for memory complaint validation (e.g., measuring event-based prospective memory while under divided attention when prospective cues are presented).

In general, however, definitive tests of the ecological validity explanation for low correlations of memory beliefs with memory performance require better assessment of memory failures as experienced in the natural ecology. There have been efforts towards using virtual environments and simulated complex tasks to better approximate remembering in natural contexts and to foster training of executive control in everyday life (e.g., Levine et al., 2007). It is yet unknown whether memory complaints will predict memory failures in such task environments. There is tantalizing evidence that subjective reports of attention issues and cognitive failures, as measured by more specific subjective reports of attentional deficits when driving, correlate with driving errors in driving simulators (Wickens, Toplak, & Wiesenthal, 2008).

An alternative perspective on the poor predictive validity of memory complaints focuses on the process by which questionnaire responses are generated. Memory self-ratings can be influenced by internalized implicit theories and stereotypes about age-related memory decline (e.g. Cavanaugh, Feldman, & Hertzog, 1998; McDonald-Miszczak, Hertzog, & Hultsch, 1995). For instance, age differences in self-rated memory ability vary depending upon whether people are asked (1) to rate themselves without an explicit standard of comparison being provided, (2) to rate themselves relative to people of all ages, or (3) to rate themselves relative to people of all ages (Lineweaver & Hertzog, 1998). Age differences in self-rated memory were most likely when ratings were requested relative to persons of all ages and were not reliable when ratings were to one's same-aged peers, and fell in between when no explicit standard was provided. This pattern suggests that consideration of one's age occurs for some individuals absent an explicit age standard.

Individuals may have internalized a self-schema of memory decline that is accessed when the individual is queried about memory problems (Cavanaugh et al., 1998). The negative memory self-schema is also apt to be continually reinforced by an attributional process in which experienced everyday memory failures, common at all ages, are interpreted in the context of concerns about possible age-related memory loss.

An implicit theory account challenges the assumption that reported memory problems are based on accurate monitoring of memory successes and failures in everyday life. In principle, it could be possible to enhance self-report validity with manipulations that discourage memory complaints responses based on self-schemas and encourage access to valid sources of information (such as memories for actual failures and successes when remembering).

The behavioral specificity hypothesis

Consistent with this view, Hertzog, Park, Morrell, and Martin (2000) offered an ecologically based hypothesis about predictive validity of memory complaints termed the behavioral specificity hypothesis. It states that predictive validity will be maximized when reports of memory problems are specifically linked to observable behaviors. The root causes of limited predictive validity are seen as both (1) a property of how questions are framed in typical complaints scales (not specific to actual behaviors) and (2) the criterion variable employed (task performance, rather than actual behaviors).

Hertzog et al. (2000) evaluated the behavioral specificity hypothesis by assessing medication adherence in a cross-sectional sample of rheumatoid arthritis patients. Each participant completed the MFQ, multiple cognitive tasks (including tests of episodic memory and prospective memory), and an interview about medication usage. Subsequent medication adherence was monitored for one month by using microelectronic-chip bottle caps to record the date and time the bottle was opened, the actual behavior of interest.

Another critical feature of the study was the nature of the medication interview. Participants brought all prescription drugs to the interview, answering questions about each one. A critical question, similar to the MFQ Frequency of Forgetting scale items, asked, "How often over the last month did you forget to take this medicine as prescribed?" Medication adherence complaints were scaled as the mean rating of problems across all medications.

Actual medication adherence errors three and four weeks after the interview correlated .35 and .42, respectively, with the reported adherence complaints. However, this measure did not correlate appreciably with any of the cognitive tasks in the measurement battery, including a prospective memory task. Conversely, the MFQ Frequency of Forgetting scale correlated between .20 and .35 with the different laboratory cognitive measures, but not with actual medication adherence errors. This dissociation was consistent with the behavioral specificity hypothesis. Interview-based adherence complaints predicted only subsequent medication adherence, whereas the MFQ did not.

It is likely, then, that the validation of memory complaints with respect to memory failures in everyday life can be improved by using measures that are designed to create a supportive retrieval context (Fisher, Amador, & Geiselman, 1989) that facilitates access to relevant instances in memory. Regarding memory behaviors, modern technology may help mitigate some of the inherent difficulties in ecological sampling in future studies through techniques such as virtual reality simulations, mobile-phone use for time sampling, and web-based data collection (e.g., Wickens et al., 2008).

Functional effects of negative memory beliefs

An interesting question about memory complaints is whether they have any functional impact on everyday cognition and behavior. As noted earlier, memory complaints do not always lead to seeking treatment for memory problems. Another important issue is whether concerns about memory function lead to compensatory behaviors to maintain memory functioning. Correlations among self-report scales from memory questionnaires support the argument that low perceived memory ability and higher complaints are associated with reports of greater uses of mnemonics and external aids to support everyday remembering (e.g., Hertzog, Hultsch, & Dixon, 1989). Dixon and colleagues developed and validated the Memory Compensation Questionnaire (MCQ) to study multiple aspects of this

construct, showing longitudinal age-related increases in compensatory behaviors in midlife and beyond that were related to worse objective memory performance (e.g., Dixon & de Frias, 2007). Apparently they have not explicitly studied the linkage of memory complaints to shifts in these compensatory behaviors. Garrett, Grady, and Hasher (2010) found reliable prediction of MCQ scales by memory complaints in a sample of older adults. Parisi et al. (2011) examined longitudinal changes in the MFQ Strategy scale, finding no connection of level or change in use of external memory aids with objective memory performance. Hence it is still an open question as to whether compensatory memory-related behaviors change in reaction to experienced memory failures and resulting memory complaints, or are instead proactive and anticipatory in nature, perhaps being linked to general concerns about aging and beliefs about age-related memory decline.

Stress and intraindividual variability in memory complaints

Given the strong relationship of negative affect to memory complaints, an interesting question is whether intraindividual (within-person) fluctuations in emotional states and reactions might also produce intraindividual fluctuations in memory complaints. Previous work on questionnaire measures of memory self-concept (self-efficacy) indicated a high degree of stability of individual differences in these scales (e.g., McDonald-Mizsczak et al., 1995), which could indicate that these kinds of constructs are more trait-like than state-like.

However, one cannot generalize from long-term longitudinal studies of change to the issue of within-person variability. Sliwinski, Smyth, Hofer, and Stawski (2006) showed that response times in a measure of working memory manifested substantial within-person variability across days. Whereas stable individual differences in this aspect of working memory bore little relation to individual differences in self-reported stress, within-person variation in stress and working memory were reliably coupled. When stress levels went up, working memory performance went down. Greater intraindividual variability in cognition and physiology has been found to predict long-term cognitive decline and mortality in old age (e.g., Ram, Gerstorf, Lindenberger, & Smith, 2011).

Studies of intraindividual variability in memory complaints could move the field in an entirely new direction, given three disparate sets of relevant findings. First, recent studies have identified links between memory complaints, stress levels, stress reactions (including circulating cortisol levels), and actual memory performance (e.g., Wolf et al., 2005). Individual differences in chronic exposure to stress and elevated cortisol are associated with reduced cognitive function in old age (Marin, Lord, Andrews, Juster, & Lupien, 2011; but see Sindi, Juster, Wan, Nair, Ying Kin, & Lupien, 2012).

Second, sleep disturbances, a somatic symptom of depression and a manifestation of disorders such as adult sleep apnea, are associated with greater subjective stress and with elevated subjective cognitive problems, including memory complaints in working adults (e.g., Van der Linden, Keijsers, Eling, & van Schaijk, 2005). Willert, Thulstrup, Hertz, and Bonde (2010) reported that a stress-reduction intervention, using a combination of mindfulness and cognitive behavioral therapy, reduced stress, improved sleep, and reduced reported cognitive problems, as measured by the CFQ. Garrett et al. (2010) reported that perceived stress moderated the relationship of memory complaints to compensatory behaviors as measured by the MCQ. Highly stressed individuals (who are typically also high in neuroticism) engaged in compensatory behaviors regardless of their level of memory complaint. Low-stress older individuals only reported memory compensation when they had high memory complaints.

Third, reliable intraindividual variability in memory complaints has been reported.

Neupert, Almeida, Mroczek, and Spiro (2006) adapted the EMQ into a daily diary format, following older adults over an eight-day period. Daily within-person variation in memory complaints was predicted by the number of reported daily stressors; days with higher numbers of stressor also manifested more memory complaints. Follow-up analyses demonstrated that neuroticism amplified the relationship between stress and increased memory complaints (Neupert, Mroczek, & Spiro, 2008). Neurotic individuals were more likely to report higher memory complaints on their stressful days. Whitbourne, Neupert, and Lachman (2008) found that day-to-day variability in leisure activity and exercise covaried with reported memory failures. These studies demonstrate that memory complaints fluctuate according to variability in everyday life demands, activities, and stressors.

Further research on within-person variations in situational influences, including daily stressors, may illuminate the contexts of everyday memory failures by revealing how and when such failures are translated into memory complaints. Whereas between-person differences in memory complaints may be more a function of stable trait neuroticism, actual reactivity to stress may fluctuate within persons according to the context and consequences of experienced memory failures and their correlates (such as stress, intrusive thoughts, and cognitive load). The magnitude of intraindividual variability in memory complaints and its coupling to actual cognitive failures and their real-world consequences may be a better long-term predictor of negative outcomes than the overall level of memory complaints.

CONCLUSION

We believe it is safe to say that we no longer need further studies that merely correlate memory complaints scales with memory test performance and other variables. It is well-established that memory complaints are weakly correlated with memory test performance and more strongly associated with emotional instability, depression, and negative affect. A more pressing question is: What can or should be done about the limited predictive validity of these scales?

There are a number of interesting suggestions in the field regarding how measurement of memory complaints can be improved and how the robust relationships of personality, depression, and complaints can be explained. In our view, research identifying individual differences in the processes and sources of information engaged when responding to complaints questions will be critical for advancing our understanding of complaints. The field would also benefit from additional longitudinal data that evaluate how changes in objective and subjective memory influence each other as people grow older. We would also argue that better techniques for assessing intraindividual fluctuations in everyday memory and memory complaints, such as intensive time sampling designs, have great potential for enriching our understanding of memory failures as they occur in everyday life.

There are also critical issues about how our understanding of memory complaints might advance differential diagnosis and treatment of older adults with concerns about their memory. We began the chapter by noting that there is a major difference between studying those who do and do not present at memory clinics complaining about memory problems, and studying memory complaints with questionnaires in typical samples. Yet the field has paid scant attention to the problem of self-referrals for memory problems and what it implies. What, specifically, are people actually concerned about as they complain about memory? What are the barriers to help-seeking by people with complaints even when those complaints are valid? Translational research in this domain is, at present, sorely lacking. The stage seems to be set for new and valuable advances in both basic and applied research questions about older adults' memory complaints.

ACKNOWLEDGMENT

Work on this chapter was facilitated by the authors' tenure as visiting scientists at the Max Planck Institute for Human Development, Berlin, in 2011 and 2012.

REFERENCES

Alexander, M .P., Stuss, D. T., & Fansabedian, N. (2003). California Verbal Learning Test: Performance by patients with focal frontal and non-frontal lesions. *Brain, 126*, 1493–1503.

Antikainen, R., Honkalampi, K., Hänninen, T., Koivumaa-Honkanen, H., Tanskanen, A., Haatainen, K., & Viinamäki, H. (2004). A decrease in memory complaints is associated with mood improvement: A twelve-month follow up-study of depressed patients. *The European Journal of Psychiatry, 18*, 143–152.

Antonell, A., Fortea, J., Rami, L., Bosch, B., Balasa, M., Sánchez-Valle, R., & Lladó, A. (2011). Different profiles of Alzheimer's disease cerebrospinal fluid biomarkers in controls and subjects with subjective memory complaints. *Journal of Neural Transmission, 118*, 259–262.

Ayalon, L. (2011). The IQCODE versus a single-item informant measure to discriminate between cognitively intact individuals and individuals with dementia or cognitive impairment. *Journal of Geriatric Psychiatry & Neurology, 24*, 168–173.

Bandura, A. (1997). *Self-efficacy: The exercise of control.* New York: W H Freeman/Times Books/Henry Holt & Co.

Barnes, L. L., Schneider, J. A., Boyle, P. A., Bienias, J. L., & Bennett, D. A. (2006). Memory complaints are related to Alzheimer disease pathology in older persons. *Neurology, 67*, 1581–1585.

Beaudoin, M., & Desrichard, O. (2011). Are memory self-efficacy and memory performance related? A meta-analysis. *Psychological Bulletin, 137*, 211–241.

Berry, J. M., & West, R. L. (1993). Cognitive self-efficacy in relation to personal mastery and goal setting across the life span. *International Journal of Behavioral Development, 16*, 351–379.

Broadbent, D. E., Cooper, P. F., FitzGerald, P., & Parkes, K. R. (1982). The Cognitive Failures Questionnaire (CFQ) and its correlates. *British Journal of Clinical Psychology, 21*, 1–16.

Bruce, D. (1985). The how and why of ecological memory. *Journal of Experimental Psychology: General, 114*, 78–90.

Buckley, T., Norton, M. C., Deberard, M., Welsh-Bohmer, K. A., & Tschanz, J. T. (2010). A brief metacognition questionnaire for the elderly: Comparison with cognitive performance and informant ratings The Cache County Study. *International Journal of Geriatric Psychiatry*, *25*, 739–747.

Bunce, D., Anstey, K. J., Cherbuin, N., Burns, R., Christensen, H., Wen, W., & Sachdev, P. S. (2010). Cognitive deficits are associated with frontal and temporal lobe white matter lesions in middle-aged adults living in the community. *PLOS ONE*, *5*(10), e13567.

Cacchione, P. Z., Powlishta, K. K., Grant, E. A., Buckles, V. D., & Morris, J. C. (2003). Accuracy of collateral source reports in very mild to mild dementia of the Alzheimer type. *Journal of the American Geriatrics Society*, *51*, 819–823.

Camp, C. J., West, R. L., & Poon, L. W. (1989). Recruitment practices for psychological research in gerontology. In M. P. Lawton and A. R. Herzog (Eds.), *Special research methods for gerontology.* (pp. 163–189). Amityville, NY: Baywood Publishing Co.

Cavallini, E., Bottiroli, S., Fastame, M. C., & Hertzog, C. (2013). The role of culture in aging stereotypes: Implicit theory and personal beliefs about memory. *Journal of Aging Studies*, *27*, 71–81.

Cavanaugh, J. C. (2000). Metamemory from a social-cognitive perspective. In D. Park and N. Schwarz (Eds.), *Cognitive aging: A primer* (pp. 115–130). Philadelphia, PA: Psychology Press.

Cavanaugh, J. C., Feldman, J. M., & Hertzog, C. (1998). Memory beliefs as social cognition: A reconceptualization of what memory questionnaires assess. *Review of General Psychology*, *2*, 48–65.

Cavanaugh, J. C., Grady, J. G., & Perlmutter, M. (1983). Forgetting and use of memory aids in 20 to 70 year olds' everyday life. *The International Journal of Aging & Human Development*, *17*, 113–122.

Chaytor, N., & Schmitter-Edgecombe, M. (2003). The ecological validity of neuropsychological tests: A review of the literature on everyday cognitive skills. *Neuropsychology Review*, *13*, 182–197.

Chung, J. C., & Man, D. K. (2009). Self-appraised, informant-reported, and objective memory and cognitive function in mild cognitive impairment. *Dementia & Geriatric Cognitive Disorders*, *27*, 187–193.

Corner, L., & Bond, J. (2004). Being at risk of dementia: Fears and anxieties of older adults. *Journal of Aging Studies*, *18*, 143–155.

Crane, M. K., Bogner, H. R., Brown, G. K., & Gallo, J. J. (2007). The link between depressive symptoms, negative cognitive bias and memory complaints in older adults. *Aging & Mental Health*, *11*, 708–715.

Crook, T. H., Bartus, R. T., Ferris, S. H., & Whitehouse, P. (1986). Age-associated memory impairment: Proposed diagnostic criteria and measures of clinical change: Report of a NIMH work group. *Developmental Neuropsychology*, *2*, 261–276.

Crook, T. H., & Larrabee, G. J. (1990). A self-rating scale for evaluating memory in everyday life. *Psychology & Aging*, *5*, 48–57.

Crook, T. H., Feher, E. P., & Larrabee, G. J. (1992). Assessment of memory complaint in age-associated memory impairment: The MAC-Q. *International Psychogeriatrics*, *4*, 165–176.

Cutler, S. J., & Grams, A. E. (1988). Correlates of self-reported everyday memory problems. *Journals of Gerontology*, *43*, S82–S90.

Cutler, S. J., & Hodgson, L.G. (1996). Anticipatory dementia: A link between memory appraisals and concerns about developing Alzheimer's disease. *The Gerontologist*, *36*, 657–664.

Cuttler, C., & Graf, P. (2007). Personality predicts prospective memory task performance: An adult lifespan study. *Scandinavian Journal of Psychology*, *48*, 215–231.

Cuttler, C., Graf, P., Pawluski, J. L., & Galea, L. M. (2011). Everyday life memory deficits in pregnant women. *Canadian Journal of Experimental Psychology*, *65*, 27–37.

Debreuil, P., Adam, S., Bier, N., & Gagnon, L. (2007). The ecological validity of traditional memory evaluation in relation with controlled memory processes and routinization. *Archives of Clinical Neuropsychology*, *22*, 979–989.

Dixon, R. A., & de Frias, C. M. (2007). Mild memory impairments differentially affect 6-year changes in compensatory strategy use. *Psychology and Aging*, *22*, 632–638.

Dixon, R. A., & Hultsch, D. F. (1983). Structure and development of metamemory in adulthood. *Journal of Gerontology*, *38*, 682–688.

Dixon, R. A., de Frias, C. M., & Bäckman, L. (2001). Characteristics of self-reported memory compensation in older adults. *Journal of Clinical & Experimental Neuropsychology*, *23*, 630–661.

Elfgren, C., Gustafson, L., Vestberg, S., & Passant, U. (2010). Subjective memory complaints, neuropsychological performance and psychiatric variables in memory clinic attendees: A 3-year follow-up study. *Archives of Gerontology & Geriatrics*, *51*, e110–e114.

Erk, S., Spottke, A., Meisen, A., Wagner, M., Walter, H., & Jessen, F. (2012). Evidence of neuronal compensation during episodic memory in subjective memory impairment. *Archives of General Psychiatry*, *68*, 845–852.

Farias, S., Mungas, D., & Jagust, W. (2005). Degree of discrepancy between self and other-reported everyday functioning by cognitive status: Dementia, mild cognitive impairment, and healthy elders. *International Journal of Geriatric Psychiatry*, *20*, 827–834.

Fisher, R. P., Amador, M., & Geiselman, R. E. (1989). Field-test of the cognitive interview – Enhancing the recollection of actual victims and witnesses of crimes. *Journal of Applied Psychology*, *74*, 722–727.

Garrett, D. D., Grady, C. L., & Hasher, L. (2010). Everyday memory compensation: The impact of cognitive reserve, subjective memory, and stress. *Psychology and Aging*, *25*, 74–83.

Gilewski, M. J., & Zelinski, E. M. (1986). Questionnaire assessment of memory complaints. In L. W. Poon, T. Crook, K. L. Davis, C. Eisdorfer, B. J. Gurland, A. W. Kasznik, and L. W. Thompson (Eds.), *Handbook for clinical memory assessment of older adults* (pp. 93–107). Washington, DC: American Psychological Association.

Gilewski, M. J., Zelinski, E. M., & Schaie, K. W. (1990). The Memory Functioning Questionnaire for assessment of memory complaints in adulthood and old age. *Psychology & Aging*, *5*, 482–490.

Gruneberg, M. M., Morris, P. E., & Sykes, R. N. (1991). The obituary on everyday memory and its practical applications is premature. *American Psychologist*, *46*(1), 74–76.

Guerdoux, E., Dressaire, D., Martin, S., Adam, S., & Brouillet, D. (2012). Habit and recollection in healthy aging, mild cognitive impairment, and Alzheimer's disease. *Neuropsychology*, *26*, 517–533.

Gunning-Dixon, F. M., Brickman, A. M., Cheng, J. C., & Alexopoulos, G. S. (2009). Aging of cerebral white matter: A review of MRI findings. *International Journal of Geriatric Psychiatry*, *24*, 109–117.

Haley, A. P., Eagan, D. E., Gonzalez, M. M., Biney, F. O., & Cooper, R. A. (2011). Functional magnetic resonance imaging of working memory reveals frontal hypoactivation in middle-aged adults with cognitive complaints. *Journal of the International Neuropsychological Society*, *17*, 915–924.

Hänninen, T., Reinikainen, K. J., Helkala, E.-L., & Koivisto, K. (1994). Subjective memory complaints and personality traits in normal elderly subjects. *Journal of the American Geriatrics Society*, *42*, 1–4.

Hannon, R., Adams, P., Harrington, S., Fries-Dias, C., & Gipson, M. T. (1995). Effects of brain injury and age on prospective memory self-rating and performance. *Rehabilitation Psychology*, *40*(4), 289–298.

Herrmann, D. J. (1982). Know thy memory: The use of questionnaires to assess and study memory. *Psychological Bulletin*, *92*, 434–452.

Hertzog, C., & Hultsch, D. F. (2000). Metacognition in adulthood and old age. In F. I. M. Craik and T. A. Salthouse (Eds.), *The handbook of aging and cognition* (2nd ed.) (pp. 417–466). Mahwah, NJ: Lawrence Erlbaum Associates Publishers.

Hertzog, C., Dixon, R. A., & Hultsch, D. F. (1990). Relationships between metamemory, memory predictions, and task performance in adults. *Psychology & Aging*, *5*, 215–227.

Hertzog, C., Dunlosky, J., & Robinson, A. E. (2009). Intellectual abilities and metacognitive beliefs influence spontaneous use of effective encoding strategies. Unpublished Manuscript.

Hertzog, C., Hultsch, D. F., & Dixon, R. A. (1989). Evidence for the convergent validity of two self-report metamemory questionnaires. *Developmental Psychology*, *25*, 687–700.

Hertzog, C., Park, D. C., Morrell, R. W., & Martin, M. (2000). Ask and ye shall receive: Behavioural specificity in the accuracy of subjective memory complaints. *Applied Cognitive Psychology*, *14*, 257–275.

Herzog, A. R., & Rodgers, W. L. (1989). Age differences in memory performance and memory ratings as measured in a sample survey. *Psychology and Aging*, *4*, 173–182.

Hohman, T. H., Beason-Held, L. L., Lamar, M., & Resnick, S. B. (2011). Subjective cognitive complaints and longitudinal changes in memory and brain function. *Neuropsychology*, *25*, 125–130.

Holsinger, T., Deveau, J., Boustani, M., & Williams, J. W., Jr. (2007). Does this patient have dementia? *JAMA: Journal of the American Medical Association*, *297*, 2391–2404.

Hultsch, D. F., Hertzog, C., & Dixon, R. A. (1987). Age differences in metamemory: Resolving the inconsistencies. *Canadian Journal of Psychology*, *41*, 193–208.

Hurt, C. S., Burns, A., Brown, R. G., & Barrowclough, C. (2012). Why don't older adults with subjective memory complaints seek help? *International Journal of Geriatric Psychiatry*, *27*, 394–400.

Isella, V. V., Villa, L. L., Russo, A. A., Regazzoni, R. R., Ferrarese, C. C., & Appollonio, I. M. (2006). Discriminative and predictive power of an informant report in mild cognitive impairment. *Journal of Neurology, Neurosurgery & Psychiatry*, *77*, 166–171.

Jessen, F., Feyen, L., Freymann, K., Tepest, R., Maier, W., Heun, R., & Scheef, L. (2006). Volume reduction of the entorhinal cortex in subjective memory impairment. *Neurobiology of Aging*, *27*, 1751–1756.

Jopp, D., & Hertzog, C. (2007). Activities, self-referent memory beliefs, and cognitive performance: Evidence for direct and mediated relations. *Psychology & Aging, 22*, 811–825.

Jorm, A. F. (2004). The Informant Questionnaire on Cognitive Decline in the Elderly (IQCODE): A review. *International Psychogeriatrics, 16*, 275–293.

Jorm, A. F., Butterworth, P. P., Anstey, K. J., Christensen, H. H., Easteal, S. S., Maller, J. J., & Sachdev, P. P. (2004). Memory complaints in a community sample aged 60–64 years: Associations with cognitive functioning, psychiatric symptoms, medical conditions, APOE genotype, hippocampus and amygdala volumes, and white-matter hyperintensities. *Psychological Medicine: A Journal of Research in Psychiatry & the Allied Sciences, 34*, 1495–1506.

Jorm, A. F., Scott, R., & Jacomb, P. A. (1989). Assessment of cognitive decline in dementia by informant questionnaire. *International Journal of Geriatric Psychiatry, 4*, 35–39.

Kahn, R. L., Zarit, S. H., Hilbert, N. M., & Niederehe, G. (1975). Memory complaint and impairment in the aged: The effect of depression and altered brain function. *Archives of General Psychiatry, 32*, 1569–1573.

Kaszniak, A. W. (1990). Psychological assessment of the aging individual. In J. E. Birren and K. W. Schaie (Eds.), *Handbook of the psychology of aging* (3rd ed., pp. 427–445). New York: Academic Press.

Kliegel, M., & Jäger, T. (2006). Can the Prospective and Retrospective Memory Questionnaire (PRMQ) predict actual prospective memory performance? *Current Psychology, 25*(3), 182–191.

Kverno, K. S. (2000). Trait anxiety influences on judgments of frequency and recall. *Personality & Individual Differences, 29*, 395–404.

La Rue, A., Small, G., McPherson, S., & Komo, S. (1996). Subjective memory loss in age-associated memory impairment: Family history and neuropsychological correlates. *Aging, Neuropsychology, & Cognition, 3*, 132–140.

Lachman, M. E., Bandura, M., Weaver, S. L., & Elliott, E. (1995). Assessing memory control beliefs: The Memory Controllability Inventory. *Aging & Cognition, 2*(1), 67–84.

Lane, C. J. & Zelinski, E. M. (2003). Longitudinal hierarchical linear models of the Memory Functioning Questionnaire. *Psychology & Aging, 18*(1), 38–53. doi: 10.1037/0882-7974.18.1.38

Leshikar, E. D., Duarte, A., & Hertzog, C. (2012). Task-selective memory effects for successfully implemented encoding strategies. *PLoS:ONE, 7*(5), e38160

Levine, B., Stuss, D. T., Winocur, G., Binns, M. A., Fahy, L., Mandich, M., Bridges, K., & Robertson, I. H. (2007). Cognitive rehabilitation in the elderly: Effects on strategic behavior in relation to goal management. *Journal of the International Neuropsychological Society, 13*, 143–152.

Levy, B., & Langer, E. (1994). Aging free from negative stereotypes: Successful memory in China and among the American deaf. *Journal of Personality & Social Psychology, 66*, 989–997.

Lineweaver, T. T., & Hertzog, C. (1998). Adults' efficacy and control beliefs regarding memory and aging: Separating general from personal beliefs. *Aging, Neuropsychology, & Cognition, 5*, 264–296.

Loewenstein, D. A., Argüelles, S., Bravo, M., Freeman, R. Q., Argüelles, T., Acevedo, A., & Eisdorfer, C. (2001). Caregivers' judgments of the functional abilities of the Alzheimer's disease patient: A comparison of proxy reports and objective measures. *The Journals of Gerontology: Series B: Psychological Sciences, 56B*, P78–P84.

Mäntylä, T. (2003). Assessing absentmindedness: Prospective memory complaint and impairment in middle-aged adults. *Memory & Cognition, 31*, 15–25.

Mäntylä, T., & Göran-Nilsson, L. (1997). Remembering to remember in adulthood: A population-based study on aging and prospective memory. *Aging, Neuropsychology, & Cognition, 4*, 81–92.

Mäntylä, T., Rönnlund, M., & Kliegel, M. (2010). Components of executive functioning in metamemory. *Applied Neuropsychology, 17*, 289–298.

Marin, M-F., Lord, C., Andrews, J., Juster, R-P., & Lupien, S. J. (2011). Chronic stress, cognitive functioning, and mental health. *Neurobiology of Learning and Memory, 96*, 583–595.

Mascherek, A., & Zimprich, D. (2011). Correlated change in memory complaints and memory performance across 12 years. *Psychology & Aging, 26*, 884–889.

Mascherek, A., Zimprich, D., Rupprecht, R., & Lang, F. R. (2011). What do cognitive complaints in a sample of memory clinic outpatients reflect? *GeroPsych: The Journal of Gerontopsychology & Geriatric Psychiatry, 24*, 187–195.

McDonald-Miszczak, L., Hertzog, C., & Hultsch, D. F. (1995). Stability and accuracy of metamemory in adulthood and aging: A longitudinal analysis. *Psychology & Aging, 10*, 553–564.

McFarland, C., Ross, M., & Giltrow, M. (1992). Biased recollections in older adults: The role of implicit theories of aging. *Journal of Personality & Social Psychology, 62*(5), 837–850.

McGlynn, S. M., & Schacter, D. L. (1989). Unawareness of deficits in neuropsychological syndromes. *Journal of Clinical & Experimental Neuropsychology, 11*(2), 143–205.

Minett, T. S. C., Dean, J. L., Firbank, M., English, P., & O'Brien, J. T. (2005). Subjective memory complaints, white-matter lesions, depressive symptoms, and cognition in elderly patients. *The American Journal of Geriatric Psychiatry*, *13*(8), 665–671.

Neupert, S. D., Almeida, D. M., Mroczek, D. K., & Spiro, A. (2006). Daily stressors and memory failures in a natural setting: Findings from the VA Normative Aging Study. *Psychology and Aging*, *21*, 424–429.

Neupert, S. D., Mroczek, D. K., & Spiro, A. (2008). Neuroticism moderates the daily relation between stressors and memory failures. *Psychology and Aging*, *23*, 287–296.

Niederehe, G,. & Yoder, C. (1989). Metamemory perceptions in depressions of young and older adults. *The Journal of Nervous & Mental Disease*, *177*, 4–14.

Okada, K., Vilberg, K. L., & Rugg, M. D. (2012). Comparison of the neural correlates of retrieval successes in tests of cued recall and recognition memory. *Human Brain Mapping*, *33*, 523–533.

Pannu, J. K., & Kaszniak, A. W. (2005). Metamemory experiments in neurological populations: A review. *Neuropsychology Review*, *15*, 105–130.

Parisi, J. M., Gross, A. L., Rebok, G. W., Saczynski, J. S., Crowe, M., Cook, S. E., & Unverzagt, F. W. (2011). Modeling change in memory performance and memory perceptions: Findings from the ACTIVE study. *Psychology & Aging*, *26*(3), 518–524.

Park, D. C., Hertzog., C., Leventhal, H., Morrell, R. W., Leventhal, E., Birchmore, D., Martin, M., & Bennett, J. (1999). Medication adherence in rheumatoid arthritis patients: Older is wiser. *Journal of the American Geriatric Society*, *47*, 172–183.

Pearman, A. (2009). Predictors of subjective memory in young adults. *Journal of Adult Development*, *16*(2), 101–107.

Pearman, A., & Storandt, M. (2004). Predictors of subjective memory in older adults. *The Journals of Gerontology: Series B: Psychological Sciences & Social Sciences*, *59B*, P4–6.

Pearman, A., & Storandt, M. (2005). Self-discipline and self-consciousness predict subjective memory in older adults. *The Journals of Gerontology: Series B: Psychological Sciences & Social Sciences*, *60B*, P153–157.

Pearman, A., Gerstorf, D., & Hertzog, C. (2013). Subjective memory complaints in the oldest old: Cross-sectional and longitudinal findings. Unpublished manuscript.

Perrotin, A., Mormino, A. C., Madison, C. M., Hayenga, A. O., & Jagust, W. J. (2012). Subjective cognition and amyloid deposition imaging: A Pittsburgh Compound B Positive Emission Tomography study in normal elderly individuals. *Archives of Neurology*, *69*, 223–229.

Petersen, R. C., Smith, G. E., Waring, S. C., Ivnik, R. J., Tangalos, E. G., & Kokmen, E. (1999). Mild cognitive impairment: Clinical characterization and outcome. *Archives of Neurology*, *56*, 303–308.

Plassman, B., Langa, K., Fisher, G., Heeringa, S., Weir, D., Ofstedal, M., & Wallace, R. (2008). Prevalence of cognitive impairment without dementia in the United States. *Annals of Internal Medicine*, *148*, 427–434.

Plotkin, D. A., Mintz, J., & Jarvik, L. F. (1985). Subjective memory complaints in geriatric depression. *The American Journal of Psychiatry*, *142*, 1103–1105.

Ponds, R. & Jolles, J. (1996). Memory complaints in elderly people: The role of memory abilities, metamemory, depression, and personality. *Educational Gerontology*, *22*, 341–357.

Rabbitt, P. & Abson, V. (1990). 'Lost and found': Some logical and methodological limitations of self-report questionnaires as tools to study cognitive ageing. *British Journal of Psychology*, *81*, 1–16.

Rabbitt, P., Maylor, E., McInnes, L., & Bent, N. (1995). What goods can self-assessment questionnaires deliver for cognitive gerontology? *Applied Cognitive Psychology*, *9*, S127–152.

Ram, N., Gerstorf, D., Lindenberger, U., & Smith, J. (2011). Developmental change and intraindividual variability: Relating cognitive aging to cognitive plasticity, cardiovascular lability, and emotional diversity. *Psychology and Aging*, *26*, 363–371.

Ramakers, I. B., Visser, P., Bittermann, A. N., Ponds, R. M., van Boxtel, M. J., & Verhey, F. J. (2009). Characteristics of help-seeking behaviour in subjects with subjective memory complaints at a memory clinic: A case-control study. *International Journal of Geriatric Psychiatry*, *24*, 190–196.

Rasmusson, D. X., Rebok, G. W., Bylsma, F. W., & Brandt, J. (1999). Effects of three types of memory training in normal elderly. *Aging, Neuropsychology, & Cognition*, *6*, 56–66.

Rast, P., Zimprich, D., van Boxtel, M., & Jolles, J. (2009). Factor structure and measurement invariance in the Cognitive Failures Questionnaire across the adult life span. *Assessment*, *16*, 145–158.

Roberts, J. L., Clare, L., & Woods, R. T. (2009). Subjective memory complaints and awareness of memory functioning in mild cognitive impairment: A systematic review. *Dementia and Geriatric Cognitive Disorders*, *28*(2), 95–109.

Rönnlund, M., Vestergren, P., Mäntylä, T., & Göran-Nilsson, L. (2011). Predictors of self-reported prospective and retrospective memory in a population-based sample of older adults. *The Journal of Genetic Psychology: Research and Theory on Human Development, 172,* 266–284.

Ryan, E. B. & Kwong See, S. (1993). Age-based beliefs about memory changes for self and others across adulthood. *Journals of Gerontology, 48,* P199–201.

Salthouse, T. A., Berish, D. E., & Siedlecki, K. L. (2004). Construct validity and age sensitivity of prospective memory. *Memory & Cognition, 32,* 1133–1148.

Schleser, R., West, R. L., & Boatwright, L. K. (1986). A comparison of recruiting strategies for increasing older adults' initial entry and compliance in a memory training program. *The International Journal of Aging & Human Development, 24,* 55–66.

Schmand, B., Jonker, C., Gerrlings, M. I., & Lindeboom, J. (1997). Subjective memory complaints in the elderly: depressive symptoms and future dementia. *British Journal of Psychiatry, 171,* 373–376.

Schofield, P. W., Jacobs, D., Marder, K., Sano, M., & Stern, Y. (1997). The validity of new memory complaints in the elderly. *Archives of Neurology, 54,* 756–759.

Schoonenboom, N. S. M., Reesink, F. E., Verwey, N. A., Kester, M. I., Teunissen, C. E., van de Ven, P. M., &van der Flier, W. M. (2012). Cerebrospinal fluid markers for differential dementia diagnosis in a large memory clinic cohort. *Neurology, 78,* 47–54.

Scogin, F., Storandt, M., & Lott, L. (1985). Memory-skills training, memory complaints, and depression in older adults. *Journal of Gerontology, 40,* 562–568.

Scott, S. & Walter, F. (2010). Studying help-seeking for symptoms: The challenges of methods and models. *Social & Personality Psychology Compass, 4*(8), 531–547.

Sims, R. C., Whitfield, K. E., Ayotte, B. J., Gamaldo, A. A., Edwards, C. L., & Allaire, J. C. (2011). Subjective memory in older African Americans. *Experimental Aging Research, 37,* 220–240.

Sindi, S., Juster, R-P., Wan, N., Nair, N. P. V., Ying Kin, N., & Lupien, S. J. (2012). Depressive symptoms, cortisol, and cognition during human aging: The role of negative aging perceptions. *Stress, 15,* 130–137.

Slavin, M. J., Brodaty, H., Kochan, N. A., Crawford, J. D., Trollor, J. N., Draper, B., & Sachdev, P. S. (2010). Prevalence and predictors of 'subjective cognitive complaints' in the Sydney Memory and Ageing Study. *The American Journal of Geriatric Psychiatry, 18,* 701–710.

Sliwinski, M. J., Smyth, J. M., Hofer, S. M., & Stawski, R. J. (2006). Intraindividual coupling of stress and cognition. *Psychology and Aging, 21,* 545–557.

Smith, G., Sala, S., Logie, R. H., & Maylor, E. A. (2000). Prospective and retrospective memory in normal ageing and dementia: A questionnaire study. *Memory, 8,* 311–321.

Smith, R. E. (2003). The cost of remembering to remember in event-based prospective memory: Investigating the capacity demands of delayed intention performance. *Journal of Experimental Psychology: Learning, Memory, & Cognition, 29,* 347–361.

Snitz, B. E., Morrow, L. A., Rodriguez, E. G., Huber, K. A., & Saxton, J. A. (2008). Subjective memory complaints and concurrent memory performance in older patients of primary care providers. *Journal of the International Neuropsychological Society, 14,* 1004–1013.

Stewart, R., Godin, O., Crivello, F., Maillard, P., Mazoyer, B., Tzourio, C., & Dufouil, C. (2011). Longitudinal neuroimaging correlates of subjective memory impairment: 4-year prospective community study. *British Journal of Psychiatry, 198,* 199–205.

Strunk, D. R., & Adler, A. D. (2009). Cognitive biases in three prediction tasks: A test of the cognitive model of depression. *Behaviour Research & Therapy, 47,* 34–40.

Strunk, D. R., Lopez, H., & DeRubeis, R. J. (2006). Depressive symptoms are associated with unrealistic negative predictions of future life events. *Behaviour Research & Therapy, 44,* 861–882.

Sunderland, A., Watts, K., Baddeley, A. D., & Harris, J. E. (1986). Subjective memory assessment and test performance in elderly adults. *Journal of Gerontology, 41,* 376–384.

Taylor, J. L., Miller, T. P., & Tinklenberg, J. R. (1992). Correlates of memory decline: A 4-year longitudinal study of older adults with memory complaints. *Psychology & Aging, 7,* 185–193.

Uttl, B., & Kibreab, M. (2011). Self-report measures of prospective memory are reliable but not valid. *Canadian Journal of Experimental Psychology, 65,* 57–68.

van der Flier, W. M., Pijnenburg, Y. A. L., Schoonenboom, S. N. M., Dik, M. G., Blankenstein, M. A., & Scheltens, P. (2008). Distribution of APOE genotypes in a memory clinic cohort. *Dementia & Geriatric Cognitive Disorders, 25,* 433–438.

Van der Linden, D., Keijsers, G. P. J., Eling, P., & van Schaijk, R. (2005). Work stress and attentional difficulties: An initial study on burnout and cognitive failures. *Work & Stress, 19,* 23–36.

van Norden, A. W., Fick, W. F., de Laat, K. F., van Uden, I. M., van Oudheusden, L. B., Tendolkar, I. I., Zwiers, & de Leeuw, F. E. (2008). Subjective cognitive failures and hippocampal volume in elderly with white matter lesions. *Neurology, 71,* 1152–1159.

Verma, S. K., Pershad, D. D., Kaur, R., & Bhagat, K. (1996). Personality correlates of perceived memory disturbances. *Journal of Personality & Clinical Studies*, *12*, 33–36.

Vestergren, P., & Nilsson, L-G. (2011). Perceived everyday memory problems in a population sample aged 25–99. *Applied Cognitive Psychology*, *25*, 641–646.

Volz-Sidiropoulou, E., & Gauggel, S. (2012). Do subjective measures of attention and memory predict actual performance? Metacognition in older couples. *Psychology and Aging*, *27*, 440–450.

Whitbourne, S. B., Neupert, S. D., & Lachman, M. E. (2008). Daily physical activity: Relation to everyday memory in adulthood. *Journal of Applied Gerontology*, *27*, 331–349.

Wickens, C. M., Toplak, M. E., & Wiesenthal, D. L. (2008). Cognitive failures as predictors of driving errors, lapses, and violations. *Accident Analysis and Prevention*, *40*, 1223–1233.

Willert, M. V., Thulstrup, A. M., Hertz, J., & Bonde, J. P. (2010). Sleep and cognitive failures improved by a three-month stress management intervention. *International Journal of Stress Management*, *17*, 193–213.

Winblad, B., Palmer, K., Kivipelto, M., Jelic, V., Fratiglioni, L., Wahlund, L., & Petersen, R. (2004). Mild cognitive impairment – beyond controversies, towards a consensus: Report of the International Working Group on MCI. *Journal of Internal Medicine*, *256*, 240–246.

Wolf, O. T., Dziobek, I., McHugh, P., Sweat, V., de Leon, M. J., Javier, E., & Convit, A. (2005). Subjective memory complaints in aging are associated with elevated cortisol. *Neurobiology of Aging*, *26*, 1357–1363.

Zarit, S. H., Gallagher, D., & Kramer, N. (1981). Memory training in the community aged: Effects on depression, memory complaint, and memory performance. *Educational Gerontology*, *6*, 11–27.

Zelinski, E. M., & Gilewski, M. J. (2004). A 10-item Rasch modeled memory self-efficacy scale. *Aging & Mental Health*, *8*, 293–306.

Zelinski, E. M., Gilewski, M. J., & Anthony-Bergstone, C. R. (1990). Memory Functioning Questionnaire: Concurrent validity with memory performance and self-reported memory failures. *Psychology & Aging*, *5*, 388–399.

25

Understanding People's Metacognitive Judgments: An Isomechanism Framework and Its Implications for Applied and Theoretical Research

John Dunlosky and Sarah K. Tauber

People think about their thoughts and decisions a lot, such as when they judge how well they are performing a task or evaluate the quality of their decision processes and products. The accuracy of such judgments is important, because inaccurately judging progress on a task or the quality of a decision can lead to non-optimal behavior and decisions. Consider two illustrations. When students are preparing for an upcoming exam, they intermittently ask themselves, "Do I know this information well enough to correctly answer questions about it on the exam?" Overconfidence in making these judgments of learning can lead to premature termination of study and in turn to underachievement (Dunlosky & Rawson, 2012; for further details, see Metcalfe, Chapter 26, this volume). Likewise, when radiologists evaluate a radiographic image, they often judge how confident they are in their evaluation, with lower levels of confidence leading them to ask another expert for advice or to obtain another image. Inaccurate judgment about the quality of the diagnosis obviously can be devastating, and poor judgment can also undermine performance in many other occupations and for many activities.

More generally, the accuracy of people's monitoring can be crucial for effective control, and hence understanding how people monitor and evaluate their cognitive processes can provide insight into improving both the accuracy of their monitoring and effectiveness of their self control (e.g., Bailey, Dunlosky, & Hertzog, 2010; Lane, Roussel, Villa, & Morita, 2007). Thus, in the present chapter, we describe how people judge their on-going cognitive processes and products, which has generally been termed *metacognitive monitoring*. Metacognitive monitoring is ubiquitous, so it is not surprising that people's monitoring has been investigated in the context of many activities; a short list includes monitoring of memory, learning, reading, writing, emotion, language, tutoring, teaching, and problem solving (Hacker, Dunlosky, & Graesser, 2009). Despite the obvious differences among these activities, we offer a new perspective on metacognitive judgments from the lens of the isomechanism framework, which states that all metacognitive judgments made within all activities are based on the same processes. Before describing this framework, we first provide a brief history of research on metacognitive judgments. The remainder of the chapter is dedicated to discussing the framework, processes for judgments, and implications for guiding future applied and theoretical research.

EARLY RESEARCH ON METACOGNITIVE MONITORING: GENERAL QUESTIONS, ISSUES, AND MEASURES

Joseph Hart (1965) published one of the most influential papers on metacognitive judgments (for definitions of this judgment and other classical judgments, see Table 25.1). Hart's (1965) innovation was to empirically estimate the accuracy of people's judgments of their subjective experiences. Hart noted that often participants were asked to introspect about their memories, but yet these feeling-of-knowing (FOK) judgments were taken at face value:

> the early investigators took the phenomenon as given and tried to study how subjects retrieved or searched for information they did not have but felt they knew … [but] asking how FOK memories are

retrieved presupposes that the FOK experience is an accurate indicator of what is in memory. (Hart, 1965, p. 208)

To sidestep this problem, Hart (1965) had participants attempt to answer trivia questions ("Which planet is the largest in our solar system?"), make a yes/no FOK judgment (a "yes" indicated that the participant knew the answer but was unable to retrieve it at the moment), and then take a multiple-choice test over the same questions. Hart used this final test to validate the FOK judgments, and the judgments were higher for questions in which participants later recognized the correct answer than for questions in which they did not. That is, their judgments demonstrated above chance accuracy.

Not long after Hart's groundbreaking research, other researchers began evaluating how well people could monitor different aspects of memory. For instance, to measure how well people could monitor the difficulty of learning new materials, Underwood (1966) had college students judge how quickly they could learn to recall trigrams (e.g., CES), and these ease-of-learning judgments were significantly correlated with the actual difficulty of learning. To measure how well people could monitor their learning of simple associations during study, Arbuckle and Cuddy (1969) had students study paired associates (e.g., S – 88, W – 12), and immediately after studying each one, they made a yes/no judgment of learning (JOL), by predicting whether or not they would recall the correct target number when later shown the letter cue. Their JOLs demonstrated above chance

Table 25.1 Names and common definitions of classical metacognitive judgments

Judgment label	Definition
Ease of learning	Prediction of how easy to-be-studied items will be to learn
Judgments of learning	Prediction of the likelihood of remembering recently studied items on an upcoming test
Feeling of knowing	Prediction of the likelihood of recognizing currently unrecallable answers on an upcoming test
Confidence in retrieved answers	Judgments of the likelihood that a response on a test is correct. Often referred to as retrospective confidence judgments

accuracy, and Arbuckle and Cuddy (1969) also evaluated one intriguing explanation for the results – that the JOLs were accurate because the students simply remembered their initial JOLs, and then only provided an answer if their initial JOL had been "yes." They ruled out this self-fulfilling-prophecy hypothesis and hence further established the validity of people's judgments. Research on other judgments was forthcoming, and within two decades after Hart (1965), several different metacognitive judgments were being actively explored (for a more detailed history, see Dunlosky & Metcalfe, 2009).

In 1990, Nelson and Narens published a framework that unified the metacognitive judgments (for an adaptation, see Figure 25.1). The framework includes judgments made during various phases of self-regulated study that largely focus on judging one's memory and/or retrieval. These judgments are most closely related to any applied context in which someone needs to monitor and control his or her own learning and retrieval. A short-list includes students preparing for classes, accountants studying to get licensed, and older adults who are learning a new hobby (e.g., bird watching or scuba diving). People also can judge their cognitive processes and products while they are engaged in numerous everyday activities, such as reading, problem solving, writing a news story, developing a speech or argument, to name a few. Importantly, although many of our examples and discussion focus on the applied area relevant to people's self-regulated learning, the ideas posed in this chapter could be applied to people's metacognitive judgments made in any applied context.

We also highlight some judgments that have been introduced since the Nelson and Narens (1990) framework was published. The names of these judgments – along with their definitions and a relevant citation – are presented in Table 25.2. These judgments are arguably different varieties of a standard judgment of learning; they are all made during study and typically for individual items, yet the prompt for the judgment changes. For instance, the prompt for judgments of forgetting is meant to focus the learner on the likelihood of forgetting, whereas the prompt for judgments of retention is meant to focus the learner on the duration of retention. Despite these differences, one question continues to concern us. Namely, with each new variation on standard JOLs, are we simply investigating the same processes with different window dressing? More generally, will we need a different theory for each metacognitive judgment? With respect to applications, will we need

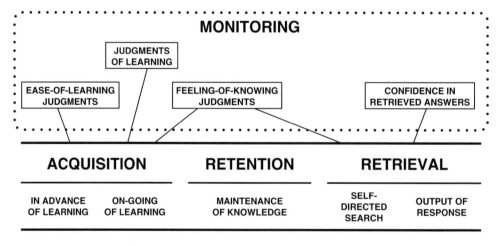

Figure 25.1   Framework of memory monitoring judgments as proposed by (and adapted from) Nelson and Narens (1990).

Table 25.2   Some metacognitive judgments introduced since Nelson and Narens (1990)

Judgment label	Definition	Citation
Judgment of prospective memory (JPM)	Prediction about the likelihood of remembering to complete an intended activity in the future	Schnitzspahn et al. (2011)
Judgment of forgetting (JOF)	Prediction of the likelihood that a recently studied item will be forgotten prior to the criterion test	Finn (2008)
Judgment of retention (JOR)	Prediction about the duration of time that a recently studied item will be retained	Tauber & Rhodes (2012)
Quality of encoding judgment (QUE)	Rating of how well a recently studied item had been encoded during study	Dunlosky et al. (2003)
Judgment of remember/know (JORK)	Prediction of the likelihood that an item will be remembered versus just known during the criterion test	McCabe & Soderstrom (2011)
Judgment of improvement (JOI)	Prediction about how much one's memory performance improved after another study trial	Townsend & Heit (2011)

Note. These judgments are variations on the standard judgments of learning (JOLs), which typically pertain to predicting the likelihood of success on an upcoming test.

a different approach and theory for understanding how students evaluate their learning and the quality of their test performance versus how radiologists judge the quality of their decisions? Or, are the basic principles that underlie the judgments similar, so learning about how people make one kind of judgment in a particular context will be relevant to other metacognitive judgments made in different applied contexts?

AN ISOMECHANISM FRAMEWORK OF METACOGNITIVE JUDGMENTS

Toward answering these questions, our specific interest is to further consider the cognitive processes and states that underlie all metacognitive judgments. Fortunately, an intriguing idea falls naturally from Nelson and Narens' (1990) framework, because it illustrates how all the judgments are interrelated via the phases of self-regulated study. The idea is simply that all metacognitive judgments are based on the same mechanism. We refer to this idea as the *isomechanism framework*, and we are using the term mechanism in its literal sense; namely, it is a system of parts working together. This *isomechanism*

framework of metacognitive judgments may seem intuitively plausible – given that all the judgments involve evaluating cognitive processes or products, why wouldn't they all be made in the same manner? If you agree with this intuition, then you may find it surprising that it is challenged by evidence from Leonesio and Nelson (1990), who argued that the judgments "do not tap memory in the same way" (p. 464). The evidence is provocative. College students studied 20 paired associates and made several metacognitive judgments, but for our current purposes, we will focus on only two. Namely, before study, the participants made an EOL judgment for each pair. Then, the pairs received repeated study-test trials until each one reached a learning criterion: half the pairs continued until they were correctly recalled once (called *learned items*), and the other half continued until they were correctly recalled four times (*overlearned items*). After a given pair met the criterion, a JOL was made, and then the item was dropped from further study. Each participant's EOLs and JOLs were correlated, and in contrast to an expectation from the isomechanism framework, the mean correlation (across participants) was only .19, suggesting a close-to-nil level of empirical overlap in the two judgments.

Although this evidence may curtail one's enthusiasm for the isomechanism framework, our own perspective is that this framework should be taken seriously. One reason is that the framework provides a plausible explanation for why different judgments may not be highly correlated (as in Leonesio & Nelson, 1990), which we discuss in further detail in a later section. Also, if the judgments are made in an identical manner, it would have implications for improving people's judgments across many domains and for the nature of the questions that would guide future research. With respect to application, if researchers discover a general principle that can improve people's judgment accuracy in one domain, this principle presumably could be used to help people make accurate judgments in other domains. With respect to guiding future research, some of the following questions should receive more attention. Assuming that all the judgments are made in the same manner, why do they behave differently under some contexts, such as established by the low correlation between EOLs and JOLs (Leonesio & Nelson, 1990)? And, why do different prompts for judgments (e.g., as listed in Table 25.2) influence how processes are recruited when making any given judgment? We hope that the current chapter will prove useful in directing future research to answer these questions.

The isomechanism framework claims that all metacognitive judgments are based on the same system of processes, which we discuss in the next section. To foreshadow, we do not equally emphasize all processes. Many heuristics would naturally apply to all judgments (Serra & Metcalfe, 2009), and noise in the judgment process would presumably also influence them all (e.g., Benjamin, Diaz, & Wee, 2009; Erev, Wallsten, & Budescu, 1994). We do not pursue these processes further (although we do consider the anchoring-and-adjustment heuristic below). Instead, we emphasize some of the shared processes that (a) seem the least controversial, even if all the details in how the processes operate are not entirely understood, (b) could

explain empirical dissociations among the judgments, and (c) have implications for improving people's judgment accuracy in real-world contexts.

ALL METACOGNITIVE JUDGMENTS ARE INFERENTIAL IN NATURE

People do not have direct access to underlying states of cognition when making metacognitive judgments. Instead, all judgments are inferential (for overviews, see Koriat, 1993; Schwartz, Benjamin, & Bjork, 1997). That is, when judging their on-going performance for a task, people use available cues to infer target performance, regardless of whether the task involves learning, problem solving, decision making, etc. The idea that all judgments are inferential gains further explanatory power when considered in the context of Egon Brunswik's (1956) model of human perception and judgment. Brunswik argued that people's perceptual judgments (e.g., about distance) are based on available cues, and hence the accuracy of the judgments is a function of the degree to which available cues influence those judgments and the degree to which those cues are predictive of target performance (which he called *ecological validity*).

Available cues here refer to any dimension – either objective or subjective – that differs across to-be-judged materials, whether they are differences in paired associates in JOL experiments or differences in radiographic images used to explore the accuracy of radiologists' confidence in their decisions. The number of possible dimensions that could vary across materials is unbounded, but fortunately, few dimensions likely vary systematically in any given context. In most experiments on metacognitive judgments, only one or two dimensions are varied and the experimenters do their best to control for others. For instance, to study how students judge their learning, Rhodes and Castel (2008) had college students study words that were printed in a large font (48 point) or a smaller font (18 point), and immediately after studying each word, they made a JOL. Finally, the students were asked to recall all the words. As shown in Figure 25.2, JOLs were significantly higher for words printed in large than smaller font, but recall did not differ as a function of font size. This cue had no ecological validity in these experiments and hence would not support accurate judgments. Similarly, in the experiment by Leonesio and Nelson (1990) described above, the learning criterion during study-test trials was varied, and JOLs were higher for items that were overlearned (i.e., four correct recall trials to reach criterion) than for items learned to a criterion of one correct recall. This cue was predictive of eventual recall and hence its higher ecological validity would support higher levels of judgment accuracy. Most important, the focal outcomes from both studies illustrate that people's JOLs are entrained by cues that are available when the judgments are made.

According to the isomechanism framework, all metacognitive judgments are based on inferences made about available cues. This framework provides a natural explanation for the lack of a relationship (or dissociation)

among judgments. In particular, low relationships (or dissociations) among metacognitive judgments are expected when (a) the available cues differ across judgments or (b) the judgment context changes the weight a particular cue is given when a judgment is constructed. We discuss cue availability next, and then turn to changes in cue weighting.

Figure 25.3 reorients the classical judgments into a framework that includes the availability of some possible cues for each one. The judgments can be made for any kinds of material or item under scrutiny; a non-exhaustive list includes paired associates (e.g., foreign language vocabulary), sentences, texts, speeches, pictures, and faces. What perhaps is most obvious from Figure 25.3 is that the cues that are available differ across the judgments. So, for instance, when studying paired associates (e.g., dog–spoon, table–chair), an EOL judgment can be based on the perceived relatedness of the pair, but it cannot be based on the fluency of retrieving the response; these later cues are available only to FOK and confidence judgments (and delayed JOLs, which are delayed well after study and can be based on retrieval from long-term memory, see Rhodes & Tauber, 2011).

As noted before, the judgments in Figure 25.3 are most relevant to self-regulated learning, but the main points emphasized by this figure – that people use cues to make metacognitive judgments and available cues can differ across contexts – holds for people's judgments made in other domains. To illustrate, we have compiled some occupations and activities in Table 25.3, which also includes an example metacognitive judgment that could be made in each case along with possible cues that could be available for the judgment. For some of these domains, the corresponding entries are based on speculation because research is not available to inform which cues are available and influential. Even so, our aim here is to merely demonstrate that one could apply the current framework to exploring how people make metacognitive judgments in any applied domain. Namely, for any given domain, the

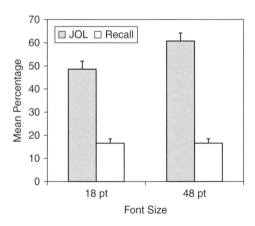

Figure 25.2 Mean judgment of learning (JOL) and recall performance for items presented in either a relatively small font (18 point) or a larger font (48 point) during study. From Rhodes and Castel (2008)

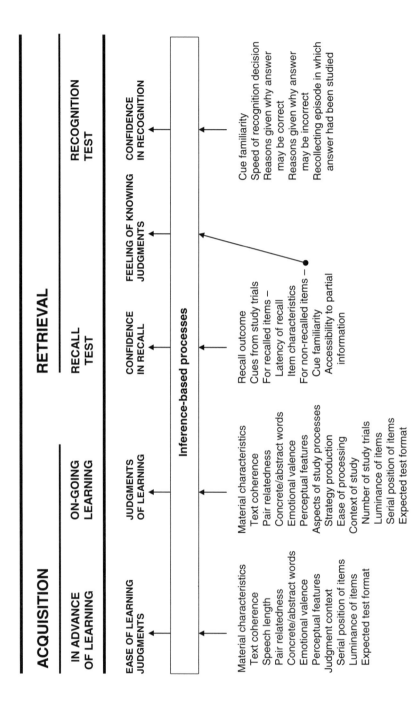

Figure 25.3   Classical metacognitive judgments along with some possible cues available for inference-based processing in single trial learning. Judgments of learning refer to those made immediately after studying a given item. Adapted from Dunlosky (2004)

Table 25.3 A few examples of metacognitive judgments from applied domains

Occupation or activity	Example metacognitive judgment	Example cues available
Public Speaking	Predicting the quality of the public speech	Fluency of giving practice talks
		Perceived quality of prior public speeches
Radiology	Confidence that a diagnosis is correct	Ease of making diagnosis
		Similiarity of current case to prior ones
Problem Solving	Predicting how one will solve transfer problems (e.g., math or physics)	Speed of solving new problems
		Past success on transfer tests
Teaching	Judging student's skill level about a particular topic	Memory for student's past performance
		Student's speed at answering practice questions
News writing	Confident that written content matches intended content	Ease of writing the passage
		Amount of experience writing about the topic

approach should be to discover the cues that are (or can be) available in any given context, and then evaluate both the degree to which people use the cues when making the relevant judgment as well as the degree to which those cues can and do support high levels of judgment accuracy.

One major point from Figure 25.3 (and Table 25.3) is merely that people's judgments may not be highly related (and even show dissociations) across some contexts, even though the isomechanism framework could explain the dissociation. To appreciate this point, recall the design of the study used by Leonesio and Nelson (1990). To collect EOL judgments, the 20 noun–noun pairs were presented in a circular array, and "without being informed that they would later learn the items, the subjects were instructed to examine the array and to indicate the item that they believed would be easiest to learn" (p. 465). For EOL judgments, the available cues would be any item characteristics that differ across the pairs and perhaps differences in the ease of reading them. By contrast, at the time of JOLs, a new cue was available, because the pairs were learned to different criteria, and these differences in criteria had a substantial influence on their JOLs. Thus, the low relationship between EOL judgments and JOLs in this study is naturally explained by the isomechanism framework. It also predicts that if the available cues overlap more, then these two judgments will be more highly related.

This prediction has been confirmed in one experiment (Dunlosky & Matvey, 2001, Experiment 1) in which the focal cue was the relatedness between two words in a paired associate: some pairs were related (e.g., table–chair) and some were unrelated (e.g., dog–spoon). In the first phase, college students made EOL judgments for all the pairs. In the next phase, each item was individually presented for 5 sec for study, and immediately after each one was presented, a JOL was made. A cued recall test was administered, which verified that related pairs were better recalled than were unrelated pairs. Most important, the relatedness cue was available for both EOL judgments and JOLs, and as predicted, judgments in this context were highly related (mean correlations between individual participants' EOL and JOLs was approximately .68, which is considerably higher than the .19 value reported by Leonesio & Nelson, 1990).

The isomechanism framework can be used to generate testable hypotheses about the degree to which different metacognitive judgments will be related. Most generally, it predicts that an available cue that influences one metacognitive judgment will typically influence any other, assuming the cue is available (in the environment or in working memory) at the time both judgments are made. We qualified the prediction above with "typically" because even within the isomechanism framework, a cue may not consistently influence a given judgment. Consider three examples. The first example involves cue overshadowing (Price & Yates, 1993). In particular, assume that one cue (call it cue A) overlaps between EOL judgments and JOLs. This cue may influence EOL judgments but not JOLs, if a different cue (B) available to only JOLs overshadows the use of the shared cue (A). The second example pertains to *how* cues influence judgments. For instance, inferences about how cues influence target performance are sometimes based on people's theories about how a cue influences target performance. As we discuss in the next section, the prompts for metacognitive judgments may influence which theories people use and hence how they may weigh different cues in making the judgments. When different prompts encourage people to use different theories, then the judgments will also dissociate; but even here, an isomechanism framework still provides a unified account for how people make the judgments.

Finally, the third example about when a cue is available for two judgments but only influences one of them involves people's beliefs about (or folk theories of) the task. In terms of a simple learning task, the influence of a cue on judgments can be mediated by a person's belief that the cue will influence memory. For instance, college students believe that diagrams (or pictures) generally improve their learning of text materials, and their JOLs are higher when texts are presented with diagrams than when they are not presented. This effect of diagrams on JOLs even occurs when the diagrams do not influence criterion test performance (Serra & Dunlosky, 2010). In some contexts, such a belief may develop through task experience, so that a cue may not influence judgments made earlier in the task (prior to the development of that belief) but will influence judgments made after the belief has developed. The idea here is that people can update their knowledge about cues through task experience and hence the newly acquired knowledge can influence later judgments.

Such *knowledge updating* and its influence on metacognitive judgments have been investigated using multiple study-test trials in which a focal cue is available on both trials (e.g., Bieman-Copland & Charness, 1994; Dunlosky & Hertzog, 2000; Hertzog, Price, Burpee, Frentzel, Feldstein, & Dunlosky, 2009; Tauber & Rhodes, 2010). Consider results from Tauber and Rhodes (2010, Experiment 3). During the first trial, participants studied face–noun pairs, which were presented individually for 4 sec each. After studying a pair, they made a JOL by predicting the likelihood of recalling the noun when later shown the face. The cue pertained to the kind of noun, which was either proper (Mr. *Baker*) or common (occupation is a *baker*). After studying and judging 20 pairs (10 with each kind of noun), a cued recall test was administered in which each face was shown and the target noun had to be recalled (in this case, Mr. *Baker* or employment as a *baker*). As shown on the left side of Figure 25.4, recall performance on the first trial was greater when the noun was an occupation than a name. However, this cue did not influence JOLs. Focal questions from this experiment were, will participants learn about the effect of this cue from experience during this first trial, and will this updated knowledge influence JOLs on the second trial? The second trial itself included all new face–noun pairs, so that any changes in JOLs on the second trial could not be attributed to monitoring of memory for the specific pairs on the first trial. Most important on the second trial (right side of Figure 25.4), the focal cue did influence JOLs in the expected direction, with JOLs being higher for occupations than for names. What is impressive is that the same judgment (a JOL) was not influenced by an available cue during the first study-test trial but was influenced on the second trial. Certainly, the same processes underlie JOLs made on both trials, but in this context, the cue had differential effects on the same judgment because people's beliefs changed with task experience.

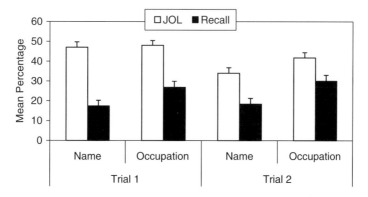

Figure 25.4 Mean judgments of learning (JOLs) and recall performance for names and occupations in each of two study-test trials. From Tauber and Rhodes (2010, Experiment 3)

INFERENCES ABOUT CUES CAN BE ANALYTIC OR NONANALYTIC

A given cue presumably can influence a judgment in multiple ways. Different processes for these influences have been proposed, and most proposals have included some form of dichotomy that parallels analytic versus nonanalytic processing. *Analytic inferences* are based on theories or beliefs about how a given cue influences the target memory performance. *Nonanalytic inferences* are based on subjective experiences people have as they perform a task. For instance, Kelley and Jacoby (1996) had college students judge how difficult anagrams would be for others to solve, and in one condition, the students solved the problems before they judged difficulty for others. Higher judgments of solution difficulty were related to slower solution latencies, leading Kelley and Jacoby (1996) to conclude that the students "used their subjective experience of anagram difficulty as a basis for judging for others" (p. 163). In this case, judging anagram difficulty presumably involved a nonanalytic inference based on subjective experience instead of the conscious use of a theory about how various cues might be related to solution difficulty. Other theories of how cues influence metacognitive judgments offer similar distinctions to analytic and nonanalytic processes, which include (respectively) theory- and

experience-based judgments (e.g., Koriat, Nussinson, Bless, & Shaked, 2008), theory- and mnemonic-based judgments (Koriat & Bjork, 2006), and dual-process frameworks that include controlled and automatic processes (Toth, Daniels, & Solinger, 2011). As noted by Koriat and Bjork (2006), the important distinction is between basing judgments on the deliberate deduction from rules (i.e., an analytic inference) versus relying on "internal cues that are used automatically and unconsciously to give rise to sheer subjective feelings" (p. 1134; i.e., a nonanalytic inference).

Poor judgment accuracy then could arise from an over-reliance on incorrect rules (beliefs), the influence of nonanalytic inferences that are based on cues with low ecological validity, or merely the lack of ecologically valid cues. Discovering which inference dominates a particular judgment should offer insight into improving people's judgment accuracy because remediation of poor accuracy can be more closely linked to its underlying cause. For example, if highly trained professionals are shown to over-rely on nonanalytic cues that can reduce their judgment accuracy (as in radiologists, see Brooks, Norman, & Allen, 1991), then perhaps they could be trained to ignore those cues and to rely on more diagnostic ones that are available in the judgment context (see Koriat & Bjork, 2006). Unfortunately, despite decades of research on metacognitive judgments, we know very little about which inferences dominate people's metacognitive judgments.

For any given cue, which inference dominates: analytic or nonanalytic?

A challenge is to discover how these inferences mediate the relationship between available cues (bottom portion of Figure 25.3) and the various judgments; the challenge becomes obvious when one realizes just a few of the simplest ways that these inferences may mediate the influence of a given cue. To illustrate, consider this equation, which undoubtedly oversimplifies yet is just meant to illustrate some subtle, but important, points:

$$j = n(q) \qquad (1)$$

j stands for a judgment for a given item, q refers to the available cue in question, and the function n stands for a nonanalytic inference based on subjective experience that mediates the relationship between the cue and the judgment. In this case, it is assumed that people are not aware of such nonanalytic inferences (that is what makes them nonanalytic) or how variability in the cue is translated into different subjective experiences.

Contrast Equation 1 with the following:

$$j = a(q) \qquad (2)$$

For Equation 2, a refers to an analytic inference based on theories about how the cue in question influences memory. In this case, one would expect people to be aware of the cue and to explicitly state that the cue is diagnostic of target performance as specified by the person's folk theory of memory.

When considering these simple equations, several alternatives become evident, but we will focus on only one here:

$$j = a[n(q)] \qquad (3)$$

For Equation 3, the person uses an analytic inference about subjective experiences (i.e.,

nonanalytic inferences) to inform his or her judgment. So, the person may think, "When I have this internal experience, it typically means that I'm going to remember, so I'll make a higher judgment for this item." We doubt that Equation 3 is what most (if any) theorists were considering when proposing the dichotomy between analytic and nonanalytic inferences, but its possibility (if not plausibility) cannot be denied.

Empirically distinguishing between which process (as embodied by equations 1–3) mediates the influence of any given cue will likely be challenging enough,[1] but the challenge is magnified further by the implicit assumption that subjective experiences (which are not measured but pertain to unobservable constructs) are correlated with observable cues. In fact, it is the relationship between these observable cues and judgments that supports the conclusion that subjective experience mediates the effect of a given cue on judgments, which further complicates efforts to discover how cues influence people's judgments. How this relationship complicates matters is illustrated by the following hypothetical experiment. During study, participants are presented with pairs of antonyms, but they are not presented with the entire target. Instead, they are presented with the cue (hot) and the first letter of the target (c _ _ _) and must generate the target from memory. Participants type each response (in this case, "cold") on a computer keyboard, and the latency of the first key press is recorded. After generating the target, they then predict the likelihood of recalling the target when shown the cue on the upcoming test (i.e., a JOL). Each participant's generation latencies and JOLs are correlated across items, and in this hypothetical experiment, generation latencies are negatively correlated with JOLs; that is, longer latencies are related to less confidence that an item will be remembered. Such evidence is often interpreted as supporting the following conclusions: (a) that generation fluency (i.e., a cue measured by generation latency) influences people's JOLs, and also, (b) that this relationship is mediated by a nonanalytic inference. That is, as per Equation 1, differences in generation fluency across items produce different subjective experiences, which in turn directly mediate the effect of generation fluency on JOLs. Although the first conclusion is relatively convincing (despite the correlational nature of the evidence), the latter conclusion is rather speculative.

The conclusion that the effect is mediated by a nonanalytic inference is reasonable, but other possibilities seem just as reasonable. To understand why, we have illustrated some of the ideas from this hypothetical experiment in Figure 25.5, where generation fluency and subjective experience are unobservables and generation latency and JOLs are observables. The top panel illustrates the aforementioned conclusion in which path "a" between subjective experience (nonanalytic inference) and JOLs is causal; that is, Equation 1 holds and differences in generation fluency (the cue) are mediated by subjective experience. By contrast, path "b" is dashed to emphasize that the relationship between generation latency and JOLs is considered epiphenomenal – the former is merely an indicator of the underlying subjective experience, which itself directly causes changes in JOLs. Compare this panel with the bottom one,

where now path "b" is considered causal in that people are using a theory about generation latency to make the judgment (i.e., "the harder I work to generate an item, the less likely I'll remember it"); that is, Equation 2 holds, where differential fluency produces differences in response latency, which in turn is used in conjunction with folk theories (or beliefs) about memory to infer the likelihood of recalling the target.

An empirical relationship between objective measures of many kinds of processing fluency (e.g., reading, retrieval, or generation fluency) and judgments has been established in many contexts (Alter & Oppenheimer, 2009), yet it is safe to say that no one is sure whether this relationship is mediated by analytic or nonanalytic processes. The reason for such uncertainty lies simply in the fact that very little empirical evidence is available to establish the contribution of analytic versus nonanalytic inferences to metacognitive judgments for any given cue presented in Figure 25.3. In the case of processing fluency, it is our sense from reading the literature that the Zeitgeist is that the effects of fluency on metacognitive judgments are mediated by a nonanalytic inference. Nevertheless, there is evidence suggesting that Equation 2 may provide a better account, at least in one

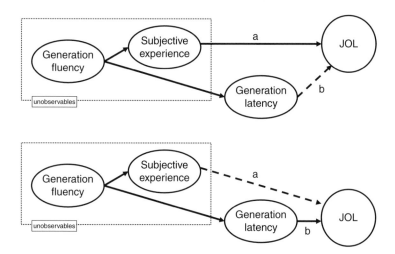

Figure 25.5   Influence of generation fluency mediated by a nonanalytic inference (top panel) and by an analytic inference (bottom panel). See text for details

context. Matvey, Dunlosky, and Guttentag (2001) used a method similar to the hypothetical experiment described above: College students were asked to generate targets given various cues (e.g., rhyme: cave – s _ _ _) and then made a JOL. As latencies increased, JOLs decreased, which would typically be interpreted as the influence of a cue (in this case, retrieval fluency) that is mediated by a nonanalytic inference. This interpretation is called into question, however, by results from another group. In particular, an observer group made predictions about how well learners would remember the targets. Namely, each observer unobtrusively watched a learner (standard JOL group) generate the targets, and then the observer made a JOL predicting the learner's performance. The correlation between the learner's generation latencies and the observer's JOLs were also negative and of the same magnitude of the learner's latency-JOL correlations. This equivalence occurred despite the fact that observers could not themselves generate the targets, so they had absolutely no subjective experience of generating, but could use only retrieval latency as a cue for their judgments. These findings are consistent with the conclusion that fluency effects are partly mediated by an analytic inference and hence should shed some doubt as to whether all fluency effects are by fiat mediated by a nonanalytic inference.

To conclude this section, we acknowledge that much research has been conducted to establish the kinds of cues that influence metacognitive judgments (for reviews, see Dunlosky & Metcalfe, 2009), and researchers are still hot in pursuit of discovering new cues that make a difference. We applaud these endeavors, but we also want to emphasize the value of developing new methods to explore the degree to which nonanalytic and analytic inferences contribute to the influence of any given cue (or combinations of cues). Such methodological advances will be critical for making further progress toward understanding metacognitive states and how people can improve their judgment accuracy.

Prompts for judgments may influence how cues are weighted

Not only may the influence of cues on judgments be mediated by analytic and nonanalytic inferences, the judgments may draw on various cues differentially as the context of the judgment changes. These contexts change and the influence they have on which cues will be influential is well illustrated by changes in prompts to JOLs (Table 25.2). An outcome from Rawson, Dunlosky, and McDonald (2002, Experiment 2) demonstrates how a simple change in the prompt can influence which cues learners attend to when they construct judgments. In particular, college students studied pairs of sentences; each pair was designed to express a different principle (e.g., why viruses are not believed to cause cancer), and the students were instructed to do their best to understand the central principles. After studying a given pair, the students either (a) judged how well they understood the principle or (b) judged the likelihood that they would correctly answer a question about the principle on an upcoming test. Importantly, regardless of whether participants were judging their current learning or were predicting future performance, they were led to believe that half of the pairs would be tested after a short delay (15 min) and half would be tested after a longer delay (two weeks). The change in judgment prompt (from an evaluation of current learning to a prediction of future performance) was expected to shift participants' cue use in a straightforward fashion. Namely, the focal cue (retention interval) was expected to influence *predictions* about test performance, because most college students (and even children) believe that forgetting occurs over time; by contrast, this belief was not expected to be activated when the college students merely judged how well the sentence pairs had been learned. As shown in Figure 25.6, this prediction was supported. The main point here is that the fundamental processes underlying the two judgments are identical, but the prompt about future test

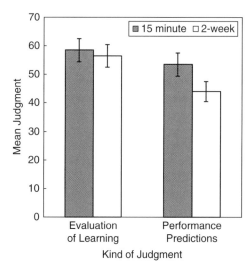

Figure 25.6   Mean judgment when participants were anticipating either a short (15-min) or longer (2-week) retention interval. From Rawson, Dunlosky, and McDonald (2002)

performance increased the likelihood that participants would attend to the retention interval cue when making the judgments (for similar evidence, see Koriat, Bjork, Sheffer, & Bar, 2004).

These observations also suggest some important questions to drive research in the field. For instance, "Exactly how do different prompts shift people's sampling of available cues?", and, "Why is the same judgment (e.g., a JOL) influenced by a cue in one context but not in another?" As we explore further in the "Future directions" section, we suspect that systematically investigating answers to these kinds of question will provide much insight into the nature of how people construct metacognitive judgments.

ANCHORING AND ADJUSTMENT

Many of the metacognitive judgments are made on some form of rating scale, such as percent likelihood of success (0–100 percent) or a Likert rating scale (0–10). According to

the isomechanism framework, the processes that influence people's use of these scales will influence all metacognitive judgments. For instance, when uncertain, people are expected to anchor their judgments near the middle of the scale, especially in the context of laboratory experiments. As Keren (1991) noted, "the laboratory setting creates an expectation of an intermediate level of difficulty. The two extremes, namely a task that is either so difficult that performance is on a chance level or a task that is so easy that performance will always be perfect or close to perfect, are assumed unlikely" (p. 255). This insight can be illustrated with JOLs: When people study a list of relatively homogeneous items, the mean judgment of learning is typically around 40 to 50 percent. Importantly, note that this use of a mid-point of the rating scale (i.e., a JOL value of 40 to 50 percent) does not mean that the learner believes there is a 40 to 50 percent chance of recall; instead, the value means the person is uncertain about his or her memory. Consistent with this claim, when people are asked to judge their confidence in their JOLs, they rate middle-of-the-scale JOLs with the least amount of confidence and JOLs nearer either end point of the scale (closer to 0 or 100 percent) with higher levels of confidence (Dunlosky, Serra, Matvey, & Rawson, 2005).

Based on the anchoring-and-adjustment heuristic, such anchors of uncertainty are adjusted given the presence of various cues that suggest an item is more (or less) likely to be recalled, as alluded to above. This proposal also provides some clarity into why cues that are manipulated *between* participants often have a minimal influence on people's judgments. For example, like Rawson et al. (2002), Koriat et al. (2004) manipulated retention interval; in contrast to Rawson et al. (2002), however, in some experiments, retention interval was manipulated between participants. Each group presumably used the appropriate anchor for the experimental context, yet would not adjust for the various levels of retention interval because they did not experience those levels (for a detailed theory on why verbal reports typically would not be influenced by between-participant manipulations, see Ericsson & Simon, 1980). By contrast, when Koriat et al. (2004) manipulated retention interval within each participant, the judgments differentiated between items slated for longer versus shorter retention intervals. Just because a person experiences all levels of the cue and believes a particular cue will influence memory, however, does not mean it will necessarily influence the person's judgments. For instance, college students presumably believe that their memory will be better if they restudy materials than if they study them only once. Nevertheless, when the number of study-test trials is manipulated within each participant, it sometimes fails to influence their judgments, with JOLs being no greater for items studied twice than items studied once (Kornell & Bjork, 2009; Kornell, Rhodes, Castel, & Tauber, 2011). Such null effects are mysterious and suggest that people's item-by-item judgments are not always sensitive to beliefs about memory.

Most important, the various heuristics, which include anchoring and adjustment, have been successfully applied to understanding how people make a variety of metacognitive judgments (e.g., for a review, see Serra & Metcalfe, 2009), and according to the isomechanism framework, these heuristics are expected to influence all judgments in a similar manner across domains.

FUTURE DIRECTIONS

We have discussed the isomechanism framework with other researchers who have been investigating how metacognitive judgments are made. Their responses have consistently fallen into one of two camps: either "of course this framework is correct, because how else could it be" or "the isomechanism framework is ludicrous; of course the judgments are at least partly different." At different times developing this framework, we have even found ourselves arguing for both camps. Moreover, as a general framework that includes multiple processes, a creative researcher can likely use it to explain any set of findings in a post hoc manner. Nevertheless, the explanations it provides for any set of data can be used to derive testable hypotheses that themselves can be disconfirmed. For instance, a post hoc explanation for results from Leonesio and Nelson (1990) was developed from this framework and a new prediction (that greater cue overlap will better align EOLs and JOLs) was developed that could have failed to pass an empirical test. Perhaps most important, we did not propose this framework as an alternative to other theories of judgments, which typically are more highly specified and focus on an individual judgment. Instead, we proposed this framework to stimulate further thought and discussion about (the possible) unified nature of metacognitive judgments, and we also find it useful for providing directions for future applied and theoretical research. Some of these directions come from the isomechanism claim itself, and others are based more on the processes that have been proposed to underlie people's judgments.

DIRECTIONS FOR APPLIED RESEARCH ON METACOGNITION

A major reason for the interest in metacognitive states and judgments is that people often use these judgments to control their subsequent thoughts and behavior. Poor judgment accuracy would also limit the effectiveness of self control (for reviews, see Dunlosky, Hertzog, Kennedy, & Thiede, 2005; Koriat & Goldsmith, 1996). Thus, if one understands how people make metacognitive judgments, perhaps techniques can be developed to improve their judgment accuracy. One implication of the isomechanism framework – or any framework that focuses on cue-based inferences – is that to obtain higher levels of judgment accuracy, we need either (a) to discover the available cues that have high ecological validity (Brunswik, 1956) in a given applied context (e.g., see Table 25.3) and then train learners to use these cues or (b) to develop contexts or activities that will produce cues with high ecological validity. Perusal of Figure 25.3 suggests two reasons why the second approach may be more fruitful with regard to improving students' judgment accuracy. First, many of the most highly diagnostic cues listed in Figure 25.3 will not be consistently available in day-to-day learning contexts. For instance, when a student is preparing for an exam on foreign-language vocabulary (e.g., cheval–horse), many of the diagnostic cues that are manipulated in experiments (e.g., the relatedness of words in a pair) would likely not be available. Second, many cues that are regularly available (e.g., processing ease, perceptual features, etc.) typically have low ecological validity.

One common activity where good cues are not consistently available is in reading. For instance, when students are reading a chapter from a textbook, they may judge how well they understand the content of each paragraph (which is simply a metacognitive judgment about text materials, e.g., see Figure 25.3, under "Material characteristics"). The accuracy of these judgments is notoriously poor (Dunlosky & Lipko, 2007; Thiede, Anderson, & Therriault, 2003). Such poor accuracy should not be too surprising because it is not evident which cues students should be using as a basis for their judgments. Another potential problem when students are trying to predict their performance on upcoming tests is that they generally do not yet know the makeup of the exam (does it tap memory or comprehension?), so practice with the expected test may help them either generate or identify more valid cues. This possibility has recently been confirmed by Thiede, Wiley, and Griffin (2011), who told college students to expect an inference test (and gave them practice examples), which enhanced their ability to accurately predict their comprehension of text materials. So, in this case, ecologically valid cues are not immediately available, but students presumably have some success at identifying valid cues when they better understand the goal for reading and how they will be tested.

Unfortunately, situations in which good cues are not immediately available are common in everyday contexts. Accordingly, one goal for future research should be to discover activities or forms of external support that will produce valid cues and consistently high levels of judgment accuracy. Applied research along these lines has already shown promise for identifying techniques that improve the accuracy of most of the classical judgments (for overviews, see Dunlosky & Metcalfe, 2009). These techniques in some way allow people to more effectively scrutinize their cognitive processes by helping them to sample cues that have high ecological validity. Two examples will help to illustrate. The first concerns improving people's learning of health materials by providing external support to improve their judgment accuracy, and the second concerns improving older adults' source memory by instructing them how to use valid cues. For the former, Rawson, O'Neil, and Dunlosky (2011) had participants study texts on how to effectively manage diabetes. Participants regulated their own study, and one group was provided with a computer interface that helped them more accurately judge how well they had learned about various aspects of diabetes and how to manage it (for details, see figure 6 in Rawson et al., 2011). Final test performance was higher for those making judgments with this interface, and secondary analyses attributed their higher test performance both to higher levels of accuracy and to better control of learning (see also, Thomas & McDaniel, 2007). For the latter example, older adults sometimes have difficulties accurately judging the source of a memory, and Multhaup (1995) found that part of their difficulty is that they do not rely on the retrieval of cues that would help them infer the source. Thus, when older adults were instructed to rely more on recollections about the possible sources of a memory, the accuracy of their source monitoring judgments increased to the level of younger adults (Multhaup, 1995).

Developing techniques, instructions, or external support to help people use valid cues is not the only way to change how people make metacognitive judgments and to improve their accuracy. Another avenue is to give learners experience with various tasks and to provide feedback about their metacognitive biases. For instance, people's JOLs are higher for related paired associates (e.g., dog–cat) than for unrelated ones (e.g., table–collar); in fact, relative to other cues, pair relatedness has one of the largest and most robust effects on JOLs. However, the influence of this cue on JOLs occurs even when recall is low for related pairs. For instance, a pair may be related (e.g., rain–umbrella) and hence receive an inflated JOL, but the likelihood of recalling "umbrella" when later shown "rain" is low (i.e., the forward association from rain to umbrella is normatively low and hence does not help cued recall performance). Koriat and Bjork (2006) gave students a practice study-test trial with these tricky pairs. As expected, their JOLs were inflated as compared with their lower level of recall performance. After the test, students were given feedback about the actual rates of recall and were encouraged to think about the discrepancy between their JOLs and actual performance. On the next study-test trial, new pairs were presented, and now students' JOLs were lower for the tricky pairs. Thus, the test experience with feedback debiased students' judgments so that they aligned better with the influence of this cue on performance. Whether task experience with feedback can be used more generally to help learners focus on valid cues across different judgments is an open issue.

DIRECTIONS FOR THEORY-FOCUSED RESEARCH ON METACOGNITION AND MEMORY

One avenue for theory-focused research that becomes immediately evident from considering the isomechanism framework is to demonstrate that different processes underlie two or more metacognitive judgments; that is, to set out to disconfirm the primary assumption of the isomechanism framework. Such endeavors would likely prove informative, because they would necessitate a comparative approach among different metacognitive judgments (e.g., Costermans, Lories, & Ansay, 1992; Dunlosky & Hertzog, 2000; Kelemen, Frost, & Weaver, 2000; Leonesio & Nelson, 1990).

One comparative approach that shows much promise involves systematically comparing different *prompts* for judgments. Little is known about how these prompts operate, even though different prompts for JOLs (Table 25.2) can lead to different conclusions about how people evaluate their cognitive processes and products. For instance, in one experiment (Koriat et al., 2004, Experiment 1), participants studied paired associates and judged that they would recall 50 percent of them a week after study. By contrast, when participants were asked how long they would remember the same kinds of item (Tauber & Rhodes, 2012), they reported that most of them would be forgotten after 15 minutes! The former experiment demonstrates the inaccuracy of people's judgments and suggests they underestimate forgetting, whereas the latter suggests people understand how quickly they can forget. Given how quickly people often forget materials, it seems reasonable to encourage students to ask, "How soon will I forget?", which could lead to more accurate judgments. Moreover, this paradox raises some interesting questions for future research. Exactly how do changes in judgment prompts influence people's monitoring? Which prompts are most likely to improve the accuracy of metacognitive judgments, and why? Answers to these questions could be attained through comparing how different prompts and cues influence the different metacognitive judgments; taking such a comparative approach to exploring metacognitive judgments is perhaps the most obvious recommendation from the isomechanism framework.

CONCLUSION

People judge the quality of their cognitive processes and products in many everyday contexts. Students use the judgments to make decisions about how much more to study, and they use self testing to judge whether they know the class materials well enough for an upcoming exam. When asked a question (e.g., "How does one find one's way to a local event?"), one may evaluate the quality of their knowledge and elect not to respond to the question if their confidence is low. When doctors are evaluating a recent diagnosis, if their initial confidence in the decision was high, they likely would not spend further time on that particular case. More generally, in many occupations and activities, people rely on their judgments and evaluations to make decisions about how to think or behave. Thus, it is important to understand how people judge and evaluate on-going cognitive processes and the quality of the products that arise from them. Much progress has been made in the past 40 years since Hart (1965) published his seminal article on the measurement of FOK accuracy, but yet many mysteries still remain, such as when analytic versus nonanalytic inferences influence judgments and how changing the prompts for judgments provoke people to use different (or more valid) cues. We look forward to future research that attempts to solve these mysteries, and we hope that the isomechanism framework, which highlights the similarities among metacognitive judgments, will be helpful to such endeavors.

ACKNOWLEDGMENTS

This research was supported by the James S. McDonnell Foundation 21st Century Science Initiative in Bridging Brain, Mind, and Behavior Collaborative Award. We thank Michael Serra, Asher Koriat, and Matt Rhodes for constructive comments about this chapter.

NOTE

1 As we discuss later in the text, some of the implications of these equations are testable. However, we mainly described these equations to clarify the challenges that arise when one attempts to understand the influence of analytic and nonanalytic inferences. Even our analysis underestimates the challenge, because it seems likely that the two kinds of inference may combine to mediate the influence of any given cue (or multiple cues) on metacognitive judgments; and, if so, more complex equations would be required to describe these processes and how they are weighted in making a given judgment.

REFERENCES

Alter, A. L., & Oppenheimer, D. M. (2009). Uniting the tribes of fluency to form a metacognitive nation. *Personality and Social Psychology Review, 13*, 219–235. doi: 10.1177/1088868309341564

Arbuckle, T. Y., & Cuddy, L. L. (1969). Discrimination of item strength at time of presentation. *Journal of Experimental Psychology, 81*, 126–131. doi: 10.1037/h0027455

Bailey, H., Dunlosky, J., & Hertzog, C. (2010). Metacognitive training at home: Does it improve older adults' learning? *Gerontology, 56*, 414–420. doi: 10.1159/000266030

Benjamin, A. S., Diaz, M., & Wee, S. (2009). Signal detection with criterion noise: Applications to recognition memory. *Psychological Review, 116*, 84–115. doi: 10.1037/a0014351

Bieman-Copland, S., & Charness, N. (1994). Memory knowledge and memory monitoring in adulthood. *Psychology and Aging, 9*, 287–302. doi: 10.1037/0882-7974.9.2.287

Brooks, L. R., Norman, G. R., & Allen, S. W. (1991). Role of specific similarity in a medical diagnostic task. *Journal of Experimental Psychology: General, 120*, 278–287. doi: 10.1037/0096-3445.120.3.278

Brunswik, E. (1956). *Perception and representative design of psychological experiments.* Berkeley, CA: University of California Press.

Costermans, J., Lories, G., & Ansay, C. (1992). Confidence level and feeling of knowing in question answering: The weight of inferential processes. *Journal of Experimental Psychology: Learning, Memory, and Cognition, 18*, 142–150. doi: 10.1037/0278-7393.18.1.142

Dunlosky, J. (2004). Metacognition. In R. R. Hunt and H. C. Ellis (Eds.), *Fundamentals of cognitive psychology* (7th edn.). New York: McGraw-Hill College.

Dunlosky, J., & Hertzog, C. (2000). Updating knowledge about strategy effectiveness: A componential analysis of learning about strategy effectiveness from task experience. *Psychology & Aging, 15*, 462–474. doi: 10.1037/0882-7974.15.3.462

Dunlosky, J., Hertzog, C., Kennedy, M., & Thiede, K. (2005). The self-monitoring approach for effective learning. *Cognitive Technology, 10*, 4–11.

Dunlosky, J., Kubat-Silman, A. K., & Hertzog, C. (2003). Effects of aging on the magnitude and accuracy of quality-of-encoding judgments. *American Journal of Psychology, 116*, 431–454. doi: 10.2307/1423502

Dunlosky, J., & Lipko, A. R. (2007). Metacomprehension: A brief history and how to improve its accuracy. *Current Directions in Psychological Science, 16*, 228–232. doi: 10.1111/j.1467-8721.2007.00509.x

Dunlosky, J., & Matvey, G. (2001). Empirical analysis of the intrinsic-extrinsic distinction of judgments of learning (JOLs): Effects of relatedness and serial position on JOLs. *Journal of Experimental Psychology: Learning, Memory, and Cognition, 27*, 1180–1191. doi: 10.1037/0278-7393.27.5.1180

Dunlosky, J., & Metcalfe, J. (2009). *Metacognition.* Beverly Hills, CA: Sage.

Dunlosky, J., & Rawson, K. A. (2012). Overconfidence produces underachievement: Inaccurate self evaluations undermine students' learning and retention. *Learning and Instruction, 22*, 271–280.

Dunlosky, J., Serra, M. J., Matvey, G., & Rawson, K. A. (2005). Second-order judgments about judgments of learning. *Journal of General Psychology, 132*, 335–346. doi: 10.3200/GENP.132.4.335-346

Erev, I., Wallsten, T. S., & Budescu, D. V. (1994). Simultaneous over- and underconfidence: The role of error in judgment processes. *Psychological Review, 101*, 519–527. doi: 10.1037/0033-295X.101.3.519

Ericsson, K. A., & Simon, H. A. (1980). Verbal reports as data. *Psychological Review, 87*, 215–251. doi: 10.1037/0033-295X.87.3.215

Finn, B. (2008). Framing effects on metacognitive monitoring and control. *Memory & Cognition, 36*, 813–821. doi: 10.3758/MC.36.4813

Hacker, D., Dunlosky, J., & Graesser, A. (Eds.) (2009). *Handbook of metacognition in education.* New York: Psychology Press.

Hart, J. T. (1965). Memory and the feeling-of-knowing experience. *Journal of Educational Psychology, 56*, 208–216.

Hertzog, C., Price, J., Burpee, A., Frentzel, W. J., Feldstein, S., & Dunlosky, J. (2009). Why do people show

minimal knowledge updating with task experience: Inferential deficit or experimental artifact? *Quarterly Journal of Experimental Psychology, 62*, 155–173. doi: 10.1080/17470210701855520

Kelemen, A. L., Frost, P. J., & Weaver, C. A. (2000). Individual differences in metacognition: Evidence against a general metacognitive ability. *Memory & Cognition, 28*, 92–107. doi: 10.1037/0278-7393.32.5.1133

Kelley, C. M., & Jacoby, L. L. (1996). Adult egocentrism: Subjective experience versus analytic bases for judgment. *Journal of Memory & Language, 35*, 157–175. doi: 10.1006/jmla.1996.0009

Keren, G. (1991). Calibration and probability judgments: Conceptual and methodological issues. *Acta Psychologica, 77*, 217–273. doi: 10.1016/0001-6918(91)90036-Y

Koriat, A. (1993). How do we know that we know? The accessibility model of the feeling of knowing. *Psychological Review, 100*, 609–639. doi: 10.1037/0033-295X.100.4.609

Koriat, A., & Bjork, R. A. (2006). Mending metacognitive illusions: A comparison of mnemonic-based and theory-based procedures. *Journal of Experimental Psychology: Learning, Memory, and Cognition, 32*, 1133–1145. doi: 10.1037/0278-7393.32.5.1133

Koriat, A., Bjork, R. A., Sheffer, L., & Bar, S. K. (2004). Predicting one's own forgetting: The role of experience-based and theory-based processes. *Journal of Experimental Psychology: General, 133*, 646–656. doi: 10.1037/0096-3445.133.4.643

Koriat, A., & Goldsmith, M. (1996). Monitoring and control processes in the strategic regulation of memory accuracy. *Psychological Review, 103*, 490–517. doi: 10.1037/0033-295X.103.3.490

Koriat, A., Nussinson, R., Bless, H., & Shaked, N. (2008). Information-based and experience-based metacognitive judgments: Evidence from subjective confidence. In J. Dunlosky and R. A. Bjork (Eds.), *Handbook of metamemory and memory.* (pp. 117–136). New York: Psychology Press..

Kornell, N., & Bjork, R. A. (2009). A stability bias in human memory: Overestimating remembering and underestimating learning. *Journal of Experimental Psychology: General, 138*, 449–468. doi: 10.1037/a0017350

Kornell, N., Rhodes, M. G., Castel, A. D., & Tauber, S. K. (2011). The ease-of-processing heuristic and the stability bias: Dissociating memory, memory beliefs, and memory judgments. *Psychological Science, 22*, 787–794. doi: 10.1177/0956797611407929

Lane, S. M., Roussel, C. C., Villa, D., & Morita, S. K. (2007). Features and feedback: Enhancing metamnemonic knowledge at retrieval reduces source-monitoring errors. *Journal of Experimental Psychology: Learning, Memory, and Cognition*, *33*, 1131–1142. doi: 10.1037/0278-7393.33.6.1131

Leonesio, R. J., & Nelson, T. O. (1990). Do different metamemory judgments tap the same underlying aspects of memory? *Journal of Experimental Psychology: Learning, Memory, and Cognition*, *16*, 464–470. doi: 10.1037/0278-7393.16.3.464

Matvey, G., Dunlosky, J., & Guttentag, R. (2001). Fluency of retrieval at study affects judgments of learning (JOLs): An analytic or nonanalytic basis for JOLs? *Memory & Cognition*, *29*, 222–232.

McCabe, D. P., & Soderstrom, N. C. (2011, June). Recollection-based prospective metamemory judgments are more accurate than those based on confidence: Judgments of Remembering and Knowing (JORKs). *Journal of Experimental Psychology: General*. Advance online publication. doi: 10.1037/a0024014

Metcalfe, J., & Finn, B. (2008). Evidence that judgments of learning are causally related to study choice, *Psychonomic Bulletin & Review*, *15*, 174–179. doi: 10.3758/PBR.15.1.174

Multhaup, K. S. (1995). Aging, source, and decision criteria: When false fame errors do and do not occur. *Psychology and Aging*, *10*, 492–497. doi: 10.1037/0882-7974.10.3.492

Nelson, T. O., & Narens, L. (1990). Metamemory: A theoretical framework and new findings. In G. H. Bower (Ed.), *The psychology of learning and motivation*, vol. 26, (pp. 125–173). New York: Academic Press.

Price, P. C., & Yates, J. F. (1993). Judgmental overshadowing: Further evidence of cue interaction in contingency judgment. *Memory & Cognition*, *21*, 561–572.

Rawson, K. A., Dunlosky, J., & McDonald, S. (2002). Influences of metamemory on performance predictions for text. *Quarterly Journal of Experimental Psychology A: Human Experimental Psychology*, *55A*, 505–524. doi: 10.1080/02724980143000352

Rawson, K. A., O'Neil, R., & Dunlosky, J. (2011). Accurate monitoring leads to effective control and greater learning of patient education materials. *Journal of Experimental Psychology: Applied*, *17*, 288–302. doi: 10.1037/a0024749

Rhodes, M. G., & Castel, A. D. (2008). Memory predictions are influenced by perceptual information: Evidence for metacognitive illusions. *Journal of Experimental Psychology: General*, *137*, 615–625. doi: 10.1037/a0013684

Rhodes, M. G., & Tauber, S. K. (2011). The influence of delaying judgments of learning on metacognitive accuracy: A meta-analytic review. *Psychological Bulletin*, *137*, 131–148. doi: 10.1037/a0021705

Schwartz, B. L., Benjamin, A. S., & Bjork, R. A. (1997). The inferential and experiential bases of metamemory. *Current Directions in Psychological Science*, *6*, 132–137. doi: 10.1111/1467-8721.ep10772899

Schnitzspahn, K. M., Zeintl, M., Jager, T., & Kliegel, M. (2011). Metacognition in prospective memory: Are performance prediction accurate? *Canadian Journal of Experimental Psychology*, *65*, 19–26. doi: 10.1037/a0022842

Serra, M., & Dunlosky, J. (2010). Metacomprehension judgments reflect the belief that diagrams improve learning from text. *Memory*, *18*, 698–711. doi: 10.1080/09658211.2010.506441

Serra, M. J., & Metcalfe, J. (2009). Effective Implementation of Metacognition. In D. J. Hacker, J. Dunlosky, and A. C. Graesser (Eds.), *Handbook of metacognition in education.* (pp. 278–298). New York: Routledge.

Singer, M., & Tiede, H. L. (2008). Feeling of knowing and duration of unsuccessful memory search, *Memory & Cognition*, *36*, 588–597. doi: 10.3758/MC.36.3.588

Tauber, S. K., & Rhodes, M. G. (2010). Metacognitive errors contribute to the difficulty in remembering proper names. *Memory*, *18*, 522–532. doi: 10.1080/09658211.2010.481818

Tauber, S. K., & Rhodes, M. G. (2012). Measuring memory monitoring with judgments of retention (JORs). *Quarterly Journal of Experimental Psychology*, *65*, 1376–1396. doi: 10.1080/17470218.2012.656665

Thiede, K. W. (1999). The importance of monitoring and self-regulation during multi-trial learning. *Psychonomic Bulletin & Review*, *6*, 662–667. doi: 10.3758/BF03212976

Thiede, K. W., Anderson, M. C. M., & Therriault, D. (2003). Accuracy of metacognitive monitoring affects learning of texts. *Journal of Educational Psychology*, *95*, 66–73. doi: 10.1037/00220663.95.1.66

Thiede, K. W., Wiley, J., & Griffin, T. D. (2011). Test expectancy affects metacomprehension accuracy. *British Journal of Educational Psychology*, *81*, 264–273. doi: 10.1348/135910710X510494

Thomas, A. K., & McDaniel, M. A. (2007). Metacomprehension for educationally relevant materials: Dramatic effects of encoding-retrieval interactions. *Psychonomic Bulletin & Review*, *14*, 212–218.

Toth, J. P., Daniels, K. A., & Solinger, L. A. (2011). What you know can hurt you: Effects of age and prior knowledge on the accuracy of judgments of learning. *Psychology and Aging*, *26*, 919–931. doi: 10.1348/135910710X510494

Townsend, C. L., & Heit, E. (2011). Judgments of learning and improvement. *Memory & Cognition, 39*, 204–216. doi: 10.3758/s13421-010-0019-2

Underwood, B. J. (1966). Individual and group predictions of item difficulty for free-recall learning. *Journal of Experimental Psychology, 71*, 673–679.

26

Metacognitive Control of Study

Janet Metcalfe

The third of Descartes' four rules concerning what he considered essential for rightly conducting the reason was:

> to direct my thoughts in an orderly way; beginning with the simplest objects, those most apt to be known, and ascending little by little, in steps as it were, to the knowledge of the most complex; establishing an order in thought even when the objects had no natural priority one to another.
> (Discours de la Méthode, 1637, as given in Mathematical Quotes: http://math.furman.edu/~mwoodard/ascquotd.html)

The allocation of study time and effort, so as to optimize the outcome of the study processes, is the topic of the present chapter. There is no doubt that learning in the classroom under close instructor guidance is of great importance. Even so, starting as early as Grade 3, students are increasingly being asked to learn in an unsupervised manner (Hofferth & Sandberg, 2000). It is this self-guided learning that is the focus of the present chapter. It appears that the results of such efforts are mixed. Metacognitively guided study strategies to enhance learning are rarely taught to students (see, Graesser, MacNamara, & VanLehn, 2005), and yet students are expected to benefit from doing homework and studying for tests on their own. They are also expected to use learning strategies effectively. To a large extent, self-guided study, for young children, is labor in vain. The hours spent studying fail to contribute to learning (Cooper, 1989; Cooper, Robinson, & Patall, 2006). Furthermore, at higher grade levels, while those students who have been able to hone in on good study strategies may be rewarded by favorable learning payoffs, those who have not acquired this skill may fall by the wayside. Zimmerman and Martinez-Pons (1990) have shown that it is the older, more gifted students who use effective self-regulated learning including strategic metacognitive control of their own time allocation and information seeking. But both children and adults, gifted and less gifted, need to effectively control their study choices and time in order to maximize the learning benefit (Thiede, 1999). Thus, a double pronged approach to the study of strategic processes seems justified. Researchers need to try to formulate models of choice and time allocation that optimize the benefits of particular study strategies. They also need to investigate what people, at all ages and levels of talent, do well, using clever and effective metacognitive strategies or do poorly, falling prey to the fallacies and dysfunctional habits that may inhibit learning.

SEMINAL STUDIES OF METACOGNITIVELY GUIDED STUDY TIME AND CHOICE ALLOCATION

Atkinson (1972a, 1972b) was one of the earliest advocates of devising a theory of learning that would help people optimize study choices. Investigating the learning of English–German vocabulary items, he used computer-based models to examine the effectiveness of various strategies. The strategies that the computer provided to his participants, by selecting for them which particular items to study, were based on a learning model derived both from prior testing of other students on the particular to-be-learned materials (English–German vocabulary, in this case) as well as on students' own response patterns during the experiment he conducted. The underlying learning model was used to ascertain how well learned was each item in the set of targeted materials. Atkinson then investigated strategies for how to study these items, at various degrees of learning, by applying a three-stage Markoff model directed at the process of learning. In the Markoff model items were considered to be (1) either completely learned or permanent (P), (2) transitional (or T) or partly learned, or (3) unlearned (U). In this model, when they were studied items could go from U to T or from T to P, but they could not jump stages and go from U directly to P. Furthermore, with interference and erroneous retrieval of other items, forgetting could occur. If forgetting occurred items could drop back from Transitional to Unlearned. But once they were in P they stayed learned.

The goal of learning, then, was to get items into the permanent state, P. The assumed status of being in P, T, or U, for any particular item at any particular time during learning, was derived from the more complicated underlying learning model that employed 480 parameters related both to the individual's learning history on particular items and also to the difficulty of learning of the items themselves based on the testing results with those items from other participants

in a prior experiment. This complicated learning model determined which items, at any point in the study sequence, were purportedly in each of three states. The strategy that was considered optimal would be that which would use study opportunities – which was when items could switch states – to get as many items as possible into the P state, since only the P items were considered to be really learned.

Items in the T state are crucial within this framework. They were considered to not yet be learned, but yet to be open to learning, and potentially transferrable to the P state. They were, then, the learning-vulnerable items, in Atkinson's framework. Work on them was where progress could best be made. Interestingly, within this framework, items in the T state were recallable during the learning procedure. They were assigned to the T state not because they could not be immediately accessed but rather because they were deemed to still be vulnerable to forgetting or interference. Only P state items were thought to be able to survive a one-week interval, which was when the criterion test would be given assessing learning. T state items were the ones that the three stage Markoff model indicated were the ones that needed to be studied, and that would result in optimal learning payoffs. Learning was evaluated, in the experiment Atkinson subsequently conducted, by contrasting how many of the total pool of items could be recalled at a one-week delay, as a function of the learning strategy.

Several strategies were investigated. The first was a random strategy of having the computer present all items equally for study. This was a default, of course, and was not expected to produce highly favorable results. While random study might be better than no study at all, no learning theory, and certainly not Atkinson's theory, would expect it to be optimal. If the goal is to get as many items as possible into the P or learned state, the random strategy has an obvious problem. Items that were already permanently learned would not benefit from further study, since they *were* already in the P state. So studying them would be a waste of time. And, it would leave less time available for studying other items that were not yet learned and might benefit from study.

The second strategy investigated was called the "equal" strategy. In this case, items that were in the P state were removed from contention, and only items that were not yet in P were presented. This should cut down on the time wasted on items that would obviously fail to benefit from the study opportunity. But once these already-learned items were eliminated, items in both the T state and the U state were chosen with equal probability for study. Whether this strategy would turn out to be optimal or not depended on whether Atkinson's assumption about the special status of the T items was correct, or not.

Finally, the third strategy that was considered was the "unequal" strategy. This third strategy focused study on items that were in the T state. The P items were ignored. But in addition, the items that were in the T state and thought to be most able to be transferred to a permanent learning state were the items that were explicitly chosen for study. The completely unlearned items were not selected.

The experiment used English–German vocabulary pairs. In four conditions, participants had an equal number of study trials in which they were given the cue of an English word, and then tried to produce the German translation. Following attempted generation of the target they were then given the correct answer as feedback. Then they went on to the next item. The difference in the between participant conditions was which items were selected for query and feedback, conforming to the Random, Equal, Unequal strategies, or allowing the participant to select whatever item they wanted. In all conditions, the goodness of learning was assessed by performance one week later on all of the vocabulary items.

In the Random condition, initial performance, measured by how well people did during the study trials, was the best in large part because items that were in the P state already were included indiscriminately in this condition. People did well on these items. However, performance at a week's delay in the random condition was poor.

In the Equal condition the computer eliminated from the study-test-feedback procedure the items that were already in the P state, based on their past history and the model-based item difficult assessments. It then gave equal study opportunity to all of the remaining items, regardless of whether they were in the T or the U state. When people studied on this schedule they were worse during the study procedure than were people in the Random condition, since the easiest well-learned items had been eliminated. But they greatly outperformed the people in the random condition, on the final test one week later.

In the Unequal condition, the computer not only did not present items in the P state, but it also differentiated among the T and the U items, allocating selective study to the T items. Once the items that were closest to being mastered had entered the P state (again, as determined by the underlying learning model) the program chose the next most learned transitional item. Thus, the computer selected the materials in an orderly fashion from easiest-as-yet-unlearned items to more and more difficult as-yet-unlearned items – an order that Descartes would, no doubt, have appreciated. Performance during study was the worst in this condition of all the conditions. The learning results exhibited one week later, though, were about twice as good as the already favorable results shown in the "equal" condition, and 108 percent better than those observed in the random condition.

But what about the fourth condition? In addition to the computer controlled conditions described above, Atkinson (1972b) had included a "self study" condition. Presumably this condition allows examination of the effects of people's own metacognitively guided choice. In the self-study condition people did about as well as in the "equal" condition, but not nearly as well as in the more nuanced "unequal" condition. The poor showing of people (in this case, Stanford University students) studying on their own led Atkinson to argue vociferously against the idea that if we just let people make their own study choices themselves they will get it right.

Unquestionably there is a need for models of study optimization, and people of all stripes including even college students can fall prey to metacognitive illusions. Even so, it is not clear that Atkinson's data provide a solid basis for the conclusion that the students' skills were as inadequate as they seemed, or as Atkinson claimed they were. As we shall see shortly, in studies that include conditions similar to Atkinson's nuanced "unequal" model condition, Metcalfe and Kornell (2003, 2005) have shown that college students perform very well. So what happened with Atkinson's participants? It seems likely that his instructions mitigated against them using their best strategies. Rather than telling them to do everything they could to optimize later memory, they were "instructed that it was best to test and study on words they did not know rather than on ones already mastered" (p. 930, Atkinson, 1972a). It seems likely that the participants interpreted these instructions – coming from a renowned learning specialist – as telling them to study *equally* all of the items that they had not yet mastered, a strategy that would have been similar to that in the "equal" computer condition. And, indeed, the data from the computer-guided "equal" condition were virtually identical to those in the self-guided study condition. These early unfavorable results might seem, at first, to reflect poorly upon even the brightest college students' abilities to effectively self-regulate their study time allocation. However, they may have resulted, instead, because the students were simply compliant with the instructions. But those instructions pointed to the use of a suboptimal strategy.

WHAT DO PEOPLE CHOOSE TO STUDY?

Many experiments have shown that most people do not choose randomly, when they select what they want to study. Son and Metcalfe (2000), in a review of the literature, found that people tended to choose to study items to which they assigned low judgments of learning. A more recent analysis of people's study choices – but one that reaches much the same conclusions – has been provided by Dunlosky and Ariel (2011). Judgments of learning (JOLs) are metacognitive assessments made by the individuals concerning the extent to which they believe they have learned particular items. While these judgments are not always completely accurate, and can be subject to biases, nevertheless, Dunlosky and Nelson (1992) have shown that if the judgments are made at some time delay after learning and without the target of the learning being present, they are extremely accurate. These judgments of learning, especially when made in the manner Dunlosky and Nelson recommend, are something like an internalized version of the 480 parameter learning model that Atkinson used to determine the state of learning of each item in the set. And like Atkinson's model, JOLs could provide the information people need to allow them to make strategic study choices. Thus, the finding that people's choices of what to study were related to their JOLs is important.

Typically, such results have been reported as a negative correlation between judgments of learning (JOLs) and study choice or study time. Items with higher JOLs (the items that people thought that they knew) tended not to be chosen for study or allocated much time, whereas items with lower JOLS (i.e., the items that people believed they didn't know very well) tended to be chosen for study and/or allocated more study time. That there is a relation between JOLs and study time allocation suggests that people were using a strategy. Exactly what strategy this negative correlation implicates, however, is contentious. A negative correlation would be obtained, of course, if people chose to simply eliminate the items they knew they knew (which, by the way, are the P items, if their metacognitions are accurate). If they chose randomly among the remaining items, as in Atkinson's "Equal" condition, a negative correlation would be found. Furthermore, it would obtain even if people were using Atkinson's "Unequal" strategy, as long as there were quite a few "know that they know" items that were eliminated from study or given very little time. It would also obtain if people were choosing to study, selectively, the very most difficult items. This last interpretation of the relation between study time allocation and judgments of learning was adopted in a model that became known as the Discrepancy Reduction model of study time allocation, which was proposed by Nelson (1990), elaborated by Dunlosky and Hertzog (1998), and modified and delimited by Dunlosky and Thiede (1998), and Thiede and Dunlosky (1999).

THE DISCREPANCY REDUCTION MODEL

A strategy that gives priority to the most difficult items – those items with the lowest JOLs – would, of course, result in strong negative correlations. Such a correlation is consistent with system models that postulate that there is a desired degree of learning, and that items are selected, and allocated study time, to reduce the discrepancy between the perceived current state of learning, over all items, and the desired state of learning. The notion is that people will continue studying each item until the discrepancy between it and the learning goal has been reduced to zero. More difficult, or lower JOL, items require more time than less difficult or higher JOL items, which are nearer to the chosen learning threshold to begin with. The net result will be that more time is allocated to the more difficult items. The selectivity for difficult items is applied to study choice as well as time according to most views. The negative correlation, so frequently found, falls out of this discrepancy reduction strategy in a natural way.

There are some problems with this model, however. One is that favoring only the most difficult items for study, before other easier items that could yield up learning benefits more quickly, could be far from optimal if there were any time constraints on the learning. It could result in items that could be mastered with little time and effort being left unstudied and unlearned. Much "low hanging fruit" would be missed. Furthermore, much time and effort might be spent to little avail on items that were so difficult as to be essentially unlearnable. Nelson and Leonesio (1988, and see also Mazzoni & Cornoldi, 1993) described such an effect as "labor in vain." They found that additional study time – even large amounts of study time – could result in little to no learning gains when that study time was devoted primarily to the most difficult items. But while this labor in vain effect undoubtedly occurs in some cases, there is also little doubt that more difficult items *require* more study time than do easier items, a key intuition of the discrepancy reduction model. If the learning task is such that all items need to be mastered, and time is unbounded, then it would be necessary to allocate time in this way. Furthermore, if items were presented one at a time, and the learners have no choice about revisiting items later, they will almost inevitably take more time on the difficult items, since they will learn the easy items in short order. In most situations, though, obsessive allocation of time to the most difficult items, at the expense of the easier items, would seem to be a suboptimal strategy.

ALTERNATIVE INTERPRETATIONS OF STUDY CHOICE JOL CORRELATIONS

Alternative interpretations of the negative correlation between study time/choice and JOLs are possible. For one thing, the correlations are typically far from −1. As noted above, such modest negative correlations could result if people were doing no more than eliminating the already mastered items, and giving equal study time/choice to all as-yet-unlearned items, as in Atkinson's "equal" condition. The correlation would be negative by virtue of the choice not to study the already-learned items, which would have very high JOLs. Furthermore, modest negative correlations could even be observed if the individual were eliminating the P items that they knew had already been mastered (with very high JOLs), and then focusing on the easiest as-yet-unlearned items first – the T items. This strategy is that of the "unequal" condition in Atkinson's experiment. As long as there were some proportion of high JOL items that were already mastered in the set, these would skew the correlation in a negative direction. Of course, if these already-mastered items were eliminated from the set of to-be-learned items, the correlation would be expected to go to zero, if people were using the "equal" strategy, or become positive, if they were using the unequal strategy. But only under these special conditions would a non-negative correlation be expected. Furthermore, if the correlation were to study time rather than order of choice, then even under conditions in which people employed the equal or unequal strategy in terms of their choice of items to study, the correlation might still be negative. No theorist or model has ever postulated that more difficult items require less study time than easier items.

The indeterminacy in the interpretation of the meaning of the negative correlation between JOL and study time/choice allocation has implications for using the magnitude of this correlation as a measure of whether individuals are or are not using good metacognitive strategies. The simplest view is that the stronger the negative correlation, the more strategically were the people behaving. More advanced learners, being more metacognitive (as Zimmerman, 2001 and Zimmerman & Schunk, 2001, noted), should, if this were true, show stronger negative correlations. People exhibiting weaker negative correlations between JOLs and study time allocation would be thought to

be exhibiting poorer metacognitive control. Consistent with this view, it has been found that more accomplished learners do have more negative correlations than do younger and weaker learners (Son & Metcalfe, 2000). The exceptions to negative correlations have been observed with learning disabled teenagers (Belmont & Butterfield, 1971), young children (Bizanz, Vesonder, & Voss, 1978; Dufresne, & Kobasigawa, 1989; Masur, McIntyre, & Flavell, 1973; Metcalfe, 2002), and people with acquired brain injury (Kennedy, Carney, & Peters, 2003). These learners might be expected to have impaired metacognitive/control skills, ostensibly supporting the idea that the more negative the correlation the more strategic the individual.

Metcalfe and Kornell (2003, 2005) challenged this view. They proposed, instead, that people – even including the people with low correlations – *may* have been behaving very strategically. But they may have used a strategy that echoed the optimal strategy of Atkinson (1972a, 1972b) and which did not predict a strong negative correlation in all circumstances.

THE REGION OF PROXIMAL LEARNING MODEL

The Region of Proximal Learning model (Metcalfe, 2002, 2009, 2010; Metcalfe & Kornell, 2003, 2005) draws on the foundational work of Atkinson (1972), and is in fundamental agreement with that view. Even so, there are some areas of disagreement. The first is that Atkinson felt it necessary to resort to a 480 parameter mathematical model to evaluate the degree of learning of each item. This assessment of learning was fed into a choice model that optimized selections for study. The Region of Proximal Learning view holds that instead of needing to use such a complex and possibly intractable external mathematical model to assess the degree of learning, people may, instead, be able to rely on their own JOLs to do the job. Second, in Atkinson's experiment, people did not seem to make the optimal choices. Indeed, they appeared to use an "equal" rather than an "unequal" strategy. It turns out, as will be reviewed below, that not all people – even those with excellent metacognitions – do use an optimal strategy. However, in contrast to Atkinson's contention, it will be argued that some do.

The Region of Proximal Learning model uses people's metacognitive judgments of learning to order the to-be-learned materials from those that the learner feels are completely mastered, through various intermediate JOLs, down to those he or she thinks are completely unlearned. The model proposes that people endeavor to set a cutoff for study whereby they will decline study of items that they know they have already mastered. Once those items have been eliminated, they attempt to study in an order from highest JOL item that has not yet been learned, down to lowest. The items that are near to being learned are considered to be in the individual's Region of Proximal Learning. A small amount of study time and effort will suffice to allow learning of those items. As such, they are in a privileged learning sweet spot.

The exact value given to the cutoff threshold is important, since items that are slightly below the appropriately set threshold are in the Region of Proximal Learning and receive the maximum benefit from even a small amount of study. Studying items that are slightly above an appropriately set threshold, though, is a waste of time. People who are either overconfident or underconfident may set this threshold incorrectly, resulting in inefficacious study. For example, a person who is overconfident may fail to study items that would have required only a small amount of effort to master. They later miss those items on the test. A person who is underconfident may obsess over items that he or she already knows well, wasting time that could have been spent to greater effect. The model also proposes that manipulations that alter people's confidence can have a large effect on the efficacy of self-guided study strategies. They may cause people to

set this threshold inappropriately. Potentially, though, such manipulations could also be used to good end by an astute educator to correct an individual's threshold setting and result in more effective learning. Notice that, although the highest as-yet-unlearned JOL items are considered to be those in the person's Region of Proximal Learning and should be favored for study, the model also indicates that the amount of time that needs to be devoted to them is small. The optimal items to choose to study are not those items that will take the most time to master, but rather those that will require the least.

Once an item has been chosen for study, the model requires that while the person studies he or she also monitors the *rate* of learning. The person continues studying if they perceive learning to be proceeding apace. But if the individual perceives that learning is not progressing at an acceptable rate he or she discontinues study of that item. The rate of perceived learning may approach zero – triggering the stop rule – for one of two different reasons: (1) because the item has already been learned and no additional learning is perceived to be occurring, or (2) because the item is too difficult to allow perceptible learning and no headway is being made. When either of these things happens study of that item terminates.

To return to the question of the correlation between study choice and JOL, we may ask: If learners were choosing appropriately to study in their own Region of Proximal Learning then what should the correlation be? Presumably, highly expert learners or people who were highly skilled in a domain would, appropriately, choose to study items that were extremely difficult, just because they would already know all of the easier items. Choosing the most difficult items preferentially would result in a strong negative correlation between JOLs and study choice for them. Learners who were less skilled or accomplished should not select items of such extreme difficulty, because they would not yet know the easier items. Being less accomplished, the items that would be most vulnerable to learning by them, then, would be easier. Those easier items would, therefore, be the right choice for them. If less skilled learners did choose easier items (presumably because they knew or thought that those were the items out of which they would derive the most learning gain) their correlations would be less negative than those of the more skilled learners. But a less negative correlation would not necessarily mean the person is being less strategic. Furthermore, a teacher or experimenter might carefully remove from the respective sets of the highly expert and less expert learner all of the items that they, respectively, knew already. In that case, both should show a positive correlation. Given the possibility that a model similar to the Region of Proximal Learning model might be correct, and point to an optimal strategy, we simply cannot tell whether people are behaving strategically from the correlations alone.

Although it is important to determine whether children are behaving strategically in their study choices, the meaning of the finding that young children often give less priority to the more difficult items than do older children or adults is difficult to interpret. The smaller negative correlation between study choice and JOL shown by the young children might have resulted because the children were choosing less discriminately than the older or more expert people. They may have been showing poorer metacognitive control. Alternatively, it might have arisen because they were choosing correctly for them and the easier materials were in their Region of Proximal Learning. Because of this uncertainty about what the magnitude and the direction of the correlation means, researchers have increasingly turned to a new method of assessing whether learners are making effective metacognitively informed study choices.

THE HONOR-CHOICE PARADIGM

A method of evaluating whether people are choosing appropriately is the so-called "honor-choice" paradigm (Kornell, 2005; Kornell & Metcalfe, 2006; Metcalfe & Kornell, 2005; Son, 2010). In this paradigm, participants are asked to choose items that they would like to study in order to optimize their later memory performance. Typically they are also asked for judgments of learning, and typically, but not always, they are asked to choose exactly half of the items. Then, following choice, they are given items to restudy. The items could be (a) those they chose themselves (the honor-choice condition), (b) those they declined (the dishonor-choice condition), or (c) items that are determined on theoretical grounds. As well as allowing assessment of theoretical positions and contrasts of these positions with people's actual choices, this paradigm allows assessment of whether people's choices were good. If people were making good choices then they should do better when those choices are honored as compared with when they are dishonored.

Most studies show that adult college student participants make good study choices: honoring their choices results in better learning than does dishonoring their choices (Metcalfe, 2009). Kornell and Metcalfe (2006) conducted studies both when all of the items from a to-be-learned list were included, and also when only items that had not yet been learned were included. When both known and unknown items were included, the items that people chose to restudy were, in general, the lower JOL items. This finding is consistent with much of the literature on the correlation between JOLs and study choices. Furthermore, people performed better when these choices were honored, as compared with when they were dishonored – indicating that their choices had been efficacious.

The results were different when the items that people knew were eliminated from consideration. Kornell and Metcalfe (2006) intervened a test between original study and the choice for restudy phase of the experiment. They had the computer eliminate from restudy choice all items that the participant got right on the test. Then participants were allowed to choose among items, all of which they had failed to recall. When the choices allowed were among only items that people got wrong on this test, they chose the higher JOL items (i.e., the easier items) rather than the lower JOL items. The correlation between study choice and JOL was positive rather than negative. This result is a direct reversal of the correlations seen in the experiments summarized above, but a finding consistent with the Region of Proximal learning model, and with Atkinson's work. Participants performed better when those high JOL choices were honored than when they were dishonored – indicating that these choices were efficacious. This honor/dishonor paradigm, can, thus, sometimes provide results concerning the efficacy of choices that are directly conflicting with what would be expected if one took the strength of the negative correlation as the indicator of whether the choices people made were efficacious.

The honor/dishonor paradigm can be applied not only to evaluate people's choices of which items to study, but also to other study strategies. There is a long history (Bahrick & Hall, 2005) suggesting that spacing repetitions of particular items, by intervening other items between presentations, rather than clustering those repetitions in a massed manner with no other items intervening, usually results in enhanced memory. However, if the items have not been fully encoded or if the interleaving breaks the flow of a narrative (Mandler, 1978), massed practice may be as good as or better than spaced practice (Kornell & Metcalfe, 2006; Waugh, 1970). Son (2004) has found that college students often choose to space practice – a seemingly good decision in most cases. However, they sometimes choose to mass practice. The question that arises is whether they make these choices to mass or space appropriately and in a manner that improves memory. To address this issue, Son (2010) used the honor/dishonor paradigm, both with adults and children. Her results indicated that when adults' choices either to space or (more

interestingly) to mass practice were honored rather than dishonored, their later memory performance was enhanced. They apparently chose appropriately, even when that choice was to mass practice.

CHILDREN'S METACOGNITION AND STUDY CHOICES

Although Son's (2010) data indicated that the adults chose to mass or space their practice in a manner that enhanced memory, such was not the case with children. First, the children nearly always chose to mass practice. When the children's choices were to space practice, and those choices were honored, their performance was better than when those choices were dishonored. However, when their choices were to mass practice, they were better off having their choices dishonored. These results indicate that massing practice is a dysfunctional strategy in children. But it is also the strategy that the children themselves adopted.

The honor-choice paradigm has also recently been used to revisit children's study choice strategies. As noted above, there has long been a suspicion that a problem in metacognition or in the manner in which children make their study choices underlies the failure of their time allocated to self-guided study to favorably impact their grades. The smaller negative correlations between JOLs and choices observed in children as compared with adults had been taken as indicating such a possibility. But those correlations are untrustworthy indicators. Accordingly, Metcalfe and Finn (2012) conducted a series of six experiments with children in grades 3 and 5 to investigate their metacognition and control.

The first three experiments revealed a very simple result. Over a variety of materials, when the children at both grade levels used the delayed judgment of learning procedure recommended by Dunlosky and Nelson (1992) they made highly accurate JOLs.

There was nothing wrong with their meta-cognition.

The last three experiments asked whether the children used those metacognitions to make effective study choices, as indicated by the honor/dishonor paradigm. In the first choice experiment the children studied, made JOLs, and then later were given sextets of items, arranged in a circle, and were asked to choose exactly three items from each sextet for later study. Their choices were either honored or dishonored. The correlations between JOL and study choices for the grade 3 children were not different from zero, though those of the grade 5 children were negative, suggesting that the younger children were choosing randomly while the older children were choosing to study the items with the lower JOLs. However, in neither grade did honoring their choices make any difference to final recall performance.

A second experiment was structured such that the children were tested between the initial study and restudy choice. Again, they were given a sequence of sextets of items and had to make choices of which three items they wanted to have a chance to restudy. Exactly three of the items in each sextet were items on which they were correct on the test, and three were items on which they had given no response or were wrong. Again, the younger children chose randomly. The older children tended to choose the items they had gotten wrong. Honoring rather than dishonoring the choices of the grade 3 children had no effect on their recall performance. Honoring the choices of the grade 5 children, though, helped their performance. We also included in this experiment a computer based "good" strategy, which was to present for restudy the items that the children had gotten wrong. Implementing the computer selected "good" strategy helped performance of both the grade 3 and the grade 5 children.

Finally, in the last experiment, children made JOLS on a set of items, and then took a test. All of the items that they got right on the test were eliminated from the choice possibilities. This left a range of JOL items all

of which had not yet been learned. The computer then constructed sextets, each of which spanned the full range of each individual child's JOLs. The children made choices of three items from the sextets. The computer then either honored or dishonored their choices. Additionally, there were two computer controlled restudy conditions. In one, the highest three JOL items from each sextet were presented for restudy. These were the items that the Region of Proximal Learning model says should be the best ones to study. In the other condition, the lowest three JOL items were given to the children for restudy. These were the items that the Discrepancy Reduction model claims should be the best items to restudy.

As in the previous two experiments, the grade 3 children chose randomly. There was no difference between the mean JOLs for the items they chose as compared with the items they declined. Honoring their choices had no effect on memory performance. The grade 5 students did not choose randomly. Instead they tended to choose the low JOL items, consistent with the Discrepancy Reduction model. Thus, a distinct strategy was emerging by grade 5. Was it a good strategy? The answer appears to be no. Honoring their choices gave no benefit. In fact, the mean recall for the honored items was 3 percent lower than for the dishonored items. When the computer gave people the high JOL items to study – the "good" items indicted by the Region of Proximal Learning model – both the grade 3 and the grade 5 children showed large increases in performance.

The honor-choice results were revealing. While all of the children exhibited good metacognition, the younger children in all three experiments chose randomly. Honoring their choices made no difference. If they were provided with the correct items to study, though, they benefited. But they did not make these choices, or any other strategic choices, themselves.

The older children were beginning to use a strategy. They showed a preference to restudy items with lower JOLs. But they did this regardless of the situation. The success of this strategy was spotty. It was effective when the choices were between learned items and unlearned items. However, in the other situations, where the distinction was not so clear, the strategy was ineffective.

EXTENSIONS OF THE HONOR-CHOICE PARADIGM

In theory, the honor-choice paradigm could be applied to other memorial strategies, such as whether to read or generate answers, whether to take a chance on making a mistake that will be corrected or to choose error free learning, whether to use retrieval practice or not (see Karpicke, 2009), whether to use large font print or small font print, whether to hear or see materials, and any number of other variables on which people's judgments about what will optimize their own learning may vary. This paradigm also allows performance based on people's own choices to be contrasted to what happens when the strategy choice is theory based. Theories may have, demonstrably, better strategies than people do. Knowing when they do could help researchers and educators devise methods to allow people to improve the efficiency of their learning.

EXTENUATING FACTORS

Although all theories agree that people should not study already learned items, there are a number of other variables that have been explored recently that also modulate effective learning. One such variable is the amount of study time available for individual items. Short study times may cut off processing before an item is fully encoded. When there is not enough time to complete encoding it is better for the person to study that item again immediately, or to mass practice, rather than breaking off study before full

encoding has occurred (Toppino & Cohen, 2010). Pyc and Dunlosky (2010) showed that item difficulty is an important factor determining whether there will be enough time (and see also Son, 2004, 2005). If there is sufficient time in the individual study event, though, so that information intake of the event is complete, then it is better to return to that item later, that is, to space study.

The distribution of optimal study time allocation also changes as the total study time changes. When people are allowed more study time they can turn to more difficult items. When study time is severely limited performance is enhanced if the time is spent on the easier items, as shown by Thiede and Dunlosky (1999; Dunlosky & Thiede, 2004). They called this effect STEM, or the shift to easier materials. Son and Metcalfe (2000), using a different paradigm, found the same relation between allowed study time and the choice of items.

But while these variables are important, so, too, are other variables, including the motivation of the participants, the value attached to the to-be learned materials, and the processing costs of metacognition and choice. These complex relations suggest that more contextually grounded models of strategic study are needed.

EVOLUTIONARILY AND CONTEXTUALLY RELEVANT NEW MODELS OF STUDY TIME ALLOCATION

Several new models have focused on non-metacognitive and sometimes far-reaching aspects of students' learning situations. There is a trend toward taking environmental conditions as well as the goals of the learner into account. For instance, some models have considered students' learning situations to be analogous to foraging situations (Metcalfe & Jacobs, 2009; Pirolli & Card, 1999). Such information foraging models take into account many factors that are not considered in more simplified models, including the value of individual items, the person's overall goals, the incentives, the energy expenditure in strategy implementation, and the costs of switching from one item to another. Importantly people may choose not to study simply because other aspects of their lives may be more important at the time.

Although most models of study time allocation are test focused, in the wild, the test may not always be of paramount importance to the individual. A student may be doing an experiment on study time allocation, for example, to get credit for a course. He or she may not care about performance on the test. Such a student may use automatic responding and not engage metacognitive strategies. Another student, because of his own goals and motivations, may care about the nominal test in the experiment. The latter may engage strategies the former could, but does not, use.

Furthermore, metacognitive decisions, like other decisions (see Busemeyer & Townsend, 1993) may be expensive in terms of cognitive energy expended. If they are too expensive, it may be justified to skip them, and use, instead, habitual automatic response patterns. Models such as foraging models raise the suggestion, then, that there may be times when the cognitive energy required for metacognitive deliberation might be better expended on actual study of the to-be-learned materials. They provocatively suggest that there are times when automatized responses, some of which will be discussed later in this chapter, are optimal. Their emphasis on broad goals as well as on cognitive and environmental constraints extends the purview of study time allocation models. These views are also consistent with more global models of metacognitive control such as those of Winnie (2005) and Winnie and Hadwin (1998).

One of the main variables of importance from the information foraging perspective is the value of the to-be-learned materials. Highly valuable, interesting, or important materials should have incentive value, and hence increase motivation and along with it study time and effort. In foraging terms,

food sources that are rich in nutrients count for more than those that are poor. But global incentives sometimes fail to have an effect. For instance, Lockl and Schneider (2004) conducted an experiment in which one group of 7- and 9- year-old children were given no incentive for remembering items in a list while others were given five cents for each item remembered. This incentive made no difference to either study time or later performance. However, it is possible that the children did not care about the incentive. Alternatively, they may have been unable to ramp up their study time or attention to accommodate it. Since this was a between participants variable, the children were not in a position to give more attention or study to more valuable items and less study to items that were less valuable.

In a number of experiments by Castel and his colleagues (Castel, Benjamin, Craik, & Watkins, 2002; Castel, Farb, & Craik, 2007), differential point values were given to different items within a to-be-learned list. People consistently learned the high point items better than the low point items. Castel et al. (2007) showed that both younger and older adults selectively remembered words as a function of assigned numeric point values. Furthermore, both groups exhibited control by not recalling negatively valued information. Castel, Humphreys, Lee, Galvan, Balota, and McCabe (2011) showed that people from age 5 to 96 have the ability to strategically remember important information, that is, to remember in a value-directed manner. A selectivity task was used in which participants were asked to study and recall items worth different point values in an effort to maximize their score. This procedure allowed for assessment of memory quantity/capacity (number of words recalled) as well as memory efficiency/selectivity (the recall of high-value items relative to low-value items). Age-related differences were found for memory capacity, with young adults recalling more words, overall, than the other groups. Of more interest for the present concern was that the selectivity of younger and older adults was higher than that of the adolescents and children. The elders were particularly selective.

Similar differences play out directly in study time allocation experiments. For example, Dunlosky and Thiede (1998) showed that as the norm of study was increased, more time was allocated for self-paced study. Study time was also greater for high point-value items. When a penalty was levied for increasing the time spent studying, study time decreased. Study time on particular items also increased with increases in the likelihood that an item would be on the test.

A newly emerging perspective on meta-cognitively guided study, which appears to be compatible with foraging notions, is the agenda-based regulation framework of Dunlosky and Ariel (2011; Ariel, Dunlosky, & Bailey, 2009; Ariel, Al-Harthy, Was, & Dunlosky, 2011; Dunlosky, Ariel, & Thiede, 2011). Dunlosky et al. (2011) proposed that learners develop a study agenda in an effort to increase the likelihood that task goals will be efficiently met (Thiede & Dunlosky, 1999). While incorporating most of the Region of Proximal Learning model's metacognitive/study choice assumptions, the agenda-based regulation framework also includes people's goals and constraint structures. The agenda-based regulation model weaves differential payoffs for memory for different items into the fabric of the strategies that should be used. It does a particularly good job of value-directed remembering. Differential processing of items with different values is explicit in the model. As such, this model is highly compatible with Castel's empirical work on this variable discussed previously. This environmentally determined differential processing seems highly strategic, metacognitive, and important.

The agenda-based regulation model also includes a number of non-metacognitive, automatic processing variables. For example, left to right reading habits are important in determining what people will do, even though they are not metacognitively determined (Ariel et al., 2009). There is no doubt that automatic processing variables have an effect on human behavior at all levels. It is not clear, of course, whether such habitual patterns of study time/choice help or hurt learning, so inclusion of such variables might not be justified if the model is intended to be prescriptive, rather than descriptive. In many (but not all) situations this kind of automatic responding would seem to be suboptimal – to contravene effective metacognitive strategies. For example, if a child were using the automatic response of simply studying all items, or studying items in the to-be-remembered items from left to right this would probably be considered non-strategic and suboptimal. But nevertheless, people sometimes do this.

If metacognitive strategy implementation were very costly, though, it might make sense to sometimes strategically engage automatic processes instead of metacognitive processes. Suppose, for example, that it was very difficult to determine whether an item had already been learned or not. It might take some considerable time and effort to make the metacognitive assessment for each item. Suppose, further, that the time spent deciding whether one should study each item were subtracted from the time that could be allocated to actual study of the items. The cognitive time/energy costs of the metacognitive strategy might be at the expense of actual learning. In such a case, it might be preferable to forego metacognitive choice. In short, if the child had a total limited amount of time, but if all or much of that time were taken up with deciding what strategy to use little time might be left to do the actual studying. But even though it is possible to imagine particular cases where automatic processing could be efficient, there are nevertheless strong correspondences between skilled self-regulated learning and effective learning (Zimmerman & Martinez-Pons, 1990). It seems likely that the routine use of automatic responding modes points to poor rather than good self-regulation and to poor rather than good learning.

CONCLUSION

There is a caveat that needs to be addressed in closing: sometimes study time and choice allocation can be metacognitively guided but still be suboptimal. The way in which the individual uses his or her metacognitions can be faulty of course. A person might believe that a particular ineffective study strategy works, but be wrong. Such difficulties could, in principle, be overcome with training or experience.

However, as has been extensively documented elsewhere, people's metacognitions, themselves, are sometimes faulty. Metacognitive biases and inaccuracies are commonplace. Indeed, there are only a few methods that give rise to accurate and reliable judgments, such as the delayed JOL paradigm (Dunlosky & Nelson, 1992). While Thiede, Anderson, and Therriault (2003) have shown that use of such accurate metacognitive judgments can lead to enhanced restudy choices, if the judgments themselves were biased or faulty (see, Bjork, 1994) this should influence study choices.

Overconfidence, for example, is a pervasive metacognitive illusion (Metcalfe, 1998), and one that is likely to result in suboptimal study. If people act on their overconfidence, they will decline to study those items they believe, wrongly, that they already know. Finn (2008) provided such demonstration. As was found by Koriat, Bjork, Sheffer, and Bar (2004), people's judgments of learning are much higher when they are asked whether they will remember something later as compared with their judgments of learning when asked the equivalent question of whether they will forget it. Finn (2008) found that people made their study choices based on these JOLs. If they had been asked for their judgment of learning with the forget probe they were much more likely to ask to restudy items than when they had been asked with the remember probe. Metcalfe and Finn (2008) have provided other instances in which, even with underlying memory held constant, people's choices are biased by faulty metacognition.

If an individual is following what they think are trustworthy metacognitions that turn out to be illusory, their study time allocation – even though it is metacognitively guided rather than based on automatic, or habitual default processes – is likely to go awry. Thus, to use metacognitive strategies to optimize study, it is not only necessary to determine good strategies that are effective in enhancing learning, it is also necessary to ensure that the metacognitive knowledge itself be free of destructive biases and illusions.

REFERENCES

Ariel , R., Al-Harthy, I. S., Was, C. A., & Dunlosky, J. (2011). Habitual reading biases in the allocation of study time. *Psychonomic Bulletin and Review, 18,* 1015–1021.

Ariel , R., Dunlosky, J., & Bailey , H. (2009). Agenda-based regulation of study-time allocation: When agendas override item-based monitoring. *Journal of Experimental Psychology: General, 138,* 432–447.

Atkinson, R. C. (l972a). Ingredients for a theory of instruction. *American Psychologist, 72,* 921–931.

Atkinson, R. C. (l972b). Optimizing the learning of a second-language vocabulary, *Journal of Experimental Psychology, 96,* 124–129.

Bahrick, H. P., & Hall, L. K. (2005). The importance of retrieval failures to long-term retention: A metacognitive explanation of the spacing effect. *Journal of Memory and Language, 52,* 566–577.

Belmont, J. M., & Butterfield, E. C. (1971). Learning strategies as determinants of memory deficiencies. *Cognitive Psychology, 2,* 411–420.

Bisanz, G. L., Vesonder, G. T., & Voss, J. F. (1978). Knowledge of one's own responding and the relation of such knowledge to learning: A developmental study. *Journal of Experimental Child Psychology, 25,* 116–128.

Bjork, R. A. (1994). Memory and metamemory considerations in the training of human beings. In J. Metcalfe and A. Shimamura (Eds.), *Metacognition: Knowing about knowing* (pp. 185–206). Cambridge, MA: MIT Press.

Busemeyer, J. R., & Townsend, J. T. (1993), Decision field theory: A dynamic-cognitive approach to decision making in an uncertain environment. *Psychological Review, 102,* 432–459.

Calfee, R, C. (1970). The role of mathematical models in optimizing instruction. *Scientia: Revue International de Synthese Scientifique, 105,* 1–25.

Castel, A. D., Benjamin, A. S., Craik, F. I. M., & Watkins, M. J. (2002). The effects of aging on selectivity and control in short-term recall *Memory & Cognition, 30,* 1078–1085.

Castel, A. D., Farb, N. A. S., & Craik, F. I. M. (2007). Memory for general and specific value information in younger and older adults: Measuring the limits of strategic control. *Memory & Cognition, 35,* 689–700.

Castel, A. D., Humphreys, K. L., Lee, S. S., Galvan, A., Balota, D. A., & McCabe, D. P. (2011). The development of memory efficiency and value-directed remembering across the life span: A cross-sectional study of memory and selectivity. *Developmental Psychology, 47,* 1553–1564.

Cooper, H. (1989). *Homework.* White Plains, NY: Longman.

Cooper, H., Robinson, J. C., & Patall, E. A. (2006). Does homework improve academic achievement? A synthesis of research. *Review of Educational Research, 76,* 1–62.

Dufresne, A., & Kobasigawa, A. (1989). Children's spontaneous allocation of study time: Differential and sufficient aspects. *Journal of Experimental Child Psychology, 47,* 274–296.

Dunlosky, J., & Ariel, R. (2011). The influence of agenda-based and habitual processes on item selection during study. *Journal of Experimental Psychology: Learning, Memory, and Cognition, 37,* 899–912.

Dunlosky, J., Ariel, R., & Thiede, K. W. (2011). Agenda-based regulation of study-time allocation. In P. A. Higham and J. P. Leboe (Eds.), *Constructions of Remembering and Metacognition: Essays in Honour of Bruce Whittlesea* (pp. 182–198). Basingstoke, UK: Palgrave MacMillan.

Dunlosky, J., & Hertzog, C. (l998). Training programs to improve learning in later adulthood: Helping older adults educate themselves. In D. J. Hacker, J. Dunlosky, and A. C. Graesser (Eds.), *Metacognition in Educational Theory and Practice,* pp. 249–276.

Dunlosky, J., & Nelson, T. O. (1992). Importance of the kind of cue for judgments of learning (JOL) and the delayed-JOL effect. *Memory & Cognition, 20,* 374–380.

Dunlosky, J., & Thiede, K. W. (1998). What makes people study more? An evaluation of factors that affect people's self-paced study and yield "labor-and-gain" effects. *Acta Psychologica, 98,* 37–56.

Dunlosky, J., & Thiede, K. W. (2004). Causes and constraints of the shift-to-easier-materials effect in the control of study. *Memory & Cognition, 32,* 779–788.

Finn, B. (2008). Framing effects on metacognitive monitoring and control. *Memory & Cognition, 36,* 815–821.

Flavell, J. H., Frederichs, A. G., & Hoyt, J. D. (1970). Developmental changes in memorization processes. *Cognitive Psychology, 1,* 324–340.

Graesser, A. C., & McNamara, D. S., & Van Lehn, D. (2005). Scaffolding deep comprehension strategies through Point&Query, AutoTutor, and iSTART. *Educational Psychologist, 40,* 225–234.

Hofferth, S. L., & Sandberg, J. F. (2000). How American children spend their time. *Journal of Marriage and Family, 63,* 295–308.

Karpicke, J. D. (2009). Metacognitive control and strategy selection: Deciding to practice retrieval during learning. *Journal of Experimental Psychology: General, 138,* 469–486.

Kennedy, M. R. T., Carney, E., & Peters, S. M. (2003). Predictions of recall and study strategy decisions after diffuse brain injury. *Brain Injury, 17,* 1043–1064.

Koriat, A., Bjork, R. A., Sheffer, L., & Bar, S. K. (2004). Predicting one's own forgetting: The role of experience-based and theory based processes. *Journal of Experimental Psychology: General, 133,* 643–656.

Kornell, N., (2005). *The Effectiveness of Study and the Region of Proximal Learning.* Ph.D. Dissertation, Columbia University.

Kornell, N., & Metcalfe, J. (2006). Study efficacy and the Region of Proximal Learning framework. *Journal of Experimental Psychology: Learning, Memory, and Cognition, 32,* 609–622.

Lockl, K., & Schneider, W. (2004) The effects of incentives and instructions on children's allocation of study time. *European Journal of Developmental Psychology, 1,* 153–169.

Mandler, J. M. (l978) A code in the node: The use of a story schema in retrieval. *Discourse Processes, 1,* 14–35.

Masur, E. F., McIntyre, C. W., & Flavell, J. H. (1973). Developmental changes in apportionment of study time among items in a multitrial free recall task. *Journal of Experimental Child Psychology, 15,* 237–246.

Mazzoni, G., & Cornoldi, C. (1993). Strategies in study-time allocation: Why is study time sometimes not effective? *Journal of Experimental Psychology: General, 122,* 47–60.

Metcalfe, J. (l998). Cognitive optimism: Self deception or memory-based processing heuristics? *Personality and Social Psychological Review, 2,* 100–110.

Metcalfe, J. (2002). Is study time allocated selectively to a region of proximal learning? *Journal of Experimental Psychology: General, 131,* 349–363.

Metcalfe, J. (2009). Metacognitive judgments and control of study. *Current Directions in Psychological Science, 18,* 159–163.

Metcalfe, J. (2010). Desirable difficulties and studying in the Region of Proximal Learning. In A. S. Benjamin (Ed.), *Successful Remembering and Successful Forgetting: A Festschrift in Honor of Robert A. Bjork.* London: Psychology Press.

Metcalfe, J., & Finn, B. (2008). Evidence that judgments of learning are causally related to study choice. *Psychonomic Bulletin Review, 15,* 174–179.

Metcalfe, J., & Finn, B. (2012). Metacognition and control of study choice in children. *Metacognition and Learning, 22,* 253–261.

Metcalfe, J., & Jacobs, W. J. (2010). People's study time allocation and its relation to animal foraging. *Behavioral Processes, 83,* 213–221.

Metcalfe, J., & Kornell, N. (2003). The dynamics of learning and allocation of study time to a Region of Proximal Learning. *Journal of Experimental Psychology: General, 132,* 530–542.

Metcalfe, J., & Kornell, N. (2005). A Region of Proximal Learning model of study time allocation. *Journal of Memory and Language, 52,* 463–477.

Nelson, T. O. (1990). Judgments of learning and the allocation of study time. *Journal of Experimental Psychology: General, 112,* 269–273.

Nelson, T. O., Dunlosky, J., Graf, P. A., & Narens, L. (1994). Utilization of metacognitive judgments in the allocation of study during multitrial learning. *Psychological Science, 5,* 207–213.

Nelson, T. O., & Leonesio, R. J. (1988). Allocation of self-paced study time and the "labor-in-vain effect." *Journal of Experimental Psychology: Learning, Memory and Cognition, 14,* 676–686.

Pirolli, P., & Card, S. (1999). Information foraging. *Psychological Review, 106,* 643–675.

Price, J., Hertzog, C., & Dunlosky, J. (2009). Self-regulated learning in younger and older adults: Does aging affect metacognitive control? *Aging, Neuropsychology, and Cognition, 17,* 329–359.

Pyc, M. A., & Dunlosky, J. (2010). Toward an understanding of students' allocation of study time: Why do they decide to mass or space their practice? *Memory & Cognition, 38,* 431–440.

Son, L. K. (2004). Spacing one's study: Evidence for a metacognitive control strategy. *Journal of Experimental Psychology: Learning, Memory, and Cognition, 30,* 601–604.

Son, L. K. (2005). Metacognitive control: Children's short-term versus long-term study strategies. *Journal of General Psychology, 132,* 347–363.

Son, L. K. (2010). Metacognitive control and the spacing effect. *Journal of Experimental Psychology: Learning, Memory, and Cognition, 36,* 255–262.

Son, L. K., & Metcalfe, J. (2000). Metacognitive and control strategies in study-time allocation. *Journal of Experimental Psychology: Learning, Memory, and Cognition, 26,* 204–221.

Thiede, K. W. (1999). The importance of monitoring and self-regulation during multitrial learning. *Psychonomic Bulletin & Review, 6,* 662–667.

Thiede, K. W., Anderson, M. C. M., & Therriault, D. (2003). Accuracy of metacognitive monitoring affects learning of texts. *Journal of Educational Psychology, 95,* 66–75.

Thiede, K. W., & Dunlosky, J. (1999). Toward a general model of self-regulated study: An analysis of selection of items for study and self-paced study time. *Journal of Experimental Psychology: Learning, Memory, and Cognition, 25,* 1024–1037.

Toppino, T. C., & Cohen, M. S. (2010). Metacognitive control and spaced practice: Clarifying what people do and why. *Journal of Experimental Psychology: Learning, Memory and Cognition, 36,* 1480–1492.

Waugh, N. C. (1970). On the effective duration of a repeated word. *Journal of Verbal Learning and Verbal Behavior, 16,* 465–478.

Winnie, P. H. (2005). A perspective on state-of-the-art research on self-regulated learning. *Instructional Science, 33,* 559–565.

Winne, P. H., & Hadwin, A. F. (1998). Studying as self-regulated learning. In D. J.Hacker, J. Dunlosky, and A. C. Graesser (Eds.), *Metacognition in Educational Theory and Practice.* (pp. 277–304). Hillsdale, NJ: LEA.

Zimmerman, B. J. (2001). Theories of self-regulated learning and academic achievement: An overview and analysis. In B. J. Zimmerman and D. H. Schunk (Eds.), *Self-regulated Learning and Academic Achievement: Theoretical Perspectives* (2nd ed.) (pp. 1–37). Mahwah, NJ: Erlbaum.

Zimmerman, B. S., & Martinez-Pons, M. (1990). Student differences in self-regulated learning: Relating grade, sex, and giftedness to self-efficacy and strategy use. *Journal of Educational Psychology, 82,* 51–59 .

Zimmerman, B. J., & Schunk, D. H. (2001). Reflections on theories of self-regulated learning and academic achievement. In B. J. Zimmerman and D. H. Schunk (Eds.), *Self-regulated Learning and Academic Achievement: Theoretical Perspectives* (2nd ed.) (pp. 289–308). Mahwah, NJ: Erlbaum.

27

Metacognitive Control of Memory Reporting

Morris Goldsmith, Ainat Pansky, and Asher Koriat

Two eyewitnesses are asked to pick the perpetrator of a crime out of a police lineup. One witness is told to keep in mind that the actual perpetrator may not be present in the lineup, and that it is perfectly acceptable to respond "don't know." The other witness is simply told to indicate whether one of the persons standing in the lineup is the perpetrator. If you were a falsely accused suspect, in which of these lineups would you prefer to appear? If you are a judge, faced with two different suspects picked out in the different lineups, which of the two witnesses' judgments would you put more faith in?

Two students take a 5-alternative multiple-choice exam under formula scoring, in which a ¼ point penalty is paid for each wrong answer. One student answers all 100 questions but 20 of those answers are wrong. The other answers only 75 questions, all of which are correct. Both students, then, will receive the same score on the exam (75). Nevertheless, is there perhaps a substantial difference between the abilities of these two students that the equivalent test score might be hiding? Two other students take a law exam. One writes long and relatively detailed answers, but many of the added details are wrong. The other is more careful in monitoring the correctness of her answers, providing less detailed responses, but all of the provided information is correct. Which student would you prefer to hire as a law clerk in your firm?

These examples illustrate the important role played by metacognitive processes that intervene between the retrieval of information from memory and the decision to volunteer that information and perhaps act on it (for a review of metacognitive contributions to retrieval itself, see Koriat, Goldsmith, & Halamish, 2008). After reading this chapter, it should become clear that the amount and accuracy of the knowledge and information that people convey from memory depend not only on memory processes per se, but also on the operation of metacognitive monitoring and control processes that are used in the strategic regulation of memory reporting.

In what follows, we present an overview of a metacognitive framework that was developed for investigating this regulation. We then use this framework as a backdrop for a selective review of experimental work on the control of memory reporting – its mechanisms and performance consequences – in both theoretical and applied research contexts, with a special focus on the area of eyewitness memory. Finally, we point to some further directions in which the framework might be extended and applied.

A METACOGNITIVE FRAMEWORK OF MEMORY REPORTING

The storehouse metaphor of memory, which has guided much of traditional memory research (Koriat & Goldsmtih, 1996a), implies a clear goal for the rememberer: to reproduce as much of the originally stored information as possible. This is the essence of the instructions provided to participants in typical list-learning experiments. Growing interest in real-life memory phenomena over the past few decades, however, has led to a greater emphasis on the functions of memory in real-life contexts and on the active role of the rememberer in putting memory to use in the service of personal goals (e.g., Neisser, 1988, 1996). The goals of remembering in everyday life are complex and varied, and may be partially or wholly conflicting. Hence, a great deal of skill and sophistication may be required of the rememberer in negotiating between the different goals and in finding an expedient compromise.

Two prominent and generally conflicting memory goals are informativeness (to provide as much information as possible) and accuracy (to avoid providing wrong information). Consider, for example, a courtroom witness who has sworn "to tell the whole truth and nothing but the truth." To avoid false testimony, the witness may choose to refrain from providing information that she feels unsure about. This, however, will tend to reduce the amount of information that she provides the court, thereby compromising the oath to tell the "whole" truth. Alternatively, she may choose to phrase her answers at a level of generality at which they are unlikely to be wrong (Neisser, 1988). Once again, however, the increased accuracy will come at the expense of informativeness. This example illustrates two general means by which rememberers regulate their memory reporting in the wake of generally competing demands for accuracy and informativeness (Goldsmith & Koriat, 2008): The first, *control of report option*, involves the decision to volunteer or withhold particular items of information, with the option to respond "don't know" to specific questions. The second, *control of grain size*, involves choosing the level of precision or coarseness of an answer when it is provided. Each of these will be considered in turn.

Control of report option

Koriat and Goldsmith (1996b) put forward a simple model of how metamemory processes are used to regulate memory accuracy and quantity performance under free-report conditions, that is, when one is free to choose which items of information to report and which to withhold (see Figure 27.1). The model is deliberately schematic, focusing on the manner in which metacognitive processes at the reporting stage affect the ultimate memory performance. Thus, in addition to an unspecified retrieval mechanism, a monitoring mechanism is used to subjectively assess the correctness of potential memory responses, and a control mechanism then determines whether or not to volunteer the best available candidate answer. The control mechanism operates by setting a report criterion on the monitoring output: The answer is volunteered if its assessed probability of being correct passes the criterion, but is withheld otherwise. The criterion is set on the basis of implicit or explicit payoffs, that is, the perceived gain for providing correct information relative to the cost of providing wrong information.

The basic implication of the model is that when given the opportunity to do so, rememberers can enhance the accuracy of the information that they report by withholding answers that are likely to be wrong. Such enhancement, however, is subject to a *quantity–accuracy trade-off*: In general, raising the report criterion should result in fewer volunteered answers, a higher *percentage* of which are correct (increased accuracy), but a lower *number* of which are correct (decreased quantity). Because of this trade-off, the strategic control of memory performance

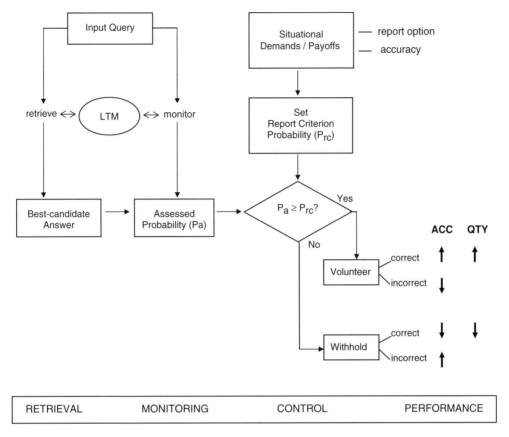

Figure 27.1 A schematic model of the strategic regulation of memory accuracy and memory quantity performance, utilizing the option of free report. The upward and downward pointing arrows on the right of the figure signify positive and negative performance outcomes. Adapted from Koriat and Goldsmith, 1996b

requires the rememberer to weigh the relative payoffs for accuracy and quantity in reaching an appropriate criterion setting.

Although the model is quite simple, its implications for the determinants of free-report memory performance are not. According to the model, such performance should depend not only on "memory" per se, but also on the operation and effectiveness of the metacognitive monitoring and control processes that mediate between the retrieval of information on the one hand, and the reporting (or withholding) of that information on the other. Before we can flesh out these implications and the empirical evidence to support them, we first briefly describe the basic research paradigm and

assessment methodology that was developed to examine the individual cognitive and metacognitive components of the model.

Quantity–Accuracy Profile (QAP) methodology

The Koriat and Goldsmith (1996b) framework was developed together with a special experimental paradigm and procedure that combines free and forced reporting with the elicitation of confidence judgments to isolate and assess the cognitive and metacognitive components postulated by the model. In a typical experiment using this paradigm, participants are presented with a series of questions (or retrieval cues) in either a recall or recognition format, and for each question they are asked: (1) to answer the question (forced report), (2) to assess the likelihood that their answer is correct (confidence judgment), and finally, (3) to decide whether or not to report the answer under either an implicit or explicit "payoff" schedule. For example, participants might be told that they will receive one point for each correct reported answer, but lose one point for each wrong reported answer, with points neither gained nor lost for withheld answers.

Rather than evaluating memory performance in terms of a single overall measure (e.g., percent correct), this basic procedure and its variants (see Goldsmith & Koriat, 2008; Higham, 2007) yields a rich profile of measures, including the joint levels of free-report quantity and accuracy performance, and the underlying determinants of this performance: memory retrieval, metacognitive monitoring, and report control. *Memory retrieval* is indexed by the percentage of correct answers under forced report instructions. Metacognitive *monitoring effectiveness* is indexed in terms of both *calibration bias* (over/under-confidence) and monitoring *resolution* (or discrimination accuracy) – the correlation between confidence in one's answers and the actual correctness of those answers. *Control sensitivity* – the extent to which a person's reporting behavior is guided by the output of his or her monitoring process – is indexed by the correlation between confidence in an answer and the decision to report it. Finally, *control policy* (report criterion level) can be estimated by identifying the confidence level above which the participant reports her answers, and below which she withholds them.

A similar methodological approach, based on the same experimental paradigm but using a Type-2 signal-detection framework to conceptualize and measure the monitoring and control aspects, has been put forward by Higham and colleagues (e.g., Higham, 2002, 2007; Higham, Perfect, & Bruno, 2009). A recent exchange on the advantages and disadvantages of each method can be found in Goldsmith (2011) and Higham (2011).

Empirical findings and conclusions: Report option

We now summarize and discuss some of the main findings and conclusions that have emerged with regard to the control of report option.

Rememberers are reasonably successful in monitoring the correctness of their best-candidate answers

A great deal of work has been conducted on the accuracy of metacognitive monitoring from various different perspectives (see Dunlosky & Metcalfe, 2009; Koriat, 2007). For the purpose of choosing which answers to report and which to withhold, the aspect of monitoring that is most crucial for the effective exercise of report option is *monitoring resolution* – the extent to which a person's confidence judgments successfully discriminate correct from incorrect answers. Under experimental conditions in which there has been no deliberate attempt to impair memory monitoring (e.g., by providing post-event misinformation or using misleading/deceptive/unanswerable questions; see section on "critical role of monitoring" below), monitoring resolution is generally moderate to high, as indexed by the within-participant Kruskal–Goodman gamma correlation between confidence and actual correctness. This correlation is generally somewhat higher for recall testing than for recognition testing (e.g., Koriat & Goldsmith, 1996b; Robinson, Johnson, & Herndon, 1997). Presumably, recall testing provides the remberer with an additional effective cue that is diagnostic of accuracy – retrieval fluency. Another reason is that answers held with low confidence may often be correct simply because of the baseline probability of guessing the right answer (see Schwartz & Metcalfe, 1994 for analysis and discussion).

A second aspect of monitoring effectiveness is *calibration bias* (over/under-confidence; Lichtenstein, Fischhoff, & Phillips, 1982) or *absolute* monitoring accuracy (Nelson, 1996). The ubiquitous finding is that remembers are generally overconfident, with the mean assessed probabilities of people's answers substantially higher than the actual proportion correct (see Hoffrage, 2004). The consequences of this for report option are that although answers held with high confidence are more likely to be correct than those held with low confidence (reflecting good monitoring resolution), the high-confidence answers may still be more likely to be wrong than the person realizes, thereby lowering the accuracy of the answers that are ultimately reported.

Memory monitoring guides the report control decisions

Consistent with the model, rememberers rely heavily on their subjective confidence in deciding whether to volunteer or withhold an answer. Control sensitivity – the relationship between one's level of confidence and the report decision – has been found to be very strong, with within-participant gamma correlations typically on the order of .95 or higher (e.g., Koriat & Goldsmith, 1996b; Mintzer, Kleykamp, & Griffiths, 2010; Pansky, Goldsmith, Koriat, & Pearlman-Avnion, 2009). Interestingly, this relationship continues to be strong even in cases in which the effectiveness of memory monitoring is poor (e.g., Kelly & Sahakyan, 2003; Koriat, 2011; Koriat & Goldsmith, 1996b, Experiment 2; Rhodes & Kelley, 2005; and see section on "critical role of monitoring" below). Rememberers rely blindly on their confidence possibly because they have no access to the diagnosticity of their monitoring or because they have no better alternative.

At the same time, however, control sensitivity has been found to be systematically lower in specific populations such as older adults (Pansky et al., 2009; but see Kelly & Sahakyan, 2003) and people with schizophrenia (Danion, Gokalsing, Robert, Massin-Krauss, & Bacon, 2001; Koren, Seidman,

Goldsmith, & Harvey, 2006). Interestingly, control sensitivity was found to correlate with measures of executive functioning (Pansky et al., 2009) and measures of clinical awareness and competence to consent (Koren et al., 2006), suggesting a link between control sensitivity and overall levels of metacognitive and executive functioning. The inclusion of control sensitivity as a theoretical component underlying free-report performance, and the examination of potential group and situational differences in such sensitivity, distinguishes the metacognitive approach from the related signal-detection approach (Type-1 or Type-2), in which use of the subjective evidence continuum as the basis for the response decision is axiomatic, and possible variance in control sensitivity is essentially ignored.

Performance consequences: By regulating their own reporting, rememberers substantially enhance the accuracy of the information that they report. This accuracy increase is often achieved at a relatively small cost in the amount of correct reported information (quantity–accuracy trade-off).

Perhaps the most basic and robust finding with regard to the consequences of report option for memory performance is that rememberers can in fact enhance their free-report accuracy substantially, relative to forced report (e.g., Higham, 2002; Koriat & Goldsmith, 1994, 1996b; Kelley & Sahakyan, 2003). They do so by withholding candidate answers that are likely to be wrong. The potential accuracy gain is particularly high when forced-report accuracy is low. Thus, for example, Koriat and Goldsmith (1996b), using general-knowledge tests of differing difficulty, observed accuracy increases of 29 percentage points (from 47 percent to 76 percent) and 47 percentage points (from 28 percent to 75 percent) in the recall conditions of their Experiments 1 and 2, respectively.

The improved accuracy generally comes at a relatively small decrease in the quantity of correct reported information (e.g., 9 percentage points and 6 percentage points, respectively, in the two recall conditions just mentioned). However, both simulation analyses (Higham, 2011; Koriat & Goldsmith, 1996b) and empirical results indicate that for typical levels of monitoring effectiveness, enhancing one's accuracy becomes relatively costly in terms of quantity performance as the criterion level is raised. Thus, simply giving a person the option of free report may allow a fairly large accuracy improvement to be achieved without much loss of quantity (e.g., Koriat & Goldsmith, 1994, 1996b; Perfect & Weber, 2012; Roebers, Moga, & Schneider, 2001), but placing a larger premium on accuracy leads to a more serious quantity reduction relative to the increased gain in accuracy (e.g., Koriat & Goldsmith, 1994, 1996b; Koriat, Goldsmith, Schneider, & Nakash-Dura, 2001).

The use of report option in the control of memory reporting is strategic

The basic dynamic of a quantity–accuracy trade-off requires rememberers to weigh the potential gain of reporting correct information against the potential penalty for providing wrong information in arriving at an appropriate report criterion for the specific reporting context. In experimental contexts, these incentives are often manipulated in terms of explicit payoffs and penalties for correct and incorrect reported answers. Several studies have found that participants do indeed adjust their report criterion according to the operative payoff matrix, setting a more strict report criterion when the motivation for accuracy is higher (e.g., Higham, 2007; Koriat & Goldsmith, 1996b; Koriat et al., 2001).

The critical role of monitoring: Both the accuracy benefits and the quantity costs of self-regulated reporting depend greatly on monitoring effectiveness

Another key implication of the metacognitive model of report control concerns the crucial role of monitoring effectiveness in determining the joint levels of free-report memory accuracy and quantity performance. Clearly some ability to distinguish between correct and incorrect candidate answers is necessary for the control of memory reporting to yield any benefits at all. Moreover, as this ability improves, greater increases in accuracy can be achieved at lower costs in quantity, so that at the extreme, when monitoring effectiveness is perfect, there is no quantity–accuracy trade-off at all. On the other hand, when monitoring ability is poor, the exercise of report option may yield little or no benefit in accuracy, and merely reduce the quantity of correct reported information. In fact, there may even be situations in which participants' monitoring is counterdiagnostic, with a negative correlation between subjective confidence and actual accuracy (see Benjamin, Bjork, & Schwartz, 1998; Koriat, 2012). Though presumably rare, in such cases the reporting and withholding of answers on the basis of subjective confidence would be expected to lower both quantity and accuracy.

The crucial role of monitoring effectiveness for the effective use of report option has been elucidated both in simulation analyses (Higham, 2011; Koriat & Goldsmith, 1996b) and in empirical results. For example, Koriat and Goldsmith (1996b, Experiment 2) manipulated participants' monitoring effectiveness by using two different sets of general-knowledge recall questions: One set consisted of standard items for which the participants' monitoring was expected to be effective, whereas the other set consisted of "deceptive" items for which the participants' ability to monitor the correctness of their answers was expected to be poor (e.g., "Who composed the Unfinished Symphony"?; see Koriat, 1995). In fact, monitoring resolution for the two sets of items averaged .90 for the standard items versus .26 for the deceptive items. Overconfidence was also much greater for the deceptive items (20 percentage points) than for the standard items (3 percentage points). Because of these differences in monitoring effectiveness, the option of free report allowed participants to increase their accuracy from 28 percent to 75 percent for the standard items, whereas for the deceptive items there was only a negligible increase, from 12 percent to 21 percent. Note that for the latter set, about 80 percent of the participants' freely reported answers were wrong! Even when the overall difficulty of the standard items was matched to that of the deceptive items, the accuracy increase was still about five times greater (from 11 percent to 63 percent) than the respective increase for the deceptive items (for a similar pattern using an associate interference manipulation, see Kelly & Sahakyan, 2003; Rhodes & Kelly, 2005).

Of particular importance is the demonstration that monitoring effectiveness can affect memory performance independent of memory "retrieval." Even when retrieval, as indexed by forced-report performance, is equated, free-report accuracy is far superior when monitoring resolution is high than when it is low. Clearly, then, free-report memory performance depends on the effective operation of metacognitive processes that are simply not tapped by forced-report performance.

Control of grain size

The basic theoretical model and results discussed so far have focused on how people regulate their memory performance when given the option to withhold individual items of information or entire answers about which they are unsure. Control of report option, however, is just one means by which people can regulate their memory reporting. In most real-life memory situations, people do not just have the choice of either volunteering a substantive answer or else responding "don't know." They can provide an answer but indicate that they are not entirely sure about it. They can also control the "graininess" or level of precision or coarseness of the information that they provide (e.g., describing the assailant's height as "around 6 feet" or

"fairly tall" rather than "5 feet 11 inches"). In attempting to explain the surprisingly superior accuracy of recall over recognition in his naturalistic study, Neisser (1988), for example, noted that the recall participants tended to choose "a level of generality at which they were not mistaken" (p. 553).

The considerations and mechanisms underlying the choice of grain size in memory reporting appear to be similar to, though somewhat more complex than, those underlying the exercise of report option. Let us return to the earlier example of a witness who wants to fulfill her vow to "tell the whole truth and nothing but the truth." How should she proceed? On the one hand, a very coarsely grained response (e.g., "between noon and midnight") will always be the wiser choice if accuracy is the sole consideration. However, such a response may not be very informative, falling short of the goal to tell the whole truth. On the other hand, whereas a very fine-grained answer (e.g., 5.23 p.m.) would be much more informative, it is also much more likely to be wrong. A similar conflict is often faced by students taking open-ended essay exams: Should one attempt to provide a very precise informative answer, but risk being wrong, or try to "hedge one's bet" by providing a coarser, less informative answer, and risk being penalized for vagueness? In both of these examples, control over grain size can be seen to involve an accuracy–informativeness trade-off (see Yaniv & Foster, 1995, 1997) similar to the accuracy–quantity trade-off observed with regard to the control of report option.

How does one find an appropriate compromise between accuracy and informativeness in choosing a grain size for one's answers? A simple strategy is to provide the most finely grained (precise) answer that passes some preset confidence criterion. Thus, for example, a witness might try to answer the question to the nearest minute, to the nearest 5 minutes, 10 minutes, 15 minutes, and so forth, until she is, say, at least 90 percent sure that the specified answer is correct. Goldsmith, Koriat, and Weinberg-Eliezer

(2002) called this the *satisficing model* of the control of grain size: The rememberer strives to provide as precise-informative an answer as possible (without being overly precise; cf. Grice, 1975), as long as its assessed probability of being correct satisfies some reasonable minimum level. Note that this model is similar to the one presented earlier with regard to report option: The assessed probability correct of each answer that is volunteered must pass a report criterion, and the setting of the criterion level should depend on the relative incentives for accuracy and informativeness in each particular situation.

Research paradigm and methodology: Control of grain size

As in the study of report option, the challenge in the study of the control of grain size is to find a way to allow participants to control the grain size of their answers while also obtaining information about the underlying metacognitive mechanisms and performance consequences. A productive approach has been to adapt the "free-forced" paradigm used for report option.

In the basic paradigm, participants are exposed to a stimulus event and later asked to answer a set of questions that pertain to quantitative values, such as the time of an accident, the speed of a car, the height of an assailant, and so forth (for an extension to non-quantitative values, see Weber & Brewer, 2008). Alternatively, participants might be asked to answer a set of general-knowledge questions that pertain to quantitative-numeric information: date, age, height, distance, and so forth. For each question, participants are required to provide an answer at both a fine-precise grain size (e.g., to the nearest minute, mile per hour, inch, etc.) and a coarse grain size (e.g., to the nearest half hour, 20-mph interval, 10-yard, etc.). Confidence judgments are also elicited for each answer at each grain size. Finally, participants are given the option to choose which of the two alternative answers for each item (i.e.,

which of the two grain sizes) they prefer to actually provide under an implicit or explicit incentive for accuracy and informativeness. For example, participants might be offered five points for each correct precise answer, one point for each correct coarse answer, and penalized one point for each incorrect answer (Goldsmith et al., 2002, Experiment 3). More naturalistically, participants might be instructed to choose the answer they would prefer to provide, assuming that "you are the only eyewitness of this crime and the police need information that is very likely to be correct" (high accuracy – low informativeness incentive), or that "there were several eyewitnesses to this crime and the police are in the initial stages of the investigation looking for leads" (high informativeness – low accuracy incentive; Higham, Luna, & Bloomfield, 2011).

In an adaptation of this basic paradigm, participants may be allowed to determine for themselves the grain size of the answer that they provide, rather than selecting from the grain sizes specified in advance by the experimenter (e.g., Evans & Fisher, 2010; Goldsmith, Koriat, & Pansky, 2005, Experiment 2; Pansky, 2012; Pansky & Nemets, 2012). This additional freedom, however, requires a method for quantifying the grain size (or informativeness) of the provided answers, either as a function of the width of the provided answer interval (for quantitative information; see Goldsmith et al., 2005, Experiment 2; Yaniv & Foster, 1995), or on the basis of subjective ratings by independent judges of the precision or informativeness of the answer (e.g., Evans & Fisher, 2010; Pansky, 2012; Pansky & Nemets, 2012).

Empirical findings and conclusions: Control of grain size

We now summarize and discuss some of the main findings and conclusions that have emerged with regard to the control of grain size in memory reporting.

Rememberers are able to monitor the correctness of their best-candidate answers at different grain sizes, but differences in grain size appear to be tied to systematic differences in monitoring effectiveness

Depending on the complexity of the theoretical model that is assumed (see following point), the effective control of memory grain size requires that people be able to monitor the correctness of their candidate answers at different grain sizes. In general, monitoring resolution has been found to be moderately high for both fine-grained and coarse-grained answers, with a tendency for lower resolution for the coarse-grained answers (e.g., Goldsmith et al., 2005; Luna, Higham, & Martin-Luengo, 2011). In addition, although the general finding of overconfidence applies to the monitoring of precise answers, people tend to be much less overconfident and sometimes even underconfident in the correctness of their coarse-grained answers (e.g., Goldsmith et al., 2002; Luna et al., 2011; Weber & Brewer, 2008). In a recent generalization of grain control to multiple-choice testing (called "plurality option"; see below), Luna et al. (2011) found that although reported coarse-grained answers were more likely to be correct than reported fine-grained answers, confidence in the former answers was lower than in the latter, yielding an apparent dissociation between confidence and accuracy across grain sizes.

One account of this pattern is that participants do not sufficiently adjust their subjective probability assessments to accommodate differences in the baseline probabilities that an answer will be correct at the different grain sizes (cf. Tversky & Kahneman, 1974). This is suggested by the typical shape of the calibration plots for fine-grained and coarse-grained answers (e.g., Figure 1 in Goldsmith et al., 2002; Figure 2 in Luna et al., 2011), in which the actual proportions correct for the coarse-grained answers are higher than the corresponding proportions correct for the fine-grained answers across the range of subjective probability categories. Thus, when participants feel that they possess precise knowledge regarding the question, they may tend to underrate the likelihood that a volunteered fine-grained answer is nevertheless wrong, and conversely, when they feel that they lack precise knowledge, they may tend to underrate the likelihood that a chosen coarse-grained answer is nevertheless correct. Such a tendency would be expected to hinder the effectiveness of the grain control process, biasing it toward the choice of fine-grained answers.

Memory monitoring guides the grain control decisions

As with the control of report option, the basic assumption of the metacognitive model of grain control is that the choice of grain size is based on subjective confidence in the correctness of one's candidate answers. Indeed, in line with the satisficing model described earlier, high correlations have been found between confidence in one's best-candidate fine-grained answer and the decision to provide that answer rather than a more coarse-grained answer (e.g., mean gamma correlations ranging between .74 and .85; Goldsmith et al., 2002, 2005; Weber & Brewer, 2008). Of course the grain control decision could conceivably be based not only on confidence in one's fine-grained candidate answer but also on confidence in alternative coarse-grained candidate answers, or perhaps on the relative gain in confidence when moving from the fine-grained to a more coarse-grained answer. Results indicate that when given the opportunity to provide either a fine-grained or a more coarse-grained answer, the grain control decision is based primarily on confidence in the fine-grained answer, in line with the simple satisficing model (Goldsmith et al., 2002, 2005; Weber & Brewer, 2008). It is possible, however, that when the choice of grain size is less constrained, the control process will be more complex.

Control over grain size enhances the accuracy of reported information, at a cost in the informativeness of the reported information (accuracy–informativeness trade-off)

Perhaps the most basic finding is that when given the option to choose the appropriate grain size for their answers, participants are not guided solely by the desire to be correct – in which case they would always choose to provide a coarse-grained answer, nor solely by the desire to be informative – in which case they would have always choose to provide a precise/fine-grained answer. Instead, participants tend to choose the coarse-grained answer when the more precise answer is unlikely to be correct. By sacrificing informativeness in this calculated manner, participants generally improve their accuracy substantially compared with what they would have achieved by providing the fine-grained answers throughout (e.g., Goldsmith et al., 2002, 2005; Luna et al., 2011; Pansky & Nemets, 2012; Weber & Brewer, 2008). The control of grain size is far from optimal, however, apparently because of imperfect monitoring: There are still many cases in which fine-grained answers are provided even though they are wrong, and coarse-grained answers are provided even though the fine-grained answer is correct.

The control of grain size in memory reporting is strategic

A key assumption of the metacognitive model of grain control is that the grain size of reported information is determined not only by the grain size of the information that is available and accessible in memory, but also on strategic control: Holding the quality of the accessible information constant, people may choose to report the information either more precisely or more coarsely, and they do so based on their subjective assessment of the likely correctness of the information and in light of implicit or explicit incentives for accuracy and informativeness. In support of this idea, studies manipulating the incentives for accuracy and informativeness have found that participants do in fact strategically adjust their grain control criterion, requiring lower levels of confidence for reporting fine-grained answers and providing more of such answers when a premium is placed on informativeness, and vice versa when the premium is placed on accuracy (e.g., Goldsmith et al., 2002, 2005; Higham et al., 2011).

The control of grain size is constrained by a minimum-informativeness criterion: When respondents are unable to provide an answer that is both sufficiently accurate and sufficiently informative, they prefer to withhold the answer entirely (if a report option is available), or violate the confidence criterion, if necessary, to provide a reasonably informative answer

According to social and pragmatic norms of communication, people are expected not only to be accurate in what they report, but also to be reasonably informative (Grice, 1975). What, then, should a rememberer do if achieving the desired level of likely correctness requires her to provide a ridiculously coarse answer such as "the assailant was between 5 and 7 feet tall" or "the French revolution occurred sometime between the years 1000 and 2000"? Ackerman and Goldsmith (2008) examined the control of grain size in answering either easy or very difficult general-knowledge questions, and found that when knowledge of the answer was very poor, such that a minimum-confidence criterion and a minimum-informativeness criterion could not be jointly satisfied, respondents tended to violate the minimum-confidence criterion, choosing to provide relatively precise but low-confidence answers. Relatedly, Yaniv and Foster (1995) observed that recipients of quantitative information often prefer an estimate that is precise but somewhat inaccurate to one that is completely accurate but so coarse as to be uninformative. However, in the Ackerman and Goldsmith (2008, Experiment 4) study, when rememberers were allowed simultaneous control over both grain size and report option, they utilized the "don't know" option to avoid violating either the minimum-confidence or minimum-informativeness criterion, though some precise low-confidence answers were still reported.

Ackerman and Goldsmith (2008) speculated that there may also be social-pragmatic norms that prohibit overuse of the "don't know" option, because this too may be seen as being uninformative or uncooperative. Several other studies have also examined the joint control of grain size and report option, and the division of labor between them (e.g., Evans & Fisher, 2010; Weber & Brewer, 2008).

Applied research contexts: Focus on eyewitness memory

The strategic control of memory reporting is an important topic of research in its own right, but is also of interest because of the role that such control plays in a variety of memory research domains and topics. The application of the metacognitive framework to examine how rememberers regulate their memory reporting, as well as the performance consequences of such regulation, has yielded new insights with regard to several important memory topics and phenomena, such as (a) the effectiveness of different questioning and testing procedures in eliciting accurate memory reports (e.g., Koriat & Goldsmith, 1994; Evans & Fisher, 2010; Luna et al., 2011; Pansky & Nemets, 2012; Perfect & Weber, 2012; Weber & Perfect, 2012), (b) the credibility of children's witness testimony (e.g., Koriat et al., 2001; Roebers & Fernandez, 2002; Roebers & Schneider, 2005; Waterman & Blades, 2011), (c) memory decline in old age (e.g., Huff, Meade, & Hutchison, 2011; Kelley & Sahakyan, 2003; Pansky et al., 2009; Rhodes & Kelley, 2005), (d) cognitive

and metacognitive impairments related to schizophrenia and psychoactive medication (e.g., Danion et al., 2001; Koren et al., 2006; Mintzer et al., 2010), (e) encoding–retrieval interactions and the encoding specificity principle (e.g., Higham, 2002; Higham & Tam, 2005), and (f) psychometric and scholastic testing (e.g., Higham, 2007; Higham & Arnold, 2007; Notea-Koren, 2006).

A systematic review of the work in each of these areas is beyond the scope of this chapter (for a summary review, see Goldsmith & Koriat, 2008). Instead, we will focus here on some illustrative applications and extensions of the metacognitive report-control framework in the study of eyewitness memory.

Perhaps nowhere is the potential importance of metacognitive report control more clear than in the domain of eyewitness research, in which there has been enormous interest in the effects of different questioning formats and procedures on the amount and accuracy of information that can be elicited from witnesses to a crime. Thus, for example, it is established wisdom in eyewitness research that witnesses should first be allowed to tell their story in their own words (i.e., in a free-narrative format) before being subjected to more directed questioning, and that, even then, greater faith should be placed in the accuracy of the former type of testimony (e.g., Milne & Bull, 1999; Neisser, 1988). This wisdom has been incorporated, for instance, into the Cognitive Interview technique (Fisher, Schreiber Compo, Rivard, & Hirn, Chapter 31, this volume; Fisher & Geiselman, 1992), and into various government documents concerning the proper way to interview witnesses such as the Memorandum of Good Practice (1992), the National Institute of Child Health and Human Development (NICHD) protocol for interviewing children (Orbach, Hershkowitz, Lamb, Sternberg, Esplin, & Horowitz, 2000), and others (see Wells, Malpass, Lindsay, Fisher, Turtle, & Fulero, 2000). An important component of the Cognitive Interview and other structured interview protocols is establishing clear "communication rules" to enable the witness to regulate his or her responses in an appropriate manner – for example, clarifying the level of detail that is forensically relevant and emphasizing to the witness that it is perfectly acceptable to respond "don't know" or "don't remember" when applicable (see, e.g., Powell, Fisher, & Wright, 2005, Table 2). This appears to be especially crucial with child witnesses (e.g., Roebers and Fernandez, 2002; see below).

In an early attempt to clarify the role of report option in "open-ended" reporting, Koriat and Goldsmith (1994) examined what they called the "recall-recognition paradox": Whereas the general finding from decades of laboratory research (e.g., Brown, 1976) is that recognition testing is superior to recall testing in eliciting a greater quantity of correct information from memory, the established wisdom in eyewitness research is that recognition is inferior to recall in eliciting accurate information from rememberers (e.g., Milne & Bull, 1999). Koriat and Goldsmith (1994) showed that this seeming inconsistency stems from the common confounding in research practice between test format (recall versus recognition) and report option (free versus forced): Typically, in recognition testing, participants are forced either to choose between several alternatives or to make a yes–no decision regarding each and every item (i.e., forced report), whereas in recall testing participants have the freedom to withhold information that they are unsure about (free report). Comparing performance on a free-recognition test to a free-recall test, Koriat and Goldsmith (1994) found that recognition quantity performance was still superior to recall, but now recognition accuracy was as high as or even higher than recall accuracy. Thus, although the superior memory quantity performance of forced-recognition over free-recall testing does appear to stem from the test-format difference, the generally superior accuracy of free recall over forced recognition appears to stem entirely from report option (for a similar pattern in a developmental study, see Koriat et al., 2001).

The implication is that recognition testing and other forms of directed questioning may yield information that is highly reliable, as long as witnesses are clearly instructed regarding the legitimacy of responding "don't know" (see also Perfect & Weber, 2012; Weber & Perfect, 2012, discussed below). Nevertheless, free-narrative reporting still appears to yield the most reliable information, as it allows simultaneous control over both grain size and report option (see Evans & Fisher, 2010, discussed below). However, more structured free-report formats that include both report option and grain size should be considered as well (e.g., Higham et al., 2011; Hope, Gabbert, & Brewer, 2011; Weber & Brewer, 2008). For example, Luna et al. (2011) have put forward a "plurality option" questioning format that allows rememberers to select more than one response alternatives on a multiple-choice test, thereby increasing the likelihood that the response is correct, but reducing its informativeness (see also Notea-Koren, 2006, who examined this procedure together with the simultaneous control of report option).

A second topic that is of great relevance for eyewitness memory research is the role of report control in regulating the decline of memory accuracy and informativeness over time. Although a decline in the accessibility of memories over time will almost inevitably lead to a decline in the amount of correct information that can be reported, conceivably the effective use of the option of free report and/or control over grain size could allow rememberers to avoid a decline in memory accuracy over time by withholding or coarsening information that is likely to be wrong. Ebbesen and Rienick (1998), for example, found that although the number of correct statements reported about an experienced event decreased dramatically over a four-week period, the accuracy of those statements remained stable (at about 90 percent). Essentially the same pattern was obtained by Flin, Boon, Knox, and Bull (1992) in comparing the number and accuracy of propositions about a staged event made either one day or five months after the event. These, as well as other studies, found stable accuracy using open-ended questioning procedures that gave participants control over what information to report, and at what grain size to report it.

The idea that rememberers might use control over grain size and/or report option to maintain a stable accuracy rate over time has been examined in several studies. Goldsmith et al. (2005) had participants read a mock crime witness transcript and then asked them to answer specific questions about the described events at either a precise or coarse grain size, "to help the investigator reproduce the facts of the case." As predicted, participants provided more coarse-grained answers after 24 hours than at immediate testing, thereby maintaining a high and stable accuracy rate at the cost of reduced informativeness. After a one-week delay, even more coarse-grained answers were provided, but now there was a drop in accuracy, though much less steep a drop than would have occurred without the use of grain control. Part of the reason for the reduced accuracy was that without report option, participants could not, in some cases, avoid providing coarse-grained answers that were likely – both subjectively and objectively – to be wrong. Recently, Pansky and Nemets (2012) found that allowing participants control both over what information to report, and at what grain size to report it, enabled them to maintain stable accuracy over a retention interval of 48 hours, at the cost of a reduction in both the number and the informativeness of the answers.

The most comprehensive investigation to date was conducted by Evans and Fisher (2010), who questioned participants about details from a mock crime video using one of three questioning formats – free narrative, specific questioning (cued recall), or yes–no recognition – after either ten minutes or one week. The free-narrative and specific-questioning formats allowed participants control over both whether to report an item of information and at what level of precision,

whereas the yes–no recognition format allowed control of report option only. For the specific questioning and recognition formats, forced-report answers were elicited after each initial "don't know" response, providing information about the performance that would be observed in the absence of report control. As expected, there was a significant decrease in the amount of correct information and in the precision of the information that was reported at delayed compared with immediate testing. This was also so when the forced-report responses were included, indicating a significant drop in information accessibility. At the same time, however, there was only a negligible (3 percentage points; only approaching significance) drop in free-report accuracy over this same time period. The level of accuracy attained (and maintained) was about 10 points higher for the free-narrative format (94 percent) than for the other two formats (84 percent), which did not differ from each other.

Another interesting finding in the Evans and Fisher (2010) study is that in comparing the use of the "don't know" option between the specific-questioning and yes–no recognition formats, participants tended to respond "don't know" more often to the recognition questions, possibly because the option for control of grain size was unavailable (for related results implying a "division of labor" in employing the joint control of grain size and report option, see Ackerman & Goldsmith, 2008; Weber & Brewer, 2008).

Although the studies discussed so far have focused on verbal witness reports, Weber and Perfect (Weber & Perfect, 2012; Perfect & Weber, 2012) recently demonstrated the importance of report control for eyewitness identifications as well. Weber and Perfect (2012) examined whether single-suspect ("show up") identification accuracy could be improved by providing an explicit "don't know" response option. When the "don't know" option was left implicit, it was rarely used spontaneously, with 98 percent of the participants providing a substantive yes or no response; hence performance in this condition was indistinguishable from the forced-report condition. Making the "don't know" option explicit increased the rate of "don't know" responses, thereby increasing the diagnosticity of the responses considerably: Compared with the forced-report condition, including an explicit "don't know" response option reduced the proportion of false identifications by almost 50 percent, with no reduction in the proportion of correct identifications. This was so both on immediate testing and after a three-week delay.

Similarly, Perfect and Weber (2012) found that including an explicit "don't know" option increased the overall diagnosticity of both suspect identifications and lineup rejections (suspect-absent responses) in a simultaneous lineup situation, again with no loss of diagnostic information stemming from exclusion of the "don't know" responses. In this study, report option was manipulated within participants, with the free-report decision elicited either before or after the forced-report decision. The results indicated that a "one-step" free-report procedure yielded the most diagnostic witness decisions (best ratio of hits to false alarms), with no additional diagnostic information provided by forcing the witness to guess after an initial "don't know" response.

These results have important implications regarding not only the diagnosticity of eyewitness identification responses, but also regarding their *output-bound* accuracy (Koriat & Goldsmith, 1994, 1996a) – the extent to which they can be relied upon to be correct. The conditional probability that an eyewitness identification response is correct, given that it was freely volunteered under conditions in which there is an explicit "don't know" response option, is much higher than the probability correct under forced-report conditions. This higher conditional probability should be of great interest to law enforcement officials, judges, and juries (cf. Deffenbacher, Bornstein, McGorty, & Penrod, 2008; and see Koriat, Pansky, & Goldsmith, 2011, for a related analysis and discussion of output-bound accuracy).

The increased reliability of the identification responses in the two studies by Perfect and Weber, just described, with no cost in diagnostic information stemming from the exercise of report option, is important practically, but also theoretically: It indicates that, at least in these two studies, the participants made very effective use of their metacognitive monitoring and control processes, using the "don't know" option only when their ability to identify the suspect, or correctly reject the foil suspects' lineups, was at chance levels.

Of even greater theoretical importance is the extension of the metacognitive report control model to what is essentially a yes–no recognition memory situation. This situation involves not only the decision about whether one is confident enough that the target is *present* to volunteer an *identification* response, but also about whether one is confident enough that the target is *absent* to volunteer a suspect or lineup *rejection* response. Perfect and Weber (2012) modeled this situation by assuming a single-threshold (Type-1) signal-detection model for the forced-report (yes–no) decision, and a double-threshold (Type-2) signal-detection model for the free-report (volunteer-withhold) decision. Using this model, they were able to show, for example, that participants adopted a more conservative (Type-1) forced-report criterion, reflecting a tendency to reject the lineup rather than identify a suspect, when the forced-report decision was made first, compared with when this decision followed an initial free-report decision. A plausible explanation is that, ordinarily, a witness who is uncertain will prefer to err by wrongly rejecting a lineup rather than falsely accusing an innocent suspect. However, a witness who has just made a "don't know" response and is then asked to make a guess may feel less wary of making a false identification, having already indicated his or her uncertainly in the preceding "don't know" response. Interestingly, such "pragmatic" social-communicative considerations (see further discussion later) appear to have influenced the placement of the Type-1, yes–no criterion, with no effect on the placement of the double-threshold Type-2, volunteer-withhold criteria.

The final area of application to be mentioned is the regulation of responses to misleading or unanswerable questions. In a developmental study, Roebers and Fernandez (2002) (followed up by Roebers & Schneider, 2005) had children (six- to eight-year-olds) and adult participants view a short video and then answer a set of questions that included "answerable" questions in either an unbiased (e.g., "What did the girl hold in her hand?") or biased-misleading (e.g., "The girl held a bouquet of flowers in her hand, didn't she?") format, as well as questions that were "unanswerable" because the pertinent information was not contained in the video, again in either an unbiased or biased format. Report option was manipulated either with or without an additional accuracy incentive. With regard to the answerable questions, adults utilized the option of free report to increase report accuracy for both biased and unbiased questions, regardless of accuracy incentive. For the children, however, only the free-report option combined with incentives was effective in causing them to utilize the "don't know" option to increase report accuracy for the misleading questions (for similar results in a lineup study, see Brewer, Keast, & Sauer, 2010). Roebers and Fernandez (2002) speculate that in the free-report condition without explicit accuracy incentives, the children may have treated the biased questioning format as similar to forced report – presenting implicit pressure to provide a substantive response (cf. Koriat et al., 2001).

With regard to the unanswerable questions, when these were asked in an unbiased manner, children and adults were both able to appropriately admit their lack of knowledge by utilizing the "don't know" option, somewhat more often in the incentives condition (77 percent) than in the no-incentives condition (64 percent). When such answers were asked in a biased format, however, children in the no-incentives condition utilized the "don't know" option much less adequately (30 percent) than did adults (57 percent). Note that in the case of unanswerable questions, "don't know" is treated by researchers as a "correct" response, whereas for answerable questions, it is treated as an "omission" that presumably reflects subjective lack of knowledge.

Pointing to this difference, Scoboria, Mazzoni, and Kirsch (2008) (see also Waterman & Blades, 2011) argue that "don't know" responses are essentially ambiguous, and that in addition to the possibility that they conceal no information at all, any given "don't know" response might in fact reflect an unstated assertion that (a) the question is unanswerable (i.e., it refers to something that did not occur or was not originally witnessed) or (b) the question is answerable (i.e., the event did occur and was witnessed) but the respondent's memory of the solicited details is insufficient to provide a confident answer. Using a post-report procedure to clarify the intended meanings of participants' "don't know" responses to a mixed set of answerable and unanswerable questions, Scoboria et al. (2008) found that a substantial number of initial "don't know" responses could in fact be recoded as substantive assertions about "presence" or "absence," which could then be scored as either correct or wrong.

The consideration of how witnesses deal with unanswerable questions poses challenges to the metacognitive model of report control that resemble those mentioned earlier with respect to report regulation in suspect lineup identifications (e.g., Perfect & Weber, 2012). Faced with a question about a witnessed event, a witness may have to decide not only whether she is confident enough to provide her best-candidate answer, but if no such candidate arises, she may also have to decide whether she is confident enough to assert that such an event never occurred or was not witnessed. Insufficient confidence in either decision would then lead to a "don't know" response, the intended meaning of which might later need to be clarified. Of course, one would expect that the rememberer's monitoring processes and control decisions with respect to potentially unanswerable questions would be strongly guided by pragmatic assumptions regarding the state of knowledge of the questioner, and the likelihood that he or she would be asking an unanswerable question in a particular research or real-world context.

CONCLUSION

Interest in "real-life" remembering over the past few decades has brought with it a myriad of challenging metatheoretical, theoretical, and methodological issues (e.g., Koriat & Goldsmith, 1996a; Koriat, Goldsmith, & Pansky, 2000; Cohen & Conway, 2008), including a functional approach that views memory as a multifaceted tool used in the service of achieving personal and social goals (e.g., Neisser, 1988, 1996). As Neisser has eloquently argued, remembering is like "doing" (Neisser, 1996), and hence, any complete theory of memory "retrieval" will need to deal with "the reason for retrieval … with persons, motives, and social situations" (Neisser, 1988, p. 553).

The metacognitive framework and associated research presented in this chapter has focused on situations in which the rememberer's goals are presumably served by providing both informative and accurate memory reports. However, as should be clear by now, depending on the effectiveness of memory monitoring, it is generally not possible to be both maximally informative and completely accurate – to tell the whole truth and nothing but the truth. Thus, rememberers are generally faced with a dilemma: Should they attempt to provide more information, taking a chance that it is wrong, or provide less information but increase the likelihood that it is correct? Much theoretical work has been directed at understanding how rememberers attempt to resolve this dilemma, and the mechanisms that they use to regulate the accuracy and quantity of the information that they report. This understanding has then been applied to examine the consequences of such regulation, as well as potential situational and group differences, in a variety of different domains, some of which were mentioned earlier (see also Goldsmith & Koriat, 2008).

Of course there is still much work that remains to be done to reach a more complete understanding of the metacognitive regulation of memory reporting and its theoretical and applied implications. Perhaps most fundamentally, it should be worthwhile to try to extend the metacognitive framework to encompass a greater range of potential goals and means of control, such as those studied by researchers taking a social-communication approach to memory (see Ackerman & Goldsmith, 2008). This approach emphasizes the cooperative pragmatic principles and assumptions involved in the explicit and implicit communication that is served by memory reporting in specific social contexts. Relevant studies have shown that people's answers to questions are guided by pragmatic considerations and tacit assumptions relating to the background and existing knowledge of the questioner, his or her purpose in asking the question, personal goals, self expectations, and so forth (e.g., Gibbs & Bryant, 2008; Smith & Clark, 1993). Thus, for example, people have been found to adjust the detail of the information they convey according to their perception of how much the listener needs to know (Gibbs & Bryant, 2008), to focus more on story details and narrative structure in recalling a story to an experimenter than when conveying it to a peer (Hyman, 1994), to include fewer details and verbatim quotes in recounting events when the goal was to entertain than when accuracy was emphasized (Dudukovic, Marsh, & Tversky, 2004), and to convey less detailed information to inattentive than to attentive listeners (Pasupathi, Stallworth, & Murdoch, 1998).

Another general direction for future theoretical development concerns the division of labor and potential interactions between metacognitive processes involved in report regulation and those involved in controlling the retrieval process itself. A useful way of conceptualizing this interaction is the "manufacturing" metaphor promoted by Jacoby and colleagues (e.g., Jacoby, Shimizu, Daniels, & Rhodes, 2005): Quality control in manufacturing can be achieved either by a post-production screening process, which identifies and screens out defective products at the "back end," or by improving the production techniques at the "front end," so that fewer defective products are produced in the first place. Likewise, the processes used by rememberers in controlling the quality of their memory outputs presumably involve a complex interplay of cognitive and metacognitive processes that operate both to guide retrieval (front-end) and to guide reporting (back-end).

To isolate and examine both front-end and back-end components, Halamish, Goldsmith, and Jacoby (2011) developed a refined version of the QAP methodology described earlier, in which recall participants record the candidate answers that come to mind in response to a recall cue, choose from among these a best-candidate answer, rate their confidence in that answer, and, finally, decide whether to report the answer for points. Using this procedure, Halamish et al. (2011) found that rememberers use metacognitive knowledge about source encoding conditions not only to monitor the accuracy of the retrieved candidate answers, but also to control the mode of retrieval itself, mentally reinstating the relevant encoding operation to enhance the quality of produced answer-candidates ("source-constrained recall"; cf. Jacoby et al., 2005). A similar approach and methodology was used by Thomas and McDaniel (2012) to examine the effects of testing and error feedback on retrieval and report processes. A recent discussion and organizing framework for research on front-end and back-end control processes in remembering can be found in Koriat et al. (2008).

Finally, there are many further applied topics for which the metacognitive framework for the study of monitoring and control

of performance could be useful. For example, returning to the anecdotal examples that appeared in the introduction to this chapter, do law exams, medical exams, business exams, and so forth evaluate the metacognitive as well as cognitive abilities of the examinees? Should they?

Higham and colleagues (Higham, 2007; Higham & Arnold, 2007; Higham & Gerrard, 2005) have examined the contribution of metacognitive monitoring and report control processes to performance on free-report scholastic tests (in which examinees decide which questions to answer and which to skip), pointing out that the overall (formula-scored) test score conceals what is in fact an amalgamation of cognitive and metacognitive abilities. Taking a similar approach, Notea-Koren (2006) applied the QAP procedure to separately assess the cognitive and metacognitive contributions to performance on a free-report multiple-choice aptitude test, finding that a component measure of metacognitive ability, monitoring resolution, contributed unique variance in predicting first-year university grades, beyond the predictive power of the free-report formula score (or the forced-report performance score) alone. Such results emphasize the need to consider carefully the potential contributions of metacognitive monitoring and control processes to performance not only on scholastic and psychometric tests, but also on the "real-world" criterion tasks, and attempt to devise ways to isolate and assess those contributions in an effective manner.

REFERENCES

Ackerman, R., & Goldsmith, M. (2008). Control over grain size in memory reporting – with and without satisficing knowledge. *Journal of Experimental Psychology: Learning, Memory, and Cognition, 34,* 1224–1245.

Benjamin, A. S., Bjork, R. A., & Schwartz, B. L. (1998). The mismeasure of memory: When retrieval fluency is misleading as a metamnemonic index. *Journal of Experimental Psychology: General, 127,* 55–68.

Brewer, N., Keast, A., & Sauer, J. D. (2010). Children's eyewitness identification performance: Effects of a Not Sure response option and accuracy motivation. *Legal and Criminological Psychology, 15*, 261–277.

Brown, J., (Ed.) (1976). *Recall and recognition.* London: Wiley.

Cohen, G., & Conway, M. A. (2008). *Memory in the real world* (3rd ed.). Hove, UK: Psychology Press.

Danion, J. M., Gokalsing, E., Robert, P., Massin-Krauss, M., & Bacon, E. (2001). Defective relationship between subjective experience and behavior in schizophrenia. *American Journal of Psychiatry, 158*, 2064–2066.

Deffenbacher, K. A., Bornstein, B. H., McGorty, E. K., & Penrod, S. D. (2008). Forgetting the once-seen face: Estimating the strength of an eyewitness's memory representation. *Journal of Experimental Psychology: Applied, 14*, 139–150.

Dudukovic, N. M., Marsh, E. J., & Tversky, B. (2004). Telling a story or telling it straight: the effects of entertaining versus accurate retellings on memory. *Applied Cognitive Psychology, 18*, 125–143.

Dunlosky, J., & Metcalfe, J. (2009). *Metacognition.* Thousand Oaks, CA: Sage.

Ebbesen, E. B., & Rienick, C. B. (1998). Retention interval and eyewitness memory for events and personal identifying attributes. *Journal of Applied Psychology, 83*, 745–762.

Evans, J. R., & Fisher, R. P. (2010). Eyewitness memory: Balancing the accuracy, precision, and quantity of information. *Applied Cognitive Psychology, 25*, 501–508.

Fisher, R. P., & Geiselman, R. E. (1992). *Memory enhancing techniques for investigative interviewing: The Cognitive Interview.* Springfield, IL: Charles C. Thomas.

Flin, R., Boon, J., Knox, A., & Bull, R. (1992). The effect of a five-month delay on children's and adults' eyewitness memory. *British Journal of Psychology, 83*, 323–336.

Gibbs, R. W., & Bryant, G. A. (2008). Striving for optimal relevance when answering questions. *Cognition, 106*, 345–369.

Goldsmith, M. (2011). Quantity-accuracy profiles or type-2 signal detection measures? Similar methods toward a common goal. In P. A. Higham and J. P. Leboe (Eds.), *Constructions of remembering and metacognition: Essays in honor of Bruce Whittlesea* (pp. 128–136). Basingstoke: Palgrave-MacMillan.

Goldsmith, M., & Koriat, A. (2008). The strategic regulation of memory accuracy and informativeness. In A. Benjamin and B. Ross (Eds.), *Psychology of learning and motivation,* Vol. 48: Memory use as skilled cognition (1–60). San Diego, CA: Elsevier.

Goldsmith, M., Koriat, A., & Pansky, A. (2005). Strategic regulation of grain size in memory reporting over time. *Journal of Memory and Language, 52*, 505–525.

Goldsmith, M., Koriat, A., & Weinberg-Eliezer, A. (2002). Strategic regulation of grain size memory reporting. *Journal of Experimental Psychology: General, 131*, 73–95.

Grice, H. P. (1975). Logic and conversation. In P. Cole and J. L. Morgan (Eds.), *Syntax and semantics: Vol. 3. Speech acts* (pp. 41–58). New York: Academic Press.

Halamish, V., Goldsmith, M., & Jacoby, L. L. (2011). Source-constrained recall front-end and back-end control of retrieval quality. *Journal of Experimental Psychology: Learning, Memory, and Cognition, 38*, 1–15.

Higham, P. A. (2002). Strong cues are not necessarily weak: Thomson and Tulving (1970) and the encoding specificity principle revisited. *Memory & Cognition, 30*, 67–80.

Higham, P. A. (2007). No special K! A signal detection framework for the strategic regulation of memory accuracy. *Journal of Experimental Psychology: General, 136*, 1–22.

Higham, P.A. (2011). Accuracy discrimination and type-2 signal detection theory: Clarifications, extensions, and an analysis of bias. In P. A. Higham and J. P. Leboe (Eds.), Constructions of remembering and metacognition. *Essays in honour of Bruce Whittlesea* (pp. 109–127). Basingstoke, UK: Palgrave Macmillan.

Higham, P. A., & Arnold, M. M. (2007). How many questions should I answer? Using bias profiles to estimate optimal bias and maximum score on formula-scored tests. *European Journal of Cognitive Psychology, 19*(4–5), 718–742.

Higham, P. A., & Gerrard, C. (2005). Not all errors are created equal: Metacognition and changing answers on multiple-choice tests. *Canadian Journal of Experimental Psychology, 59*, 28–34.

Higham, P. A., Luna, K., & Bloomfield, J. (2011). Trace-strength and source-monitoring accounts of accuracy and metacognitive resolution in the misinformation paradigm. *Applied Cognitive Psychology, 25*, 324–335.

Higham, P. A., Perfect, T. J., & Bruno, D. (2009). Investigating strength and frequency effects in recognition memory using Type-2 signal detection theory. *Journal of Experimental Psychology: Learning, Memory and Cognition, 35*, 57–80

Higham, P. A., & Tam, H. (2005). Generation failure: estimating metacognition in cued recall. *Journal of Memory and Language, 52*, 595–617.

Hoffrage, U. (2004). Overconfidence. In R. F. Pohl (Ed.), *Cognitive illusions: Fallacies and biases in thinking, judgment, and memory* (pp. 235–254). Hove, UK: Psychology Press.

Hope, L., Gabbert, F., & Brewer, N. (2011). *Regulating memory: Increasing output quantity and diagnosing accuracy with a Grain Size approach.* Paper presented at the 5th International Conference on Memory, York, UK.

Huff, M. J., Meade, M. L., & Hutchison, K. A. (2011). Age-related differences in guessing on free and forced recall tests. *Memory, 19,* 317–330.

Hyman, I. E. (1994). Conversational remembering: Story recall with a peer versus for an experimenter. *Applied Cognitive Psychology, 8,* 49–66.

Jacoby, L. L., Shimizu, Y., Daniels, K. A., & Rhodes, M. (2005). Modes of cognitive control in recognition and source memory: Depth of retrieval. *Psychonomic Bulletin and Review, 12,* 852–857.

Kelley, C. M., & Sahakyan, L. (2003). Memory, monitoring, and control in the attainment of memory accuracy. *Journal of Memory and Language, 48,* 704–721.

Koren, D., Seidman, L. J., Goldsmith, M., & Harvey, P. D. (2006). Real-world cognitive – and metacognitive – dysfunction in schizophrenia: A new approach for measuring (and remediating) more "right stuff". *Schizophrenia Bulletin, 32,* 310–326.

Koriat, A. (1995). Dissociating knowing and the feeling of knowing: Further evidence for the accessibility model. *Journal of Experimental Psychology: General, 124,* 311–333.

Koriat, A. (2007). Remembering: Metacognitive monitoring and control processes. In H. L. Roediger, III, Y. Dudai, and S. M. Fitzpatrick (Eds.), *Science of memory: Concepts* (pp. 243–246). New York: Oxford University press.

Koriat, A. (2011). Subjective confidence in perceptual judgments: A test of the self-consistency model. *Journal of Experimental Psychology: General, 140,* 117–139.

Koriat, A. (2012). The self-consistency model of subjective confidence. *Psychological Review, 119,* 80–113.

Koriat, A., & Goldsmith, M. (1994). Memory in naturalistic and laboratory contexts: Distinguishing the accuracy-oriented and quantity-oriented approaches to memory assessment. *Journal of Experimental Psychology: General, 123,* 297–316.

Koriat, A., & Goldsmith, M. (1996a). Memory metaphors and the real-life/laboratory controversy: Correspondence versus storehouse conceptions of memory. *Behavioral and Brain Sciences, 19,* 167–188.

Koriat, A., & Goldsmith, M. (1996b). Monitoring and control processes in the strategic regulation of memory accuracy. *Psychological Review, 103,* 490–517.

Koriat, A., Goldsmith, M., & Halamish, V. (2008). Controlled processes in voluntary remembering. In J. H. Byrne, H. Eichenbaum, R. Menzel, H. Roediger and D. Sweatt (Eds.), *Learning and memory: A comprehensive reference* (pp. 307–324). Oxford: Academic Press.

Koriat, A., Goldsmith, M., & Pansky, A. (2000). Toward a psychology of memory accuracy. *Annual Review of Psychology, 51,* 481–537.

Koriat, A., Goldsmith, M., Schneider, W., & Nakash Dura, M. (2001). The credibility of children's testimony: Can children control the accuracy of their memory reports? *Journal of Experimental Child Psychology, 79,* 405–437.

Koriat, A., Pansky, A., & Goldsmith, M. (2011). An output-bound perspective on false memories: The case of the Deese–Roediger–McDermott (DRM) paradigm. In A. Benjamin (Ed.), *Successful remembering and successful forgetting* (pp. 302–332). New York: Psychology Press.

Lichtenstein, S., Fischhoff, B., & Phillips, L. D. (1982). Calibration of probabilities: The state of the art to 1980. In D. Kahneman, P. Slovic, and A. Tversky (Eds.), *Judgment under uncertainty: Heuristics and biases* (pp. 306–334). New York: Cambridge University Press.

Luna, K., Higham, P. A., & Martín-Luengo, B. (2011). Regulation of memory accuracy with multiple answers: The plurality option. *Journal of Experimental Psychology: Applied, 17,* 148–158.

Memorandum of good practice. (1992). London: Her Majesty's Stationary Office.

Milne, R., & Bull, R. (1999). *Investigative interviewing: Psychology and practice.* Chichester, UK: Wiley.

Mintzer, M. Z., Kleykamp, B. A., & Griffiths, R. R. (2010). Dose effects of triazolam and scopolamine on metamemory. *Experimental and Clinical Psychopharmacology, 18*(1), 17–31.

Neisser, U. (1988). Time present and time past. In M. M. Gruneberg, P. Morris, and R. Sykes (Eds.), *Practical aspects of memory: Current research and issues* (Vol. 2, pp. 545–560). Chichester, UK: Wiley.

Neisser, U. (1996). Remembering as doing. *Behavioral and Brain Sciences, 19,* 203–204.

Nelson, T. O. (1996). Gamma is a measure of the accuracy of predicting performance on one item relative to another item, not of the absolute performance on an individual item. Comments on Schraw (1995). *Applied Cognitive Psychology, 10,* 257–260.

Notea-Koren, E. (2006). *Performance accuracy and quantity in psychometric testing: An examination and assessment of cognitive and metacognitive components.* Unpublished doctoral dissertation, University of Haifa, Israel.

Orbach, Y., Hershkowitz, I., Lamb, M. E., Sternberg, K. J., Esplin, P. W., & Horowitz, D. (2000). Assessing the value of structured protocols for forensic interviews of alleged child abuse victims. *Child Abuse & Neglect*, *24*, 733–752.

Pansky, A. (2012). Inoculation against forgetting: Advantages of immediate versus delayed initial testing due to superior verbatim accessibility. *Journal of Experimental Psychology: Learning, Memory, and Cognition*, *38*, 1792–1800.

Pansky, A., Goldsmith, M., Koriat, A., & Pearlman-Avnion, S. (2009). Memory accuracy in old age: Cognitive, metacognitive, and neurocognitive determinants. *European Journal of Cognitive Psychology*, *21*, 303–329.

Pansky, A., & Nemets, E. (2012). Enhancing the quantity and accuracy of eyewitness memory via initial memory testing. *Journal of Applied Research in Memory and Cognition* , *1*, 2–11.

Pasupathi, M., Stallworth, L. M., & Murdoch, K. (1998). How what we tell becomes what we know: Listener effects on speakers' long-term memory for events. *Discourse Processes*, *26*, 1–25.

Perfect, T. J., & Weber, N. (2012, May 7). How should witnesses regulate the accuracy of their identification decisions: One step forward, two steps back? *Journal of Experimental Psychology: Learning, Memory, and Cognition.* Advance online publication, doi: 10.1037/a0028461

Powell, M. B., Fisher. R. P., & Wright, R. (2005). Investigative interviewing. In N. Brewer and K. Williams (Eds.), *Psychology and law: An empirical perspective* (pp. 11–42). New York: Guilford.

Rhodes, M. G., & Kelley, C. M. (2005). Executive processes, memory accuracy, and memory monitoring: An aging and individual difference analysis. *Journal of Memory and Language*, *52*, 578–594.

Robinson, M. D., Johnson, J. T., & Herndon, F. (1997). Reaction time and assessments of cognitive effort as predictors of eyewitness memory accuracy and confidence. *Journal of Applied Psychology*, *82*, 416–425.

Roebers, C. M., & Fernandez, O. (2002). The effects of accuracy motivation and children's and adults' event recall, suggestibility, and their answers to unanswerable questions. *Journal of Cognition and Development*, *3*, 415–443.

Roebers, C. M., Moga, N., & Schneider, W. (2001). The role of accuracy motivation on children's and adults' event recall. *Journal of Experimental Child Psychology*, *78*, 313–329.

Roebers, C. M., & Schneider, W. (2005). The strategic regulation of children's memory performance and suggestibility. *Journal of Experimental Child Psychology*, *91*, 24–44.

Schwartz, B. L., & Metcalfe, J. (1994). Methodological problems and pitfalls in the study of human metacognition. In J. Metcalfe and A.P. Shimamura (Eds.), *Metacognition: Knowing about knowing* (pp. 93–113). Cambridge, MA: MIT Press.

Scoboria, A., Mazzoni, G., & Kirsch, I. (2008). "Don't know" responding to answerable and unanswerable questions during misleading and hypnotic interviews. *Journal of Experimental Psychology: Applied*, *14*, 255–265.

Smith, V. L., & Clark, H. H. (1993). On the course of answering questions. *Journal of Memory and Language*, *32*, 25–38.

Thomas, R. C., & McDaniel, M. A. (2012, June 25). Testing and feedback effects on front-end control over later retrieval. *Journal of Experimental Psychology: Learning, Memory, and Cognition.* Advance online publication, doi: 10.1037/a0028886.

Tversky, A., & Kahneman, D. (1974). Judgment under uncertainty: Heuristics and biases. *Science*, *185*, 1124–1131.

Waterman, A. H., & Blades, M. (2011). Helping children correctly say "I don't know" to unanswerable questions. *Journal of Experimental Psychology: Applied*, *17*, 396–405.

Weber, N., & Brewer, N. (2008). Eyewitness recall: Regulation of grain size and the role of confidence. *Journal of Experimental Psychology: Applied*, *14*, 50–60.

Weber, N., & Perfect, T. J. (2012). Improving eyewitness identification accuracy by screening out those who say they don't know. *Law and Human Behavior*, *36*, 28–36.

Wells, G. L., Malpass, R. S., Lindsay, R. C. L., Fisher, R. P., Turtle, J. W., & Fulero, S. M. (2000). From the lab to the police station: A successful application of eyewitness research. *American Psychologist*, *55*, 581–598.

Yaniv, I., & Foster, D. P. (1995). Graininess of judgment under uncertainty: An accuracy-informativeness trade-off. *Journal of Experimental Psychology: General*, *124*, 424–432.

Yaniv, I., & Foster, D. P. (1997). Precision and accuracy of judgmental estimation. *Journal of Behavioral Decision Making*, *10*, 21–32.

28

Involuntary Autobiographical Memories in Daily Life and in Clinical Disorders

Dorthe Berntsen and Lynn A. Watson

Involuntary autobiographical memories are spontaneously arising memories of personal events. In contrast to voluntary (deliberately retrieved) memories, involuntary memories come to mind with no preceding attempt directed at their retrieval. They simply "pop up" during our activities in daily life, usually facilitated by some content overlap with the current situation. Thus, they are subjectively experienced as unintended recollections.

Consider the following example from a diary study of this phenomenon (Berntsen, 1996). The participant is sitting in a crowded auditorium, attending a lecture. She describes that the packed auditorium is hot and the air is bad. She is sitting next to a female friend and she notices a particular smell of perfume, after which the following recollection spontaneously comes to mind:

> It was one of the last days of a vacation in Spain. The weather had been quite bad, but on this last day the sun was shining and it was really hot. All my friends and I were laying together by the pool, trying to get a tan, before we had to fly home – it was our last chance. There was a heavy smell of a particular sun lotion, which everyone used. I didn't like the smell.
> (Berntsen, 2009, p. 121).

Such involuntary autobiographical memories have been described in literature (e.g.,

Proust, 1928–1956) and by early pioneers of memory research. In the very beginning of his groundbreaking book on memory, Ebbinghaus (1885) identified three basic modes of remembering: a voluntary mode, an involuntary mode, and a non-conscious mode. He described involuntary memories as occurring when "mental states once present in consciousness return to it with apparent spontaneity and without any act of the will" (p. 2). This was opposed to voluntary memories described as when "we call back into consciousness by an exertion of the will directed to this purpose the seemingly lost states" (p. 1). Further, voluntary and involuntary memory were distinguished from non-conscious memory, which he described as when "the vanished mental states give indubitable proof to their continuing existence even if they themselves do not return to consciousness at all" (p. 2).

Ebbinghaus' taxonomy implies a distinction between conscious versus non-conscious awareness and intentional versus unintentional retrieval, which allows a category of memories that are both unintentionally retrieved and consciously recollected – that is, involuntary conscious memories. In contrast to Ebbinghaus, twentieth-century cognitive psychology has tended to view remembering as a goal-directed process. There are many historical reasons for this, one being the emphasis on feedback models, which originally dominated cognitive psychology, and thus the view that behavior is goal-oriented and controlled (see Berntsen, 2009, for a review). The neglect of involuntary memories has been both empirical and conceptual. For example, in his seminal book on episodic memory, Tulving (1983) stated that: "Access to, or actualization of, information in the episodic system tends to be deliberate and usually requires conscious effort" (p. 46). He also observed that "few things that we perceive make us think of previous happenings in our own lives … many stimuli that could potentially serve as reminders or cues, even if prominently displayed to person, will have no such effect" (p. 169). Thus, according to Tulving (1983), episodic remembering is generally voluntary (see also Tulving, 2002).

Although research on implicit memory deals with automatic and thus uncontrolled processes, it too has tended to ignore involuntary conscious memories. According to its original definition, implicit memory was the facilitation of the performance on a certain task by an earlier experience, in the absence of conscious recollection of this experience (Schacter, 1987). However, many scholars considered this definition as problematic, because it was unclear whether the notion of conscious recollection should refer to intentional retrieval or to phenomenological awareness of the study episode (e.g., Kinoshita, 2001; Richardson-Klavehn, Gardiner, & Java, 1994; Schacter, Bowers, & Booker, 1989). Schacter et al. (1989) therefore recommended a definition in terms of retrieval intentionality rather than in terms of conscious awareness, so that implicit memory was defined in terms of its unconscious retrieval strategy. Obviously, this left little room for involuntary – but nonetheless conscious – memories (e.g., Kinoshita, 2001; Richardson-Klavehn et al., 1994).

In contrast to mainstream cognitive psychology, research on daydreaming, which emerged in the 1960s (Singer, 1966), attempted to study the flow, or stream, of consciousness (James, 1880, 1882) as it unfolds more or less spontaneously in daily life. The definition of daydreaming used by its pioneer Jerome Singer (Singer, 1966) was simply a shift in attention away from an ongoing task (and external stimuli) towards internal sources of stimuli. Task-unrelated-thoughts (e.g., Giambra, 1989) and mind wandering (e.g., Smallwood & Schooler, 2006) are more recent variants of the same idea, the latter being defined as "a situation in which executive control shifts away from a primary task to the processing of personal goals" (p. 946). Thus, daydreaming (or mind wandering) encompasses many kinds of mental contents, and is thus not limited to involuntary autobiographical memories. Although such memories may occasionally show up in the ongoing stream of thoughts, they are not directly targeted by this line of research (see Berntsen, 2009, for a review).

In spite of the fact that involuntary memories clearly are a cognitive phenomenon, central to our understanding of memory (e.g., Berntsen, 2009; Hintzman, 2011), historically they have received much more attention in the field of clinical psychology. This attention has almost always been in relation to negative and stressful experiences. For example, it is often observed that individuals who have experienced traumatic events suffer from disturbing involuntary recollections that involve high levels of conscious reliving of the stressful experience. Such intrusive trauma recollections have been considered as a key symptom of Posttraumatic Stress Disorder (PTSD; American Psychiatric Association, 2000) since this diagnosis was introduced in 1980. More recently, intrusive involuntary memories have been described in relation to a range of other emotional disorders, including depression, social phobia, bipolar disorder, psychosis, and agoraphobia (e.g., Holmes & Bourne, 2008; Steel, Fowler, & Holmes, 2005; Williams & Moulds, 2010). Later in this chapter, we will review key findings on intrusive memories in clinical disorders.

The fact that involuntary conscious remembering has been studied extensively in clinical settings, while being largely ignored by cognitive psychologists, has helped nourish the view that involuntary autobiographical memories are closely related to emotional distress and that they therefore are rare in the daily life of healthy individuals. Recently, however, an accumulating amount of evidence (e.g., Ball & Little, 2006; Berntsen, 1996, 2001; Berntsen & Hall, 2004; Kvavilashvili & Mandler, 2004; Mace, 2004; Rubin, Boals, & Berntsen, 2008; Schlagman & Kvavilashvili, 2008; for reviews, see Mace, 2007; Berntsen, 2009, 2010) refutes this idea and instead suggests (consistent with Ebbinghaus) that involuntary autobiographical memories are indeed a basic mode of remembering .

In the present chapter, we first elaborate on the claim that involuntary autobiographical memories form a basic mode of remembering (Berntsen, 2009, 2010). We next address which mechanisms may be responsible for their activation, as well as how involuntary memories differ from autobiographical memories retrieved in a goal-directed manner. We then review findings on involuntary intrusive memories in clinical disorders and their similarities and differences with everyday involuntary memories. We state at the outset that we are here solely concerned with involuntary *autobiographical* (or *episodic*) memories – that is, spontaneous memories of past personal events.

Other forms of involuntary conscious memories exist, such as involuntary musical imagery – for example, having a "tune on the brain" (Bailes, 2007; Beaman & Williams, 2010) – or random words or sentences popping into mind (Kvavilashvili & Mandler, 2004). Little research has been conducted on these highly interesting phenomena and they are beyond the scope of this chapter.

INVOLUNTARY AUTOBIOGRAPHICAL MEMORIES AS A BASIC MODE OF REMEMBERING

The position that involuntary memories form a basic mode of remembering has the

following implications (also see Berntsen, 2010, 2012): First, involuntary autobiographical memories are universal, which means that everyone with intact autobiographical memory has them. Claims of universality cannot be proved, but may eventually be refuted. So far this has not happened. Consistent with the universality claim, large, non-selective samples of subjects are, with very few exceptions, capable of reporting involuntary memories as they occur in their daily life (e.g., Ball & Little, 2006). Survey studies with large stratified samples (e.g., Berntsen & Rubin, 2002; Rubin & Berntsen, 2009) also suggest that involuntary autobiographical memories are well known to most people.

Second, involuntary autobiographical memories are frequent in daily life, but frequency estimates of involuntary autobiographical memories vary depending on the methods used. When interviewed subsequent to their participation in a diary study (e.g., Berntsen, 1996), most participants retrospectively assessed that they had about five to six involuntary memories per day, but they also stated that this varied greatly as a function of their overall level of duties and activity. On more dull and quiet days they would have (or at least notice) more involuntary memories than on days with many tasks and obligations. Because frequency was not the focus of these diary studies and the estimates were done retrospectively, these numbers should be considered with caution. Only one study (Rasmussen & Berntsen, 2011) has involved on-line recording of the frequency on involuntary versus voluntary autobiographical memories on a daily basis. The participants were carefully instructed that they had to record memories of past events. In the involuntary memory condition, they were explained that the memories had to come to mind spontaneously, without any conscious search. In the voluntary memory condition, the memories had to be the result of a consciously initiated search. A surprising dominance of involuntary recollections was seen. The average number of involuntary autobiographical memories was around

20 per day whereas voluntary autobiographical recollections were reported on the average only seven times a day. However, these numbers should be considered with some caution. Because involuntary memories are unexpected, often involve more emotional impact, and often occur during periods of unfocused attention, they may be more easily noticed as compared with their voluntary counterparts, which often come to mind as part of problem solving and social sharing (Rasmussen & Berntsen, 2011). In a survey study, Rubin and Berntsen (2009) asked large stratified samples of Danes to assess how often they had involuntarily as well as voluntarily thought about a self-chosen important event from the last week as well as an important childhood event selected by the experimenter. The participants reported the involuntary remembering of the events to have taken place about as frequently as the voluntary counterpart. Thus, across different methodologies, involuntary remembering of past events takes place at least as frequently as voluntary remembering of past events, consistent with the idea that involuntary remembering forms a basic mode of remembering.

Third, involuntary autobiographical memories operate on the same episodic memory system as do voluntary memories. This means that they are subject to the same basic encoding mechanisms, but differ with respect to the way in which they are brought to mind (Berntsen, 2009). We shall elaborate on this claim shortly in the section addressing how involuntary memories are activated.

Fourth, involuntary autobiographical memories are as functional and adaptive as are voluntary memories. One important function is to provide an obligatory rehearsal of personal memories in ongoing situations with a distinctive feature overlap with the memory content. This allows potentially relevant episodic information to be transferred from the past to the present situation, which may lead to a change in ongoing behavior and/or the extraction of regularities, contributing to the construction of a mental model of the particular social and physical environment of the individual (e.g., whom to trust, where to buy groceries). These functional aspects of involuntary memories may have maladaptive consequences after highly negative/traumatic events, for example in terms of spontaneous recollections or flashbacks of the traumatic event in neutral situations, as observed in relation to PTSD (American Psychiatric Association, 2000). Later in this chapter we shall discuss how findings on the mechanisms underlying normal involuntary memory activation may have important implications for our understanding of maladaptive involuntary memories in emotional disorders.

THE ACTIVATION OF INVOLUNTARY AUTOBIOGRAPHICAL MEMORIES

One of the most intriguing questions related to involuntary autobiographical memories is: How do they come to mind? The naturalistic conditions for the activation of involuntary memories have been examined through diary studies in which the participants make records of the memory and the retrieval context immediately when they have become aware of having an involuntary memory. In many studies, the participant also retrieves a voluntary (word cued) memory for each involuntary memory as part of the same diary, in order to allow a comparison between the two types of recall (e.g., see Berntsen & Hall, 2004, for details).

Diary studies conducted in different laboratories yield consistent findings regarding the activation of involuntary autobiographical memories (see Berntsen, 2009, for an overview). First, involuntary autobiographical memories most frequently arise when the person is not concentrated and engaged in a particular task (Berntsen, 1998; Kvavilashvili & Mandler, 2004; Rasmussen & Berntsen, 2011). This agrees with laboratory studies on daydreaming and mind wandering showing that the frequency of task independent thoughts is negatively correlated with the level of attentional demands posed by an ongoing task (e.g., Singer, 1993; Smallwood & Schooler, 2006). One possible explanation is that focusing attention on a specific task may interfere with the automatic associative processes that lead to the formation of an involuntary memory (McVay & Kane, 2010; Mandler, 1994, 2007). Alternatively, the construction of an involuntary memory may require some executive processes, which are taken up by the parallel task (Smallwood & Schooler, 2006). For example, it may be that the initial activation is associative and automatic, whereas more elaborative processes are needed in order to contextualize the activated episode more broadly in time and space (Moscovitch, 1995).

Second, the great majority of the memories have identifiable cues in the retrieval situation in terms of some overlapping features between the retrieval situation and the memory as illustrated by the example at the beginning of this chapter. When participants are asked to classify the cues as external (present in the physical surroundings), internal (only present in thoughts), or mixed (a combination of external and internal features), external cues are generally more frequent than internal cues (see Berntsen, 2009, for a review). Thus, features of the environment are more frequently experienced as triggers for involuntary autobiographical memories than are features of thoughts and emotions. The cue is often a central (rather than a peripheral) feature of the memory and thus distinctive for the memory content.

Third, involuntary memories are more rapidly retrieved as compared with voluntary memories, consistent with the idea that the former involves less executive control. Schlagman and Kvavilashvili (2008) examined involuntary autobiographical memories arising in response to verbal cues during a signal detection task in a laboratory setting. They found that the retrieval time for involuntary memories was markedly shorter than the one for a comparable sample of voluntary memories. Similar findings were recently obtained in a series of experiments conducted in our laboratory, controlling both the encoding and retrieval of involuntary episodic memories (Berntsen, Staugaard, & Sørensen, 2013, but see Kompus, Eichele, Hugdahl, & Nyberg, 2011).

Fourth, a study using Positron Emission Tomography (PET) recording of neural activity has shown that both involuntary and voluntary recall activate brain areas associated with retrieval success (the medial temporal lopes, the precuneus, and the posterior cingulate gyrus), whereas voluntary compared with involuntary recall shows enhanced activity in areas in the right prefrontal cortex that are known to be involved in strategic retrieval (Hall, Gjedde, & Kupers, 2008). Similarly, using fMRI and ERP recordings of brain activity, Kompus et al. (2011) found that voluntary compared with involuntary retrieval was associated with increased activation in dorsolateral prefrontal cortex, whereas retrieval success was associated with increased activation in the same areas for both conditions (the hippocampus, precuneus, and ventrolateral prefrontal cortex). These findings agree with the idea that voluntary recall is a goal-directed process that requires executive control to initiate and monitor the search, whereas involuntary recall is an associative process that takes place with little executive control and therefore relies less on frontal lobe structures in comparison with the voluntary mode.

Taken together, these findings suggest that involuntary autobiographical memories reflect an associative, context sensitive mode of constructing memories, which requires fewer executive control processes than voluntary autobiographical recall. This raises the important question as to how exactly it is possible to recollect a past event with no deliberate monitoring of the search process. Many theorists have invoked the notion of encoding specificity in order to explain this (see Berntsen, 2009, for a review). According to this principle, the probability of successfully retrieving a memory increases by increasing overlap between the information present at retrieval (i.e., the cue) and the information stored in memory (Tulving & Thomson, 1973). However, the adherence to the encoding-retrieval match leaves several questions unresolved (Nairne, 2002). Notably, explanations based on the encoding-retrieval match fail to explain why we are not constantly flooded by involuntary episodic memories. Any moment in our lives seems to include an almost endless number of potential memory cues in terms of features that were also part of our past experiences. Thus, if having involuntary autobiographical memories were simply a matter of an encoding-retrieval match, it would seem that we should be flooded by such memories throughout our waking life (Berntsen, 2009).

In order to resolve this problem, the encoding-specificity principle has to be supplemented by the principle of cue overload stating that "The probability of recalling an item declines with the number of items subsumed by its functional retrieval cue" (Watkins & Watkins, 1975, p. 442). In other words, the likelihood of a cue providing access to a given target memory depends on the extent to which this cue is uniquely associated with the target. Its strength declines to the extent it is associated with other memories as well. A recent series of experiments provides evidence that the uniqueness of the associative link between the cue and the target (memory) is decisive for the activation of involuntary memories (Berntsen et al., 2013), at least for emotionally neutral targets. Thus, the activation of involuntary autobiographical memories depends at least in part on mechanisms of associations that are well known from studies on (voluntary) episodic memories, for example, cue overload. However, whereas involuntary remembering is assumed to rely almost exclusively on such associative mechanisms, voluntary recall of autobiographical events also engages a top-down schema-based search. These differences concerning the retrieval of involuntary versus voluntary memories help to explain some of the differences between the characteristics of the two types of memories.

DIFFERENCES BETWEEN INVOLUNTARY AND VOLUNTARY AUTOBIOGRAPHICAL MEMORIES

In a number of studies, involuntary memories sampled in diary studies have been compared with voluntary memories retrieved in response to word cues as part of the same diary study. Two consistent differences have been found regarding the characteristics of these memories. One is that involuntary autobiographical memories more often than their voluntary counterparts refer to memories of specific episodes – that is, experiences that took place at a specific time and place in the participant's life, in contrast to memories extracting the essence of many similar occasions (Berntsen, 1998; Berntsen & Hall, 2004; Berntsen & Jacobsen, 2008; Finnbogadottir & Berntsen, 2011; Johannessen & Berntsen, 2010; Mace, 2007; Schlagman & Kvavilashvili, 2008; Schlagman, Kliegel, Schultz, & Kvavilashvili, 2009; Watson, Berntsen, Kuyken, & Watkins, 2013). The only exceptions from this pattern are studies where participants are limited to recording specific episodes (Rubin et al., 2008; Rubin, Dennis, & Beckham, 2011). The other relatively consistent difference is that involuntary autobiographical memories more often than their voluntary counterparts are accompanied by an identifiable mood impact (Berntsen, 1998; Berntsen & Hall, 2004; Berntsen & Jacobsen, 2008; Finnbogadottir & Berntsen, 2011; Johannessen & Berntsen, 2010; Rubin et al., 2008, 2011; Watson, Berntsen, Kuyken, & Watkins, 2012), although in some cases this effect is found only for negative mood impact (Berntsen & Jacobsen, 2008; Johannessen & Berntsen, 2010).

The most likely explanation for these differences is that they are caused by the disparate retrieval mechanisms underlying the two types of autobiographical memories. For an involuntary memory to occur, the cue has to provide an informational overlap with a past event that is sufficiently distinct to discriminate this event from alternatives (Berntsen et al., 2013). Voluntary retrieval of autobiographical events, on the other hand, is a relatively slow process involving search descriptions generated from schematized autobiographical knowledge, which are elaborated and monitored throughout the retrieval process, according to most accounts (e.g., Conway & Pleydell-Pearce, 2000). As a consequence of their different retrieval mechanisms, the two types of remembering sample slightly different events from the same underlying autobiographical memory system. The enhanced frequency of specific episodes among involuntary memories is likely to be due to the associative retrieval process favoring memories with distinctive (non-repeated) features because such features can provide a unique associative link with features in the ongoing situation. Distinctive features are more likely to be maintained in memories of specific events than in general event representations, because the latter focus on conceptual similarities across several events and represent a more semantic level of autobiographical knowledge (e.g., Conway & Pleydell-Pearce, 2000). In addition, involuntary recall is less tied to generic autobiographical knowledge, because this type of recall involves no search description generated from higher-order autobiographical memory, consistent with studies showing that involuntary memories tend to be rated as less relevant to the person's life story and identity (Rubin et al., 2008; Johannessen & Berntsen, 2010).

This explanation is supported by findings on involuntary and voluntary autobiographical memory in relation to aging (Schlagman et al., 2009). It is well established that old people have more difficulties recalling specific episodes as compared with young people, when their retrieval is measured through standard voluntary recall tasks (Levine et al., 2002). This is assumed to reflect an age-related deficit in the executive control processes that normally monitor retrieval. In a diary study, Schlagman et al. (2009) compared involuntary and voluntary memories among old and young participants and showed that the young participants as

compared to old participants, as expected, recorded more specific episodes in voluntary recall. However, this difference was absent for the involuntary memories, for which the old and the young participants recorded an equal number of specific events. This suggests that involuntary remembering accesses specific episodes through processes that require little executive control, which is consistent with the claim that the increased level of specificity among involuntary memories may be due to the associative retrieval process favoring such memories. Similar findings were recently obtained in a study on involuntary and voluntary autobiographical memories in depression (Watson et al., 2013).

The fact that involuntary memories more often than voluntary memories are accompanied by a detectable mood impact is likely to reflect the fact that the involuntary memories come to mind rapidly and automatically in response to situational cues for which reason the retrieval process leaves little room for antecedent-focused emotion regulation, which refers to emotion regulation strategies that come into play before a full-blown emotional reaction has been formed (Gross, 2001). One important form of antecedent-focused emotion regulation is to reevaluate (or reappraise) a potentially emotional situation in such a way that it is less likely to influence us. Voluntary retrieval may involve such antecedent-focused emotion regulation through the construction of the search description guiding the memory retrieval. However, because involuntary memories come to mind with no conscious monitoring of the retrieval process, such reevaluations are unlikely to precede the recollection (Berntsen, 2009).

The idea that these two key differences between involuntary versus voluntary memories reflect the way in which the memories are retrieved (rather than factors at encoding) is supported by two studies showing that similar differences are found for involuntary versus voluntary episodic future thoughts. Not only past events, but also images of possible future events, often come to mind spontaneously (Berntsen & Jacobsen, 2008).

Indeed, just like memories for past events, images of possible future events typically spring to mind in response to situational cues (Berntsen & Jacobsen, 2008; Finnbogadottir & Berntsen, 2011). Such involuntary future projections also show enhanced frequency of specific episodes as well as more pronounced mood impact relative to voluntary future projections (Berntsen & Jacobsen, 2008; Finnbogadottir & Berntsen, 2011). Because the future events have not yet taken place, but are construed on the basis of schematized knowledge and/or information extracted from past events (D'Argembeau, 2012), pure encoding factors are unlikely to account for these differences. More likely they appear to reflect mechanisms that come into play at the time of retrieval.

SIMILARITIES BETWEEN INVOLUNTARY AND VOLUNTARY AUTOBIOGRAPHICAL MEMORIES

There are a number of similarities between involuntary and voluntary autobiographical memories that agrees with the view that they are two different manifestations of the same underling episodic memory system (Berntsen, 2009, 2010). They show the same forgetting function and the same distribution across the life span (Berntsen, 2009). Both types of memories are predominantly positive in healthy individuals (Berntsen, 2009) consistent with a general positivity bias in autobiographical remembering (Walker et al., 2003). They are similarly affected by emotion at the time of encoding. Hall and Berntsen (2008) obtained recordings of emotional reactions to aversive pictures at an encoding session preceding a diary study. During the diary study the participants recorded involuntary and voluntary memories of the emotional pictures. A comparison of individual ratings, obtained during encoding of pictures that were recalled involuntarily and voluntarily, showed that emotional stress at encoding increased overall accessibility, independent

of whether subsequent recall was voluntary or involuntary (for similar findings, see Ferree & Cahill, 2009). Interestingly, involuntary and voluntary remembering are also similarly affected by trauma. In a diary study of undergraduates with either high or low levels of PTSD symptoms, Rubin et al. (2008) found that individuals with high levels of PTSD symptoms recorded more memories related to their trauma. However they did so for both voluntary and involuntary memories. Similar findings were more recently obtained in a clinical sample (Rubin et al., 2011). Involuntary and voluntary memories also appear to be similarly affected by current concerns (Johannessen & Berntsen, 2010). In short, involuntary remembering does not appear to more easily access negative and stressful material as compared with voluntary remembering. The only mental conditions that appear to differentially affect the two forms of remembering seem to be conditions that influence executive functioning, for example, aging and depression, as reviewed above. In such conditions, voluntary recall is hampered whereas involuntary remembering appears to be left relatively intact. However, much more data are needed in order to arrive at definitive conclusions concerning these interactions.

INVOLUNTARY AND INTRUSIVE MEMORIES DURING CLINICAL DISORDERS

As in studies of involuntary memory retrieval in the general population, clinical psychologists have repeatedly identified that involuntary memories are commonly experienced as part of everyday life during psychopathology (Moulds & Holmes, 2011). Such studies have identified that intrusive memories, which come to mind involuntarily, are present across a range of both mood and anxiety disorders and rely on similar underlying cognitive processes (Brewin, Gregory, Lipton, & Burgess, 2010; Williams &

Moulds, 2010). Important questions for the present chapter are then what qualities do intrusive and involuntary memories share? How are they different and, to what extent can intrusive memories be explained by the concept of involuntary memories as a basic mode of remembering? The second section of this chapter will address these questions by reviewing the characteristics of intrusive memories identified both in studies of posttraumatic stress disorder and depression. The relationship between intrusive memories during psychopathology will then be considered in relation to the model of involuntary autobiographical memories as a basic mode of remembering.

THE DEFINITION OF INTRUSIVE RECOLLECTIONS

Empirically, the study of intrusive memories arose from clinical observations that some individuals experience "unintended or intrusive thoughts, images and emotions" following stressful, traumatic, or negative events and that extreme forms of these intrusive recollections are associated with prolonged stress syndromes such as posttraumatic stress disorder (Horowitz & Becker, 1971; Horowitz, Wilner, Kaltreider, & Alvarez, 1980; American Psychiatric Association, 1980; see Brewin et al., 2010, for a recent review). A second line of clinically orientated research identified that healthy individuals also experience recurrent, unbidden, and unusually intense images following exposure to stressful or traumatic films (see Holmes & Bourne, 2008, for a review).

Early clinical researchers argued that these unbidden or unintended images come to mind following events that are beyond normal cognitive processing capabilities (Horowitz, 1975). It was argued that these images remain in a raw or unprocessed form in short-term memory and that they remain accessible for re-entry into consciousness. Horowitz and Becker (1971) stated that these images come to consciousness when they become associated with external or internal events. Horowitz and Becker (1971) labeled this associative priming. However, using modern terminology, we would label this as cuing. When such cueing occurs, these unbidden recollections, which are usually inhibited, break through impulse-defences and therefore are subjectively experienced as intrusive. It is beyond the scope of this chapter to review current theoretical models of intrusive memories. However, it is important to note that although current models of intrusive memories do not adhere to this impulse-defence view (see Brewin, 2010; Ehlers, 2010; Williams & Moulds, 2010, for current theoretical models) the term *intrusive memory* or *memory intrusion* is commonly employed within clinical research.

Based on this early definition of intrusive memories, the core feature of these memories is that they come to mind spontaneously, unbidden or unintended. Ehlers and colleagues also define intrusive memories in this way: as spontaneously triggered and unwanted (Ehlers, Hackmann, & Michael, 2004; Hackmann, Ehlers, Speckens, & Clark, 2004). Importantly, Ehlers and colleagues also emphasize that, although intrusive memories come to mind unbidden, they are not necessarily accompanied by emotional distress. Second, intrusive memories have been found to be present both in healthy individuals and individuals experiencing psychopathology (Horowitz, 1975; Brewin, Hunter, Carroll, & Tata, 1996; Michael, Ehlers, Halligan, & Clark, 2005; Newby & Moulds, 2011). Consequently, although the theoretical underpinnings of intrusive memories and involuntary memories are very different, this most basic definition of intrusive memories as an unbidden or spontaneous cognition parallels the definition of involuntary memories studied in the general population (Krans, Näring, & Becker, 2009; Pearson, Ross, & Webster, 2012). Furthermore, present in both definitions is a shared understanding that spontaneous memory retrieval is universal in that it occurs in both healthy and clinical populations.

One way in which the study of involuntary and intrusive memories has differed is in terms of the types of life events studied during retrieval. According to the view that involuntary autobiographical memories form a basic mode of remembering, potentially any autobiographical event can be retrieved spontaneously. Consequently, in studies of involuntary memory individuals are asked to record any autobiographical event that comes to mind. During involuntary memory studies individuals retrieve spontaneous memories of both stressful events and non-stressful events (Berntsen, 1996, 2009). Initial definitions of intrusive memories suggested that memory intrusions only occur for stressful events that our cognitive processing system is not capable of dealing with (Horowitz, 1975). Current models of intrusive memory also focus on stressful events. Although clinicians recognize that spontaneous retrieval does occur for both stressful and non-stressful life events, clinical models maintain that stressful events sometimes have a deleterious effect on the autobiographical memory system (Brewin et al., 2010). Early researchers defined stress, not in terms of the emotional valence of the event, but in terms of the extent to which the event upsets the homeostatic balance of the cognitive system: "roller coaster rides are stress events," "death wishes are stress events" (Horowitz & Becker, 1971, p. 262). One early study investigated intrusive memories following traumatic, erotic, and neutral films (Horowitz & Becker, 1972). It was found that both types of arousing films led to similar levels of intrusive and repetitive thought but varying affective responses; the traumatic film leading to greater negative affect and the erotic film leading to greater positive affect. Despite evidence from this study that intrusions take a similar form following positive and negative arousing material, subsequent research on intrusive memories has focused mainly on memories for negative events. Consequently, more recent studies of intrusive memories tend to define stressful events, whether implicitly or explicitly, as events

that were also highly emotionally negative at the time of occurrence (Brewin et al., 2010; Krans, Woud, Näring, Becker, & Holmes, 2010). Encouragingly, some research into the involuntary retrieval of positive material is now beginning to emerge (Davies, Malik, Pictet, Blackwell, & Holmes, 2012).

In line with this, studies of intrusive memories have mainly focused on investigating the spontaneous retrieval of highly negative or traumatic events (Moulds & Holmes, 2011). Studies of PTSD have tended to focus on spontaneous memories of traumatic events leading to a clinical diagnosis of PTSD and studies of depression have focused on negative life events more generally (Williams & Moulds, 2010) .[1] Despite the difference in methodologies used to study intrusive and involuntary memories, the terms *involuntary* and *intrusive memories* are sometimes used interchangeably within the literature (Brewin et al., 2010; Holmes & Bourne, 2008). In the present chapter, the term *intrusive memory* will refer to studies that investigated spontaneous retrieval of highly traumatic or negative events, whereas the term *involuntary memory* will refer to studies that investigated spontaneous memory retrieval for any type of autobiographical events. This separation serves to facilitate the integration of research findings across studies of involuntary and intrusive memories and highlight potentially fruitful areas of future research both in relation to adaptive and maladaptive cognition. See Andrade (Chapter 6, this volume) for a discussion of intrusive thoughts.

PRESENCE AND FREQUENCY

As stated earlier, intrusive memories for traumatic, stressful, or negative events have been found to be present during PTSD, in traumatized individuals without PTSD, during depression, in individuals who have recovered from depression, and in healthy controls (Michael et al., 2005; Spenceley & Jerrom, 1997; Newby & Moulds, 2011).

These populations also report involuntary memories for everyday life events (Rubin et al., 2011; Watson et al., 2012). Taken together, these findings provide evidence to support the view that spontaneous memory retrieval occurs following a variety of events and represents a basic mode of remembering during both healthy and disordered cognition.

In line with this, the presence and frequency of intrusive memories have been found to be poor predictors of psychopathology. Across two studies, Michael et al. (2005) assessed the characteristics of intrusive memories in assault victims with and without a diagnosis of PTSD. They identified that intrusion frequency explained less than 10 percent of the variance of PTSD symptoms both concurrently and at six months following the initial interview. Williams and Moulds (2007) also found that characteristics of intrusive memories such as emotional reactions to memory intrusions and intrusion-related distress predicted dysphoria over and above intrusion frequency. Furthermore, Newby and Moulds (2011) found no significant differences in the presence of intrusive memories or the frequency of these memories over a period of a week in depressed, recovered depressed, and never depressed individuals.

Although the presence and frequency of intrusive memories are poor predictors of psychopathology, some authors suggest that intrusive memories have an important role to play in the onset and maintenance of psychological disorders. Brewin et al. (2010) suggest that intrusive memories are involved in the onset of posttraumatic stress disorder and this view is consistent with the fact that intrusive recollection is one of the criteria necessary in order to obtain a diagnosis of PTSD (American Psychological Association, 2000). In terms of maintenance, Brewin, Reynolds, and Tata (1999) found that the presence of intrusive memories at an initial interview significantly contributed to the presence of depressive symptoms in depressed participants six months later, even when initial symptoms of depression were controlled for. Therapeutic intervention studies have also found that imaginal exposure and imagery rescripting lead to a reduction in the frequency of specific intrusions and improvements in levels of psychopathology (Brewin et al., 2009; Kandris & Moulds, 2008; Wheatley et al., 2007). One possible explanation for this is that factors other than the presence and frequency of spontaneous retrieval are driving the relationship between intrusive memories and psychopathology. The following two sections will examine the phenomenological characteristics of intrusive memories and the cognitive and behavioural strategies employed by individuals during psychopathology.

CHARACTERISTICS OF INTRUSIVE MEMORIES

According to many definitions, intrusive memories refer to specific episodic events (Brewin et al., 2010). Involuntary memories are also highly specific (see differences between involuntary and voluntary autobiographical memory section of this chapter). Intrusive memories are also found to contain high levels of sensory detail. Ehlers, Hackmann, Steil, Clohessy, Wenninger, and Winter (2002) found that 90 percent of survivors of childhood sexual abuse, 87 percent of ambulance staff, and between 70 and 83 percent of survivors of road traffic accidents report visual images as part of their intrusive memories. Individuals in these studies also consistently reported other sensory experiences, such as sounds and smells at a lower frequency than visual images. Studies of involuntary memories in healthy individuals have shown that these types of memories also possess high levels of sensory information (see Table 28.1). As in studies of intrusive memories, individuals in these studies reported that their involuntary memories contain high levels of visual information and that other sensory information is also

Table 28.1   Participant ratings of the sensory qualities of involuntary memories

Memory type	Rubin et al. (2008)		Rubin et al. (2011)		Finnbogadottir and Berntsen (2011)	
	Involuntary	Involuntary	Involuntary	Involuntary	Involuntary	Involuntary
Participant group	High PTSD symptoms	Low PTSD symptoms	PTSD diagnosis	No PTSD diagnosis	High Worriers	Low Worriers
Visual	5.45	5.32	5.95	5.85	5.36	5.38
Auditory	4.31	3.96	4.74	4.01	3.03	3.75
Olfactory	1.82	1.96	2.44	1.92	2.03	2.51
Verbal	3.72	3.11	3.64	3.26	2.83	2.68

Note: Participants rated the extent to which their memories contained sensory information on a scale of 1–7, 1 = low in sensory detail, 7 = high in sensory detail.

present to a lesser extent than visual imagery. Furthermore, when the same individuals are asked to retrieve specific autobiographical memories during voluntary retrieval, the levels of sensory information reported during voluntary memory retrieval follow a similar pattern (Rubin et al., 2008, 2011).

In the three studies presented in Table 28.1, no significant group differences were identified in the ratings of visual, auditory, olfactory, and verbal information. Group comparisons of the sensory qualities of intrusive memories reveal similar findings. Michael et al. (2005) found no significant differences in the frequency of sensory information between individuals with and without a diagnosis of PTSD, and Newby and Moulds (2011) found no significant differences in the sensory qualities of intrusive memories across depressed, recovered depressed, and never depressed individuals. Due to differences in the types of events studied and to the differences in measurements employed it is not possible to make direct comparisons between the sensory qualities of intrusive and involuntary memories; however, taken together, the findings suggest that spontaneous memories for stressful and everyday events both contain high levels of sensory information. The similarities in the relative predominance of visual information over auditory and olfactory information potentially suggest that the associative processes that operate during both involuntary and intrusive memories access sensory information in similar ways.

Studies of intrusive memories during PTSD and depression have repeatedly identified that individuals experiencing high levels of psychopathology experience strong emotional and physical reactions in response to their intrusive memories (Horowitz et al., 1980; Kuyken & Brewin, 1994). Reynolds and Brewin (1999) identified that in individuals with PTSD or depression intrusive memories are highly distressing and are associated with negative emotions. Patel, Brewin, Wheatley, Wells, Fisher, and Myers (2007) found that, during depression, intrusive autobiographical memories are accompanied by high levels of emotional and physical sensations. They also identified that the two most common emotions associated with these memories were sadness and anger, and that intrusive memories were highly distressing, uncontrollable, and interfered with daily activities. Newby and Moulds (2011) found that although the intrusive memories of depressed, recovered depressed, and never depressed individuals share striking characteristics, depressed individuals reported higher levels of intrusion-related distress, negative emotions, and interference with daily activities.

When memory retrieval is not limited to negative events, individuals with psychopathology continue to report stronger emotional and physical reactions in response to both involuntary and voluntary retrieval. Rubin et al. (2008, 2011) found that, compared with individuals not experiencing symptoms of PTSD, those with PTSD symptoms reported significantly more intense emotional reactions, more negative emotions, stronger physical reactions, greater mood change, and higher numbers of trauma-related memories during involuntary memory retrieval. Similarly, Watson et al. (2012) identified that depressed individuals experience more frequent physical reactions, more negative mood-change, and higher levels of negative emotions following involuntary memory retrieval than never depressed individuals (see ratings of emotional and physical reactions in Table 28.2). The three studies also found that individuals with high levels of psychopathology rate their involuntary memories as more central to their life-story when compared with healthy controls (see ratings of centrality in Table 28.2).

The findings suggest that individuals with high levels of psychopathology experience stronger and more negative emotional and physical reactions following both intrusive memories and the retrieval of autobiographical memories more generally. These findings provide evidence that strong reactions during psychopathology are not limited to the spontaneous retrieval of stressful or negative events but in fact represent a more generalized negative response bias evident during cognitive processing. Such biases have also been identified during voluntary memory retrieval (Clark & Teasdale, 1982; Fogarty & Hemsley, 1983; Lloyd & Lishman, 1975) and across a number of domains other than autobiographical memory retrieval, i.e., when making attributions (Sweeny, Anderson, & Scott, 1986) and processing self-relevant information (Watson, Dritshcel, Jentzsch, & Obonsawin, 2007). It is important to determine whether these strong reactions present during psychopathology represent a specialized feature of spontaneous memory retrieval or if they form part of a more generalized tendency towards negative and self-referential emotional processing. In order to investigate this further, the studies presented in Table 28.2 directly compared involuntary and voluntary memory retrieval in clinical and non-clinical populations.

All three studies identified differences in physical reaction following memory retrieval;

Table 28.2   Participant ratings of emotional and physical reactions to involuntary memories

Participant group	Rubin et al. (2008)		Rubin et al. (2011)		Watson et al. (2012)	
	High PTSD symptoms	Low PTSD symptoms	PTSD diagnosis	No PTSD diagnosis	Depressed	Never depressed
Involuntary memories						
Intensity	3.29	2.80	4.00	2.82	–	–
Physical reaction	2.53	2.91	3.29	2.38	0.20 [b]	0.04 [b]
Mood-change	3.72	3.11	4.30	3.05	0.03 [a]	0.35 [a]
Emotions [a]	0.11	0.64	-0.29	0.31	0.27	0.85
Centrality	2.37	1.79	4.05	2.85	2.45	1.96
Trauma-related [b]	0.18	0.08	0.44	0.28	–	–
Voluntary memories						
Intensity	3.23	2.64	3.78	2.63	–	–
Physical reaction	2.69	2.24	3.10	2.16	0.12 [b]	0.03 [b]
Mood-change	3.28	2.69	3.97	2.86	-0.10 [a]	0.21 [a]
Emotions [a]	0.35	0.61	0.07	0.41	0.03	0.64
Centrality	2.50	2.14	4.18	2.89	2.54	2.05
Trauma-related [b]	0.18	0.09	0.42	0.26	–	–

Note: Participants' ratings reported on a seven-point likert-scale: 1 = minimal reaction, 7 = strong reaction, a = reported on a rating scale of −3 to +3: −3 = negative, +3 = positive, b = rated as a proportion of total memories reported.

Note: [a] In studies that asked participants to record any memory which came to mind spontaneously, only negative events are included in the statistical analyses.

regardless of diagnostic status, all groups reported stronger or more frequent physical reactions following involuntary than voluntary memories. Rubin et al. (2008, 2011) and also found that all groups reported stronger mood change following involuntary, rather than voluntary, memories. Futhermore, main effects of group were identified in all three studies for all variables listed in Table 28.2, suggesting that individuals with high levels of psychopathology experience stronger emotional and physical reactions regardless of the mode in which the memories were retrieved. No interactions were identified across these variables in any of the three studies. The findings of these studies have a number of important implications. First, individuals with high levels of psychopathology show a number of generalized response tendencies: (1) they report stronger emotional and physical reactions, (2) they show a bias towards negative information, and (3) they are more likely to report information as being central to their identity or life-story. Second, the extent to which these generalized tendencies are activated can be influenced by the mode in which memories are retrieved. When intrusive memories are considered within this context it is plausible that the general tendency towards strong emotional and physical reactions, which is generally active during psychopathology, is further enhanced when autobiographical memories of negative events come to mind spontaneously due to the associative cognitive processes involved in this type of retrieval. Consequently, it is proposed that intrusive memories represent a subset of autobiographical memories that can become particularly distressing during involuntary memory retrieval in the extent to which they activate a number of generalized response tendencies, which are frequently present during high levels of psychopathology.

COPING STRATEGIES AND COGNITIVE STYLE

Two areas that have begun to receive attention in the study of intrusive memories

are 1) the way which individuals emotionally appraise their intrusive memories and 2) the cognitive and behavioural strategies that individuals employ to cope with distressing and intrusive memories. Ehlers and Steil (1995) proposed that negative interpretations of intrusive memories predict symptom persistence in PTSD and similar models have also been applied to account for symptoms of depression (Williams & Moulds, 2010). These cognitive models purport that individuals who negatively appraise their intrusive memories (i.e., "this memory means I am going crazy") are also more likely to report intrusion-related distress and show increased use of strategies such as rumination, avoidance, and thought suppression to control their intrusions. Evidence for this model has been found both in relation to PTSD (Steil & Ehlers, 2000; Ehlers, Mayou, & Bryant, 1998) and depression (Starr & Moulds, 2006; Newby & Moulds, 2010).

One important question that needs to be addressed is the extent to which these negative appraisals and cognitive and behaviour strategies are employed during other forms of autobiographical memory retrieval. Studies of voluntary memory retrieval have shown that cognitive strategies, such as rumination and avoidance, are associated with increased recall of overgeneral memories (see Williams et al., 2007) suggesting that these strategies influence both spontaneous and voluntary memory retrieval. Watson et al. (2012) assessed the extent to which depressed and never depressed individuals reported rumination and avoidance following involuntary and voluntary memory retrieval. They found that depressed individuals reported higher levels of rumination and avoidance than never depressed individuals following retrieval of both involuntary and voluntary memories. Furthermore, levels of rumination were equivalent following both involuntary and voluntary memory retrieval, suggesting that levels of rumination are not influenced by the mode in which autobiographical memories are retrieved. In terms of avoidance, both groups reported lower levels of avoidance following involuntary, rather than voluntary, memories; however, involuntary memories were also rated as more positive than voluntary memories in this study. Therefore, it is possible that the lower levels of avoidance reported during involuntary retrieval in this study were the result of the higher frequency of positive involuntary memories. Although these results are preliminary they suggest that investigating the relationship between mode of memory retrieval, negative appraisals, cognitive/behavioural strategies, and psychopathology may present a fruitful area of research. Combining these strands of research further highlights that it is not just the spontaneous or deliberate nature of retrieval that needs to be considered when thinking about autobiographical memory but also how individuals respond to these memories during and following both modes of retrieval.

INVOLUNTARY AND INTRUSIVE AUTOBIOGRAPHICAL MEMORIES

Many similarities can be seen between everyday involuntary memories and intrusive memories as observed in clinical disorders: both arise spontaneously in response to situational cues; both are sensory vivid with a dominance of visual imagery; both involve more emotional impact at the time of recall than strategically retrieved memories; both can be persistent and appear repetitive in response to reinstated cues (Berntsen & Rubin, 2008). The main difference between the two appears to be their emotional content or how they have been emotionally appraised. Involuntary autobiographical memories can refer to all kinds of personal events, whereas intrusive memories are frequently referred to in terms of unpleasant and stressful experiences. Currently, intrusive memories may therefore be most parsimoniously viewed as a subclass of involuntary autobiographical memories with an emotionally negative content, which therefore may be associated with avoidance attempts.

Following this view, there are at least two reasons why intrusive memories may occur.

One is simply that the individual has encountered one or more highly emotional event(s) that, due to its emotionality and personal significance, remains highly accessible in memory for which reason it may come to mind spontaneously in response to a variety of cues. This may form part of the explanation for intrusive memories in PTSD (see Berntsen, 2009; Berntsen & Rubin, 2008; Rubin et al., 2008, 2011, for elaborations and support for this view). The same explanation may also in part account for intrusive memories observed in depression, since such memories are also often about specific negative events (e.g., Brewin & Kuyken, 1994). Another factor may be the cognitive style of the individual; certain individuals may be more prone to employing avoidance coping-strategies such as rumination, cognitive avoidance, or thought suppression, and some may have difficulties with inhibiting disruptive spontaneous images and memories. Only a few studies have been conducted so far on individual differences in relation to involuntary or intrusive memories. They have found trait dissociation to be correlated with the frequency of such memories (Brewin & Soni, 2011; Hall & Berntsen, 2008). More research is needed to disentangle how individual dispositions may interact with stressful encounters to generate intrusive memories.

Strong arguments for the position that intrusive memories are best viewed as a dysfunctional subclass of everyday involuntary memories are provided by studies showing that involuntary (intrusive) memories in clinical disorders, such as depression and PTSD, are not more frequently about negative, stressful events than are strategically retrieved autobiographical memories in the same populations (Rubin et al., 2008, 2011; Watson et al., 2012). These studies suggest that in such disorders autobiographical memory in general is colored by negative emotion rather than this effect being limited to involuntary (intrusive) recollections. Again, this coloring may be due to an interaction between negative encounters in the past in combination with individual dispositions.

In short, the growing research on involuntary autobiographical memories in both healthy and clinical populations is likely to significantly add to our understanding of negative intrusive memories during clinical disorders. The alternative position that everyday involuntary memories can be understood based on observations of negative intrusive memories in clinical disorders – that is both are stress responses (Horowitz, 1975) – cannot be maintained in the face of the last two decades of research on this topic. Involuntary autobiographical memories are generally a functional (not dysfunctional) mode of remembering, which may become dysfunctional when applied to negative events. Exactly why and when this happens are important questions for future research.

ACKNOWLEDGMENTS

Both authors contributed equally to this work and therefore share joint first authorship. This work was supported by the Danish Research Council for the Humanities and the Danish National Research Foundation (DNRF93).

NOTE

1 In studies that asked participants to record any memory which came to mind spontaneously, only negative events are included in the statistical analyses.

REFERENCES

American Psychiatric Association (1980). *Diagnostic and statistical manual of mental disorders,* (3rd ed.), Washington, DC: American Psychiatric Association.

American Psychiatric Association (2000). *Diagnostic and statistical manual of mental disorders* (th ed. text revision). Washington, DC: American Psychiatric Association.

Andrade, J. (2014). Working memory beyond the laboratory. In T. J. Perfect & D. S. Lindsay (Eds.), *The SAGE Handbook of Applied Memory* (pp 92-109). London: Sage Publications Ltd.

Bailes, F. (2007). The prevalence and nature of imagined music in the everyday lives of music students. *Psychology of Music, 35,* 555–570.

Ball, C. T., & Little, J. R. (2006). A comparison of involuntary memory retrievals. *Applied Cognitive Psychology, 20,* 1167–1179.

Beaman, C. P., & Williams, T. I. (2010). Earworms (stuck song syndrome): Towards a natural history of intrusive thoughts. *British Journal of Psychology, 101,* 637–653.

Berntsen, D. (1996). Involuntary autobiographical memories. *Applied Cognitive Psychology, 10,* 435–454.

Berntsen, D. (1998). Voluntary and involuntary access to autobiographical memory. *Memory, 6,* 113–141.

Berntsen, D. (2001). Involuntary memories of emotional events. Do memories of traumas and extremely happy events differ? *Applied Cognitive Psychology, 15,* 135–158.

Berntsen, D. (2009). *Involuntary autobiographical memories. An introduction to the unbidden past.* Cambridge: Cambridge University Press.

Berntsen, D. (2010). The unbidden past: Involuntary autobiographical memories as a basic mode of remembering. *Current Directions in Psychological Science, 19,* 138–142.

Berntsen, D. (2012). Spontaneous recollections: Involuntary autobiographical memories as a basic mode of remembering. In D. Berntsen and D. C. Rubin (Eds.), *Understanding autobiographical memory: Theories and approaches* (pp. 290–310). Cambridge: Cambridge University Press.

Berntsen, D., & Hall, N. M. (2004). The episodic nature of involuntary autobiographical memories. *Memory & Cognition, 32,* 789–803

Berntsen, D., & Jacobsen, A. S. (2008). Involuntary (spontaneous) mental time travel into the past and future. *Consciousness & Cognition, 17,* 1093–1104.

Berntsen, D., Staugaard, S. R., & Sørensen, M. L. (2013). Why am I remembering this now? Predicting the occurrence of involuntary (spontaneous) episodic memories. *Journal of Experimental Psychology: General, 142,* 426–444.

Berntsen, D., & Rubin, D. C. (2002). Emotionally charged autobiographical memories across the lifespan: The recall of happy, sad, traumatic, and involuntary memories. *Psychology and Aging, 17,* 636–652.

Berntsen, D., & Rubin, D. C. (2008). The reappearance hypothesis revisited: Recurrent involuntary memories after traumatic events and in everyday life. *Memory & Cognition, 36,* 449–460.

Brewin, C. R., Gregory, J. D., Lipton, M., & Burgess, N. (2010). Intrusive images in psychological disorders: Characteristics, neural mechanisms, and treatment implications. *Psychological Review, 117,* 210–232. doi:10.1037/a0018113

Brewin, C. R., Hunter, E., Carroll, F., & Tata, P. (1996). Intrusive memories in depression: An index of schema activation? *Psychological Medicine, 26,* 1271–1276.

Brewin, C. R., & Sone, M. (2011). Gender, personality and involuntary autobiographical memory. *Memory, 19,* 559–565.

Brewin, C. R., Reynolds, M., & Tata, P. (1999). Autobiographical memory processes and the course of depression. *Journal of Abnormal Psychology, 3,* 511–517.

Brewin, C. R., Wheatley, J., Patel, T., Fearon, P., Hackmann, A., Wells, A., Fisher, P., & Myers, S. (2009). Imagery re-scripting as a brief stand alone treatment for depressed patients with intrusive memories. *Behaviour, Research and Therapy, 47,* 569–576.

Clark, D. M., & Teasdale, J. D. (1982). Diurnal variations in clinical depression and accessibility of memories of positive and negative experiences. *Journal of Abnormal Psychology, 91,* 87–95.

Conway, M. A., & Pleydell-Pearce, C. W. (2000). The construction of autobiographical memory in the Self-Memory system. *Psychological Review, 107,* 261–288.

D'Argembeau, A. (2012). Autobiographical memory and future thinking. In D. Berntsen and D. C. Rubin (Eds.), *Understanding autobiographical memory: Theories and approaches* (pp. 311–330). Cambridge: Cambridge University Press.

Davies, C., Malik, A., Pictet, A., Blackwell, S. E., & Holmes, E. A. (2012). Involuntary memories after a positive film are dampened by a visuospatial task: Unhelpful in depression but helpful in mania? *Clinical Psychology & Psychotherapy, 19,* 341–351. doi: 10.1002/cpp.1800

Ebbinghaus, H. (1885/1964). *Memory. A contribution to experimental psychology.* New York: Dover Publications.

Ehlers, A. (2010). Understanding and treating unwanted trauma memories in Posttraumatic Stress Disorder. *Journal of Psychology, 21, 8,* 141–145.

Ehlers, A., Hackmann, A., Steil, R., Clohessy, S., Wenninger, K., & Winter, H. (2002). The nature of intrusive memories after trauma: the warning signal hypothesis. *Behaviour, Research and Therapy, 40,* 995–1002.

Ehlers, A., Mayou, R. A., & Bryant, B. (1998). Psychological predictors of chronic posttraumatic stress disorder after motor vehicle accidents. *Journal of Abnormal Psychology, 107,* 508–519.

Ehlers, A., & Steil, R. (1995). Maintenance of intrusive memories in posttraumatic stress disorder: a cognitive approach: *Behavioural and Cognitive Psychotherapy, 23,* 217–249.

Ferree, N. K., & Cahill, L. (2009). Post-event spontaneous intrusive recollections and strength of memory for emotional events in men and women. *Consciousness and Cognition, 18,* 126–134.

Finnbogadottir, H., & Berntsen, D. (2011). Involuntary mental time travel in high and low worriers. *Memory, 19,* 625–640.

Fogarty, S. J., & Hemsley, D. R. (1983). Depression and the accessibility of memories. *British Journal of Psychiatry, 142,* 232–237.

Giambra, L. M. (1989). Task-unrelated-thought frequency as a function of age: A laboratory study. *Psychology and Aging, 4,* 136–143.

Gross, J. J. (2001). Emotion regulation in adulthood: Timing is everything. *Current Directions in Psychological Science, 10,* 214–219.

Hackmann, A., Ehlers, A., Speckens, A., & Clark, D. M. (2004). Characteristics and content of intrusive memories in PTSD and their changes with treatment. *Journal of Traumatic Stress, 17,* 231–240.

Hall, N. M., Gjedde, A., & Kupers, R. (2008). Neural mechanism of voluntary and involuntary recall: A PET study. *Behavioural Brain Research, 186,* 261–272.

Hintzman, D. L. (2011). Research strategy in the study of memory: Fads, fallacies, and the search for the "coordinates of truth". *Perspectives on Psychological Science, 6,* 253–271.

Holmes, E. A., & Bourne, C. (2008). Inducing and modulating intrusive emotional memories: A review of the trauma film paradigm, *Acta Psychologica, 127,* 553–556. doi: 10.1016/j.actpsy.2007.11.002

Horowitz, M. J. (1975). Intrusive and repetitive thought after experimental stress. *Archives of General Psychiatry, 32,* 1457–1463.

Horowitz, M. & Becker, S. (1971). Cognitive responses to stress: Experimental studies of a "compulsion to repeat trauma". *Psychoanalysis and Contemporary Science, 1,* 258–305.

Horowitz, M. & Becker, S. (1972). Cognitive response to erotic and stressful films. *Archives of General Psychiatry, 29,* 81–84.

Horowitz, M. J., Wilner, N., Kaltreider, N., & Alvarez, W. (1980). Signs and symptoms of posttraumatic stress disorder. *Archives of General Psychiatry, 37,* 85–92.

James, W. (1890). *The principles of psychology.* Vol I. New York: Henry Holt & Co.

James, W. (1892). *Psychology. The briefer course.* New York: Henry Holt & Co.

Johannessen, K. B., & Berntsen, D. (2010). Current concerns in involuntary and voluntary autobiographical memories. *Consciousness & Cognition, 19,* 847–860.

Kandris, E., & Moulds, M. L. (2008). Can imaginal exposure reduce intrusive memories in depression? A case study. *Cognitive Behaviour Therapy, 37,* 216–220.

Kinoshita, S. (2001). The role of involuntary aware memory in the implicit stem and fragment completion task: A selective review. *Psychonomic Bulletin & Review, 8,* 58–69.

Kompus, K., Eichele, T., Hugdahl, K., & Nyberg, L. (2011). Multimodal imaging of incidental retrieval: The low route to memory. *Journal of Cognitive Neuroscience, 23,* 947–960.

Krans, J., Woud, M. L., Näring, G., Becker, E. S., & Holmes, E. A. (2010). Exploring involuntary recall in posttraumatic stress disorder from an information-processing perspective: intrusive images of trauma. In J. H. Mace (Ed.), *Act of remembering: Toward an understanding of how we recall the past.* Oxford: Blackwell Publishing.

Krans, J., Näring, G., & Becker, E. S. (2009). Count out your intrusions: effects of verbal encoding on intrusive memories. *Memory, 17,* 809–815.

Kuyken, W., & Brewin, C. R. (1994). Intrusive memories of childhood abuse during depressive episodes. *Behaviour, Research and Therapy, 32,* 525–528.

Kvavilashvili, L., & Mandler, G. (2004). Out of one's mind: A study of involuntary semantic memories. *Cognitive Psychology, 48,* 47–94.

Levine, B., Svoboda, E., Hay, J. F., Winocur, G., & Moscovitch, M. (2002). Aging and autobiographical memory: Dissociating episodic from semantic retrieval. *Psychology and Aging, 17,* 677–689.

Lloyd, G. G., & Lishman, W. A. (1975). The effects of depression on the speed of recall of pleasant and unpleasant experiences. *Psychological Medicine, 5,* 173–180.

Mace, J. H. (2004). Involuntary autobiographical memories are highly dependent on abstract cueing. The Proustian view is incorrect. *Applied Cognitive Psychology, 18,* 893–899.

Mace, J. H. (2007) (Ed.), *Involuntary memory.* Malden: Blackwell.

Mandler, G. (1994). Hypermnesia, incubation, and mind-popping: On remembering without really trying. In C. Umilta and M. Moscovitch (Eds.), *Attention and performance. Conscious and unconscious information processing* (pp. 3–33) Cambridge, MA: MIT Press.

Mandler, G. (2007). Involuntary memory: Variations on the unexpected. In John H. Mace (Ed.), *Involuntary memory* (pp. 208–223). Malden: Blackwell.

McVay, J. C., & Kane, M. J. (2010). Does mind wandering reflect executive function or executive failure?

Comment on Smallwood and Schooler (2006) and Watkins (2008). *Psychological Bulletin, 136,* 188–197.

Moscovitch, M. (1995). Recovered consciousness: A hypothesis concerning modularity and episodic memory. *Journal of Clinical and Experimental Neuropsychology ,17,* 276–290.

Moulds, M. L., & Holmes, E. A. (2011). Intrusive imagery in psychopathology: A commentary. *International Journal of Cognitive Therapy, 4,* 197–207.

Michael, T., Ehlers, A., Halligan, S. L., & Clark, D. M. (2005). Unwanted memories of assault: What intrusion characteristics are associated with PTSD? *Behaviour, Research and Therapy, 46,* 573–580.

Nairne, J. S. (2002). The myth of the encoding-retrieval match. *Memory, 10,* 389–395.

Newby, J. M., & Moulds, M. L. (2010). Negative intrusive memories in depression: the role of maladaptive appraisals and safety behaviours. *Journal of Affective Disorders, 126,* 147–154.

Newby, J. M., & Moulds, M. L. (2011). The characteristics of intrusive memories in a community sample of depressed, recovered depressed and never depressed individuals. *Behaviour Research and Therapy, 49,* 234–243.

Patel, T., Brewin, C. R., Wheatley, J., Wells, A., Fisher, P., & Myers, S. (2007). Intrusive images and memories in major depression. *Behaviour, Research and Therapy, 45,* 2573–2580.

Pearson, D. G., Ross, F. D. C., & Webster, V. L. (2012). The importance of context: Evidence that contextual representations increase intrusive memories. *Journal of Behavioural Therapy and Experimental Psychiatry, 43,* 573–580.

Proust, M. (1928–1956). Swann's way. In *Remembrance of things past* (vol. 1). Translated by C. K. Scott Moncrieff. New York: Random House.

Rasmussen, A. S., & Berntsen, D. (2011). The unpredictable past: Spontaneous autobiographical memories outnumber memories retrieved strategically. *Consciousness & Cognition, 20,* 1842–1846.

Reynolds, M., & Brewin, C. R. (1999). Intrusive memories in depression and post-traumatic stress disorder. *Behaviour Research and Therapy, 37,* 201–215.

Richardson-Klavehn, A., Gardiner, J. M., & Java, R. I. (1994). Involuntary, conscious memory and the method of opposition. *Memory, 2,* 1–29.

Rubin, D. C., & Berntsen, D. (2009). The frequency of voluntary and involuntary autobiographical memories across the lifespan. *Memory & Cognition, 37,* 679–688.

Rubin, D. C., Dennis, M. F., & Beckham, J. C. (2011). Autobiographical memory for stressful events: The role of autobiographical memory in posttraumatic stress disorder. *Consciousness and Cognition, 20,* 840–856.

Rubin, D. C., Boals, A., & Berntsen, D. (2008). Memory in posttraumatic stress disorder: Properties of voluntary and involuntary, traumatic and non-traumatic autobiographical memories in people with and without PTSD symptoms. *Journal of Experimental Psychology: General, 137,* 591–614.

Schacter, D. L. (1987). Implicit memory: History and current status. *Journal of Experimental Psychology: Learning, Memory and Cognition, 13,* 501–518.

Schacter, D. L., Bowers, J., & Booker, J. (1989). Intention, awareness and implicit memory: The retrieval intentionality criterion. In S. Lewandowsky, J.C. Dunn, and K. Kirsner (Eds.), *Implicit memory. Theoretical issues* (pp. 47–65). Hillsdale, NJ: Lawrence Erlbaum.

Schlagman, S., Kliegel, M., Schulz, J., & Kvavilashvili, L. (2009). Effects of age on involuntary and voluntary autobiographical memory. *Psychology and Aging, 24,* 397–411.

Schlagman, S., & Kvavilashvili, L. (2008). Involuntary autobiographical memories in and outside the laboratory: How different are they from voluntary autobiographical memories? *Memory & Cognition, 36,* 920–932.

Singer, J. L. (1966). *Daydreaming. An introduction to the experimental study if inner experience.* New York: Random House.

Singer, J. L. (1993). Experimental studies of ongoing conscious experience. In C. R. Bock and J. Marsch (Eds.), *Experimental and theoretical studies of consciousness* (pp. 100–122). Chichester, UK: Wiley.

Smallwood, J., & Schooler, J. W. (2006). The restless mind. *Psychological Bulletin, 132,* 946–958.

Spenceley, A., & Jerrom, B. (1997). Intrusive traumatic childhood memories in depression: A comparison between depressed, recovered and never depressed women. *Behavioural and Cognitive Psychotherapy, 25,* 309–318.

Starr, S., & Moulds, M. L. (2006). The role of negative interpretations of intrusive memories in depression. *Journal of Affective Disorders, 93,* 125–132.

Steel, C., Fowler, D., & Holmes, E. A. (2005). Trauma-related intrusions and psychosis: An information processing account. *Behavioural and Cognitive Psychotherapy, 33,* 139–152.

Steil, R., & Ehlers, A. (2000). Dysfunctional meaning of posttraumatic intrusions in chronic PTSD. *Behaviour Research and Therapy, 38,* 537–558.

Sweeny, P. D., Anderson, K., & Scott, B. (1986). Attributional style in depression: A meta-analytic review. *Journal of Personality and Social Psychology, 50,* 974–991.

Tulving, E. (1983). *Elements of episodic memory.* New York: Oxford University Press.

Tulving, E. (2002). Episodic memory: From mind to brain. *Annual Review of Psychology, 53,* 1–25.

Tulving, E., & Thomson, D. M. (1973) Encoding specificity and retrieval processes in epsodic memory. *Psychological Review, 80*(5), 352–373.

Walker, W. R., Skowronski, J. J., & Thompson, C. P. (2003). Life is pleasant – and memory helps to keep it that way! *Review of General Psychology, 7,* 203–210.

Watkins, O. C., & Watkins, M. J. (1975). Build up of proactive inhibition as a cue-overload effect. *Journal of Experimental Psychology. Human Learning and Memory, 1,* 442–452.

Watson, L. A., Berntsen, D., Kuyken, W., & Watkins, E. R. (2012). The characteristics of involuntary and voluntary autobiographical memories in depressed and never depressed individuals. *Consciousness and Cognition, 21,* 1382–1392.

Watson, L. A., Berntsen, D., Kuyken, W., & Watkins, E. R. (2013). Involuntary and voluntary autobiographical memory specificity as a function of depression. *Journal of Behaviour Therapy and Experimental Psychiatry, 44,* 7–13.

Watson, L.A., Dritschel, B., Jentzsch, I. & Obonsawin, M. C. (2008). Changes in the relationship between self-reference and emotional valence as a function of dysphoria. *British Journal of Psychology, 99,* 143–152.

Wheatley, J., Brewin, C. R., Patel, T., Hackmann, E. A., Wells, A., Fisher, P., et al. (2007). "I'll believe it when I can see it": Imagery re-scripting of intrusive sensory memories in depression. *Journal of Behavior Therapy and Experimental Psychiatry, 38,* 371–385.

Williams, A. D., & Moulds, M. L. (2007). An investigation into the cognitive and experiential features of intrusive memories in depression. **Memory, 5,** 912–920.

Williams, A. D., & Moulds, M. L. (2010). The content, nature, and persistence of intrusive memories in depression. In J. H. Mace (Ed.), **Act of remembering: Toward an understanding of how we recall the past**. Oxford: Blackwell Publishing,

Williams, J. M. G., Barnhofer, T., Crane, C., Hermans, D., Raes. F., Watkins, E., & Dalgleish, T. (2007). Autobiographical memory specificity and emotional disorder. **Psychological Bulletin, 113,** 122–148.

29

Epistemic Feelings and Memory

Chris J. A. Moulin and Celine Souchay

OVERVIEW

This chapter brings together several disparate literatures to illustrate a few infrequent and striking experiences in our daily mental lives, such as the feeling of knowing, the tip of the tongue state and déjà vu. Since many of the illustrations and theoretical insights rest on cases of brain damage or intoxication, an alternative title might have been *Disorders of Memory Experience*. However, because we wish to appeal to an emerging literature that considers low-level feelings and the phenomenology of reflective memory processing – what Koriat (2007) has described as *experience-based metacognition* – we chose a title that reflected our theoretical allegiances. In short, this chapter will outline that: a) memory is guided by feelings and experiences; b) these feelings are most apparent when they are distorted, damaged, or dissociated from the goals of processing; and c) these feelings usually have some value to cognition, and when they malfunction, so does processing more generally. The central theme of this chapter is that people are not passive conduits for information processing: "… the person is not a mere medium through which information flows" (Koriat, 2007; p. 292).

AN INTRODUCTION TO EPISTEMIC FEELINGS

William James, whose quotes often grace the pages of textbooks, once declared that he had had a profound insight into the nature of being: "There are no differences but differences of degree between different degrees of difference and no difference"(James, 1882, p. 207). He was high on nitrous oxide – laughing gas – when he noted this thought, and described that it produced a "delirium of theoretic rapture" (James, 1882, p. 207). This remark was interpreted by William James as an important insight. It *felt like* it was a profound understanding of the world.

A second anecdote comes from the *Metro* newspaper, which ran a short, sad article on Thursday, 10 January 2008 about a 43-year-old, Michael Toye, who was "Killed proving spirit 'isn't flammable".[1] Toye had had an argument with a friend after a drinking session, and asserted that White Spirit – an organic solvent formed from paraffin – was not flammable. To prove his point, he poured some over himself and set it alight with a cigarette lighter. His friend managed to extinguish the flames, but did not call for help after Toye refused medical attention, stating: "I'm alright, I just want a fag and a beer". The next day he went to hospital, where he died six days later as a consequence of his injuries.

These two stories strike at the same critical issue. William James and Michael Toye were united in having an erroneous feeling about the contents of cognition. William James felt he had a profound insight, and Michael Toye was so sure that white spirit is not flammable that he is willing to risk death by proving himself right. His certainty that white spirit was not flammable was at odds with the facts and had a fatal cost.

There is a theoretical point to William James's bizarre statement. James (1882) writes: "I strongly urge others to repeat the experiment, which with pure gas is short and harmless enough … the keynote of the experience is the tremendously exciting sense of an intense metaphysical illumination." Once sober, he wrote: "what possible ecstasies of cognitive emotion might have bathed these tattered fragments of thought when they were alive?" It is this notion of "cognitive emotion" or feelings of knowing (and not knowing) that is critical. William James is saying that the thoughts he experiences while intoxicated are given significance by a feeling that accompanies them. This feeling was somewhat artificial, since, in the cold light of day, the feeling is no longer there. James (1902), then, argues that feelings guide our thoughts and beliefs. Without getting too metaphysical, these feelings are special in that they give a sense of truth to a belief, or ascribe some meaning to our cognitive processing. Like with emotions more generally, it is rather crude to think of these feelings as "right" or "wrong" – there are times when we cannot (and should not) objectively say whether someone is "correct" to feel sad. But having reported a feeling of knowing an answer or having had some epiphany, we can at least ask what the answer is, what the feeling is "about".

Such feelings are described as "epistemic", which means that they relate to knowledge or cognition. Broadly speaking, they amount to the subjective experiences that arise when confronted with a particular cognitive task. For a philosophical debate about the nature of these epistemic feelings see Proust (2007) and Carruthers (2009). For a handbook of applied cognition, these sensations, experiences and feelings are critical because they can drive our real-world behaviours, as do other forms of subjective beliefs and evaluations. Epistemic feelings include feelings of certainty, pastness, insight and mental effort (see de Sousa, 2009). Arguably, they are fast-acting, reflective and guide processing in the same way that emotional feelings do, but much like an emotion, they don't carry any content – they are just a signal.

Most pertinent to this chapter is the debate about metacognition and epistemic feelings (see Arango-Muñoz, 2011). Metacognition is covered elsewhere in this handbook, and covers much of the same issues as here: it is a reflective capacity that helps govern and co-ordinate cognition. Largely based on Koriat's view (e.g., Koriat, 2000, 2007), Arango-Muñoz (2011) suggests that metacognition can be split into two levels, one that is metarepresentational, and involves "thinking about thinking". As an example, this might include making predictions of future performance based on our understanding of the pronouncability of words, the parameters of the memory task and our general dispositional characteristics and tendencies ("I'm good with mental arithmetic" or "I'm useless at remembering people's names"). In this way, metacognition concerns humans turning their ability to predict other people's intentions and behaviours on themselves (e.g., Flavell, 2004).

The second level that Arango-Muñoz discusses is a quick-acting intuitive process, which is based more on how things feel rather than an assessment based on stored representations and problem-solving heuristics. It is these lower-level epistemic feelings, also described as experience-based metacognition, that we wish to emphasise here. These two levels of metacognition map nicely onto relatively recent developments in reasoning and judgement, most notably Evans' dual-processing account (Evans, 2008; see also

Kahneman, 2011). This dual-processing account distinguishes between cognitive processes that are fast and automatic, and those that are slower and deliberative. At least in the reasoning and decision-making literature, there is empirical support for the idea of a two-stage metacognitive evaluation. For instance, Thompson, Prowse Turner, and Pennycook (2011) have examined the role of fast, intuitive "feelings of rightness" while people are solving complex, real-world problems. Participants were encouraged to make fast, intuitive responses, and then report a "feeling of rightness" while solving problems. Their initial feeling then correlated with subsequent behaviours – participants allocated more time to problems that they initially felt had lower levels of "rightness".

EPISTEMIC FEELINGS AND METACOGNITION

The literature on epistemic feelings in memory is rather underdeveloped, but the concept neatly maps onto a set of phenomena and paradigms that are rather better researched and understood. Epistemic feelings are possibly easiest to describe in instances where there is a mismatch or dissociation between the processing and the contents of cognition. Two commonly experienced dissociations are the tip-of-the-tongue (ToT) state and déjà vu. The ToT state occurs when there is a feeling that a piece of information is known, but is not available for conscious report. Déjà vu is a mental experience whereby a place (for example) *feels* as if it has been visited before, whereas it is *known* that it is the first time it has been visited. In ToT and déjà vu there is evidence for the existence of epistemic feelings in that a feeling about cognitive processing has become divorced from the material being processed. Normally, when epistemic feelings are in concert with the goals of processing, we are not so aware of them.

The literature on metacognition (see various chapters, this volume) is rather well developed and with a clear applied focus. There is research into eyewitness testimony, student education and memory rehabilitation, for instance, which all consider the relationship between judgements about performance, actual performance and, most critically, the extent to which someone can *do something* based on their self-appraisal. As a general principle, metacognitive judgements relate to behaviour. Studies have shown that people spend more time learning words previously judged as difficult to remember, for instance (Nelson & Leonesio, 1988).

We are therefore separating metacognitive experiences/states/feelings from analytic judgements/inferences in the manner described in the philosophy literature (Arango-Muñoz, 2011; de Sousa, 2009). These states describe obligatory and consciously experienced configurations of the cognitive system (see, eg., Conway, 2009), which signal to the experient the nature of the processing being carried out. They contrast with introspections about the nature of processing. For instance, during the attempted retrieval of a temporarily inaccessible target, one can make introspective evaluations of the likelihood of retrieval, and report the content of other thoughts and deal with the problem consciously and strategically. On the other hand, one can also find oneself in a state of retrieval failure, with the feeling that something that is known cannot be retrieved.

Tulving's contribution: subjective experiences of retrieval success

One area in which subjective reports have been extensively researched is the recollective experience paradigm. Tulving (1985) claimed that phenomenological experience is one of the ways of distinguishing different memory systems. He characterised episodic memory as "autonoetic" (self-knowing). Semantic memory, on the other hand, often described as memory for facts, was "noetic". Tulving asked participants to make subjective reports of the feelings associated with retrieval. His shift in attention from the result of a decision-making process to the process itself emphasised the importance of subjective experience in decision-making about the contents of memory.

The recollective experience paradigm asks participants to distinguish between sensations of "remembering" and "knowing", (or finding familiar, e.g., Conway, Gardiner, Perfect, Anderson, & Cohen, 1997). Remembering is the act of bringing something to mind with recollective experience: It includes a subjective state of pastness, and knowledge about the memory's context and source, often referred to as "mental time travel". Familiarity or "just knowing", on the other hand, relates to a state where the experient cannot retrieve any contextual information and can only report whether or not an item has been encountered recently. There are many approaches for researching these differences – for a review see Yonelinas (2002). In brief, recollection and familiarity can be indexed either by retrieval of objectively verifiable information such as the source of the item, or by subjective reports about the quality of retrieval, and experience. The application of such a theory of memory function has led to better categorisation and description of memory disorders following disease or damage (eg., "remembering" is selectively impaired in Alzheimer's disease; Souchay & Moulin, 2009).

Other applications abound. In a study examining over 200 students completing psychology modules, Conway et al. (1997) measured recollective experience in a multiple-choice test immediately after the students' lecture course, and then following final exam assessment. Conway et al. found that, initially, high-performing students reported higher levels of "remember" than "know" responses. However, in the later exam, these same students reported higher levels of knowing. This "remember to know (R-to-K) shift", was stronger in high-performing students, and was proposed to reflect the change in information from an episodic to semantic nature, and the formation of knowledge. The R-to-K shift is only apparent in subjective reports of feelings at retrieval, not traditional objective measures of behaviour.

In fact, the field of remembering and knowing is divided as to whether the two processes are quantitatively or qualitatively different. On the one hand, some researchers suggest that remembering and familiarity are functionally and neuroanatomically separate whereas others suggest that they lie along a continuum, and remembering is reflective of a strong trace at retrieval and merely finding familiar reflects a weaker underlying trace strength (for critical debates from opposing viewpoints see Diana, Reder, Arndt, & Park 2006, and Wixted & Stretch, 2004). Those who argue that remembering and familiarity lie on a continuum and reflect just one memory system at play suggest that the two differ along one dimension, usually captured as subjective confidence. Participants report higher levels of confidence for events that are remembered than for those which are just familiar (see Dunn, 2004). Confidence is a subjective report, which is critical in applied cognition research – for instance, jurors may well trust the account of a crime from a witness who reports that he feels certain in his memory of events; they will feel less convinced by someone who reports that they are less than sure. There is in fact a large literature on the confidence–accuracy relation in eyewitness testimony (e.g., see Wells, Olson, & Charman, 2002).

SUBJECTIVE EXPERIENCES OF RETRIEVAL FAILURE

Memory retrieval is not an all-or-nothing process. There are a number of different feelings and states that can be experienced when trying to retrieve information, ranging from fast, automatic "ecphoric" retrieval of facts to a complete failure of retrieval. In many instances, memory retrieval will be strategic, and information and feelings generated during failed recall will be useful for the experient and guide processing. In some cases, of course, nothing will come to mind when desired. Even this is beginning to garner research interest, described as the "blank-in-the-mind" state (Efklides, 2010). We presumably do not need to search memory in order to know whether we know the answer to every question – in this way there is a difference between failing to retrieve something and knowing that we don't know it. For instance, you can very quickly answer questions like "Have you ever been to *Place Darcy* in Dijon, France?" without setting up an exhaustive search of French cities and their parks (see Kolers & Palef, 1976).

Here, we want to focus on the subjective states accompanying retrieval failure that are discussed in the feeling-of-knowing (FOK, Hart, 1965) and tip-of-the-tongue (ToT) literatures. These two entities rest on similar paradigms that present test materials and ask participants to make subjective reports at the point at which they cannot retrieve information. These reports may entail a prediction of subsequent performance on the same question, the retrieval of "partial information" related to the to-be-sought item, or a simple assessment of whether the item feels like it is on "the tip of the tongue". The extent to which both of these experiences are epistemic feelings as opposed to metacognitive evaluations is discussed below, although it is worth noting that de Sousa (2009) and Arango-Muñoz (2011) both characterise these experiences as epistemic feelings.

The tip-of-the-tongue state

Brown and McNeil (1966) defined the tip-of-the-tongue (ToT) state as "the state of mind in which a person is unable to think of a word that he is certain he knows, the state of mind in which a word seems to be on the tip of one's tongue" (p. 327). From a linguistic perspective, when in a ToT state, semantic information is available but the phonological representation is not successfully accessed. The recall of related information, such as the first letter of the word or the number of syllables (e.g. Koriat & Lieblich, 1974) that often accompanies ToTs, is thus perceived as a failure to phonologically retrieve the word. (This related, associated information is variously referred to as peripheral or partial information, and for the purposes of this chapter the terms can be thought of as interchangeable.) The ToT can therefore be defined as a breakdown occurring in the lexical retrieval process or a failure to access the correct phonological word form. Unsurprisingly, in memory and language disorders there has been a lot of research into the ToT state, as presented in Table 29.1.

What is the name of Batman's butler?[2] Such questions (in this case taken from Nelson & Narens, 1980; about 32 per cent of their sample could answer this question correctly) can be compiled into difficult general knowledge tests, which can be expected to generate a handful of ToT experiences in all, or nearly all, participants. This has been an effective paradigm for bringing ToT into the laboratory (perhaps too effective given the incidence of ToT in the laboratory compared with in real life – an idea we develop below).

Most of such research into the ToT considers it to be metacognitive in a way that resonates with our view of epistemic feelings (Bacon, Schwartz, Paire-Ficout, & Izaute, 2007). From this viewpoint, ToTs are feelings that are distinct from the retrieval failure itself; ToTs have a functional significance and guide our behaviours. For example, ToTs influence retrieval, as evidenced by a longer period spent attempting to retrieve ToT items compared with non-ToT items (Gollan & Brown, 2006). Schwartz (2002) suggested that ToTs can be classified on different quantitative and qualitative dimensions of experience. For example, ToTs can be described as being either automatic or effortful. In support of this idea, several studies have shown that ToT resolution can either be very fast (five to seven seconds; Riefer, Kevari, & Kramer, 1995) or can happen quite some time after

Table 29.1   Examples of research into the tip-of-the-tongue experience in memory impairment and psychological disorder

Authors	Population/cause	Finding
Juncos-Rabadan et al. (2011)	Mild cognitive impairment	Phonological access (but not semantic) is impaired in ToT
Langfit & Rausch (1996)	Post surgery epilepsy patients	Left temporal lobectomy leads to increased word-finding difficulties, with ToT errors being the most frequent
Astell & Harley (1996)	Probable Alzheimer's disease	People with AD enter into a ToT state but cannot provide any phonological information related to which they are searching
Hanly et al. (2010)	Dyslexia	Children with dyslexia have more ToTs, proportionately more for phonological access, and for longer and low-frequency words
Bacon et al. (2007)	Anxiolytic drug Lorazepam	"Commission" ToTs produced more frequently on the drug: i.e. recall of incorrect facts associated with a ToT

cue presentation. These latter ToTs, also called "retrospective ToTs", occur for 22 per cent of questions, while brief and fast ToTs only account for 9 per cent (Schwartz, 2001). ToTs also differ in whether or not partial or peripheral information is retrieved. A distinction has been made between objective ToTs (associated with the retrieval of partial information) and subjective ToTs (without the retrieval of partial information) thus suggesting that ToTs might not always been associated with the retrieval of partial information (e.g., Perfect & Hanley, 1992).

The ToT state has been extensively researched in the healthy aging process, and this work speaks to the retrieval of related information during the retrieval process; examining what else comes to mind in a ToT. For example, one way to measure ToT accuracy is to consider the retrieval of partial information; whether the information retrieved whilst participants experience a TOT state is correct. In aging, the presence of peripheral information declines significantly with age (Brown & Nix, 1996; Burke, MacKay, Worthley, & Wade, 1991). Combined with the common finding of more ToTs reported in older adults, these findings suggest that there are more empty ToTs in older adults. Furthermore, age differences in resolution processes applied to solve ToTs

have been reported. Older adults attempt to search for the information less often and rely more on pop-ups (Burke et al., 1991; Cohen & Faulkner, 1986). Older adults may be more prone to enter into ToT states when failing to retrieve information, therefore, but also they may fail to resolve the ToT later, and to retrieve any related or helpful information. This could suggest that either the older adult is entering into a state where material cannot be retrieved, a "terminal ToT", or perhaps erroneous ToTs are being generated when information was never known.

Aging studies propose that ToTs have different levels, and that there are qualitative differences between ToTs in young and old experients. In this context, Widner, Otani and Winkelman (2005) suggested a two-stage model of the ToT. The first stage involves an "automatic feeling of availability" (which we would characterise as familiarity), while the second represents an effortful memory search. This two-stage model is neatly captured in the two levels of metacognition. We argue that the automatic, and fast-acting, feeling is the epistemic *experience-based* component of the ToT. The later inferences, which are higher-level and metarepresentational, according to the literature will either be based on familiarity with the cue that has generated the ToT, general domain knowledge (Metcalfe, Schwartz, & Joaquim, 1993) or the accessibility of peripheral information (e.g. Koriat, 1993). Older adults seem to generate more automatic, low level feelings during failed retrieval, but then either fail to act strategically on them, or have a memory failure that prevents the retrieval of appropriate peripheral information. They are left with a signal of unrecalled knowledge, but do not generate any extra information.

The feeling of knowing

The feeling of knowing term is only applied to situations in which, like in the ToT, the person cannot currently retrieve the "known" information. Within the metacognition literature, feeling-of-knowing *judgements* are predictions of subsequent recognition of currently non-recalled information (Hart, 1965). In this way they operationalise the proposed relationship between the subjective feeling that something is known and an objectively verifiable consequence of that feeling. In a typical experiment, participants are tested with either the cues from previously learned paired associates (episodic memory task) or general knowledge (GK) questions such as "Who was the author of the comic strip Tintin?" (semantic memory task). If they cannot recall the appropriate answer, they are asked to predict whether or not they will later correctly retrieve the non-recalled information on a second criterion test. This prediction is a FOK judgement. Unsurprisingly, these judgements have been of interest in memory impairment (see Table 29.2).

There is clearly a lot more than just an epistemic feeling captured in FOK judgements. Since they are predictions typically made on a rating scale, they are likely to involve a number of different inferential processes based on different types of information, rather than a report of whether one or not is in a particular state or not (for a thorough review see Koriat, 2000). In particular, several findings suggest that FOKs drive memory search: participants spend more time searching for items that they think are available in memory as judged by FOK predictions (Barnes, Nelson, Dunlosky, Mazzoni, & Narens, 1999). Litman, Hutchins and Russon. (2005) investigated the relationship between feelings of curiosity and subsequent memory behaviours in a feeling-of-knowing paradigm. This study is notable for its measuring of epistemic curiosity as an individual differences variable, and it is a rare study that looks to reconcile strategic behaviours and lower level feelings, asking participants to rate how curious they were to see the answer to a question that they could not answer. Despite being identified as a critical feeling by philosophers (e.g., de Sousa, 2009) there is little in the metacognition literature on curiosity, or how it guides information acquisition. In short, Litman et al. (2005) found an association between the level of curiosity to know an answer and the extent to which their participants had a feeling of knowing the answer. Curiosity was low when participants

Table 29.2 Examples of research into the Feeling-of-Knowing in memory impairment and psychological disorder

Authors	Population/cause	Finding
Janowsky et al. (1989)	Frontal lobe patients and Korsakoffs	Frontal processes are involved in the FOK, with frontal and Korsakoffs patients showing inaccuracy for episodic materials. Semantic FOK unimpaired
Nelson et al. (1986)	Alcohol consumption	Alcohol impairs memory, but not FOK accuracy
Souchay et al. (2002)	Alzheimer's disease	Impaired episodic FOK accuracy
Souchay et al. (2006)	Parkinson's disease	Impaired episodic FOK accuracy
Souchay et al. (2006)	Schizophrenia	Impaired episodic memory but intact accuracy of episodic FOK

reported that they knew the answer to a question. Loewenstein (1994)[3] suggests that when very close to answering a question and resolving a feeling of knowing, epistemic curiosity peaks; we are motivated by the gap in our knowledge to answer the question.

Explaining the accuracy of judgements such as FOKs has been at the centre of metacognition research and has taken its lead from memory theory, in particular on the processes of recollection and familiarity. Both the attempt to recollect the forgotten information (e.g., Souchay, Moulin, Clarys, Taconnat, & Isingrini, 2007) and familiarity with cues influence FOK accuracy (e.g., Hosey, Peynircioglu, & Rabinovitz, 2009). Critically, the way these processes interact and interface with memory retrieval possibly illuminates a little how epistemic feelings are integrated into strategic retrieval processes more generally.

Koriat (2001) proposed that different processes are at play in a FOK in a cascaded manner. Rapid preliminary FOK is affected by cue familiarity. When the question evokes a very low sense of familiarity, a fast "don't know" response may be issued. In contrast, when familiarity is high enough to induce a positive preliminary FOK, memory search is initiated. FOKs then derive from target accessibility, described as the amount of partial information related to the target retrieved while searching for the item (Koriat, 1993, 2008). For example, FOK studies show that participants successfully retrieve structural-phonological partial information, such as the initial letter (Blake, 1973), or semantic related information, such as the connotative meaning (e.g., Schwartz, 2002; Koriat, 1993; Schacter & Worling, 1985). The amount of accessible partial information can then be used to update the initial FOK. At this point, the cues operate as an "undifferentiated mass" (Jacoby & Brooks, 1984). In Koriat's (2001) interactive hypothesis, two different FOKs are distinguished: a preliminary FOK based on the cue familiarity and a post-retrieval FOK influenced by the results of the retrieval attempt. In line with our view,

the first preliminary FOK might be thought of as an epistemic feeling – some researchers would even characterise this feeling as a ToT. It is a fast, non-introspective assessment based on a feeling of familiarity, without the retrieval of specific information.

A more recent development in the FOK literature suggests that the contextual information associated to the target, such as the source, could be among the information that contributes to guide FOK states (Cook, Marsh, & Hicks, 2006). Recent studies have demonstrated that the retrieval of source information had an influence on the magnitude of FOKs (Brewer, Marsh, Clark-Foos, & Meeks, 2010; Thomas, Bulevich, & Dubois, 2011). Furthermore, there is evidence supporting the idea that recollection defined as the explicit retrieval of contextual information regarding the encoding episode may be central to FOK states (Brewer et al., 2010; Hicks & Marsh, 2002; Souchay et al., 2007; Thomas et al., 2011). Hicks and Marsh (2002) showed that high FOK predictions were associated with "remember" responses in a recognition memory task. Souchay et al. (2007) demonstrated a relationship between FOK accuracy and recollection by showing significant correlations between FOK accuracy scores and the proportion of "remember" responses.

We suggest that recollection-mediated retrieval processes are critical in episodic FOK but not semantic FOK (e.g., Souchay et al., 2007). In an episodic task, to make an evaluation of FOK it is necessary to access information based on retrieval of the specific study episode of the materials in question. Thus, episodic FOK tasks involve another kind of partial information regarding how and where the information was acquired. The partial information guiding FOK states could thus be of different types: sensory/perceptual information (noetic), spatial and temporal information (autonoetic), semantic detail (noetic) and affect (autonoetic). The use of noetic partial information would lead to a judgement based on familiarity while the use of autonoetic partial information would lead to a judgement based on recollection (Souchay & Moulin, 2009; See Metcalfe & Son, 2012, for a similar argument).

This new framework explains why a deficit in FOK accuracy is observed in some clinical populations (see Table 29.2). For example, the studies in clinical populations such as frontal lobe patients, Alzheimer's disease or schizophrenia have also demonstrated clear dissociations between preserved semantic FOKs and impaired episodic FOKs (see Souchay, 2007, and Pannu & Kaszniak, 2005, for reviews). These studies thus suggest that epistemic feelings associated with episodic retrieval are impaired in patients presenting with recollection deficits. But note that an FOK accuracy deficit is not an inevitable given memory impairment. Patients with schizophrenia perform significantly worse than do controls on tests of episodic memory, but are not impaired in terms of metacognitive accuracy (Souchay et al., 2006).

As with the ToT state, much has been learned from the study of healthy aging. Several studies have also shown that aging has little or no effect on the resolution of semantic FOKs (Allen-Burge & Storandt, 2000; Marquie & Huet, 2000). However, a number of studies have also found that the resolution of episodic FOKs is impaired in aging (Souchay, Isingrini, & Espagnet, 2000; Souchay et al., 2007; Thomas et al., 2011, but see Perfect & Stollery, 1993; MacLaverty & Hertzog, 2009). To explain these findings, we suggest that the deficit in episodic FOK resolution in older adults is related to a lack of recollection; older adults fail to use the contextual information related to the target to make their judgements. Whether or not this is due to a failure in the epistemic feeling of recollection, or some other cue that motivates the search for contextual information, or merely a forgetting of partial information, is something that should be assessed. Unlike the ToT, there is little research into the partial information accompanying FOK judgements.

In summary, FOK judgements and ToT states are similar in that they both relate to

information that is not currently available. Despite the obvious similarity, one major difference between these two epistemic feelings is that the ToT is "experienced" by the participants as it happens, while FOK judgements are requested by the experimenter. However, similar theories have been used to interpret these states. In brief, both FOKs and ToTs rely to some extent on cue familiarity and partial information accessibility (Koriat & Levy-Sadot, 2001). For example, Metcalfe et al. (1993) showed that both ToT and FOK were increased by cue familiarity.

Research has tried to determine whether or not the processes underlying FOK and ToT are the same. On one hand, studies have showed significant correlations between ToTs and FOKs (Schwartz, Travis, Castro, & Smith, 2000; Yaniv & Meyer, 1987) but on the other hand behavioural differences have been found between these two feelings (e.g., Schwartz, 2008). For example, Widner, Smith and Gaziano (1996) showed that a demand characteristic (telling participants that the material presented is either easy or difficult) had an influence on ToTs only. More recently, Schwartz (2008) found that working memory load differentially affects ToTs and FOKs. ToT rates decreased under working memory load, whereas FOK rates increased or remained the same. One prominent view is that a ToT state is the epistemic feeling at the core of the FOK. Thus, a feeling of knowing might involve a ToT, but not the other way around. Of course, this depends not only on your theoretical viewpoint, but on the nomenclature you use.

DÉJÀ EXPERIENCES

The FOK and ToT are states triggered when the sought for material is not accessed, but a feeling signals that the material is available. On the whole, FOKs and ToTs are researched as prima facie evaluations of the state of knowledge, and although they can be incorrect, they are most often assumed to be correct.

In contrast, the déjà vu experience is often encountered as a *false* epistemic feeling. It is a transitory mental state whereby a novel experience, such as arriving for the first time at an airport in a new city, feels as if it is familiar. Here, we take the view that déjà vu is a memory-based illusion, originating from the erroneous activation of the epistemic feeling of familiarity. The déjà vu experience strikes at the core issues of this chapter – it is a situation where an automatic, low-level signal (familiarity) clashes with a higher-level metacognitive evaluation (the awareness that this feeling is false). It might be thought of as a situation in which the epistemic feeling and its interpretation are at odds with each other.

Déjà vu occurs when the feeling of familiarity is dissociated either from the actual experience of an unfamiliar stimulus or when familiarity is felt for material for which the prior experience is forgotten or unknown; what is referred to as the decoupled familiarity hypothesis (Illman, Souchay, Butler, & Moulin, 2012). For a full review of déjà experiences in neurology, psychiatry and healthy participants, see O'Connor and Moulin (2010) – a few key studies are summarised in Table 29.3. The resulting mismatch is an erroneous feeling of familiarity for a stimulus that is simultaneously known by the experient to be unfamiliar. This

second part, of *knowing that the feeling is wrong* is critical for the experience – feelings of false familiarity that are unopposed by the knowledge that they are false would merely be termed a "false positive".

The nearest laboratory analogue for our account of déjà vu is "recognition without identification" (RWI) – a line of reasoning begun by Brown and Marsh (2008). In their study, participants shallowly processed pictures of visual scenes and were one week (Experiment 1) and three weeks (Experiment 2) later asked to report the likelihood that they had visited the places. They were able to influence the degree to which people reported having visited places before, which the participants were not aware of, and some participants compared this to déjà vu.

In a development of this idea, Cleary and Reyes (2009) have produced a déjà vu-like experience in healthy participants by arranging for them to process materials during encoding in such a way that they are able to "recognise" materials but not know from where they encountered the information, a process akin to source amnesia (Schacter, Harbluk, & McLachlen, 1984). For instance, participants may perceive a set of scenes in a study phase, and see very similar scenes in a test phase. There is sufficient overlap that the participants feel that they have encountered the scene but cannot pinpoint

Table 29.3 Causes of pathological and clinical cases of déjà vu

Authors	Population/cause	Finding
Adachi et al. (2007)	Schizophrenia	People with déjà vu report fewer instances of déjà vu than do controls
Taiminen & Jaaskelainen (2001)	(SC) Flu medication: amantadine and phenylpropanolamine	Intense and prolonged experiences of déjà vu
Kalra et al. (2007)	(SC) Treatment for platal tremor: carbidopa and 5-hydroxytryptophan	Intense protracted déjà vu lasting for several hours; case shut herself in a darkened room
Singh (2007)	(SC) Drug abuse: Salvia	After long-term use, paranoid and debilitating déjà vu is experienced without concurrent hallucinations
Adachi et al. (2010)	Temporal lobe epilepsy	Normal déjà vu experiences are no different in TLE, and not experienced more frequently, but a seizure-related form exists

Note: SC = Single case (or case series report).

the source of this feeling. There are similar accounts of déjà vu historically. Knight (1895) experienced déjà vu whilst in Tibet, and later concluded that this was due to the vivid descriptions of Laputa in Swift's *Gulliver's Travels*, creating a similarity with Tibet that was not retrieved at the time of the déjà vu. Cleary proposes a similarity hypothesis of déjà vu. Deja vu arises from familiarity with a scene caused by an overlap with a previous experience, a similarity that is undetected. Most recently, this has been demonstrated with carefully manipulated virtual reality environments (Cleary, Brown, Sawyer, Nomi, Ajoku, & Ryals, 2012).

These theories of déjà vu rest heavily on the epistemic feeling of familiarity, an entity that is relatively well understood in the brain (Yonelinas, 2002). Recollection and familiarity are critical for the neuroscience of memory since they pertain to different brain areas – the hippocampus and a network of associated brain regions mainly within the medial temporal lobe (MTL) are responsible for recollection, and a more isolated perirhinal region is responsible for familiarity (Eichenbaum, Yonelinas, & Ranganath, 2007). Our view of déjà vu has been largely influenced by this understanding of the brain. In particular, we have stressed that déjà vu – even in healthy people – is a meaningless, top-down error based on the inappropriate activation of neural circuitry involved in the epistemic feelings surrounding memory processing (O'Connor & Moulin, 2008). This is a view which has overlaps with Penfield's seminal work on the 'interpretative illusions' seen in artificial stimulation of the temporal lobe in temporal lobe epilepsy (e.g., Penfield and Perot, 1963).

Note that the RWI literature (e.g., Cleary & Reyes, 2009) assumes that déjà vu is essentially a bottom-up process: similarities between a scene and a previously encountered scene lead to the sensation of familiarity in the absence of knowing the source of the familiarity. To differentiate this account from a false positive, we need the knowledge that this familiarity is wrong. Perhaps this

is achieved by some aspects of the scene appearing novel, or perhaps we can experience familiarity in a context we know to be new. In this way, a novel location might trigger a stored representation, without awareness of where that location is. An extension of the RWI account is that we might expect that sometimes, as with the ToT, the feeling of familiarity with a scene may actually later be resolved: 'I know ... this bend in the road here reminds me of a place I visited close to my Grandma's old house when I was a child'. Whilst daily life is constantly triggering such memories (reviewed briefly below) the relationship between memories being triggered like this and déjà vu is not known, and aside of Knight's valiant attempt with Tibet, not many cases of the resolution of déjà vu have been presented.

A major problem in the déjà vu literature is that, despite all researchers converging on the notion of erroneous familiarity, it is actually rather difficult to produce in the laboratory. In this way, the ToT and déjà vu experiences are rather similar. Although reports of ToTs are somewhat easier to produce in the laboratory than déjà vu, we must be careful how we interpret such reports. Experimental studies often produce multiple reports of a ToT state in a single test, whereas diary studies indicate that such experiences occur only about once a week in real life. For example, Heine et al. (1999) examined diary ToT and laboratory ToT rates in the same groups of participants. In the laboratory, their group of young adults generated 23 ToTs on a 112-item test, but only reported a mean of 5.21 ToTs in the real world over a four-week period. Either cognitive psychologists are very good at producing materials that generate ToTs, or participants are very poor at reporting real-world ToTs, or the two measures are measuring something very different from one another.

We imagine that similar things happen in studies of déjà vu, too. Cleary and Reyes (2009) report an experimental procedure that leads to 87 per cent of participants (33 of 38) reporting at least one incidence of déjà vu during the study. This is striking in that the generation of déjà vu appears almost as frequent as the generation of the ToT, which was reported by 97 per cent of participants in the same experiment. Given that only 60 per cent of the population have ever experienced déjà vu in their lives (Brown, 2003), and that the estimates of the frequency of occurrence normally peak at twice a year, such high rates of reporting déjà vu must be treated cautiously. The fact that déjà vu is not generally documented in the multitude of studies eliciting familiarity without recollection published each year should also give pause for thought. Elsewhere we have also expressed caution in that demand characteristics may be behind these high rates of experience (O'Connor & Moulin, 2010). Our feeling from our own laboratory studies of déjà vu is that if we really were successful in recreating that peculiar and intense sensation of déjà vu as it is in the real world, we would have a long queue of undergraduates lined up willing to take place in our research. Studies that attempt to reconcile rates of déjà vu in the laboratory and in the real world are a priority.

In general, the déjà vu literature needs to develop in the manner of the ToT and FOK literatures, which share a generally accepted definition, and a central paradigm behind which researchers can align themselves. The ToT and FOK literatures have the advantage that there are behavioural consequences to the feeling (such as allocation of study time), whereas it is difficult to see what the behavioural consequences of a déjà vu experience are. One promising idea is to examine the after-effects of the déjà vu eliciting trial. If the experimenter really has produced an attention-grabbing experience, one might expect a cost to processing on the next trial (or possibly on a dual task). Schwartz (2011) has shown that ToTs are less likely to occur in the trial after a ToT has been reported, with the interpretation being that the high level of resources required to generate a metacognitive evaluation have been depleted, and take a while to recover. This occurs even though recall is not affected for the subsequent trial.

CONCLUSION

Theoretical implications

Thus far we have described some feelings and experiences that we think are non-inferential and automatic, which guide memory processes. When they are in concert with the goals of top-down processing and the products of memory they go unnoticed, or we merely act upon them, without reflecting on their significance. When these feelings go awry, they lead to sensations of déjà vu. When memory fails, the experient may be left with elevated levels of frustrating ToT and FOK feelings. Moreover, if the processes associated with and interpretations of the epistemic feelings fail, people may end up making incorrect metacognitive evaluations of their memory.

We aimed to differentiate lower level feelings and higher order inferential processes, but, in fact, in all of the examples summarised above, the feelings themselves cannot be experienced separately from their interpretation. The epistemic feelings, by their very definition have some value and some meaning. Because of this interplay between feelings and judgements, many researchers have pointed out the need to describe interactions between the two levels of metacognition. Koriat (2000), for example, suggests that feelings of knowing "serve to interface between implicit-unconscious-automatic process on the one hand, and explicit-conscious-controlled processes on the other" (p. 152).

One view of metacognition is that it involves expectations and evaluations in order to make sense of lower level feelings (e.g., Whittlesea, 1997). In Whittlesea's SCAPE theory (1997), memory processing is described in terms of a Selective Construction and Preservation of Experience. This theory emphasises the experiences associated with memory function, but does not crudely delineate them into recollection and familiarity in the way proposed by Tulving. Whittlesea's proposal is that feelings arise in a very non-specific way, and essentially have no meaning, until experienced in the context of a particular task or according to a conceptual framework according to expectations. A review of these ideas can be found in Ansons and Leboe (2010).

Perhaps the neatest illustration of this theory is Goldinger and Hansen's (2005) celebrated buzz chair experiment. In this experiment, participants were presented with a subliminal buzz through the chair they were sitting on. During a recognition memory test, participants were more likely to respond that a word was old when accompanied by a buzz. The buzz also increased their confidence in false alarms. One cannot argue for any adaptive or epistemic value to the subliminal buzz sensed by participants per se. According to a Whittlesea interpretation, in the context of a memory test, the buzz is interpreted as meaningful. The expectations and ongoing task demands lead the subliminal buzz to be experienced as a memory-relevant feeling. A subliminal buzz to the rear, outside the context of a memory experiment will not presumably trigger a false memory (or if it did it would make bus rides so much more rewarding). Such findings extend to other metacognitive illusions, such as the finding that predictions of performance are higher for words written in a larger font when presented at study, even when font size has no effect on memory (Rhodes & Castell, 2008).[4] A small handful of experiments have begun to consider how people may correct their subjective assessments once they know they have been altered (e.g., Nussinson & Koriat, 2008) and this would be of interest when trying to understand the relation between the proposed two levels of metacognition.

Whittlesea and Williams (1998) asked why strangers, but not friends, induce feelings of familiarity. The idea is that familiarity is sensed when it is unexpected, and not when it is in keeping with processing. This view resonates with our idea of the interplay between two levels of metacognition, and could explain why ToT and déjà vu are so much more intense in the real world: in the laboratory we are just expecting that the experimenter is tinkering with our memory system. To have a strong déjà vu, for instance, necessitates that we do not understand the source of the familiarity.

Finally, while Whittlesea's views resonate with our own, one point of departure would be the nature of the feelings. Whittlesea's account suggests that the feelings are rather indeterminate and fundamental, as meaningless as a subliminal buzz, whereas we have suggested that the feelings that are generated during cognition may be intrinsically epistemic. Unfortunately, Whittlesea's theory has seldom been invoked in the context of memory impairment, and this remains a research priority, alongside tackling the nature (and significance) of epistemic feelings. Whittlesea's approach stresses that there might be relatively abstract and generic feelings that guide performance, and one obvious feeling central to most of the examples presented here would be certainty (e.g., Burton, 2008). Perhaps elemental feelings like certainty of not having being somewhere before (in déjà vu) or certainty of prior experience (in recollection) are critical for our understanding of subjective experience in cognition.

Future applications

> Once seized of any random belief, I would have no motive to undertake any further inquiry if I were incapable of experiencing doubt.
> (de Sousa, 2009, p. 149)

For a contribution to a book on applied cognition, we have been a little light on application, and we present three applications of epistemic feelings to everyday life and memory failure (there will be others) in order to stress the possible future utility of this approach:

The control and monitoring of memory in memory impairment

A primary goal of our research is to contribute to the rehabilitation of memory in neuropsychological groups. Such rehabilitation relies upon the proficient co-ordination of memory processes through effective control and monitoring. One of our earliest papers on metacognition in memory impairment (Alzheimer's disease; Moulin, Perfect, & Jones, 2000) showed that while patients were able to allocate study time (a measure of control) in an appropriate fashion according to repetition, the explicit judgements of performance were not sensitive to this manipulation. The advantage of considering two levels of metacognition is that we can better understand such data: study time may be allocated appropriately on the basis of lower-level feelings that are not well captured in explicit judgements of performance (which may be differentially impaired in neuropsychological groups). Thus a more complete understanding of memory impairment and metacognitive failure may be achieved through understanding epistemic feelings as well as explicit predictions of performance.

Delusions and confabulations

One of the themes that we have developed elsewhere (O'Connor, Lever, & Moulin, 2010) is that epistemic feelings permit confabulators and those with delusions to experience perceptual and cognitive anomalies as "real", an idea that stems from Langdon and Coltheart's (2000) two-factor model of delusion. Langdon and Coltheart posit that there is an interaction of two factors in the formation of a delusion. First, a neuropsychological deficit alters perceptual or emotional processing and disrupts "perceived reality'". Second, damage to a system of belief evaluation occurs that is responsible for the person's failure to reject the erroneous belief. Delusions may be thought of as a dramatic and pathological breakdown between the beliefs and feelings associated with cognition – in that sense they are an exaggeration of the déjà vu experience. We have published a series of cases whose main problem is that they feel like the whole of their life is repeating (which their carers describe as like persistent déjà vu; e.g., O'Connor et al., 2010). These patients act on the strong delusional

feelings they encounter during processing, and are resistant to rational attempts to explain their feelings. This is a central feature of delusion: the beliefs are immune to reason, even where there are logical impossibilities and inconsistencies – the idea of epistemic feelings (as distinct from rationally held beliefs) has explanatory power in such cases.

Obsessive-compulsive and post-traumatic stress disorders

Several authors have posited a role for epistemic feelings in obsessive- compulsive-disorder (e.g., de Sousa, 2009), especially in repeated checking behaviours. The cognitions generated in obsessive-compulsive disorder (OCD) and post-traumatic stress disorder (PTSD) are similar in that they are not unlike everyday experiences and errors of the healthy population, but are made more severe by their emotional significance and frequency. One account of superstitious behaviours in PTSD is that, just like with William James's earlier quote, meaningless actions are imbued with some erroneous feeling of significance. In the case of repeated checking, people with OCD have a fundamental distrust of their memory, which may stem from a metacognitive problem (e.g., Exner, Kohl, Zaudig, Langs, Lincoln, & Rief, 2009) or they fail to generate the appropriate feelings of certainty (de Sousa, 2009) despite being able to encode what they just did.

To conclude, it is worth reminding the reader of the wealth of subjective experiences, illusions and mental events that remain to be fully investigated by the memory researcher. They are difficult to research as a consequence of their subjectivity, but also because experiences like déjà vu have no behavioural corollary. But in memory impairment and psychological dysfunction more generally, we have found that it is often difficult to investigate and remediate dysfunction without taking note of the subjective experiences at the core of the dysfunction. One patient described it to one of us like this: "If someone has a broken arm, it is apparent and obvious from the x-ray, and people can sympathise accordingly, but what's happening in my head, no-one can know how that is."

NOTES

1 http://metro.co.uk/2008/01/10/killed-proving-spirit-isn-t-flammable-498126/ (last accessed 26 June, 2013).

2 Alfred.

3 This study also illustrates the lack of precision in terminology in the various paradigms and across authors. Litman et al. describe an FOK judgement with three points on the scale: "I don't know the answer", "The answer is on the tip of my tongue" and "I know the answer".

4 Who knows how our subjective experiences are being altered on a daily basis? Recent research has even shown that the physical distance between the participant (leaning forward or leaning back) and the problem on a computer monitor, influence the reported level of difficulty – problems feel easier if you lean back in your chair (Thomas & Tsai, 2011).

REFERENCES

Adachi, N., Adachi, T., Akanuma, N., Matsubara, R., & Ito, M. (2007). Déjà vu experiences in schizophrenia: Relations with psychopathology and antipsychotic medication. *Comprehensive psychiatry, 48*, 592–596.

Adachi, N., Akanuma, N., Ito, M., Adachi, T., Takekawa, Y., Adachi, Y., Matsuura, M., et al. (2010). Two forms of déjà vu experiences in patients with epilepsy. *Epilepsy & behavior, 18*(3), 218–222.

Allen-Burge, R., & Storandt, M. (2000). Age *equivalence in Feeling-of-Knowing experiences. Journal of Gerontology: Psychological Sciences, 55*, 214–223.

Ansons, T. L., & Leboe, J. P. (2010). The constructive nature of recollection. In P. Higham and J. P. Leboe (Eds.), *Constructions of remembering and metacognition: Essays in honor of Bruce Whittlesea.* London: Palgrave MacMillan.

Arango-Muñoz, S. (2011). Two levels of metacognition. *Philosophia, 39*, 71–82.

Astell, A. J., & Harley, T. A. (1996). Tip-of-the tongue states and lexical access in dementia. *Brain and Language, 54*, 196–215.

Bacon, E., Schwartz, B. L., Paire-Ficout, L., & Izaute, M. (2007). Dissociation between the cognitive process

and the phenomenological experience of TOT: Effect of the anxiolytic drug lorazepam on TOT states. *Consciousness & Cognition, 16*, 360–373.

Barnes, A. E., Nelson, T. O., Dunlosky, J., Mazzoni, G., & Narens, L. (1999). An integrative system of metamemory components involved in retrieval. *Attention And Performance Xvii – Cognitive Regulation of Performance: Interaction of Theory And Application, 17*, 287–313.

Blake, M. (1973). Prediction of recognition when recall fails: Exploring the feeling of knowing phenomenon, *Journal of Verbal Learning and Verbal Behavior, 12*, 311–319.

Brewer, G. A., Marsh, R. L., Clark-Foos, A., & Meeks, J. T. (2010). Noncriterial recollection influences metacognitive monitoring and control processes. *Quarterly Journal of Experimental Psychology, 63*, 1936–1942.

Brown, A. S. (2003). A review of the déjà vu experience. *Psychological Bulletin, 129*, 394–413.

Brown, A. S. (2012). *The tip of the tongue state.* New York: Psychology Press

Brown, A. S., & Marsh, E. J. (2008). Evoking false beliefs about autobiographical experience. *Psychonomic Bulletin and Review, 15*, 186–190.

Brown, A. S., & Nix, L. A. (1996). Age-related changes in the tip-of-the-tongue experience. *American Journal of Psychology, 109*, 79–91.

Brown, R., & McNeill, D. (1966). Tip of the tongue phenomenon. *Journal of Verbal Learning and Verbal Behavior, 5*, 325.

Burke, D. M., MacKay, D. G., Worthley, J. S., & Wade, E. (1991). On the tip-of-the tongue: What causes word finding failures in young and older adults? *Journal of Memory & Language, 30*, 542–579.

Burton, R. A. (2008). On being certain: Believing you are right even when you're not. New York: St. Martin's Press.

Carruthers, P. (2009). How we know our own minds: The relationship between mindreading and metacognition. *Behavioural and Brain Sciences, 32*, 121–138.

Cleary, A. M., & Reyes, N. L. (2009). Scene recognition without identification. *Acta Psychologica, 131*, 53–62.

Cleary, A. M., Brown, A. S., Sawyer, B. D., Nomi, J. S., Ajoku, A. C., & Ryals, A. J. (2012). Familiarity from the configuration of objects in 3-dimensional space and its relation to déjà vu: A virtual reality investigation. *Consciousness and Cognition, 21*, 969–975.

Cohen, G., & Faulkner, D. (1986). Memory for proper names: Age differences in retrieval. *British Journal of Developmental Psychology, 4*, 187–197.

Conway, M. A. (2009). Episodic memories. *Neuropsychologia, 47,* 2305–2313.

Conway, M. A., Gardiner, J. M., Perfect, T. J., Anderson, S. J., & Cohen, G. M. (1997). Changes in memory awareness during learning: The acquisition of knowledge by psychology undergraduates. *Journal of Experimental Psychology – General, 126,* 393–413.

Cook, G. I., Marsh, R. L., Hicks, J. L. (2006). Source memory in the absence of successful cued recall. *Journal of Experimental Psychology: Learning, Memory and Cognition, 32*(4), 828–835.

Diana, R. A., Reder, L. M., Arndt, A., & Park, H. (2006). Models of recognition: A review of arguments in favor of a dual-process account. *Psychonomic Bulletin & Review, 13,* 1–21.

de Sousa, R. (2009). Epistemic feelings. *Mind & Matter, 7*(2), 139–161.

Dunn, J. C. (2004). Remember–know: A matter of confidence. *Psychological Review, 111*(2), 524–542.

Efklides, A. (2010). Prospective memory failure and the metacognitive experience of "blank in the mind". *Trends and Prospects in Metacognition Research, 1,* 105–126.

Eichenbaum, H., Yonelinas, A. P., & Ranganath, C. (2007). The medial temporal lobe and recognition memory. *Annual Review of Neuroscience, 30,* 123–152.

Evans, J. St. B. T. (2008). Dual-processing accounts of reasoning, judgement and social cognition. *Annual Review of Psychology, 59,* 255–278.

Exner, C. Kohl, A., Zaudig, A., Langs, G., Lincoln, T. M., & Rief, W. (2009). Metacognition and episodic memory in obsessive-compulsive disorder. *Journal of Anxiety Disorders, 23,* 624–631.

Flavell, J. H. (2004). Theory-of-mind development: Retrospect and prospect. *Merrill-Palmer Quarterly, 50,* 274–290.

Goldinger, S. D., & Hansen, W. A. (2005). Remembering by the seat of your pants. *Psychological Science, 16,* 525–529.

Gollan, T. H., & Brown, A. S. (2006). From Tip-of-the-tongue (TOT) data to theoretical implications in two steps: When more ToTs means better retrieval. *Journal of Experimental Psychology: General, 135,* 462–483.

Hanly, S., & Vandenberg, B. (2010). Tip-of-the-tongue and word retrieval deficits in dyslexia. *Journal of Learning Disability, 43*(1), 15–23.

Hart, J. T. (1965). Memory and the feeling-of-knowing experiments. *Journal of Educational Psychology, 56,* 208–216.

Heine, M. K., Ober, B. A., & Shenaut, G. K. (1999). Naturally occurring and experimentally induced tip-of-the-tongue experiences in three adult age groups. *Psychology and Aging, 14,* 445–457.

Hicks, J. L., & Marsh, R. L. (2002). On predicting the future states of awareness for recognition of unrecallable items. *Memory and Cognition, 30,* 60–66.

Hosey, L. A., Peynircioglu, Z. F., & Rabinovitz, B. E. (2009). Feeling of Knowing for names in responses to faces. *Acta Psychologica, 130,* 214–224.

Illman, N. A., Butler, C. R., Souchay, C., & Moulin, C. J. A. (2012). Déjà experiences in temporal lobe epilepsy. *Epilepsy research and treatment,* vol. 2012, Article ID 539567, 15 pages, doi:10.1155/2012/539567

Jacoby, L. L., & Brooks, L. (1984). Nonanalytic cognition: Memory, perception and concept learning. In G. H. Bower (Ed.), *The psychology of learning and motivation: Advances in research and theory, 18,* 1–47. San Diego, CA: Academic Press.

James, W. (1882). On some Hegelisms. *Mind, 7,* 186–208.

James, W. (1902). *The varieties of religious experience, a study in human nature,* retrieved from www.gutenberg.org/ebooks/621 on 25 June 2012

Janowsky, J. S., Shimamura, A. P., & Squire, L. R. (1989). Memory and metamemory –comparisons between patients with frontal-lobe lesions and amnesic patients. *Psychobiology, 17,* 3–11.

Juncos-Rabadán, O., Rodriguez, N., Facal, D., Cuba, J., & Pereiro, A. (2011). Tip-of-the-tongue for proper names in mild cognitive impairment: Semantic or post-semantic impairments? *Journal of Neurolinguistics, 24*(6), 636–651.

Kahneman, D. (2011). *Thinking, fast and slow.* New York: Macmillan.

Kalra, S., Chancellor, A., & Zeman, A. (2007). Recurring déjà vu associated with 5-hydroxytryptophan. *Acta Neuropsychiatrica, 19,* 311–313.

Knight, E. F. (1895). *Where three empires meet: A narrative of recent travel in Kashmir, Western Tibet, Gilgit and the adjoining countries.* London: Longmans, Green & Co.

Kolers, P. A., & Palef, S. R. (1976). Knowing not. *Memory & Cognition, 4*(5), 553–558.

Koriat, A. (1993). How do we know that we know? The accessibility model of the feeling of knowing. *Psychological Review, 100,* 609–639.

Koriat, A. (2000). The feeling of knowing: Some metatheoretical implications for consciousness and control. *Consciousness and Cognition, 9,* 149–171.

Koriat, A. (2007). Metacognition and consciousness. In P. D. Zelazo, M. Moscovitch, and E. Thompson, *The Cambridge handbook of consciousness.* Cambridge: Cambridge University Press.

Koriat, A. (2008). Easy comes, easy goes? The link between learning and remembering and its exploitation in metacognition. *Memory & Cognition, 36*(2), 416–428.

Koriat, A., & Levy-Sadot, R. (2001). The combined contributions of the cue-familiarity and accessibility heuristics to feelings-of-knowing. *Journal of Experimental Psychology: Learning, Memory and Cognition, 27,* 34–53.

Koriat, A., Levy-Sadot, R., Edry, E., & de Marcas, G. (2003). What do we know about what we cannot remember? Accessing the semantic attributes of words that cannot be recalled. *Journal of experimental Psychology: Learning, Memory and Cognition, 29,* 1095–1105.

Koriat, A., & Lieblich, I. (1974) What does a person in a TOT state know that a person in a "don't know" state doesn't know? *Memory and Cognition, 2,* 647–655.

Langdon, R., & Coltheart, M. (2000). The cognitive neuropsychology of delusions. *Mind and Language, 15,* 183–216.

Langfitt, J. T., & Rausch, R. (1996). Word-finding deficits persist after left anterotemporal lobectomy. *Archives of Neurology, 53,* 72–76.

Litman, J. A., Hutchins, T. L., & Russon, R. K. (2005). Epistemic curiosity, feeling-of-knowing, and exploratory behaviour. *Cognition and Emotion, 19,* 559–582.

Loewenstein, G. (1994). The psychology of curiosity: A review and reinterpretation. *Psychological Bulletin, 116,* 75–98.

MacLaverty, S. N. & Hertzog, C. (2009). Do age-related differences in episodic feeling of knowing accuracy depend on the timing of the judgment? *Memory, 17,* 860–873.

Marquie, J. C., & Huet, N. (2000). Age differences in feeling-of-knowing and confidence judgments as a function of knowledge domain. *Psychology and Aging, 15,* 451–461.

Metcalfe, J., Schwartz, B. L., & Joaquim, S. G. (1993). The cue-familiarity heuristic in metacognition. Journal of Experimental *Psychology–Learning Memory and Cognition, 19,* 851–861.

Metcalfe, J., & Son, L. (2012). Anoetic, noetic and autonoetic metacognition. In M. J. R. Beran, J. Brandl, J. Perner, and J. Proust (Eds.), *The foundations of metacognition.* Oxford: Oxford University Press.

Moulin, C. J. A., Perfect, T. J., & Jones, R. W. (2000). The effects of repetition on allocation of study time and judgements of learning in Alzheimer's Disease. *Neuropsychologia, 38,* 748–756.

Nelson, T., & Leonesio, J. (1980). Norms of 300 general-information questions: Accuracy of recall, latency of recall , and Feeling-of-Knowing ratings. *Journal of Verbal Learning and Verbal Behavior, 19,* 338–368.

Nelson, T. O., & Leonesio, R. J. (1988). Allocation of self-paced study time and the "labor-in-vain effect". *Journal of Experimental Psychology, Learning, Memory, and Cognition, 14,* 676–686.

Nelson, T. O., & Narens, L. (1980). Norms of 300 general-information questions: Accuracy of recall, latency of recall, and felling-of- knowing ratings. *Journal of Verbal Learning and Verbal Behavior, 19,* 338–368.

Nelson, T. O., McSpadden, M., Fromme, K., & Marlatt, G. A. (1986). Effects of alcohol intoxication on metamemory and on retrieval from long-term memory. *Journal of Experimental Psychology–General, 115,* 247–254.

Nussinson, R., & Koriat, A. (2008). Correcting experience-based judgments: the perseverance of subjective experience in the face of the correction of judgment. *Metacognition and Learning, 3*(2), 159–174. doi:10.1007/s11409-008-9024-2

O'Connor, A. R., Lever, C., & Moulin, C. J. A. (2010). Novel insights into false recollection: A model of déjà vécu. *Cognitive Neuropsychiatry, 15,* 118–144.

O'Connor, A. R., Moulin, C. J. A. (2008). The persistence of erroneous familiarity in an epileptic male: Challenging perceptual theories of déjà vu activation. *Brain and Cognition, 68,* 144–147.

O'Connor, A. R., & Moulin, C. J. A. (2010). Recognition without identification, erroneous familiarity, and déjà vu. *Current Psychiatry Reports, 12,* 165–173.

Pannu, J. K., & Kaszniak, A.W. (2005). Metamemory experiments in neurological populations: A review. *Neuropsychological Review, 15,* 105–130.

Penfield, W., & Perot, P. (1963). The brain's record of auditory and visual experience: A final summary and discussion. *Brain, 86,* 595–696.

Perfect, T. J., & Hanley, J. R. (1992). The tip-of-the tongue phenomenon: Do experimenter-presented interlopers have any effect? *Cognition, 45,* 55–75.

Perfect, T. J., & Stollery, B. (1993). Memory and metamemory performance in older adults: One deficit or two? *Quarterly Journal of Experimental Psychology (A), 46*(1), 119–135.

Proust, J. (2007). Metacognition and metarepresentation: Is a self-directed theory of mind a precondition for metacognition? *Synthese, 159,* 271–295.

Rhodes, M. G., & Castel, A. D. (2008). Memory predictions are influenced by perceptual information: Evidence for metacognitive illusions. *Journal of Experimental Psychology: General, 137,* 615–625.

Riefer, D. M., Kevari, M. K., & Kramer, D. L. (1995). Name that tune: Eliciting the tip-of-the tongue experience using auditory stimuli. *Psychological Reports, 77,* 1379–1390.

Schacter, D. L., Harbluk, J. L., & McLachlan, D. R. (1984). Retrieval without recollection: An experimental analysis of source amnesia. *Journal of Verbal Learning and Verbal Behaviour, 23*(5), 593–611.

Schacter, D. L., & Worling, J. R. (1985) Attribute information and the feeling of knowing. *Canadian Journal of Psychology, 39,* 467–475.

Schwartz, B. L. (2001). The relationship of tip-of-the tongue states and retrieval time. *Memory and Cognition, 29,* 117–126.

Schwartz, B. L. (2002). The strategic control of retieval during tip-of-the tongue states. *The Korean Journal of Thinking & Problem Solving, 12,* 27–37.

Schwartz, B. L. (2008). Working memory load differentially affect tip-of-the tongue states and feeling-of-knowing judgments. *Memory and Cognition, 36,* 9–19.

Schwartz, B. L. (2011). The effect of being in a tip-of-the-tongue state on subsequent items. *Memory & Cognition, 39,* 245–250.

Schwartz, B. L., Travis, D. M., Castro, A. M., & Smith, S. M. (2000). The phenomenology of real and illusory tip-of the tongue states. *Memory and Cognition, 28,* 18–27.

Singh, S. (2007). Adolescent salvia substance abuse. *Addiction, 102*(5), 823–824.

Souchay, C., Bacon, E., Danion, J- M. (2006). Metamemory in Schizophrenia: An exploration of the feeling-of-knowing state. *Journal of Clinical and Experimental Neuropsychology, 28*(5), 828–840.

Souchay, C., Isingrini, M., & Espagnet, L. (2000). Aging, episodic memory feeling-of knowing, and frontal functioning. *Neuropsychology, 14,* 299–309.

Souchay, C., Isingrini, M., & Gil, R. (2002). Alzheimer's disease and feeling-of-knowing in episodic memory. *Neuropsychologia, 40,* 2386–2396.

Souchay, C., & Moulin, C. J. A. (2009). Memory and consciousness in Alzheimer's disease. *Current Alzheimer Research, 6,* 186–195.

Souchay, C., Moulin, C. J. A., Clarys, D., Taconnat, L., & Isingrini, M. (2007). Diminished episodic memory awareness in older adults: Evidence from feeling of knowing and recollection. *Consciousness and Cognition, 16,* 769–784.

Taiminen, T., & Jääskeläinen, S. K. (2001). Intense and recurrent déjà vu experiences related to amantadine and phenylpropanolamine in a healthy male. *Journal of clinical neuroscience: Official journal of the Neurosurgical Society of Australasia, 8*(5), 460–462.

Thomas, A. K., Bulevich, J. B., & Dubois, S. J. (2011). Context affects feeling-of-knowing accuracy in younger and older adults. *Journal of Experimental Psychology: Learning, Memory and Cognition, 37,* 96–108.

Thomas, M., & Tsai, C. I. (2011). Psychological distance and subjective experience: How distancing reduces the feeling of difficulty. *Journal of Consumer Research, 39*(2), 324–340. doi:10.1086/663772

Thompson, V. A., Prowse Turner, J. A., & Pennycook, G. (2011). Intuition, reason, and metacognition. *Cognitive Psychology, 63,* 107–140.

Tulving, E. (1985). Memory and consciousness. *Canadian Psychology–Psychologie Canadienne, 26,* 1–12.

Tulving, E. (1989). Remembering and knowing the past. *American Scientist, 77*(4), 361–367.

Wells, G. L., Olson, E. A., & Charman, S. D. (2002). The confidence of eyewitnesses in their identifications from lineups. *Current Directions in Psychological Science, 11*(5), 151–154.

Whittlesea, B. W. A. (1997). Production, evaluation, and preservation of experiences: Constructive processing in remembering and performance tasks. In D. L. Medlin (Ed.), *Psychology of learning and motivation* (Vol. 37, pp. 211–264). New York: Academic Press.

Whittlesea, B. W. A., & Williams, L. D. (1998). Why do strangers feel familiar, but friends don't? A discrepancy-attribution account of feelings of familiarity. *Acta Psychologica, 98,* 141–165.

Widner, R. L., Otani, H., & Winkelman, S. E. (2005). Tip-of-the tongue experiences are not merely strong feeling-of-knowing experiences. *The Journal of General Psychology, 132,* 392–407.

Widner, R. L., Smith, S. M., & Gaziano, W. G. (1996). The effects of demand characteristics on the reporting of tip-of-the tongue and feeling-of-knowing states. *American Journal of Psychology, 109,* 525–538.

Wixted, J. T., & Stretch, V. (2004). In defense of the signal detection interpretation of remember/know judgments. *Psychonomic Bulletin & Review, 11*(4), 616–641.

Yaniv, I., & Meyer, D. E. (1987). Activation and metacognition of inaccessible stored information: Potential bases for incubation effects in problem solving. *Journal of Experimental Psychology: Learning,* Memory and Cognition, 13, 187–205.

Yonelinas, A. P. (2002). The nature of recollection and familiarity: A review of 30 years of research. *Journal of Memory and Language, 46,* 441–517.

Eyewitness Memory

30

Eyewitness Recall: An Overview of Estimator-Based Research

Pär Anders Granhag, Karl Ask, and Erik Mac Giolla

Popular fiction and the so-called "CSI effect" (Goodman-Delahunty & Tait, 2006) create the impression that most crimes are solved by DNA evidence and sophisticated offender profiles. This impression is grossly misleading. In fact, the overwhelmingly most frequent type of evidence in criminal cases is testimony from witnesses (de Poot, Bokhorst, van Koppen, & Muller, 2004). Eyewitness testimony is not only the most frequent and important form of evidence; it is also particularly susceptible to various forms of debilitating influences. In this chapter, we will review research on factors that affect the completeness and reliability of eyewitness recall. This chapter, and the three that follow, are structured around Wells' (1978) distinction between estimator and system variables in the study of eyewitness testimony. Estimator variables concern parameters that are naturally associated with the witnessing of an event, and that may influence the reliability of eyewitness memory. Examples of such variables range from the simple (e.g., viewing distance) to the psychologically complex (e.g., stress). By definition, these variables are beyond the control of the legal system, and their influence can, at best, only be estimated after the fact. System variables, in contrast, are parameters that are under the control of

the legal system. For instance, the police can influence the reliability of eyewitness testimony through their use of more or less appropriate interviewing techniques. We will limit our review to topics related to estimator variables. Moreover, we will only cover research with its main focus on eyewitness recall; that is, how estimator variables relate to the reliability of eyewitness reports. Topics related to system variables and eyewitness identifications will be covered in subsequent chapters.

A LOOK OVER THE SHOULDER

Seminal studies conducted in Germany by William Stern and his colleagues at the beginning of the twentieth century, examining variables such as retention interval and stress, are a testament to the early considerations given to the effects of estimator variables on eyewitness recall (Stern, 1939). Further evidence for this early interest can be found in Whipple's many reviews, in which the effects of individual differences, cultural influences, environmental conditions, stimulus features, and attention on the reliability of testimony are addressed (e.g., Whipple, 1909). Interestingly, many of the issues raised in this initial wave of eyewitness research have resurfaced in the contemporary literature. For instance, Whipple's (1914) observations concerning the attention-grabbing potential of unusual objects have reemerged, some 80 years later, as a novel explanation of the "weapon-focus effect" (Mitchell, Livosky, & Mather, 1998; Pickel, 1998; see below), and cultural phenomena mentioned by researchers a century ago, such as the "cross-race effect" (Feingold, 1914), are now subjects of intense empirical enquiry (Brigham, Bennett, Meissner, & Mitchell, 2007).

The decades that followed this initial productive era saw a considerable decline in eyewitness research in general (Wells, Memon, & Penrod, 2006), while more specific research relating to estimator variables seems to have been virtually nonexistent (for rare exceptions, see Hastorf & Cantrill, 1954; Sommer, 1959). The "renaissance" of eyewitness research is said to have begun in the mid-to-late 1970s, with the works of psychologists like Elizabeth Loftus garnering considerable attention and being published in high-impact journals (Wells et al., 2006). Along with this came a resurgence of interest in estimator variables and their effects on recall. For example, Seigel and Loftus (1978) examined the effects of anxiety on recall, while Clifford and Scott (1978) investigated the role of individual and environmental influences (e.g., the nature of the crime, type of information to be recalled) on witness testimony. This period also saw researchers go beyond the laboratory and into the archives of police records (e.g., Kuehn, 1974), complementing experimental findings with real-life statistics. Since the 1970s, the literature on eyewitness testimony has undergone a rapid expansion, and is now one of the largest subfields of applied memory research.

Below we will review current research examining estimator variables' effects on recall. This section will be divided into two main parts, focusing on *event-related* and *witness-related* variables, respectively. Then a more critical analysis of the state of the field will be provided, before we conclude with suggestions for future research.

WITNESS-RELATED VARIABLES

Stress

The influence of emotion on eyewitness memory has received an enormous amount of attention in the last three decades, evident in the large number of reviews and books on the topic published during this period (e.g., Christianson, 1992; Deffenbacher, 1983; Deffenbacher, Bornstein, Penrod, & McGorty, 2004; Fiedler & Hütter, Chapter 9, this volume; Holland & Kensinger, 2010; Levine & Pizarro, 2004; Reisberg & Hertel, 2003; Reisberg & Heuer, 2007; Uttl, Ohta, & Siegenthaler, 2006). For the sake of brevity, we will limit our discussion to the influence of "experienced stress" rather than the broader topic of emotion. In line with Deffenbacher et al. (2004), "experienced stress" refers here to the degree of cognitive stress or anxiety experienced by the witness while observing the to-be-remembered stimuli. This excludes studies where the stressfulness of the stimuli is varied (e.g., images of a car crash versus a leisurely drive), but where witnesses' experienced stress need not vary correspondingly (e.g., Christianson & Loftus, 1987; Christianson, Loftus, Hoffman, & Loftus, 1991).

Research on stress and eyewitness recall has produced mixed findings. A growing body of research attests to the impairing effects of stress on memory (for a review, see Deffenbacher et al., 2004). For example, using a novel stress-inducing method, Valentine and Mesout (2009) examined witnesses' ability to describe an individual seen during a visit to the London Dungeon – a tourist attraction designed to evoke fear and anxiety in visitors. Valentine and Mesout found that increased anxiety was significantly correlated with increased description errors.

As pointed out by Reisberg and Heuer (2007), however, such results stand in stark contrast to the superior accuracy and longevity often observed for memories of traumatic, and most likely stress-inducing, events (e.g., Parker, Bahrick, Fivush, & Johnson, 2006; Peace & Porter, 2004; Peterson & Whalen, 2001). It seems that these discrepancies can only be resolved with further research. In their comprehensive review, Reisberg and Heuer (2007) identified important limitations of both strands of research, and highlighted critical areas for future studies.

One possible approach is to focus on individual differences. For example, a highly stress-inducing situation for some individuals may not be at all stressful for others, and may thus have diverse effects on memory. This approach is exemplified in the above-mentioned study by Valentine and Mesout (2009) who divided witnesses into a high-stress and a low-stress group based on witnesses' self-reported state anxiety. Interestingly, in that study, description accuracy was uncorrelated with measures of trait anxiety, further underscoring the importance of situation-specific individual differences. A second possible approach would be to investigate, in more detail, which specific type of information is remembered more or less accurately as a result of stress. For example, studies showing impairing effects of stress have focused largely on person descriptors, whereas studies of traumatic events have focused more broadly on memory for the event itself (Reisberg & Heuer, 2007).

Witness age

Witnesses' age is one of the most extensively researched individual differences in relation to eyewitness recall, with an abundance of studies on both child witnesses (see Principe, Greenhoot & Ceci, Chapter 35, this volume; Pozzulo, 2007) and elderly witnesses (see Bartlett, Chapter 36, this volume; Bartlet & Memon, 2007; Mueller-Johnson & Ceci, 2007). Although developmental issues such as language proficiency and knowledge are likely to influence children's recall ability (Pipe, Thierry, & Lamb, 2007), research indicates that children of a very young age may be capable of producing coherent and accurate testimonies. This finding is, however, qualified by a number of issues. First, while they may be accurate, children's testimonies are often quite brief, and younger children tend to produce shorter reports than do older children (Pipe, Lamb, Orbach, & Esplin, 2004). Second, child witnesses are especially prone to description errors for certain types of details. For instance, specific person descriptors, such as weight, age, and height, tend to be more inaccurately reported by children than by adults (Pozzulo, 2007). This finding is probably due, at least partly, to children's inexperience in making such judgments. Third, child witnesses are more susceptible to suggestions compared with adult witnesses (for a review, see Melnyk, Crossman, & Scullin, 2007). In light of these issues, it is quite understandable that contemporary research on child eyewitnesses focuses largely on interview techniques designed to maximize the accuracy and completeness of children's testimonies (for more on this topic, see Lamb, La Rooy, Malloy, & Katz, 2011; Gronlund & Carson, Chapter 33, this volume).

At the other end of the lifespan, the cognitive and perceptual consequences of aging can influence the elderly witness (Bartlett, Chapter 36, this volume). For instance, aging is associated with impairments in attentional resources, vision, hearing, and long-term memory storage (Mueller-Johnson & Ceci, 2007). As would be expected, these deficits negatively influence eyewitness testimony. Research indicates that elderly witnesses perform more poorly than younger adults both in terms of the completeness and accuracy of general memory recall (Mueller-Johnson & Ceci, 2007), but also with regards to perpetrator descriptions (Bartlett & Memon, 2007). The detrimental consequences of aging appear to be mitigated by several factors, however, including the witness's degree of education, verbal ability, familiarity with the setting, and the proximity in age between the perpetrator and the witness (Bartlett & Memon, 2007; Mueller-Johnson & Ceci, 2007).

Effects of alcohol consumption

Witnesses to crimes are often under the influence of alcohol, both when viewing the incident and in subsequent police interviews (Evans, Schreiber Compo, & Russano, 2009). A great deal of research has examined the effects of alcohol on memory (e.g., Acheson, Stein, & Swartzelder, 1998; Bisby, Leitz, Morgan, & Curran, 2010; Curran & Hildebrandt, 1999; Maylor & Rabbitt, 1993; Ryback, 1971; White, 2003), with the general conclusion that increased consumption results in increased memory impairment (Soraci et al., 2007). Very little of this research, however, is directly applicable to eyewitness recall. For example, studying memory for stimuli like word lists (e.g., Maylor, Rabbitt, & Kingstone, 1987; Tracy & Bates, 1999) is unlikely to illuminate the specific effects of alcohol on eyewitness memory for a complex scene (Evans et al., 2009). Here we will focus exclusively on the few existing studies directly applicable to eyewitness recall. (See Valentine, Chapter 32, this volume, for a discussion of alcohol and recognition.)

Yuille and Tollestrup (1990) compared the recall ability of sober and intoxicated witnesses of a staged crime, both immediately after the crime and one week later. In the immediate interview, alcohol intoxication reduced the quantity of details reported, whereas the accuracy of the reported details was unaffected. In the follow-up interview one week later, however, the intoxicated group performed worse with regards to both amount of details and accuracy compared with their sober counterparts. These results are in line with the traditional assumption that alcohol generally impairs eyewitness testimony.

Recent findings from our laboratory, however, qualify this notion. For example, Dahlgren, Roos af Hjelmsäter, Granhag, Fahlke, and Söderpalm-Gordh (2013) let a high-dose group, a moderate-dose group, and a sober control group watch a filmed crime. When interviewed one week later, witnesses in the high-dose condition reported significantly fewer details than did participants in the moderate-dose group (no other group differences were significant). Importantly, however, there were no differences in the accuracy of the reported details. Other researchers have found that alcohol impairs recall primarily for peripheral (versus central) details (Schreiber Compo et al., 2011a), or have found no impairing effects of alcohol on witness testimony at all (Schreiber Compo et al., 2011b). The latter findings have been explained in light of *alcohol myopia theory* (Steele & Josephs, 1990), holding that the cognitive impairment of alcohol restricts attention to central details of an event, at the expense of peripheral ones, thereby reducing accuracy for peripheral details while leaving central details relatively intact.

The emerging picture is further complicated in view of the results of a recent field study. Van Oorsouw and Merckelbach (2011) recruited participants with no, intermediate, or high blood alcohol levels from bars, and had them watch a staged crime. When tested a few days after the event, participants in the intermediate and high alcohol groups had considerably poorer recall than their sober counterparts. In contradiction to alcohol myopia theory, however, this impairment was shown for both central and peripheral event details; in fact, memory for central details seemed to be especially impaired. In sum, although alcohol intoxication appears to have a generally detrimental influence on eyewitness recall, the discrepant findings reported in the literature indicate more research on the topic is needed.

Intellectual disabilities

Traditionally, individuals with intellectual disabilities (IDs) have been regarded as unreliable witnesses (Ternes & Yuille, 2008;

Valenti-Hein & Schwartz, 1993), and they are often met with skepticism when attempting to report a crime to the police (Sharp, 2001). This increases their vulnerability to crime, as perpetrators can act without fear of retribution. The skepticism towards witnesses with IDs has been suggested as one of the main reasons for the overrepresentation of this population in sexual assault cases (Perlman, Ericson, Esses, & Isaacs, 1994).

Although basic memory research shows impaired encoding, storage, and recall for individuals with IDs (Brown & Geiselman, 1990), specific research on eyewitness testimony paints a more hopeful picture. Individuals with IDs, during free recall, have accuracy rates that compare quite favorably with those of the general population, although their statements tend to be significantly shorter (Agnew & Powell, 2004; Brown & Geiselman, 1990; Perlman et al., 1994; Ternes & Yuile, 2008). In other words, compared with the general population, individuals with IDs are more likely to make errors of omission but have comparable error rates for commissions (Kebbell & Hatton, 1999; Milne & Bull, 2001). Such results are encouraging, as they suggest that individuals with IDs are capable of producing reliable, albeit short, witness reports. However, a number of qualifications are necessary. For instance, there exists great variation within the spectrum of intellectual disabilities, ranging from mild (or high functioning) to severe (or low functioning; American Psychiatric Association, 1994). All the studies mentioned above involved individuals with mild intellectual disabilities; intelligence quotients (IQs), when reported, ranged from 53 to 80. Because participants must fulfill the requirements for informed consent, participation in psychological studies is typically restricted to the more mild forms of disabilities (Ternes & Yuile, 2008). It is doubtful whether such studies generalize to individuals with more severe intellectual disabilities. For example, Gudjonsson, Murphy, and Clare (2000) found that individuals with low-functioning IDs had considerable

difficulties in accurately recalling a narrative, if at all able to produce a report. Other concerns specific to witnesses with IDs include the finding that such individuals display heightened suggestibility (Gudjonsson, 1990), and that specialized interview techniques may be necessary (Cardon & Dent, 1996; Milne & Bull, 2001).

Other witness-related variables

Victims versus bystanders

Intuitively, there are a number of reasons to expect that victims and bystanders would differ with regards to their reports of an incident. For instance, victims are likely to have closer and more prolonged contact with the perpetrator, both of which are factors facilitative of recall. Furthermore, victims are likely to experience relatively more stress than bystanders, which is thought to influence encoding and recall (Deffenbacher et al., 2004).

Empirical findings appear to support this intuitive assumption. Victims, or witnesses with more personal involvement, recall events and describe individuals more accurately than do uninvolved bystanders. This claim has been supported by experimental (Hosch & Bothwell, 1990; Yuille, Davies, Gibling, Marxsen, & Porter, 1994; but see Kassin, 1984) and archival evidence (Fahsing, Ask, & Granhag, 2004), and field studies (Nachson & Slavutskay-Tsukerman, 2010). In the study by Nachson and Slavutskay-Tsukerman (2010), victims of a discotheque bombing had better recall for both central and peripheral details, in comparison with uninjured bystanders and a control group who had merely received information about the incident from the media. Witness role also appears to produce qualitative differences in the content of witness reports. A study by Manzanero, El-Astal, and Aróztegui (2009) showed that differences in *imagined* personal involvement are sufficient to qualitatively alter the nature of reports; personally involved individuals tended to focus more on emotional and autobiographical elements of an incident than did uninvolved individuals.

Other individual differences

A host of individual differences, other than those treated in previous sections, can act as powerful moderators of situational variables. Consider, for instance, findings showing that stressful and nonstressful situations have different impacts on memory (Deffenbacher et al., 2004; see above). Given that individuals differ in their tendency to experience stress, memory performance may vary greatly between witnesses of the same event (Valentine & Mesout, 2009). Thus, straightforward application of general findings, without consideration of individual differences, may produce misleading conclusions.

Furthermore, individual differences among perpetrators and witnesses can influence subsequent recall more directly. In terms of perpetrator characteristics, higher attractiveness and distinctiveness have been shown to increase perpetrator identifications (Brigham, 1990). Even seemingly irrelevant factors like accented speech have been shown to affect person descriptions; the extra cognitive demand of processing accented speech appears to draw resources from other cognitive activities critical for accurate visual descriptions (Pickel & Staller, 2012).

A particularly interesting individual-difference variable is witnesses' degree of self-monitoring. High self-monitors, as opposed to low self-monitors, are more concerned with presenting themselves appropriately in social situations, which necessitates a more thorough appraisal of the situation and the actors within it (Snyder, 1974). It has therefore been hypothesized that high self-monitors will show superior memory for key persons in a situation, thus making them better witnesses (Hosch, Leippe, Marchioni, & Cooper, 1984). Studies on eyewitness identification have supported this hypothesis (for a review, see Hosch, 1994). Although similar findings should be expected for recall accuracy, this is yet to be examined empirically.

EVENT-RELATED VARIABLES

Optimality of encoding and retention

The witnessing of criminal events varies naturally along numerous fundamental dimensions, such as the time available to view the critical stimuli (i.e., exposure duration), viewing distance, lighting conditions, and the delay between encoding and recall (i.e., retention interval). Intuitively, one would predict that shorter exposure, longer retention intervals, longer viewing distances, and poorer lighting conditions would impair eyewitness recall. By and large, the extant literature supports these notions. The pervasive influence of exposure duration has been confirmed in archival (Fahsing et al., 2004), experimental (Memon, Hope, & Bull, 2003), and field (Yarmey, Jacob, & Porter, 2002) studies; shorter exposure to the event consistently results in poorer recall. The robustness of this finding is generally agreed upon by leading witness psychology researchers (Kassin, Tubb, Hosch, & Memon, 2001). Although deviations from this general pattern have been reported (e.g., Memon et al., 2003), there is little doubt that memory recall in general benefits from increased encoding time.

With regards to the effects of viewing distance and illumination, intuitive predictions again seem to harmonize well with research findings. Meissner, Sporer, and Schooler's (2007) review of archival studies on the topic shows that longer distances and poorer illumination generally impair recall. Of course, at the extremes (i.e., complete darkness, very long distances) such variables must have a significant impact for quite trivial reasons. More interesting, from a psychological and legal perspective, is at what point such variables start becoming a problem. Due to a paucity of experimental research, meaningful conclusions are difficult to draw in this regard. Loftus (2010) provides compelling arguments that distances as short as 40 m (126 ft) and 82 m (271 ft) can drastically impair viewing conditions of small objects and faces, respectively. Relatedly, a recent experimental study found that increased viewing distance (ranging from 5 to 50 m), significantly impaired estimates of the height and weight of a target, but not estimates of age (Lindsay, Semmler, Weber, Brewer, & Lindsay, 2008). Although consistent with the detrimental influence of distance, the latter findings suggest that all person descriptors may not be equally sensitive to variations in distance.

Longer retention intervals tend to deteriorate the quality of witness reports. Both omission and commission errors become more likely as the delay between encoding and recall increases (Meissner et al., 2007). Research shows, however, that the influence of delay is contingent on a number of factors. For instance, mnemonic techniques ranging from simple rehearsal (Read & Connolly, 2007) to more complex metacognitive strategies (Evans & Fisher, 2011) can protect memory from gradual deterioration. Moreover, not all types of information are equally prone to forgetting. For instance, schema-consistent information seems better able to withstand the effects of time than does schema-inconsistent or schema-irrelevant information (Tuckey & Brewer, 2003b). Similarly, it is likely that memory for central information is more long-lasting than peripheral information (Read & Connolly, 2007).[1] Finally, longer delays generally make individuals more susceptible to the damaging effects of suggestibility and post-event information (Meissner et al., 2007).

Weapon-focus effect

The *weapon-focus effect* refers to the impairment in witnesses' memory and recall, most notably for the perpetrator, due to the presence of a weapon. The effect is a well-documented experimental finding, consistently showing impaired recall for perpetrators carrying weapons (see Steblay, 1992; Pickel, 2007, for reviews), and increasingly accepted among leading witness psychology researchers as a reliable phenomenon (Kassin et al., 2001). Furthermore, the effect has been demonstrated with a wide variety of weapons (e.g., Davies, Smith, & Blincoe, 2008; Kramer, Buckhout, & Eugenio, 1990; Pickel, 2009), in diverse populations (e.g., Davies, Smith, & Blincoe, 2008; Pickel, Narter, Jameson, & Lenhardt, 2008; O'Rourke, Penrod, Cutler, & Stuve, 1989; Shaw & Sholnick, 1999), and with different presentation modes, including pictorial slides (e.g., Loftus, Loftus, & Messo, 1987), videos (e.g., Pickel, 1999), and staged events (e.g., Maass & Köhnken, 1989).

It seems that the weapon-focus effect is dependent on attentional mechanisms; weapons attract a disproportionate amount of witnesses' attention at the expense of other stimuli in the environment (Pickel, 2007). This was demonstrated by Loftus et al. (1987), who were able to show that participants made more and longer eye fixations on a weapon compared with a control object (a check). The precise reason for the attention-grabbing potential of weapons, however, remains a contested issue.

Two differing theoretical accounts exist for the weapon-focus effect. The first, known as the "Easterbrook hypothesis" (derived from Easterbrook, 1959), holds that it is the inherent threat of a weapon that attracts our attention. More specifically, the anxiety or arousal caused by the presence of a weapon results in a narrowing of attention on the source of the arousal (i.e., the weapon), impairing the encoding of peripheral details like physical characteristics of the perpetrator. Recent studies support the Easterbrook account of the weapon-focus effect (e.g., Davies et al., 2008; Hope & Wright, 2007).

The second account suggests that it is the unusualness or novelty of the weapon that attracts our attention (Mitchell, Livosky, & Mather, 1998). A more specific version of this account is derived from script and schema theory (Abelson, 1981). A weapon will be seen as unusual, and hence attract our attention, whenever it is incongruent with the current contextual script (e.g., a gun at a shooting range is contextually congruent, but a gun at a baseball game is incongruent;

Pickel, 1999) or person schema (e.g., a chef carrying a knife is congruent, but a mailman carrying a knife is incongruent; Pickel, 2008). In favor of the unusualness account, as opposed to the Easterbrook hypothesis, a number of studies have shown that the weapon-focus effect is independent of perceived threat (e.g., Pickel, 1998, 2009; Shaw & Skolnick, 1999).

The threat and unusualness explanations need not be seen as contradictory, but instead as complementary. In fact, due to the existing support for both sides, the joint influence of anxiety and novelty is suggested as a likely cause by a number of researchers (e.g., Hope & Wright, 2007; Pickel, 2007).

A review of the literature on the weapon-focus effect reveals a notable absence of conclusive archival research on the topic. Although a number of archival studies have approached the issue (e.g., Behrman & Davey, 2001; Wagstaff, MacVeigh, Boston, Scott, Brunas-Wagstaff, & Cole, 2003), these studies are marred by methodological problems related specifically to the detection of weapon-focus effects (see Pickel, 2007, for a comprehensive review of these problems). Because, in our opinion, no study to date has successfully managed to isolate the weapon-focus effect through archival analysis, this should be an important objective for future studies.

Cross-race effect

The *cross-race effect* (also known as the *own-race bias* or *other-race effect*) refers to the robust finding that individuals show a higher ability to recognize people of their own ethnic background, as opposed to other ethnic groups (for reviews, see Brigham et al., 2007; Meissner & Brigham, 2001; Sporer, 2001; Valentine, Chapter 32, this volume). The vast body of literature supporting this claim has focused, as the definition implies, almost exclusively on the effects of race on recognition ability. In contrast, very few studies have addressed the effect of race

on person descriptions and recall. However, some empirically grounded assumptions suggest that the cross-race effect may be curbed or nonexistent during recall (Brigham et al., 2007).

The argument advanced by Brigham et al. (2007) rests on three assumptions. First, our impressive ability to recognize faces is likely due, in part, to *holistic* or *configural* encoding (Farah, Wilson, Drain, & Tanaka, 1998; Yin, 1969). That is, the face is processed and recognized as a gestalt, rather than as a composite of individual features (Maurer, Le Grand, & Mondloch, 2002). Second, expertise is associated with an increased ability for configural processing (Diamond & Carey, 1986). Hence, the encoding of same-race faces (expert encoding) should rely on relatively more configural processing than the encoding of other-race faces (novice encoding). Recently, a flurry of studies have supported this claim (Michel, Caldara, & Rossion, 2006a; Michel, Rossion, Han, Chung, & Caldare, 2006b; Rhodes, Hayward, & Winkler, 2006; Sangiroli & de Schonen, 2004; Tanaka, Kiefer, & Bukach, 2004; see also Rhodes, Brake, Taylor, & Tan, 1989; Fallshore & Schooler, 1995; but see Buckout & Regan, 1988; Valentine & Bruce, 1986). Third, the verbalization of thoughts encoded configurally may be more difficult than the verbalization of thoughts encoded featurally (Wells & Turtle, 1987). Therefore, it is possible that same-race descriptions may, paradoxically, be disrupted by the superior configural encoding that improves same-race recognition.

Although the veracity of Brigham and colleagues' (2007) argument remains to be tested empirically, two important qualifications can be made already at this point. First, research shows that the encoding of same-race (versus other-race) faces is superior not only for configural aspects, but also for featural information (Hayward, Rhodes, & Schwaninger, 2008; Rhodes et al., 2006). Second, the relative reliance on configural and featural encoding is unlikely to be the only contributing factor to the cross-race effect (Michel et al., 2006b; Mondloch et al., 2010; for a proposed multiply determined model, see Hugenberg, Young, Bernstein, & Sacco, 2010). Hence, the argument, even if proven valid, does not entirely rule out the possibility of a cross-race effect in recall and descriptions.

Some clues as to whether a cross-race effect would emerge in perpetrator descriptions comes from research on people's strategies when describing or viewing same-race and other-race faces. In an often-cited study, Elis, Deregowski, and Shepherd (1975) found that people employ the same strategies to describe other-race individuals as they do to describe same-race individuals. Because some descriptors (e.g., eye color, hair color) are informative about members of some ethnic groups (e.g., Caucasians) but not of others (e.g., Afro-Americans), such an indiscriminate application of common description strategies may produce cross-race effects. More recent research, using eye-tracking technology, shows that Western Caucasians and East Asians attend to different areas when encoding faces (e.g., focusing on the eye region and central region, respectively; Blais, Jack, Scheepers, Fiset, & Caldera, 2008). The inflexible application of description strategies, paired with cultural differences in attentional preference, may be reason to expect a cross-race effect in perpetrator descriptions.

Of course, only studies directly investigating cross-racial descriptions will provide conclusive evidence on the topic. Using a *communication accuracy paradigm*, where judges made identifications based on other people's descriptions, Fallshore and Schooler (1995) found that identification accuracy was almost identical for same-race and other-race descriptions. Similar results were reported by Dore, Brigham, and Buck (2005). The more recent findings of McQuiston-Surrett and Topp (2008), however, were somewhat more mixed. Gauging both a *matching task* (similar to the communication accuracy paradigm) and an objective measure of description accuracy, Hispanic participants were equally accurate when describing Hispanic (same-race) and White (other-race) faces. In a follow-up experiment, with Black faces in the other-race condition, a cross-race effect was found on the matching task (but not on the objective accuracy measure). Hispanic participants' descriptions of same-race faces led to significantly more correct matches than did their descriptions of other-race faces. One explanation for these mixed findings is that the Hispanic participants are likely to have had more exposure to White than to Black populations, and White targets may thus not have represented a true other-race group (McQuiston-Surret & Topp, 2008).

Other event-related variables

Level of violence

Criminal events differ greatly in the extent to which they involve violence. Experimental research indicates that increased violence leads to decreased accuracy of recall of the event and of person descriptions (Clifford & Hollin, 1981; Clifford & Scott, 1978). These results are partially supported by archival studies. For instance, Kuehn (1974) found that more violent types of crime were associated with less complete reports. Similarly, Fahsing et al. (2004) found that witnesses of bank robberies involving guns produced less complete perpetrator descriptions than did witnesses of robberies involving knives, arguably because guns are capable of inflicting more injury. In contrast to experimental studies, however, crimes involving guns (versus knives) were associated with *more accurate* descriptions. Possibly, this discrepancy can be explained by obvious methodological differences. In the experimental studies (Clifford & Hollin, 1981; Clifford & Scott, 1978), violent crimes were compared with nonviolent crimes, while in the study by Fahsing et al. (2004) all of the crimes were violent, differing only with regards to degree of violence.

Number of perpetrators

Another significant aspect in which crimes naturally differ relates to the complexity of the event. Specifically, some crimes are committed by single perpetrators, whereas others are carried out by multiple offenders. This creates important differences in the amount of information that witnesses need to encode. As would be expected, both experimental (Clifford & Hollin, 1981) and archival studies (Fashing et al., 2004) show that the accuracy of eyewitness recall decreases as the number of perpetrators increases. Most likely, this occurs because more than one perpetrator requires witnesses to divide their attention, thus reducing the depth of encoding of any single individual (Megreya & Bindemann, 2011).

Crime schemas and crime typicality

Schemas and scripts help us organize, synthesize, and remember information. People have script-based memory representations for typical crimes, like they do for other social events (Holst & Pezdek, 1992; List, 1986). For instance, although most people lack firsthand experience of such an event, most of us can easily imagine what typically happens during a bank robbery. Because people tend to organize event memories around existing scripts, recollection of events that differ in some regard from the script may be distorted; that is, people may recall things as they expected them to be rather than as they were.

This was elegantly demonstrated in a now classic study by Loftus and Palmer (1974, Experiment 2). Participants were shown a film of a car accident, and were immediately questioned about the contents of the film. The phrasing of a critical question was subtly manipulated, such that some participants were asked about how fast the cars were going when they "smashed" into each other, whereas others were asked to estimate the speed when the cars "hit" each other. Consistent with the script for a serious accident, participants who received the "smashed" verb estimated the speed to be significantly higher than did participants who

received the "hit" verb. Furthermore, when questioned about the film one week later, participants in the "smashed" condition were much more likely to falsely report having seen broken glass (32 percent) than were participants in the "hit" condition (14 percent). Clearly, the activation of a script can distort the recollection of an event in a script-consistent manner (Loftus & Palmer, 1974).

Subsequent studies have further bolstered this claim. For example, memory reports relating to highly typical (versus atypical) aspects of an incident have been found to be at the same time more detailed *and* less accurate (List, 1986; Migueles & García-Bojas, 2004). Thus, for typical aspects, witnesses tend to report details generated from scripted memory representations, leading to an increase in commission errors. Similarly, in studies requiring "yes/no" or "occurred/did not occur" responses from witnesses, information of high (versus low) typicality is associated with both more correct hits *and* more false alarms (Greenberg, Westcott, & Bailey, 1998, Luna & Migueles, 2008; Migueles & García-Bojas, 2004). Such "schema intrusions" are more likely to occur when the to-be-remembered information is ambiguous (Tuckey & Brewer, 2003b) or unclear (Greenberg et al., 1998), as the scripts can be used to fill gaps in the witnesses' memory of the event.

Although most of the above research highlights detrimental consequences, it should be noted that schemas and scripts can also have a positive influence on witness reports. If the actual event is consistent with the activated schema, the amount of information correctly recalled may increase. Furthermore, it seems that schemas can safeguard correct schema-relevant information from both retrieval-induced forgetting (García-Banjos, Migueles, & Anderson, 2009; Migueles & García-Banjos, 2006) and general memory decay (Tuckey & Brewer, 2003a).

Familiarity and expertise

Closely related to crime typicality is the witness's familiarity with, or knowledge about, the various components of a crime. For instance, familiarity with the suspect, weapon, or getaway car is likely to improve the specific recall of these factors, while an understanding of the event itself is likely to improve episodic memory more generally. The first claim needs little explanation: Past familiarity and experience results in better memory of stimuli (Baddeley, 1990). Therefore, for example, if a witness is acquainted with the suspect, his or her memory and recall should be better than if the suspect was a stranger.

The more general positive influence of knowledge on memory can be inferred from the memory literature comparing experts and novices. A quintessential study in this field examined expert chess players' memory of the positioning of chess pieces compared with that of novices (Chase & Simon, 1973). Results showed that experts were superior in reconstructing a given board from memory, but only if the pieces were positioned in a game-consistent manner (versus randomly). Such results attest to an expert's ability to encode the to-be-remembered information in a more systematic and meaningful way, conducive of subsequent recall.

Translated to the witness setting, it could be argued that better knowledge and understanding of a crime may result in a more systematic and meaningful encoding of the event. This reasoning is supported by research on young children, showing that knowledge or understanding of an event can moderate the typical negative effects associated with lower witness age (see Pipe et al., 2007).

ANALYSIS AND EVALUATION

From our review of the contemporary literature it is clear that the conclusiveness of the existing research varies considerably from topic to topic. The topics marred by the largest gaps are those that have received minimal attention, generated inconclusive results, and

host competing and/or contradictory theories. The effects of alcohol and cross-race descriptions on eyewitness recall are pertinent examples. For instance, some studies point to the conclusion that alcohol is universally detrimental for accurate recall (Yuille & Tollestrup, 1990), while other studies are closer in line with the alcohol myopia theory (Schreiber Compo et al., 2011a). Similarly, empirical support exists for both the more traditional claim that cross-race descriptions will be less accurate than same-race descriptions (McQuiston-Surrett & Topp, 2008) and the contradictory claim that cross-race descriptions may in fact be more accurate, or equally as accurate, as same-race descriptions (Fallshore & Schooler, 1995). The conflicting theories and results, and sparse number of studies, make it difficult to draw any meaningful conclusions with regards to these topics either from a theoretical or practical perspective.

Other topics pose other challenges. For instance, although there is no shortage of studies on the effects of experienced stress, there appears to be an experiment–reality dichotomy (Reisberg & Heuer, 2007); experimental research strongly attests to the negative impact of stress on recall (Deffenbacher et al., 2004), whereas studies of eyewitness reports of real-life traumatic events often document highly accurate and long-lasting memories (e.g., Parker et al., 2006). This dichotomy poses serious questions as to the applied value of the extant laboratory-based research. If the gap cannot be bridged in the future, the conclusions reached by laboratory research may have little merit in the real world (see Yuille, Ternes, & Cooper, 2010, for a discussion of this issue).

As for the weapon-focus effect, the main issue is not whether the phenomenon exists, as it has been experimentally replicated on numerous occasions, but rather why it occurs. There is an ongoing debate over what causes the weapon-focus effect – threat, novelty, or both. Even if a consensus may be reached on these matters, there is still a notable paucity of archival or field studies (Pickel, 2007;

Yuille et al., 2010). There are obvious differences between laboratory and real-life incidents in which weapons are brandished (e.g., stress, scene complexity), and the ability to generalize the existing research is therefore uncertain (Yuille et al., 2010). This, again, highlights the experiment–reality dichotomy. A similar problem exists for research on the effects of violence and crime typicality, and for studies on individual differences that may interact with such factors.

The remaining topics, though often lacking in direct research, appear to be converging towards a consensus. Basic situational conditions such as illumination (Meissner et al., 2007), viewing distance (Loftus, 2010), and exposure duration (Memon et al., 2003) are all likely to influence encoding and subsequent recall in predictable ways. Moreover, it can be rather confidently concluded that increased personal involvement improves witnesses' memory for an event (Fashing et al., 2004; Nachson & Slavutskay-Tsukerman, 2010); that an increased number of perpetrators leads to decrements in recall accuracy (Clifford & Hollin, 1981; Fashing et al., 2004); and that familiarity with and understanding of the witnessed event is facilitative of recall (Pipe et al., 2007).

Estimator-based research has shed important light on the reliability of particularly vulnerable witnesses. Under optimal conditions, it seems individuals with high-functioning intellectual disabilities (Agnew & Powell, 2004), children of a very young age (Pozzulo, 2007), and elderly witnesses (Mueller-Johnson & Ceci, 2007) are all capable of providing accurate eyewitness reports. On the other hand, such witnesses are particularly susceptible to a range of detrimental influences (e.g., suggestion). Hence, in order to elicit reliable information from these groups, great care must be taken to use appropriate interview methods and memory-enhancing techniques (see Fisher, Schreiber Compo, Rivard, & Hirn, Chapter 31, this volume).

A common critique of estimator-based eyewitness research concerns its relevance and applicability to individual cases (e.g.,

Egeth, 1993; McCloskey & Egeth, 1983; Yuille et al., 2010). It has been argued that research findings on general human tendencies offer little guidance for how to evaluate the reliability of a specific, isolated testimony. Although such criticism is difficult to refute altogether, we believe that the value of this research should not be assessed in terms of its helpfulness in single cases, but rather in terms of its potential to improve the average decision quality across many cases. In other words, although research on eyewitness recall cannot guarantee correct decisions in any particular case, it can systematically increase the likelihood of making a correct decision. Considering the sheer number of decisions that practitioners (e.g., judges, prosecutors, police officers) make during their careers, the long-term benefits of applying estimator-based eyewitness research should be substantial.

CONCLUSION

The chapter began by acknowledging that statements from eyewitnesses are the most frequent and important form of evidence in criminal cases. A recurring theme throughout the chapter, however, was the gross underrepresentation of research on eyewitness recall in comparison with issues related to eyewitness recognition performance. This imbalance is particularly notable given the rarity of police investigations reaching the identification phase without first availing of witness reports. We therefore request more basic eyewitness recall research on most of the topics reviewed (e.g., effects of alcohol/drug use, cross-race descriptions, individual differences, viewing conditions).

Although research on single factors has obvious methodological advantages, we believe that it may be time to move beyond the isolated study of particular topics. As an illustrative example, let us consider two situations in which a prejudiced witness, believing that other-race individuals are more disposed than own-race individuals to engage in violent crimes, observes a violent crime committed by an other-race perpetrator or by an own-race perpetrator. According to the novelty account of the weapon-focus effect (Pickel, 1998, 1999; see above), the effect may be weaker in the other-race (versus own-race) situation, because the presence of a weapon would then be more consistent with the witness's contextual crime script. This quite plausible example contains the diverse themes of individual differences (i.e., prejudice), schema theory, cross-race descriptions, and weapon focus, and illustrates that outside of the laboratory individual topics are unlikely to act independently on a witness.

This brings us to another pressing concern for future research, namely, to bridge the experiment–reality gap. As mentioned above, and highlighted most notably by Yuille et al. (2010), the serious issue of how best to apply laboratory-based research on eyewitness recall remains at large. A step in the right direction would be to increase the number of field, case, and archival studies, where more rigorous attempts are made to isolate specific variables in real-life settings. Alternatively, experimental studies can be designed with a more ecologically valid bent. A pertinent example comes from the topic of stress and recall ability, where Morgan, Doran, Steffian, Hazlett, and Southwick (2006) were able to study memory under high stress, induced using high-intensity military training procedures. More studies of this kind are essential if research on estimator variables is to gain an applied value comparable with that of research on system variables.

Judges, jurors, and other legal practitioners are faced daily with the challenge of judging the impact of estimator variables on the reliability of witness recall. Without guidance from applied memory research, these judgments may draw on common-sense beliefs or popular misconceptions about human memory, and risk ending up grossly inaccurate. Hence, the research covered in this chapter addresses a pressing practical need for knowledge with many critical gaps to be filled. It is our firm belief that research along the lines outlined here has great potential for improving the quality of legal judgments.

NOTE

1 Information centrality, however, is largely subjective to the individual witness. Hence, forensically relevant information need not be considered as central by witnesses (Read & Connolly, 2007).

REFERENCES

Abelson, R. P. (1981). Psychological status of the script concept. *American Psychologist, 36*, 715–729.

Acheson, S., Stein, R., & Swartzelder, H. S. (1998). Impairment of semantic and figural memory by acute ethanol: Age-dependent effects. *Alcoholist: Clinical and Experimental Research, 47*, 1437–1442.

Agnew, S. E., & Powell, M. B. (2004). The effect of intellectual disability on children's recall of an event across different question types. *Law and Human Behavior, 28(3)*, 273–294.

American Psychiatric Association (1994). *Diagnostic and statistical manual of mental disorders* (4th ed.). Washington, DC: Author.

Baddeley, A. D. (1990). *Human memory: theory and practice*. London: Erlbaum.

Bartlett, J. C., & Memon, A. (2007). Eyewitness memory in young and older eyewitnesses. In R. C. L. Lindsay, D. F. Ross, J. D. Read, and M. P. Toglia (Eds.), *The handbook of eyewitness psychology Vol. II. Memory for people* (pp. 309–338). Mahwah, NJ: Erlbaum.

Behrman, B. W., & Davey, S. L. (2001). Eyewitness identification in actual criminal cases: An archival analysis. *Law and Human Behavior, 25*, 475–491.

Bisby, J. A., Leitz, J. R., Morgan, C. J. A., & Curran, H. V. (2010). Decreases in recollective experience following acute alcohol: A dose-response study. *Psychopharmacology, 208*, 67–74. doi: 10.1007/s00213-009-1709-y.

Blais, C., Jack, R. E., Scheepers, C., Fiset, D., & Caldara, R. (2008). Culture shapes how we look at faces. *PLoS One, 3*, e3022. doi:10.1371/journal.pone.0003022

Brigham, J. C. (1990). Target person distinctiveness and attractiveness as moderator variables in the confidence-accuracy relationship in eyewitness identifications. *Basic and Applied Social Psychology, 11*, 101–115.

Brigham, J. C., Bennett, L. B., Meissner, C. A., & Mitchell, T. L. (2007). The influence of race on eyewitness memory. In R. Lindsay, D. Ross, J. Read, and M. Toglia (Eds.), *Handbook of eyewitness psychology Vol. II. Memory for people* (pp. 257–281). Mahwah, NJ: Erlbaum.

Brown, C. L., & Geiselman, R. E. (1990). Eyewitness testimony of the mentally retarded: Effect of the cognitive interview. *Journal of Police and Criminal Psychology, 6(2)*, 14–22.

Buckhout, R., & Regan, S. (1988). Explorations in research on the other-race effect in face Recognition. In M. M. Gruneber, P. E. Morris, and R. N. Skyes (Eds.), *Practical aspects of Memory: Current research and issues: Vol. 1. Memory in everyday life* (pp. 40–46). NewYork: John Wiley & Sons.

Cardon, D., & Dent, H. (1996). Memory and interrogative suggestibility: The effects of modality of information presentation and retrieval conditions upon the suggestibility scores of people with learning disabilities. *Legal and Criminological Psychology, 1*, 165–177.

Chase, G. W., & Simon, H. A. (1973). Perception in chess. *Cognitive Psychology, 4*, 55–81.

Christianson, S.-Å., (1992). Emotional stress and eyewitness memory: A critical review. *Psychological Bulletin, 112*, 284–309.

Christianson, S.-Å., & Loftus, E. F. (1987). Memory for traumatic events. *Applied Cognitive Psychology, 1*, 225–239.

Christianson, S. Å., Loftus, E. F., Hoffman, H., & Loftus, G. R. (1991). *Eye fixations and memory for emotional events, 17*(4), 693–701.

Clifford, B. R., & Hollin, C. R. (1981). Effects of the type of incident and the number of perpetrators on eyewitness memory. *Journal of Applied Psychology, 66*(3), 364–370.

Clifford, B. R., & Scott, J. (1978). Individual and situational factors in eyewitness testimony. *Journal of Applied Psychology, 63*(3), 352–359.

Curran, V. H., & Hildebrandt, M. (1999). Dissociative effects of alcohol on recollective Experience. *Consciousness and Cognition, 8*, 497–509.

Dahlgren, A., Roos af Hjelmsäter, E., Granhag, P. A., Fahlke, C., & Söderpalm-Gordh, A. (2013). Bottled memories: On how alcohol affects eyewitness recall. *Scandinavian Journal of Psychology, 54*, 188–195. doi: 10.1111/sjop.12035

Davies, G. M., Smith, S., & Blincoe, C. (2008). A "weapon focus" effect in children. *Psychology, Crime & Law, 14*(1),19–28.

de Poot, C. J., Bokhorst, R. J., van Koppen, P. J., & Muller, E. R. (2004). *Rechercheportret: Over Dilemma's in de Opsporing.* Alphen aan den Rijn: Kluwer. In Dutch.

Deffenbacher, K. A. (1983). The influence of arousal on reliability of testimony. In S. M. A. Lloyd-Bostock and B. R. Clifford (Eds.), *Evaluating witness evidence* (pp. 235–251). Chichester, UK: Wiley.

Deffenbacher, K. A., Bornstein, B. H., Penrod, S. D., & McGorty, E. K. (2004). A meta-analytic review of the effects of high stress on eyewitness memory. *Law and Human Behavior, 28*, 687–706.

Diamond, R., & Carey, S. (1986). Why faces are and are not special: An effect of expertise. *Journal of Experimental Psychology: General, 115*(2), 107–177.

Dore, H. A., Brigham, J. C., & Buck, J. (2005). *Is there an "other race effect" in the accuracy of descriptions of people?* Unpublished manuscript, Florida State University.

Easterbrook, J. A. (1959). The effect of emotion on the utilization and organization of behavior. *Psychological Review, 66*, 183–201.

Egeth, H. E. (1993). What do we not know about eyewitness identification? *American Psychologist, 48*, 577–580.

Ellis, H. D., Deregowski, J. B., & Shepherd, J. W. (1975). Descriptions of white and black faces by white and black subjects. *International Journal of Psychology, 10*(2), 119–123.

Evans, J. R., & Fisher, R. P. (2011). Eyewitness memory: Balancing the accuracy, precision and quantity of information through metacognitive monitoring and control. *Applied Cognitive Psychology, 25*, 501–508.

Evans, J. R., Schreiber Compo, N., & Russano, M. B. (2009). Intoxicated witnesses and suspects: Procedures and prevalence according to law enforcement. *Psychology, Public Policy, and Law, 15*, 194–221.

Fahsing, I. A., Ask, K., & Granhag, P. A. (2004). The man behind the mask: Accuracy and predictors of eyewitness offender descriptions. *Journal of Applied Psychology, 89*, 722–729.

Fallshore, M., & Schooler, J. W. (1995). Verbal vulnerability of perceptual expertise. *Journal of Experimental Psychology: Learning, Memory and Cognition, 21*, 1608–1623.

Farah, M. J., Wilson, K. D., Drain, M., & Tanaka, J. W. (1975). What is "special" about face perception? *Psychological Review, 105*, 482–498.

Feingold, G. A. (1914). The influence of environment on the identification of persons and things. *Journal of Criminal Law and Political Science, 5*, 39–51.

García-Banjos, E., Migueles, M., & Anderson, M. C. (2009). Script knowledge modulates retrieval-induced forgetting for eyewitness events. *Memory, 17*, 92–203.

Goodman-Delahunty, J., & Tait, D. (2006). DNA and the changing face of justice. *Australian Journal of Forensic Sciences*, *38*, 97–106.

Greenberg, M. S., Westcott, D. R., & Bailey, S. E. (1998). When believing is seeing: The effect of Scripts on eyewitness memory. *Law and Human Behavior*, *22*, 685–694.

Gudjonsson, G. H. (1990). The relationship of intellectual skills to suggestibility, compliance and acquiescence. *Personality and Individual Differences*, *11*, 227–231.

Gudjonsson, G. H., Murphy, G. H., & Clare, I. C. H. (2000). Assessing the capacity of people with intellectual disabilities to be witnesses in court. *Psychological Medicine*, *30*, 307–314.

Hastorf, E. M., & Cantril, H. (1954). They saw a game: A case study. *Journal of Abnormal and Social Psychology*, *49*, 129–134.

Hayward, W. G., Rhodes, G., & Schwaninger, A. (2008). An own-race advantage for components as well as configurations in face recognition. *Cognition*, *106*, 1017–1027.

Holland, A. C., & Kensinger, E. A. (2010). Emotion and autobiographical memory. *Physics of Life Reviews*, *7*, 88–131.

Holst, V. F., & Pezdek, K. (1992). Scripts for typical crimes and their effects on memory for eyewitness testimony. *Applied Cognitive Psychology*, *6*, 573–587.

Hope, L., & Wright, D. (2007). Beyond unusual? Examining the role of attention in the weapon focus effect. *Applied Cognitive Psychology*, *21*, 951–961.

Hosch, H. M. (1994). Individual differences in personality and eyewitness identification. In D. Ross, D. Read, and M. Toglia (Eds.), *Adult eyewitness testimony* (pp. 329–346). Cambridge: Cambridge University Press.

Hosch, H. M., & Bothwell, R. K. (1990). Arousal, description and identification accuracy of victims and bystanders. *Journal of Social Behavior & Personality*, *5*(5), 481–488.

Hosch, H. M., Leippe, M. R., Marchioni, P. M., & Cooper, D. S. (1984). Victimization, self-monitoring, and eyewitness identification. *Journal of Applied Psychology*, *69*(2), 280–288.

Hugenberg, K., Young, S. G., Bernstein, M. J., & Sacco, D. F. (2010). The categorization-individuation model: An integrative account of the other-race recognition deficit. *Psychological Review*, *117*(4), 1168–1187.

Kassin, S. (1984). Eyewitness identification: Victims versus bystanders. *Journal of Applied Social Psychology*, *14*, 519–529.

Kassin, S. M., Tubb, V. A., Hosch, H. M., & Memon, A. (2001). On the "general acceptance" of Eyewitness testimony research: A new survey of the experts. *American Psychologist*, *56*, 405–416.

Kebbell, M. R. & Hatton, C. (1999). People with mental retardation as witnesses in court: A review. *Mental Retardation*, *37*, 179–187.

Kramer, T. H., Buckhout, R., & Eugenio, P. (1990). Weapon focus, arousal and eyewitness memory: Attention must be paid. *Law and Human Behavior*, *14*, 167–184.

Kuehn, L. (1974). Looking down a gun barrel: Person perception and violent crime. *Perceptual and Motor Skills*, *39*, 1159–1164.

Lamb, M. E., La Rooy, D. J., Malloy, L. C., & Katz, C. (Eds.) (2011). *Children's testimony: A handbook of psychological research and forensic practice* (2nd ed.). Hoboken, NJ: John Wiley & Sons.

Levine, L. J., & Pizarro, D. A. (2004). Emotion and memory research: A grumpy overview. *Social Cognition*, *22*, 530–554.

Lindsay, R. C. L., Semmler, C., Weber, N., Brewer, N., & Lindsay, M. R. (2008). How variations in distance affect eyewitness reports and identification accuracy. *Law and Human Behavior*, *32*, 526–535.

List, J. A. (1986). Age and schematic differences in the reliability of eyewitness testimony. *Developmental Psychology*, *22*, 50–57.

Loftus, E. F., Loftus, G. R., & Messo, J. (1987). Some facts about "weapon focus." *Law and Human Behavior*, *11*, 55–62.

Loftus, E. F., & Palmer, J. (1974). Reconstruction of automobile destruction: An example of the interaction between language and memory. *Journal of Verbal Learning and Verbal Behaviour*, *13*, 585–589.

Loftus, G. R. (2010). What can a perception–memory expert tell a jury? *Psychonomic Bulletin & Review*, *17*, 143–148.

Luna, K., & Migueles, M. (2008). Typicality and misinformation: Two sources of distortion. *Psicológica*, *29*, 171–187.

Maass, A., & Köhnken, G. (1989). Eyewitness identification: Simulating the "weapon effect". *Law and Human Behavior*, *13*, 397–408.

Manzanero, A. L., El-Astal, S., & Aróztegui, J. (2009). Implication degree and delay on recall of events: an experimental and HDV study. *The European Journal of Psychology Applied to Legal Context*, *1*, 183–203.

Maurer, D., Le Grand, R., & Mondloch, C. J. (2002). The many faces of configural processing. *Trends in Cognitive Sciences*, *6*, 255–260.

Maylor, E. A., & Rabbitt, P. M. (1993). Alcohol, reaction time and memory: A meta-analysis. *British journal of Psychology*, *84*, 301–317.

Maylor, E. A., Rabbitt, P. M., & Kingstone, A. (1987). Effects of alcohol on word categorization and recognition memory. *British Journal of Psychology, 78*, 233–239.

McCloskey, M., & Egeth, H. E. (1983). What can a psychologist tell a jury? *American Psychologist, 38*, 550–563.

McQuiston-Surrett, D., & Topp, L. D. (2008). Externalizing visual images: Examining the Accuracy of facial descriptions versus composites as a function of the own-race bias. *Experimental Psychology, 55*, 195–202.

Megreya, A. M., & Bindemann, M. (2011). Identification accuracy for single- and double-perpetrator crimes: Does accomplice gender matter? *British Journal of Psychology.* doi: 10.1111/j.2044-8295.2011.02084.x

Meissner, C. A., & Brigham, J. C. (2001). Thirty years of investigating the own-race bias in memory for faces: A meta-analytic review. *Psychology, Public Policy, and Law, 7*, 3–35.

Meissner, C. A., Sporer, S. L., & Schooler, J. W. (2007). Person descriptions as eyewitness evidence. In R. C. L. Lindsay, D. F. Ross, J. D. Read, and M. P. Toglia (Eds.), *The handbook of eyewitness psychology Vol. II. Memory for people* (pp. 3–34). Mahwah, NJ: Erlbaum.

Melnyk, L., Crossman, A. M., & Scullin, M. H. (2007). The suggestibility of children's testimony. In M. P. Toglia, J. D. Read, D. F. Ross, and R. C. L. Lindsay (Eds.), *Handbook of eyewitness psychology: Vol. I: Memory for events* (pp. 401–427). Mahwah, NJ: Erlbaum Associates.

Memon, A., Hope, L., & Bull, R. (2003). Exposure duration: Effects on eyewitness accuracy and confidence. *British Journal of Psychology, 94*, 339–354.

Michel, C., Caldara, R., & Rossion, B. (2006a). Same-race faces are perceived more holistically than other-race faces. *Visual Cognition, 14*(1), 55–73.

Michel, C., Rossion, B., Han, J., Chung, C-. S., & Caldara, R. (2006b). Holistic processing is finely tuned for faces of one's own race. *Psychological Science, 17*(7), 608–615.

Migueles, M., & García-Bajos, E. (2004). This is a stick-up! Biases of typicality in eyewitness memory. *Estudios de Psicología, 25*(3), 331–342.

Migueles, M., & García-Bajos, E. (2006). Influence of the typicality of the actions in a mugging script on retrieval-induced forgetting. *Psicológica, 27*, 119–135.

Milne, R., & Bull, R. (2001). Interviewing witnesses with learning disabilities for legal purposes: A review. *British Journal of Learning Disabilities, 29*, 93–97.

Mitchell, K. J., Livosky, M., & Mather, M. (1998). The weapon focus effect revisited: The role of novelty. *Legal and Criminological Psychology, 3*, 287–303.

Mondloch, C. J., Elms, N., Maurer, D., Rhodes, G., Hayward, W. G., Tanaka, J. W., & Zhou, G. (2010). Processes underlying the cross-race effect: An investigation of holistic, featural, and relational processing of own-races versus other-race faces. *Perception, 39*(8), 1065–1085.

Morgan, C. A., III, Doran, A., Steffian, G., Hazlett, G., & Southwick, S. M. (2006). Stress-induced deficits in working memory and visuo-constructive abilities in special operations soldiers. *Biological Psychiatry, 60*, 722–729.

Mueller-Johnson, K., & Ceci, S. J. (2007). The elderly eyewitness: A review and prospectus. In M. P. Toglia, J. D. Read, D. F. Ross, and R. C. L. Lindsay (Eds.), *Handbook of eyewitness psychology: Vol. I: Memory for events* (pp. 577–603). Mahwah, NJ: Erlbaum Associates.

Nachson, I., & Slavutskay-Tsukerman, I. (2010). Effect of personal involvement in traumatic events on memory: The case of the Dolphinarium explosion. *Memory, 18*(3), 241–251.

Oue, W., Hakoda, Y., & Onuma, N. (2008). The pointed shape of a knife influences eyewitness perception. *Asian Criminology, 3*, 193–200.

O'Rourke, T. E., Penrod, S. D., Cutler, B. L., & Stuve, T. E. (1989). The external validity of eyewitness identification research: Generalizing across subject populations. *Law and Human Behavior, 13*(4), 385–395.

Parker, J. F., Bahrick, L. E., Fivush, R., & Johnson, P. (2006). The impact of stress on mothers' memory of a natural disaster. *Journal of Experimental Psychology: Applied, 12*, 142–154.

Peace, K. A., & Porter, S. (2004). A longitudinal investigation of the reliability of memories for trauma and other emotional experiences. *Applied Cognitive Psychology, 18*, 1143–1159.

Perlman, N. B., Ericson, K. I., Esses, V. M., & Isaacs, B. J. (1994). The developmentally handicapped witness: Competency as a function of question format. *Law and Human Behavior, 18*(2), 171–187.

Peterson, C., & Whalen, N. (2001). Five years later: Children's memory for medical emergencies. *Applied Cognitive Psychology, 15*(7), 7–24.

Pickel, K. L. (1998). Unusualness and threat as possible causes of "weapon focus". *Memory, 6*(3), 277–295.

Pickel, K. L. (1999). The influence of context on the "weapon focus" effect. *Law and HumanBehavior, 23*(3), 299–311.

Pickel, K. L. (2007). Remembering and identifying menacing perpetrators: Exposure to violence and the weapon focus effect. In R. C. L. Lindsay, D. F. Ross, J. D. Read, and M. P. Toglia (Eds.), *The handbook of* eyewitness psychology Vol. II. Memory for people (pp. 339–360). Mahwah, NJ: Erlbaum.

Pickel, K. L. (2009). The weapon focus effect on memory for female versus male perpetrators. *Memory*, *17*(6), 664–678.

Pickel, K. L., Narter, D. B., Jameson, M. M., & Lenhardt, T. T. (2008). The weapon focus effect in child eyewitnesses. *Psychology, Crime & Law*, *14*(1), 61–72.

Pickel, K. L., & Staller, J. B. (2012). A perpetrator's accent impairs witnesses' memory for physical appearance. *Law and Human Behavior*, *36*, 140–150.

Pipe, M.-E., Lamb, M. E., Orbach, Y., Esplin, P. W. (2007). Recent research on children's testimony about experienced and witnessed events. *Developmental Review*, *24*, 440–468.

Pipe, M.-E., Thierry, K. L., & Lamb, M. E. (2007). The development of event mamory: Implications for child witness testimony. In M. P. Toglia, J. D. Read, D. F. Ross, and R. C. L. Lindsay (Eds.), *Handbook of eyewitness psychology: Vol. I: Memory for events* (pp. 453–478). Mahwah, NJ: Erlbaum Associates.

Pozzulo, J. (2007). Person description and identification by child witnesses. In R. C. L. Lindsay, D. F. Ross, J. D. Read, and M. P. Toglia (Eds.), *The handbook of eyewitness psychology Vol. II. Memory for people* (pp. 283–307). Mahwah, NJ: Erlbaum.

Read, J. D., & Connolly, D. A. (2007). The effects of delay on long-term memory for witnessed events. In M. P. Toglia, J. D. Read, D. F. Ross, and R. C. L. Lindsay (Eds.), *Handbook of eyewitness psychology: Vol. I: Memory for events* (pp. 117–155). Mahwah, NJ: Erlbaum Associates.

Reisberg, D., & Hertel, P. (Eds.) (2003). *Memory and emotion*. New York: Oxford University Press.

Reisberg, D., & Heuer, F. (2007). The influence of emotion on memory in forensic settings. In M. P. Toglia, J. D. Read, D. F. Ross, and R. C. L. Lindsay (Eds.), *Handbook of eyewitness psychology: Vol. I: Memory for events* (pp. 81–116). Mahwah, NJ: Erlbaum Associates.

Rhodes, G., Brake, S., Taylor, K., & Tan, S. (1989). Expertise and configural coding in face recognition. *British Journal of Psychology, 80*, 313–331.

Rhodes, G., Hayward, W. G., & Winkler, C. (2006). Expert face coding: Configural and component coding of own-race and other-race faces. *Psychonomic Bulletin & Review*, *13*(3), 499–505.

Ryback, R. S. (1971). The continuum and specificity of the effects of alcohol on memory: A review. *Quarterly Journal of Studies on Alcohol*, *32*, 995–1016.

Sangrigoli, S., & de Schonen, S. (2004). Effect of visual experience on face processing: A developmental study of inversion and non-native effects. *Developmental Science*, *7*(1), 74–87.

Schreiber Compo, N., Evans, R. J., Carol, R. N., Villalba, D., Ham, L. S., Garcia, T., & Rose, S. (2011a). Intoxicated eyewitnesses: Better than their reputation? *Law and Human Behaviour*. doi: 10.1007/s10979-011-9273-5

Schreiber Compo, N., Evans, R. J., Carol, R. N., Kemp, D., Villalba, D., Ham, L. S., & Rose, S. (2011b). Alcohol intoxication and memory for events: A snapshot of alcohol myopia in a real-world drinking scenario. *Memory*, *12*, 202–210.

Sharp, H. (2001). Steps toward justice for people with learning disabilities as victims of crime: The important role of the police. *British Journal of Learning Disabilities*, *29*, 88–92.

Shaw, J. I., & Skolnick, P. (1999). Weapon focus and gender differences in eyewitness accuracy: Arousal versus salience. *Journal of Applied Social Psychology*, *29*(11), 2328–2341.

Siegel, J. M., & Loftus, E. F. (1978). Impact of anxiety and life stress upon eyewitness testimony. *Bulletin of the Psychonomic Society*, *12*(6), 479–480.

Snyder, M. (1984). Self-monitoring of expressive behavior. *Journal of Personality and Social Psychology*, *30*, 526–537.

Sommer, R. (1959). The new look on the witness stand. *The Canadian Psychologist*, *8*, 94–99.

Soraci, S. A., Carlin, M. T., Read, J. D., Wakeford, Y., Pogoda, T., Cavanaug, S., & Shin, L. (2007). Psychological impairment, eyewitness testimony, and false memories: Individual differences. In M. P. Toglia, J. D. Read, D. F. Ross, and R. C. L. Lindsay (Eds.), *Handbook of eyewitness psychology: Vol. I: Memory for events* (pp. 261–297). Mahwah, NJ: Erlbaum Associates.

Sporer, S. L. (2001). Recognizing faces of other ethnic groups: An integration of theories. *Psychology, Public Policy, and Law*, *7*(1), 36–97.

Steblay, N. M. (1992). A meta-analytic review of the weapon focus effect. *Law and Human Behaviour*, *16*(4), 413–424.

Steele, C. M., & Josephs, R. A. (1990). Alcohol myopia: Its prized and dangerous effects. *American Psychologist*, *45*, 921–933.

Stern, L. W. (1939). The psychology of testimony. *Journal of Abnormal and Social Psychology*, *34*, 3–20.

Tanaka, J. W., Kiefer, M., & Bukach, C. M. (2004). A holistic account of the own-race effect in the face recognition: Evidence from a cross-cultural study. *Cognition*, *93*, B1–B9.

Ternes, M., & Yuille, J. C. (2008). Eyewitness memory and eyewitness identification Performance in adults with intellectual disabilities. *Journal of Applied Research in Intellectual Disabilities, 21*, 519–531.

Tracy, J. I., & Bates, M. E. (1999). The selective effects of alcohol on automatic and effortful Memory processes. *Neuropsychology, 13*, 282–290.

Tuckey, M. R., & Brewer, N. (2003a). How schemas affect eyewitness memory over repeated retrieval attempts. *Applied Cognitive Psychology, 17*, 785–800.

Tuckey, M. R., & Brewer, N. (2003b). The influence of schemas, stimulus ambiguity, and interview schedule on eyewitness memory over time. *Journal of Experimental Psychology: Applied, 9*(2), 101–118.

Uttl, B., Ohta, N., & Sigenthaler, A. L. (Eds.) (2006). *Memory and emotion: Interdisciplinary perspectives.* Malden, MA: Blackwell Publishing.

Valenti-Hein, D. C., & Schwartz, L. D. (1993). Witness competency in people with mental retardation: Implications for prosecution of sexual abuse. *Sexuality and Disability, 11*(4), 287–294.

Valentine, T., & Bruce V. (1986). The effect of race, inversion, and encoding activity upon face recognition. *Acta Psychologica, 61*, 259–273.

Valentine, T., & Mesout, J. (2009). Eyewitness identification under stress in the London Dungeon. *Applied Cognitive Psychology, 23*, 151–161.

Van Oorsouw, K., & Merckelbach, H. (2011). The effects of alcohol on crime-related memories: A field study. *Applied Cognitive Psychology.* doi: 10.1002/acp.1799

Wagstaff, G. F., MacVeigh, J., Boston, R., Scott, L., Brunas-Wagstaff, J., & Cole, J. (2003). Can laboratory findings on eyewitness testimony be generalized to the real world? An archival analysis of the influence of violence, weapon presence, and age on eyewitness accuracy. *Journal of Psychology, 137*, 17–28.

Wells, G. L. (1978). Applied eyewitness-testimony research: System variables and estimator variables. *Journal of Personality and Social Psychology, 36*, 1546–1557.

Wells, G. L., Memon, A., & Penrod, S. D. (2006). Eyewitness evidence: Improving its probative value. *Psychological Science in the Public Interest, 7*, 45–75.

Wells, G. L., & Turtle, J. W. (1987). What is the best way to encode faces? In M. M. Gruneberg, P. E. Morris, and R. N. Sykdes (Eds.), *Practical aspects of memory: Current research & issues Vol. 1* (pp. 163–168). New York: Wiley.

Whipple, G. M. (1909). The observer as reporter: A survey of the 'psychology of testimony'. *Psychology Bulletin, 6*, 153–170.

Whipple, G. M. (1914). Psychology of testimony and report. *Psychological Bulletin, 11*, 245–250.

White, A. M. (2003). What happened? Alcohol, memory blackouts, and the brain. *Alcohol Research & Health, 27*, 740–746.

Wigmore, J. H. (1909). Professor Muensterberg and the psychology of testimony. *Illinois Law Review, 3*, 399–445.

Yarmey, A. D., Jacob, J., & Porter, A. (2002). Person recall in field settings. *Journal of Applied Social Psychology, 32*, 2354–2367.

Yin, R. K. (1969). Looking at upside-down faces. *Journal of Experimental Psychology, 81*, 141–145.

Yuille, J. C., Davies, G., Gibling, F., Marxsen, D., & Porter, S. (1994). Eyewitness memory of police trainees for realistic role plays. *Journal of Applied Psychology, 79*, 931–936

Yuille, J. C., Ternes, M., & Cooper, B. S. (2010). Expert testimony on laboratory witnesses. *Journal of Forensic Psychology Practice, 10*, 238–251.

Yuille, J. C., & Tollestrup, P. A. (1990). Some effects of alcohol on eyewitness memory. *The Journal of Applied Psychology, 75*, 268–273.

31

Interviewing Witnesses

Ronald P. Fisher, Nadja Schreiber Compo,
Jillian Rivard, and Dana Hirn

In Hollywood movies and television programs, investigators solve crimes by conducting hi-tech analyses of spent bullets, blood stains, barely visible fingerprints and fingernails, and other such exotic sources; in reality, police solve crimes more mundanely, by interviewing cooperative witnesses and asking, "What happened?" How do – and, more important, how should – police investigators interview victims and witnesses to elicit extensive and accurate information to solve real-world crime? We open this chapter with a brief historical overview of typical forensic methods of interviewing and the consequence of these methods. We then describe in detail two theoretically grounded interview protocols that have been developed to enhance the quantity and quality of information elicited from adult and child witnesses. After examining the laboratory and field studies that empirically test these protocols, we explore several methodological and theoretical issues that are critical for understanding and evaluating the extant literature and for planning new research. Next, we assess the research from a practical perspective, in an attempt to understand real-world constraints that are imposed on forensic interviews. Finally, we describe some innovative reforms that are being considered

to maximize the utility of forensic interviews and several new ideas for future research.

Despite the importance of proper interviewing for eliciting witness information, training in interviewing has historically been sparse. Note, for instance, the lack of coverage on interviewing in many standard monographs on police work (e.g., Palmiotto, 2003; Steverson, 2008). Furthermore, many police and investigative training academies provided their trainees with a scant few hours on how to conduct interviews with cooperative witnesses; instead, the bulk of their training is devoted to interrogating suspects and the legal aspects of police work (see Fisher & Schreiber, 2007, for a more detailed description). With such limited guidance, one might expect police interviews to be less than professional. Indeed, in a few notorious police investigations, the interviewing procedures were so amateurish that they led to innocent people being arrested. Highly publicized examples in the US include the McMartin preschool case in Manhattan Beach, California and the Kelly Michaels case in Maplewood, New Jersey (both of which involved child witnesses). Outside the US, other notorious cases were reported, such as the investigation of the Birmingham six in the UK (Ceci &

Bruck, 1993; Gudjonsson, 1992, 2008), the "Montessori-Prozess" in Münster, Germany (Köhnken, 1995), the Oude Pekela case in the Netherlands (Jonker & Jonker-Bakker, 1991), and the Martensville, Saskatchewan case in Canada (Nathan & Snedeker, 1995). These profound interviewer-induced errors were covered extensively by the news media and ultimately led to government commissions being charged to ameliorate the problem – and ultimately a major impetus for scientific research on interviewing (Ceci & Bruck, 1995; Nathan & Snedeker, 1995).

The first systematic assessments of police interviews were conducted by Fisher, Geiselman, and Raymond (1987) and George and Clifford (1992), who described interviewing protocols of small samples of American and British police, respectively. Their characterization of police was, to say the least, discouraging. The typical interview opened with a perfunctory effort to establish rapport and then one (and often the only) open-ended request, "Tell me what happened." This was followed by a series of short-answer questions on the order of: How old was he? How tall was he? How much did he weigh? Each question elicited (or failed to elicit) a brief answer, and the remainder of the interview was a series of question-answer, question-answer mini-episodes. Sprinkled within these specific questions was an occasional suggestive or leading question, for example, "Was he wearing a green T- shirt?" In one particularly illuminating exchange, when the witness started to narrate in detail the perpetrator's appearance, the police investigator exerted control and said "Let me ask the questions, and you give me the answers." In brief, the interviews were unsophisticated, ineffective, and seemingly not grounded in any formal scientific framework. We note with a sigh of renewed discouragement that similar patterns of poor interviewing procedures were found in more recent analyses of small samples of German, Canadian, and American police interviews (Berresheim & Weber, 2003; Snook & Keating, 2011; Schreiber Compo, Hyman Gregory, & Fisher,

2012, respectively). The commonality of style across nationalities (and also kinds of investigation, for example, transportation, military, and industrial accidents) suggests to us that investigators often follow an intuitive approach, whereby they isolate the specific facts that they want to elicit, and then direct specific questions toward each of these facts. That this pattern occurs across several domains of investigation merely indicates that the problem of poor interviewing is not limited to forensic interviews.

METHODS TO IMPROVE INTERVIEWING

Psychologists' efforts to improve interviewing followed two distinct paths, depending on whether the respondent was a child or an adult. This division reflects important differences in (a) the criminal conditions in adult and child investigations, (b) the underlying psychological processes mediating adults' and children's reporting, and (c) interviewers' expectations of the difficulties associated with interviewing adults and children. In the cases involving adult witnesses that have sparked concern, the culprit was unfamiliar to the victim, whereas the controversial cases with child witnesses usually involved allegations against individuals close to the children (e.g., family members, teachers) whom the child may be motivated to protect. Other differentiating characteristics include adults' and children's comfort when speaking to strangers (adult police officers), their awareness of the differences between truthful and fabricated experiences, their mastery of the language, their understanding of the law and the purpose of the interview, and their susceptibility to influence by other people. Finally, differences exist within the police officers who interview adults (where interviewers are often not aware that interviewing cooperative witnesses requires more than just asking specific questions) versus children (where it is obvious that special skills are required to conduct the interview properly). In keeping with these differences, we separate the research on interviewing adults and children.

INTERVIEWING ADULTS: THE COGNITIVE INTERVIEW

Most training provided to police about interviewing adults revolved around interrogating suspects, who often either hide or distort their knowledge. In keeping with this view, procedures like Conversation Management (Shepherd, 1988) evolved to combat suspects' deceptive, evasive, and confrontational schemes. Little thought was given to developing procedures to interview cooperative adults as this was perceived to be a relatively simple and straightforward task. (Other investigative domains, e.g., industrial and vehicular accidents, also have few effective guidelines for interviewing cooperative adults, e.g., Benner, 1985, although note that survey researchers have developed many effective guidelines: see Belli, Chapter 21, this volume.) Given the many errors that police seemed to make when conducting interviews with cooperative witnesses (e.g., Fisher et al., 1987), apparently the task is more difficult than police realized. In an attempt to provide police investigators with better interview skills, various evidence-based interviewing protocols were developed, including the Cognitive Interview and the Memorandum of Good Practice (later renamed Achieving Best Evidence: Home Office, 2002). We focus here on the Cognitive Interview, because it has been the most thoroughly researched and tested.

The Cognitive Interview is based on three underlying psychological processes: the social dynamics between the witness and interviewer, the cognitive processes engaged by both the witness and interviewer, and communication between the witness and interviewer. Below is a brief overview of the Cognitive Interview; for a more detailed description, see Fisher and Geiselman (1992).

Social dynamics

Police interviews with witnesses entail two people interacting closely with one another, and the success of the interview hinges on mutual trust and cooperation. Interviewers must communicate that they are sincerely interested in the personal welfare of the witness (and especially of a victim) and are not merely information-gatherers. Second, the police investigator must engineer the social dynamics of the interview so that the witness sees his or her role as an information generator and not merely a question answerer.

Developing rapport

Witnesses, and especially victims, are often asked to provide detailed descriptions of highly personal experiences to police officers whom they have never met before. Eliciting such information freely requires establishing personal rapport at the very outset of the interview (Collins, Lincoln, & Frank, 2002), a phase often overlooked by police (Fisher et al., 1987).

Active witness participation

For a police interview to be effective, the witness needs to generate information actively by supplying richly detailed narrations. As we noted earlier, police interviewers often discourage such behaviors by asking many closed, short-answer questions, which elicit only brief answers. Interviewers can facilitate witnesses actively generating information by (a) explicitly instructing them to output their knowledge without waiting for questions, (b) asking mainly open-ended questions, which afford witnesses the opportunity to generate rich narratives, and (c) not interrupting witnesses during their narrations.

Cognition

Witnesses and interviewers have cognitively demanding tasks: Witnesses are asked to recall and describe in detail complex events that may have occurred in the distant past, and interviewers must listen to and notate witnesses' responses and formulate hypotheses to account for the crime. Completing such demanding tasks requires that interviewers and witnesses use their cognitive skills as efficiently as possible.

Context reinstatement

According to the encoding specificity principle, recall should be most effective when the context of the original crime event is reinstated during the interview (Smith & Vela, 2001; Tulving & Thomson, 1973). Interviewers can implement this principle by instructing their witnesses to mentally recreate the cognitive, emotional, and environmental context that existed at the time of the crime.

Limited mental resources

Both interviewers and witnesses have only limited resources to process information (Kahneman, 1973). Interviewers can help to overcome witnesses' limited mental resources by instructing them to close their eyes, a technique known to facilitate concentration (Perfect et al., 2008; Vredeveldt, Hitch, & Baddeley, 2011). Asking fewer questions, and proportionally more open-ended questions, also allows witnesses to make better use of their limited resources. Asking open-ended questions, and thereby promoting longer, narrative responses, also makes the task easier for the interviewer by obviating the need to formulate questions constantly.

Multiple and varied retrieval

Searching through memory repeatedly should yield some new recollections on later memory probes that were not recalled initially (Oeberst, 2012). This seems to violate common sense, which suggests that memories should become less available, not more available, with the passage of time. Nevertheless it is almost always observed that repeated testing yields new information on the later tests (reminiscence: Gilbert & Fisher, 2006). Interviewers can take advantage of this phenomenon by interviewing witnesses repeatedly or by asking them to describe the critical event several times during an interview – although care must be exercised so as not to communicate that the interviewer is dissatisfied with the original response. If witnesses are interviewed or probed for information more than once, the second interview/probe should generate more reminiscence if it differs from the first interview (see Anderson & Pichert, 1978). For instance, the first probe might ask witnesses to think about the visual properties of the crime, and the second probe about the auditory properties. There is some difference of opinion about whether all instantiations of this principle are effective, as some researchers have found that asking witnesses to switch from recalling in chronological order to recalling in reverse order is effective (Geiselman & Callot, 1990) whereas others have found it to be ineffective (Dando, Ormerod, Wilcock, & Milne, 2011).

Minimizing guessing

To maintain high accuracy, interviewers should explicitly instruct witnesses not to guess, but, preferably, to indicate that they "don't know" (Evans & Fisher, 2011; Koriat & Goldsmith, 1996). Similarly, interviewers should not apply social pressure on witnesses to volunteer responses if they are uncertain.

Minimizing constructive recall

Witnesses may construct memories by incorporating information conveyed by the interviewer either verbally or non-verbally. Interviewers should therefore avoid leaking information to witnesses either by asking leading or suggestive questions or non-verbally, by smiling or paying increased attention when the witness makes a particular statement. These last two principles are particularly important when interviewing children (Ceci & Bruck, 1995), as we develop later in the chapter.

Communication

Interviewers must convey their investigative needs to the witness, and, conversely, witnesses must communicate their knowledge of the crime to the interviewer. Ineffective communication will encourage witnesses to withhold valuable information or to provide inappropriate or incorrect answers.

Promoting extensive, detailed responses

Witnesses frequently withhold information simply because they do not know what is important for police investigations. Interviewers should therefore instruct witnesses to report everything they think about, whether it is trivial, out of chronological order, or even if it contradicts an earlier statement. This should not be taken as a license to guess, as Memon, Wark, Bull, and Köhnken (1997) mistakenly concluded.

Non-verbal output

Interviewers and respondents often communicate using only the verbal medium. Some objects and events, however, are better described non-verbally (Leibowitz, Guzy, Peterson, & Blake, 1993). Interviewers can assist witnesses by allowing them to use non-verbal methods to express their knowledge. For instance witnesses may be able to describe the spatial layout of the crime scene better by drawing a sketch than by describing it verbally (Dando, Wilcock, & Milne, 2009).

Flexibility within the Cognitive Interview

The Cognitive Interview is not a recipe, but rather a collection of techniques only some of which are used in any one interview. Furthermore, the techniques must be adapted to meet the demands of the specific interview. If time is short, then the interviewer may delete some of the time-consuming techniques, e.g., asking witnesses to describe the event in reverse order after having described it chronologically (Dando, Wilcock, Milne, & Henry, 2009; Davis, McMahon, & Greenwood, 2005). Also, some techniques may not work with all individuals. For instance, a witness

may be uncomfortable to close his/her eyes. In such a case, the interviewer can either omit or modify the instruction, for example, by instructing the witness to keep his/her eyes open but to focus on a blank field such as a table or the floor. The skill of conducting an interview is to know which techniques can be implemented, given the specific conditions of the interview, and how best to implement the techniques. This flexibility and the concomitant decision-making are advantageous yet costly, in that the interviewer must be more fully engaged in the interview process and must make more on-line decisions. As a consequence of the Cognitive Interview's greater complexity and flexibility, it is more difficult to learn and to implement, but it yields considerably more information than does the comparison interview.

Empirical testing of the Cognitive Interview

The Cognitive Interview has been examined in approximately 100 laboratory tests, most of which were conducted in the United States, England, Germany, or Australia. We shall only summarize these findings, as they have been reviewed in detail elsewhere (see Fisher, Ross, & Cahill, 2010, and Holliday, Brainerd, Reyna, & Humphries, 2009, for recent reviews, and Köhnken, Milne, Memon, & Bull, 1999, and Memon, Meissner, & Fraser, 2010, for meta-analyses). In these laboratory tests, volunteer witnesses typically observed either a videotape of a simulated crime or a live, non-threatening event. Later, the witnesses were interviewed either via the Cognitive Interview or a comparison interview that was modeled after either a typical police interview or a "structured interview," which incorporates generally accepted principles of interviewing. Across these studies, the Cognitive Interview has typically elicited between 25 to 50 percent more correct statements than the comparison interview. Furthermore, the effect is extremely reliable: Of the 59 experiments in Memon et al.'s (2010) meta-analysis, 58 experiments found that the Cognitive Interview elicited more correct information than did the comparison interview (weighted mean effect size d = 1.20). Equally important, accuracy (as measured by the proportion of all witness statements that are correct) was comparable for the Cognitive Interview and comparison interview. Finally, the basic finding, that the Cognitive Interview increases the amount of correct information, is very robust: It holds across types of event (criminal and non-criminal) and types of witness (children, young adults, and the elderly; "normal" and cognitively impaired – although, see Maras & Bowler's (2010) study with children of autism spectrum disorder).

Although the Cognitive Interview has been found to be beneficial in laboratory studies, practitioners are more concerned with its value in actual criminal investigations. To examine the Cognitive Interview in a criminal investigation, Fisher, Geiselman, and Amador (1989) trained experienced robbery detectives to conduct the Cognitive Interview and then compared their tape recorded interviews (of victims and other witnesses) with those of interviews conducted by either untrained (but experienced) detectives or their own interviews conducted prior to training. The trained detectives elicited 63 percent more information than the untrained investigators, and 47 percent more information than in their own pre-trained interviews. Moreover, for those elicited witness statements that were corroborable (compared with statements made by a second witness to the same crime), the corroboration rates were high, and slightly higher for the Cognitive Interviews than the untrained interviews. Clifford and George (1996) and George and Clifford (1992) conducted a similar study with British police officers and found comparable results (55 percent increase in information).

Ultimately, to establish the value of the Cognitive Interview in police investigations, evidence is needed that it facilitates police solving criminal cases, (which we report

shortly when describing National Institute of Child Health and Human Development (NICHD) interviews in children's investigations) and not merely that it elicits more information. Presumably, gathering more information should help to solve more cases, but currently that remains more of an assumption than a demonstrated fact. Police and other investigators have described several cases that they believe were aided by using the Cognitive Interview (see Fisher & York, 2009, and Geiselman & Fisher, 1997, for descriptions), but ultimately these are only anecdotes, with their attendant limitations. Nevertheless, the converging pattern of results across controlled laboratory research, field studies, and police anecdotes does provide good reason to expect that the Cognitive Interview will help police to solve real criminal cases.

CHILD WITNESS INTERVIEWING: NICHD PROTOCOL

Since the early daycare abuse cases of the 1980s and 1990s, much has been learned about investigative interviewing of (vulnerable) child witnesses, and, in particular, young children. In fact, the number and quality of field and laboratory studies that have focused on child witness memory and interviewing in the last 30 years is nothing short of impressive (see Bruck, Ceci, & Principe, 2006; Ceci & Bruck, 1995; Lamb, Orbach, Hershkowitz, Esplin, & Horowitz, 2007, for detailed reviews). As a result, several important policy-level advances have been made in the field of child interviewing including the establishment of centers specialized in interviewing children, known as Child Advocacy Centers (CACs), and the widely accepted practice of videotaping child interviews. In addition, several evidence-based, child-interviewing guidelines have been developed and modified. These guidelines include the Step-Wise Interview (Yuille, Hunter, Joffe, & Zaparniuk, 1993), the Narrative Elaboration Procedure (Saywitz & Snyder, 1996), Finding Words or RATAC (Rapport, Anatomy Identification, Touch Inquiry, Abuse and Closure: Walters, Holmes, Bauer, & Vieth, 2003) and, as previously mentioned, the NICHD Investigative Interview (e.g., Orbach, Hershkowitz, Lamb, Sternberg, Esplin, & Horowitz, 2000). Of these guidelines for interviewing children, the NICHD protocol is the most extensively researched, with at least five independent field studies conducted in four different countries (e.g., Orbach et al., 2000). As such, we discuss in detail the NICHD protocol in the following section.

Similar to the Cognitive Interview, the NICHD protocol was developed to elicit extensive and accurate information, but was more responsive to children's limited cognitive and metacognitive abilities. Thus, the NICHD protocol provides more direction to facilitating children's willingness and ability to communicate experiences and to minimizing interviewer suggestiveness. Furthermore, the NICHD protocol is unique in that it assesses the child's credibility as a competent witness within the boundaries of his or her developmental limitations. For a detailed review of developmental limitations impacting children's ability to communicate see, for example, Lamb, La Rooy, Malloy, and Katz (2011).

Overcoming hurdles to disclosure

Rapport building

As children are frequently interviewed as victims in the context of child sexual abuse investigations, building rapport is a critical component of the NICHD protocol. Research suggests that children are reluctant to disclose abuse in a formal interviewing context (London, Bruck, Ceci, & Shuman, 2005, 2007). Therefore, interviewers must create a relaxing physical and social environment in which victims are comfortable disclosing adults' wrong-doings despite fear of the perpetrator, desires to protect family members, or embarrassment talking about such

private experiences. Compared with no rapport, child witnesses who experience social support and rapport are likely to report more information and more accurate information (e.g., Carter, Bottoms, & Levine, 1996; Hershkowitz, Orbach, Lamb, Sternberg, & Horowitz, 2006; Moston & Engelberg, 1992; Quas, Wallin, Papini, Lench, & Scullin, 2005; but see Hershkowitz, 2009; Imhoff & Baker-Ward, 1999; Teoh & Lamb, 2010) and may be less susceptible to misinformation (Davis & Bottoms, 2002).

Sensitivity to social influence and suggestibility

Knowledge and power differentials

In order to facilitate children to be active reporters of information, child interviewers must overcome perceived knowledge and power differentials inherent to adult–child relationships. Telling the child that he or she knows more than the interviewer helps to break down the child's assumption that omnipotent adults already know what happened. Interviewers can further empower the child by encouraging the child to correct the interviewer if he or she makes a mistake (Orbach et al., 2000). Similar to the Cognitive Interview, the NICHD protocol also aims to encourage the child to take a more active role in the interview by (a) explicitly telling the child that he or she knows more about what happened than the interviewer, (b) asking primarily open-ended questions, and (c) not interrupting the child (Orbach et al., 2005).

Suggestibility

Research has generally shown that, compared with adults, children are more suggestible (e.g., Poole & Lamb, 1998), are more likely to answer affirmatively to yes/no questions (e.g., McBrien & Dagenbach, 1998), and are more likely to change their answer in response to repeated closed questions within an interview (e.g., Memon & Vartoukian,

1996; Poole & White, 1991). Parallel to the Cognitive Interview, the NICHD therefore recommends cautionary instructions at the beginning of the interview that (a) discourage the child from guessing and (b) explain that it is okay to say "I don't know" (Orbach et al., 2000). In addition, the NICHD protocol recommends that interviewers inform the child witness that if the interviewer does not understand a statement, he/she may ask the child to explain (Orbach et al., 2000). This helps to communicate to the child that follow-up questions reflect the interviewer's lack of understanding, rather than dissatisfaction with the child's previous answer, although some research does not support the notion that children change their answers for this reason (Howie, Kurukulasuriya, Nash, & Marsh, 2009; Howie, Nash, Kurukulasuiya, & Bowman, 2012).

Open-ended questions

A plethora of research suggests that open-ended questions elicit the most accurate information from child witnesses compared with any other question style (see, e.g., Lamb, Hershkowitz, Orbach, & Esplin, 2008; although note our later comment about the difficulty of interpreting these findings). As such, open-ended questions are recommended as the question of choice across all empirically based child witness interviewing guidelines. However, it is important to point out that preschool-aged children typically provide only little information in free narratives, which can be at odds with legal requirements associated with bringing sexual abuse charges forward. Therefore, forensic interviewers are often faced with the difficult task of asking specific follow-up questions (e.g., about touching versus penetration) without being suggestive or leading. This challenge presents another strong reason to invest in extensive forensic interviewer training and adherence to best-practice guidelines.

Videotaping child interviews

Because children are particularly sensitive to various forms of suggestive influence, many jurisdictions require that investigative interviews with children be videotaped. This electronic record is believed to encourage adherence to accepted interviewing protocols, allow identification of poor interviewing techniques that could unduly influence the child's statement and, perhaps most importantly, limit the number of times a child must recount the (traumatic) event. In addition, videotaped, freely elicited child witness accounts of abuse can become a powerful piece of evidence during a trial.

Assessing competency and credibility

Developmental considerations

In contrast to adult witness interviewing guidelines, the NICHD protocol recommends that interviewers ask children to describe a recent, neutral event prior to discussing the forensically relevant event(s) to have the child "practice" giving a detailed narrative response. This introductory narrative also serves to build rapport by showing interest in the child's life and assessing the child's language and communication abilities. It also places the child in the role of the knowledgeable information source in the interaction. Research suggests that such practice increases the quality and quantity of details reported by the child during the substantive phase of the interview, which focuses on the alleged crime itself (Price, Roberts, & Collins, 2013).

The importance of truth-telling

Due to documented cases of false allegations and the frequent lack of corroborating physical evidence in child sexual abuse investigations, it is important to address the credibility of an alleged child victim's statements in the formal, forensic interview context. One such method is for interviewers to test the child's understanding of the importance of telling the truth and comprehension of the various instructions of what is expected of him or her. For example, establishing ground rules to tell the truth typically involves a "truth–lie ceremony" during which the interviewer educates or clarifies the difference between what is true and what is not true (e.g., asking the child to explain what he or she means, telling the child that the truth is "what actually happened") and then testing the child's knowledge with examples (e.g., "If I said my shirt was green, would that be true or not true?"). Similarly, when child interviewers instruct the child not to guess, that it is okay to say "I don't know," and that it is okay to correct the interviewer, additional test questions are used (e.g., "If I ask you, 'What did I have for breakfast?' what would you say?" Or "What would you say if I made a mistake and said you were a boy?"). However, research has demonstrated that children's understanding of the meaning of truth and lie and the consequences of telling a lie are not necessarily predictive of subsequent truth-telling or statement accuracy with their own transgressions and those of adults (Lyon, Malloy, Quas, & Talwar, 2008; Talwar, Lee, Bala, & Lindsay, 2002), particularly in the face of suggestive questions or coaching to provide false reports (Lyon et al., 2008). This version of the "truth-lie ceremony" may instead serve to enhance the credibility of the child rather than foster truth-telling. Alternatively, the interviewer can ask the child to take an oath to tell the truth, known as "truth induction," instead of or in addition to the truth-lie ceremony. This "truth induction" can indeed reduce lying and enhance the accuracy and detail of their accounts, suggesting that having child witnesses promise to tell the truth during an investigative interview is a powerful tool to supplement the NICHD protocol and minimize lying (Lyon et al., 2008; Talwar et al., 2002; Talwar, Lee, Bala, & Lindsay, 2004).

Empirical testing of the NICHD protocol

Many field studies support the use of the NICHD protocol (e.g., Cyr, Lamb, Pelletier,

Leduc, & Perron, 2006; Lamb, Orbach, Hershkowitz, Esplin, & Horowitz, 2007; Orbach, Hershkowitz, Lamb, Sternberg, Esplin, & Horowitz, 2000; Sternberg, Lamb, Orbach, Esplin, & Mitchell, 2001). Interviewers who follow the protocol improve the quality of their investigative interviews, that is, they use three times the number of open-ended prompts and significantly fewer suggestive leading questions, compared with interviewers who conduct a standard interview. Eighty percent of initial disclosures of sexual abuse reported by child witnesses who are interviewed using the NICHD protocol were elicited by open-ended questions (Lamb et al., 2007). With better quality interviews being conducted, field research comparing pre- and post-introduction of the NICHD protocol also suggests that it generates more investigative leads (Darwish, Hershkowitz, Lamb, & Orbach, 2005, 2008) and results in more charges, particularly when the suspect is an adult and is an immediate family member (Pipe, Orbach, Lamb, Abbott, & Stewart, 2008). Pipe and colleagues' research also demonstrates that for those cases that went to trial, guilty verdicts occurred significantly more often in cases occurring after the protocol was introduced, compared with the previously used, standard method.

Additional child interviewing techniques

Although not specifically recommended in the NICHD protocol, current child interviewing practice often involves the use of "supplementary" techniques (e.g., props, toys, drawings, or dolls), some of which have stirred considerable debate. Many practitioners argue that these investigative interviewing aids may assist child witnesses in responding in a non-verbal fashion. Clinicians and interviewers are concerned that, due to motivational, language, and cognitive hurdles, a significant portion of child witnesses will not disclose and/or coherently describe an abusive event – a hurdle that they attempt to circumvent using anatomically correct dolls, for example. However, research does not support the notion that anatomically correct dolls increase the number of accurately reported details (Poole, Bruck, & Pipe, 2011). In fact, despite some encouraging findings (Saywitz, Goodman, Nicholas, & Moan, 1991), most experimental studies suggest that children interviewed using dolls report a higher proportion of fantastic details than children interviewed without dolls (Thierry, Lamb, Orbach, & Pipe, 2005). Other studies confirm this increase in errors when children are interviewed using anatomically correct dolls (Bruck, Ceci, & Francoeur, 2000; Pipe & Salmon, 2009).

Body diagrams are often used in forensic interviews to assist children with naming body parts or describing locations and specific actions pertaining to abuse allegations. Although some research suggests that using body diagrams can result in children recalling additional details, some controlled laboratory studies find no differences between accuracy rates in interviews with and without body diagrams (Salmon, Pipe, Malloy, & Mackay, 2012) whereas other studies suggest that introducing body diagrams can increase false reports of touching (Poole & Dickinson, 2011). Taken together, there is no strong empirical evidence that interviewing props elicit any additional accurate information beyond the use of verbal techniques (Poole et al., 2011). In addition, the potential benefits of supplemental techniques are not without risks, and the utility of these techniques varies as a function of (a) the child's age and (b) how the props are introduced and used in the interview (see Brown, 2011, for a detailed review).

In sum, a wealth of research has provided child interviewers with the knowledge and tools necessary to enhance the completeness and accuracy of children's accounts. Researchers' early focus on limitations of child witnesses and victims in the wake of highly publicized false allegations of sexual abuse has since shifted to the ways in which interviewers can accommodate the specific needs of child witnesses (e.g., addressing motivational hurdles of reporting, requiring heightened sensitivity to power and knowledge differentials, and incorporating "tests" of the child's competence and credibility). If interviewed properly, child witnesses as young as three years can effectively convey a significant amount of accurate, forensically relevant information in criminal investigations.

METHODOLOGICAL AND THEORETICAL CONCERNS

Research on interviewing has been conducted in several laboratories, and hence there is no one standard methodology. Rather, different laboratories use different methods to assess the interviews and different designs to examine the efficacy of the interview. We examine some of these issues.

Measuring accuracy

Although researchers generally agree how to measure the quantity of information gathered – typically, they count the number of correct statements – researchers disagree about how to measure accuracy. Some researchers count the number of incorrect statements made per witness and other researchers compute the proportion of all witness statements that are correct (accuracy *rate*). As we have argued elsewhere (Fisher, 1996; although see Memon & Stevenage, 1996, for an alternative argument), we believe that accuracy rate is the better measure of accuracy as it is less influenced by the total number of statements a witness generates. As such, it is a purer measure of the credibility of the witness's statement (Koriat & Goldsmith, 1996). A simple numerical example will illustrate the difference between number of inaccurate statements and accuracy rate as measures of accuracy. Compare two witnesses: One witness provides 100 statements, of which two are incorrect (the other 98 being correct); the other witness provides two statements, of which one is incorrect (the other being correct). Clearly, even though the first witness makes more incorrect statements (2) than the second witness (1), the first witness's testimony (98 percent accuracy rate) is considerably more trustworthy than the second (50 percent). If a researcher reported number of errors, as many researchers do, readers might be misled into thinking that the second witness (one error) was more accurate than the first witness (two errors). As such, we encourage researchers to report their data in terms of the observed accuracy rates – in addition to reporting the amount of information gathered.

Componential analysis

Both the Cognitive Interview and the NICHD protocol are collections of individual component elements, and so we would like to know, not only whether the overall technique is effective, but also which elements are the most effective (e.g., Milne & Bull, 2002). Whereas this seems like a simple question, and is open to experimental analysis, the solution is more complex than initially seems apparent. Consider the following difficulties. First, some elements were intended to be used in concert with other elements (e.g., not interrupting the witnesses' responses is appropriate but only when interviewers ask open-ended questions) and so it is not appropriate to test some elements in isolation. And even if an element was not intended initially to be used in combination with others, the element's effectiveness may be influenced by other interviewing components (e.g., the value of asking open-ended questions is influenced by whether witnesses are instructed to generate rich narrative responses; if witnesses are not so instructed, even open-ended questions may produce incomplete narrations). Second, some elements may be more effective in one situation than in another (e.g., reinstating the encoding context should be more effective when interviews are conducted after a longer interval of time) so it may not be possible to make global claims about *the* effectiveness of a component, but rather that a component's effectiveness depends on the test conditions. Third, what should the targeted element be compared to? Should the comparison interview simply not contain that element or should the comparison interview have a "free recall" option instead of the targeted element? For instance, Dando et al. (2011) found that, after requesting a free-recall narration, adding the instruction to recall in reverse order generated several pieces of new information and at a high accuracy rate, which seemingly showed that the reverse-order instruction was helpful; however, even more new information was generated, and at a higher accuracy rate, if witnesses were simply asked to do an additional free-recall narration, which seemingly showed that the reverse-order instruction was not helpful.

Comparing open-ended and closed questions

There is a general belief that open-ended questions yield more accurate responses than do closed questions, but that closed questions yield more information than open-ended questions. Although many people believe this assertion – and it may be true – it is impossible to determine the absolute amount of information and the accuracy of responses generated to open-ended and closed questions. The problem is that the difficulty of each question and the total number of questions asked can vary widely from one situation to another, and there is no established norm that one can use for comparison. For instance, although asking 100 closed questions is likely to generate more information than asking one open-ended question, asking only one closed question will likely generate less information than asking one open-ended question. Similarly, asking an open-ended question typically yields more accurate recollections than asking a closed question; however, if the closed question is easy enough (e.g., Was there a fight? Was it a man or a woman?), then answers to closed questions might be extremely accurate, and more accurate than answers to difficult open-ended questions (How were the punches thrown during the fight?). Thus, although responses to open-ended questions may typically be more accurate than those to closed questions, and closed questions can be used judiciously to increase the amount of information gathered, the lack of standardization of questions makes it difficult or impossible to verify the overall accuracy and quantity of information elicited to open-ended and closed questions (see Fisher, 1995 for a more thorough discussion).

Dependent measures of effectiveness

Many of the research studies on the Cognitive Interview and NICHD protocols measured the number of facts collected within an interview. This is a reasonable starting point, as the assumption is that the more facts that are gathered, the better is the quality of the interview. However, the research community should broaden its scope somewhat to (a) give more (or exclusive) weight to facts that are investigatively or forensically relevant than to less relevant facts, and (b) assess the ultimate value of investigations (whether cases are solved correctly). In line with those goals, Geiselman, Fisher, MacKinnon, and Holland (1985) asked prosecutors to list the 20 most relevant facts (toward a successful prosecution) and rescored the data (originally in terms of the total number of facts recalled) to include only those 20 most relevant facts. (They found similar results to the analysis of all recalled facts.) Second, as indicated earlier, Pipe et al. (2008) conducted a study of the effectiveness of NICHD training in child-abuse investigations and examined the number of cases in which charges were filed, defendants pled guilty, and the number of convictions. Obviously, these

non-traditional measures are more resource-demanding to assess than the conventional laboratory measures – and hence the preponderance of studies that assess the number of facts collected. Nevertheless, if the research community wants its findings to be taken up by practitioners, researchers should make an effort to measure behavior in ways that are more commensurate with the needs of the practitioner community. This will require researchers to work more closely with practitioners, but that cooperation is likely to pay off in the long run.

PRACTICAL CONCERNS

Police reactions

Despite the general success of the Cognitive Interview, British police officers have expressed some reservations. Line officers report that the Cognitive Interview often requires more time than police have available, and especially those police who handle high-volume cases, such as petty theft (Dando, Wilcock, & Milne, 2008). Laboratory studies bear out the claim that the Cognitive Interview often requires more time than the comparison interview. It may be appropriate, then, to use the full Cognitive Interview only in the most important cases (e.g., murder, rape, robbery), where police investigators are afforded more time and resources to conduct interviews. Another solution is to develop a shortened version of the Cognitive Interview (e.g., Davis et al., 2005) to be used for those cases where time is at a premium.

Some British police have also expressed their discomfort when implementing (or choosing not to implement) two specific techniques: Change-Order (asking witnesses to describe the event both chronologically and in reverse order) and Change-Perspective (asking witnesses to describe the event from their perspective and also from another perspective: Dando et al., 2008). Although we are sensitive to police interviewers' concerns, we think their concern reflects a misunderstanding of the Cognitive Interview. The Change-Order and Change-Perspective techniques are merely two instantiations of the more general principle, Varied Retrieval (any variation in how witnesses are asked to search through memory). The general principle can be implemented in many ways, for example, probing for visual, auditory, and other sensory modalities; describing a room's contents from left-to-right and also from right-to-left; thinking about an event in terms of time and location, etc. We encourage police trainers to think in terms of the more general principle, Varied Retrieval, so that if investigators are uncomfortable implementing some specific instantiations (e.g., Change-Order and Change-Perspective), they can use the principle in other ways. Furthermore, we strongly recommend that researchers not be so focused on testing the Change-Order and Change-Perspective techniques, which we note occupies one paragraph of the 200-page manual describing the Cognitive Interview (Fisher & Geiselman, 1992).

Self-administered interviews

Obviously, it is preferable to interview witnesses shortly after a crime has occurred, as with the passage of time, (a) memory fades, (b) witnesses are exposed to the corrupting elements of speaking with one another and exposure to the media, and (c) memory becomes more of a constructive process. However, sometimes it is impossible for police to interview witnesses immediately, because too many witnesses are present at the crime scene and not enough police investigators are available to interview everyone, as might happen if a riot breaks out at a popular sporting event or outdoor concert. If police investigators have to wait several days before they conduct face-to-face interviews with all of the witnesses, some information will be lost and memories will become distorted. As a partial solution to the problem of delayed interviewing, Gabbert,

Hope, and Fisher (2009) developed an interview protocol that witnesses can administer themselves immediately after the crime. This self-administered interview is in the form of a booklet that can be distributed by police to many witnesses at the crime scene. Witnesses read the instructions in the booklet and then record their responses in the spaces provided. The instructions incorporate many elements of the Cognitive Interview, including reinstating the context, instructions to recall everything, varied retrieval, a sketch of the scene, and specific questions about normatively important details associated with the crime (e.g., perpetrator's appearance, actions, weapons). Thus far, laboratory testing has demonstrated that such a self-administered preliminary test (a) generates more information than merely asking witnesses to freely recall the event, (b) reduces the deleterious effects of post-event misinformation, and, most important, (c) reduces the amount of forgetting (as measured by recall in a face-to-face interview conducted one week later) that would have occurred had such a preliminary interview not be conducted (see Hope, Gabbert, & Fisher, 2011, for a review). Currently, several police departments in England and northern Europe have volunteered to try the procedure on a limited basis, and their feedback has been extremely supportive. As reported by the police, the procedure saves time and resources, and has been credited with solving at least one crime (see Hope et al., 2011).

FUTURE DIRECTIONS

We have made considerable progress in improving the quality of the investigative interview over the past 30 years, elevating it from the status of an untrained skill that was uninfluenced by scientific principles to a more sophisticated, appreciated skill that is guided by research in social, cognitive, and developmental psychology. We sense, though, that the discipline has reached a plateau, with not many advances being made in the past five years. In our view, this has occurred because researchers have focused too much of their time conducting validation studies on the Cognitive Interview and the NICHD protocol rather than developing new interviewing techniques that might advance the field even further. As such, we put out a call here to encourage researchers to ply current theories of psychology and generate new methods to enhance memory and communication. Similarly, researchers skilled in developmental psychology should strive to create new theory-driven techniques to assist children to remember episodes or report evidence.

One such theory-driven approach is directed toward improving the accuracy of witness testimony. Most of the research on the Cognitive Interview shows that it enhances the quantity of information elicited, but that it has only minimal or no effect on accuracy. Recent studies, however, show that various metacognitive manipulations can be exercised to increase the accuracy of recall, including the option not to reply (e.g., say "I don't know") and the option to describe an event at a coarse level of precision (e.g., rather than describe an event as occurring at 3.10 pm, one can describe the time more coarsely, e.g., "in the afternoon.") Both of these methods are known to preserve accuracy (Evans & Fisher, 2011; Goldsmith, Koriat, & Weinberg-Eliezer, 2002). We should explore these and other metacognitive control mechanisms to increase accuracy. Similarly, there are known "signatures" associated with accurate and inaccurate responses, for example, responses given to open-ended questions are typically more accurate than responses to closed questions. Hence, we can use these signatures after the interview has been conducted to determine which elements of the witness's statement are more or less likely to be correct (see Fisher, 1995 for a more thorough analysis). Finding additional signatures of accuracy and inaccuracy will surely enhance our ability to assess witness reports and "create" accurate witness testimony.

Several procedural aspects of interviewing also beg to be addressed:

- Response modality: What is the difference between respondents speaking their answer or writing their answer? Although speech is undoubtedly faster than writing, thus allowing respondents to keep pace with their thoughts, perhaps the slower pace of writing will encourage respondents to probe their memories deeper and provide more details. Certainly the advantage of each modality will vary across situations and people, and so we might even develop a multi-modal interview format, asking witnesses to report some information via speech and other via writing.
- Telephones, Skype: How might these various technologies be used optimally to improve interviews? Whereas face-to-face interviewing permits greater opportunities for rapport, it is logistically more difficult to arrange a face-to-face interview than a telephone or Skype interview. Perhaps telephones and Skype also excel in other areas, for example, allowing witnesses to concentrate on their thoughts better because of the greater personal space afforded by the absence of a physically intrusive interviewer.
- Using props: Neutral props (e.g., maps or diagrams of the crime scene; catalogues of weapons and cars) should have the potential to enhance memory and/or communication – assuming that they are used judiciously and not to imply the existence of an unnamed object. When should the props be presented? Before or after the witness provides a free narrative? Providing props before the free narrative may assist by reinstating the context of the original event, but it may also impair a witness's free narrative because it disrupts his or her unique, idiosyncratic way of representing the crime.

Thus far, interviews have been used primarily to elicit respondents' knowledge about the factual details of a crime: perpetrators, weapons, cars, actions, etc. Another potential use of interviewing is to facilitate people's recall of decisions they made during the crime. For instance, police are debriefed regularly about their decisions to shoot or not to shoot, or strategies they adopted to control the crime area, or to interrogate suspects, or even to engage in negotiations with hostage-takers. Similarly, we may learn something valuable by debriefing cooperative criminals about decisions they made before or during the commission of a crime, or why they confessed. What methods do we currently have to interview people about their earlier decisions? One such method is the Critical Decision Method (Crandall, Klein, & Hoffman, 2006), which has been used to debrief experts about a variety of domains, including military operations (Kaempf, Wolf, Thordsen, & Klein, 1992). Might the Critical Decision Method be combined with the Cognitive Interview to improve on its knowledge-eliciting capabilities? A recent study by Hirn, Fisher, and Carol (2012) showed that a hybrid interviewing technique that combined the two procedures has considerable potential (increasing more than two-fold the amount of relevant information in comparison with a more direct method of asking about respondents' decisions). We encourage researchers to explore this novel area of research, as much can be learned by debriefing police, suspects, and convicted criminals about their decisions. One can easily imagine the potential utility of such an interviewing protocol in related areas: military, clinical, scientific investigation, medicine, etc.

Training investigators to conduct interviews properly requires not only a well-designed interview protocol, but also an effective method of delivering the message. Unfortunately, relatively little systematic research has been published on effective training procedures for interviewing skills – although see several interesting training studies by Martine Powell and her associates (e.g., Powell, Fisher, & Wright, 2005). Based on the current authors' experiences of conducting such training sessions, we believe that the critical elements for successful training include: (a) distributing training across multiple sessions rather than massed training (Donovan & Radosevich, 1999) – although note the logistic difficulties this may impose; (b) selecting trainees who are motivated to invest their personal resources

to learn the trained skills (Ericsson, Krampe, & Tesch-Romer, 1993); (c) including many exercises for trainees to practice the learned skills and providing immediate feedback on their performance (e.g., Cyr, Dion, McDuff, & Trotier-Sylvain, 2012); (d) explaining the underlying rationale behind the various techniques, rather than presenting the skills in cookbook form, so that trainees will be able to adapt the requisite skills in novel situations; (e) showing examples of good and poor interviewing techniques, so that trainees have clear models of what behaviors to emulate (and not emulate) and (f) providing post-training refresher courses, and especially for trainees who will not have frequent opportunities to ply the learned skills after training. Perhaps the best working model of a formal system to develop interviewing skills is that used in the UK, where police officers work their way through a tiered system, so that all officers receive some basic training in interviewing, and then only the most talented officers progress through more sophisticated levels of training and are placed in police roles requiring the greatest level of skills, for example, interviewing rape victims (see Fisher, Milne, & Bull, 2011, and Griffiths & Milne, 2005, for descriptions).

Finally, we describe an ongoing discussion within the New Zealand justice system about how to utilize well-conducted police investigations in the courtroom. (Thanks to Nina Westera for informing us about this matter.) Many New Zealand police officers are trained to conduct Cognitive Interviews with victims and witnesses. Some of their interviews are also videotaped. The Court is now deciding whether to show the original videotaped Cognitive Interview with a victim or witness in lieu of having the witness testify in court. (The witness would be available for cross-examination.) The major advantages of such a novel approach are (a) the witness's initial, pristine memory of the event would be preserved on the videotape rather than having the witness testify in court several months or years after the crime occurred, with a concomitant loss of detail and distortion arising from exposure to post-event information, and (b) the police, who are trained to conduct the Cognitive Interview, are likely to be more efficient and less biased interviewers than the prosecuting and defense attorneys who would interview (via direct and cross-examination) the witness in court. The major drawback of showing to the jurors the original videotaped interview is that it would likely contain much irrelevant information, which might lengthen the in-court process, in comparison with the crisper style of in-court interviewing. That problem might be dealt with by court officials editing the videotape so as to retain only the relevant testimony. At the time of this writing, the Court is still debating the issue. That the Court is even considering such an issue speaks to the elevated status that proper interviewing has finally reached after years (centuries) of languishing.

CONCLUSION

As victims and witnesses are the main sources for solving crimes, eliciting information from them must be done professionally and with a high degree of skill (Yuille, Marxsen, & Cooper, 1999). Police investigators must be trained properly and the discipline itself must be constantly seeking to improve itself. This will happen only through the concerted efforts of both the research and practitioner communities, and most important, their sharing ideas and information with one another (Oxburgh, Walsh, & Milne, 2011). Fortunately, we have seen such increased cooperation between practitioners and researchers, as exemplified by organizations like the International Investigative Interviewing Research Group (iIIRG). We trust that, after many years of having overlooked the critical skill of interviewing, the advances made in the past 20 to 30 years will set the tone for even further progress in the years to come.

REFERENCES

Anderson, R. C., & Pichert, J. W. (1978). Recall of previously unrecallable information following a shift in perspective. *Journal of Verbal Learning and Verbal Behavior, 17,* 1–12.

Benner, L. (1985). Rating accident models and investigation methodologies. *Journal of Safety Research , 16,* 105–126.

Berresheim, A., & Weber, A. (2003). Structured witness interviewing and its effectiveness. *Kriminalistik, 57,* 757–771.

Brown, D. A. (2011). The use of supplementary techniques in forensic interviews with children. In M. E. Lamb, D. J. La Rooy, L. Malloy, and C. Katz (Eds.), *Children's testimony: A handbook of psychological research and forensic practice* (2nd ed., pp. 217–249). Chichester, UK: John Wiley & Sons, Ltd.

Bruck, M., Ceci, S. J., & Francoeur, E. (2000). A comparison of three and four year old children's use of anatomically detailed dolls to report genital touching in a medical examination. *Journal of Experimental Psychology: Applied, 6,* 74–83.

Bruck, M., Ceci, S. J., & Principe, G. F. (2006). The child and the law. In *Handbook of child psychology* (6th ed.) Hoboken, NJ: John Wiley & Sons Inc.

Carter, C. A., Bottoms, B. L., & Levine, M. (1996). Linguistic and socioemotional influences on the accuracy of children's reports. *Law and Human Behavior, 20,* 335–358.

Ceci, S. J., & Bruck, M. (1995). *Jeopardy in the courtroom: A scientific analysis of children's testimony.* Washington, DC: American Psychological Association.

Clifford, B. R., & George, R. (1996). A field evaluation of training in three methods of witness/victim investigative interviewing. *Psychology, Crime & Law, 2*(3), 231–248.

Collins, R., Lincoln, R., & Frank, M. G. (2002). The effect of rapport in forensic interviewing. *Psychiatry, Psychology and Law, 9*(1), 69–78.

Crandall, B., Klein, G., & Hoffman, R. R. (2006). *Working minds: A practitioner's guide to cognitive task analysis.* Cambridge, MA: MIT Press.

Cyr, M., Dion, J., McDuff, P., & Trotier-Sylvain, K. (2012). Transfer of skills in the context of non-suggestive investigative interviews: Impact of structured interview protocol and feedback. *Applied Cognitive Psychology, 26,* 516–524.

Cyr, M., Lamb, M. E., Pelletier, J., Leduc, P., & Perron, A. (2006). Assessing the effectiveness of the NICHD Investigative Interview protocol in Francophone Quebec. Paper presented at the Second International

Investigative Interviewing Conference, Portsmouth, UK.

Dando, C. J., Ormerod, T. C., Wilcock, R., & Milne, R. (2011). When help becomes hindrance: Unexpected errors of omission and commission in eyewitness memory resulting from change temporal order at retrieval? *Cognition, 121*(3), 416–421.

Dando, C., Wilcock, R., & Milne, R. (2008). The cognitive interview: Inexperienced police officers' perceptions of their own witness/victim interviewing practices. *Legal and Criminological Psychology, 13,* 59–70.

Dando, C., Wilcock, R., & Milne, R. (2009). The cognitive interview: The efficacy of a modified mental reinstatement of context procedure for frontline police investigators. *Applied Cognitive Psychology, 23*(1), 138–147.

Dando, C. J., Wilcock, R., Milne, R., & Henry, L. (2009). An adapted Cognitive Interview procedure for frontline police investigators. *Applied Cognitive Psychology, 23,* 698–716.

Darwish, T., Hershkowitz, I., Lamb, M. E., & Orbach, Y. (2005). The effect of the NICHD interview protocol on the elicitation of investigative leads in child sexual abuse investigations. Paper presented at The Annual Conference of the Society of Research in Memory and Cognition, Wellington, New Zealand.

Darwish, T., Hershkowitz, I., Lamb, M. E., & Orbach, Y. (2008). The effect of the NICHD interview protocol on the elicitation of investigative leads in child sexual abuse investigations. Paper presented at the meeting of the American Psychology-Law Society Conference, Jacksonville, FL.

Davis, M. R., McMahon, M., & Greenwood, K. M. (2005). The efficacy of mnemonic components of the cognitive interview: Towards a shortened variant of for time-critical investigations. *Applied Cognitive Psychology, 19,* 75–93.

Davis, S. L., & Bottoms, B. L. (2002). Effects of social support on children's eyewitness reports: A test of the underlying mechanism. *Law and Human Behavior, 26,* 185–215.

Donovan, J. J., & Radosevich, D. J. (1999). A meta-analytic review of the distribution of practice effect: Now you see it, now you don't. *Journal of Applied Psychology, 84,* 795–805.

Ericsson, K. A., Krampe, R. T., & Tesch-Romer, C. (1993). The role of deliberate practice in the acquisition of expert performance. *Psychological Review, 100,* 363–406.

Evans, J. R., & Fisher, R. P. (2011). Eyewitness memory: Balancing the accuracy, precision, and quantity of information through metacognitive monitoring and control. *Applied Cognitive Psychology, 25*(3), 501–508.

Fisher, R. P. (1995). Interviewing victims and witnesses of crime. *Psychology, Public Policy, and Law, 1,* 732–764.

Fisher, R. P. (1996). Misconceptions in design and analysis of research with the cognitive interview. *PSYCOLOQUY, 7*(6), witness-memory. 12. fisher. (electronic journal).

Fisher, R. P., & Geiselman, R. E. (1992). *Memory-enhancing techniques for investigative interviewing: The cognitive interview*. Springfield, IL: Charles C. Thomas.

Fisher, R. P., Geiselman, R. E., & Amador, M. (1989). Field test of the cognitive interview: Enhancing the recollection of actual victims and witnesses of crime. *Journal of Applied Psychology, 74,* 722–727.

Fisher, R. P., Geiselman, R. E., & Raymond, D. S. (1987). Critical analysis of police interviewing techniques. *Journal of Police Science and Administration, 15,* 177–185.

Fisher, R. P., Milne, R., & Bull, R. (2011). Interviewing cooperative witnesses. *Currrent Directions in Psychological Science, 20,* 16–19.

Fisher, R. P., Ross, S. J., & Cahill, B. S. (2010). Interviewing witnesses and victims. In P. A. Granhag (Ed.), *Forensic psychology in context: Nordic and international approaches.* (pp. 56–74). Portland, OR: Willan Publishing.

Fisher, R. P., & Schreiber, N. (2007). Interview protocols for improving eyewitness memory. In M. P. Toglia, J. D. Read, D. F. Ross, and R. C. L. Lindsay (Eds.), *The handbook of eyewitness psychology, Vol I: Memory for events* (pp. 53–80). Mahwah, NJ: Lawrence Erlbaum Associates Publishers.

Fisher, R. P., & York, R. M. (2009). Enhancing eyewitness memory with the cognitive interview. In M. St-Yves and M. Tanguay (Eds.), *The psychology of criminal investigations: The search for the truth* (pp. 41–62). Toronto: Carswell.

Gabbert, F., Hope, L., & Fisher, R. P. (2009). Protecting eyewitness evidence: Examining the efficacy of a self-administered interview tool. *Law and Human Behavior, 33*(4), 298–307.

Geiselman, R. E., & Callot, R. (1990). Reverse versus forward recall of script-based texts. *Applied Cognitive Psychology, 4,* 141–144.

Geiselman, R. E., & Fisher, R. P. (1997). Ten years of cognitive interviewing. In D. G. Payne and R. G. Conrad (Eds.), *A synthesis of basic and applied approaches to human memory* (pp. 291–310). Hillsdale, NJ: Erlbaum.

Geiselman, R. E., Fisher, R. P., MacKinnon, D. P., & Holland, H. L. (1985). Eyewitness memory enhancement in the police interview: Cognitive retrieval mnemonics versus hypnosis. *Journal of Applied Psychology, 70*(2), 401–412.

George, R., & Clifford, B. (1992). Making the most of witnesses. *Policing, 8,* 185–198.

Gilbert, J. A. E., & Fisher, R. P. (2006). The effects of varied retrieval cues on reminiscence in eyewitness memory. *Applied Cognitive Psychology, 20,* 723–739.

Goldsmith, M., Koriat, A., & Weinberg-Eliezer, A. (2002). Strategic regulation of grain size memory reporting. *Journal of Experimental Psychology: General, 131,* 73–95.

Gudjonsson, G. H. (1992). The psychology of interrogations, confessions and testimony. Oxford: John Wiley & Sons.

Gudjonsson, G. H. (2008). *The psychology of interrogations and confessions: A handbook.* Chichester, UK: John Wiley & Sons, Ltd.

Griffiths, A., & Milne, R. (2005). Will it all end in tiers? Police interviews with suspects in Britain. In T. Williamson. (Ed.), *Investigative interviewing: Rights, research, regulation* (pp. 167–189). Cullompton: Willan Publishing.

Hershkowitz, I. (2009). Socioemotional factors in child abuse investigations. *Child Maltreatment, 14*(2), 172–181.

Hershkowitz, I., Orbach, Y., Lamb, M. E., Sternberg, K. J., & Horowitz, D. (2001). The effects of mental context reinstatement on children's accounts of sexual abuse. *Applied Cognitive Psychology, 15,* 235–248.

Hershkowitz, I., Orbach, Y., Lamb, M. E., Sternberg, K. J., & Horowitz, D. (2006). Dynamics of forensic interviews with suspected abuse victims who do not disclose abuse. *Child Abuse & Neglect, 30,* 753–769.

Hirn, D. E., Fisher, R. P., & Carol, R. N. (2012). Use of a hybrid interview method to retrieve memories created during decision. Paper presented at the meeting of the American Psychology-Law Society, San Juan, Puerto Rico.

Holliday, R. E., Brainerd, C. J., Reyna, V. F., & Humphries, J. E. (2009). The cognitive interview: Research and practice across the lifespan. In R. E. Holliday, C. J. Brainerd, V. F. Reyna, and J. E. Humphries (Eds.), *Handbook of psychology of investigative interviewing: Current developments and future directions* (pp. 137–160). Chichester, UK: Wiley-Blackwell.

Home Office (2002). *Achieving best evidence in criminal proceedings: Guidance for vulnerable and intimidated witnesses, including children.* London, Home Office.

Hope, L., Gabbert, F., & Fisher, R. P. (2011). From laboratory to the street: Capturing witness memory using the self-administered interview. *Legal and Criminological Psychology, 16,* 211–226.

Howie, P., Kulasuriya, N. K., Nash, L., & Marsh, A. (2009). Inconsistencies in children's recall of witnessed events: The role of age, question format and perceived reason for question repetition. *Legal and Criminological Psychology, 14*(2), 311–329.

Howie, P., Nash, L., Kurukulasuiya, N., & Bowman, A. (2012). Children's event reports: Factors affecting responses to repeated questions in vignette scenarios and event recall interviews. *British Journal of Developmental Psychology, 30*(4), 550–568.

Imhoff, M. C., & Baker-Ward, L. (1999). Preschoolers' suggestibility: Effects of developmentally appropriate language and interviewer supportiveness. *Journal of Applied Developmental Psychology, 20,* 407–429.

Jonker, F., & Jonker-Bakker, I. (1991). Experiences with ritualist child sexual abuse: A case study from The Netherlands. *International Journal on Child Abuse and Neglect, 15* (3), 191–196.

Kaempf, G. L., Wolf, S., Thordsen, M. L., & Klein, G. (1992). Decision making in the AEGIS combat information center (Tech. Report Contract N66001-90-C-6023, Naval Command, Control, and Ocean Surveillance Center). Fairborn, OH: Klein Associates, Inc.

Kahneman, D. (1973). *Attention and effort.* Englewood Cliffs, NJ: Prentice-Hall.

Köhnken, G. (1995). *Wissenschaftliches Gutachten zur Glaubwürdigkeitsbeurteilung an das Landgericht Münster.* Unpublished manuscript.

Köhnken, G., Milne, R., Memon, A., & Bull, R. (1999). The cognitive interview: A meta-analysis. *Psychology, Crime and Law, 5,* 3–28.

Koriat, A., & Goldsmith, M. (1996). Monitoring and control processes in the strategic regulation of memory accuracy. *Psychological Review, 103*(3), 490–517.

Lamb, M. E., Hershkowitz, I., Orbach, Y., & Esplin, P. W. (2008). *Tell me what happened: Structured investigative interviews of child victims and witnesses.* Chichester, UK: Wiley.

Lamb, M. E., La Rooy, D. J., Malloy, L. C., & Katz, C. (2011). *Children's testimony: A handbook of psychological research and forensic practice.* Chichester, UK: John Wiley & Sons.

Lamb, M. E., Orbach, Y., Hershkowitz, I., Esplin, P. W., & Horowitz, D. (2007). Structured forensic interview protocols improve the quality and informativeness of investigative interviews with children: A review of research using the NICHD investigative interview protocol. *Child Abuse and Neglect, 31,* 1201–1231.

Leibowitz, H. W., Guzy, L. T., Peterson, E., & Blake, P. T. (1993). Quantitative perceptual estimates: Verbal versus nonverbal retrieval techniques. *Perception, 22*(9), 1051–1060.

Loftus, E. F. (1975). Leading questions and the eyewitness report. *Cognitive Psychology, 7,* 560–572.

London, K., Bruck, M., Ceci, S. J., & Shuman, D. W. (2005). Disclosure of child sexual abuse: What does the research tell us about the ways that children tell? *Psychology, Public Policy, and the Law, 11,* 194–226.

London, K., Bruck, M., Ceci, S. J., & Shuman, D.W. (2007). Disclosure of child sexual abuse: A review of the contemporary empirical literature. In M. E. Pipe, M. E. Lamb, Y. Orbach, and A. C. Cederborg (Eds.), *Child sexual abuse: disclosure, delay and denial* (pp. 11–40). Mahwah, NJ: Erlbaum.

Lyon, T. D., Malloy, L. C., Quas, J. A., & Talwar, V. A. (2008). Coaching, truth induction, and young maltreated children's false allegations and false denials. *Child Development, 79,* 914–929.

Maras, K. L., & Bowler, D. M. (2010). The cognitive interview for eyewitnesses with autism spectrum disorder. *Journal of Autism and Developmental Disorders, 40,* 1350–1360.

McBrien, C. M., & Dagenbach, D. (1998). The contributions of source misattributions, acquiescence, and response bias to children's false memories. *The American Journal of Psychology, 111*(4), 509–528.

Memon, A., Meissner, C. A., & Fraser, J. (2010). The cognitive interview: A meta-analytic review and study space analysis of the past 25 years. *Psychology, Public Policy, and Law, 16*(4), 340–372.

Memon, A., & Stevenage, S.V. (1996). Interviewing witnesses: What works and what doesn't? PSYCOLOQUY 7(6) witness-memory.1.memon.

Memon, A., & Vartoukian, R. (1996). The effects of repeated questioning on young children's eyewitness testimony. *British Journal of Psychology, 87*(3), 403–415.

Memon, A., Wark, L., Bull, R., & Köhnken, G. (1997). Isolating the effects of the cognitive interview techniques. *British Journal of Psychology, 88*(2), 179–197.

Milne, R., & Bull, R. (2002). Back to basics: A componential analysis of the original cognitive interview mnemonics with three age groups. *Applied Cognitive Psychology, 16*(7), 743–753.

Moston, S., & Engelberg, T. (1992). The effects of social support on children's eyewitness testimony. *Applied Cognitive Psychology, 6*(1), 61–75.

Nathan, D., & Snedeker, M. (1995). *Satan's silence: Ritual abuse and the making of a modern American witch hunt.* New York: HarperCollins Publishers.

Oeberst, A. (2012). If anything else comes to mind … better keep it to yourself? Delayed recall is discrediting – unjustifiably. *Law and Human Behavior, 36*(4), 266–274.

Orbach, Y., Hershkowitz, I., Lamb, M. E., Sternberg, K. J., Esplin, P. W., & Horowitz, D. (2000). Assessing the value of structured protocols for forensic interviews of alleged child abuse victims. *Child Abuse and Neglect, 24,* 733–752.

Oxburgh, G. E., Walsh, D., & Milne, B. (2011). The importance of applied research in investigative interviews: A real-life perspective. *Journal of Investigative Psychology and Offender Profiling, 8*(2), 105–109.

Palmiotto, M. (Ed.) (2003). *Policing and training issues.* Upper Saddle River, NJ: Prentice Hall.

Perfect, T. J., Wagstaff, G. F., Moore, D., Andrews, B., Cleveland, V., Newcombe, S., et al. (2008). How can we help witnesses to remember more? It's an (eyes) open and shut case. *Law and Human Behavior, 32*(4), 314–324.

Pipe, M.-E., Orbach, Y., Lamb, M., Abbott, C. B., & Stewart, H. (2008). Do best practice interviews with child abuse victims influence case processing? Retrieved November 27, 2000, from National Criminal Justice Reference Service: www.ncjrs.gov/pdffiles1/nij/grants/224524.pdf

Pipe, M. E., & Salmon, K. (2009). Dolls, drawings, body diagrams and other props: A role in investigative interviews. In K. Kuehnle and M. Connell (Eds.), *Critical issues in child sexual abuse assessment* (pp. 365–395). Hoboken, NJ: John Wiley & Sons, Inc.

Poole, D. A., Bruck, M., & Pipe, M. (2011). Forensic interviewing aids: Do props help children answer questions about touching? *Current Directions in Psychological Science, 20*(1), 11–15.

Poole, D. A., & Dickinson, J. J. (2011). Evidence supporting restrictions on uses of body diagrams in forensic interviews. *Child Abuse & Neglect, 35*(9), 659–669.

Poole D.A., & Lamb M. E. (1998). *Investigative interviews of children: A guide for helping professionals.* Washington, DC: American Psychological Association.

Poole, D. A., & White, L. T. (1991). Effects of question repetition on the eyewitness testimony of children and adults. *Developmental Psychology, 27,* 975–986.

Powell, M. B., Fisher, R. P., & Wright, R. (2005). Investigative interviewing. In N. Brewer and K. Williams (Eds.), *Psychology and Law: An empirical perspective* (pp. 11–42). New York: Guilford.

Price, H. L., Roberts, K. P., Collins, A. (2013). The quality of children's allegations of abuse in investigative interviews pertaining to practice narratives. *Journal of Applied Research in Memory and Cognition, 2,* 1–6.

Quas, J. A., Wallin, A. R., Papini, S., Lench, H., & Scullin, M. H. (2005). Suggestibilty, social support, and memory for a novel experience in young children. *Journal of Experimental Child Psychology, 91,* 315–341.

Salmon, K., Pipe, M-E., Malloy, A., & Mackay, K. (2012). Do non-verbal aids increase the effectiveness of "best practice" verbal interview techniques? An experimental study. *Applied Cognitive Psychology, 26,* 370–380.

Saywitz, K. J., Goodman, G. S., Nicholas, E., & Moan, S. F. (1991). Children's memories of a physical examination involving genital touch: Implications for reports of child sexual abuse. *Journal of Consulting and Clinical Psychology, 59*(5), 682–691.

Saywitz, K., & Snyder, L. (1996). Narrative elaboration: Test of a new procedure for interviewing children. *Journal of Counseling and Clinical Psychology, 64,* 1347–1357.

Schreiber Compo, N., Hyman Gregory, A. R., & Fisher, R. P. (2012). Interviewing behaviors in police investigators: A field study of a current U.S. sample. *Psychology, Crime and Law, 18*(3–4), 359–375.

Shepherd, E. (1988). Developing interview skills. In P. Southgate (Ed.), *New directions in police training* (pp. 170–188). London: HMSO.

Smith, S. M., & Vela, E. (2001). Environmental context-dependent memory: A review and meta-analysis. *Psychonomic Bulletin & Review, 8*(2), 203–220.

Snook, B., & Keating, K. (2011). A field study of adult witness interviewing practices in a Canadian police organization. *Legal and Criminological Psychology, 16,* 160–172.

Sternberg, K. J., Lamb, M. E., Orbach, Y., Esplin, P. W., & Mitchell, S. (2001). Use of a structured investigative protocol enhances young children's responses to free-recall prompts in the course of forensic interviews. *Journal of Applied Psychology, 86,* 997–1005.

Steverson, L. A. (2008). *Policing in America: A reference handbook.* Santa Barbara, CA: ABCCLIO.

Talwar, V., Lee, K., Bala, N., & Lindsay, R. C. L. (2002). Children's conceptual knowledge of lying and its relation to their actual behavior: Implications for court competence evaluations. *Law and Human Behavior, 26,* 395–415.

Talwar, V., Lee, K., Bala, N., & Lindsay, R. C. L. (2004). Children's lie-telling to conceal a parent's transgression: Legal implications. *Law and Human Behavior, 28,* 411–435.

Teoh, Y. S., & Lamb, M. E. (2010). Preparing children for investigative interviews: Rapport-building, instruction, and evaluation. *Applied Developmental Science, 14,* 154–163.

Thierry, K. L., Lamb, M. E., Orbach, Y., & Pipe, M. (2005). Developmental differences in the function and use of anatomical dolls during interviews with alleged sexual abuse victims. *Journal of Consulting and Clinical Psychology, 73*(6), 1125–1134.

Tulving, E., & Thomson, D. M. (1973). Encoding specificity and retrieval processes in episodic memory. *Psychological Review, 80,* 352–373.

Vredeveldt, A., Hitch, G. J., & Baddeley, A. D. (2011). Eye-closure helps memory by reducing cognitive load and enhancing visualisation. *Memory & Cognition, 39*(7), 1253–1263.

Walters, S., Holmes, L., Bauer, G., & Vieth, V. (2003). *Finding words: Half a nation by 2010: Interviewing children and preparing for court.* Alexandria, VA: National Center for Prosecution of Child Abuse.

Yuille, J. C., Hunter, R., Joffe, R., & Zaparniuk, J. (1993). Interviewing children in sexual abuse cases. In G. S. Goodman and B. L. Bottoms (Eds.), *Child victims, child witnesses: Understanding and improving testimony* (pp. 95–115). New York: Guilford Press.

Yuille, J. C., Marxsen, D., & Cooper, B. (1999). Training investigative interviewers: Adherence to the spirit, as well as the letter. *International Journal of Law and Psychiatry, 22*(3–4), 323–336.

32

Estimating the Reliability of Eyewitness Identification

Tim Valentine

Around 10 o'clock at night on 7 March 2002 Tracy McAlroy was with her younger sister in the kitchen of her new house about 5 miles from Glasgow, Scotland. Tracy's husband, Justin McAlroy, was expected home soon. Suddenly, they heard three or four loud bangs outside. Both women ran to the front door. Tracy looked through the windows at the top of the door. She saw a man at the top of her driveway, running away. It was dark but he passed under a street light. The fleeing man had been waiting for Justin to return home. As Justin got out of the car he was shot several times and later died of his injuries. Within 30 minutes of the murder Tracy gave a statement to the police. She described the gunman as aged in his late twenties or early thirties, medium build, 5' 10" tall, wearing a blue or green hooded bomber jacket with the hood up. His nose and mouth were covered. Her statement ended by saying: "I cannot identify the man who ran off."

In a court, almost two years later, Tracy McAlroy identified William Gage as the gunman. Although she accepted that she was not 100 per cent sure of her identification, she said "I'll never forget the eyes". Other witnesses saw the gunman getting into a white car. One witness, who saw the gunman without his hood and face-covering, described

a face shape and hair. His description did not match William Gage. The defendant was linked by DNA evidence to clothing found in a white car abandoned that evening, about 15 minutes' drive from the crime scene. Apart from its colour and Tracy McAlroy's identification of the clothing, nothing else directly linked that car to the crime scene. The clothing did not closely resemble the description of the killer's clothing given by several witnesses, including Tracy McAlroy. One witness said the car was a Volvo. The car recovered was a Saab. Despite these inconsistencies in the evidence, William Gage was convicted and sentenced to life imprisonment. The first appeal was unsuccessful, but eight years later the Scottish Criminal Cases Review Commission referred the case back to the Court of Appeal on the grounds that the judge misdirected the jury on the identification evidence. The Appeal Court ruled that expert testimony on eyewitness identification evidence was inadmissible (Gage v. HMA, 2011). The appeal was rejected (Gage v. HMA, 2012).

William Gage's case raises a number of questions about how the circumstances of the crime affect the accuracy of eyewitness testimony. Was the reliability of Tracy McAlroy's identification affected by the distance, lighting and her opportunity to view the gunman?

Was her recollection affected by the emotional distress of her husband's murder? Factors such as these are known as *estimator* variables, and their effect on eyewitness identification forms the focus of this chapter. The effect of estimator variables on witnesses' verbal recall is the subject of a separate chapter in this volume (Granhag, Ask, & Giolla, Chapter 30). The Gage case also raises some issues about the conduct of the police investigation, for example the decision to rely on an identification of the accused in the courtroom. Factors that are under the control of the criminal justice system are known as *system* variables and their effect on eyewitness identification and recall are the subject of separate chapters by Gronlund and Carlson (Chapter 33, this volume) and Fisher, Schreiber Compo, Rivard and Hirn (Chapter 31, this volume) respectively.

To fully understand the role of estimator variables on eyewitness identification it is necessary to consider evidence from experimental laboratory studies; field studies carried out in more realistic settings relevant to the typical situation an eyewitness may face; and analyses of archival data from real cases. Laboratory studies allow careful control to isolate the effect of individual variables. Field studies show effects that persist in an everyday setting. Archival data allow the performance of real eyewitnesses to be studied in the wide range of circumstances found in real crimes. By combining these approaches, behaviour of real eyewitnesses can be interpreted using theoretical models of human memory tested in both the laboratory and the field. A sound theoretical understanding can allow the performance of eyewitnesses under various conditions to be predicted and interpreted appropriately.

THE RANGE OF ESTIMATOR VARIABLES

The reliability of eyewitness identification can be affected by the characteristics of the crime event (e.g., the time available to view the culprit); the characteristics of the perpetrator (e.g., use of a disguise); the characteristics of the witness (e.g., age), and characteristics of the identification procedure (e.g., the delay before the identification procedure). Research on variables within each of these groups is reviewed below. The selection of variables is guided by the availability of recent research and the significance of the variable's influence on identification.

CRIME EVENT CHARACTERISTICS

Time to view

In laboratory studies of face recognition participants are asked to distinguish photographs of many faces presented once, a few minutes previously, from pictures of faces not seen before. Usually the same photographs of the target faces are presented again at test, making the task one of picture recognition rather than of recognising faces across the changes of view, pose and appearance that occur in everyday life. Generally, laboratory studies show that faces presented for a longer duration are better recognised than faces presented briefly. A meta-analysis of eight studies found that faces seen for longer were more likely to be recognised, but the time viewed did not affect the number of mistaken identifications made (Shapiro & Penrod, 1986). The mean time to view faces in the studies analysed was 12 seconds with a standard deviation of 19 seconds. However there are a few exceptions in which longer exposure durations led to more mistaken identifications (e.g., Read, Vokey, & Hammersley, 1990).

There have been few studies that have systematically investigated the time to view the culprit using an eyewitness paradigm, in which a perpetrator is seen in a staged event and subsequently the witness is asked to identify the perpetrator, if present, from a lineup. Read (1995) found that shop sales staff who interacted with an experimenter for 4 to 12 minutes were more likely to choose from a lineup than participants who interacted for 30–60 seconds. Witnesses who interacted for longer made more correct identifications when the shopkeeper was present in the lineup, but made more mistaken identification from target-absent lineups. Thus, longer exposure increased the willingness of the witness to make an identification. Memon, Hope and Bull (2003) found that witnesses who viewed the face of a target person in a video for 45 seconds were more likely to recognise the face than witnesses who saw the face for only 12 seconds. The witnesses who saw the perpetrator for 45 seconds made more correct identifications from target-present lineups and, contrary to Read (1995), fewer mistaken identifications from target-absent lineups. Witnesses and victims of real crimes were more likely to identify the police suspect (who is not necessarily the perpetrator in all cases) from a live lineup if they reported seeing the perpetrator for more than a minute (Valentine, Pickering, & Darling, 2003). In summary, evidence from experimental and archival studies generally supports the contention that faces seen in a fleeting glance are less likely to be identified than faces seen for an extended time. However, in some circumstances, a longer viewing time can lead to more mistaken identifications from target-absent lineups.

Distance and lighting

Distance affects the ability of a witness to see sufficient detail of a perpetrator's face to be able to recognise the face later. Over what distance can an unfamiliar face be seen sufficiently clearly to be recognisable? There are too important issues to note. First, the clarity of the view depends on the available lighting as well as distance. Under good outdoor lighting a face can be seen adequately to be identified at a greater distance than under low levels of lighting (Wagenaar & Van der Schrier, 1996). Second, the ability to identify

a face declines in an approximately linear function with the distance from which it was viewed. There is no sudden drop-off in performance, and therefore no critical minimum distance for viewing (Lindsay, Semmler, Weber, Brewer, & Lindsay, 2008). The available evidence shows that under good lighting identification of faces starts to decline when viewed from about 10 metres, and is significantly reduced for faces viewed from 15 metres or more (Lindsay et al., 2008; Loftus & Harley, 2005; Wagenaar & Van der Schrier, 1996). These distances will be shorter under anything less than ideal lighting conditions. Recognition of familiar faces (e.g., celebrities) is affected in the same way (De Jong, Wagenaar, Wolters, & Verstijnen, 2005), as would be expected if the adequacy of face perception for recognition is the limiting factor (Loftus & Harley, 2005).

Weapon focus

Weapon focus refers to a phenomenon in which the attention of a witness is captured by a weapon (e.g., when threatened by a perpetrator wielding a knife or a gun). Under these circumstances there is believed to be a narrowing of attention to the central details and, therefore, less attention paid to peripheral details. As a result, eyewitnesses are very capable of describing the knife or gun, but may be less able to describe or recognise the perpetrator. The reliability of the weapon focus effect has become established in laboratory studies that compare eyewitness memory for a "weapon" condition with a "no weapon" or "neutral" object condition. For example, in one of the first experiments on weapon focus, Loftus, Loftus, and Messo (1987) compared memory for a perpetrator in a fast food outlet who produced a gun or a cheque book when he approached the cashier. Steblay (1992) reported a systematic analysis of 19 tests of the hypothesis and found a reliable but small effect on identification accuracy of .13 (using a weighted mean effect size for proportions recommended by Cohen, 1977) and a moderate effect size ($d = .55$) for description accuracy. Witnesses were less accurate in describing and identifying a perpetrator when a weapon was present.

A weapon may capture a witness' attention because of the threat it poses or because it is unexpected in the context. Pickel (1998) found that the ability to describe a target person was affected by the unusualness of the object held but not the threat posed. There was no effect of either unusualness or threat on the accuracy of identifying the target in a photograph lineup. Pickel (1999) manipulated the context of an event to show that an unexpected object captures attention resulting in impaired description (but not recognition) of a target person. A gun did not produce a weapon focus effect in the context of a shooting range in which participants might expect to see a gun, and it would pose little threat in this context. Similarly an object that was inconsistent with a gender role stereotype produced a greater reduction in witness description accuracy than an object consistent with the target person's gender (Pickel, 2009). Hope and Wright (2007) argued that both the novelty (unusualness) and perceived threat of an object capture the attention of witnesses and therefore contribute to the weapon focus effect. However, Pickel, Ross, and Truelove (2006) showed that the capture of attention is not automatic because it can be consciously controlled. Participants forewarned not to attend to the weapon were protected against the weapon focus effect.

Field or archival studies of real criminal cases in both the UK and the United States have investigated whether the use of a weapon during a crime reduces the likelihood that the police suspect will be identified from a lineup. None of these studies found an effect of weapon focus (Behrman & Davey, 2001; Pike, Brace, & Kyman, 2002; Tollestrup, Turtle, & Yuille, 1994; Valentine et al., 2003). This result is perhaps unsurprising because the cases involved in these studies included a wide range of circumstances and the weapon focus effect on identification

has been found to be small in laboratory studies (Steblay, 1992). Studies published since Steblay's meta-analysis have generally not found a reliable weapon focus effect on identification.

Witness characteristics

Stress
One night in 1984 a man broke into Jennifer Thompson's apartment and raped her. She said that during her ordeal she "studied every single detail of the rapist's face". Later that day she recognised the man from a photograph she was shown by the police. She said: " I knew this was the man. I was completely confident. I was sure." Jennifer Thompson's identification of Ronald Cotton was proved to be mistaken by new DNA evidence obtained after Ronald Cotton had served 11 years in prison for a crime he did not commit. Did the extreme stress of the attack that Jennifer Thompson endured affect her ability to recognise her attacker?

The effect of stress is difficult to study. Extreme stress cannot be induced in experimental participants due to ethical considerations. For this reason stress in laboratory studies has been rather mild, and some results supported the contention that stress can enhance memory (Christianson, 1992). In contrast, Catastrophe Theory predicts that heightened stress can cause a catastrophic failure of memory (Deffenbacher, Borstein, Penrod, & McGorty, 2004). Heightened stress is defined as sufficient to induce a physiological response, for example increased heart rate, muscle tension or respiration rate. In a meta-analysis of the literature, Deffenbacher et al. (2004) found that high stress impaired the ability to identify a target person from a lineup. There was no effect of stress on mistaken identifications made from a lineup when the target person was not present.

Two field studies published since Deffenbacher et al.'s (2004) meta-analysis add further support to the view that high stress impairs face identification. Morgan et al. (2004) used a counter-balanced experimental design to examine soldiers' ability to recognise an interrogator after spending 12 hours in a mock prisoner of war camp. Each soldier underwent two interrogations: a high stress interrogation involving physical confrontation, and a low stress interrogation. When present in the lineup, the soldiers more often correctly identified the low-stress interrogator (67 per cent) than the high-stress interrogator (29 per cent). There was no significant difference in the number of mistaken identifications when an interrogator was not present in a lineup.

Valentine and Mesout (2009) tested eyewitness identification of an actor who was encountered in the dark, disorienting environment of the Horror Labyrinth of the London Dungeon. A pilot study established that the horror labyrinth was sufficiently stressful to raise participants' heart rate. Furthermore, the increase in heart rate was highly correlated with a self-report questionnaire measure of anxiety used in the main study. Seventy-five per cent of visitors who experienced less anxiety in the labyrinth were able to identify the actor from a photograph lineup. In contrast only 18 per cent of visitors who reported feeling more anxious whilst in the labyrinth identified the actor.

A third approach, in addition to laboratory and field studies, has been to analyse the effect of stress or emotional impact on memory for real crimes (Christianson & Hubinette, 1993; Odinot, Wolters, & Van Koppen, 2009; Woolnough & McCleod, 2001; Yuille & Cutshall, 1986). Multiple witnesses were interviewed and their testimonies compared to data from police reports and in some cases CCTV imagery. Yuille and Cutshall (1986) interviewed witnesses to a shooting. Comparison with police interviews showed that their reports were highly consistent over a long period of time. Self-report of stress from the witnesses suggested that stress did not affect their memory. Similar results were reported by Christianson and Hubinette (1993), who found no relationship between the number of details reported by witnesses of a bank robbery and self-reported stress. Woolnough and MacLeod (2001) compared CCTV imagery of incidents with police statements given by victims and bystanders. Witnesses' recall was highly accurate, although in some aspects they were incomplete. Woolnough and MacLeod (2001) found that bystanders (but not victims) recalled more action details in the incidents that were rated as higher in emotional impact. Odinot, Wolters, and van Koppen (2009) interviewed witnesses to an armed robbery approximately three months after the event. Accuracy was checked against CCTV imagery. As found in previous studies, witnesses' recall was highly consistent with police statements made previously. Witnesses were split into two groups according to the level of emotional impact they self-reported. The groups did not differ in the amount recalled but those reporting more emotional impact were more accurate.

Analyses of the recall of witnesses and victims of real crimes offer a fascinating opportunity to study memory in the real world. Generally these studies have shown either no effect or a small advantage in the completeness or accuracy of witnesses who report, or are judged to have experienced, high emotional impact of the crime. However, there are many shortcomings and confounding factors in these archival studies. The self-report of emotional impact is not recorded at the time of the crime but up to many months later. Witnesses' ratings may be influenced by a long-term impact that may be associated with thinking or talking about the event. Witnesses who felt most threatened by the events may have been closer or paying more attention to the events. Witnesses who reported low emotional impact may not have realised they were witnessing a crime until later. Low statistical power may contribute to null results.

In summary, the results from studies of real crime are difficult to interpret, but they appear to suggest either little impact or a positive impact of emotional stress on the accuracy of eyewitness testimony. In contrast, the field studies discussed above (Morgan et al., 2004: Valentine & Mesout, 2009) used accuracy of selecting the perpetrator from a lineup as a dependent variable rather than recall of the events. There is good evidence from well-controlled field studies and from laboratory studies that a threat that induced sufficiently heightened stress to provoke a physiological response impaired eyewitness identification of the perpetrator.

Alcohol intoxication

Many violent crimes are committed when the perpetrator and/or potential witnesses are intoxicated. In 50 per cent of all violent crimes in Britain during 2009–10 the victim believed the offender was under the influence of alcohol (Flatley, Kershaw, Smith, Chaplin, & Moon, 2010). Violent crime committed by a stranger is the category of crime in which eyewitness identification evidence is most likely to be disputed. However, few studies have examined the effect of alcohol on eyewitness identification. Yuille and Tollestrup (1990) found that alcohol reduced the number of correct details, and increased the number of incorrect details, recalled by witnesses of a live event. However, there was no effect of alcohol on identification accuracy from target-present or target-absent photograph lineups. Read, Yuille, and Tollestrup (1992) examined the effect of alcohol on the recollections of participants in a staged robbery. In one experiment alcohol impaired the amount of information recalled but did not affect identification accuracy from either target-present or target-absent photograph lineups. In a second experiment there was no effect of alcohol on the accuracy of recalled information. But alcohol did reduce identification accuracy from target-present photograph lineups only for participants in a low arousal condition.

Participants in the Yuille and Tollestrup (1990) and Read et al. (1992) studies consumed alcohol prior to witnessing or participating in a staged event. Their recall and recognition was assessed one week later when the participants were sober. Dysart, Lindsay, MacDonald, and Wicke (2002) examined the situation in which an intoxicated witness identified a suspect at the scene of the crime when still intoxicated. Dysart et al. argued that in these circumstances it is likely that the witness would participate in a showup. In a showup the witness is shown a single person and asked whether this person is the perpetrator. Participants drinking in a bar were recruited and subsequently their recognition of the person who recruited them a few minutes earlier was tested. Alcohol did not affect the accuracy of identifying the recruiter when their picture was presented in a showup. However, participants who had drunk alcohol were more likely than sober participants to make a mistaken identification of an innocent suspect seen in a showup. Using a similar procedure, Valentine, Cullasy, Fantham, and Davis (2012) found that participants who had consumed alcohol made fewer correct identifications from a target-present lineup (a small effect size, $\varphi = .21$), and more mistaken identifications from target-absent lineups (a large effect size, $\varphi = .55$). The confidence of sober witnesses was higher for correct identifications than for inaccurate identifications. However, intoxicated witnesses showed the same level of high confidence for their correct and incorrect identifications.

In summary, there is very little evidence that alcohol intoxication impairs eyewitness identification made a week after the event when the witness is sober, but there is evidence that alcohol impairs recall of the event a week later. If an identification is made by an intoxicated witness, an innocent suspect is at greater risk of mistaken identification.

Witness age: older adults

Laboratory studies of face recognition have shown that age affects face recognition accuracy. Older people are less likely to correctly identify a face they have seen before (e.g., Bartlett & Fulton, 1991). Identification accuracy decreases from about 50 years of age (O'Rourke, Penrod, & Cutler, 1989). Older witnesses make more mistaken

identifications as well as fewer correct identifications (Searcy, Bartlett, & Memon, 1999,
2000; Searcy, Bartlett, Memon, & Swanson,
2001). See Bartlett (Chapter 36, this volume)
for a comprehensive review of the effect of
age on eyewitness memory. It is important to
note that analysis of the outcome of identification attempts from live lineups organised
by the British police found that witness under
30 were more likely to identify the police
suspect than were older witnesses (Pike et al.,
2002; Valentine et al., 2003). In summary a
decline in eyewitness identification accuracy
in older adults is a robust finding from laboratory and field studies.

Witness age: children

Laboratory studies of face recognition show
that children of up to 12–13 years of age are
less accurate than adults in their ability to indicate which faces from a list have been seen a
few minutes previously. In a meta-analysis of
face recognition and eyewitness identification
studies, Shapiro and Penrod (1986) found a
significant effect of age. Children were less
likely than adults to identify faces correctly as
having been seen before ($d = 1.10$), but more
likely to mistakenly indicate that a new face
was presented previously ($d = 0.66$).

Pozzulo and Lindsay (1998) reported a
meta-analysis of eyewitness studies, in which
children under five years old were less likely
than adults to correctly identify the target
person when present in a lineup. But older
children were as likely to correctly identify the
target from a lineup. When the target person
was not in the lineup, children of 4–13 years
were more likely than adults to make a mistaken identification. There were rather few
studies available for Pozzulo and Lindsay's
(1998) meta-analysis. Although statistically
significant, the effects were mostly rather
slight and should be interpreted with caution.

The tendency of young children to select
from a target-absent lineup has been replicated
in several studies since (e.g., Keast, Brewer,
& Wells, 2007). Zajac and Karageorge (2009)
and Karageorge and Zajac (2011) found that
including a wildcard, which depicts a silhouette

with a question mark, serves to remind children aged 5–11 years that making no identification may be the correct answer, and
substantially reduced the number of mistaken
identifications children made from target-
absent lineups. Principe, Follmer Greenhoot,
and Ceci (Chapter 35, this volume) provide a
comprehensive review of children's eyewitnesses recall, but do not address their lineup
identification performance.

Ethnicity

Witnesses tend to be less accurate in recognising people of an ethnic origin different from their own (Meissner & Brigham,
2001). The effect is well established in
laboratory-based studies. In full cross-over
designs, participants of both ethnicities typically show greater proficiency in recognising
faces of their own ethnicity (e.g., Chiroro &
Valentine, 1995; Valentine & Endo, 1992).
The effect of cross-ethnicity identification
is of a moderate size and accounts for about
15 per cent of the variance in face recognition performance (Meissner & Brigham,
2001). Observers are more likely to recognise a previously seen face of their own ethnicity and less likely to mistakenly identify
a new face of their own ethnicity. Poorer
performance in cross-ethnicity identification
has also been established in field studies
using lineup methods to test performance
(e.g., Wright, Boyd, & Tredoux, 2001 used
a cross-over design). The effect of ethnicity
depends on the experience of the witness.
Wright, Boyd, and Tredoux (2003) found an
association between self-rated contact with
the other ethnic group and cross-ethnicity
recognition. Chiroro and Valentine (1995)
found that experience of people of a different ethnic origin in daily life may reduce
or eliminate any effect of ethnicity, but not
necessarily so. The quality of the social
contact appears to be an important mediating
factor. This conclusion was supported using
an experimental, laboratory manipulation of
the quality of experience. Tanaka and Pierce
(2009) found that learning to individuate
photographs of faces of another ethnicity

produced better recognition of the faces than did an equivalent amount of practice categorising the faces according to their ethnicity. The effect of ethnicity on face recognition can be interpreted within the Face-Space framework, in which individual faces are recognised by their distinctive qualities in relation to the population of faces experienced in one's lifetime (Valentine, 1991; Valentine & Endo, 1992).

Archival studies of police identification procedures have shown mixed results on the effect of ethnicity. In the United States, Behrman and Davey (2001) found that more police suspects of the same ethnicity as the witness were identified than when the suspect's and witness' ethnicity differed. In the UK, Horry, Memon, Wright, and Milne (2012), Pike et al. (2002) and Valentine et al. (2003) found no difference in the rate of identification of police suspects of the same ethnicity as the witness and of a different ethnicity from the witness.

Perpetrator characteristics

Disguise

The courts recognise that a perpetrator who wears a disguise (e.g., hat, sunglasses, mask) is less likely to be recognised by a witness than a culprit who does not. Laboratory research has shown an effect of disguise on face recognition (Cutler, Penrod, O'Rourke, & Martens, 1986; Patterson & Baddeley, 1977). Patterson and Baddeley (1977) found that effects of wearing a wig and a false beard were substantial. Wearing a wig and a beard led to fewer people recognising the face than when either disguise alone was worn. Disguise also affects matching of faces when there is no memory component. Davis and Valentine (2009) found an effect of disguise (sunglasses or hat) on the accuracy of matching a photograph of a face to a perpetrator in a video. As a face becomes familiar through repeated exposure, we learn to recognise better the internal features (eyes, nose, mouth) and perhaps their configuration. For faces

seen once the external features are relatively more important (Ellis, Shepherd, & Davies, 1979). Therefore disguises that occlude the external features (hairstyle, face shape) are likely to be particularly effective in disrupting recognition by a witness to whom the culprit is unknown. Davies and Flin (1984) showed that a stocking mask is an effective disguise mainly because it disguises the external features of the face. Recognition was improved if the faces were also masked at test, suggesting that the overlap of cues available during encoding and test is important, as predicted by the encoding specificity principle (Tulving & Thompson, 1973).

Facial distinctiveness and distinguishing marks

Distinctiveness is an important variable in laboratory studies of face recognition, and has played a central role in the Face-Space model of face processing (e.g., Valentine, 1991, 2001; Wenger & Townsend, 2001). Laboratory research has shown that faces rated as distinctive or unusual in appearance are more likely to be recognised and less likely to be mistakenly recognised than are faces rated as typical in appearance (Valentine, 1991). It is widely recognised that a suspect should not stand out in a lineup compared with the foils (e.g., Technical Working Group for Eyewitness Evidence, 1999). Methods to select appropriate foils and to measure the fairness of lineups have been developed (see Gronlund & Carlson, Chapter 33, this volume). However, the effect of facial distinctiveness has been neglected in the context of eyewitness identification research. In experiments designed to investigate the advantage of sequential presentation (see Gronlund & Carlson, Chapter 33, this volume), fewer mistaken identifications were made to target-absent lineups when the target face was distinctive (Carlson, 2011; Carlson & Gronlund, 2011). Carlson (2011) found that more correct identifications from target-present simultaneous lineups were made to distinctive targets faces than to typical faces, but Carlson and Gronlund

(2011) found no effect of distinctiveness on the outcome of target-present lineups. Witnesses were more likely to report that they experienced conscious "recollection" when they correctly identified a distinctive face in a lineup, or correctly rejected a target-absent lineup when looking for a distinctive target. There were fewer "recollection" responses to non-distinctive faces (Carlson & Gronlund, 2011).These data support the hypothesis that witnesses can use a "recall-to-reject" strategy more effectively when attempting to identify a distinctive face from a target-absent lineup (Rotello & Heit, 2000). Both Carlson (2011) and Carlson and Gronlund (2011) used a rather artificial laboratory task in which participants' memory for several faces was tested, and many faces were presented during the task. Further research is needed to study the effects of the distinctiveness of the perpetrator's face in more realistic eyewitness settings.

One way in which a suspect's face may stand out is by the presence of a distinguishing mark (e.g., a scar, tattoo, or mole) that may have been mentioned in a witness' description (Carlson, 2011; Zarkadi, Wade, & Stewart, 2009). If the suspect is the only person in the lineup with a scar or tattoo, he will stand out in comparison with the foils rendering the lineup unfair. There are two solutions to this problem. For video lineups used in the UK the most frequent procedure is to conceal the area of the distinguishing feature on the face of the suspect and the foils. The alternative strategy is to replicate the distinguishing mark on the faces of the foils. Surprisingly, over 30 per cent of lineups recorded in England are digitally manipulated to conceal or replicate a feature (Zarkadi et al., 2009). A large majority involve concealment of the feature. This raises the question of whether is it better to conceal or replicate. Zarkadi et al. (2009) found that replicating the distinctive feature produced more correct identifications of the culprit than removal of the feature, without increasing the number of mistaken identifications from culprit-absent lineups.

This pattern of results is consistent with the encoding specificity principle and was modelled using the hybrid-similarity model of recognition (Nosofsky & Zaki, 2003). This model has previously been applied to modelling the effects of distinctiveness in face recognition.

Multiple perpetrators

Many crimes are carried out by more than one perpetrator, yet most studies of eyewitness memory focus on memory for a single perpetrator. The few studies that have examined multiple perpetrator crime scenarios have found identification accuracy is lower for perpetrators who were seen with another person. This effect was observed even when viewing time was equated, and memory for only one culprit was tested (Clifford & Hollin, 1981; Megreya & Burton, 2006). To identify multiple offenders seen by the same witness, the British police place each suspect in a separate lineup. The witness is shown the first lineup. If an identification is made, the witness is asked what role the person played. The witness is then shown the next lineup, continuing for each suspect. In an experimental study, Hobson and Wilcock (2011) found that when three perpetrators seen in a video event were included in separate lineups, witnesses who view multiple lineups were more accurate if they viewed all of the lineups before making any identification decision, than if they made an identification after each lineup. This result suggests that remembering "who did what" is easier with the modified procedure. Identification of multiple perpetrators is clearly an issue of great relevance to the courts and requiring more attention from eyewitness researchers.

Identification procedure characteristics

Delay

There has been some controversy over the effect of delay on eyewitness identification (Dysart & Lindsay, 2007). The nature of forgetting is well established from laboratory studies of memory. Forgetting can be described mathematically by a negatively accelerating exponential function. Initially forgetting is rapid, giving a steep decline with delay. The rate of forgetting slows exponentially so that as the delay increases, performance reaches an asymptote and relatively little further decline is observed with long delays. However, many studies of eyewitness identification show little, if any, effect of delay. Clifford, Havard, Memon, and Gabbert (2011) tabulated experimental, archival and meta-analytic studies to show that about half of the studies show no effect of delay on identification. However, in a meta-analysis of 18 face recognition and eyewitness identification studies, Shapiro and Penrod (1986) reported an effect of delay on both correct identifications ($d = 0.43$) and mistaken identifications ($d = 0.33$). The delay in the studies analysed had a mean of 4.5 days with a standard deviation of 21 days. In a systematic review of the effect of delay on eyewitness identification, Deffenbacher, Bornstein, McGorty, and Penrod (2008) demonstrated that there is a reliable effect of delay and that it can be modelled by an exponential function as predicted by standard theories of forgetting.

The length of delay between a crime and the identification of a suspect from a lineup in some court cases is much longer than the delays typically studied in most eyewitness experiments. Shepherd (1983) reported data for much longer delays than most studies. He found that 65 per cent of unfamiliar faces were recognised after one week, 55 per cent after a month, 50 per cent after three months and 10 per cent after 11 months. In contrast there was no effect of delay on mistaken identifications.

Witness description

Laboratory research suggests that the quality of a verbal description is not strongly associated with the accuracy of a subsequent identification (e.g., Pozzulo & Warren, 2003). However, in a field study of police lineups, Valentine et al. (2003) found that the detail of the witness' first description was associated with the probability that the police suspect was identified. Witnesses who gave a detailed description were more likely to identify the suspect than were witnesses who gave an average description or one with few details. Note that the finding referred to the number of details given (i.e., the completeness of description) and not to any measure of the degree to which the description matched the appearance of the suspect. The effect may have been found in a study of real cases because the witnesses will have seen the culprits under very widely ranging circumstances. In laboratory experiments all participants typically view the target person under the same conditions. Therefore there is a greater variety of viewing conditions in the real world and therefore more variance in the detail of descriptions and ability to identify offenders. This difference may account for an association being observed in the field that is not observed in the laboratory. (See the section on "Confidence" below for a related argument made by Lindsay, Read, and Sharma (1998) and Lindsay, Nilsen, and Read (2000) with reference to the confidence–accuracy relationship.)

Speed of identification

Laboratory studies have shown that witnesses who made fast identifications from a lineup are more likely to be correct than witness who chose more slowly (Sporer, 1992, 1993, 1994). Dunning and Perretta (2002) argued that identifications made within 10 to 12 seconds were more likely to be accurate. Re-analysis of data from over 3000 participants in a number of published studies confirmed that decision speed is a predictor of accuracy but did not support the 10–12 second rule. Several factors affected the absolute speed of decisions across studies (Weber, Brewer, Wells, Semular, & Keast, 2004). A field study found that 87 per cent of witnesses who made fast identifications when they attended a live police lineup identified the police suspect compared with

38 per cent of witnesses who chose with average speed. The speed of identification was rated on a scale (fast/average/slow) by the police lineup administrator (Valentine et al., 2003). In summary, both laboratory and field data suggest that fast identifications are more likely to be accurate than slow identifications. The effect may be explained by appeal to the distinction between recollection and familiarity as a basis for responding. Witnesses who have a strong memory trace they are likely to experience conscious recollection or recognition of the target face as soon as they see it, and so have no need to compare faces in a lineup. If an identification is made on the basis of a feeling of familiarity in the absence of a strong recollection of the face it may be necessary to compare lineup members to reach a decision.

Confidence

Research on eyewitness identification has mainly focused on accuracy as a dependent variable. Typically scientists can set up experiments in which they know whether the "culprit" is present in a lineup or not. However, in court, some basis is required to judge whether a witness is accurate in their identification. Careful consideration of estimator variables will help a judge or jury reach a view of whether an identification is plausible, but the confidence or demeanour of a witness may be used to judge the accuracy of their identification. A confident eyewitness may provide compelling evidence and be highly influential. Therefore the question arises of whether confidence is a reliable cue to accuracy.

Many studies of eyewitness identification have suggested that the relationship between confidence and accuracy is low (Bothwell, Deffenbacher, & Brigham, 1987), leading psychologists to conclude that witness confidence is an unreliable means to assess accuracy. It has been appreciated for a long time that a confident witness may be mistaken. In English courts a warning to this effect must be given to the jury in cases that

involve disputed eyewitness identification (R v. Turnbull, 1976).

In recent years our understanding of the confidence–accuracy relationship has become more sophisticated. One factor that may have restricted the relationship in experimental studies is that participants usually view a live or video mock crime under identical conditions. The relationship is stronger when a wide range of viewing conditions is considered (Lindsay, Read, & Sharma, 1998; Lindsay, Nilsen, & Read, 2000). Furthermore, the correlation is stronger if only witnesses who identify somebody from a lineup are considered; the correlation is lower amongst witnesses who reject the lineup (Sporer, Penrod, Read, & Cutler, 1995). The effect size of the confidence–accuracy correlation of witnesses who chose from a lineup can be moderate, but nevertheless it is far from a perfect relationship. Confident but mistaken eyewitnesses may frequently give evidence in court. Wells, Olsen, and Charman (2002) point out that the confidence–accuracy relationship is similar to the strength of the correlation between height and sex. If we attempted to guess a person's sex from knowing only their height, tall women and short men would be at risk of misclassification. Similarly if we attempted to judge the accuracy of an identification from knowing only the confidence of a witness, many errors would be made.

It matters when confidence is measured. A statement of confidence taken immediately after an identification procedure is a better indicator of accuracy than confidence measured before an identification (Cutler & Penrod, 1989; Bothwell, Deffenbacher, & Brigham, 1987). It is extremely important that confidence measured after the lineup should be taken before there is any possibility of the witness receiving feedback. Being told that you have identified the police suspect or that another witness identified the same person inflates witnesses' confidence in their identification, and also inflates their estimates of how long the culprit was seen for, how close they were and how much attention the witness paid (Wells & Bradfield, 1998).

The utility of confidence as a dependant variable, and by extension its utility to a court, has been evaluated for several estimator variables. Experimental conditions expected to enhance memory strength yield higher confidence ratings. Witnesses make more confident identifications after long exposure durations to the target face (Bothwell et al., 1987), after a short retention interval, and to distinctive faces (Sauer, Weber, & Brewer, 2012).

A more informative measure of the confidence–accuracy relationship than the point-biserial correlation has been developed. Juslin, Olsson, and Winman (1996) introduced "calibration" of the accuracy of identification by plotting the mean accuracy of groups of witnesses against the different levels of confidence they expressed. Both accuracy and confidence were measured on a 0–100 per cent scale. Calibration revealed that even with a modest correlation, witnesses who expressed greater confidence were generally more likely to be accurate than witnesses who expressed lower confidence. Witnesses who were required to reflect on the encoding and test conditions after seeing a lineup showed more accurate calibration of their confidence judgments than did witnesses in a control condition who were not invited to reflect on the encoding and test conditions (Brewer, Keast, & Rishworth, 2002).

Measuring calibration provides a measure of over-confidence or under-confidence. For example, if only 40 per cent of witnesses who expressed 70 per cent confidence were correct, they would be over-confident. Alternatively if 70 per cent of witnesses who expressed 40 per cent confidence made a correct identification, they would be under-confident. Calibration has been used to investigate further the effect of confirming feedback on the accuracy–confidence relationship. Semmler, Brewer, and Wells (2004) reported that confirming feedback led witnesses to become over-confident, so that they expressed more confidence

in their identification than was warranted. The danger in the criminal justice system is that by the time witnesses give evidence in court they are likely to have received confirming feedback, and if so, their testimony given in court is liable to distortion by the feedback.

CONCLUSION

Over the last 30 years much has been learned about the factors that affect eyewitness identification and the theoretical basis for these effects. Useful applied knowledge has been established in recent theoretical-motivated investigations and analyses of estimator variables. For example, theoretical models have been applied to investigations of viewing distance, stress and delay. Progress in research has been recognised by the courts in a recent judgment that evaluated the influence of many estimator variables (State v. Henderson, 2001). Research has helped us to appreciate how Tracy McAlroy's memory may have been affected by a number of estimator variables when, on the night of 7 March 2002, she looked through the glass in her front door at her husband's murderer. The lighting conditions and the distance from which she saw his face are likely to have impaired her ability to recognise his face. The hood and face covering would have made recognition yet more difficult. The very considerable emotional stress of the witness is also likely to have impaired memory for his appearance. Was William Gage the killer? Psychological science cannot tell us whether a witness on a particular occasion was correct or incorrect in the identification she made. It can only help us understand the probabilities of correct identification across a group of observers under relevant conditions. The challenge for the courts is to apply our knowledge of the abilities and limitations of human perception and memory to the facts of a case, and to form an opinion of whether a particular witness's evidence is reliable.

REFERENCES

Bartlett, J. C., & Fulton, A. (1991). Familiarity and recognition of faces in old age. *Memory & Cognition, 19,* 229–238.

Behrman, B. W., & Davey, S. L. (2001). Eyewitness identification in actual criminal cases: An archival analysis. *Law and Human Behavior, 25,* 475–491.

Bothwell, R. K., Deffenbacher, K. A., & Brigham, J. C. (1987). Correlations of eyewitness accuracy and confidence: Optimality hypothesis revisited. *Journal of Applied Psychology, 72,* 691–695.

Brewer, N., Keast, A., & Rishworth, A. (2002). The confidence-accuracy relationship in eyewitness identification: The effects of reflection and disconfirmation on correlation and calibration. *Journal of Experimental Psychology: Applied, 8,* 44–56.

Carlson, C. A. (2011). Influence of a perpetrator's distinctive facial feature on eyewitness identification from simultaneous versus sequential lineups. *Applied Psychology in Criminal Justice, 7,* 77–92.

Carlson, C. A., & Gronlund, S. D. (2011). Searching for the sequential line-up advantage: A distinctiveness explanation. *Memory, 19,* 916–929.

Cutler, B. L., & Penrod, S. D. (1989). Forensically-relevant moderators of the relationship between eyewitness identification accuracy and confidence. *Journal of Applied Psychology, 74,* 650–652.

Chiroro, P., & Valentine, T. (1995). An investigation of the contact hypothesis of the own-race bias in face recognition. *Quarterly Journal of Experimental Psychology, 48A,* 879–894.

Christianson, S-Å. (1992). Emotional stress and eyewitness memory: A critical review. *Psychological Bulletin, 112,* 284–309.

Christianson, S-Å., & Hubinette, B. (1993). Hands up! A study of witnesses' emotional reactions and memories associated with bank robberies. *Applied Cognitive Psychology, 7,* 365–379.

Clifford, B. R., Havard, C., Memon, A., & Gabbert, F. (2011). Delay and age effects on identification accuracy and confidence: An investigation using a video identification parade. *Applied Cognitive Psychology, 26,* 130–139.

Clifford, B. R., & Hollin, C. (1981). Effects of type of incident and the number of perpetrators in eyewitness memory. *Journal of Applied Psychology, 66,* 364–370.

Cohen, J. (1977). *Statistical power analysis for the behavioral sciences* (revised edition). New York: Academic Press.

Cutler, B. L., Penrod, S. D., O'Rourke, T. E., & Martens, T. K. (1986). Unconfounding the effects of contextual cues on eyewitness identification accuracy. *Social Behaviour, 1,* 113–134.

Davies, G., & Flin, R. (1984). The man behind the mask – disguise and face recognition. *Human Learning: Journal of Practical Research & Applications, 3,* 83–95.

Davis, J. P., & Valentine, T. (2009). CCTV on trial: Matching video images with the defendant in the dock. *Applied Cognitive Psychology, 23,* 482–505.

Deffenbacher, K. A., Bornstein, G. H., McGorty, E. K., & Penrod, S. D. (2008). Forgetting the once-seen face: Estimating the strength of an eyewitness's memory representation. *Journal of Experimental Psychology: Applied, 14,* 139–150.

Deffenbacher, K. A., Bornstein, B. H., Penrod, S. D., & McGorty, K. (2004). A meta-analytic review of the effects of high stress on eyewitness memory. *Law and Human Behavior, 28,* 687–706.

De Jong, M., Wagenaar, W. A., Wolters, G., & Verstijnen, I. M. (2005). Familiar face recognition as a function of distance and illumination: A practical tool for use in the courtroom. *Psychology, Crime & Law, 11,* 87–97.

Dunning, D., & Perretta, S. (2002). Automaticity and eyewitness accuracy: A 10- to 12-second rule for distinguishing accurate from inaccurate positive identifications, *Journal of Applied Psychology, 87,* 951–959.

Dysart, J. E., & Lindsay, R. C. L. (2007). The effect of delay on eyewitness identification accuracy. Should we be concerned? In In R. C. L. Lindsay, D. F. Ross, J. D. Read, and M. P. Toglia (Eds.), *Handbook of eyewitness psychology: Vol. 2. Memory for people* (pp. 361–376). Mahwah, NJ: Lawrence Erlbaum Associates.

Dysart, J. E., Lindsay, R. C. L., MacDonald, T. K., & Wicke, C. (2002). The intoxicated witness: Effects of alcohol on identification accuracy from show-ups. *Journal of Applied Psychology, 87,* 170–175.

Ellis, H. D., Shepherd, J. W., & Davies, G. M. (1979). Identification of familiar and unfamiliar faces from internal and external features: Some implications for theories of face recognition. *Perception, 8,* 431–439.

Flatley, J., Kershaw, C., Smith, K., Chaplin, R., & Moon, D. (2010). *Crime in England and Wales 2009/10: Findings from the British Crime Survey and police recorded crime.* Home Office Statistical Bulletin 12/10. Downloaded on 10-25-2012 from: http://rds.homeoffice.gov.uk/rds/pdfs10/hosb1210.pdf

Gage v. HMA (2011). HCJAC 40. Downloaded 10-25-2012 from: www.scotcourts.gov.uk/opinions/2011HCJAC40.html

Gage v. HMA (2012). HCJAC 14. Downloaded 10-25-2012 from: www.scotcourts.gov.uk/opinions/2012HCJAC14.html

Hobson, Z., & Wilcock, R. (2011). Eyewitness identification of multiple perpetrators. *International Journal of Police Science & Management, 13,* 286–296.

Hope, L., & Wright, D. (2007). Beyond unusual? Examining the role of attention in the weapon focus effect. *Applied Cognitive Psychology, 21,* 951–961.

Horry, R., Memon, A., Wright, D. B., & Milne, R. (2012). Predictors of eyewitness identification decisions from video lineups in England: A field Study. *Law and Human Behaviour, 36,* 257–265.

Juslin, P., Olsson, N., & Winman, A. (1996). Calibration and diagnosticity of confidence in eyewitness identification: Comments on what can be inferred from low confidence-accuracy correlation. *Journal of Experimental Psychology: Learning, Memory & Cognition, 22,* 1304–1316.

Karageorge and Zajac (2011). Exploring the effects of age and delay on children's person identifications: Verbal descriptions, lineup performance, and the influence of wildcards. *British Journal of Psychology, 102,* 161–183.

Keast, A., Brewer, N., & Wells, G. L. (2007). Children's metacognitive judgments in an eyewitness identification task. *Journal of Experimental Child Psychology, 97,* 286–314.

Lindsay, R. C. L., Semmuler, C., Weber, N., Brewer, N., & Lindsay, M. R. (2008). How variations in distance affect eyewitness reports and identification accuracy, *Law and Human Behavior, 32,* 526–535.

Lindsay, D. S., Nilsen, E., & Read, J. D. (2000). Witnessing-condition heterogeneity and witnesses' versus investigators' confidence in the accuracy of witnesses' identification decisions. *Law and Human Behavior, 24,* 685–697.

Lindsay, D. S., Read, J. D., & Sharma, K., (1998). Accuracy and confidence in person identification: The relationship is strong when witnessing conditions vary widely. *Psychological Science, 9,* 215–218.

Loftus, G., & Harley, E. M. (2005). Why is it easier to identify someone close than far away? *Psychonomic Bulletin & Review, 12,* 43–65.

Loftus, E. F., Loftus, G. R., & Messo, J. (1987). Some facts about "weapon focus". *Law and Human Behavior, 11,* 55–62.

Megreya, A. M., & Burton, A. M. (2006). Recognising faces seen alone or with others: When two heads are worse than one. *Applied Cognitive Psychology, 20,* 957–972.

Meissner, C. A., & Brigham, J. C. (2001). Thirty years of investigating the own-race bias in memory for faces. *Psychology, Public Policy and Law, 7,* 3–35.

Memon, A., Hope, L., & Bull, R. (2003). Exposure duration: Effects on eyewitness accuracy and confidence. *British Journal of Psychology, 94,* 339–354.

Morgan, C. A., Hazlett, G., Doran, A., Garrett, S., Hoyt, G., Thomas, P., Baranoski, M., & Southwick, S. M. (2004). Accuracy of eyewitness memory for persons encountered during exposure to highly intense stress. *International Journal of Law and Psychiatry, 27,* 265–279.

Nosofsky, R. M., & Zaki, S. R. (2003). A hybrid-similarity exemplar model for predicting distinctiveness effects in perceptual old–new recognition. *Journal of Experimental Psychology: Learning, Memory, and Cognition, 29,* 1194–1209.

Odinot, G., Wolters, G., & van Koppen, P. J. (2009). Eyewitness memory of a supermarket robbery: A case study on accuracy and confidence after 3 months. *Law and Human Behavior, 3,* 506–514.

O'Rourke, T. E., Penrod, S. D., & Cutler, B. L. (1989). The external validity of eyewitness identification research: Generalizing across subject populations. *Law and Human Behavior, 13,* 385–397.

Patterson, K. E., & Baddeley, A. D. (1977). When face recognition fails. *Journal of Experimental Psychology: Human Learning & Memory, 3,* 406–417.

Pickel, K. L. (1998). Unusualness and threat as possible causes of "weapon focus". *Memory, 6,* 277–295.

Pickel, K. L. (1999). The influence of context on the "weapon focus" effect. *Law and Human Behavior, 23,* 299–311.

Pickel, K. L. (2009). The weapon focus effect on memory for female versus male perpetrators *Memory, 17,* 664–678.

Pickel, K. L., Ross, S. J., & Truelove, R. S. (2006). Do weapons automatically capture attention? *Applied Cognitive Psychology, 20,* 871–893.

Pike, G., Brace, N., & Kyman, S. (2002). *The visual identification of suspects: procedures and practice.* Briefing note 2/02, Policing and Reducing Crime Unit, Home Office Research Development and Statistics Directorate. Downloaded 10-25-2012 from: www.homeoffice.gov.uk/rds/prgbriefpubs1.html

Pozzulo, J. D., & Lindsay, R. C. L. (1998). Identification accuracy of children versus adults: A meta analysis. *Law and Human Behavior, 22,* 549–570.

Pozzulo, J. D., & Warren, K. L. (2003). Descriptions and identifications of strangers by child and adult witnesses. *Applied Cognitive Psychology, 88,* 315–323.

R v. Turnbull (1976) 3 All ER 549.

Read, J. D. (1995). The availability heuristic in person identification – the sometimes misleading consequences of enhanced contextual information. *Applied Cognitive Psychology, 9,* 91–121.

Read, J. D., Vokey, J. R., & Hammersley, R. H. (1990). Changing photos of faces: Effects of exposure duration and photo similarity on recognition and the accuracy-confidence relationship. *Journal of Experimental Psychology: Learning, Memory, and Cognition, 16,* 870–882.

Read, J. D., Yuille, J. C., & Tollestrup, P. (1992). Recollections of a robbery. *Law and Human Behavior, 16,* 425–446.

Rotello, C. M., & Heit, E. (2000). Associative recognition: A case of recall-to-reject processing. *Memory & Cognition, 28,* 907–922.

Sauer, J. D., Weber, N., & Brewer, N. (2012). Using euphoric confidence ratings to discriminate seen from unseen faces: The effects of retention interval and distinctiveness. *Psychonomic Bulletin & Review, 19,* 490–498.

Searcy, J. H., Bartlett, J. C., & Memon, A. (1999). Age differences in accuracy and choosing in eyewitness identification and face recognition. *Memory & Cognition, 27,* 538–552.

Searcy, J. H., Bartlett, J. C., & Memon, A. (2000). Relationships of availability, lineup conditions, and individual differences to false identification by young and older eyewitnesses. *Legal and Criminological Psychology, 5,* 219–236.

Searcy, J. H., Bartlett, J. C., Memon, A., & Swanson, K. (2001). Ageing and lineup performance at long retention intervals. Effects of metamemory and context reinstatement. *Journal of Applied Psychology, 86,* 207–214.

Semmler, C., Brewer, N., & Wells, G. L. (2004). Effects of postidentification feedback on eyewitness identification and nonidentification confidence. *Journal of Applied Psychology, 89,* 334–346.

Shapiro, P. N., & Penrod, S. (1986). Meta-analysis of facial identification studies. *Psychological Bulletin, 100,* 139–156.

Shepherd, J. W. (1983). Identification after long delays. In S. M. A. Lloyd-Bostock and B. R. Clifford (Eds.), *Evaluating eyewitness evidence* (pp. 173–187). Chichester, UK: Wiley.

Sporer, S. (1992). Post-dicting accuracy: Confidence, decision times and person descriptions of choosers and non-choosers. *European Journal of Social Psychology,* 22, 157–180.

Sporer, S. (1993). Eyewitness identification accuracy, confidence and decision times in simultaneous and sequential lineups. *Journal of Applied Psychology, 78,* 22–33.

Sporer, S. (1994). Decision times and eyewitness identification accuracy in simultaneous and sequential lineups. In D. F. Ross, J. D. Read, and M. P. Toglia (Eds.), *Adult eyewitness testimony: Current trends and developments* (pp. 300–327). Cambridge: Cambridge University Press.

Sporer, S., Penrod, S., Read, D., & Cutler, B. L. (1995). Choosing, confidence and accuracy: A meta-analysis of the confidence-accuracy relations in eyewitness identification studies, *Psychological Bulletin, 118,* 315–327.

State v. Henderson (2011). 208 N.J. 208, Lexis 927, 8/24/11.

Steblay, N. K. (1992). A meta-analytic review of the weapon focus effect. *Law and Human Behavior, 16,* 413– 423.

Tanaka, J. W., & Pierce, L. J. (2009). The neural plasticity of other-race face recognition. *Cognitive, Affective and Behavioral Neuroscience, 9,* 122–131.

Technical Working Group for Eyewitness Evidence (1999). *Eyewitness Evidence: A Guide for Law Enforcement.* Washington: US Department of Justice Downloaded 10-25-2011 from: www.nij.gov/pubs-sum/178240.htm

Tollestrup, P. A., Turtle, J. W., & Yuille, J. C. (1994). Actual victims and witnesses to robbery and fraud: An archival analysis. In: D. F. Ross, J. D. Read, and M. P. Toglia (Eds.), *Adult eyewitness testimony: Current trends and developments* (pp. 144–160). Cambridge: Cambridge University Press.

Tulving, E., & Thomson, D. M. (1973). Encoding specificity and retrieval processes in episodic memory. *Psychological Review, 80,* 352–373.

Valentine, T. (1991). A unified account of the effects of distinctiveness, inversion and race in face recognition. *Quarterly Journal of Experimental Psychology, 43A,* 161–204.

Valentine, T. (2001). Face-space models of face recognition. In M.J. Wenger and J.T. Townsend (Eds.), *Computational, geometric, and process perspectives on facial cognition: Contexts and challenges* (pp. 83–113). Mahwah, NJ: Lawrence Erlbaum Associates.

Valentine, T., Cullasy, F., Fantham, V., & Davis, J. P. (2012). *Accuracy and confidence of identification by intoxicated eyewitnesses.* Paper presented at the Conference of the European Association for Psychology and Law, Nicosia.

Valentine, T., & Endo, M. (1992). Towards an exemplar model of face processing: The effects of race and distinctiveness. *Quarterly Journal of Experimental Psychology, 44A,* 671–703.

Valentine, T., & Mesout, J. (2009). Eyewitness identification under stress in the London Dungeon. *Applied Cognitive Psychology, 23,* 151–161.

Valentine, T., Pickering, A., & Darling, S. (2003). Characteristics of eyewitness identification that predict the outcome of real lineups. *Applied Cognitive Psychology, 17,* 969–993.

Wagenaar, W. A., & Van der Schrier, J. (1996). Face recognition as a function of distance and illumination: A practical tool for use in the courtroom. *Psychology, Crime & Law, 2,* 321–332.

Weber, N., Brewer, N., Welles, G. L., Semmler, C., & Keast, A. (2004). Eyewitness identification accuracy and response latency: The unruly 10–12 second rule. *Journal of Experimental Psychology: Applied, 10,* 137–149.

Wells, G. L., & Bradfield, A. L. (1998). "Good you identified the suspect": Feedback to eyewitnesses distort their reports of the witnessing experience. *Journal of Applied Psychology, 66,* 688–696.

Wells, G. L., Olson, E. A., & Charman, S. D. (2002). The confidence of eyewitnesses in their identifications from lineups. *Current Directions in Psychological Science, 11,* 151–154.

Wenger, M. J., & Townsend, J. T. (2001) (Eds.), *Computational, geometric, and process perspectives on facial cognition: Contexts and challenges.* Mahwah, NJ: Lawrence Erlbaum Associates.

Woolnough, P. S., & MacLeod, M. D. (2001). Watching the birdie watching you: Eyewitness memory for actions using CCTV recordings of actual crimes. *Applied Cognitive Psychology, 15,* 395–411.

Wright, D. B., Boyd, C. E., & Tredoux, C. G. (2001). A field study of own-race bias in South Africa and England. *Psychology, Public Policy and Law, 7,* 119–133.

Wright, D. B., Boyd, C. E., & Tredoux, C. G. (2003). Inter-racial contact and the own-race bias for face recognition in South Africa and England. *Applied Cognitive Psychology, 17,* 365–373.

Yuille, J. C., & Cutshall, J. L. (1986). A case study of eyewitness memory of a crime. *Journal of Applied Psychology, 71,* 291–301.

Yuille, J. C., & Tollestrup, P. (1990). Some effects of alcohol on eyewitness memory. *Journal of Applied Psychology, 75,* 268–273.

Zajac, R., & Karageorge, A. (2009). The wildcard: A simple technique for improving children's lineup performance. *Applied Cognitive Psychology, 23,* 358–368.

Zarkadi, T., Wade, K. A., & Stewart, N. (2009). Creating fair lineups for suspects with distinctive features. *Psychological Science, 20,* 1448–1453.

33

System-based Research on Eyewitness Identification

Scott D. Gronlund and Curt A. Carlson

We have known at least since the publication of *On the Witness Stand* by Hugo Münsterberg (1908) that eyewitness identification can be faulty. DNA exonerations by the Innocence Project[1] have made the entire world aware of this problem. A national registry has recently been released that chronicles 1000 wrongful convictions since 1989.[2] Researchers have studied 873 of these cases in detail. The website indicates that faulty eyewitness identification was a contributing factor in 43 percent of these cases; it played a role in approximately 80 percent of the sexual assault cases.

What can we do about this problem? Given the kind of memory system that we have evolved, one ill-equipped to do the job required of an eyewitness, an argument could be made for the elimination of eyewitness evidence from the criminal justice system. Our memory system did not evolve to retain verbatim representations of events and it does not operate like a video recorder, despite what the general public believes (Simons & Chabris, 2011). Despite these shortcomings of memory, are there procedures that the criminal justice system can use to collect and evaluate eyewitness evidence that could enhance its accuracy and thereby partially compensate for the memory system

we have? An examination of these procedures is the focus of this chapter.

Wells (1978) introduced a distinction between two classes of variables that affect eyewitness identification: estimator and system variables. Estimator variables, the topic of Chapter 30 in this volume, are variables that influence the accuracy of eyewitness identification but are not under the control of the criminal justice system (for an earlier review, see Wells, Memon, & Penrod, 2006). They involve factors such as a race mismatch between the victim and the perpetrator (Meissner & Brigham, 2001), the presence of a distinctive feature on the perpetrator's face (Carlson, 2011), and the presence of a weapon (e.g., Carlson & Carlson, 2012; Loftus, Loftus, & Messo, 1987). Extreme stress adversely affects memory (Morgan et al., 2004), as does poor illumination, greater distance, or shorter exposure (Loftus, 2010). To the extent that these factors produce a weak memory representation, the reconstructive nature of memory becomes even more problematic and the accuracy of an eyewitness even more dubious.

System variables involve factors that are under the control of the criminal justice system. These variables come into play after the occurrence and initial encoding of an event. System variables often are divided into two broad categories: interviewing the eyewitness and asking the witness to identify the suspect. Chapter 31 in this volume considers the former topic; we focus on the latter. In particular, we will discuss three different identification procedures: the mugbook, a showup, and especially the construction and administration of a lineup. Factors to consider regarding lineups include how to construct a lineup, how to instruct a witness, who should administer the lineup, and how the lineup members should be presented. After describing these system variables and examining the data in support of their effectiveness, we will close with a discussion of alternative procedures and future directions that look promising for the next generation of system-variable research.

We begin before the police even have a suspect, with a search for the suspect through a mugbook. Of course, like any identification procedure, just because a witness has chosen someone does not mean that the witness is correct, even if a witness professes to be 150 percent confident.[3] In more sedate situations, people often fail to see what is right in front of their eyes if their attention is focused elsewhere (see the "Gorillas in our Midst" demonstration of Simons & Chabris, 1999).[4] No identification procedure can outperform the memory system on which we must rely.

MUGBOOK

Police sometimes present a series of photos to a witness in the hope that the witness may identify the perpetrator from among those viewed. A potential problem arises when an eyewitness is subsequently shown a lineup that includes an individual whose mugshot the witness previously selected. Deffenbacher, Bornstein, and Penrod (2006) showed that exposure to mugshots can produce a variety of negative effects including a decrease in correct identifications (failure to select the actual guilty suspect) and an increase in false identifications (the selection of an innocent suspect). Misplaced familiarity and commitment are two explanations offered to account for the negative influence of mugshot exposure on subsequent lineup performance (Goodsell, Neuschatz, & Gronlund, 2009).

Misplaced familiarity is a recurrent contributor to faulty eyewitness identifications. Someone in a lineup can be familiar for any number of reasons besides being the perpetrator, including being an innocent bystander (Buckhout, 1974), having been seen in the newspaper or on TV, or from having been previously seen in a mugbook. This problem can be understood in terms of the source-monitoring framework (Johnson, Hashtroudi, & Lindsay, 1993; Lindsay, Chapter 4, this volume).

Our memory system is not good at keeping track of why something is familiar. We often weakly encode the source of a memory because the source seldom is important. Consequently, witnesses have difficulty discriminating between separate memory traces (e.g., an innocent bystander versus the perpetrator) and may not realize that a feeling of familiarity is due to an innocuous past exposure (from a mugbook or a photo in the newspaper) rather than from witnessing the crime. For example, participants are more likely to make a false identification of an individual viewed in the mugshot phase compared with photographs of individuals that had not been seen before (e.g., Brown, Deffenbacher, & Sturgill, 1977; Davies, Shepherd, & Ellis, 1979).

Although simply viewing someone in a mugbook can make that person familiar in a subsequent lineup, incorrectly choosing someone from a mugbook can be an even greater problem. In the identification context, this is called "commitment" and can take two forms: (1) committing to a previously selected individual or (2) committing to a selection strategy. Gorenstein and Ellsworth (1980) proposed that once an eyewitness has chosen someone from a mugbook, he or she is likely to choose that same person again in a later identification task (see also Dysart, Lindsay, Hammond, & Dupuis, 2001; Haw, Dickinson, & Meissner, 2007; Memon,

Hope, Bartlett, & Bull, 2002). Alternatively, a witness can commit to a response strategy whereby a witness who failed to choose from a mugbook will stay committed to that response strategy and fail to select anyone from the lineup, even when the perpetrator is included (see Experiment 2 in Goodsell et al., 2009). Goodsell et al. disentangled familiarity and commitment, which often are confounded, and found that more faulty identifications arose from commitment errors when mugbooks were utilized.

Should the use of mugbooks be discontinued? Not if it might provide a lead when there is little else to go on. But their use becomes problematic when an individual (incorrectly) selected from a mugbook is included in a subsequent lineup, because the selection of that same individual from a lineup is viewed as independent, corroborating evidence. One remedy is to limit a witness to just a single identification attempt. Goodsell (2009) proposed an alternative that might limit the deleterious effect of commitment. Some participants were told to find individuals from a 50-photo perpetrator-absent mugbook that "looked like the perpetrator." Others received traditional mugbook search instructions to pick out *the* perpetrator. The former were just as able to pick the actual guilty suspect from a subsequent lineup as were the participants in a control condition, and better than those participants who completed the traditional mugbook search. Moreover, the mugbook search participants were twice as likely to incorrectly pick their mugbook selection from the lineup compared with those participants who picked out "look-alikes." Although promising, it is important to replicate this study, and to include a perpetrator-present mugbook to determine how often the set of mugshots that look like the perpetrator actually include him.

SHOWUPS

There is no need to have a witness view a mugbook if the police find a suspect near the scene of the crime. In these cases the police often conduct a showup, a one-person identification procedure. Dysart and Lindsay (2007) found that showups are the most common form of eyewitness identification. But showup identifications have been repudiated as less reliable than lineup identifications by the US Supreme Court (Stoval v. Denno, 1967; United States v. Wade, 1967), state courts (Bradley v. State, 1980; Commonwealth v. Carter, 1979; State v. Dubose, 2005), and social science researchers (meta-analyses by Clark & Godfrey, 2009; Steblay, Dysart, Fulero, & Lindsay, 2003). Kassin, Tubb, Hosch, and Memon (2001) reported that 74 percent of eyewitness identification experts endorsed the statement that showups increased the likelihood of a false identification relative to lineups. Nevertheless, Goodsell, Wetmore, Neuschatz, and Gronlund (2013) concluded that the extant data comparing showups to lineups were not conclusive.

Showups are thought to be suggestive because they are difficult to administer in a blind manner, and there are no foils that could be chosen by a witness who is merely guessing. Showups tend to foster a higher choosing rate than do lineups (Behrman & Davey, 2001; Meissner, Tredoux, Parker, & MacLin, 2005),[5] in part because there may be greater social pressure to choose from a showup, something that is difficult to simulate in a laboratory study (Dysart, Lindsay, & Dupuis, 2006). Another complicating factor involves the measures used to compare showups with lineups. Clark (2012a), Clark, Erickson, and Breneman (2011), and Wixted and Mickes (2012) showed that performance measures based on the ratio of correct to false identifications are negatively correlated with choosing rates. Consequently, showup performance is adversely affected because showups have a higher choosing rate than lineups.

To demonstrate this problem, Gronlund, Andersen, and Perry (2013) fit the WITNESS model (Clark, 2003) to the summary data from Table 5 in Clark, Howell, and Davey

(2008). WITNESS is a direct-access matching model (see Clark & Gronlund, 1996) designed to simulate the processes occurring in an eyewitness identification task. Gronlund et al. simulated four variants of the summary data; two in which participants were more willing to choose than in the standard data and two in which participants were less willing to choose than in the standard data. They accomplished this by adjusting the response criteria in WITNESS but holding memory (the remaining parameters) constant. The problem is that identification (ID) diagnosticity (correct IDs/false IDs or C/F)[6] increases as the willingness to choose decreases despite memory being held constant. The same problem arises for similar ratio measures ($\log(C/F)$ and $C/(C + F)$). Consequently, the use of these ratio measures makes it difficult to determine if an identification procedure is superior because it results in better performance or because it induces more conservative choosing, or both.

It is easy to determine which identification (ID) procedure produces better performance if one ID procedure yields both fewer false IDs and more correct IDs. But when one ID procedure yields fewer false IDs and fewer correct IDs, the choice is not straightforward. Wixted and Mickes (2012) argued that the solution to this problem is to compare performance using ROC analysis (Egan, 1958) to determine which testing procedure is more accurate. ROC analysis is grounded in signal detection theory (Green & Swets, 1966; Swets, Dawes, & Monahan, 2000). An ROC curve plots the proportion of correct IDs versus the proportion of false IDs at various discrimination thresholds or at different levels of response confidence. All points on the ROC reflect the same level of performance, but if C/F is computed at each confidence level, it reveals that the ratio increases as response confidence increases (i.e., as the discrimination threshold becomes more conservative). The medical profession reached the same conclusion years ago and abandoned the use of ratio measures in favor of ROC analysis (Lusted, 1971a, 1971b;

Metz, 1978; Pisano et al., 2005). A similar change is needed in the field of eyewitness memory.

Gronlund et al. (2012a) compared identification accuracy between showups and simultaneous lineups using ROC analyses and found clear evidence in support of the superiority of simultaneous lineups. It appears that the US Supreme Court was correct regarding its recommendation that the use of showups should be minimized.

LINEUPS

Lineups allow us to address several of the factors that make showups suggestive. Because lineups are not conducted at the scene of the crime, in the heat of the moment, with the suspect potentially standing next to the police officer in handcuffs, the pressure for a witness to choose can be reduced. Moreover, a lineup administrator can be made blind to the suspect's identity. Also, the presence of multiple foils in the lineup provides some protection from a witness with a poor memory of the perpetrator. We will review each of these recommendations, which follow the recommendations made by Wells et al. (1998). But we begin with a discussion of the factors to consider before putting a suspect at risk in a lineup.

Whether to conduct a lineup

Due to the unreliability of eyewitness identification under even the best of circumstances, one of the potentially most important variables under the control of the criminal justice system is when to conduct a lineup. Wells and Olson (2002) suggested that the police should have probable cause before putting someone at risk in a lineup. If a lineup identification is utilized early in an investigation before the police have probable cause, confirmation biases (Nickerson, 1998) can work to contaminate and distort subsequent evidence. A set of guidelines also could be developed for determining the likelihood that an eyewitness's identification could be accurate. For example, a close interaction between the eyewitness and the perpetrator, of a long duration, in bright sunlight, warrants a lineup test more than does an eyewitness who observed a crime from afar, at night, from a passing car. Can we develop guidelines to diagnose a situation to see if an identification attempt is warranted? Loftus (2010; see also De Jong, Wagenaar, Wolters, & Verstijnen, 2005) offered a framework for evaluating several physical variables that could help estimate the quality of a witness's memory for an event. The police could incorporate factors such as measures of the likely illumination, event duration, and distance from the witness to the perpetrator, into an actuarial model that could estimate the quality of a witness's memory. The model also could incorporate qualitative variables (e.g., confidence, did or did not see suspect's photo on TV, disguise worn). The output of this actuarial model could be used to help investigators decide if a witness should even view a lineup, thereby eliminating low-diagnosticity identifications. Of course, any such actuarial model must be developed alongside sufficient empirical validation to support the underlying assumptions.[7]

There also are individual differences that characterize an eyewitness that might make the police more or less willing to present that witness a lineup. For example, Morgan et al. (2007) (see also Jones, Scullin, & Meissner, 2011) showed that eyewitness accuracy was positively correlated with performance on the Weschler Face Test (1997), a simple face recognition test. Bindemann, Brown, Koyas, and Russ (2012) determined that an eyewitness's performance on a face recognition test could postdict their previous identification accuracy from a simultaneous lineup. However, this effect was limited to those who chose from the lineup. The criminal justice system would be well served to exclude as an eyewitness any individual judged to be unlikely to be able to accurately identify a perpetrator

due to the circumstances of the encounter or the capabilities of the eyewitness.

Another way to separate reliable from unreliable eyewitnesses is to present a "blank" lineup of known-innocents prior to the lineup that contains the police suspect (Wells, 1984). Wells showed that participants who incorrectly chose from a blank lineup were more likely to incorrectly reject the subsequent second lineup that contained the perpetrator (note that no faces repeated). More recently, Palmer, Brewer, and Weber (2012) explored the cognitive factors responsible for the poorer second lineup performance of those who chose from the blank lineup. They found that cognitive biases (confirmation bias and commitment effects) were to blame. In addition, those participants who made a choice from the blank lineup tended to have poorer memories for the perpetrator. The blank lineup is a promising and simple-to-implement practice that can enhance the reliability of eyewitness evidence. Palmer et al. (2012) concluded with a detailed summary of the policy implications surrounding the use of the blank lineup.

Lineup construction

Given the difficulty of constructing even one fair lineup, the police may have reservations about having to construct two lineups to implement the blank lineup procedure. What factors are relevant to constructing a lineup and selecting the foils?

The first step is to ensure that only one suspect is in the lineup (Wells & Turtle, 1986). The more suspects present in the lineup, the greater the likelihood that an eyewitness's choice, even based on something other than their memory (e.g., bias, guessing), would implicate someone. In contrast, if there is only one suspect in the lineup and an eyewitness chooses an innocent foil, this provides evidence that their memory for the perpetrator is not strong. In other words, selection of a foil can be diagnostic of the strength of the eyewitness's memory (see Clark, 2012b).

The issue of foil selection has become a complex one in the literature. Two alternatives have been considered: (a) select foils based on the description of the perpetrator provided by the eyewitness(es) or (b) select foils based on their similarity to the apprehended suspect. But suspect-matched fillers can backfire against the innocent suspect (Clark & Tunnicliff, 2001), and a witness's description of the suspect may not be detailed enough to construct a reasonable lineup. The National Institute of Justice (NIJ, 1999) recommends the selection of foils matched to the description rather than to the suspect. In a review of the literature comparing the description-matched with the suspect-matched approach, Clark, Rush, and Moreland (2013) found no evidence that description-matched is better. Rather, they recommended some combination of the two, which appears to be what many police departments currently do (Wise, Safer, & Maro, 2011). More work is needed to determine how best to select foils for a lineup, and how similar those foils should be to the suspect.

There are two additional issues concerning lineup construction that can influence the accuracy of an identification. First, after police have selected foils, the suspect must be placed somewhere in the lineup. Recent research indicates that suspect position can interact with other system variables, such as presentation method (e.g., simultaneous versus sequential lineup, see section below). For example, if the suspect is placed earlier in a sequential lineup, there is evidence that this harms performance relative to a simultaneous lineup (Gronlund, Carlson, Dailey, & Goodsell, 2009; Gronlund et al., 2012a). The second issue involves distinctiveness. What if the description of the perpetrator includes one or more distinctive features? For example, if the perpetrator had a black eye, should an attempt be made to conceal this or replicate the black eye across all foils (e.g., with makeup for a live lineup or Photoshop for a photo lineup)? Zarkadi, Wade, and Stewart (2009) (see also Carlson, 2011) addressed this question using several distinctive features (e.g., black eye, piercing, tattoo), and found that replicating the feature across all lineup members increased correct IDs of the perpetrator when present, and reduced foil IDs from a perpetrator-absent lineup, compared with concealing the feature. Finally, Clark et al. (2013) argued for more research on the adverse effect of pictorial distinctiveness on making a suspect's photo stick out in a simultaneous lineup (e.g., because it is the only crooked photo, or the only one cropped a certain way). Gronlund, Goodsell, and Andersen (2012b) discussed a case relevant to this issue involving Kevin Keith. Kevin Keith was convicted and sentenced to death for the murder of three and the shooting of three others. Ohio Governor, Ted Strickland, subsequently commuted his sentence to life without parole.[8] Approximately 80 percent of naive participants picked Keith's photo from a simultaneous lineup given the witness's description of a "big black man." This raises concerns about the quality of the eyewitness evidence in this case.

Instructions

Some witnesses may view it as their job to select someone from a lineup, and view it as a failure if they cannot. After all, witnesses may surmise that the police would not conduct a lineup unless it included the person the police believe committed the crime. Therefore, it is very important how the police instruct witnesses. Malpass and Devine (1981) were the first to evaluate the effectiveness of giving unbiased instructions: "The perpetrator may or may not be present." Since then, many (e.g., Cutler, Penrod, & Martens, 1987; O'Rourke, Penrod, Cutler, & Stuve, 1989; see meta-analysis by Steblay, 1997) have concluded that unbiased instructions produce decreased choosing from a perpetrator-absent lineup without decreasing correct IDs from a perpetrator-present lineup. Clark (2012a) called this the no-cost view because unbiased instructions appear to produce benefits (reduced false IDs) with little to no cost in reduced correct IDs. But a meta-analysis by Clark that showed that unbiased instructions produce a trade-off between costs and benefits, a pattern that holds across a number of reforms, including two that we will take up shortly, double-blind lineup administration and sequential lineup presentation.

If biased versus unbiased instructions simply affect choosing rates but not accuracy (i.e., the costs and benefits tradeoff), does it matter how we instruct a witness? Instructions matter little if the increased choosing gets spread out across all lineup members. However, biased instructions are a problem if the bias is directed at a particular individual. In the Kevin Keith case the detective gave the witness biased instructions, telling him to "pick him out." Because Keith stood out in the lineup, the use of biased instructions was problematic because the increased likelihood of choosing was directed at one individual. Keith remains in prison. It is because of matters like his unfair lineup and the use of biased instructions that some people have doubts about his guilt.

Unbiased instructions are not the only reform of instructions that has been suggested. For example, reforms recently enacted in the state of Texas[9] include several additional factors, including that the investigation will continue whether the witness makes an identification or not, that some physical characteristics are easy to change (e.g., facial hair), and that it is important to exclude the innocent as well as implicate the guilty. Although sensible, the impact of these instructions on witness behavior is unknown.

We now have reviewed what we know about how foils should be selected for the lineup and about how to instruct the witness. The next step is to examine who should administrate the lineup.

Lineup administration

The lineup administrator can influence eyewitnesses in two primary ways: (a) verbal or nonverbal influence during the lineup that affects the likelihood of choosing (Clark, 2005; Clark, Marshall, & Rosenthal, 2009; Greathouse & Kovera, 2009; Haw & Fisher, 2004) and (b) post-identification feedback that can affect eyewitness confidence in a decision (e.g., Wells & Bradfield, 1998; see meta-analysis by Douglass & Steblay, 2006). The first means of influence can occur via explicit verbal cues ("Take another look at number 2") or in a more subtle fashion. The best way to avoid such influence is to use an administrator who is blind as to whether the suspect is the perpetrator and to the suspect's location in the lineup. However, Clark et al. (2009) found that, even when unbiased instructions were provided by a blind administrator, statements such as "take your time" can influence choosing rates and identification accuracy. Notably, participant-witnesses who were affected by such influence typically did not report being aware of it.

The value of double-blind testing in other scientific areas and in the medical profession intimates that it will be of value to secure more reliable eyewitness identifications. Nevertheless, it also is important to conduct research that firmly establishes the superiority of this method in the eyewitness domain. Clark (2012a) examined the issue of double-blind lineup administration in the eyewitness identification literature, and found just one study (Greathouse & Kovera, 2009) that explicitly compared double-blind with single-blind administration for both perpetrator-present and -absent lineups. Greathouse and Kovera found that when biasing factors were present (e.g., biased instructions), single-blind lineup administration increased a participant's inclination to guess. This is a good start, but more studies must be conducted to place the recommendation for double-blind testing on firm empirical ground.

A related procedural reform is the certainty reform, which involves securing a certainty statement at the time of the identification and prior to events like post-identification feedback that contaminate witness certainty (see Dysart, Lawson, & Rainey, 2012). It is important to limit the lineup administrator, or anyone else, from conveying information to the witness about the lineup decision. Wells and Bradfield found that even a seemingly innocuous statement like "Good, you identified the suspect" dramatically increased eyewitness confidence in a choice, heightened confidence in the memory of the original event (e.g., that they got a better look at the perpetrator than they really did), and even enhanced the willingness to testify in court. Of course, these all are bad for an innocent suspect, particularly because jurors place great weight on confident eyewitness testimony (e.g., Cutler, Penrod, & Dexter, 1990). The post-identification feedback effect has been replicated many times (Douglass & Steblay, 2006) and has been found for real eyewitnesses (Wright & Skagerberg, 2007).

Should a lineup consist of actual individuals (a live lineup), videos of these individuals, or static photos? How should the lineup members be presented to the witness, all at once (simultaneous) or one at a time (sequential)? We turn next to lineup presentation methods.

Lineup presentation methods

Lineup members in the US are presented either as static images/mugshots or live (Valentine, Darling, & Memon, 2007). In the UK it has become common practice to present moving images (see Horry, Memon, Wright, & Milne, 2012; Wilcock & Kneller, 2011). A 15-second video clip of each lineup member is presented, in which a frontal, left-facing, and right-facing view is seen. Valentine et al. (2007) listed several advantages of these video lineups over live lineups, including: (a) dramatically reduced delay between crime and lineup (the UK uses VIPER – Video Identification Procedure Electronically Recorded – which can be presented within two hours); (b) large databases of video clips lead to the construction of fairer lineups (Valentine & Heaton, 1999); (c) viewing the lineup is less threatening to victim-eyewitnesses who do

not have to potentially encounter an attacker, and (d) they are portable, such that a laptop can be brought to an eyewitness if he or she cannot come to the police station. But so far, experiments have not revealed any advantage of video lineups over those with static images (Darling, Valentine, & Memon, 2008; Valentine et al., 2007). Kerstholt, Koster, and van Amelsvoort (2004) compared live, video, and photo lineups and found no differences in the rate of correct identifications. These findings are surprising given that more cues are available in a live lineup (Cutler, Berman, Penrod, & Fisher, 1994). Of course, it is likely that to benefit from the availability of more and richer cues in a live lineup a witness must have had a good look at the perpetrator. A live lineup likely would not benefit a witness who only got a fleeting glimpse of a pickpocket. Also, live lineups are not very practical and likely are difficult to construct fairly. The State of New York mandates live lineups followed by photo lineups (R. J. Masters, personal communication, June 18, 2012). Aforementioned source monitoring difficulties raise concerns about this practice.

In the US, lineup members typically are presented as photospreads in a simultaneous array or six-pack (Wogalter, Malpass, & McQuiston, 2004). However, the last few decades have seen the development and implementation of a popular alternative, the sequential lineup. In a sequential lineup, each member is presented alone, outside the context of the other members. Wells (1984) proposed that many of the errors involving eyewitness identification arose from witnesses making relative judgments. A relative judgment can lead to the selection of the individual in the lineup who most resembles the perpetrator. If the police have an innocent suspect, this is a problem. Presenting lineup members sequentially is supposed to limit relative judgments and facilitate absolute comparisons of each lineup member to memory, thereby reducing false identifications.

Sequential lineups are conducted differently in different countries. In the US, an eyewitness typically is not informed of how many lineup members will be presented, no member is shown a second time, and if one is chosen, no more are presented (for a notable exception see Wells, Steblay, & Dysart, 2012). In the UK, following from the Police and Criminal Evidence (PACE) act, an eyewitness must view the sequential lineup twice, and can view members more times if requested. Wilcock and Kneller (2011) found an advantage in correct ID rates (and no difference in false ID rates) for this variation of the sequential lineup, compared with the "strict" version popular in the US. However, Valentine et al. (2007) found a reduced choosing rate for the strict sequential lineup compared with the PACE version.

Over the past few decades, a great deal of system-variable research has been focused on simultaneous versus sequential lineups.[10] Lindsay and Wells (1985) conducted the first empirical test, finding that, although both correct IDs and false IDs (of the innocent suspect) decreased when the sequential lineup was used, the decrease in the false ID rate was larger. Subsequent research replicated this pattern, culminating in two meta-analyses supporting the "sequential superiority effect" (Steblay, Dysart, Fulero, & Lindsay, 2001; Steblay, Dysart, & Wells, 2011). The sequential procedure is now required in several states and jurisdictions (e.g., New Jersey, North Carolina, Ohio, Texas, Virginia). But recent research has raised questions about the robustness of the sequential superiority effect (Gronlund et al., 2009). A meta-analysis by Clark (2012a) tells the story of an ID procedure that makes an eyewitness less likely to choose (see also Palmer & Brewer, 2012). One problem with the earlier research was that performance was assessed by ratio lineup measures, which are negatively correlated with choosing rates. Consequently, the more conservative sequential procedure appeared to produce superior performance. But recent experiments using ROC analysis suggest that sequential lineups do not result in superior performance (see also Palmer & Brewer, 2012). Although Gronlund et al. (2009)

reported that a sequential advantage occurred only when a suspect (guilty or innocent) was placed late in the sequential lineup (fifth position), Gronlund et al. (2012a) reanalyzed these data using ROC analysis and found that late suspect position merely raised sequential performance up to the level of the simultaneous lineup. In fact, early sequential suspect position (second position) was no better than a showup. Mickes, Flowe, and Wixted (2012) found evidence for a simultaneous lineup advantage using ROC analysis.

In sum, the sequential lineup does protect the innocent via a reduction of choosing, but this comes with the cost of reduced choosing when a guilty suspect is in the lineup. Some might argue that it is worth the risk of releasing the guilty in order to protect the innocent, given the number of wrongful convictions where faulty eyewitness evidence played a role. But the fact that the benefits and the costs tradeoff makes a decision regarding the adoption of sequential lineups complex, and makes such a decision dependent on the base rate that innocent suspects are placed into lineups (which no one knows) and the utilities assigned to the various response options (see Swets et al., 2000). If we assume that the vast majority of suspects placed in lineups are guilty, then one might hesitate to adopt a lineup procedure that reduces the choosing rate. However, if we follow Blackstone's ratio that it is better that ten guilty people escape than one innocent suffer, the more conservative sequential lineup is the answer. Although an analysis of base rates and utilities is beyond the scope of this chapter, we point the interested reader to a discussion of these issues in Clark (2012a).

We are of the opinion that whether a lineup is presented simultaneously or sequentially makes little difference to the level of performance achieved, and that the other reforms discussed hold greater potential for enhancing eyewitness identification accuracy. Too much time and research effort has been devoted to the controversy surrounding the sequential superiority effect. The time is now to examine other ways to collect eyewitness evidence that might be superior to either of these presentation methods. We turn to these ideas next.

ALTERNATIVE PROCEDURES AND FUTURE DIRECTIONS

Researchers have explored several modest modifications to simultaneous and sequential lineup presentation. Dillon, McAllister, and Vernon (2009) examined hybrid lineups that include both simultaneous and sequential elements but found no differences in the correct or false identification rates as a function of how the lineup was conducted. Pozzulo and Lindsay (1999) proposed an "elimination" procedure whereby a witness first chooses the person most resembling the perpetrator from a simultaneous lineup, and then answers a second question regarding whether this person is the perpetrator (Humphries, Holliday, & Flowe, 2011; Pozzulo & Balfour, 2006; Pozzulo et al., 2008). Pryke, Lindsay, Dysart, and Dupuis (2004) proposed the use of multiple lineups, each assessing a different type of information. For example, there could be a lineup of faces, followed by a lineup of voice samples, a lineup of clothing, and so on. The more times a witness selected the suspect (his face, voice, clothing) rather than a foil, the more likely the suspect was guilty. Nairne (2002), however, provided a different view of this procedure. The effectiveness of a retrieval cue is determined by the extent to which it provides diagnostic (distinctive) information about a target. In other words, we are more likely to retrieve the memory we are searching for if we use the available cues in a multiplicative manner to focus the search rather than in an additive manner. However, it is possible that the piecemeal approach might provide more protection for an innocent suspect, as any mismatching factor could result in a correct rejection.

A different approach to trying to enhance the reliability of eyewitness evidence is to have the eyewitness perform a preparatory task prior to the lineup. For example, Macrae and Lewis (2002; see also Perfect, Dennis, & Snell, 2007) presented Navon (1977) stimuli prior to a lineup. An example of a Navon stimulus is a large capital letter A made up of several small letter S's. Participants instructed to focus on the global level (the A) performed better viewing the lineup than those instructed to focus on the local level (the S's). Macrae and Lewis explained these results with reference to the face processing literature (Farah, Wilson, Drain, & Tanaka, 1998). Because global processing is similar to the natural configural/holistic processing we undertake when viewing faces, it enhances face identification from a lineup. In contrast, local processing encourages featural processing of faces, which contrasts with natural face processing and thereby reduces lineup performance. See Perfect, Weston, Dennis, and Snell (2008) for an alternative explanation. More work is needed to explore these pre-identification procedures.

Alternatives to binary lineup decisions

There are alternative ways to gather information regarding an eyewitness's lineup decision. It is common to assess confidence after an eyewitness's binary (identifying someone as the perpetrator or not) decision, and recent studies have shown that confidence can be a reasonable indicator of accuracy for eyewitnesses who choose a lineup member (Brewer & Wells, 2006; Sauerland & Sporer, 2009; Sporer, 1992; Sporer, Penrod, Read, & Cutler, 1995). In particular, choosers' identification diagnosticity is high for very confident choosers (Sauer, Brewer, Zweck, & Weber, 2010). This is good news, as prosecutors are more likely to place highly confident eyewitnesses on the stand at trial, and jurors base their decisions in large part on eyewitness confidence (Cutler et al., 1990). The US Supreme Court supports the use of eyewitness confidence in assessing the veracity of eyewitness testimony (Neil v. Biggers, 1972), though ironically, this decision was reached long before the empirical research supported it.

Based on this newfound potential for confidence as an indicator of eyewitness identification accuracy, a confidence-based means of assessing eyewitness identifications recently has arisen. Brewer, Weber, Wootton, and Lindsay (2012 see also Sauer, Brewer, & Weber, 2008) asked participants to provide a confidence assessment (0–100 percent) within three seconds for each of the sequentially presented lineup members. Both group- and participant-level analyses showed that the level of performance obtained using these confidence judgments exceeded that of binary identification decisions. It appears that a witness knows more than a simple binary decision reveals.

Another approach to increasing eyewitness accuracy could be to add an explicit "don't know" response for eyewitnesses prior to a lineup. Weber and Perfect (2012; see also Warnick & Sanders, 1980) recently explored the implications of providing eyewitnesses with this option. Weber and Perfect presented participants with a showup of either the perpetrator or an innocent suspect. They examined three report conditions. In a free-report condition, participants could respond "don't know" as to whether the showup contained the perpetrator; in a forced-choice condition participants had to indicate whether the showup contained the perpetrator or not; and a spontaneous free report condition – mimicking real world police strategy – allowed, but did not explicitly state, the possibility for a "don't know" response. Results showed that participants rarely made a "don't know" response in the spontaneous condition. However, when explicitly provided with the option, approximately 20 percent of participants reported "don't know." Importantly, the removal of participants reporting "don't know" significantly improved the diagnosticity of showup decisions by reducing incorrect decisions (false identifications of the innocent suspect

and incorrect rejections of the perpetrator). An important next step, as Weber and Perfect acknowledged, is to see if these results will generalize to lineups. Steblay and Phillips (2011) addressed this issue by presenting a "not sure" response option to participants viewing a simultaneous or sequential lineup. Having this option decreased overall choosing, but only from sequential lineups. Nevertheless, research on meta-memory and the strategic deployment of memory (e.g., Benjamin, 2008) suggests that there is additional information to exploit about a witness's memory for a perpetrator if we adopt alternative response formats and procedures.

Postdictors

Aspects of an eyewitness's decision other than confidence can "postdict" the accuracy of a lineup decision. For example, Dunning and Perretta (2002) reported that identification decisions lasting 10–12 seconds or less were more accurate than decisions taking longer. However, Weber, Brewer, Wells, Semmler, and Keast (2004) found no evidence for this window, although they did support the robust negative correlation between lineup response latency and identification accuracy (e.g., Dunning & Stern, 1994; Smith, Lindsay, Pryke, & Dysart, 2001; Sporer, 1992): Quicker identification decisions tend to be more accurate (Sporer, 1993). In addition, Weber et al. (2004) found that the combination of relatively short response latency (i.e., under 10 seconds), and high confidence, was an excellent postdictor of identification accuracy.

In addition to response latency and confidence, police might be able to postdict eyewitness identification accuracy based on subjective aspects of the eyewitness's memory report (Dunning & Stern, 1994; Lindsay & Bellinger, 1999; Palmer, Brewer, McKinnon, & Weber, 2010). For example, Palmer et al. (2010) applied a popular phenomenological measure of recognition memory – Remember-Know judgments (Tulving, 1985) – to eyewitness identification decisions (see also Carlson & Gronlund,

2011). Palmer et al. found that an identification was more accurate when participants followed the identification decision by stating that they *Remembered* details from the simulated crime, compared with participants who indicated that they simply *Knew* without recollecting any details. But these judgments were not good postdictors above and beyond confidence. Therefore, Palmer et al. also subdivided Remember judgments into those with more or less perpetrator-associated details (as opposed to contextual details that would not necessarily aid an identification). Indeed, the more relevant details reported by their participants after choosing someone from a lineup, the more likely that the choice was correct.

Two other techniques attempt to capitalize on secondary measures of identification performance: eye movements and memory for lineup foils. Hannula, Baym, Warren, and Cohen (2012) recorded participants' eye movements while viewing a lineup and found that differences in the time spent viewing various lineup members might be more indicative of recognition accuracy than explicit decisions. Charman and Cahill (2012) found that an eyewitness's memory for the foils in a simultaneous lineup was as useful a postdictor of eyewitness accuracy as the actual lineup identifications. They argued that better memory for the foils was indicative of a more deliberative relative judgment process as opposed to a more automatic absolute judgment. The former process had been shown to be susceptible to reducing identification accuracy (e.g., Lindsay & Bellinger, 1999).

CONCLUSION

Eyewitness identification will never be perfect. That is not the goal of the system-variable research we reviewed. But prior research has identified procedural modifications that can enhance the reliability of eyewitness evidence. Some of these recommendations

are well established; others await additional empirical testing and theoretical validation. But future research on these and other recommendations must be conducted using sufficient sample sizes. Maxwell (2004) argued that many psychology studies are underpowered, and this especially is an issue for eyewitness research because these studies often collect only a single observation per participant. Meta-analysis of a large corpus of studies is one way to address this issue, but Kraemer, Gardner, Brooks, and Yesavage (1998) showed that meta-analyses that include underpowered studies can produce biased effect size estimates if the availability of studies depends on the likely role of publication biases favoring statistically significant results. Kraemer et al. (1998) recommended excluding underpowered studies from meta-analyses. Perhaps the inclusion of underpowered studies plays a role in the opposing conclusions sometimes reached by meta-analyses in the eyewitness domain (e.g., Clark, 2012a vs. Steblay et al., 2011).

As of this writing, here are the guidelines as we see them: An eyewitness should make only a single identification attempt. An individual repeated in a second identification attempt might be judged familiar from the first identification exposure rather than from the event in question. The identification attempt should take place using a lineup rather than a showup. Of course, this assumes that it has been determined that the witness had a reasonable opportunity to view the perpetrator, and that the police have probable cause implicating this individual. If not, it is unwise to conduct a lineup. The suspect plus five or more foils should be placed into a lineup. Although the literature is not yet clear on how those foils should be selected, and on just how much or how little they should resemble the perpetrator, the suspect should not stand out. If the suspect is in some way particularly distinctive (e.g., a facial tattoo), that characteristic should be replicated across the foils. An administrator, blind to the suspect's identity, should instruct the witness that the perpetrator may or may not be present. A certainty estimate should be collected once a (relatively quick) decision is reached. Finally, the criminal justice system should acknowledge that a positive suspect ID, a foil selection, or a rejection decision, all can provide evidence regarding the guilt *or innocence* of a suspect (see Clark et al., 2008; Wells & Lindsay, 1980). We find the evidence promoting the superiority of sequential lineups lacking and believe more can be gained by moving beyond the simultaneous-sequential debate to an exploration of promising alternative response formats (especially confidence) and various postdictors.

Confidence in the criminal justice system will be enhanced by continued system-variable research. Not only can system-variable research reduce the tragedy of false identifications, but more reliable eyewitness evidence also can reduce the diversion of resources expended on investigating truly guilty individuals. If Kevin Keith is innocent, the unreliable eyewitness evidence contributed to a tragedy. But if Kevin Keith is guilty, the poor quality of his eyewitness evidence raised unnecessary questions about his guilt.

To conclude, it is important to reiterate that the empirical support and theoretical validity of many of the recommendations we reviewed are not yet secure. We especially lament the lack of theoretical progress (see also Brewer, Weber, & Semmler, 2007) regarding system-variable research and eyewitness research more generally. We believe (as did McQuiston-Surrett, Malpass, & Tredoux, 2006) that system-variable research should be theoretically oriented and buttressed by quantitative modeling (e.g., Clark, 2008; Clark et al., 2011; Goodsell, Gronlund, & Carlson, 2010; Wells, 2008). Only when applied research is firmly grounded in psychological theories (Lane & Meissner, 2008) can seemingly disparate findings be tied together and policy recommendations be given the grounding they need. Without that grounding, it is unclear what the data are telling us, which obscures the path forward.

ACKNOWLEDGMENTS

The authors appreciate the helpful suggestions of Steve Lindsay and Neil Brewer.

NOTES

1 See: www.innocenceproject.org (last accessed June 1, 2013).

2 The National Registry of Exonerations, see: www.law.umich.edu/special/exoneration (last accessed June 1, 2013).

3 Retrieved May 22, 2012: www.psychology.iastate.edu/~glwells/hutchingscase.htm

4 See "selective attention test": www.youtube.com/watch?v=vJG698U2Mvo (last accessed June 1, 2013).

5 An increased choosing rate would not be a problem if the base rate of the police presenting innocent suspects in showups was very low.

6 Correct IDs involve choosing the guilty suspect out of a perpetrator-present lineup; false IDs involve choosing the innocent suspect out of a perpetrator-absent lineup.

7 The authors acknowledge Colton Perry's contributions to this idea.

8 See: www.nytimes.com/2010/09/03/us/03ohio.html (last accessed June 1, 2013).

9 See: www.lemitonline.org/publications/ewid.html (last accessed June 1, 2013).

10 A comprehensive discussion of simultaneous versus sequential lineups would push this chapter beyond its maximum length requirement, but we direct the reader to a chapter by Gronlund, Anderson, and Perry (2013) for a fuller treatment of the subject matter.

REFERENCES

Behrman, B. W., & Davey, S. L. (2001). Eyewitness identification in actual criminal cases: An archival analysis. *Law and Human Behavior*, *25*, 475–491. doi:10.1023/A:1012840831846

Benjamin, A. S. (2008). Memory is more than just remembering: Strategic control of encoding, accessing memory, and making decisions. In A. S. Benjamin and B. H. Ross (Eds.), *The psychology of learning and motivation: Skill and strategy in memory use* (Vol. 48; pp. 175–223). London: Academic Press.

Bindemann, M., Brown, C., Koyas, T., & Russ, A. (2012). Individual differences in face identification postdict eyewitness accuracy. *Journal of Applied Research in*

Memory and Cognition, 1, 96–103. doi:10.1016/j.jarmac.2012.02.001

Bradley v. State, 264 SD.E.2d 332 (Ga. App. 1980).

Brewer, N., Weber, N., & Semmler, C. (2007). A role for theory in eyewitness identification research. In R. C. L. Lindsay, D. F. Ross, J. D. Read, and M. P. (Eds.), *The handbook of eyewitness psychology, Vol II: Memory for people*. Mahwah, NJ: Lawrence Erlbaum Associates Publishers.

Brewer, N., Weber, N., Wootton, D., & Lindsay, D. S. (2012). Identifying the bad guy in a lineup using deadlined confidence judgments. *Psychological Science*, 23, 1208–1214. doi:10.1177/0956797612441217

Brewer, N., & Wells, G. L. (2006). The confidence–accuracy relationship in eyewitness identification: Effects of lineup instructions, foil similarity, and target-absent base rates. *Journal of Experimental Psychology: Applied*, 12, 11–30.

Brown, E., Deffenbacher, K., & Sturgill, W. (1977). Memory for faces and the circumstances of encounter. *Journal of Applied Psychology*, 62, 311–318. doi:10.1037/0021-9010.62.3.311

Buckhout, R. (1974). Eyewitness testimony. *Scientific American*, 231, 23–31.

Carlson, C. A. (2011). Influence of a perpetrator's distinctive facial feature on eyewitness identification from simultaneous versus sequential lineups. *Applied Psychology in Criminal Justice*, 7, 77–92.

Carlson, C.A., & Carlson, M.A. (2012). A distinctiveness-driven reversal of the weapon focus effect. *Applied Psychology in Criminal Justice*, 8, 36–53.

Carlson, C. A., & Gronlund, S. D. (2011). Searching for the sequential lineup advantage: A distinctiveness explanation. *Memory*, 19, 916–929. doi:10.1080/09658211.2011.613846

Charman, S. D., & Cahill, B. A. (2012). Witnesses' memories for lineup fillers postdicts their identification accuracy. *Journal of Applied Research in Memory and Cognition*, 1, 11–17. doi:10.1016/j.jarmac.2011.08.001

Clark, S. E. (2003). A memory and decision model for eyewitness identification. *Applied Cognitive Psychology*, 17, 629–654. doi:10.1002/acp.891

Clark, S. E. (2005). A re-examination of the effects of biased lineup instructions in eyewitness identification. *Law and Human Behavior*, 29, 395–424. doi:10.1007/s10979-005-5690-7

Clark, S. E. (2008). The importance (necessity) of computational modelling for eyewitness identification research. *Applied Cognitive Psychology*, 22, 803–813. doi:10.1002/acp.1484

Clark, S. E. (2012a). Costs and benefits of eyewitness identification reform: Psychological science and public policy. *Perspectives on Psychological Science*, 7, 238–259. doi:10.1177/1745691612439584

Clark, S. E. (2012b). Eyewitness identification reform: Data, theory, and due process. *Perspectives on Psychological Science*, 7, 279–283. doi:10.1177/1745691612444136

Clark, S. E., Erickson, M. A., & Breneman, J. (2011). Probative value of absolute and relative judgments in eyewitness identification. *Law and Human Behavior*, 35(5), 364–380. doi:10.1007/s10979-010-9245-1

Clark, S. E., & Godfrey, R. D. (2009). Eyewitness identification evidence and innocence risk. *Psychonomic Bulletin & Review*, 16, 22–42. doi:10.3758/PBR.16.1.22

Clark, S. E., & Gronlund, S. D. (1996). Global matching models of recognition memory: How the models match the data. *Psychonomic Bulletin & Review*, 3(1), 37–60.

Clark, S. E., Howell, R. T., & Davey, S. L. (2008). Regularities in eyewitness identification. *Law and Human Behavior*, 32, 187–218. doi:10.1007/s10979-006-9082-4

Clark, S. E., Marshall, T. E., & Rosenthal, R. (2009). Lineup administrator influences on eyewitness identification decisions. *Journal of Experimental Psychology: Applied*, 15, 63–75. doi:10.1037/a0015185

Clark, S. E., Rush, R. A., & Moreland, M. B. (2013). Constructing the lineup: Law, reform, theory, and data. In B. Cutler (Ed.), *Reform of eyewitness identification procedures*. Washington, DC: APA Publications.

Clark, S., & Tunnicliff, J. L. (2001). Selecting lineup foils in eyewitness identification experiments: Experimental control and real-world simulation. *Law and Human Behavior*, 25, 199–216. doi:10.1023/A:1010753809988

Commonwealth v. Carter, 414 A.2d 369 (Pa. Super. Ct. 1979).

Cutler, B. L., Berman, G. L., Penrod, S., & Fisher, R. P. (1994). Conceptual, practical, and empirical issues associated with eyewitness identification test media. In D. F. Ross, J. D. Read and M. D. Toglia (Eds.), *Adult eyewitness testing: Current trends and developments*. New York: Cambridge University Press.

Cutler, B. L., Penrod, S. D., & Dexter, H. R. (1990). Juror sensitivity to eyewitness identification evidence. *Law and Human Behavior*, 14, 185–191. doi:10.1007/BF01062972

Cutler, B. L., Penrod, S. D., & Martens, T. K. (1987). The reliability of eyewitness identification: The role of system and estimator variables. *Law and Human Behavior, 11*, 233–258. doi:10.1007/BF01044644

Darling, S., Valentine, T., & Memon, A. (2008). Selection of lineup fillers in operational contexts. *Applied Cognitive Psychology, 22*, 159–169. doi:10.1002/acp.1366

Davies, G., Shepherd, J., & Ellis, H. (1979). Effects of interpolated mugshot exposure on accuracy of eyewitness identification. *Journal of Applied Psychology, 64*, 232–237. doi:10.1037/0021-9010.64.2.232

Deffenbacher, K.A., Bornstein, B. H., & Penrod, S. D. (2006). Mugshot exposure effects: Retroactive interference, mugshot commitment, source confusion, and unconscious transference. *Law and Human Behavior, 30*, 287–307. doi:10.1007/s10979-006-9008-1

De Jong, M., Wagenaar, W. A., Wolters, G., & Verstijnen, I. M. (2005). Familiar face recognition as a function of distance and illumination: A practical tool for use in the courtroom. *Psychology, Crime, & Law, 11*, 87–97. doi:10.1080/10683160410001715123

Dillon, J. M., McAllister, H. A., & Vernon, L. L. (2009). The hybrid lineup combining sequential and simultaneous features: A first test. *Applied Psychology in Criminal Justice, 5*, 90–108.

Douglass, A. B., & Steblay, N. (2006). Memory distortion in eyewitnesses: A meta-analysis of the post-identification feedback effect. *Applied Cognitive Psychology, 20*, 859–869. doi:10.1002/acp.1237

Dunning, D., & Perretta, S. (2002). Automaticity and eyewitness accuracy: A 10- to 12-second rule for distinguishing accurate from inaccurate positive identifications. *Journal of Applied Psychology, 87*, 951–962. doi:10.1037/0021-9010.87.5.951

Dunning, D., & Stern, L. B. (1994). Distinguishing accurate from inaccurate eyewitness identifications via inquiries about decision processes. *Journal of Personality and Social Psychology, 67*, 818–835. doi:10.1037/0022-3514.67.5.818

Dysart, J. E., Lawson, V. Z., & Rainey, A. (2012). Blind lineup administration as a prophylactic against the post-identification feedback effect. *Law and Human Behavior, 36*, 312–319. doi:10.1037/h0093921

Dysart, J. E., & Lindsay, R. C. L. (2007). Show-up identifications: Suggestive technique or reliable method? In R. C. L. Lindsay, D. F. Ross, J. D. Read, and M. P. (Eds.), *The handbook of eyewitness psychology, Vol II: Memory for people.* Mahwah, NJ: Lawrence Erlbaum Associates Publishers.

Dysart, J. E., Lindsay, R. C. L., & Dupuis, P. R. (2006). Show-ups: The critical issue of clothing bias. *Applied Cognitive Psychology, 20*, 1009–1023. doi:10.1002/acp.1241

Dysart, J. E., Lindsay, R. C. L., Hammond, R., & Dupuis, P. (2001). Mug shot exposure prior to lineup identification: Interference, transference, and commitment effects. *Journal of Applied Psychology, 86*, 1280–1284. doi:10.1037/0021-9010.86.6.1280

Egan, J. P. (1958). *Recognition memory and the operating characteristic* (Technical Note AFCRC-TN-58-51, AO-152650). Bloomington, IN: Indiana University Hearing and Communication Laboratory.

Farah, M. J., Wilson, K. D., Drain, M., & Tanaka, J. N. (1998). What is "special" about face perception? *Psychological Review, 105*, 482–498. doi:10.1037/0033-295X.105.3.482

Goodsell, C. A. (2009). *Contributions of memory and decision processes to lineup identifications following mugshot exposure* (Unpublished doctoral dissertation). University of Oklahoma, Norman, OK.

Goodsell, C. A., Gronlund, S. D., & Carlson, C. A. (2010). Exploring the sequential lineup advantage using WITNESS. *Law and Human Behavior, 34*, 445–459. doi:10.1007/s10979-009-9215-7

Goodsell, C. A., Neuschatz, J. S., & Gronlund, S. D. (2009). Effects of mugshot commitment on lineup performance in young and older adults. *Applied Cognitive Psychology, 23*, 788–803. doi:10.1002/acp.1512

Goodsell, C. A., Wetmore, S., Neuschatz, J. S., & Gronlund, S. D. (2013). Showups vs. lineups: A review of two identification techniques. In B. Cutler (Ed.), *Reform of eyewitness identification procedures.* Washington, DC: APA Publications.

Gorenstein, G. W., & Ellsworth, P. C. (1980). Effect of choosing an incorrect photograph on a later identification by an eyewitness. *Journal of Applied Psychology, 65*, 616–622. doi:10.1037/0021-9010.65.5.616

Greathouse, S. M., & Kovera, M. B. (2009). Instruction bias and lineup presentation moderate the effects of administrator knowledge on eyewitness identification. *Law and Human Behavior, 33*, 70–82. doi:10.1007/s10979-008-9136-x

Green, D. M., & Swets, J. A. (1966). *Signal detection theory and psychophysics.* Oxford: John Wiley.

Gronlund, S. D., Andersen, S. M., & Perry, C. (2013). Presentation methods. In B. Cutler (Ed.), *Reform of eyewitness identification procedures.* Washington DC: APA.

Gronlund, S. D., Carlson, C. A., Dailey, S. B., & Goodsell, C. A. (2009). Robustness of the sequential lineup advantage. *Journal of Experimental Psychology: Applied, 15(2)*, 140–152. doi:10.1037/a0015082

Gronlund, S. D., Carlson, C. A., Neuschatz, J. S., Goodsell, C. A., Wetmore, S., Wooten, A., & Graham, M. (2012a). Showups versus lineups: An evaluation using ROC analysis. *Journal of Applied Research in Memory and Cognition, 1*, 221–228. doi:10.1016/j.jarmac.2012.09.003

Gronlund, S. D., Goodsell, C. A., & Andersen, S. M. (2012b). Lineup procedures in eyewitness identification. In L. Nadel and W. Sinnott-Armstrong (Eds.), *Law and neuroscience* (pp. 59–83). New York: Oxford University Press.

Hannula, D. E., Baym, C. L., Warren, D. E., & Cohen, N. J. (2012). The eyes know: Eye movements as a veridical index of memory. *Psychological Science, 23*, 278–287. doi:10.1177/0956797611429799

Haw, R. M., Dickinson, J. J., & Meissner, C. A. (2007). The phenomenology of carryover effects between show-up and line-up identification. *Memory, 15*, 117–127. doi:10.1080/09658210601171672

Haw, R. M., & Fisher, R. P. (2004). Effects of administrator-witness contact on eyewitness identification accuracy. *Journal of Applied Psychology, 89*(6), 1106–1112. doi:10.1037/0021-9010.89.6.1106

Horry, R., Memon, A., Wright, D. B., & Milne, R. (2012). Predictors of eyewitness identification decisions from video lineups in England: A field study. *Law and Human Behavior, 36*, 257–265. doi:10.1037/h0093959

Humphries, J. E., Holliday, R. E., & Flowe, H. D. (2011). Faces in motion: Age-related changes in eyewitness identification performance in simultaneous, sequential, and elimination video lineups. *Applied Cognitive Psychology, 26*, 149–158. doi:10.1002/acp.1808

Johnson, M. K., Hashtroudi, S., & Lindsay, L. D. (1993). Source monitoring. *Psychological Bulletin, 114*, 3–28. doi:10.1037/0033-2909.114.1.3

Jones, R. L., Scullin, M. H., & Meissner, C. A. (2011). Evidence of differential performance on simultaneous and sequential lineups for individuals with autism-spectrum traits. *Personality and Individual Differences, 51*, 537–540. doi:10.1016/j.paid.2011.04.013

Kassin, S. M., Tubb, V. A., Hosch, H. M., & Memon, A. (2001). On the "general acceptance" of eyewitness testimony research: A new survey of the experts. *American Psychologist, 56*(5), 405–416. doi:10.1037/0003-066X.56.5.405

Kerstholt, J. H., Koster, E. R., & van Amelsvoort, A. G. (2004). Eyewitnesses: A comparison of live, video,

and photo line-ups. *Journal of Police and Criminal Psychology, 19*, 15–22.

Kraemer, H. C., Gardner, C., Brooks, J. O., & Yesavage, J. A. (1998). Advantages of excluding underpowered studies in meta-analysis: Inclusionist versus exclusionist viewpoints. *Psychological Methods, 3*, 23–31.

Lane, S. M., & Meissner, C. A. (2008). A "middle road" approach to bridging the basic-applied divide in eyewitness identification research. *Applied Cognitive Psychology, 22*, 779–787.

Lindsay, R. C. L., & Bellinger, K. (1999). Alternatives to the sequential lineup: The importance of controlling the pictures. *Journal of Applied Psychology, 84*, 315–321. doi:10.1037/0021-9010.84.3.315

Lindsay, R. C., & Wells, G. L. (1985). Improving eyewitness identifications from lineups: Simultaneous versus sequential lineup presentation. *Journal of Applied Psychology, 70*(3), 556–564. doi:10.1037/0021-9010.70.3.556

Loftus, G. R. (2010). What can a perception–memory expert tell a jury? *Psychonomic Bulletin & Review, 17*, 143–148. doi:10.3758/PBR.17.2.143

Loftus, E. F., Loftus, G. R., & Messo, J. (1987). Some facts about "weapon focus." *Law and Human Behavior, 11*, 55–62. doi:10.1007/BF01044839

Lusted, L. B. (1971a). Signal detectability and medical decision-making. *Science, 171*, 1217–1219.

Lusted, L. B. (1971b). Decision-making studies in patient management. *New England Journal of Medicine, 284*, 416–424.

Macrae, C. N., & Lewis, H. L. (2002). Do I know you? Processing orientation and face recognition. *Psychological Science, 13*, 194–196. doi:10.1111/1467-9280.00436

Malpass, R. S., & Devine, P. G. (1981). Eyewitness identification: Lineup instructions and the absence of the offender. *Journal of Applied Psychology, 66*, 482–489. doi:10.1037/0021-9010.66.4.482

Maxwell, S. E. (2004). The persistence of underpowered studies in psychological research: Causes, consequences, and remedies. *Psychological Methods, 9*, 147–163.

McQuiston-Surrett, D., Malpass, R. S., & Tredoux, C. G. (2006). Sequential vs. simultaneous lineups: A review of methods, data, and theory. *Psychology, Public Policy, and Law, 12*, 137–169.

Meissner, C. A., & Brigham, J. C. (2001). A meta-analysis of the verbal overshadowing effect in face identification. *Applied Cognitive Psychology, 15*, 603–616. doi:10.1002/acp.728

Meissner, C. A., Tredoux, C. G., Parker, J. F., & MacLin, O. H. (2005). Eyewitness decisions in simultaneous and sequential lineups: A dual-process signal detection theory analysis. *Memory & Cognition, 33*, 783–792. doi:10.3758/BF03193074

Memon, A., Hope, L., Bartlett, J., & Bull, R. (2002). Eyewitness recognition errors: The effects of mugshot viewing and choosing in young and old adults. *Memory & Cognition, 30,* 1219–1227. doi:10.3758/BF03213404

Metz, C. E. (1978). Basic principles of ROC analysis. *Seminars in Nuclear Medicine, 8,* 283–298.

Mickes, L., Flowe, H. D., & Wixted, J. T. (2012). Receiver operating characteristic analysis in the assessment of lineup-based eyewitness memory. *Journal of Experimental Psychology: Applied, 18,* 361–376. doi:10.1037/a0030609

Morgan, C. A., Hazlett, G., Baranoski, M., Doran, A., Southwick, S., & Loftus, E. (2007). Accuracy of eyewitness identification is significantly associated with performance on a standardized test of face recognition. *International Journal of Law and Psychiatry, 30,* 213–223. doi:10.1016/j.ijlp.2007.03.005

Morgan, C. A., Hazlett, G., Doran, A., Garrett, S., Hoyt, G. Thomas, P., Baranoski, M., & Southwick, S. M. (2004). Accuracy of eyewitness memory for persons encountered during exposure to highly intense stress. *International Journal of Law and Psychiatry, 27,* 265–279. doi:10.1016/j.ijlp.2004.03.004

Münsterberg, H. (1908). *On the witness stand.* New York: McClure.

Nairne, J. S. (2002). The myth of the encoding-retrieval match. *Memory, 10,* 389–395. doi:10.1080/09658210244000216

National Institute of Justice (NIJ) (1999). *Eyewitness evidence: A guide for law enforcement.* Washington, DC: US Department of Justice.

Navon, D. (1977). Forest before trees: The precedence of global features in visual perception. *Cognitive Psychology, 9,* 353–383. doi:10.1016/0010-0285(77)90012-3

Neil v. Biggers, 409 US 188 (1972).

Nickerson, R. S. (1998). Confirmation bias: A ubiquitous phenomenon in many guises. *Review of General Psychology, 2,* 175–220.

O'Rourke, T. E., Penrod, S. D., Cutler, B. L., & Stuve, T. E. (1989). The external validity of eyewitness identification research: Generalizing across subject populations. *Law and Human Behavior, 13,* 385–395. doi:10.1007/BF01056410

Palmer, M. A., & Brewer, N. (2012). Sequential presentation encourages less biased criterion setting but does not improve discriminability. *Law and Human Behavior, 36,* 247–255. doi: 10.1037/h0093923

Palmer, M. A., Brewer, N., McKinnon, A. C., & Weber, N. (2010). Phenomenological reports diagnose accuracy of eyewitness identification decisions.

Acta Psychologica, 133, 137–145. doi:10.1016/j.actpsy.2009.11.002

Palmer, M. A., Brewer, N., & Weber, N. (2012). The information gained from witnesses' responses to an initial "blank" lineup. *Law and Human Behavior, 36,* 439–447. doi:10.1037/h0093939

Perfect, T. J., Dennis, I., & Snell, A. (2007). The effects of local and global processing orientation on eyewitness identification performance. *Memory, 15,* 784–798. doi:10.1080/09658210701654627

Perfect, T. J., Weston, N. J., Dennis, I., & Snell, A. (2008). The effects of precedence on Navon-induced processing bias in face recognition. *The Quarterly Journal of Experimental Psychology, 61,* 1479–1486. doi:10.1080/17470210802034678

Pisano, E. D., Gatsonis, C., Hendrick, E., Yaffe, M., Baum, J. K., Acharyya, S., Conant, E. F., et al. (2005). Diagnostic performance of digital versus film mammography for breast-cancer screening. *New England Journal of Medicine, 353,* 1773–1783.

Pozzulo, J. D., & Balfour, J. (2006). Children's and adults' eyewitness identification accuracy when a culprit changes his appearance: Comparing simultaneous and elimination lineup procedures. *Legal and Criminological Psychology, 11,* 25–34. doi:10.1348/135532505X52626

Pozzulo, J. D., Dempsey, J., Corey, S., Girardi, A., Lawandi, A., & Aston, C. (2008). Can a lineup procedure designed for child witnesses work for adults? Comparing simultaneous, sequential, and elimination lineup procedures. *Journal of Applied Social Psychology, 38,* 2195–2209. doi:10.1111/j.1559-1816.2008.00387.x

Pozzulo, J. D., & Lindsay, R. C. L. (1999). Elimination lineups: An improved identification procedure for child eyewitnesses. *Journal of Applied Psychology, 84,* 167–176. doi:10.1037/0021-9010.84.2.167

Pryke, S., Lindsay, R. C. L., Dysart, J. E., & Dupuis, P. (2004). Multiple independent identification decisions: A method of calibrating eyewitness identifications. *Journal of Applied Psychology, 89,* 73–84. doi:10.1037/0021-9010.89.1.73

Sauer, J. D., Brewer, N., & Weber, N. (2008). Multiple confidence estimates as indices of eyewitness memory. *Journal of Experimental Psychology: General, 137,* 528–547. doi:10.1037/a0012712

Sauer, J. D., Brewer, N., Zweck, T., & Weber, N. (2010). The effect of retention interval on the confidence–accuracy relationship for eyewitness identification. *Law and Human Behavior, 34,* 337–347. doi:10.1007/s10979-009-9192-x

Sauerland, M., & Sporer, S. L. (2009). Fast and confident: Postdicting eyewitness identification accuracy in a field study. *Journal of Experimental Psychology: Applied*, *15*, 46–62.doi:10.1037/a0014560

Simons, D. J., & Chabris, C. F. (1999). Gorillas in our midst: Sustained inattentional blindness for dynamic events. *Perception*, *28*, 1059–1074. doi:10.1068/p2952

Simons, D. J., & Chabris, C. F. (2011). What people believe about how memory works: A representative sample of the US population. *PLoS ONE*, *6*, e22757.

Smith, S. M., Lindsay, R. C. L., Pryke, S., & Dysart, J. E. (2001). Postdictors of eyewitness errors: Can false identifications be diagnosed in the cross-race situation? *Psychology, Public Policy, and Law*, *7*, 153–169. doi:10.1037/1076-8971.7.1.153

Sporer, S. L. (1992). Post-dicting eyewitness accuracy: Confidence, decision-times and person descriptions of choosers and non-choosers. *European Journal of Social Psychology*, *22*, 157–180. doi:10.1002/ejsp.2420220205

Sporer, S. L. (1993). Eyewitness identification accuracy, confidence, and decision times in simultaneous and sequential lineups. *Journal of Applied Psychology*, *78*, 22–33.

Sporer, S. L., Penrod, S., Read, D., & Cutler, B. (1995). Choosing, confidence, and accuracy: A meta-analysis of the confidence–accuracy relation in eyewitness identification studies. *Psychological Bulletin*, *118*, 315–327. doi:10.1037/0033-2909.118.3.315

State v. Dubose, WI 126, No. 2003AP1690-CR (2005).

Steblay, N. M. (1997). Social influence in eyewitness recall: A meta-analytic review of lineup instruction effects. *Law and Human Behavior*, *21*, 283–297. doi:10.1023/A:1024890732059

Steblay, N. K., Dysart, J., Fulero, S., & Lindsay, R. C. L. (2001). Eyewitness accuracy rates in sequential and simultaneous lineup presentations: A meta-analytic comparison. *Law and Human Behavior*, *25*, 459–474.

Steblay, N., Dysart, J., Fulero, S., & Lindsay, R. C. L. (2003). Eyewitness accuracy rates in police showup and lineup presentations: A meta-analytic comparison. *Law and Human Behavior*, *27*, 523–540. doi:10.1023/A:1025438223608

Steblay, N. K., Dysart, J. E., & Wells, G. L. (2011). Seventy-two tests of the sequential lineup superiority effect: A meta-analysis and policy discussion. *Psychology, Public Policy, and Law*, *17*, 99–139. doi:10.1037/a0021650

Steblay, N. K., & Phillips, J. D. (2011). The not sure response option in sequential lineup practice. *Applied Cognitive Psychology*, *25*, 768–774.

Stovall v. Denno, 388 US 293 (1967).

Swets, J. A., Dawes, R. M., & Monahan, J. (2000). Psychological science can improve diagnostic decisons. *Psychological Science in the Public Interest*, *1*, 1–26. doi:10.1111/1529-1006.001

Tulving, E. (1985). Memory and consciousness. *Canadian Psychology*, *26*, 1–12. doi:10.1037/h0080017

United States v. Wade, 388 US 218 (1967).

Valentine, T., Darling, S., & Memon, A. (2007). Do strict rules and moving images increase the reliability of sequential identification procedures? *Applied Cognitive Psychology*, *21*, 933–949. doi:10.1002/acp.1306

Valentine, T. & Heaton, P. (1999). An evaluation of the fairness of police line-ups and video identifications. *Applied Cognitive Psychology*, *13*, S59–S72. doi:10.1002/(SICI)1099-0720(199911)13:1+<S59::AID-ACP679>3.0.CO;2-Y

Warnick, D. H., & Sanders, G. S. (1980). Why do eyewitnesses make so many mistakes? *Journal of Applied Social Psychology*, *10*, 362–366. doi:10.1111/j.1559-1816.1980.tb00716.x

Weber, N., & Brewer, N. (2006). Positive versus negative face recognition decisions: Confidence, accuracy, and response latency. *Applied Cognitive Psychology*, *20*, 17–31. doi:10.1002/acp.1166

Weber, N., Brewer, N., Wells, G. L., Semmler, C., & Keast, A. (2004). Eyewitness identification accuracy and response latency: The unruly 10–12-second rule. *Journal of Experimental Psychology: Applied*, *10*, 139–147. doi:10.1037/1076-898X.10.3.139

Weber, N., & Perfect, T. J. (2012). Improving eyewitness identification accuracy by screening out those who say they don't know. *Law and Human Behavior*, *36*, 28–36. doi:10.1037/h0093976

Wechsler, D. (1997). *Wechsler Memory Scale – Third Edition Manual*. San Antonio, TX: The Psychological Corporation.

Wells, G. L. (1978). Applied eyewitness-testimony research: System variables and estimator variables. *Journal of Personality and Social Psychology*, *36*, 1546–1557. doi:10.1037/0022-3514.36.12.1546

Wells, G. L. (1984). The psychology of lineup identifications. *Journal of Applied Social Psychology*, *14*, 89–103. doi:10.1111/j.1559-1816.1984.tb02223.x

Wells, G. L. (2008). Theory, logic and data: Paths to a more coherent eyewitness science. *Applied Cognitive Psychology*, *22*, 853–859. doi:10.1002/acp.1488

Wells, G. L., & Bradfield, A. L. (1998). "Good, you identified the suspect": Feedback to eyewitnesses distorts their reports of the witnessing experience. *Journal of Applied Psychology*, *83*, 360–376. doi:10.1037/0021-9010.83.3.360

Wells, G. L., & Lindsay R. C. L. (1980). On estimating the diagnosticity of eyewitness nonidentifications. *Psychological Bulletin, 88*, 776–84.

Wells, G. L., Memon, A., & Penrod, S. D. (2006). Eyewitness evidence: Improving its probative value. *Psychological Science in the Public Interest, 7*, 45–75. doi:10.1111/j.1529-1006.2006.00027.x

Wells, G. L., & Olson, E. A. (2002). Eyewitness identification: Information gain from incriminating and exonerating behaviors. *Journal of Experimental Psychology: Applied, 8*, 155–167. doi:10.1037/1076-898X.8.3.155

Wells, G. L., Small, M., Penrod, S., Malpass, R. S., Fulero, S. M., & Brimacombe, C. A. E. (1998). Eyewitness identification procedures: Recommendations for lineups and photospreads. *Law and Human Behavior, 22*, 603–647. doi:10.1023/A:1025750605807

Wells, G. L., Steblay, N. M., & Dysart, J. E. (2012). http://www.ajs.org/wc/ewid/ewid_report.asp

Wells, G. L., & Turtle, J. W. (1986). Eyewitness identification: The importance of lineup models. *Psychological Bulletin, 99*, 320–329. doi:10.1037/0033-2909.99.3.320

Wilcock, R., & Kneller, W. (2011). A comparison of presentation methods of video identification parades. *Applied Cognitive Psychology, 25*, 835–840. doi:10.1002/acp.1754

Wise, R. A., Safer, M.A., & Maro, C. M. (2011). What US law enforcement officers know and believe about eyewitness factors, eyewitness interviews and identification procedures. *Applied Cognitive Psychology, 25*, 488–500.

Wixted, J. T., & Mickes, L. (2012). The field of eyewitness memory should abandon "probative value" and embrace Receiver Operating Characteristic analysis. *Perspectives on Psychological Science, 7*, 275–278. doi:10.1177/1745691612442906

Wogalter, M. S., Malpass, R. S., & McQuiston, D. E. (2004). A national survey of US police on preparation and conduct of identification lineups. *Psychology, Crime & Law, 10*, 69–82. doi:10.1080/10683160410001641873

Wright, D. B., & Skagerberg, E. M. (2007). Postidentification feedback affects real eyewitnesses. *Psychological Science, 18*, 172–178. doi:10.1111/j.1467-9280.2007.01868.x

Zarkadi, T., Wade, K. A., & Stewart, N. (2009). Creating fair lineups for suspects with distinctive features. *Psychologial Science, 20*, 1448–1453. doi:10.1111/j.1467-9280.2009.02463.x

34

Social Influences on Eyewitness Memory

Amy Bradfield Douglass and Lorena Bustamante

When eyewitnesses are the foundation of prosecution cases, mistaken eyewitness identifications or erroneous reports of crime details can contribute to wrongful convictions that punish the innocent and leave the perpetrator free to reoffend (e.g., Garrett, 2011). For that reason, psychological scientists have examined a wide range of variables implicated in negatively affecting eyewitness memory reports. This chapter focuses on the extent to which social variables affect the integrity of eyewitness memory reports, including memory for event details, identification decisions, and confidence. The potential for interaction between social variables and memory was first noted by one of the forefathers of psychology who wrote, "the very form and style of recall [varies] with changes in the social background" (Bartlett, 1932, p. 253).

Although Bartlett's theoretical insights and empirical observations presaged many contemporary experiments, there was a considerable lag between his 1932 book and a concerted emphasis on how social influences affect remembering. As late as 2001, cognitive psychologist Mary Susan Weldon lamented that "Bartlett's argument that remembering is social has received little

serious treatment in psychology, and has had no perceptible influence on how memory has been conceptualized or investigated in mainstream experimental work" (Weldon, 2001, p. 67). In spite of this dim view of cognitive psychologists' response to Bartlett, social psychologists, perhaps by virtue of their field's questions about human behavior, have been more attentive to social influences on memory (e.g., see Hirst, Coman, & Coman, Chapter 16, this volume, Wyer, Chapter 17, this volume). In particular, the interface of psychology and law is a real-world context in which social influences on memory are critically important precisely because errors have disastrous effects.

Experimental psychologists use a range of methodologies to study the effect of social variables on eyewitnesses. In design, these paradigms range from purely cognitive to purely social. For example, in a typical cognitive experiment participants study a set of stimuli and then make old/new judgments about those stimuli in a test phase (e.g., Reysen, 2005). Some of these experiments also include questions asking participants to indicate whether they "remember" or "know" the stimuli to be old (e.g., Tulving, 1985). Social influence is tested by manipulating confederate co-witness responses in the constrained setting of the old/new response paradigm (e.g., Meade & Roediger, 2002) or measuring the effect of collaborative recall (e.g., Henkel & Rajaram, 2011). In a typical social paradigm, the interaction between participants is more free-flowing with realistic stimuli such as slide shows of crime scenes (e.g., Wright, Self, & Justice, 2000) or live staged events (e.g., Shaw & McClure, 1996). Both cognitive and social paradigms provide clear evidence that social factors have profound and lasting effects on eyewitness memory reports. Throughout the remainder of this chapter, we incorporate relevant literature from both cognitive and social perspectives in the context of the following fictitious eyewitness scenario.

A WITNESSED EVENT

Knoxville, Tennessee, 1.00 am
College students Annie and Sarah stepped quietly into their off-campus apartment building. Before they closed the door, a man came running down the stairs, violently pushed Sarah aside and escaped outside. Just then, they heard a woman screaming upstairs.

In a perfect world, memory reports would be collected immediately to prevent contamination from external sources. However, real witnesses are likely to encounter many social influences that could contaminate the details they remember, any identification decision, and their confidence. The vulnerability of witness reports to decay and influence supports the argument from many psychological scientists that memory reports should be considered trace evidence.

Typically, the trace evidence label is reserved exclusively for physical remnants of a crime (e.g., blood stains and DNA samples). However, experimental psychologists argue that memory evidence deserves to share that label because it can be contaminated in much the same way as physical evidence (e.g., Wells, 1995). Although

this conceptualization appeals to experimental psychologists, it should be noted that it was explicitly rejected in a recent appellate decision in the United States. As described in the New Jersey Supreme Court's decision,

the criminal justice system collects and evaluates trace evidence and eyewitness identification evidence differently. Unlike vials of blood, memories cannot be stored in evidence lockers. Instead, we must strive to avoid reinforcement and distortion of eyewitness memories from outside effects, and expose those influences when they are present.
(State v. Henderson, 2011, p. 122)

The Court's method for "exposing those influences" was to recommend increased opportunities for pre-trial hearings on eyewitness evidence and enhanced jury instructions. We return to the question of whether these solutions are likely to be successful in the concluding sections of this chapter. First, we discuss some of the influences to which the Court referred by following the witnesses introduced above in the immediate aftermath of the fictitious crime.

REPORTING THE EVENT

As soon as the man disappeared, Sarah pulled out her cell phone and dialed 9-1-1: "My sister and I are at our apartment and we just saw a man running out of the building. Someone upstairs is screaming that she's been raped and we think we saw who did it."

The choice of who made the 9-1-1 call may have been a simple function of which sister had easiest access to her cell phone. However, research suggests that response order has profound implications for the nature of memory conformity. In one recent set of experiments, participants took an old/new recognition test for 50 studied line drawings (Wright & Carlucci, 2011). Participants responded in groups of three where two participants were confederates whose answers were presented on a video. When the two confederates disagreed on whether the stimulus was old or new, the participant was most likely to conform to whichever confederate spoke first. This effect occurred regardless of whether order was determined by the confederates themselves (Experiment 1), or arbitrarily by a light signaling each person's turn (Experiment 2). Importantly, response order dictated influence regardless of the confederate's actual accuracy (see also, Gabbert, Memon, & Wright, 2006, but see also Lindsay, 2007).

Even more troubling, research suggests that initial conformity to co-witness reports can impair subsequent recognition. In one experiment, participants studied a list of 100 words, completed a joint test phase in which they identified words as old or new, and then completed an individual recognition test. In the joint test phase, participants were exposed to responses from a virtual confederate who provided answers via computer (Reysen, 2005). When the confederate responded first, the data showed clear conformity to the confederate's response; inaccurate confederate responses decreased participants' own accuracy (compared with participants' accuracy when answering first) and correct confederate responses increased participants' accuracy. In a second experiment, participants' accuracy on the individual recognition test was lower for items on which they had responded second, compared with items on which they responded first – regardless of the accuracy of the confederate's answer.

Another study demonstrated that response order was a stronger influence on conformity than were natural differences in power. In this study, pairs of siblings responded to a power questionnaire including questions such as "If you and your sibling disagree about what you want to do, who is more likely to decide in the end?" (Skagerberg & Wright, 2009a, p. 103). Responses indicated that older siblings were seen as having more power in the relationship by both members of the sibling pair. However, that power differential had no impact on which sibling conformed to the other's memory report. The only significant

effect was for response order: whichever sibling responded first elicited conformity from his or her sibling partner (Skagerberg & Wright, 2009a).

Other studies suggest that power differentials can sometimes shape the joint report produced, even if that context is highly artificial. In one example of such a demonstration, pairs of participants saw 50 faces and then were randomly assigned to a low power role (the designer of a restaurant) or a high power role (the judge of the restaurant design, Skagerberg & Wright, 2008a). Participants later engaged in a facial recognition task in which one person had to answer before the other. Individuals in the low power condition were more likely to be influenced by their partner's responses than those in the high power condition, again regardless of accuracy.

Other studies manipulate power by creating different levels of expertise within the experiment. In one clever design, experimenters manipulated participants' expectations of visual acuity by telling them "what we do is degrade people's acuity by different amounts using our different acuity glasses" (French, Garry, & Mori, 2011, p. 121). Participants were randomly assigned to "optimal" or "moderately degraded" visual acuity conditions; participants' glasses did not actually affect their vision. After learning about the "acuity" of their partner, participants watched a videotaped event with that partner, discussed the video, and completed an independent memory report.

There are two interesting findings from this study. The first is that participants who expected their visual acuity to be degraded compared with their partner actually performed better on the memory test than their "optimal acuity" partner, presumably because participants in the degraded condition marshaled extra resources while watching the videotaped event. However, superior performance among participants in the degraded acuity condition only occurred when they expected to be at a relative disadvantage, not when their partner's acuity was also degraded. The second interesting finding also happened among pairs with different levels of acuity: Participants with higher acuity were less likely to incorporate misinformation into their independent memory report compared with participants who had lower acuity (French et al., 2011).

Taken together, these findings highlight the key role of social context in dictating the extent to which people actively encode a scene and conform to their partner's description of that scene. An innocuous decision about who places the 9-1-1 call could have lasting implications for the silent co-witness's own reports about the witnessed event, especially if there are meaningful power differentials between co-witnesses (e.g., differences in visual acuity). One troubling feature of all of these studies is that influence transmitted between witnesses is independent of accuracy; witnesses have no apparent ability to discriminate between accurate and errant information, making the evaluation of information from witnesses who report events together extremely difficult. In the next section, we describe research showing that social influence is not just a function of mere response order, but also of detailed conversations among co-witnesses.

TALKING WITH A CO-WITNESS

"Did you see his face?" Annie asked after hanging up with the police. The girls immediately started comparing details with one another.

Co-witnesses frequently discuss what they have seen after a crime occurs. In one field study, 58 percent of real co-witnesses discussed the crime with a fellow witness, with the number of fellow witnesses averaging approximately four (Skagerberg & Wright, 2008b). The percentage of witnesses who reported conversations with a co-witness is even higher (86 percent) among a sample of undergraduates who reported witnessing

real instances of serious crime (Paterson & Kemp, 2006).

Although some co-witness discussions are a non-strategic outcome of sharing an unusual event, other discussions might occur because people think they can produce a superior memory if they collaborate as they recall event details. For example, in a recall task involving remembering lists of words, both young adults (mean age 20.25 years) and older adults (mean age 79.15 years) reported that collaboration was better than working alone, especially if there were more people rather than fewer (Henkel & Rajaram, 2011). This pattern was especially strong among participants who had actually engaged in collaborative recall prior to answering questions about whether collaborative recall enhances memory accuracy.

Among the two age groups, older and younger adults had different opinions about which categories of people would enhance their recall. Older adults' perception of the benefit of collaboration was independent of whether they expected strangers or friends to serve as collaboration partners; younger adults expected collaboration with close friends to help produce more accurate recall than collaboration with strangers (Henkel & Rajaram, 2011). Research with older children supports this assumption: among 15-year-olds, collaborative recall accuracy is higher among friend dyads than among dyads of non-friends. Interestingly, this same research shows that collaborative recall in younger children (seven years old) does reduce accuracy compared with individual recall, perhaps suggesting that the ability to take another's perspective present in older children is a mechanism through which the negative effects of collaboration can be mitigated (Andersson, 2001). In other studies, the effect of collaboration is not so positive: among adults, collaborative recollection is worse when individuals are paired with a romantic partner versus a stranger (French, Garry, & Mori, 2008; see also Hope, Ost, Gabbert, Healey, & Lenton, 2008).

General belief in the benefits of collaborative recall are striking in light of survey data indicating that people do not believe joint interviews of eyewitnesses are desirable. In a survey of 1000 Norwegian adults, researchers asked the following question: "Sometimes two or more persons are witnesses to the same event. A police investigator may interview the witnesses together or separately. When do you think he will obtain the most information?" (Magnussen et al., 2006, p. 608). Even though some police officers believe joint interviews can be beneficial (Paterson & Kemp, 2005), almost 70 percent of adults in Magnussen et al.'s study indicated that separate interviews would produce the most information; fewer than 20 percent said that a joint interview would produce the most information.

Consistent with people's impressions about forensic interviews, collaboration during recall actually results in inferior performance under some circumstances. *Collaborative inhibition* is widely studied within cognitive psychology (e.g., Rajaram & Pereira-Pasarin, 2010; Weldon, 2001). In one demonstration of this phenomenon, participants heard a story called *War of the Ghosts* from Bartlett (1932). Subsequently, they recalled details of the story either individually or in collaborative groups of three. To test the impact of collaborative recall, researchers compared the number of accurate details produced by individuals, collaborative groups, and nominal groups created by combining the unique details recalled by participants in the individual recall condition. Nominal groups provide information about the maximum information that collaborative groups should have been able to recall. Although collaborative groups did recall more details than did individuals, their performance was significantly worse than that of nominal groups (Weldon & Bellinger, 1997), even with monetary rewards for accuracy (Weldon, Blair, & Huebsch, 2000).

Collaboration harms recall because it "disrupts [individuals'] own idiosyncratic organization of the material" (Weldon, 2001, p. 95).

This fact was demonstrated in an experiment in which researchers manipulated the extent to which idiosyncratic organization of to-be-recalled material was possible by creating two conditions of stimulus materials: fifteen six-item categories or six 15-item categories. When the categories had only six items each, there was not much variability in how participants organized and then recalled the information; collaborative recall did not impair performance (compared with the nominal group condition). However, with six 15-item categories, the high number of items in each category facilitated idiosyncratic organization of the material, allowing each participant to create his or her own system for recalling the information. In that condition, collaborative recall did impair performance (Basden, Basden, Bryner, & Thomas, 1997; see also Rajaram, 2011).

These data have implications for real witnesses' joint recall attempts. Because there is no standard way of encoding a face or crime details, the opportunity for idiosyncratic organization of the complex information available in encoding a perpetrator's face or crime details seems high. If co-witnesses then attempt to collaborate in producing a joint description, the data described above suggest that these attempts would be less effective than if witnesses tried to produce descriptions on their own.

REPORTING SPECIFIC DETAILS

"Tall, white male with dark hair and a goatee," said Annie. "A goatee?" thought Sarah, puzzled. Annie confidently continued her description. Sarah ultimately concluded, "That's right, tall, white male with dark hair and a goatee!"

Suppose Annie's description of the perpetrator was incorrect; there was no goatee. A host of experimental research provides specific predictions about how and when witnesses' reports will be affected by misinformation of this type. Across several decades, misinformation has been presented in the context of post-event questionnaires (e.g., Loftus, Miller, & Burns, 1978), co-witness conversations (e.g., Zajac & Henderson, 2009), experimenter information (e.g., Luus & Wells, 1994), and written materials (e.g., Paterson & Kemp, 2006). In all cases, it is surprisingly easy to contaminate witness reports, especially if the misinformation is introduced after a delay (Paterson, Kemp, & Forgas, 2009). One constraint appears to be that witnesses are only persuaded by co-witnesses if they see them as a credible source of information (e.g., Hoffman, Granhag, See, & Loftus, 2001).

In comparison with misinformation originating from another source, co-witness misinformation is particularly influential on recognition tests. In one experiment, those who heard misinformation from a co-witness during discussion were more likely to incorporate it into a subsequent memory report; witnesses who heard misinformation from a leading question or a media report performed at the same level as the control group. In a free recall test, co-witness misinformation produced the same number of errors as did misinformation embedded in media reports (Paterson & Kemp, 2006). Because eyewitnesses are typically engaged in free recall tasks rather than recognition tasks, these data suggest that misinformation from either source will impair witness reports equally.

In another study, researchers ensured that witnesses had access to different information by showing co-witnesses two different videos of the same event (Gabbert, Memon, & Allan, 2003). The different versions of the event were created by filming the same sequence of events from two different angles, simulating the different perspectives two witnesses might have. Half of the witnesses then discussed the video in pairs, having been led to believe that their partner watched the exact same video. Finally, all witnesses completed an individual memory test, which included a free recall component and four critical questions asking about items that were visible from one perspective but not the other (e.g., a book title). Witnesses were cautioned to "think back to what they could remember

witnessing from the event" (Gabbert et al., 2003, p. 536). Details reported by a co-witness were likely to appear in witnesses' final report of the event, even when those details were unseen by witnesses in the original video. The tendency to incorporate information from a co-witness appeared equally for both younger witnesses (mean age 20 years) and older witnesses (mean age 69 years).

The extent of co-witness influence extends beyond changing mere details of memory reports to changing fundamental aspects of what was witnessed. In one example, witnesses completely invented (or ignored) the presence of a central player in the witnessed event. In this study, witnesses discussed a slide show with a partner (Wright et al., 2000). In each group of two witnesses, one member of the pair saw a slide show containing an accomplice; the other partner saw the same slide show, but without an accomplice. Even though witnesses' reports were accurate when they were tested alone, in 19 of 20 pairs the witnesses produced a joint report about the slide show in which they agreed about the presence (or absence) of the accomplice. Individual post-discussion questionnaires demonstrated that their actual beliefs about the presence (or not) of an accomplice did indeed change as a result of the conversation with their co-witness. Not surprisingly, whichever witness was more confident in his/her recall of the accomplice's presence (or absence) dictated the content of the joint report (see also, e.g., Schneider & Watkins, 1996).

In the same way, witnesses with low confidence are particularly vulnerable to social influence (e.g., Wright, London, & Waechter, 2000), witnesses who find their task difficult – and important – are at increased risk of changing their reports as a function of social influence. The combined effect of difficulty and importance in dictating vulnerability to social influence was creatively demonstrated in a task modeled after Asch's (1951) classic line-judging experiment (Baron, Vandello, & Brunsman, 1996). In Baron et al.'s experiment, witnesses provided an identification decision in groups of three participants, two of whom were confederates who provided incorrect identifications on critical trials, with the real participant always providing a decision last on the critical trials.

Participants saw a line drawing of a figure and made an identification from "lineup" of four line drawings of figures having seen each for 5 seconds (easy) or 500 milliseconds (hard). Participants were told that the experiment was a pilot project for the researchers (low importance) or a test that would be used in the forensic process (high importance). In the low importance condition, witnesses conformed on an equal number of trials, regardless of task difficulty. Thus, they conformed even when they knew the answer was wrong (i.e., in the easy task condition), suggesting that conformity was driven by normative influence (cf. Deutsch & Gerard, 1955).

In the high importance condition, task difficulty moderated conformity. Participants didn't conform when they knew the confederates' answers were wrong (i.e., the easy task condition) but did when they did not know the right answer themselves (i.e., the difficult task condition). Therefore, the high importance condition demonstrated informational influence rather than normative influence (cf. Deutsch & Gerard, 1955). In a more general test of this idea in the specific context of co-witness discussions, eyewitness responses reflected memory blend (i.e., informational influence) rather than memory conformity (i.e., normative influence), possibly because the accuracy of the task was more important than standing out from the crowd (see also Wright et al., 2010).

This distinction between normative and informational influence is common in research on social influence and provides an important mechanism for distinguishing among people's motivations. Interestingly, Morton Deutsch wrote in 1980 that he "did not think that [the distinction between normative and informational influence] was a particularly important one … it was mainly a commonsense protest against some intellectual sloppiness about 'group" influences … I have been surprised by its popularity"

(Deutsch, 1980, p. 235). In spite of Deutsch's objections, the distinction between normative and informational influence is likely to continue serving as a useful framework for research understanding the impact of social variables on eyewitness behavior and memory reports.

BEING INTERVIEWED

> The sisters were interviewed separately. Before beginning the interview, the officers gave each sister specific instructions about how to report her memories, including a warning to focus only on what she actually remembered herself, not on any information her sister might have provided.

The opportunity for social influence in the interaction between a police investigator and an eyewitness is clear. Interviewers must encourage accurate reporting from eyewitnesses without soliciting inaccurate information. Some police manuals encourage interviewers to achieve that balance by "continually reward[ing] the interviewee with feedback" (Ord, Shaw, & Green, 2008, p. 45). In contrast, empirically validated protocols focus on limiting interviewers' behavior to the delivery of a specific set of instructions. The most well-known of these protocols is the Cognitive Interview in which interviewers lead witnesses through a specific set of prompts, including that witnesses should remember the event from different perspectives and "report everything" (see e.g., Fisher, Schreiber Compo, Rivard, & Hirn, this volume; Memon, Meissner, & Fraser, 2010). A new Self-Administered Interview has adapted the Cognitive Interview protocol for use at the scene of a crime where face-to-face exchanges may not be possible (e.g., Gabbert, Hope, & Fisher, 2009).

The Cognitive Interview aims for standardization across interviewer–interviewee pairs, where the interviewer's influence is limited to extracting the most information and most accurate information possible. Even so, there are opportunities for flexibility in the social relationship that develops. For example, investigators and eyewitnesses often begin an interview with different goals. An eyewitness might be interested in providing only those details known to be accurate, for fear of eventual contradiction. In contrast, an investigator might hope that the lone eyewitness provides information about any detail recalled, so as to guide the nascent investigation. Recent research manipulating the goals for investigators and eyewitnesses in a mock forensic interview demonstrates that this asymmetry has significant implications for the outcome of the interview. In particular, when investigators' and eyewitnesses' goals matched each other (versus mismatched), eyewitnesses reported more accurate information, regardless of the actual content of the instructions (Douglass, Brewer, Semmler, Bustamante, & Hiley, 2013).

Some researchers have tested whether warnings can actually ameliorate the effect of misinformation. For example, Paterson, Kemp, and Ng (2011) had participants watch two versions of the same video and discuss what they saw. After approximately one week, all participants were interviewed individually about what they saw in the video. Half of the participants were explicitly told that their partner might have seen a different video, so they should only report what they remembered themselves. The warning had no effect: 28 percent of participants who received a warning reported at least one piece of misinformation compared with 32 percent of unwarned participants.

On occasion, warnings do work. Meade and Roediger (2002) presented participants with slides of household scenes (e.g., bathroom, kitchen). After seeing six slides of these scenes, participants completed a minute filler task and then recalled items from the scenes with a confederate. Each individual alternated giving their response, with the confederate introducing some misinformation items. Finally, each participant completed an individual free recall test, indicating for each item whether they "remembered" it or "knew" it (cf. Tulving, 1985).

Before the free recall test, half of the participants were warned that their conversation partner may have introduced inaccurate information. Participants who were warned were significantly less likely to report misinformation items.

Another study also found that warning participants successfully inoculated them against misinformation effects. This study used the staged crime video from Gabbert et al. (2003) in which the same event is filmed from two perspectives. In one condition, participants discussed the video in dyads, assuming that their partner watched the exact same video. In Experiment 2, participants were warned to "report only details they had personally witnessed" (Bodner, Musch, & Azad, 2009, p. 1073). In the dyad condition, this warning did eliminate reporting of non-witnessed critical details compared with a condition in which participants only read another participant's report containing misinformation. However, in spite of the warning, the dyad groups were more likely to report other kinds of non-critical inaccurate details, perhaps because the warning introduced a response bias (see also Wright, Gabbert, Memon, & London, 2008).

The studies reviewed here indicate that warnings sometimes inoculate participants against misinformation effects. Importantly, delay seems to moderate the effectiveness of warnings. For example, in Paterson et al. (2011), participants were interviewed after a one-week delay; the warning did not reduce the effect of misinformation. In contrast, a warning was effective in Bodner et al. (2009) where participants were interviewed immediately after discussing a crime video with a co-witness. To the extent that Paterson et al.'s paradigm more accurately captures the experience a real witness might have, researchers should be cautious about assuming that warnings are effective in protecting witnesses against incorporating misinformation into their own memory reports.

In addition to delay, another key feature distinguishing successful warning manipulations from unsuccessful ones might rest in the ability of witnesses to accurately identify the source of the to-be-recalled information. For example, misinformation effects can be eliminated when the recall instructions specifically encourage participants to consider the source of the detail (i.e., whether the detail came from the pictures, the text describing the pictures, neither, or both, Lindsay & Johnson, 1989, p. 352). Although this represents a promising solution to memory conformity effects, it relies on a witness's ability to accurately remember the source of any information. Data showing that witnesses forget the source of the information (e.g., Gabbert, Memon, & Wright, 2007) speak to the difficulty in relying on this technique as a panacea for memory conformity effects, especially if source monitoring instructions come after a delay, when participants have forgotten the source of the information, but not the information gleaned from that source (e.g., Paterson et al., 2011).

MAKING AN IDENTIFICATION

In separate identification procedures, each sister selected the same photo. After one identification, one of the police officers exclaimed, "That is exactly who we thought committed the crime!"

Both identification decisions and memories of the witnessed event can be affected by seemingly insignificant variations in the identification procedure. For example, witnesses are more likely to identify the lineup administrator's suspect when the administrator is sitting close to the witness, compared with sitting out of the witness's sight (Haw & Fisher, 2004). Similarly, a simple reassurance from the police officer that the identification was correct can have profound effects on a wide swath of judgments related to witnesses' memory. In experiments testing this effect, participants watch a videotaped event and make an identification from a target-absent photospread, ensuring that any resulting identification is incorrect. Participants then receive feedback about their

identification and complete a questionnaire containing testimony-relevant items. These paradigms find that comments suggesting a witness's identification was accurate (e.g., "good, you identified the actual suspect") inflate witnesses' memory of how confident they were at the time of their identification, how good their view was, how willing they are to testify, and how good their basis was for making an identification, among several other judgments (e.g., Wells & Bradfield, 1998; see Douglass & Steblay, 2006 for a meta-analysis). The same pattern of distortion occurs in real witnesses (Wright & Skagerberg, 2007).

The striking feature of the post-identification feedback phenomenon is that the social interaction between the witness and experimenter is so brief. It consists of a simple comment, delivered by a stranger. Even so, this interaction is sufficient to create profound memory distortions in judgments highly relevant to a defendant's fate. Most troubling, perhaps, is that these inflated judgments come from inaccurate witnesses who produce highly compelling collections of reports, including statements that they were confident at the time of the identification. Witnesses who have received feedback are evaluated more positively even if observers see the actual feedback delivered and are warned to avoid using it in judging the eyewitness (Douglass, Neuschatz, Imrich, & Wilkinson, 2010).

One experiment directly compared investigator post-identification feedback with corroborating information from co-witnesses. After participants made an identification, they heard either (a) that they had identified the police's suspect (e.g., typical post-identification feedback) or (b) that 92 percent of the witnesses had identified the same person (e.g., corroborating co-witness information). Participants then responded to several testimony-relevant questions such as confidence and certainty in the identification, quality of view of the culprit, and willingness to testify in court. In this context, post-identification feedback has a stronger effect on witnesses' judgments than does a co-witness's corroboration, for both confirming and disconfirming information (Skagerberg & Wright, 2009b, see also Semmler, Brewer, & Wells, 2004). Few variations on this manipulation have been tested (i.e., manipulating the percentage of fellow witnesses who made the same identification), leaving the generalizability of this pattern unclear at this point. What we do know is that witnesses are not completely blind to the source of the feedback and that memory distortion effects only occur if witnesses attribute the feedback to a highly credible source (e.g., police officers) rather than a source with less credibility (e.g., children, Skagerberg & Wright, 2009b).

PREPARING TO TESTIFY

Before appearing in court, the sisters met with the district attorney to discuss their testimony and privately rehearsed what they were going to say over and over again.

Although witnesses are likely to rehearse their testimony, doing so can actually have negative ramifications (e.g., Wells, Ferguson, & Lindsay, 1981). In one study, participants observed a staged interruption during a college classroom and were then questioned multiple times during the next five weeks (Experiment 1) or during the next five days (Experiment 2). During the final questioning session, participants reported a higher confidence level for the items that were asked repeatedly compared with the items that were asked only once (Shaw & McClure, 1996).

The fact that confidence reports are malleable as a function of simple techniques like repeated questioning provides some useful insight into how confidence judgments are formed. One school of thought is that they are based on the degree to which a stimulus matches one's memory (i.e., degree of ecphoric similarity, Tulving, 1985). A high degree of match between the stimulus (i.e., photospread member) and a witness's memory of the perpetrator's face might exist because the opportunity to view was exceptionally good; a low degree of match might exist because time has passed since encoding or the original stimulus quality was poor. Under this simple ecphoric similarity analysis, high degrees of match translate into high confidence; poor degrees of match translate into low confidence.

Although this analysis is intuitively appealing, it fails to account for the influence of external, social variables on confidence reports. As one way to explain this, Charman and colleagues propose a Selective Cue Integration Framework where witnesses infer confidence judgments from available external sources of information when the internal memory cue is weak (Charman, Carlucci, Vallano, & Gregory, 2010). This framework usefully explains the appeal of external variables, such as feedback, to witnesses trying to answer testimony-relevant questions.

TESTIFYING IN COURT

The next morning, Annie took the stand and the district attorney began asking her questions.

Once in court, Annie's and Sarah's confidence levels about both event details and identification accuracy have an enormous influence on the jury. Jurors are more likely to believe confident witnesses, even those whose confidence is a function of practicing their testimony rather than identification accuracy (e.g., Wells et al., 1981). The reliance on assumptions about the confidence–accuracy relationship to discriminate accurate from inaccurate witnesses persists among jurors, even when experiments include judicial safeguards such as judges' instructions (e.g., Cutler, Dexter, & Penrod, 1990) and expert testimony (e.g., Penrod & Cutler, 1995). Because confidence is such a critical element of witness testimony, scholars of psychology and law have devoted many years to understanding the relationship between confidence and accuracy (e.g., Sporer, Penrod, Read, & Cutler, 1995). These investigations clearly indicate that eyewitness confidence is tied to memory quality. For example, witnesses who have poor views of the culprit (and lower accuracy) report reliably lower confidence levels than witnesses with good views of the culprit (Lindsay, Read, & Sharma, 1998). Although there is a non-trivial relationship between confidence and memory accuracy, social variables can intervene to mask the forensic utility of the relationship.

Traditionally, most research has measured the relationship between confidence and accuracy with a simple point-biserial correlation (e.g., Sporer et al., 1995). These analyses measure the extent to which the overall confidence rating is associated with an accurate or inaccurate response. Newer research investigates the relationship as a function of the calibration between confidence and accuracy (e.g., Juslin, Olsson, & Winman, 1996). In this analysis, witnesses' confidence judgments are plotted against the percent correct. This analysis allows researchers to assess the departure from perfect calibration, in which witnesses who are 100 percent confident would have 100 percent of items correct and witnesses who are not at all confident would have no correct items (e.g., Brewer, 2006). Calibration analyses require witnesses to provide confidence assessments as numerical values (e.g., 85 percent certain) rather than verbal statements (e.g., "I'm pretty certain"). Directly comparing witnesses' ratings on numerical scales (0 percent–100 percent) with ratings on verbal scales ("impossible" to "certain") reveals highly similar distributions of ratings, suggesting that the numerical requirement of a calibration analysis does not interfere with witnesses' ability to report a confidence judgment (Weber, Brewer, & Margitich, 2008).

Although calibration analyses provide a useful addendum to the traditional point-biserial correlations, there are two challenges in using calibration analyses. First, calibration analyses require data across instances and across individuals, making them difficult to complete in typical eyewitness experiments where individuals make single identification decisions with one accompanying confidence judgment. If calibration analyses are to be conducted from these paradigms, the required sample size is extremely large (cf. Weber & Brewer, 2004). Second, it is not clear that calibration analyses will help jurors evaluate eyewitnesses appropriately. Given jurors' reticence to incorporate technical information into verdicts (e.g., Bornstein, 2004), calibration analyses might not solve the problem of jurors' overbelief in eyewitnesses (e.g., Cutler, Penrod, & Dexter, 1990).

Even paradigms that do not allow for calibration analyses still provide extremely useful information about the relationship between social factors and relevant forensic variables. For example, a series of experiments indicates that confidence appears highly susceptible to two social factors: the setting in which testimony is given and whether contradiction from co-witnesses is possible. First, witnesses who give statements in public have lower confidence in their reports than do witnesses who give their statements in private, even though the accuracy rates in the two conditions are identical (Shaw, Zerr, & Woythaler, 2001). Subsequent studies revealed that this pattern is moderated by the possibility of contradiction. If co-witnesses can contradict a report, public confidence is lower than private confidence, presumably because witnesses want to avoid the embarrassment of contradiction (cf. Schlenker, 2003). In contrast, if co-witnesses cannot contradict one's report, public confidence is higher than private confidence (Shaw, Appio, Zerr, & Pontoski, 2007). For all four experiments reported in Shaw et al. (2007), the public/private manipulation did not affect participants' actual accuracy, further demonstrating the malleability of confidence reports independent of accuracy.

Differences between public and private confidence levels among eyewitnesses might also be moderated by social anxiety. This supposition is based on a recent study of adolescents who studied faces in pairs and then indicated, still in pairs, whether test faces were old or new. Those participants classified as socially anxious, as defined by scores on the Social Anxiety Scale for Adolescents (La Greca & Lopez, 1998), conformed to peers more than did adolescents who were socially avoidant. For the socially anxious teens, the cost of disagreeing was more severe than the cost of making an error. For the socially *avoidant* teens, their decreased tendency to conform is presumably explained by their relative inattention to social information (Wright et al., 2010).

Finally, witness confidence–accuracy relationships can also be manipulated at trial by the type of questions posed by lawyers. For example, lawyers occasionally ask confusing questions such as those with double negatives, e.g., "Would you not say that the woman did not scream?" (Kebbell & Giles, 2000, p. 132). Even though the number of "absolutely sure" responses remained the same regardless of the questioning format (confusing versus simplified form), the "absolutely sure" answers to simple questions were almost always correct, whereas accuracy levels in complex questioning were comparatively poor. This result is independent of the age of the witness (kindergarten, fourth grade, ninth grade, and college), indicating that lawyers confuse children, adolescents, and young adults equally (Perry, McAuliff, Tam, Claycomb, Dostal, & Flanagan, 1995).

ANALYSIS OF CURRENT STATE OF KNOWLEDGE

A review of the extant literature reveals a wide variety of social variables that influence individual recall. Three critical problems make social influences on eyewitness memory especially serious. First, people are almost completely incapable of correctly assessing when they have been influenced by social variables. In the original post-identification feedback experiment, for example, participants were asked whether the experimenter's comment influenced their

responses to the testimony-relevant judgments. Participants who said "no" were just as likely to produce inflated judgments compared with participants who said "yes" (Wells & Bradfield, 1998).

Second, extant data provide no clues as to how researchers can uncover an untainted memory if evidence of contamination by social influence is present. Even worse, there is substantial research suggesting that social influence variables are more pernicious when memory quality is weak. For example, both post-identification feedback effects and misinformation effects are stronger when initial memory quality is weak (cf. Charman et al., 2010). As another example, participants who form strong memories for a stimulus (e.g., by lingering over a reading) are less likely to incorporate misinformation into a memory test, presumably because their encoding of the original stimulus is strong (e.g., Tousignant, Hall, & Loftus, 1986, see also Paterson et al., 2009).

These data suggest some crude techniques for evaluating witness reports. For example, courts might refuse to allow eyewitness reports taken after a delay because the memory has weakened enough to make the risk of distortion as a function of social influence too severe. In general, to the extent that objective features of a witness's experience are available (e.g., time between witnessed event and memory report), courts might find them useful in assessing the risk of influence as a function of social variables. Although this suggestion has a certain appeal, it is problematic in the sense that judges' assessments could vary considerably. Unfortunately, relying on witnesses themselves to provide information with which to evaluate their vulnerability to social influences is completely impractical (see Wells & Quinlivan, 2009 for a discussion of this problem).

Finally, research on variables designed to prevent social influence effects has an uneven track record of producing successful interventions. For example, forensically relevant warnings to disregard feedback do not protect against post-identification feedback inflation (e.g., "If you were an actual witness in court you would be asked to disregard any feedback you received and rely entirely on your own independent recollection of the event. In answering the questions that follow, we want you to rely only on your own memory. Ignore any feedback you received, and answer the questions on your own best recollections of the events." Lampinen, Scott, Pratt, Leding, & Arnal, 2007, p. 1048). The ineffectiveness of this realistic warning to inoculate witnesses against post-identification feedback suggests that feedback effects will continue to contaminate witness reports, even if a warning happens to be issued.

Nevertheless, when suspicion is introduced, participants are comparatively immune to the effects of feedback on memory reports. In one post-identification feedback experiment, before completing the final questionnaire, participants encountered another experimenter who suggested that the original feedback was bogus by saying, "did [the experimenter] tell you that you picked the right person, (s)he's telling everyone that." (Neuschatz et al., 2007, p. 235). People can also ignore feedback when they hear it was randomly generated from a computer (Lampinen et al., 2007).

Witnesses can also be successfully inoculated against post-identification feedback when they are required to think about their testimony-relevant judgments before hearing feedback. In the original test of this intervention, participants witnessed an event, and then were instructed to think about testimony-relevant judgments (e.g., certainty, view, attention) before completing the dependent measures questionnaire. Before responding to the final questionnaire, participants received feedback about their identification. Because participants had a clear memory for how confident they were before hearing feedback, their reports on the questionnaire could rely on that memory, rather than intuiting a judgment after having heard feedback (Wells & Bradfield, 1999).

Based on the inoculation attempts described above, eyewitnesses are able to disregard feedback under two general conditions: when they think about testimony-relevant judgments before hearing feedback or when they have a reasonable justification for ignoring the feedback. The fact that establishing a pre-feedback trace for testimony-relevant judgments successfully inoculates witnesses against feedback suggests that witnesses do not consider their responses to questions about certainty and other measures until asked by the experimenter. Therefore, these judgments reflect a retrospective process, rather than a process whereby witnesses naturally generate judgments while the events are unfolding. This pattern also suggests that confidence and other judgments are not inflated in response to impression management concerns among witnesses (cf. Bradfield & Wells, 2005). If witnesses were interested in creating an image of themselves as skilled decision makers, they might have engaged in augmenting (Kelley, 1973) in which they articulated barriers to success. Doing so makes the accurate decision even more impressive (e.g., "Even though I couldn't see very well, I still made an accurate identification.").

The second category of variables able to prevent post-identification feedback relies on witnesses to have a reasonable justification for ignoring the feedback. In this category, witnesses are able to ignore feedback when they learn that the experimenter is acting unethically by telling all participants they were correct (Neuschatz et al., 2007) or that the feedback was randomly generated (Lampinen et al., 2007). Indeed, when participants are explicitly asked in a counterfactual paradigm to imagine themselves not having received feedback, they generate responses to testimony-relevant judgments that reflect an awareness of the potential for feedback to bias their responses (Charman & Wells, 2008). In contrast, when they are implored to "rely on [their] own memory," feedback is not ignored (Lampinen et al., 2007).

This pattern of adjusting judgments appropriately when justification is available exists in other domains. For example, mock jurors will ignore a confession if it is ruled inadmissible because the interrogation recording is garbled, but not if it is ruled inadmissible due to a legal technicality (Kassin & Sommers, 1997). In a similar pattern, observers tend to ignore evidence of a witness's confidence inflation unless there is an unsatisfactory explanation for it. If witnesses are clearly inflating their confidence as a strategy to implicate the defendant, evidence of confidence inflation produces lower guilt ratings of the defendant, compared with a condition where there is no explanation for the inflation (Jones, Williams, & Brewer, 2008).

DIRECTIONS FOR FUTURE RESEARCH

Throughout this chapter, we have presented data from experimental paradigms derived from both social and cognitive perspectives. For some research questions, the conclusions from the two paradigms are nearly identical. For example, we know that other people's responses are influential from both social contagion (i.e., cognitive) experiments and memory conformity (i.e., social) experiments (e.g., Roediger, Meade, & Bergman, 2001; Wright et al., 2000, respectively). For other questions, the results from cognitive paradigms directly contradict those from social paradigms. For example, Meade and Roediger (2002) found that warnings reduce the effect of misinformation; Paterson et al. (2011) found that warnings were ineffective in preventing distortions as a function of misinformation (but see Bodner et al., 2009). It is tempting to assume that the procedural differences between the studies are solely responsible for the contradictory effects of warning in the two experiments. Future research will be required to uncover the variables that might explain differences between cognitive and social paradigms.

Given the vast array of social variables that influence eyewitnesses, one potential solution is to warn juries that social factors may have inappropriately affected witnesses' testimony. Unfortunately, juries have a lackluster record in reacting appropriately to expert testimony in both eyewitness domains (e.g., Martire & Kemp, 2011) and forensic science domains (e.g., Jenkins & Schuller, 2007). More specifically, warnings to disregard evidence are often unsuccessful. For example, in post-identification feedback research, observers were completely unaffected by warnings to disregard feedback delivery when evaluating a witness's accuracy (Douglass et al., 2010). These data suggest that the solutions of jury instructions and expert testimony as recommended by the New Jersey Supreme Court will not adequately address the issues of bias present in eyewitness testimony (State v. Henderson, 2011). Perhaps successful interventions require tailoring the jury instructions or expert testimony so that they articulate justification for jurors to consider social influences in evaluating the witness's testimony.

As described earlier, mock jurors can appropriately discount an inadmissible confession when they have a good reason to do so (i.e., the interrogation recording is difficult to hear, Kassin & Sommers, 1997) and adjust evaluations of a witness with inflated confidence when the justification seems unreasonable (i.e., the witness is trying to implicate the defendant, Jones et al., 2008). These two studies suggest a general approach to helping jurors appropriately evaluate eyewitness evidence when social influence variables might have affected reports: providing justification for skepticism. One example of this might be to make available videotaped evidence of the identification procedure. In one experiment, observers saw the videotaped identification procedure (where confidence was low) and the testimony at trial (where confidence was high). In that condition, observers rated the defendant as less guilty compared with a condition in which an eyewitness testifying at trial read her prior statement (where confidence was low) but testified at trial that her confidence was high (Douglass & Jones, 2013).

Fruitful avenues for future research could also come from attempts to understand how individual difference variables might combine with procedural features of identification attempts to enhance (or eliminate) social influence on witnesses. For example, social anxiety moderates reactions to conformity attempts (Wright et al., 2010). In addition, the context in which memory reports are provided moderates eyewitness confidence (e.g., Shaw et al., 2007). Taken together, these studies might suggest that socially anxious individuals will produce a closer calibration of confidence and accuracy for reports provided in private rather than in public. If that pattern is broadly true for all individuals, it suggests a concrete recommendation for when and how to record confidence statements.

Although research on individual difference variables is theoretically valuable, using those variables to dictate procedural choices is risky, precisely because individual difference variables are probabilistic. Not every member of the socially anxious category, for example, will behave the same way in all situations. Therefore, research should especially focus on systemic, procedural changes that can protect all witnesses from contaminating effects of social influence. For example, the Cognitive Interview prevents witnesses from providing wrong information when queried with leading questions (Geiselman, Fisher, Cohen, & Holland, 1986; see also Holliday, 2003), presumably by creating a stronger memory for the witnessed event through the standard prompts used to solicit information (Memon, Zaragoza, Clifford, & Kidd, 2010).

To the extent possible, future research should directly compare existing paradigms that have produced contradictory results, striving to isolate the variables that might moderate observed patterns. For example, Paterson et al. (2011) found no effect of warning on witnesses' tendency to incorporate misinformation into reports; Bodner et al. (2009) did find an effect. As noted above, one possible explanation for this difference is delay, used by Paterson et al., but not Bodner et al. Until these issues are resolved, the more

ecologically valid paradigms (e.g., Paterson et al., 2011) should inform practical suggestions for how to treat eyewitness evidence. When different paradigms do produce the same recommendation, converging validity will enhance the recommendation's support.

CONCLUSION

In the 80 years since Bartlett (1932) wrote *Remembering*, empirical research in psychology has confirmed many of his assumptions about the social nature of recall. With modern experimental designs and data analytic techniques, it is abundantly clear that memory is strongly affected by social variables. In particular, social influences on memory produce inaccurate reports (e.g., Wright et al., 2000), mistaken identifications (e.g., Haw & Fisher, 2004), and inflated judgments (e.g., Wells & Bradfield, 1998) in a domain where errors are disastrous. In the worst case scenario, these errors can result in decades-long wrongful incarcerations or the death of innocent individuals (see Innocence Project)[1]. The only practical solution is to extract and record memory reports from witnesses as quickly and privately as possible, ideally before any conversation transpires with co-witnesses or prior to any other external influences.

NOTE

1 See: www.innocenceproject.org (last accessed June 1, 2013).

REFERENCES

Andersson, J. (2001). Net effect of memory collaboration: How is collaboration affected by factors such as friendship, gender and age? *Scandinavian Journal of Psychology, 42*, 367–375. doi: 10.1111/1467-9450.00248

Asch, S. E. (1951). Effects of group pressure upon the modification and distortion of judgments. In

H. Guetzkow and H. Guetzkow (Eds.), *Groups, leadership and men: Research in human relations* (pp. 177–190). Oxford: Carnegie Press.

Baron, R. S., Vandello, J. A., & Brunsman, B. (1996). The forgotten variable in conformity research: Impact of task importance on social influence. *Journal of Personality and Social Psychology, 71*, 915–927. doi:10.1037/0022-3514.71.5.915

Bartlett, F. (1932). *Remembering: A study in experimental and social psychology*. New York: Cambridge University Press.

Basden, B. H., Basden, D. R., Bryner, S., & Thomas, R. (1997). A comparison of group and individual remembering: Does collaboration disrupt retrieval strategies? *Journal of Experimental Psychology: Learning, Memory, and Cognition, 23*, 1176–1189. doi:10.1037/0278-7393.23.5.1176

Bodner, G. E., Musch, E., & Azad, T. (2009). Reevaluating the potency of the memory conformity effect. *Memory & Cognition, 37*, 1069–1076. doi:10.3758/MC.37.8.1069

Bornstein, B. H. (2004). The impact of different types of expert scientific testimony on mock jurors' liability verdicts. *Psychology, Crime & Law, 10*, 429–446. doi: 10.1080/1068316030001629292

Bradfield, A. L., & Wells, G. L. (2005). Not the same old hindsight bias: Outcome information distorts a broad range of retrospective judgments. *Memory & Cognition, 33*, 120–130. doi: 10.3758/BF03195302

Brewer, N. (2006). Uses and abuses of eyewitness identification confidence. *Legal and Criminological Psychology, 11*,3–23.doi:10.1348/135532505X79672

Charman, S. D., Carlucci, M., Vallano, J., & Gregory, A. (2010). The selective cue integration framework: A theory of postidentification witness confidence assessment. *Journal of Experimental Psychology: Applied, 16*, 204–218. doi:10.1037/a0019495

Charman, S. D., & Wells, G. L. (2008). Can eyewitnesses correct for external influences on their lineup identifications? The actual/counterfactual assessment paradigm. *Journal of Experimental Psychology: Applied, 14*, 5–20. doi: 10.1037/1076-898X.14.1.5

Cutler, B. L., Dexter, H. R., & Penrod, S. D. (1990). Nonadversarial methods for sensitizing jurors to eyewitness evidence. *Journal of Applied Social Psychology, 20*, 1197–1207. doi: 10.1111/j.1559-1816.1990.tb00400.x

Cutler, B. L., Penrod, S. D., & Dexter, H. R. (1990). Juror sensitivity to eyewitness identification evidence. *Law and Human Behavior, 14*, 185–191. doi: 10.1007/BF01062972

Deutsch, M. (1980). This Week's Citation Classic, 27, 235.

Deutsch, M., & Gerard, H. B. (1955). A study of normative and informational social influences upon individual judgment. *The Journal of Abnormal and Social Psychology, 51*, 629–636. doi:10.1037/h0046408

Douglass, A. B., Brewer, N., Semmler, C. Bustamante, L. V., & Hiley, A. (2013). The dynamic interaction between eyewitnesses and investigators: The impact of differences in perspective on memory reports and interviewer behavior. Law and Human Behavior, 37(4), 290–301. doi: 10.1037/lhb0000034

Douglass, A. B., & Jones, E. J. (2013). Confidence inflation in eyewitnesses: Seeing is not believing. *Legal and Criminological Psychology, 18*(1), 152-167. doi: 10.1111/j.2044-8333.2011.02031.x

Douglass, A., Neuschatz, J. S., Imrich, J., & Wilkinson, M. (2010). Does post-identification feedback affect evaluations of eyewitness testimony and identification procedures? *Law and Human Behavior, 34*, 282–294. doi: 10.1007/s10979-009-9189-5

Douglass, A., & Steblay, N. (2006). Memory distortion in eyewitnesses: A meta-analysis of the post-identification feedback effect. *Applied Cognitive Psychology, 20*, 859–869. doi:10.1002/acp.1237

French, L., Garry, M., & Mori, K. (2008). You say tomato? Collaborative remembering leads to more false memories for intimate couples than for strangers. *Memory, 16*, 262–273. doi:10.1080/09658210701801491

French, L., Garry, M., & Mori, K. (2011). Relative – not absolute – judgments of credibility affect susceptibility to misinformation conveyed during discussion. *Acta Psychologica, 136*, 119–128. doi:10.1016/j.actpsy.2010.10.009

Gabbert, F., Hope, L., & Fisher, R. P. (2009). Protecting eyewitness evidence: Examining the efficacy of a Self-Administered Interview tool. *Law & Human Behavior, 33*, 298–307. doi: 10.1007/s10979-008-9146-8

Gabbert, F., Memon, A., & Allan, K. (2003). Memory conformity: Can eyewitnesses influence each other's memory for an event? *Applied Cognitive Psychology, 17*, 533–543. doi: 10.1002/acp.885

Gabbert, F., Memon, A., & Wright, D. B. (2006). Memory conformity: Disentangling the steps toward influence during a discussion. *Psychonomic Bulletin & Review, 13*, 480–485. doi: 10.3758/BF03193873

Gabbert, F., Memon, A., & Wright, D. B. (2007). I saw it for longer than you: The relationship between perceived encoding duration and memory conformity. *Acta Psychologica, 124*, 319–331. doi: 10.1016/j.actpsy.2006.03.009

Garrett, B. L. (2011). *Convicting the innocent: When criminal prosecutions go wrong.* Cambridge, MA: Harvard University Press.

Geiselman, R., Fisher, R. P., Cohen, G., & Holland, H. (1986). Eyewitness responses to leading and misleading questions under the cognitive interview. *Journal of Police Science & Administration, 14,* 31–39.

Haw, R. M., & Fisher, R. P. (2004). Effects of administrator-witness contact on eyewitness identification accuracy. *Journal of Applied Psychology, 89,* 1106–1112. doi:10.1037/0021-9010.89.6.1106

Henkel, L. A., & Rajaram, S. (2011). Collaborative remembering in older adults: Age-invariant outcomes in the context of episodic recall deficits. *Psychology and Aging, 26,* 532–545. doi:10.1037/a0023106

Hoffman, H., Granhag P. A., See S., & Loftus, E. F. (2001). Social influences on reality-monitoring decisions. *Memory & Cognition, 29,* 394–404. doi: 10.3758/BF03196390

Holliday, R. E. (2003). Reducing misinformation effects in children with cognitive interviews: Dissociating recollection and familiarity. *Child Development, 74,* 728–751. doi:10.1111/1467-8624.00565

Hope, L., Ost, J., Gabbert, F., Healey, S., & Lenton, E. (2008). "With a little help from my friends …": The role of co-witness relationship in susceptibility to misinformation. *Acta Psychologica, 127,* 476–484. doi: 10.1016/j.actpsy.2007.08.010

Jenkins, G., & Schuller, R. A. (2007). The impact of negative forensic evidence on mock jurors' perceptions of a trial of drug-facilitated sexual assault. *Law and Human Behavior, 31,* 369–380. doi: 10.1007/s10979-006-9068-2

Jones, E. E., Williams, K. D., & Brewer, N. (2008). "I had a confidence epiphany!": Obstacles to combating post-identification confidence inflation. *Law and Human Behavior, 32,* 164–176. doi: 10.1007/s10979-007-9101-0

Juslin, P., Olsson, N., & Winman, P. (1996). Calibration and diagnosticity of confidence in eyewitness identification: Comments on what can be inferred from the low confidence–accuracy correlation. *Journal of Experimental Psychology: Learning, Memory, and Cognition, 22,* 1304–1316. doi: 10.1037/0278-7393.22.5.1304

Kassin, S. M., & Sommers, S. R. (1997). Inadmissible testimony, instructions to disregard, and the jury: Substantive versus procedural considerations. *Personality and Social Psychology Bulletin, 23,* 1046–1054. doi: 10.1177/01461672972310005

Kebbell, M. R., & Giles, D. C. (2000). Some experimental influences of lawyers' complicated questions on eyewitness confidence and accuracy. *Journal of Psychology: Interdisciplinary and Applied, 134,* 129–139. doi:10.1080/00223980009600855

Kelley, H. H. (1973). The processes of causal attribution. *American Psychologist, 28,* 107–128. doi: 10.1037/h0034225

La Greca, A. M., & Lopez, N. (1998). Social anxiety among adolescents: Linkages with peer relations and friendships. Journal of Abnormal Child Psychology: An Official Publication of the International Society for Research in Child and Adolescent Psychopathology, 26, 83–94. doi:10.1023/A:1022684520514

Lampinen, J., Scott, J., Pratt, D., Leding, J. K., & Arnal, J. D. (2007). "Good, you identified the suspect … but please ignore this feedback": Can warnings eliminate the effects of post-identification feedback? *Applied Cognitive Psychology, 21,* 1037–1056. doi: 10.1002/acp.1313

Lindsay, D. S., (2007). Order effects in collaborative memory contamination? Comment on Gabbert, Memon, & Wright (2006). *Psychonomic Bulletin & Review, 14,* 1010. doi: 10.3758/BF03194137

Lindsay, D. S., & Johnson, M. K. (1989). The eyewitness suggestibility effect and memory for source. *Memory & Cognition, 17,* 349–358. doi: 10.3758/BF03198473

Lindsay, D. S., Read, J., & Sharma, K. (1998). Accuracy and confidence in person identification: The relationship is strong when witnessing conditions vary widely. *Psychological Science, 9,* 215–218. doi:10.1111/1467-9280.00041

Loftus, E. F., Miller, D. G., & Burns, H. J. (1978). Semantic integration of verbal information into a visual memory. *Journal of Experimental Psychology: Human Learning and Memory, 4,* 19–31. doi:10.1037/0278-7393.4.1.19

Luus, C., & Wells, G. L. (1994). The malleability of eyewitness confidence: Co-witness and perseverance effects. *Journal of Applied Psychology, 79,* 714–723. doi:10.1037/0021-9010.79.5.714

Magnussen, S., Andersson, J., Cornoldi, C., De Beni, R., Endestad, T., Goodman, G. S., et al. (2006). What people believe about memory. *Memory, 14,* 595–613. doi: 10.1080/09658210600646716

Martire, K. A., & Kemp, R. I. (2011). Can experts help jurors to evaluate eyewitness evidence? A review of eyewitness expert effects. *Legal and Criminological Psychology, 16,* 24–36. doi: 10.1348/135532509X477225

Meade, M. L., & Roediger, H. (2002). Explorations in the social contagion of memory. *Memory & Cognition, 30,* 995–1009. doi: 10.3758/BF03194318

Memon, A., Meissner, C. A., & Fraser, J. (2010). The Cognitive Interview: A meta-analytic review and study space analysis of the past 25 years. *Psychology, Public Policy, and Law, 16*(4), 340–372. doi: 10.1037/a0020518

Memon, A., Zaragoza, M., Clifford, B., & Kidd, L. (2010). Inoculation or antidote? The effects of cognitive interview timing on false memory for forcibly fabricated events. *Law and Human Behavior, 34*, 105–117. doi: 10.1007/s10979-008-9172-6

Neuschatz, J. S., Lawson, D. S., Fairless, A. H., Powers, R. A., Neuschatz, J. S., Goodsell, C. A., & Toglia, M. P. (2007). The mitigating effects of suspicion on post-identification feedback and on retrospective eyewitness memory. *Law and Human Behavior, 31*, 231–247. doi: 10.1007/s10979-006-9047-7

Ord, B., Shaw, G., & Green, T. (2008). *Investigative interviewing explained* (2nd ed.). Chatswood, New South Wales, Australia: LexisNexis Butterworths.

Paterson, H. M., & Kemp, R. I. (2005). Co-witness discussion: a survey of police officers' attitudes, knowledge, and behaviour. *Psychiatry, Psychology and Law, 12*, 424–434. doi:10.1375/pplt.12.2.424

Paterson, H. M., & Kemp, R. I. (2006). Co-witnesses talk: A survey of eyewitness discussion. *Psychology, Crime & Law, 12*, 181–191. doi:10.1080/10683160512331316334

Paterson, H. M., Kemp, R. I., & Forgas, J. P. (2009). Co-witnesses, confederates, and conformity: Effects of discussion and delay on eyewitness memory. *Psychiatry, Psychology and Law, 16*, S112–S124. doi:10.1080/13218710802620380

Paterson, H. M., Kemp, R. I., & Ng, J. R. (2011). Combating co-witness contamination: Attempting to decrease the negative effects of discussion on eyewitness memory. *Applied Cognitive Psychology, 25*, 43–52. doi:10.1002/acp.1640

Penrod, S., & Cutler, B. (1995). Witness confidence and witness accuracy: Assessing their forensic relation. *Psychology, Public Policy, and Law, 1*, 817–845. doi:10.1037/1076-8971.1.4.817

Perry, N. W., McAuliff, B. D., Tam, P., Claycomb, L., Dostal, C., & Flanagan, C. (1995). When lawyers question children: Is justice served? *Law and Human Behavior, 19*, 609–629. doi:10.1007/BF01499377

Rajaram, S. (2011). Collaboration both hurts and helps memory: A cognitive perspective. *Current Directions in Psychological Science, 20*, 76–81. doi:10.1177/0963721411403251

Rajaram, S., & Pereira-Pasarin, L. P. (2010). Collaborative memory: Cognitive research and theory. *Perspectives on Psychological Science, 5*, 649–663. doi:10.1177/1745691610388763

Reysen, M. B. (2005). The effects of conformity on recognition judgements. *Memory, 13*, 87–94. doi:10.1080/09658210344000602

Roediger, H., Meade, M. L., & Bergman, E. T. (2001). Social contagion of memory. *Psychonomic Bulletin & Review, 8*, 365–371. doi: 10.3758/BF03196174

Schlenker, B. R. (2003). Self-presentation. In M. R. Leary and J. P. Tangney (Eds.), *Handbook of self and identity* (pp. 492–518). New York: Guilford.

Schneider, D. M., & Watkins, M. J. (1996). Response conformity in recognition testing. *Psychonomic Bulletin & Review, 3*, 481–485. doi: 10.3758/BF03214550

Semmler, C., Brewer, N., & Wells, G. L. (2004). Effects of postidentification feedback on eyewitness identification and nonidentification confidence. *Journal of Applied Psychology, 89*, 334–346. doi:10.1037/0021-9010.89.2.334

Shaw, J., Appio, L. M., Zerr, T. K., & Pontoski, K. E. (2007). Public eyewitness confidence can be influenced by the presence of other witnesses. *Law and Human Behavior, 31*, 629–652. doi:10.1007/s10979-006-9080-6

Shaw, J. S., & McClure, K. A. (1996). Repeated postevent questioning can lead to elevated levels of eyewitness confidence. *Law and Human Behavior, 20*, 629–653. doi: 10.1007/BF01499235

Shaw, J., Zerr, T. K., & Woythaler, K. A. (2001). Public eyewitness confidence ratings can differ from those held privately. *Law and Human Behavior, 25*, 141–154. doi: 10.1023/A:1005641314083

Skagerberg, E. M., & Wright, D. B. (2008a). Manipulating power can affect memory conformity. *Applied Cognitive Psychology, 22*, 207–216. doi:10.1002/acp.1353

Skagerberg, E. M., & Wright, D. B. (2008b). The prevalence of co-witnesses and co-witness discussions in real eyewitnesses. *Psychology, Crime & Law, 14*, 513–521. doi: 10.1080/10683160801948980

Skagerberg, E. M. & Wright, D. B. (2009a). Sibling differentials in power and memory conformity. *Scandinavian Journal of Psychology, 50*, 101–107. doi:10.1111/j.1467-9450.2008.00693

Skagerberg, E. M. & Wright, D. B. (2009b). Susceptibility to postidentification feedback is affected by source credibility. *Applied Cognitive Psychology, 23*, 506–523. doi: 10.1002/acp.1470

Sporer, S., Penrod, S., Read, D., & Cutler, B. (1995). Choosing, confidence, and accuracy: A meta-analysis of the confidence-accuracy relation in eyewitness identification studies. *Psychological Bulletin, 118*, 315–327. doi: 10.1037/0033-2909.118.3.315

State of New Jersey v. Henderson, 2011 WL 3715028 (N.J. August 24, 2011)

Tousignant, J. P., Hall, D., & Loftus, E. F. (1986). Discrepancy detection and vulnerability to misleading postevent information. *Memory & Cognition, 14,* 329–338. doi: 10.3758/BF03202511

Tulving, E. (1985). Memory and consciousness. *Canadian Psychology, 26,* 1–12. doi: 10.1037/h0080017

Weber, N., & Brewer, N. (2004). Confidence–accuracy calibration in absolute and relative face recognition judgments. *Journal of Experimental Psychology: Applied, 10,* 156–172. doi: 10.1037/1076-898X.10.3.156

Weber, N., Brewer, N., & Margitich, S. (2008). The confidence–accuracy relation in eyewitness identifications: Effects of verbal versus numerical confidence scales. In K. H. Kiefer (Ed.), *Applied psychology research trends* (pp. 103–118). Hauppauge, NY: Nova Science Publishers.

Weldon, M. (2001). Remembering as a social process. In D. L. Medin (Ed.). *The psychology of learning and motivation: Advances in research and theory, Vol. 40* (pp. 67–120). San Diego, CA: Academic Press.

Weldon, M., & Bellinger, K. D. (1997). Collective memory: Collaborative and individual processes in remembering. *Journal of Experimental Psychology: Learning, Memory, and Cognition, 23,* 1160–1175. doi: 10.1037/0278-7393.23.5.1160

Weldon, M., Blair, C., & Huebsch, P. (2000). Group remembering: Does social loafing underlie collaborative inhibition? *Journal of Experimental Psychology: Learning, Memory and Cognition, 26,* 1568–1577. doi: 10.1037/0278-7393.26.6.1568

Wells, G. L. (1995). Scientific study of witness memory: Implications for public and legal policy. *Psychology, Public Policy, and Law, 1,* 726–731. doi:10.1037/h0092727

Wells, G. L. & Bradfield, A. L. (1998). "Good, you identified the suspect": Feedback to eyewitnesses distort their reports of the witnessing experience. *Journal of Applied Psychology, 83,* 360–376. doi: 10.1037/0021-9010.83.3.360

Wells, G. L., & Bradfield, A. L. (1999). Distortions in eyewitnesses' recollections: Can the post-identification feedback effect be moderated? *Psychological Science, 10,* 138–144. doi: 10.1111/1467-9280.00121

Wells, G. L., Ferguson, T. J., & Lindsay, R. C. (1981). The tractability of eyewitness confidence and its implications for triers of fact. *Journal of Applied Psychology, 66,* 688–696. doi: 10.1037/0021-9010.66.6.688

Wells, G. L., & Quinlivan, D. S. (2009). Suggestive eyewitness identification procedures and the Supreme Court's reliability test in light of eyewitness science: 30 years later. *Law and Human Behavior, 33,* 1–24. doi: 10.1007/s10979-008-9130-3

Wright, D. B., & Carlucci, M. E. (2011). The response order effect: People believe the first person who remembers an event. *Psychonomic Bulletin & Review, 18,* 805–812. doi: 10.3758/s13423-011-0089-6

Wright, D. B., Gabbert, F., Memon, A., & London, K. (2008). Changing the criterion for conformity in free recall and recognition. *Memory, 16,* 137–148. doi: 10.1080/09658210701836174

Wright, D. B., London, K., & Waechter, M. (2010). Social anxiety moderates memory conformity in adolescents. *Applied Cognitive Psychology, 24,* 1034–1045. doi: 10.1002/acp.1604

Wright, D. B., Self, G., & Justice, C. (2000). Memory conformity: Exploring misinformation effects when presented by another person. *British Journal of Psychology, 91,* 189–202. doi: 10.1348/000712600161781

Wright, D. B., & Skagerberg, E. M. (2007). Postidentification feedback affects real eyewitnesses. *Psychological Science, 18,* 172–178. doi: 10.1111/j.1467-9280.2007.01868.x

Zajac, R., & Henderson, N. (2009). Don't it make my brown eyes blue: Co-witness misinformation about a target's appearance can impair target-absent line-up performance. *Memory, 17,* 266–278. doi: 10.1080/09658210802623950

35

Young Children's Eyewitness Memory

Gabrielle F. Principe, Andrea Follmer Greenhoot,
and Stephen J. Ceci

An analysis of children as witnesses requires a consideration of their abilities to remember and report on their past experiences, especially stressful or traumatic experiences. Thirty years of research on children's event memory have produced a substantial literature on how well children of different ages remember salient, personally experienced events and those factors that can induce errors in children's recollections. In the sections that follow, we review the research on children's autobiographical memory and reporting of salient life events, beginning with an overview of basic memory development, followed by a discussion of the literature on children's memory for stressful and traumatic events. We then explore studies examining factors that can influence the accuracy of children's reports of their experiences. Finally, we turn to a discussion of the difficulties of distinguishing the accuracy of the statements of child witnesses. There are, of course, other bodies of work relevant to discussions of young witnesses, such as children's courtroom experiences, trial preparation, and legal reforms intended to accommodate children. These issues, however, are beyond the scope of this chapter given our focus on memory and testimony.

CHILDREN'S AUTOBIOGRAPHICAL MEMORY ABILITIES

Research on early memory development shows that children's ability to provide coherent verbal recollections emerges between two and three years of age (e.g., Fivush, Gray, & Fromhoff, 1987; Howe, 2000; Nelson & Fivush, 2000). Although children show behavioral indications of memory in infancy and toddlerhood through paradigms such as habituation, conditioning, and deferred imitation, the interpretation of these behaviors as indications of memory are heavily dependent on both context and the interviewer's knowledge of the child's experiences. Furthermore, there is little evidence that children spontaneously translate preverbal memories into verbal form once they acquire language, at least not without repeated exposure or discussions with adults who have previous knowledge of the event (Bauer, Wenner, & Kroupina, 2002; Morris & Baker-Ward, 2007; Simcock & Hayne, 2002). Therefore, it is unlikely that children or adults could independently provide informative and valid reports about events that they witnessed or experienced when they were younger than two or two and a half years of age.

Even after the emergence of autobiographical memory, the ability to attend to, encode, retrieve, and report information improves significantly across childhood (e.g., Baker-Ward, Ornstein, Gordon, Larus, & Clubb, 1993). With increasing age, developmental changes in prior knowledge about events and in fundamental information processing skills (e.g., speed of encoding) all have implications for what can be remembered (Bender, Wallsten, & Ornstein, 1996; Howe & Brainerd, 1989); given similar exposure to an event, older children form stronger, more organized memory traces that are more readily retrievable than those of younger children. For instance, a series of studies on 3- to 7-year-olds' memories for medical experiences suggests that compared with older children, younger children remember less, are more dependent on specific memory prompts, show greater confusion between what happened and what *could* have happened, and forget their experiences more rapidly (e.g., Baker-Ward et al., 1993; Ornstein, Gordon, & Larus, 1992). Similarly, an extensive literature on parent–child reminiscing shows that from early to middle childhood children increasingly contribute to conversations with their parents about shared past events (e.g., Fivush & Nelson, 2004). Overall then, the younger the child, the weaker the memory representation, the greater the reliance on adult guidance in remembering, and the more vulnerable the memory will be to forgetting and influences due to lack of knowledge, intervening events, and other people.

Finally, many autobiographical memories that are remembered early in childhood are not retained into later childhood and adulthood, resulting in the phenomenon of "childhood amnesia." Although the underlying mechanisms are still under debate, it is well established that adults rarely retain memories of events experienced in the first three to five years of life (Sheingold & Tenney, 1982; Usher & Neisser, 1993) and recent research with children shows that most early memories begin to fade by middle childhood (e.g., Peterson, Grant, & Boland, 2005). A major implication here is that many events that occur early in life will be forgotten over extensive delays, through processes related to memory development and childhood amnesia.

CHILDREN'S MEMORIES FOR STRESSFUL AND TRAUMATIC EVENTS

Models of stressful and traumatic memory have been the subject of vigorous scientific and public debate for three decades. At issue are questions about the accuracy and robustness of memories of highly stressful events, and whether trauma activates specific memory mechanisms (e.g., repression, dissociation) that operate independently of standard memory processes (e.g., Freyd, DePrince, & Zurbriggen, 2001; McNally, 2006; Ornstein, Ceci, & Loftus, 1998a; van der Kolk, 1994). A profusion of research on memory for stressful and traumatic events now suggests that the core of such events tends to be remembered quite well but that these memories are far from indelible and are susceptible to alteration due to suggestion. The vast majority of these investigations focus on memory for acute one-time traumas, such as a parent's murder or a natural disaster. Both clinical observations and large-scale studies illustrate that children produce vivid and detailed recollections of these events several years after they have occurred (e.g., Ackil, Van Abbema, & Bauer, 2003; Fivush, Sales, Goldberg, Bahrick, & Parker, 2004; Najarian, Goenjian, Pelcovitz, Mandel, & Najarian, 1996; Pynoos & Eth, 1984; Terr, 1983). Although these memories are not typically externally validated, these patterns are corroborated by investigations of memory for distressing medical experiences, which permit precise documentation. For instance, 3- to 7-year-olds are able to recall the majority of a medically indicated invasive radiological procedure, a voiding cystourethrogram (VCUG), although older children remember more than younger children (Merritt, Ornstein, & Spicker, 1994; Quas, Goodman, Bidrose, Pipe, Craw, & Ablin, 1999). Similarly, children who were older than two years when they experienced a traumatic injury and emergency room treatment have robust recollections even after five years (Burgwyn-Bailes, Baker-Ward, Gordon, & Ornstein, 2001; Peterson & Whalen, 2001).

Nonetheless, like nontraumatic memories, memories for stressful and traumatic events are subject to both distortion and forgetting. For instance, Pynoos and Nader (1989) found that children who were directly exposed to a sniper attack on their elementary school playground tended to distort their recall so as to reduce their degree of life threat, whereas those who were not directly exposed tended to increase their proximity to the danger in recall, including claims to have been present even though they were absent the day of the attack. Further, children sometimes forget single traumatic events altogether, especially when they occur at a young age. Thirty percent of Quas et al.'s (1999) sample of children who experienced a VCUG evidenced no memory of it when questioned 8 to 69 months later. Consistent with research on childhood amnesia, almost all of the "forgetters" were under five years at the time of the VGUC, and none of those who were two at the time of the VCUG recalled it; the two who were five or older were interviewed after delays of four and five years.

The degree of forgetting and distortion in traumatic memories also appears to vary with the level of stress experienced by the child, although there is little consistency in the types of stress-memory patterns that have been documented. Both positive (e.g., Peterson & Whalen, 2001) and negative associations (e.g., Merritt et al., 1994; Quas et al., 1999) have been observed. More complex patterns were documented by Bahrick, Parker, Fivush, and Levitt (1998), who found that 3- to 4-year-olds with either low or severe exposure to Hurricane Andrew remembered less about it months later than

children with moderate exposure. After a six-year delay this group difference disappeared, although the severely exposed group did require more memory prompting (Fivush et al., 2004). Given these inconsistencies, it may be that memory for stressful events can be best understood in conjunction with several moderating variables, such as the level of stress, and how it is measured, and the timing of the assessments. Recent work, for example, suggests that stress has facilitative effects at encoding but detrimental effects at retrieval (Quas & Lench, 2007). The relation between stress and memory also seems to depend on behavioral responses and coping (e.g., Salmon, Price, & Pereira, 2002; Quas et al., 1999). For instance, crying and distraction during a VCUG predict poorer memory than talking about the procedure.

In sum, research on children's memories for one-time acute stressors suggests that most children have enduring memories of the core components of these events, but that distortion and even complete forgetting are not unusual. These memories, moreover, behave in ways that are generally consistent with principles from the basic memory literature. It is important to note, however, that this work focuses on memories for single stressors in otherwise normal and healthy children. Many children who participate in the legal system are victims of child maltreatment and are victimized repeatedly or chronically. Maltreatment may differ from events like natural disasters and medical experiences on several dimensions with implications for remembering, including event repetition or chronicity and family and community roles in discussing and coping with the event (Connolly & Lindsay, 2001). Furthermore, abuse is associated with atypical patterns of social, emotional, and cognitive development (e.g., Arata, Langhinrichsen-Rohling, Bowers, & O'Farrill-Swails, 2005; Coster, Gersten, Beeghly, & Cicchetti, 1989; Hoffman Plotkin & Twentyman, 1984), leading some researchers to argue that research with healthy children may not be applicable to children who are chronically stressed or maltreated. We turn to the literature on maltreated children's memory in the next section.

MEMORY AND CHILD MALTREATMENT

Children's memories for maltreatment

The literature on memory for maltreatment is much sparser than that on memory for one-time traumas. For many years clinical observations provided the only information about children's memories for maltreatment. For instance, Terr's (1988) clinical reports on five young sexual abuse victims indicated that all of the children had either very sparse or no recall of the abuse. As would be predicted by research on childhood amnesia, however, all of the children were under three years of age when the abuse occurred. Terr also reported that all of the children exhibited behavioral indications of their traumas, but as mentioned above the interpretation of nonverbal indicators in the absence of verbal memory is highly dependent on context and the evaluator's knowledge of the event in question. More objective data on memory for maltreatment are offered by large scale empirical studies of children's forensic reports of sexual abuse. This work shows that older children provide more detail about abuse experiences than younger children, and victims of multiple incidents report more than those who are victims of single incidents (e.g., Orbach, Hershkowitz, Lamb, Esplin, & Horowitz, 2000; Sternberg, Lamb, & Hershkowitz, 1996). The major limitation of this work, however, is that it does not yield information about accuracy and forgetting. These studies do not include external documentation of the abuse, or follow-up interviews to track memory changes over time.

The best data on memory for child maltreatment are provided by prospective longitudinal investigations of memory for documented child abuse. But such studies are few and far between and most focus on adult recollections of childhood abuse. These latter studies show that a sizeable minority of people with childhood histories of physical or sexual abuse completely forget or fail to report their abuse (Goodman et al., 2003; Williams, 1994; Widom & Morris, 1997). Forgetting is predicted by variables such as younger age at the time of the abuse, a perpetrator known to the victim, lower abuse severity, and lack of maternal support, all of which are quite consistent with patterns in the basic memory literature. For instance, both intrafamilial abuse and lack of maternal support may reduce the likelihood that abuse is discussed or rehearsed.

No prospective studies have looked at preadolescent children's memories for abuse, but Greenhoot, McCloskey, and Glisky (2005) examined adolescents' memories for family violence that was documented six years earlier. Most of the teens remembered witnessing or being targets of family violence when they were children, but they failed to report many of the details of their experiences (40 to 50 percent), particularly when their mothers were the victims. As in the adult studies, some participants failed to recall any childhood family violence, and this was unrelated to a measure of nondisclosure tendency. Participants exposed to the most severe violence (e.g., kicking, burning) were the least likely to show complete forgetting, although they tended to not report the severest acts. Several other predictors of memory, including older age and recent exposure to family violence, were consistent with the traditional memory literature. Importantly, memory for family violence was also predicted by memory for nontraumatic salient events, suggesting that memories for abusive and nonabusive events draw on the same underlying processes. Measures of nontraumatic event memory have also been shown to predict consistency in children's accounts of sexual abuse over time (Ghetti, Goodman, Eisen, Qin, & Davis, 2002). In sum, the literature suggests that the factors that influence memory for child abuse and for one-time stressors are similar, although more research is needed to evaluate the retention of memories of maltreatment *during childhood*.

Child maltreatment and memory functioning

In contrast to research on memory for child maltreatment per se, considerably more work addresses the proposal that maltreatment, chronic trauma exposure, or associated psychopathology might produce general changes in children's memory functioning. Some interest in this issue was stimulated by reports in the clinical literature of global memory losses for the period of time around a trauma (e.g., Herman & Schatzow, 1987). Further, research on nonhuman animals indicates that elevated levels of the stress hormone cortisol may damage the hippocampus and impair cognitive and memory functioning (Gould, Tanapat, McEwen, Flugge, & Fuchs, 1998; Sapolsky & McEwen, 1986). Some findings with human adults are also consistent with this hypothesis (Bremner, Vermetten, Afzal, & Vythilingam, 2004; Stein, Koverola, Hanna, Torchia, & McClarty, 1997), but differences between people with and without trauma histories may be attributable to trauma-related psychopathology rather than trauma per se (e.g., Kitayama, Vaccarino, Kutner, Weiss, & Bremner, 2005).

Evidence for maltreatment-related differences in children's declarative memory functioning has not been forthcoming despite several studies addressing this possibility (e.g., Chae, Goodman, Eisen, & Qin, 2011; Eisen, Goodman, Qin, Davis, & Crayton, 2007; Howe, Toth, & Cicchetti, 2011). A large literature on "overgeneral memory" does show that adults and adolescents with childhood trauma histories may be less able or willing to recall specific personal memories in response to cue words, but overgenerality fluctuates with the remembering conditions (e.g., Bunnell & Greenhoot, 2012; Johnson, Greenhoot, Glisky, & McCloskey, 2005), thus specific memories are available

for retrieval. Moreover, the tendency to avoid specific memories may be more directly linked to posttraumatic stress symptoms rather than the trauma itself (e.g., Bunnell & Greenhoot, 2012; Goodman, Quas, & Ogle, 2009). Differences between people with and without trauma histories also seem to be more quantitative than qualitative, as there is quite a bit of variability in specificity among nontraumatized individuals (e.g., Williams et al., 2007). Finally, to date, no one has documented trauma-related memory specificity problems in children. Overall, then, there is currently little evidence of fundamental differences in the memory abilities of children with histories of abuse or chronic trauma as compared with nontraumatized children.

There are several legal implications of research on children's memory for salient and stressful experiences. First, children are unlikely to be able to remember past events that occurred during infancy or toddlerhood, whether they were traumatic or not. Second, most children exposed to stressful or traumatic events after the preverbal period continue to remember their experiences over long delays, but like memories of ordinary events these memories are vulnerable to forgetting of details and distortion. Moreover, it should not be seen as extraordinary for a child to completely forget an aversive experience, especially if he or she was very young at the time of the event or not re-exposed to reminders over time. Third, there appears to be considerable overlap in the processes involved in traumatic and nontraumatic memories, and in the memory abilities of individuals with and without maltreatment histories, indicating that the vast literature on children's memory and suggestibility is quite relevant to a consideration of children as witnesses.

THE SUGGESTIBILITY OF CHILDREN'S MEMORY

The previous section on children's autobiographical memory offers ample evidence that even very young witnesses can provide accurate reports of their experiences, even those that are stressful or traumatic. However, just because children *can* accurately relay the past to others does not mean that they always *do*. The literature on children's suggestibility reveals a range of internal and external factors that can distort children's event reports and complicate fact-finders' judgments of testimonial accuracy. Below we review these factors. The majority of this work centers on preschool- and early elementary school-aged children – a focus driven largely by applied concerns regarding the testimonial abilities of young witnesses. However, older children and adults also are vulnerable to a range of suggestive influences (e.g., Ceci, Papierno, & Kulkofsky, 2007), indicating that suggestibility is not something that children outgrow but rather something for which younger children are disproportionately more prone under most conditions.

Internal factors

Knowledge is the most widely studied internal factor influencing children's autobiographical memory. Generally, relevant event knowledge leads to inferences and elaborations that facilitate the generation of a well-organized, elaborate representation in memory. However, when expectations are inconsistent with what was experienced, individuals may be prone to condense, embellish, or distort information to reflect their beliefs and expectations (Kulkofsky, Wang, & Ceci, 2008). For example, what preschool-aged children already know about routine physical examinations can enhance their recall of the medical procedures that occurred during a specific visit to the doctor (Ornstein, Baker-Ward, Gordon, Pephrey, Tyler, & Gramzow, 2006). However, young children's knowledge can lead to errors in memory when their expectations differ from what actually happened. To illustrate, after undergoing a mock physical examination in which some highly expected procedures

were omitted (e.g., listening to the heart with a stethoscope), most children subsequently reported experiencing at least one expected-but-omitted procedure (Ornstein, Merritt, Baker-Ward, Furtado, Gordon, & Principe, 1998). Even fantasy beliefs can affect the ways in which children filter reality. For instance, Smith and Principe (2007, 2008) found that children who truly believed in the reality of the Tooth Fairy were likely to interpret ambiguous sights and sounds on the night of a tooth loss in line with the myth. For these children, a shadow under the bedroom door or a creaking of the stairway on the night of a tooth loss was misinterpreted and subsequently misremembered as caused by the Tooth Fairy.

Just as internal factors can affect encoding, they can also influence storage and retrieval processes, particularly over long delays as details are lost and expectations and inferences are used as a guide for filling in gaps in memory (Ross, 1989; Trabasso & van den Broek, 1985). To illustrate, Principe, Guiliano, and Root (2008) exposed children to contextual clues that were designed to induce inferences about the causes of two unresolved components of an earlier experienced event. For instance, after seeing a magician fail to pull a rabbit out of his hat, children found carrot ends with "teeth marks" in their classrooms. This "clue" was expected to induce an inference about the cause of the failed trick, namely that the rabbit had escaped in the school rather than appearing in the hat. When later interviewed about the event, many children wrongly recalled their inferences as actual experiences. Other work by Greenhoot (2000) demonstrates that changes in relevant knowledge after an event is experienced can lead to corresponding reconstructive changes of information already in memory.

External factors

In addition to internal factors, there are a range of external influences that also can contaminate memory. Given that children's testimony is elicited in interviews – and because analyses of real world cases have shown that forensic interviewers, at least at times, rely on suggestive questions to elicit disclosures from young witnesses (e.g., Lamb et al., 1996) – much of this literature has centered on mnemonic effects of suggestive interviewing techniques. This body of work has demonstrated that a range of commonly used suggestive practices, such as repetition of misleading questions, stereotype induction (e.g., telling the child that the suspected perpetrator does "bad things"), negative or accusatory emotional tone (e.g., urging the child to keep the defendant in jail), guided imagery (e.g., prompting the child to generate a mental image of an event and to think about its details), peer pressure (e.g., telling children that their peers have already told), and positive reinforcement for desired answers (e.g., praising the child for disclosing information consistent with the interviewer's beliefs) can lead to serious distortions and even induce entirely fictitious accounts of the past (see Bruck, Ceci, & Hembrooke, 2002; Bruck, Ceci, & Principe, 2006, for reviews).

The use of nonverbal props, such as anatomical dolls (Bruck, Ceci, & Francouer, 2000) and human figure drawings (Bruck, 2009), also can induce false claims. These are particularly suggestive influences among younger children because many do not yet recognize dolls or drawings as symbols of themselves (DeLoache & Marzolf, 1995) and they may be tempted to treat these props in ways that adults construe as inappropriate touch even when none occurred.

Although experimental work demonstrates that each of these techniques boosts children's proneness to memory errors, the most mnemonic damage is done when children come up against a biased interviewer who holds a priori beliefs about what occurred and uses a combination of suggestive procedures to prompt accounts that are consistent with his or her own beliefs (see Bruck et al., 2006, for a review). Of greatest concern

are interviewers who make single-minded attempts to elicit only belief-consistent statements and steer clear of any lines of questioning that might produce dissenting information. Biased interviewers tend to sparsely use open-ended questions and instead center their questioning on repeated specific probes, such as yes/no and forced choice questions, that collectively communicate their beliefs. This strategy is particularly worrisome because not only are young children less accurate following specific questions than open-ended prompts (e.g., Baker-Ward et al., 1993; Peterson & Bell, 1996), they also have a bias to produce "yes" responses and rarely say, "I don't know" (e.g., Peterson & Grant, 2001). Further, young children are prone to change their answer when they are repeatedly asked the same specific questions (e.g., Cassel, Roebers, & Bjorklund, 1996; Poole & White, 1991). Some may reason that their initial answer must be wrong, otherwise the interviewer would not be asking the question again. However, Howie, Nash, Kurukulasuriya, and Bowman (2012) offer evidence that younger children, who are especially prone to give inconsistent answers to repeated questions, are less likely than older children to interpret question repetition as an implicit request for answer change. This finding suggests that there likely are multiple reasons for younger children's vulnerability to switch their responses when asked the same question multiple times. In an examination of high-profile sex abuse cases, Bruck and Ceci (2012) reported that interviewer bias is characterized by:

- The child is given little opportunity to say in her own words what, if anything, happened.
- Interviewers quickly resort to using questions that require monosyllabic responses.
- Interviewers' statements and questions contain sexual content and details that are beyond the child's initial knowledge.
- Questions are repeated within and across interviews.
- Interviews continue or are repeated until the child provides information consistent with the interviewer's suspicion of sexual abuse.

An especially relevant paradigm to investigate interviewer bias involves a situation in which an interviewer is asked to question a group of children, all but one of whom experienced the same event. The sole child who did not experience it affords a close look at what happens when an interviewer develops a suspicion in the course of conducting multiple interviews and, based on this experience, attempts to cajole the nonconforming child into making a disclosure. Bruck, Ceci, Melnyk, and Finkelberg (1999) staged a surprise birthday party for preschool children. In groups of three and with the guidance of a research assistant, the children surprised a second research assistant, played games, ate food, and watched magic tricks. Other children did not attend the birthday party but, in groups of two, they colored a picture with the two research assistants. These children were told that it was the first research assistant's birthday. Interviewers were asked to question four children about what had happened when the special visitors came to the school. They were not told about the events but were simply told to find out from each child what had happened. The first three children that each interviewer questioned attended the birthday party and the fourth child attended the coloring event. Bruck et al. found that the fourth children (those who attended the coloring event and were interviewed last) produced twice as many errors as the children who attended the birthday party; 60 percent of the children who only colored made false claims that involved a birthday party. This result suggests that the interviewers had built up a bias that all the children had attended a birthday party. By the time they interviewed the fourth child, their interviews were arranged to elicit claims consistent with this hypothesis. These findings demonstrate that when interviewers develop a belief that all the children they are interviewing have experienced a certain event, nonparticipants may be at risk to make such claims. Interestingly, even when the fourth child denied attending a birthday party, 84 percent of their interviewers later reported that all the children they interviewed had told them attended a birthday party. These results suggest that regardless of what children actually say, biased interviewers are prone to inaccurately report the child's claims, making them consistent with their own hypotheses.

Collectively, this body of work suggests that young children's reporting accuracy is largely dependent on the interviewer's interrogation style, such that one can have greater confidence in the veracity of statements elicited in a neutral context than those made only after biased or suggestive interviews. In response to this line of research, a number of research groups have developed forensic interviewing protocols designed to minimize errors stemming from suggestive techniques, such as the Revised Cognitive Interview or the National Institute of Child Health and Human Development Investigative Interview (see e.g., Lamb, Hershkowitz, Orbach, & Esplin, 2008).

Admittedly, however, the effects of biased interviewing are not so straightforward. For example, even in studies with robust suggestibility effects, there are invariably some children who consistently resist even repeated and aggressive attempts to convince them that a false event occurred. In other investigations, some children quickly incorporate erroneous suggestions into their accounts, even after only a single mildly leading interview. And even under maximally supportive interviewing conditions, there are occasionally a few children who report nonexperienced events (e.g., Baker-Ward et al., 1993). Thus, although one can have more confidence in a child's report when he or she has not undergone suggestive interviews, the use of nonsuggestive questioning does not guarantee a veridical account.

These patterns illustrate that not all false reports surface as the result of biased questioning but can be due to false information picked up from other sources. A growing number of studies have demonstrated a range of experiences outside of the formal interviewing context that can produce errors in remembering, even when children are questioned in an optimally nonsuggestive manner. For instance, studies have shown that exposure to misleading information about an earlier experience from story books (Poole & Lindsay, 2001) and television (Principe, Ornstein, Baker-Ward, & Gordon, 2000) can produce distortions in memory.

Related work demonstrates that natural interactions with peers also can induce false reports. For example, Principe and Ceci (2002) had some preschoolers witness events in their classrooms that others did not and then allowed them to interact naturally with one another. When the nonwitness children later were interviewed, many reported seeing, rather than merely hearing about, nonexperienced events that were consistent with their classmates' experiences. These findings demonstrate that the content of conversations with peers can infiltrate later memory. In another study, Principe and colleagues (Principe, Kanaya, Ceci, & Singh, 2006) exposed some children within preschool classrooms to an errant rumor about a shared experience and then had them interact naturally with their peers. When later asked for their memory, those children who heard the rumor directly or picked it up from their peers were as likely to report experiencing the rumored-but-nonexperienced event as other children who actually experienced the event suggested by the rumor. Further, the rumor was more mnemonically damaging than a suggestive interview. Compared with children for whom the false information was suggested in a highly coercive interview, those exposed to the rumor gave more errant reports, were more likely to wrongly recall actually seeing the suggested event, and embellished their accounts with a generous degree of fictitious detail in line with the suggestion. These findings demonstrate not only the serious potential of rumor to contaminate children's memory, but also that exposure to rumor can be more detrimental than the most widely studied source of error in the suggestibility literature, namely biased interviewing.

Even parents can serve as a source of report distortion when they hold beliefs that are false. Principe, DiPuppo, and Gammel in (2013) found that when mothers were exposed to misinformation about an event that their preschool-aged children experienced and were then asked to discuss the event in a natural manner with their children, children later were prone to report details that were nonexperienced but suggested to their mothers. Earlier work has shown that parents can be a source of memory error when they suggest experimenter-provided scripted nonoccurrences (e.g., Poole & Lindsay, 2001), but this is the first study to demonstrate that misinformation encountered by parents can leak into children's later accounts when they are not asked to suggest the nonevent to their children, but merely to talk with their children in a natural manner. Interestingly, Principe et al. also found that children whose mothers took on a highly elaborative conversational style when discussing the event were more likely than children with low elaborative mothers to later report nonevents consistent with suggestions to their mothers. This finding is noteworthy because it suggests that the high elaborative maternal style usually associated with more skilled autobiographical remembering (see Fivush, Haden, & Reese, 2006, for a review) is also linked with increases in children's memory errors when mothers are exposed to misinformation about their children's experiences.

Examination of the mother–child conversations provides some insight into why the children of high elaborative mothers may have been particularly likely to report nonexperienced details in line with the maternal misinformation. For instance, in their conversations with their children, high elaborative mothers mentioned more than three times the amount of details consistent with the theme of the misleading information compared with low elaborative mothers. Children of high elaborative mothers also behaved differently. Compared with children of low elaborative mothers, they were more likely to accept their mother's very first suggestion in line with the misinformation and they acquiesced to a higher proportion of their mother's total suggestions. Further, during the subsequent interview, children of high elaborative mothers seemed particularly influenced by their mother's contributions during their earlier conversations. Among those children who made false reports of the misinformation, those with high elaborative mothers were more likely to embellish their accounts with the very suggestions made earlier by their mothers, whereas the children of low elaborative mothers were more likely to invent new details on the fly. These maternal and child patterns suggest that, compared with low elaborative mothers, high elaborative mothers created (likely unwittingly) a suggestible memory sharing environment and that their persistence in providing multiple elaborations in line with the suggestion led to higher levels of acquiescence during the mother–child conversation and consequently higher error rates during the interview.

In sum, this body of work provides ample evidence that children's retention of events can be influenced dramatically by a range of internal and external factors that occur outside of the formal interview context. Importantly, such factors complicate efforts to obtain accurate testimony because these sources of suggestibility are eliminated by the procedures currently used to minimize reporting errors in forensic interviews, especially among young children (see e.g., Poole & Lindsay, 2002).

It is important to note that in any study of suggestibility rarely do 100 percent of the children fall prey to 100 percent of the suggestions. Thus, suggestive interviews and extra-interview suggestive influences do not inevitability lead to false reports by children. Given that not all children are vulnerable to suggestive influences, investigators have begun to search for individual difference variables that could be used to alert legal professional to children who are especially prone or resistant to suggestion. Individual differences in a range of cognitive and social factors, such as metacognitive understanding, intelligence, verbal abilities, maternal attachment style, and temperament, have been linked

with suggestibility proneness (see Bruck & Melnyk, 2004, for a review). However, none of these effects are large or powerful enough to reliably inform the court of the probability that a particular child would make a false report. For instance, Clark-Stewart, Malloy, and Allhusen (2004) entered the single best predictors of suggestibility (i.e., measures of language skills, adaptive/inhibitory control, and parental relationship quality) into a regression model and found that the combination of these variables accounted for 32 percent of the variance in children's vulnerability to be misled. While 32 percent is a statistically impressive number, these sorts of studies cannot be used in any logical or statistical fashion to determine the truth or accuracy of any particular child's testimony. If one were to use any of these factors, or even a combination of them, to predict accuracy, there would be many misdiagnoses.[1]

Chronological age is a powerful predictor of suggestibility proneness. Children become less likely to be misled as they get older (see Bruck et al., 2006). However, there is much variability within age groups and there are some conditions under which there are no developmental effects. This is the case with both interviewer-induced suggestibility (Finnila, Mahlberga, Santtilaa, Sandnabbaa, & Niemib, 2003) as well as suggestibility due to extra-interview factors (Principe et al., 2007). Further, there are conditions that produce reverse developmental trends, making older children more suggestibility prone than younger children. For example, Principe and colleagues (2008) showed that 5- and 6-year-olds were more likely than 3- and 4-year-olds to mistakenly report inferences about the causes of ambiguous events as actual experiences. Presumably this effect occurred because the older children were more likely than the younger children to generate plausible inferences that could be misinterpreted as memories for the observed event. Likewise, Ornstein and colleagues (1998b) found that when asked to recall the details of a physical examination that excluded some scripted medical procedures (e.g., listening to the heart with a stethoscope), 6-year-olds were subsequently more likely than 4-year-olds to wrongly recall expected-but-nonexperienced medical procedures. This genre of knowledge-driven memory effects was presaged by Michelene Chi in several of her classic experiments (see Chi & Ceci, 1987 for review).

Given these sorts of findings demonstrating reversed developmental trends, Brainerd and colleagues argue for a more nuanced view of age differences. Specifically, this view holds that on both theoretical and empirical grounds, there are situations in which reverse developmental trends should be expected, and indeed the empirical literature seems to support this claim (Brainerd, Reyna, & Ceci, 2008). In situations in which older children possess more meaning-connectedness knowledge and where the suggestion interacts with such knowledge, then younger children actually may be less suggestible. For example, in the Deese–Roediger–McDermott (DRM) task, in which lists of semantically related words (e.g., *bed*, *rest*, *awake*, *tired*, *dream*) are read aloud, older children are more likely than younger children to later claim to have heard non-presented words that are strong semantic associates of the presented words (i.e., *sleep*; Brainerd et al., 2008). Mistaken reports of nonpresented but semantically related words arise developmentally because older children have more extensive semantic networks than younger children. Consequently, the DRM items induce greater activation of semantically related words among older children and thereby increase the chance that semantic associates become confused with original words. This line of work brings in the powerful role of knowledge and how it is represented.

In a series of studies, it has been shown that the way that knowledge is represented in memory can affect not only recall and recognition but even the subprocesses that underpin them, such as metamemory (Ceci, Fitneva, & Williams, 2010; Ceci et al., 2007). When some material is represented more elaborately by younger children (more dimensions and greater semantic similarity between items such as *Sesame Street* characters) and some material is represented more elaborately by older children (e.g., items that belong to categories such as predacity, citrus, dairy), then targeted predictions were confirmed whereby those who possessed more elaborate representations of the items (which sometimes was younger and sometimes older children) were more suggestible. Thus, depending on how they represented the materials, children were differentially suggestible and their metamemory was differentially effective. When older children's representation of material was related to a false suggestion, they were more suggestible than were younger children whose representation was not close to the suggestion. And the reverse was true of items whose representations were related to the suggestion of younger children (see Table 1 of Ceci et al., 2007, for targeted predictions that were confirmed for both age trends and reverse age trends as a result of how older and younger children represented the same material). The bottom line is that the nature and richness of the way events are represented influences suggestibility-proneness, and sometimes this can lead to the expectation that older individuals will be more suggestible than younger ones and sometimes it will lead to the opposite expectation.

EVALUATING THE ACCURACY OF CHILDREN'S TESTIMONY

The literatures on autobiographical memory and suggestibility demonstrate that even though children can provide accurate and compelling reports of the past, their reports can be contaminated by various internal and external forces. These constructive tendencies of memory complicate fact finders' judgments of testimonial accuracy. In fact, adults are notoriously poor at determining the accuracy of children's event reports. For instance, when Ceci and his colleagues (Ceci, Crotteau-Huffman, Smith, & Loftus, 1994; Ceci, Loftus, Leichtman, & Bruck, 1994; Leichtman & Ceci, 1995) asked professionals in psychology, law enforcement, social work, and psychiatry who attended a forensic conference to view selected videotaped or transcribed portions of interviews with children, they could not reliability discriminate between children who were providing accurate reports of past experiences from those who were describing nonexperienced events that had been suggested to them. Related work shows that even when professionals are given extensive case material, they have difficulty reaching consensus regarding the accuracy of children's statements (Horner, Guyer, & Kalter, 1993a, 1993b). Even when children are coached to deliberately lie, neither laypeople (Crossman & Lewis, 2012) nor professionals, such as police officers and customs officers, have been shown to detect truthful statements with significant accuracy (Leach, Talwar, Lee, Bala, & Lindsay, 2004; see Vrij, Chapter 37, this volume). There are also multiple demonstrations, among professionals as well as lay people, that confidence in one's judgments of the accuracy of children's accounts is not linked with children's veracity (Leach et al., 2004; Shao & Ceci, 2011).

Admittedly, the judges in these studies relied merely on subjective qualities of children's accounts to make decisions about accuracy. Might more objective measures be more successful at distinguishing true from false reports? Indeed, experts in cases involving children as witnesses often testify that is it easy to recognize accurate statements because they have certain features that distinguish them from erroneous accounts (see Bruck, Ceci, Kulkofsky, Klemfuss, & Sweeney, 2008). Below, we discuss the effectiveness of several qualities of children's narratives that have been proposed as markers of accuracy by experts. Some of these qualities seem intuitively diagnostic of accuracy and others have some theoretical grounding, but, on the whole, empirical work examining these

qualities shows little support for their use in legal situations as markers of truthfulness.

PROPOSED MARKERS OF TRUE VERSUS FALSE REPORTS

Spontaneity

One commonly held belief is that spontaneously reported events generally are accurate, whereas statements elicited by prompts are more prone to error. In support of this assumption, dozens of investigations have shown that spontaneous recall tends to yield more accurate, albeit less complete, information than children's responses to specific questions (e.g., Kulkofsky et al., 2008; Peterson & Bell, 1996). For instance, Ornstein and his colleagues have found that although children as young as three years of age are able to provide generally accurate, but limited, spontaneous accounts of a recent pediatric examination (Baker-Ward, Gordon, Ornstein, Larus, & Clubb, 1993), their recall in response to yes/no questions (Gordon & Follmer, 1994) and recognition cues (Myers, Gramzow, Ornstein, Wagner, Gordon, & Baker-Ward, 2003) is highly inaccurate.

However, it is not the case that children's spontaneous statements are always accurate, even when children are interviewed under optimally nonsuggestive conditions. There are a range of suggestive influences outside of the interview context that can induce high rates of spontaneous errors. For instance, books read by parents can lead young children to freely recall experiencing activities that were mentioned only in the story (Poole & Lindsay, 1995), and television programs can promote spontaneous intrusions of activities that were nonexperienced but seen on television (Principe, Ornstein, Baker-Ward, & Gordon, 2000). Natural conversations with peer witnesses who experienced a slightly different version of a shared event (Principe & Ceci, 2002) and adults who uttered a false rumor about a past experience also can engender false claims during free recall (Principe, Kanaya, Ceci, & Singh, 2006). Further, internal processes, such as expectations generated by prior knowledge (Ornstein, Merritt, Baker-Ward, Gordon, Furtado, & Principe, 1998b), fantasy beliefs (Principe & Smith, 2008), and causal inferences (Principe, Guiliano, & Root, 2008) can induce claims of expected but nonexperienced occurrences in response to open-ended probes.

Elaborative recall

Another proposed indicator of veridicality is abundant elaborative detail. There is, however, no scientific evidence that the number of details reported by children is diagnostic of their accuracy. When young children are exposed to suggestive influences, their subsequent reports often contain false details that go above and beyond the literal suggestions but nonetheless are consistent with them (e.g., Poole & Lindsay, 2001; Principe, 2004). To illustrate, Leichtman and Ceci (1995) found that when 3- to 6-year-old children were told that an upcoming classroom visitor was clumsy, some later invented new details consistent with this quality and described how this person spilled, ripped, soiled, and broke things during his visit. Other work shows that young children's false reports are often as detailed as their true reports, if not more so (e.g., Bruck et al., 2002; Powell, Jones, & Campbell, 2003; Principe & Ceci, 2002; Scullin, Kanaya, & Ceci, 2002). For instance, Principe et al. (2006) found that after overhearing a false rumor about a nonoccurring event, 3- to 5-year-old children's errant reports of this nonevent were twice as voluminous as those of other children who actually experienced the event suggested by the rumor. Further correlational studies have demonstrated an inverse relationship between narrative volume and accuracy. When Kulkofsky and her colleagues (2007) asked children to recollect a recently experienced event, those children

who described the event in more detail also produced proportionately more inaccurate narratives, demonstrating that better, more elaborated stories are not always the most accurate.

Narrative coherence

Another possible index of accuracy is the inclusion of features that bring coherence to the organization of children's true event narratives. These include temporal markers, such as chronological time (then, first, next, before, later), conditional statements (if/then, when, since), references to causal relations (because, so), and dialogue statements (reproductions of portions of conversations). These features become increasingly common in children's descriptions of experienced events with age (Reese, Haden, Baker-Ward, Bauer, Fivush, & Ornstein, 2011) and some legal experts have assumed that highly coherent narratives are indicative are truthfulness (Honts, 1994; Raskin & Esplin, 1991). However, when Kulkofsky and colleagues (2007) explored the coherence–accuracy link directly in preschool-aged children's accounts of a recent experience, they found that increased coherency, as measured in terms of temporal markers or dialogue statements, was related to higher accuracy only when the length of children's narratives was controlled. Further work that directly contrasted 3- to 5-year-old children's reports of experienced and suggested-but-nonexperienced events revealed more references to temporal and causal relations in their false than their true accounts and equal levels of dialogue statements in the two sorts of narratives (Bruck et al., 2002). Studies exploring the mnemonic effects of nonevents suggested during natural conversations demonstrate that pre-school aged children's false narratives can contain high levels of dialogue statements overheard from others as well as those uttered by themselves (Principe, Cherson, DiPuppo, & Schindewolf, 2012).

Fantastic details

Some experts have suggested that the inclusion of fantastic details suggests exposure to aggressively coercive interviews and therefore are indicative of fabrication. This belief comes from several high profile daycare center child abuse cases in the 1990s where children underwent repeated highly suggestive interviews and consequently made a range of bizarre and unfounded claims, such as eating feces, sacrificing babies, setting children on fire, and swimming with sharks (Ceci & Bruck, 1995). However, studies comparing children's reports of experienced versus nonexperienced events have found that fantastic claims ensure neither accuracy nor inaccuracy. For example, Bruck and her colleagues (2002) found that although false narratives following suggestion were more likely to contain fantastic details than were true narratives, children's true accounts also often contained fantastic elements. Thus the inclusion of fantastic statements in and of themselves does not signify that all of the report is errant. Supporting this claim is research by Principe and Smith (2007, 2008), which shows that children's truthful reports of actual events can be peppered with fantastic details when their beliefs lead them to interpret certain aspects of experienced events in fantastic terms.

Consistency

The degree to which the same details are repeated consistently across interviews is another criterion used by professionals as an index of accuracy. In support of this claim is research showing that, with repeated retellings, children tend to include more new information in false than true reports, and correspondingly are more likely to repeat consistent details in true versus false accounts (Bruck et al., 2002). Longitudinal work confirms this pattern even over lengthy delays (i.e., one or two years; Peterson, Moores, & White, 2001; Salmon & Pipe, 2000) and

shows that new information reported for the first time after a delay is much more likely than repeated information to include fictitious statements and should be treated with caution. However, other work shows that entirely false accounts can be consistent over time. For instance, Principe et al. (2012) found children's false accounts engendered by rumor to be quite consistent across interviews. Likewise, Huffman, Crossman, and Ceci (1997) showed that some false memories created by asking children to repeatedly imagine nonevents persisted after a one-year delay, and Scullin et al. (2002) reported that by the third interview, true and false statements did not differ in consistency. Even among adults, consistency does not necessarily predict accuracy (Brewer, Potter, Fisher, Bond, & Lusczc, 1999).

Confidence

In mock trials, the single most important factor affecting jurors' beliefs about the credibility of testimony (of those assessed) is the confidence that witnesses expressed about their reports (Leippe & Eisenstadt, 2007). Young children, however, tend to be overly confident in the accuracy of their recall. Not only do they typically give very high confidence ratings after both correct and incorrect responses (Pressley, Levin, Ghatala, & Ahmad, 1987), they also tend to experience particular difficulties when questioned on suggested-but-nonexperienced information (Roebers & Howie, 2003). Some have argued that this is likely because young children do not yet realize that one can hold a belief that is false (Welch-Ross, 1999), nor do they believe that their memories are susceptible to distortion from misinformation that has been suggested by others (O'Sullivan, Howe, & Marche, 1996). Instead, they presume that their memories are always accurate, and that the only way for information to get into memory is through direct experience (O'Sullivan & Howe, 1995). In fact, even when children in suggestibility studies are told that their memories have been induced experimentally via false suggestions, many continue to insist in the veracity of their fictitious memories (Ceci et al., 1994; Principe, Haines, Adkins, & Guiliano, 2010). Thus, when false information becomes incorporated into memory, young children's naive beliefs about the invulnerability of memory to errors often lead to high confidence in their recollections – a confidence that is likely interpreted by many adults as diagnostic of accuracy.

Corroboration

In cases of multiple witnesses, corroboration might seem to signal accuracy. It is likely compelling hearing child after child tell the same story, especially if one believes that each child has arrived at the same storyline independently. But the exact opposite might be the case. The story may have been arrived at in a collaborative manner among peers who initially had very different representations of the event. Demonstrating this possibility is research by Principe, Daley, and Kauth (2010) showing that high levels of corroboration can occur even when none of the witnesses are accurate. In this study, 3- to 5-year-old children overheard an errant rumor about a shared event and then were allowed to interact naturally with one another. When later interviewed individually, many provided accounts that were consistent with the rumor but inconsistent with what actually happened. This and related work with both children (Bruck et al., 1999; Principe & Ceci, 2002) and adults (Wright, Self, & Justice, 2000) shows that corroboration among co-witnesses should not be interpreted as evidence of accuracy but can occur as the result of opportunities to interact with co-witnesses.

Collectively, this literature has revealed some factors that are more characteristic of true than false reports. Given, however, evidence that false accounts can have qualities associated with veridicality, such as spontaneous productions, narrative detail,

and confidence, the presence of one or even a combination of them cannot be used as an infallible index for judging whether a particular child's report is accurate or inaccurate. Even when experts attempt to apply more systematic techniques to determine true accounts, their decisions are not reliable. Statement validity analysis, or more specifically criterion-based content analysis (CBCA), has been developed as an objective means to distinguish true from false reports. CBCA involves coding children's accounts on the basis of criteria presumed to be indicative of truthfulness, such as abundant details, reproductions of dialogue statements, contextual embedding, and shifts in focus. There is some evidence that CBCA can identify truthful statements from deliberate lies at above-chance (albeit far from perfect) levels (Vrij, 2005). CBCA cannot, however, distinguish accurate accounts from false accounts produced as the result of suggestive influences (Erdmann, Volbert, & Bohm, 2004; Shao & Ceci, 2011; Stromwell, Bengtsson, Leander, & Granhag, 2004), particularly when individuals have become convinced that suggested events actually occurred (Blandon-Gitlin, Pezdek, Lindsay, & Hagen, 2009). Other work shows that coaching children on CBCA criteria can boost their scores and consequently lower judges' ability to identify false reports (Vrij, Akehurst, Soukara, & Bull, 2002).

The implications of these findings are quite sobering, especially considering the gravity of distinguishing between accurate and inaccurate statements made by children in many legal situations. Nonetheless, these data reveal an important reality of memory reporting both to professionals who deal with young witnesses and to researchers who explore facets of children's remembering – children's accounts of nonexperienced events, even though they are inaccurate, can become so elaborate, organized, and compelling that they are indistinguishable from children's true reports of actual experiences. The same is doubtlessly true of adults, but the body of work presented in this chapter demonstrates that children, and especially 3- to 6-year-old children, are particularly prone to experience compelling false memories. In fact, in some cases, decreases in accuracy are accompanied by increases in proposed indicators of credibility (Bruck et al., 2002; Principe & Ceci, 2002; Principe, Daley, & Kauth, 2010), thus making fictitious reports seem more believable than accurate accounts. Communicating this information to fact finders is important, as surveys reveal that laypeople as well as licensed psychologists and legal professionals are generally unaware of this line of research.

CONCLUSION

Despite the many strengths of children's memory abilities, one consistent theme throughout this chapter concerns the fallibility of children's (and especially young children's) recollections. We have also highlighted the consequent challenges encountered by those who must make legally relevant decisions based on the testimony of young witnesses. Indeed, this account of children's memory and testimony leaves us with many problems and with many challenges. Given that performance varies as a function of many factors, any "diagnostic" conclusion about an individual child's memory for a given event must be referenced to the particular constellation of individual difference, interviewing, and contextual variables in operation (see also Poole & Lindsay, 1998). Memory is a dynamic process, changing over time in response to events both internal and external to the individual, and accuracy is affected by infinite factors that undoubtedly vary with age along with numerous other individual difference factors. Empirical work could never hope to capture each of these variables into a single research design or to mirror the precise factors involved in a particular legal case. Nor should it. It is not the job of memory researchers to arbitrate truthfulness in individual cases. That is the job of finders of fact. The best that memory researchers can do is to provide those who work with children in the legal system an understanding of factors that raise or lower the potential for accuracy.

NOTES

1 Such efforts would also have to make assumptions about the base rates of true and false allegations (as laid out in Poole & Lindsay, 1998). Also see Ceci–Friedman, utility functions plotting reduction of correct and false identifications as a function of the base rate of guilt, p(G) in Clark (2012).

2 In these studies, hundreds of psychologists, social workers, and psychiatrists who attended professional meetings were unable to reliably discriminate between true and false accounts of ten videos (five true, five false), including in one analysis the arguably top four forensic experts in statement validity analysis (see p. 315 of Ceci et al., 1994a, and p. 398 of Ceci et al., 1994b for description of samples). The video clips were selected from Leichtman and Ceci (1995), but the specific ten videos differed for each sample.

REFERENCES

Ackil, J. K., Van Abbema, D. L., & Bauer, P. J. (2003). After the storm: Enduring differences in mother–child recollections of traumatic and nontraumatic events. *Journal of Experimental Child Psychology*, *84*(4), 286–309.

Arata, C. M., Langhinrichsen-Rohling, J., Bowers, D., & O'Farrill-Swails, L. (2005). Single versus multitype maltreatment: An examination of the long-term effects of child abuse. *Journal of Aggression, Maltreatment & Trauma*, *11*, 29–52.

Bahrick, L., Parker, J. F., Fivush, R., & Levitt, M. (1998). Children's memory of Hurricane Andrew. *Journal of Experimental Psychology: Applied*, *4*, 308–331.

Baker-Ward, L., Gordon, B. N., Ornstein, P. A., Larus, D. M., & Clubb, P. A. (1993). Young children's long-term retention of a pediatric examination. *Child Development*, *64*, 1519–1533.

Bauer, P. J., Wenner, J. A., & Kroupina, M. G. (2002). Making the past present: Later verbal accessibility of early memories. *Journal of Cognition and Development. Special issue in honor of Katherine Nelson*, *3*(1), 21–47.

Bender, R. H., Wallsten, T. S., & Ornstein, P. A. (1996). Age differences in encoding and retrieving details of a pediatric examination. *Psychonomic Bulletin and Review, 3*, 188–198.

Blandon-Gitlin, I., Pezdek, K., Lindsay, D. S., & Hagen, L. (2009). Criteria-based content analysis of true and suggested accounts of events. *Applied Cognitive Psychology, 23*, 901–917.

Brainerd, C., Reyna, V., & Ceci, S. J. (2008). Developmental reversals in false memory: A review of data and theory. *Psychological Bulletin, 134*, 334–375.

Bremner, J. D., Vermetten, E., Afzal, N., & Vythilingam, M. (2004). Deficits in verbal declarative memory function in women with childhood sexual abuse-related posttraumatic stress disorder. *Journal of Nervous and Mental Disease, 192*, 643–649.

Brewer, N., Potter, R., Fisher, R. P., Bond, N., & Luszcz, M. A. (1999). Beliefs and data on the relationship between consistency and accuracy of eyewitness testimony. *Applied Cognitive Psychology, 13*, 297–313.

Bruck, M. (2009). Human figure drawings and children's recall of touching. *Journal of Experimental Psychology: Applied, 15*, 361–374.

Bruck, M., & Ceci, S. J. (2012). Forensic developmental psychology in the courtroom. In D. Faust and M. Ziskin (Eds.), *Coping with psychiatric and psychological testimony* (Chapter 33). New York: Cambridge University Press.

Bruck M., Ceci S. J., & Francouer E. (2000). A comparison of three and four year old children's use of anatomically detailed dolls to report genital touching in a medical examination. *Journal of Experimental Psychology: Applied, 6*, 74–83.

Bruck, M., Ceci, S. J., & Hembrooke, H. (2002). The nature of children's true and false narratives. *Developmental Review, 22*, 520–554.

Bruck, M., Ceci, S. J., & Principe, G. F. (2006). *The child and the law.* In K. A. Renniger and I. E. Sigel (Eds.), *Handbook of child psychology: vol. 4. child psychology in practice* (6th ed.). (pp. 776–816). New York: Wiley.

Bruck, M., & Melnyk, L. (2004). Individual differences in children's suggestibility: A review and synthesis, *Applied Cognitive Psychology, 18*, 947–958.

Bruck, M., Ceci, S. J., Kulkofsky, S. C., Klemfuss, J. Z., & Sweeney, C. (2008). Unwarranted assumptions about children's testimonial accuracy. In M. Rutter, D. Bishop, et al. (Eds.), *Rutter's handbook of child and adolescent psychiatry* (5th ed.). Oxford: Blackwell.

Bunnell, S. L., & Greenhoot, A. F. (2012). When and why does Abuse predict reduced autobiographical memory specificity? *Memory*, 20, 121–137.

Burgwyn-Bailes, E., Baker-Ward, L., Gordon, B. N., & Ornstein, P. A. (2001). Children's memory for emergency medical treatment after one year: The impact of individual difference variables on recall and suggestibility. *Applied Cognitive Psychology. Special Issue: Trauma, stress, and autobiographical memory, 15*(7), S25–S48.

Cassel, W. S., Roebers, C. E. M., & Bjorklund, D.F. (1996). Developmental patterns of eyewitness responses to repeated and increasingly suggestive questions. *Journal of Experimental Child Psychology, 61*(2), 116–133.

Ceci, S. J., & Bruck, M. (1995). *Jeopardy in the courtroom: A scientific analysis of children's testimony.* Washington, DC: American Psychological Association.

Ceci S. J., Crotteau-Huffman M., Smith E., & Loftus E. W. (1994b). Repeatedly thinking about nonevents. *Consciousness and Cognition, 3*, 388–440.

Ceci, S. J., Fitneva, S. A., & Williams, W. M. (2010). Representational constraints on the development of memory and metamemory: A developmental-representational-theory. *Psychological Review, 117*, 464–495.

Ceci, S. J., Loftus, E. W., Leichtman, M., & Bruck, M. (1994a). The role of source misattributions in the creation of false beliefs among preschoolers. *International Journal of Clinical Experimental Hypnosis, 62*, 304–320.

Ceci, S. J., Papierno, P. B., & Kulkofsky, S. C. (2007). Representational constraints on children's memory and suggestibility. *Psychological Science, 18*, 503–509.

Chae, Y., Goodman, G. S., Eisen, M. L., & Qin, J. (2011). Event memory and suggestibility in abused and neglected children: Trauma-related psychopathology and cognitive functioning. *Journal of Experimental Child Psychology, 110*, 520–583.

Chi, M. T. H., & Ceci, S. J. (1987). Content knowledge: Its representation and restructuring in memory development. In H.W. Reese and L .Lipsett (Eds.), *Advances in Child Development and Behavior, 20*, 91–146.

Clark, S. E. (2012). Costs and benefits of eyewitness identification reform: Psychological science and public policy. *Perspectives in Psychological Science, 7*, 238–259.

Clarke-Stewart, K. A., Malloy, L. C., & Allhusen, V. D. (2004). Verbal ability, self-control, and close relationships with parents protect children against misleading suggestions. *Applied Cognitive Psychology, 18*, 1037–1058.

Connolly, D. A., & Lindsay, D. S. (2001). The influence of suggestions on children's reports of a unique experience versus an instance of a repeated experience. *Applied Cognitive Psychology, 15,* 205–223.

Coster, W. J., Gersten, M. S., Beeghly, M., & Cicchetti, D. (1989). Communicative functioning in maltreated toddlers. *Developmental Psychology, 25*(6), 1020–1029.

Crossman, A., & Lewis, M. (2012). Adults' ability to detect children's lying. *Behavioral Sciences & the Law, 24,* 703–715.

DeLoache, J. S., & Marzolf, D. P. (1995). The use of dolls to interview young children: Issues of symbolic representation. *Journal of Experimental Child Psychology. Special Issue: Early memory, 60*(1), 155–173.

Eisen, M. L., Goodman, G. G., Jianjian, Q., Davis, S., & Crayton, J. (2007). Maltreated children's memory: Accuracy, suggestibility and psychopathology. *Developmental Psychology, 43*(6), 1275–1294.

Erdmann, K., Volbert, R., & Bohm, C. (2004). Children report suggested events even when interviewed in a nonsuggestive manner: What are the implications for credibility assessment? *Applied Cognitive Psychology, 18,* 589–611.

Finnila K., Mahlberga N., Santtilaa P., Sandnabbaa K., & Niemib, P. (2003). Validity of a test of children's suggestibility for predicting responses to two interview situations differing in their degree of suggestiveness. *Journal of Experimental Child Psychology, 85,* 32–49.

Fivush, R., Gray, J. T., & Fromhoff, F. A. (1987). Two-year-olds talk about the past. *Cognitive Development, 2,* 393–409.

Fivush, R., Reese, E., & Haden, C. A. (2006). Elaborating on elaborations: Role of maternal reminiscing style in cognitive and socioemotional development. *Child Development, 77*(6), 1568–1588.

Fivush, R., & Nelson, K. (2004). Culture and language in the emergence of autobiographical memory, *Psychological Science, 15*(9), 573–577.

Fivush, R., Sales, J. M., Goldberg, A., Bahrick, L., & Parker, J. (2004). Weathering the storm: Children's long-term recall of Hurricane Andrew. *Memory, 12*(1), 104–118.

Freyd, J. J., DePrince, A. P., & Zurbriggen, E. L. (2001). Self-reported memory for abuse depends upon victim-perpetrator relationship. *Journal of Trauma & Dissociation, 2*(3), 5–16.

Ghetti, S., Goodman, G. S., Eisen, M. L., Qin, J., & Davis, S. L. (2002). Consistency in children's reports of sexual and physical abuse. *Child Abuse & Neglect, 26,* 977–995.

Goodman, G. S., Ghetti, S., Quas, J. A., Edelstein, R. S., Alexander, K. W., Redlich, A. D., Cordon, I. M., & Jones, D. P. (2003). A prospective study of memory for child sexual abuse: New findings relevant to the repressed-memory controversy. *Psychological Science, 14*(2), 113–118.

Goodman, G. S., Ogle, C. M., Block, S. D., Harris, L. S., Larson, R. P., August, E., Cho, Y. I., Beber, J., Timmer, S., & Urquiza, A. (2011) False memory for trauma-related Deese–Roediger–McDermott lists in adolescents and adults with histories of child sexual abuse. *Development and Psychopathology, 23,* 423–438.

Goodman, G. S., Quas, J. A., & Ogle, C. M. (2009). Child maltreatment and memory. *Annual Review of Psychology, 61,* 325–351.

Gordon, B. N., & Follmer, A. (1994). Developmental issues in judging the credibility of children's testimony. *Journal of Clinical Child Psychology, 23,* 283–294.

Gould, E., Tanapat, P., McEwen, B. S., Flugge, G., & Fuchs, E. (1998). Proliferation of granule cell precursors in the dentate gyrus of adult monkeys is diminished by stress. *Proceedings of the National Academy of Sciences USA, 95,* 3168–3171.

Greenhoot, A. F. (2000). Remembering and understanding: The effects of changes in underlying knowledge on children's recollections. *Child Development, 71,* 1309–1328.

Greenhoot, A. F., McCloskey, L., & Glisky, E. (2005). A longitudinal study of adolescents' recollections of family violence. *Applied Cognitive Psychology, 19*(6), 719–743.

Herman, J. L., & Schatzow, E. (1987). Recovery and verification of memories of childhood sexual trauma. *Psychoanalytic Psychology, 4*(1), 1–14.

Hoffman Plotkin, D., & Twentyman, C. T. (1984). A multimodal assessment of behavioral and cognitive deficits in abused and neglected preschoolers. *Child Development, 55*(3), 794–802.

Honts, C. R., (1994). Psychophysiological detection of deception. *Current Directions in Psychological Science, 3*(3), 77–82.

Horner, T. M., Guyer, M. J., & Kalter, N. M. (1993a). The biases of child sexual abuse experts: Believing is seeing. *Bulletin of the American Academy of Psychiatry and Law, 21,* 281–292.

Horner, T. M., Guyer, M. J., & Kalter, N. M. (1993b). Clinical expertise and the assessment of child sexual abuse. *Journal of the American Academy of Child and Adolescent Psychiatry, 32,* 925–931.

Howe, M. L. (2000). *The fate of early memories: Developmental science and the retention of childhood experiences.* Washington, DC: American Psychological Association.

Howe, M. L., & Brainerd, C. J. (1989). Development of children's long-term retention. *Developmental Review, 9,* 301–340.

Howe, M. L., Toth, S. L., & Cicchetti, D. (2011). Can maltreated children inhibit true and false memories for emotional information? *Child Development*, *82*(3), 967–981.

Howie, P., Nash, L., Kurukulasuriya, N., & Bowman, A. (2012). Children's event reports: Factors affecting responses to repeated questions in vignette scenarios and event recall interviews. *British Journal of Developmental Psychology*, *30*, 550–568.

Huffman, M. L. C., Crossman, A. M., & Ceci, S. J. (1997). "Are false memories permanent?": An investigation of the long-term effects of source misattributions. *Consciousness and Cognition*, *6*, 482–490.

Johnson, R. J., Greenhoot, A. F., Glisky, E., & McCloskey, L. A. (2005). The relations among abuse, depression, and adolescents' autobiographical memory. *Journal of Clinical Child and Adolescent Psychology*, *34*(2), 235–247.

Kitayama, N., Vaccarino, V., Kutner, M., Weiss, P., & Bremner, J. D. (2005). Magnetic resonance imaging (MRI) measurement of hippocampal volume in posttraumatic stress disorder: A meta-analysis. *Journal of Affective Disorders*, *88*(1), 79–86.

Kulkofsky, S. C, Wang, Q., & Ceci, S. J. (2008). Do better stories make better memories? Narrative quality and memory accuracy in preschool children. *Applied Cognitive Psychology*, *22*, 21–38.

Lamb, M. E., Hershkowitz, I., Orbach, Y., & Esplin, P.W. (2008). *Tell me what happened*. Chichester, UK and Hoboken, NJ: Wiley.

Lamb, M. E., Hershkowitz, I., Sternberg, K. J., Esplin, P.W., Hovav, M., Manor, T., & Yudilevitch, L. (1996). Effects of investigative utterance types of Israeli children's responses. *International Journal of Behavioral Development*, *19*(3), 627–637.

Leach, A-M., Talwar, V., Lee, K., Bala, N., & Lindsay, R.C.L. (2004). "Intuitive" lie detection of children's deception by law enforcement officials and university students. *Law and Human Behavior*, *28*, 661–685.

Leippe, M. R., & Eisenstadt, D. (2007). Eyewitness confidence and the confidence–accuracy relationship in memory for people. In R. C. L. Lindsay, D. F. Ross, J. D. Read, and M. P. Toglia (Eds.), *Handbook of eyewitness psychology* (Vol. 2, pp. 377–425). Mahwah, NJ: Erlbaum.

Leichtman, M. D., & Ceci, S. J. (1995). The effects of stereotypes and suggestions on preschoolers' reports. *Developmental Psychology*, *31*, 568–578.

McNally, R. J. (2006). Let Freud rest in peace. *Behavioral and Brain Sciences*, *29*(5), 526–527.

Merritt, K., Ornstein, P.A., & Spiker, B. (1994). Children's memory for a salient medical procedure: Implications for testimony. *Pediatrics*, *94*, 17–23.

Morris, G., & Baker-Ward, L. (2007). Fragile but real: Children's capacity to use newly acquired words to convey preverbal memories. *Child Development*, *78*, 448–458.

Myers, J., Gramzow, E., Ornstein, P. A., Wagner, L., Gordon, B. N., & Baker-Ward, L. (2003). Children's memory of a physical examination: A comparison of recall and recognition assessment protocols. *International Journal of Behavioural Development*, *27*, 66–73.

Najarian, L. M., Goenjian, A. K., Pelcovitz, D., Mandel, F., & Najarian, B. (1996). Relocation after a disaster: Posttraumatic stress disorder in Armenia after the earthquake. *Journal of the American Academy of Child & Adolescent Psychiatry*, *35*, 374–383.

Nelson, K., & Fivush, R. (2000). Socialization of memory. In E. Tulving (Ed.), *Oxford handbook of memory* (pp. 283–295). Oxford: Oxford University Press.

Orbach, Y., Hershkowitz, I., Lamb, M. E., Esplin, P. W., & Horowitz, D. (2000). Assessing the value of structured protocols for forensic interviews of alleged child abuse victims. *Child Abuse & Neglect*, *24*(6), 733–752.

Ornstein, P. A., Baker-Ward, L., Gordon, B. N., Pelphrey, K. A., Tyler, C. S., & Gramzow, E. (2006). The influence of prior knowledge and repeated questioning on children's long-term retention of the details of a pediatric examination. *Developmental Psychology*, *42*, 332–344.

Ornstein, P. A., Gordon, B. N., & Larus, D. (1992). Children's memory for a personally experienced event: Implications for testimony. *Applied Cognitive Psychology*, *6*(1), 49–60.

Ornstein, P. A., Ceci, S. J., & Loftus, E. F. (1998a). Adult recollections of childhood abuse: Cognitive and developmental perspectives. *Psychology, Public Policy, and Law*, *4*, 1025–1051.

Ornstein, P. A., Merritt, K. A., Baker-Ward, L., Gordon, B. N., Furtado, E., & Principe, G. (1998b). Children's knowledge, expectation, and long-term retention. *Applied Cognitive Psychology*, *12*, 387–405.

O'Sullivan, J. T., & Howe, M. L. (1995). Metamemory and memory construction. *Consciousness and Cognition: An International Journal*, *4*(1), 104–110.

O'Sullivan, J. T., Howe, M. L., & Marche, T. A. (1996). Children's beliefs about long-term retention. *Child Development*, *67*(6), 2989–3009.

Peterson, C. (2011). Children's memory reports over time: Getting both better and worse. *Journal of Experimental Child Psychology*, *109*, 275–293.

Peterson, C., & Bell, M. (1996). Children's memory for traumatic injury. *Child Development*, *67*(6), 3045–3070.

Peterson, C., & Grant, M. (2001). Forced-choice: Are forensic interviewers asking the right questions? *Canadian Journal of Behavioural Science/Revue canadienne des sciences du comportement, 33*(2), 118–127.

Peterson, C., Grant, V. V., & Boland, L. D. (2005). Childhood amnesia in children and adolescents: Their earliest memories. *Memory, 13*(6), 622–637.

Peterson, C., Moores, L., & White, G. (2001). Recounting the same events again and again: Children's consistency across multiple interviews. *Applied Cognitive Psychology, 15*(4), 353–371.

Peterson, C., & Whalen, N. (2001). Five years later: Children's memory for medical emergencies. *Applied Cognitive Psychology. Special Issue: Trauma, stress, and autobiographical memory, 15*(7), S7–S24.

Poole, D. A., & Lindsay, D. S. (1995). Interviewing preschoolers: Effects of nonsuggestive techniques, parental coaching, and leading questions on the reports of nonexperienced events. *Journal of Experimental Child Psychology, 60*, 129–154.

Poole, D. A., & Lindsay, D. S. (1998). Assessing the accuracy of young children's reports: Lessons from the investigation of child sexual abuse. *Journal of Applied and Preventative Psychology, 7*, 1–26.

Poole, D. A., & Lindsay, D. S. (2001). Children's eyewitness reports after exposure to misinformation from parents. *Journal of Experimental Psychology: Applied, 7*, 27–50.

Poole, D. A., & Lindsay, D. S. (2002). Reducing child witnesses' false reports of misinformation from parents. *Journal of Experimental Child Psychology, 81*, 117–140.

Poole, D. A., & White, L.T. (1991). The effects of question repetition on the eyewitness testimony of children and adults. *Developmental Psychology, 27*(6), 975–986.

Powell, M. B., Jones, C. H., & Campbell, C. (2003). A comparison of preschoolers' recall of experienced versus non-experienced events across multiple interviewers. *Applied Cognitive Psychology, 17*, 935–952.

Pressley, M., Levin, J. R., Ghatala, E. S., & Ahmad, M. (1987). Test monitoring in young grade school children. *Journal of Experimental Child Psychology, 43*(1), 96–111.

Principe, G. F. (2004). If at first you don't remember, try, try again: The role of initial encoding in children's false reports. *Journal of Cognition and Development, 5*, 337–362.

Principe, G. F., & Ceci, S. J. (2002). "I saw it with my own ears": The influence of peer conversations and suggestive questions on preschoolers' event memories. *Journal of Experimental Child Psychology, 83*, 1–25.

Principe, G. F., Cherson, M., DiPuppo, J., & Schindewolf, E. (2012). Children's natural conversations following exposure to a rumor: Linkages to later false reports. *Journal of Experimental Child Psychology, 113*, 383–400.

Principe, G. F., Daley, L., & Kauth, K. (2010). Social processes affecting the mnemonic consequences of rumors on children's memory. *Journal of Experimental Child Psychology, 107*, 479–493.

Principe, G. F., DiPuppo, J., & Gammel, J. (2013). Effects of mothers' conversation style and receipt of misinformation on children's event reports. *Cognitive Development, 28*, 260–271.

Principe, G. F., Guiliano, S., & Root, C. (2008). Rumormongering and remembering: How rumors originating in children's inferences can affect memory. *Journal of Experimental Child Psychology, 99*, 135–155.

Principe, G. F., Haines, B., Adkins, A., & Guiliano, S. (2010). False rumors and true belief: Memory processes underlying children's errant reports of rumored events. *Journal of Experimental Child Psychology, 107*, 407–422.

Principe, G. F., Kanaya, T, Ceci, S. J., & Singh, M. (2006). Believing is seeing: How rumors can engender false memories in preschoolers. *Psychological Science, 17*, 243–248.

Principe, G. F., Ornstein, P. A., Baker-ward, L., & Gordon, B. N. (2000). The effects of intervening experiences on children's memory for a physical examination. *Applied Cognitive Psychology, 14*, 59–80.

Principe, G. F., & Smith, E. (2007). The tooth, the whole tooth, and nothing but the tooth: How belief in the Tooth Fairy can engender false memories. *Applied Cognitive Psychology, 21*, 1–18.

Principe, G. F., & Smith, E. (2008). Seeing things unseen: Fantasy beliefs and false reports. *Journal of Cognition and Development, 9*, 1–23.

Principe, G. F., Tinguely, A., & Dobkowski, N. (2007). Mixing memories: The effects of rumors that conflict with children's experiences. *Journal of Experimental Child Psychology, 98*, 1–19.

Pynoos, R. S., & Eth, S. (1984). The child as witness to homicide. *Journal of Social Issues, 40*(2), 87–108.

Pynoos, R. S., & Nader, K. (1989). Children's memory and proximity to violence. *Journal of the American Academy of Child & Adolescent Psychiatry, 28*(2), 236–241.

Quas, J. A., Goodman, G. S., Bidrose, S., Pipe, M.-E., Craw, S., & Ablin, D. S. (1999). Emotion and memory:

Children's long-term remembering, forgetting, and suggestibility. *Journal of Experimental Child Psychology, 72*(4), 235–270.

Quas, J. A., & Lench, H. C. (2007). Arousal at encoding, arousal at retrieval, interviewer support, and children's memory for a mild stressor. *Applied Cognitive Psychology, 21*(3), 289–305.

Raskin, D. C., & Esplin, P. W. (1991). Statement validity assessment: Interview procedures and content analysis of children's statements of sexual abuse. *Behavioral Assessment, 13(3)*, 265–291.

Reese, E., Haden, C. A., Baker-Ward, L., Bauer, P., Fivush, R., & Ornstein, P. A. (2011). Coherence of personal narratives across the lifespan: A multidimensional model and coding method. *Journal of Cognition and Development, 12*, 424–462.

Roebers, C. M., & Howie, P. (2003). Confidence judgments in event recall: Developmental progression in the impact of question format. *Journal of Experimental Child Psychology, 95*(4), 352–371.

Ross, M. (1989). Relation of implicit theories to the construction of personal histories. *Psychological Review, 96*, 341–357.

Salmon, K., Price, M., & Pereira, J. K. (2002). Factors associated with young children's long-term recall of an invasive medical procedure: A preliminary investigation. *Journal of Developmental & Behavioral Pediatrics, 23*(5), 347–352.

Salmon, K., & Pipe, M. E. (2000). Recalling an event one year later: The impact of props, drawing, and a prior interview. *Applied Cognitive Psychology, 14*(2), 99–120.

Sapolsky, R. M., & McEwen, B. S. (1986). Stress, glucocorticoids, and their role in degenerative changes in the aging hippocampus. In T. Crook, R. T. Bartus, S. Ferris, and S. Gershon (Eds.), *Treatment development strategies for Alzheimer's disease* (pp. 151–171). Madison, CT; Mark Powley Associates.

Scullin, M., Kanaya, T., & Ceci, S. J. (2002). Measurement of individual differences in children's suggestibility across situations. *Journal of Experimental Psychology: Applied, 8*, 233–246.

Shao, Y., & Ceci, S. J. (2011). Adult credibility assessments of misinformed, deceptive and truthful children. *Applied Cognitive Psychology, 25*, 135–145. DOI: 10.1002/acp.1652.

Sheingold, K., & Tenney, Y. J. (1982). Memory for a salient childhood event. In U. Neisser (Ed.), *Memory observed* (pp. 201–212). New York: Freeman.

Simcock, G., & Hayne, H. (2002). Breaking the barrier? Children fail to translate their preverbal memories into language. *Psychological Science, 13*(3), 225–231.

Stein, M. B., Koverola, C., Hanna, C., Torchia, M. G., & McClarty, B. (1997). Hippocampal volume in women victimized by childhood sexual abuse. *Psychological Medicine, 27*, 951–959.

Sternberg, K. J., Lamb, M. E., & Hershkowitz, I. (1996). Child sexual abuse investigations in Israel. *Criminal Justice and Behavior, 23*, 322–337.

Stromwell, L. A., Bengtsson, L., Leander, L., & Granhag, P. A. (2004). Assessing children's statements: The impact of a repeated experience on CBCA and RM ratings. *Applied Cognitive Psychology, 18*, 653–668.

Terr, L. (1983). Chowchilla revisited: The effects of psychic trauma four years after a school-bus kidnapping. *American Journal of Psychiatry, 140*(12), 1543–1550.

Terr, L. (1988). What happens to early memories of trauma? A study of twenty children under age five at the time of documented traumatic events. *Journal of the American Academy of Child & Adolescent Psychiatry, 27*(1), 96–104.

Trabasso, R., & van den Broek, P. (1985). Causal thinking and the representation of narrative events. *Journal of Memory and Language, 24*(5), 612–630.

Usher, J. A., & Neisser, U. (1993). Child amnesia and the beginnings of memory for four early life events. *Journal of Experimental Psychology: General, 122*(2), 155–165.

van der Kolk, B. A. (1994). The body keeps the score: Memory and the emerging psychobiology of posttraumatic stress. *Harvard Review of Psychiatry, 1*, 253–265.

Vrij, A. (2005). Criteria-based content analysis: A qualitative review of the first 37 studies. *Psychology, Public Policy, and Law, 11*(1), 3–41.

Vrij, A., Akehurst, L., Soukara, S., & Bull, R. (2002). Will the truth come out? The effect of deception, age, status, coaching, and social skills on CBCA scores. *Law and Human Behavior, 26*(3), 261–283.

Welch-Ross, M. (1999). Preschoolers' understanding of mind: Implications for suggestibility. *Cognitive Development, 14*(1), 101–131.

Widom, C. S., & Morris, S. (1997). Accuracy of adult recollections of childhood victimization, Part 2: Childhood sexual abuse. *Psychological Assessment, 9*(1), 34–46.

Williams, J. M. G., Barnhofer, T., Crane, C., Herman, D., Raes, F., Watkins, E., & Dalgleish, T. (2007). Autobiographical memory specificity and emotional disorder. *Psychological Bulletin, 133*(1), 122–148.

Williams, L. M. (1994). Recall of childhood trauma: A prospective study of women's memories for child sexual abuse. *Journal of Consulting and Clinical Psychology, 62*(6), 1167–1176.

Wright, D. B., Self, G., & Justice, C. (2000). Memory conformity: Exploring misinformation effects when presented by another person. *British Journal of Psychology, 91*, 189–202.

36

The Older Eyewitness

James C. Bartlett

The importance of research on the older eye-witness, along with its sparseness, has been noted for some time (Yarmey & Kent, 1980). Fortunately, the sparseness problem is being addressed. The seminal two-volume *Handbook of Eyewitness Psychology*, published in 2007, includes four chapters on older eyewitnesses (Bartlett & Memon, 2007; LaVoie, Mertz, & Richmond, 2007; Moulin, Thompson, Wright, & Conway, 2007; Mueller-Johnson & Ceci, 2007). A thorough reading of all four reveals that a significant literature had emerged by that time. Together with a more recent chapter by Wilcock (2010), and a number of reviews found in the Introduction sections of recent research reports, these papers have established a number of important and sometimes surprising findings that fall into two general areas: (1) The older eyewitness and performance in lineups and (2) the older eyewitness and verbal testimony. The two major sections of this chapter review the key findings in each of these areas, briefly summarizing what was known in 2007, examining more recent findings that appear to be of particular note, and discussing implications for both theory and practice.

THE OLDER EYEWITNESS AND THE LINEUP TASK

It was well known by 2007 that performance in the standard lineup task, which is a critical source of evidence used in courts around the world, is highly subject to error. Indeed, DNA exonerations of persons wrongly convicted of crimes, often based partly if not entirely on a "positive ID" in a lineup, had become common knowledge by that time (Scheck, Neufeld, & Dwyer, 2000, and see websites for the Innocence Project [www.innocenceproject.org] and National Registry of Exonerations [www.law.umich.edu/special/exoneration]). These exonerations date back to 1989 and numbered 325 at the end of 2012, averaging 13.5 per year. Because every erroneous conviction means that the guilty party walks free (at least temporarily), we cannot deny that false identification errors in the lineup task are both disturbingly frequent and consequential.

When we consider in addition the aging populations in many developed countries, including the US and Britain, another concern arises. Many witnesses to crime, both now and in the future, are what I will refer to as "older adults," persons aged 60 and over. Could it be that older adults are even more prone to error, and in particular to false identifications, than are younger persons?

There has long been reason to suspect that this is so. The lineup task is an example of a face recognition test, and it is well established that older persons perform less accurately than young adults in laboratory tests of face recognition. This age-related deficit often takes a particular form: While young and older adults are similar with respect to *correct* recognitions of previously viewed faces, older adults make more *false* recognitions of faces that are "new" (i.e., not previously seen in an experiment, Smith & Winograd, 1978; see Searcy, Bartlett, & Memon, 1999, for a review).

Many of the relevant studies use the standard "old/new" paradigm in which a study "list" of ten or more photographs of faces is followed by a test in which the task is to recognize old faces (copies of study-list face-photographs) and to reject new faces (photographs of faces not shown previously). However, the pattern of near age-invariance in correct recognition and an age-related increase in false recognition holds up well in more naturalistic studies modeled on the lineup task. Bartlett and Memon (2007) assembled 19 data sets comparing young and older participants in such lineup studies, separately examining performance with both target-present lineups (lineups containing a previously seen face) and target-absent lineups (containing only new faces). We examined the rate of correct identifications (i.e., "hits") with target-present lineups as well as the rate of correct rejections with target-absent lineups (the correct-rejection rate with target-absent lineups is 1 minus the false-recognition rate). The correct identification rates in target-present lineups averaged .41 and .37 for young and older adults, respectively, and this difference was shown in only 6 of 15 data sets. By contrast, the correct rejection rates with target-absent lineups averaged .53 and .31 for younger and old adults, respectively, and the difference was

shown in 16 of 17 data sets. The implications are obvious and disturbing: Older adults are prone to false alarms in the lineup task, even more than young adults.

The remainder of this section will review what we have learned and what still is not known about: (a) when in the lifespan age-related deficits in face recognition appear, (b) whether performance of older eyewitnesses can be improved through changes in testing procedures, and (c) why, in terms of theory, older as well as younger eyewitnesses are so subject to error.

Face recognition across the adult lifespan

There is no question that the young-adult/old-adult comparison used in the bulk of cognitive aging research is crude at best, and there is evidence that "old-old" adults (typically viewed as those over 70 or 75) show stronger deficits in face recognition and lineup performance than do "young-old" participants (typically viewed as those between 60 and 70 years old, see Bäckman, 1991; Memon, Gabbert, & Hope, 2004; Wright & Holiday, 2007). Accepting, however, that a simple dichotomy between young and old adults might mask important effects, a trichotomy between young-adults, young-old adults and old-old adults might be insufficient and possibly misleading as well. From both theoretical and applied perspectives, the critical issue is not whether old-old persons – defined as those exceeding an arbitrary cut-off age such as 70 or 75 – perform more poorly than younger old adults. A more important issue is when in the lifespan age-related declines begin, and whether such declines are simply linear in nature or show inflection points at which the rate of decline is substantially changed. To address this issue, we need data from large numbers of participants of many different ages, such as those collected in a web-based study reported by Germine, Duchaine, and Nakayama (2011).

Germine et al. (2011) examined face recognition ability in over 60,000 participants aged from the early teens to the late sixties. They conducted three web-based experiments, two using old/new recognition tasks, and one using the standardized Cambridge Face Recognition Test (CFMT, Duchane & Nakayama, 2006). The CFMT requires participants to study six faces and then attempt to distinguish them from foils in conditions of varying difficulty. In all three experiments, Germine et al. found an inverted-U-shaped function such that face recognition improved from early adolescence to the early-thirties and then declined in a roughly linear fashion thereafter. Across the three experiments, this inverted-U-shaped function was found to generalize from young-adult faces to children's faces, and so the surprisingly late peak in face recognition in the early thirties is not easily attributable to "own-age bias" (a phenomenon discussed subsequently). Regrettably, performance with old-adult faces was not examined, and so we do not know if a still later peak might be attained with such stimuli. Interestingly, neither name recognition nor inverted-face recognition showed a performance peak in the early thirties. Rather, name recognition and inverted-face recognition appeared to peak in the late teens, or early twenties, dropping after that. This difference between faces and other stimuli is taken up subsequently.

Web-based studies lack important controls, but broadly consistent data have been reported in a laboratory study by Hildebrandt, Wilhelm, Schmiedk, Herzmann, and Sommer (2011) using 448 adults from 18 to 82 years of age. Because their sample lacked early adolescents, Hildebrandt et al.'s data do not speak to the question of whether face memory peaks in the early thirties. However, Hildebrandt et al. did find a roughly linear decline in performance from the thirties to the eighties, though the rate of decline appeared to increase slightly after age 65. Importantly, Hildlebrandt et al. employed three different face-memory tasks along with several other cognitive tasks, and were able to show that age-related deficits in face

memory remained strong after taking general cognitive functioning into account.

Another large-scale study (Bowles et al., 2009) employed two tests of face processing and developmental prosopagnosia: The Cambridge Face Memory Test (CFMT), and the Cambridge Face Perception Test (CFPT). The two tasks differ in memory load and several other factors, but they are robustly correlated ($r = .61$ with an estimated maximum .81) and they arguably converge on the same face processing construct. Like Germine et al. (2011) and Hildebrandt et al. (2011), Bowles et al. observed approximately linear declines in CFMT and CFPT performance from the mid-thirtiess through the late eighties that did not appear attributable to general intellectual decline.

From the standpoint of research on the older eyewitness, these studies of the adult lifespan trajectory of face recognition have several limitations, including their use of laboratory paradigms that differ from the lineup task and that do not provide separate measures of false recognition and correct recognition. However, when these lifespan studies are viewed alongside the lineup experiments comparing young and older adults, they suggest there may be a gradual, roughly linear decline in lineup performance beginning as early as the mid-thirties. Such a decline is consistent with archival studies by Valentine, Pickering, and Darling (2003) and Horry, Memon, Wright, and Milne (2012), who conducted archival studies of eyewitness performance in lineups administered in Britain. A youthful witness (under 30) was one of a handful of factors linked to identification of the suspect in both field studies (though Horry et al., 2012, noted that older adults tended not to choose from lineups). This is clearly reminiscent of the findings of Germine et al. (2011) and Hildebrandt et al. (2011).

If the approximately linear decline in face recognition after the early thirties proves to generalize to the lineup task, it should be considered by expert witnesses testifying in courtrooms about the reliability of older eyewitnesses. For example, if the decline proves linear or approximately so, it would be questionable to testify that just because a witness is past a certain age, his or her lineup performance should not be believed. Rather, such testimony should be more nuanced, and to the effect that the older the eyewitness, the less their judgment in the lineup should be weighed. Another implication pertains to future applied research. If performance in tests such as the CFMT and CPFT proves to correlate with correct recognition and/or false recognition lineup performance, it will be important to examine whether such tests can be used to identify poor face-recognizers – and possibly also "super" face recognizers (see Russell, Duchaine, & Nakayami, 2009) – at all age levels. This would allow the legal community to weigh lineup evidence in accordance with the abilities of the witness, rather than just her age. Such a possible scenario is tantalizing, but making it real depends on much work to determine precisely which face recognition tests are most predictive of lineup performance. Again, given the limited data provided from individual participants in a lineup experiment, large-scale, web-based studies will doubtlessly contribute to progress in this area.

Procedures for enhancing lineup performance

Given that erroneous lineup decisions appear even more likely among older persons than among young adults, can we help the older eyewitness? Research on this question is bearing some fruit. It has been known for some time that "non-biased" lineup instructions, which clearly state that the perpetrator may or may not be present, can reduce false identifications in target-absent lineups (Malpass & Devine, 1981). However, the benefit of such instructions depends on their being remembered by the witness, and older participants are impaired in this respect (Rose, Bull, & Vrij, 2003, 2005), even when the

instructions have been elaborated to enhance their memorability (Wilcock, Bull, & Vrij, 2005). In a recent addition to this line of research, Wilcock and Bull (2010) examined whether older witnesses' performance might be improved by preceding the lineup with an extensive set of questions and statements emphasizing that the perpetrator might not be present and that lineup identifications often are wrong. This pre-lineup-questions condition reduced the older participants' false identifications with target-absent lineups, but it also appeared to reduce their correct identifications with target-present lineups. This of course is problematic from the standpoint of application.

Another condition appeared more promising: The critical lineup was preceded by a practice lineup containing famous female faces, and the participant was asked whether one was the British Queen (none were). In two experiments, this practice lineup condition reduced false identifications (from a target-absent lineup), with no such reduction in correct identifications (from a target-present lineup). Furthermore, the practice lineup condition improved memory for the unbiased instructions, and recall of these instructions was correlated with performance. There is a caveat, however: These findings were convincingly supported only with a young-adult lineup (in which both suspect and foils were young). They were at best only weakly supported with an old-adult lineup, suggesting either that: (a) face-age is a moderating variable, or (b) these findings are unreliable across different lineups. With only one young lineup and one old lineup, it is impossible to tell.

To demonstrate an effect of a pre-lineup procedure with a single lineup is not to demonstrate it will be consistently helpful with all or even most lineups. Therefore, it is essential to test the effects of any such procedures across multiple lineups with faces that vary in age, distinctiveness, familiarity, and other relevant variables. This is another area where large-scale, web-based studies may prove extremely useful.

Explanations for adult age differences in lineup performance

Finding new ways to improve performance of older eyewitnesses – as well as that of young adults and children – is likely to benefit from an improved understanding of why age-related differences occur. Three possible explanations are discussed in this section, one of which appeals to "own-age bias" in face recognition. A second hypothesis derives from a wealth of new evidence that a type of information called "holistic-configural" is more important for recognition of faces than other visual objects. A third idea springs from well-established age differences in recollection of details and contextual information about prior experiences in episodic memory tasks.

Own-age bias

According to an own-age bias account, face recognition differences related to *participant*-age are moderated by *face*-age such that: (a) people are better at recognizing faces of people the same age as them as compared with younger or older faces, and, in consequence, (b) age-related deficits in face recognition are reduced if not eliminated when the faces are older. Indeed, "own age bias" (or an "other-age effect") in face recognition has been reported in standard laboratory paradigms for over 25 years (see Bäckman, 1991; Bartlett & Leslie, 1986; Fulton & Bartlett, 1991; Mason, 1986). The literature on the topic continues to expand, moving Rhodes and Anastasi (2012) to conduct a meta-analysis aimed at assessing the strength of the effect, and how it might vary across different age groups, tasks, and measures. Their analysis indicated that, overall, the effect is reliable, though small, on both correct recognitions and false recognitions, and stronger on a discrimination measure (*d'*) derivable from correct and false recognition rates in standard laboratory tasks , but not in the lineup task. Should these effects generalize to lineup tasks, they would call for special caution in evaluating lineup identifications of

"other-age" faces (i.e., young-adult faces in the case of older eyewitnesses). However, it is not clear that they do.

Rhodes and Anastasi (2012) found a marginally reliable effect of type-of-recognition task on the magnitude of the own-age bias effect on correct recognitions, and it appeared to be due to the lineup task *not* showing this effect. The moderating effect of task was not reliable in the analysis of false recognitions, but, nonetheless, own-age bias did not reliably affect false recognitions when lineup studies were examined separately. Matthew Rhodes (personal communication, December, 2011) kindly provided the mean hit rates and false alarm rates for young and old participants and young and old faces for the seven lineup studies included in the Rhodes and Anastasi review. Across these lineup studies, the young adults' correct recognition rates averaged .50 for young faces and .55 for old faces, while the old adults' correct recognition rates averaged .32 for young faces and .35 for old faces. Own-age bias is clearly *not* shown by the young-adult data and is negligible (though in the predicted direction) in the old-adult data. The young adults' false recognition rates averaged .19 for young faces and .30 for old faces while the old adults' false recognition rates averaged .49 for young faces and .47 for old faces. These false recognition data suggest own-age bias in the young-adult group, but it is once again negligible (a .02 difference) in the older adult group.

The lineup data analyzed by Rhodes and Anastasi (2012) were taken from target-present lineups. However, a similar conclusion is reached in analyses of a smaller set of studies examining (a) correct recognitions with target-present lineups and (b) false recognitions – or correct rejections – with target-absent lineups. Bartlett and Memon (2007) were able to locate only two studies (Memon, Bartlett, Rose, & Gray, 2003; Perfect & Harris, 2003) in which young and older adults over 60 were tested with young and older faces in both target-present and target-absent lineups. The findings on correct recognitions in target-present lineups were mixed, but the studies agreed in suggesting own-age bias with target-absent lineups. However, four recent studies question this conclusion, as shown in Table 36.1. Looking first at the data from target-present lineups, one of the four studies showed own-age bias with young adults while three of four showed own-age bias with old adults. This result might be viewed as promising, with the caveat that when own-age bias is shown in only one of two age groups, face-age may be confounded with other variables (e.g., distinctiveness). Turning to the data from target-absent lineups, only two of four studies showed the effect with young adults, and only one of four showed the effect with old adults. This is not promising at all.

It is instructive to examine Table 36.1 again, this time with a focus on the age-related deficit in lineup performance in each of the various conditions (compare data rows 1 and 4, 2 and 5, 7 and 10, and 8 and 11).

All 16 comparisons suggest an age-related deficit, and the average size of this deficit across the four studies is .16 and .22 for young and old faces in target-present lineups, and .26 and .19 with young and old faces in target-absent lineups. With due consideration for the fact that individual studies with limited samples can fail to support effects that are real, these data carry a clear implication: Own-age bias does not always occur in lineup tasks, or, if it does, it is smaller and/or less reliable than is the main effect of age. The main effect of age cannot easily be attributed to own-age bias.

It also is instructive to view the four studies in Table 36.1 in the context of the larger corpus of data on age-differences in lineup performance now available to us. Figure 36.1 shows scatter plots for performance by young and older participants in target-present lineups (top) and target-absent lineups (bottom) for the data sets reported in Bartlett and Memon (2007, Table 13.1 and

Table 36.1 Hit rates in target-present lineups and correct-rejection rates in target-absent lineups by young and old participants with young and old lineups in four studies

Study	Havard & Memon (2009)	Wilcock et al. (2007)	Rose et al. (2005)	Wilcock et al. (2005)	Mean
n per cell	22	24	24	24	
Target-present hit rates: Young participants					
Young Faces	0.55	0.48	0.54	0.54	0.53
Old Faces	0.44	0.65	0.67	0.75	0.63
Difference	0.11	−0.17	−0.13	−0.21	−0.10
Target-present hit rates: Old participants					
Young Faces	0.23	0.35	0.50	0.38	0.37
Old Faces	0.24	0.56	0.29	0.54	0.41
Difference	−0.01	−0.21	0.21	−0.16	−0.04
Target-absent correct rejection rates: Young participants					
Young Faces	0.78	0.83	0.58	0.54	0.68
Old Faces	0.36	0.46	0.75	0.67	0.56
Difference	0.42	0.37	−0.17	-0.13	0.12
Target-absent correct rejection rates: Old participants					
Young Faces	0.48	0.34	0.37	0.50	0.42
Old Faces	0.22	0.29	0.54	0.42	0.37
Difference	0.26	0.05	-0.17	0.08	0.05

Figure 13.1) and for the four newer studies just reviewed. Also included are the results from each of three conditions of a recent study using young lineups only by Wilcock and Bull (2010, Experiment 1, described previously in this chapter). Again, correct-rejection rates are reported for target-absent lineups so that higher scores always reflect better performance. Points falling below the diagonals reflect age-related deficits (or trends in that direction), and it is clear that such deficits have been suggested in the majority (19 out of 26) of the target-present

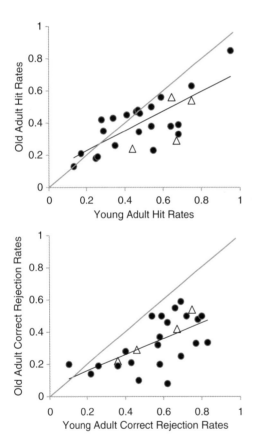

data sets and nearly all (26 out of 27) of the target-absent data sets. The data also suggest that age differences tend to be larger in conditions in which the young participants do better, as previously noted by Bartlett and Memon (2007). For present purposes, the main point concerns the four triangles shown in each plot. These reflect performance with old-face lineups in the four studies in Table 36.1. The regression lines were fitted to the circles only, but note that the triangles never fall much above those lines, and sometimes fall below them. This implies age-related deficits in lineup performance are not consistently lessened with old faces, contrary to a general own-age bias effect.

The preceding observations are not meant to deny own-age bias in old/new recognition – which was confirmed by Rhodes and Anastasi (2012) – nor to deny it in the lineup task under some conditions. Both Memon et al. (2003) and Perfect and Harris (2003) reported own-age bias with target-absent lineups using a one-week retention interval between the original event and the subsequent lineup task. A one-week interval is longer than that used in most lineup studies, though of course retention intervals of one week or more occur in real life. Own-age bias may depend on a delay between encoding and test, and/or on interference produced by viewing many faces between encoding and test (note that many different faces are seen during a week).[1]

Future research on own-age bias should consider that other face attributes besides face-age can affect recognition performance, and that some of these attributes (e.g., familiarity, typicality) might be confounded with face-age among young and/or old participants. For example, in Bartlett and Fulton (1991), younger adults but not older adults rated younger faces (of strangers) as more familiar than older faces, whereas older adults but not younger adults showed a correlation between rated familiarity of faces and recognition judgments (both correct and false) in an old/new recognition test. The familiarity/recognition correlation among

Figure 36.1 Scatter Plots showing the relationship between young adult performance and old adult performance for hit rates in target-present lineups (upper plot) and correct-rejection rates with target-absent lineups (lower plot) across 22 data sets. Triangles represent performance with older adult lineups in the four studies listed in Table 36.1.

older persons is considered below. The point for now is that one must consider effects of face-age along with those of other mnemonically relevant attributes that can be confounded with it. Given the limitations of the lineup paradigm, particularly with regard to the small number of faces used in any lineup study, it is likely that web-based approaches will be needed to adequately examine the effect of various facial attributes on lineup performance.

Future research should also consider that own-age bias can "explain" age differences in face recognition in only a very limited sense, as own-age bias is itself a phenomenon that needs to be explained. In their review of the literature, Rhodes and Anastasi (2012) considered the dominant accounts of own-age bias, favoring the view that one's greater recent experience with own-age faces allows for more distinctive encoding. However, they concluded that a complete account must recognize that social-cognitive factors – such as an initial categorization of a face as an "other group" member – can produce a deficit in distinctive encoding (Sporer, 2001), possibly due to reduced looking time (He, Ebner, & Johnson, 2011). Note that both of these accounts might be applied to the *general* deficit in lineup performance shown by older adults, *apart* from own-age bias. For example, some older persons with limited social worlds may be out of practice at learning new faces, and may regard most new faces, regardless of age, as "other group" members. Both factors could contribute to non-distinctive encoding and poor recognition, even for same-age faces.

A holistic-processing deficit hypothesis

As noted earlier, Germine et al. (2011) found that recognition performance peaks at a later point in life with upright faces than with inverted faces or proper names. This finding is aligned with evidence for "special" aspects of upright-face processing not found with names or even inverted faces. It is known that our ability to recognize upright faces is based

partly on "holistic" or "holistic-configural" information, rather than entirely on piecemeal feature- or part-based information used with many other objects including inverted faces (see Tanaka & Gordon, 2011; McKone & Robbins, 2011, for reviews). People differ with respect to holistic face processing and those who use it more show higher face recognition performance (Richler, Cheung, & Gauthier, 2011; Wang, Li, Fang, & Tian, 2012). Such data raise the question of whether age-related declines (after the early thirties) in face recognition are due to deficits in holistic processing unique to upright faces.

This is an intriguing hypothesis, but several findings suggest that it is wrong. First, in the Germine et al. (2011) study, the decline in face recognition performance after the early thirties appeared similar in magnitude and linearity to that with inverted faces and names. Second, several studies have found that while performance is worse with inverted faces as compared to upright faces, the size of the facial inversion effect – which is often taken as a measure of face-specific holistic processing – holds up well in old age (Germine et al., 2011; Bowles et al., 2009; Perfect & Moon, 2005; Chaby, Narme, & George, 2011).[2]

A third relevant finding was provided by Edmonds, Glisky, Bartlett, and Rapcsak (2011). They used a variant of the old/new paradigm in which the recognition test includes not only study-list faces and entirely new faces, but two additional types of difficult lures: (a) familiarized lures, which were not presented in the study list but had been seen by participants and rated for personality traits prior to the study list, and (b) conjunction lures, each of which combined the inner portion of one study list face and the outer portion of another, as shown in Figure 36.2. The young and old participants did not differ in correct recognitions ($Ms = .69$ and $.71$, respectively), though the older participants made slightly more false recognitions of entirely new faces ($Ms = .09$ and $.15$, respectively), as in many prior studies.[3]

Of greater importance, young and old participants differed strongly in false recognitions

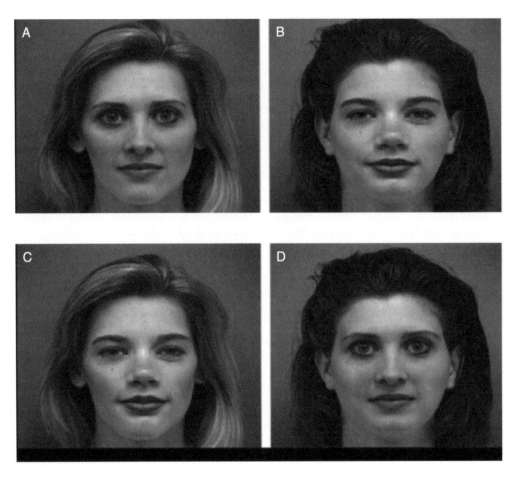

Figure 36.2   Two original faces (A and B) and two conjunctions made from them (C and D), used by Edmonds et al. (2011).

with familiarized lures (Ms = .38 and .71, respectively), but not with conjunction lures (Ms = .41 and .45, respectively). In light of prior evidence that holistic processing supports discrimination between study-list faces and conjunction lures (old/conjunction discrimination is markedly impaired by inversion, see McKone & Peh, 2006; Bartlett, Shastri, Abdi, & Neville-Smith, 2009), the lack of age differences in both correct recognitions and in conjunction false alarms rules against holistic processing as a locus of age-related deficits. At the same time, the large age-related increase in false recognition of familiarized lures converges with a wealth of evidence from the cognitive aging literature that older persons have difficulty with the

controlled retrieval of "source" information that can specify the context in which stimuli were encoded. Thus, young and old adults appear not to differ in upright-face-specific, holistic, processing that is important for face recognition. Rather, they appear to suffer in more domain-general memory processes such as retrieval of context.

A recollection deficit and familiarity-based responding

It may seem surprising that old and young adults in the Edmonds et al. (2011) study did not differ in either correct recognitions of old faces or in false recognitions of conjunction faces, suggesting age-invariance in old/conjunction discrimination. This result is not a one-time fluke (see Searcy et al., 1999), and yet it contradicts the well-replicated finding of pronounced age differences in old/conjunction discrimination (often called "associative recognition") with words and other stimuli (Naveh-Benjamin, 2000). A resolution is suggested by evidence that while old/conjunction discrimination often depends on conscious recollection of contextual or "source" information, with holistically processed or "unitized" stimuli, old/conjunction discrimination can be based on familiarity. Familiarity is a graded, strength-like process that – unlike recollection – is well maintained in old age (Jacoby & Rhodes, 2006; Yonelinas, 2002; Yonelinas, Kroll, Dobbins, & Soltani, 1999). Viewed in this light, the Edmonds et al. (2011) findings converge with other evidence that age-related increases in false facial recognition are due to: (a) older persons' deficits in conscious recollection, and (b) their resultant tendency to base recognition judgments on general familiarity (or "gist," a related concept, see Brainerd & Reyna, 2005).

For example, Bartlett and Fulton (1991) showed that, in standard laboratory tasks, rated familiarity of faces affects the overall tendency for older participants to judge these faces as previously studied or "old," whether or not they had been previously studied (i.e., among older participants, rated face-familiarity was positively correlated with both correct recognitions of study-list faces and false recognitions of lure faces). This biasing effect of face-familiarity was not found among young adult participants, suggesting that older persons rely more on general, context-free familiarity, and less on detailed, context-specific information, in recognizing faces as compared with young adults (see Bartlett, 1993, and Reyna & Brainerd, 2005, for reviews).

However, as was the case with the own-age bias and holistic face processing hypotheses, we know very little about whether impaired recollection – and an increased reliance on familiarity – is the cause of age differences in the lineup task. Three relevant studies have used variants of the lineup task designed to examine "unconscious transference." Unconscious transference is the false identification of a lineup foil who was not the perpetrator in a previously viewed event, but who was previously seen in another context (Memon, Hope, Bartlett, & Bull, 2002; Perfect & Harris, 2003; Goodsell, Neuschatz, & Gronlund, 2009). In each of these three studies, the lineup contained a "critical foil" who had been previously presented in a set of mugshots. In the Memon et al. (2002) study, the older participants were more likely to falsely identify one of the mugshot faces, and were also more likely to identify foils in the target-absent lineup that followed. Further, participants who identified a mugshot face were more likely to identify the critical foil (even when it was not the face they picked in the mugshot test). Finally, the age difference in lineup performance disappeared when the age difference in mugshot identification was statistically removed. This pattern suggested that: (a) a familiarity strategy is likely to lead to a false identification in a mugshot set as well as in a lineup, and (b) a greater proportion of older participants used this familiarity strategy.

Perfect and Harris (2003) obtained clear evidence for an age-related increase in false mugshot selections and unconscious-transference errors in the subsequent lineup. However, the age-related increase in unconscious transference was found only with young adult faces, and was restricted to cases in which the critical foil had been previously selected in the mugshot task. Thus, the age-related increase in unconscious transference may have been the result of identity confusions in the mugshot task, as opposed to a familiarity strategy in the lineup task.

The Goodsell et al. (2009) study differed from the other two in finding no age differences in either false identifications in the mugshot task or unconscious transference. Null effects in experiments with limited power are always difficult to interpret. It is noteworthy, however, that a very large number of mugshots that were shown (50, as compared with 12 in Memon et al., 2002, and 8 or 16 in Perfect & Harris, 2003), and there was a high rate of mugshot choosing overall (about 74 percent of the participants wrongly identified a mugshot face). With such a large mugshot set, a critical foil in the subsequent lineup may have appeared no more familiar than any other foil, especially since the mugshots and lineup foils were selected to resemble the original perpetrator, and doubtlessly resembled each other. In such a case, a familiarity strategy would not lead to an increase unconscious transference errors. Indeed, several findings suggested that the unconscious transference errors in this experiment were due to identity confusions during the mugshot task and a "commitment" strategy of sticking with one's prior judgment. A familiarity strategy may not have been involved.

The mugshot paradigm has been useful in demonstrating that, regardless of the age of the witness, preceding a lineup with a mugshot book is a dangerous practice (see discussions in Memon et al., 2002; Goodsell et al., 2009; Gronlund & Carlson, Chapter 33, this volume). However, due to complexities such as identity confusions and commitment strategies, this paradigm is probably not ideal for testing a recollection-deficit view of age-related differences in lineup performance. One alternative is a correlational approach using tasks that assess recollection ability and use of familiarity strategy. Memon et al. (2003) took this approach, finding that a measure of context recollection with facial stimuli was reliably correlated with lineup performance in both young and old adults. Unfortunately, this approach has not been taken further since.

THE OLDER EYEWITNESS AND VERBAL TESTIMONY ABOUT CRIMES

We previously argued that age-related deficits in face recognition likely involve general processes of memory as opposed to face-specific mechanisms. There currently are a number of theoretical notions that attempt to characterize these domain-general processes

involved in age-related deficits, but all must address the undisputed fact that conscious recollection of detailed information about a prior event is often impaired in old age (Luo & Craik, 2008). And it is not just that older persons show lower levels of correct recollection – they also are more subject to false recollection and so-called "illusions of memory" whereby they recollect things in an altered form, or even recollect things that did not occur at all (Roediger & McDaniel, 2007). This raises a second concern with the older eyewitness, one in addition to their well-documented tendency for false recognition of faces discussed in the first section: When police interview eyewitnesses to crime, what they want is detailed and accurate recollection of information about the crime event. If older persons are impaired in such recollection – both because they recall fewer correct details and recall more erroneous details – this should impair their usefulness as eyewitnesses.

Fortunately, things are not as bad as they might appear at first, because recollection depends on a host of factors, including person characteristics such as verbal intelligence and real-world knowledge that hold up well in old age (Park, Lautenschlager, Hedden, Davidson, Smith, & Smith (2002). Indeed, Bartlett and Memon (2007) reviewed several eyewitness studies in which verbal recall by older persons was equally good if not better than verbal recall by younger adults (e.g., Mello & Fisher, 1996). They concluded that such cases are those in which the older persons were more highly educated, relative to their cohort, than were the young adults, and/or the older persons were higher in intelligence and verbal ability. While such studies might be criticized as having confounded age with intellectual function, they nonetheless make an important point: The verbal recall of an older eyewitness who is well educated and intelligent may be as good as or better than that of a much younger witness who is lower on such variables.

Progress in the last several years has been made along two fronts: First, we know more than before about the effectiveness of several interviewing techniques deriving from the Cognitive Interview, a technique for enhancing eyewitnesses' reports (Fisher & Geiselman, 1992). Second, we now have an improved theoretical understanding of why older adults often show increases in false recollection, as well as decreases in correct recollection. We treat these two topics in turn, and then examine some new lines of research and theory that offer promise for understanding and ameliorating age differences in eyewitness testimony.

The cognitive interview and the older eyewitness

The original Cognitive Interview (CI) instructs the interviewee to: (1) mentally reinstate the physical and personal context surrounding a previously experienced event, (2) report everything possible about that event, including incomplete fragments of questionable relevance, (3) recall the event from a variety of perspectives, and (4) recall the event not only from the start to the end, but in other temporal orders as well. Among the several variants of the original CI (see Holliday et al., 2011; Memon, Meissner, & Fraser, 2010, for reviews) is the "Enhanced Cognitive Interview" (ECI), which has additional elements designed to ensure good rapport and communication between the interviewer and the interviewee, and to allow the interviewee to better control the flow of the conversation through the use of open-ended questions and the avoidance of interruptions. A second variant is the "Modified Cognitive Interview" (MCI), which shortens and simplifies the procedure through removing the varied-perspectives instruction and sometimes the different-temporal instruction as well. In fact, several different versions of the MCI exist. The MCIs are growing in popularity due to their efficiency and ease of use, particularly with children. In much of the research on the MCI and its variants, especially in more recent years, the control condition is a Structured Interview (SI), in which the participant is first asked to recall the event in his/her own words, is subsequently asked if he/she can recall anything more, and finally is asked a set of open-ended and closed questions about details she/he had reported in the free recall phase.

An impressive corpus of evidence supports the effectiveness of CI techniques as means of interviewing young adult eyewitnesses to crimes. A recent meta-analysis by Memon et al. (2010) updated a prior effort published some 13 years ago (Köhnken, Milne, Memon, & Bull, 1999), and reported that CI techniques produce large and significant increases in recall of correct details ($d = 1.21$) along with only a very slight increase in recall errors ($d = 0.29$) among young-adult participants in over 40 experiments. This of course is encouraging, and the analyses conducted by Memon et al. (2010) suggest that the effect with older adults may be even greater ($ds = 1.99$ and 1.17 for correct details and errors, respectively). Unfortunately, Memon et al. could locate only five studies using the CI or one of its variants with older adults, and could use only four of these in their meta-analysis. Furthermore, one of these four studies failed to find a positive effect of the CI (McMahon, 2000), possibly due to a very small n. This left only three studies showing positive effects (Dornburg & McDaniel, 2006; Mello & Fisher, 1996; Wright & Holliday, 2007).

More recently, Holliday et al. (2011) compared a MCI and the SI with young and old adults in a "misinformation paradigm" initiated by Loftus and Palmer (1974) and discussed further in the next section. Young and older participants viewed a film of a purse theft, followed the next day by a post-event narrative that included six misleading details about the video and later received either a MCI or SI about the original event. Both the MCI and SI included a free recall phase followed by a question phase in which participants were asked for more details about things mentioned in free recall. A final recognition test contained six details from the film and six "misled" items (false details contained in the post-event narrative).

The results were intriguing but complex: One finding concerned "completeness" of detail recall (the number of details recalled by each participant divided by the number of different details recalled across all participants). Completeness scores were higher with the MCI than with the SI in the young-adult group (*M*s = .21 and .14, respectively), but not in the old-adult group (*M*s = .16 and .15, respectively). Similarly, the total number of correct details recalled across the two phases of the interviews (free recall and follow-up questions) was higher with the MCI than with the SI, but this effect was larger among the younger participants.

Data pertaining to the misinformation effect showed a different pattern. Young adults showed no such effect as, puzzlingly, their accuracy did not differ between misled and control items regardless of condition. However, the older adults showed a misinformation effect in the SI condition, but not in the MCI condition. Hence, the MCI increased correct recall primarily among the young, but it reduced misinformation effects among the old.

What can be concluded about the effectiveness of the CI and its variants with the older eyewitness? The weight of the evidence suggests that they improve aspects of performance, but it is not yet clear exactly how or why, particularly in the misinformation paradigm. Thinking positively, we still have only a handful of studies of the technique with older adults, and its effects on various measures appear to be either positive or simply not there. There are no established cases of negative effects. Thus, the technique holds promise with the older eyewitness, perhaps especially with respect to false recall and recognition.

Age-related increases in false recollection

In the early 2000s, the evidence was mixed on the question of whether the older eyewitness

is more subject to false recollection in forensically relevant verbal memory tasks (see Bartlett & Memon, 2007; Mueller-Johnson & Ceci, 2007). Then and now, the most popular paradigm for examining this question is the Loftus and Palmer (1974) "misinformation paradigm" in which a depiction of a crime or accident is followed by verbal information (often a narrative or a set of questions) that includes erroneous as well as accurate information about the previous event. Participants often incorporate some of the misinformation into their subsequent recollections of the event in verbal recall and recognition tests (more so than in control conditions, where no misinformation is given). When considering whether there are age differences in this misinformation effect, Roediger and Geraci (2007) pointed out that three outcomes are possible – a reduced misinformation effect among older participants, an increased misinformation effect among older participants, and no age differences in the misinformation effect. And they further observed that each of these three outcomes had been observed in at least one study.

To clarify the picture, Roediger and Geraci (2007) performed two experiments, one focused on the testing procedures and a second focused on characteristics of the older participants. In their first experiment, a slide show of an event was followed by post-event narratives in which several items of misinformation were embedded either one or three times. The final recognition test was of two different types. One type was a yes/no test in which participants simply judged statements as true or false of the original event, and, in this condition, the older adults showed a stronger misinformation effect than did the young adults. However, the other was a source-monitoring test in which participants judged each item in the test as presented in the event, presented in the post-event narratives, both, or neither. In this latter condition no age difference in the misinformation effect was found. The pattern demonstrates that while older persons can be more prone to false memories, a task that calls attention to the source of such memories may reduce their false remembering to the same level as shown by young adults. However, such tasks might not work for all older persons, as suggested by a second experiment.

In their second experiment, Roediger and Geraci (2007) partitioned their older adults into two groups, based on their performance on a battery of tests that tap frontal lobe function assembled by Glisky, Polster, and Routhieaux (1995). While there were several interesting results, a key finding was that the "low-frontal" elderly appeared more subject to the misinformation effect not only in the yes/no test, but in the source-memory test as well. In fact, the age-related deficit was clearer in the source-memory test. The implication here is that good testing procedures – those that encourage participants to "consider the source" – can take us only so far in reducing false remembering in older adults. Older persons with low frontal function may prove highly subject to false remembering, even with better tests.

One possible view of the Roediger and Geraci (2007) findings is that age-related increases in false remembering – and perhaps in accurate remembering as well – are mediated by deficits in frontal-lobe processing. That is, these age-related deficits might pertain only to a subset of older persons who have frontal lobe dysfunction. This "frontal hypothesis" will be discussed in light of new research on the cognitive neuroscience of memory at the end of this chapter. However, it should be noted here that caution is required in drawing this conclusion, as Roediger and Geraci did not examine differences between high-frontal persons and low-frontal persons within the young adult group. This comparison has been made in another experiment by Chan and McDermott (2007), using a task that assessed false recall of pragmatic inferences of previously studied sentences. They compared subsets of both young and old participants who scored high versus low on the Glisky et al. (1995) frontal-lobe battery. The clearcut result was that both age and frontal-lobe function were

correlated with correct recall (positively) as well as false recall (negatively), and these correlations were independent of each other. These data are empirically consistent with the Roediger and Geraci findings, but they tend to weigh against a simple form of the frontal hypothesis. Rather, they suggest that age and frontal function make separable contributions to correct memory as well as false memory.

While it clearly is important to examine the conditions that determine whether the older eyewitness is more highly subject to false memory errors, equally important are the factors that determine the confidence of older as well as younger persons when they make such errors. Rather low correlations between accuracy and confidence in eyewitness memory have been noted for some time. However, a related but somewhat different observation has been published only recently: In some conditions, older persons make a higher proportion of highly confident false memory errors than do young adults. Moreover, this effect can occur even when experiments are designed such that overall performance levels – apart from confidence – do not differ for young and old adults.

To my knowledge, the first report of this effect was made by Dodson and Kreuger (2006) who used a standard misinformation paradigm in which both young-adult and old participants viewed a video depicting a crime followed by a set of yes/no questions, some of which contained misleading information. The design included a group of young-adult participants who experienced a two-day delay between the questions and the final test (which was similar to the source memory test of Roediger & Geraci, 2007). As intended, recall performance in this young-adult/delay group was similar to that in the older group. However, while young adults made more low-confidence errors than high-confidence errors, older adults made more high-confidence errors than low-confidence errors. Subsequent studies by Dodson, Bawa, and Slotnick (2007) and Dodson, Bawa, and Krueger (2007) replicated and extended these findings using converging measures involving calibration and signal detection analyses. Along these same lines, Aizpurua, Garcia-Bajos, and Migueles (2009) compared young and older adults' recognition of actions, people, and visual details seen in a video of a robbery. They found that older participants made about twice as many false "remember" judgments (which are generally high in confidence) to foil actions and people, as compared with young adults.

Explanations for adult age differences in verbal testimony

This final section could be either quite long, covering the several long-standing hypotheses for why recollection is decreased in older persons, or it could be quite short, dealing only with the newest theoretical developments that appear of greatest relevance to the next round of research. A long final section would be redundant with many recent, excellent reviews (e.g., Luo & Craik, 2008; Park & Rueter-Lorenz, 2009), and, moreover, is precluded by page limitations. So I will take the latter course.

The misrecollection hypothesis

In considering their finding that older adults can be surprisingly confident about their false memories, Dodson and Krueger (2006) proposed a "misrecollection hypothesis," which holds that age-related deficits in detailed recollection are not simply the result of *reduced memory* in old age. Rather, older persons suffer deficits in associating or "binding" together the elements of events, and therefore are susceptible to miscombining these elements at the time of retrieval. The basic ideas of miscombination errors and age-related deficits in binding processes were proposed some time ago (Henkel, Johnson, & De Leonardis, 1998; Naveh-Benjamin, 2000; Kroll, Knight, Metcalfe, Wolf, & Tulving, 1998). However, the issue of confidence with respect to these errors has not been given detailed consideration in the cognitive

aging or eyewitness testimony literatures. This issue deserves more attention because the misrecollection theory is interesting and might, if successful, suggest new methods for interviewing the older eyewitness. And regardless of whether the theory survives, the phenomenon it addresses – highly confident misrecollections in old age – is critical to study due to its obvious and alarming implications for interviewing the older eyewitness. For example, if experimental evidence continues to suggest that older adults are more prone to highly confident false recollections, research should examine whether subjective assessments other than confidence might be more diagnostic of accuracy (see Marchie, Brainerd, & Reyna, 2010).

Reduced specificity at retrieval

Another alternative to the *reduced memory* hypothesis is that retrieval by older individuals is impaired in proportion to the *specificity* of the information that is needed in the task. This basic idea is aligned with fuzzy trace theory (Brainerd & Reyna, 2005), which proposes larger age differences in memory for "verbatim" information than in memory for "gist." However, Luo and Craik (2009) have proposed that specificity of memory exists on a continuum from generic, context-free knowledge and the phenomenology of "knowing" to context-specific, detailed information and the phenomenology of "remembering." They performed three experiments and found an increase in age-related deficits when more specific information was required in a source memory task. They also found that when young adults' attention was divided at test, they showed reduced specificity of recollection like that found in old adults. That conditions prevailing at the time of a test can affect the specificity of a person's recall is forensically relevant, as such conditions can be controlled (to an extent) by interviewers of witnesses. Of course, we need to know about conditions that *improve* specificity among older adults, as opposed to those that *reduce* specificity among young adults (as in the Luo & Craik,

2009, experiment). Hopefully, such manipulations are possible to devise.

Stereotype threat and the older eyewitness

It is well known in western cultures that we have unflattering stereotypes concerning older persons (e.g., they are viewed as slow and forgetful). A new line of research indicates that older persons themselves are susceptible to effects of these stereotypes, performing more poorly on a variety of tasks, including memory tasks, if such stereotypes are primed or activated in their minds (Chasteen, Bhattacharyya, Horhota, Tam, & Hasher, 2005; Hess, Auman, Colcombe, & Rahhal, 2003; and see Meisner, 2011, for a meta-analysis and review). These findings are relevant to the older eyewitness, as it is reasonable to suspect that ageist stereotypes can be aroused in the course of eyewitness interviews and lineup administration. In fact, there are concerns that some versions of the Cognitive Interview might unintentionally activate stereotype threat through the interviewer speaking to the older witness in an especially slow and careful way, although this has not been empirically confirmed (Memon et al., 2010). Of particular relevance for eyewitness research is a recent study by Thomas and Dubois (2011), who induced stereotype threat after the study list but prior to the test in the well-known DRM paradigm – a paradigm known to produce large numbers of false recognition judgments. The results indicated that ageist stereotype threat – induced by a passage concerning older persons' poor memory and a description of the test as a memory test – increased false recognition errors by the older adults. This effect was not found among young adults. Moreover, stereotype activation in the older adults not only increased their false recognition errors, it also increased their confidence in these errors, a finding reminiscent of the Dodson and Krueger (2007) study described above. One explanation is that activation of ageist stereotypes worked to reduce the attentional resources available to support controlled recollection of information

needed to avoid false recognition errors. This interpretation requires more testing, but the basic finding has applied importance apart from this particular hypothesis. If stereotype threat at the time of retrieval is shown to consistently increase false memory – and to increase confidence at the same time – this will be important for interviewers and lineup administrators to know.

Cognitive neuroscience theories

Research using neuroimaging techniques is enriching our understanding of neural factors underlying age differences in memory and cognition, significantly expanding on the "frontal hypothesis" of age-related memory deficits considered previously in this chapter. Park and Reuter-Lorenz (2009) have recently proposed a "scaffolding theory of aging and cognition" (STAC). STAC takes as its starting point the discovery that, while older persons suffer in frontal-lobe-mediated memory tasks, they often show increased frontal-lobe activation during performance of these tasks (see also Davis, Dennis, Daselaar, Fleck, & Cabeza, 2007). According to STAC, increased frontal activation among older adults reflects the development of new neural circuits that work to maximize performance in the face of various forms of neural deficit such as (a) reduced volume of brain structures involved in memory and cognition such as the hippocampus and the lateral prefrontal cortex, and (b) thinning of the cortical mantle and loss of white-matter integrity in frontal as well as occipital brain areas. According to STAC, the age-related deterioration in occipital brain regions is in line with older evidence that age-related declines in visual function are linked to those in cognitive tasks known to be frontally mediated (Baltes & Lindenberger, 1997). Specifically, perceptual deficits in occipital brain regions may trigger compensatory "scaffolding" in frontal brain regions that help to maximize performance, though often not to the extent that young-adult levels of performance are achieved. Indeed, recent neuroimaging studies are supporting age-related neural "dedifferentiation" in certain brain regions such as those specialized for face processing (Goh, Suzuki, & Park, 2010). Neural deterioration in these regions might require the recruitment of more domain-general, frontal regions for perceptual processing, depleting the attentional resources available for higher-level, controlled, processes such as recollection of context or source.

A particularly exciting line of research is using PET imaging to measure a well-known marker of Alzheimer disease (AD) – beta-amyloid protein deposition – in healthy younger and older adults. One recent project (Rodrigue et al. (2012) sampled 137 adults aged from 30 to 89, all carefully screened for dementia and other factors linked to cognitive impairments. They found a strikingly linear increase with age in amyloid deposition in several brain regions, except for a minority of the older participants with substantially greater amyloid than a linear function would predict. Further, among these older, high-amyloid participants, there were reliable correlations between the overall amount of amyloid deposition and behavioral performance in tests of working memory, processing speed, and reasoning. There was no reliable correlation with episodic memory, though, as the authors point out, this may have been due to the tasks that were used (memory for lists of words).

Can we look forward to a day when the older eyewitness can be examined for healthy brain function and neural integrity in order to assess how reliable she or he might be? Perhaps, but according to STAC, it will be important to examine not only various measures of neural health and deterioration, but also neural and/or behavioral signs of compensatory scaffolding. By this theory, it is those older persons with neural impairments as well as poor compensatory scaffolding whose verbal testimony and lineup performance are most prone to error.

Considering the state of research on the older eyewitness in 2007, in 2013 we have good news and better news. The good news is that we have learned a few things that might improve testimony – or the proper use of testimony – by the older eyewitness,

at least to a degree. These include the use of practice target-absent lineups along with unbiased lineup instructions, the avoidance of language or behavior that might evoke ageist "stereotype threat," and our recognition of the significant probability that highly confident recollections by older eyewitnesses may be in error. There is also cause for encouraging the use of cognitive interview techniques with older eyewitnesses as well as young adults. This is all well and fine, but the really good news is that the research emerging in recent years provides a much improved foundation for new investigations that promise more substantial improvements in our treatment of the older eyewitness. We now have tests of face recognition ability with excellent psychometric properties, setting the stage for work that will validate these tests – and modifications of them – with respect to lineup performance. We also have a rapidly improving understanding of the cognitive, affective, and social processes underlying age-related changes in perception and memory, and of individual differences in these changes. This has opened the door for a new generation of research on how to improve the performance of older eyewitnesses through procedural changes and cognitive training. In addition, we have a rapidly evolving and expanding set of neuroimaging tools that will help us understand how memory failures can emerge, and can help us identify older eyewitnesses whose neurocognitive function is likely to compromise their competence as witnesses. Finally, advances in web-based technology and service will enable the completion of large-scale research projects that are essential to establishing the generality and robustness of our findings across people, stimuli, and situational contexts. It is enough to make this (somewhat) older eyewitness wish he were young again.

NOTES

1 Additionally, Perfect and Harris used a variant of the lineup task that challenges the participant to avoid "unconscious transference," that is, false

recognition of a lineup foil that the witness saw previously (e.g., in a mugshot book) but not at the crime. Such tasks might require recollection of context and this may be subject to own-age bias. In line with this view, a recent ERP study (Wiese, Schweinberger, & Hansen, 2008) found a reduced parietal old/new effect for older faces compared with younger faces in young adult participants. The parietal old/new effect has been linked to recollection in prior ERP studies.

2   Germine et al. (2011) reported that the inversion effect actually increased with age. The other cited studies did not find an increase, but nonetheless confirmed that the effect is *not* reduced.

3   This difference was smaller than usual, but nonetheless reliable (p < .05) by a one-tailed test.

REFERENCES

Aizpurua, A., Garcia-Bajos, E., & Migueles, M. (2009). False memories for a robbery in young and older adults. *Applied Cognitive Psychology, 23*, 174–187.

Bäckman, L. (1991). Recognition memory across the adult lifespan: The role of prior knowledge. *Memory & Cognition, 19*, 63–71.

Bales, P. B., & Lindenberger, U. (1997). Emergence of a powerful connection between sensory and cognitive functions across the adult lifespan: A new window to the study of cognitive aging? *Psychology and Aging, 12*(1), 12–21.

Bartlett, J. C. (1993). Limits on losses in face recognition. In J. Cerella, J. Rybash, W. Hoyer, and M. L. Commons (Eds.), *Adult information processing: Limits on loss.* New York: Academic Press.

Bartlett, J. C., & Fulton, A. (1991). Familiarity and recognition of faces: The factor of age. *Memory & Cognition, 19*, 229–238.

Bartlett, J. C., & Leslie, J. E. (1986). Aging and memory for faces versus pictures of faces. *Memory & Cognition, 14*, 371–381.

Bartlett, J. C., & Memon, A. (2007). Eyewitness memory in young and older eyewitnesses. In R. C. L. Lindsay, D. F. Ross, J. D. Read, and M. P. Toglia (Eds.), *The handbook of eyewitness psychology, Volume II: Memory for people.* Mahwah, NJ: Erlbaum.

Bartlett, J. C., Shastri, K. K., Abdi, H., & Neville-Smith, M. (2009). Component structure of individual differences in true and false recognition of faces. *Journal of Experimental Psychology: Learning, Memory and Cognition, 35*(5), 1207–1230.

Bowles, D. C., McKone, E., Dawel, A., Duchaine, B., Palermo, R., Schmalzl, L., Revolta, D., Wilson, C. E., & Yovel, G. (2009). Diagnosing prosopagnosia: Effects of ageing, sex, and participant-stimulus ethnic match on the Cambridge Face Memory Test and Cambridge Face Perception Test. *Cognitive Neuropsychology, 26*, 423–455.

Brainerd, C. J., & Reyna, V. (2005). *The science of false memory.* London: Oxford.

Chaby, L., Narme, P., & George, N. (2011). Older adults' configural processing of faces: Role of second-order information. *Psychology and Aging, 26*, 71–79.

Chan, J. C., & McDermott, K. B. (2007). The effects of frontal lobe functioning and age on veridical and false recall. *Psychonomic Bulletin and Review, 13*(5), 770–775.

Chasteen, A. L., Horhota, M., Tam, R., & Hasher, L. (2005). How feelings of stereotype threat influence older adults' memory performance. *Experimental Aging Research, 31*, 235–260.

Davis, S. W., Dennis, N. A., Daselaar, S. M., Fleck, M. S., & Cabeza, R. (2008). Cerebral *Cortex, 18*, 1201–1209.

Dodson, C. S., Bawa, S., & Krueger, L. E. (2007). Aging, metamemory and high-confidence errors: A misrecollection account. *Psychology and Aging, 22*, 122–133.

Dodson, C. S., Bawa, S., & Slotnick, S. D. (2007). Aging, source memory and misrecollections. *Journal of Experimental Psychology: Learning, Memory and Cognition, 33*, 169–181.

Dodson, C. S., & Krueger, L. E. (2006). I misremember it well: Why older adults are unreliable eyewitnesses. *Psychonomic Bulletin and Review, 13*(5), 770–775.

Dornberg, C. C., & McDaniel, M. A. (2006). The cognitive interview enhances long-term free recall in older adults. *Psychology and Aging, 21*(1), 196–200.

Duchane, B., & Nakayama, K. (2006). The Cambridge Face Memory Test: Results for neurologically intact individuals and an investigation of its validity using inverted face stimuli and prosopagnosic participants. *Neuropsychologia, 44*(4), 576–585.

Edmonds, E. C., Glisky, E. L., Bartlett, J. C., & Rapcsak, S. Z. (2011). Cognitive mechanisms of false facial recognition in older adults, *Psychology and Aging.* Advanced online publication, doi:10.1037/a0024582.

Fisher, R. P., & Geiselman, R. E. (1992). *Memory enhancing techniques for investigative interviewing: The cognitive interview.* Springfield, IL: Charles C. Thomas.

Fulton, A., & Bartlett, J. C. (1991). Young and old faces in young and old heads: The factor of age in face recognition. *Psychology and Aging, 6*, 623–630.

Germine, L. T., Duchaine, B., & Nakayama, K. (2011). Where cognitive development and aging meet: Face learning ability peaks after age 30. *Cognition, 118,* 201–210. doi:10.1016/j.cognition.2011.11.002

Glisky, E. L., Polster, M. R., & Routhieaux, B. C. (1995). Double dissociaton between item and source memory. *Neuropsychology, 9,* 229–235.

Goh, J. O., Suzuki, A., & Park, D. C. (2010). Reduced neural selectivity increases fMRI adaptation with age during face discrimination. *Neuroimage, 51,* 336–344.

Goodsell, C. A., Neuschatz, J. S., & Gronlund, S. D. (2009). Effects of mugshot commitment on lineup performance in young and older adults. *Applied Cognitive Psychology, 23,* 788–803.

Havard, C., & Memon, A. (2009). The influence of face age on identification from a video line-up: A comparison between older and younger adults. *Memory, 17*(8), 847–859.

He, Y., Ebner, N. C., & Johnson, M. K. (2011). What predicts own-age bias in face recognition memory? *Social Cognition, 29*(1), 97–109.

Henkel, L. A., Johnson, M. K., & De Leonardis, D. M. (1998). Aging and source monitoring: Cognitive processes and neuropsychological correlates. *Journal of Experimental Psychology: General, 127,* 251–168.

Hess, T. M., Auman, C., Colcombe, S. J., & Rahhal, T. A. (2003). The impact of stereotype threat on age differences in memory performance. *Journal of Gerontology: Psychological Sciences, 58B,* 3–11.

Hildebrandt, A., Wilhelm, O., Schmiedek, F., Herzmann, G., & Sommer, W. (2011). On the specificity of face cognition compared with general cognitive functioning across adult age. *Psychology and Aging, 26,* 701–715.

Holliday, R. E., Humphries, J. E., Milne, R., Memon, A., Houlder, L., Lyons, A., & Bull, R. (2011). Reducing misinformation effects in older adults with cognitive interview mnemonics. *Psychology and Aging.* Advance online publication. Doi: 10.1037/a0022031

Horry, R., Memon, A., & Wright, D. B. (2012). Predictors of eyewitness identification decisions from video lineups in England: A field study. *Law and Human Behavior, 36*(4), 257–265. Doi: 10.1007/S10979-011-9279-z

Jacoby, L. L., & Rhodes, M. G. (2006). False remembering in the aged. *Current Directions in Psychological Science, 15,* 49–53. doi:10.1111/j.0963-7214.2006.00405.x

Köhnken, G., Milne, R., Memon, A., & Bull, R. (1999). A meta-analysis on the effects of the Cognitive Interview. *Psychology, Crime and Law, 5,* 3–27.

Kroll, N., Knight, R. T., Metcalfe, J., Wolf, E. S., & Tulving, E. (1998). Cohesion failure as a source of memory illusions. *Journal of Memory and Language, 35,* 176–196.

LaVoie, D. J., Mertz, H. K., & Richmond, T. L. (2007). False memory susceptibility in older adults: Implications for the elderly eyewitness. In M. P. Toglia, J. D. Read, D. F. Ross, and R. C. L. Lindsay (Eds.), *Handbook of eyewitness psychology, Volume 1: Memory for events,* (pp. 605–626). Mahwah, NJ: Erlbaum.

Loftus, E., & Palmer, J. (1974). Reconstruction of automobile destruction: An example of the interaction between language and memory. *Journal of Verbal Learning and Verbal Behavior, 13,* 585–589.

Luo, L., & Craik, F. I. M. (2008). La *Revue canadienne de psychiatrie, 53,* 346–353.

Luo, L., & Craik, F. I. M. (2009). Age differences in recollection: Specificity effects at retrieval. *Journal of Memory and Language, 60,* 421–436.

Malpass, R. S., & Devine, P. G. (1981). Eyewitness identification: Lineup instructions and the absence of the offender. *Journal of Applied Psychology, 66,* 482–489.

Marchie, T. A., Brainerd, C. J., & Reyna, V. F. (2010). Distinguishing true from false memories in forensic contexts: Can phenomenology tell us what is real? *Applied Cognitive Psychology, 24,* 1168–1182.

Mason, S. E. (1986). Age and gender as factors in facial recognition and identification. *Experimental Aging Research, 12,* 151–154.

McKone, E., & Peh, Y. X. (2006). Memory conjunction errors for realistic faces are consistent with configural processing. *Psychonomic Bulletin and Review, 13*(1), 106–111.

McKone, E., & Robbins, R. (2011). Are faces special? In A. J. Calder, G. Rhodes and M. Johnson (Eds.), *Oxford handbook of face perception* (pp. 149–176). Oxford: Oxford University Press.

Mello, E. W., & Fisher, R. P. (1996). Enhancing older adult eyewitness memory with the cognitive interview. *Applied Cognitive Psychology, 10,* 403–417.

Memon, A., Bartlett, J. C., Rose, R., & Gray, C. (2003). The aging eyewitness: The effects of face-age and delay upon younger and older observers. *Journal of Gerontology: Psychological and Social Sciences, 58,* 338–345.

Memon, A., Gabbert, F., & Hope, L. (2004). The aging eyewitness. In J. Adler (Ed.), *Forensic psychology: Debates, concepts and practice* (pp. 96–112). Uffcolme, Devon: Willan Publishing.

Memon, A., Hope, L., Bartlett, J. C. & Bull, R. (2002). Eyewitness recognition errors: The effects of mugshot viewing and choosing in young and old adults. *Memory & Cognition, 30,* 1219–1227.

Memon, A., Meisner, C. A., & Fraser, J. (2010). The cognitive interview: A meta-analytic review and study space analysis of the past 25 years. *Psychology, Public Policy and Law, 16*(4), 340–372.

Meisner, B. A. (2011). A meta-analysis of positive and negative age stereotype priming effects on behavior among older adults. *Journal of Gerontology: Psychological Sciences*, 10.1093/geronb/gbr062

Moulin, C. J. A., Thompson, R. G., Wright, D., & Conway, M. A. (2007). Eyewitness memory in older adults. In M. P. Toglia, J. D. Read, D. F. Ross and R. C. L. Lindsay (Eds.), *Handbook of eyewitness psychology, Volume 1: Memory for events*, (pp. 627–625). Mahwah, NJ: Erlbaum.

Mueller-Johnson, K., & Ceci, S. J. (2007). The elderly eyewitness: A review and a prospectus. In M. P. Toglia, J. D. Read, D. F. Ross and R. C. L. Lindsay (Eds.), *Handbook of eyewitness psychology, Volume 1: Memory for events* (pp. 577–603). Mahwah, NJ: Erlbaum.

Naveh-Benjamin, M. (2000). Adult age differences in memory performance: Tests of an associative deficit hypothesis. *Journal of Experimental Psychology: Learning, Memory and Cognition, 26*, 1170–1187.

Perfect, T. J., & Harris, L. J. (2003). Adult age differences in unconscious transference: Source confusion or identity blending? *Memory & Cognition, 31*, 570–580.

Perfect, T. J. & Moon, H. C. (2005). The own-age effect in face recognition. In J. Duncan and P. McLeod (Eds.), *Measuring the mind: Speed, control, age* (pp. 317–340). Oxford, Oxford University Press.

Park, D. C., Lautenschlager, G., Hedden, T., Davidson, N. S,, Smith, A. D., & Smith, P. K. (2002). Models of visuospatial and verbal memory across the adult lifespan. *Psychology and Aging, 17*(2), 299–320.

Park, D. C., & Reuter-Lorenz, P. (2008). The adaptive brain: Aging and neurocognitive scaffolding. *Annual Review of Psychology, 60*, 21.1–21.24.

Rhodes, M. G., & Anastasi, J. S. (2012). The own-age bias in face recognition: A meta-analytic and theoretical review. *Psychological Bulletin, 138*(1), 146–174.

Richler, J. J., Cheung, O. S., & Gauthier, I. (2011). *Holistic processing predicts face recognition. Psychological Science, 22*(4), 464–471.

Rodrigue, K. M., Kennedy, K. M., Devous, M. D., Rieck, J. R., Hebrank, A, C., Diaz-Arrastia, R., Mathews, D., & Park, D. C. (2012). Amyloid burden in healthy aging: Regional distribution and cognitive consequences. *Neurology, 78*, 387–395.

Roediger, H. L., & Geraci, L. (2007). Aging and the misinformation effect: A neuropsychological analysis. *Journal of Experimental Psychology: Learning, Memory and Cognition, 33*(2), 321–334.

Roediger, H. L., & McDaniel, M. A. (2007). Illusory recollection in older adults: Testing Mark Twain's conjecture. In M. Garry and H. Hayne, *Do justice and let the sky fall*, Mahwah, NJ: Erlbaum.

Rose, R. A., Bull, R., & Vrij, A. (2003). Enhancing older witnesses' identification performance: Context reinstatement is not the answer. *Canadian Journal of Police and Security Services, 58*, 338–345.

Rose, R. A., Bull, R., & Vrij, A. (2005). Non-biased lineup instructions do matter – a problem for older eyewitnesses. *Psychology, Crime and Law, 11*(2), 147–159.

Russell, R., Duchaine, B., & Nakayama, K. (2009). Super recognizers: People with extraordinary face recognition ability. *Psychonomic Bulletin and Review, 16*(2), 252–257.

Scheck, B., Neufeld, P., & Dwyer, J. (2000). *Actual innocence: Five days to execution and other dispatches from the wrongly convicted.*, New York: Doubleday.

Searcy, J. H., Bartlett, J. C., & Memon, A. (1999). Age differences in accuracy and choosing rates in face recognition and eyewitness identification tasks. *Memory & Cognition, 27*, 538–552.

Smith, A. D., & Winograd, E. (1978). Adult age differences in remembering faces. *Developmental Psychology, 14*, 443–444.

Sporer, S. L. (2001). Recognizing faces of other ethnic groups. *Psychology, Public Policy, and Law, 7*, 36–97. doi: 10.1037/1076-8971.7.1.36

Tanaka, J. W., & Gordon, I. (2011). Features, configuration and holistic face processing, In A. J. Calder, G. Rhodes and M. Johnson (Eds.), *Oxford handbook of face perception* (pp. 177–194). Oxford: Oxford University Press.

Thomas, A. K., & Dubois, (2012). Reducing the burden of stereotype threat eliminates age differences in memory distortion. *Psychological Science, 22*(12), 1515–1517.

Valentine, T., Pickering, A., & Darling, S. (2003). Characteristics of eyewitness identification that predict the outcome of real lineups. *Applied Cognitive Psychology, 17*, 969–993.

Wang, R., Li, J., Fang, H., & Tian, M. (2012). Individual differences in holistic processing predict face recognition ability. *Psychological Science*, published online DOI: 10.1177.

Wiese, H., Schweinberger, S. R., & Hansen, K. (2008). The age of the beholder: ERP evidence of an own-age bias in face memory. *Neuropsychologia, 46*, 2973–2985.

Wilcock, R. (2010). The aging eyewitness. In J. Adler and J. Gray. (Eds.), *Forensic psychology: Concepts, debates and practice* (pp. 162–180). Uffcolme, Devon: Willan Publishing.

Wilcock, R., & Bull, R. (2010). Novel lineup methods for improving the performance of older eyewitnesses. *Applied Cognitive Psychology, 24*, 718–736.

Wilcock, R., Bull, R., & Vrij, A. (2005). Aiding the performance of older eyewitnesses: Enhanced, non-biased lineup instructions and lineup presentation. *Psychiatry, Psychology and Law, 12*, 129–140.

Wilcock, R., Bull, R., & Vrij, A. (2007). Are old eyewitnesses always poorer eyewitnesses? Identification accuracy, context reinstatement, own-age bias. *Psychology, Crime & Law, 13*(3), 305–316.

Wright, A. M., & Holliday, R. E. (2007). Enhancing the recall of young, young-old, and old-old adults with cognitive interviews. *Applied Cognitive Psychology, 21*, 19–43.

Yarmey, A. D., & Kent, J. (1980). Eyewitness identification by elderly and young adults. *Law and Human Behavior, 3*, 359–371.

Yonelinas, A. P. (2002). The nature of recollection and familiarity: A review of 30 years of research. *Journal of Memory and Language, 46*, 441–517. doi:10.1006/jmla.2002.2864.

Yonelinas, A. P., Kroll, N. E. A., Dobbins, I. G., & Soltani, M. (1999). Recognition memory of faces: When familiarity supports associative recognition judgments. *Psychonomic Bulletin & Review, 6*, 654–661.

37

Eliciting Verbal and Nonverbal Cues to Deceit by Outsmarting the Liars

Aldert Vrij

INTRODUCTION

The year 2003 may well turn out to have been a crucial turning point in deception research. First, Bella DePaulo and her colleagues published a meta-analysis revealing that verbal and nonverbal cues to deceit are typically faint and unreliable. Second, the American National Research Council (NRC) published their report stating that no convincing theoretical rationale exists as to why truth tellers would be less anxious during questioning than liars. DePaulo et al.'s meta-analysis opened the way to a new approach in deception research. If cues to deception are weak, interviewers need to play a more active role and need to attempt to actively *elicit* such cues during their interviews via specific interview techniques (Vrij, Granhag, & Porter, 2010). The NRC report makes clear that developing anxiety-based interview techniques aimed at eliciting cues of anxiety in liars will be problematic as no one question can be asked that systematically makes liars more anxious than truth tellers. Therefore, researchers started to investigate whether questions could be asked that are more difficult to answer for liars than for truth tellers, and, hence, whether such questions can elicit cognitive cues to deceit. This

chapter presents these latter research efforts. It shows that this new wave of cognitive – outsmarting the liars – lie detection research bears fruit.

Prior to discussing this research, the history of verbal and nonverbal cues to deception will be outlined. This section contains discussions of the three dominant theoretical approaches as to why verbal and nonverbal cues to deception may occur, and of the most well-known verbal and nonverbal lie detection tools used to date.

The final part of this chapter presents ideas for future research, including a plea for exploring new domains of deception, such as lying about intentions or lying in street-based interview settings. Such research is relevant when dealing with threats that characterise the twenty-first century, such as terrorism. The current forensic deception research predominantly examines lying about past activities in police interview settings.

This chapter concentrates on nonverbal and verbal cues that can be discerned by human perceivers without the aid of equipment. The relevant question is whether people can detect lies when observing someone's nonverbal behaviour or analysing their speech. Such "low-tech" lie detection tools could be used in virtually all circumstances, as examinees do not have to be hooked up to a machine, and time-consuming analyses of complex data are not required. The use of equipment and complicated analyses are two characteristics of "high-tech" lie detection tools, such as the polygraph, P300 and fMRI. Comprehensive reviews of the polygraph (Iacono, 2008b, 2008c; Kleiner, 2002; Verschuere, Ben-Shakhar, & Meijer, 2011), P300 (Rosenfeld, 2011; Rosenfeld, Ben-Shakhar, & Ganis, in press) and fMRI (Christ, Van Essen, Watson, Brubaker, & McDermott, 2009; Gamer, 2011; Ganis & Rosenfeld, in press; Langleben, 2008; Rosenfeld et al., in press; Spence, 2008) are available elsewhere.

THEORETICAL PERSPECTIVES ABOUT (NON)VERBAL CUES TO DECEPTION

Different theoretical approaches exist that predict nonverbal and verbal cues to deception, in particular the leakage and deception cues approach (Ekman & Friesen, 1969), the multi-factor model (Zuckerman, DePaulo, & Rosenthal, 1981), the emotion approach (Ekman, 1985/2009), Interpersonal Deception Theory (Buller & Burgoon, 1996), and the self-presentational perspective (DePaulo, 1992; DePaulo, Lindsay, Malone, Muhlenbruck, Charlton, & Cooper, 2003). Three elements that these approaches have in common have influenced verbal and nonverbal lie detection in particular: The notion that, compared with truth tellers, liars may (i) experience higher levels of cognitive load; (ii) experience stronger emotions (particularly fear as a result of detection apprehension); and (iii) are inclined to use more and different strategies to make a convincing impression on others.

Cognitive load

Several aspects of lying may make it cognitively more demanding than truth telling. First, formulating the lie itself may be cognitively demanding. Liars need to invent a story and monitor their fabrication so that it is plausible and adheres to everything the questioner knows or might find out. In addition, liars must remember what they have said to whom in order to maintain consistency. Liars should also avoid making slips of the tongue and refrain from providing new leads (Vrij, 2008).

A second aspect of lying that adds to mental load is that liars are typically less likely than truth tellers to take their credibility for granted (DePaulo et al., 2003; Gilovich, Savitsky, & Medvec, 1998; Kassin, 2005; Kassin & Gudjonsson, 2004; Kassin & Norwick, 2004; Vrij, Mann, & Fisher, 2006b). As such, liars will be more inclined than truth tellers to monitor and control their demeanour so that they will appear honest to the lie detector (DePaulo & Kirkendol, 1989). This should add cognitive demand for liars. Third, because liars do not take credibility for granted, they may monitor the *interviewer's* reactions more carefully in order to assess whether they are getting away with their lie (Buller & Burgoon, 1996; Schweitzer, Brodt, & Croson, 2002). Carefully monitoring the interviewer also requires cognitive resources. The final four reasons all relate to the fact that truth is a default response and that lies are more difficult to access than truths, which adds to cognitive load. Fourth, liars may be preoccupied by the task of reminding themselves to act and role-play (DePaulo et al., 2003), which requires extra cognitive effort. Fifth, liars need to justify to themselves why they lie, whereas truth telling does not require a justification (Levine, Kim, & Hamel, 2010). Sixth, the truth occurs to liars spontaneously, and they have to suppress this first before they can start lying (Spence, Farrow, Herford, Wilkinson, Zheng, & Woodruff, 2001). Finally, whereas the truth occurs spontaneously, activating a lie is more intentional and deliberate (Gilbert, 1991; Walczyk, Roper, Seemann, & Humphrey, 2003; Walczyk, Schwartz, Clifton, Adams, Wei, & Zha, 2005).

Obviously, lying is not always more cognitively demanding than truth telling, and these seven reasons given as to *why* lying is more cognitively demanding could give us insight into *when* it is more cognitively demanding. That is, lying is more cognitively demanding to the degree that these six principles are in effect. For example, lying is likely to be more demanding than truth telling only when interviewees are motivated to be believed. Only under those circumstances can it be assumed that liars take their credibility less for granted than truth tellers and hence will be more inclined than truth tellers to monitor their own behaviour and/or the interviewer's reactions. Second, for lying to be more cognitively demanding than truth telling, liars must be able to retrieve their truthful activity easily and have a clear image of it. Only when liars' knowledge of the truth is easily and clearly accessed will it be difficult for them to suppress the truth. On the other side of the equation, truth tellers also need to have easy access to the truth for the task to be relatively undemanding. If truth tellers have to think hard to remember the target event (e.g., because it was not distinctive or it occurred long ago), their cognitive demands may exceed the cognitive demands that liars require for fabricating a story.

Emotions

Regarding emotions, it has been argued that telling a lie is associated most commonly with three different emotions: guilt, fear or delight (Ekman, 1985/2009). Liars might feel guilty because they are lying, might be afraid of getting caught or might be excited at having the opportunity of fooling someone. The strength of these emotions depends on the personality of the liar and on the circumstances under which the lie takes place (Ekman, 1985/2009; Vrij, 2008).

Control

As discussed above, liars take their credibility less for granted than truth tellers.

They therefore may attempt to control their behaviour and speech more than truth tellers. In particular, they may wish to avoid exhibiting behaviours or speech that they believe will make a dishonest impression on others and try instead to show behaviours or speech that they believe will appear credible (Hocking & Leathers, 1980; Köhnken, 1996; Leary & Kowalski, 1990). These control activities are cognitively demanding and have also been reported in the cognitive load section above. However, it is important to distinguish control from cognitive load as they predict different behavioural patterns. For example, the cognitive load approach predicts that liars will stutter more than truth tellers, whereas the control approach predicts that liars will actively try to suppress such stutters because they will think that stuttering will make a suspicious impression.

EVIDENCE FOR THE THEORETICAL APPROACHES

Nonverbal and verbal cues to deception

DePaulo and her colleagues published the most comprehensive meta-analysis of nonverbal and verbal cues to deception to date (DePaulo et al., 2003). They considered 158 verbal and nonverbal cues to deception, within 120 studies. The striking finding of that meta-analysis was that cues to deception are typically faint and unreliable. For example, of the 50 cues that were examined in six or more studies, 14 (28 per cent) showed a significant relationship with deception (DePaulo et al., 2003, Table 8). The average effect size of those 14 diagnostic cues was $d = .25$, which is considered a small effect (Cohen, 1988). Cohen argued that a small effect is barely perceptible, such as the difference in height between 15- and 16-year-old girls (Cohen, 1988; Rice & Harris, 2005).

Accuracy rates in nonverbal and verbal lie detection

Perhaps more relevant than a discussion of (non)verbal cues to deceit is how accurate observers are in detecting truths and lies when they pay attention to people's behaviour or speech. Research has shown that people are not good at this task. Bond and DePaulo (2006) reviewed the lie detection literature, and their meta-analysis included 206 studies in which a total of 24,483 observers participated. These observers achieved an average accuracy rate of 54 per cent, whereas just tossing a coin would lead to 50 per cent. Vrij (2008) examined whether professionals, such as law enforcement personnel, were any better at this task than laypersons (typically college students). The results of 79 studies that included laypersons as observers and 28 studies that included professionals as observers were assessed. There was no difference between the two groups. The laypersons achieved an accuracy rate of 54.27 per cent whereas the professionals achieved a 55.91 per cent accuracy rate. The professionals, however, were more confident in their veracity judgements than lay persons (Vrij, 2008).

These low accuracy rates, particularly those of professionals, may seem surprising. It is important to consider the context in which lie detection research is normally conducted. In a typical lie detection experiment observers are given short video fragments of people they do not know who are either telling the truth or lying. They typically do not know those people (called senders) and are not given any background information about the senders and their statements, so the only source of information available to them is the nonverbal and verbal behaviour displayed by these senders. Compared with real life this is a somewhat unusual way of detecting lies, because observers often have background information and compare the statements with this information (Park, Levine, McCornack, Morrison, & Ferrara, 2002). Judging whether someone contradicts facts is probably an easier way to detect deceit than analysing someone's speech or behaviour.

Specific lie detection tools

Specific nonverbal and verbal lie detection tools have been developed to detect truth tellers and liars, and I will discuss the five most well-known tools. Two of those tools (Micro-expressions and Behavior Analysis Interview) concentrate on nonverbal behaviours, and they are both based on the emotion approach. The other three tools (Criteria-Based Content Analysis, Reality Monitoring and Scientific Content Analysis) are based on a combination of the cognitive and control approaches and on memory theory. As this section demonstrates, there is evidence that only two of the five tools (Criteria-Based Content Analysis and Reality Monitoring) can discriminate between truth tellers and liars well above the level of chance.

Micro-expressions

Over the years Paul Ekman has argued that facial expressions of emotion betray liars (Ekman, 1985/2009). According to Ekman, aspects of facial communication are beyond control and can betray a deceiver's true emotion via micro-expressions (lasting 1/25 to 1/5 of a second) of that emotion. Ekman has claimed that his system of lie detection can achieve accuracy of more than 95 per cent (*Washington Post*, 29 October 2006). However, Ekman has never published empirical data to back up this claim. That is, he has never published data showing that observers achieve this accuracy; neither has he published data showing that facial expressions of emotions are a diagnostic indicator of deceit. Regarding the latter, Porter and ten Brinke (2008) found that micro-expressions only occurred in 14 out of the 697 analysed expressions, and that 6 of those 14 expressions were displayed by truth tellers. Those findings suggest that the micro-expressions lie detection tool is largely ineffective.

Behavior Analysis Interview

The second nonverbal lie detection tool is the Behavior Analysis Interview (BAI; Inbau, Reid, Buckley, & Jayne, 2013). Blair and Kooi (2004) claimed that over 150,000 police personnel have been trained in the use of BAI throughout the world, and the tool is frequently used in the United States (Vrij, Mann, & Fisher, 2006a). BAI investigators examine nervous behaviours and the BAI can therefore be classified as an emotion-based tool. However, there are other theoretical assumptions (Horvath, Blair, & Buckley, 2008), such as liars' lack of understanding of how truth tellers actually behave and liars' reluctance to share much information out of fear that it will lead to deception detection.

The BAI protocol includes an open-ended question that invites suspects to describe their activities during a specific period of time (e.g., "What did you do between 3 pm and 4 pm?"), which is then followed by a series of standardised questions, such as "Did you take the money?" (in the case of an alleged theft of money) and "Do you know who took the money?" Inbau et al. (2013) report that liars feel less comfortable than truth tellers during an investigative interview. As a result, guilty suspects are more likely to display nervous and anxiety reducing behaviour, such as crossing their legs, shifting about in their chair and performing grooming behaviour while answering the question, whereas innocent suspects are more likely to lean forward, establish eye contact and use illustrators to reinforce their confidence in their statements. In addition, according to Inbau et al., guilty suspects are more likely to answer quickly, and their answers will sound less sincere.

Horvath, Jayne, and Buckley (1994) tested the efficiency of BAI in a field study. Their study included 60 videotaped interviews with real suspects in which the BAI protocol was employed. When inconclusive outcomes were disregarded (N = 9), an overall accuracy rate of 86 per cent was obtained. This is an impressive accuracy rate, but the study had an important limitation. The ground truth in the study was unclear. That is, it could not be established with certainty that the innocent suspects were truly innocent and the guilty suspects were truly guilty. A lack of ground truth is a well-documented and widespread problem in deception field studies (Iacono, 2008a). In fact, Horvath et al. (1994) reported that the ground truth was established by "incontrovertible evidence" in only *two* of the 60 cases that they analysed. They concluded that "If it were possible to develop ground truth criteria in a large number of cases such as occurred in these two instances, the interpretation of findings would be less problematic" (p. 805). This conclusion probably does not go far enough. The results of a study in which the ground truth is established in only 3 per cent of the cases (two out of 60 cases) are simply uninterpretable.

The alternative to field research is laboratory research where ground truth problems do not exist. Practitioners are often against such research because they believe that it does not accurately reflect how they interview in real life (Buckley, 2012; Horvath et al., 2008; Mann, Vrij, Fisher, & Robinson, 2008). We tested the BAI in a controlled laboratory experiment, and our results directly refuted Inbau et al.'s (2013) predictions: Liars were *less* likely to cross their legs and *less* likely to shift posture than truth tellers (Vrij, Mann, & Fisher, 2006a). In a subsequent lie detection experiment, we showed observers these videotaped BAI interviews. The observers were unable to distinguish the truth tellers from the liars (Vrij, Mann, Kristen, & Fisher, 2007). Moreover, in Kassin and Fong's (1999) experiment half of the observers received training in the visual BAI cues. The trained observers' performance on a subsequent lie detection test was worse than that of untrained participants. In other words, there is evidence that endorsing the information about visual cues to deception discussed in the BAI protocol is counterproductive and makes people worse lie detectors.

Criteria-based content analysis

The first verbal lie detection tool to be discussed, Criteria-Based Content Analysis (CBCA), combines the "cognitive" and "control" theoretical approaches. CBCA originates from Sweden (Trankell, 1963) and Germany (Undeutsch, 1967) and was designed to assess the statements of children in alleged sexual abuse cases. CBCA is the core of Statement Validity Assessment (SVA), and SVA assessments are accepted as evidence in court in several West European countries including Germany, the Netherlands and Sweden. CBCA is a list of 19 verbal criteria that are assumed to occur more frequently in truthful than in deceptive accounts (Köhnken & Steller, 1988; Steller & Köhnken, 1989). According to CBCA theory, some criteria are likely to indicate genuine experiences because these criteria are typically too difficult to fabricate (Köhnken, 1996, 2004). Therefore, statements that are coherent and consistent (*logical structure*), in which the information is not provided in a chronological time sequence (*unstructured production*) and that contain a significant amount of detail (*quantity of detail*) are more likely to be true. Other indicators of truthfulness include if the child reports details that are not part of the allegation but are related to it (*related external associations*, e.g., a witness who describes that the perpetrator talked about various women he had slept with and the differences between them), when the witness describes his or her feelings or thoughts experienced at the time of the incident (*accounts of subjective mental state*), or describes their interpretation of the perpetrator's feelings, thoughts or motives during the incident (*attribution of perpetrator's mental state*).

Other criteria are said to be more likely to occur in truthful statements for motivational reasons. It is assumed that truthful persons will not be as concerned with impression management as deceivers. Compared with truth tellers, deceivers will be keener to construct a report that they believe will make a credible impression on others, and will leave out information that, in their view, will damage their image of being a sincere person (Köhnken, 1996, 2004). As a result, a truthful statement is more likely to contain information that is inconsistent with the stereotypes of truthfulness. The CBCA list includes five of these so-called "contrary-to-truthfulness-stereotype" criteria (Ruby & Brigham, 1998), including: *spontaneous corrections* (corrections made without prompting from the interviewer) and *admitting lack of memory* (expressing concern that some parts of the statement might be incorrect: "I think", "Maybe", "I am not sure", etc.).

CBCA has been widely researched and more than 50 empirical studies about this method have been published to date (Vrij, 2008). Those studies demonstrate that CBCA analyses can be useful for lie detection purposes. In 20 studies researchers computed total CBCA scores and compared these scores for truth tellers and liars. In 16 out of 20 studies (80 per cent) the hypothesis that truth tellers will obtain significantly higher total CBCA scores than liars was supported. Only in one of the 20 studies (5 per cent), did truth tellers obtain lower CBCA scores than liars (Ruby & Brigham, 1998), but the protocol used in that study differed in several ways from the typical CBCA approach, including that assessments were based on watching videos rather than reading transcripts. In that respect, Ruby and Brigham's (1998) study is not a fair test of the CBCA method. Regarding the individual criteria, Criterion 3, *quantity of details*, received the most support. The amount of details was calculated in 29 studies and in 22 of those (76 per cent) truth tellers included significantly more details in their accounts than did liars. Moreover, in not a single study did truth tellers include significantly fewer details in their statements than did liars. Finally, in 24 studies the extent to which CBCA analyses can discriminate liars from truth tellers was examined. The average accuracy rate in these studies was 71 per cent. In other words, there is evidence that CBCA can be effective in discriminating between truths and lies.

Whether CBCA scores (and SVA assessments) should be admissible in criminal courts is a different matter. The United States Supreme Court provided a set of guidelines for admitting expert scientific evidence in (American) federal courts. These guidelines were presented in the *Daubert v. Merrel Dow Pharmaceuticals, Inc.* (1993) case, and one of these guidelines refers to the known error rate. The known error rate in CBCA research is 29 per cent, which is probably too high to be accepted in criminal courts.

Reality monitoring

A second verbal lie detection approach is Reality Monitoring (RM). It is not used by professional lie detectors, but by scientific researchers. RM is based on memory theory. The core of RM is that memories of experienced events differ in quality from memories of imagined events (Johnson & Raye, 1981, 1998). Memories of real experiences are obtained through perceptual processes and are therefore likely to contain, among other things, *perceptual information*: details of sound, smell, taste, touch or visual details and *contextual information*: spatial details (details about where the event took place and about how objects and people were situated in relation to each other, e.g., "He stood behind me"), and temporal details (details about the time order of events, e.g., "First he switched on the video-recorder and then the TV" and about the duration of events). These memories are usually clear, sharp and vivid. Accounts of imagined events are derived from an internal source and are therefore likely to contain *cognitive operations*, such as thoughts and reasoning ("She is the girlfriend of the driver so must have been in our car as well"). They are usually vaguer and less concrete. Although RM is not developed for lie detection purposes, it is used as such by researchers. Their claim is that "experienced events" reflect truth telling whereas "imagined events" reflect deception. Obviously, this is not always the case. A person who gives a false alibi by describing something he truly experienced albeit at a different time from the time he claims to have done so is also describing an experienced event when he lies. Nevertheless, when Masip, Sporer, Garrido, and Herrero (2005) and Vrij (2008) reviewed the Reality Monitoring deception research (all laboratory studies), they found that lie and truth accuracy rates were similar to those obtained with CBCA research. That is, in the ten studies in which RM was used to discriminate liars from truth tellers, the average accuracy rate was 69 per cent. In terms of individual criteria in particular, the idea that truth tellers recall more perceptual information and contextual embeddings received support. In sum, research findings suggest that RM can be effective in discriminating between truths and lies.

Scientific content analysis

A third verbal lie detection tool is Scientific Content Analysis (SCAN), developed by the former Israeli police lieutenant and polygraph examiner Avinoam Sapir. SCAN is very popular amongst practitioners but has not been researched much (Nahari, Vrij, & Fisher, 2012). In the SCAN procedure, the examinee is asked to write down in detail all his/her activities during a critical period of time in such a way that a reader without background information can determine what actually happened. The handwritten statement is then analysed by a SCAN expert on the basis of a list of predetermined criteria. Sapir (1987/2000) claims that some SCAN criteria are more likely to occur in truthful than in deceptive statements (e.g., denial of allegations, use of self-references), whereas other criteria are more likely to occur in deceptive than in truthful statements (e.g., change in language, missing information), but does not provide a theoretical rationale for his assumptions.

SCAN users refer to Driscoll's (1994) field study as evidence that SCAN works, and, indeed, the accuracy rate obtained in that study was high at 83 per cent. However, a serious limitation of the study was that the ground truth could not be established. Nahari, Vrij, and Fisher (2012) tested the efficiency of SCAN in a laboratory experiment. Truth tellers truthfully wrote down their activities during the last half hour, whereas liars were asked to fabricate a story. The statements were analysed with SCAN and, by way of comparison, also with RM. SCAN did not distinguish truth tellers from liars above the level of chance but RM did. With RM analyses 71 per cent of truth tellers and liars were correctly classified.

There is some overlap between SCAN and CBCA in the criteria that are examined. For example, the criteria "spontaneous corrections", "lack of memory" and "extraneous information" appear on both lists. Intriguingly, the predictions about how these criteria vary between truth tellers and liars differ. In CBCA the occurrence of those cues are perceived as indictors of truth whereas in SCAN the same criteria are seen as indicators of deceit. Research regarding these individual criteria gives support only to the CBCA assumptions (Vrij, 2008). In sum, although SCAN is popular amongst practitioners and widely used, there is no evidence that it works.

Reflection on the lie detection tools

Two of the five lie detection tools discussed above appear to be able to discriminate between truths and lies. Both tools, CBCA and RM, analyse speech content. There is very little evidence that either of the two tools examining nonverbal behaviour (microexpressions and BAI) work. It could be that nonverbal cues are simply not diagnostic enough to be used in veracity assessments (Levine, Shaw, & Shulman, 2010). Indeed, research has shown that nonverbal cues are typically less diagnostic of deceit than verbal cues (DePaulo et al., 2003; Vrij, 2008), which can, at least in part, be explained by taking truth tellers' and liars' strategies into account. Truth tellers and liars appear to use the *same nonverbal* strategies but *different verbal* strategies, as two studies examining strategies revealed (Hartwig, Granhag, Strömwall, & Doering, 2010; Vrij, Mann,

Leal, & Granhag, 2010). Regarding nonverbal strategies, both truth tellers and liars believed that signs of nervousness would appear suspicious. They therefore reported that they would try to suppress displaying signs of nervousness during the interview. Regarding verbal strategies, truth tellers were mainly concerned with giving as much detail about what had happened as possible. In contrast, liars were keen not to give too much detail because to do so increases the chance of saying something that the interviewer knows or can find out to be untrue. The result of these different verbal strategies is that truth tellers' stories are likely to be more detailed than liars' stories, and research supports this claim (DePaulo et al., 2003; Vrij, 2008).

Of course, not all verbal lie detection tools work, and only those that are based on sound theory will do so (CBCA and RM). In other words, an essential element for cues to deception to occur is that they are based on sound theory. A limitation of the two emotion-based tools (micro-expressions and BAI) is that the underlying assumption that liars are more uncomfortable and nervous than truth tellers appears to be unfounded (National Research Council, 2003). Indeed, truth tellers may also be anxious when they are interviewed, as a consequence of being suspected of wrongdoing or out of fear of not being believed (Bond & Fahey, 1987; DePaulo et al., 2003; Heath, 2009; Kassin, Appleby, & Torkildson-Perillo, 2010; Ofshe & Leo, 1997). Because questioning may have a similar effect in terms of anxiety on truth tellers as on liars, it will be difficult to ask questions that will evoke anxiety in liars but not in truth tellers (National Research Council, 2003). As was argued above, liars often experience more cognitive load than do truth tellers. The issue arises of whether questions can be asked that are more difficult for liars to answer than truth tellers and/or that address the differences in the strategies truth tellers and liars use in interview settings. Research has shown that this is possible, as outlined in the next two sections.

INTERVIEWING TO DETECT DECEPTION

Imposing cognitive load

An investigator could exploit the differential levels of cognitive load that truth tellers and liars experience to discriminate more effectively between them. Liars who require more cognitive resources than truth tellers for the act of storytelling will have fewer cognitive resources left over than truth tellers. This makes liars vulnerable and so if cognitive demand is further raised, which could be achieved by making additional requests, liars may not be as good as truth tellers in coping with these additional requests.

One way to impose cognitive load on interviewees is by asking them to tell their stories in reverse order. This increases cognitive load because (a) it runs counter to the natural forward-order coding of sequentially occurring events (Gilbert & Fisher, 2006; Kahana, 1996) and (b) it disrupts the reconstructing of events from a schema (Geiselman & Callot, 1990). In one experiment, half of the liars and truth tellers were requested to recall their stories in reverse order, whereas no instruction was given to the other half of participants (Vrij, Mann, Fisher, Leal, Milne, & Bull, 2008). More cues to deceit emerged in this reverse order condition than in the control condition. More importantly, observers who watched these videotaped interviews could distinguish between truths and lies better in the reverse order condition than in the control condition. In the control condition only 42 per cent of the lies were correctly classified, well below what is typically found in a lie detection experiment, suggesting that the lie detection task in this experiment was particularly difficult. Yet, in the experimental condition, 60 per cent of the lies were correctly classified, which is slightly more than typically found in lie detection research. The difference between the two deception conditions (18 per cent) represents a medium effect size ($d = .40$).

Another way to increase cognitive load is by instructing interviewees to maintain eye contact with the interviewer. This should increase cognitive load (Beattie, 1981) because when people have to concentrate on telling their stories, which is likely when they are requested to recall what has happened, they are inclined to look away from their conversation partner every now and then (typically to a motionless point), because maintaining eye contact with a conversation partner is distracting (Doherty-Sneddon, Bruce, Bonner, Longbotham, & Doyle, 2002; Doherty-Sneddon & Phelps, 2005; Glenberg, Schroeder, & Robertson, 1998).When interviewees are instructed to maintain eye contact continuously their concentration on telling their stories is therefore likely to be compromised, and since lying is more mentally taxing than truth telling, this should impair the storytelling of liars more than the storytelling of truth tellers. In an experiment, half of the liars and truth tellers were requested to maintain eye contact with the interviewer continuously throughout the interview, whereas no instruction was given to the other half of participants (Vrij, Mann, Leal, & Fisher, 2010). It was again found that more cues to deceit emerged in the Eye Contact condition than in the control condition and that observers who watched these videotaped interviews could discriminate between truths and lies only in the Eye Contact condition.

An experiment with children reveals a third type of additional request that can be made: Asking event-irrelevant questions (Quas, Davis, Goodman, & Myers, 2007). Children played individually with a male confederate who touched each child twice on their stomach, nose and neck. In the subsequent interview, children were asked to tell the truth or lie when asked questions about the touching. They were also asked a series of questions about the event, which were unrelated to body touch, and were asked to answer those questions truthfully. The children who lied about the body touch answered these unrelated questions less accurately than did the children who told the truth about the body touch. Quas and colleagues argued that remembering and rehearsing the lie required cognitive resources, and by devoting their resources to the lie, children had difficulty in conducting an adequate memory search for other event details.

Unanticipated questions

A consistent finding in deception research is that liars prepare themselves when anticipating an interview (Hartwig, Granhag, & Strömwall, 2007). Planning makes lying easier, and planned lies typically contain fewer cues to deceit than spontaneous lies (DePaulo et al., 2003). However, the positive effects of planning will only emerge if liars correctly anticipate which questions will be asked. Investigators can exploit this limitation by asking questions that liars do not anticipate. Though liars can refuse to answer unanticipated questions, such "I don't know" or "I can't remember" responses will create suspicion if the questions are about central (but unanticipated) aspects of the target event.

To test the unanticipated questions technique, pairs of liars and truth tellers were interviewed individually about having had lunch together at a restaurant (Vrij et al., 2009). While the truth tellers did have lunch together, the liars were instructed to pretend that they had. All pairs were given the opportunity to prepare for the interview together. The interviewer asked conventional opening questions (e.g., "What did you do in the restaurant?"), followed by questions about spatial (e.g., "In relation to where you sat, where were the closest diners?") and temporal issues (e.g., "Who finished their food first, you or your friend?"). Furthermore, they were asked to sketch the layout of the restaurant. The spatial questions and drawing requests came as a surprise to interviewees (this was established after the interview). Based on the overlap in responses between the two pair members to the anticipated questions, the liars and truth tellers were

not classified above chance level. However, based on the responses to the unanticipated questions, up to 80 per cent of pairs of liars and truth tellers were correctly classified (i.e., the answers to spatial questions and the answers to drawings were less alike for the pairs of liars than pairs of truth tellers). Asking unanticipated questions about central topics therefore elicited cues to deceit.

Comparing the answers to anticipated and unanticipated questions can also be used to detect deceit in individual liars, as two recent experiments demonstrated. In the first experiment truth tellers and liars were interviewed about their alleged activities in a room (Lancaster, Vrij, Hope, & Waller, 2013). Expected questions (e.g., "Tell me in as much detail as you can what you did in the room") were followed by unexpected spatial and temporal questions. In the second experiment truth tellers and liars were interviewed about their alleged forthcoming trip (Warmelink, Vrij, Mann, Jundi, & Granhag, 2012). Expected questions about the purpose of the trip (e.g., "What is the main purpose of your trip?"), were followed by unexpected questions about transport (e.g., "How are you going to travel to your destination?"), planning ("What part of the trip was easiest to plan?") and the core event ("Keep in mind an image of the most important thing you are going to do at this trip. Please describe this mental image in detail"). Liars are likely to have prepared answers to the expected questions and may therefore be able to answer them in considerable detail. Liars will not have prepared answers for the unexpected questions and may therefore struggle to generate detailed answers to them. Indeed, in both experiments, compared with truth tellers, liars gave significantly more detail to the expected questions and significantly less detail to the unexpected questions. This resulted in a larger decline in detail between anticipated and unanticipated answers in liars than in truth tellers.

Another way of using the unanticipated question technique with individuals is by asking the same question twice (Leins,

Fisher, Vrij, Mann, & Leal, 2011). When liars have not anticipated the question, they have to fabricate an answer on the spot. A liar's memory of this fabricated answer may be more unstable than a truth teller's memory of the actual event. Therefore, liars may contradict themselves more than truth tellers. This approach probably works best if the questions are asked in different formats. Truth tellers will have encoded the topic of investigation along more dimensions than liars. Truth tellers should therefore be able to recall the event more flexibly (along more dimensions) than liars. Leins, Fisher, and Vrij (2012 found support for this hypothesis. In their experiment, truth tellers entered a room and performed several tasks, whereas liars did not enter the room or perform the tasks but attempted to convince an interviewer that they did. Truth tellers and liars were interviewed twice about the room and tasks, and were asked to express their answers either the same way on both interviews (e.g., verbally at Times 1 and 2 or drawing a sketch at Times 1 and 2) or in different ways (e.g., verbally at Time 1, but drawing a sketch at Time 2 or drawing a sketch at Time 1, but verbally at Time 2). Liars' reports were less consistent than truth tellers' reports, but only when the report modality changed from the first to the second interview.

Vrij et al. (2009) were the first researchers to use drawings as a lie detection tool. Two further experiments have demonstrated that drawings have potential as a lie detection tool. More so than a verbal request, the request to sketch forces the interviewee to convey spatial information. That is, including an object within a drawing requires that object to be spatially located. By comparison, verbally describing an object in a room can be done without indicating its spatial location. If a liar has not experienced an item in a particular location, s/he may still verbally describe the object but will do so without referring to its location to avoid the risk of misplacing it. Such a "masking strategy" is not possible when asked to sketch. As a result, a liar may instead decide against sketching the object.

In an experiment, truth tellers discussed their real occupation whereas liars discussed an occupation they pretended to have. When asked to *verbally describe* the layout of their office, truth tellers' and liars' answers were equally detailed. However, when asked to *sketch* the layout of their office, liars' drawings were less detailed than truth tellers' drawings (Vrij, Mann, Leal, & Fisher, 2012).

In a second drawings experiment, 31 "agents" were sent on a mission during which they had to collect a decoder from another agent (Vrij, Leal, et al., 2010). After delivering the decoder, they were asked to (i) *verbally describe* and later to (ii) *sketch* what they could see at the location where they had received the decoder. Half of the agents were requested to lie and half to tell the truth. The liars were asked to pretend to have been on a different mission whereby they received the decoder at a different location. Only two out of 16 (12.5 per cent) liars included the agent from whom they had received the decoder in their drawing, whereas 12 out of 15 truth tellers (80 per cent) did so. This difference was statistically significant. In their verbal descriptions, again two out of 16 (12.5 per cent) liars mentioned the other agent, whereas eight out of 15 (53 per cent) truth tellers did so. In other words, like the occupations experiment, truth tellers' and liars' drawings differed more from each other than truth tellers' and liars' verbal recalls. Liars were inclined to omit the agent from the sketch and verbal description for two possible reasons: First, the agent had not been present at the location they sketched/described, and they forgot to include him/her. Second, liars may be reluctant to include people in their drawings/descriptions in case they trigger further questions (about clothing, appearance, etc.).

The strategic use of evidence

Lying and truth telling suspects enter police interviews with different mental states (Granhag & Hartwig, 2008). Guilty suspects will often have unique knowledge about the crime, which, if recognised by the interviewer, makes it obvious that they are the perpetrator. Their main concern will be to ensure that the interviewer does not gain that knowledge. In contrast, innocent suspects face the opposite problem, fearing that the interviewer will not learn or believe what they did at the time of the crime. These different mental states result in different counter-interrogation strategies for liars and truth tellers (Hartwig et al., 2007). Guilty suspects are inclined to use avoidance strategies (e.g., in a free recall avoid mentioning that they were at a certain place at a certain time) or denial strategies (e.g., denying having been at a certain place at a certain time when directly asked). In contrast, innocent suspects neither avoid nor escape but are forthcoming and "tell the truth like it happened" (Granhag & Hartwig, 2008).

When investigators possess critical and possibly incriminating background information (evidence) in a case, they can exploit these differential truth tellers' and liars' strategies by introducing the available evidence during the interview in a strategic manner (the Strategic Use of Evidence technique, SUE). When questions about the evidence are asked, the forthcoming innocent suspects will be more consistent with the available evidence than the avoidant/denying guilty suspects.

Hartwig, Granhag, Strömwall, and Kronkvist (2006) tested the SUE technique at a Swedish police academy. All participants (university students) were asked to go to a bookshop. Half of the participants were instructed to steal a wallet from a briefcase that was situated on top of a box of stationery. The other half were instructed to buy something that was in the box of stationery underneath the briefcase. In other words, both liars and truth tellers left fingerprints on the briefcase. Swedish police trainees interviewed the mock suspects and were told that the suspect's fingerprints had been found on the briefcase. Prior to the interviews, half of the interviewers were trained how to use the

SUE technique and were asked to use this technique in the subsequent interview. The other half of the interviewers did not receive training and were instructed to interview the suspects in the manner of their own choice. The untrained interviewers obtained 56.1 per cent accuracy rate, which is similar to that typically found in nonverbal and verbal deception detection research. SUE trained interviewers, however, obtained 85.4 per cent accuracy rate. In addition, the liars' answers were more inconsistent with the evidence than the truth tellers' answers.

The SUE-technique has a strategic and a tactical level (Granhag, Strömwall, Willén, & Hartwig, in press). The strategic level is abstract, and contains the case-independent general principles underlying the SUE-technique (e.g., guilty suspects are avoidant or deny and innocent suspects are forthcoming). The tactical level is concrete, and contains specific tactics that are case-dependent. There are three groups of SUE-tactics: (i) Evidence tactics, (ii) Question tactics and (iii) Disclosure tactics. The evidence tactics are used primarily to assess the evidence in the planning phase; the question tactics are used systematically to exhaust the alternative explanations that a suspect may have to account for the evidence; and the disclosure tactics are used to maximise the diagnostic value of the evidence. Granhag et al. (in press) introduced and tested the so-called Evidence Framing Matrix, which is an example of a disclosure tactic. This matrix suggests that when one piece of evidence is disclosed, two dimensions are particularly helpful in illuminating the different framing alternatives that exist: the *strength of the source* of the evidence, which can vary from weak to strong, and the *degree of precision* of the evidence, which can vary from low to high. The source and specificity dimensions can be related orthogonally, resulting in a matrix explicating the different alternatives regarding how a singular piece of evidence can be framed at the point of disclosure. Granhag et al. (in press) found that using this matrix to reveal the evidence in a stepwise manner moving from the most indirect form of framing (weak source/low specificity, for example "We have information telling us that you recently visited the central station") to the most direct form of framing (strong source/high specificity, for example, "We have CCTV footage showing that you collected a package from a deposit box at the central station, ground floor level, on the 24th of August at 7.30 pm") elicited more and stronger cues to deception than using the most direct form of framing only. In other words, it was found that both *when* and *how* the evidence was disclosed moderated the effectiveness of disclosure. It was most effective to disclose the evidence late rather than early in the interview, and it was most effective when the evidence became progressively stronger and more precise.

The SUE-technique has been found to be successful in eliciting cues to deception for lying adults (Hartwig et al., 2011) and lying children (Clemens, Granhag, & Strömwall, 2011), for lying single suspects (Hartwig, Granhag, Strömwall, & Vrij, 2005) and lying multiple suspects (Rangmar, Granhag, & Strömwall, (in press, and for suspects lying about their past actions (Hartwig et al., 2005) and lying about their intentions (Clemens et al., 2011).

FUTURE RESEARCH

This section presents five important avenues for future research. Most forensic deception research to date has been carried out in a police interview setting where (mock) suspects discuss their past activities. However, other contexts are also important, and three will be introduced in this section: lying about intentions, lying by groups of suspects, and the use of undercover interviewing to detect deceit. Two avenues deal with issues that have been largely neglected in deception research but that are important: cross-cultural deception and the strategies used by truth tellers and liars. The final issue deals with the

importance of developing "within subjects" lie detection tools.

Intentions

The first suggestion for future research is to examine lying about future actions (intentions). Situations calling for assessments of whether a person is lying or truth telling about his or her intentions occur frequently, such as in stated reasons for crossing a border. To be able to detect such lies is important, as they include addressing the issue of preventing crimes from occurring. Deception research about intentions has commenced with the publication of six experimental studies (Clemens et al., 2011; Granhag & Knieps, 2011; Vrij, Granhag, Mann, & Leal, 2011; Vrij, Mann, Jundi, Hope, & Leal, 2012; Vrij, Leal, Mann, & Granhag, 2011; Warmelink et al., 2011). The pattern that emerges from these experiments is that intentions reveal different verbal cues to deceit from those of past activities. For example, the verbal criterion "detail", a diagnostic cue to deceit when interviewees discuss their past activities, has not yet emerged as a cue to deceit when interviewees discuss their future activities. One aspect that often makes truth tellers' stories about past activities more detailed than liars' is that there is a wealth of perceptual details that truth tellers have experienced during these past activities that they can recall (if they still remember them). In contrast, when discussing their intentions about a forthcoming activity, truth tellers have not yet experienced anything that restricts the amount of detail in their recall of intentions.

There may be a diagnostic cue to deceit that is uniquely related to lying about intentions: the elicitation of mental images. In Granhag and Knieps' (2011) experiment, participants who told the truth about their intentions more frequently agreed that planning their future actions evoked mental images than did participants who lied about their intentions. In addition, liars who claimed to have activated a mental image during the planning phase provided verbal descriptions of it that were less rich in detail than truth tellers'. Those findings are in alignment with the concept of episodic future thought, which represents the ability to mentally pre-experience a one-time personal event that may occur in the future (Schacter & Addis, 2007). People who make up a plan for a future event that they intend to execute seem to activate a more concrete (detailed) mental image of the upcoming scenario than do those who adopt a plan that they do not intend to execute (Watanabe, 2005).

Undercover interviewing

At the intentions stage, no crime has yet been committed, and a formal interview may therefore be inappropriate. Furthermore, in some investigative contexts, law enforcement and security personnel may have good reason to extract information from suspects without them actually being aware that they are under investigation. In particular, law enforcement officers working in an undercover capacity and interacting with potential suspects in informal settings will not wish to draw attention to themselves or to arouse suspicion about their motives by using direct question formats. For example, in settings where an undercover officer has become embedded within a criminal gang or is required to interact with suspects in order to collect intelligence, the ability to elicit relevant and usable information without detection is critical. In addition, in the UK, the police were accused of misuse of terror laws when they stopped innocent photographers taking pictures of tourist attractions (see *The Independent,* 3 December 2009 and *The Evening Standard*, 27 November 2009). A possible solution is to conduct interviews without the suspect actually knowing they are being interviewed (so-called undercover interviewing). For example, an undercover interviewer could pose as a tourist pretending to take pictures of tourist attractions. Undercover interviewing may shed light on

whether an individual has criminal intentions without arousing their suspicion in such circumstances. Undercover interviewing to detect deception is virtually unknown terrain with only one experiment having been carried out in this area (Vrij, Mann, Jundi et al., 2012. Encouragingly, that experiment demonstrated that undercover interviews can reveal deceit. Liars were instructed to run a crime-related reconnaissance mission to a nearby island and were further instructed to generate an innocent cover-up story to hide their criminal intentions. On arrival at the hovercraft terminal an undercover agent, acting in the role of either a doctoral student or an amateur photographer, approached the liars and asked apparently innocuous questions about their forthcoming trip. Actual tourists using the hovercraft terminal served as a control group. The questions were designed in the knowledge that liars tend to avoid and escape, and do not expect spatial questions; and that truth tellers have detailed representations of intentions they are about to execute. In support of the hypotheses, liars were less willing to be photographed, less accurate in identifying the places they planned to visit and less concrete and more uncertain when describing their intentions.

Lying by networks

A third line of research that merits attention is lying by networks. Most deception research addresses individual truth tellers and liars but criminals often act in pairs or larger groups. Research could focus on the development of interview tools that can successfully discriminate between pairs of truth tellers and pairs of liars. Probably the dominant interview strategy to date is to interview each member of the group individually and compare the answers they give. If the members give consistent answers they are considered truth tellers and if they give contradicting answers they are considered liars. This strategy is limited as it appears to ignore the fact that liars tend to prepare their alibis together, and are therefore likely to give the same answers when asked about these alibis. As noted earlier, the strategy works if questions are asked that the liars have not anticipated, as in that case they cannot give their prepared answers (Vrij, Leal, et al., 2009). Thus, examining contradictions could work but only in answers to unanticipated questions. There is no evidence that professionals make this crucial distinction between anticipated and unanticipated questions when they interview multiple suspects.

Several street-based situations are better suited to interviewing suspects collectively rather than individually. For example, police performing stop and search, or road border controls where cars containing several people are checked. In such situations interviewers can examine how group members communicate with each other when lying or telling the truth. A first experiment in this area revealed differences between truth tellers and liars (Vrij, Mann, Jundi et al., 2012). As mentioned before, research into the strategies used by truth tellers and liars has revealed that, when asked to recall an event, truth tellers reconstruct the event from memory and prefer a "tell it all" approach, aiming to provide a detailed description of what happened. In contrast, liars do not reconstruct a story but report their planned alibi. In terms of detail, they prefer a "keep it simple" approach, incorporating enough detail to avoid raising suspicion but avoiding giving too much detail for fear that it may contradict something the interviewer knows or could subsequently find out (Hartwig et al. 2007). The different approaches of truth tellers and liars result in different group interactions when being interviewed simultaneously, as Vrij, Mann, Jundi et al.'s (2012) experiment revealed. When truth tellers were asked about a shared experience, they started to reconstruct the event, and interacted with each other. They shared the telling of these experiences, and compared and corrected each other's recall. Liars' interacted less when giving their rehearsed answers. Thus, compared with liars, truth tellers interrupted each other more, added more information to each other's accounts and corrected each other's answers more.

Cross-cultural research

A fourth line of important future research is carrying out cross-cultural studies. In this era of globalisation people from different cultural backgrounds increasingly interact with each other, and so do people who do not speak each other's language well. Research in this area is scarce (Beune, Giebels, & Taylor, 2010; Bond & Atoum, 2000; Bond, Omar, Mahmoud, & Bonser, 1990; Bond & Rao, 2004; Da Silva & Leach, 2013). The existing research findings suggest that observers are best at lie detection when they share the native language of the persons they observe. However, for example, in intelligence interviews, investigators and interviewees often have different mother tongues and the investigator little to no understanding of the interviewee's native language. Interviewing and detecting deceit in those interviews can be challenging. In this context research about how truth tellers and liars make drawings (discussed above) is relevant as sketching does not require an interviewee to speak. Also relevant is how the aid of interpreters will affect lie detection and rapport building in such interviews.

Strategies

A fifth line of fruitful and important research is examining the strategies used by truth tellers and liars when they are interviewed. As we have argued in the present chapter, effective lie detection interview techniques take advantage of the distinctive psychological processes and requirements of truth tellers and liars. In order to design new interview strategies we need further insight into truth tellers' and liars' strategies through research. A new stream of interview strategies that could be developed are interview strategies based on memory. As time passes between the event occurring and being recalled, memory becomes vaguer and story-telling less detailed. In addition, during repeated interviews, truthful statements will follow the basic principles of "reconstructive memory" (e.g., Baddeley, 1990). That is, some details will be lost (omission errors) and some details will be added (commission errors). How do liars, who recall their alibis, deal with this? If their alibis are well rehearsed their memory of them is unlikely to become vaguer over time, yet liars need to become vaguer over time and need to include omission and commission errors in order to mirror truth tellers.

Within-subjects designs

A sixth line of deception research is the importance of developing within-subjects lie detection tools. With such tools the responses within an interviewee are compared during two parts of the test. An example of a within-subjects test is the Concealed Information Test (Lykken, 1959, 1960), a polygraph test. The CIT utilises a series of multiple-choice questions, each having one relevant alternative (e.g., a feature of the crime under investigation that should be known only to the criminal) and several neutral (control) alternatives, chosen so that an innocent suspect would not be able to discriminate them from the relevant alternative (Lykken, 1998). Liars are thought to show stronger physiological responses to the relevant alternatives than to the control alternatives, whereas no such differences are expected in truth tellers. Within-subjects tests allow investigators to establish clear norms or cut-off points. In a CIT, a stronger response to the relevant alternative than the control alternatives means lying and all other patterns indicate truth telling. Many lie detection tools, such as CBCA, do not contain within-subjects comparisons and norms and cut-off points cannot be established. It makes the decision making process in real life much more difficult. For example,

what does a CBCA total score of "9" actually mean: is the person telling the truth or lying? Research discussed above has shown that truth tellers typically obtain higher CBCA scores than liars, but such a finding tells us little about individual cases. The development of lie detection tools where cut-off points can be established is thus desirable.

CONCLUSION

For many years deception research has presented a gloomy picture. Verbal and nonverbal cues to deception are faint and unreliable; people are not good at discriminating between truths and lies; and from the five most well-known verbal and nonverbal lie detection tools only two seem to reliably work to some extent.

More recently, researchers have started to examine whether lie detection can be improved by letting interviewers employ cognitive interventions aimed at eliciting cues to deceit. This research into "imposing cognitive load", asking "unanticipated questions", and the "Strategic Use of Evidence" has shown that interviewers can indeed elicit cues to deceit via specific questioning and therefore improve their ability to detect deceit.

Most of the forensic lie detection research is narrowly focused on detecting lies told by individual suspects in police interviews about their past activities. It is important to widen this research and to examine situations that practitioners frequently deal with, such as assessing the veracity of people who discuss their intentions.

REFERENCES

Baddeley, A. (1990). *Human memory. Theory and practice.* Hove, UK: Lawrence Erlbaum.

Beattie, G. W. (1981). A further investigation of the cognitive interference hypothesis of gaze patterns during conversation. *British Journal of Social Psychology, 20,* 243–248.

Beune, K., Giebels, E., & Taylor, P. J. (2010). Patterns of interaction in police interviews: The role of cultural dependency. *Criminal Justice and Behavior, 37,* 904–925.

Blair, J. P., & Kooi, B. (2004). The gap between training and research in the detection of deception. *International Journal of Police Science and Management, 6,* 77–83.

Bond, C. F., & Atoum, A. O. (2000). International deception. *Personality and Social Psychology Bulletin, 26,* 385–395.

Bond, C. F., & DePaulo, B. M. (2006). Accuracy of deception judgements. *Personality and Social Psychology Review, 10,* 214–234.

Bond, C. F., & Fahey, W. E. (1987). False suspicion and the misperception of deceit. *British Journal of Social Psychology, 26,* 41–46.

Bond, C. F., Omar, A., Mahmoud, A., & Bonser, R. N. (1990). Lie detection across cultures. *Journal of Nonverbal Behavior, 14,* 189–205.

Bond, C. F., & Rao, S. R. (2004). Lies travel: Mendacity in a mobile world. In P. A. Granhag and L. A. Strömwall (Eds.), *Deception detection in forensic contexts* (pp. 127–147). Cambridge: Cambridge University Press.

Buckley, J. P. (2012). Detecting of deception researchers need to collaborate with experienced practitioners. *Journal of Applied Research in Memory and Cognition, 1,* 126–127.

Buller, D. B., & Burgoon, J. K. (1996). Interpersonal deception theory. *Communication Theory, 6,* 203–242.

Christ, S., E., Van Essen, D. C. Watson, J. M., Brubaker, L. E., & McDermott, K. B. (2009). The contributions of prefrontal cortex and executive control to deception: Evidence from activation likelihood estimate meta-analyses. *Cerebral Cortex, 19,* 1557–1566. doi:10.1093/cercor/bhn189.

Clemens, F., Granhag, P. A., & Strömwall, L. (2011). Eliciting cues to false intent: A new application of strategic interviewing. *Law and Human Behavior, 35,* 512–522.

Clemens, F., Granhag, P.A., Strömwall, L.A. Vrij, A., Landström, S., Roos af Hjelmsäter, E., & Hartwig, M. (2010). Skulking around the dinosaur: Eliciting cues to children's deception via strategic disclosure of evidence. *Applied Cognitive Psychology, 24,* 925–940.

Cohen, J. (1988). *Statistical power analysis for the behavioral sciences* (2nd ed.). Hillsdale, NJ: Erlbaum.

Da Silva, C. S., & Leach, A. M. (2013). Detecting deception in second-language speakers. *Legal and Criminological Psychology, 18,* 115–127.

DePaulo, B. M. (1992). Nonverbal behavior and self-presentation. *Psychological Bulletin, 111,* 203–243.

DePaulo, B. M., & Kirkendol, S. E. (1989). The motivational impairment effect in the communication of deception. In J. C. Yuille (Ed.), *Credibility assessment* (pp. 51–70). Dordrecht, the Netherlands: Kluwer.

DePaulo, B. M., Lindsay, J. L., Malone, B. E., Muhlenbruck, L., Charlton, K., & Cooper, H. (2003). Cues to deception. *Psychological Bulletin, 129,* 74–118.

Doherty-Sneddon, G., Bruce, V., Bonner, L., Longbotham, S., & Doyle, C. (2002). Development of gaze aversion as disengagement of visual information. *Developmental Psychology, 38,* 438–445.

Doherty-Sneddon, G., & Phelps, F. G. (2005). Gaze aversion: A response to cognitive or social difficulty? *Memory and Cognition, 33,* 727–733.

Driscoll, L. N. (1994). A validity assessment of written statements from suspects in criminal investigations using the SCAN technique. *Police Studies, 17,* 77–88.

Ekman, P. (1985/2009). *Telling lies: Clues to deceit in the marketplace, politics and marriage.* New York: W.W. Norton. (Reprinted in 1992 and 2001 and 2009.)

Ekman, P. (2006, October 29). How to spot a terrorist on the fly. *Washington Post.* (http://washington post.com).

Ekman, P., & Friesen, W. V. (1969). Nonverbal leakage and clues to deception. *Psychiatry, 32,* 88–106.

Gamer, M. (2011). Detection of deception and concealed information using neuroimaging techniques. In B. Verschuere, G. Ben-Shakhar, and E. Meijer (Eds.), *Memory detection: Theory and application of the concealed information test* (pp. 90–113). Cambridge: Cambridge University Press.

Ganis, G., & Rosenfeld, J. P. (2011). Neural correlates of deception. In J. Illes and B. J. Sahakian (Eds.), *Oxford handbook of neuroethics* (pp. 101–118). Oxford: Oxford University Press.

Geiselman, R. E., & Callot, R. (1990). Reverse and forward order recall of script based text. *Applied Cognitive Psychology, 4,* 141–144.

Gilbert, D. T. (1991). How mental systems believe. *American Psychologist, 46,* 107–119.

Gilbert, J. A. E., & Fisher, R. P. (2006). The effects of varied retrieval cues on reminiscence in eyewitness memory. *Applied Cognitive Psychology, 20,* 723–739.

Gilovich, T., Savitsky, K., & Medvec, V. H. (1998). The illusion of transparency: Biased assessments of others' ability to read one's emotional states. *Journal of Personality and Social Psychology, 75,* 332–346.

Glenberg, A. M., Schroeder, J. L., & Robertson, D. A. (1998). Averting the gaze disengages the environment and facilitates remembering. *Memory & Cognition, 26*, 651–658.

Granhag, P. A., & Hartwig, M. (2008). A new theoretical perspective on deception detection: On the psychology of instrumental mind-reading. *Psychology, Crime & Law, 14*, 189–200.

Granhag, P. A., & Knieps, M. (2011). Episodic future thought: Illuminating the trademarks of forming true and false intentions. *Applied Cognitive Psychology, 25*, 274–280.

Granhag, P. A., Strömwall, L. A., Willén, R., & Hartwig, M. (in press). Eliciting cues to deception by tactical disclosure of evidence: The first test of the Evidence Framing Matrix. *Legal and Criminological Psychology.*

Granhag, P. A. & Vrij, A. (2010). Interrogating suspects: Deception detection. In P. A. Granhag (Ed.). *Forensic psychology in context: Nordic and international approaches* (pp. 75–93). Cullompton, Devon: Willan Publishing.

Hartwig, M., Granhag, P. A., Strömwall, L. (2007). Guilty and innocent suspects' strategies during interrogations. *Psychology, Crime, & Law, 13*, 213–227.

Hartwig, M., Granhag, P. A., Strömwall, L, & Doering, N. (2010). Impression and information management: On the strategic self-regulation of innocent and guilty suspects. *The Open Criminology Journal, 3*, 10–16.

Hartwig, M., Granhag, P. A., Strömwall, L., & Kronkvist, O. (2006). Strategic use of evidence during police interrogations: When training to detect deception works. *Law and Human Behavior, 30*, 603–619.

Hartwig, M., Granhag, P. A., Strömwall, L. A., Wolf, A., Vrij, A., & Roos af Hjelmsäter, E. (2011). Detecting deception in suspects: Verbal cues as a function of interview strategy. *Psychology, Crime, & Law, 17*, 643–656.

Heath, W. (2009). Arresting and convicting the innocent: The potential role of an "inappropriate" emotional display in the accused. *Behavioral Sciences and the Law, 27*, 313–332.

Hocking, J. E., & Leathers, D. G. (1980). Nonverbal indicators of deception: A new theoretical perspective. *Communication Monographs, 47*, 119–131.

Horvath, F., Blair, J. P., & Buckley, J. P. (2008). The Behavioral Analysis Interview: Clarifying the practice, theory and understanding of its use and effectiveness. *International Journal of Police Science and Management, 10*, 101–118.

Horvath, F., Jayne, B., & Buckley, J. (1994). Differentiation of truthful and deceptive criminal suspects in behavioral analysis interviews. *Journal of Forensic Sciences, 39*, 793–807.

Iacono, W. G. (2008a). Accuracy of polygraph techniques: Problems using confessions to determine ground truth. *Physiology & Behavior, 95*, 24–26.

Iacono, W. G. (2008b). Effective policing: Understanding how polygraph tests work and are used. *Criminal Justice and Behavior, 35*, 1295–1308.

Iacono, W. G. (2008c). Polygraph testing. In E. Borgida and S. T. Fiske (Eds.), *Beyond common sense: Psychological Science in the Courtroom* (pp. 219–235). Oxford: Blackwell Publishing.

Inbau, F. E., Reid, J. E., Buckley, J. P., & Jayne, B. C. (2013). *Criminal interrogation and confessions, (5th ed.).* Burlington, MA: Jones & Bartlett Learning.

Johnson, M. K., & Raye, C. L. (1981). Reality monitoring. *Psychological Review, 88*, 67–85.

Johnson, M. K., & Raye, C. L. (1998). False memories and confabulation. *Trends in Cognitive Sciences, 2*, 137–146.

Kahana, M. J. (1996). Associate retrieval processes in free recall. *Memory & Cognition, 24*, 103–109.

Kassin, S. M. (2005). On the psychology of confessions: Does innocence put innocents at risk? *American Psychologist, 60*, 215–228.

Kassin, S. M., Appleby, S. C., & Torkildson-Perillo, J. (2010). Interviewing suspects: Practice, science, and future directions. *Legal and Criminological Psychology, 15*, 39–56.

Kassin, S. M., & Fong, C. T. (1999). "I'm innocent!": Effects of training on judgments of truth and deception in the interrogation room. *Law and Human Behavior, 23*, 499–516.

Kassin, S. M., & Gudjonsson, G. H. (2004). The psychology of confessions: A review of the literature and issues. *Psychological Science in the Public Interest, 5*, 33–67.

Kassin, S. M., & Norwick, R. J. (2004). Why people waive their Miranda rights: The power of innocence. *Law and Human Behavior, 28*, 211–221.

Kleiner, M. (2002). *Handbook of polygraph testing.* San Diego, CA: Academic Press.

Köhnken, G. (1996). Social psychology and the law. In G. R. Semin and K. Fiedler (Eds.), *Applied social psychology* (pp. 257–282). London: Sage Publications.

Köhnken, G. (2004). Statement validity analysis and the "detection of the truth". In P. A. Granhag and L. A. Strömwall (Eds.), *Deception detection in forensic contexts* (pp. 41–63). Cambridge: Cambridge University Press.

Köhnken, G., & Steller, M. (1988). The evaluation of the credibility of child witness statements in German procedural system. In G. Davies and J. Drinkwater (Eds.), *The child witness: Do the courts abuse children?* (Issues in Criminological and Legal

Psychology, no. 13) (pp. 37–45). Leicester, United Kingdom: British Psychological Society.

Lancaster, G. L. J., Vrij, A., Hope, L., & Waller, B. (2013). Sorting the liars from the truth tellers: The benefits of asking unanticipated questions on lie detection. *Applied Cognitive Psychology*, *27*(1), 107–114.

Langleben, D. D. (2008). Detection of deception with fMRI: Are we there yet? *Legal and Criminological Psychology*, *13*, 1–10.

Leary, M. R., & Kowalski, R. M. (1990). Impression management: A literature review and two-component model. *Psychological Bulletin*, *107*, 34–47.

Leins, D., Fisher, R., & Vrij, A. (2012). Drawing on liars' lack of cognitive flexibility: Detecting deception through varying report modes. *Applied Cognitive Psychology*, *26*, 601–607.

Leins, D., Fisher, R. P., Vrij, A., Leal, S., & Mann, S. (2011). Using sketch-drawing to induce inconsistency in liars. *Legal and Criminological Psychology*, *16*, 253–265.

Levine, T. R., Kim, R. K., & Hamel, L. M. (2010). People lie for a reason: Three experiments documenting the principle of veracity. *Communication Research Reports*, *27*, 271–285.

Levine, T. R., Shaw, A., & Shulman, H. C. (2010). Increasing deception detection accuracy with strategic questioning. *Human Communication Research*, *36*, 216–231.

Lykken, D. T. (1959). The GSR in the detection of guilt. *Journal of Applied Psychology*, *43*, 385–388.

Lykken, D. T. (1960). The validity of the guilty knowledge technique: The effects of faking. *Journal of Applied Psychology*, *44*, 258–262.

Lykken, D. T. (1998). *A tremor in the blood: Uses and abuses of the lie detector*. New York: Plenum Trade.

Mann, S., Vrij, A., Fisher, R. & Robinson, M. (2008). See no lies, hear no lies: Differences in discrimination accuracy and response bias when watching or listening to police suspect interviews. *Applied Cognitive Psychology*, *22*, 1062–1071.

Masip, J., Sporer, S. L., Garrido, E., & Herrero, C. (2005). The detection of deception with the Reality Monitoring approach: A review of the empirical evidence. *Psychology, Crime, & Law*, *11*, 99–122.

Nahari, G., Vrij, A., & Fisher, R. P. (2012). Does the truth come out in the writing? SCAN as a lie detection tool. *Law & Human Behavior*, 36, 68–76.

National Research Council (2003). *The polygraph and lie detection*. Committee to Review the Scientific Evidence on the Polygraph. Washington, DC: The National Academic Press.

Ofshe, R. J., & Leo, R. A. (1997). The decision to confess falsely: Rational choice and irrational action. *Denver University Law Review*, *74*, 979–1112.

Park, H. S., Levine, T. R., McCornack, S. A., Morrisson, K., & Ferrara, M. (2002). How people really detect lies. *Communication Monographs*, *69*, 144–157.

Porter, S., & ten Brinke, L. (2008). Reading between the lies: Identifying concealed and falsified emotions in universal facial expressions. *Psychological Science*, *19*, 508–514.

Quas, J. A., Davis, E. L., Goodman, G. S., & Myers, J. E. B. (2007). Repeated questions, deception, and children's true and false reports of body touch. *Child Maltreatment*, *12*, 60–67.

Rangmar, J., Granhag, P. A., & Strömwall, L. A. (2012). *Cells of suspects: Interviewing strategically to elicit cues to deception and truth*. Manuscript in preparation.

Rice, M., & Harris, G. T. (2005). Comparing effect sizes in follow-up studies: ROC Area, Cohen's *d*, and *r*. *Law & Human Behavior*, *29*, 615–620.

Rosenfeld, J. P. (2011). P300 in detecting concealed information. In B. Verschuere, G. Ben-Shakhar, and E. Meijer (Eds.), *Memory detection: Theory and application of the concealed information test* (pp. 63–89). Cambridge: Cambridge University Press.

Rosenfeld, J. P., Ben Shakhar, G., & Ganis, G. (in press): Physiologically based methods of concealed memory detection. In W. Sinnott-Armstrong, F. Schauer, and L. Nadel (Eds.), *Neuroscience, philosophy and law*. Oxford: Oxford University Press.

Ruby, C. L., & Brigham, J. C. (1998). Can Criteria-Based Content Analysis distinguish between true and false statements of African-American speakers? *Law and Human Behavior*, *22*, 369–388.

Sapir, A. (1987/2000). The LSI course on scientific content analysis (SCAN). Phoenix, AZ: Laboratory for Scientific Interrogation.

Schacter, D. L., & Addis, R. D. (2007). The cognitive neuroscience of constructive memory: Remembering the past and imagining the future. *Philosophical Transactions of the Royal Society*, *392*, 773–786.

Schweitzer, M. E., Brodt, S. E., & Croson, R. T. A. (2002). Seeing and believing: Visual access and the strategic use of deception. *The International Journal of Conflict Management*, *13*, 258–275.

Spence, S. (2008). Playing devil's advocate: The case against fMRI lie detection. *Legal and Criminological Psychology*, *13*, 11–26.

Spence, S. A., Farrow, T. F. D., Herford, A. E., Wilkinson, I. D., Zheng, Y., & Woodruff, P. W. R. (2001). Behavioural and functional anatomical correlates of deception in humans. *Neuroreport: For Rapid Communication of Neuroscience Research*, *12*, 2849–2853.

Sporer, S. L. (2004). Reality monitoring and detection of deception. In P. A. Granhag and L. A. Strömwall

(Eds.), *Deception detection in forensic contexts* (pp. 64–102). Cambridge: Cambridge University Press.

Steller, M., & Köhnken, G. (1989). Criteria-Based Content Analysis. In D. C. Raskin (Ed.), *Psychological methods in criminal investigation and evidence* (pp. 217–245). New York: Springer-Verlag.

Trankell, A. (1963). *Vittnespsykologins Arbetsmetoder.* Stockholm, Sweden: Liber.

Undeutsch, U. (1967). Beurteilung der Glaubhaftigkeit von Aussagen. In U. Undeutsch (Ed.), *Handbuch der Psychologie Vol. 11: Forensische Psychologie* (pp. 26–181). Göttingen, Germany: Hogrefe.

Verschuere, B., Ben-Shakhar, G., & Meijer, E. (2011). *Memory detection: Theory and application of the concealed information test.* Cambridge: Cambridge University Press.

Vrij, A. (2005). Criteria-Based Content Analysis: A qualitative review of the first 37 studies. *Psychology, Public Policy, and Law, 11,* 3–41.

Vrij, A. (2008). *Detecting lies and deceit: Pitfalls and opportunities* (2nd ed.). Chichester, UK: John Wiley and sons.

Vrij, A., Granhag, P. A., Mann, S., & Leal, S. (2011). Lying about flying: The first experiment to detect false intent. *Psychology, Crime, and Law, 17,* 611–620.

Vrij, A., Granhag, P. A., & Porter, S. B. (2010). Pitfalls and opportunities in nonverbal and verbal lie detection. *Psychological Science in the Public Interest, 11,* 89–121.

Vrij, A., Jundi, S., Hope, L., Hillman, J., Gahr, E., Leal, S., Warmelink, L., Mann, S., & Granhag, P. A. (2012). Collective interviewing of suspects. *Journal of Applied Research in Memory and Cognition, 1*(1), 41–44.

Vrij, A., Leal, S., Granhag, P. A., Mann, S., Fisher, R. P., Hillman, J., & Sperry, K. (2009). Outsmarting the liars: The benefit of asking unanticipated questions. *Law and Human Behavior, 33,* 159–166.

Vrij, A., Leal, S., Mann, S., & Granhag, P. A. (2011). A comparison between lying about intentions and past activities: Verbal cues and detection accuracy. *Applied Cognitive Psychology, 25,* 212–218.

Vrij, A., Leal, S., Mann, S., Warmelink, L., Granhag, P. A., & Fisher, R. P. (2010). Drawings as an innovative and successful lie detection tool. *Applied Cognitive Psychology, 4,* 587–594.

Vrij, A., Mann, S., & Fisher, R. (2006a). An empirical test of the Behaviour Analysis Interview. *Law and Human Behavior, 30,* 329–345.

Vrij, A., Mann, S., & Fisher, R. (2006b). Information-gathering vs accusatory interview style: Individual

differences in respondents' experiences. *Personality and Individual Differences, 41,* 589–599.

Vrij, A., Mann, S., Fisher, R., Leal, S., Milne, B., & Bull, R. (2008). Increasing cognitive load to facilitate lie detection: The benefit of recalling an event in reverse order. *Law and Human Behavior, 32,* 253–265.

Vrij, A., Mann, S., Jundi, S., Hope, L., & Leal, S. (2012). Can I take your picture? Undercover interviewing to detect deception. *Psychology, Public Policy, & Law, 18,* 231–244.

Vrij, A., Mann, S., Kristen, S., & Fisher, R. (2007). Cues to deception and ability to detect lies as a function of police interview styles. *Law and Human Behavior, 31,* 499–518.

Vrij, A., Mann, S., Leal, S., & Fisher, R. (2010). "Look into my eyes": Can an instruction to maintain eye contact facilitate lie detection? *Psychology, Crime, & Law, 16,* 327–348.

Vrij, A., Mann, S., Leal, S., & Fisher, R. (2012). Is anyone out there? Drawings as a tool to detect deception in occupations interviews. *Psychology, Crime, & Law, 18,* 377–388.

Vrij, A., Mann, S., Leal, S., & Granhag, P. A. (2010). Getting into the minds of pairs of liars and truth tellers: An examination of their strategies. *The Open Criminology Journal, 3,* 17–22.

Walczyk, J. J., Roper, K. S., Seemann, E., & Humphrey, A. M. (2003). Cognitive mechanisms underlying lying to questions: Response time as a cue to deception. *Applied Cognitive Psychology, 17,* 755–744.

Walczyk, J. J., Schwartz, J. P., Clifton, R., Adams, B., Wei, M., & Zha, P. (2005). Lying person-to-person about live events: A cognitive framework for lie detection. *Personnel Psychology, 58,* 141–170.

Warmelink, L., Vrij, A., Mann, S., Jundi, S., & Granhag, P. A. (2012). Have you been there before? The effect of experience and question expectedness on lying about intentions. *Acta Psychologica, 141,* 178–183.

Warmelink, L., Vrij, A., Mann, S., Leal, S., Forrester, D., & Fisher, R. P. (2011). Thermal imaging as a lie detection tool at airports. *Law & Human Behavior, 35,* 40–48.

Watanabe, H. (2005). Semantic and episodic predictions of memory for plans. *Japanese Psychological Research, 47,* 40–45.

Zuckerman, M., DePaulo, B. M., & Rosenthal, R. (1981). Verbal and nonverbal communication of deception. In L. Berkowitz (Ed.), *Advances in experimental social psychology,* volume 14 (pp. 1–57). New York: Academic Press.

Name Index

Subject Index